Basic Marketing Research

5^e

Gilbert A. Churchill, Jr.
University of Wisconsin

Tom J. Brown
Oklahoma State University

THOMSON

SOUTH-WESTERN

Australia · Canada · Mexico · Singapore · Spain · United Kingdom · United States

THOMSON ™
SOUTH-WESTERN

Basic Marketing Research, 5e
Gilbert A. Churchill, Jr. & Tom J. Brown

VP/Editorial Director:
Jack W. Calhoun

VP/Editor-in-Chief:
Michael P. Roche

Publisher:
Melissa S. Acuña

Acquisitions Editor:
Steven W. Hazelwood

Marketing Manager:
Nicole C. Moore

Developmental Editor:
Rebecca von Gillern

Sr. Production Editor:
Elizabeth A. Shipp

Media Developmental Editor:
Peggy Buskey

Media Production Editor:
Pam Wallace

Photography Manager:
Deanna Ettinger

Photo Researcher:
Terri Miller/E-Visual Communications, Inc.

Production House:
Stratford Publishing Services

Sr. Design Project Manager:
Michelle Kunkler

Internal and Cover Designer:
Kim Torbeck/Imbue Design
Cincinnati, OH

Cover Images:
© Bruce Ayres/Stone, © PhotoDisc, Inc.,
and © Sparky/The Image Bank

Manufacturing Coordinator:
Diane Lohman

Printer:
R.R. Donnelley
Willard, Ohio

To our grandchildren

Kayla Marie
Johnathan Winston
Kelsey Lynn
Sean Jeffrey
Ethan Thomas
Averie Mae
(Gilbert A. Churchill, Jr.)

To *DiAnn, Drew, Taylor, and Avery*
(Tom J. Brown)

Contents in Brief

Contents

Part 2

Research Design   87

Types of Research Design and Exploratory Research   88

Descriptive and Causal Research Designs   108

Part 3

Data Collection Methods   159

7 Secondary Data   160

8 Standardized Marketing Information Services   187

Part 4

Data Collection Forms   279

12 Designing the Questionnaire or Observation Form   280

13 Measurement Basics   320

14 Measuring Attitudes, Perceptions, and Preferences 345

18 Collecting the Data: Nonsampling Errors and Response Rate Calculation   470

Part 7

Research Reports   657

22   The Research Report   658

Preface

DESIGNED FOR THE INTRODUCTORY, UNDERGRADUATE COURSE in marketing research, *Basic Marketing Research, 5e* can be used either in one- or two-quarter sequences or in semester courses.

Marketing research can be a complex topic. It involves a number of questions that need to be answered and a number of decisions that need to be made in order to make the best choice of techniques when solving the research problem. This text provides a framework for these choices, preventing students from becoming lost in a maze when they focus on the bits and pieces to the point that they fail to see the interrelationships of the parts to the whole. An understanding of these interrelationships is essential both to the aspiring manager and the aspiring researcher.

Decisions made in one stage of the research process have consequences for other stages. Managers and marketing researchers both need an appreciation of the subtle and pervasive interactions among the parts of the research process so that they can have confidence in a particular research result.

This book attempts to serve both aspiring managers and aspiring researchers by breaking the research process down into the basic stages that must be completed when answering a research question. These stages are

1. Formulate problem.
2. Determine research design.
3. Determine data-collection method.
4. Design data collection forms.
5. Design sample and collect data.
6. Analyze and interpret the data.
7. Prepare the research report.

The organization of the book parallels these stages in the research process. Thus, the book is organized into seven corresponding parts. Each part (or stage) is then broken into smaller parts, so that a given stage is typically discussed in multiple chapters. This modular treatment allows students to negotiate the maze. It also allows instructors some latitude with respect to the order in which they cover topics.

Organization

Part 1 consists of four chapters. Chapter 1 provides an overview of marketing research and describes the kinds of problems for which it is used, who is doing research, and why it is important to study marketing research. Chapter 1 also provides a perspective on career opportunities available in marketing research. Chapter 2 provides an overview of the various ways of gathering marketing intelligence. It emphasizes the increasingly important role played by decision support systems and the Internet in providing business and competitive intelligence. Chapter 3 then overviews the research process, and includes a discussion of ethics in marketing research. Chapter 4 discusses the problem-formulation stage of the research process and explains the issues that must be addressed in translating a marketing decision problem into one or more research problems that research can address productively. It also covers the preparation of the research request agreement and the research proposal.

Part 2 concerns the choice of research design and consists of two chapters. Chapter 5 overviews the role of various research designs and discusses one of the basic types, the exploratory design. Chapter 6 then discusses the two other basic types, descriptive and causal designs.

Part 3 discusses the general issue of selecting a data collection method and contains five chapters and an appendix. Chapter 7 focuses on secondary data as an information resource, while the appendix to Chapter 7 discusses the many sources of secondary data. Chapter 8 discusses the operations of and data supplied by standardized marketing information services. Chapter 9 describes the issues involved when choosing between the two primary means by which marketing information can be collected—through observing or questioning subjects. Chapter 10 then describes the main alternatives and the advantages and disadvantages of each when subjects are to be questioned. Chapter 11 does the same for observational techniques.

Part 4 addresses the actual design of the data collection forms that will be used in a study. Chapter 12 discusses a sequential procedure that can be used to design a questionnaire or observation form, and Chapter 13 then discusses some basic measurement issues that researchers and managers need to be aware of so that they will neither mislead others nor be misled themselves when interpreting the findings. Chapter 14 describes some of the most popular techniques marketers currently use to measure customers' attitudes, perceptions, and preferences. It also discusses the importance of developing norms for interpreting measures.

Part 5, which consists of four chapters, examines sample design and the actual collection of data needed to answer questions. Chapter 15 gives an overview of the main types of samples that can be used to determine the population elements from which data should be collected. It also describes the main types of nonprobability samples and simple random sampling, the most basic probability sampling technique. Chapter 16 discusses the use of stratified sampling and cluster sampling, which are more sophisticated probability sampling techniques. Chapter 17 addresses the question of how many population elements need to be sampled for research questions to be answered with precision and confidence in the results. Chapter 18 discusses data collection and the many errors that can occur in completing this task from a perspective that allows managers to better assess the quality of information they receive from research. It also presents the appropriate methods for calculating survey response rates.

Once the data have been collected, the research process logically turns to analysis, which is a search for meaning in the collected information. The search for meaning involves many questions and several steps, and the three chapters in Part 6 give an overview of these steps and questions. Chapter 19 reviews the preliminary analysis steps of editing and coding, plus building the codebook and data file. Chapter 20 discusses the procedures that are appropriate for analyzing individual variables, along with the basics of hypothesis testing. Chapter 21 describes the statistical procedures that can be used when multiple variables are considered at the same time.

Part 7, which consists of one chapter and an epilogue, discusses the last, yet critically important, part of the research process: the research report. Because it often becomes the standard by which any research effort is judged, the research report—whether in written or oral format—must contribute positively to that evaluation. Chapter 22 discusses the criteria a written research report should satisfy and a form it can follow so that it does contribute positively to the research effort. A similar perspective is provided for oral reports. Finally, this chapter also discusses some graphic techniques that can be used to more forcefully communicate the important findings. The epilogue ties together the elements of the research process by demonstrating their interrelationships in overview fashion.

Organizing the material in this book around the stages in the research process has several significant benefits. First, it allows the subject of marketing research to be broken into very digestible bites. Second, it demonstrates and continually reinforces how the individual bits and pieces of research technique fit into a larger whole. Students can see readily, for example, the relationship between statistics and marketing research, or where they might pursue additional study to become research specialists. Third, the organization permits the instructor some flexibility with respect to the order in which the parts of the marketing research process may be covered.

Changes in the Fifth Edition

This newest edition of *Basic Marketing Research* brings with it several major changes. While the structure of the book remains largely the same, we have gone to great lengths to make the information in it more accessible and appealing to twenty-first century undergraduate students. At the same time, we maintain the scholarly standards the book has built over its four previous editions. We have focused our efforts on the practical aspects of conducting marketing research—the general "how-to," including key issues and possible problems and their solutions. Through extensive examples, we demonstrate how the concepts and techniques presented are put into practice.

Here are a few highlights of the changes we've made.

- In Chapter 1, we make an even greater effort to communicate to students why organizations need marketing research, as well as why they personally need to study the topic.
- Chapter 2 includes new information about the types of data companies hold in their MIS and DSS systems, as well as a discussion of customer relationship management.
- We have streamlined the discussion of marketing research ethics in Chapter 3, and in the process eliminated an appendix that had appeared in prior editions. Under the "less is more" axiom, we think that students will be more likely to absorb the information in its new format.
- One of the most extensive changes we made involves the problem definition/formulation process. Chapter 4 now centers on a new process for defining problems that adds considerable structure to what has traditionally been a mostly abstract process in marketing research. Here, students are introduced to the notion of discovery- vs. strategy-oriented research.
- Consistent with ongoing trends in the industry, we have added to Chapter 6 a discussion of online panel research conducted via the Internet, as well as new examples of test marketing and an exhibit detailing the relative advantages and disadvantages of different types of test markets.
- In Chapter 8, we've included new information on the NAICS classification system as well as current information about UPC codes. We've also added a Technically Speaking box on how the Nielsen television ratings are computed, which should be of interest to many students, given that almost all will have heard of these ratings. We also briefly discuss syndicated measurement for Internet Web sites.
- In Chapters 13 and 14, we've streamlined much of the discussion of measurement and the assessment of attitudes and preferences, added a Research Window on how marketing research is used in Hollywood, and provided an example from BizRate.com of online attitude ratings for online companies. We've also added new sections on considerations in scale design and on the importance of developing norms for interpreting rating scale scores.
- Chapters 15 through 17, which cover sampling and sample size calculation, have been streamlined to make the presentation more straightforward. Some of the more technical material has been shifted to Technically Speaking boxes.
- Chapter 18 has been completely restructured, with large amounts of new material on sources of error, calculating response rates for different types of data collection, and improving response rates. New exhibits detail methods for detecting nonresponse error and the percentages, for two new studies, of respondents contacted by number of telephone calls.
- Chapter 19 demonstrates our effort to focus on practical aspects of marketing research, with new material on coding two kinds of open-ended responses, building the data file and codebook, cleaning the data file, and an expanded discussion of how to handle missing data. Exhibits 19.1 through 19.4 use an ongoing example to demonstrate how to take responses from the questionnaire to the data file.

- We have completely rewritten and restructured Chapters 20 and 21, the analysis chapters, from earlier editions. We have placed a premium on application and interpretation of the various techniques, with less focus on how many of the statistics are calculated. Our goal is to emphasize to students that analysis is actually quite straightforward when we know (a) the level of measurement of the variable(s) being analyzed, and (b) whether a variable is being analyzed in isolation or simultaneously with other variables. Accordingly, Chapter 20 deals with univariate analyses (and the basics of hypothesis testing) and Chapter 21 addresses multivariate analyses. In some examples, we also present SPSS output and guide students toward the relevant statistics in the output. Relevant information from three appendices (for example, the analysis of variance) appearing in earlier editions has been moved directly into the text.
- Chapter 22 provides and updates material on presenting the results of the research project, both in written and oral format. This chapter condenses material that had previously appeared as two separate chapters.
- A total of eleven cases are new to the text for this edition, with significant revisions to numerous other cases. In addition, the end-of-chapter materials including review questions, discussion questions, problems, and projects have been revised—sometimes quite substantially—to reflect the revised content of the chapters.

Key Features

Basic Marketing Research has several special features that deserve mention. The general approach employed when discussing topics is not only to provide students with the pros and cons of the various methods used to address a research problem, but also to develop an appreciation of why these advantages and disadvantages occur. The hope is that through this appreciation students will be able to creatively apply and critically evaluate the procedures of marketing research. Other important features include the following:

Learning Objectives. A set of learning objectives highlights the most important topics discussed in the chapter. The learning objectives are repeated in the margins in the chapter where the topics are discussed. The chapter summary then recaps the learning objectives point by point.

Looking Ahead/Looking Back Cases. A specific research scenario, Looking Ahead, opens each chapter. These scenarios are adapted from actual situations and should prove to be very interesting to students. Furthermore, an end-of-chapter continuation of the scenario, Looking Back, illustrates how the scenario can be brought into sharper focus using the methods described in the chapter.

Key Terms with Definitions. A running glossary appears throughout the text. Key terms in each chapter are boldfaced, and their definitions appear in the margin where the terms are discussed. A complete glossary is also included.

Research Windows. The Research Windows provide a view of what is happening in the world of marketing research. Research Windows describe what is going on at specific companies and offer some specific how-to tips. Like the Looking Ahead/Looking Back features, they serve to breathe life into the subject and strongly engage the students' interest.

Technically Speaking Boxes. These provide interested students with more detailed information about some of the topics presented in the text.

Photos and Cartoons. These provide visual reinforcement to important concepts. Throughout the book, photos provide students with a tangible understanding of how various aspects of the research process are conducted.

End-of-Chapter Materials. Discussion questions, problems, and/or projects are found at the end of each chapter. This feature allows students the opportunity to apply the chapter topics to focused situations, thereby honing their analytical skills and developing firsthand knowledge of the strengths and weaknesses of various research techniques.

End-of-Part Features

1. A **complete research project** at the end of each part concerns retailers' attitudes toward advertising in various media. The project represents an actual situation faced by a group of radio stations in one community. It begins with a description of the radio stations' concerns and objectives. Each of the sections then describes how the research was designed and carried out, demonstrating the interrelationships of the stages in the research process and providing students with a real, hands-on perspective as to how research is actually conducted. Discussion questions are included with each section of this case.

2. **End-of-Part Cases for Parts 1 through 6** deal with each stage in the research process. These cases assist students in developing their own evaluation and analytical skills. They are also useful in demonstrating the universal application of marketing research techniques. Marketing research methods can be used not only by manufacturers and distributors of products, as is commonly assumed, but also by the private and public sectors to address other issues. Cases include such diverse entities or issues as the Big Brothers program, education, banking, and theater, among others. All cases represent actual situations, although some of them have been disguised to protect the proprietary nature of the information.

Raw Data

Data are provided for several of the cases to allow students to perform their own analyses to answer questions. These data are available to adopters both on an Instructor's Resource CD-ROM and on the Web site for this text: **http://churchill.swlearning.com.**

Real-World Case. The text also contains the description, questionnaire, coding form, and raw data for a ground coffee study conducted by NFO. This study was used to generate a number of discussion questions and problems for the chapters, which give students the opportunity to work with "live" data. This should develop their skills in translating research problems into data analysis issues and in interpreting computer output. Moreover, the database is rich enough for instructors to design their own application problems and exercises for their classes, thereby allowing even more opportunity for hands-on learning.

Supplements

Instructor's Resource CD-ROM

This brand-new supplement to this edition includes everything you need for teaching the marketing research course. On the CD you'll find complete files for the Instructor's Manual, the Test Bank, the Examview Testing Software, and the PowerPoint Presentation.

Web Site

Completely new for this edition of the text, you'll find complete Instructor's Resources as well as an Interactive Study Center for students that includes quizzing, crossword puzzles, a summary of the learning objectives for each chapter, and Infotrac citations and exercises. Visit us today at: **http://churchill.swlearning.com.**

Video Cases

For this edition of the text you'll find a video case that uses an original script and professional actors that allows students to view short segments illustrating the points being discussed. There is a special icon at the end of the chapters in the Instructor's Manual that indicates questions that might be asked after students view a segment of the video case. The video case makes for a lively and interactive learning experience.

Acknowledgments

This book has benefited immensely from the many helpful comments received along the way from interested colleagues. We especially wish to acknowledge the following people who reviewed the manuscript for this or one of the earlier editions. While much of the credit for the strength of this book is theirs, the blame for any weaknesses is strictly ours. Thank you one and all for your most perceptive and helpful comments.

David Andrus	Dhruv Grewal	Roland Jones	Pradeep A. Rau
Joseph Ballenger	Thomas S. Gruca	Ram Kesavan	Debra Ringold
Edward Bond	D. S. Halfhill	Richard H. Kolbe	Abhijit Roy
Donald Bradley	James E. Hansz	Elizabeth K. La Fleur	Bruce Stern
Terry Childers	Doug Hausknecht	Subhash Lonial	R. Sukumar
James S. Chow	Vince Howe	Daulatram Lund	John H. Summey
C. Anthony Di Benedetto	Deborah Roedder John	Douglas Mac Lachlan	David Urban
		Tridib Mazumdar	Gerrit H. van Bruggen
Elizabeth Ferrell	Glen Jarboe	Donald J. Messmer	Joe Welch
David Gourley	Leonard Jensen	Thomas Noordewier	

My colleagues at the University of Wisconsin have my thanks for the intellectual stimulation and psychological support they have always provided.

I also wish to thank Janet Christopher, who did most of the typing of the manuscript. She was efficient in her efforts and patient with mine. I also wish to thank students Beth Bubon, Jennifer Markkanen, Joseph Kuester, Jayashree Mahajan, Kay Powers, and David Szymanski for their help with many of the tasks involved in completing this book. I would like to thank the editorial and production staff of South-Western/Thomson Learning for their professional efforts on my behalf. I am also grateful to the Literary Executor of the late Sir Ronald A. Fisher, F.R.S; to Dr. Frank Yates, F.R.S; and to Longman Group Ltd., for permission to reprint Table III from their book *Statistical Tables for Biological, Agricultural and Medical Research* (6th Edition, 1974).

Finally, I once again owe a special debt of thanks to my wife, Helen, and our children. Their unyielding support and generous love not only made this book possible but also worth doing in the first place.

Gilbert A. Churchill, Jr.

Madison, Wisconsin
March 2003

I want to thank my colleagues at Oklahoma State University, as well as my various research colleagues, for their support, friendship, and patience while I've focused attention on this text. Thanks also to Janet Christopher, for all the support and diligent efforts on the text and Instructor's Manual. Amy Sallee did an incredible job helping out with Chapter 7 as well as with questions for the test bank. John Phillips and, especially, Steve Locy of OSU's Edmon Low Library were instrumental in seeing that the information on secondary data sources in Chapter 7 (and appendix) was as current as possible. I appreciate their efforts on our behalf. I also want to thank the editorial and production staffs at South-Western/Thomson Learning and Stratford Publishing Services for their efforts on the book; we're really proud of the final result.

I also want to say thanks to Gil Churchill for everything he's taught me over the years, his friendship and support, and for the opportunity to join him in this endeavor. Watching him for a few years at the University of Wisconsin was a privilege and I learned a great deal from his example. Thanks, Gil; I'll try to pass it on to my students.

Projects like this require lots of time, effort, and motivation. My wife, DiAnn, has been a lovely source of inspiration throughout the process. I will forever appreciate her patience and love. I also thank my children for the wonderful way they help keep my attention where it really needs to be.

Tom J. Brown

Stillwater, Oklahoma
March 2003

About the Authors

Gilbert A. Churchill, Jr., received his DBA from Indiana University in 1966 and joined the University of Wisconsin faculty upon graduation. Professor Churchill was named Distinguished Marketing Educator by the American Marketing Association in 1986, the second individual so honored. This lifetime achievement award recognizes and honors a living marketing educator for distinguished service and outstanding contributions in the field of marketing education. Professor Churchill was also awarded the Academy of Marketing Science's lifetime achievement award in 1993 for his significant scholarly contributions. In 1996, he received a Paul D. Converse Award, which is given to the most influential marketing scholars, as judged by a national jury drawn from universities, businesses, and government. Also in 1996, the Marketing Research Group of the American Marketing Association established the Gilbert A. Churchill, Jr., lifetime achievement award, which is to be given each year to a person judged to have made significant lifetime contributions to marketing research. In 2002, he received the Charles Coolidge Parlin lifetime achievement award from the American Marketing Association for his substantial contributions to the ongoing advancement of marketing research practice.

Professor Churchill is a past recipient of the William O'Dell Award for the outstanding article appearing in the *Journal of Marketing Research* during the year. He has also been a finalist for the award five other times. He is a coauthor of the most and third most influential articles of the past century in sales management as judged by a panel of experts in the field. He has served as consultant to a number of companies including Oscar Mayer, Western Publishing Company, and Parker Pen.

Professor Churchill's articles have appeared in such publications as the *Journal of Marketing Research, Journal of Marketing, Journal of Consumer Research, Journal of Retailing, Journal of Business Research, Decision Sciences, Technometrics,* and *Organizational Behavior and Human Performance,* among others.

In addition to *Basic Marketing Research,* he is the coauthor of several other books, including *Marketing Research: Methodological Foundations,* 8th ed. (Fort Worth, TX: Harcourt College Publishers, 2002), *Marketing: Creating Value for Customers,* 2nd ed. (Burr Ridge, IL: Irwin/McGraw-Hill, 1998), *Sales Force Management: Planning, Implementation, and Control,* 6th ed. (Burr Ridge, IL: Irwin/McGraw-Hill, 2000), and *Salesforce Performance* (Lexington, MA: Lexington Books, 1984). He is a former editor of the *Journal of Marketing Research* and has served on the editorial boards of the *Journal of Marketing Research* and *Journal of Marketing,* among others. Professor Churchill is a past recipient of the Lawrence J. Larson Excellence in Teaching Award.

Tom J. Brown, received his Ph.D. from the University of Wisconsin-Madison in 1994. Prior to joining the marketing faculty at Oklahoma State University, he served on the faculty at Southern Methodist University. Professor Brown has taught marketing research to undergraduate students every semester since receiving his Ph.D., and has supervised dozens of student research projects for industry clients ranging from not-for-profit service organizations (such as Voice of Hope Ministries) to *Fortune* 500 companies (such as Lucent Technologies).

Professor Brown's articles have appeared in such publications as the *Journal of Marketing Research,* the *Journal of Marketing,* the *Journal of Consumer Research,* the *Journal of the Academy of Marketing Science,* the *Journal of Retailing,* the *Journal of Service Research,* the *Journal of Services Marketing, Marketing Health Services,* the *Cornell Hotel and Restaurant Administration Quarterly,* and *Corporate Reputation Review.* His research interests include the development of corporate image and its influences on various constituent groups, as well as aspects of services marketing. He has served on the editorial review board of the *Journal of the Academy of Marketing Science* and is cofounder of the Corporate Associations/Identity Research Group. He was the recipient of a Richard D. Irwin Foundation Doctoral Dissertation Fellowship while at the University of Wisconsin and the Kenneth D. and Leitner Greiner Teaching Award at Oklahoma State University.

© PhotoDisc/Getty Images

Part 1

Introduction to Marketing Research and Problem Definition

Part 1 gives an overview of marketing research. Chapter 1 looks at the role of marketing research in the organization, the kinds of problems for which marketing research is used, and who is doing it. Chapter 2 discusses alternative ways of providing marketing intelligence: through marketing information systems, decision support systems, or projects designed to get at specific issues. Chapter 3 provides an overview of the research process, which serves as the backbone in structuring this book. Chapter 4 discusses in detail problem formulation, the first stage in the research process.

1

Role of Marketing Research

© PhotoDisc/Getty Images

Learning Objectives

1   *Define marketing research.*

2   *Discuss different kinds of firms that conduct marketing research.*

3   *List some of the skills that are important for careers in marketing research.*

4   *List three reasons for studying marketing research.*

Sarah yawned, Erik twisted in his chair, Kelli slammed her book shut, and Paul sighed. All four were ready for a study break. "When I finish school," Kelli announced, "I'm not going to hunt for some corporate job. I'm going to start my own company—like that handbag company in Virginia."

"What handbag company?" asked Paul.

"That one I was telling Sarah about this morning. I heard this girl got $500 when she graduated from college, and she used it to start a business that makes handcrafted handbags. She sells them online."

"You mean like purses?"

"Not just ordinary purses, Paul," explained Sarah, "Beautiful hand-sewn bags. I found her Web site—Pilgrim Designs. I bookmarked it to show you, Kelli." Sarah began clicking to the site on her laptop. "Look, hand-dyed silks."

"Hey," said Paul, looking over her shoulder. "She even won a couple of awards for her Web site. I guess that's one way to get some buzz."

"Well," said Erik, knowingly, "You can start a business if you want, Kelli, but I sure wouldn't. My cousin tried that about eight years ago. He got a degree in history and decided to start a business offering guided tours of museums in Boston, where he was living. Also virtual tours of historical sites online."

"What happened?" asked Paul.

"He went bankrupt. He was going to get rich in e-commerce, but he went broke. My mom said he just wasn't very businesslike about his business. He tried to get my mom to invest, and when she asked to see his plans, he just said, 'This is e-commerce, Aunt Diane. The rules have changed.'"

"So what!" persisted Kelli. "I know I have to plan. My business is going to succeed. It's going to be a translation service, translating documents for businesses."

"You'll have to do marketing research," said Erik.

"Customer surveys? No, I'm just going to sell to businesses. I won't have to do surveys. Anyway, I can't afford all that."

"Not just customer surveys, Kelli," said Sarah. "I had my first marketing research class today, and that's what the instructor kept saying: 'There's a lot more to good marketing research than doing a survey.' So there has to be more to it."

"Test marketing?" suggested Paul. "That could be research. You always hear about companies testing their new product before the national rollout."

"It still sounds expensive," grumbled Kelli. "I don't see how it applies to starting a business."

"Well, what my cousin did was expensive, too," said Erik. "He maxed out all his credit cards. Maybe he could have tried to find out something about who his customers would be."

"Yeah, Erik's right," agreed Paul. "You have to know what your customers want, or you'll just be wasting your time."

Discussion Issues

1. Why is marketing research important to business success?

2. What are some basic questions marketing research can answer?

3. How should a start-up company approach marketing research, compared with the approach of a large, established company? ∎

Marketing research is a much broader activity than most people realize. Most of us have probably completed surveys on paper or over the telephone, but there is much more to marketing research than just asking consumers how they think or feel about a product or an ad. This chapter introduces the broad role of marketing research within a company or organization. In addition, different types of companies that conduct marketing research and three important reasons that business students should develop a working knowledge of marketing research will be presented.

The Problem: Marketers Need Information

Define marketing research.

Regardless of the types of products or services offered, all businesses or organizations share a common problem: they need information in order to target their audience appropriately. Consider the following examples:

Example   When Danny Meyer, a successful New York City restaurateur, decided to open a new barbecue restaurant in Manhattan, he and his team traveled across the country to cities like Memphis, Kansas City, and Austin to gather information about how to prepare *real* barbecue. After numerous stops at barbecue joints to sample the local fare, Meyer and his team took what they learned (along with a few extra pounds) back to Manhattan and opened the Blue Smoke, to great acclaim.

Example   When Kroger opens new Signature food stores, the shelf selection for each store is based largely on information obtained from surveys sent to residents in surrounding neighborhoods before the new store is opened. A new store opened recently in the Dallas area with 860 varieties of produce, many of which were requested by the nearby Asian-American population. By paying attention to such details, the chain hopes to be able to compete effectively against price-oriented competitors like Wal-Mart.

Example   The Girl Scouts use research to better understand young girls and their interests and concerns. In 2000, the Girl Scout Research Institute was founded to study the "healthy development of girls" according to Dr. Harriet S. Mosatche, who oversees the development of new badges. A recent study identified stress and anxiety among pre-teen girls from the pressure to grow up quickly as a key problem area. The "Stress Less" badge was recently introduced on the basis of this study.

Example   When Julia Knight launched Growing Healthy, Inc., to sell a line of frozen baby food, she was an experienced marketing executive but not a parent. She gained a mom's perspective by personally conducting research into how parents shop. Knight cruised the aisles of supermarkets, often accompanied by friends and their children. She observed children complaining about the cold in the frozen-food aisle and saw parents rush them through that section of the store. Knight therefore developed a marketing strategy that included convincing supermarket managers to put cutaway freezers in the warmer environs of the baby food section. Her attention to buying habits helped Knight build Growing Healthy into a $2.8 million firm.

Example   In the United Kingdom, Levi's coupled industry and population data with its own consumer studies to identify a need for change in its marketing strategy. The company observed that the market for denim, and Levi's share of that market, peaked in 1996 and then declined. In addition, population trends indicated that the size of the company's core age group of 18- to 25-year-olds has been declining in Europe. Levi's research into attitudes revealed a possible cause of the decline in market share: Young adults in the U.K. want more innovation from the company. Levi's responded by setting up groups to develop new products for each of three markets, called "urban opinion formers," "extreme sports," and "regular girls and guys."[1]

As these examples illustrate, different companies need different kinds of information, and the information they need can be gathered in many different ways. Salespeople use the results of marketing research studies to better sell their products. Politicians use marketing research to plan campaign strategies. Even clergy use marketing research to determine when to hold services! The point is that marketing research is an essential activity that can take many forms, but its basic function is to gather information needed to help managers make better decisions. The accompanying advertisement shows how Gerber used market research to develop a new line of products.

You may recall from your introductory course in marketing that the principal task of marketing is to create value for customers, where customer value is the difference between customer perceptions of the benefits they receive from

© 1998 Gerber Products Company

purchasing and using products and services, and their perceptions of the costs they incur to exchange for them. Customers who are willing and able to make exchanges will do so when (1) the benefits of exchanges exceed the costs of exchanges and (2) the products or services offer superior value compared with alternatives.[2]

In their attempts to create customer value, marketing managers generally focus their efforts on the four Ps—namely, the *p*roduct or service, its *p*rice, its *p*lacement or the channels in which it is distributed, and its *p*romotion or communications mix.

The marketing manager's essential task is to develop a marketing strategy that combines the marketing mix elements in such a way that they complement each other and positively influence customers' value perceptions and behaviors. This task would be much simpler if all the elements that affect customers' perceptions of value were under the manager's control and if customer reaction to any contemplated change could be predicted. Usually, however, a number of factors affecting the success of the marketing effort, including economic, political and legal, social, natural, technological, and competitive environments, are beyond the marketing manager's control, and the behavior of individual customers is largely unpredictable.

Figure 1.1 summarizes the task of marketing management. Customers are the target because they are the focus of the firm's activities. Their satisfaction is achieved through simultaneous adjustments in the elements of the marketing mix, but the results of these adjustments are uncertain because the marketing task takes place within an uncontrollable environment (see Figure 1.2). Consequently, as director of the firm's marketing activities, the marketing manager has an urgent need for information—and marketing research is

The Task of Marketing Management

Figure 1.1

Source: Gilbert A. Churchill, Jr., and J. Paul Peter, *Marketing: Creating Value for Customers,* 2nd ed. (Burr Ridge, Ill.: Irwin/McGraw-Hill, 1998), p. 22.

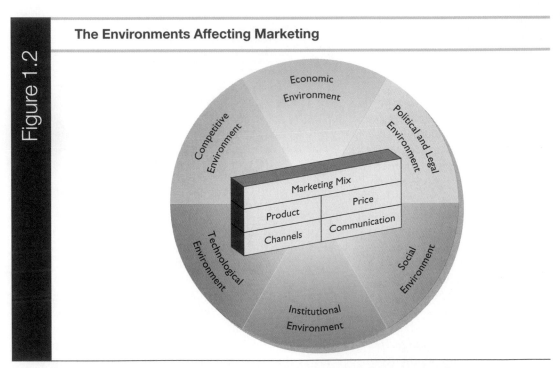

The Environments Affecting Marketing

Figure 1.2

Source: Gilbert A. Churchill, Jr., and J. Paul Peter, *Marketing: Creating Value for Customers,* 2nd ed. (Burr Ridge, Ill.: Irwin/McGraw-Hill, 1998), p. 29.

marketing research
The function that links the consumer to the marketer through information—information used to identify and define marketing problems; generate, refine, and evaluate marketing actions; monitor marketing performance; and improve understanding of marketing as a process.

traditionally responsible for providing it. Marketing research is the firm's formal communication link with the environment. Through marketing research, the firm gathers and interprets data from the environment for use in developing, implementing, and monitoring the firm's marketing plans.

The formal definition of **marketing research** emphasizes its information-linkage role.

Marketing research is the function that links the consumer, customer, and public to the marketer through information—information used to identify and define marketing opportunities and problems; generate, refine, and evaluate marketing actions; monitor marketing performance; and improve our understanding of marketing as a process.[3]

Marketing research provides information to the organization for use in at least four areas:

1. The generation of ideas for marketing action, including the identification of marketing problems and opportunities.
2. The evaluation of marketing actions.
3. The comparison of performance versus objectives.
4. The development of general understanding of marketing phenomena and processes.

Marketing research is also involved with all phases of the information-management process, including (1) the specification of what information is needed, (2) the collection and analysis of the information, and (3) the interpretation of that information with respect to the objectives that motivated the study in the first place.

Another way of looking at the function of marketing research is to consider how management uses it. Some marketing research is used for planning, some for problem solving, and some for control. When used for planning, it deals largely with determining which marketing opportunities are viable and which are not promising for the firm. Also, when viable opportunities are uncovered, marketing research provides estimates of their size and scope, so that marketing management can better assess the resources needed to develop them. Problem-solving marketing research focuses on the short- or long-term decisions that the firm must make with respect to the elements of the marketing mix. Control-oriented marketing research helps management isolate trouble spots and keep abreast of current operations. The kinds of questions marketing research can address with regard to planning, problem solving, and control decisions are listed in Exhibit 1.1. The relationship between each of these questions and a marketing manager's area of responsibility is easy to see.

The communication link that marketing research serves is becoming increasingly critical and difficult as the world moves to a global economy. What works in one environment

Exhibit 1.1

Kinds of Questions Marketing Research Can Help Answer

I. Planning
   A. What kinds of people buy our products? Where do they live? How much do they earn? How many of them are there?
   B. Are the markets for our products increasing or decreasing? Are there promising markets that we have not yet reached?
   C. Are the channels of distribution for our products changing? Are new types of marketing institutions likely to evolve?

II. Problem Solving
   A. Product
      1. Which of various product designs is likely to be the most successful?
      2. What kind of packaging should we use?
   B. Price
      1. What price should we charge for our products?
      2. As production costs decline, should we lower our prices or try to develop higher-quality products?
   C. Place
      1. Where, and by whom, should our products be sold?
      2. What kinds of incentives should we offer the trade to push our products?
   D. Promotion
      1. How much should we spend on promotion? How should it be allocated to products and to geographic areas?
      2. What combination of media—newspapers, radio, television, magazines, the Internet—should we use?

III. Control
   A. What is our market share overall? In each geographic area? By each customer type?
   B. Are customers satisfied with our products? How is our record for service? Are there many returns?
   C. How does the public perceive our company? What is our reputation with the trade?

Example An American manufacturer of cornflakes tried to introduce its product in Japan but failed miserably. Since the Japanese were not interested in the general concept of breakfast cereals, how could the manufacturer expect them to purchase cornflakes?

Example After learning that ketchup was not available in Japan, a U.S. company is reported to have shipped the Japanese a large quantity of its popular brand-name ketchup. Unfortunately, the firm did not first determine why ketchup was not already marketed in Japan. The large, affluent Japanese market was so tempting that the company feared any delay would permit its competition to spot the "opportunity" and capture the market. A marketing research study would have revealed the reason behind the lack of availability of ketchup: Soy sauce is the preferred condiment in Japan.

Example Unilever was forced to withdraw temporarily from one of its foreign markets when it learned the hard way that the French were not interested in frozen foods.

Example CPC International met some resistance when it first tried to sell its Knorr soups in the United States. The company had test-marketed the product by serving passersby a small portion of its already prepared warm soup. After the taste test, the individuals were questioned about buying the product. The research revealed U.S. interest, but sales were very low once the packages were placed on grocery store shelves. Further investigation uncovered that the market tests had not taken into account the American tendency to avoid dry soups. During the testing, those individuals interviewed were unaware that they were tasting a dried soup. Finding the taste quite acceptable, the interviewees indicated they would be willing to buy the product. Had they known that the soup was sold in a dry form and that the preparation required 15 to 20 minutes of occasional stirring, they would have lost interest in the product. In this case, the soup's method of preparation was extremely important to the consumer, and the company's failure to test for this unique product difference resulted in an unpredicted sluggish market.

Example Warner encountered difficulties when it tried to sell cinnamon-flavored Freshen-Up gum in Chile. Because the gum's taste was unacceptable there, the product fared poorly in the marketplace. Coca-Cola also had little success in marketing a product in Chile. When the company attempted to introduce a new grape-flavored drink, it soon discovered that the Chileans were not interested. Apparently, the Chileans prefer wine as their grape drink.

Example Chase and Sanborn met resistance when it tried to introduce its instant coffee in France. In the French home, the consumption of coffee plays a more significant role than in the English home. Since the preparation of "real" coffee is a ritual in the life of the French consumer, he or she will generally reject instant coffee because of its impromptu characteristics. ∎

Source: David A. Ricks, *Blunders in International Business, 3rd edition* (Cambridge, Mass.: Blackwell Publishers, 1999), pp. 139–147.

does not necessarily work in another, as the examples in Research Window 1.1 illustrate. Firms operating in the international arena often use marketing research to get a perspective on what it is like to do business in specific countries. For example, marketing research helped McDonald's adjust its positioning as attitudes toward the company changed in the United Kingdom. When the company first crossed the Atlantic in the mid-1970s, customers were drawn in by its American origins and the novelty of fast food. Reflecting this appeal, McDonald's first U.K. ad slogan announced, "There's a difference at McDonald's you'll enjoy."

The fast-food giant used consumer research to keep tabs on opinions as the market matured. Fifteen years after McDonald's began serving the British market, consumers were describing McDonald's as inflexible and arrogant—a negative take on the efficiency consumers associated with the company's American heritage. McDonald's therefore adjusted its ad campaigns to use softer messages depicting McDonald's at the center of British family life.

The company's ability to detect and adapt to changing customer attitudes helps it maintain an impressive 75 percent share of the U.K. hamburger market.[4]

Who Does Marketing Research?

While individuals and organizations have practiced marketing research for centuries—the need for information has always existed—the formal practice of marketing research can be traced to the nineteenth century:

Discuss different kinds of firms that conduct marketing research.

> More by accident than foresight, N. W. Ayer & Son applied marketing research to marketing and advertising problems. In 1879, in attempting to fit a proposed advertising schedule to the needs of the Nichols-Shepard Company, manufacturers of agricultural machinery, the agency wired state officials and publishers throughout the country requesting information on expected grain production. As a result, the agency was able to construct a crude but formal market survey by states and counties. This attempt to construct a market survey is probably the first real instance of marketing research in the United States.[5]

The Curtis Publishing Company is generally given credit for forming the first formal marketing research department back in 1911, while ACNielsen (now a division of VNU, Inc.), still a world leader in the marketing research industry, began operation in 1934. The notion of marketing research as an important business function really took off around the end of World War II, as competition for customers heightened.[6]

The three major categories of firms that conduct marketing research are: (1) the producers of products and services, (2) advertising agencies, and (3) marketing research companies.

Producers of Products and Services

Marketing research really began to grow when firms found they could no longer sell all they could produce, but instead had to gauge market needs and produce accordingly. Marketing research was called upon to estimate these needs. As consumers began to have more choices in the marketplace, marketing began to assume a more dominant role and production a less important one. The marketing concept emerged, and along with it a reorganization of the marketing effort. Many marketing research departments were born in these reorganizations.

Although the growth in the number of new marketing research departments has slowed recently, the firm that does not have a formal department, or at least a person assigned specifically to the marketing research activity, is now the exception rather than the rule. Marketing research departments are very prevalent among industrial and consumer manufacturing companies. These companies conduct research designed to develop and market the products they manufacture. For example, producers such as Goodyear, Pillsbury, Kraft, and Oscar Meyer either have or have had their own marketing research departments.

Marketing research departments also exist in other types of companies. Publishers and broadcasters, for example, do a good deal of research. They attempt to measure the size of the market reached by their message and construct a demographic profile of this audience. These data are then used to sell advertising space or time. Large retailers such as Sears and JC Penney have operated marketing research departments to gather information about consumer preferences, store image, etc. Financial institutions such as banks and brokerage houses do research involving forecasting, measurement of market potentials, determination of market characteristics, market share analyses, sales analyses, location analyses, and product-mix studies. For example, one major home mortgage lender wanted to understand how to best serve first-time home buyers. The research team conducted one-on-one interviews followed by concept tests that allowed the company to better understand the needs of these buyers.

Many companies use marketing research to regularly track customer satisfaction and customer usage patterns. For example, the marketing research department at Silver Dollar City, a popular theme park located in Branson, Missouri, routinely surveys guests to determine their demographics, behavior, and levels of satisfaction. Researchers found that visitors from over 301 miles away (outer market) took three times longer to plan their trips to Silver Dollar City than did guests who lived less than 100 miles away (core market). Based upon these findings the marketing department altered their strategy. They started their advertising in outer markets several weeks before beginning those same ads in the core market. This resulted in more efficient advertising purchasing and the message was presented to those visitors at the time they were making plans to visit. This shift accounted in part for an extra 60,000 guests that visited the park that year. Research Window 1.2 presents an overview of the various kinds of research conducted or used by Silver Dollar City, Inc., which owns or operates entertainment properties in several different locations across the U.S.

RESEARCH *Window* 1.2

Marketing Research at Silver Dollar City, Inc.

Silver Dollar City, Inc. (SDC) has one of the most comprehensive databases of primary and secondary entertainment-related research in the industry. This library of guest, theme park, tourism, and consumer information is largely the foundation of SDC's long-term strategic plans and marketing strategies.

Guest Research, Profiling, and Analysis
Every property in the SDC, Inc. family has an ongoing (in-house) guest survey program designed to gather customer demographics, geographic origin, behavior, and level of satisfaction. Depending on the property, these surveys are conducted in person or by telephone interview. In the second phase of the testing program, they are implementing surveys via the Web.

This enormous database of guest information has been processed, reported, and analyzed seasonally and by customer segment for the past decade. In addition to measuring each customer segment's size and attendance trend, this research is also used to analyze the impact of capital additions and the economic impact by customer segment.

Market Research, Profiling, and Analysis
In addition to profiling specific customer segments and monitoring attendance patterns over time, tourists from each destination in which SDC operates are also profiled and analyzed on a regular basis. Such market

research provides insight into destination trends as well as a better understanding of the type of tourists who are *not* visiting SDC properties. This information includes but is not limited to: tourists profiles, visitor counts, resident market size and demographics, market performance, etc.

Empirical Data Analysis Empirical data such as attendance, sales revenue, and per capita spending are also blended together with primary research efforts in order to provide a seamless and complete understanding of the SDC, Inc. guest experience. Other types of empirical data used include census information. Census data are used to profile and measure resident population and characteristics in the destinations in which SDC operates.

Research and Analysis Designed to Address a Specific Issue In addition to these regularly scheduled research activities, each property in the company frequently invests in research and analysis designed to answer specific marketing or management questions. Examples of these kinds of efforts include Estimates of Market Potential, How Area Visitors Use Their Leisure Time at Home and in Our Markets, Feasibility Studies, Analysis of Synergy Between Branson Properties, Guest Psychographic Profiles Assessed Using PRIZM, etc.

Advertising Agencies

Much of the research conducted by advertising agencies deals directly with creating the advertisement itself. This may involve testing alternative approaches to the wording or art used in the ad or investigating the effectiveness of various celebrity spokespersons. However, many agencies also do marketing research for their clients to determine the market potential of a proposed new product or the client's market share.

Ad agencies also do research to better understand consumers, their interests, and behaviors, in order to serve their corporate clients. For instance, Dentsu, one of the world's largest agencies, conducted research on the psychological effect of colors among women. Among other findings, they discovered that 39% of the women in their sample focused on color when making a purchase; that women in their 40s were more sensitive to the color of products than were younger women; that women were most sensitive to color in the clothing and accessories product category; and that women under the age of 30 were more likely than other women to focus on color for its psychological effects in helping create a mood or project a personality image.[7]

Competitive Research Competitive research is another avenue in which a great amount of time is invested. In addition to monitoring local competition and competitive destinations, a large database of top-50-theme-park information has been developed. This database includes theme park attendance history, pricing history, history of capital additions and estimated capital investments, overnight domestic leisure visitors to each park's home market, resident population, resident income, resident age, year the park opened, size of the park, number of coasters installed, etc. The purpose of maintaining this information is to be able to measure attendance impacts based upon multiple variables such as installation of coasters by price of the coaster, or size of the park, or by the number of coasters already existing at the park.

Other Research and Statistical Analysis

Other research and analysis activities that are frequently used include lifetime value analysis, season passholder decay probability/retention studies, commonality analysis, regression forecasting models, etc. Such statistical analyses help in the understanding of the potential value (or lack thereof) of specific customer segments or market programs being considered.

HOW CONSUMER AND LEISURE TRENDS ARE BEING TRACKED

Silver Dollar City, Inc. closely monitors trends from a variety of industries in an effort to evolve with their customers' changing needs, wants, and behaviors. Specifically, the demographic and behavioral trends of each of the properties' guests are tracked. Guests' ages, party composition, last visit, incomes, crossover with other properties, etc. are closely monitored. Such changes are taken into account as future strategic decisions and marketing plans are created.

Consumer trends are also of great concern. Through books, periodicals, syndicated research studies, and conferences, social, demographic, technological, economic, and commerce trends are monitored extensively.

Trends in the theme park industry are also tracked. In addition to attendance, pricing, and capital trends mentioned above, SDC researches the stock prices of publicly traded theme parks, the consolidation in the industry, new theme park queue line technologies being introduced, new types of ride-technologies, and marketing promotions.

Tourism trends also impact SDC, Inc. and are being followed closely. Secondary research is gathered through the Travel Industry Association's Outlook Forum, *Yankelovich National Leisure Monitor,* Plog's *American Traveler Survey*, and other tourism-related resources. Whether it's an increase in shorter trips, an increased interest in outdoor recreation, the combining of business and leisure trips, or increased sales of timeshare properties, numerous trends and evaluation of potential impact on SDC, Inc. properties nationwide are being watched.

These are just a few of the categories of trends being followed by the SDC Research Department. Literally hundreds of resources are evaluated and analyzed every year for the purpose of determining how such trends might impact the company. ■

Source: Adapted from "Corporate Research Activity Brief," Silver Dollar City, Inc., (undated).

© AP/Wide World Photos

Marketing researchers at Silver Dollar City, Inc., use marketing research to profile guests, measure satisfaction, analyze markets, and much more for their entertainment properties around the United States.

Before the 2002 World Cup soccer tournament, McCann-Erickson WorldGroup conducted extensive research on attitudes about soccer, collecting data from men and women in 39 countries around the world. U.S. respondents indicated that they did not follow soccer as closely as other sports, although the majority knew that the U.S. was competing in the 2002 World Cup and about half knew where the games were being held (Asia). Non-Hispanic respondents who were interested in the games seemed to focus more on the athletic ability of the participants; Hispanic respondents were also interested in athletic prowess, but indicated an important social dimension as well—the enjoyment of watching the games with family and friends. Overall, U.S. respondents believed the World Cup to be much less commercial than U.S. sporting events such as the Super Bowl. The group best able to correctly identify World Cup sponsors included younger (mostly in their teens) Hispanic consumers.[8] Basic research such as that conducted by Dentsu and McCann-Erickson and other agencies is important to the process of carrying out effective advertising campaigns for clients.

Marketing Research Companies

Many companies specialize in conducting marketing research. In the U.S., marketing research is a $5.5 billion industry—that's about $20 spent on research each year for every man, woman, and child in the U.S.[9] Worldwide, total revenues for the marketing research industry exceed $15 billion.[10] (And don't forget that these numbers don't reflect the research done by producers and advertising agencies.)

Although most specialized marketing research firms are small, a few are sizable enterprises. Research Window 1.3 shows the names, home countries, and revenues of the 10 largest marketing research firms in the world. Some firms provide syndicated research; they collect certain information on a regular basis, which they then sell to interested clients. The syndicated services include such operations as VNU Inc., which provides product-movement data for grocery stores and drugstores through its ACNielsen division, and Arbitron, which measures U.S. radio audiences. Such services are distinguished by the fact that their research is not custom designed except in the limited sense that the firm will perform special analyses for a client from the data it regularly collects. Other firms, though, specialize in custom-designed research. Some of these provide only a field service; they collect data and return the data-collection instruments directly to the research sponsor. Some are limited-service firms, which not only collect the data but also analyze them for the client. And some are full-service research suppliers, which help the client in the design of the research as well as in collecting and analyzing data. For example, GfK Custom Research Inc. (CRI) provides full-service customized research services for numerous *Fortune* 500 clients. CRI can conduct large-scale qualitative or quantitative studies from start to finish, utilizing a range of traditional techniques as well as online data collection.

Other organizations that provide or conduct marketing research include government agencies, trade associations, and universities. Government agencies provide much marketing information in the form of published statistics. In fact, the federal government is the largest producer of marketing facts through its various censuses and other publications. Trade associations often collect and share data gathered from members. Much university-sponsored research of interest to marketers is produced by the marketing faculty or by the bureaus of business research found

The World's 10 Largest Marketing Research Firms

Rank/Organization	Parent Country	Global Research Revenues (U.S. $ in millions)
1. VNU NV	Netherlands	$2,400.0
2. IMS Health, Inc.	U.S.	1,171.0
3. WPP plc	U.K.	1,006.9
4. Taylor Nelson Sofres plc	U.K.	813.2
5. Information Resources, Inc.	U.S.	555.9
6. GfK Group	Germany	479.6
7. NFO Worldgroup Inc.	U.S.	452.9
8. Ipsos Group SA	France	429.9
9. NOP World	U.K.	324.7
10. Westat, Inc.	U.S.	285.8

Source: Developed from information in "Honomichl Global Top 25," *Marketing News* (August 19, 2002), pp. H1–H28. This report also describes the services provided by these and the remaining 25 largest research organizations.

in many schools of business. Faculty research is often reported in marketing journals, while research bureaus often publish monographs on various topics of interest.

Job Opportunities in Marketing Research

Employment opportunities for those interested in a career in marketing research continue to be good. Employment is expected to grow faster than the average for all occupations through 2010. Why is this? The demand for information continues to grow—and so will the demand for individuals who can collect, analyze, and interpret this information. In general, however, opportunities will be stronger for those with graduate degrees than for those with only undergraduate degrees. Competition is usually stiff for the relatively limited number of entry-level positions available for which those without graduate degrees will qualify.[11]

3 List some of the skills that are important for careers in marketing research.

Types of Jobs in Marketing Research

There are many different kinds of tasks that a marketing researcher might perform. Depending upon whether one works for a producer, an advertising agency, a marketing research firm, or some other type of organization, the type and scope of jobs available can vary greatly. In smaller companies, researchers are likely to be exposed to a greater variety of tasks, simply out of necessity. In larger firms, the work may tend to be more specialized for each employee. The responsibilities of a marketing researcher could range from the simple tabulation of questionnaire responses to the management of a large research department. Research Window 1.4 lists some common job titles and the functions typically performed by persons in these positions.

As shown in these job descriptions, there are opportunities in marketing research for people with a variety of skills. There is room for technical specialists, such as statisticians, as well as for research generalists, whose skills are relevant to managing the people and resources needed for a research project rather than the mathematical detail any study may involve. The skills required to perform each job satisfactorily will, of course, vary.

In consumer-goods companies, the typical entry-level position is research analyst, usually for a specific brand. While learning the characteristics and details of the industry, the analyst will receive on-the-job training from a research manager. The usual career path for an analyst is to advance to senior analyst, then research supervisor, and on to research manager for a specific brand. At that time the researcher's responsibilities often broaden to include a group of brands.

Courtesy of President, Teenage Research Unlimited

Peter Zollo is president of Teenage Research Unlimited. Zollo assists the marketing departments in companies such as MTV, Nike, and Procter & Gamble by selling insights on the teen mind. He claims that teenagers are not a homogenous group but are highly stratified into groups—the "edge" teens, who set trends but have no interest in anything mainstream; the "influencers," who edit the trends of the edgy teens; and the "conformers" or the mainstream teens, the biggest group, who follow the trends set by the influencers.

Among research suppliers, the typical entry-level position is research trainee, a position in which the person will be exposed to the types of studies in which the supplier specializes and to the procedures required for completing them. Quite often, trainees will spend some time actually conducting interviews, coding completed data-collection forms, or possibly even assisting with the analysis. The goal is to expose trainees to the processes the firm follows so that when they become account representatives, they will be familiar enough with the firm's capabilities to respond intelligently to clients' needs for research information.

The requirements for entering the marketing research field include human-relations, communication, conceptual, and analytical skills. Marketing researchers need to be able to interact effectively with others and they need to be good communicators, both orally and in writing. They need to understand business in general and marketing processes in particular. When dealing with brand, advertising, sales, or other types of managers, they need to have some understanding of the issues with which these managers contend and the types of mental models the managers use to make sense of situations. Marketing researchers also should have basic numerical and statistical skills, or at least they should have the capacity to develop those skills. They must be comfortable with numbers and with the techniques of marketing research. Their growth as professionals and their advancement within their organization will depend upon their use of these skills and acquiring other technical, management, and financial skills.

For marketing researchers working for producers, it is not uncommon to switch from research to product or brand management at some point in the career path. One advantage these people possess is that after working so closely with marketing intelligence, they often know more about the customers, the industry, and the competitors than anyone in the company with the same years of experience. Note, though, that researchers desiring such a switch need to develop more knowledge about marketing and business in general than those who plan to stay in marketing research, although all researchers need a good foundation of business and marketing knowledge if they are going to succeed.

Successful marketing researchers tend to be proactive rather than reactive; that is, they tend to identify and lead the direction in which the individual studies and overall programs go rather than simply respond to explicit requests for information. Successful marketing researchers realize that marketing research is conducted for one primary reason—to help make better marketing decisions. Thus, they are comfortable in the role of staff person making recommendations to others rather than having responsibility for the decisions themselves.

Why Study Marketing Research?

List three reasons for studying marketing research.

Almost all business schools offer courses in marketing research, and many require students who are completing majors in marketing to take a marketing research course. Why is this the case?

There are at least three important reasons for a business student to be exposed to marketing research training. First, some students will discover that marketing research can be rewarding and fun. For these students, initial training in how to be an "information detective" may lead to further study and a career in marketing research. These students usually develop an immediate appreciation for the power and responsibility involved in taking pre-existing or

1. **Research Director/Vice President of Marketing Research:** This is the senior position in research. The director is responsible for the entire research program of his company. Accepts assignments from superiors, from clients, or may, on own initiative, develop and propose research undertakings to company executives. Employs personnel and executes general supervision of research department. Presents research findings to clients or to company executives.

2. **Assistant Director of Research:** This position usually represents a defined "second in command," a senior staff member having responsibilities above those of other staff members.

3. **Statistician/Data Processing Specialist:** Duties are usually those of an expert consultant on theory and applications of statistical technique to specific research problems. Usually responsible for experimental design and data processing.

4. **Senior Analyst:** Usually found in larger research departments. Participates with superior in initial planning of research projects, and directs execution of projects assigned. Operates with minimum supervision. Prepares or works with analysts in preparing questionnaires. Selects research techniques, makes analyses, and writes final report. Budgetary control over projects and primary responsibility for meeting time schedules rests with the senior analyst.

5. **Analyst:** The analyst usually handles the bulk of the work required for execution of research projects. Often works under senior analyst's supervision. The analyst assists in questionnaire preparation, pretests them, and makes preliminary analyses of results. Most of the library research or work with company data is handled by the analyst.

6. **Junior Analyst:** Working under rather close supervision, junior analysts handle routine assignments. Editing and coding of questionnaires, statistical calculations above the clerical level, and simpler forms of library research are among their duties. A large portion of the junior analyst's time is spent on tasks assigned by superiors.

7. **Librarian:** The librarian builds and maintains a library of reference sources adequate to the needs of the research department.

8. **Clerical Supervisor:** In larger departments, the central handling and processing of statistical data are the responsibilities of one or more clerical supervisors. Duties include work scheduling and responsibility for accuracy.

9. **Field Work Director:** Usually only larger departments have a field work director, who hires, trains, and supervises field interviewers.

10. **Full-time Interviewer:** The interviewer conducts personal interviews and works under direct supervision of the field work director. Few companies employ full-time interviewers.

11. **Tabulating and Clerical Help:** The routine, day-to-day work of the department is performed by these individuals. ■

Source: Thomas C. Kinnear and Ann R. Root, *1994 Survey of Marketing Research,* 1995, p. 93. Reprinted with permission from American Marketing Association, Chicago, Ill. 60606.

new data and converting them into information that can be used by marketing managers to make important decisions. Thus, for some students at least, the study of marketing research will be directly relevant to their careers.

Most students will not go on to careers in marketing research; why should they study marketing research? We are all consumers of marketing and public opinion research, almost on a daily basis. The second important reason for studying marketing research, therefore, is to learn to be a *smart* consumer of marketing research results. Businesspeople are often exposed to research results, usually by someone trying to convince them to do something. Suppliers will use research to promote the virtues of their particular products and services; advertising agencies will use research to encourage a company to promote a product in particular media vehicles; product managers inside a firm will use research to demonstrate the likely demand for the products they are developing to get further funding. Effective managers, however, do not take research results at face value, but instead know the important questions to ask to determine the likely validity of the results.

A third key reason for studying marketing research is to gain an appreciation of the process, what it can and cannot do. As a manager, you will need to know what to expect marketing research to be able to deliver. While marketing research is an essential business function, the process of gathering data and generating information is full of opportunities for error to slip into the results. Thus, no research is perfect, and managers must take this into account when making decisions. Managers also need to understand what they are asking of researchers when requesting marketing research. The process is detailed, time-consuming, and requires great amounts of thought and effort. As a result, marketing research is costly to an organization and should *not* be undertaken on trivial issues or to support decisions that have already been made.

looking back...

Erik and Paul were correct to say that learning about customers is important to a business's success. During the dot-com boom and bust of the last decade, many of the companies that failed had never adequately researched and tested their ideas. Often, e-commerce start-ups got funding because of investors' eagerness to profit from the Internet boom, but many of these companies didn't last because they lacked a profitable level of customer interest. Now, in an economy that has slowed, the only successful companies are the ones that build and maintain strong customer relationships. Such relationships require information about customers.

Marketing research can answer some of the most basic questions related to business success: Does our business strategy meet a need? Who are our customers? Where are they? What do they care about? How much will they pay? Where will they shop? Do the people our company serves see and hear our advertising? Are buyers satisfied with our company's products and customer service? What do they think about our competitors?

Kelli is correct to think that answering such questions can be expensive. Large companies, especially consumer products giants, need to learn about a national and international customer base. They hire full-service marketing research firms to help them answer these questions in detail. However, as future chapters will discuss, marketing research includes a wide variety of activities. Some of these are practical even for the owner of a small business. Large and small companies alike need managers who can apply the most appropriate marketing research alternatives.

As Kelli talked with her friends, she began to appreciate the potential of marketing research.

"What I was planning to do," she explained, "is to find out which businesses have a lot of international activity. I think I can find information about that on the Web. And I was going to learn about those businesses and try to figure out which departments and which positions would need the most help with translations."

"You can also try to find out what their pet peeves are," suggested Sarah. "Then you can tell them why your service will be better."

"So you *are* going to do research," said Paul. "You're talking about researching companies online and interviewing potential customers."

"I just never thought of that as marketing research," replied Kelli. "Sarah, let me know if that marketing research course turns out to be a good one. It sounds like that's a course I'll be needing, too." ∎

Sources: Leigh Buchanan, "Early to Web," *Inc.* (December 2002), pp. 80-82, 84, 86; PilgrimDesigns Web site (http://www.pilgrimdesigns.com), downloaded January 31, 2003; Jerry W. Thomas, "Skipping MR a Major Error," *Marketing News* (March 4, 2002), p. 50; Keith Malo and Mark Marone, "Corporate Strategy Requires Market Research," *Marketing News* (January 21, 2002), p. 14.

Summary

Learning Objective 1
Define marketing research.
Marketing research is the function that links the consumer to the marketer through information. The information is used to identify and define marketing problems; generate, refine, and evaluate marketing actions; monitor marketing performance; and improve understanding of marketing as a process.

Learning Objective 2
Discuss different kinds of firms that conduct marketing research.
Producers of products and services often have marketing research departments and gather information relevant to the particular products and services they produce and the industry in which they operate. Advertising agencies often conduct research, primarily to test advertising and measure its effectiveness. Marketing research companies are in business to conduct research; some focus on very specific topics or aspects of the research process, while others are more general in focus.

Learning Objective 3
List some of the skills that are important for careers in marketing research.
Most positions in marketing research require analytical, communication, and human-relations skills. In addition, marketing researchers must be comfortable working with numbers and statistical techniques, and they must be familiar with a great variety of marketing research methods.

Learning Objective 4
List three reasons for studying marketing research.
(1) Some students pursue careers in marketing research; (2) almost everyone is a consumer of marketing research in one way or another and needs to be able to know how to evaluate the likely validity of the research; and (3) managers must understand what marketing research can and cannot do, as well as what is involved in the process of conducting research.

Key Term

marketing research (page 6)

Review Questions

1. What is marketing management? What is the task of marketing research? Is there any relation between these two?
2. How is marketing research defined? What are the key elements of this definition?
3. Who does marketing research? What are the primary kinds of research done by each enterprise?
4. Why did marketing research begin to experience real growth after World War II?
5. In a large research department, who would be responsible for specifying the objective of a research project? For deciding on specific procedures to be followed? For designing the questionnaire? For analyzing the results? For reporting the results to top management?
6. What are the necessary skills for employment in a junior or entry-level marketing research position? Do the skills change as one changes job levels? If so, what new skills are necessary at the higher levels?

Discussion Questions, Problems, and Projects

1. Indicate whether marketing research is relevant to each of the following organizations and, if so, how each might use it.
   (a) Pepsico, Inc.
   (b) Your university
   (c) CitiBank
   (d) The American Cancer Society
   (e) A small dry cleaner

2. Specify some useful sources of marketing research information for the following situation. Ethan Moore has worked for several years as the head chef in a restaurant specializing in ethnic cuisine. Dissatisfied with his income, he has decided to start his own business. Based on his experiences in the restaurant, he recognizes a need for a local wholesale distributor specializing in hard-to-find ethnic foodstuffs. He envisions starting a firm that will handle items commonly used in Asian and African recipes.

   With the help of a local accountant, Moore prepared a financial proposal that revealed the need for $150,000 in start-up capital for Ethan's Ethnic Foods. The proposal was presented to a local bank for review by their commercial loan committee, and Moore subsequently received the following letter from the bank:

   Mr. Moore:

   We have received and considered your request for start-up financing for your proposed business. While the basic idea seems sound, we find that your sales projections are based solely on your own experience and do not include any hard documentation concerning the market potential for the products you propose to carry. Until such information is made available for our consideration, we must reject your loan application.

   Bitten hard by the entrepreneurial bug, Moore views this rejection as a minor setback. Given his extremely limited financial resources, where and how might he obtain the needed information? (Hint: First determine what types of information would be useful.)

3. What do the following two research situations have in common?

   Situation I: The Bugs-Away Company marketed successful insect repellents. The products were effective and leaders in the market. They were available in blue aerosol cans with red caps. The instructions, in addition to a warning to keep the product away from children, were clearly specified on the container. Most of the company's range of products were also produced in similar containers by competitors. The CEO of Bugs-Away was worried because of declining sales and shrinking profit margins. Another issue of concern was that companies such as hers were being severely criticized by government and consumer groups for their use of aerosol cans. The CEO contacted the company's advertising agency and requested that it do the necessary research to find out what was happening.

   Situation II: In early 1990 the directors of Adams University were considering an expansion of the business school due to increasing enrollments over the past 10 years. Their plans included constructing a new wing, hiring five new faculty members, and increasing the number of scholarships from 100 to 120. The funding for this ambitious project was to be provided by some private sources, internally generated funds, and the state and federal governments. A prior research study (completed in 1981), using a sophisticated forecasting methodology, indicated that student enrollment would peak in 1989. Another study, conducted in November 1983, indicated that universities could expect gradual declining enrollments during the mid-1990s. The directors were concerned about the results of the later study and the talk it stimulated about budget cuts by the government. A decision was made to conduct a third and final study to determine likely student enrollment.

4. What do the following two research situations have in common?

   Situation I: The sales manager of Al-Can, an aluminum can manufacturing company, was delighted with the increase in sales over the past few months. He wondered whether the company's new cans, which would be on the market in two months, should be priced higher than the traditional products. He confidently commented to the vice president of marketing, "Nobody in the market is selling aluminum cans with screw-on tops. We can get a small portion of the market and yet make substantial profits." The product manager disagreed with this strategy. In fact, she was opposed to marketing these new cans. The cans might present problems in preserving the contents. She thought to herself, "Aluminum cans are recycled, so nobody is going to keep them as containers." There was little she could do formally because these cans were the president's own idea. She strongly recommended to the vice president of marketing that the cans should be priced in line with the other products. The vice president thought a marketing research study would resolve this issue.

Situation II: A large toy manufacturer was in the process of developing a tool kit for children in the five-to-10-year age group. The tool kit included a small saw, screwdriver, hammer, chisel, and drill. This tool kit was different from the competitors', as it included an instruction manual with "101 things to do." The product manager was concerned about the safety of the kit and recommended the inclusion of a separate booklet for parents. The sales manager recommended that the tool kit be made available in a small case, as this would increase its marketability. The advertising manager recommended that a special promotional campaign be launched in order to distinguish it from the competitor's products. The vice president thought that all the recommendations were worthwhile but that the costs would increase drastically. He consulted the marketing research manager, who further recommended that a study be conducted.

5. List the key attributes that an individual occupying the following positions must possess. Why are these attributes essential?
   (a) Senior analyst
   (b) Full-time interviewer
   (c) Research director

6. Suppose that you have decided to pursue a career in the field of marketing research. In general, what types of courses should you take in order to help yourself achieve your goal? Why? What types of part-time jobs and/or volunteer work would look good on your resume? Why?

Suggested Additional Readings

For a discussion of what is happening in the world of marketing research, see Jack Honomichl, "Honomichl Top 50: Annual Business Report on The Marketing Research Industry," *Marketing News* (June 10, 2002), pp. H1–H44.

Jack Honomichl, "Honomichl Global Top 25," *Marketing News* (August 19, 2002), pp. H1–H28.

Chapter 2

Gathering Marketing Intelligence

Learning Objectives

1   *Explain the difference between a project emphasis in research and a systems emphasis.*

2   *Define what is meant by a marketing information system (MIS) and a decision support system (DSS).*

3   *Describe the networking of modern information systems.*

4   *Identify the components of a decision support system.*

5   *Discuss trends in the gathering of marketing intelligence.*

E stella reflected on the presentation she had just left. Stan, her company's chief information officer, had described the benefits of installing customer relations management software—CRM for short. That system would collect data about every customer contact, from sales calls through payments. Estella recalled Stan's conclusion: "Today, Total Insurance is lagging behind the business world in information technology. But with CRM, we can surpass our competitors in becoming customer focused."

Although the system was expensive, thought Estella, it would be a powerful source of information. With CRM, Total's employees would really know their customers. The system would add to the database whenever an agent visited a prospect, whenever a claim was filed, and whenever a client called with a question or applied for a policy. Stan had called these encounters with customers "touch points." According to Stan, insurance companies have more touch points than businesses in many other industries. For example, agents and other employees visit Total's largest commercial accounts several times a year. Logically, they should use these interactions as an opportunity to learn about customers.

Estella could see many uses for CRM data. Authorized employees could use CRM to answer questions ranging from which advertising campaigns produce more sales to which policies customers tend to buy as a package. Still, Estella wondered about Stan's recommendation that Total's own employees handle customer service calls, so customers' questions and problems could be included in the CRM system. Under her direction last year, Total had outsourced customer service to a call center, saving $2 million a year. Could collecting data about customers offer benefits of that magnitude?

Estella also recalled Stan's claim that a CRM system could help Total develop profitable new products, such as insurance policies serving the needs of particular industries. Using her Internet portal's link to industry news, she searched for articles about new insurance products. Other companies certainly had some innovations. American International Group had introduced coverage of risks related to e-commerce, and Hartford had even put together a property and liability policy for fish farmers. Estella realized that to be equally innovative, Total must be able to sort data by industry, and she doubted that the company's existing information systems could do so.

Estella left a message for Philip, her sales vice president. Later that afternoon, he called from the airport. After telling Philip about Stan's presentation, she asked, "If you had a system like that, how much do you think it would help?"

"A lot!" said Philip. "We could improve our use of time and get some hard data on performance. But don't you think CRM is missing some of the most important customer data?"

looking ahead...

Discussion Issues

1. How might a company use data about every customer interaction to support its marketing strategy?

2. From which people does a CRM system gather data? From what other important groups of people does the system *not* gather information?

3. How can other forms of research complement the use of a CRM system? ■

The preceding chapter suggested that the fundamental purpose of marketing research is to help managers make decisions they face each day in their various areas of responsibility. Marketing managers urgently need information, or marketing intelligence, as they carry out the firm's marketing activities. They might need to know about the changes that can be expected in customer purchasing patterns, which of several alternative product designs might be the most successful, the shape of the firm's demand curve, or any of a number of other issues that could affect the way they plan, solve problems, or evaluate and control the marketing effort. We suggested that marketing research is traditionally responsible for this intelligence function. As the formal link with the environment, marketing research generates, transmits, and interprets feedback regarding the success of the firm's marketing plans and the strategies and tactics used in implementing those plans.

Marketing research can meet the need for marketing intelligence in two basic ways:

1. By developing and executing projects that answer a specific problem;
2. By establishing systems that provide marketing intelligence and guide decision making on an ongoing basis.

Most of this book describes the first approach, called the project approach. The following chapter provides an overview of the steps involved in using research to address a specific problem. The remainder of the book then explores each step in detail. In contrast, this chapter examines the second approach, typically called the systems approach. The chapter begins by distinguishing a systems approach to marketing research from a project approach. The remainder of the chapter describes the kinds of systems marketers use for obtaining information and making decisions.

The Project Approach and the Systems Approach

1 Explain the difference between a project emphasis in research and a systems emphasis.

2 Define what is meant by a marketing information system (MIS) and a decision support system (DSS).

marketing information system (MIS)
A set of procedures and methods for the regular, planned collection, analysis, and presentation of information for use in making marketing decisions.

decision support system (DSS) A coordinated collection of data, systems, tools, and techniques with supporting software and hardware, by which an organization gathers and interprets relevant information from business and the environment and turns it into a basis for marketing decisions.

Although most discussions of marketing research focus on the project approach, both approaches are valuable. Both contribute information, but in different ways. Robert J. Williams, who created the first recognized marketing information system, described the difference this way: both sources of marketing intelligence illuminate the darkness, but the project approach is like a flashbulb, and the systems approach is like a candle.[1] A marketing research project can shed intense light on a particular issue at a particular time. In contrast, a marketing information system rarely shows all the details of a particular situation, but its glow is continuous, even as conditions change.

As this analogy suggests, one of the problems of the project emphasis is its nonrecurring nature. Often projects are devised in times of crisis and carried out with urgency. This pattern has led to an emphasis on data collection and analysis instead of the development of pertinent information on a regular basis. One suggestion for closing the gap is to think of management in terms of an ongoing process of decision making that requires a flow of regular input rather than in terms of waiting for crises. Today the usual mechanisms for doing this are some form of marketing information system and/or decision support system.

The earliest attempts at providing a steady flow of information input (that is, candlelight) were **marketing information systems (MIS).** An MIS is "a set of procedures and methods for the regular, planned collection, analysis, and presentation of information for use in making marketing decisions."[2] The key word in the definition is *regular,* because the emphasis in an MIS is to produce information on a steady basis rather than on the basis of one-time research studies.

In contrast to an MIS, which emphasizes the preparation of routine reports, a **decision support system (DSS)** includes software that allows managers to more fully utilize the available information to assist in making decisions. Formally defined, a DSS is "a coordinated collection of data, systems, tools, and techniques with supporting software and hardware, by which an organization gathers and interprets relevant information from business and the environment and turns it into a basis for marketing decisions."[3] Thus, besides storing information, the DSS provides models for analyzing that information—for example, creating tables or graphs of key data and seeing how a forecast changes if assumptions are changed.

DSSs and MISs are both concerned with improving information processing to enable better marketing decisions. A DSS differs from an MIS, though, in a number of ways:

PART 1:
Introduction to Marketing Research and Problem Definition

- A DSS tends to be aimed at the less well structured, underspecified problems that managers face rather than at problems that can be investigated using a relatively standard set of procedures and comparisons.
- A DSS combines the use of models and analytical techniques and procedures with the more traditional data access and retrieval functions of an MIS.
- A DSS specifically incorporates features that make it easy to use in an interactive mode by noncomputer people. These features include menu-driven procedures for doing an analysis and graphic display of the results. Regardless of how the interaction is structured, the systems can respond to users' information requests in real time, so that information is available when managers need it to make decisions.
- A DSS emphasizes flexibility and adaptability. It can accommodate different decision makers with diverse styles as well as changing environmental conditions.

Ideally, a marketing information system regularly provides the information marketers need for making decisions. Designers of such an MIS start with a detailed analysis of each decision maker who might use the system. They attempt to secure an accurate, objective assessment of each manager's decision-making responsibilities, capabilities, and style. They identify types of decisions each decision maker routinely makes, the types of information needed to make those decisions, the types of information the individual receives regularly, and the special studies that are periodically needed. The analysis also considers the improvements decision makers would like in the current information system, not only in the types of information they receive but also in the form in which they receive it.

Given these information specifications, system designers then attempt to specify, get approval for, and subsequently generate a series of reports that would go to the various decision makers. To complete these tasks, systems designers need to specify the data to be input into the system, how to secure and store the data, how to access and combine the data, and what the report formats will look like. Only after these analysis and design steps are completed can the system be constructed. Programmers write and document the programs, making data retrieval as efficient as possible in terms of computer time and memory. When all the procedures are debugged, it is put on-line, so managers with authorized access can request a report.

Limitations of Marketing Information Systems

When they were first proposed, MISs were regarded as the solution for information problems inside the firm. The reality, however, often fell short of the promise. Effective MIS or DSS systems are often difficult to implement, for several reasons. People tend to resist change, and with an MIS the changes are often substantial. Also, many decision makers are reluctant to disclose to others what factors they use and how they combine these factors when making a decision about a particular issue, and without such disclosure it is next to impossible to design reports that will give them the information they need in the form they need it.

Even when managers are willing to disclose their decision-making process and information needs, there are problems. Different managers typically emphasize different things and, consequently, have different data needs. There are very few report formats that are optimal for a variety of users. Either the developers have to design "compromise" reports that are satisfactory for a number of users, although not ideal for any single user, or they have to engage in the laborious task of programming to meet each user's needs, one at a time.

Moreover, the costs and time required to establish such systems are often underestimated, due to underestimating the size of the task, changes in organizational structure, key personnel, and electronic data-processing systems they require. By the time these systems can be developed, the personnel for which they are designed often have different responsibilities or the economic and competitive environments around which they are designed have changed. Thus, they are often obsolete soon after being put on-line, meaning that the whole process of analysis, design, development, and implementation has to be repeated.

Another fundamental problem with MISs is that the systems do not lend themselves to the solution of the kinds of problems managers typically face. Many of the activities performed by managers cannot be programmed, nor can they be performed routinely or delegated, because they involve personal choices. Because a manager's decision making is often ad hoc and involves unexpected choices, standardized reporting systems lack the necessary scope and flexibility to be useful. Nor can managers specify in advance what they want from programmers and model builders, because decision making and planning are often exploratory. As decision makers and their staffs learn more about a problem, their information needs and methods of analysis evolve. Further, decision making often involves exceptions and qualitative issues that are not easily programmed.

A final problem common to both MISs and DSSs is that they are limited to the data available in the system. No matter how colorful the report is or how easy the system is to use, if the right kinds of data are not collected in the first place, the system will be ineffective for guiding a current marketing decision. To some extent this problem is unavoidable; managers are constantly learning new things and applying them to their businesses. Before we know the value of various kinds of information, it is unlikely that we will include them in our databases. Sometimes, however, limited data availability indicates that MIS managers may not have done a thorough enough job of identifying the kinds of data that managers need to make good decisions.

Networking Information Systems

3 *Describe the networking of modern information systems.*

In the earliest days of MISs, managers obtained reports by requesting them from the company's computer or information systems department. Someone in the department would print the report and deliver it to the manager. Modern computer systems allow authorized users at all levels of an organization to get the information themselves, usually through some form of computer network. This empowers decision makers to get the information they need, when they need it, even if they suddenly and unexpectedly face new situations with new information requirements.

The older computer networks linked terminals or personal computers to a database in a mainframe. Such networks still exist in many companies, especially those with massive databases. Today's computer networks may also link a series of smaller computers within the company as well as connect to the Internet.

The *Internet*—an extensive global network of computers at government agencies, universities, businesses, and Internet access providers—was once limited to academicians and government employees sharing technological information. It has grown explosively in terms of the number of users and the kinds of information available. The Internet links

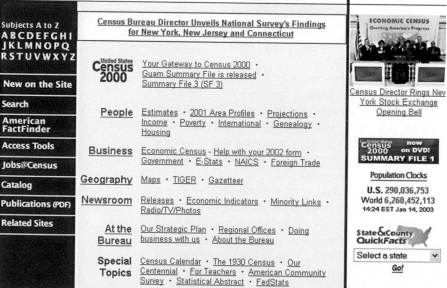

Courtesy of U.S. Census Bureau

The U.S. Census Bureau maintains a Web site at http://www.census.gov. At this site, users can access online data as well as order printed reports.

more than 440 million people from many countries.[4] Its popularity is due in part to the fact that access requires only a personal computer with the right software and modem plus an account with a service provider such as America Online.

Many Internet users browse the *World Wide Web,* a hypertext system that allows users to receive text, graphics, video, and sound. *Hypertext* allows one to jump to text and graphics by clicking on highlighted words and images. The Web's hypertext links may send users from the documents of one organization to those of another, perhaps in another part of the world. The World Wide Web boasts over 8 million Web sites, a number that continues to grow rapidly.[5]

The familiarity and capabilities of the Internet have inspired many organizations to apply its tools to their own computer networks. A growing number of organizations are setting up *intranets,* which apply such Web tools as hypertext links to internal computer networks. Similarly, *extranets* link authorized users in the organization, its suppliers, and customers, allowing them to share information as easily as they browse the World Wide Web. With both intranets and extranets, users can look up a variety of company data, from the past week's sales or the inventory level of a particular product to the production status of a particular order. The search engines that have been designed to search the Web have proven to be so useful that many companies have begun using them to manage their intranets and extranets. Companies use software called "firewalls" to prevent unauthorized computer users from accessing confidential data in the network. However, those using the intranet or extranet can use links that carry them outside the firewall to the rest of the Internet.

The Internet, and its intranet and extranet offspring, have given a whole new meaning to the idea of an information system. Today's computer users can look up not only data stored on the company's proprietary system but an astounding variety of free data from the government and, usually for a fee, data from industry and trade groups, publishers, and many other sources. Chapter 7 offers a more detailed look at some of these sources of data.

Decision Support Systems

As the problems with traditional MISs became more apparent, the emphasis in regularly supplied marketing intelligence changed from the production of preformatted batch reports to a decision support system (DSS). A DSS combines data systems, model systems, and dialog systems that can be used interactively (see Figure 2.1).

Identify the components of a decision support system.

Data Systems

The **data system** in a DSS includes the processes used to capture and store data coming from marketing, finance, and manufacturing, as well as information coming from any number of external or internal sources. The typical data system has modules containing customer information, general economic and demographic information, competitor information, and industry information, including market trends. Where do the data in a DSS originate? One recent survey of *Fortune* 500 companies indicated that 62% of the data come from internal accounting and data processing sources, with the remainder coming from marketing research and intelligence.[6]

Exhibit 2.1 shows the percentage of companies with marketing information systems that collect various types of information. In addition, it shows how much of the data is maintained in computerized form versus some other format. For example, of the companies that have marketing information systems, 82% collected information about the federal government. Sixty-three percent (63%) of the companies maintained information about the federal government in computer databases. The most common categories of data held relate to existing customers, prospective customers, competitors, and suppliers.

The exponential growth in computing power and the emergence of increasingly sophisticated data processing capabilities has led to a commensurate increase in the size of databases. While historically a business's databases contained current information, many new ones contain historical information as well. These "data warehouses" literally dwarf those available even a few years ago. For example, Wal-Mart has a data warehouse storing transaction information about each of Wal-Mart's over 4,000 stores in nine countries. Wal-Mart uses the information to select products that need replenishment, analyze seasonal buying patterns, examine customer buying trends, select markdowns, and react to merchandise volume and movement.[7]

data system
The part of a decision support system that includes the processes used to capture and the methods used to store data coming from a number of external and internal sources.

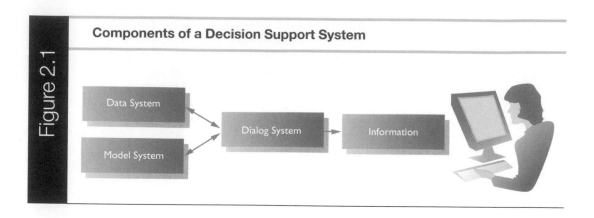

Figure 2.1

Components of a Decision Support System

Data System

Model System

Dialog System

Information

Exhibit 2.1

Percent of Firms Collecting Various Types of Data

Type of Data	Maintained in Computer	Maintained, but Not Computerized*	Total
Existing customers	97	3	100
Competitors	68	29	97
Suppliers	77	10	87
Prospects	71	16	87
Federal Government	63	19	82
Local Government	54	27	81
State Government	54	27	81
National Economy	42	33	75
State Economy	26	39	65
Local Economy	32	32	64
Global Economy	20	40	60
Foreign Governments	18	36	54

*Percent of companies that report maintaining an MIS/DSS.
Source: Reprinted from *Information & Management,* 38, Eldon Y. Li, Raymond McLeod Jr., and John C. Rogers, "Marketing Information Systems in *Fortune* 500 Companies: A Longitudinal Analysis of 1980, 1990, and 2000," (2001), p. 313, with permission of Elsevier.

Besides company data, the data system may retrieve information from online databases. A significant trend affecting DSSs is the explosion in the number of such databases. Thousands of databases can now be accessed online via computer, as compared with less than nine hundred in 1980. The insights managers can gather from commercially available databases are mind-boggling, and dwarf the possibilities of even a half-dozen years ago. Research Window 2.1, for example, highlights some of the information available on the Internet.

Lycos and IntelliSeek teamed up to offer Internet users access to over 7,400 databases and other information sources. To retrieve information with this service, called Invisible Web Catalog, you visit their Web site (http://www.invisibleweb.com) and type in the terms you want to look up. The service then displays a list of documents and databases containing that term. Invisible Web Catalog differs from other Internet search engines in its use of IntelliSeek's technology for indexing databases with formats that had not previously been indexable (for example, those with a proprietary format).[8]

As the number of databases has expanded, so too has public concern with the issue of privacy and if, and how, people's right to privacy is being violated in the generation and sharing of these databases. Research Window 2.2 describes the controversy over automated generation

From the U.S. Bureau of the Census to Dun & Bradstreet, most of the traditional suppliers of marketing and other business information now provide access to that information on the Internet. Some of the information can be downloaded free. You can download other data in exchange for a subscription fee or item-by-item charges. In still other cases, you can order print publications or CDs and have them shipped to you.

Web Portals   Most visitors to the Internet start at a Web portal, an indexing and search site where users enter the World Wide Web. Examples include the Microsoft Network (http://www.msn.com), Netscape Netcenter (http://home.netscape.com/), and Yahoo! (http://www.yahoo.com). At the portal, you can type in the URL (Internet "address") for a Web site you want to visit or use hypertext links to selected information sources. You can also use a search engine such as Google or Lycos to find information about particular companies or topics.

CEO Express   A portal designed especially for businesspeople is CEO Express (http://www.ceoexpress.com). This site is especially helpful for novice Internet researchers, because it lists a wealth of links to major business-related sites such as these:

- Newspapers, news magazines, television networks, and news wires
- Business and technology magazines
- Search engines for researching particular topics or locating organizations' Web sites
- Sources of company data, including annual reports, listings of the *Fortune* 500 and *Inc.* 100, rating services, and stock quotes
- Government agencies, including the Patent and Trademark Office, Internal Revenue Service, and Library of Congress
- Reports of research into Internet usage and on-line marketing.

Yellow Pages   To find names and addresses of companies, such as competitors or potential distributors, you can visit an on-line yellow pages. For example, at the Netscape Netcenter's yellow pages service (at http://yp.netscape.com), you can look up addresses and phone numbers by company name or category (for example, autos or computers). You can also specify that the search be limited to a particular geographic region (city, state, country).

Securities and Exchange Commission   If you want information about particular companies, you can start with the reports they file with the Securities and Exchange Commission. Visit the SEC's Web site (http://www.sec.gov).

Dun and Bradstreet   For more company details—including facts about privately held companies, which don't have to file documents with the SEC—visit the Dun & Bradstreet Web site (http://www.dnb.com). You can order CD-ROMs and directories drawn from D&B's database on more than 15 million U.S. companies or from its global database on more than 70 million companies worldwide. D&B also offers publications on a variety of topics, including marketing and particular industries.

Moody's   Rating firms such as Moody's Investors Service examine company performance and industry trends and rate companies for investment purposes. You can get ratings and other information from Moody's at its Web site (http://www.moodys.com).

Patents and Trademarks   If you are developing a new product, you will need information about patents and trademarks. You can get reports, forms, and other information from the U.S. Patent and Trademark Office at its Web site (http://www.uspto.gov).

The Census Bureau   Vast amounts of data collected from the various U.S. Censuses are available on-line at http://www.census.gov or by placing an order at the Web site. Want to know the number of pharmacies in Rankin County, Mississippi? You can find the number here. Also contains updated reports since the last census. ∎

Courtesy of Warren Roos/Executive Technology

RF (radio frequency) systems are a wireless form of data capture that is evolving rapidly. The systems, attached to lift trucks or wrists, pinpoint deliveries, control inventories, and provide marketing information better than ever before. Shoppers can use portable scanners to record purchases as they fill their carts.

of detailed data about individuals' Internet usage. Much of this controversy arises because people are asked to provide data without full information about how it will be used. Yahoo! recently angered customers by informing them that unless a customer specifically instructed them not to do it, the company would assume that the customer wanted to receive advertising via email, regular mail, or telephone. As a result of privacy concerns that result from actions like this, legislative efforts are underway in the U.S. and Europe to tighten online privacy.[9]

The privacy problem is not limited to consumers, either. Companies in extranets and other information-sharing arrangements routinely share detailed data. Like consumers, they do not always know every use to which the data are put.

Boston-based Newbury Comics depends on its forward-looking knowledge of music to keep its music stores competitive with the retailing giants. Mike Dreese, co-owner of the business, was therefore shocked to learn that he was inadvertently sharing his insights. He was reporting each store's weekly sales, by label and artist, to SoundScan, a firm that specializes in gathering such data from most of the music retailers in the United States. Retailers providing data to SoundScan receive more favorable treatment from the recording companies. Dreese knew that SoundScan uses the data to prepare reports for recording labels, promoters, and managers. What surprised him were comments from a rack jobber (a type of intermediary), boasting that his company was buying detailed data from SoundScan to support giant retailers like Wal-Mart and Kmart by stocking what would be the hottest albums in particular regions. Especially because of its position as a trendsetter, Newbury Comics was apparently providing data that helped its toughest competitors. After some hard thinking about the consequences, Dreese decided that Newbury Comics would no longer provide data to SoundScan.[10]

Beyond protection of privacy, an important criterion for adding a particular piece of data to a database is whether it is useful for marketing decision making. The basic task of a DSS is to capture relevant marketing data in reasonable detail and to put those data in a truly accessible form. It is crucial that the database management capabilities built into the system can logically organize the data the same way a manager does, regardless of the form that organization assumes.

Model Systems

model system
The part of a decision support system that includes all the routines that allow the user to manipulate the data so as to conduct the kind of analysis the individual desires.

The **model system** in a DSS includes all the routines that allow the user to manipulate the data in order to conduct the kind of analysis he desires. Whenever managers look at data, they have a preconceived idea of how something works and, therefore, what is interesting and worthwhile in the data. These ideas are called *models*.[11] Most managers also want to manipulate data to gain a better understanding of a marketing issue. These manipulations are called *procedures*. The routines for manipulating the data may run the gamut from summing a set of numbers, to conducting a complex statistical analysis, to finding an optimization strategy using some kind of nonlinear programming routine. At the same time, "the most frequent

Too Much Marketing Intel-ligence?

Privacy advocates howled when Intel launched its Pentium III computer chips. The chips were designed to contain so-called processor serial numbers that could uniquely identify each computer's online communications.

Intel expected that the 96-digit serial number would be a boon to marketers by providing extra security, because it could be used to verify computer users' identity. The company also thought consumers might be glad to get the feature. The serial number could prevent problems arising from mistakes when the consumer enters personal information. It could also discourage fraudulent use of consumers' credit card numbers or passwords. In addition, Intel thought the serial number would help organizations manage their computer networks.

Nevertheless, many consumers were up-set that they would be providing information about themselves without first being asked for it. Intel quickly responded to the deluge of criticism. It modified its chip to enable users to deactivate the ID system.

A spokesperson for the American Civil Liberties Union praised Intel's decision. Still, the criticism has continued in other quarters. The Center for Democracy and Technology filed a complaint with the Federal Trade Commission. The center and other privacy advocates worry that popular Web sites may deny access to computers with a deactivated ID. They also contend that consumers may get so used to the idea of the serial numbers that they may eventually treat them as a routine aspect of life in cyberspace—disclosing their online habits without much thought. ■

Sources: Robert O'Harrow, Jr., and Elizabeth Corcoran, "Intel Drops Plans to Activate Chip IDs," *Washington Post* (January 26, 1999, downloaded from the Washington Post Internet archives, http://search.washingtonpost.com, February 9, 1999); James Lardner, "Intel Even More Inside," *U.S. News & World Report* (February 8, 1999), p. 43; Dan Goodin, "More Support for Pentium III Complaint," CNET News.com (April 8, 1999, downloaded from CNET Web site, http://www.news.com, June 7, 1999).

operations are basic ones: segregating numbers into relevant groups, aggregating them, taking ratios, ranking them, picking out exceptional cases, plotting and making tables."[12]

The BayCare Health System, an alliance of not-for-profit community hospitals in west central Florida, developed a decision support system designed to provide managers (corporate and medical) with key information for making decisions about specific healthcare programs for the communities it served. The system tracks a large number of indicators, ranging from community socioeconomic indicators to behavioral risk factors and has been used to identify specific problem areas among the communities covered by the program. For example, several communities with unusually high levels of deaths due to stroke were identified. When follow-up research indicated the problem of lack of transportation among the elderly, minority, and low-income populations in these areas, a Mobile Medical Unit was developed to deliver medical services and prevention/education services to the affected groups.[13]

More sophisticated models for manipulating data are being developed all the time, often for relatively specific purposes. For example, decision support systems have been developed to enable brand managers to make better marketing mix decisions for their brands; to help bankers make stronger credit management decisions; to guide managers when they make new product development decisions; and to assess alternative marketing plans for motion pictures before they are released.[14]

The explosion in recent years in the number of databases available and the size of some of them has triggered a commensurate need for ways to efficiently analyze them. For example, store scanners provide massive amounts of data to marketing managers in packaged goods companies. The huge amounts of data require a great amount of time for even a well-trained analyst to come up with simple summaries that show the major trends. In response, a number of firms have developed **expert systems**—computer-based, artificial intelligence systems that attempt to model how experts in the area process information to solve the problem at hand.[15]

expert system
A computer-based, artificial intelligence system that attempts to model how experts in the area process information to solve the problem at hand.

Dialog Systems

dialog system
The part of a decision support system that permits users to explore the databases by employing the system models to produce reports that satisfy their particular information needs. Also called language system.

The element of a DSS that clearly differentiates it from an MIS is its **dialog system,** also called a *language system.* Dialog systems permit managers who are not programmers themselves to explore the databases by using the system models to produce reports that satisfy their own particular information needs. The reports can be tabular or graphic, and the formats can be specified by individual managers. The dialog systems can be passive, which means that the analysis possibilities are presented to the decision makers for selection via menu, a few simple keystrokes, light pen, or a mouse, or they can be active, requiring the users to state their requests in a command mode.

A key feature is that managers and employees, instead of funneling their data requests through a team of programmers, can conduct their analyses by themselves sitting at a computer using the dialog system. This allows them to target the information they want and not be overwhelmed with irrelevant data. They can ask a question and, on the basis of the answer, ask a subsequent question, and then another, and another, and so on.

As the availability of online databases has increased, so too has the need for better dialog systems. The dialog systems are what puts data at the decision maker's fingertips. While that sounds simple enough, it is in fact a difficult task because of the large amount of data available, the speed with which they hit a company, and the fact that they come from a variety of sources.

One way to handle these problems is distributed network computing. Such systems make use of a common interface or server. Through that server, the analyst can do data entry, data query, spreadsheet analysis, plots, statistical analysis, or even report preparation, all through simple commands (see Figure 2.2). The technical term for this capability is *data mining,* and businesses hope it will allow them to boost sales and profits by better understanding their customers.

A typical approach to data mining uses a supercomputer to link a number of personal computers. Decision makers at their PCs pose their questions, and the supercomputer tackles

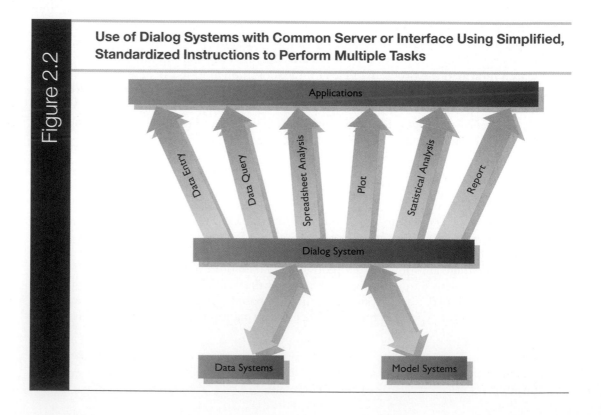

Figure 2.2

Use of Dialog Systems with Common Server or Interface Using Simplified, Standardized Instructions to Perform Multiple Tasks

Applications

Data Entry · Data Query · Spreadsheet Analysis · Plot · Statistical Analysis · Report

Dialog System

Data Systems   Model Systems

them with parallel processing, which breaks down questions into smaller computational tasks to perform simultaneously. A computer using parallel processing can readily work through trillions of pieces of data, slashing problem-solving time from weeks or months to days or hours. For example, Fingerhut Companies, a Minnetonka, Minnesota, catalog retailer, used data mining to target a promotional effort. The company's computer sorted through six trillion characters of data to learn which of its 25 million customers had recently purchased outdoor furniture and thus might also be interested in a new gas grill.[16]

Trends in Obtaining Marketing Intelligence

There is no question that the explosion in databases, computer hardware and software for accessing those databases, and the Internet are all changing the way marketing intelligence is obtained. Not only are more companies building DSSs, but those that have them are becoming more sophisticated in using them for general business and competitive intelligence.

5 Discuss trends in the gathering of marketing intelligence.

Chief Information Officers and Chief Knowledge Officers

The sophistication in the design and uses of decision support systems opens up access to so much data that higher-level management of information becomes critical. An executive in charge of information can ensure that it is used in support of strategic thinking. In many organizations, this function is now the responsibility of a chief information officer, or CIO.

The CIO's major role is to run the company's information and computer systems like a business. The CIO serves as the liaison between the firm's top management and its information systems department. He or she is responsible for planning, coordinating, and controlling the use of the firm's information resources, and is much more concerned with the firm's outlook than with the daily activities of the department. CIOs typically know more about the business in general than the managers of the information system departments, who are often stronger technically. In many cases, the managers of the information system department report directly to the CIO.

When falling sales awakened Levi Strauss to the need to build closer ties to consumers, CIO Linda Glick and her team evaluated the ways in which individual consumers interact directly with the company—at its Web site and through its Original Spin service, which allows customers in stores to have their measurements taken so that they can order individually customized jeans. In addition, Glick oversaw the restructuring of the information technology divisions in North America, Europe, and Asia so that its people worked more directly with Levi's employees in business departments such as design and marketing. The objective of the restructuring was to have IT employees act as internal consultants to the departments.[17] This example demonstrates both the increasingly important role of information in the management of a company and the increasing power of those who manage the information collection and dissemination process.

A growing number of companies are extending the idea of information systems management to include management of the knowledge that resides inside its employees' heads. One of an organization's greatest assets can be what its people know about customers, its products, and its marketplace. However, few companies yet have a way to make that information widely available to those who can use it. **Knowledge management** is an effort to systematically collect that information and make it accessible to others.

Oil giant BP Amoco has documented hundreds of millions of dollars in savings from applying knowledge management. Its strategy is to identify projects that can most benefit from the effort and then to apply a variety of tactics. Before launching a project, the company conducts a two-day meeting at which people who have done a similar project describe what they have learned. After the project, brief and in-depth reviews analyze what happened and what was learned. Information from the meeting and reviews go into a Web-based folder that includes

knowledge management
The systematic collection of employee knowledge about customers, products, and the marketplace.

© Richard Shock/Index Stock Imagery

After a marketing research project is completed, many companies meet to review and analyze what was learned from the endeavor. The knowledge they gain can be shared with other employees and applied to future projects. A CKO is often responsible for leading this effort.

hypertext links to people who have relevant information to share. In addition, the company's intranet offers an in-house yellow pages of people who have volunteered to share information on specific topics.[18]

Companies that adopt knowledge management may assign responsibility for the effort to a chief knowledge officer, or CKO. Typically, a CKO is responsible for the ways an organization manages and shares, not just explicit information, but also those bits of knowledge that experienced people may use without giving much conscious thought to them. Carrying out this type of information sharing requires getting the organization's people to recognize and communicate what they know. Thus, it is not surprising that a study by the London Business School found that technological skills are less important to a CKO than to a traditional CIO, and people-related skills are more important.[19]

Linking Marketing Intelligence to Other Business Intelligence

Another way in which powerful information systems are influencing the direction of marketing intelligence is in the blurring of distinctions between types of information management. When an organization's computer could handle only enough data for a single function's decision support system, each function needed a separate system with a separate database. However, today more and more companies are enjoying the benefits of sharing data among the various functions and levels of the organization.

For example, an enterprise resource planning (ERP) system monitors and controls all of an organization's resource requirements, such as inventory, human resources, and production capacity. This sophisticated software system tracks financial data, schedules, inventory levels, and more, all in an effort to ensure that the organization has just the resources it needs to meet anticipated demand as efficiently as possible. Marketing intelligence can support ERP by helping managers prepare accurate sales forecasts. In addition, a promotional effort or new-product launch will affect all of an organization's functions and many of its resource needs. ERP can support marketing efforts by providing information about a marketing decision's impact on the entire organization.

Another meaningful development in the cross-functional use of information stored in a company's databases is customer relationship management (CRM). As detailed in Research Window 2.3, CRM attempts to gather all relevant information about a company's customers—everything from demographic data to sales data to service records and more. The goal is to better understand customers' needs and behaviors and to put this information in the hands of those who interact with customers.

Intelligence Gathering in the Organization of the Future

Although one might expect they would, the explosion in databases and the emergence of DSSs have not eliminated traditional marketing research projects for gathering marketing intelligence. This is because the two activities are not competitive mechanisms for marketing intelligence but, rather, complementary ones. For one thing, many of the project-oriented techniques discussed in this book are used to generate the information that goes into the databases that businesses use in their DSSs. Thus, the value of the insights gained from these databases depends directly on the quality of the underlying data, and users need to be able to assess their quality. For another, while DSSs provide valuable input for broad strategic decisions, allow managers to stay in tune with what is happening in their external environments, and serve as excellent early-warning systems, they sometimes do not provide enough information as to what to do in specific instances, such as when the firm is faced with introducing a new product, changing distribution channels, evaluating a promotional campaign, and so on. When actionable information is required to address specific marketing problems or opportunities, the research project will likely continue to play a major role.

In sum, both traditional, or project-based, and DSS-based approaches to marketing intelligence can be expected to remain important. In an increasingly competitive world, information is vital, and a company's ability to obtain and analyze information will largely determine its future. The light from both flashbulbs and candles is necessary.

What Is CRM?

CRM stands for Customer Relationship Management. It is a strategy used to learn more about customers' needs and behaviors in order to develop stronger relationships with them. After all, good customer relationships are at the heart of business success. There are many technological components to CRM, but thinking about CRM in primarily technological terms is a mistake. The more useful way to think about CRM is as a process that will help bring together lots of pieces of information about customers, sales, marketing effectiveness, responsiveness and market trends.

What is the goal of CRM?

The idea of CRM is that it helps businesses use technology and human resources to gain insight into the behavior of customers and the value of those customers. If it works as hoped, a business can:

- provide better customer service
- make call centers more efficient
- cross sell products more effectively
- help sales staff close deals faster
- simplify marketing and sales processes
- discover new customers
- increase customer revenues

That sounds rosy. How does it happen?

It doesn't happen by simply buying software and installing it. For CRM to be truly effective, an organization must first decide what kind of customer information it is looking for and it must decide what it intends to do with that information. For example, many

financial institutions keep track of customers' life stages in order to market appropriate banking products like mortgages or IRAs to them at the right time to fit their needs.

Next, the organization must look into all of the different ways information about customers comes into a business, where and how these data are stored and how they are currently used. One company, for instance, may interact with customers in a myriad of different ways including mail campaigns, Web sites, brick-and-mortar stores, call centers, mobile sales force staff and marketing and advertising efforts. Solid CRM systems link up each of these points. The data flow between operational systems (like sales and inventory systems) and analytical systems that can help sort through these records for patterns. Company analysts can then comb through the data to obtain a holistic view of each customer and pinpoint areas where better services are needed. For example, if someone has a mortgage, a business loan, an IRA and a large commercial checking account with one bank, it behooves the bank to treat this person well each time it has any contact with him or her.

Are there any indications of the need for a CRM project?

Not really. But one way to assess the need for a CRM project is to count the channels a customer can use to access the company. The more channels you have, the greater need there is for the type of single centralized customer view a CRM system can provide.

How long will it take to get CRM in place?

A bit longer than many software salespeople will lead you to think. Some vendors even claim their CRM "solutions" can be installed and working in less than a week. Packages like those are not very helpful in the long run because they don't provide the cross-divisional and holistic customer view needed. The time it takes to put together a well-conceived CRM project depends on the complexity of the project and its components.

How much does CRM cost?

A recent (2001) survey of more than 1,600 business and IT professionals, conducted by The Data Warehousing Institute found that close to 50% had CRM project budgets of less than $500,000. That would appear to indicate that CRM doesn't have to be a budget-buster. However, the same survey showed a handful of respondents with CRM project budgets of over $10 million.

What are some examples of the types of data CRM projects should be collecting?

- Responses to campaigns
- Shipping and fulfillment dates
- Sales and purchase data
- Account information
- Web registration data
- Service and support records
- Demographic data
- Web sales data

What are the keys to successful CRM implementation?

- Break your CRM project down into manageable pieces by setting up pilot programs and short-term milestones. Start with a pilot project that incorporates all the necessary departments and groups that gets projects rolling quickly but is small enough and flexible enough to allow tinkering along the way.
- Make sure your CRM plans include a scalable architecture framework.
- Don't underestimate how much data you might collect (there will be LOTS) and make sure that if you need to expand systems you'll be able to.
- Be thoughtful about what data are collected and stored. The impulse will be to grab and then store EVERY piece of data you can, but there is often no reason to store data. Storing useless data wastes time and money.
- Recognize the individuality of customers and respond appropriately. A CRM system should, for example, have built-in pricing flexibility.

Which division should run the CRM project?

The biggest returns come from aligning business, CRM and IT strategies across all departments and not just leaving it for one group to run.

What causes CRM projects to fail?

Many things. From the beginning, lack of communication between everyone in the customer relationship chain can lead to an incomplete picture of the customer. Poor communication can lead to technology being implemented without proper support or buy-in from users. For example, if the sales force isn't completely sold on the system's benefits, they may not input the kind of demographic data that is essential to the program's success. One *Fortune* 500 company is on its fourth try at a CRM implementation, primarily because its sale force resisted all the previous efforts to share customer data. ■

Source: Stewart Deck, "What is CRM?" downloaded from the CIO.com Web site (http://www.cio.com), November 4, 2002.

looking back...

More and more organizations are using customer relationship management systems to gather ongoing market intelligence. As Estella realized, CRM would give her organization detailed data about many kinds of customer behavior, including inquiries, applications, renewals, and claims. The system would let her company sort data by individual customer or customer segment, geographic region, type of product, and so on. The customer data could be related to data about selling and promotions to see which activities produce the best results. Also, because CRM focuses on customer relationships, it collects longitudinal data—data about behavior over the course of time. In contrast, most surveys collect one-time data.

But Estella's vice president of sales raised an important issue. No matter how extensive CRM data may be, this type of information gathering cannot replace other marketing research. The reasons involve the kinds of data CRM can collect and the population from which it collects data.

A CRM system gathers data about customer activities but generally not about customer beliefs and attitudes. It answers questions about who customers are and what they do, but not about why they act or don't act. For example, a system might record that a customer called with a question about his policy and received an answer from a particular service representative. However, the system typically would not gather information about the customer's attitudes toward the company, which might affect future purchasing behavior. Data about beliefs and attitudes are often essential to identifying opportunities or correcting problems.

Another shortcoming of CRM is the lack of data gathered from people who are not already interacting with the company. Suppose a strategy of Total Insurance is to increase its market share in the Southwest. The company needs data about *potential* customers in its southwestern target market. What is their opinion of Total Insurance? Have they even heard of the company? What product and service characteristics do they value? Gathering such data will require research methods like surveys or focus groups, described in later chapters.

When Estella asked Philip why he thought CRM might miss important customer data, he pointed out these limitations. She agreed and determined that she should ask her chief information officer to develop a plan for a system that merges the best of CRM and problem-oriented marketing research. For example, the same system should provide information about transactions and the results of focus groups, attitude surveys, and similar research. Such a system would tell the company how customer behavior changes when the company tries to apply what it learns about customers' beliefs and attitudes. ■

Sources: This case is based on ideas and trends drawn from Wesley Sprinkle, "In Sync with Customers," *Best's Review* (April 2002), pp. 104–106; Doug Grisaffe, "See About Linking CRM and MR Systems," *Marketing News* (January 21, 2002), p. 13; Lawrence A. Crosby, Sherre L. Johnson, and Richard T. Quinn, "Is Survey Research Dead?" *Marketing Management* 11(3) (Summer 2002), downloaded from EBSCOhost, May 2, 2002.

Summary

Learning Objective 1
Explain the difference between a project emphasis in research and a systems emphasis.
The difference between the project emphasis to research and the marketing information system (MIS) or decision support system (DSS) emphasis is that both of the latter rely on the continual monitoring of the firm's activities, competitors, and environment, while the former emphasizes the in-depth, but nonrecurring, study of some specific problem or environmental condition.

Learning Objective 2
Define what is meant by a marketing information system (MIS) and a decision support system (DSS).
A marketing information system is a set of procedures and methods for the regular, planned collection, analysis, and presentation of information for use in making marketing decisions. A decision support system expands the capabilities of an MIS to include tools that assist in decision making. A DSS is a coordinated collection of data, systems tools, and techniques with supporting software and hardware, by which an organization gathers

and interprets relevant information from business and the environment and turns it into a basis for marketing action. A DSS encompasses data systems, model systems, and dialog systems.

Learning Objective 3
Describe the networking of modern information systems.
Modern information systems are usually linked in a network that allows decision makers at personal computers to get information themselves, without making requests through an information systems department. The data may reside in a central computer, in personal computers, or on the Internet. Many networks incorporate Internet search tools and data into an intranet (for internal users only) or an extranet (for internal users and authorized external users such as customers or suppliers).

Learning Objective 4
Identify the components of a decision support system.
A decision support system has three major components: a data system, a model system, and a dialog system. The data system collects and stores data from internal and external sources. The model system consists of routines that allow the user to manipulate data in order to analyze it as desired. Software in the model system may include expert systems, which make information-processing deci-

sions based on models of how experts solve similar problems. Finally, the dialog system permits marketers to use the system models to produce reports based on criteria they specify themselves.

Learning Objective 5
Discuss trends in the gathering of marketing intelligence.
So much information is readily available from modern information systems and decision support systems that managing it has become a strategic challenge. Many organizations have placed a chief information officer (CIO) in charge of how the organization gathers data and makes it available to support decision making. Others have broadened this role to the gathering and management of all the organization's knowledge, sometimes under the oversight of a chief knowledge officer (CKO). In addition, many organizations are creating information and decision support systems that serve entire organizations, linking the various functions. Systems such as enterprise resource planning (ERP) systems show decision makers how their decisions affect the organization's resource levels and needs. Customer relationship management (CRM) attempts to gather all relevant information about a company's customer into a system that can put this information into the hands of those who interact with customers.

Key Terms

marketing information system (MIS) (page 22)
decision support system (DSS) (page 22)
data system (page 25)
model system (page 28)

expert system (page 29)
dialog system (page 30)
knowledge management (page 31)

Review Questions

1. How does a project emphasis in marketing research differ from a systems emphasis?
2. What are the steps in developing an MIS?
3. What are the main differences between a marketing information system and a decision support system?
4. In a decision support system, what is a data system? A model system? A dialog system? Which of these is most important? Why?
5. How does knowledge management expand the concept of an information system? What additional kinds of marketing intelligence can it provide?

PART 1:
Introduction to Marketing Research and Problem Definition

Discussion Questions, Problems, and Projects

1. How is the growth in the Internet and the World Wide Web changing the way researchers use management information systems and decision support systems? Consider opportunities and challenges of researching on the Internet, as opposed to using a traditional marketing information system.

2. You have been requested to design a DSS for a manufacturer of automotive parts.
   (a) What data should be included in the system (e.g., sales by sales area or by product line, age, and type of automobile driven)?
   (b) What data sources might be used to create the information system?
   (c) How will you structure the system conceptually, including the elements you will build into each of the subsystems?

3. You are responsible for deciding whether to adopt an MIS or a DSS for the following situations. Which system approach would you choose? Why?
   (a) Production of profit and loss statements for Kool Aid sugar-free flavored drink mixes.
   (b) Introduction of a new product line extension for Smucker's preserves and jellies.
   (c) Determination of seasonal pricing schedules for Johnson outboard motors.
   (d) Identification of the amount of time spent on hold by consumers on a toll-free, customer-service assistance telephone line.

4. Arrange an interview with a manager of a local business to discuss a DSS, intranet, extranet, or knowledge management system.
   (a) Complete the following:
   Name of the company: _____
   Name and title of the manager you interviewed: _____
   (b) Briefly describe the system that the company is currently using, emphasizing especially the functions that are served by it (e.g., production, sales management, etc.).
   (c) Write a brief assessment of the manager's familiarity with the concept. Is the manager more concerned with the technical questions (e.g., how information is stored) or with the overall concept and its impact on the organization's decision-making capabilities?
   (d) Briefly describe the company's use of the system, including how it determines who gets what access to what data and how, its experience with the system, and so on.

5. Your company is in the process of installing its first DSS. The system has been designed and the hardware installed, and it is due to be up and running in two weeks. Your task is to provide system users with orientation and training. It is your feeling that the company's people initially will resist using the DSS. To help overcome this resistance, what specific capabilities of the DSS will you emphasize in your initial orientation presentations?

Suggested Additional Readings

For useful discussions of the structure and use of decision support systems, see Robert C. Blattberg, Rashi Glazer, and John D. C. Little, eds., *The Marketing Information Revolution* (Boston: Harvard Business School Press, 1994).

Louis Moutinho, Bruce Curry, Fiona Davies, and Paulo Rita, *Computer Modeling and Expert Systems in Marketing* (New York: Routledge, 1994).

Chapter 3

Process of Marketing Research

© PhotoDisc/Getty Images

Learning Objectives

1 *Explain the difference between a program strategy and a project strategy in marketing research.*

2 *Outline the steps in the research process and show how the steps are interrelated.*

3 *Cite the most critical error in marketing research.*

4 *Highlight the main differences between the teleological and deontological ethical frameworks.*

Tempers flared within the expensively appointed, oak-paneled offices of Waring, Weatherell & Hough in Chicago. Management of the 400-attorney international law firm was debating the merits of spending money to learn more information about the firm's clients.

"This is a wholly inappropriate use of funds," growled Bernard Lowenthal, who, as head of the firm's finance committee, held the purse strings. It was Lowenthal who last month had attempted to discontinue the firm's traditional year-end bonuses for nonattorney personnel—this despite the fact that WW&H was on the way to its most profitable year ever. Lowenthal had been overruled on the bonuses by Charles "Chip" Shepherd, the firm's managing partner. Now, Shepherd disagreed with the tightfisted tax attorney regarding marketing research.

"Bernie, I'm going to be blunt: Sometimes you can be pretty ignorant," Shepherd asserted. "Just how much longer do you think we can sustain profitability without learning everything we can about our clients? Right now, we know almost nothing. Let's bite the bullet, for heaven's sake, and begin the research before this whole thing gets any further out of hand.

"You and I both know that some people here are spending marketing dollars without any rationale. When we know more about our clients, we'll be able to impose stricter controls on that spending," Shepherd added.

"Setting aside costs for the moment," interrupted trial attorney Janet Lathrop, "I agree that we should know more about our clients. But specifically, what is it we hope to learn from this research? How will we go about it? And who will conduct it?

"I hope you don't think that my attorneys have time to do this sort of thing, Chip. With caseloads being what they are, we can barely keep our heads above water now."

"No, Janet," Shepherd began, massaging his brow wearily, "this is not a project for attorneys. I don't know exactly how we'll go about it. But I think, at a minimum, we ought to be able to create some profiles of our most typical clients—how much they're spending with us, how many and what types of matters they're giving us, which other firms they use and why.

"I suggest we ask Lauren how to start. I don't know if this is a project she can handle by herself, but she can get it going."

Shepherd was referring to Lauren Greene, the firm's marketing director. Greene, WW&H's first marketing director, came from a Big Six accounting firm the year before. When she arrived, she discovered an organization in disarray: a few gung-ho marketers spending money without a rationale or any thought to measurement; some lawyers vehemently condemning marketing—and her; and others in the middle, knowing little about marketing but willing to learn as long as it didn't require any commitment on their part.

"So, it's settled," Shepherd stated. "I'll talk to Lauren first thing in the morning."

Discussion Issues

1. If you were Lauren Greene, what would you tell Chip Shepherd when he asks you for advice on marketing research?

2. Does Waring, Weatherell & Hough have a research strategy? Does it need one?

3. What would you tell the lawyers to assure them of the value of marketing research to the firm? ∎

1
Explain the difference between a program strategy and a project strategy in marketing research.

program strategy
A company's philosophy of how marketing research fits into its marketing plan.

project strategy
The design of individual marketing research studies that are to be conducted.

research process
The sequence of steps in the design and implementation of a research study, including problem formulation, determination of research design, determination of data collection method, design of data collection forms, design of the sample and collection of the data, analysis and interpretation of the data, and preparation of the research report.

Chapter 1 highlighted the many kinds of problems that marketing research can be used to solve. It emphasized that marketing research is a firm's communication link with the environment and can help the marketing manager in planning, problem solving, and control. Every company has its own way of using marketing research. Some use it on a continuous basis to track sales or to monitor the firm's market share. Others resort to it only when a problem arises or an important decision—such as the launching of a new product—needs to be made.

A company's overall philosophy of how marketing research fits into its marketing plan determines its **program strategy** for marketing research.[1] A program strategy specifies the types of studies that are to be conducted and for what purposes. It might even specify how often these studies are to take place. Program strategy typically answers such questions as "Should we do marketing research?" and "How often?" and "What kind?"

How the individual studies are designed is the basis of a firm's **project strategy.** Project strategy addresses the issue of "Now that we've decided to go ahead with marketing research, how should we proceed? Should we use in-store surveys, self-administered printed questionnaires, or perhaps electronically administered questionnaires? Should we question more people or fewer? More often or less often?" In sum, project strategy deals with how a study should be conducted, whereas program strategy addresses the question of what type of studies the firm should conduct.

Research Window 3.1 outlines the kinds of studies that constitute the Gillette Company's program strategy for marketing research. As you can see, each type of study is planned to meet a certain objective. The design of individual studies defines the firm's project strategy—for example, the use of personal interviews in the national consumer studies, mail questionnaires in the brand-tracking studies, and telephone interviews when measuring brand awareness. The goal of all this research is to help Gillette maintain its 60 percent share of the blade and razor market.

All research problems require their own special emphases and approaches. Since every marketing research problem is unique in some ways, the research procedure is usually custom tailored. Nonetheless, there is a sequence of steps called the **research process** (see Figure 3.1), which can be followed when designing the research project. This chapter overviews the research process, and the remaining chapters discuss the stages in the process in more detail.

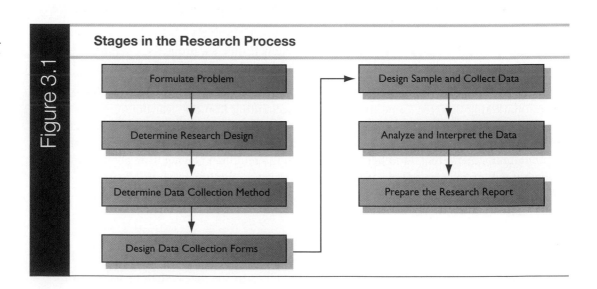

Figure 3.1

Stages in the Research Process

Formulate Problem → Determine Research Design → Determine Data Collection Method → Design Data Collection Forms → Design Sample and Collect Data → Analyze and Interpret the Data → Prepare the Research Report

Major Thrusts of Marketing Research at the Gillette Company

1. Annual National Consumer Studies

The objectives of these annual studies are to determine what brand of razor and blade was used for the respondents' last shave, to collect demographic data, and to examine consumer attitudes toward the various blade and razor manufacturers. These studies rely on personal interviews with national panels of male and female respondents, who are selected using probability sampling methods.

2. National Brand-Tracking Studies

The purpose of these studies is to track the use of razors and blades so as to monitor brand loyalty and brand switching tendencies over time. These studies are also conducted annually and use panels of male and female shavers. However, the information is collected via mail questionnaires.

3. Annual Brand-Awareness Studies

These studies are aimed at determining the "share of mind" Gillette products have. This information is collected by annual telephone surveys that employ unaided as well as aided recall of brand names and advertising campaigns.

4. Consumer-Use Tests

The key objectives of the use-testing studies are to ensure that "Gillette remains state of the art in the competitive arena, that our products are up to our desired performance standards, and that no claims in our advertis-

ing, packaging, or display materials are made without substantiation." At least two consumer-use tests are conducted each month by Gillette. In these tests, consumers are asked to use a single variation of a product for an extended period of time, at the end of which their evaluation of the product is secured.

5. Continuous Retail Audits

The purpose of the retail audits is to provide top management with monthly market share data, along with information regarding distribution, out-of-stock, and inventory levels of the various Gillette products. This information is purchased from the commercial information services providing syndicated retail sales data. The information is supplemented by special retail audits that Gillette itself conducts, which look at product displays and the extent to which Gillette blades and razors are featured in retailer advertisements.

6. Laboratory Research Studies

These studies are designed to test the performance of existing Gillette products and to help in the design of new products. They include having people shave with Gillette and competitor products and measuring the results, as well as determining the number of whiskers on a man's face, how fast whiskers grow, and how many shaves a man can get from a single blade. ◼

Sources: Adapted from "Mature Products Remain as the Mainstays in the Gillette Company," *Marketing News* 17 (June 10, 1983), p. 17; Lourdes Lee Valeriano, "Marketing: Western Firms Poll Eastern Europeans to Discern Tastes of Nascent Consumers," *The Wall Street Journal* (April 27, 1992), p. B1; Lawrence Ingrassia, "Gillette Holds Its Edge by Endlessly Searching for a Better Shave," *The Wall Street Journal* (December 10, 1992), pp. A1, A6; Barbara Carton, "To Make Gillette Bristle, Ask about the Razor's Edge," *The Wall Street Journal* (July 30, 1996), p. A1; James Surowlecki, "The Billion Dollar Blade," *Management Today* (August 1998), pp. 32–36.

Sequence of Steps in Marketing Research

Formulate Problem

One of the more valuable roles of marketing research is to help define the marketing problem to be solved. Only when the problem is precisely defined can research be designed to provide pertinent information. Part of the process of problem definition includes specifying the *objectives* of the specific research project or projects that might be undertaken. Each project should have one or more objectives, and the next step in the process should not be taken until these can be explicitly stated.

Outline the steps in the research process and show how the steps are interrelated.

Determine Research Design

The choice of research design depends on how much is known about the problem. If relatively little is known about the phenomenon to be investigated, *exploratory research* will be warranted. Typically, exploratory research is used when the problem to be solved is broad or vague. It may involve reviewing published data, interviewing knowledgeable people, conducting focus

Nissan Comes Up with a SUT for Sore Eyes

Source: Copyright Nissan (1999). Nissan and the Nissan logo are registered trademarks of Nissan.

Nissan Design International, Inc. used new technology and effective marketing research to design a new type of vehicle. The Nissan sport-utility truck (SUT) is designed for people who need the passenger space of an SUV but also occasionally need extra cargo space. Focus groups liked the SUT concept so much that the company gave the OK for production.

secondary data
Statistics not gathered for the immediate study at hand but for some other purpose.

primary data
Information collected specifically for the investigation at hand.

groups, or investigating trade literature that discusses similar cases. In any event, one of the most important characteristics of exploratory research is its flexibility. Since researchers know little about the problem at this point, they must be ready to follow their intuition about possible areas and tactics of investigation.

If, instead of being broad or vague, a problem is precisely and unambiguously formulated, *descriptive* or *causal* research is needed. In these research designs, data collection is not flexible but rigidly specified, both with respect to the data collection forms and the sample design. The descriptive design emphasizes determining the frequency with which something occurs or the extent to which two variables covary. The causal design uses experiments to identify cause-and-effect relationships between variables.

Determine Data Collection Method

Often the information that a firm needs to solve its problem already exists in the form of **secondary data,** or data that have already been collected for some purpose other than the question at hand. Such data may exist in the firm's own internal information system as feedback on warranty cards, call reports from the sales force, or orders from wholesalers. If the firm itself does not have the necessary information, it may be readily available from a good business library, in the form of government statistics or trade association reports. Finally, if neither of these sources proves fruitful, the data may have been collected already by a commercial research supplier. Although the firm must pay for such information, the fee is usually less than the cost of an original study. In any case, for reasons of both cost and time, researchers should always look first at existing sources of data before launching a research project.

If the information needed is not readily available, or if it is available only in a form unsuitable for the problem at hand, then the research must depend on **primary data,** which are collected specifically for the study. The research questions here are several, including: Should the data be collected by observation or questionnaire? How should these observations be made—personally or electronically? How should the questions be administered—in person, over the telephone, through the mail, or perhaps by Fax or email?

Design Data Collection Forms

Once the researchers have settled on the method to be used for the study, they must decide on the type of observation form or questionnaire that will best suit the needs of the project. Suppose a questionnaire is being used. Should it be structured as a fixed set of alternative answers, or should the responses be open-ended, to allow respondents to reply in their own words? Should the purpose be made clear to the respondents, or should the study objectives be disguised? Should some kind of rating scale be used? What type?

Design Sample and Collect Data

After determining how the needed information will be collected, the researchers must decide what group will be observed or questioned. Depending on the study, this group might be homemakers, preschoolers, sports car drivers, Pennsylvanians, or tennis players. The particular subset of the population chosen for study is known as a *sample.*

In designing the sample, researchers must specify (1) the **sampling frame,** which is the list of population elements from which the sample will be drawn, (2) the sample-selection process, and (3) the size of the sample. Although people often assume the frame is implicit in the research problem and thus take it for granted, that assumption can be dangerous.

> Take the case of the manufacturer of dog food . . . who went out and did an intensive market study. He tested the demand for dog food; he tested the package size, the design, the whole advertising program. Then he launched the product with a big campaign, got the proper distribution channels, put it on the market and had tremendous sales. But two months later, the bottom dropped out—no follow-up sales. So he called in an expert, who took the dog food out to the local pound, put it in front of the dogs—and they would not touch it. For all the big marketing study, no one had tried the product on the dogs.[2]

As this old but classic example illustrates, the dog population was not part of the sampling frame, probably because it is people who buy dog food and not the dogs themselves. Nevertheless, the careless specification of population elements had dire consequences. Although the consequences may be less dire in other cases, it is important to realize that when we sample from, say, a phone book or a mailing list, we are not sampling from the population as a whole, but only from people whose names appear in the phone book or on the mailing list. Answers to a questionnaire on frequency of air travel would clearly be quite different if the sample were selected from the New York City phone book than if it were selected from the book covering rural West Virginia.

The sample-selection process requires that the form of the sample be specified. Will it be a **probability sample,** in which each member of the population has a known nonzero chance of being selected? Or will it be a **nonprobability sample,** in which the researchers subjectively decide which particular group will be part of the study?

Sample size addresses the issue of how many institutions or subjects it is necessary to use in the project in order to get reliable answers without exceeding the time and money budgeted for it.

Once the dimensions of the sample design are specified, data collection can begin. Data collection requires a field force of some type, although field methods are largely dictated by the data collection method, the kinds of information to be obtained, and the sampling requirements. The use of personnel to collect data raises a host of questions with respect to selection, training, and control of the field staff. For example, what kind of background should interviewers have in order to glean the most information from respondents? What specific training is necessary to ensure that interviewers administer the questionnaires accurately? How often, and in what way, should the accuracy of the answers on the questionnaires be checked by validation studies? These questions should be anticipated in designing the research.

Analyze and Interpret the Data

Researchers may amass a mountain of data, but it is useless unless the findings are analyzed and the results interpreted in light of the problem at hand. Data analysis generally involves several steps. First, the data collection forms must be scanned to be sure that they are complete and consistent and that the instructions were followed. This process is called **editing.** After being edited, the forms must be **coded,** which involves assigning numbers to each of the answers so that they may be analyzed by a computer. The final step in analyzing the data is **tabulation.** This refers to the orderly arrangement of data in a table or other summary format achieved by

sampling frame
The list of sampling units from which a sample will be drawn; the list could consist of geographic areas, institutions, individuals, or other units.

probability sample
A sample in which each population element has a known, nonzero chance of being included in the sample.

nonprobability sample
A sample that relies on personal judgment somewhere in the element selection process and therefore prohibits estimating the probability that any population element will be included in the sample.

editing
Inspection and correction, if necessary, of each questionnaire or observation form.

coding
The technical procedure by which data are categorized; it involves specifying the alternative categories or classes into which the responses are to be placed and assigning code numbers to the classes.

tabulation
The procedure by which the cases that fall into each of a number of categories are counted.

counting the frequency of responses to each question. At this point the data may also be cross-classified by other variables. Suppose researchers asked women if they like a certain new cosmetic. Their responses may be cross-classified by age-group, income level, and so forth.

The editing, coding, and tabulation functions are common to most research studies. Any statistical tests applied to the data are generally unique to the particular sampling procedures and data collection instruments used in the research. These tests should be anticipated before data collection is begun, if possible, to ensure that the data and analyses will be appropriate for the problem as specified.

Prepare the Research Report

The research report is the document submitted to management that summarizes the research results and conclusions. It is all that many executives will see of the research effort, and it becomes the standard by which that research is judged. Thus, it is imperative that the research report be clear and accurate, since no matter how well all previous steps have been completed, the project will be no more successful than the research report. Simply put, the research report is one of the most important factors affecting whether the research will be used and the changes based on it implemented.

Additional Comments on Marketing Research Steps

While the above discussion should provide some understanding of the steps in the research process, six additional points need to be made. First, each step in the process is more complex than the above discussion suggests. Each involves a number of issues rather than a single decision or even a few decisions. Exhibit 3.1 lists some of the typical questions that need to be resolved at each stage.

Second, although the stages have been presented as if one would proceed through them in a lockstep fashion when designing a research project, nothing could be further from the truth. Rather, Figure 3.1 could be drawn with a number of feedback loops suggesting a possible need to rethink, redraft, or revise the various elements in the process as the study proceeds. The process would begin with problem formulation and could then take any direction. The problem may not be specified explicitly enough to allow the development of the research design, in which case the researchers would need to return to stage one to define the research objectives more clearly. Alternatively, the process may proceed smoothly to the design of the data collection forms, the pretest of which may require a revision of the research objectives or the research design. Still further, the sample necessary to answer the problem as specified may be prohibitively costly, again requiring a revision of the earlier steps. Once the data are collected, no revision of the procedure is possible. It is possible, though, to revise the earlier steps on the basis of the *anticipated* analysis, so it is critical that the methods used to analyze the data be determined before the data are collected.

Although it is hard for beginning researchers to understand, the steps in the research process are highly interrelated. A decision made at one stage will affect decisions at each of the other stages, and a revision of the procedure at any stage often requires modifications of procedures at each of the other stages. Unfortunately, it seems that this lesson is understood only by those who have experienced the frustrations and satisfactions of being involved in an actual research project.

Cite the most critical error in marketing research.

Third, the important error to be concerned about when designing a research project is the *total error* likely to be associated with the project. All the steps are necessary and vital, and it is dangerous to emphasize one to the exclusion of one or more others. Many beginning students of research, for example, argue for large sample sizes. What they fail to realize is that an increase in the sample size to reduce sampling error can often lead to an increase in the total error of the research effort, since other errors increase more than proportionately with sample size. For example, a study may require researchers to call people from a list of randomly selected phone numbers. Even if the numbers themselves represent an excellent cross section of the population, a funny thing may happen on the way to the study's results.

Exhibit 3.1

Questions Typically Addressed at the Various Stages of the Research Process

Stage in the Process	Typical Questions
Formulate problem	What is the purpose of the study—to solve a problem? Identify an opportunity? Is additional background information necessary? What information is needed to make the decision at hand? How will the information be utilized? Should research be conducted?
Determine research design	How much is already known? Can a hypothesis be formulated? What types of questions need to be answered? What type of study will best address the research questions?
Determine data collection method	Can existing data be used to advantage? What is to be measured? How? What is the source of the data to be collected? Are there any cultural factors that need to be taken into account in designing the data collection method? What are they? Are there any legal restrictions on data collection methods? What are they? Can objective answers be obtained by asking people? How should people be questioned? Should the questionnaires be administered in person, over the phone, through the mail, via Fax, on the Internet, or through email? Should electronic or mechanical means be used to make the observations?
Design data collection forms	Should structured or unstructured items be used to collect the data? Should the purpose of the study be made known to the respondents? Should rating scales be used in the questionnaires? What specific behaviors should the observers record?
Design sample and collect data	Who is the target population? Is a list of population elements available? Is a sample necessary? Is a probability sample desirable? How large should the sample be? How should the sample be selected? Who will gather the data? How long will the data gathering take? How much supervision is needed? What operational procedures will be followed? What methods will be used to ensure the quality of the data collected?
Analyze and interpret the data	Who will handle the editing of the data? How will the data be coded? Who will supervise the coding? Will computer or hand tabulation be used? What tabulations are called for? What analysis techniques will be used?
Prepare the research report	Who will read the report? What is their technical level of sophistication? What is their involvement with the project? Are managerial recommendations called for? What will be the format of the written report? Is an oral report necessary? How should the oral report be structured?

Researchers working a nine-to-five day will doubtlessly have trouble connecting with families in which both spouses work or with households made up of single working people. If this potential error is not accounted for, the study may overly represent the homebound—the elderly, families with a baby or an invalid, or the unemployed. The larger the sample size, of course, the larger would be the weight of this group's opinions. The magnitude of the error caused by a large sample would then have a significant effect on the total error associated with the project.

Total error, rather than errors incurred in any single stage, is the important error in research work, except insofar as those individual errors increase total error. Quite often, *part error*, or *stage error*, will be increased so that total error may be decreased. Questions such as those in Exhibit 3.1 must be addressed so that total error can be minimized.

Fourth, the stages in the research process serve to structure the remainder of this book. The next chapter, for example, discusses the first stage, problem formulation, while each of the remaining stages warrants a special section in the book.

Fifth, the stages in the research process can also be used to direct additional study in research method. The aspiring research student needs more sophistication in at least some of the stages than this book could possibly provide. The sections and chapters will indicate where in-depth study might be most useful.

Sixth, while much of this text discusses the techniques for doing marketing research, the art of choosing a particular technique many times will involve an implicit judgment about the ethics of the proposed procedure, which must be considered by the marketing researchers. The remainder of this chapter highlights the major ethical issues researchers face.

Marketing Research Ethics

ethics
A concern with the development of moral standards by which situations can be judged; applies to all situations in which there can be actual or potential harm of any kind to an individual or group.

marketing ethics
The principles, values, and standards of conduct followed by marketers.

Ethics are the moral principles and values that govern the way an individual or group conducts its activities. Ethics apply to all situations in which there can be actual or potential harm of any kind (e.g., economic, physical, or mental) to an individual or group. **Marketing ethics** are the principles, values, and standards of conduct followed by marketers.

Many researchers (and managers as well) fail to confront the issue of whether it is morally acceptable to proceed in a particular way or whether they are acting in a socially responsible manner by doing so. Many take the view that if it is legal, it is ethical. They fail to appreciate that there can be differences between what is ethical and what is legal. Even among those who do appreciate the distinction, there is often a reluctance to evaluate the ethical implications of their decisions, because they feel ill-equipped to do so.

Marketing researchers need to recognize that the effective practice of their profession depends a great deal on the goodwill of and participation by the public, and that the American public is becoming more and more protective of its privacy. This makes it more difficult and costly to approach, recruit, and survey participants. "Bad" research experiences that violate the implicit trust of the participants in a study can only accentuate the trend. In addition to moral fairness issues, self-preservation issues dictate that marketing researchers develop a sense for the ethical issues involved in particular choices. The fact that good ethics is good business is one reason associations whose members are involved in marketing research have developed codes of ethics to guide the behaviors of their members. Exhibit 3.2 contains the marketing research code of ethics for the American Marketing Association.

Marketing researchers can face ethical issues when dealing with: (1) research participants, (2) the client for whom the research is being conducted, and (3) the research team itself.

Research Participants

Highlight the main differences between the teleological and deontological ethical frameworks.

Whether a researchers' interactions with research participants are ethical or unethical can depend on the moral reasoning framework that researcher embraces. Currently, there are

Exhibit 3.2

AMA Marketing Research Code of Ethics

The American Marketing Association, in furtherance of its central objective of the advancement of science in marketing and in recognition of its obligation to the public, has established these principles of ethical practice of marketing research for the guidance of its members. In an increasingly complex society, marketing management is more and more dependent upon marketing information intelligently and systematically obtained. The consumer is the source of much of this information. Seeking the cooperation of the consumer in the development of information, marketing management must acknowledge its obligation to protect the public from misrepresentation and exploitation under the guise of research.

Similarly, the research practitioner has an obligation to the discipline and to those who provide support for it—an obligation to adhere to basic and commonly accepted standards of scientific investigation as they apply to the domain of marketing research.

For Research Users, Practitioners, and Interviewers

1. No individual or organization will undertake any activity which is directly or indirectly represented to be marketing research, but which has as its real purpose the attempted sales of merchandise or services to some or all of the respondents interviewed in the course of the research.
2. If respondents have been led to believe, directly or indirectly, that they are participating in a marketing research survey and that their anonymity will be protected, their names shall not be made known to anyone outside the research organization or research department, or used for other than research purposes.

For Research Practitioners

1. There will be no intentional or deliberate misrepresentation of research methods or results. An adequate description of methods employed will be made available upon request to the sponsor of the research. Evidence that fieldwork has been completed according to specifications will, upon request, be made available to buyers of the research.
2. The identity of the survey sponsor and/or the ultimate client for whom a survey is being done will be held in confidence at all times, unless this identity is to be revealed as part of the research design. Research information shall be held in confidence by the research organization or department and not used for personal gain or made available to any outside party unless the client specifically authorizes such release.
3. A research organization shall not undertake marketing studies for competitive clients when such studies would jeopardize the confidential nature of client-agency relationships.

For Users of Marketing Research

1. A user of research shall not knowingly disseminate conclusions from a given research project or service that are inconsistent with or not warranted by the data.
2. To the extent that there is involved in a research project a unique design involving techniques, approaches, or concepts not commonly available to research practitioners, the prospective user of research shall not solicit such a design from one practitioner and deliver it to another for execution without the approval of the design originator.

For Field Interviewers

1. Research assignments and materials received, as well as information obtained from respondents, shall be held in confidence by the interviewer and revealed to no one except the research organization conducting the marketing study.
2. No information gained through a marketing research activity shall be used, directly or indirectly, for the personal gain or advantage of the interviewer.
3. Interviews shall be conducted in strict accordance with specifications and instructions received.
4. An interviewer shall not carry out two or more interviewing assignments simultaneously, unless authorized by all contractors or employers concerned.

Members of the American Marketing Association will be expected to conduct themselves in accordance with the provisions of this code in all of their marketing research activities.

Reprinted with permission from the American Marketing Association.

two ethical frameworks that tend to dominate ethical reasoning in general and marketing ethics in particular: **teleology** and **deontology.**

The most well known branch of teleological ethics is *utilitarianism,* which focuses on society as the unit of analysis and stresses the consequences of an act on all those directly or indirectly affected by it. The utilitarian perspective holds that the correct course of action is the one that promotes "the greatest good for the greatest number." Utilitarianism requires that a social cost/benefit analysis be conducted for the contemplated action. All benefits and costs to all persons affected by the particular act need to be considered to "the degree possible and summarized as the net of all benefits minus all costs. If the net result is positive, the act is morally acceptable; if the net result is negative, the act is not."[3] Net benefits can be assessed by reviewing the questions in Exhibit 3.3.

Deontological ethics focus on the welfare of the individual and emphasize means and intentions for justifying the act. Deontologists believe that every individual has a right to be treated in ways that ensure the person's dignity, respect, and autonomy. The deontological model is thus sometimes referred to as the rights, or entitlements, model. Probably most people in the United States would argue, for example, that every person has a right to safety, to be informed, to choose, and to be heard. Exhibit 3.4 depicts the types of questions that need to be asked to apply the rights model.

When the two frameworks lead to the same judgment as to the ethicality of an act, the decision as to whether to go ahead is easy. When they lead to different ethical judgments, the marketing researcher's decision as to the appropriate way to proceed becomes clouded. The following chapters contain various ethical scenarios which should serve to highlight ethical dilemmas faced by marketing researchers when dealing with research participants as well as with other constituencies.

© Grantpix/Index Stock Imagery

The American public has become more protective of its privacy, making it increasingly difficult for marketing researchers to find consumers willing to participate in surveys and studies. Following strict ethical guidelines in research can help gain the trust of the public.

Clients

Regarding the client, the marketing researcher must be careful to maintain confidentiality and technical and administrative integrity. Marketing researchers must not reveal one client's affairs to another client who is a competitor, and in some circumstances, must not reveal the sponsor of the research to participants. Violations of research integrity can range from designing studies without due care through the unnecessary use of complex analytical procedures, to the deliberate fudging of data. It cannot be emphasized enough that researchers must maintain the strictest technical integrity if they are to have credibility as professional experts. It is not only unethical but also shortsighted business sense to take advantage of the client's lack of expertise in research design and methodology, because where trust fails, funding eventually does also. Specific recommendations include choosing the simplest appropriate methodology, as opposed to unnecessarily sophisticated and costly techniques; expressing oneself in simple and generally accessible language rather than in intimidating jargon; making explicit mention of the limitations of the research; and refusing any project in which personal problems or conflicts will lead to inadequate performance. Administrative integrity covers issues such as not passing on hidden charges to the client.

PART 1:
Introduction to Marketing Research and Problem Definition

Exhibit 3.3

Questions That Need Asking to Apply the Utilitarian (Teleological) Model

- What are the viable courses of action available?
- What are the alternatives?
- What are the harms and benefits associated with the course of action available?
- Can these harms and benefits be measured?
- How long will these harms and benefits last?
- When will these harms begin?
- Who is directly harmed? Who is indirectly harmed?
- Who is directly benefited? Who is indirectly benefited?
- What are the social and/or economic costs attached to each alternative course of action?
- Which alternatives will most likely yield the greatest net benefit to all individuals affected by the decision? Or if no alternative yields a net benefit, which one will lead to the least overall harm?

Source: Robert A. Cooke, *Ethics in Business: A Perspective* (Chicago: Arthur Anderson, 1988), p. 5.

Exhibit 3.4

Questions That Need Asking to Apply the Rights (Deontological) Model

- Does the research violate the participants' anonymity?
- Does the research expose the participants to mental stress?
- Does the research ask participants questions detrimental to their self-interest?
- Does the research involve special equipment and does the use of the special equipment violate any basic rights of the participants?
- Does the research involve participants without their knowledge?
- Does the research use deception?
- Does the research use coercion in any way, obvious or subtle?
- Does the research deprive participants of their right to self-determination?

The Research Team

Finally, there are considerations regarding the research team itself. For example, when subordinates are acting according to instructions, the supervisor is partly responsible for their ethical conduct. Moreover, in addition to the official hierarchy, an unofficial sphere of influence exists that renders every team member partially responsible for the others' moral behavior. In particular, studies of organizational culture (such as in marketing research firms) show that actions of top management have been found to be the best predictor of perceived ethical problems for marketing researchers. The source of the boss's influence probably resides in subordinates' fear of reprisals for not conforming and in their acceptance of legitimate authority. As a consequence of the poor examples they see, marketing practitioners do not see themselves as being under pressure to improve their own ethics. See Research Window 3.2 to get a better understanding of the kinds of ethical issues that confront marketing researchers.

Source: John R. Sparks and Shelby D. Hunt, "Marketing Researcher Ethical Sensitivity: Conceptualization, Measurement, and Exploratory Investigation," based on *Journal of Marketing* 62 (April 1998), pp. 92–109.

RESEARCH *Window* 3.2

Marketing Researchers' Own Perceptions of the Difficult Ethical Problems They Face

Ethical Issues to Which Practitioners Are Most Sensitive:

1. Maintaining their research integrity: for example, deliberately withholding information, falsifying figures, altering research results, misusing statistics, ignoring pertinent data.
2. Treating outside clients fairly: for example, passing hidden charges to clients, overlooking violations of the project requirements when subcontracting parts of the project.
3. Maintaining research confidentiality: for example, sharing information among subsidiaries in the same corporation, using background data developed in a previous project to reduce the cost of a current project.

Factors That Predict Sensitivity to Ethical Issues:

1. Organizational socialization (for example, "I know the rules associated with my job" and "I know what's considered appropriate behavior in my company").
2. Ability to empathize (such as, "Generally, I find it easy to see things from the other person's perspective"). ■

looking back...

Shepherd called Lauren Greene into his office in the morning. "Lauren," he began, "we're going to do some marketing research. We need to know more about who our clients are. How do we begin?"

Greene replied, "You and I have had many discussions about research, Chip, so forgive me if today I go back to the beginning. We need first to articulate the problem: Specifically, what do we need to know and why do we need to know it? Then, let's outline what we hope to achieve with the research."

"Well, as you know, Lauren, some of our partners are spending money on marketing activities without any idea of whether it's effective. We need to get control of these expenditures, and fast.

"Obviously, we've got some accounting controls in place, but that doesn't do much to help us understand the value of the expenditure. To really get a handle on our marketing effort, we need to obtain as complete a picture of our clients as possible. That will help us determine whether we're spending money intelligently on some of these marketing projects," her boss answered.

"And," Greene interjected, "it will give us a yardstick for the marketing activities we want to undertake in the future."

"OK, so how do we go about this?" asked Shepherd.

"There are all kinds of research possibilities," Greene began. "Let's look first at what we can learn from the data the firm already maintains. I'm talking about our financial information, Chip. We have a wealth of secondary data stored in our billing system, and we've never really tapped it for marketing purposes.

"We can extract and organize this information and learn a lot about who our biggest clients are, how often they use us, and how many of our practice groups they use. We can also create profiles on the types of clients we have, all from information we can pull from the billing system.

"Depending on how detailed our attorneys or their secretaries have gotten with the 'Comments' section of the billing system, we may also be able to spot patterns in other things, such as which firms are getting the business we can't handle. For example, when there's a conflict of interest, we may be able to determine what business is being lost and to which firms we are losing it.

"At some point in the process, we'll want to collect some primary data as well. We'll obtain that kind of information from clients themselves. There are many ways to do this. For now, however, let's assess what's on hand and how we can learn from it."

The discussion continued, with Greene and Shepherd identifying the research problem and outlining the objectives of proposed research. Greene agreed to prepare a memo summarizing their discussion, which Shepherd would use in a report to management on how the research program would proceed. ∎

Summary

Learning Objective 1

Explain the difference between a program strategy and a project strategy in marketing research.

A company's overall philosophy of how marketing research fits into its marketing plan determines its program strategy for marketing research. A program strategy specifies the types of studies that are to be conducted, and for what purposes. It might even specify how often these studies are to take place. The design of the individual studies themselves constitutes the firm's project strategy.

Learning Objective 2

Outline the steps in the research process and show how the steps are interrelated.

The steps in the research process are: (1) formulate the problem, (2) determine the research design, (3) determine the data collection method, (4) design the data collection forms, (5) design the sample and collect the data, (6) analyze and interpret the data, and (7) prepare the research report. These steps are highly interrelated in that a decision made at one stage will affect decisions

in every other stage, and a revision of the procedure in any stage often requires modification of procedures in every other stage.

Learning Objective 3

Cite the most critical error in marketing research.

Total error, rather than the size of an error that occurs in any single stage, is the most critical error in research work.

Learning Objective 4

Highlight the main difference between the teleological and deontological ethical frameworks.

Teleological ethics focuses on society as the unit of analysis and stresses the consequences of an act on all those directly or indirectly affected by it. If the benefits of the act to society exceed its costs, the act is ethical; if the net benefits are negative, the act is unethical. Deontological ethics focus on the individual as the unit of analysis and specifically on the rights to which every individual is entitled. Activities which violate an individual's basic rights are considered unethical.

Key Terms

program strategy (page 40)
project strategy (page 40)
research process (page 40)
secondary data (page 42)
primary data (page 42)
sampling frame (page 43)
probability sample (page 43)
nonprobability sample (page 43)

editing (page 43)
coding (page 43)
tabulation (page 43)
ethics (page 46)
marketing ethics (page 46)
teleology (page 48)
deontology (page 48)

Review Questions

1. What is the difference between a program strategy for research and a project strategy?
2. What is the research process?
3. What is the most important error in research? Explain.
4. What are the main differences between the teleological and deontological ethical frameworks?

Discussion Questions, Problems, and Projects

1. What advantages are gained by marketing researchers who follow the research process illustrated in Figure 3.1?

2. For each of the situations described below, which type of research design is most appropriate? Why?

   (a) Frank's Flies is a fishing lure manufacturer. Frank's management has decided to enter the lucrative market for trout flies, an area in which the company has little experience. The fly development department has decided that it needs more information concerning trout fishing in general before it can begin designing the new product line.

   (b) The management team at Aardvark Audio strongly suspects that the company's current advertising campaign is not achieving its stated goal of raising consumer awareness of the company's name to a 75 percent recognition level in the target market. The team has decided to commission a research project to test the effectiveness of the various ads in the current campaign.

   (c) Ace Fertilizer Company is trying to decide where advertisements for its vegetable garden fertilizers should be placed. Management is contemplating a research project to determine which publications home gardeners read on a regular basis.

3. Using the steps of the research process to structure your thinking, evaluate the following marketing research effort.

   The FlyRight Airline Company was interested in altering the interior layout of its aircraft to suit the tastes and needs of an increasing segment of its market—businesspeople. Management was planning to reduce the number of seats and install small tables to enable businesspeople to work during long flights. Prior to the renovation, management decided to do some research to ensure that these changes would suit the needs of the passengers. To keep expenses to a minimum, the following strategy was employed.

Questionnaires were completed by passengers during flights. Due to the ease of administration and collection, the questionnaires were distributed only on the short flights (those less than one hour). The study was conducted during the second and third week of December, as that was when flights were full. To increase the response rate, each flight attendant was responsible for a certain number of questionnaires. Management thought this was a good time to acquire as much information as possible; hence, the questionnaire included issues apart from the new seating arrangement. As a result, the questionnaire took 20 minutes to complete.

4. Schedule an interview with the marketing research director of a firm near your home or where you go to school. In the interview, try to develop an exhaustive list of the general types of studies the firm conducts and for what purposes. Pick two of the studies and secure as much detail as you can on their specifics, such as the type and size of the sample, the data collection instruments used, what is done with the data after they are collected, and so on. Report on what you find, organizing that report according to the firm's program and project strategies for research.

Suggested Additional Readings

For an empirical investigation of the extent to which marketing researchers rely on teleological versus deontological ethics to guide their decision making, see John Pallister, Clive Nancarrow, and Ian Brace, "Navigating the Righteous Course: A Quality Issue," *Journal of the Market Research Society*, 41 (July 1999), pp. 327–342

For in-depth discussion of the major ethical issues that arise when dealing with research participants, see Dan Toy, Lauren Wright, and Jerry Olson, "A Conceptual Framework for Analyzing Deception and Debriefing Effects on Marketing Research," *Psychology & Marketing*, 18 (July 2001), pp. 691–719.

Allan J. Kemmel and N. Craig Smith, "Deception in Marketing Research: Ethical, Methodological, and Disciplinary Implications," *Psychology & Marketing*, 18 (July 2001), pp. 663–689.

Problem Formulation

© PhotoDisc/Getty Images

Chapter 4

Learning Objectives

1. *Specify the key steps in problem formulation.*

2. *Discuss two objectives of the initial meeting with the research client.*

3. *Discuss the two general sources of marketing problems/opportunities.*

4. *Explain why the researcher must be actively involved in problem formulation.*

5. *Describe the ALCA Model.*

6. *Distinguish between two types of decision problems.*

7. *Distinguish between a decision problem and a research problem.*

8. *Describe the Research Request Agreement.*

9. *Outline the various elements of the research proposal.*

10. *Describe types of research that should be avoided.*

Elizabeth Silver didn't like what she was hearing from her ad agency, BBDO Worldwide. Silver, senior vice president of advertising at Visa USA, had asked BBDO to run focus groups to learn consumers' image of the Visa credit card. What they said was a little embarrassing.

Charles Miesmer, vice chairman and senior executive creative director of BBDO, put it this way: "We heard 'garden hose.'" In other words, people thought of Visa when it came time to pay for mundane items.

Silver, Miesmer, and their teams agreed that this was not an image that served the company well.

They wanted the brand to stand apart from its major rival, MasterCard. They wanted people to think of using a Visa card in more situations. And they wanted people to feel good about using their Visa card—not to feel awkward pulling it out on a special date or with an important client.

To fulfill those plans, Visa needed a makeover—a more exciting image.

Silver and Miesmer agreed that their strategy would be to reposition Visa. They wanted Visa to be more prestigious, even potentially a card that businesses would issue to their executives and salespeople. "But how can we tell people that Visa is something different?" mused a member of Silver's group.

Miesmer promised that his team would soon be back with a proposal. He already had an idea.

Discussion Issues

1. What is the decision problem Elizabeth Silver faces?

2. What specific research problems emerge from this decision problem?

3. How should the Visa and BBDO teams proceed? ■

Problem Formulation

A business executive once remarked that he had spent his entire career climbing the ladder of success only to discover when he got to the top that the ladder was leaning on the wrong building. He regretted that he hadn't devoted more of his time to the things that really mattered. If we aren't careful, the same thing can happen with marketing research: we can take all the necessary steps and get perfectly valid answers—only to discover that we've been asking the wrong questions.

The Coca-Cola Company's experience with New Coke in the 1980s is a classic example of how not defining the problem correctly can lead to disastrous results.[1] Coca-Cola's market share had shrunk from 60% in the mid-1940s to less than 24% in 1983. At the same time, Pepsi, the product's chief rival, had continued to gain market share. It was easy for Coca-Cola's managers to see that a problem existed. Stung by Pepsi-Cola's "Pepsi Challenge" promotional campaign, which showed consumers consistently preferring the taste of Pepsi to Coke in blind taste tests, company researchers, managers, and executives became convinced that Coca-Cola had a "taste problem."[2]

© Terri L. Miller/E-Visual Communications, Inc.

Marketing research can only be of value if the problem is defined correctly. The Coca-Cola Company learned this lesson the hard way in the 1980s when they introduced New Coke. It had been thoroughly researched, but ultimately was a failure because the company didn't take into account consumers' loyalty to the original product.

Coca-Cola Company researchers proceeded to conduct extensive marketing research—including 190,000 blind taste tests with consumers, costing $4 million—to compare the taste of a new version of Coca-Cola with that of Pepsi and regular Coke. The new formulation was preferred by a majority of consumers. Further research demonstrated that the results held—in fact, were stronger—when consumers were allowed to glimpse the labels to see what they were tasting. Managers were confident that they had developed a product that would successfully solve the taste problem. On the basis of the research, the company introduced New Coke to the world in April 1984, replacing the original formula.

The decision to replace the original product with New Coke has become infamous as one of the biggest marketing blunders in history.[3] The company performed an about-face less than three months later with the reintroduction of the original Coca-Cola product. What happened? The research was technically sound; it is quite likely that people actually preferred the sweeter taste of New Coke. A far greater issue than taste for many consumers, however, was the idea that the original Coca-Cola—with a century's worth of history and imagery—was being tampered with, discontinued. Although Coca-Cola managers recognized in advance that some consumers would probably not accept a change in the brand, they continued to focus on the "taste problem," which led to disastrous results.

Many other companies have stumbled because of research with misguided problem formulation. For example, many people do not know that the Miller Brewing Co. did not invent Lite beer. Rather, it was first developed by Meister Bräu.[4] Initial taste tests indicated that people liked the newly developed beer, but it failed miserably when Meister Bräu introduced it to the marketplace. The frustrated company in turn sold it to Miller, who defined the marketing research problem more broadly than simply consumer taste preferences. Miller's research encompassed consumer perceptions of the new type of beer and found that the very concept of a diet beer connoted "wimp," while big beer drinkers tried to project macho images. Based on their research, Miller's emphasis became one of changing the image of the brand through its use of famous sports personalities.

Another instance of poor problem definition involved RJR Nabisco's attempt to develop a smokeless cigarette. After much hard work to develop a cigarette with an acceptable taste but no visible smoke, the company launched Eclipse. Unfortunately, smokers didn't care to buy the product; they liked the smoke of a cigarette. Cigarettes' smokiness was a problem only for nonsmokers—and they, by definition, were not the company's target market. The company's $100 million development effort went to correct something its customers didn't view as a problem by developing a product they didn't want.[5]

How does one avoid the trap of researching the wrong problem? The best way is to delay research until the problem is properly defined. Too often the researcher's initial step is to write a proposal describing the methods that will be used to conduct the research. Instead, the researcher—in cooperation with managers—must take the time necessary to fully understand the situation. Even well designed and executed research can't rescue a project (and the resulting business decisions and consequences) if researchers have failed to define the problem correctly. An old adage says, "A problem well defined is half solved." This is especially true in marketing research, for it is only when the problem has been clearly defined and the objectives of the research precisely stated that research can be designed properly.

Problems versus Opportunities

When we talk about "defining the problem" or "problem formulation" we simply mean a process of trying to identify specific areas where additional information is needed about the marketing environment. A manager may be confronted with a situation that has obvious neg-

PART 1:
Introduction to Marketing Research and Problem Definition

ative ramifications for the organization (e.g., sharply reduced revenues compared with earlier periods for a retailer; chronic shortage of volunteers to support an ongoing civic organization; lack of evidence of market demand to persuade investors to "buy in" to an entrepreneur's idea for a new kind of product). These kinds of situations are normally thought of as "problems."

On the other hand, a manager might face a situation with potentially positive results for the organization (e.g., the organization's research department has invented a new chemical compound that promises to revolutionize the production process for many kinds of products; brand managers think they have identified a market segment of consumers whose needs are not being met adequately by competitors). Managers must often decide how to exploit these "opportunities," if it all.

Although it is sometimes useful to distinguish between problems and opportunities, it is often better to think of problems and opportunities more as two sides of the same coin. Regardless of perspective, both situations require good information about the marketing environment before managers make important decisions. And today's opportunity is tomorrow's problem if a company fails to take advantage of the opportunity while competitors do. Similarly, a company that successfully deals with a problem before its competitors do has created an opportunity to move ahead in the industry. For these reasons, we usually refer to a "problem" as something that needs information regardless of whether the organization originally viewed the situation as a problem or an opportunity.

The Problem Formulation Process

Exhibit 4.1 presents the six key steps in problem formulation. Defining the problem correctly is critical to the success of the project. Problem formulation is among the most difficult—and certainly most important—aspects of the entire marketing research process. The difficulty is primarily due to the uniqueness of every situation a manager may encounter. Although we provide some fairly specific directions, problem formulation involves more art than science and must be approached with great care.

Specify the key steps in problem formulation.

Step One: Meet with Client

The first step toward defining the problem correctly is to meet with the manager(s) requesting marketing research. This should be done at the earliest stages of the project for two important reasons. First, it is essential that managers and researchers are able to communicate openly with one another, and this likely won't happen unless the parties develop an initial rapport and a relationship built on mutual trust. To the extent possible, researchers need to

Discuss two objectives of the initial meeting with the research client.

Exhibit 4.1

Key Steps in Problem Formulation

Meet with client to obtain (a) management statement of problem/opportunity; (b) background information; (c) management objectives for research; and (d) possible managerial actions to result from research.

Clarify the problem/opportunity by questioning managerial assumptions and gathering additional information from managers and/or others as needed. Perform exploratory research as necessary.

State the manager's decision problem, including source (planned change or unplanned change in environment) and type (discovery- or strategy-oriented).

Develop full range of possible research problems that would address the manager's decision problem.

Select research problem(s) that best address the manager's decision problem, based on an evaluation of likely costs and benefits of each possible research problem.

Prepare and submit Research Request Agreement to client. Revise in consultation with client.

keep the client engaged and actively participating in the process, especially during problem formulation, but also at later stages. This requires strong two-way communication. During problem formulation, researchers must communicate to managers what marketing research can and cannot accomplish. At the same time, managers must be able to communicate the nature of the problem as well as the information they need to be able to deal with it.

The second reason to meet with the client is straightforward. The researcher must get as much information as possible from the manager with respect to the problem/opportunity at hand. In particular, the researcher needs to obtain a clear understanding of the problem from the manager's viewpoint, along with all relevant background information. Questions such as "What caused you to notice the problem?" "What factors do you think have created this situation?" and "What is likely to happen if nothing changes in the next 12 months?" are appropriate at this point. The researcher also needs to understand exactly what the manager hopes to accomplish, what s/he wants to learn through marketing research. In order to make sure that the information developed through marketing research is useful, it is very important to also have the manager requesting the research provide specific actions that they plan to take depending upon the results of the project. If the manager doesn't know what actions

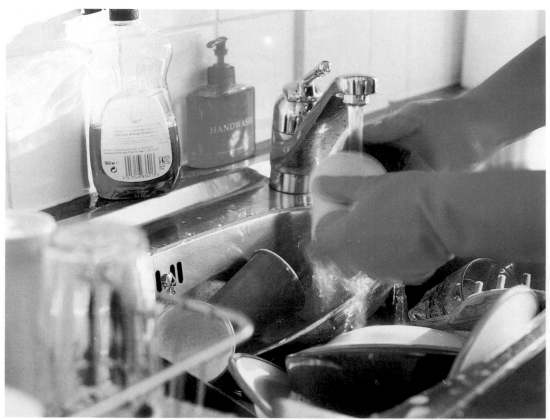

Customer complaint letters led Rubbermaid executives to an unexpected product opportunity in developing the one-piece dish drainer

PART 1:
Introduction to Marketing Research and Problem Definition

would be taken based on the range of possible results, then there is a good chance that the problem hasn't been defined carefully enough.

During the initial meeting with the client the researcher should also try to get managers' insights into the fundamental source of the problem/opportunity at hand. In general, there are only two basic sources of marketing problems: (1) unanticipated changes in the marketing environment, and (2) planned changes in the marketing environment. Understanding the basic source of the problem will provide clues about the nature of the problem and the type of research that is needed.

There are many elements in a firm's external environment that can unexpectedly create problems or opportunities. These environmental elements include demographic, economic, technological, competitive, political, and legal changes that can impact, often significantly, the marketing function. How the firm responds to new technology or a new product introduced by a competitor or a change in demographics or lifestyles largely determines whether the change turns out to be a problem or an opportunity. In recent years, many change-driven problems and opportunities have resulted from the widespread adoption of Internet technology. For example, the executives and editors of the business world's prestigious *Fortune* magazine noticed a growing amount of advertising in online rivals such as *Business 2.0* and *Red Herring*. They conducted an analysis and found that three-quarters of that advertising came from advertisers that don't buy space in *Fortune*. The magazine's management therefore began evaluating whether to launch the company's own cyberpublication.[6]

A slightly different form of unplanned change is serendipity, or chance ideas. An unexpected new idea might come from a customer in a complaint letter or by some other means. For example, Rubbermaid makes its executives read customer letters to find out how people like the company's products. These letters often lead to new product ideas. For example, complaints about the difficulty of storing traditional rack-and-mat sets because of their bulk led the company to develop a one-piece dish drainer for washing dishes by hand. Strict attention to detail, including suggestions like this, has allowed the company to introduce hundreds of new products a year; over 30 percent of the company's sales in recent years have come from new products.[7] Marketing research plays an important role in the company's development process. Besides customers, other sources of good ideas are salespeople and their call reports.

Not all change is unanticipated. Much of it is planned. Most firms want to increase their business and contemplate various marketing actions for doing so. These actions include the introduction of new products, improved distribution, more effective pricing, and advertising. Planned change is oriented more toward the future, while unanticipated change is oriented more toward the past. The former is more proactive, while the latter is more reactive. Planned change is change that the firm wishes to bring about—the basic issue is how. The role of marketing research here is to investigate the feasibility of the alternatives being considered.

3 Discuss the two general sources of marketing problems/ opportunities.

Step Two: Clarify the Problem/Opportunity

During the first step in problem formulation, the primary task of the researcher is to listen carefully as managers provide their perspective of the problem, its background and source (planned vs. unplanned change), and what they hope to learn through marketing research. Step Two involves helping managers get precisely to the heart of the problem. This may seem odd at first—after all, shouldn't managers have a better understanding of the problem than the researcher? Good researchers, however, are proactive at this stage to ensure that usable results are ultimately obtained. If you conduct the research based on the client's definition of the problem and the results cannot be used, who do you think will be blamed? That's right; more often than not, the researcher will take the fall. Even worse, the actual problem still will not have been defined, much less solved.

Thus, researchers must avoid simply responding to managers' requests for information. To do so is like a doctor letting a patient perform his or her own diagnosis and prescribe the treatment as well. Instead, the researcher needs to work with the manager much like a doctor works with a patient; both need to communicate openly in translating symptoms into underlying causal factors.

There is a general tendency to assume that managers have a clear understanding of the problems they face and that the only real difficulty lies in communicating that understanding. This assumption is false. To many managers, the problem is primarily a lack of important facts, which they tend to define as a broad area of ignorance. "They say in effect: 'Here are some things I don't know. When the results come in, I'll know more. And when I know more, then I can figure out what to do.'"[8] Research results based on such a mode of operation often turn out to be "interesting," but not very actionable. Good marketing research derives from a clear understanding of what information is needed and how that information will be used to address the problem at hand.

At this stage of the research, one of the most important things a researcher can do is to provide a different perspective of the problem/opportunity. Many managers, particularly those who have been with a company for a long time, become afflicted with what might be termed "normal thinking." That is, they have adopted a routine way of looking at the business and responding to different situations. In many ways this is a good thing; the presence of normal operating procedures allows great efficiency through the development of standards and routines. As we have seen, some forms of marketing research (e.g., marketing information system) are by nature routine and standardized. When a manager needs marketing research on a project basis to address a particular problem/opportunity, however, the normal ways of thinking and approaching situations should be discarded in favor of a fresh approach. It is the duty of the researcher to provide the new perspective, even though the client may not appreciate it at first.

The following example might help you begin to think creatively. There is an old story of a factory worker who left the factory to walk home each night pushing a wheelbarrow piled high with trash and scraps left over from the production process. At the factory gate, the security guard would tip his hat, say "good evening," and wonder to himself why anybody would want to take that stuff home. But since the scraps held no value to the company, the guard let him pass each night. Years later, after both the security guard and the factory worker had left the company, the former guard happened to run into the worker at a shopping mall. After they exchanged greetings, the guard pulled the worker aside and said, "Say, now that we're both retired, there's something I've just got to know. What did you want with all that trash you took home every night?" The worker looked at him and smiled. "I didn't want the trash," he said. "I was stealing wheelbarrows!"

The security guard in this story was guilty of normal thinking. He was focused on the contents of the wheelbarrow—right where his focus "should" be, at least under normal conditions—and failed to consider any other perspectives. Similarly, if you ask 100 people which way a clock's hands move, 99 or more of them will say "clockwise." Which is true, unless you take the clock's perspective; then, the hands move counterclockwise. Again, at this stage of the project, one of the researcher's primary tasks is to ensure that managers are focused on the true problem.

Bringing a new perspective to a problem may sound like a good idea, but how is it actually done? How could the Coca-Cola Company have known to define its problem a bit more broadly than as simply one of taste? To be honest, it's tough. Because the researcher doesn't deal with the manager's issues on a daily basis, s/he is automatically less likely to fall victim to normal thinking. In general, at this stage researchers should follow the **ALCA Model**—*A*sk, *L*isten, *C*larify, and *A*nalyze. Until the problem/opportunity is properly formulated, researchers must be asking key questions, listening carefully to the answers to those questions, asking more questions to clarify the situation further, and at all times carefully thinking about, or analyzing, the situation.

After gathering and reviewing all relevant background information on Step One, including the manager's statement of the problem, the researcher should develop a list of questions for the manager or others involved in the project. Researchers at times must adopt the role of

---

4 *Explain why the researcher must be actively involved in problem formulation.*

5 *Describe the ALCA Model.*

ALCA Model
A model especially useful in early stages of problem formulation in which researchers *ask* questions, *listen* carefully to responses, *clarify* the situation by asking additional questions, and *analyze* available information about the situation.

PART 1:
Introduction to Marketing Research and Problem Definition

The Best-Laid Models of Mice and Men . . .

The late Bob Keith, while president of the Pillsbury Company, was once persuaded by Pillsbury's operations researchers to review one of his major marketing decisions using a formal decision model. He agreed to the outcomes, their values, and their probabilities, and chose the decision rule he felt most appropriate. The computer then calculated the expectations, compared them, and reported the alternative that should be chosen according to that rule. Keith disagreed, noting that another alternative was obviously the only correct choice—indeed, it was the choice that had been made not long before. "How can that be?" the researchers asked. "You accepted all the values and probabilities and chose the decision rule yourself. The rest is just arithmetic." "That's fine," Keith replied, "but you forgot to ask me about a few other things that were more important."

Source: Adapted from Charles Raymond, *The Art of Using Science in Marketing* (New York: Harper and Row, 1974), p. 17.

detective in order to uncover the hidden agendas, information, and decision alternatives lurking beneath the surface in any marketing research situation. If a critical piece of information remains undiscovered, even the most sophisticated research techniques cannot solve the problem. Attempting to impress the company president, researchers at Pillsbury discovered this fact belatedly—to their embarrassment (Exhibit 4.2). It is unfortunate, but true, that managers sometimes fail to explicitly state their objectives in conducting research.

> Despite a popular misconception to the contrary, objectives are seldom given to the researcher. The decision maker seldom formulates his objectives accurately. He is likely to state his objectives in the form of platitudes which have no operational significance. Consequently, objectives usually have to be extracted by the researcher. In so doing, the researcher may well be performing his most useful service to the decision maker.[9]

Sometimes it is necessary to challenge managers on their pre-existing assumptions. For example, in the case of a new service that hasn't lived up to revenue expectations, perhaps there was never any evidence of consumer need for that type of service. It is also sometimes useful to probe managers as to why the problem is important: "Why do you want to measure customer satisfaction? Have you seen signs that customers may not be satisfied? Are you concerned about a new competitor that's entered the market? Are you planning to upgrade service and want a baseline level of satisfaction?" The point isn't to put a manager on the spot or to demonstrate superior intellect; the point is to help the manager understand the true nature of the problem. Asking hard questions is much easier if you have demonstrated your professionalism and have begun to develop a rapport with the client.

One way to ensure that the true problem is addressed in the research is through the use of scenarios that attempt to anticipate the contents of the final report. The researcher is primarily responsible for preparing the scenarios. Based on his or her understanding of the situation, the researcher tries to anticipate what the final report could look like and prepares hypothetical elements, admittedly in relatively crude form. The researcher then confronts the decision maker with tough questions like, "If I came up with this cross tabulation with these numbers in it, what would you do?"[10] One of the biggest payoffs that comes from this exercise is improved communication between researcher and manager as to the exact parameters of the study. For example, one large electronics company wished to determine the knowledge of and preferences for stereo components among young consumers. It was only after the researchers prepared mock tables showing preference by age and sex that the client's wishes became truly clear. Based on their prior discussions, the researchers specified the age breakdowns for the tables as 13 to 16 and 17 to 20. Only after presenting this scenario to the company's managers did the researchers learn that to the client, "young" meant children age 10 or older. The client further believed that preteens are very volatile and undergo radical changes from year to year, especially as they approach puberty. Thus, not only was the contemplated research wrong from the standpoint of starting age it would attempt to access, but the planned age categories were wrong for capturing the client's basic concerns. Without the scenarios, the client's expectations may not have surfaced until the research was too far underway to change it.

It is often advisable to conduct exploratory research at this stage, particularly when managers have seen evidence of a problem (e.g., falling sales revenue, increasing complaints from customers), but don't know the underlying causes. As we discuss in the following chapter, exploratory research can be used to help pinpoint the problem.

Step Three: State the Manager's Decision Problem

6 *Distinguish between two types of decision problems.*

decision problem
The problem facing the decision maker for which the research is intended to provide answers.

discovery-oriented decision problem
A decision problem that typically seeks to answer "what" or "why" questions about a problem/opportunity. The focus is generally on generating useful information.

At this point, the researcher should be able to state the manager's **decision problem,** which is simply the basic problem/opportunity facing the manager for which marketing research is intended to provide answers. A well-stated decision problem takes the manager's perspective, is as simple as possible, and takes the form of a question. For example, consider a new coffee shop near a university campus that has been open for about 6 months, but has yet to make a profit. Costs have been held as low as possible; sales revenue simply hasn't materialized as quickly as expected. While the owner no doubt has many questions about her business, its lack of success, and how to move forward successfully, her initial decision problem might best take the form "Why are store revenues so low?" This situation was certainly unanticipated, so the problem has originated from unplanned change.

The decision problem facing the coffee shop owner is an example of a **discovery-oriented decision problem.** Discovery-oriented problems are common with unplanned changes in the marketing environment. In these situations, managers often simply need basic information about "what is going on?" and "why is it going on?" and the researcher is asked primarily to provide facts that decision-makers can use in formulating strategies in dealing with the unanticipated situation. For instance, researchers could provide information about customer satisfaction (perhaps the shop doesn't consistently offer a quality product), or the overall awareness level among the target market (maybe most people don't know about the shop), or consumer perceptions of competing coffee shops (perhaps a nearby coffee shop is perceived as a better value for the money). In each case, the researcher can offer facts and figures that help shed light on the basic problem. Note, however, that discovery-oriented research rarely solves a problem in the sense of providing actionable results. This form of research aims simply to provide some of the insights and the building blocks necessary for managers to make better decisions.

Discovery-oriented decision problems may also apply to situations of planned change, particularly in early stages of planning when the issue is to identify possible courses of action (as opposed to choosing a preferred course of action). In this situation, key questions are likely to include "what options are available?" or "why might this option be effective?"

strategy-oriented decision problem
A decision problem that typically seeks to answer "how" questions about a problem/opportunity. The focus is generally on selecting alternative courses of action.

A second form of manager's decision problem, the **strategy-oriented decision problem,** aims more directly at making decisions. This type of decision problem is commonly used with planned change, with an emphasis on how the planned change should be implemented. It is also appropriate for problems originating from unplanned change, provided that enough is known about the situation (perhaps through discovery-oriented research) so that strategic decisions are warranted. Suppose that initial research for the coffee shop indicated that only 38% of the customers in its target market were aware that the coffee shop existed. An appropriate decision problem at this point might be "How do we increase awareness?" and researchers might determine the effectiveness of two proposed advertising campaigns at generating awareness. Notice that the output from the research process in this situation will be a recommendation about which of two specific alternatives to choose. The key distinction between discovery-oriented and strategy-oriented decision problems is the latter's focus on actionable results.

Where possible, researchers should attempt to conduct strategy-oriented research. As noted earlier, providing additional "facts" through discovery research may not get managers much closer to a good decision. And many companies place a preference on strategy-oriented

PART 1:
Introduction to Marketing Research and Problem Definition

research. At General Mills, for example, the emphasis is on research that evaluates alternatives. Thus, instead of asking the question, "What proportion of potato chips is eaten at meals?" General Mills would ask, "How can we advertise our potato chips for meal consumption?" or "Will a 'meal commercial' sell more chips than our present commercial?" (both strategy-oriented questions). Still, there are times when discovery-oriented research is absolutely essential, particularly when managers are confronted with unplanned changes in the environment.

Strategy-oriented decision problems are by nature more specific than discovery-oriented decision problems. Strategy-oriented decision problems are designed to select one alternative course of action over other available options. Research can be properly designed only when the alternative courses of action being considered are known. The more obvious ones are typically given to the researcher by the decision maker, and the researcher's main task is to determine whether the list provided indeed exhausts the alternatives. Quite often the researcher will not be informed of some of the options being considered. The researcher should check to see that all options have been made explicit, since it is important that the research be relevant to all alternatives.

As an example of the types of alternative courses of action that a company may weigh, consider the Campbell Soup Company, which has a strong commitment to keeping pace with consumer and technological trends. As part of its ongoing research, the company's product managers team up with in-house and outside researchers to probe for openings in the market. Research teams have investigated the preferences and eating habits of growing consumer market segments and noted the preference for easy-to-prepare items. Thus, some of the company's newest products are based on convenient packaging: tomato soup in resealable plastic bottles and microwaveable soup in single-serving containers. The company is also testing a type of vending machine for soup, which could be installed in convenience stores.[11]

Step Four: Develop Possible Research Problems

The manager's decision problem describes the manager's view of the problem/opportunity. A **research problem,** on the other hand, is essentially a restatement of the decision problem in research terms, from the researcher's perspective. A research problem states specifically what research can be done to provide answers to the decision problem. Consider again the coffee shop owner facing the discovery-oriented decision problem of "Why are store revenues so low?" As is true of most discovery-oriented problems, there are several avenues of research that might provide insights into the problem, including "investigate current customer satisfaction," "assess target market perceptions of the coffee shop and its competitors," and "determine target market awareness." Each of these possible research problems begins with an

7 *Distinguish between a decision problem and a research problem.*

research problem
A restatement of the decision problem in research terms.

© 1990 Norm Bendell. Bendell Studio represented by David Goldman Agency, New York City, NY

It is of the utmost importance that the problem to be investigated is precisely defined before research is carried out. Sophisticated technique cannot overcome poor problem specification.

action word and describes, without getting into methodological detail, the specific information to be uncovered that might help solve the decision problem. Also, a myriad of possible research problems may be associated with a particular decision problem, particularly in the case of discovery-oriented problems. At this stage, the researcher's primary task is to develop the full range of research problems for a given decision problem. Exhibit 4.3 provides examples of the relationship between decision problems and research problems.

With strategy-oriented decision problems there are typically fewer possible research problems, because the focus has shifted onto making a choice among selected alternatives. At least, that's the way it's supposed to work. When the coffee shop owner shifted to the strategy-oriented decision problem "How do we increase awareness?" there were still several strategic options available including improved signage, increased levels of sales promotion, the introduction of an advertising campaign, and so on. Research problems might have included "which style of lettering is most readable on outdoor signage," "investigate the effectiveness of alternative coupon designs," or "determine consumer response to two proposed advertising campaigns." Presumably, the manager's experience, available budget, and/or discovery-oriented research led her to decide that advertising was the best area to consider for further research. (Don't forget that defining the problem is often more art than science.) At that point, the manager's decision problem might well have shifted to "Which advertising campaign should I select?" with a single associated research problem.

Where does the researcher get ideas about possible research problems? Usually, from the client during the process of clarifying the problem. Sometimes, however, new ideas will be uncovered through exploratory research or as a result of the researcher's experience. In any

Exhibit 4.3

Examples of the Relationship between Decision Problems and Research Problems

Decision Problems	Possible Research Problems
Discovery-Oriented (What? Why?)	
Why are store revenues so low?	Investigate current customer satisfaction.
	Assess target market perceptions of store and competitors.
	Determine target market awareness.
What needs do our customers have that are currently not being met?	Investigate customer lifestyles.
	Determine customer problems with existing products.
	Measure customer satisfaction.
Strategy-Oriented (How?)	
How do we increase store traffic?	Investigate effectiveness of different sales promotions.
	Determine consumer response to two proposed ad campaigns.
	Measure consumer preferences for new store layouts.
How should we introduce a new product?	Run test market to determine consumer preferences for different package sizes.
	Determine if at least 80% of test market purchasers are satisfied with product.
	Determine if product sampling promotion leads to 15% initial purchase rate.

case, the key point at this stage of problem formulation is to specify the full range of potential research problems.

Step Five: Select Research Problem(s) to be Addressed

Especially with discovery-oriented decision problems, there are likely to be many possible research problems that would provide useful information to the manager. As we have seen, even strategy-oriented problems will often have many associated research problems. The trick is to figure out which research problem(s) to pursue given the normal resource constraints facing managers. Only in rare cases will decision makers opt to fund research on all possible research problems. At this point, the researcher must carefully review each identified research problem in terms of the trade-off between the information to be obtained versus the costs of obtaining that information. The costs may include money, time, and effort.

It is particularly important to note from whom information would be gathered with each possible research problem. Gathering information from multiple populations means multiple data collection procedures, which in turn multiplies the overall cost of the project. For example, we noted three of the possible research problems for the coffee shop owner facing the discovery-oriented decision problem "Why are store revenues so low?" Investigating customer satisfaction will require gathering information from current customers. Assessing target market perceptions of the store and its competitors, as well as determining the target market's overall level of awareness of the store require collecting data from the target market, many of whom are obviously not current customers. Thus, to address all three research problems adequately would be costly. In this situation, the researcher would work closely with the coffee shop owner to determine the most likely problem area(s) and, in turn, the most profitable areas of research. (Again, more art than science.) If there are known problems with customer dissatisfaction, that may be the most appropriate research problem to address. On the other hand, the other two research problems involve the same respondents and might be accomplished in a single data collection procedure, bringing sizable benefit for the costs involved. If the researcher has done a thorough job at previous stages in the problem definition process, the selection of research problems should be relatively straightforward. Straightforward or not, the researcher must be able to justify the selection of the research problem(s) chosen.

It is important to note at this point that it is better to address one or two research problems fully than to try to tackle multiple issues and do a half-baked job on each. Our experience is that novice researchers, in their enthusiasm to do a good job, tend to believe that they can accomplish much more in a single project than is actually possible. The researcher usually cannot do all the research s/he would like to do because of budget considerations, which makes the choice of research problems so critical.

Step Six: Prepare Research Request Agreement

The researcher must ensure that the client understands and agrees with the problem as defined by the researcher (and that the researcher truly understands the problem confronting the manager). One useful mechanism for making sure that the client and the researcher are in agreement is to prepare a written **Research Request Agreement.**[12] The Research Request Agreement essentially summarizes the problem formulation process and should include, but is not limited to, the following items:

1. *Origin:* The events that led to the manager's decision problem. While the events may not directly affect the research that is conducted, they help the researcher understand more deeply the nature of the problem.
2. *Decision Problem:* The underlying question confronting the manager. A brief discussion of the source of the problem (i.e., planned vs. unplanned change) should be included. Importantly, whether the problem is discovery-oriented or strategy-oriented must be specified.
3. *Research Problem(s):* The range of research problems that would provide input to the decision problem. An overview of costs and benefits of each research problem should be

8 *Describe the Research Request Agreement.*

Research Request Agreement
The initial step that sets the research process in motion; this statement, which is prepared by the researcher after meeting with the decision maker, summarizes the problem and the information that is needed to address it.

included. The final choice of research problem(s) to be addressed must be indicated and justified.

4. *Use:* The way each piece of information will be used. For discovery-oriented decision problems, indicate key information to be obtained and how managers will use the information. For strategy-oriented decision problems, indicate the way the information will be used to help make the action decision. Supplying logical reasons for each piece of the research ensures that the research problem(s) make sense in light of the decision problem.

5. *Targets and their subgroups:* The groups from whom the information must be gathered. Specifying these groups helps the researcher design an appropriate sample for the research project.

6. *Logistics:* Approximate estimates of the time and money that are available to conduct the research. Both of these factors will affect the techniques finally chosen.

This written statement should be submitted to the decision maker for his or her approval. The approval should be formalized by having the decision maker initial and date the entire document or each section. Initialing the statement commits the manager and the researcher to an agreement that is much stronger than a verbal agreement. Lawrence Blagman, the director of marketing research for MasterCard International, found this out early in his research career. As he reports: "I learned a very big lesson once when conducting a communication test. The objectives for testing were not written. The results of the test came back, and when I proceeded to show how and why the advertising failed to communicate the intended message, the agency and marketing group were quick to point out all the other things that were communicated. Now although these other issues were of lesser importance and were not the purpose of the advertising, marketing proclaimed the test to be a success."[13] Consequently, the research department at MasterCard International requires those requesting research to sign the research request form prepared by the researchers before the department will even undertake the formal development of the procedures of the research.

The Research Proposal

9 *Outline the various elements of the research proposal.*

research proposal
A written statement that describes the marketing problem, the purpose of the study, and a detailed outline of the research methodology.

Once the purpose and scope of the research are agreed upon, researchers can turn their attention to the techniques that will be used to conduct the research. The decision maker should be informed of these techniques before the research begins. Typically, this is done via a formal **research proposal,** which also gives the researcher another opportunity to make sure the research being contemplated will provide information needed to address the decision maker's problem.

Some research proposals are very long and detailed, running 20 pages or more. Others are as short as a single page. Regardless of their length, however, most proposals contain the following elements:[14]

I. **Tentative project title**

II. **Statement of the problem**
One or two sentences describing the general problem under consideration.

III. **Define and delimit the problem**
Here the writer states the purpose(s) and scope of the problem. *Purpose* refers to goals or objectives. Closely related to this is *justification.* Sometimes this is a separate step, depending on the urgency of the task. *Scope* refers to the limits of the research effort; in other words, what *is* and what *is not* going to be investigated. Here is the point where the researcher spells out the various hypotheses to be investigated or the questions to be answered.

IV. **Outline**
Generally, this is a tentative framework for the entire project. It should be flexible enough to accommodate unforeseen difficulties, show statistical tables in outline form, and also show planned graphs.

PART 1:
Introduction to Marketing Research and Problem Definition

V. **Method and data sources**

The types of data to be sought (primary, secondary) are briefly identified. A brief explanation of how the necessary information or data will be gathered (e.g., surveys, experiments, library sources) is given. *Sources* refer to the actual depositories for the information, whether from government publications, company records, actual people, and so forth. If measurements are involved, such as consumers' attitudes, the techniques for making such measurements are stated. The relevance of all techniques (qualitative and quantitative) should be discussed. The nature of the problem will probably indicate the types of techniques to be employed, such as factor analysis, depth interviews, or focus groups.

VI. **Sample design**

This provides a description of the population to be studied and how it will be defined. The researcher specifies the population, states the desired sample size, and discusses how nonresponse and missing data are to be handled. If a nonrandom sample is to be used, the justification and type of sampling strategy to be employed, such as convenience sample, are stated.

VII. **Data collection forms**

The forms to be employed in gathering the data are discussed here. For surveys, this involves either a questionnaire or an interview schedule. For other research, the forms could include inventory forms, psychological tests, and so forth. The plan should state how these instruments have been or will be validated, and the reader should be given any evidence of their reliability and validity.

VIII. **Personnel requirements**

This provides a complete list of all personnel who will be required, indicating exact jobs, time duration, and expected rate of pay. Assignments should be made indicating each person's responsibility and authority.

IX. **Phases of the study with a time schedule**

This is a detailed outline of the plan to complete the study. The study should be divided into workable pieces. Then, considering the persons involved in each phase, their qualifications and experience, and so forth, the time for the job is estimated. Some jobs may overlap. This plan will help in estimating the time required.

Illustration:

1. Preliminary investigation—two weeks.
2. Final test of questionnaire—one week.
3. Sample selection—one week.
4. Mail questionnaires, field follow-up, and so forth—two months.
5. Additional tasks.

X. **Analysis plans**

This is a discussion of editing and proofreading of questionnaires, coding instructions, and the type of data analysis. An outline of some of the major tables that will appear in the report should be presented.

XI. **Cost estimate for doing the study**

Personnel requirements are combined with time on different phases to estimate total personnel costs. Estimates on travel, materials, supplies, drafting, computer charges, and printing and mailing costs must also be included. If an overhead charge is required, it should be calculated and added to the subtotal of the above items.

Once the decision maker has read and apporoved the proposal, he or she should formalize acceptance of it by signing and dating the document. Exhibit 4.4 contains a portion of an actual research plan, with some authorization and budget information removed, which was prepared by the research department at General Mills. Note the clearly stated criteria that will be used to interpret the results and the carefully crafted action standards specifying what will be done depending upon what the research results indicate. The effort expended by the marketing research department in translating information requests into specific, action-oriented

A Sample Proposal from General Mills for Protein Plus

1. Problem and Background. Protein Plus has performed below objectives in test-market. New product and copy alternatives are being readied for testing. Three alternative formulations—Hi Graham (A), Nut (B), and Cinnamon (C)—that retain the basic identity of current Protein Plus but have been judged to be sufficiently different and of sufficient potential for separate marketing have been developed for testing against the current product (D).

2. Decision Involved. Which product formulations should be carried into the concept fulfillment test?

3. Method and Design. An in-home product test in which one product is tested at a time. Each of the four test-products will be tested by a separate panel of 150 households. Each household will have purchased adult ready-to-eat cereal within the past month and will be interested in the test-product, as evidenced by their selection of Protein Plus as one or more of the next ten cereal packages they say they would like to buy. They will be exposed to Protein Plus in a booklet that will also contain an ad for several competitive products such as Product 19, Special K, Nature Valley, and Grape Nuts. A Protein Plus ad will be constructed for each of the four test-products, differing primarily in the kind of taste appeal provided. Exposure to these various executions will be rotated so that each of the four test-panels is matched on ready-to-eat cereal usage. The study will be conducted in eight markets. Product will be packaged in the current Protein Plus package flagged with the particular taste appeal for that product.

    The criterion measure will be the homemakers' weighted share after their exposure to the product, adjusted to reflect the breadth of interest in the various Protein Plus taste appeals that have been promoted.

    Rather than trust a random sampling procedure to represent the population at large, a quota will be established to ensure that the sample of people initially contacted for each panel will conform as closely as possible to the division of homemakers under 45 (56 percent) and over 45 (44 percent) in the U.S. population.

4. Criteria for Interpretation. Each formulation generating a higher weighted homemaker share than standard will be considered for subsequent testing. If more than one formulation beats standard, each will be placed in concept fulfillment test unless one is better than the other(s) at odds of 2:1 or more.

5. Estimated Project Expense: within ± 500: $22,000

6. Individual who must finally approve recommended action:#_____

7. Report to be delivered by #_____ if authorized by #_____# and test materials shipped by# _____

Source: Used with permission of General Mills.

statements like this helps account for the wide acceptance of and enthusiatic support for the research function at General Mills.

Research to Avoid

Although there are many benefits of marketing research, it is not without its drawbacks, especially when used inappropriately. It is even worse when researchers know that their actions are inappropriate or even unethical. Stealing competitors' documents in the name of competitive intelligence, falsifying data or results to please a client or manager, conducting advocacy research in which the goal is to support a particular position with pseudo-scientific results rather than search for the truth, attempting to sell products or services or ideas after telling respondents you are conducting marketing research (a process known as "sugging") are all blatantly unethical uses of marketing research. Unfortunately, these offenses and many others occur all too often. Several organizations offer guidelines or codes of ethics prohibiting unethical practices.[15]

Besides unethical research, there are other types of research that should be avoided. Sometimes a decision maker will have preset ideas about a particular situation, and surprisingly, his or her position may not change, regardless of what is found by the researcher. Research merely represents "conscience money" in these cases. The results are readily accepted when they are consistent with the decision the individual wants to make, or with the person's perceptions of the environment or the consequences of alternative actions. Otherwise, the results are questioned at best, or discarded as being inaccurate at worst. The reason, of course, is that the decision maker's view of the situation is so strongly held that the research will do little to change it. When this is the case, research would be a waste of the firm's resources.

The manager in the previous situation might be described as closed-minded, although his or her motives may be pure. Unfortunately, some managers take it a step further to "suggest" what the results should be when the project is completed, another form of advocacy research. In this case, however, the manager is probably setting up an alibi in case the advertising campaign fails or the new product never catches on (e.g., "But the research results were all positive . . ."). This is a manager to avoid if possible.

Research should also be avoided when resources such as time and budget are lacking to do the research appropriately. This may seem strange, in that some research ought to be better than none at all, but this isn't always the case. The danger is that managers will use preliminary or exploratory research as justification for important decisions. Not all research has to be expensive or take a lot of time, but important decisions should be supported by adequate research. Too often, managers are willing to take shortcuts.

ETHICAL dilemma 4.2

A manufacturer of bolts and screws approaches you and outlines the following problem: "My friend owns a hardware store, and you used a technique called multidimensional scaling to produce what I think he called a 'perceptual map,' which positioned his operation in relation to his competitors and showed him where there was space in the market to expand his business. I don't understand the details of it, but I was very impressed with the map and I want you to do the same for me."

- *What have you learned about the manufacturer's research problem?*
- *Is it likely that the development of a perceptual map will be useful to the manufacturer of bolts and screws?*
- *Is it ethical to agree to his proposal?*

Feeling pressed for time, these managers typically ask researchers to run a few focus groups, make 100 telephone calls to test a concept, or undertake one of the many other popular conventional techniques we refer to as "death wish" research. These techniques seem reasonable to the time-challenged
because they're quick, low-cost, and often corroborate what the marketer already thought.

They may take less time and cost less money, but death wish research techniques offer little in the way of value. What companies usually get is more misinformation than information, which then contributes to the failure of marketing programs. As a result, not surprisingly, executives' confidence in marketing research has declined.[16]

Even when done correctly, there are situations in which marketing research either cannot provide the answers a company seeks or poses disadvantages that outweigh its possible advantages. For example, the benefits of marketing research must always be weighed against the risks of tipping off a competitor, who can then rush into the market with a similar product at perhaps a better price or with an added product advantage. Moreover, when the product is truly innovative, it may be difficult for consumers to assess accurately how they would ultimately use it. For example, the telephone answering machine and computer mouse were both panned by the consumers who were first exposed to them.[17] Some companies will forgo test marketing if there is little financial risk associated with a new product introduction. The best strategy is to examine the potential benefits from the research and to make sure they exceed the anticipated costs, both financial and otherwise.

Choosing and Using a Research Supplier

Most sizable business organizations today have formal marketing research departments. However, except for the very largest consumer products companies, these departments tend to be small—sometimes consisting of one person. In such cases, the firm's researcher may spend less time conducting actual research than supervising projects undertaken by research suppliers hired by the firm. Marketing managers in many large companies also use outside suppliers.

There are many advantages to using research suppliers. If the research work load tends to vary over the course of the year, the firm may find it less expensive to hire suppliers to conduct specific projects when needed than to staff an entire in-house department that may sit idle between projects. Also, the skills required for various projects may differ. By hiring outside suppliers, the firm can match the project to the vendor with the greatest expertise in the particular area under investigation. In addition, hiring outside suppliers allows the sponsoring company to remain anonymous, and it avoids problems that might arise with regard to internal politics.

Although it has become increasingly common to buy marketing research, many managers are uncertain as to how to select a research supplier. The first step is to decide when research is really necessary. Although there is no simple formula for assessing this need, most managers turn to research when they are unsure about their own judgment and other information sources seem inadequate. Before contacting research suppliers, it is important for the manager to identify the most critical areas of uncertainty and the issues that would benefit most from research.

Once a manager has determined the most critical area for research, he or she is ready to seek the right supplier for the job. The selection process is not easy, for there are thousands of qualified marketing research companies in the United States. Some are full-service "generalist" companies; others are specialists in qualitative research, advertising-copy testing, concept testing, and so on, and still others are services that only conduct interviews, process data, or work with statistics.

It is important that the manager carefully evaluate the capabilities of suppliers in light of the company's research needs. Some issues require small-scale qualitative studies while others require large-scale quantitative research projects. It is essential that the vendor selected understand the firm's information needs and have the expertise required to conduct the research.

Experts suggest that managers seek proposals from at least three companies. They also urge that the research user talk with the persons at the supplier company who will be processing and analyzing the data, writing the report, supervising the interviewers, and making presentations to management. Marketing research benefits from heavy involvement of senior research professionals, who provide insights that come only from years of training and experience. The most important asset of a research firm is the qualifications of the research professional(s) who will be involved in the design, day-to-day supervision, and interpretation of the research.

The research user's responsibility is to communicate effectively with the prospective vendor and provide the necessary background and objectives for the study. Research users should also ask about the supplier's quality control standards. Most research firms are pleased when clients show concern about the quality of their work and will gladly explain their quality control steps in the areas of field work, coding, and data processing.

After reading the proposals and meeting key personnel, the manager should perform a comparative analysis. He or she should use the proposals to evaluate each vendor's understanding of

One possible, but not recommended, method for choosing a research supplier: "All right, Miss Burton, start the music and take away another chair."

PART 1:
Introduction to Marketing Research and Problem Definition

the problem, how each will address it, and the cost and time estimates of each. In making this evaluation, the manager needs to keep in mind that the value of the information to be produced is determined by its use, not its mere presence. Thus, the manager needs to be forthright in addressing how he or she would use the information provided by executing the various proposals.

Many firms have formal evaluation systems with specified criteria for evaluating research suppliers.[18] This is particularly true among those companies who use suppliers on a regular basis. One well-known dairy producer, for example, uses the criteria shown in Exhibit 4.5 to evaluate the research suppliers it uses. The company has a formal set of written guidelines that it shares with potential research suppliers, spelling out these criteria in more detail. Further, at the completion of each project, a research analyst, the manager, or the research director evaluates the supplier in terms of whether the provider was excellent, very good, good, fair, or poor in terms of each of the criteria. There is also a comment section for each criterion, where the evaluator can explain the basis of the evaluation. The firm applies as many of these criteria as it can when evaluating the proposals of new suppliers.

When evaluating suppliers that seem equally competent, a manager must rely on his or her intuitive assessment regarding the soundness of the research design proposed, the supplier's responsiveness to the manager's specific questions, and the vendor's understanding of the subtler aspects of the marketing problem.

An increasingly popular way for firms to work with marketing research suppliers is to form long-term partnering relationships with a few select firms. In a typical collaborative partnership, the client and research firm work together on an on-going basis on those projects for which the research firm has the necessary expertise, instead of the client relying on project-by-project bids to select suppliers for specific projects. In some situations, research firm staff may actually work at the client's premises on a regular basis. For example, many ACNielsen employees work directly at the offices of firms purchasing its scanner data, performing data analysis tasks that might have been done formerly by the client. The arrangements between firms and their research partners are often referred to as "preferred relationships," and may be captured by an informal understanding or formalized in a contract. The net result of partnering relationships is that both sides work with fewer companies, while the research firm

Exhibit 4.5

Criteria Used by Dairy Producer to Evaluate Research Suppliers

General attitude and responsiveness: enthusiastic, helpful, prompt replies on cost estimates, proposals, etc.
Marketing insight: informative, understands study objectives, has ability to analyze data, provides recommendations
Fundamental design: questionnaire, study instructions, test plan, etc.
Questionnaire construction: format, order and wording of questions, appropriate scales
Tabulation design: format, accuracy
Day-to-day serving: responsive and informative on study progress, problems, etc.
Analysis: thorough, relates to objectives
Quality of report writing: concise, clear, accurate, executive summary
Presentation: well planned, concise, materials organized, verbal skills
Delivery time: topline, tables, report
Cost: over, under, justified

Overall performance

Excellent: outstanding performance in all phases of the project
Very good: acceptable performance on all phases of the project
Good: work is satisfactory; however, could improve performance in one or two phases of the project
Fair: performance fell short in one or more phases of the project
Poor: performance and quality of the work is unacceptable

becomes an additional resource that extends the client's information-gathering and analysis capabilities. Over time, the research firm becomes more familiar with the client's business and issues. This has allowed those in client firms to spend more time on managerial functions, including problem definition, design, interpretation and recommendations, and less time on the nuts and bolts of a typical study.[19]

looking back...

For BBDO's Charles Miesmer, the key to a successful advertising strategy lay in additional insights gathered from the focus groups. Specifically, consumers indicated that they thought of American Express as the top card in terms of image but believed it wasn't widely accepted. The BBDO team got to work on an advertising campaign that would portray Visa as a card people could use in those situations where merchants wouldn't accept American Express. This enabled the ads to associate Visa with fun situations while also pointing out an important strength of the card: its wide acceptance.

When the BBDO team made its presentation to Visa, Silver and her group were positive, but they were most excited by the last idea presented: a campaign built on the slogan "Everywhere you want to be." Each ad profiles a fun, small retailer that accepts Visa but not American Express—places like Performance Bicycle, Fog City Diner in San Francisco, and Rosalie's, an Italian restaurant off the beaten path in Marblehead, Massachusetts.

The Visa team agreed that BBDO would test the campaign. If test audiences began to associate the brand with special life experiences rather than routine shopping chores, they would roll out the campaign nationwide. Then they would watch the company's market share and brand image.

Many years later, Visa is still using the same tag line. Although the company spends more on marketing than chief rival MasterCard, it stands behind what is now a $200 million campaign. Its executives credit the marketing strategy with boosting the brand's market share from 44 percent to 53 percent of annual credit card transactions in the United States.

The ads have helped the company's relationships with another group of customers: the retailers who accept the card. Initially, retailers were unsure they wanted to appear in the ads, but they saw that the first brave business owners to be featured became local celebrities. Before long, merchants were writing to Visa, urging that they be selected.

"It's everywhere you want to be" has also turned out to be very adaptable as Visa's business climate has changed. The company is more aggressively seeking business clients. Perhaps even more significantly, Visa is positioning itself to be with its customers in cyberspace. The company is not only advertising on the World Wide Web but is working with online merchants to accept electronic Visa transactions.

"Everywhere you want to be" today is as likely to be a hot Web site as a charming restaurant. ∎

Source: The Visa case is based on information from Mercedes M. Cardona, "Visa Still Gets Charge out of Campaign," *Advertising Age* (May 31, 1999), p. 6; Jennifer Kingson Bloom, "Visa Says Data Show That Brand Promotion Efforts Are Paying Off," *American Banker* (May 13, 1999, downloaded from Dow Jones Publications Library Web site, accessed at http://www.dowjones.com, July 27, 1999); Daintry Duffy, "Chief Executives Who Get IT," *CIO Enterprise* (July 15, 1999, downloaded from CIO Web site, http://www.cio.com, July 27, 1999); Paul Beckett, "Visa Is Loosening Its Grip on Credit-Card Development," *The Wall Street Journal* (June 11, 1999, downloaded from Dow Jones Publications Library, accessed from http://www.dowjones.com, July 27, 1999); Visa International Web site (http://www.visa.com, downloaded July 27, 1999).

PART 1:
Introduction to Marketing Research and Problem Definition

Summary

Learning Objective 1

Specify the key steps in problem formulation.
The six key steps are (1) meet with client, (2) clarify the problem/opportunity, (3) state the manager's decision problem, (4) develop full range of possible research problems, (5) select research problem(s), and (6) prepare and submit Research Request Agreement.

Learning Objective 2

Discuss two objectives of the initial meeting with the research client.
The two goals are (1) to develop rapport and open communication lines, and (2) to obtain as much information as possible about the problem/opportunity.

Learning Objective 3

Discuss the two general sources of marketing problems/opportunities.
The two sources of marketing problems, and consequently research problems, are (1) unanticipated change and (2) planned change. Research on planned change tends to be proactive, while research on unanticipated, or unplanned, change tends to be reactive.

Learning Objective 4

Explain why the researcher must be actively involved in problem formulation.
Researchers play a key role in problem formulation because they bring a new perspective to the problem/opportunity situation. Managers often fall into routine ways of seeing the business and its environment; researchers can help them get to the heart of the problem.

Learning Objective 5

Describe the ALCA Model.
When working with managers to define the problem, researchers should follow the ALCA Model: Ask, Listen, Clarify, and Analyze.

Learning Objective 6

Distinguish between two types of decision problems.
A decision problem is the basic problem or opportunity facing the manager. Discovery-oriented decision problems typically ask "what" or "why"

and generate information that can be used by managers to make important decisions. Strategy-oriented decision problems are usually directed at "how" planned change should be implemented and focus on making decisions.

Learning Objective 7

Distinguish between a decision problem and a research problem.
A decision problem is the problem/opportunity as seen by managers. Research problems restate the decision problem in research terms, from the researcher's perspective.

Learning Objective 8

Describe the Research Request Agreement.
The Research Request Agreement summarizes the problem formulation process in written form and is submitted to managers for approval. It includes the following sections: origin, decision problem, research problem(s), use, targets and their subgroups, and logistics.

Learning Objective 9

Outline the various elements of the research proposal.
Most research proposals contain the following elements: tentative project title, statement of the marketing problem, purpose and limits of the project, outline, data sources and research methodology, estimate of time and personnel requirements, and cost estimates.

Learning Objective 10

Describe types of research that should be avoided.
Several types of research should be avoided, including unethical research (e.g., sugging, advocacy research); research to support a decision that has already been made; research for which adequate resources are unavailable; and research in which the costs involved outweigh the benefits to be obtained.

Key Terms

ALCA Model (page 60)
decision problem (page 62)
discovery-oriented decision problem
(page 62)
strategy-oriented decision problem
(page 62)

research problem (page 63)
Research Request Agreement (page 65)
research proposal (page 66)

Review Questions

1. What does it mean when we say that problems and opportunities are two sides of the same coin?
2. What are the sources of marketing problems or opportunities? Are different sources typically associated with different research objectives? Explain.
3. What is "normal thinking"? Why is it a problem when defining the marketing problem/opportunity?
4. What is involved in using scenarios to help define the decision problem?
5. What is the basic nature of a decision problem?
6. What are the fundamental characteristics of the two types of decision problems?
7. What is a research problem? Why is it important to develop the full range of possible research problems?
8. What is involved in a Research Request Agreement? What is included in the written statement?
9. How does the research proposal differ from the Research Request Agreement?
10. What is "death wish" research? Why should it be avoided?
11. What factors should be considered when choosing a research supplier?

Discussion Questions, Problems, and Projects

1. Identify one possible research problem for each of the following decision problems. Tell whether the decision problems are discovery- or strategy-oriented.
   (a) Why have sales of my brand decreased?
   (b) Is my advertising working?
   (c) What pricing strategy should I choose for a new product?
   (d) Should I increase the level of expenditures on print advertising?
   (e) How can I increase in-store promotion of existing products?
   (f) Should I change the sales force compensation package?

2. Given the following research problems, identify corresponding decision problems which might provide useful information.
   (a) design a test market to assess the impact on sales volume of a particular discount theme
   (b) evaluate the stock level at the different warehouses
   (c) evaluate the sales and market share of grocery stores in a particular location
   (d) develop sales forecasts for a particular product line
   (e) assess the level of awareness among students, faculty, and staff about the benefits of a new software package
   (f) assess attitudes and opinions of customers toward existing theme restaurants

3. Briefly discuss the difference between a decision problem and a research problem.

4. In each of the following situations, identify the fundamental source of the marketing problem or opportunity, a decision problem arising from the marketing problem or opportunity, and a possible research problem.

(a) Apex Chemical Supply is a manufacturer of swimming pool maintenance chemicals. Recently, a malfunction of the equipment that mixes anti-algae compound resulted in a batch of the product that not only inhibits algae growth but also causes the pool water to turn a beautiful shade of light blue (with no undesirable side effects).

(b) State University's director of recruitment for the MBA program recently extended offers to 20 promising students. Only five offers were accepted. In the past, acceptance rates averaged 90 percent.

(c) Montgomery Candy Company has enjoyed great success in its small regional market. Management attributes much of this success to Montgomery's unique distribution system, which ensures twice weekly delivery of fresh product to retail outlets. The directors of the company have instructed management to expand Montgomery's geographical market if it can be done without altering the twice weekly delivery policy.

5. Schedule an interview with the marketing manager of a firm near your home or your school. In the interview, attempt to isolate a problem with which the manager is wrestling and for which research information would be helpful. Explore each of the parts of a Research Request Agreement with the manager. After the interview, prepare a short report that summarizes your discussion with respect to actions being considered, origin of the problem, information that would be useful to solve it, how each bit of information might be used in its solution, and the targets and subgroups for the study. Submit your report to the manager and secure an evaluation from him or her as to whether your report effectively captures the situation confronting the firm.

6. You are the marketing manager of a mid-size manufacturing firm. Recently you solicited proposals for an upcoming research project from three outside marketing research suppliers. You have the formal proposals in hand and must choose which supplier to use. In general, what criteria should you use in making your decision?

7. Describe three situations in which marketing research should not be undertaken. Explain why this is true.

Suggested Additional Readings

For useful discussions on how to translate decision problems into research problems, see Alan R. Andreasen, "'Backward' Market Research," *Harvard Business Review* 63 (May/June 1985), pp. 176, 180, 182.

Randall G. Chapman, "Problem-Definition in Marketing Research Studies," *Journal of Consumer Marketing* 6 (Spring 1989), pp. 51–59.

Paul W. Conner, "'Research Request Step' Can Enhance Use of Results," *Marketing News* 19 (January 4, 1985), p. 41.

William F. O'Dell, Andrew C. Ruppel, Robert H. Trent, and William J. Kehoe, *Marketing Decision Making: Analytic Framework and Cases,* 4th ed. (Cincinnati: South-Western Publishing Co., 1988).

For more detailed treatment of the content of the various parts of a research proposal and some sample proposals, see Ron Tepper, *How to Write Winning Proposals for Your Company or Client* (New York: John Wiley, 1989).

In the following description of an actual research project, note the kind of background information the researchers received when they first met their client, a group of radio station managers. Subsequent sections in this book will show how the researchers tackled the project and will analyze what they did well—or could have done better or differently.

In a small midwestern city, radio station owners and operators banded together to form a group called the Centerville Area Radio Association (CARA) to promote radio advertising. Station managers in the group were interested in finding out what their customers—specifically the local businesses who advertised on their stations—liked and disliked about radio advertising. They decided to commission a marketing research study to investigate the situation.

Members of CARA hoped the study would uncover ways that they could compete more effectively with the other major media: television and newspapers. They also hoped that the research could show them how they might better satisfy customers and thus increase their advertising sales volume.

When the study began, radio held a 13.5 percent share of the market in the Centerville area. CARA data showed that radio's sales volume had been growing at an annual rate of 9 to 10 percent for the past several years, and group members expected that this level of growth would continue for the foreseeable future.

CARA members thought that radio offered some advantages over newspapers and television. The group was especially proud of its sales philosophy, which embodied the marketing concept at its best. "The client comes first," was the watchword with CARA. CARA members thought that this philosophy, combined with their "consultant-sell" sales approach, made customers perceive radio sales representatives as more concerned, more cooperative, and better trained than other media reps. Hence, it was CARA's opinion that radio sales reps had a better image in the business than sales reps from other media. These opinions, while widely held by CARA members, had never been tested for accuracy.

The groups that interested CARA the most were local businesspeople who were already their customers or those whom they would like to have as customers. Businesses that were not yet advertisers were included in the study if they showed an interest in using one of the three major media in the future.

Finally, CARA wanted to know (1) if the amount of money a given business spent every year on advertising had any effect on its attitudes toward media and sales representatives and (2) what characteristics businesspeople sought in these representatives.

The researchers formulated a number of hypotheses or conjectures from the information presented them by CARA managers. For example, it was hypothesized that there would be differences in businesspeoples' attitudes toward television, radio, and newspaper, and that differences would also be found in attitudes toward sales representatives of each of the media. The various characteristics of the advertising media, as well as the attributes of the salespeople for each medium, were hypothesized to vary in importance to businesspeople. It was also hypothesized that the attitudes of businesspeople who were not managers or owners, and who were not involved in buying advertising, would differ from those of the population of interest.

After further probing, researchers were able to translate these hypotheses into problems that could be addressed by research. Specifically, they restated the decision problem in the form of two research problems:

1. Identify business decision makers' attitudes toward the advertising media of newspaper, radio, and television.
2. Identify business decision makers' attitudes toward the advertising sales representatives of newspaper, radio, and television.

They pointed out to CARA members that the information acquired from investigating these two areas could subsequently be used to make informed choices about what strategy to pursue in competing with other media.

Discussion Issues

It is, of course, too early to know what the actual results of the study might be. However, we can speculate on how varying results might affect management decisions.

1. What might management want to do if the study showed that businesspeople had a negative opinion of radio advertising?
2. What might they do if they found that advertisers liked their sales approach?
3. Using the steps in the research process as a guide, how would you suggest the research proceed?

Case • 1.1

Big Brothers of Fairfax County

Big Brothers of America is a social service program designed to meet the needs of boys ages six to 18 from single-parent homes. Most of the boys served by the program live with their mothers and rarely see or hear from their fathers. The purpose of the program is to give these boys the chance to establish a friendship with an interested adult male. Big Brothers of America was founded on the belief that association with a responsible adult can help program participants become more responsible citizens and better adjusted young men.

The program was started in Cincinnati in 1903. Two years later, the organization was granted its first charter in New York State through the efforts of Mrs. Cornelius Vanderbilt. By the end of World War II, there were 30 Big Brothers agencies. Today there are 300 agencies across the United States, and more than 120,000 boys are matched with Big Brothers.

The Fairfax County chapter of Big Brothers of America was founded in Fairfax in 1966. In 1971, United Way of Fairfax County accepted the program as part of its umbrella organization and now provides about 85 percent of its funding. The remaining 15 percent is raised by the local Big Brothers agency.

Information about the Big Brothers program in Fairfax County reaches the public primarily through newspapers (feature stories and classified advertisements), radio, public service announcements, posters (on buses and in windows of local establishments), and word-of-mouth advertising. The need for volunteers is a key message emanating from these sources. The agency phone number is always included so that people wanting to know more about the program can call for information. Those calling in are given basic information over the telephone and are invited to attend one of the monthly orientation sessions organized by the Big Brothers program staff. At these meetings, men get the chance to talk to other volunteers and to find out what will be expected of them should they decide to join the program. At the end of the session, prospective volunteers are asked to complete two forms. One is an application form and the other is a questionnaire in which the person is asked to describe the type of boy he would prefer to be matched with, as well as his own interests.

The files on potential Little Brothers are then reviewed in an attempt to match boys with the volunteers. A match is made only if both partners agree. The agency stays in close contact with the pair and monitors its progress. The three counselors for the Big Brothers program serve as resources for the volunteer.

The majority of the inquiry calls received by the Fairfax County agency are from women who are interested in becoming Big Sisters or from people desiring information on the Couples Program. Both programs are similar to the Big Brothers program and are administered by it. In fact, of 55 calls concerning a recent orientation meeting, only five were from males. Only three of the five callers actually attended the meeting, a typical response.

Although the informational campaigns and personal appeals seemed to have some effect, the results were generally disappointing and did little to alleviate the shortage of volunteer Big Brothers. There are currently 250 boys waiting to be matched with Big Brothers, and the shortage grows weekly.

Big Brothers of Fairfax County believed that a lack of awareness and accurate knowledge could be the cause of the shortage of volunteers. Are there men who would volunteer if only they were made aware of the program and its needs? Or is the difficulty a negative program image? Do people think of Little Brothers as problem children, boys who have been in trouble with the law or who have severe behavioral problems? Or could there be a misconception of the type of man who would make a good Big Brother? Do people have stereotypes with respect to the volunteers—for example, that the typical volunteer is a young, single, professional male?

Questions

1. What are some possible marketing decision problems? State whether the decision problems are discovery- or strategy-oriented.
2. What are some relevant marketing research problems for the decision problems you have identified?
3. What types of information would be useful to answer these questions?
4. How would you go about securing this information?

Case • 1.2

Transitional Housing, Inc. (A)[1]

Transitional Housing, Inc. (THI), is a local nonprofit organization located in Madison, Wisconsin. THI provides assistance to homeless and very low income individuals and families in finding emergency shelter, food, employment, transitional housing, and affordable apartment housing. These services are provided through four basic THI programs (see Exhibit 1 for details):

1. The Drop-In Shelter: An emergency drop-in shelter for men located at Grace Episcopal Church.
2. The Hospitality House: A day shelter for homeless and very low income men and women.
3. The Transitional Housing Program: Provides transitional living arrangements for families and single men for six months or more depending on the needs of the individual/family and the unit.
4. The Housing Opportunity Program: Helps families in obtaining a lease.

As part of its planning, the board of directors of THI was interested in determining ways to improve the organization's services. Their original thought was to conduct a survey of the organization's paid staff, volunteers, and guests (the homeless staying at THI or using its facilities or services), to determine which programs of THI they found particularly useful, which should be revised, and what other programs or services might be of more assistance to guests.

However, the analysis of THI's internal statistics and other published data indicated the need for THI to narrow its focus. Specifically, internal information indicated that the number of agencies serving the male homeless population was decreasing, and the number of homeless families was increasing. Moreover, THI was currently the only Madison shelter that served the male homeless population, and this community appeared to be underserved. In fact, the

---

Exhibit 1

Programs Offered by Transitional Housing, Inc.

Drop-In Shelter

Located at the Grace Episcopal Church in the downtown area, the Drop-In Shelter (DIS) is a 46-person-capacity emergency drop-in shelter for men. Overflow capacity for 20 additional people is provided at St. John's Lutheran Church from October through April. The basic services provided at DIS are shelter, food, personal grooming supplies, and counseling. Medical and legal services are also provided once a week through volunteers. The shelter is open to all men who are not incapacitated by drugs or alcohol and agree to abide by the rules of DIS. Operating hours are from 8:00 P.M. to 8:00 A.M. seven days per week, 365 days per year. Both dinner and breakfast are provided for DIS guests through the support of approximately 1,200 volunteers (churches, community groups, and other interested individuals) who offer their help to DIS.

Hospitality House

Hospitality House (HH), located on the near west side, is a day shelter and resource center for homeless and very low income men, women, and children. HH is generally regarded as a warm, safe place for the homeless to congregate, where services are provided but are not mandatory. The basic services provided at HH are: assistance with finding employment and housing, help for obtaining benefits from other social service agencies, and mental health services. Telephones are available for the guests' use, and guests may also use HH as a mailing address while they are staying at DIS.

Transitional Housing Program

The Transitional Housing Program (THP) operates 15 traditional housing sites throughout Dane County. There are 20 family units and 39 single units. Residents of THP may stay in the units for a period of six months to "permanent," depending on the unit and the needs of the individual or family. Services provided to the residents of the THP include money management, employment counseling, case management, and referrals to agencies involved in providing services needed by the individual or family. DIS is often the first step in the process of single men involved in THP.

Housing Opportunity Program

The Housing Opportunity Program (HOP) is a service provided by THI that is designed to aid families in obtaining a lease in their own name and living at the site on a permanent basis. THI leases apartments from area landlords and subleases the units to homeless families, who are referred to THI through area shelters. During this time, THI assumes responsibility for any unpaid rent or repairs that may accrue. Maintenance checks are performed monthly, and outreach services are provided to families involved in the program.

PART 1:
Introduction to Marketing Research and Problem Definition

number of homeless men staying at THI's Drop-In Shelter had increased 89 percent, from 607 three years ago to 1,146 the past year. This was partly due to the closing of other Madison male shelters in the last three years. Finally, the THI shelter was filled beyond its capacity of 66 men per night. During the winter, there were frequently more than 90 men staying at the Drop-In Shelter on any given night, with many of them sleeping on the hallway floor.

Given this information, the board of directors decided to use the organization's limited resources to focus first on the Drop-In Shelter. More specifically, the board asked for an evaluation of THI's current facilities and the services for the homeless as well as a determination of what future services and facilities it should try to provide.

Questions

1. What is the decision problem? Is this decision problem discovery- or strategy-oriented?
2. What are some relevant research problems?
3. Discuss in general terms how you would address the board of directors' concerns. Specifically, who would you obtain information from and how would you access these people?

[1]The contributions of Monika Wingate to the development of this case are gratefully acknowledged.

Case • 1.3

Supervisory Training at the Management Institute

University of Wisconsin–Extension is the outreach campus of the University of Wisconsin system. Its mission is to extend high-quality education to people who are not necessarily "college students" in the usual sense. The Management Institute is one of the departments within UW–Extension. It conducts programs aimed at providing education and training in at least a dozen areas of business and not-for-profit management.

The supervisory training area within the Management Institute designs and conducts continuing education training programs for first-level supervisors. The training programs are designed to improve a trainee's managerial, communication, decision-making, and human-relations skills. They consequently cover a broad range of topics.

A continuing decline in enrollments in the various programs during the past several years had become a problem of increasing concern to the three supervisory program directors. They were at a loss to explain the decline, although informal discussions among the supervisors raised a number of questions to which they did not know the answers. Have people's reasons for attending supervisory training programs changed? What are their reasons for attending them? Was the decline caused by economic factors? Was it because of increased competition among continuing education providers? Was it due to the content or structure of the programs themselves? Was it because of the way the programs were structured or promoted? Were the programs targeted at the right level of supervisor?

Typically, the major promotion for any program involved mailed brochures that described the content and structure of the course. The mailing list for the brochures included all past attendees of any supervisory training program conducted by the Management Institute.

Questions

1. What is the manager's decision problem? Is this problem discovery- or strategy-oriented?
2. What are some relevant research problems?
3. Which research problem would you recommend pursuing? Why?
4. How would you recommend the Management Institute go about addressing this research problem? That is, what data would you collect and how might those data be used to answer the research question posed?

Case • 1.4

Wisconsin Power & Light (A)[1]

Recent changes in the utility industry have led to a more deregulated and competitive environment. In response, Wisconsin Power & Light (WP&L) has been shifting its focus from that of a product-driven company to one of a market- and information-driven company. Management has increasingly relied on information from marketing studies and has been incorporating the external data in their decision-making processes. WP&L's espousal of a market-sensitive mentality has helped shape the company's overall business strategies. One current area of concern for WP&L involves environmental issues, so much so that one of the company's goals is "to be a responsible corporate citizen, promoting the social, economic, and environmental well-being of the communities that it serves."

WP&L, in an effort to realize its environmental goals, developed several programs for its residential, commercial, and industrial customers to foster the conservation of energy. The programs, which were classified under the BuySmart umbrella of WP&L's Demand-Side Management Programs, consisted of such specific programs as Appliance Rebates, Energy Analysis, Weatherization Help, and the Home Energy Improvement Loan (HEIL) program. All previous marketing research and information gathering focused primarily on issues from the customer's perspective, such as an evaluation of net energy savings, an estimation of the number of individuals who would have undertaken the conservation actions even if there was no program in place, and an evaluation of customer attitudes and opinions concerning the design, implementation, features, and delivery of the residential programs. Having examined the consumer perspective, WP&L's current goal is to focus on obtaining information from other participants in the programs, namely employees and lenders.

The next task for the management of WP&L to undertake is a study of the Home Energy Improvement Loan (HEIL) program of the BuySmart umbrella. The HEIL program was designed to make low-interest-rate financing available to residential gas and electric WP&L customers for conservation and weatherization measures. The low-interest guaranteed loans are delivered through WP&L account representatives in conjunction with participating financial institutions and trade allies. The procedures for obtaining a loan begin with an energy "audit" of the interested customer's residence to determine the appropriate conservation measures. Once the customer decides on which measures to have installed, the WP&L representative assists in arranging the low-interest-rate financing through one of the participating local banking institutions. At the completion of the projects, WP&L representatives conduct an inspection of the work by checking a random sample of participants. Conservation measures eligible under the HEIL program include the installation of natural gas furnaces/boilers, automatic vent dampers, intermittent ignition devices, heat pumps, and heat pump water heaters. Eligible structural improvements include the addition of attic/wall/basement insulation, storm windows and doors, sillbox insulation, window weatherstripping, and caulking.

Purpose

The primary goal of the current study is to identify ways of improving the HEIL program from the lenders' point of view. Specifically, the following issues need to be addressed:

- Identify the lenders' motivation for participating in the program.
- Determine how lenders get their information regarding various changes/updates in the program.
- Identify how lenders promote the program.
- Assess the current programs with respect to administrative and program features.
- Determine the type of credit analysis conducted by the lenders.
- Identify ways of minimizing the default rate from the lenders' point of view.
- Identify lenders' opinions of the overall program.
- Assess the lenders' commitment to the program.
- Identify if the reason for loan inactivity in some lending institutions is due to lack of a customer base.

Question

1. Prepare a Research Request Agreement that will address WP&L's study objectives.

[1]The contributions of Kavita Maini and Paul Metz to the development of this case are gratefully acknowledged, as is the permission of Wisconsin Power & Light to use the material included.

Case • 1.5

Telecard.com (A)

Teresa Morgan was having a bad day. One year ago, she and two other partners started Telecard.com, a new Internet venture selling prepaid long distance telephone services. So far, the company had yet to show much increase in revenues, much less turn a profit. Worse yet, the venture's start-up capital—money Teresa and her partners had scraped together from savings and what they could borrow from friends and family—was all but gone. She figured that if she and her partners continued to draw no salaries, the company could probably hold out another three months at most. Prospects for additional cash inflows were almost nonexistant because of their poor operating results from the first 12 months. So, instead of celebrating the company's one-year anniversary, Teresa was trying desperately to devise a new plan for the company.

The Company and Its Services

Telecard.com was the brainchild of three close friends who worked together at a large advertising agency located just outside Chicago. Teresa Morgan was an account representative who had been with the agency for about eight years. Her friend Steve Morrison was director of the agency's computing and information services department and had joined the agency two years ago after working with another ad agency for several years. Maria Carlotti managed the agency's media scheduling department; Teresa had known Maria since college. The friends regularly ate lunch together and sometimes socialized on weekends with each other's families.

One day at lunch, Teresa, Steve, and Maria were talking about the Internet and the way it had changed business practices for several of their clients. During the same lunch, Maria complained about having to drive to a nearby shopping center on a break to purchase a prepaid long distance calling card to use for personal business while at work. As the conversation continued, Steve pointed out that the plastic calling card wasn't really necessary to use prepaid long distance; only the numbers on the card mattered. And if the card itself wasn't needed, then distribution of the service would not be limited to retail store locations. Thus, the basic idea of Telecard.com was born: the venture would purchase blocks of long distance telephone service from telecommunications companies and resell it over the Internet in the form of prepaid long distance. Within three months, the new partners had gathered start-up capital, designed an attractive and user-friendly Web page and placed the service online. Because of the uncertainty of the new venture, all three partners kept their jobs at the agency and spent most of their "free" time after work and on weekends working on Telecard.com.

Compared to traditional forms of prepaid long distance, the partners believed that Telecard.com was amazingly simple. A customer accesses the Telecard.com Web site and chooses (a) the number of prepaid minutes they want to purchase, and (b) the pricing plan that best fits their calling needs (see below). Using a secure payment system, the customer then provides a credit card number and an e-mail address. Within minutes, the purchase is verified and an access number is mailed electronically to the customer. The prepaid long distance is then used exactly like any other type of prepaid long distance service, except that no tangible card is ever produced. The elimination of the plastic card greatly reduces the cost of the service, and these savings are passed on to the customer in the form of lower prices.

Three different calling plans are available to meet different calling needs. The first plan offers long distance at $0.025 per minute with a $0.90 per call surcharge and is ideal for calls over ten minutes in length. The second plan is available at $0.039 per minute and a $0.20 per call surcharge. The third plan offers a $0.089 per minute rate with no surcharge; this plan is best for shorter calls or when there is a strong likelihood of getting an answering machine.

Target Market and Promotion

Initially, Telecard.com offered its services to anyone who logged into its Web site. That is, in their haste to get the service online, the partners paid little attention to identifying potential market segments, although they implicitly assumed that the customers would be business professionals much like themselves who needed a convenient way to make personal long distance calls when away from home (e.g., at the office; while traveling). Working with an extremely limited promotion budget, the partners had left much of the promotion of the service to word-of-mouth, although they had managed to get a little local publicity through a feature story in the business section of one of the daily newspapers.

The Problem

So far, results have been much worse than Teresa had hoped. During the first 11 months of operation the company had total revenues of $4,110, based on sales of 39,918 minutes of prepaid long distance across 1438 customers. During the same time period, the costs (including

Internet access fees, development costs, cost of services sold, and depreciation of hardware) amounted to $18,768. The company Web site had been accessed (i.e., "hit") 3793 times. From some of the comments and questions that customers left on the "comments" section of the Web site, it was clear that at least a few customers really liked the service and were accessing the site multiple times. The partners recognized that almost all new ventures experience lean times in the beginning, but they didn't know how much longer they could hold out.

The more Teresa thought about the situation, the more confused she became about what to do next. One of her friends in the research department of the ad agency suggested conducting marketing research and offered to help, but Teresa wasn't sure that it would do any good.

Questions

1. State the manager's decision problem. Is this decision problem the result of planned or unplanned change? Is it discovery- or strategy-oriented? Under the circumstances, which do you believe is more appropriate: a discovery or a strategy orientation? Why?

2. State five (5) possible research problems related to the decision problem. How would you decide which research problem(s) to pursue?

part 1 cases

Case • 1.6

Hand-to-Hand Against Palm (A)

An electronics and personal computing firm has been closely watching the success of the Palm Pilot and seeks to introduce a competitive device, beta-named "Organize My Life!" or OML for short. The OML marketing manager has gathered some intelligence on the Palm Inc. sales and believes that, for all its success, some potential markets are being underserved.

Handheld personal digital assistants (PDAs) were introduced unsuccessfully at first by Apple in 1993. Some analysts argue that the Newton, Apple's market offering, was not clearly positioned to the consumers; others argue that they were simply ahead of their time. 3Com's Palm Computing focused the PDA, limiting its functionality to calendars and appointments, contact directory information, and to-do lists, so as to convey its technological benefits more clearly to the potential user. In only five years, Palm achieved more than two-thirds of the global market to support this claim.[1] Over 5.5 million devices have been sold, and sales continue to show strong growth (sales are expected to reach 13 million in the next two years).

Competitors offer Internet access, including wireless variants, but the OML group has data that indicate only 17 percent of PDA users would pay extra for this feature—these users already have PC Internet access and view the PDA's access version as redundant, and worse, likely to be slow. OML is considering conducting research to investigate whether other features, like voice recognition capabilities, stereo quality sound systems for downloading music, video and digital photographic abilities, and global positioning mapping ("u r here") software would be of value.

In addition to seeking data on features, OML is considering the attractiveness of this technology to another segment. Its data indicate that the typical Palm Pilot user is a male in his early 40s, college-educated, and a white-collar professional with a relatively high income. OML is interested in serving the university student market. An important concern is that the typical student will have fewer discretionary funds than the current PDA purchaser profile. Thus, OML marketing discussions revolve around questions like these: What is the price point beyond which students would be unable to purchase this device? If the device were priced at, say, $299 or less, which features would be prohibitive to continue to offer? What are the students' priorities in terms of the functions and features they would like to see bundled into the PDA? Would the benefits sought depend on whether this device were targeted to undergraduates "in general" compared with engineering and computer science students and compared with MBA graduate students? How do we choose the features to offer and the segments to target?

Questions

1. What is the decision problem?
2. What is (are) the research problem(s)?
3. What recommendations would you make to the OML marketing manager to address the research problem(s)? That is, what data would you collect and how might those data be used to answer the research question(s) posed?

[1]See David Rynecki, "Is Palm's IPO Really the One to Catch?" *Fortune* (February 2, 2000), pp. 213–214.

Case • 1.7

E-Food and the Online Grocery Competition (A)

When everybody's busy, something's got to give. The relatively new service industry of online groceries (that is, grocery shopping online and home delivery of the purchased items) has grown to address today's consumer demands of convenience and time savings. Perhaps the best-known provider in the industry is Peapod.com, an operation that began outside Chicago. Since its founding in 1989, it has expanded to nearly a dozen metropolitan markets, serving over 100,000 households. Other competitors sense the market potential, and many firms share space in the marketplace, including groceronline.com (which uses UPS and Federal Express rather than local delivery operators); or netgrocer.com (which covers towns and rural areas, with no annual fee and makes available merchandise such as books and CDs); as well as many as-yet-local providers. Industry experts predict continued strong growth (although their numbers vary wildly, home food shopping is expected to grow to anywhere from $5 billion to $80 billion in the next three to five years).

These online grocery services provide virtual stores through which the electronic visitor navigates, as if pushing a shopping cart in a traditional grocer. The user clicks on items to purchase, which are placed in the user's cart. When complete, the user is "checked out," specifying a delivery date and time (paying a premium for narrower windows of delivery time, such as from 1 to 1:30 compared to 1 to 4 P.M.). Users pay annual dues and delivery costs proportionate to each shopping bill.

The software allows the user to store his or her preferences in a personal shopping list that can be altered, adding or deleting items as necessary with each e-visit. Across the various providers, the software also usually allows facile consumer comparison; for example, the SKUs in a particular category may be sorted by brand name, by price, by value (price per ounce, for example), by what is on "feature" (sale and point-of-purchase promotions), by various dietetic goals (such as "healthy," "low fat"), and so on. The user may write in "notes," to specify in more detail, for example, "Please pick up green (unripe) bananas, not yellow ones," or "If Fancy Feast is out of beef, please get turkey instead," which instruct the professional shopper as to the user's particular preferences. Categories of items that can be purchased are continually expanding, from foods to drugstore items and other merchandise.

Most users are women, employed full-time, and married, with household incomes that exceed $100,000.

Online grocery providers tend to conduct the online business very well, if customers' satisfaction, repeat visits, and word-of-mouth are any indicators. That is, the software provided, the merchandise selected, the delivery reliability, etc., are valued by the customer, with few complaints. However, home delivery of food is not a particularly profitable industry. One of the major paths to profit is in selling the data that result from the visitors' trips to the Web site.

Ashley Sims is an MBA student, taking her last term of classes, and thinking about starting up a local online grocer. She's certain that by learning from the templates of the current providers in other markets, she too can run the logistics of the business. However, she hopes that, given her contacts of computer experts, she can create a competitive advantage in the software setup, if she understands the consumers' mind-set as they travel through the e-grocery stores. She wants to know just what a user is thinking from the first click onto the Web site to the last "Done Shopping" click off the site. This knowledge would allow her to offer better advice to her software developers in terms of what features would facilitate the visitors' traversal of the grocery store. Data like these would help improve the system, and it would also lend great insight to the consumers' decision processes.

Questions

1. What is the decision problem?
2. What is (are) the research problem(s)?
3. Prepare a research proposal to submit to an online grocer on behalf of your research team.

© Digital Vision/Getty Images

Part 2

Research Design

Part 2 deals with the general issue of designing research so that it addresses the appropriate questions efficiently. Chapter 5 provides an overview of various research designs and discusses the exploratory design at some length. Chapter 6 then discusses descriptive and causal designs, two other primary types of research design.

Chapter 5

Types of Research Design and Exploratory Research

© Digital Vision/Getty Images

Learning Objectives

1	*Explain what a research design is.*
2	*List the three basic types of research design.*
3	*Describe the major emphasis of each type of research design.*
4	*Cite the crucial principle of research.*
5	*Describe the basic uses of exploratory research.*
6	*Specify the key characteristic of exploratory research.*
7	*Discuss the various types of exploratory research and identify the characteristics of each.*
8	*Identify the key person in a focus group.*

"Now what?" Dan asked Emily, the representative of the marketing research firm his company had employed. "We did the focus groups. Your moderator led three groups of eight parents through discussions of our product, and all we know is that we need to overhaul the product—somehow." Dan was marketing director for a parenting program sponsored by a national religious organization. His employer wanted to offer guidance in child rearing, but feedback from parents suggested only that they weren't being helped by the existing program.

"Well," replied Emily, "As a marketing professional yourself, you know that exploratory research often leads us from one question to another question, not to an answer. We're still at the idea-generating stage. I have some ideas that might help you. But first, I'd like to hear your thoughts about our report."

"It's an excellent summary of what our members say our program isn't doing for them. Clearly, we need to know what kinds of changes will meet our members' needs, but I'm wondering if we can afford to find out how they'll react to the changes we're proposing. Another round of focus groups would be expensive. And it isn't just the money. As we've discussed, it's hard to put together a group of busy parents who will take time to sit down and discuss the program. I don't blame parents for saying, 'No, thanks.' I have teenagers myself, and believe me, time is precious."

Emily smiled. "It sure is. I have a three-year-old and a five-year-old, and I hear it doesn't get any easier. That's one of the issues my plan addresses. I propose that we use the Internet to get feedback on some possible program features."

"An online survey?"

"Not quite. I'm proposing a variation of online focus groups: a bulletin board focus group."

"How would it work?"

"We have a relationship with a research specialist called Itracks. They'd set up an online bulletin board devoted to your program. We'd recruit groups of about 40 people to visit the bulletin board at their convenience, in their own homes, and post their comments. A specially trained moderator posts questions and keeps the discussion moving for two weeks; that gives everyone plenty of time to participate. In general, we've found that bulletin board focus groups generate huge amounts of data. Participants are more willing to be included because they can choose when to post their comments. Also, they can type at their own rate, without anyone interrupting, so we tend to get longer responses—sometimes more thoughtful responses."

"Then let's try it."

Discussion Issues

1. How would a company benefit from a type of research that, in Emily's words, "leads from one question to another question"?

2. What are advantages of talking to customer groups in person, rather than online? What are advantages of an online discussion?

3. Other than parents, what customer groups might be open to participating in an online discussion of a product? ■

Research Design as a Plan of Action

1 *Explain what a research design is.*

research design
The framework or plan for a study that guides the collection and analysis of the data.

A **research design** is simply the framework or plan for a study used as a guide in collecting and analyzing data. It is the blueprint that is followed in completing a study. It resembles the architect's blueprint for a house. While it is possible to build a house without a detailed blueprint, the final product will more than likely be somewhat different from what was originally envisioned by the buyer. A certain room is too small; the traffic pattern is poor; some things really wanted are omitted; other, less important things are included; and so on. It is also possible to conduct research without a detailed blueprint. The research findings are also likely to differ widely from what was desired by the consumer or user of the research. "These results are interesting, but they do not solve the basic problem" is a common lament. Further, just as the house built without a blueprint is likely to cost more because of midstream alterations in construction, research conducted without a research design is likely to cost more than research properly executed using a research design.

2 *List the three basic types of research design.*

Thus, a research design ensures that the study (1) will be relevant to the problem and (2) will use economical procedures. It would help the student learning research methods if there was a single procedure to follow in developing the framework or if there was a single framework to be learned. Unfortunately, this is not the case. Rather, there are many research design frameworks, just as there are many unique house designs. Fortunately though, just as house designs can be broken into basic types (ranch, split-level, two-story), research designs can be classified into some basic types. One very useful classification is in terms of the fundamental objective of the research: exploratory, descriptive, or causal.[1]

Types of Research Design

3 *Describe the major emphasis of each type of research design.*

exploratory research
Research design in which the major emphasis is on gaining ideas and insights; it is particularly helpful in breaking broad, vague problem statements into smaller, more precise subproblem statements.

The major emphasis in **exploratory research** is on the discovery of *ideas* and *insights*.[2] The soft drink manufacturer faced with decreased sales might conduct an exploratory study to generate possible explanations. **Descriptive research** is typically concerned with determining the *frequency* with which something occurs or the relationship between two variables. It is typically guided by an initial hypothesis. An investigation of the trends in the consumption of soft drinks with respect to such characteristics as age, sex, and geographic location would be a descriptive study.

A **causal research** design is concerned with determining cause-and-effect relationships. Causal studies typically take the form of experiments, since experiments are best suited to determine cause and effect. For instance, a soft drink manufacturer may want to determine which of several different advertising appeals is most effective. One way to proceed would be to use different ads in different geographic areas and investigate which ad generated the highest sales. In effect, the company would perform an experiment, and if it was designed properly, the company would be in a position to conclude that one specific appeal caused the higher rate of sales.

4 *Cite the crucial principle of research.*

descriptive research
Research design in which the major emphasis is on determining the frequency with which something occurs or the extent to which two variables covary.

Although it is useful to divide research designs into these neat categories—exploratory, descriptive, and causal—as a way of helping to explain the research process, three warnings are in order. First, the distinctions among the three are not absolute. Any given study may serve several purposes. Nevertheless, certain types of research designs are better suited for some purposes than others. The crucial principle of research is that *the design of the investigation should stem from the problem*. Each of these types is appropriate to specific kinds of problems.

Second, in the remainder of this chapter and in the next chapter, we discuss each of the design types in more detail. The emphasis will be on their *basic characteristics* and *generally fruitful approaches*. Whether the designs are useful in a given problem setting depends on how imaginatively they are applied. Architects can be taught basic design principles; whether they then design attractive, well-built houses depends on how they apply these principles. So it is with research. The general characteristics of each design can be taught. Whether they are productive in a given situation depends on how skillfully they are applied. There is no single best way to proceed, just as there is no single best floor plan for, say, a ranch-type house. It all depends on the specific problem to be solved. Research analysts, then, need an understanding of the basic designs so that they can modify them to suit specific purposes.

causal research
Research design in which the major emphasis is on determining cause-and-effect relationships.

Finally, the three basic research designs can be viewed as stages in a continuous process. Figure 5.1 shows the interrelationships. Exploratory studies are often seen as the initial step. When researchers begin an investigation, it stands to reason that they lack a great deal of knowledge about the problem. Consider, for example, the following problem: "Brand X's share of the disposable diaper market is slipping. Why?" This statement is too broad to serve as a guide for research. To narrow and refine it would logically be accomplished with exploratory research, in which the emphasis would be on finding possible explanations for the sales decrease. These tentative explanations, or hypotheses, would then serve as specific guides for descriptive or causal studies.

© Josef Astor

Suppose the tentative explanation that emerged was that "Brand X is an economy-priced diaper, originally designed to compete with low-cost store-brand diapers. Families with children have more money today than when the brand was first introduced and are willing to pay more for higher quality baby products. It stands to reason that our market share would decrease." These tentative explanations, or hypotheses that families with small children have more real income to spend and that a larger proportion of that money is going toward baby products could be examined in a descriptive study of trends in the baby products industry.

Suppose that the descriptive study did support the hypothesis. The company might then wish to determine whether parents were, in fact, willing to pay more for higher quality diapers and, if so, what features (such as better fit or greater absorbency) were most important to them. This might be accomplished through a test market study, a causal design.

Each stage in the process thus represents the investigation of a more detailed statement of the problem. Although we have suggested that the sequence would be from exploratory to descriptive to causal research, alternative sequences might occur. The "families with small children have more money to spend on baby products" hypothesis might be so generally accepted that the sequence would go from exploratory directly to causal. The potential also exists for conducting research in the reverse direction. If a hypothesis is disproved by causal research (for example, the product bombs in the test market), the analyst may then decide that another descriptive study, or even another exploratory study, is needed. Also, not every research problem will begin with an exploratory study. It depends on how specific researchers are in formulating the problem before them. A general, vague statement leads naturally to exploratory work, whereas a specific cause-effect hypothesis lends itself to experimental work.

Leonard Riggio, chief executive of Barnes & Noble, is the man who made bookstores fun, turning them into modern village greens where people flock as much for the entertainment value as the huge selection. Barnes & Noble, whose stores have been reported to ring up one in eight books sold in America, has a huge online presence. Riggio sees the Internet as much more than just another place to sell books. He envisions it as a place to meet all types of consumer needs: a book research center, a database, an ad vehicle, and, most of all a tool to help people weed through an onslaught of information.

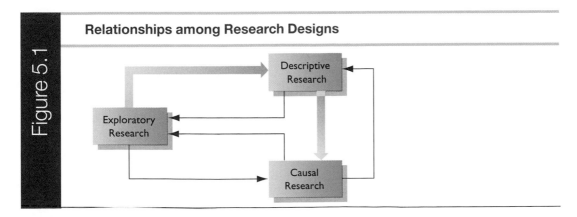

Relationships among Research Designs

Figure 5.1

Exploratory Research → Descriptive Research → Causal Research

5 *Describe the basic uses of exploratory research.*

6 *Specify the key characteristic of exploratory research.*

hypothesis
A statement that specifies how two or more measurable variables are related.

As previously stated, the general objective in exploratory research is to gain insights and ideas. The exploratory study is particularly helpful in breaking broad, vague problem statements into smaller, more precise subproblem statements, ideally in the form of specific hypotheses. In effect, a **hypothesis** is a statement that specifies how two or more measurable variables are related.[3]

In the early stages of research, we usually lack sufficient understanding of the problem to formulate a specific hypothesis. Further, there are often several tentative explanations for a given marketing phenomenon. For example, sales are off because our price is too high, our dealers or sales representatives are not doing the job they should, or our advertising is weak, and so on. Exploratory research can be used to establish priorities in studying these competing explanations. Top priority would usually be given to whichever hypothesis appeared most promising in the exploratory study. Priorities may also be established according to the feasibility of researching the hypotheses. Exploratory studies should help eliminate ideas that are not practical.

An exploratory study is also used to increase the analyst's familiarity with a problem. This is particularly true when the analyst is new to the problem arena—for example, a marketing research consultant working for a company for the first time.

The exploratory study may also be used to clarify concepts. For instance, if management is considering a change in service policy intended to increase dealer satisfaction, an exploratory study could be used to (1) clarify what is meant by dealer satisfaction and (2) develop a method by which dealer satisfaction could be measured.

When Congress discusses revising the tax code in order to make it "more fair" (so as to increase taxpayer compliance), a problem that often surfaces is determining what fairness in the tax code means. Is it tax enforcement that bothers people? Tax avoidance by other people? The way tax laws are written? Tax rates? That people believe their tax dollars are being poorly spent? Exploratory research would play a particularly important role in clarifying a concept such as this.

In sum, an exploratory study is used for any or all of the following purposes:[4]

- Formulating a problem for more precise investigation
- Developing hypotheses
- Establishing priorities for further research
- Gathering information about the practical problems of carrying out research on particular issues
- Increasing the analyst's familiarity with the problem
- Clarifying concepts

In general, exploratory research is appropriate for any problem about which little is known. It becomes the foundation for a good study.

Because so much is typically unknown at the beginning of an inquiry, exploratory studies are gen-

ETHICAL dilemma 5.1

Marketing Research Insights was asked to carry out the data collection and analysis procedures for a study designed by a consumer goods company. After studying the research purpose and design, a consultant for Marketing Research Insights concluded that the design was poorly conceived. First, she thought that the design was more complex than was necessary since some of the data could be obtained through secondary sources, precluding the necessity of much primary data collection. Second, the proposed choice of primary data collection would not produce the kinds of information sought by the company.

Although the consultant advised the company of her opinions, the company insisted on proceeding with the proposed design. Marketing Research Insights' management was reluctant to undertake the study, as it believed that the firm's reputation would be harmed if its name were associated with poor research.

- *What decision would you make if you were a consultant for Marketing Research Insights?*
- *In general, should a researcher advance his or her opinion of a proposed design, or should the researcher remain silent and simply do the work?*
- *Is it ethical to remain silent in such situations?*

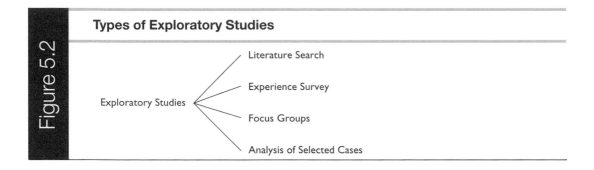

Figure 5.2

Types of Exploratory Studies

Exploratory Studies
- Literature Search
- Experience Survey
- Focus Groups
- Analysis of Selected Cases

erally very flexible with regard to the methods used for gaining insight and developing hypotheses. Exploratory studies rarely use detailed questionnaires or involve probability sampling plans. Rather, investigators frequently change the research procedure as the vaguely defined initial problem is transformed into one with more precise meaning. Investigators often follow their intuition in an exploratory study. Ingenuity, judgment, and good luck inevitably play a part in leading to the one or two key hypotheses that, it is hoped, will account for the phenomenon. While exploratory research may be conducted in a variety of ways, experience has shown that literature searches, experience surveys, focus groups, and the analysis of selected cases are particularly productive (see Figure 5.2).

Literature Search

One of the quickest and least costly ways to discover hypotheses is in the work of others, through a **literature search.** The search may involve conceptual literature, trade literature, or, quite often, published statistics. The literature that is searched depends naturally on the problem being addressed. Miller Business Systems, Inc., of Dallas, for example, routinely monitors trade literature in order to keep track of its competitors. The information on each competitor is entered into the "competitor profiles" it keeps in its database. The company regularly scans these profiles for insights on what the competition might be doing. One such scan indicated that a competitor had hired nine furniture salespeople in a ten-day period. This was a tip-off to a probable push by the competitor in the office-furniture market. With this early notice, Miller was able to schedule its salespeople to make extra calls on their accounts, thereby blunting the competitor's sales drive.[5]

Sometimes conceptual literature is more valuable than trade literature. For example, a firm with a dissatisfied field sales force would probably begin its study with a search of literature on concepts and ideas related to satisfaction in such personnel. The search might include research studies in psychology, sociology, and personnel management, as well as studies in marketing journals. The focus would be on the factors determining employee satisfaction and dissatisfaction. The analyst would be alert for those factors also found in the company's environment. The question of how to measure an employee's satisfaction would be researched at the same time.

Suppose a firm's problem was one that typically triggers much marketing research: "Sales are off. Why?" Exploratory insights into this problem could easily and inexpensively be gained by analyzing published data and trade literature. Such an analysis would quickly indicate whether the problem was an industry problem or a firm problem. Very different research is in order if the firm's sales are down but (1) the company's market share is up, since industry sales are down further; (2) the company's market share has remained stable; or (3) the company's market share has declined. The last situation would trigger an investigation of the firm's marketing mix variables, while the first would prompt an analysis to determine why industry sales are off.

A company's own internal data should be included in the literature examined in exploratory research, as Mosinee Paper Company found to its pleasant surprise. The company was contemplating dropping one of its products because of its dismal sales performance.

Discuss the various types of exploratory research and identify the characteristics of each.

literature search
A search of statistics, trade journal articles, other articles, magazines, newspapers, and books for data or insight into the problem at hand.

Before doing so, however, the company tallied sales of the product per salesperson and found that only a single salesperson was selling that specific grade of industrial paper. Upon further investigation, Mosinee discovered how the buyers were using the paper—an application that had been known only to the one salesman and his customers. This information enabled management to educate the rest of its sales force as to the potential market for the paper, and sales rose substantially.

It is important to remember that in a literature search, as in any exploratory research, the major emphasis is on the discovery of ideas and tentative explanations of the phenomenon and not on demonstrating which explanation is *the* explanation. The demonstration is better left to descriptive and causal research. Thus, the analyst must be alert to the hypotheses that can be derived from available material, both published material and the company's internal records.

Experience Survey

experience survey
Interviews with people knowledgeable about the general subject being investigated.

Sometimes called the *key informant survey,* the **experience survey** attempts to tap the knowledge and experience of those familiar with the general subject being investigated. For example, a San Francisco builder focused on architects and designers when trying to get a handle on its competitors. The company asked these people to describe the traits of builders that tended to turn off buyers of expensive homes. Some of the answers included bad manners, workers who tracked dirt across carpets, and beat-up construction trucks, which buyers objected to having parked in their driveways. The company used these insights for a major repositioning of its business to the Bay Area's upper crust. The company bought a new truck, had its estimators wear jackets and ties, and made sure its work crews were impeccably polite. For example, the crews began rolling protective runners over carpets before they entered clients' homes. In less than two years, the company's annual revenue more than quintupled.

In studies concerned with the marketing of a product, anyone who has any association with the marketing effort is a potential source of information. This would include the top executives of the company, the sales manager, product manager, and sales representatives. It would also include wholesalers and retailers who handle the product, as well as consumers who use the product. It might even include individuals who are not part of the chain of distribution but who might possess some insight into the phenomenon. For example, a children's book publisher gained valuable insights into the reason for a sales decline by talking with librarians and schoolteachers. These discussions indicated that an increased use of library facilities, both public and school, coincided with the product's drop in sales. The increase in library usage was, in turn, traced to an increase in federal funds, which had enabled libraries to buy more books for their children's collections. Similarly, when designing the Louisville, a medium-duty conventional truck intended for beverage distribution among other things, Ford Motor Company sought feedback from fleet owners, mechanics, and drivers.[6]

Usually, many people know something about the general subject of any given problem. However, not all of them should be contacted.

> Research economy dictates that the respondents in an experience survey be carefully selected. The aim of the experience survey is to obtain insight into the relationships between variables rather than to get an accurate picture of current practices or a simple consensus as to best practices. One is looking for provocative ideas and useful insights, not for the statistics of the profession. Thus the respondents must be chosen because of the likelihood that they will offer the contributions sought. In other words, a selected sample of people working in the area is called for.[7]

Never, therefore, should a probability sample, in which respondents are chosen by some random process, be used in an experience survey. Moreover, it is a waste of time to interview those who have little competence or little relevant experience in the subject under investigation. It is also a waste of time to interview those who cannot articulate their experience and knowledge. It is important, however, to include people with differing points of view. The children's book publisher mentioned earlier interviewed company executives, key people in the product group, sales representatives, managers of retail outlets in which the books were sold, teachers, and librarians in the process of investigating the sales decline.

The interviews were all unstructured and informal. The emphasis in each interview among those immediately concerned with the distribution of the product was, "How do you explain the sales decrease? In your opinion, what is needed to reverse the downward slide?"[8] Most of the time in each interview was then devoted to exploring in detail the various rationales and proposed solutions. A number of sometimes conflicting hypotheses emerged. This provided the researchers with an opportunity to "bounce" some of the hypotheses off groups with differing vantage points and, in the process, get a feel for which of the hypotheses would be most fruitful to research. The interviews with librarians and teachers approached the problem from a different angle. Here the emphasis was on discovering changes in children's reading habits.

The respondents were given a great deal of freedom in choosing the factors to be discussed. This is consistent with the notion that the emphasis in exploratory research is on developing tentative explanations and not on demonstrating the viability of a given explanation.

Focus Groups

Focus groups are another useful method for gathering ideas and insights. In a **focus group,** a small number of individuals are brought together to talk about some topic of interest to the focus group sponsor. The discussion is directed by a moderator. The moderator attempts to follow a rough outline of issues while simultaneously having the comments made by each person considered in group discussion. Each individual is thereby exposed to the ideas of the others and submits his or her ideas to the group for consideration.

Focus groups are one of the more frequently used techniques in marketing research; they have proved to be productive for a variety of purposes, including:

- Generating hypotheses that can be further tested quantitatively.
- Generating information helpful in structuring consumer questionnaires.
- Providing overall background information on a product category.
- Securing impressions on new product concepts.

When Brendan Boyle and Fern Mandelbaum pooled their marketing experience to start Skyline Products, a company that develops and licenses children's toys, they wanted to get regular feedback directly from children. Their solution was to set up focus groups in the form of six-week-long play groups. Parents were happy to sign up their children in exchange for the one-hour break each week; in fact, they pay $30 for the privilege. The groups meet at a local park or school. Boyle and Mandelbaum show up with toys and watch the children play, observing which toys they choose and which are hard to handle. During the session they also ask children why they prefer one toy over another. Afterward, they follow up with parents to learn what the children said they liked. Mandelbaum credits the focus groups with helping them develop a "kid sense" that has enabled the company to license 70 products in its first few years.[9] In designing its Z3 roadster, BMW conducted focus groups in Japan, the United States, the United Kingdom, and Germany; the Americans' influence is visible in the dual cupholders, the coinholder, and the third brake light.[10] Research Window 5.1 discusses the insights Harley-Davidson gleaned from focus groups.

Although focus groups vary in size, most consist of eight to twelve members. Smaller groups are too easily dominated by one or two members; with larger groups, frustration and boredom can set in, as individuals have to wait their turn to respond or get involved. Respondents are generally selected so that the groups are relatively homogeneous, minimizing both conflicts among group members on issues not relevant to the study objectives and differences in perceptions, experiences, and verbal skills. Differences that are too great with respect to any of these characteristics can intimidate some of the group participants and stifle discussion.

focus group
An interview conducted among a small number of individuals simultaneously; the interview relies more on group discussion than on directed questions to generate data.

Experience of Harley-Davidson with Focus Groups

After making a remarkable comeback in the 1980s, motorcycle manufacturer Harley-Davidson had buyers on two-year-long waiting lists all over the country. But that success placed the company in a familiar quandary: Should Harley expand and risk a market downturn, or should it stay the course, content with its good position in the industry?

"To invest or not to invest, that was the question," said Frank Cimermancic, Harley's director of business planning. "Dealers were begging us to build more motorcycles," he said. "But you have to understand our history. One of the things that caused past problems was a lack of quality, and that was the result of a too-rapid expansion. We did not want to relive that situation."

The company's dilemma was complicated by the fact that the market for heavyweight bikes was shrinking. "We were doing fine, but look at the market," Cimermancic said. "Maybe, we thought, we could reverse these trends and become an industry leader, something we hadn't been for a long time."

A new kind of customer seemed to hold the keys to market growth. White-collar motorcycle enthusiasts, or "Rubbies" (Rich Urban Bikers), started to shore up Harley sales in the middle '80s, adding to the company's success and image. But whether these Lenos and Forbeses were reliable, long-term customers was another question.

"Are those folks going to stay with us, or are they going to move on when the next fad comes along?" Cimermancic asked. "If we got the answer right, we could become a force in the industry. If we got it wrong, we would go right back to the early '80s. Nobody wanted to make the wrong decision and watch 20 percent of our employees walk away with their possessions in a cardboard box."

Harley also needed to know if it should market its products differently to different audiences. A core clientele of traditional "bikers" had kept Harley afloat during its leanest years, and they could not be alienated. "We had to understand the customer mindset," Cimermancic said. "Was there a universal appeal to owning a Harley?"

To find out, the company first invited focus groups made up of current owners, would-be owners, and owners of other brands to make cut-and-paste collages that expressed their feelings about Harley-Davidsons. Whether long-time Harley riders or fresh prospects, common themes emerged in the artwork: enjoyment, the great outdoors, freedom.

Harley-Davidson then mailed more than 16,000 surveys "with a typical battery of psychological, sociological, and demographic questions you typically see in studies," Cimermancic said, as well as subjective questions such as "Is Harley typified more by a brown bear or a lion?" The questionnaire got a 30 percent response rate, with no incentive for return.

From the responses, Harley identified seven core customer types: the Adventure-Loving Traditionalist, the Sensitive Pragmatist, the Stylish Status-Seeker, the Laid-Back Camper, the Classy Capitalist, the Cool-Headed Loner, and the Cocky Misfit. All of them appreciated Harley-Davidson products for the same reasons.

"Independence, freedom, and power were universal Harley appeals," Cimermancic said. "It didn't matter if you were the guy who swept the floor of the factory or if you were the CEO at that factory, the attraction to Harley-Davidson was very similar. We were surprised by a tremendous amount of loyalty across the board."

That loyalty meant the company could build and sell more motorcycles, without having to overextend itself. In 1990, Harley-Davidson expanded to build 62,800 bikes; last year, it built more than 105,000. Based on research, and the fact that names are again piling up on waiting lists, Harley expects its phenomenal growth to continue. ∎

Source: Ian P. Murphy, "Aided by Research, Harley Goes Whole Hog," *Marketing News* 30 (December 2, 1996), pp. 16–17. See also Ted Shelsby, "Harley Sales Go Hog Wild," *The Baltimore Sun* (November 25, 2001), p. 1c.

Most firms conducting focus groups use screening interviews to determine the individuals who will compose a particular group. One type they try to avoid is the person who has participated before in a focus group, since some of these people tend to behave as "experts." Their presence can cause the group to behave in dysfunctional ways as experienced participants continually try to make their presence felt. Firms also try to avoid groups in which some of the participants are friends or relatives, because this tends to inhibit spontaneity in the discussion as the acquaintances begin talking to each other.

Given that the participants in any one group should be reasonably homogeneous, how can a firm ensure that it is getting a wide spectrum of insights? The key way is by having multiple groups. Not only can the characteristics of the participants vary across groups, but so can the issue outline. Ideas discovered in one group session can be introduced in subsequent group sessions for reaction. A typical project has four groups, but some may have up to twelve. The guiding criterion is whether the later groups are generating additional insight into the phenomenon under study. When they show diminishing returns, the groups are stopped.

© Eyewire/Getty Images

The typical focus group session lasts from 1½ to 2 hours. Most groups are held at facilities designed especially for them, although they can be held at other places.[11] One advantage of these facilities is that they can incorporate the latest in technology because of the large number of groups held there. For example, videoconferencing technology can be used to link groups in different locations, allowing participants at the various locations to interact directly with each other.

The moderator in the focus group has a key role.[12] For one thing, the moderator typically translates the study objectives into a discussion guide. To do so, he or she needs to understand the background of the problem and the most important information the client hopes to glean from the research process. The moderator also needs to understand the parameters of all the focus groups in terms of their number, size, and composition, as well as how they might be structured to build on one another. Moreover, the moderator must lead the discussion so that all objectives of the study are met and do so in such a way that *interaction* among the group members is stimulated and promoted. The focus group session should not be allowed to dissolve into nothing more than a set of concurrent interviews in which the participants each take turns responding to a predetermined set of questions. The moderator role is extremely delicate. It requires someone who is intimately familiar with the purpose and objectives of the research and at the same time possesses good interpersonal communication skills. One important measure of a focus group's success is whether the participants talk to each other, rather than the moderator, about the items on the discussion guide.

Some of the key qualifications moderators must have are described in Exhibit 5.1. Moderating an industrial focus group is even more difficult than moderating one involving a consumer product. A moderator for a consumer good typically knows something about the product or service at issue. After all, moderators are consumers too. Not so with many industrial goods. This means that the moderator's briefing for an industrial product has to be longer and more detailed. It also means that many of the group participants will know a great deal more about the product or service being discussed than the moderator. Directing group discussion under these conditions can be a taxing job.

Sponsors can realize several advantages from the proper conduct of focus groups. For one thing, they allow for serendipity. Ideas can simply drop "out of the blue" during a focus

Market researchers can take advantage of groups that meet in natural settings—such as children's play groups—to get feedback on new products on a regular basis.

8 *Identify the key person in a focus group.*

Exhibit 5.1

Seven Characteristics of Good Focus Group Moderators

Superior Listening Ability. It is essential that the moderator be able to listen to what the participants are saying. A moderator must not miss the participants' comments because of lack of attention or misunderstanding. The effective moderator knows how to paraphrase, to restate the comments of a participant when necessary, to ensure that the content of the comments is clear.

Excellent Short-Term Auditory Memory. The moderator must be able to remember comments that participants make early in a group, then correlate them with comments made later by the same or other participants. A participant might say that she rarely watches her weight, for example, then later indicate that she always drinks diet soft drinks. The moderator should remember the first comment and be able to relate it to the later one so that the reason for her diet soft drink consumption is clarified.

Well Organized. The best moderators see things in logical sequence from general to specific and keep similar topics organized together. A good moderator guide should be constructed logically, as should the final report. An effective moderator can keep track of all the details associated with managing the focus group process, so that nothing "falls through the cracks" that impacts negatively on the overall quality of the groups.

A Quick Learner. Moderators become intimately involved in a large number of different subject areas—and for only a very short time in each. An effective moderator is able to learn enough about a subject quickly in order to develop an effective moderator guide and conduct successful group sessions. Moderators normally have only a short period of time to study subject areas about which they will be conducting groups. Therefore, the most effective moderators can identify the key points in any topic area, then focus on them, so that they know enough to listen and/or probe for the nuances that make the difference between an extremely informative and an average group discussion.

High Energy Level. Focus groups can be very boring, both for the participants and for the client observers. When the tenor of a group gets very laid back and lifeless, it dramatically lowers the quality of the information that the participants generate. The best moderators find a way to inject energy and enthusiasm into the group so that both the participants and the observers are energized throughout the session. This ability tends to be most important during the second group of an evening (the eight to ten o'clock session), when observers and participants are frequently tired because of the late hour, and can become listless if they are not motivated to keep their energy and interest levels high. The moderator must be able to keep his or her own energy level high so that the discussion can continue to be very productive to the end.

Personable. The most effective moderators are people who can develop an instant rapport with participants, so that the people become actively involved in the discussion in order to please the moderator. Participants who don't establish rapport with the moderator are much less likely to "open up" during the discussion, and the output from the group is not as good.

Well-Above-Average Intelligence. This is a vital characteristic of the effective moderator, because no one can plan for every contingency that may occur in a focus group session. The moderator must be able to think on his or her feet: to process the information that the group is generating, then determine what line of questioning will most effectively generate further information needed to achieve the research objectives.

Source: Thomas L. Greenbaum, *The Handbook for Focus Group Research,* 2nd ed. (Thousand Oaks, Calif.: Sage Publications, 1998), pp. 77–78.

group discussion. Further, the group setting allows ideas to be developed to their full significance, because it allows for snowballing. A comment by one individual can trigger a chain of responses from other participants. Often after a brief introductory warm-up period, respondents can "turn on" to the discussion. They become sufficiently involved that they want to express their ideas and expose their feelings. Some feel more secure in the group environment than if they were being interviewed alone, since they soon realize that they can expose an idea without necessarily having to defend or elaborate on it. Consequently, responses are often more spontaneous and less conventional than they might be in a one-on-one interview.

Group interviews do offer certain benefits not obtainable with individual depth interviews (Exhibit 5.2), but they also have weaknesses. Although they are easy to set up, they are diffi-

Exhibit 5.2

The Advantages/Disadvantages of Individual Depth Interviews versus Focus Groups

Advantages of Individual Depth Interviews versus Focus Groups

■ They permit the interviewer to delve much deeper into a topic, because all the attention during the 1½-hour session is concentrated on one individual rather than a group of ten.

■ They allow more candid discussion on the part of the interviewee, who might be intimidated to talk about a particular topic in a group of his or her peers. This is particularly true for sensitive topics such as personal-care products, financial behavior, or attitudes toward sex, religion, and politics.

■ They eliminate negative group influences that can occur in a focus group. Because there is only one person being interviewed in the room, it is not possible for the individual's comments to be influenced by others.

■ They are essential for certain situations where competitors would otherwise be placed in the same room. For example, it might be very difficult to do an effective focus group with managers from competing department stores or restaurants. Therefore, research with these people must be done on a one-on-one basis.

Limitations of Individual Depth Interviews versus Focus Groups

■ They are typically much more expensive than focus groups, particularly when viewed on a per-interview basis. This is because the time of the moderator, which is the biggest cost in qualitative research, is the same for a two-hour focus group as it is for two hours of one-on-ones. Thus, for the same budget, the client gains input from significantly more people in a focus group.

■ They generally do not get the same degree of client involvement as focus groups. It is difficult to convince most clients to sit through multiple hours of a one-on-one interview; this can be a problem if one of the objectives is to get the clients to view the research so they benefit firsthand from the information.

■ They are physically exhausting for the moderator, so it is difficult to cover as much ground in one day as can be covered with groups. Most moderators will not do more than four or five interviews in a day, yet in two focus groups they can cover 20 people.

■ Focus groups give the moderator the ability to leverage the dynamics of the group to obtain reactions that might not otherwise be generated in a one-on-one session.

Source: Adapted from Thomas L. Greenbaum, "Focus Groups vs. One-on-Ones: The Controversy Continues," *Marketing News* 25 (September 2, 1991), p. 16. Reprinted with permission of American Marketing Association. See also Thomas L. Greenbaum, *Moderating Focus Groups: A Practical Guide for Group Facilitation* (Thousand Oaks, CA.: Sage Publications, 2000), Chapter 3.

cult to moderate and to interpret. It is easy to find evidence in one or more of the group discussions that supports almost any preconceived position. Because executives have the ability to observe the discussions through one-way mirrors or the opportunity to listen to tape recordings of the sessions, focus groups seem more susceptible to executive and even researcher biases than do other data collection techniques.

There seems to be a tendency among those seeing a session firsthand to forget that the discussion, and consequently the results, are greatly influenced by the moderator and the specific direction he or she provides. Moderators possessing all of the desired skills listed in Exhibit 5.1 are extremely rare. One has to remember that the results are not representative of what would be found in the general population and thus are *not* projectable. Further, the unstructured nature of the responses makes coding, tabulation, and analysis difficult. Focus groups should *not* be used, therefore, to develop head counts of the proportion of people who feel a particular way. Focus groups are better for generating ideas and insights than for systematically examining them.

With the increasing tendency of companies to offer their products and services for sale worldwide, many U.S. companies are relying on foreign focus groups to research global markets. Firms considering doing so need to be aware of some of the more important differences between focus groups conducted in foreign countries versus those held in the United States and Canada. See Research Window 5.2.

Major Differences between Focus Groups Held in Foreign Countries and Those Held in the United States and Canada

■ **Timeframe.** Whereas many companies are accustomed to developing a project on a Monday and having it completed by the end of the following week, this is almost impossible to do in foreign countries. Lead times tend to be much longer, especially in the Far East. If it takes two weeks to set up groups in the United States, expect almost double that in most of Europe and even more than that for Asia.

■ **Structure.** Eight to ten people in a group is a large number for most foreign groups, which often consist of four to six people. Further, the length of groups outside the United States can be up to four hours. Be very specific when arranging for international focus groups. Most foreign research organizations seem to adapt well to our format if properly informed and supervised.

■ **Recruiting and recreating.** In general, the United States is much more rigid in adhering to specifications both in recruiting and screening. These processes must be monitored very carefully.

■ **Approach.** Foreign moderators tend to be much less structured and authoritative, which can result in a great deal of down time during the sessions. Foreign moderators feel this is necessary to make group members feel comfortable with each other and build the rapport necessary to get the desired information.

Also, they tend to use fewer writing exercises and external stimuli such as concept boards and photos. This must be considered when planning foreign sessions.

■ **Project length.** Projects can take much longer to execute. In the United States we are accustomed to doing two, sometimes three or four, groups a day, but in many overseas markets, one group is the limit because of the time they are scheduled, the length of the sessions, or the demands of the moderators. Also, some moderators have a break in the middle of the group, which would be very unusual in U.S. sessions.

■ **Facilities.** The facility environment outside the United States and Canada is much like the setup here 20 years ago. For example, it is more common than not to watch a group in a residential setting on a television that is connected to the group room by cable. Further, many of the facilities with one-way mirror capabilities simply do not have the amenities we are accustomed to in the United States.

■ **Costs.** Although costs vary considerably by region and country, it would not be unusual to pay almost twice as much per group for sessions conducted in Europe and almost three times as much for many areas in Asia. ■

Source: Thomas L. Greenbaum, "Understanding Focus Group Research Abroad," *Marketing News* 30 (June 30, 1996), pp. H14, H36.

Analysis of Selected Cases

analysis of selected cases
Intensive study of selected examples of the phenomenon of interest.

Sometimes referred to as the analysis of *insight-stimulating examples,* the **analysis of selected cases** involves the intensive study of selected cases of the phenomenon under investigation. Researchers may examine existing records, observe the phenomenon as it occurs, conduct unstructured interviews, or use any one of a variety of other approaches to analyze what is really happening in a given situation. The focus may be on entities (individual people or institutions) or groups of entities (sales representatives or distributors in various regions).

The method is characterized by several features.[13] First, the researcher must be careful to record all relevant data, not just data that support any initial hypotheses he or she already formed. As with all forms of exploratory research, the goal is to gain insights, not to test explanations. By remaining neutral, it will be easier for the researcher to make the frequent changes in direction that are necessary as new information emerges. For example, he or she may first have to search for new cases or gather more data from previously contacted cases as the need arises. Second, the success of all forms of case analysis depends upon the researcher's ability to interpret the diverse mass of information that is eventually collected from one (or usually more) cases. The researcher must be able to sort through the data and see the "big picture," or insights that apply across multiple cases, not just details that apply only to individual cases. Third, the data collection and analysis requirements of most forms of analysis of selected cases can be intense. In general, the researcher wants to obtain enough information to understand both the unique features of the case being studied and the features it has in common with other cases.

A case in point is a study aimed at improving the productivity of the sales force of a particular company. In this case, the investigator chose to study intensively several of the best salespeople and to compare them to several of the worst. While a comparison of their backgrounds and experience revealed little, the time spent making sales calls with them suggested the hypothesis that the sales people who checked the stock of retailers and pointed out items on which they were low seemed to most clearly differentiate the successful and poor representatives.

The following situations are particularly productive of hypotheses:

1. *Cases reflecting changes and, in particular, abrupt changes.* For example, the way a market adjusts to the entrance of a new competitor can reveal a great deal about the structure of an industry.

2. *Cases reflecting extremes of behavior.* The case of the best and worst sales representatives just cited is an example. Similarly, to determine the factors responsible for the differences in sales performance among a company's territories, one could learn more by comparing the best and worst territories than by looking at all territories.

3. *Cases reflecting the order in which events occurred over time.* For example, in the case of the differing sales performance by territory, it may be that in one territory a branch office replaced a manufacturer's agent, while in another it replaced an industrial distributor.

Which cases will be most valuable depends, of course, on the problem in question. It is generally true, however, that cases that display sharp contrasts or have striking features are most useful. This is because minute differences are usually difficult to discern. Thus, instead of trying to determine what distinguishes the average case from the slightly above-average case, it is better to contrast the best and worst and thereby magnify whatever differences may exist.

A frequently used example of the use of selected cases to develop insights is benchmarking. **Benchmarking** involves identifying one or more organizations that excel at carrying out some function and using their practices as a source of ideas for improvement. For example, L. L. Bean is noted for its excellent order fulfillment. Even during the busy Christmas season, the company typically fills over 99 percent of its orders correctly. Therefore, other organizations have sought to improve their own order fulfillment by benchmarking L. L. Bean.

ETHICAL dilemma 5.2

Prompted by an increasing incidence of homes for sale by owner, the president of a local real estate company asks you to undertake exploratory research to ascertain what kind of image Realtors enjoy in the community. Unbeknownst to your current client, you undertook a similar research study for a competitor two years ago and, based on your findings, have formed specific hypotheses about why some homeowners are reluctant to sell their houses through Realtors.

- *Is it ethical to give information obtained while working for one client to another client who is a competitor? What should you definitely not tell your current client about the earlier project?*

- *Is it ethical to undertake a research project when you think that you already know what the findings will be? Can you generalize findings from two years ago to today?*

- *Should you help this company define its problem, and if so, how?*

benchmarking
Using organizations that excel at some function as sources of ideas for improvement.

© Stephen Saks/Index Stock Imagery

L. L. Bean is often studied and used as a benchmark by other companies for its consistent excellence in order fulfillment.

ethnographic methods
The detailed observation of consumers during their ordinary daily lives using direct observations, interviews, and video and audio recordings.

Organizations carry out benchmarking through activities such as reading about other organizations, visiting or calling them, and taking apart competing products to see how they are made. The process of benchmarking varies according to the information needs of the organization and the resources available.

Benchmarking is most useful for learning about existing rather than new products and about business practices, including ways of providing better value to customers. Benchmarked organizations are less likely to reveal information about new products or to disclose their strategies to competitors.

Xerox is widely credited with the first benchmarking project in the United States. In 1979, Xerox studied Japanese competitors to learn how they could sell midsize copiers for less than what it cost Xerox to make them. Today many companies including AT&T, Eastman Kodak, and Motorola use benchmarking as a standard research tool. Pittsburgh's Mellon Bank started benchmarking to improve the way it handled customer complaints about its credit card billing. Mellon benchmarked seven companies, including credit card operations, an airline, and a competing bank, by visiting three companies and phoning four. By applying what it learned, the bank cut its complaint-resolution time from an average of 45 days to 25 days.[14]

Ethnographic methods, which are being used increasingly by marketers, provide another example of the selected case approach to develop insights. These procedures, which have been adapted from anthropology, involve the detached and prolonged observation of consumers' emotional responses, cognitions, and behaviors during their ordinary daily lives. Unlike anthropologists, however, who might live in the group being studied for months or years, ethnographers use a combination of direct observations, interviews, and video and audio recordings to make their observations more quickly. For example, ethnographers at Intel played a large part in the development of the "couch pad," a hand-held flat-screen display that shows Web pages related to TV programs. The ethnographer's inspiration came from watching real people watch Web TV and squabble over how much of the screen should be devoted to data from the Web. The hand-held display, which shows a Web page related to the TV program being viewed, allows one person to look at Web sites while another views TV.[15] Research Window 5.3 provides more insights into the philosophy behind and methods used in ethnographic research.

Imagine being a fly on the wall at your consumers' homes: You would know exactly what products the consumer was using, when, and how. No more guessing about what a consumer wants.

That's why more and more companies are using ethnographic research as a tool to better understand how products fit into the context of consumers' lifestyles and, in turn, provide a basis for generating innovative new-product concepts. Ethnography allows one to observe consumer behavior where the person uses the product, whether it is in the home, on the go, at school, or in the office.

Ethnography is an anthropologic view of the marketplace. It deals with the scientific description of contemporary cultures. It uses anthropology to understand what the consumer needs but cannot adequately articulate. It records insights into the consumer experience with the product.

With ethnography, a consumer is viewed using products in his or her natural environment. For example, an ethnographer with a video camera becomes an observer at a consumer's home, perhaps "viewing" the inside of kitchen cabinets or the freezer compartment to get an accurate assessment of storage products' uses.

It should be obvious that this procedure shifts the focus to what consumers actually do, versus what they say they do. It draws hypotheses from the activities or behavior of the consumer rather than from their expressed attitudes. By closely observing and evaluating these patterns of behavior, we are able to draw conclusions for potential new-product ideas.

Perhaps the greatest benefit of such an ethnographic approach is the marketers' ability to view the consumer actually using the product, taking the concept of a "taste test" to a whole new realm. Rather than having a consumer test a product and provide feedback, consumers are using the product where and when they are most comfortable.

This exactness of ethnography is appealing. Consumers can't alter their response to a question about a product if they are being videotaped.

Among the most important approaches to ethnography are (1) in-home observation of consumers, (2) having consumers photograph usage occasions or environments, and (3) in-field observation of consumers.

In-home observation is most desired when the product's use is home-related. An interviewer and videographer might enter the respondent's home and ask specific questions under the watchful eye of the camera.

The second method involves having a consumer videotape or photograph the product in the home. For storage containers, for instance, the consumer might take pictures or videotape her cabinets, freezer, refrigerator, pantry, or any other place storage containers are used, providing a comprehensive photographic record of the product in use.

In the third method, in-field observation, a videographer, interviewer, and anthropologist go out to the field—a supermarket, picnic area, or daycare facility—to view the intended product.

While skeptics feel the presence of a camera hinders respondents from behaving naturally there are ways to structure the observation so that it seems as though the camera isn't even there.

There are many other methods to obtain a record of consumers' attitudes and behaviors. One involves having consumers take photographs of products throughout their homes. These allow consumers to express in a visual way the impact of products on specific parts of their lives. These photographs then are brought to an "ideation" session for generating new-product ideas.

In another method, consumers keep diaries of their responses to products, how they use certain products, when, and where. The diary is kept for a specified time and is used as a written recording of consumers' interaction with products. ■

Source: Adapted from Marvin Matises, "Send Ethnographers Into New—SKU Jungle," *Brandweek* 41 (September 25, 2000), pp. 32–33.

Emily's research team used Itracks' software to run two bulletin board focus groups of 40 people each. Participants received samples of the revised parenting program. They posted their reactions online and supplemented that feedback with responses to a mail survey. Because the focus groups took place over the Internet, the researchers could use a nationwide sample—something that would have been impractical with traditional focus groups.

From the extensive data and well-written report supplied by Emily, Dan could readily see how to set up his organization's parenting program. In addition, he could see *why* he should set up the program that way, and he had some data that would help in pricing the program and forecasting initial demand. He was so delighted with these practical results that he budgeted money for pretesting other products the same way.

Of course, the Internet is not ideal for all focus groups. Online moderators lack the cues provided by participants' tone of voice, facial expressions, and body language. Moderators need special training to notice subtle cues such as the length of responses and the way participants refer to themselves. Also, the questions the moderator posts to a bulletin board should stimulate deep reflection rather than quick response. Careful wording is essential for online discussions, because the moderator can't probe for details while a person is answering. Another challenge of online groups is that participants can't physically handle items unless the company provides them ahead of time, as in the example of Dan's company. Still, the Internet does allow the viewing of audio and video clips—a practical option if most participants have high-speed connections. With these challenges, online focus groups, including bulletin board focus groups, amount to no more than 15 percent of budgets for qualitative research.

Despite the drawbacks, online focus groups fill an important niche. They are especially useful for customer groups who are pressed for time and share a common passion. Just as many parents like to discuss the joys and frustrations of that role, professionals such as doctors or engineers may appreciate a chance to discuss an issue of genuine professional interest. Online discussions also may be appropriate for issues that are complex (because participants have time to reflect on questions and answers) and sensitive (because participants feel anonymous). Add to these uses the fact that online research lets companies bring together participants in far-flung locations, and it is not surprising that a growing share of companies are doing their qualitative research online. ■

Source: Based on "Bulletin Board Focus Group Brings Together National Sample: Busy Parents Provide Feedback on New Membership Program," posted in the "Press Room" section of the Itracks Web site, http://www.itracks.com, downloaded February 5, 2003. Additional background from Steve Jarvis and Deborah Szynal, "Show and Tell," *Marketing News* (November 19, 2001), pp. 1, 13; Nino DeNicola and Samantha Kennedy, "Quality Inter(net)action," *Marketing News* (November 19, 2001), p. 14; Deborah Szynal, "Big Bytes," *Marketing News* (March 18, 2002), p. 3; and Dana James, "This Bulletin Just In," *Marketing News* (March 4, 2002).

Summary

Learning Objective 1
Explain what a research design is.
A research design is the framework or plan for a study and guides the collection and analysis of data.

Learning Objective 2
List the three basic types of research design.
One basic way of classifying designs is in terms of the fundamental objective of the research: exploratory, descriptive, or causal.

Learning Objective 3
Describe the major emphasis of each type of research design.

The major emphasis in exploratory research is on the discovery of ideas and insights. Descriptive research is typically concerned with determining the frequency with which something occurs or the relationship between variables. A causal research design is concerned with determining cause-and-effect relationships.

Learning Objective 4
Cite the crucial principle of research.

The crucial principle of research is that the design of the investigation should stem from the problem.

Learning Objective 5
Describe the basic uses of exploratory research.

Exploratory research is basically "general picture" research. It is quite useful in becoming familiar with a phenomenon, in clarifying concepts, in developing but not testing "if-then" statements, and in establishing priorities for further research. The output from exploratory research is ideas and insights, not answers.

Learning Objective 6
Specify the key characteristic of exploratory research.

Exploratory studies are characterized by their flexibility.

Learning Objective 7
Discuss the various types of exploratory research and identify the characteristics of each.

Among the various types of exploratory research are literature searches, experience surveys, focus groups, and analyses of selected cases. Literature searches may involve conceptual literature, trade literature, or, quite often, published statistics. Experience surveys, sometimes known as key informant surveys, attempt to tap the knowledge and experience of those familiar with the general subject being investigated. Focus groups are in a sense personal interviews conducted among a small number of individuals, normally 8 to 12, simultaneously. However, the interview relies more on group discussion than on a series of directed questions to generate data. The analysis of selected cases is sometimes referred to as the analysis of insight-stimulating examples. By either label, the approach involves the intensive study of selected cases of the phenomenon under investigation.

Learning Objective 8
Identify the key person in a focus group.

The moderator is key to the successful functioning of a focus group. The moderator must not only lead the discussion so that all objectives of the study are met but must do so in such a way that interaction among group members is stimulated and promoted.

Key Terms

research design (page 90)
exploratory research (page 90)
descriptive research (page 90)
causal research (page 91)
hypothesis (page 92)
literature search (page 93)

experience survey (page 94)
focus group (page 95)
analysis of selected cases (page 100)
benchmarking (page 101)
ethnographic methods (page 102)

Review Questions

1. What is a research design? Is a research design necessary to conduct a study?
2. What are the different types of research designs? What is the basic purpose of each?
3. What is the crucial tenet of research?
4. What are the basic uses for exploratory research?
5. What is the key characteristic of exploratory research?
6. What are some of the more productive types of exploratory research? What are the characteristics of each type?

Discussion Questions, Problems, and Projects

1. The Communicon Company was a large supplier of residential telephones and related services in the southeast United States. The Department of Research and Development recently designed a prototype with a memory function that could store the number of calls and the contents of the calls for a period of 48 hours. A similar model, introduced by Communicon's competitor three months earlier, was marginally successful. However, both models suffered from a technical flaw. It was found that a call lasting for over 20 minutes would result in a loss of the dial tone for 90 seconds. This was mainly attributable to the activation of the memory function. Notwithstanding the flaw, management was excited about the efforts of the research and development department. They decided to do a field study to gauge consumer reaction to the memory capability. A random sample of 1,000 respondents was to be chosen from three major metropolitan centers in the Southeast. The questionnaires were designed to find out respondents' attitudes and opinions toward this new instrument.

   In this situation, is the research design appropriate? If yes, why? If no, why not?

2. A medium-sized manufacturer of high-speed copiers and duplicators was introducing a new desktop model. The vice president of communications had to decide between two advertising programs for this product. He preferred advertising program Gamma and was sure it would generate more sales than its counterpart, advertising program Beta. The next day he was to meet with the senior vice president of marketing to plan an appropriate research design for a study that would aid in the final decision as to which advertising program to implement.

   What research design would you recommend? Justify your choice.

3. A local mail-order firm was concerned with improving its service. In particular, management wanted to assess if customers were dissatisfied with current service and the nature of this dissatisfaction.

   What research design would you recommend? Justify your choice.

4. The Write-It Company was a manufacturer of writing instruments such as fountain pens, ballpoint pens, soft-tip pens, and mechanical pencils. Typically, these products were sold through small and large chains, drugstores, and grocery stores. The company had recently diversified into the manufacture of disposable cigarette lighters. The distribution of this product was to be restricted to drugstores and grocery stores because management believed that its target market of low- and middle-income people would use these outlets. Your expertise is required in order to decide on an appropriate research design to determine if this would indeed be the case.

   What research design would you recommend? Justify your choice.

5. Feather-Tote Luggage is a producer of cloth-covered luggage, one of the primary advantages of which is its light weight. The company distributes its luggage through major department stores, mail-order houses, clothing retailers, and other retail outlets such as stationery stores, leather goods stores, and so on. The company advertises rather heavily, but it also supplements this promotional effort with a large field staff of sales representatives, numbering around 400. The number of sales representatives varies, and one of the historical problems confronting Feather-Tote Luggage has been the large number of resignations. It is not unusual for 10 to 20 percent of the sales force to turn over every year. Since the cost of training a new person is estimated at $5,000 to $10,000, not including the lost sales that might result because of a personnel switch, Mr. Harvey, the sales manager, is rightly concerned, and has been conducting exit interviews with each departing sales representative. On the basis of these interviews, he has concluded that the major reason for this high turnover is general sales representatives' dissatisfaction with company policies, promotional opportunities, and pay. But top management has not been sympathetic to Harvey's pleas regarding the changes needed in these areas of corporate policy. Rather, it has tended to counter Harvey's pleas with arguments that too much of what he is suggesting is based on his gut reactions and little hard data. Before it would be willing to make changes, top management wants more systematic evidence that job satisfaction, in general, and these dimensions of job satisfaction, in particular, are the real reasons for the high turnover. Harvey has called on the Marketing Research Department at Feather-Tote Luggage to assist him in solving his problem.

(a) As a member of this department, identify the general hypothesis that would guide your research efforts.

(b) What type of research design would you recommend to Harvey? Justify your answer.

6. Cynthia Gaskill is the owner of a clothing store that caters to college students. Through informal conversations with her customers, she has begun to suspect that a video-rental store specifically targeting college students would do quite well in the local market. While her conversations with students have revealed an overall sense of dissatisfaction with existing rental outlets, she hasn't been able to isolate specific areas of concern. Thinking back to a marketing research course she took in school, Gaskill has decided that focus group research would be an appropriate method to gather information that might be useful in deciding whether to pursue further development of her idea to open a video rental store (e.g., a formal business plan, store policies, etc.).

(a) What is the decision problem and resulting research problem apparent in this situation?

(b) Who should Gaskill select as participants for the focus group?

(c) Where should the focus group session be conducted?

(d) Who should be the moderator of the focus group?

(e) Develop a discussion outline for the focus group.

7. The exploratory techniques of focus group research and experience surveys are similar in many ways, yet each offers distinct advantages, depending on the objectives of the research project. What are some of the similarities and differences in these techniques?

Suggested Additional Readings

For a discussion of the different types of research designs, their basic purposes, and generally fruitful approaches, see David A. deVaus, *Research Design in Social Research* (Thousand Oaks, CA.: Sage Publications, 2001).

For more detailed discussion of the techniques used in exploratory research, see David Carson and Audrey Gilmore, *Qualitative Marketing Research* (Thousand Oaks, CA.: Sage Publications, 2001).

For detailed discussion on conducting focus groups, see Thomas L. Greenbaum, *The Handbook for Focus Group Research,* 2nd ed. (Thousand Oaks, Calif.: Sage Publications, 1998).

Holly Edmunds, *The Focus Group Research Handbook* (Chicago: American Marketing Association, 1999).

For discussion of how to conduct ethnographic research, see John D. Brewer, *Ethnography* (Philadelphia: Open University Press, 2000).

Chapter 6

Descriptive and Causal Research Designs

© Digital Vision/Getty Images

Learning Objectives

1. Cite three major purposes of descriptive research.

2. List the six specifications of a descriptive study.

3. Explain what a dummy table is.

4. Discuss the difference between cross-sectional and longitudinal designs.

5. Explain what is meant by a panel in marketing research and explain the difference between a continuous panel and a discontinuous panel.

6. Describe the emphasis in sample surveys.

7. Clarify the difference between laboratory experiments and field experiments.

8. Explain which of the two types of experiments has greater internal validity and which has greater external validity.

9. List the three major problems in test-marketing.

10. Distinguish between a standard test market and a controlled test market.

11. Discuss the advantages and disadvantages of simulated test-marketing.

How do you talk to your friends and family when you're away from home? Suppose you're running late and don't want your friends to worry. Or say you get lost on your way to an appointment and need directions. Or what if your little brother or sister wants to call Mom or Dad for a ride home after a school activity? How do you leave a message or get the help you need? For a large and growing share of Americans, the answer is as obvious as the cell phone tucked into a pocket or backpack.

Not surprisingly, then, corporations are spending millions on research to learn about the cell phone features and benefits that consumers value. Who wants text messaging? How important is phone size? What pricing packages are most attractive and most profitable? These areas of research are logical, but what might come as a surprise is that one phone company recently researched an alternative from days gone by: the pay phone. In Boston, Verizon Communications took a fresh look at its pay-phone service to see whether it could boost the profitability of this old-fashioned product.

The freedom to set prices for pay phones is a relatively recent development in Massachusetts. Until the late 1990s, regulators in that state set the price of a pay phone call at 10 cents (a rate that callers in most other states could only dream of). When the state lifted regulations in 1997, the company raised the price of a call to 25 cents. A year later, Verizon announced that it would raise rates to 35 cents for a five-minute call. In 2000, Verizon raised rates again, to 50 cents for a call of any length. During this same time period, cell phones became popular, and the idea of carrying around coins for a phone call became a quaint notion from the past. Therefore, in spite of price increases, revenues from Verizon's pay phones fell.

In cities around the United States, pay phones have been disappearing, but Verizon's managers wondered whether there might be an alternative. They wondered if some consumers might prefer to use a pay phone for a quick call if the cost were low enough. In terms of research, the company wanted to predict how people in their service area would behave. If the price of a call were very low, would they choose a pay phone over a cell phone?

Verizon decided to try to answer this question. The company's task was to develop a research design that would be practical and would give a reliable answer.

Discussion Issues

1. What research design is appropriate for predicting consumers' response to a price reduction?

2. What variables would Verizon want to study?

3. Why should (or shouldn't) Verizon test a sample of consumers' responses, rather than reducing prices on all pay phones? ■

In the preceding chapter we learned that research designs typically fall into one of three categories: exploratory, descriptive, or causal research. We examined exploratory research and noted that one of its primary uses is to generate ideas and insights for additional, more targeted research. In this chapter we introduce some basic ideas about descriptive research. We then look at how causal research might be used to test the validity of the hypotheses that exploratory studies generate.

Descriptive Research Designs

Cite three major purposes of descriptive research.

A great deal of marketing research can be considered descriptive research, which is used for the following purposes:

1. To describe the characteristics of certain groups. For example, based on information gathered from known users of a particular product, we might attempt to develop a profile of the "average user" with respect to income, sex, age, educational level, and so on.
2. To estimate the proportion of people in a specified population who behave in a certain way. We might be interested, for example, in estimating the proportion of people within a specified radius of a proposed shopping complex who would shop at the center.
3. To make specific predictions. We might want to predict the level of sales for each of the next five years so that we could plan for the hiring and training of new sales representatives.

Descriptive research can be used to accomplish a wide variety of research objectives. However, a well-designed descriptive study is more than a simple fact-gathering expedition. Of themselves, facts are of little use unless they lead to better decisions:

> Our training as researchers and as businesspeople has always told us that more data is good. While it is no surprise that data comes at a cost, data is most valuable when it informs a decision. Suppose we are trying to find out how people shop. If the range of possible outcomes of this research will not alter any decision we will make, the research should not be done. Unfortunately, much non-diagnostic research is conducted every day. It usually begins with someone saying, "Wouldn't it be interesting to know . . ." The problem is that when the resulting crosstabs, bar chart, or pie chart is presented, part of that year's research budget is gone and managers are not any wiser than they were prior to the research.[1]

List the six specifications of a descriptive study.

Descriptive data become useful for solving problems only when their collection is guided by one or more specific hypotheses and much thought and effort. The hypotheses guide the research in specific directions. In this respect, a descriptive study design is very different from an exploratory study design. While an exploratory study is characterized by its flexibility, descriptive studies can be considered rigid. They require a clear specification of the who, what, when, where, why, and how of the research.

Suppose a chain of convenience food stores is planning to open a new store, and the company wants to determine how people usually come to patronize a new store. Consider some of the questions that would need to be answered before data collection for this descriptive study could begin. Who is to be considered a patron? Anyone who enters the store? What if they do not buy anything but just participate in the grand-opening prize giveaway? Perhaps a patron should be defined as anyone who purchases anything from the store.

Should patrons be defined on the basis of the family unit, or should they be defined as individuals, even though the individuals come from the same family? What characteristics of these patrons should be measured? Are we interested in their age and sex, or in where they live and how they came to know about the store? When shall we measure them—while they are shopping or later? Should the study take place during the first weeks of operation of the store, or should it be delayed until the situation has stabilized somewhat? Certainly if we are interested in word-of-mouth influence, we must wait at least until that influence has a chance to operate.

Where shall we measure the patrons? Should it be in the store, immediately outside the store, or should we attempt to contact them at home? Why do we want to measure them? Are we going to use these measurements to plan promotional strategy? In that case the emphasis might be on measuring how people become aware of the store. Or are we going to use these measurements as a basis for locating other stores? In that case the emphasis might shift more to determining the trading area of the store.

How shall we measure the patrons? Shall we use a questionnaire, or shall we observe their purchasing behavior? If we use a questionnaire, what form will it take? Will it be highly structured? Will it be in the form of a scale? How will it be administered? By telephone? By mail? Perhaps by personal interview?

These questions are not the only ones that would be or should be asked. Certainly, some of the answers will be implicit in the hypothesis or hypotheses that guide the descriptive research. Others, however, will not be obvious. The researcher will be able to specify them only after much thought or even after a small pilot or exploratory study. In either case, the researcher should delay data collection until hypotheses are developed and clear judgments of the who, what, when, where, why, and how of descriptive research are made.

The researcher should also delay data collection until it has been clearly determined how the data are to be analyzed. Ideally, a **dummy table** should be prepared before beginning the collection process. A dummy table is used to catalog the data that are to be collected. It shows how the analysis will be structured and conducted. Complete in all respects save for filling in the actual numbers, it contains a title, headings, and specific categories for the variables making up the table. All that remains after collecting the data is to count the number of cases of each type. Exhibit 6.1 shows a dummy table that might be used by a women's specialty store preparing to investigate whether its customers are predominantly from one age group and, if so, how that group differs from the customers who frequent competitors' stores.

Note that the table lists the age segments the store's owner wishes to compare. It is crucial that the exact variables and categories to be investigated be specified before researchers begin to collect the data. The statistical tests that will be used to uncover the relationship between age and store preference in this case should also be specified before data collection begins. Inexperienced researchers often question the need for such hard, detailed decisions before collecting the data. They assume that delaying these decisions until after the data are collected will somehow make the decisions easier. Just the opposite is true, as any experienced researcher will attest.

3 *Explain what a dummy table is.*

dummy table
A table that will be used to catalog the collected data.

© Terri L. Miller/E-Visual Communications, Inc.

Most difficult for the beginning researcher to anticipate will be the analytical problems he may face after the data are gathered. He tends to believe that a wide variety of facts will be enough to solve anything. Only after struggling with sloppy, stubborn, and intractable facts, with data not adequate for the testing of hypotheses and with data that are interesting but incapable of supporting practical recommendations for action will he be fully aware that the big "mistakes" of research usually are made in the early stages. Each definition of a problem or problem variable will create different facts or findings, and a formulation once made serves to restrict the scope of analysis. No problem is definitively formulated until the researcher can specify how he will make his analysis and how the results will contribute to a practical solution.[2]

Descriptive studies can help retail companies determine how consumers become patrons of a new store or a new location of a familiar store.

Once the data have been collected and analysis is begun, it is too late to say, "If only we had collected information on that variable," or "If only we had measured that variable using a different scale." Correcting such mistakes at this time is next to impossible. Instead, the analyst

Exhibit 6.1

Dummy Table: Store Preference by Age

		Store Preference	
Age	Prefer A	Prefer B	Prefer C
Less than 30			
30–39			
40 or over			

cross-sectional study
Investigation involving a sample of elements selected from the population of interest that are measured at a single point in time.

4 *Discuss the difference between cross-sectional and longitudinal designs.*

longitudinal study
Investigation involving a fixed sample of elements that is measured repeatedly through time.

5 *Explain what is meant by a panel in marketing research and explain the difference between a continuous panel and a discontinuous panel.*

continuous panel
A fixed sample of respondents who are measured repeatedly over time with respect to the same variables.

must take such considerations into account when planning the study. The researcher should specify in advance the objective each question addresses, the reason the question is included in the study, the particular analysis in which the question will be used, and the way the results might appear using dummy tables. Dummy tables are particularly valuable in providing clues on how to phrase the individual questions and code the responses.

Figure 6.1 is an overview of various types of descriptive studies. The basic distinction is between cross-sectional designs, which are the most common and most familiar, and longitudinal designs. Typically, a **cross-sectional study** involves researching a sample of elements from the population of interest. Most characteristics of the elements, or sample members, are measured only once.

A **longitudinal study,** on the other hand, involves a panel, which is a fixed sample of elements. The elements may be stores, dealers, individuals, or other entities. The panel, or sample, remains relatively constant through time, although members may be added to replace dropouts or to keep it representative. The sample members in a panel are measured repeatedly, in contrast with the one-time measurement in a cross-sectional study. Both cross-sectional and longitudinal studies have weaknesses and advantages.

Longitudinal Analysis

There are two types of panels: continuous panels (sometimes called true panels) and discontinuous panels (sometimes called omnibus panels). **Continuous panels,** which are older, rely on repeated measurements of the same variables. Nielsen maintains panels consisting of more than 155,000 households across 21 countries. Most panel households use a handheld scanner to record every UPC-coded item they purchase. They simply pass the scanner across the Universal Product Codes on the packages of the purchased items when they return from shopping and then answer a programmed set of questions (e.g., store where purchased, price

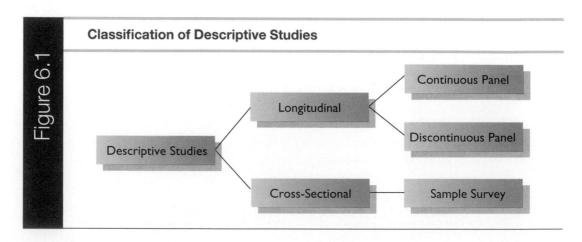

Figure 6.1 — Classification of Descriptive Studies

paid) by responding to a series of prompts from the machine. Taylor, Nelson, Sofres, a large marketing research company headquartered in London, maintains continuous panels in Great Britain and 19 other countries around the world. The NPD Group offers the NPD Online Panel, with over 900,000 individual members who provide tracking services for a number of different industries. The operations of panels will be detailed in the section on standardized marketing information services in Chapter 8. The important point to note now is that each panel member is measured with respect to the same characteristics at each time—purchases.

In recent years, another type of panel, called a **discontinuous panel,** has been developed. The information collected from the members selected for this type of panel varies. At one time, it may be attitudes with respect to a new product. At another time, the panel members might be asked to evaluate alternative advertising copy. In each case, a sample might be selected from the larger group, which is in turn a sample of the population. The subsample might be drawn randomly. More likely, however, participants with the desired characteristics will be chosen from a total panel. For example, the Parker Pen Company maintains a panel of 1,100 individuals who were chosen because they expressed some interest in writing instruments and, of course, because of their willingness to participate. Parker Pen uses selected members of this panel to evaluate new writing instruments. If the new instrument is a fountain pen, the company will probably choose individuals who prefer fountain pens to test the product. Those chosen and the information sought varies from project to project.

Several large marketing research companies also operate discontinuous panels. For example, Market Facts Inc. offers a discontinuous panel with over 600,000 households. NFO Worldgroup and Ipsos Group S.A. also operate large discontinuous consumer panels.

The distinction between the traditional continuous panel and the discontinuous panel is important. True longitudinal analysis, also called *time series analysis,* can be performed only on the first type of data, repeated measurements of the same variables for the same entities over time. This is a real advantage compared with discontinuous panels and cross-sectional studies. Technically Speaking 6.1 demonstrates the analytic advantages of continuous panels.[3]

In many respects, the other advantages and disadvantages of both types of panels compared with cross-sectional studies are about the same. For example, a panel provides some advantages in the kind of information it yields. Panels are probably a researcher's best format for collecting classification information, such as respondents' incomes, ages, education levels, and occupations. And this information allows a more sophisticated analysis of a study's results. Cross-sectional studies are limited in this respect, since respondents being contacted for the first and only time are rarely willing to give lengthy, time-consuming interviews. Panel members are usually compensated for their participation, so their interviews can be longer and more exacting, or there can be several interviews. Further, the sponsoring firm can afford to spend more time and effort securing accurate classification information, as this information can be used in a number of studies.

Panel data are also believed to be more accurate than cross-sectional data, particularly when it comes to measuring things like purchasing behavior and watching and listening to media outlets. With cross-sectional designs, respondents are asked to remember and report their past behaviors, a process that inevitably leads to error because people tend to forget, partly because time has elapsed, but partly for other reasons. In particular, research has shown that events and experiences are forgotten more readily if they are inconsistent with attitudes or beliefs that are important to the person or that threaten the person's self-esteem. If, for example, subjects are asked how often they brush their teeth, they might overstate the number of times—either because they genuinely do not remember or because they fear the interviewer will think less of them for brushing too seldom. In a panel, on the other hand, behavior is recorded as it occurs, so less reliance is placed on a respondent's memory. When diaries are used to record purchases, the problems should be virtually eliminated because the respondent is instructed to record the purchases immediately upon returning home. When

discontinuous panel
A fixed sample of respondents who are measured repeatedly over time but on variables that change from measurement to measurement.

PROBABLY THE SINGLE MOST IMPORTANT ADVANTAGE OF TRUE PANEL DATA IS THE way it lends itself to analysis. Suppose that we can obtain consumer purchase data from a panel of 1,000 families, and that we manufacture a laundry detergent, which we will call Brand A. Our brand has two main competitors, Brands B and C, and a number of other smaller competitors, which we will classify together in the single category Brand D.

We have recently changed the package design of our product, and are interested in determining what impact the new design has on sales. Let us consider the performance of our brand before the change (time period t_1) and after the package change (time period t_2).

We could perform several types of analyses on these data. We could look at the proportion of those in the panel who bought our brand in period t_1. We could also calculate the proportion of those who bought our brand in period t_2. Suppose these calculations generated the data shown in Exhibit A, which indicates that the package change was successful. Brand A's market share increased from 20 percent to 25 percent. Further,

Brand A seemed to make its gain at the expense of its two major competitors, whose market shares decreased.

But that is not the whole story. Because we can identify panel participants and we have repeated measures from those participants, we can count the number of families who bought Brand A in both periods, those who bought the other brands in both periods, and those who switched brands between the two periods. Suppose the information in Exhibit B was a result of these tabulations. This table, which is a turnover table, or a brand-switching matrix, contains the same basic information as Exhibit A. That is, we see that 200, or 20 percent, of the families bought Brand A in period t_1, while 250, or 25 percent, did so in period t_2. But Exhibit B also shows that Brand A did not make its market share gains at the expense of Brands B and C, as originally suggested, but rather captured some of the families who previously bought one of the miscellaneous brands; 75 families switched from Brand D in period t_1 to Brand A in period t_2. And, as a matter of fact, Brand A lost some of its previous users to Brand B during the period; 25 families switched from Brand A in period t_1 to Brand B in period t_2.

Exhibit A

Number of Families in Panel Purchasing Each Brand

Brand Purchased	During First Time Period (t_1)	During Second Time Period (t_2)
A	200	250
B	300	270
C	350	330
D	150	150
Total	1,000	1,000

Exhibit B

Number of Families in Panel Buying Each Brand in Each Period

		During Second Time Period (t_2)			
		Bought A	Bought B	Bought C	Bought D	Total
During First Time Period (t_1)	Bought A	175	25	0	0	200
	Bought B	0	225	50	25	300
	Bought C	0	0	280	70	350
	Bought D	75	20	0	55	150
	Total	250	270	330	150	1,000

Exhibit C

Brand Loyalty and Brand-Switching Probabilities among Families in Panel					
	During Second Time Period (t₂)				
	Bought A	Bought B	Bought C	Bought D	Total
During First Time Period (t₁) Bought A	.875	.125	.000	.000	1.000
Bought B	.000	.750	.167	.083	1.000
Bought C	.000	.000	.800	.200	1.000
Bought D	.500	.133	.000	.367	1.000

Exhibit 2 also allows the calculation of brand loyalty. Consider Brand A, for example: 175 of the 200, or 87.5 percent, of those who bought in period t_1 remained "loyal to it" (bought it again) in period t_2. By dividing each cell entry by the row or previous period totals, one can assess these brand loyalties. Exhibit C, produced by such calculations, suggests, for example, that among the three major brands, Brand A exhibited the greatest buying loyalties and Brand B the least. This is important to know because it indicates whether families like the brand when they try it.

Whether we can conclude that those who switched from one of the miscellaneous brands to Brand A were prompted to do so by the package change is open to question, for reasons we will discuss later. The point is that turnover, or brand-switching, analysis can be performed only when there are repeated measures over time for the same variables for the same subjects. It is not appropriate for discontinuous panel data, in which the variables being measured are constantly changing, nor is it appropriate for cross-sectional studies, even if successive cross-sectional samples are taken.

Thus, the unique advantage of true longitudinal analysis is that since it reveals changes in individual members' behavior, researchers can determine the effect of a change in a particular marketing variable—a package design, for example—better than if they had conducted separate studies using samples made up of different individuals. Had two different groups been used to study a change in a particular variable, it would not be clear whether variations in the data were due to changes in the marketing variable or to differences between the two groups. ■

other behaviors, such as television viewing, are of interest, actual viewing behaviors can be recorded electronically as they occur, thus minimizing the possibility that they will be forgotten or distorted when they are eventually asked about. Exhibit 6.2 shows a page from an Arbitron radio listening diary. These diaries, which are used to determine radio station listening audiences, are used by stations to make programming decisions and by advertisers to determine which programs to sponsor. Every person over the age of 12 in each of the participating households receives a new diary for each week they participate. A key advantage of the diary is that it is completely portable and can be filled out anywhere, which tends to increase its accuracy.

The main disadvantage of panels is that they are nonrepresentative. The agreement to participate involves a commitment on the part of the designated sample member, and many individuals do not want to make this commitment. They do not wish to be bothered with testing products, evaluating advertising copy, or filling out consumer diaries. Because these activities require a sizable time commitment, families in which both husband and wife work, for example, may be less well represented than those in which one partner works and the other is at home. Most consumer panels have cooperation rates of 50% or less—and that is among households that agreed to participate in the panel. A large percentage of consumers choose not to join a panel in the first place. As might be expected, cooperation rates tend to be higher when consumers find the topic interesting or when less work is required of them (for

Exhibit 6.2

Arbitron Radio Listening Diary

THURSDAY

	Time		Station			Place			
			Call letters, dial setting or station name *Don't know? Use program name.*	*Mark (X) one*		*Mark (X) one*			
	Start	Stop		AM	FM	At Home	In a Car	At Work	Other Place
Early Morning (from 5 AM)	:	:							
	:	:							
	:	:							
	:	:							
Midday	:	:							
	:	:							
	:	:							
	:	:							
Late Afternoon	:	:							
	:	:							
	:	:							
	:	:							
Night (to 5 AM Friday)	:	:							
	:	:							
	:	:							

If you didn't hear a radio today, please mark (X) here. ☐

Source: © 2000 The Arbitron Company

example, using a Nielsen television meter versus keeping a diary by hand of all grocery purchases).[4]

The better ongoing panel operations select prospective participants very systematically. They attempt to generate and maintain panels that are representative of the total population of interest with respect to such characteristics as age, occupation, education, and so on. Quite often, to create a representative panel, they will use quota samples, in which the proportion of sample members possessing a certain characteristic is approximately the same as the proportion possessing that characteristic in the general population. As a very simplified example of this, consider an organization that wishes to study sports car owners. If the organization knows that in the general population of interest, 52 percent are men and 48 percent are women, then it will want its quota sample to reflect that percentage.

All the research organization can do, however, is designate families or respondents to be included in the sample. Researchers cannot force anyone to participate, nor can they require continued participation from those who initially agreed to cooperate. True, they often encourage participation by offering some premium or by paying panel members for their cooperation. Nevertheless, a significant percentage of the individuals the organization may have hoped to include often do not cooperate—or drop out quickly once the panel has begun. Some individuals are lost to the panel because they move away or die. Depending on the type of cooperation needed, the refusal and mortality, or drop-out, rate might run over 50 percent. Then the question arises as to whether the panel is still representative of the population. Further, the payment of a reward for cooperation raises the question of whether particular types of people are attracted to such panels. It is generally accepted, for example, that panel samples underrepresent African Americans, persons with poor English language skills, and those at the extremes of the socioeconomic spectrum.[5] In addition, evidence suggests that cooperation is generally lower for households with only one or two members, households with wives in older age groups, and households with lower degrees of education. Online panels, in which members are contacted via email or access online surveys via the Web, are assumed to exhibit the same representation differences identified for online users—a tendency toward overrepresentation of younger, professional men. As Internet penetration increases, however, differences between online panels and the general public should decrease.[6] Lack of unrepresentativeness may not be a problem in every study. It depends on the purpose of the study and the particular variables of interest. Research Window 6.1 considers the merits of traditional vs. online panels.

In a series of studies investigating the "representativeness" of a continuing household panel, Market Facts compared data gathered from a mail panel against data gathered from randomly selected telephone samples. Research Window 6.2 displays some of the results of its findings with respect to such characteristics as product ownership, lifestyle, and leisure activities. As the sample of comparisons suggest, the evidence led Market Facts to conclude that "mail panels are likely to parallel the population in most, if not all, dimensions of leisure activity and lifestyle."[7] The studies did, however, identify differences between survey and panel data in some instances. Thus, while panels can be incredibly useful, the researcher must be aware of potential problem areas, particularly with respect to unrepresentative panels. The trouble with bias due to "unrepresentativeness" is that we never know in advance whether it will affect the results, much less how.

Cross-Sectional Analysis

Despite the advantages of longitudinal analysis, in actual practice cross-sectional designs are the best known and most important descriptive designs. The cross-sectional study has two distinguishing features. First, it provides a snapshot of the variables of interest at a single point in time, as contrasted with the longitudinal study, which provides a series of pictures that, when pieced together, provide a movie of the situation and the changes that occur. Second, in the cross-sectional study, the sample of elements is typically selected to be representative of some known universe, or population. Therefore, a great deal of emphasis is placed on selecting sample members, usually with a probability sampling plan. That is one reason the technique is often called **sample survey**. The probability sampling plan allows the determination of the sampling error associated with the statistics, which are generated from the sample but used to describe the population. Most sample surveys involve enough observations to allow for cross-classification of the variables.

The objective of cross-classification analysis is to establish categories such that classification in one category implies classification in one or more other categories. The method of cross-classification analysis will be detailed later. For the moment, simply note that it involves counting the simultaneous occurrence of the variables of interest. For example, suppose management feels that occupation is an important factor in determining consumption of its product. Fur-

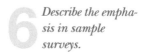

Describe the emphasis in sample surveys.

sample survey
Cross-sectional study in which the sample is selected to be representative of the target population and in which the emphasis is on the generation of summary statistics such as averages and percentages.

Sorting Out the Offline (Traditional) vs. Online Decision

For some situations and some questions, offline panels are the obvious choice. For other types of questions, online panels are obvious. The difficulty lies in the gray areas. Each method has its benefits and each has its self-selection biases. The crucial concern with an online panel is that it is presently the least favorable choice for research in terms of accuracy, according to Karl Irons, president of NPD Online Research.

Online panels can have some tremendous benefits when the population is accurately sampled. Online panels are fast, they can generate large samples, they can be inexpensive (no mailing and printing costs and lower labor costs), they can show graphics and video, and they can provide seamless international coordination. Furthermore, they can reduce in-house errors associated with interviewer bias or coding and data entry errors.

Despite these benefits, there are concerns that Internet-savvy consumers are not representative of the general population. While no method offline or online is perfectly representative of the population being studied, there is a sizable concern that online panels are psychographically biased toward progressive technology innovators, and demographically biased toward young male professionals. If this is true, then the typical grocery shopper is probably represented more accurately by offline panels then online panels. In this case, the decision of which type of panel to use to study grocery shopping would

involve a trade-off: the speed and savings of online or the increased accuracy of an offline panel. For certain questions, accuracy is less important than others.

Yet the representativeness of online panels to the general population of consumers is only important if you are actually interested in the general population of consumers. There are situations where the population of interest—for instance, people who purchase on the Internet—is best captured by an online panel. Presently, items that can easily be bought using the Internet (books, compact discs, airline tickets, magazine subscriptions, home banking, investment services, and software, etc.) are probably good candidates for online consumer panels.

Furthermore, there are subgroups within the population that may be better represented through Internet than through other methods. Teenagers, for instance, have been an elusive group with respect to consumer panels prior to online consumer panels. This is also true for consumers who are single and for well-educated audiences, such as doctors, lawyers, and other professionals, and it may also be true for working mothers.

In summary, the online vs. offline decision depends on the products and the populations you are studying and on the level of accuracy that you need. As Internet use increases, biases will decrease, and online panels will be better able to access a more general population. ■

Source: Brian Wansink and Seymour Sudman, "Selecting a Consumer Panel Service," *Quirk's Marketing Research Review* (May 2002), pp. 35–36.

ther, suppose the proposition to be examined is that white-collar workers are more apt to use the product than blue-collar workers. If this hypothesis was examined in a cross-sectional study, measurements would be taken from a representative sample of the population with respect to occupation and use of the product. In cross tabulation, researchers would count the number of cases that fell in each of the following classes:

- White-collar and use the product
- Blue-collar and use the product
- White-collar and do not use the product
- Blue-collar and do not use the product

That is, the emphasis would be on the relative frequency of occurrence of the joint phenomenon "white-collar occupation and user of the product." If the hypothesis is to be supported by the sample data, the proportion of white-collar workers using the product should exceed the proportion of blue-collar workers using the product.

Although the sample survey is commonly used, it has several disadvantages. These include superficial analysis of the phenomenon, high cost, and the technical sophistication required

Comparison of Responses of the Market Facts Mail Panel and a Randomly Selected Telephone Sample

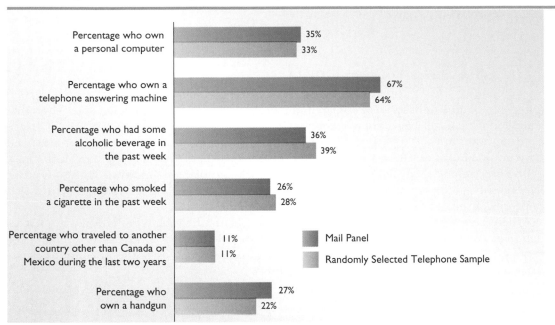

Percentage who own a personal computer — 35% / 33%

Percentage who own a telephone answering machine — 67% / 64%

Percentage who had some alcoholic beverage in the past week — 36% / 39%

Percentage who smoked a cigarette in the past week — 26% / 28%

Percentage who traveled to another country other than Canada or Mexico during the last two years — 11% / 11%

Percentage who own a handgun — 27% / 22%

■ Mail Panel
■ Randomly Selected Telephone Sample

Source: "Mail Panels vs. General Samples: How Similar and How Different," *Research on Research,* No. 59 (Chicago: Synovate, formerly Market Facts, Inc., undated).

to conduct survey research. Let us consider each disadvantage in turn.

One common criticism of survey data is that they typically do not penetrate very deeply below the surface, since breadth is often emphasized at the expense of depth. There is ordinarily an emphasis on the calculation of statistics that efficiently summarize the wide variety of data collected from the sometimes large cross section of subjects. Yet the very process of generating summary statistics to describe the phenomenon suggests that the eventual "average" might not accurately describe any individual entity making up the aggregate. The situation is much like that of "the guy who slept with his feet in the refrigerator and his head in the stove and who, on the average, was comfortable."

Second, a survey is expensive in terms of time and money. It will often be months before a single hypothesis can be tested because of necessary preliminaries so vital to survey research. The entire research process—from problem definition through measuring instrument development, design of the sample, collecting the data, and editing, coding, and tabulating the data—must be executed before an analyst can begin to examine the hypotheses that guide the study. As will be shown in subsequent chapters, each of these tasks can be formidable in its own right. Each can require large investments of time, energy, and money.

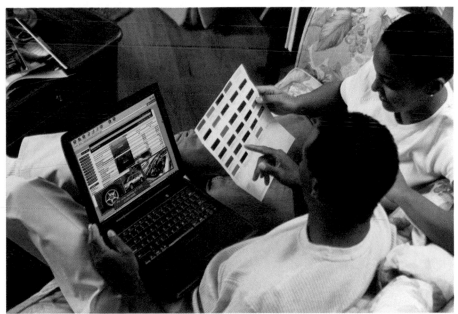

© Jon Riley/Index Stock Imagery

Surveying consumers via online panels can be particularly effective when researchers are studying products frequently purchased via the Internet.

CHAPTER 6:
Descriptive and Causal Research Designs

119

Survey research also requires a good deal of technical skill. The research analyst must either have the technical skills required at each stage of the process or have access to technical consultants. Only rarely will a person be able both to develop an attitude scale and to design a complex probability sample.

Causal Research Designs

Often exploratory or descriptive research will turn up several cause-and-effect hypotheses that a marketing manager may want to examine. For example, if a price change is planned, a manager may want to test this hypothesis: "A 5 percent increase in the price of the product will have no significant effect on the amount of the product that customers will buy." If the marketing department is considering a change in packaging, planners may first want to test this hypothesis: "A redesign of the cereal package so that it is shorter and less likely to tip over will improve consumer attitudes toward the product."

When the research question can be stated this explicitly, the researcher is dealing with a situation in which causal analysis would be the method of choice. Descriptive research is fine for testing hypotheses about relationships between variables, but it is not as effective as causal designs for testing cause-and-effect relationships.

Concept of Causality

Everyone is familiar with the general notion of causality, the idea that one thing leads to the occurrence of another. The scientific notion of causality is quite complex, however, and a detailed discussion of it is beyond the scope of this book. An important point to recognize at this stage is that we can never really prove that one thing causes another. As discussed in Technically Speaking 6.2, establishing that variable X causes variable Y requires meeting a number of conditions, including the elimination of all other possible causes of Y. Because we can never know for certain that we have eliminated all other possible causes, no matter how carefully we have planned and conducted our research, we can never say with certainty that X causes Y.

Does this mean that researchers should not bother trying to establish causal relationships? Not at all! Although we cannot prove with certainty that a change in one variable produces a change in another, we can conduct research that helps us narrow down the likely causal relationship between two variables by eliminating other possible causes that we can recognize. With typical descriptive research designs we do this by measuring the other variables and attempting to control their effects on the outcome variable via statistical techniques. With causal research designs, we work toward establishing possible causal relationships through the use of experiments.

Experimentation as Causal Research

experiment
Scientific investigation in which an investigator manipulates and controls one or more indepent variables and observes the degree to which the dependent variables change.

An **experiment** can provide more convincing evidence of causal relationships than an exploratory or descriptive design can because of the control it gives investigators. For this reason, experiments are often called causal research. In an experiment, a researcher manipulates, or sets the levels of, one or more causal variables to examine the effect on one or more outcome variables while attempting to account for the effects of all other possible causal variables. The variables manipulated by the researcher are referred to as independent variables, and the outcome variables are called dependent variables. Because investigators are able to control the levels of the independent variable(s), they can be more confident that the relationships discovered are so-called true relationships.

PART 2:
Research Design

Evidence of Causality

THREE CONDITIONS MUST BE MET BEFORE CONCLUDING "X CAUSED Y."[a] THE FIRST condition is concomitant variation—that is, the extent to which a cause, X, and an effect, Y, occur together or vary together in the way predicted by the hypothesis.

Consider a car manufacturer who wants to test the relationship between the quality of its dealers and the company's market share in an area. The manufacturer's hypothesis is, "The success of our marketing efforts is highly dependent upon the degree of service quality offered by our dealers. Where we have high service quality dealers, we have good market penetration, and where we have poor service quality dealers, we have unsatisfactory market penetration." Now if X is to be considered a cause of Y, we will find the following: In territories where our dealers receive high marks for service quality, we should have satisfactory market shares, while in territories with poor service quality dealers, we should have unsatisfactory market shares. However, if we find that in a large number of territories with good service quality dealers we also have unsatisfactory market shares, we must conclude that either our hypothesis is faulty or that there are additional factors involved.

Suppose that when we analyzed the relationship between X and Y, we found evidence of concomitant variation. All we can conclude is that the association makes the hypothesis more likely; it does not prove it. We are always inferring, rather than proving, that a causal relationship exists. Similarly, the lack of an association between X and Y cannot be taken as conclusive evidence that there is no causal relationship between them.

The second condition for establishing causality involves the time order of occurrence of the variables. That is, if a change in one variable is supposed to cause a change in another variable (e.g., improving dealer service quality will lead to improved market share), the change in the cause variable (i.e., improving dealer service quality) must normally occur prior to the change in the effect variable (i.e., improvement in market share):

> One event cannot be considered the "cause" of another if it occurs after the other event. The occurrence of a causal factor may precede or may be simultaneous with the occurrence of an event; by definition, an effect cannot be produced by an event that occurs only after the effect has taken place. However, it is possible for each term in the relationship to be both a "cause" and an "effect" of the other term.[b]

Although this condition seems simple enough, it is sometimes difficult to establish the time sequence in practice. For example, consider the relationship between a firm's annual advertising expenditures and its sales. Marketing managers often attribute a sales increase to an increase in spending on advertising. However, some companies follow a rule of thumb that uses past sales as a guide to allocating resources to advertising. For example, an amount equal to 10 percent of last year's sales may be earmarked for this year's advertising budget. This practice confuses the issue of which event is the cause and which is the effect. Does advertising lead to higher sales, or do higher sales lead to an increased ad budget? An intimate understanding of the way the company establishes the ad budget should resolve the dilemma in this situation.

The final condition for establishing causality is also the most difficult to meet. To fully establish causality, the researcher must eliminate all other possible causes for the outcome variable. The elimination of other possible causal factors is very much like the Sherlock Holmes approach to analysis. Just as Sherlock Holmes holds that "when you have eliminated the impossible, whatever

Technically SPEAKING

6.2

[a] See Claire Selltiz, Lawrence S. Wrightsman, and Stuart W. Cook, *Research Methods in Social Relations,* rev. ed. (New York: Holt, Rinehart and Winston, 1959), pp. 80–82, for a brief but helpful discussion of the differences between the commonsense and scientific notions of causality. See also David A. Kenny, *Correlation and Causality* (New York: John Wiley, 1979); Earl R. Babbie, *The Practice of Social Research,* 7th ed. (Belmont, Calif.: Wadsworth Publishing, 1995).
[b] Selltiz, Wrightsman, and Cook, *Research Methods,* p. 85.

remains, however improbable, must be the truth,"[c] this condition for causality focuses on the elimination of possible explanations other than the one being studied. This may mean physically holding other factors constant, or it may mean adjusting the results to remove the effects of other possible causal factors. Unfortunately, we can never be certain that we have eliminated all other possible causes of an effect.

Take the situation of the divisional manager of a chain of supermarkets investigating the effects of end-of-aisle displays on orange sales. Suppose that the manager found that per-store sales of oranges increased during the past week and that a number of stores were using end-of-aisle displays for oranges. To establish that the end displays were likely to be the factor responsible for the sales increase, the manager would need to eliminate other possible variables, such as price, size of store, and orange type and quality. This might involve looking at orange sales for stores of approximately the same size, checking to see if prices were the same in stores having an increase in sales and stores with no increase, and determining if the type and quality of oranges were consistent with the previous week's. Even if the manager could conclude that none of these additional variables led to the increased sales of oranges, however, we cannot be certain that some other, perhaps presently unknown, variable has caused the change in sales.

Thus, as a practical matter it is impossible to prove that a change in one variable has caused a change in another. Even though concomitant variation and temporal ordering can often be established, we can never be certain that all other possible causes of the outcome variable have been eliminated. ■

[c] Arthur Conan Doyle, "The Sign of the Four," in *The Complete Sherlock Holmes* (Garden City, N.Y.: Garden City Publishing Company, 1938), p. 94.

There are two basic types of experiments—laboratory experiments and field experiments. Each has its own advantages and disadvantages, and research analysts need to be familiar with both.

A **laboratory experiment** is one in which an investigator creates a situation with the desired conditions and then manipulates some variables while controlling others. By holding other variables constant while manipulating the independent variable(s), the investigator is able to observe and measure the effect of the manipulation of the variables while the effect of other factors is minimized.

In one laboratory experiment designed to measure the effect of price on the demand for coffee and cola, for example, 135 homemakers in a small town in Illinois were asked to take part in simulated shopping trips.[8] On each of the eight simulated trips, which were conducted in subjects' homes, the homemakers could choose their favorite brands from a full assortment of coffees and colas listed on index cards. The only change on each trip was the products' prices. Each homemaker was free to switch brands to obtain the best product for the money. In this respect, the trial purchase was not unlike an actual purchase. In other respects, however, this trial was unlike conditions in a real supermarket. In the laboratory experiment, the homemakers were free from the distractions of other variables such as packaging, position on the shelf, and in-store promotions; each of these variables was held constant.

A **field experiment** is a research study in a realistic or natural situation, although it, too, involves the manipulation of one or more variables under as carefully controlled conditions as the situation will permit. The field experiment differs from the laboratory experiment primarily in terms of environment. The degree of control and precision allowed by each individual field or laboratory experiment varies.[9]

A similar investigation to test the effect of price on the demand for coffee and cola was also conducted in a field experiment. In this case, the experiment was conducted in two small towns in Illinois, ten miles apart. The manipulations here involved actual changes in price for

7 *Clarify the difference between laboratory experiments and field experiments.*

laboratory experiment
Research investigation in which investigators create a situation with exact conditions in order to control some variables, and manipulate others.

field experiment
Research study in a realistic situation in which one or more independent variables are manipulated by the experimenter under as carefully controlled conditions as the situation will permit.

PART 2:
Research Design

the respective brands. Four supermarkets were used in all, two from each town. The stores in one town were designated as control stores, where the price of each brand was maintained at its regular level throughout the experiment. In the experimental town, the prices were systematically varied in the two stores during the experiment. Prices were marked on the package of each brand so as to be clearly visible but not unusually obvious. After each price change, a cooling-off period was introduced to offset any surplus accumulated by consumers. The impact of the price change was monitored by recording weekly sales for each brand. This allowed brand market shares for each price condition to be determined. No displays, special containers, or other devices were used to draw consumer attention to the fact that the relative prices of the brands had been altered. All other controllable factors were also held as constant as possible.

Note the distinction between the two studies. In the field experiment, no attempt was made to set up special conditions. Manipulation of the experimental variable—price—was imposed in a natural environment. The laboratory experiment, on the other hand, was contrived. Subjects were told to behave as if they were actively shopping for the product. The prices of the respective brands were varied for each of these simulated shopping trips.

The results of the two experiments were consistent for one product and inconsistent for the other. The laboratory experiment generated reasonably valid estimates of consumers' reactions to real-world (field experiment) price changes for brands of cola. However, the data for coffee from the laboratory experiment was considered invalid since it tended to overstate the effects of the price changes.

Online retailers have been able to use experimentation quite successfully. Binney & Smith wanted to investigate ways of attracting potential customers to its Crayola.com Web site and getting them to purchase products from its online store. After experimentally varying a number of elements of the email messages sent to prospective customers, the company was able to identify one message that was three times as effective as others at getting individuals to visit the Web site. "For converting these visitors into buyers, the best combinations converted nearly four times as many shoppers into buyers and nearly doubled revenues per buyer."[10] The company credits its online experimentation with helping to make its online efforts profitable. In this situation, the research would be categorized as a field experiment because the company was working with actual shoppers (and buyers) in the actual online shopping environment.

ETHICAL dilemma 6.1

The regional sales manager for a large chain of men's clothing stores asks you to establish whether increasing her salespeople's commission will result in better sales performance. Specifically, she wants to know whether increasing the commission on limited lines of clothing will result in better sales on those lines but with the penalty of fewer sales on the remaining lines, and whether raising the commission on all lines will produce greater sales on all lines. Suppose that you think the best way to investigate the issue is through a field experiment in which some salespeople receive increased commission on a single line, others receive increased commission across the board, and still others make up a control group, whose members receive no increase in commission.

- *Are there ethical problems inherent in such a design?*
- *Is the control group being deprived of any benefits?*

Internal and External Validity of Experiments

Certain advantages and disadvantages result from the differences in laboratory and field experiments. The laboratory experiment typically has the advantage of greater **internal validity** because of the greater control of the variables that it affords. To the extent that we are successful in eliminating the effects of other factors that may obscure or confound the relationships under study, either by physically holding the other factors constant or by allowing for them statistically, we may conclude that the observed effect was due to the manipulation of

Explain which of the two types of experiments has greater internal validity and which has greater external validity.

internal validity

A criterion by which an experiment is evaluated; the focus is on obtaining evidence demonstrating that the variation in the dependent variable was the result of exposure to the treatment, or experimental, variable.

external validity

A criterion by which an experiment is evaluated; the extent to which the observed experimental effect can be generalized to other populations and settings.

the experimental variable. That is, we may conclude the experiment is internally valid. Thus, internal validity refers to our ability to attribute the effect that was observed to the experimental variable and not to other factors. In the pricing experiment, internal validity focused on the need to obtain data demonstrating that the variation in the criterion variable—brand demanded—was the result of exposure to the experimental variable—relative price of the brand—rather than to other factors, such as advertising, display space, store traffic, and so on. These other factors were nonexistent in the simulated shopping trips.

While laboratory experiments have the advantage in internal validity, the field experiment has the advantage in **external validity,** which focuses on how well the results of the experiment can be generalized, or extended, to other situations. The artificiality of laboratory experiments limits the extent to which the results can be generalized to other populations and settings.[11] In the simulated shopping trips, no real purchases took place. Further, by calling attention to the price the researcher may have caused people to be more price conscious than they would have been in a supermarket. They may have attempted to act more "rationally" than they normally would. Further, those who agreed to participate in the laboratory experiment may not be representative of the larger population of shoppers, either because the location of the study was not typical or because those who willingly participated in such a study may be different in some significant way from those who declined to participate. Such problems would seriously jeopardize the external validity of the findings.

The controls needed for internal validity often conflict with those needed for external validity. A control or procedure required to establish internal validity may lessen the ability to generalize the results. The conditions needed to establish external validity may cast doubt on a study's internal validity. Both internal and external validity are matters of degree rather than all-or-nothing propositions.

So, which type of validity is more important? The answer is that both types are important. A study with little internal validity is worthless; on the other hand, a study with little external validity won't help a marketing manager very much either. One possible strategy is to conduct both types of experiments. The laboratory experiment can be used to establish the basic cause and effect relationship between one or more independent variables and the dependent variable(s), and the field experiment can be used to confirm the effect in a more natural environment, thus providing some evidence of external validity.

ETHICAL dilemma 6.2

The promotions manager of a soft drink company asks you to help him run an experiment to determine whether he should start advertising in cinemas showing movies rated R or NC-17. He explains that he has read a journal article indicating that viewers' responses to upbeat commercials are more favorable if the commercials follow very arousing film clips, and he believes that his soft drink commercial will stimulate more sales of the drink in the cinema if it follows previews of very violent or erotic films, such as are shown before the feature film.

- *If you ran a laboratory experiment for this client, what kinds of manipulations would you use, and what are the ethical issues involved in their use?*

- *Is it feasible to run a field experiment, and would the ethical issues change if a field experiment were run rather than a laboratory experiment?*

- *If you found that increasing viewers' arousal levels did indeed make them more favorably disposed toward products advertised through upbeat commercials, what are the ultimate ethical implications for influencing television programming?*

Role of Experimentation in Marketing Research

Experiments in marketing were rare before 1960, but their growth since then has been steady. One of the most significant growth areas has been in **market testing,** or test-marketing. Although some writers make a distinction between the terms, the essential feature of the market test is that "it is a controlled experiment, done in a limited but carefully selected part of the marketplace, whose aim is to predict the sales or profit consequences, either in absolute or relative terms, of one or more proposed marketing actions."[12] Very often the action in question is the marketing of a new product or an improved version of an old product. For example, in 1999 Blockbuster Video launched test marketing of CD-ROM rentals. At stores in Anchorage, Alaska, and Austin, Texas, Blockbuster began offering ten computer games on CD-ROM to complement its rentals of movies and Nintendo and Sony PlayStation games. Consumers who rented the CD-ROMs received a coupon that they activated online, permitting them to play the game for three days. They could keep the CD-ROM and choose to renew the rental or buy the game.[13]

Even if a company has performed previous tests of the product concept, the product package, the advertising copy, etc., the test market is still the final gauge of consumer acceptance of the product. ACNielsen data, for example, indicate that roughly three out of four products that have been test-marketed succeed, while four out of five that have not been test-marketed fail.[14] The benefits to be gained from test marketing are illustrated in the experience of Pillsbury in developing its Oven Lovin' refrigerated cookie dough, which was packaged in resealable tubs. In focus groups, consumers raved about Oven Lovin', which was loaded with Hershey's chocolate chips, Reese's Pieces, or Brach's candies. Based on the rave reactions, the company omitted test marketing and immediately rolled out the product, supporting it with heavy television advertising and some 200 million coupons. Sales took off like a rocket, rising from zero to almost $6 million a month. After three months, however, sales began to crumble and were almost nonexistent two years later. While consumers still maintained they liked the product and resealable package, "many shoppers found they ended up baking the entire package at once—or gobbling up leftover raw dough instead of saving it—eliminating the need for the . . . package." In sum, the package provided a benefit consumers didn't really need, particularly given the fact that it contained only 18 ounces of dough, compared with 20 ounces in a tube of Pillsbury Best dough that was priced comparably.[15]

Test-marketing is not restricted to testing the sales potential of new products; it has been used to examine the sales effectiveness of almost every element of the marketing mix. General Motors, for example, used its Cadillac car division to test market a proposed alteration in the distribution strategy for all its car lines. The Florida test involved keeping 1,200 new cars at a regional distribution center in Orlando for delivery to the state's 42 dealerships within 24 hours of an order. The approach was intended to whittle down the costly inventory that dealers have to maintain, improve manufacturing efficiency, and increase sales by allowing consumers to take quick possession of precisely the Cadillac model they wanted. GM and most other car makers have long been criticized for the waste associated with their typical practice of loading up dealership lots with an assortment of cars they think people will buy. This practice saddles dealers with high-cost inventory and does little to encourage just-in-time production practices at the factory level. Moreover, dealers often find themselves stuck with models that customers really don't want and short of the ones in demand.[16]

Market tests have also been used to measure the sales effectiveness of new displays, the responsiveness of sales to shelf-space changes, the impact of changes in retail prices on market shares, the price elasticity of demand for products, the effect of different commercials on sales of products, and the differential effects of price and advertising on demand.

Experimentation is not restricted to test-marketing. It can also be used whenever a manager has some specific mix alternatives to consider—for example, package design A versus B—and when a researcher can control the conditions sufficiently to allow an adequate test of the alternatives. Experiments are often used, therefore, when testing product or package concepts and advertising copy, although they have also been used for such things as determining the optimal number of sales calls to be made upon industrial distributors.[17]

Future and Problems of Experimentation

Although marketing experiments will continue to be used, particularly when the research problem is one of determining which is the best of an available set of limited marketing alternatives, experimentation is not without its problems. Test-marketing, which has been described as a double-edged sword, is a useful vehicle for illustrating these problems. As Larry Gibson, former

market testing (test-marketing)
A controlled experiment done in a limited but carefully selected sector of the marketplace; its aim is to predict the sales or profit consequences, either in absolute or relative terms, of one or more proposed marketing actions.

9 *List the three major problems in test-marketing.*

director of corporate marketing research for General Mills, once described test marketing: "It costs a mint, tells the competition what you're doing, takes forever, and is not always accurate. . . . For the moment, it's the only game in town."[18] Although Gibson was referring specifically to test-marketing, similar problems exist for other types of experiments as well. Three of the more critical problems of experimentation in general, and test-marketing in particular, are cost, time, and control.

Cost   Always a major consideration in test-marketing, the cost includes the normal research costs associated with designing the data-collection instruments and the sample, the wages paid to the field staff that collects the data, and several other indirect expenses as well. General Mills, for example, spent $2.8 million testing and refining its chain of Olive Garden restaurants.[19] Moreover, the test market should reflect the marketing strategy to be used on the national scale if the results are to be useful. So the test also includes marketing costs for advertising, personal selling, displays, etc.

With new product introductions, there are also the costs associated with producing the merchandise. To produce the product on a small scale is typically inefficient. Yet to gear up immediately for large-scale production can be tremendously wasteful if the product proves a failure.

Time   The time required for an adequate test market can also be substantial. In the 1960s, Procter & Gamble spent eight years testing Pampers disposable diapers before launching the product in the United States. In today's faster-paced global environment, this approach simply leaves a company much too vulnerable to attack from more agile competitors.

There is pressure to extend the period of test-marketing because the empirical evidence indicates that a test market's accuracy increases directly with time. Experiments conducted over short periods do not allow the cumulative impact of marketing actions. Consequently, a year is often recommended as a minimum before any kind of "go–no go" decision is made. The year allows researchers to account for possible seasonal variations and to study repeat-purchasing behavior. Such lengthy experiments are costly, however, and raise additional problems of control and competitive reaction. Procter & Gamble has committed itself to speeding product introductions worldwide. Its test marketing of the Dryel home dry-cleaning kit and the Swiffer sweeper system each took less than a year and a half. Furthermore, the test markets were international—Columbus, Ohio, and Ireland for Dryel and Iowa and France for Swiffer. This enables the company to launch products globally, rather than waiting for U.S. success before moving overseas.[20]

Control   The problems associated with control manifest themselves in several ways. First, there are the control problems in the experiment itself. What specific test markets will be used? How will product distribution be organized in those markets? Can the firm elicit the necessary cooperation from wholesalers? From retailers? Can the test markets and control cities be matched sufficiently to rule out market characteristics as the primary reason for different sales results? Can the rest of the elements of the marketing strategy be controlled so as not to cause unwanted aberrations in the experimental setting? Too much control can often be as much a problem as too little. Precisely because the product is being test-marketed, it may receive more attention than it would ever receive on a national scale. In the test market, for example, store shelves may be better stocked, the sales force more diligent, and the advertising more prominent than would normally be the case.

One example of this phenomenon is Pringle's potato chips, which were very successful in the test market but initially bombed nationally. Their failure has often been attributed to a decline in quality that occurred when the product had to be produced in quantities large enough for national distribution.

There are control problems associated with competitive reaction, too. Although the firm might be able to coordinate its own marketing activities, and even those of intermediaries in the distribution channel, so as not to contaminate the experiment, it can exert little control over its

PART 2:
Research Design

competitors. Competitors can, and do, sabotage marketing experiments by cutting the prices of their own products, gobbling up quantities of the test marketer's product—thereby creating a state of euphoria and false confidence on the part of the test marketer—and by other devious means. Test-marketing has been called the most dangerous game in all of marketing because of the great opportunity it affords for misfires, as shown by the examples in Exhibit 6.3.

Exhibit 6.3

Examples of Misfires in Test-Marketing

- A few years ago, Snell (Booz Allen's design and development division, which does product development and work under contract) developed a nonliquid temporary hair coloring that consumers used by inserting a block of solid hair dye into a special comb. "It went to market and it was a bust," a company manager recalled. On hot days when people perspired, any hair dye excessively applied ran down their necks and foreheads. "It just didn't occur to us to look at this under conditions where people perspire," he says.
- Frito-Lay test marketed its Max potato, corn, and tortilla chips containing the Olestra fat substitutes in Grand Junction, Colorado; Eau Claire, Wisconsin; and Cedar Rapids, Iowa. A TV crew sampled the chips and succumbed to diarrhea, and then broadcast a report about it, creating lots of bad publicity for the chips.
- When Campbell Soup first test-marketed Prego spaghetti sauce, Campbell marketers say they noticed a flurry of new Ragu ads and cents-off deals that they feel were designed to induce shoppers to load up on Ragu and to skew Prego's test results. They also claim that Ragu copied Prego when it developed Ragu Homestyle spaghetti sauce, which was thick, red, flecked with oregano and basil, and which Ragu moved into national distribution before Prego.
- Procter & Gamble claims that competitors stole its patented process for Duncan Hines chocolate chip cookies when they saw how successful the product was in test market.
- A health and beauty aids firm developed a deodorant containing baking soda. A competitor spotted the product in test market, rolled out its own version of the deodorant nationally before the first firm completed its testing, and later successfully sued the product originator for copyright infringement when it launched its deodorant nationally.
- When Procter & Gamble introduced its Always brand sanitary napkin in a test market in Minnesota, Kimberly-Clark Corporation and Johnson & Johnson countered with free products, lots of coupons, and big dealer discounts, which caused Always not to do as well as expected.
- Campbell Soup spent 18 months developing a blended fruit juice called Juiceworks. By the time the product reached the market, three competing brands were already on store shelves. Campbell dropped its product.
- Spurred by its incredible success with Fruit 'N' Juice Bars, Dole worked hard to create a new fruity ice cream novelty product with the same type of appeal. Company officials expected that the product that resulted from this development activity, Fruit and Cream Bars, which it test-marketed in Orlando, Florida, would do slightly less well because it was more of an indulgence-type product. However, the test market results were so positive that Dole became the number-one brand in the market within three months. The company consequently shortened the test market to six months. When it rolled out the product, however, the company unhappily found four unexpected entrants in the ice cream novelty category. Due to the intense competition, Fruit and Cream sales fell short of expectations.
- In a move to speed products to market, Procter & Gamble decided to reserve the use of test marketing mainly to new products that would require investing in new plants and equipment. As a result, the company failed to test Pampers Rash Guard, a premium diaper, only to see the product fail to meet sales goals.

Source: Example 1—Roger Recklefs, "Success Comes Hard in the Tricky Business of Creating Products," *The Wall Street Journal* (August 23, 1978), pp. 1, 27; Example 2—Annetta Miller and Karen Springen, "Will Fake Fat Play in Peoria?" *Newsweek* (June 3, 1996), p. 50; Example 3—Betty Morris, "New Campbell Entry Sets Off a Big Spaghetti Sauce Battle," *The Wall Street Journal* (December 2, 1982), p. 31; Example 4—Eleanor Johnson Tracy, "Testing Time for Test Marketing," *Fortune* 110 (October 29, 1984), pp. 75–76; Example 5—Kevin Wiggins, "Simulated Test Marketing Winning Acceptance," *Marketing News* 19 (March 1, 1985), pp. 15, 19; Example 6—Damon Darden, "Faced with More Competition, P&G Sees New Products as Crucial to Earnings Growth," *The Wall Street Journal* (September 13, 1983), pp. 37, 53; Example 7—Annetta Miller and Dody Tsiantor, "A Test for Market Research," *Newsweek* 110 (December 28, 1987), pp. 32–33; Example 8—Leslie Brennan, "Test Marketing Put to the Test," *Sales and Marketing Management* 138 (March 1987), pp. 65–68; Example 9—Jack Neff, "Is Testing the Answer?" *Advertising Age* (July 9, 2001), p. 13.

One could argue that the misfires reflected in the first two examples in Exhibit 6.3 represent one fundamental reason that test markets are desirable. Indeed, it seems better to find out about product performance problems like this in a test market than after a product is introduced nationally. Consider, for example, the losses in company prestige that would have resulted if the following problems had not been discovered in test markets.[21]

- Sunlight dishwashing liquid was confused with Minute Maid lemon juice by at least 33 adults and 45 children, who became ill after drinking it.
- When a large packaged goods company set out to introduce a squirtable soft drink concentrate for children, it held focus groups to monitor user reaction. In the sessions children squirted the product neatly into cups. Yet once at home, few could resist the temptation to decorate their parents' floors and walls with colorful liquid. After a flood of parental complaints, the product was withdrawn from development.

Other companies, however, could not avoid embarrassment when they implemented faulty plans nationwide. A mid-1990s effort to merge television and computers flopped when NetTV was offered at $3,000 for a 29-inch monitor coupled with a personal computer. Consumers couldn't imagine why they wanted a computer in their living room, especially considering how frustrating a computer can be to operate.[22] Apple Computer's notorious mistake was introducing an early palmtop computer, the Newton, which failed miserably at one of its featured tasks: reading the user's handwriting. Newton quickly became the butt of jokes, and although Apple later improved the product, it sank under the weight of poor publicity.[23]

The simple point is that the marketing manager contemplating a market test must weigh the costs of such a test against its anticipated benefits. While it may serve as the final yardstick for consumer acceptance of the product, in some cases it may be less effective and more expensive than a carefully controlled laboratory or in-home test.

Types of Test Markets

10 *Distinguish between a standard test market and a controlled test market.*

standard test market
A test market in which the company sells the product through its normal distribution channels.

There are three general categories of test markets: standard, controlled, and simulated. In a **standard test market** approach, such as those we've been describing, a company develops a product and then attempts to sell it through the normal distribution channels in a number of test market cities. The potential success of the product can be gauged, and different elements of the marketing mix for the product can be experimentally varied with an eye toward developing the best marketing mix combination for the product. The results are typically monitored by one of the standard distribution services discussed in Chapter 8. A key distinguishing feature of a standard test market is that the producer must sell the product to distributors, wholesalers, and/or retailers just like it would any other product.

Figure 6.2 shows some traditionally popular standard test market cities. What makes some cities better than others for standard test markets? Several factors are involved. While specific criteria differ across situations, there are a number of general requirements that companies must consider. First, the proposed test market city needs to be demographically representative of the larger market in which the product will ultimately be sold. Most of the popular test market cities are reasonably representative of the overall U.S. population, although some are more representative than others. If the product is geared more toward a specific segment of the population, however, then markets should be chosen with high representation of that segment. For example, for products targeted toward Hispanic consumers, test markets with higher proportions of Hispanic residents are obviously desirable.

Popular standard test market cities also possess other features prized by researchers. The test market should be large enough that it has multiple media outlets (e.g., newspapers and radio and television stations) of its own, which allow tests of advertising and promotion. It must also be large enough to have a sufficient number of the right kind of retail outlets. When Taco Bell was looking for a test market for its Grilled Stuft Burrito, for example, it was important to find a market with a good mix of company and franchise-owned restaurants; Fresno, California fit the bill as discussed in Research Window 6.3. It is also important that test markets be geographically isolated from other cities in order to avoid "spillover" effects from

PART 2:
Research Design

Figure 6.2

Some Popular Standard Test Markets

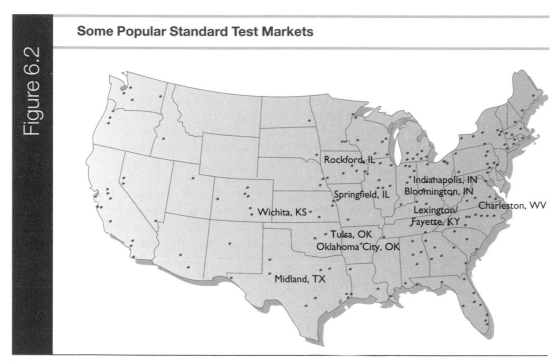

Source: Steve Lohr, "Test It in Tulsa, It'll Play in Peoria," *Chicago Tribune* (June 7, 1992), sec. 7, p. 1. See also Judith Waldrop, "Markets with Attitude," *American Demographics* (July 1994), pp. 22–33 for the "most typical" and "most surveyed" American cities.

RESEARCH *Window*

6.3

Taco Bell's Use of Test Marketing for the Grilled Stuft Burrito

Laurie Gannon, director of public relations for Taco Bell, said the Grilled Stuft Burrito was tested in Fresno in February 1999, and was quite successful. "We made some modifications, then tested it in a few other markets and rolled it out nationally at the end of this past April [2001]."

Gannon says when testing a product, Taco Bell looks for regional representation, picking test markets on the West Coast, in the northeast and in the central part of the country. "We also look for markets with a good mix of company and franchise-owned restaurants. And we look for markets that are cost effective. Because it's a local test, we have to cut-in over the national media with our local spot. Some markets like Los Angeles or New York would be cost prohibitive."

Gannon says adding a new item to the menu is a long and expensive procedure. She declined to state how much the Grilled Stuft Burrito cost to launch, but said Taco Bell spends a substantial amount of money on market research and testing. "In this market test we had to install new grills and provide employee training. It took two years to bring the Grilled Stuft Burrito to the national market. We refine the product and set up for another market test. We check the packaging and all kinds of variables before it's ready. We look at the results and try to determine what the product would do nationally. Obviously, the Grilled Stuft Burrito did well in Fresno and made it to the national market."

The burrito went through a complete market test in Fresno. "We had local TV commercials, in-store point of purchase materials and we trained our employees before the product was offered to the public," said Gannon. She said the test lasted from four to six weeks. "We do in-store consumer research where people physically come into the store and talk to customers. We want to check things like: Are they aware of the commercial? Is it filling? How's the taste, the texture and price?" ■

Source: Don A. Wright, "The Perfect Place for a Test Market," *The Business Journal* (May 21, 2001), p. 12.

controlled test market
An entire test program conducted by an outside service in a market in which it can guarantee distribution.

nearby markets where testing is not taking place. Such spillover effects might include advertising and other promotion or a significant percentage of consumers in the test market traveling outside the test market to shop.

An alternative to the standard test market is the **controlled test market,** sometimes called the forced-distribution test market. In the controlled test market, the entire test program is conducted by an outside service. The service pays retailers for shelf space and can therefore guarantee distribution to those stores that represent a predetermined percentage of the marketer's total food store sales volume. A number of research firms operate controlled test markets, including GfK AG, a large research company based in Germany, and Information Resources, Inc.

An increasingly popular variation of the controlled test market is the electronic test market, in which providers of the electronic services recruit a panel of households in the test market area from which they secure a great deal of demographic information. These households are given identification cards, which they show when checking out at participating retailers. Everything they purchase from these retailers is automatically recorded and associated with the household. Through the use of hand-held scanners, it is also possible to have consumers record purchases of products from nonparticipating retailers. Second, suppliers of the electronic services also have the capability to monitor each household's television-viewing behavior—and in some cases deliver different test commercials to different households. Thus they can correlate exposure to test commercials to purchase behavior, which in turn allows users of the electronic services to test not only consumer acceptance of a new or modified product but also various other parts of the marketing program. Del Monte, for example, uses electronic test markets for media-weight, pricing, and promotion tests, in addition to new product evaluations. Leading suppliers of electronic test-marketing services include Nielsen and IRI's BehaviorScan. Research Window 6.4 illustrates how the link between the demographic information of households and their purchase behavior can be used to advantage.

RESEARCH
Window

6.4

Use of an Electronic Test Market by Ocean Spray

In an attempt to be perceived more broadly, Ocean Spray developed a totally new fruit beverage, Mauna La'i Hawaiian Guava Drink. The product represented a significant departure for Ocean Spray, in that it was different in color, taste, and aroma from any other fruit drink on the market.

Concerned about how consumers might respond to the product, Ocean Spray decided to test-market it using BehaviorScan's facilities in Eau Claire, Wisconsin, and Midland, Texas. Ocean Spray believed that the target market for Mauna La'i was similar to that for its cranberry drink: older children and adults with average education and income.

After six months in test market, initial trial for Mauna La'i was good, but the rate of re-purchase was far below what was needed to be profitable. It did not appear that Mauna La'i would survive the test to go national. But on analyzing BehaviorScan's data more closely, Ocean Spray found a few surprises: (1) the buyer base was smaller than ex-

pected, but these consumers were buying the product more frequently than was projected; (2) the product was not selling to the target market—yuppies (young urban professionals) were buying the Mauna La'i.

After analyzing this pattern for nearly a year, Ocean Spray decided that it would be profitable to market the product as long as it was marketed toward the heavily beverage-consuming yuppies. Mauna La'i's media plan was altered to reach the more upscale market, and the juice was rolled out nationally. After only three months in the national market, consumer demand was so high that Ocean Spray started to produce a 64-ounce size. John Tarsa, Ocean Spray's manager of marketing research, believes that the use of an electronic test market was key to Mauna La'i's success. "In a traditional test market, we wouldn't be rolling with Mauna La'i at all, because our repeat number was no good. The electronic test market was instrumental in helping us decide what we needed to change to make it a success." ■

Source: Leslie Brennan, "Test Marketing Put to the Test," *Sales and Marketing Management* 138 (March 1987), p. 68. Electronic test markets are also used to test the effects of advertising strategy. See Leonard M. Lodish, et al., "How TV Advertising Works: A Meta-Analysis of 389 Real World Split Cable T.V. Advertising Experiments," *Journal of Marketing Research* 32 (May 1995), pp. 125–139 for an integration of the findings.

PART 2:
Research Design

Another variation in test-marketing is the **simulated test market (STM).** A simulated test market differs from standard and controlled test markets in that consumers do not purchase the product (or service) being tested from a retail store. In fact, in many cases, the product has not even been put into production. Instead, researchers will typically recruit consumers to participate in the simulated study, either in shopping malls or via the Internet. Consumers are shown the new product or product concept and asked to rate its features. They may be shown commercials for it and for competitors' products. Often, in a simulated store environment, they are then given the opportunity to buy the product, perhaps at a discounted rate. If the product is in tangible form (often sent in advance to those recruited via the Internet), researchers may followup with participating consumers after a predetermined use period to assess their reactions to the product and likely repeat-purchase intentions.

All the information is fed into a computer model, which has equations for the repeat purchase and market share likely to be achieved by the test model. The key to successful simulation is the equations built into the computer model. Studies have indicated that in 90 percent of the cases, STM models can come within 20 percent of actual results in the marketplace.[24]

Nielsen is a leading provider of simulated test markets through its BASES simulation approach. Reporting an 83 percent drop in the number of completed surveys obtained using mall intercepts from the 1970s to the 1990s, the company began exploring the possibility of using the Internet for simulated test markets several years ago and is reporting encouraging results. Members of an online panel are recruited for participation in a particular study by letter and email, which contain a password that will allow access to an online survey. A $5 incentive and product samples are mailed directly to the participant.[25] In addition, producers sometimes conduct their own simulated test markets. For example, Procter & Gamble recently launched an online STM called ConsumerAisles.com.[26]

Choosing a Test-Market Procedure

Marketers who need to test market a new product or to fine-tune an element of a marketing program must choose which type of test market to use. One way to view that choice is to look at the alternatives as stages in a sequential process, with simulated test markets preceding controlled test markets, which in turn come before standard test markets (Figure 6.3). The sequence is not always as pictured, however. A very promising STM or controlled test market can cause a firm to skip one or more intermediate stages, and perhaps to move directly to national rollout.

A prime advantage of simulated test markets is the protection they provide from competitors. They are also good for assessing trial and repeat-purchasing behavior. They are faster and cheaper than full-scale tests and are particularly good for spotting weak products, which

simulated test market (STM)
A study in which consumer ratings are obtained along with likely or actual purchase data often obtained in a simulated store environment; the data are fed into computer models to produce sales and market share predictions.

11 Discuss the advantages and disadvantages of simulated test-marketing.

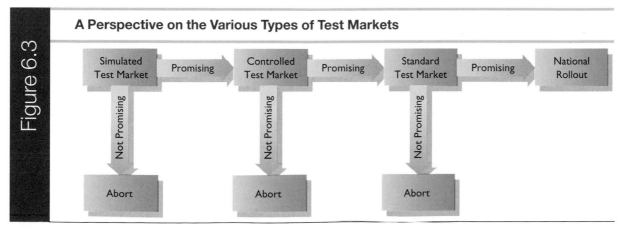

Figure 6.3

A Perspective on the Various Types of Test Markets

allows firms to avoid full-scale testing of these products. The primary disadvantage of simulated test markets is that they do not provide any information about the firm's ability to secure trade support for the product or about what competitive reaction is likely to be. Thus, they are more suited for evaluating product extensions than for examining the likely success of radically different new products.

Controlled test markets are more expensive than simulated test markets but less costly than standard test markets. One reason they cost less than standard test markets is that the research supplier provides distribution. The manufacturer does not need to use its own sales force to convince the trade that stocking the product is worthwhile. The manufacturer can rest assured that the new product will obtain the right level of store acceptance, will be positioned in the correct aisle in each store, will receive the right number of facings on the shelf, will have the correct everyday price, will not experience any out-of-stock problems, and will receive the planned level of promotional displays and price features.

This perfect implementation of the marketing plan also represents one of the weaknesses of the controlled test market. Acceptance or rejection of the new product by the trade in the "real world" is typically critical to the success of any new product. A controlled test market guarantees acceptance by the trade for the duration of the test, but acceptance will not be guaranteed during the actual marketing of the product. When a new product fits in nicely with a company's existing line, for which it already has distribution, the controlled test market is a fairly good indicator. However, the problem of overcontrol of the marketing effort during the test market does need to be taken into account. At times, the real situation will still have out-of-stocks, poor aisle locations, inadequate displays, and less-than-perfect cooperation from the trade on pricing and trade promotions. When the manufacturer has sufficient experience to account for these adjustments, the controlled test market provides a useful laboratory for testing acceptance of the product and for fine-tuning the marketing program. When the product is new or represents a radical departure for the manufacturer, the question of trade support is much more problematic, and the controlled test is much less useful under these circumstances.

The traditional, or standard, test market provides a more natural environment than either the simulated or the controlled test market. The standard test market plays a more vital role when (1) it is important for the firm to test its ability to actually sell to the trade and get distribution for the product; (2) the capital investment is significant and the firm needs a prolonged test market to accurately assess its capital needs or its technical ability to manufacture the product; and/or (3) the company is entering new territory and needs to build its experience base so that it can play for real, but wants to learn how to do so on a limited scale.

The relative advantages and disadvantages of the three basic types of test markets are shown in Exhibit 6.4.

Exhibit 6.4

Relative Advantages and Disadvantages of Different Types of Test Markets

	Simulated	Controlled	Standard
Speed	1	2	3
Cost	1	2	3
Security	1	2	3
Validity			
* Internal	1	2	3
* External	3	2	1
Prediction accuracy	3	2	1

1 = most favorable   3 = least favorable

PART 2:
Research Design

To investigate pricing of its pay phones in Boston, Verizon decided to test the hypothesis that if the price were low enough, greater demand for using the phones would increase total pay-phone revenues. The company's idea was that at a low enough price, calling from a pay phone would be attractive—for some consumers, even more attractive than using a cell phone.

To test its hypothesis, Verizon decided to set up an experiment. The company planned a 90-day market test involving 16 pay phones in the Boston area. Verizon converted nine phones at seven locations to place one-minute calls for 10 cents (compared with the usual rate of 50 cents for a call of any length). The company also converted seven phones to place calls of up to three minutes for 25 cents. In other words, the test would compare the impact on revenues of two different prices: 10 cents for one minute and 25 cents for three minutes. Included in the test market were phones located near high schools. Verizon's managers thought students might use these phones to call home for rides after school. At the end of the 90-day test period, the company planned to evaluate whether the low-priced phones were more profitable than the 50-cent phones, and if so, whether the 10-cent rate or the 25-cent rate delivered superior results.

By using an experiment rather than focus groups or surveys, Verizon had an opportunity to see how real phone users would behave if they had access to 10-cent and 25-cent pay phones. The company, with over 3,700 pay phones in Massachusetts, also was in a position to select test sites that represented good sources of possible users. At the same time, testing the new price at such a small percentage of phones presented some problems in interpreting the data. Demand for the cheaper phones might not be representative of demand throughout the state at 10 or 25 cents per call. Despite this drawback, Verizon's test was an inexpensive way to gauge market reaction. In addition, Verizon avoided an important risk of experimenting with low prices statewide. If the company had instead tried low prices on all its Massachusetts phones but demand had failed to rise to profitable levels, Verizon would have had difficulty explaining to the public a return to higher prices. Experimenting with prices was therefore a logical way for Verizon to figure out how to ring up more profits. ■

Source: Peter J. Howe, "Verizon to Test 10-Cent Pay Phones in Boston Area," *Boston Globe* (January 31, 2002), downloaded from EBSCOhost, May 3, 2002.

Summary

Learning Objective 1
Cite three major purposes of descriptive research.
Descriptive research is used when the purpose is to (1) describe the characteristics of certain groups, (2) estimate the proportion of people in a specified population who behave in a certain way, and (3) make specific predictions.

Learning Objective 2
List the six specifications of a descriptive study.
Descriptive studies require a clear specification of the answers to who, what, when, where, why, and how in the research.

Learning Objective 3
Explain what a dummy table is.
A dummy table is used to catalog the data that are to be collected. It serves as a statement of how the analysis will be structured and conducted. Complete in all respects save for filling in the actual numbers, it contains a title, headings, and specific categories for the variables making up the table.

Learning Objective 4
Discuss the difference between cross-sectional and longitudinal designs.
A cross-sectional design involves researching a sample of elements from the population of inter-

est. Various characteristics of the elements are measured once. Longitudinal studies involve panels of people or other entities whose responses are measured repeatedly over a span of time.

Learning Objective 5

Explain what is meant by a panel in marketing research and explain the difference between a continuous panel and a discontinuous panel.

A panel is a fixed sample of elements. In a continuous panel, a fixed sample of subjects is measured repeatedly with respect to the same type of information. In a discontinuous panel, a sample of elements is still selected and maintained, but the information collected from the members varies with the project.

Learning Objective 6

Describe the emphasis in sample surveys.

The sample survey involves the study of a number of cases at the same point in time. The survey attempts to be representative of some known universe, both in terms of the number of cases included and in the manner of their selection.

Learning Objective 7

Clarify the difference between laboratory experiments and field experiments.

Laboratory experiments differ from field experiments primarily in terms of environment. The analyst creates a setting for a laboratory experiment, while a field experiment is conducted in a natural setting. Both types, however, involve control and manipulation of one or more presumed causal factors.

Learning Objective 8

Explain which of the two types of experiments has greater internal validity and which has greater external validity.

The laboratory experiment typically has greater internal validity because of greater control of the

variables it affords. Field experiments are generally considered more externally valid, meaning that their results are better able to be generalized to other situations.

Learning Objective 9

List the three major problems in test-marketing.

Three of the more critical problems in experimentation in general, and in test-marketing in particular, are cost, time, and control.

Learning Objective 10

Distinguish between a standard test market and a controlled test market.

A standard test market is one in which companies sell the product through their normal distribution channels, and results are typically monitored by a standard distribution service. In a controlled test market, the entire program is conducted by an outside service. The service pays retailers for shelf space and therefore can guarantee distribution to those stores that represent a predetermined percentage of the marketer's total store sales volume.

Learning Objective 11

Discuss the advantages and disadvantages of simulated test-marketing.

Simulated test-marketing studies provide the following advantages: (1) they protect a marketer from competitors, (2) they are faster and cheaper than full-scale tests, and (3) they are particularly good for spotting weak products. However, they do have disadvantages in that they cannot provide any information about the firm's ability to secure trade support for a product, nor do they indicate what competitive reaction is likely to be.

Key Terms

dummy table (page 111)
cross-sectional study (page 112)
longitudinal study (page 112)
continuous panel (page 112)
discontinuous panel (page 113)
sample survey (page 117)
experiment (page 120)
laboratory experiment (page 122)

field experiment (page 122)
internal validity (page 124)
external validity (page 124)
market test (test-marketing) (page 125)
standard test market (page 128)
controlled test market (page 130)
simulated test market (page 131)

Review Questions

1. What are the basic uses of descriptive research?
2. What is the key characteristic of descriptive research?
3. What are the main types of descriptive studies, and what do their differences mean?
4. What are the basic types of panels, and how important are the differences between them?
5. What is the fundamental thrust of a sample survey? What are its advantages and disadvantages?
6. What types of evidence can be used to support an inference of causality?
7. What is an experiment?
8. What is the distinction between a laboratory and a field experiment?
9. What is the difference between internal and external validity?
10. How would you explain marketing's infrequent use of experimental research before 1960 and its steadily increasing use since then?
11. What is a test market? For what kinds of investigations can test markets be used? What are the problems associated with test markets?
12. What is the primary difference between a standard test market and a controlled test market?
13. How does an electronic test market work? What are its advantages compared to a traditional test market?
14. How does simulated test-marketing (STM) work? What are its main advantages and disadvantages compared to full market tests?
15. Under what conditions is a standard test market a better choice than either simulated or controlled test markets?

Discussion Questions, Problems, and Projects

1. The management of a national book club was convinced that the company's market segment consisted of individuals in the 25- to 35-year-old age group, while its major competitor's market segment seemed more widely distributed with respect to age. It attributed this difference to the type of magazines in which the competitor advertised. Management decided to do a study to determine the socioeconomic characteristics of its own market segment. Management formed a panel of 800 heads of households who had previously shown a strong interest in reading. Mail questionnaires would be sent to all the panel members. One month after receiving all the questionnaires, the company would again send similar questionnaires to all the panel members. In this situation is the research design appropriate? If yes, why? If no, why not?

2. Mr. Pennymarch, the advertising manager for *Chemistry Today* magazine, is responsible for selling advertising space in the magazine. The magazine deals primarily with chemical processing technology and is distributed solely by subscription. Major advertisers in the magazine are the producers of chemical processing equipment, since the magazine is primarily directed at engineers and other technical people concerned with the design of chemical processing units.

    Since the size and composition of the target audience for *Chemistry Today* are key concerns for prospective advertisers, Pennymarch is interested in collecting more detailed data on the readership. While he presently has total circulation figures, he feels that these understate the potential exposure of an advertisement in *Chemistry Today*. In particular, he feels that for every subscriber, there are several others in the subscriber's firm to whom the magazine is routed for their perusal. He wishes to determine how large this secondary audience is and also wishes to develop more detailed data on *Chemistry Today* readers, such as degree of technical training, level in the administrative hierarchy, etc.

    (a) Does Pennymarch have a specific hypothesis? If yes, state the hypothesis.
    (b) What type of research design would you recommend? Justify your answer.

3. The Allure Company, a large manufacturer of women's beauty aids, conducted a study in 2002 in order to assess sales of its brand of hair dye. Questionnaires were mailed to a panel of 1,260 families. The Allure brand of hair dye had three major competitors: Brand A, Brand B, and Brand C. A similar study conducted in 2001 had indicated the following market shares: Allure, 32 percent (i.e., 400 families); Brand A, 25 percent (315 families); Brand B, 33 percent (410 families); and Brand C, 11 percent (135 families). The 2002 study indicated that Allure's market share had not changed during the one-year period, although Brand B had increased its market share to 37 percent (460 families). However, this increase could be accounted for by a decrease in Brand A's and Brand C's market shares. Brand A now had a market share of 22 percent (280 families); Brand C now had a market share of 10 percent (120 families). The management of the Allure Company decided it had little to worry about.

   The 2002 study also revealed some additional facts. Over the one-year period 70 families from Brand A and 30 families from Brand C had switched to Allure. Five families from Brand B and 30 families from Brand C had switched to Brand A, while none of the Allure users had switched to Brand A. These facts further reassured management. Finally, 45 families switched from Brand B to Brand C, but none of the families using Allure or Brand A had switched to Brand C. Brand C's loyalty was estimated to be .556.

   (a) Do you think that management of the Allure Company was accurate in analyzing the situation? Justify your answer.
   (b) You are called upon to do some analysis. From the data given above, construct the brand-switching matrix. (Hint: Begin by filling in the row and column totals.)
   (c) Indicate what this matrix reveals for each of the brands over the one-year period.
   (d) Complete the following table and compute the brand loyalties.

		At Time (t_2)				
		Bought Allure	Bought A	Bought B	Bought C	Total
	Bought Allure					
	Bought A					
At Time	Bought B					
(t_1):	Bought C					
	Total					

   (e) What can be said about the degree of brand loyalty for each of the four products?

4. The Nutri Company was a medium-sized manufacturer of highly nutritional food products. The products were marketed as diet foods with high nutritional content. The company was considering marketing these products as snack foods but was concerned about its present customers' reaction to the change in the products' images. The company decided to assess customers' reaction by conducting a study using one of the established types of consumer panels. What type of panel would you recommend in this situation? Why?

5. Super Savers is a chain of department stores located in large towns and metropolitan centers in the northeastern United States. In order to improve its understanding of the market, management has decided to develop a profile of the so-called average customer. You are requested to design the study.
   (a) What kind of research design will you select? Justify your choice.
   (b) List at least ten relevant variables.
   (c) Specify at least four hypotheses. (Note: A hypothesis is a conjecture as to how two or more variables are related. You should indicate the direction of the suggested relationship and how each of the variables would be measured.)
   (d) Construct dummy tables using four of the variables that you specified in part (b) of this problem.

6. Consider the following statement: "The increase in sales is due to the new sales personnel that we recruited from the vocational school over the last several years. Sales of the new salespeople are up substantially, while sales for longer-term salespeople have not increased."
   (a) Identify the causal factor (X) and the effect factor (Y) in the above statement.

7. The research department of the company in Question 6 investigated the change in sales for each of the company's salespeople. Using criteria supplied by management, the department categorized all territory sales changes as "increased substantially," "increased marginally," or "no increase." Consider the following table, in which 260 sales personnel have been classified as old or new:

| Salesperson Assigned | Territory Sales Change | | | |
	Increased Substantially	Increased Marginally	No Increase	Total
New	75	30	5	110
Old	50	40	60	150

(a) Does this table provide evidence of concomitant variation? Justify your answer.
(b) What conclusions can be drawn about the relationship between X and Y on the basis of the preceding table?

8. Six months later, the research department in Question 6 investigated the situation once again. However, a new variable was considered in the analysis, namely, the type of territory to which the salesperson was assigned—more specifically, whether the salesperson was assigned to an essentially metropolitan or nonmetropolitan territory. The following table summarizes the research department's findings:

| Salesperson Assigned | Metropolitan Territory Territory Sales Change | | | |
	Increased Substantially	Increased Marginally	No Increase	Total
New	70	20	—	90
Old	54	16	—	70

| Salesperson Assigned | Nonmetropolitan Territory Territory Sales Change | | | |
	Increased Substantially	Increased Marginally	No Increase	Total
New	5	10	5	20
Old	20	40	20	80

(a) If the type of territory to which the salesperson was assigned is ignored, does this table provide evidence of concomitant variation between change in sales and whether the salespeople were new or old? Justify your answer.
(b) If type of territory is considered, does the table provide evidence of concomitant variation between sales changes and whether the salespeople were new or old? Justify your answer.

9. The product development team at Busby's Briquets has been working on several modifications of Busby's highly successful line of charcoal briquets. The most promising development is a new briquet that imparts a unique smoky flavor to grilled meat. Management, based on favorable feedback from a few employees who have tested the product in their homes, feels that the new briquet has the potential to become a major seller.

At a recent strategy session, the vice president of marketing suggested a test-marketing program before committing to introduction of the new briquet. He pointed out that a test market would be a good way to evaluate the effectiveness of two alternative advertising and promotional campaigns that have been proposed by Busby's ad agency. He feels that effectiveness should be evaluated in terms of the trial and repeat-purchasing behavior engendered by each program. He also wants to gauge Busby's current distributors' acceptance of the new product.

The CEO of Busby's, however, is not very enthusiastic about the idea of test-marketing. She pointed out several of her concerns, among them the fact that Busby's competitors could easily duplicate the new briquet, the fact that the company is nearing the limit of budgeted costs for developing the new briquet, and the fact that the seasonal nature of briquet sales makes it imperative to reach a "go–no go" decision on the new briquet by early April, only four months away.

The director of marketing research stated that she felt a test-marketing plan could be devised that would satisfy both the vice president of marketing and the CEO. She was instructed to submit a preliminary proposal at the next strategy session.

   (a) What information should be obtained from the test market in order to satisfy the vice president of marketing?

   (b) Under what constraints must the test-marketing plan operate in order to satisfy the CEO?

   (c) Given your answers to (a) and (b), what method of test marketing should the director recommend? Why?

10. Schedule an interview with the marketing manager of a firm near your home or your school. In the interview, discuss the use of test-marketing by the firm. Attempt to find answers to the following questions: How important is test-marketing in the firm's product-development process? Does the firm normally progress through different types of test-marketing for a specific product (as suggested in this text), or is only one type commonly used? What does your contact see as the advantages and disadvantages of various methods of test-marketing? Have successful test-marketing episodes always led to successful product introductions for the firm? What does your contact perceive as the most promising avenue for future development of test-marketing procedures?

Write a report of your interview, highlighting information that you obtained that was not discussed in the text, or that seems at odds with the textbook discussion.

Suggested Additional Readings

For discussion of the operation and the advantages and disadvantages of panels, see Frank J. R. Pol, *Issues of Design and Analysis of Panels* (Amsterdam, The Netherlands: Sociometric Research Foundation, 1989).

Seymour Sudman and Brian Wansink, *Consumer Panels,* 2d ed. (Chicago: American Marketing Association, 2002).

For an overview of the top firms in the marketing research industry, see Jack Honomichl, "Honomichl Top 50," *Marketing News* (June 10, 2002), pp. H1–H44.

For general discussion regarding the design of experiments, see Geoffrey Keppel, *Design and Analysis: A Researcher's Handbook,* 2d ed. (New York: W. H. Freeman and Company, 1995).

part 2 research project

The second stage in the research process is to determine the research design. As we have seen in Chapters 5 and 6, the design may take one of three forms, depending on the objective of the research. In these chapters we discussed the three basic types of research: exploratory, descriptive, and causal.

You will recall that the major emphasis in exploratory research is on the discovery of ideas and insights. A descriptive study is typically concerned with determining the frequency with which something occurs or the relationship between two variables, and it is generally guided by an initial hypothesis. A causal research design is concerned with determining cause-and-effect relationships.

Researchers for the Centerville Area Radio Association (CARA) decided to begin their study by conducting some exploratory research. This research consisted primarily of two types: (1) a literature review and (2) experience surveys.

They began the literature review by reading articles dealing with the positive and negative perceptions held by users of television, radio, and newspaper advertising. This secondary information was found in marketing research studies, general articles, and reference works dealing with the three major advertising media.

They found "The Radio Marketing Consultants Guide to Media," published by the Radio Advertising Bureau, to be a particularly helpful source. This source provided extensive coverage of the advantages and problems associated with each of the three major media.

They supplemented what they found in the literature review with an experience survey. They began by interviewing people who had specialized knowledge and experience with these media and then used their input to develop a revised list of advantages and problems associated with each.

Next, they discussed each of the media attribute items on the list with a group of CARA advertising sales representatives in order to obtain their input. Although the sales reps' feedback and suggestions were valued highly and weighed heavily, researchers also recognized that the group's opinions were not free of bias. Consequently, the final list of attribute items included in the study were determined by the researchers alone.

The resulting criteria that were chosen were then discussed with three local retail businesses, in order to determine the relevancy of each of the items and to make any appropriate additions, corrections, or deletions. In these interviews, it was obvious that individuals were going to have strong opinions and biases about the effectiveness of one medium versus another. However, there was virtually total agreement that the criteria chosen would be sufficient and broad enough in scope to assess the three media and respective sales representatives accurately.

The information gleaned from the literature review and experience survey was then used to develop the various hypotheses that would guide further research. A complete list of these hypotheses was given at the end of Part One. Among them were the hypotheses that there would be differences in businesspeople's attitudes toward television, radio, and newspaper, and that differences would also exist in attitudes toward sales representatives of each of the media.

As we pointed out in Chapter 3, the stages in the research process should not be viewed as discrete entities, but rather as elements in a continuous process. Information uncovered at one stage in the process is often used to refine decisions made earlier in the study. The information that researchers for CARA discovered in the course of their exploratory research may well have been used to formulate the research problem more clearly.

In this case, once the hypotheses were formed, the decision was made to test them by examining the perceptions of a cross section of retailers.

Discussion Issues

Given the hypotheses, if you were one of the researchers for CARA,

1. What kinds of information would you attempt to secure from retailers?
2. How would you go about selecting retailers to contact?

Case • 2.1

Rumstad Decorating Centers (A)

In 1929, Joseph Rumstad opened a small paint and wallpaper supply store in downtown Rockford, Illinois. For the next 45 years the store enjoyed consistent, although not spectacular, success. Sales and profits increased steadily but slowly as, to keep pace with the competition, the original line of products was expanded to include unpainted furniture, mirrors, picture framing material, and other products. In 1974, because of a declining neighborhood environment, Jack Rumstad, who had taken over management of the store from his father in 1970, decided to close the downtown store and open a new outlet on the far west side of the city. The west side was chosen because it was experiencing a boom in new home construction. In 1999, a second store was opened on the east side of the city, and the name of the business was changed to Rumstad Decorating Centers. The east side store was staffed with salesclerks, but was basically managed by Rumstad himself from the west side location. All ordering, billing, inventory control, and storage of excess inventory were concentrated at the west side store.

In 2001, the east side store was made an independent profit center. Rumstad personally took over the management of the outlet and hired a full-time manager for the west side store. With the change in accounting procedures occasioned by this organizational change, it became possible to examine the profitability of each outlet separately.

Rumstad conducted such an examination early in 2003, using the profit and loss figures shown in Exhibit 1, and became very concerned with what he discovered. Both stores had suffered losses for 2002, and, although he had anticipated incurring a loss during the first couple of years of operation of the east side store, he was not at all prepared for a second successive loss at the west side outlet. He blamed the 2001 loss on the disruptions caused by the change in organizational structure. Further, from 2001 to 2002, the east side had a 25 percent increase in net sales, a 25 percent increase in gross profits, and an 8 percent increase in total direct costs. Also, although the east side store still showed a net loss, it was 80 percent less than the previous year's loss. The west side store, on the other hand, had shown a 21 percent decrease in net sales, a 31 percent decrease in gross profit, an 11 percent decrease in direct costs, and a 136 percent increase in net loss. Rumstad is very concerned about the survival of the business and is particularly concerned with the west side store. He has called you in as a research consultant to help him pinpoint what is happening so that he might take corrective action.

West Side Store

The west side store is located in the heart of the census tract with the highest per capita income in the city. Most of the residents in the area are professional people or white-collar workers. The store is a freestanding unit located on a frontage road with the word "Rumstad" printed across the front. Since Rumstad's transfer to the east side store, there has been a succession of managers at the west side store. The first one lasted for six months and the second and third for four months. The current manager, previously a salesclerk at the store for four years, has held the job for ten months. Even though the products carried and the prices charged are the same in both stores, there is some difference in advertising emphasis. The west side store does all of its advertising in the *Shopper's World,* a weekly paper devoted exclusively to advertising, which is distributed free to all households in the community. Paper delivery is by and large door-to-door, although it is quite typical for a stack of newspapers to be placed at the entrance to apartment buildings for residents to pick up a copy.

East Side Store

The east side store is located in a small shopping center in a predominantly blue-collar area. Most of the residents in the immediate vicinity work for one of the various machine tool manufacturers that compose one of the basic industries in Rockford. The store has a large window display area with a readily visible "Rumstad Decorating Center" sign above the store. The east side store advertises periodically in the *Rockford Morning Star* in addition to its Yellow Pages advertising.

Question

1. How would you proceed to answer Rumstad's problem?

Exhibit 1

Profit and Loss Statement for Rumstad Decorating Centers

	East Side Store		West Side Store	
	2002	2001	2002	2001
Total sales	$114,461	$91,034	$87,703	$108,497
Cash sale discounts	4,347	2,971	4,165	2,930
Net sales	110,114	88,063	83,538	105,567
Beginning inventory	53,369	49,768	1,936	0
Purchases	64,654	56,528	163,740	59,366
Total	118,023	106,206	165,676	59,366
Ending inventory	51,955	53,369	115,554	1,936
Cost of sales	66,068	52,837	50,122	57,430
Gross profit or (loss)	44,046	35,226	33,416	48,137
Direct costs				
Salaries	24,068	19,836	24,549	26,583
Payroll taxes	2,025	1,814	1,764	2,060
Depreciation—furniture and fixtures	92	92	92	92
Freight	6	43	511	800
Store supplies	694	828	607	4,153
Accounting and legal expenses	439	433	439	433
Advertising	2,977	4,890	4,820	5,252
Advertising—Yellow Pages	1,007	618	1,387	956
Convention and seminar expenses	0	33	83	216
Insurance	226	139	1,271	1,643
Office expense and supplies	4,466	4,393	5,327	5,010
Personal property tax	139	139	140	140
Rent	7,000	7,000	4,900	4,900
Utilities	2,246	1,651	2,746	2,359
Total direct costs	45,385	41,909	48,636	54,597
Profit or (loss)	(1,339)	(6,683)	(15,220)	(6,460)

PART 2:
Research Design

Case • 2.2

Riverside County Humane Society (A)

The demands on the Riverside County Humane Society (RCHS) had increased rather dramatically over the past several years, while the tax dollars the society received to provide services had remained relatively unchanged. In an effort to halt further decline in the quality of its services and to provide better care for the pets at the center, the membership committee of the board of directors began making plans for a member/contributor drive. The organized drive was to be the first of its kind for the local chapter, and the committee members wanted it to be as productive as possible.

As the plans began to evolve, the committee realized that the organization had only scattered pieces of information about its current members. It did have a list of members and contributors for the last five years that had been compiled by the RCHS staff. In addition, it had access to the results of a survey done by a staff member several years previous that focused on member usage of shelter facilities and their opinions of shelter services and programs. However, the organization had only sparse knowledge of the profile of its typical member and contributor, why they belonged or contributed, how long they had been associated with the Humane Society, how the services of the Humane Society could be improved, and so on. The committee members believed that information on these issues was important to the conduct of a successful membership drive, and they commissioned some research to secure it.

One of the first things the researchers did was to contact other Humane Society chapters to determine what kinds of research they had done, particularly with respect to identifying the characteristics of their members. The researchers also interviewed key Riverside County Humane Society staff members and several board members for their thoughts and ideas regarding RCHS membership. The researchers also held a focus group among members of the Membership Committee.

These research activities produced the following general facts about membership and contributions:

1. The people who use the center's facilities are not necessarily the same people who would become members. Members love their own pets, take good care of them, and want other animals to be treated humanely.
2. Most contributors do not care about being a "member" because membership does not confer any rights or privileges, except a newsletter. Members are very different from contributors.
3. The female member of the household is probably making the decision regarding membership or contribution to the RCHS.
4. The majority of members in the RCHS are female and are at least 35 years old.
5. Many retired or elderly people are contributing to or joining the RCHS.
6. The average contribution is about $15 to $25.
7. People in the community have a generally positive perception of the RCHS.
8. An emotional appeal in a membership drive is likely to have the best chance for success.
9. Most people have heard about the RCHS primarily through education programs conducted by the society.
10. The greatest benefit associated with membership is the warm feeling that people get from belonging to the RCHS.

The research firm planned to select a sample of names from the current lists of members and contributors and to send them mail questionnaires to explore these ideas further.

Questions

1. What kind of research design is being used?
2. Is it a good choice?
3. Design a questionnaire that addresses the issues raised and that also gathers helpful demographic information on members and contributors.

Case • 2.3

HotStuff Computer Software[1]

Simpson, Edwards and Associates has had considerable success with a computer software package that it designed to enable government agencies to manage their database systems. The firm is currently developing a second product, a more specialized version of its first endeavor. Called HotStuff, its latest computer software concept is targeted at the firefighting industry. Researchers at Simpson, Edwards and Associates have a hunch that fire departments are a prime market for database software because of their extensive information-handling responsibilities—equipment inventories, building layouts, hazardous materials data, budget records, personnel files, and so on.

At this embryonic stage in the new product's development, the company is following the same game plan that helped it launch its previous success. Responsibilities have been broadly divided: Jean Edwards has assumed command of the production side and Craig Simpson has taken charge of marketing and promotion. Craig's first move was to reassemble the original team of staff members who had researched the market for government agency software. At their first orientation meeting, he submitted the following objectives for their deliberation:

1. Determine market potential.
2. Identify important product attributes.
3. Develop an effective promotional strategy.
4. Identify competitors in the market.

By the close of discussion, the group had decided that its first task would be exploratory research. Specifically, it decided to conduct experience surveys involving local fire chiefs, informal telephone interviews with state and national fire officials, and a literature search. Based on findings from this effort, the group hoped to pursue descriptive research to fulfill the four objectives.

Exploratory Research

The first finding to emerge from the exploratory research affected the target market for HotStuff. There are two broad categories of fire departments: municipal departments with full staffs of paid firefighters, and volunteer departments consisting of a paid chief and remaining members who may or may not be paid firefighters. The team quickly discovered that the two kinds of departments differ in two important ways. First, from the point of view of funding, municipal departments receive the majority of their funds from taxes, so the money is tightly controlled

and tends to be earmarked for specific uses. Volunteer fire departments, on the other hand, rely heavily on donors and special events as sources of income, to the extent that fund-raising may account for more than 50 percent of their total receipts. Since money obtained through fund-raising is not technically part of the budget, it is not subject to budgetary controls per se.

The second key difference between municipal and volunteer departments concerned purchasing procedures. Local municipal departments tended to route all purchases through a central purchasing agent, who would then apply for approval from the data-processing center at city hall before acquiring computer hardware and software. Fire chiefs interviewed in volunteer departments, however, reported that they had sole authority to purchase any hardware or software required.

Telephone calls to out-of-state fire officials indicated that these differences were consistent across the nation. As a result, Simpson, Edwards and Associates decided to restrict its target market to volunteer fire departments.

A second finding uncovered in the exploratory research concerned the extent to which the needs of the target market were already being met. Inquiries within the state revealed that only a few volunteer departments had already purchased computers. Further, those with computers had not possessed them for long and were still in the process of automating manual databases. The general feeling among fire officials was that computerization would be an inevitable development in the industry in the near future. Indeed, four specialized software packages were already being advertised in fire prevention journals: Chief's Helper, Fire Organizer, Spread Systems, and JLT Software. Spread Systems differed from the others in that it consisted of separate programs, each of which sold individually and covered a particular information type, such as inventory records or hazardous materials. The strategy followed by Spread Systems allowed fire departments to reduce their expenditure on software because they could select only the programs they needed. It was conjectured at Simpson, Edwards and Associates that specific programs for specific functions may help overcome initial consumer caution toward spending several thousand dollars for computer software, because the expenditure would not be made all at one time. It was also believed that some makers of generic software packages that perform spreadsheet or database management analysis should be included in the

---

[1]The contributions of Jacqueline C. Hitchon to the development of this case are gratefully acknowledged.

list of competitors, although users of generic software packages needed some proficiency with computers in order to tailor these basic packages to their specific applications.

A third finding of interest from the exploratory research was that the term "volunteer" was offensive to departments officially classified as volunteer because they thought it implied a lack of professionalism. In fact, their staffs were as well trained as members of municipal departments. This sentiment led the researchers to conclude that the label "volunteer" should not be used in the future promotion of HotStuff.

Based on what it had learned from the exploratory research, Simpson, Edwards and Associates decided to conduct a more formal investigation to address the following objectives:

1. Determine the market potential for its new software by
   a. establishing the incidence of computer use and planned computer purchases in volunteer fire departments, and
   b. obtaining more information about volunteer fire departments' funding and authority structures.
2. Identify important product attributes—that is, the types of information that needed to be handled by volunteer fire departments and thus incorporated into the software.
3. Secure ideas for promotional strategy by
   a. determining which fire publications are read by the target market, and
   b. determining which association conventions are most well attended by the target market.
4. Identify competitors in the market by
   a. establishing which brands of software are currently used in volunteer fire departments, and
   b. establishing how satisfactory existing software packages are perceived to be.

Study Design

Simpson, Edwards and Associates' researchers believed that the best way to address these objectives was through a national survey of volunteer fire departments. They decided on a structured–disguised telephone survey using team members as interviewers. The state fire marshall informed the group that most volunteer fire departments were located in communities with populations under 25,000. Consequently, it was decided to sample towns with populations under 25,000 that were situated within a 20-mile radius of cities of at least 100,000 people. Volunteer fire departments within those towns could then be contacted by telephone using directory assistance. Two large cities were randomly selected from each state in the United States, excluding Alaska and Hawaii, and then a town located near each city was randomly selected. An atlas and the most recent Current Population Reports were used to identify cities and towns of the right specification.

A questionnaire was devised and pretested twice. The first pretest was conducted through personal interviews and was meant to test the questionnaire; the second pretest was performed by telephone and was meant to test the mode of administration. In each case, inquiries were directed to the fire chiefs as representatives of the departments. The actual survey was conducted between April 13 and April 24. It would have taken less time to administer the survey had there not been a national fire convention the week the phone survey began. Nonetheless, the interviewer team was able to increase the response rate to 85 percent by numerous callbacks.

Questions

1. Evaluate Simpson, Edwards and Associates' decision to focus on volunteer fire departments as its target market, based on the exploratory research.
2. Do you consider that exploratory research was productive in this case? Do you think that further useful insights could have been gained without significantly greater expenditure of resources? Is so, what and how?
3. Comment on the differences between the four objectives as originally formulated and as reformulated after exploratory research.
4. Was the choice of phone interviews a good one?

Case • 2.4

Student Computer Lab (A)[1]

A major university served over 2,000 undergraduate and graduate students majoring in business administration. The large number of students enrolled in the Business School coupled with increasing use of computer technology by faculty and students created overwhelming demands on the Business School's computer center. In order to respond, the Business School decided to upgrade its computer facilities.

Rod Stevenson, director of the Student Computer Center (SCC), opened a new computer lab in the fall of 2002. The new lab offered specialized software required by student courses and the latest technology in hardware and software.

Computer Lab Project

After operating for six months, Stevenson recognized some potential problems with the new computer lab. Although the number of computers had doubled, student suggestions and complaints indicated that the demand for computers at times exceeded the available resources. To address this problem, Stevenson established a task force to investigate the level of student satisfaction with the computer lab. The task force was made up of four graduate students and was established in January 2003. The task force aimed to help the computer lab identify student needs and provide suggestions on how those needs could be most effectively met.

The first activity of the task force was to examine available information on the lab and its functions and resources. Services offered by the computer lab included network and printer access. The lab usually had three to four lab monitors to collect money for printouts and answer any of the student's questions. Lab hours were 8:00 A.M. to 9:30 P.M. on weekdays and 8:00 A.M. to 5:00 P.M. on Saturdays and Sundays.

After reviewing available information on the lab, the task force decided it needed to conduct some research before making recommendations on the services offered. Exhibit 1 displays a proposal written by the task force outlining the information to be obtained and the time frame for the research.

Focus Group Study

Stevenson received the proposal and approved it. He agreed with the task force's use of focus groups to gain a preliminary understanding of the students' attitudes. The focus groups would identify existing problems better than secondary research, although the process of collecting and analyzing the data would be more time consuming. After receiving approval, the task force posted information around the Business School to alert students that focus groups were being conducted. Free laser copies were offered as an incentive for participation. Students were selected based on their interest. The student focus group was held on March 10, 2003. Seven students participated, five graduate and two undergraduate. Transcripts are provided in Exhibit 2.

Because one of the responsibilities of the lab monitors is to assist students with questions and problems, separate focus groups were also conducted on March 9, 2003, and March 11, 2003, with eight lab monitors. Information from both the student and lab monitor focus groups was used as a guide to develop questions for the second phase, a student survey. Information from the focus groups was reduced to a list of key issues, which were then categorized. An exhaustive list of statements was devised to address potential user attitudes with respect to each issue. When the list was complete, statements were revised, combined, or eliminated to a set that succinctly covered the original key issue categories. The questionnaire was then pretested, and finally administered to a sample of students attending class in the Business School.

Questions

1. Did the moderator do an adequate job of getting the information needed by the SCC?
2. Do you think it was wise to have a group with both graduate and undergraduate students included?
3. Analyze the focus group transcript very thoroughly. Make a list of problems and ideas generated for the student computer lab.
4. What do you see as the benefits and limitations of the focus group findings? Do you think the task force plan for utilizing the focus groups is appropriate?

[1]The contributions of Monika E. Wingate to the development of this case are gratefully acknowledged.

Exhibit 1

Task Force Proposal

DATE: February 1, 2003
TO: Rod Stevenson
FROM: Computer Center Improvement Task Force
RE: Computer Lab Research Proposal

Background: In 2002, the Business School opened a new student computer lab. Through suggestions and complaints, the SCC realizes that there is a service delivery problem in that student demand for computers at times exceeds available resources. The aim of this research is to help the SCC identify student needs and provide suggestions on how those needs can be most effectively met. The results of this research will be limited to the student computer lab. Other Business School computer facilities, such as the computer classrooms and the multimedia lab, are outside the scope of this project.

Objectives: The research objectives are as follows:

- Determine overall student satisfaction with the lab
- Identify current problem areas
- Collect student recommendations for improvements

Methodology: The research design is divided into two parts, exploratory research followed by descriptive research. The exploratory research would attempt to gain a better understanding of students' perceptions of the computer lab and to identify the issues that concern them. The student survey would aim to quantify the magnitude of these problems and to develop recommendations.

Focus Groups: The task force feels that focus groups would be the most appropriate method for exploratory research. Two sets of focus groups are recommended. One set will focus on students who use the computer lab, while the other will address the lab monitors who deal with student problems on a daily basis.

Student Survey: The focus group information would be used to develop questions for a subsequent survey. Since the population of interest is students enrolled in the Business School, this survey would be administered to students attending classes within the Business School, both graduates and undergraduates.

Time Schedule	Completed By
Focus Groups	March 11
Questionnaire Design	April 2
Pretest Questionnaire	April 9
Survey	April 23
Data Analysis	May 10

Exhibit 2

Student Focus Group Transcript

Moderator: I'm Robert from Professional Interviewing. I really appreciate your participation in this group session. As you can see, I am taping this session so I can review all of your comments. We are here tonight to talk about the computer lab at the Business School. As business students, you all have access to the lab for your class assignments. How do you think the computer lab is meeting your needs?

Lisa: I think there is a problem with the lab because the folks who are using computers don't know about computers. That's been reflected in the fact that you go to one computer and you pick up a virus. These people don't know anything about viruses, they're transmitting them all over the place, nobody is scanning for viruses, and there's something that could easily be put on the systems.

Oliver: I think there has to be training for the people who are watching the computers. They are ignorant. You ask them any question and they can't answer it. It's a computer lab and this computer doesn't seem to be doing the thing that it should be doing, why? Why is this network different from the rest? How are we supposed to handle this network? They don't know.

Lisa: Not only that, they don't know any of the software.

Oliver: Absolutely!

Lisa: This is like I have Word at home and this is WordPerfect, "How do I do XYZ in WordPerfect?" They don't know. They say, let me go check with John and it takes three of them to try to answer the question.

Marion: And there are three of them!

continued

Exhibit 2

Student Focus Group Transcript (*continued*)

Lisa: I know!

Oliver: There is always a big queue so you cannot get onto a Windows machine; you have to go to Pagemaker Plus if you need to make a presentation. You cannot go to these WordPerfect machines that have just keyboard entries. But there are very few computers and a lot of lines in the peak times and they are just not equipped to handle it. They have so many staff over there, five people, all of these people, but not one of them will help anyone.

Moderator: How about you, Jennifer, have you experienced this?

Jennifer: Yeah, I even had it today. I just don't have time to wait in line to get a computer. It's a half hour sometimes to go in and get one.

Lisa: And that's now. At the end of the semester it's worse.

Jennifer: Yeah, it gets worse.

Lisa: It takes an hour and there's no sign-up. There's no regular sign-up.

Mike: They truncated the hours the last two weeks of the semester.

Jennifer: You could take these four people and turn that into one educated person, or take the four people and have one uneducated person there 24 hours a day. That would be nice. If all they're going to do is take your card and give you your copy, why do you have to have four of them? That's all they're doing. And studying.

Moderator: How about you, I didn't get your name?

Tammy: Tammy.

Moderator: Welcome, Tammy, how about you. What kind of things have you come across?

Tammy: What I'm hearing are a lot of the problems I've seen too. I just think there needs to be more computers in the lab and the hours need to be longer.

Mike: I don't think they need more computers. They just need to expand the hours and the computing labs.

Oliver: I had an idea where they don't need more computers. One suggestion I already put in the suggestion box, is to have people bring their own computers. Why doesn't a grad student who is going to be here for two years, going to interface with technology when he leaves here, spend a thousand dollars and go buy his own system? They should do that. Have your own computer here, I'm saying it's a requirement. It's a requirement at a lot of universities that you come with your own system. Then you don't have to worry, you don't need access to our labs. Now for undergraduates we still have similar problems, but it would put less stress on the system.

Moderator: What would you suggest for people who would say, okay I can get this computer system, but I have to get this software for this class, and this software for this class, and this software. That is a lot of money.

Oliver: Yeah, we can already jump into the network from home. All you need is the software.

Lisa: I don't think so.

Oliver: You can get in. I can check my mail and stuff.

Lisa: But not software.

Oliver: Oh, software. I haven't tried, so I don't know.

Tammy: Getting back to the machine. I'd love to have my own machine but I don't want to have it if I don't have to. As long as we have all these other computers, why not use what we've got?

Mike: I can't afford it. If you want to buy a good computer, a decent printer, a decent monitor, you are still going to spend between $1,600 and $2,000.

Oliver: I think while we're in school the school should support us with computers.

Mike: I think one of the reasons there aren't enough computers is that people who aren't enrolled in the Business School have access to the lab. In the old building, they always checked your ID.

Tammy: Yeah. Why don't we use the card machines? They were working, weren't they? They had the doors closed and you used a key card.

Oliver: I think the old lab was better because they controlled people coming and going.

Mike: Yeah. Gatekeeping.

Exhibit 2

Student Focus Group Transcript (*continued*)

Tammy: They had hours when only graduate students could come in. I think that's something that should be started again because they have a lot more papers to type up.

Mike: I don't see why this lab isn't open 24 hours. I really don't. Why aren't the labs open 24 hours?

Lisa: Monitor problem, they need someone to monitor them, to work with them.

Jennifer: Three people, three eight-hour shifts.

Mike: They don't have a budget to increase their hours. They need to double the hours, like not having four monitors at one time.

Moderator: There are peak hours and there are hours that there are a lot of open computers, where people don't generally come in. If there was a way to monitor those times and put a schedule up, people could come in and indicate a time when we could go there. Continually monitor that, what do you think about that?

Mike: Every hour is a peak hour, particularly at the end of the semester.

Oliver: I think it would be a good way of trying to smooth it out, because that's what you are trying to do. Have people go there when it's not so busy. But then what about times like today? I happened to get out of class one-half hour early and went downstairs and used it. But if I hadn't signed up early, there were a million folks in there. There are some trade-offs, but I think it's a great idea to try and smooth it out. This morning there were four of us in there at 8:00 or 8:15 when it opened, and I don't think anybody else showed up until 10:00.

Mike: Another problem in the lab right now, is that there are a lot of computers that are broken at one time.

Oliver: Oh yeah!

Mike: There are six of them right now that aren't working.

Oliver: That's from people not knowing what they are doing. I was sitting down there on one of the old machines and there was a gentleman sitting next to me who couldn't figure out why it wouldn't work. He took his disk out and shut the computer off. When it came back on it got a boot error. Then he got scared and he just left. He didn't go tell anyone. The monitors are looking from the other side, so they don't know there is anything wrong. Someone comes in, they just look around, and see that the computer is broken, or it's not booted up, and so on. That's why I am saying, it's the students themselves. People need to know how to use the system.

Ira: I think there should be a small note pasted next to the computers with instructions as to how to use each computer.

Marion: Even a template for the word processing.

Ira: Even a small hint for troubleshooting, please don't do this and do this.

Tammy: I think an excellent model for this are the computer labs in the dorms. The first time you use them, they scan your ID to be sure you are a dorm resident, they know if it's the first time you are using it, they ask you to make sure you know how to use the software. They have a rack with every different kind of title and anything you need to use the software. They tell you exactly what's going to come up on the machine and what you have to do. I'm sure the Business School can get copies of it all and then just copy it.

Marion: We have no reference guides for the software.

Tammy: And then they have the guides there. The little orange books.

Moderator: Are there any other concerns we haven't talked about?

Ira: Is there any way the cost for a laser print can be reduced?

Tammy: It kills me.

Ira: It should be 7 cents. It is 6 cents in the library.

Tammy: You used to have the option to go to a dot matrix printer. They changed that this semester. The only way to go to the dot matrix was to go to an AT&T machine. Don't tell me someone is looking at cost.

Ira: I think the initial cost is pretty high, that is why they're keeping it at 10 cents.

Jennifer: If they are planning on getting more printers, I think they should have at least one or two individual print stations where you can grab your stuff. If you're working on your resume and you want to print on bond paper or do envelopes, the people behind the desk won't let you do it because they don't know if other people are going to send before you do, they don't know what is going to come out.

Oliver: Or they waste your paper because they can't coordinate it.

Jennifer: So I think there should be some individual workstations.

continued

Exhibit 2

Student Focus Group Transcript (*continued*)

Oliver: I have something to say and maybe I'm the only one with this problem. I always find that when I go there and I am working alone, other groups are creating a racket, so it's really frustrating. I'm working on a project, I need to think. I don't need this kind of heavy distraction, this loud talk. I go and work in groups too, we try to whisper. There should be some kind of discipline in the computer lab. I think I may be the only one being that sensitive, but I think silence has to be maintained. It is a computer lab, it is a place for people working, if you're having a fun time go have it outside.

Moderator: How effective do you think their waiting lists system is?

Tammy: It stinks.

Ira: I didn't even know they had one.

Tammy: It would be better to set up a physical waiting list where there would be chairs or a bench or something like that.

Ira: Or like a number.

Tammy: Or six chairs in a row and you sit down next to the computers and that means you are next to get on; then if you leave the next person can move down and then you can see that no one is getting in front of you.

Oliver: It worked pretty well for me. Every time I used the waiting list I had to wait for maybe a half hour and my name was called and I could get a computer. I have no complaints. This happened every time. There was no problem. I had no problems at all.

Mike: Until now I didn't even know there was a waiting list. If there was an open computer I would just sit down.

Tammy: I found out the hard way, I went down and sat down and someone told me.

Jennifer: It's not very consistent. It's kind of whenever they feel like.

Moderator: Anything else?

Jennifer: I have one comment about the resources, since we are able to use the resources like e-mail and the Internet. The Internet's great, but if you don't know any of the numbers to call out, it's kind of a useless thing. But there are books out there with the numbers that cost about $30 and if you keep one of the books as a reference copy at the desk for people to look at, I think it would be a great resource. I looked at the bookstore once and it's incredible the different things you can search for on the Internet.

Tammy: Good point. I think they could put it down there with all the reference items.

Jennifer: I think they need more computers and longer hours. They're not meeting the demands.

Ira: At least the building hours.

Tammy: Match the library's hours. They're open 100 plus hours a week. Sunday night. They could close earlier on Friday and Saturday night (like 8:00 A.M. to 11:00 P.M.).

Jennifer: And do it during exams too—all of a sudden it's close to 5:00 and even Memorial Library is open later than that.

Moderator: We're close to wrapping up. Is there anything else?

Tammy: Oh, can I get templates? For the word processing, I don't know how to use them. You have to use control that, shift that.

Ira: They used to have them. Just photocopy them.

Moderator: Is there anything else? I want to thank all of you. Your concerns will definitely be evaluated and considered. I have some print-out cards for all of you. I knew I would give you $5.00 for each copy but as it turned out there's $9.75 on each card.

Case • 2.5

Chestnut Ridge Country Club[1]

The Chestnut Ridge Country Club has long maintained a distinguished reputation as one of the outstanding country clubs in the Elma, Tennessee, area. The club's golf facilities are said by some to be the finest in the state, and its dining and banquet facilities are highly regarded as well. This reputation is due in part to the commitment by the board of directors of Chestnut Ridge to offer the finest facilities of any club in the area. For example, several negative comments by club members regarding the dining facilities prompted the board to survey members to get their feelings and perceptions of the dining facilities and food offerings at the club. Based on the survey findings, the board of directors established a quality control committee to oversee the dining room, and a new club manager was hired.

Most recently, the board became concerned about the number of people seeking membership to Chestnut Ridge. Although no records are kept on the number of membership applications received each year, the board sensed that this figure was declining. They also believed that membership applications at the three competing country clubs in the area—namely, Alden, Chalet, and Lancaster—were not experiencing similar declines. Because Chestnut Ridge had other facilities, such as tennis courts and a pool, that were comparable to the facilities at these other clubs, the board was perplexed as to why membership applications would be falling at Chestnut Ridge.

To gain insight into the matter, the board of directors hired an outside research firm to conduct a study of the country clubs in Elma, Tennessee. The goals of the research were: (1) to outline areas in which Chestnut Ridge fared poorly in relation to other clubs in the area; (2) to determine people's overall perception of Chestnut Ridge; and (3) to provide recommendations for ways to increase membership applications at the club.

Research Method

The researchers met with the board of directors and key personnel at Chestnut Ridge to gain a better understanding of the goals of the research and the types of services and facilities offered at a country club. A literature search of published research relating to country clubs uncovered no studies. Based solely on their contact with individuals at Chestnut Ridge, therefore, the research team developed the survey contained in Exhibit 1. Because personal information regarding demographics and attitudes would be

asked of those contacted, the researchers decided to use a mail questionnaire.

The researchers thought it would be useful to survey members from Alden, Chalet, and Lancaster country clubs in addition to those from Chestnut Ridge for two reasons. One, members of these other clubs would be knowledgeable about the levels and types of services and facilities desired from a country club, and, two, they had at one time represented potential members of Chestnut Ridge. Hence, their perceptions of Chestnut Ridge might reveal why they chose to belong to a different country club.

No public documents were available that contained a listing of each club's members. Consequently, the researchers decided to contact each of the clubs personally to try to obtain a mailing list. Identifying themselves as being affiliated with an independent research firm conducting a study on country clubs in the Elma area, the researchers first spoke to the chairman of the board at Alden Country Club. The researchers told the chairman that they could not reveal the organization sponsoring the study but that the results of their study would not be made public. The chairman was not willing to provide the researchers with the mailing list. The chairman cited an obligation to respect the privacy of the club's members as his primary reason for turning down the research team's request.

The researchers then made the following proposal to the board chairman: In return for the mailing list, the researchers would provide the chairman a report on Alden members' perceptions of Alden Country Club. In addition, the mailing list would be destroyed as soon as the surveys were sent. The proposal seemed to please the chairman, for he agreed to give the researchers a listing of the members and their addresses in exchange for the report. The researchers told the chairman they had to check with their sponsoring organization for approval of this arrangement.

The research team made similar proposals to the chairmen of the boards of directors of both the Chalet and Lancaster country clubs. In return for a mailing list of the club's members, they promised each chairman a report outlining their members' perceptions of their clubs, contingent on approval from the research team's sponsoring organization. Both chairmen agreed to supply the requested list of members. The researchers subsequently met with the Chestnut Ridge board of directors. In their meeting, the researchers outlined the situation and asked

[1]The contributions of David M. Szymanski to the development of this case are gratefully acknowledged.

Exhibit 1

Questionnaire Used to Survey Alden, Chalet, and Lancaster Country Club Members

1. Of which club are you currently a member? _____

2. How long have you been a member of this club? _____

3. How familiar are you with each of the following country clubs?

Alden Country Club
_____ very familiar (I am a member or I have visited the club as a guest)
_____ somewhat familiar (I have heard of the club from others)
_____ unfamiliar

Chalet Country Club
_____ very familiar (I am a member or I have visited the club as a guest)
_____ somewhat familiar (I have heard of the club from others)
_____ unfamiliar

Chestnut Ridge Country Club
_____ very familiar (I am a member or I have visited the club as a guest)
_____ somewhat familiar (I have heard of the club from others)
_____ unfamiliar

Lancaster Country Club
_____ very familiar (I am a member or I have visited the club as a guest)
_____ somewhat familiar (I have heard of the club from others)
_____ unfamiliar

4. The following is a list of factors that may be influential in the decision to join a country club. Please rate the factors according to their importance to you in joining your country club. Circle the appropriate response, where 1 = not at all important and 5 = extremely important.

Golf facilities	1	2	3	4	5
Tennis facilities	1	2	3	4	5
Pool facilities	1	2	3	4	5
Dining facilities	1	2	3	4	5
Social events	1	2	3	4	5
Family activities	1	2	3	4	5
Number of friends who are members	1	2	3	4	5
Cordiality of members	1	2	3	4	5
Prestige	1	2	3	4	5
Location	1	2	3	4	5

5. The following is a list of phrases pertaining to Alden Country Club. Please place an X in the space that best describes your impressions of Alden. The ends represent extremes; the center position is neutral. Do so even if you are only vaguely familiar with Alden.

Club landscape is attractive.	:__:__:__:__:__:__:	Club landscape is unattractive.
Clubhouse facilities are poor.	:__:__:__:__:__:__:	Clubhouse facilities are excellent.
Locker room facilities are excellent.	:__:__:__:__:__:__:	Locker room facilities are poor.
Club management is ineffective.	:__:__:__:__:__:__:	Club management is effective.
Dining room atmosphere is pleasant.	:__:__:__:__:__:__:	Dining room atmosphere is unpleasant.
Food prices are unreasonable.	:__:__:__:__:__:__:	Food prices are reasonable.
Golf course is poorly maintained.	:__:__:__:__:__:__:	Golf course is well maintained.
Golf course is challenging.	:__:__:__:__:__:__:	Golf course is not challenging.
Membership rates are too high.	:__:__:__:__:__:__:	Membership rates are too low.

6. The following is a list of phrases pertaining to Chalet Country Club. Please place an X in the space that best describes your impressions of Chalet. Do so even if you are only vaguely familiar with Chalet.

Club landscape is attractive.	:__:__:__:__:__:__:	Club landscape is unattractive.
Clubhouse facilities are poor.	:__:__:__:__:__:__:	Clubhouse facilities are excellent.
Locker room facilities are excellent.	:__:__:__:__:__:__:	Locker room facilities are poor.

Exhibit 1

Questionnaire Used to Survey Alden, Chalet, and Lancaster Country Club Members (*continued*)

Club management is effective.	:__:__:__:__:__:	Club management is ineffective.
Dining room atmosphere is pleasant.	:__:__:__:__:__:	Dining room atmosphere is unpleasant.
Food prices are unreasonable.	:__:__:__:__:__:	Food prices are reasonable.
Food quality is excellent.	:__:__:__:__:__:	Food quality is poor.
Golf course is poorly maintained.	:__:__:__:__:__:	Golf course is well maintained.
Golf course is challenging.	:__:__:__:__:__:	Golf course is not challenging.
Tennis courts are in excellent condition.	:__:__:__:__:__:	Tennis courts are in poor condition.
There are too many tennis courts.	:__:__:__:__:__:	There are too few tennis courts.
Membership rates are too high.	:__:__:__:__:__:	Membership rates are too low.

7. The following is a list of phrases pertaining to Chestnut Ridge Country Club. Please place an X in the space that best describes your impressions of Chestnut Ridge. Do so even if you are only vaguely familiar with Chestnut Ridge.

Club landscape is attractive.	:__:__:__:__:__:	Club landscape is unattractive.
Clubhouse facilities are poor.	:__:__:__:__:__:	Clubhouse facilities are excellent.
Locker room facilities are excellent.	:__:__:__:__:__:	Locker room facilities are poor.
Club management is ineffective.	:__:__:__:__:__:	Club management is effective.
Dining room atmosphere is pleasant.	:__:__:__:__:__:	Dining room atmosphere is unpleasant.
Food prices are unreasonable.	:__:__:__:__:__:	Food prices are reasonable.
Food quality is excellent.	:__:__:__:__:__:	Food quality is poor.
Golf course is poorly maintained.	:__:__:__:__:__:	Golf course is well maintained.
Tennis courts are in poor condition.	:__:__:__:__:__:	Tennis courts are in excellent condition.
There are too many tennis courts.	:__:__:__:__:__:	There are too few tennis courts.
Swimming pool is in poor condition.	:__:__:__:__:__:	Swimming pool is in excellent condition.
Membership rates are too high.	:__:__:__:__:__:	Membership rates are too low.

8. The following is a list of phrases pertaining to Lancaster Country Club. Please place an X in the space that best describes your impressions of Lancaster. Do so even if you are only vaguely familiar with Lancaster.

Club landscape is attractive.	:__:__:__:__:__:	Club landscape is unattractive.
Clubhouse facilities are poor.	:__:__:__:__:__:	Clubhouse facilities are excellent.
Locker room facilities are excellent.	:__:__:__:__:__:	Locker room facilities are poor.
Club management is ineffective.	:__:__:__:__:__:	Club management is effective.
Dining room atmosphere is pleasant.	:__:__:__:__:__:	Dining room atmosphere is unpleasant.
Food prices are unreasonable.	:__:__:__:__:__:	Food prices are reasonable.
Food quality is excellent.	:__:__:__:__:__:	Food quality is poor.
Golf course is poorly maintained.	:__:__:__:__:__:	Golf course is well maintained.
Tennis courts are in poor condition.	:__:__:__:__:__:	Tennis courts are in excellent condition.
There are too many tennis courts.	:__:__:__:__:__:	There are too few tennis courts.
Swimming pool is in poor condition.	:__:__:__:__:__:	Swimming pool is in excellent condition.
Membership rates are too high.	:__:__:__:__:__:	Membership rates are too low.

9. Overall, how would you rate each of the country clubs? Circle the appropriate response, where 1 = poor and 5 = excellent.

Alden	1	2	3	4	5
Chalet	1	2	3	4	5
Chestnut Ridge	1	2	3	4	5
Lancaster	1	2	3	4	5

10. The following questions are designed to give a better understanding of the members of country clubs.

Have you ever been a member of another club in the Elma area?

_____yes   _____no

Approximately what is the distance of your residence from your club in miles?

_____0–2 miles   _____3–5 miles   _____6–10 miles   _____10+ miles

Age: _____21–30   _____31–40   _____41–50   _____51–60   _____ 61 or over

Sex: _____male   _____female

Marital status: _____married   _____single   _____ widowed   _____divorced

Number of dependents including yourself:

_____ 2 or less   _____3–4   _____5 or more

continued

Exhibit 1

Questionnaire Used to Survey Alden, Chalet, and Lancaster Country Club Members (*continued*)

Total family income:
_____Less than $20,000
_____$20,000–$29,999
_____$30,000–$49,999
_____$50,000–$99,999
_____$100,000 or more
_____Do not know/Refuse to answer

Thank you for your cooperation!

for the board's approval to provide each of the clubs with a report in return for the mailing lists. The researchers emphasized that the report would contain no information regarding Chestnut Ridge nor information by which each of the other clubs could compare itself to any of the other clubs in the area, in contrast to the information to be provided to the Chestnut Ridge board of directors. The report would only contain a small portion of the overall study's results. After carefully considering the research team's arguments, the board of directors agreed to the proposal.

Membership Surveys

A review of the lists subsequently provided by each club showed that Alden had 114 members, Chalet had 98 members, and Lancaster had 132 members. The researchers believed that 69 to 70 responses from each membership group would be adequate. Anticipating a 70 to 75 percent response rate because of the unusually high involvement and familiarity of each group with the subject matter, the research team decided to mail 85 to 90 surveys to each group; a simple random sample of members was chosen from each list. In all, 87 members from each country club were mailed a questionnaire (348 surveys in total). Sixty-three usable surveys were returned from each group (252 in total) for a response rate of 72 percent.

Summary results of the survey are presented in the exhibits. Exhibit 2 gives member's overall ratings of the country clubs, and Exhibit 3 shows their ratings of the various clubs on an array of dimensions. Exhibit 4 is a breakdown of attitudes toward Chestnut Ridge by the three different membership groups: Alden, Chalet, and Lancaster. The data are average ratings of respondents. Exhibit 2 scores are based on a five-point scale, where "1" is poor and "5" is excellent. The last two are based on seven-point scales in which "1" represents an extremely negative rating and "7" an extremely positive rating.

Questions

1. What kind of research design is being used? Is it a good choice?
2. Do you think it was ethical for the researchers not to disclose the identity of the sponsoring organization? Do you think it was ethical for the boards of directors to release the names of their members in return for a report that analyzes their members' perceptions toward their own club?
3. Overall, how does Chestnut Ridge compare to the other three country clubs (Alden, Chalet, and Lancaster)?
4. In what areas might Chestnut Ridge consider making improvements to attract additional members?

Exhibit 2

Average Overall Ratings of Each Club by Club Membership of the Respondent

| | Membership | | | |
Club Rated	Alden	Chalet	Lancaster	Composite Ratings Across All Members
Alden	4.57	3.64	3.34	3.85
Chalet	2.87	3.63	2.67	3.07
Chestnut Ridge	4.40	4.44	4.20	4.35
Lancaster	3.60	3.91	4.36	3.95

Exhibit 3

Average Ratings of the Respective Country Clubs across Dimensions

Dimension	Country Club			
	Alden	Chalet	Chestnut Ridge	Lancaster
Club landscape	6.28	4.65	6.48	5.97
Clubhouse facilities	5.37	4.67	6.03	5.51
Locker room facilities	4.99	4.79	5.36	4.14
Club management	5.38	4.35	5.00	5.23
Dining room atmosphere	5.91	4.10	5.66	5.48
Food prices	5.42	4.78	4.46	4.79
Food quality	[a]	4.12	5.48	4.79
Golf course maintenance	6.17	5.01	6.43	5.89
Golf course challenge	5.14	5.01	[a]	4.77
Condition of tennis courts	[b]	5.10	4.52	5.08
Number of tennis courts	[b]	4.14	4.00	3.89
Swimming pool	[b]	[b]	4.66	5.35
Membership rates	4.49	3.97	5.00	4.91

[a]Question not asked.
[b]Not applicable.

Exhibit 4

Attitudes toward Chestnut Ridge by Members of the Other Country Clubs

Dimension	Alden	Chalet	Lancaster
Club landscape	6.54	6.54	6.36
Clubhouse facilities	6.08	6.03	5.98
Locker room facilities	5.66	5.35	5.07
Club management	4.97	5.15	4.78
Dining room atmosphere	5.86	5.70	5.41
Food prices	4.26	4.48	4.63
Food quality	5.52	5.75	5.18
Golf course maintenance	6.47	6.59	6.22
Condition of tennis courts	4.55	4.46	4.55
Number of tennis courts	4.00	4.02	3.98
Swimming pool	5.08	4.69	4.26
Membership rates	5.09	5.64	4.24

Case • 2.6

Hand-to-Hand Against Palm (B)

The marketing manager for the "Organize My Life!" (OML) personal digital assistant (PDA) competitor to Palm Computing's Palm Pilot device is evaluating a number of proposals for research to be commissioned to investigate what kinds of features users of these devices might like to see in competitive and next-generation models (for example, sound, video, and so on), and to understand the particular needs of the university student segment (such as price sensitivities, special needs of different groups of students, and so on). The manager is choosing from among three proposals, each of which has been presented by different members of the brand management team.

Proposal 1 advocates exploratory research. It argues that there is insufficient knowledge about the PDA category, so it would not be useful to execute large-scale survey. Rather, this proposal suggests that students come to a central point on campus (the campuses and the meeting places on each campus to be determined), at which place the students will be asked to do a "back-pack dump." In addition to the usual textbooks and notebooks, the researchers will clearly see, using this observational technique, just what electronic equipment the student carries (for example, laptop computer, CD player, tape recorder, and so on), along with what kind of appointment book (such as electronic PDA or paper calendar) the student uses to keep track of homework assignments, friends and social events, and the like.

Proposal 2 recommends that since plenty of secondary data are available on the Palm Pilot and extant competitors, exploratory data would be a waste of time. If the OML team wants to know what the students want, the team should simply ask them. A survey has been designed comprised largely of lists of potential features for the OML PDA. The respondent would be asked to indicate the importance of each feature. For example, the features would be rated on a 10-point scale, where "0" means "I don't care about this; I would never use this feature," to "10," which means "This feature would be very important

to me; I would use it several times a day." The list of features to be rated includes a calendar, to-do list, calculator, video games, hot sync capability, digital photography storage, infrared emailing ability, and so on. Pricing could be assessed similarly, for example, "How much would you be willing to pay for this PDA? $100, $101 to $199, $200 to $299," and so on. The proponent of this research proposal reasons that the attributes that are most valued would appear as the features with the highest means on the rating scales, and that the OML developers would focus on offering the resulting combination of these important features.

Proposal 3 recommends a causal design. The idea would be to set up a "mock" store, featuring the OML with its list of attributes and price, side-by-side with the Palm and competitors (with the lists of their features and prices) and ask the student participants which PDA they would buy, how likely it is that they would buy the OML, and so on. The next group of students would see the OML with a different list of attributes and price point, with the competitors' information held constant, and they would be asked to make the same kind of choices. At the end, having cycled through different variations of the OML features, the team would know which properties were most attractive to the students, and the devices could be developed for market on this basis.

Questions

1. What are the trade-offs among the research designs being proposed? What information can each technique obtain that the others cannot?

2. Imagine role-playing as one of the OML team members and defending one of the three proposals. What strengths does your approach offer? What shortcomings must you acknowledge? What action could be taken as a result of obtaining the information in the form you seek it?

Case • 2.7

E-Food and the Online Grocery Competition (B)

Ashley Sims is an MBA student who is considering starting her own grocery online. Two weeks ago, she ran a focus group consisting of 12 of her classmates, some of whom use an online grocer. She kept the moderator questions broad, trying to get a sense of what e-visitors are looking for in their online grocery trips. Exhibit 1 contains a sampling of the verbata from that focus group.

Those data indicate various levels of satisfaction with current online grocery shopping, and even for loyal users, different levels of satisfaction with different features of the system. While people seem generally happy, there is clearly room for improvement in elements of online grocery shopping.

In addition, Sims is trying to think long-term, knowing that she wants part of her business to focus on grocery delivery, and part to grow into a profitable consumer research business, offering in-depth insight into the consumer-decision processes for grocery shopping and online shopping in general. Sims figures additional research will be required to understand how to set priorities in improving the software, and the broader questions of how to understand consumer behavior and the thought processes underlying that behavior.

Sims used this textbook in her own marketing research class, so she knows there are many research methodologies to choose from. She is fresh from her experience running the focus group that yielded the data in Exhibit 1. While it was fun and she thinks she learned a lot, she doubts that she could run another focus group that could be shaped to address these fairly specific concerns. She's thought about doing a survey—asking people, "Do you care about brands?" or "Are you price sensitive?" and so on. However, she doubts that people would admit to being overly influenced by brand or price, even though their purchases may

indicate that they are. She's also rejected an observational technique—a friend had suggested that she sit down next to someone who is about to do an online grocery run and just watch what they do and take notes. She's afraid that her presence would be off-putting and the person doing the grocery shopping might behave differently from how they normally would (for example, maybe buy asparagus rather than M&M's).

Ashley's computer friend tells her that every mouse click gets stored into a user file and that she should look at what people actually do rather than what they say. Sims is intrigued by this but understandably is having difficulty obtaining such data from current online grocery providers. She decides to invest in having a programmer create a small-scale simulation of an online grocer. She will ask participants to pretend they are grocery shopping online. She'll strip off each user file and analyze the click-stream data. She might run a survey, too, but with the click-streams, she'll know just what people did, not just what they say they would do.

Questions

1. Sims has considered a number of marketing research approaches. Do you agree with her general assessment or do you feel she was hasty in dismissing any of the techniques? Which of the methods would you recommend and why? How would you modify the technique from what she has been considering?

2. What did you learn from the focus group verbatim accounts? Was the sample suitable? When would it be important to run two different focus groups, one for users, one for nonusers?

Sampling of Verbatim Accounts from Focus Group on Online Grocery Trips

■ "It's great! I don't need a car!" (Current user)

■ "It's difficult to just browse, like if I'm not sure what I'm in the mood for." (Had tried online shopping but is no longer a user)

■ "I can't touch the fruits. I can't read the side of the box on cereals." (Current user)

■ "They chose my vegetables better than I would have!" (Current user)

■ "I wish they could pick up my dry cleaning too." (Not a user, intends to begin)

■ "It's kind of expensive. There's a big annual fee, a delivery charge each time, and you know you've got to tip the delivery guy." (Current user)

■ "This is terrific—I don't like to shop for food even if I had the time, which I certainly do not." (Current user)

■ "I guess it's okay. Thing is, there's a <name of local grocery> on my way home from work, so that's just as convenient. For me." (Non-user, does not intend to begin)

■ "Don't I get any, you know, frequent flyer points things?" (Non-user, getting used to the concept)

Exhibit 1

© Eyewire/Getty Images

Part 3

Data Collection Methods

Part 3 covers the third stage in the research process, determination of the methods used to collect data. Chapter 7 focuses on secondary data as an information resource; Chapter 8, on the data available from commercial suppliers. Chapter 9 compares the two methods marketing researchers have available for collecting marketing data—communication and observation. Chapter 10 then discusses the main alternatives if communication methods are used; Chapter 11 explains the alternatives if observation methods are used.

Secondary Data

Chapter 7

© Eyewire/Getty Images

Learning Objectives

1. Explain the difference between primary and secondary data.

2. Cite two advantages offered by secondary data.

3. Specify two problems common to secondary data.

4. List the three criteria researchers should use in judging the accuracy of secondary data.

5. State the most fundamental rule in using secondary data.

6. Explain the difference between internal and external data.

7. List some of the key sources researchers should consider in conducting a search process.

B anks are not generally known as marketing innovators. Sometimes, however, the need to change becomes impossible to ignore.

At NationsBank (now part of Bank of America), executives saw such a need when they reviewed demographic data from the federal government. They saw projections that the Hispanic segment of the U.S. population would grow by 49 percent through 2010, becoming the largest minority group in the United States. The company examined the market area it would serve along with Bank of America and determined that it already had a potential market of 20 million Hispanic consumers and over a million Hispanic-owned businesses. Furthermore, the buying power of Hispanic people has been growing faster than the national average: an 84.5 percent increase since 1990 versus 56.7 for the nation as a whole. NationsBank and Bank of America executives saw the obvious: This was a market to target.

Other bankers have been reaching similar conclusions, especially in areas of the country where the Hispanic presence is greater than average. In Texas, according to census forecasts, Hispanic people will constitute 43 percent of the population by 2030. Chase Bank executive vice president Alice Rodriguez spoke for many Texas banks when she observed, "We recognize the buying power in the minority community is significant, and we want to capture that market."

In Bethany, Oklahoma, near Oklahoma City, Peter and Chris Pierce view the Hispanic population as an untapped market for their small, privately owned bank, First Bethany Bank and Trust. Peter Pierce told a reporter, "It's like finding a city of about 80,000 people which doesn't have a local financial institution." The Pierce brothers hired Jorge Esperilla, who served for two years as director of diversity programs at Southern Nazarene University, to consult on developing a new division that would serve the area's Hispanic residents. First Bethany is betting its future on a strategy of targeting underserved niche markets, including the Hispanic population.

To Alex López Negrete, president of the marketing firm López Negrete, targeting Hispanic consumers and businesses is an immensely practical strategy. "It's common knowledge," he told a reporter. "Whoever wins the multicultural race will win, period."

But how to target that group effectively? In the past, banks have simply printed some literature in Spanish to include in their displays and perhaps hired a translator in neighborhoods with a sizable population of non-English-speaking people. However, these tactics do not really reach out beyond the bank's walls to bring in new customers.

Furthermore, the banks don't want to make mistakes based on stereotypes or misuse of data. (Even sophisticated marketers like Frito-Lay can make mistakes. Consider that company's evaluation a decade ago of data suggesting that Hispanic consumers are very brand loyal. The company decided to build Frito-Lay parks in Hispanic communities—a nice gesture, but the connection to buying corn chips was not exactly obvious to the communities' residents.)

Successfully targeting Hispanic consumers and businesses will require a great deal of information about those new markets. This is information that banks sorely lack, claims Bill Strunk, a banking consultant based in Houston: "Eighty-five percent of the growth between now and 2015 in Texas will be Hispanics, and everyone is waking up and wanting to market to this, but only a handful know how to do it."

Discussion Issues

1. What kinds of information will banks need in order to target Hispanic consumers and businesses?

2. Where can banks get such information (external sources, company data, published reports, commissioning their own research projects)?

3. Whom should the banks include in their research process? ■

secondary data
Information not gathered for the immediate study at hand but for some other purpose.

primary data
Information collected specifically for the investigation at hand.

Once the research problem is defined and clearly specified, the research effort turns to data collection. The natural temptation among beginning researchers is to begin designing a survey immediately—however, survey data should only be collected if absolutely necessary. "A good operating rule is to consider a survey akin to surgery—to be used only after other possibilities have been exhausted."[1] First attempts at data collection should focus on **secondary data,** which are statistics not gathered for the immediate study at hand but previously gathered for some other purpose. Information originated by the researcher for the purpose of the investigation at hand is called **primary data.**

If General Electric conducted a survey on the demographic characteristics of refrigerator purchasers to determine who buys the various sizes of refrigerators, this would be primary data. If, instead, the company used its existing files and compiled the same data from warranty cards its customers had returned, or if it used already-published industry statistics on refrigerator buyers, the information would be considered secondary data.

Beginning researchers usually have no idea how much secondary data are available. Exhibit 7.1 lists some of the information on people and households collected by the U.S. Bureau of the Census and readily available for use by researchers. It is important for researchers to know what is available in secondary sources, not just to avoid "reinventing the wheel," but because secondary data possess some significant advantages over primary data. Further, some types of marketing research—in particular, market analysis—rely almost exclusively on secondary data.

Exhibit 7.1

Information Available From the 22nd Census of Population and Housing

100-percent characteristics (short form): A limited number of questions were asked of every person and housing unit in the United States. Information is available on:

Household relationship	Race
Sex	Tenure (whether the home is owned or rented)
Age	Vacancy characteristics
Hispanic or Latino origin	

Sample characteristics (long form): Additional questions were asked of a sample (generally 1-in-6) of persons and housing units. Data are provided on:

Population	*Housing*
Marital status	Value of home or monthly rent paid
Place of birth, citizenship, and year of entry	Units in structure
School enrollment and educational attainment	Year structure built
Ancestry	Number of rooms and number of bedrooms
Migration (residence in 1995)	Year moved into residence
Language spoken at home and ability to speak English	Plumbing and kitchen facilities
Veteran status	Telephone service
Disability	Vehicles available
Grandparents as caregivers	Heating fuel
Labor force status	Farm residence
Place of work and journey to work	Utilities, mortgage, taxes, insurance, and fuel costs
Occupation, industry, and class of worker	
Work status in 1999	
Income in 1999	

Source: "Introduction to Census 2000 Data Products," pg. 1, downloaded from http://www.census.gov/dmd/www/products.html, January 22, 2003.

Advantages of Secondary Data

The most significant advantages of secondary data are the time and money they save the researcher. If the information being sought is available as secondary data, the researcher can simply go to the library or go online, locate the appropriate source or sources, and gather the information desired. This should take no more than a few days and involve little cost. If the same information were to be collected in a sample survey, the following steps would have to be taken: data collection form designed and pretested; field interviewing staff selected and trained; sampling plan devised; data gathered and then checked for accuracy and omissions; data coded and analyzed. As a conservative estimate, this process would take two to three months and could cost thousands of dollars, since it would include expenses and wages for a number of additional field and office personnel.

Cite two advantages offered by secondary data.

With secondary data, the expenses incurred in collecting the data have already been paid by the original compiler of the information. Even if there is a charge for using the data (unlike statistics compiled by government or trade associations, commercial data are not free), the cost is still substantially less than if the firm collected the information itself.

Given the substantial amount of time and money at stake, we offer this advice: Do not bypass secondary data. Begin with secondary data, and only when the secondary data are exhausted or show diminishing returns, proceed to primary data. Sometimes the secondary data are sufficient, especially when all the analyst needs is a ballpark estimate, which is often the case. For example, a common question that confronts marketing research analysts is: What is the market potential for the product or service? Are there enough people or organizations interested in it to justify providing it?

Exhibit 7.2 illustrates how secondary data were successfully used to answer this question, in this case by a manufacturer of pet foods to assess the potential demand for a dog food that

---

Exhibit 7.2

Use of Secondary Data by a Pet Food Manufacturer

The question was, "Is there currently a significant number of persons who mix moist or canned dog food with dry dog food?" At this early stage in the exploration of this product concept, the firm did not want to expend funds for primary research. While an actual survey of pet owners would have yielded the best answer, such a survey would have required the expenditure of several thousand dollars. In addition, further development of the idea would have required a delay of several weeks to obtain the survey results. An effort to develop an acceptable first answer to the question of demand using secondary sources was initiated.

The firm identified the following information:

1. From published literature on veterinary medicine, the firm identified the amount (in ounces) of food required to feed a dog each day by type of food (dry, semimoist, moist), age, size, and type of dog.
2. From an existing survey conducted annually by the firm's advertising agency the firm obtained information on
   (a) the percentage of U.S. households owning dogs;
   (b) the number, sizes, and types of dogs owned by each household in the survey;
   (c) the type(s) of dog food fed to the dogs; and
   (d) the frequency of use of various types of dog food.

It was assumed that dog owners who reported feeding their dogs two or more different types of dog food each day were good prospects for a product that provided premixed moist and dry food. Combining the information in the survey with the information from the literature on veterinary medicine and doing some simple multiplication produced a demand figure for the product concept. The demand exceeded 20 percent of the total volume of dog food sales, a figure sufficiently large to justify proceeding with product development and testing.

© David Young-Wolff/PhotoEdit

Source: David W. Stewart and Michael A. Kamins, *Secondary Research: Information Sources and Methods,* 2nd ed. (Thousand Oaks, CA: Sage Publications, 1993), p. 129. Reprinted by permission of Sage Publications, Inc.

included both moist chunks and hard, dry chunks. As the example indicates, when using secondary data it is often necessary to make some assumptions in order to use the data effectively (e.g., the number of owners who were good prospects). The key is to make reasonable assumptions and then to vary these assumptions to determine how sensitive a particular conclusion is to variations in them. In the dog food example, "altering the assumption regarding the number of owners who were good prospects for the new product to include as few as one-tenth of the original number did not alter the decision to proceed with the product. Under such circumstances, the value of additional information would be quite small."[2]

Although it is rare that secondary data completely solve the problem under study, they usually will (1) help the investigator to better state the problem under investigation, (2) suggest improved methods or further data that should be collected, and/or (3) provide comparative data by which primary data can be more insightfully interpreted.

Disadvantages of Secondary Data

3 *Specify two problems common to secondary data.*

Two problems that commonly arise with secondary data are (1) they do not completely fit the problem, and (2) they are not totally accurate.

Problems of Fit

Because secondary data are collected for other purposes, it is rare when they perfectly fit the problem as defined. In some cases, the fit will be so poor that the data are completely inappropriate. Usually the poor fit is due to (1) different units of measurement, (2) different class definitions, or (3) the age of the data.

The size of a retail store, for instance, can be expressed in terms of gross sales, profits, square feet, and number of employees. Consumer income can be expressed by individual, family, household, and spending unit. So it is with many variables, and a common source of frustration in using secondary data is that the source containing the basic information desired presents that information in units of measurement different from that needed.

Assuming the units are consistent, we find that the class boundaries presented are often different from those needed. If the problem demands income by individual in increments of $5,000 (0–$4,999, $5,000–$9,999, and so on), it does the researcher little good if the data source offers income by individual using boundaries $7,500 apart (0–$7,499, $7,500–$14,999, and so on).

Finally, secondary data are often out of date. The time from data collection to data dissemination is often long, sometimes as much as two to three years, as, for example, with much government census data. Although census data have great value while current, this value diminishes rapidly with time. Most marketing decisions require current, rather than historical, information.

Problems of Accuracy

4 *List the three criteria researchers should use in judging the accuracy of secondary data.*

The accuracy of much secondary data is also questionable. As this book indicates, there are a number of sources of error possible in the collection, analysis, and presentation of marketing information. When a researcher is collecting primary data, firsthand experience helps in judging the accuracy of the information being collected. But when using secondary data, the researcher's task in assessing accuracy is more difficult.[3] It may help to consider the primacy of the source, the purpose of publication, and the general quality of the data collection methods and presentation.

Primacy of Source Consider the source first. Secondary data can be secured from either a primary source or a secondary source. A **primary source** is the source that originated the data. A **secondary source** is a source that in turn secured the data from a primary source. The *Statistical Abstract of the United States,* for example, which is published each year and contains a

primary source
The originating source of secondary data.

great deal of useful information for many research projects, is a secondary source of secondary data. All of its data are taken from other government and trade sources. The researcher who stopped searching for secondary data with the *Statistical Abstract* would violate the most fundamental rule in using secondary data—always use the primary source of secondary data.

5 *State the most fundamental rule in using secondary data.*

Irene Viento violated that rule when she planned the launch of her store Grand Kids Ltd. in Pelham, New York. She thought her upscale suburb was an ideal location for a store catering to grandparents eager to spoil their grandchildren. After all, specialty stores of this type were the largest segment of the clothing market for infants and toddlers. She checked secondary data from the school district and a company that produces advertising circulars, and estimated that there were about 10,000 families in Pelham—enough, she reasoned, to support her store. But three years after the founding, she closed for lack of business. She had grossly overestimated her market. Census data recorded 12,000 residents and fewer than 3,500 families. Furthermore, less than one-third of Pelham's residents were in her targeted age group of people 50 and older.[4]

There are two main reasons for using a primary source. First and foremost, the researcher will need to search for general evidence of quality (e.g., the methods of data collection and analysis). The primary source will typically be the only source that describes the process of collection and analysis, and thus is the only source by which this judgment can be made. Second, a primary source is usually more accurate and complete than a secondary source. Secondary sources often fail to include important information such as footnotes that the original researchers included with the research results. Errors in transcription can also occur in copying data from a primary source. Once made, transcription errors seem to hold on tenaciously, as the following example illustrates.

In 1901 Napoleon Lajoie produced the highest batting average ever attained in the American League when he batted .422 on 229 hits in 543 times at bat. In setting the type for the record book after that season, a printer correctly reported Lajoie's .422 average, but incorrectly reported his hits, giving him 220 instead of 229. A short time later, someone pointed out that 220 hits in 543 at-bats yields a batting average of .405, and so Lajoie's reported average was changed. The error persisted for some 50 years, until an energetic fan checked all the old box scores and discovered the facts.[5]

Purpose of Publication A second criterion by which the accuracy of secondary data can be assessed is the purpose of publication. Consider the examples in Research Window 7.1. Would your reactions to any of the examples be different if you knew that (a) the survey in Example A was sponsored by *Prevention* magazine, which publishes health-related articles and is therefore a magazine in which prescription drug marketers advertise; (b) the survey in Example B was sponsored by *Popular Mechanics* magazine; and (c) the survey in Example C was sponsored by Bridgestone/Firestone, a tire manufacturer? Do you now have the same confidence in the objectivity of the results? Probably not, which suggests that the source is one criterion for evaluating the accuracy of secondary data.

Research that has been collected in such a way that the results will support a particular position is often referred to as advocacy research. With **advocacy research,** the goal is to support a position, not to uncover the truth about an issue. Researchers pursuing this type of research may word questions in such a way that they get the answers they want; select a nonrepresentative sample (e.g., only surveying people known to support the position the researcher wants); or any number of other unethical practices.

This doesn't mean that all data collected or sponsored by an interested party should automatically be rejected as advocacy research. Instead, we simply suggest that such data should be viewed critically by the research user. A source that publishes secondary data as its primary function deserves confidence. Companies whose primary business is to publish secondary data must maintain high quality. Inaccurate data offer such a firm no competitive advantage, and their publication represents a potential loss of confidence and eventual demise. The success of any organization supplying data as its primary purpose depends on the long-run satisfaction by its users that the information supplied is indeed accurate.

secondary source
A source of secondary data that did not originate the data but rather secured them from another source.

advocacy research
Research conducted to support a position rather than to find the truth about an issue.

Using the Source to Evaluate the Accuracy of Secondary Data

A. Advertising Medicine to Consumers

According to a recent survey, almost one-third of respondents have talked to a doctor about a treatment they saw advertised. Of those who asked their doctor for a drug they saw advertised, half were given a prescription for it. Three-quarters of respondents said ads for prescription drugs showed both the risks and benefits of the medicine. The survey was released at a time when the Food and Drug Administration was preparing new guidelines for advertising prescription drugs directly to consumers (rather than promoting them only to physicians).

B. Home Handymen

Home handymen play a significant role in millions of purchasing decisions, a new study finds. According to the study, 18 million "must-know" men affect what is bought by as many as 85 million other consumers. The study says that such men—independent do-it-yourselfers who have a compulsion to know what makes things tick and enjoy fiddling with gadgets—are sought for their advice by buyers of products in such areas as home improvement and electronics.

C. Americans and Their Cars

How strong are Americans' love affairs with their cars? A surprising 38 percent of the men surveyed recently by a Nashville research firm declared that they love their cars more than women. Nearly 8 percent of the women surveyed said that men who drove nice cars are more appealing, and roughly 15 percent of the respondents had even gone so far as to name their cars. ■

Source: Example A: David Goetzl, "Second Magazine Study Touts Value of DTC Drug Ads," *Advertising Age* (June 28, 1999), p. 22; Example B: "Just Ask the Man Who Has Taken One Apart," *The Wall Street Journal* (September 20, 1991), p. B1; Example C: "The 'Other Woman' May Be His Volvo," *The Wall Street Journal* (June 24, 1994), p. B1.

General Evidence of Quality   The third criterion by which the accuracy of secondary data can be assessed is through the general evidence of quality. One way of determining this quality is to evaluate the ability of the supplying organization to collect the data. The Internal Revenue Service, for example, has greater leverage in securing income data than an independent marketing research firm. However, researchers also have to weigh whether this additional leverage may introduce bias. Would a respondent be more likely to hedge in estimating her income in completing her tax return or in responding to a consumer survey?

In judging the quality of secondary data, a user also needs to understand how the data were collected. A primary source should provide a detailed description of the data collection process, including definitions, data collection forms, method of sampling, and so forth. If it does not, be careful! Such omissions are usually indicative of sloppy methods (at best) or advocacy research (at worst).

When the details of data collection are provided, the user of secondary data should examine them thoroughly. Was the sampling plan sound? Was this type of data best collected through questionnaire or by observational methods? What about the quality of the field force? What kind of training was provided? What kinds of checks of the fieldwork were used? What was the extent of nonresponse due to refusals, not at homes, and by item? Are these statistics reported? Is the information presented in a well-organized manner? Are the tables properly labeled, and are the data within them internally consistent? Are the conclusions supported by the data? As these questions suggest, the user of secondary data must be familiar with the research process and the potential sources of error. The remainder of this book provides much of the needed insight for evaluating secondary data. For the moment, however, let us examine some of the main types of secondary data.

Types of Secondary Data: Internal and External

The most common way of classifying data is by source, whether internal or external. **Internal data** are those found within the organization for whom the research is being done, while

external data are those obtained from outside sources. The external sources can be further split into those that regularly publish statistics and make them available to the user at no charge (e.g., the U.S. government), and those commercial organizations that sell their services to various users (e.g., ACNielsen). In the remainder of this chapter and its appendix we will review some of the main types and sources of published statistics; in the next chapter we will review some of the more important sources of commercial statistics. Together they represent some of the most commonly used sources of secondary data, the ones with which the researcher would typically begin a search. Figure 7.1 provides an overview of these sources.

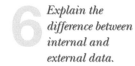

6 Explain the difference between internal and external data.

internal data
Data that originate within the organization for which the research is being done.

external data
Data that originate outside the organization for which the research is being done.

Internal Secondary Data

Internal data that were collected for some purpose other than the study at hand are internal secondary data. For example, the sales and cost data compiled in the normal accounting cycle represent promising internal secondary data for many research problems—such as evaluation of past marketing strategy or assessment of the firm's competitive position in the industry. Such data are less helpful in guiding future-oriented decisions, such as evaluating a new product or a new advertising campaign, but even here they can serve as a foundation for planning other research.

Generally, for manufacturers the one most productive source document is the sales invoice. From this, the following information can usually be extracted:

- Customer name and location
- Product(s) or service(s) sold
- Volume and dollar amount of the transaction
- Salesperson (or agent) responsible for the sale
- End use of the product sold
- Location of customer facility where product is to be shipped and/or used
- Customer's industry, class of trade, and/or channel of distribution

Figure 7.1

Types of Secondary Data

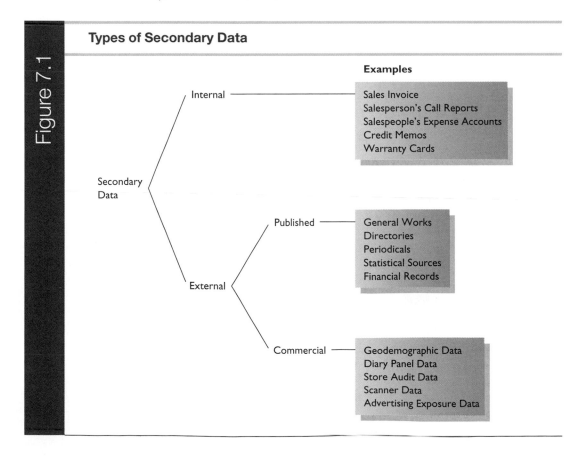

Examples

Secondary Data

Internal — Sales Invoice / Salesperson's Call Reports / Salespeople's Expense Accounts / Credit Memos / Warranty Cards

External

Published — General Works / Directories / Periodicals / Statistical Sources / Financial Records

Commercial — Geodemographic Data / Diary Panel Data / Store Audit Data / Scanner Data / Advertising Exposure Data

- Terms of sale and applicable discount
- Freight paid and/or to be collected
- Shipment point for the order
- Transportation used in shipment

Other documents provide more specialized input. Some of the more important of these are listed in Exhibit 7.3. Most companies are likely to use only two or three of these sources of sales information in addition to the sales invoice. Those used depend on the company and the types of analyses used to plan and evaluate the marketing effort. Even something as simple as a product registration card can be used to advantage for marketing intelligence, as Research Window 7.2 indicates.

Another useful, but often overlooked, source of internal secondary data is prior marketing research studies on related topics. While each study typically addresses a number of specific questions, most also involve only one or two key learnings. There can be great synergy when these key learnings are studied and combined. As Larry Stanek, while director of marketing research at Kraft, commented:

> Combining key learnings can help you develop a competitive advantage for your company. By examining your combined learnings you may discover things that other companies have yet to learn. Or you can learn to be more productive or cost effective and lower your research costs. Or you may learn something that helps you skip steps or speeds your development process.[6]

Exhibit 7.3

Some Useful Sources of Internal Secondary Data

Document	Information Provided
Cash register receipts	Type (cash or credit) and dollar amount of transaction by department by salesperson
Salesperson's call reports	Customers and prospects called on (company and individual seen; planned or unplanned calls)
	Products discussed
	Orders obtained
	Customer's product needs and usage
	Other significant information about customers
	Distribution of salesperson's time among customer calls, travel, and office work
	Sales-related activities: meetings, conventions, etc.
Salesperson's expense accounts	Expenses by day by item (hotel, meals, travel, etc.)
Individual customer (and prospect) records	Name and location and customer number
	Number of calls by company salespersons (agents)
	Sales by company (in dollars and/or units, by product or service, by location of customer facility)
	Customer's industry, class of trade, and/or trade channel
	Estimated total annual usage of each product or service sold by the company
	Estimated annual purchases from the company of each such product or service
	Location (in terms of company sales territory)
Financial records	Sales revenue (by products, geographic markets, customers, class of trade, unit of sales organization, etc.)
	Direct sales expenses (similarly classified)
	Overhead sales costs (similarly classified)
	Profits (similarly classified)
Credit memos	Returns and allowances
Warranty cards	Indirect measures of dealer sales
	Customer service

Targeting: It's in the Cards

When the Skil Corporation was launching a cordless power screwdriver, management was worried. It believed that the company had designed a useful product, but it wondered whether consumers would think the new tool was just a gimmick. Using information from product registration cards and follow-up interviews, Skil was quickly able to prove to itself that the screwdriver was not a fad.

The registration card research revealed something else, however. Although do-it-yourselfers were the primary market for the new product, a substantial portion of the purchases were elderly people for whom the screwdriver's ease of operation was the chief advantage. "We hadn't realized the arthritis implications," says Skil's Ron Techter. In response, Skil began advertising in publications geared to older Americans.

Almost everyone has filled out a product registration card. As they slip the card into the mailbox, few consumers realize that they have just completed a questionnaire. Yet for National Demographics & Lifestyles (NDL), the information from product registration cards has been pure gold. NDL compiles information from these "mini-questionnaires" to feed its comprehensive data base, which includes demographics and participation information covering 57 activities, interests, and lifestyles.

According to Jock Bickert, the company's founder, NDL data offer no special advantage at a national level, because a marketer can survey 1,500 or 2,000 consumers to obtain national projections. However, NDL's data base is very powerful when one moves down to individual markets, neighborhoods, or even postal routes.

One company that has made effective use of NDL's data is Amana Appliance. One day Bill Packard, domestic sales manager for an independent Amana Appliance distributor in Fort Lauderdale was talking with Amana's manager of marketing services, Dave Collins. Collins mentioned that Amana could provide Packard with profiles of Amana purchasers from his territory for the past year and a half based on NDL product-registration cards. When the NDL profile arrived, Packard got an idea.

He took the information to the marketing director of a Boca Raton real estate developer who was trying to decide what brand of appliances to put into his $200,000 homes. Packard pointed out that the purchaser profile of high-end Amana products perfectly matched the developer's profile of potential customers. Initially skeptical, the marketing director polled 100 potential home buyers himself. These homebuyer profiles so closely matched Amana's that the developer decided to use Amana appliances in the kitchens.

"If you look at one of our completed questionnaires," says NDL's Bickert, "you really begin to get a picture of the individual. You are able to say, 'This person is a likely candidate for these kinds of offers and promotions and appeals and is very unlikely for other kinds.' You can't do that if you are looking at demography alone." ■

Source: Wally Wood, "Targeting: It's in the Cards," *Marketing & Media Decisions* 23 (September 1988), pp. 121–122. See also Robert Bengen, "Teamwork: It's in the Bag," *Marketing Research: A Magazine of Management & Applications* 5 (Winter 1993), pp. 30–33, for discussion of how Samsonite uses warranty cards along with other information to improve its marketing.

Internal secondary data are the least costly (and most readily available) of any type of marketing research. If maintained in an appropriate form, internal sales data can be used to analyze the company's past sales performance by product, geographic location, customer, channel of distribution, and so on, while cost data help in determining how profitable these segments of the business are. This type of information typically forms the basis of a firm's marketing intelligence system. We shall not go into the details of this type of analysis here because it is a somewhat specialized topic and is extensively reported elsewhere. Most studies should begin with internal secondary data.

Searching for Published External Secondary Data

There is such a wealth of external data, that beginning researchers typically underestimate what is available. There is likely to be relevant external secondary data on almost any problem a marketer might confront. The fundamental problem is not availability; it is identifying and

ETHICAL dilemma 7.1

An independent marketing research firm was hired by a manufacturer of power equipment, including lawn mowers, snowblowers, and chain saws, to study the Minneapolis market. The manufacturer wanted to determine (1) whether there was sufficient market potential to warrant opening a new dealership, and (2) if so, where the dealership should be located in the metropolitan area. The research firm went about the task by scouring secondary data on the Minneapolis market, particularly statistics published by the Census Bureau. In less than two months, the research firm was able to develop a well-documented recommendation as to what the power equipment manufacturer should do.

Approximately six months after completing this study, the research firm has been approached by a manufacturer of electric power tools to do a similar study concerning the location of a distribution center through which it could more effectively serve the many hardware stores in the area.

- *Is it ethical for the research firm to use the information it collected in the first study to reduce its cost quote to the client in the second?*

- *Does it make any difference if the firm making electric power tools also manufactures electric lawn mowers and chain saws?*

- *Suppose some of the data were collected through personal interviews that the first client paid for. Should that affect the situation in any way?*

accessing what is there. Even researchers who do have an inkling of how much valuable secondary data exists are typically unsure of how to go about searching for it. Figure 7.2 provides some guidelines that can be used to get started on a search of secondary data on a particular topic.[7]

Step 1 The first step in the process is to identify what you want to know and what you already know about your topic. This may include relevant facts, names of researchers or organizations associated with the topic, key papers and other publications with which you are already familiar, and any other information you may have.

Step 2 A useful second step is to develop a list of key terms and authors. These terms and names will provide access to secondary sources. Unless you have a very specific topic of interest, it is better to keep this initial list long and quite general.

Step 3 In Step 3, you are ready to use the library or the Internet for the first time. It is useful to begin your search with several of the directories and guides listed in Appendix 7A or Web sites that deal with the subject. A relatively new way to identify information sources on the Internet is to start with an InfoTech Marketing Web site called "The Sales and Marketing Source" (http://www.smsource.com). It offers hundreds of links to sites that InfoTech has reviewed for relevancy to marketing issues, including published reports, newspapers and magazines, government data sources, and sources of data about specific companies. Some of the links are to free data.

Step 4 Now it is time to compile the literature you have found. Is it relevant to your needs? You may be overwhelmed by information at this point, or you may have found little that is relevant. If you need more information, rework your list of key words and authors and expand your search to include a few more years and a few additional sources. Once again, evaluate your findings. By the end of Step 4, you should have a clear idea of the nature of the information you are seeking and sufficient background to use more specialized sources.

Step 5 One very useful specialized source is a reference librarian. Reference librarians are specialists who have been trained to know the contents of many of the key information sources in a library and on the Web, as well as how to search those sources most effectively. A reference librarian can usually uncover information that is relevant to your current problem. The reference librarian will need your help, however, in the form of a carefully constructed list of key words or topics. You need to remember that the reference librarian cannot be of much help until you can provide specific details about what you want to know.

Step 6 If you have had little success or your topic is highly specialized, consult one of the general guides to information listed in Appendix 7A. These are really directories of directo-

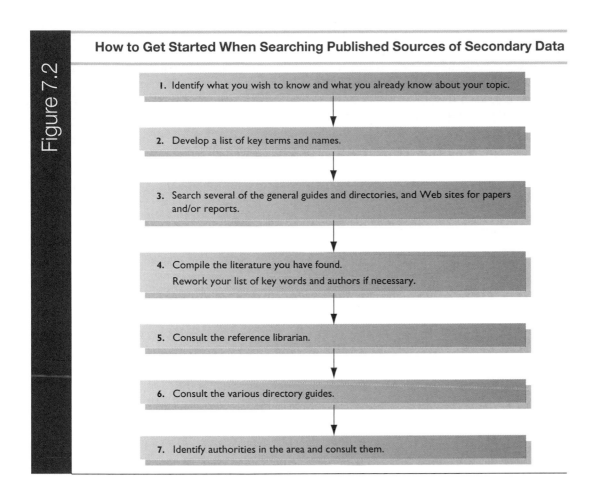

Figure 7.2

How to Get Started When Searching Published Sources of Secondary Data

1. Identify what you wish to know and what you already know about your topic.

2. Develop a list of key terms and names.

3. Search several of the general guides and directories, and Web sites for papers and/or reports.

4. Compile the literature you have found.
   Rework your list of key words and authors if necessary.

5. Consult the reference librarian.

6. Consult the various directory guides.

7. Identify authorities in the area and consult them.

ries, which means that this level of search will be very general. You will first need to identify potentially useful primary directories, which will then lead you to other sources.

Step 7 If you are unhappy with what you have found or are otherwise having trouble, and the reference librarian has not been able to identify sources, use an authority. Identify some individual or organization that might know something about the topic. The *Consultants and Consulting Organizations Directory, Encyclopedia of Associations, Industrial Research Laboratories in the United States,* or *Research Centers Directory* may help you identify sources. The Bureau of the Census puts out a list of department specialists whom users can contact for information on any of the bureau's studies. These people are often quite knowledgeable about related studies in their areas of expertise. Faculty at universities, government officials, and business executives can also be useful sources of information.

Some Key General Sources of External Secondary Data

In addition to the key role played by reference librarians, some important sources of external secondary data are associations, general guides to useful marketing information, and online computer searches.

List some of the key sources researchers should consider in conducting a search process.

Associations Most associations gather and often publish detailed information on such things as industry shipments and sales, growth patterns, environmental factors affecting the industry, operating characteristics, etc. Trade associations can often secure information from members that other research organizations cannot, because of the working relationships that exist between the association and the firms that belong to it. Two useful sources for locating associations serving a particular industry are the *Directories in Print* and the *Encyclopedia of Associations,* described in Appendix 7A.

General Guides to Secondary Data The general guides to secondary data are also described in Appendix 7A. Exhibit 7.4, for example, lists what the *Encyclopedia of Business Information Sources* says about data sources on the electronic security systems industry. Aspiring researchers should also become familiar with the more important general sources of marketing information so that they know what statistics are available and where they can be found. Many of the most important of these are listed and briefly described in Appendix 7A.

Online Computer Searches Online computer searches have become increasingly popular for locating published information and data in the past 20 years, as computer-readable storage systems for databases have come into their own. Many public libraries, as well as college and university libraries, have invested in the equipment and personnel necessary to make

---

Exhibit 7.4

Sources of Data on the Electronic Security Systems Industry

ELECTRONIC SECURITY SYSTEMS

See also: INDUSTRIAL SECURITY PROGRAMS

DIRECTORIES

Automotive Burglary Protection and Mechanical Equipment Directory. Underwriters Laboratories, Inc. • Annual. $10.00. Lists manufacturers authorized to use UL label.

National Burglar and Fire Alarm Association Members Services Directory. National Burglar and Fire Alarm Association. • Annual. Membership. Names and addresses of about 4,000 alarm security companies. Formerly *National Burglar and Fire Alarm Association-Directory of Members.*

Security Distributing and Marketing-Security Products and Services Locator. Cahners Business Information. • Annual. $50.00. Formerly *SDM: Security Distributing and Marketing-Security Products and Services Directory.*

Security: Product Service Suppliers Guide. Cahners Business Information. • Annual. $50.00. Includes computer and information protection products. Formerly *Security—World Product Directory.*

HANDBOOKS AND MANUALS

Burglar Alarm Sales and Installation. Entrepreneur Media, Inc. • Looseleaf. $59.50. A practical guide to starting a burglar alarm service. Covers profit potential, start-up costs, market size evaluation, owner's time required, pricing, accounting, advertising, promotion, etc. (Start-Up Business Guide No. E1091.).

Effective Physical Security: Design, Equipment, and Operations. Lawrence J. Fennelly, editor. Butterworth-Heinemann. • 1996. $36.95. Second edition. Contains chapters written by various U.S. security equipment specialists. Covers architectural considerations, locks, safes, alarms, intrusion detection systems, closed circuit television, identification systems, etc.

PERIODICALS AND NEWSLETTERS

9-1-1 Magazine: Public Safety Communications and Response. Official Publications, Inc. • Bimonthly. $31.95 per year. Covers technical information and applications for public safety communications personnel.

Security Distributing and Marketing. Cahners Business Information. • 13 times a year. $82.00 per year. Covers applications, merchandising, new technology and management.

Security Management. American Society for Industrial Security. • Monthly. Free to members; non-members, $48.00 per year. Articles cover the protection of corporate assets, including personnel property and information security.

Security Systems Administration. Cygnus Business Media. • Monthly. $10.00 per year.

Security: The Magazine for Buyers of Security Products, Systems and Service. Cahners Business Information. • Monthly. $82.90 per year.

TRADE/PROFESSIONAL ASSOCIATIONS

ASIS International (American Society for Industrial Security). 1625 Prince St., Alexandria, VA 22314-2818. Phone: (703)519-6200 Fax (703)519-6299. URL: http://www.asisonline.org.

Automatic Fire Alarm Association. P.O. Box 951807, Lake Mary, FL 32795-1807. Phone: (407)322-6288 Fax: (407)322-7488. • URL: http://www.afaa.org.

Central Station Alarm Association, 440 Maple Ave., Suite 201, Vienna, VA 22180-4723. Phone (703)242-4670 Fax (703)242-4675 E-mail: communications@csaaul.org.

National Burglar and Fire Alarm Association. 8300 Colesville Rd., Ste. 750, Silver Spring, MD 20910. Phone: (301)907-3202 Fax: (301)907-7897 E-mail: staff@alarm.org • URL: http://www.alarm.org.

Source: James Woy, ed., *Encyclopedia of Business Information Sources,* 16th Edition (Detroit: Gale, 2002) p. 282.

database searching available to their patrons. There are now thousands of databases to choose from, with many of them applying to business. Companies use online databases to search for journal articles, reports, speeches, marketing data, economic trends, legislation, inventions, and many other types of information on a particular topic.

When accessing a database online, users typically pay whether they get the answer or not. The more information they get, the more they pay. The overall cost of using an on-line database may include: (1) planning and executing the search, (2) telephone-line charges, (3) connect charges, and (4) citation and printing charges. The big advantage of on-line searching is time savings. Some of the more well known database vendors are Dialog (a subsidiary of Thompson), Dow Jones, Knight/Ridder, and Lexis/Nexis.

Databases are typically defined by the type of information they contain. For example, bibliographic databases provide references to magazine or journal articles. They will list the name of the article, the author, the title of the journal, and the date of publication. They are likely to include some key words that describe the contents of the article. Most bibliographic databases also provide an abstract or summary of the article. Some of the useful databases for marketers are included in Appendix 7A.

In addition to using online databases, researchers can use the Internet for general searches of the World Wide Web to locate secondary data on a subject. To do so requires Web access through an access provider and one or more search engines. Search engines are needed because the Internet contains many billions of words in documents that are not arranged for retrieval. Creators of search engines compile and index an electronic catalog of Web contents, then provide the software needed to search through the index for key words or concepts specified by the user. The most popular search engine is Google (http://www.google.com), which currently processes more than 150 million searches a day in 74 languages in 32 countries.[8]

Courtesy of Google.com.

Google, the most popular search engine, can help researchers locate secondary data.

ETHICAL dilemma 7.2

A marketing manager for a dog food manufacturer stumbled onto an important piece of competitive intelligence while visiting a local printer near her company's plant. While waiting to speak with the salesperson that handled her company's account, the manager noticed some glossy advertising proofs for one of its competitor's products. The ad highlighted some new low prices. When she mentioned the prices to the printer, she was told that they were part of a new advertising campaign. On her return to headquarters, the marketing manager called a meeting of her own company's management. As a result of that meeting, the company initiated a preemptive, price-cutting campaign of its own that effectively neutralized the competitor's strategy.

- *Did the marketing manager act ethically in reporting the information back to her own company?*

- *Would your judgment be different if the proofs were in a folder and the marketing manager casually and somewhat inadvertently opened the folder while standing there? What if she did so on purpose after noticing that the folder pertained to the competitor?*

- *Should information like this be entered into the firm's decision support system?*

For such a significant move as targeting what may become the largest minority group in the United States (Hispanic persons), banks are getting marketing research data from a variety of sources.

They are starting with government census data. This is what highlighted the opportunity in the first place, and it details where the market potential is greatest.

They are getting further insight and help from companies that specialize in marketing to Hispanics. Bank of America hired López Negrete, which is advising the company to take a three-pronged approach: identifying and providing relevant products, communicating in both English and Spanish, and "earning the right to do business with the community" through support of the community's interests.

Bank of America has also reviewed published research reports on Hispanic consumers, in particular their use of banking services. For example, the bank learned from a firm called EPM Communications that half of Hispanic consumers would use more banking services if they had a clearer understanding of their choices. Almost two-thirds of the consumers told the researchers that they wanted better financial advice from their banks.

Some of the actions Bank of America has taken include staffing a customer service line with Spanish-speaking representatives, offering a choice of language at ATMs, seeking branch employees who reflect the area's demographics, and funding scholarships for minority students at the University of Dallas.

Wells Fargo & Company, based in San Francisco, sponsored a study to learn more about the needs of Hispanic-owned businesses. The study report, titled "Latino Owned Businesses: Access to Capital," told bank management that Hispanic business owners are much less likely than other business owners to have enough capital.

The bank determined that this was a business opportunity and launched a joint program with the United States Hispanic Chamber of Commerce, in which the bank committed to lending $1 billion to Hispanic-owned businesses over a six-year period. The lending process is designed to be simple, and applications are available in a choice of English or Spanish. Wells Fargo's first year of experience with the program showed that a real demand exists. Lending through the program exceeded the bank's first-year forecast by 10 percent.

In Oklahoma, First Bethany's consultant, Jorge Esperilla, has contributed insights into Mexican culture and banking practices. (Most Hispanics in the area are of Mexican descent.) Esperilla observed that banks are less central to Hispanics than to other Americans, and that Hispanics have tended to avoid credit. Based on the results of his consulting work, and in his more recent role as president of First Bethany's new facility for Hispanic customers, Esperilla has developed a strategy. He emphasizes building ties to the local Hispanic community and educating them about the services the bank offers.

The combination of government data, published research, commissioned studies, and work by consultants and marketing specialists has equipped banks for their race to obtain a share of the important Hispanic market. ■

Sources: Barbara Powell, "Texas Banks Want to Reach Minority Markets, But Not All Know How," *Fort Worth Star-Telegram* (April 5, 1999, downloaded from Dow Jones Publications Library at the Dow Jones Web site, http://www.dowjones.com, August 5, 1999); "Bank of America Hires Ad Agencies to Target Ethnic Segments," press release (July 1, 1999, downloaded from Bank of America Web site, http://www.bankofamerica.com, August 10, 1999); "Wells Fargo Exceeds Expectations, Lends $184 Million to Hispanic Business Owners in First Year of Latino Loan Program," press release (December 1, 1998, downloaded from Wells Fargo & Company Web site, http://www.wellsfargo.com, August 10, 1999); Gregory Potts, "Banking on the Hispanic Market," *The Journal Record* (May 26, 1998, downloaded from the Northern Light Internet site, http://www.northernlight.com, August 10, 1999); Gene Taylor, "Remarks at Hispanic Association on Corporate Responsibility," President's Breakfast Keynote, speech delivered June 12, 1998, in Miami, Florida (downloaded from Bank of America Web site, http://www.bankofamerica.com, August 10, 1999); Hugh Graham, "Annals of Marketing: Don't Go Changin'," *Globe and Mail* (September 25, 1998, downloaded from Dow Jones Publications Library at the Dow Jones Web site, http://www.dowjones.com, August 10, 1999).

Summary

Learning Objective 1

Explain the difference between primary and secondary data.

Secondary data are statistics not gathered for the immediate study, but for some other purpose. Primary data are originated by the researcher for the purpose of the investigation at hand.

Learning Objective 2

Cite two advantages offered by secondary data.

The most significant advantages offered by secondary data are time savings and money savings for the researcher.

Learning Objective 3

Specify two problems common to secondary data.

Two problems that commonly arise when secondary data are used are (1) they do not completely fit the problem, and (2) they are not completely accurate.

Learning Objective 4

List the three criteria researchers should use in judging the accuracy of secondary data.

The three criteria researchers should use in judging the accuracy of secondary data are (1) the source, (2) the purpose of publication, and (3) general evidence regarding the quality of the data.

Learning Objective 5

State the most fundamental rule in using secondary data.

The most fundamental rule in using secondary data is to always use the primary source of secondary data.

Learning Objective 6

Explain the difference between internal and external data.

Internal data are those found within the organization for which the research is being done, while external data are those obtained from outside sources.

Learning Objective 7

List some of the key sources researchers should consider in conducting a search process.

The key sources researchers should keep in mind in conducting a search process are reference librarians, associations, online computer searches, and general guides to useful marketing information.

Key Terms

secondary data (page 162)
primary data (page 162)
primary source (page 164)
secondary source (page 165)

advocacy research (page 165)
internal data (page 167)
external data (page 167)

Review Questions

1. What is the difference between primary and secondary data?
2. What are the advantages and disadvantages of secondary data?
3. What criteria can be used to judge the accuracy of secondary data?
4. What is the difference between a primary source and a secondary source of secondary data? Which is preferred? Why?
5. What distinguishes internal secondary data from external secondary data?
6. How would you go about searching the secondary data on a particular topic?
7. How would you perform an online computer search? What types of information would you be hoping to find?

Discussion Questions, Problems, and Projects

1. List some major secondary sources of information for the following situations:
(a) The marketing research manager of a national soft-drink manufacturer has to prepare a comprehensive report on the soft-drink industry.
(b) Mr. Baker has several ideas for instant cake mixes and is considering entering this industry. He needs to find the necessary background information to assess its potential.
(c) Mr. Adams has heard that the profit margins in the fur business are high. The fur industry has always intrigued him, and he decides to do some research to determine if the claim is true.
(d) A recent graduate hears that condominiums are the homes of the future. She decides to collect some information on the condominium market.
(e) Owning a grocery store has been Mrs. Smith's dream, and she finally decides to make it a reality. The first step she wishes to take is to collect information on the grocery business in her hometown.

2. For many years, Home Decorating Products had been a leading producer of paint and painting-related equipment such as brushes, rollers, turpentine, and so on. The company is now considering adding wallpaper to its line. At least initially, it did not intend to actually manufacture the wallpaper but, rather, to subcontract the manufacturing. Home Decorating Products would assume the distribution and marketing functions.

Before adding wallpaper to its product line, however, Home Decorating secured some secondary data assessing the size of the wallpaper market. One mail survey made by a trade association showed that, on the average, families in the United States wallpapered two rooms in their homes each year. Among these families, 60 percent did it themselves. Another survey, which had also been done by mail but by one of the major home magazines, found that 70 percent of the subscribers answering the questionnaire had wallpapered one complete wall or more during the last 12 months. Among these families, 80 percent had done the wallpapering themselves. Home Decorating Products thus has two sets of secondary data on the same problem, but the data are not consistent.

Discuss the data in terms of the criteria one would use to determine which set, if either, is correct. Assume that you are forced to make the determination on the basis of this information. Which would you choose?

3. Assume that your school is interested in developing a marketing plan to boost sagging attendance at major athletic events, particularly home football games. As an initial step in developing the new marketing plan, the athletic department has decided that it needs demographic and lifestyle profiles of people who currently attend games on a regular (season-ticket) basis. Fortunately, the ticket office maintains a listing of all season-ticket purchasers (including names and addresses) from year to year. What potential sources of internal secondary data might the athletic department first investigate before considering the collection of primary data?

4. Using the 2001 U.S. *Statistical Abstract* answer the following questions:
(a) Which metropolitan statistical area in the United States has the largest population (based on 2000 numbers)?
(b) What is the population of this metropolitan area?
(c) What was the estimated median age of the U.S. population in 2000?
(d) Complete the following table:

Marital Status of U.S. Population	2000 (million)	Percent of Total
Total		
Never Married		
Married		
Widowed		
Divorced		

(e) Complete the following table on school enrollment for 1999.

18–19 years old	20–21 years old	25–29 years old

(f) Complete the following table:

Income Category	# All Households 1999
Under $10,000	
$10,000 to $14,999	
$15,000 to $24,999	
$25,000 to $34,999	
$35,000 to $49,999	
$50,000 to $74,999	
$75,000 and over	

(g) What was the Consumer Price Index for all items in 2000? What was the base year? What does that indicate?

5. The *Statistical Abstract* is a secondary source of secondary data. Since it is always better to use the primary source, identify the primary source for the following data:
   (a) The estimated median age of the U.S. population for 2000.
   (b) The height of males and females ages 20–29.
   (c) The Consumer Price Indexes by major groups.
   (d) The manufacturing corporations' profits, stockholders' equity, sales, and debt ratios.

6. John Smith is interested in becoming a wholesaler in household appliances. He has collected some general information but requires your help in finding answers to the following questions:
   (a) What is the North American Industry Classification System (NAICS) code for household appliance manufacturers?
   (b) How many retail establishments sell household appliances in the United States?
   (c) What are the total sales of all the retail establishments?
   Instead of attempting to handle all household appliances, John is considering specializing in household refrigerators and freezers.
   (d) What are the total number of establishments manufacturing household refrigerators and freezers?
   (e) How many wholesale establishments are there in the United States dealing in this category?
   John thinks that Dayton, Ohio, would be a profitable place to locate. He needs to know the following:
   (f) What is the total population of Dayton?
   (g) What is the total civilian labor force in Dayton?
   (h) How many persons are employed in Dayton?
   (i) In what county is Dayton, Ohio located? What is the total number of furniture and home furnishing stores within this county?
   (Hint: To complete this exercise, refer to the *Economic Census: Manufacturing Sector; Retail Trade Sector; Wholesale Trade Sector;* and *County and City Databook.*)

7. Interview representatives of your local media outlets (e.g., radio stations, television stations, and newspapers) and determine the extent to which they use sources of standardized marketing information. You may wish to use the following questions as a guideline for your interviews:
   (a) Which sources do they use?
   (b) What specific types of information do they obtain?
   (c) How do they use the information?
   (d) How important is the information in the conduct of their business?
   (e) How do they rate the accuracy of the information?
   (f) Do they supplement the standardized information with locally collected primary data?

8. Assume that you have recently begun work as a researcher with a very large management consulting organization. One of your first assignments is to prepare a thorough profile of a specific industry

based on secondary data. For a significant industry of your choosing, develop such a profile. Your report should contain industry information related to major products, largest producers, primary inputs on the supply side, NAICS codes, unions, trade magazines, and other information you feel is useful (including financial information). The information should be addressed to other business-people—not academicians—and should be presented in a readable manner using a format similar to the following:

    I Executive Summary (including a synopsis of your opinion on the state of the industry along with the reasons for your opinion)
   II Major Industry Competitors (including financial information)
  III Major Industry Products (including export information)
  IV Primary Industry Inputs (including import information)
   V Human Resource/Labor Unions
  VI Ownership Trends
 VII Technology
VIII Governmental Regulation

Include two special exhibits with your profile—a chronology showing important events in the history of the industry, especially during the past ten years; and a flowchart of a typical firm in the industry showing inputs, primary products, channels of distribution, major customers, and so on.

You are encouraged to use as many sources as possible, including financial databases, business periodicals, and government reports. Prepare a complete bibliography of all sources used in preparing your report. In addition, carefully identify all sources throughout your report, including sources for graphs and charts.

Suggested Additional Readings

For a general discussion of secondary data sources and how to go about finding secondary data, see David W. Stewart and Michael A. Kamins, *Secondary Research: Information Sources and Methods,* 2d ed. (Thousand Oaks, CA: Sage Publications, 1993).

Secondary Data Sources

There is so much published secondary data that it is impossible to mention all of it in a single appendix. Thus, we present only a representative cross section of the available material. These secondary sources are organized into six sections, according to the type of information they contain. Several sources of electronic online search services are included. First, however, a brief discussion of governmental sources of secondary data is presented.

Census Data and Other Government Publications: Overview

The Bureau of the Census of the United States Department of Commerce is the largest gatherer of statistical information in the world. The original census was the Census of Population, which was required by the Constitution to serve as a basis for apportioning representation in the House of Representatives. The first censuses were merely head counts. Not only has the Census of Population been expanded, but the whole census machinery has also been enlarged. At this point there are nine different censuses, all of which are of interest to the marketing researcher. Exhibit 7.1, for example, listed some of the most useful data on population and housing that are available in the Census of Population. Exhibit 7A.1 lists some of the most useful data that are collected in the various economic censuses described in the following sections.

Census data are of generally high quality. Further, they are quite often available on the detailed level that the researcher needs. When data are not available in this form, researchers can create their own tabulations by purchasing data from the Bureau of the Census for a nominal fee. Alternatively, researchers can contract with one of the private companies that market census-related products for information on a particular issue. Not only does this get the information tailored to one's own needs, but it is also one of the fastest ways to get census data. Further, many of the private providers update the census data at a detailed geographic level for the between-census years.

There are two major drawbacks to the use of census data: (1) censuses are not taken every year, and (2) the delay from time of collection to time of publication is quite substantial, often two years or more. This last weakness, necessary because of the massive editing, coding, and tabulation tasks involved, makes the data obsolete for many research problems. The first difficulty requires that the researcher supplement the census data with current data. Unfortunately, current data are rarely available in the detail the researcher desires. This is particularly true with

respect to detailed classifications by small geographic area, unless one takes advantage of the services of a private provider with update capability.

The federal government also collects and publishes a great deal of statistical information in addition to the censuses. Some of this material is designed to supplement the various censuses and is gathered and published for this purpose (e.g., Current Population Reports), whereas other data are generated in the normal course of operations, such as collecting taxes, social security payments, claims for unemployment benefits, and so forth.

Industry Information

Almanac of Business and Industrial Financial Ratios (Englewood Cliffs, N.J.: Prentice-Hall) This publication contains the number of establishments, sales, and selected operating ratios for various industries (e.g., food stores). The figures are derived from tax return data supplied by the Internal Revenue Service and are reported for 12 categories, based on assets, within each industry. The data thus allow the comparison of a particular company's financial ratios with competitors of similar size.

Business & Industry (Detroit: Gale Group) This database provides access to over 600 business journals and trade publications, covering over 200 countries. All articles have extensive abstracts, and over 60 percent contain the full text as well.

© PhotoDisc/Getty Images

The assistance of Steven M. Locy and John B. Phillips of Oklahoma State University's Edmon Low Library in revising this appendix is gratefully acknowledged.

Exhibit 7A.1

Information Available from Economic Censuses

	Manufacturing	Mining	Construction	Retail Trade	Wholesale Trade	Management of Companies	All Other Sectors
Number of establishments and firms							
All establishments	√	√	√	√	√	√	√
Establishments with payroll	√	√	√	√	√	√	√
Establishments without payroll (nonemployers)			√	√			√
Single-unit and multiunit establishments	√	√	√	√	√	√	√
Establishments by legal form of organization	√	√	√	√	√	√	√
Firms	√	√		√	√	√	√
Employment							
All employees	√	√	√	√	√	√	√
Production (construction) workers/hours	√	√	√				
Employment size of establishment	√	√	√	√	√	√	
Labor costs							
Payroll, entire year	√	√	√	√	√	√	√
Payroll, first quarter				√	√	√	√
Worker wages	√	√	√				
Supplemental costs	√	√	√	√	√	√	√
Cost of contract labor				√	√	√	√
Sales, receipts, or value of shipments/construction work done							
Establishments with payroll	√	√	√	√	√	√	√
By specific product, line, or type of construction	√	√	√	√	√		√
Sales/receipts size of establishments				√	√	√	√
Class of customer				√	√		
Type of structure			√				
E-commerce sales	√	√	√	√	√		√
Expenses							
Total				√	√		√
Cost of materials, parts, etc.	√	√	√	√	√	√	
Cost of fuels	√	√	√	√	√	√	√
Energy consumed	√	√					
Cost of electricity	√	√	√	√	√	√	√
Cost of other utilities				√	√	√	√
Products bought for resale	√	√		√	√		
Taxes and license fees				√	√	√	√
Cost of office supplies				√	√		√
Depreciation charges	√	√		√	√	√	
Commission expense					√		
Purchased services:							
Advertising	√			√	√	√	√
Rental payments	√	√	√	√	√	√	√
Legal services	√			√	√	√	√
Accounting services	√			√	√	√	√
Data processing services	√			√	√	√	√
Refuse removal	√						
Communications services	√	√	√	√	√	√	√
Purchased repairs	√		√	√	√	√	
Cost of contract work	√	√			√		
Assets, capital expenditures, inventories							
Capital expenditures, total	√	√	√				
Depreciable assets, gross value	√	√	√				
Value of inventories	√	√	√	√	√		

Census of Agriculture (U.S. Department of Agriculture: National Agricultural Statistics Service) The Census of Agriculture was formerly taken in the years ending in "4" and "9." Since 1982, it has been taken in years ending in "2" and "7." This census offers detailed breakdowns by state and county on the number of farms, farm types, acreage, land-use practices, employment, livestock produced and products raised, and value of products. Earlier data can be found in the *Census of Agriculture* compiled by the U.S. Bureau of the Census.

Census of Governments (U.S. Bureau of the Census: Government Printing Office) The *Census of Governments* presents information on the general characteristics of state and local governments, including such things as employment, size of payroll, amount of indebtedness, and operating revenues and costs. The census is taken at five-year intervals.

Economic Census (U.S. Bureau of the Census: Government Printing Office) The *Economic Census* provides a detailed portrait of the nation's economy, from the national to the local level. Released every five years, it is a major source of facts about the structure and functioning of the nation's economy. Statistics are classified according to the North American Industry Classification System (NAICS). Some of the more important sectors are:

- *Construction.* This census covers establishments primarily engaged in contract construction, in construction for sale, or in subdividing real property into lots. Statistics are provided for such things as value of inventories, total assets, and employment by state. Earlier data can be found in the *Census of Construction Industry.*
- *Manufacturing.* This census categorizes manufacturing establishments by type, using some 450 classes, and contains detailed industry and geographic statistics for such items as the number of establishments, quantity of output, value added in manufacture, capital expenditures, employment, wages, inventories, sales by customer class, and fuel, water, and energy consumption. The *Annual Survey of Manufacturers* covers the years between publications of the census, and *Current Industrial Reports* contains the monthly and annual production figures for some commodities. Earlier data can be located in *Census of Manufacturers.*
- *Mining.* Detailed geographic breakdowns for some 50 mineral industries on such things as the number of establishments, production, value of shipments, capital expenditures, cost of supplies, employment, payroll, power equipment, and water use are contained in this census. The *Minerals Yearbook,* published by the U.S. Geological Survey of the Department of the Interior, supplements the *Mining Sector Census* by providing annual data, although the two are not completely comparable because they use different classifications—an industrial classification for the Census Bureau data and

a product classification for the Geological Survey data. Earlier data can be found in the *Census of Mineral Industries* and the *Bureau of Mines.*

- *Retail Trade.* This census contains detailed statistics on the retail trade. Retail stores are classified by type of business, and statistics are presented on such things as the number of stores, total sales, employment, and payroll. The statistics are broken down by small geographic areas such as counties, cities, and standard metropolitan statistical areas. Current data pertaining to some of the information can be found in *Monthly Retail Trade.* Older data are located in the *Census of Retail Trade.*
- *Transportation and Warehousing.* Statistics from this census cover areas such as passenger travel, truck and bus inventory and use, and the warehousing and storage of goods. Yearly information can be found in the *Service Annual Survey.*
- *Wholesale Trade.* This census contains detailed statistics on the wholesale trade. For instance, it classifies wholesalers into over 150 business groups and contains statistics on the functions they perform, sales volume, warehouse space, expenses, and so forth. It presents these statistics for counties, cities, and standard metropolitan statistical areas. Current data can be found in *Monthly Wholesale Trade.* Older statistics can be found in the *Census of Wholesale Trade.*

Commodity Yearbook (New York: Commodity Research Bureau) Produced annually, this publication contains data on prices, production, exports, and stocks for approximately 100 individual commodities.

Guide to Industrial Statistics (Washington, D.C.: U.S. Bureau of the Census) A guide to the Census Bureau's programs relating to industry, including the types of statistics gathered and where these statistics are published.

Industry Norms and Key Business Ratios (Murray Hill, N.J.: Dun & Bradstreet) This annual publication provides industry norm statistics for over 800 types of businesses.

Information, Finance and Services USA: Industry Analyses, Statistics, and Leading Organizations (Detroit: Gale Group) This biannual volume provides comprehensive information on 320 industries engaged in the information, finance, and service sectors.

Manufacturing and Distribution USA: Industry Analyses, Statistics, and Leading Companies (Detroit: Gale Group) This three-volume set provides comprehensive information on manufacturing industries, the wholesale trade, and retail sector.

Mergent's Industry Review (New York: Mergent FIS) This publication provides financial information on 137 industry groups and compares the performance of top companies within each industry.

North American Industry Classification System (NAICS) (Washington, D.C., Executive Office of the President, Office of Management and Budget) The NAICS groups business establishments into industries based on the activities in which they are primarily engaged. Introduced in 1997 to replace the Standard Industrial Classification, the NAIC system has 1,170 industries and is used in the United States, Canada, and Mexico to facilitate country and North American economic analyses.

Predicast's Overview of Markets and Technology (PROMT) (New York: Information Access Co.) This database provides citations, abstracts, and some full-text articles from over 2,400 international business and trade journals, industry newsletters, and newspapers.

RMA Annual Statement Studies (Philadelphia: Robert Morris Associates) This volume provides composite financial data on over 400 manufacturers, wholesalers, retailers, service providers, and agricultural endeavors.

Standard & Poor's Industry Surveys (New York: Standard & Poor's Corp.) Organized by broad industry headings, this quarterly publication consists of detailed articles as well as charts and graphs depicting trends in 52 areas.

Standard Industrial Classification Manual (Springfield, Va.: Office of Management and Budget, National Technical Information Service) The *Standard Industrial Classification Manual* provides the basic system used for classifying industries into 11 major divisions. The SIC system was used for federal economic statistics classified by industry, but is being replaced with the *North American Industrial Classification System (NAICS)*.

U.S. Industry Profiles: The Leading 100 (Detroit: Gale Group) The 100 leading U.S. industries are described along with an industry outlook, the names of relevant associations, trade journals, statistical sources, and other sources of information.

Company Information

Directory of Corporate Affiliations (Wilmette, Ill.: National Register Publishing) An annual publication, the *Directory of Corporate Affiliations* provides a description of which companies own more than 114,000 U.S. and international corporations.

Fortune 500 Directory (New York: Time, Inc.) Published annually by the editors of *Fortune* magazine, this directory provides information on sales, assets, profits, invested capital, and employees for the 500 largest industrial corporations in the United States.

Hoover's Handbook of American Business (Austin, Tex.: Hoover's Business Press) This two-volume set profiles over

750 of the largest and fastest-growing companies in the United States. A useful "List-Lover's Compendium" is also included.

How to Find Information About Companies (Washington, D.C.: Washington Researchers, 1999) A useful guide to locating information about specific companies.

International Directory of Company Histories (New York: Gale Group) This multi-volume set compiles company histories for over 5,000 corporations worldwide and includes article citations for further reading.

Mergent's Manuals (New York: Mergent) Published annually, these eight sets of manuals contain balance sheets and income statements for individual companies and governmental units.

Million Dollar Directory (New York: Dun & Bradstreet) Published annually, this reference source lists the offices, products, sales, and number of employees for United States companies with sales volume of at least $9 million or 180 employees.

Standard & Poor's Corporation Records (New York: Standard & Poor's Corp.) *Corporation Records* provides current financial statistics, news items, and background information on approximately 12,000 publicly traded companies.

Standard & Poor's Register of Corporations, Directors and Executives (New York: Standard & Poor's Corp.) This annual publication lists officers, products, sales, addresses, telephone numbers, and employees for more than 75,000 United States and Canadian public companies and major international corporations.

Thomas Food and Beverage Market Place (Millerton, N.Y.: Grey House Publishing Co.) This three-volume set provides detailed information on more than 40,000 food-related companies. Also available on CD-ROM.

Thomas Register of American Manufacturers and Thomas Register Catalog File (New York: Thomas Publishing Co.) Published annually in paper and CD-ROM format, this multi-volume publication lists the specific manufacturers of individual products and provides information on their addresses, branch offices, and subsidiaries.

Value Line Investment Survey (New York: Value Line Publishing) This quarterly publication provides current information on 1,700 publicly traded companies. Although written with investors in mind, it offers concise yet comprehensive company information.

Market and Consumer Information

Aging America—Trends and Projections (U.S. Senate Special Committee on Aging and the American Association of

Retired Persons: Government Printing Office) This chartbook describes the sustained growth in America's elderly population expected during the next 30 years. Graphs and tables cover such areas as demographics, employment, health, and income.

Census of Housing (U.S. Bureau of the Census: Government Printing Office) The *Census of Housing* is published decennially for the years ending in "0." It was first taken in 1940 and lists such things as type of structure, size, building condition, occupancy, water and sewage facilities, monthly rent, average value, and equipment including stoves, dishwashers, air conditioners, and so on. For large metropolitan areas, it provides detailed statistics by city block. Approximately one of every 6 housing units in the nation are included in the census sample. The periods between publications of the *Census of Housing* are covered by the Bureau's *American Housing Survey*.

Census of Population (U.S. Bureau of the Census: Government Printing Office) The *Census of Population* is taken every ten years, in the years ending with "0." The census reports the population by geographic region. It also provides detailed breakdowns on such characteristics as sex, marital status, age, education, race, national origin, family size, employment and unemployment, income, and other demographic characteristics. The *Current Population Reports,* which are published annually and make use of the latest information on migrations, birth and death rates, and so forth, update the information in the *Census of Population.*

County and City Databook (U.S. Bureau of the Census: Government Printing Office) Published every five years, the *County and City Databook* serves as a convenient source of statistics gathered in the various censuses and provides breakdowns on a city and county basis. Included are statistics on such things as population, education, employment, income, housing, banking, manufacturing output and capital expenditures, retail and wholesale sales, and mineral and agricultural output.

County Business Patterns (U.S. Department of Commerce: Government Printing Office) This annual publication contains statistics on a number of businesses by type and their employments and payrolls broken down by county. These data are often quite useful in industrial market potential studies.

Data Sources for Business and Market Analysis, 4th ed., Nathalie D. Frank (Metuchen, N.J.: Scarecrow Press, 1994) An annotated guide to original statistical sources arranged by source of information rather than by topic.

Editor and Publisher Market Guide (New York: Editor and Publisher Co.) Published annually, this guide contains data on some 265 metropolitan statistical areas, including location, population, number of households, principal industries, retail sales and outlets, and climate.

A Guide to Consumer Markets (New York: The Conference Board) Issued annually, this publication contains data on the behavior of consumers in the marketplace. It includes statistics on population, employment, income, expenditure, and prices.

Rand McNally Commercial Atlas and Marketing Guide (Chicago: Rand McNally Company) Published annually, this atlas contains marketing data and maps for some 100,000 cities and towns in the United States. Included are such things as population, auto registrations, population projections, and retail trade.

State and Metropolitan Area Data Book (U.S. Department of Commerce: Government Printing Office) This book is a *Statistical Abstract* supplement put out by the Department of Commerce. It contains information on population, housing, government, manufacturing, retail and wholesale trade, and selected services by state and standard metropolitan statistical areas.

Survey of Buying Power and Media Markets (New York: Sales and Marketing Management) Published annually, this survey contains market data for states, a number of counties, cities, and standard metropolitan statistical areas. Included are statistics on population, retail sales, and household income, and a combined index of buying power for each reported geographic area.

General Economic and Statistical Information

Business Statistics (U.S. Department of Commerce: Government Printing Office) Published every two years, this publication provides a historical record of the data series appearing monthly in the *Survey of Current Business.*

Economic Indicators (Council of Economic Advisers: Government Printing Office) This monthly publication contains charts and tables of general economic data, such as gross national product, personal consumption expenditures, and other series important in measuring general economic activity. An annual supplement presenting historical and descriptive material on the sources, uses, and limitations of the data is also issued.

Economic Report of the President (U.S. Government: Government Printing Office) This publication results from the president's annual address to Congress about the general economic well-being of the country. The back portion of the report contains summary statistical tables using data collected elsewhere.

Federal Reserve Bulletin (Washington, D.C.: Federal Reserve System Board of Governors) Published monthly, this publication is an important source of financial data, including statistics on banking activity, interest rates, savings, the index of industrial production, an index of department store sales, prices, and international trade and finance.

Historical Statistics of the United States from Colonial Times to 1970 (U.S. Bureau of the Census: Government Printing Office) This volume was prepared by the Bureau of the Census to supplement the *Statistical Abstract*. The *Statistical Abstract* is one of the more important general sources for the marketing researcher. However, many figures are incomparable at various points in time because of the changes in definitions and classifications. *Historical Statistics* contains annual data on some 12,500 different series, using consistent definitions and going back to the inception of the series.

Monthly Labor Review (U.S. Bureau of Labor Statistics: Government Printing Office) This monthly publication contains statistics on employment and unemployment, labor turnover, earnings and hours worked, wholesale and retail prices, and work stoppages.

Standard & Poor's Statistical Service (New York: Standard & Poor's Corp.) A loose-leaf service periodically updated that includes government and non-government data in banking, production, price indexes, and stock price indexes.

Statistical Abstract of the United States (U.S. Bureau of the Census: Government Printing Office) This annual publication reproduces more than 1,500 tables originally published elsewhere that cover such areas as the economic, demographic, social, and political structure of the United States. The publication is intended to serve as a convenient statistical reference and as a guide to more detailed statistics. The latter function is fulfilled through references to the original sources in the introductory comments to each section, the table footnotes, and a bibliography of sources. The *Statistical Abstract* is a source with which many researchers begin the search for external secondary data.

Statistics of Income (Internal Revenue Service: Government Printing Office) This annual publication is prepared from federal income tax returns of corporations and individuals. There are different publications for each type of tax report—one for corporations, one for sole proprietorships and partnerships, and one for individuals. The *Corporate Income Tax Return* volume, for example, contains balance sheet and income statement statistics compiled from corporate tax returns and broken down by major industry, asset size, and so on.

Survey of Current Business (U.S. Bureau of Economic Analysis: Government Printing Office) This monthly publication provides a comprehensive statistical summary of the national income and product accounts of the United States. There are some 2,600 different statistical series reported, covering such topics as general business indicators, commodity prices, construction and real estate activity, personal consumption expenditures by major type, foreign transactions, income and employment by industry, transportation and communications activity, and so on. Most of the statistical series present data on the last four years.

United Nations Statistical Yearbook (New York: United Nations) This annual United Nations publication contains statistics on a wide range of foreign and domestic activities, including forestry, transportation, manufacturing, consumption, and education. The *Monthly Bulletin of Statistics* supplies updates.

World Almanac and Book of Facts (Mahwah, N.J.: World Almanac Education Group) Issued annually, this publication serves as a well-indexed handbook on a wide variety of subjects. Included are industrial, financial, religious, social, and political statistics for most nations.

General Guides to Business Information

American Marketing Association Bibliography Series (Chicago: American Marketing Association) Published periodically, each of the publications provides an in-depth annotated bibliography of a topic of interest in marketing.

Business Information: How to Find It, How to Use It, 2d ed., Michael R. Lavin (Phoenix, Ariz.: Oryx Press, 1992) A general guide to searching for business information, this book provides useful information for the development of search strategies.

Business Information Sources, 3d ed., Lorna M. Daniells (Berkeley: University of California Press, 1993) A guide to the basic sources of business information organized by subject area.

Census Catalog and Guide (U.S. Bureau of the Census: Government Printing Office) This annual, cumulative catalog describes all products (reports, maps, microfiche, computer tapes, diskettes, and on-line items) that the Census Bureau has issued since 1980, including information about how to order the material. Also included is an appendix that includes, among other things, a directory of telephone numbers of Census Bureau specialists by area of expertise.

Encyclopedia of Business Information Sources, 16th ed. (Detroit: Gale Research, 2002) A guide to the information available on various subjects, including basic statistical sources, associations, periodicals, directories, handbooks, and general literature.

The Federal Database Finder (Chevy Case, Md.: Information USA Inc.) This useful resource provides a directory of over 4,200 no-cost and fee-based databases and data files that are available through the federal government.

Guide to American and International Directories, 15th ed., (Nyack, N.Y.: Todd Publications, 2002) This guide provides information on directories published in the United States and worldwide, categorized under 300 technical, mercantile, industrial, scientific, and professional headings.

Guide to Foreign Trade Statistics (Washington, D.C.: U.S. Bureau of the Census, 1999) A guide to the published and unpublished sources of foreign trade statistics.

A Handbook on the Use of Government Statistics (Charlottesville, Va.: Tayloe Murphy Institute) This publication is designed to assist the businessperson with the use of government statistics. A series of brief case descriptions are presented.

Statistics Sources, 25th ed., Jacqueline Wasserman O'Brien, et al. (Detroit: Gale Group, 2001) A guide to international, federal, state, and private sources of statistics on a wide variety of subjects.

A User's Guide to BEA Information (U.S. Bureau of Economic Analysis: Government Printing Office) This booklet provides a directory for Bureau of Economic Analysis publications, diskettes, and other information sources.

Indexes

ABI/Inform (Ann Arbor, Mich.: UMI) This core business database indexes 800 scholarly, trade, and popular business and management journals. The full text of some articles is available.

American Statistics Index (Washington, D.C.: Congressional Information Service) Published annually and updated monthly, the publication is intended to serve as a comprehensive index of statistical data available to the public from any agency of the federal government.

Business Index (Foster City, Calif.: Information Access Company) The *Business Index* is an index to over 800 business periodicals, some 80 regional and national journals and newspapers, and business information from more than 3,000 general and legal periodicals.

Business Periodicals Index (Bronx, N.Y.: The H. W. Wilson Company) The *Business Periodicals Index* is a general purpose business index published monthly (with annual compilations) and is composed of subject entries covering approximately 520 business periodicals.

Communication Abstracts (Thousand Oaks, Calif.: Sage Publications) *Communication Abstracts* provides an index to communications-related articles, books, and reports. It is issued quarterly and covers such topics as marketing, advertising, and mass communication.

Dissertation Abstracts International (Ann Arbor, Mich.: University Microfilms International) Issued monthly, this publication contains descriptions of doctoral dissertations and some Master's theses from nearly 500 participating institutions in North America and around the world. The approximately 35,000 annual entries are divided into three divisions: the humanities and social sciences, the sciences and engineering, and European abstracts.

Index to International Statistics (Washington, D.C.: Congressional Information Service). Published monthly with annual cumulations, this is a selective guide to statistical publications from international intergovernmental organizations.

Journal of Marketing, "Marketing Literature Review" (Chicago: American Marketing Association) Each quarterly issue of the *Journal of Marketing* includes a "Marketing Literature Review" section that indexes a selection of article abstracts related to marketing from the ABI/Inform database. Abstracts are drawn from over 125 business journals; entries are indexed under a variety of marketing subject headings.

Social Sciences Citation Index (Philadelphia: Institute for Scientific Information) Published three times yearly, with annual cumulations, this publication indexes all articles in more than 1,725 social science periodicals and selected articles in approximately 3,300 periodicals in other disciplines.

Statistical Reference Index (Washington, D.C.: Congressional Information Service) Published monthly with annual cumulations, this publication is a selective guide to American statistical publications from private organizations and state government sources.

The Wall Street Journal Index (New York: Dow Jones) Published monthly and annually, *The Wall Street Journal Index* provides a subject index of information appearing in the Eastern edition of *The Wall Street Journal* in two sections—general news and corporate news.

Specialized Directories

American Business Locations Directory (Detroit: Gale Group) This unique directory provides 50,000 site locations for 1,000 of the largest American corporations. Sites include manufacturing plants, branch offices, R&D centers, and subsidiaries.

American Marketing Association Members and Marketing Services Directory (Chicago: American Marketing Association) This directory, produced annually, contains an international directory of AMA members and member companies as well as a guide to providers of marketing services.

Business Organizations, Agencies, and Publications Directory, 14th ed. (Detroit: Gale Research, 2002) This directory serves as a guide to approximately 42,000 organizations, agencies, and publications related to foreign and domestic business, trade, and industry.

Consultants and Consulting Organizations Directory, 24th ed. (Detroit: Gale Research, 2001) This directory lists approximately 25,000 firms and individuals who are active in consulting and briefly describes their services and fields of interest.

Directories in Print, 21st ed. (Detroit: Gale Research, 2001) This directory is a descriptive guide to over 15,500 print and nonprint directories and includes a valuable keyword index.

Encyclopedia of Associations (Detroit: Gale Group) Published annually, this encyclopedia lists the active trade, business, and professional associations, and briefly describes their activities and lists their publications. Also available on CD-ROM.

FINDEX, The Directory of Market Research Reports, Studies and Surveys (Bethesda, Md.: Cambridge Information Group) This publication indexes and provides abstracts to more than 50,000 research reports produced by top U.S. and international research firms. Also available online.

Gale Directory of Databases (Detroit: Gale Research) Published twice a year, this comprehensive guide describes more than 12,500 databases, 3,600 database producers, and 2,400 online services and vendors.

Hoover's Masterlist of Major U.S. Companies (Austin, Tex.: Hoover's Business Press) This annual volume gives brief histories and key statistics for the largest U.S. companies.

Information Industry Directory (Detroit: Gale Research) This directory lists and describes over 4,000 producers and vendors of electronic information.

International Directory of Marketing Research Houses and Services (The Green Book) (New York: American Marketing Association, New York Chapter) This publication provides an alphabetic listing of domestic and international marketing research companies. A geographic listing is also provided, along with an index of principal personnel.

Standard Directory of Advertisers (Wilmette, Ill.: National Register Publishing Company) This annual directory lists over 24,000 companies with allotments for advertising campaigns of more than $200,000. Included are individual listings containing information on type of business, address, key personnel, advertising agency relationship, products advertised, media utilized, etc. The directory is published in two editions, one by product classification and one by geographic location.

Standard Directory of Advertising Agencies (Wilmette, Ill.: National Register Publishing Company) This annual directory lists approximately 13,500 advertising agencies and provides such information as personnel by title, key accounts, addresses, and telephone numbers.

Chapter 8

Standardized Marketing Information Services

© Eyewire/Getty Images

Learning Objectives

1   List three common uses of the information supplied by standardized marketing information services.

2   *Define* geodemography.

3   *Describe the operation of a diary panel.*

4   *Describe the operation of store audits.*

5   *Define* UPC.

6   *Define* single-source measurement.

7   *Discuss the purpose and operation of people meters.*

Marcie Chandler drives an hour each way, past the region's big supermarket chains, to go grocery shopping. Her destination: the Whole Foods Market in Plano, Texas. "I'd rather drive all this way and spend more—I mean, it costs a lot more to feed your family fresher products," Chandler, a college student, told a newspaper reporter.

Driving an hour to spend more? What's going on here? The attraction for Chandler is the chance to buy what she considers the most healthful food. Whole Foods specializes in natural and certified organic products, as well as hormone-free meat and seafood that meets requirements for sustainable fishing. Chandler explained, "I have a lot of heart disease in my family. It's a big concern for me. . . . It's worth knowing that you don't have the chemicals in your products."

Consumers like Chandler have fueled impressive growth for Whole Foods. The first Whole Foods Market opened in Austin, Texas, in 1980, when fewer than half a dozen natural-food supermarkets existed in the United States. Expanding through acquisitions and construction, the chain now operates close to 140 stores. Sales of $2.7 billion in 2002 helped the store maintain its position as the market leader among natural-foods retailers. And sales in Whole Foods's comparable stores (a comparison of year-to-year performance) rose 10 percent that year, in spite of what Whole Foods CEO John Mackey called "the weakest economy the United States has seen in over 10 years." The company's plans call for continuing that pattern of growth.

Despite the struggling economy, some national trends favor Whole Foods. Its specialty—natural foods—is a fast-growing sector of the otherwise ailing retail industry. In particular, forecasts for retail sales of organic products call for annual growth of roughly 20 percent, with sales reaching $20 billion by 2005. The federal government recently enacted standards for classifying and labeling organic products, a development that is expected to increase awareness of organic products, as well as demand for them.

Of course, the robust growth attracts competitors, including mainline supermarkets, which have been adding natural and organic offerings to their product mix. As natural-foods sections have become a feature of many supermarkets, mainline retailers' share of the organic market has grown rapidly. Traditional supermarkets have had the advantage of lower prices, but this may be changing. Whole Foods once charged 30 percent more than mainstream grocers, but as it has grown and expanded distribution channels, the price difference has fallen by half. Greater competition and lower costs should further shrink the price difference.

With competition coming from the big supermarket chains, how can Whole Foods stay at the top of the heap?

Discussion Issues

1. To maintain its competitive strength, what does Whole Foods need to know about its customers?

2. What does it need to know about how its customers respond to its product selection and other marketing decisions, including pricing and advertising?

3. How can Whole Foods obtain this information? ∎

The many standardized marketing information services that are available are additional important sources of secondary data for the marketing researcher. These services are available at some cost to the user, and in this respect are a more expensive source of secondary data than published information. However, they are also typically much less expensive than primary data, because purchasers of these data share the costs incurred by the supplier in collecting, editing, coding, and tabulating them. Because it must be suitable for a number of users, however, what is collected and how the data are gathered must be uniform. Thus, the data may not always ideally fit the needs of the user, which is their main disadvantage over primary data.

This chapter describes some of the main types and sources of standardized marketing information service data.

List three common uses of the information supplied by standardized marketing information services.

Profiling Customers

Market segmentation is common among businesses seeking to improve their marketing efforts. Effective segmentation demands that firms group their customers into relatively homogeneous groups. That enables them to tailor marketing programs to the individual groups, thereby making the programs more effective. A common segmentation base for firms selling industrial goods takes into account the industry designation or designations of its customers, most typically by means of the Standard Industrial Classification (SIC) codes. The SIC codes are a system developed by the U.S. Bureau of the Census for organizing the reporting of business information, such as employment, value added in manufacturing, capital expenditures, and total sales. The original SIC code system is gradually being replaced by the more comprehensive North American Industry Classification System (NAICS). In both systems, major industry sectors are given a two-digit code number, and the types of businesses making up the industry are given additional digits. Exhibit 8.1 demonstrates how two U.S. industries are coded using the newer NAICS system.

One of the commercial services that is especially popular among industrial goods and service suppliers is Dun's Business Locator, an index that provides basic data on over 10 million U.S. businesses including the SIC code of each establishment. These records allow sales management to construct sales prospect files, define sales territories and measure territory potentials, and isolate potential new customers with particular characteristics. They allow advertising management to select potential customers by size and location; to analyze and select the media to reach them; to build, maintain, and structure current mailing lists; to generate sales leads qualified by size, location, and quality; and to locate new markets for testing. Finally, they allow marketing research professionals to assess market potential by territory, to measure market penetration in terms of numbers of prospects and numbers of customers, and to make comparative analyses of overall performance by districts and sales territories and in individual industries.

Exhibit 8.1

NAICS Hierarchy and Codes for Two Industries

Level	Code	Title	Code	Title
Sector	31–33	Manufacturing	51	Information
Subsector	334	Computer and Electronic Product Manufacturing	513	Broadcasting and Telecommunications
Industry Group	3346	Manufacturing and Reproducing of Magnetic and Optical Media	5133	Telecommunications
Industry	33461	Manufacturing and Reproducing of Magnetic and Optical Media	51332	Wireless Telecommunications Carriers (except Satellite)
U.S. Industry	334611	Reproducing of Software	513321	Paging

Source: *NAICS: New Data for a New Economy*. Economic Classification Policy Committee, Table 3, pg. 6. (October 1998).

geodemography
The availability of demographic, consumer-behavior, and lifestyle data by arbitrary geographic boundaries that are typically quite small.

Firms selling consumer goods don't normally target individual customers, because no single customer is likely to buy much of any product or service. Rather, firms need to target groups of customers. Their ability to do this has increased substantially since the 1970 census, which was the first electronic census. Since that time, the Census Bureau has made available computer tapes of the facts that have been gathered and, more recently, CD and online formats, which make the data easily usable by those with personal computers. Having the data available in electronic form allows their tabulation by arbitrary geographic boundaries, and an entire industry has developed to take advantage of this capability. The **geodemographers,** as they are typically called, combine census data with their own survey data or data that they gather from administrative records such as motor vehicle registrations or credit transactions, to produce customized products for their clients.

Mapping software, often called a geographic information system (GIS), combines various kinds of demographic data with geographic information on maps. The user can draw a map showing average income levels of a county, then zoom closer to look at particular towns in more detail. Most GIS programs on the market can show information as detailed as a single block; some programs can show individual buildings. Seeing the information on a map can be more useful than merely reading tables of numbers. At PepsiCo, a GIS enabled marketers to analyze traffic patterns and consumer demographics to identify the best sites for new Taco Bell and Pizza Hut restaurants.[1]

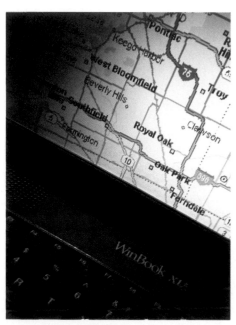

© Terri L. Miller/E-Visual Communications, Inc.

Sophisticated, inexpensive geographic information system (GIS) software that overlays demographic information on maps can help companies decide where to locate a new franchise or find a particular neighborhood to target.

Chase Manhattan Bank used GIS analysis to determine that only two-thirds of one branch's customers lived in its trade area, with the other customers working in the area but living elsewhere. Further analysis indicated that many of the customers who lived out of the area worked at nearby medical centers and that, as a group, the remote customers might represent more than half a billion dollars in potential deposits. They also discovered that a competing bank was actually in a better location to attract this potential business. Based on the GIS analysis, Chase was able to identify options for relocating the existing branch.[2]

GISs once required mainframe computers and were quite expensive, but today's applications are usually off-the-shelf programs that can run on personal computers and can be very inexpensive. Microsoft's Excel, the popular spreadsheet program, contains a GIS function. Many GIS packages are now available, including BusinessMAP (from ESRI), GeoMedia (Intergraph), Maptitude (Caliper Corporation), MapInfo (MapInfo), and MapLinx (IMSI).

Another thing that geodemographers do is regularly update the census data through statistical extrapolation. The data can consequently be used with much more confidence during the years between the censuses. Another value-added feature that has had a great deal to do with the success of the industry has been the analysis performed on the census data. Firms supplying geodemographic information have cluster-analyzed the census-produced data to produce "homogeneous groups" that describe the American population.

For example, Claritas (the first firm to do this and still one of the leaders in the industry) used over 500 demographic variables in its PRIZM (Potential Ratings for Zip Markets) system when classifying residential neighborhoods. This system breaks the 260,000 neighborhood areas in the United States into 62 types based on consumer behavior and lifestyle. Each of the types has a fancy name that theoretically describes the type of people living there, such as Country Squires, New Homesteaders, Mines and Mills, and so on. Figure 8.1 describes the Towns and Gowns cluster.

Claritas or the other suppliers will do a customized analysis for whatever geographic boundaries a client specifies. Alternatively, a client can send the zip code addresses of some customer database, and the geodemographer will attach the cluster codes. Researchers can request information, ranging from descriptions of Prizm clusters to detailed maps, by submitting requests via an online connection with Claritas. A somewhat more limited set of information is available over the Internet at the Claritas Web site.[3,4]

Figure 8.1

Sample Cluster Profile from the PRIZMSystem

Many college towns and university campus neighborhoods are divided into half locals (Towns) and half students (Gowns). Cluster 36 is primarily compsed of 18–24 year olds on limited budgets and highly-educated, but perhaps underpaid, professionals. Both of these groups have a taste for prestige products that are beyond their means.

Predominant Characteristics

- Household (%U.S.):   1,397,588 (1.39%)
- Population: 3,696,461 (1.37%)
- Demographic Caption: College Town Singles
- Ethnic Diversity: Predominantly White, High Asian
- Family Type: Singles
- Predominant Age Ranges: 18–24, 25–34
- Education: College Graduates, Some College
- Employment Level: White-Collar, Service
- Housing Type: Renter in Multi-Unit 2–9 or 10+
- Density Centile: 58 (1=Sparse, 99=Dense)
- SER/Median Income   SER 31/Lower middle $19,700

Lifestyle

Play racquetball
Go online 20+ hours per month
Go downhill skiing
Belong to BMG Music Club
Buy alternative rock music
Buy science fiction literature
Visit Europe
Be college basketball fans

Products and Services

Own an Acura/Infiniti/Lexus bought new
Shop at Banana Republic
Own a Saturn bought new
Drink Coca Cola Classic
Drink imported beer
Buy BF Goodrich tires
Buy a VCR
Buy a computer system > $1000

Radio/TV

Listen to progressive rock radio
Listen to classic rock radio
Listen to variey radio
Watch the NCAA Men's Soccer
   Championship
Watch the NCAA Basketball
   Championship

Print

Read *Spin*
Read *Skiing*
Read *Mademoiselle*
Read *Rolling Stone*
Read *Entertainment Weekly*
Read *Bicycling*
Read *Shape*
Read *Glamour*

Measuring Product Sales and Market Share

A critical need in today's increasingly competitive environment is for firms to have an accurate assessment of how they are doing. A common yardstick for that assessment is sales and market share. Firms selling industrial goods or services typically track their own sales and market shares through analyses of their sales invoices. They also obtain feedback from the sales department in terms of how they did in various product or system proposal competitions. An alternative source that companies use to measure their market share is one of the online bibliographic data sources discussed in the preceding chapter. Many times a search of an appropriate database will turn up published studies containing product, company, and market information, including market share statistics.

Manufacturers of consumer goods also monitor their sales on an account-by-account basis through the examination of sales invoices. For them, however, knowing how much product has been shipped to wholesalers and retailers doesn't provide a timely understanding of how the product is doing with consumers. Historically, there are several ways of measuring sales to final consumers, including the use of diary panels of households and the measurement of sales at the store level.

(Online) Diary Panels

3 *Describe the operation of a diary panel.*

Diary panels are an important source of information about products purchased by households. Whether recorded on paper or reported online, the key feature of a diary panel is that a representative group of individuals or households keeps track of purchases made or products consumed over a given period of time. In this way, purchasing and/or consumption behavior can be extrapolated to the larger population.

The NPD Group tracks a number of food-related trends in the U.S. For example, the National Eating Trends (NET) service has operated a household diary panel since 1980. Participants keep a record of all food and drink consumed by all household members for a period of two weeks. Participation is spread across a one-year period, with about 50 households beginning the recording process each week. During the two-week period, respondents are asked to record the name and brand of all food and drink products consumed by all members of the household. At the end of each day, respondents report that day's food consumption back to the NPD Group's offices, where they are collected and analyzed. The panel is demographically balanced, reflecting U.S. Census Bureau statistics.[5]

Similarly, the NPD Book Trends and NPD Children's Book Trends panels also use diaries to monitor the book purchasing behavior of its sample of households. The main types of information reported in the diaries are shown in Figure 8.2.

The NPD Group also offers results from a large online consumer panel. The panel offers access to around 600,000 individuals in the U.S. who have agreed to respond to surveys and to provide information on purchasing behavior. Ongoing tracking services are provided for a variety of product categories, ranging from automotive to fashion to toys.[6]

Figure 8.2

Questions Asked of NPD Book Trends Panel Members

- Whether purchased for someone under 14 (Children's Book) or over 14 (Adult Book)
- Date of purchase
- ISBN—used to determine category, publisher, format, etc.
- Book type (storybooks, coloring book, etc.)
- Price paid
- Title, name of main character
- How purchased
- Where purchased
- Age/gender of buyer/recipient
- Whether purchased as a gift or for self
- Whether a planned or impulse purchase
- Recipient relation to purchaser
- Main reason for purchasing
- Occasion

Source: Information downloaded from the NPD Group Web site (http://clientcenter.npd.com/cc/special/booktrends_methodology.htm), April 8, 2003.

PART 3:
Data Collection Methods

Store Audits

Another historically popular way of measuring sales to ultimate customers is at the store level using either store audits or scanners. Scanners reflect the new way; store audits, the old. However, audits are still used in some stores that do not as yet use scanners, primarily because the products they sell do not lend themselves to scanner processing or the stores have not made the investment in scanner equipment.

The basic concept of a store audit is very simple. The research firm sends field workers, called auditors, to a select group of retail stores at fixed intervals. On each visit the auditors take a complete inventory of all products designated for the audit. The auditors also note the merchandise moving into the store by checking wholesale invoices, warehouse withdrawal records, and direct shipments from manufacturers. Sales to consumers are then determined by the following calculation:

Beginning inventory
+ Net purchases (from wholesalers and manufacturers)
− Ending inventory
= Sales

The store audit was pioneered by ACNielsen and served as the backbone of the Nielsen Retail Index for many years. The method is still used to measure sales for small, independent grocery stores, convenience stores, and liquor stores and to gather other information. The company takes the auditing records and generates the following information for each brand of each of the products audited:

- Sales to consumers
- Purchases by retailers
- Retail inventories
- Number of days' supply
- Out-of-stock stores
- Prices (wholesale and retail)
- Special factory packs
- Dealer support (displays, local advertising, coupon redemption)

Subscribers to the ACNielsen service can get these data broken down by competitor, geographic area, or store type. ACNielsen will also provide special reports to clients for a fee. These special reports include such things as the effect of shelf facings on sales; the sales impact of different promotional strategies, premiums, or prices; or the analysis of sales by client-specified geographic areas. The stores pinpointed for inclusion in the panel are contacted personally to secure their cooperation. Further, the stores are compensated for their cooperation on a per-audit basis.

4 *Describe the operation of store audits.*

ETHICAL dilemma 8.1

Maps, Inc., is the marketing research division of a large credit card company. The division specializes in the preparation of geodemographic maps. To prepare these maps, it combines information from customers' credit card transactions with the demographic data it collected when the customers applied for a credit card. Then, with its profiles of who is purchasing what, in combination with census data on small geographic areas, Maps, Inc., is able to develop maps that display by zip code area the potential market for various types of products and services. The company in turn sells this information to various manufacturers, wholesalers, and retailers after customizing the data to the geographic boundaries specified by the client.

- *Is it ethical to use credit card transaction information in this way?*

- *Do the credit card users have a right to know this research is being conducted?*

- *Should it be necessary for Maps, Inc., to get signed releases from individual cardholders before incorporating the individuals' purchase transactions in the database? What might happen to the quality of the data with the requirement of signed releases?*

Scanners

5 *Define* UPC.

Since the late 1970s, ACNielsen has been replacing its Retail Index service with its SCAN-TRACK service. The SCANTRACK service emerged from the revolutionary development in the grocery industry brought about by the installation of scanning equipment to read Universal Product Codes (UPCs). Universal Product Codes are 12-digit numbers imprinted on products themselves or on tags attached to the products. In general, the first six digits identify the manufacturer, and the next five a particular product of the manufacturer, be it a different size, variety, or flavor. See Figure 8.3.

There is a unique 12-digit code for each product. As the bar code is read by a fixed or hand-held **scanner,** the scanner identifies the 12-digit number, looks up the price in the attached computer, and immediately prints the description and price of the item on the cash register receipt. At the same time, the computer can keep track of the movement of every item that is scanned.

Scanners are now so pervasive that the majority of retail-sales information today is based on scanner data. Using either a sample of stores to represent a channel or a census of all stores to represent a retail organization, scanning data are available across multiple outlets, including grocery, mass merchant, drug, special warehouse clubs, and selected convenience stores. Where scanning is available, weekly sales (units sold at what price) are collected from a

scanner
An electronic device that automatically reads the Universal Product Code imprinted on a product, looks up the price in an attached computer, and instantly prints the description and price of the item on the cash register receipt.

Figure 8.3

Universal Product Codes: How Do They Work?

Since the introduction of the Universal Product Code (U.P.C.) 25 years ago, the symbology has allowed supermarkets to control their inventory more efficiently, automate the task of reordering stock, provide a faster and more accurate check-out for customers, and gather information for accurate and immediate marketing studies. But when you get down to the bare bars, how exactly does the U.P.C. work?

The U.P.C. is composed of a row of 59 black and white bars that vary in width. Together these bars make up the symbology of the code. Beneath these bars is a series of numbers called a standard. There are 12 numbers in the U.P.C. standard and 13 in the European EAN-13 code. The thickness of the bars and the distance between the bars define the numbers contained in the bar code.

A set of two black bars appear at the beginning, middle and end of the symbology and are called guard patterns. These patterns provide start and stop signals to tell the scanner where it is reading within the code.

The standard of the code consists of two parts, the UCC company prefix and the item reference. The UCC company prefix, which is the first six digits, identifies the manufacturer of the product. The item number, or the five digits after the company prefix, identifies the product. A 12th digit is included in the code as a "check" digit. The digit is mathematically based on the previous 11 numbers and protects against transposition errors if the data is manually entered.

UCC Company Prefix and Item Reference

Check Digit

Source: Downloaded from the Uniform Code Council, Inc. Web site (http://www.uc-council.org/about_ucc/uc_disection_of_the_upc.html), January 22, 2003.

retailer's system. ACNielsen takes these data and matches the UPC to a description to make the information analytically useful (e.g., share of category, full fat versus low fat, etc.). In addition, other data sources can be combined with this information.

For example, causal data are collected to help explain the "causes" of sales fluctuations. Causal data include:

- Display information—stores are audited and items on display are recorded;
- Feature information—features are collected and coded to identify items being advertised;
- Price decreases—the system identifies decreases via comparisons to historical prices.

By combining the retail sales and causal data, the effectiveness of various marketing actions can be assessed. This is accomplished by estimating what "base" sales would have been without the presence of the action. The data allow clients to evaluate the effectiveness of short-term promotions, to evaluate pricing changes, to follow new product introductions, and to monitor unexpected events such as product recalls and shortages.

© Terri L. Miller/E-Visual Communications, Inc.

ACNielsen's Homescan Service tracks customer purchasing and demographic information by providing households with portable UPC scanners.

Scanners' effect on the collection of sales and market share data has been profound. Research Window 8.1 provides an example. Scanners also provide an ability to link purchase behavior with demographic information. Before the advent of scanners, the link was made using diaries. A problem with diaries is that they depend for their accuracy on the conscientiousness of those in the panel to record their purchases as they occur. Scanner data are not subject to such recording biases. Several firms have developed systems over the last few years to take advantage of this fact, including Information Resources, Inc. (IRI) and ACNielsen (the marketing information company). A key feature of the new systems is the ability to link television-viewing behavior with product-purchasing behavior to produce what has become known as **single-source data.**

The basics of single-source research are straightforward. For example, consider the operation of the IRI BehaviorScan system. In each of the markets in which BehaviorScan operates, the company has recruited more than 3,000 households to present identification cards at grocery stores or drugstores every time a household member makes a purchase. Almost all the supermarkets and drugstores in each area are provided scanners by IRI. Each household member presents his or her identification card when checking out. The card is scanned along with the purchases, allowing IRI to relate a family's purchase by brand, size, and price to the family's demographic characteristics and the household's known exposure to coupons, newspaper ads, free samples, and point-of-purchase displays. In some markets, panel households are also given handheld scanners so that they can electronically record purchases made at non-participating retailers.[7]

IRI is also able to direct different TV advertising spots to different households in cooperation with the cable television systems serving the markets. This allows the company to monitor the buying reactions to different advertisements or to the same advertisement in different types of households (e.g., whether the buying reactions to a particular ad are the same or different among past users and nonusers of the product). This targetable television capability allows IRI to balance the panel of members for each ad test within each market according to

6 *Define* single-source measurement.

single-source data
Data that allow researchers to link together purchase behavior, household characteristics, and advertising exposure at the household level.

RESEARCH
Window

8.1

An Example of the Impact of Scanners

HARTSDALE, N.Y.—TVT Records President Steve Gottlieb spends his Wednesday mornings hunched over a computer screen, studying numbers that tell him whether he's having a good week.

Most music industry executives are doing the same thing, since that's the day SoundScan transmits data showing how many albums Alanis Morissette, Stone Temple Pilots, and other artists have sold.

SoundScan, a company that didn't exist at the dawn of the 1990s, in five years has transformed the record business simply by providing an accurate accounting of how the product is selling.

Information provided by SoundScan has changed the way music is marketed, rerouted concert tours and leveled the playing field between major record companies and independents.

SoundScan's leaders, Michael Fine and Michael Shalett, formed a partnership in the late 1980s to set up focus groups of music consumers. Fine had a background in political polling and Shalett in radio and record promotion. They decided to compete with Billboard, the music industry's chief trade paper, which was trying to establish a computerized system for tracking music sales to make its record charts more accurate.

For all the money at stake, compiling the weekly Top 40 list was unscientific. Trade publications would ask selected record stores to phone in reports of their top sellers. It was susceptible to manipulation—a store owner might be persuaded to inflate the sales of a certain disc in return for, say, tickets to a hot concert.

SoundScan signed major retail chains like Musicland, Trans World, and Camelot to exclusive deals letting the company keep track of sales through bar codes. The system went on-line in January 1991.

It took until the middle of that year to establish a market. But when Sony became the first major record company to sign up for SoundScan's service, most of the others quickly followed suit. So did artist managers, concert promoters, and the ABC Radio network. Billboard abandoned its own efforts and began basing its charts on SoundScan's data.

Suddenly, the industry had a comprehensive record of what was selling and where. Not only could it tell how many discs Madonna really sold, it could also see if opera was hot in Omaha or alternative rock big in Albuquerque.

SoundScan showed that many discs sell the most copies in their first week of release, with only the true hits growing in sales as time went on. It's the sort of information that guides advertising and marketing decisions; many record stores now host events on the release date of a much-awaited album.

Record companies tend to show more patience in supporting new artists if SoundScan data shows these musicians are making an impact, said Geoff Mayfield, Billboard's charts director.

Artists such as Sheryl Crow, Hootie & the Blowfish, and Morissette might not have been a success in the pre-SoundScan era, he said.

Large record companies, no longer able to manipulate charts to help their artists, now face tougher competition from nimble independent labels like Tommy Boy, he said.

Marketers use SoundScan's information in very specific ways. Concert promoters are able to see where an artist is doing well and are using that information in scheduling tours.

SoundScan measures sales in close to 13,000 music outlets in the United States representing between 85 percent and 90 percent of the total music sold, Shalett said.

Many independent stores are missing from SoundScan's count. Mayfield's heard his share of gripes from industry officials who see this as a crucial weakness; they believe their discs are selling big in the stores not counted. He discounts most complaints as sour grapes. ■

Source: David Bauder, "Tracking Sales by Computer Transforms Music Industry," *Wisconsin State Journal* (May 28, 1996), p. 5B.

the criteria the sponsor chooses (e.g., past purchases of the product), thereby minimizing the problem of having noncomparable experimental and control groups.

ACNielsen's system is designed to measure natural consumer behavior as well as test the effects of different promotions or advertising. Its Homescan Service maintains a panel of

61,500 participating households whose purchases are measured through an electronic wand they are asked to pass over the UPC codes on products brought into the house. The electronic unit then queries them with respect to where the purchase was made, age and sex of the shopper, price paid, and deal type if any, among other things. The information from each household is downloaded each week to ACNielsen's computer system.[8] Some of the other types of analyses that are possible with Homescan are described in Exhibit 8.2.

Exhibit 8.2

Types of Analyses Possible Using ACNielsen's Homescan Service

Type	Purpose	Key measures
Market Overview/ Trend Analysis	To provide a general overview of consumer purchasing for a particular product category, its major segments, and major brands. Measures are compared between brands and over time to identify changes and developments in the marketplace. Data can be analyzed for any period, can be looked at across/within outlet types, or can be looked at for specific consumer groups (e.g., heavy buyers, microwave owners, etc.).	Volume and market share. Percentage of households purchasing (penetration). Volume per buyer (buying rate). Volume per purchase occasion. Purchase occasion per buyer (frequency). Pricing (total, deal, nondeal). Percentage of volume on deal (coupon vs. store special). Distribution of volume by outlet (e.g., grocery, drug, club warehouse, etc.).
Demographic Analysis	To target advertising and promotional efforts most effectively by determining the demographic profile of particular buyer groups (e.g., brand buyers, heavy buyers, frequent commercial viewers). By evaluating the absolute sales importance of one demographic segment versus another, along with the importance of each demographic segment relative to the general population, the overall profile of each buyer group can be identified.	Across all demographic characteristics, the following measures are produced: Distribution of buyers. Distribution of volume. Market share (within demographic group). Percentage of volume on deal (within demographic group). Buyer Index (distribution of buyers vs. distribution of population). Volume Index (distribution of volume vs. distribution of population).
Loyalty/Combination Purchase Analysis	To understand the extent; to which buyers are loyal to a brand or retailer; to determine the competitive set in which brands operate; and to identify size/flavor/form preference. The report also looks at the importance of price and dealing when buyers purchase competitive items.	Percentage of brand buyers purchasing competitive items. Percentage of brand volume accounted for by buyers who purchase competitive brands. Percentage of competitive brand volume purchased on deal by Brand A buyers. Price paid for competitive brand by Brand A buyers. Brand A buyers' total category volume (distribution). Interaction Index—index of Brand A's interaction with competitive brands versus expectations.
Brand-Shifting Analysis	To identify the sources of growth or decline in a brand's sales. By looking at changes from period to period on a household-by-household basis, we can see if volume changes were attributed to consumers switching to/from other brands, increasing/decreasing their overall category purchasing, and/or entering/leaving the market.	Brand-shifting volume. Increased/decreased category purchasing. New/lost category buyers. Percentage of shifting gains/loss. Gain/loss index. Interaction index.
Trial and Repeat Analysis	Trial measures consumer interest in a new product by evaluating the percentage of households using the product. Trial also measures the ability of a marketing plan to translate interest into purchasing. Repeat purchasing evaluates product satisfaction by determining the percentage of triers and repurchasing the brand—the ability of a product to deliver on its promise.	Cumulative trial. Cumulative repeat. Depth of repeat. Package rate (volume on trial, on repeat). Percentage volume on deal (total on trial vs. on repeat). Market share (total from trial vs. from repeat).

Source: ACNielsen

As retailers get used to single-source measurement and see a return on using it, and as companies like ACNielsen gain experience in different means of collecting the data, these services are expanding. For example, ACNielsen has adapted Homescan to cover fresh foods sold by the pound or the piece, such as produce, meat, and deli items. Consumers who participate in the Homescan Fresh Foods Consumer Index use scanners and a book of scannable codes for items sold by weight or in bulk. In addition, the company recently introduced a WalMart channel to specifically monitor purchases made at WalMart, the world's largest retailer. Using information from the Homescan consumer panel, both manufacturers and competing retailers can track products sold.[9]

The impact of single-source measurement on the conduct of marketing activities has been and promises to be so profound that it may "ultimately rival the importance of the microscope to scientists," according to a report by J. Walter Thompson USA.[10] For example, ACNielsen recruited a panel of 500 Hispanic households to use its Homescan system, thereby providing marketers with much greater insight into the buying behavior of that demographic group. Data compare purchases by Hispanic households whose preferred language is Spanish, English, or bilingual with purchases by non-Hispanic households. Early results show marketers that it is important to consider various types of Hispanic households. Spanish-speaking households are heavy buyers of diapers, cereal, and yogurt, but in Hispanic households where English is the preferred language, these items are purchased even less than in non-Hispanic households.[11]

Although single-source measurement offers the opportunity for new market insights, firms subscribing to these services need to prepare themselves for the incredible amounts of data they produce. Without proper planning, firms can literally drown in these data. That is why decision support systems for analyzing data (particularly expert systems, discussed in Chapter 2) are becoming increasingly important in marketing research.

Measuring Advertising Exposure and Effectiveness

6 *Define single-source measurement.*

Another area in which there is a great deal of commercial information available for marketers relates to the assessment of exposure to, and effectiveness of, advertising. Most suppliers of industrial goods advertise most heavily in trade publications. To sell space more effectively, the various trade publications typically sponsor readership studies that they make available to potential advertisers. Suppliers of consumer goods and services also have access to media-sponsored readership studies. In addition, a number of services have evolved to measure consumer exposure to the various media.

Television and Radio

7 *Discuss the purpose and operation of people meters.*

The Nielsen television ratings produced by Nielsen Media Research are probably the most familiar form of media research to most people. Almost everyone has heard of the Nielsen ratings and their impact on which television shows are canceled by the networks and which are allowed to continue. The ratings themselves are designed to provide estimates of the size and nature of the audience for individual television programs.

people meter
A device used to measure when a television is on, to what channel it is tuned, and who in the household is watching it.

Data needed to compute the Nielsen ratings are gathered in a variety of ways. **People meters** attempt to measure not only the channel to which a set is tuned, but who in the household is watching. Each member of the family has his or her own viewing number. Whoever turns on the set, sits down to watch, or changes the channel is supposed to enter his or her number into the people meter. All of this information is transmitted to a central computer for processing. In addition, Nielsen supplements people meter data with information collected using simple electronic meters that record what channels are being watched (but nothing about who is watching), consumer diaries, and telephone interviews.

Through the data provided by these basic records, Nielsen develops estimates of the number and percentage of all television households viewing a given television show. Nielsen also

PART 3:
Data Collection Methods

breaks down these aggregate ratings by numerous socioeconomic and demographic characteristics, including territory, education of head of house, household income, occupation of head of house, household size, etc. These breakdowns assist the television networks in selling advertising on particular programs, while they assist the advertiser in choosing programs that reach households with the desired characteristics. Technically Speaking 8.1 provides a more detailed overview of how Nielsen produces its television ratings.

Behind the Nielsen TV Ratings

"Technically SPEAKING" 8.1

CLIENTS USE NIELSEN MEDIA RESEARCH'S TELEVISION AUDIENCE RESEARCH INFORMATION to buy and sell television time as well as to make program decisions. That information is the currency in all the transactions between buyers and sellers, which adds up to more than $40 billion in national and local advertising spending in the U.S. each year. Without an independent, third-party measurement system embracing the highest standards of accuracy and integrity, the television marketplace could not function effectively. Assuring the value of this currency is the number one priority of Nielsen Media Research.

The television marketplace in the United States is broadly defined as all users of television ratings data—national broadcast and cable networks, regional networks, syndicators, television stations, local cable TV systems, satellite distributors, advertising agencies and advertisers, program producers, station representatives, and buying services.

HOW THE DATA ARE COLLECTED

National Measurement

The heart of the Nielsen Media Research national ratings service in the United States as well as in Canada is an electronic measurement system called the Nielsen People Meter. These meters are placed in a sample of 5,000 households (13,000 persons) in the U.S., randomly selected and recruited by Nielsen Media. The People Meter is placed on each TV in the sample household. The meter measures two things—what program or channel is being tuned and who is watching. The People Meter is used to collect audience estimates for broadcast and cable networks, nationally distributed syndicated programs, and satellite distributors.

Which TV source (broadcast, cable, etc.) is being watched in the sample homes is continually recorded by one part of the meter which has been calibrated to identify which station, network or satellite is carried on each channel in the home. Channel changes are electronically monitored by the meter. Nielsen Media Research gathers and maintains a database of information about source and time of telecast for TV programs, and when this information is combined with source tuning data from the sample homes, we can credit audience to specific TV programs.

Who is watching is measured by another portion of the Nielsen People Meter which uses an electronic "box" at each TV set in the home and accompanying remote control units. Each family member in the sample household is assigned a personal viewing button (identified by name or symbol) on the People Meter. The Nielsen Media Research representative who recruits the household links the assigned button to the age and gender of each person in the household. Whenever the television set is turned on a red light flashes from time to time on the meter, reminding viewers to press their assigned button to indicate if they are watching television. Additional buttons on the meter enable guests in a sample home to report when they watch TV by entering their age and gender and pushing a visitor button.

Local Measurement

In 53 of the largest markets in the U.S. (expanding to 55 in October 2002), a different metering system provides TV ratings information on a daily basis. This information is used by local television stations, local cable systems, advertisers and their agencies to make programming decisions as well as to buy and sell commercial advertising. In each of these markets, approximately 400–500 households are recruited (not the same homes as the national People Meter sample), and electronic meters are attached to each TV set in the sample home. Homes recruited for local samples are not equipped with People Meters, so the information is limited to "set tuning" information from which Nielsen Media Research can determine which channel the TV set is tuned. This information is augmented at least four months a year with demographic viewing data which are collected from separate samples of households which each maintain a paper viewing diary for one week. Household members are asked to write down what programs they and their guests watch in their home over the course of that week. Standard reports which combine the meter and diary data are issued regularly.

Diary measurement is used to collect viewing information from sample homes in every one of the *210 television markets in the United States* in November, February, May and July of each year. These measurement periods are known in the industry as "*the sweeps.*" This local viewing information provides a basis for advertising decisions and program scheduling. In some larger markets there are as many as three additional months (October, January and March) during which diaries are used to provide viewer information.

Hispanic Measurement

To help provide a total picture of viewing in all homes, Nielsen Media Research has established separate samples to capture viewing habits of Hispanic viewers to Spanish-language television. Special methods are used to elicit cooperation and ensure that the national and local samples of Hispanic households accurately reflect language usage in the community.

HOW THE DATA ARE PROCESSED

Household tuning data from both the national and local metered samples (and persons viewing data from the national sample) for each day are stored in the in-home metering system until they are automatically retrieved by Nielsen Media Research's computers each night. Data include: when the set is turned on; which channel is tuned; when the channel is changed; when the set is off; and, for the People Meter households, who is viewing, and when that person's viewing starts and stops. In addition, program lineups and station/cable carriage information are confirmed to make certain Nielsen Media Research accurately reports what is being watched.

Nielsen Media Research's Operations Center in Dunedin, Florida, processes this information each night for release to the television industry the next day. To comprehend the dimension of the task, consider that Nielsen Media Research collects information from approximately 25,000 households starting about 3 a.m. each day, processes approximately 10 million viewing minutes each day, and has more than 4,000 gigabytes of data available for customer access the next day.

SAMPLING

Any system of television measurement depends upon an audience sample to represent the entire population of viewers. A randomly selected group of households is the best known way to represent the characteristics and behavior of the population. By using randomly selected probability samples, Nielsen Media Research can make projections regarding the entire population.

Nielsen Media Research uses the U.S. Census Bureau's decennial (updated annually) census counts of all housing units in the nation. Using these data, Nielsen Media randomly selects more than 6,000 small geographic areas (blocks in urban areas and their equivalent in rural areas) and dispatches surveyors to each area to enumerate and list the housing units. Sample housing units are randomly selected within each sample area. Each occupied housing unit is a household. This sampling method is designed to give each occupied household a chance to be selected for the Nielsen People Meter Sample. Self-selected volunteers, though plentiful, do not represent the viewing of those who don't volunteer, and therefore cannot be included in the sample.

METHODOLOGY

The Nielsen People Meter measurement technique is the product of many years of experience with audience measurement. Since the reliability of the People Meter depends on the active participation of each household member and visitor as they watch TV, Nielsen Media Research's Methodological Research department is constantly studying and evaluating how people watch TV and how the Nielsen People Meter is actually used. As a result of this research, two major advances have significantly improved cooperation among sample households—that is, the proportion of households initially contacted by Nielsen Media Research who agree to participate in the People Meter Sample, as well as the continuing commitment of the people in those households to use the People Meter correctly.

The first research initiative is the introduction of the Nielsen People Meter Representative. These are specially trained recruiters who have experience in working with children and teens in order to train these younger viewers, and their families, to accurately use the People Meter. The other research initiative goes to the first step in the recruitment process—gaining the cooperation of the primary (or first choice) households randomly selected by Nielsen Media Research's statisticians. Using a concept called "Membership," the Nielsen Media Research recruiters encourage sample household members to participate in the Nielsen TV ratings in order to contribute to the accuracy of television viewing information.

ETHNIC MEASUREMENT

Although all ethnic groups are represented in Nielsen Media Research samples, the need to provide more frequent information on specific ethnic groups is increasingly important to all users of TV ratings information. In 1991, Nielsen Media Research expanded its monthly national reports to provide data on viewing among African-American households and approximately 20 African-American demographic categories. Additional information has been added to each local market rating report to identify African-American and Hispanic audiences and viewing activity.

In the fall of 1992, Nielsen Media Research launched the first national Hispanic television ratings service (Nielsen Hispanic Television Index) in the U.S. The unique viewing habits of this population group, particularly in those homes where Spanish is the only or dominant language spoken, are now reported on a national level and in more than a dozen local markets where the Hispanic portion of the population is significant. ■

Advertisers buying radio time are also interested in the size and demographic composition of the audiences they will be reaching. Radio-listening statistics are typically gathered using diaries that are placed in a panel of households. Arbitron, for example, generates telephone numbers randomly to ensure that it is reaching households with unlisted numbers. Those household members who agree to participate when called are sent diaries similar to that illustrated in Chapter 6, in which they are asked to record their radio-listening behavior for a short period. Most radio markets are rated only once or twice a year, although some of the larger ones are rated four times a year. The April/May survey is conducted in every Arbitron market and consequently is known as the "sweeps" period. Radio ratings are typically broken down by age and sex and focus more on individual than household behavior, in contrast with television ratings.

Arbitron, in conjunction with Nielsen Media Research, is experimenting with a new portable people meter, a pager-sized device to be carried by consumers. The devices sense inaudible codes embedded into programming by radio and television broadcasters (including cable TV) so that an accurate record can be made of actual exposure to media. The portable people meters are even equipped with a motion sensor to verify that the device has been moved (and presumably carried by the respondent), a basic requirement for proper use. Each night, the participants recharge the unit in a base station that also automatically sends the data collected during the day back to a central computer for processing.[12]

Print Media

There are several services that measure exposure to, and readership of, print media. For example, the Starch Ad Readership program measures the reading of advertisements in magazines and newspapers. Some 25,000 advertisements in over 400 issues are assessed each year. For each magazine issue, in-person personal interviews are conducted with 100–200 respondents who approximate the readership of the magazine.

The Starch surveys use the recognition method to assess a particular ad's effectiveness. With the magazine open, the respondent is asked to indicate whether he or she had read each ad. Four degrees of reading are recorded:

1. **Noted**—a person who remembered seeing any part of the advertisement in that particular issue.
2. **Associated**—a person who not only noted the advertisement but also saw the advertiser's name.
3. **Read Some**—a person who read any of the advertising copy.
4. **Read Most**—a person who read more than half of the advertising copy.[13]

During the course of the interview, reading data are also collected on the component parts of each ad, such as the headlines, subheadings, pictures, copy blocks, and so forth.

Interviewing begins a short time after the issue of the magazine is placed on sale. For weekly and biweekly consumer magazines, interviewing begins three to six days after the on-sale date and continues for one to two weeks. For monthly magazines, interviewing begins two weeks after the on-sale date and continues for two weeks.

Starch readership reports are compiled issue by issue and include three features: (1) labeled issue, (2) summary report, and (3) adnorm tables. The target ads in each issue are labeled to indicate overall readership level as well as the noting or reading of the major components of the ads. The summary report lists all the ads that were measured in the issue. The ads are arranged by product category and show the percentages for the three degrees of ad readership: noted, associated, and read most, allowing the comparison of the readership of each ad versus the other target ads in the issue. The adnorm tables enable one to compare the readership of an ad in a given issue with the norm for ads of the same size and color that are for the same product category for that publication.

Starch readership data allow advertisers to compare their ads with competitors' ads, current ads with prior ads, current ads against competitors' prior ads, and current ads against Starch adnorm tables. This process can be effective in assessing changes in theme, copy, layout, use of color, and so on.

Internet

Advertisers also need information about consumers' online activities. It is relatively easy to count the number of times that a site or banner ad has been accessed, along with revenues from online transactions. As with other forms of media, however, it is a

ETHICAL dilemma 8.2

Toys-4-Kids, a major toy manufacturer, wishes to monitor changes in its sales, market share, and household penetration through the establishment and maintenance of a panel of households that have children ages 12 and under. The households will be asked to record their purchases of all toys and games. Jean Blue, the marketing research director, believes it will be best to withhold the sponsor's name when recruiting households for the panel. She thinks that if the panel members know the research is being conducted by Toys-4-Kids, their reporting behavior could be biased.

- *If the panel members are volunteers, do they have a right to know who is sponsoring the panel?*

- *If they are compensated for their participation, do they have a right to know who is sponsoring the panel?*

- *Do you think a household's reporting behavior will be biased if the household knows Toys-4-Kids is sponsoring the research?*

little more complicated to determine the demographics of those accessing a Web site—and this is important for decisions about which Web sites to choose for advertising purposes. ACNielsen/NetRatings offers its Audience Measurement Service, a syndicated service that assesses Internet usage at work and at home. Regular reports detail a site's audience size and composition, time spent at the site, etc.

Multimedia Services

Simmons Market Research uses a national probability sample of about 20,000 adult respondents (plus children in the randomly selected households) and serves as a comprehensive data source allowing the cross-referencing of product usage and media exposure through their National Consumer Survey. Using single-stage stratified sampling (see Chapter 16) and random digit dialing, Simmons recruits at the household level for participation. Those agreeing to participate are sent a household survey booklet that collects information about household usage of an extensive list of products and services. In addition, each member of the household is sent a personal survey booklet that collects extensive media usage measures as well as personal information on demographics and lifestyle, product/service usage, shopping behavior, etc. By taking into account both media habits and product usage, the Simmons data allow companies to better segment, target, and communicate to the most promising groups.[14]

Courtesy of Simmons Market Research

Simmons Market Research gathers comprehensive data on household media viewing and product usage. Their data help companies pinpoint target markets.

Mediamark Research Inc. also makes available information on exposure to various media and household consumption of various products and services. Its annual survey of over 26,000 adult respondents covers more than 230 magazines, plus newspapers, radio and television stations, cable television channels, and outdoor advertising and over 500 product and service categories.[15] Information is gathered from respondents by two methods. First, a personal interview is used to collect demographics and data pertaining to media exposure. Magazine readership is measured by a recent-reading method that asks respondents to sort a deck of magazine logo cards according to whether they (1) are sure they have read, (2) are not sure they have read, and (3) are sure they have not read a given magazine within the previous six months.

Newspaper readership is measured using a yesterday-reading technique in which respondents are asked which of the daily newspapers on the list of papers that circulate in the area were read or looked at within the previous seven days. For Sunday and weekend papers, a four-week time span is used. Radio listening is determined through a yesterday-recall technique in which respondents are shown a list of five day parts and are asked how much time was spent listening to a radio during each time period on the previous day. They are then asked what stations were listened to. Television-audience data are collected in a similar manner.

On completion of the interview, interviewers then leave a questionnaire booklet with respondents. The interviewer personally picks up the booklet, which covers personal and household usage of approximately 500 product and service categories and 6,000 brands, after a short time. The 26,000 respondents for the Mediamark reports are selected using probability sampling methods.

A s the market for natural foods has expanded, so has the amount of data available to Whole Foods and its competitors.

Geodemographic data can tell Whole Foods about its customers. The company needs to locate stores near the kinds of consumers who can afford to spend a little extra and who value natural products. A logical place to start is with the PRIZM cluster called "Urban Uptown"—young, affluent, mostly single professionals, artists, executives, and students. Thus, Whole Foods's first expansion stores in Texas were in neighborhoods of Dallas, Plano, and Richardson with a high concentration of these kinds of people. As the store broadens its appeal and as organic foods become more widely demanded, the store expands into areas with young families that have rising or higher-than-average incomes.

As Whole Foods enters and serves new markets, it can work with research firms such as Claritas, the source of PRIZM data, to define the demographics of its markets. These firms can also help Whole Foods learn about the media usage and lifestyles of its target markets. The information can enable the company to target its promotional activities more efficiently.

Other sources of data can tell Whole Foods what natural and organic products sell best at its own stores and to U.S. consumers in general. For example, SPINs is a San Francisco–based marketing research firm that monitors the sales of over 80,000 products sold by natural-food stores and supermarkets. It can tell Whole Foods the fastest-growing product categories of natural foods.

SPINs also identifies regions where sales of products are growing. In the past, natural products were primarily sold in the biggest cities, like Chicago and Los Angeles, but that pattern of sales has changed, according to SPINs. Now stores in cities like Hartford and St. Louis are enjoying impressive performance.

Whole Foods can participate in research projects that gather panel data to monitor sales of particular products. ACNielsen's Homescan collects data on some of Whole Foods's mainstays: produce, bulk foods, fresh meats, and deli fare. This type of data collection helps manufacturers evaluate which advertising and promotional activities are beneficial and where products sell best. By sharing the data with Whole Foods, manufacturers and research firms can help the retailer tailor its product mix to what customers want.

As an advertiser itself, Whole Foods can obtain data from firms that specialize in testing advertising. For instance, the company can use readership reports such as the Starch service to evaluate its advertising programs.

The explosion in the demand for natural and organic products is sending Whole Foods into the big league of retailing. Fortunately, big-league researchers offer plenty of help. ∎

Sources: Len Lewis, "Natural Selection," *Progressive Grocer* (September 1998), pp. 74-75, 78, 80; Deborah L. Cohen, "Trotsky and Tofu Meet in Evanston: Shoppers Unite! Testing Lower-Cost Natural Foods Store," *Crain's Chicago Business* (August 9, 1999, downloaded from Dow Jones Publications Library at the Dow Jones Web site, http://www.dowjones.com, August 16, 1999). Whole Foods Market Web site, http://www.wholefoodsmarket.com, downloaded January 21, 2003; Whole Foods Market, "Whole Foods Market Reports Strong Fourth Quarter Results," news release, November 19, 2002, downloaded at http://www.wholefoodsmarket.com, February 10, 2003; Rudy Kortbech-Olesen, "The United States Market for Organic Food and Beverages," report of the International Trade Centre (UN Conference on Trade and Development and World Trade Organization, March 2002).

Summary

Learning Objective 1
List three common uses of the information supplied by standardized marketing information services.
The information supplied by standardized marketing information services is commonly used to (1) profile customers, (2) measure product sales and market share, and (3) measure advertising exposure and effectiveness.

Learning Objective 2
Define geodemography.
Geodemography refers to the availability of demographic, consumer-behavior, and lifestyle data by arbitrary geographic boundaries that are typically small.

Learning Objective 3
Describe the operation of a diary panel.
Diary panels are made up of families who use a preprinted diary to record the details of each purchase in a number of prespecified product categories. The details include the brand and amount bought, the price paid, whether the product was purchased on any deal and the type of deal if it was, the store where purchased, etc. Families are recruited on a regular basis, often quarterly, to keep the panel balanced demographically.

Learning Objective 4
Describe the operation of store audits.
Store audits involve sending field workers, called auditors, to a select group of retail stores at fixed intervals. On each visit the auditors take a complete inventory of all products designated for the audit. The auditors also note the merchandise moving into the store by checking wholesale invoices, warehouse withdrawal records, and direct shipments from manufacturers, and from this information determine sales to consumers.

Learning Objective 5
Define UPC.
The Universal Product Code (UPC) is a 12-digit number imprinted on products or price tags that identifies the product manufacturer and the particular product. The UPC is read by a scanner at the time of purchase.

Learning Objective 6
Define single-source measurement.
Single-source measurement refers to organizations that have the capability to monitor product-purchase data and advertising-exposure data by household, and to relate that information to the demographic characteristics of the households.

Learning Objective 7
Discuss the purpose and operation of people meters.
People meters attempt to measure which household members are watching which television channels at what times. Each member of the family has his or her own viewing number. Whoever turns on the set, sits down to watch, or changes the channel is supposed to enter his or her number into the people meter, which is an electronic device that stores and transmits this information to a central computer for processing.

Key Terms

geodemography (page 190)
scanner (page 194)

single-source data (page 195)
people meter (page 198)

Review Questions

1. What is the basic operation of a store audit?
2. Describe how a type of business can be more successfully targeted using the Dun's Business Locator.
3. What does it mean to "profile" customers or prospects? How does the process of profiling customers differ for firms selling industrial vs. consumer goods?

4. If you were a product manager for Brand X detergent and you needed up-to-date market share information by small geographical sectors, would you prefer diary panel data or store audit data? Why?
5. What are the key distinctions between diary panel data and scanner data?
6. What is the advantage of using single-source data?
7. How are Starch scores determined?
8. What is the basis for the Nielsen television ratings?
9. How do multimedia services operate?

Discussion Questions, Problems, and Projects

1. Several scenarios are presented below. In each case, there is a need for standardized marketing information. Recommend a service or services that could provide the required information. Explain your choice.
   (a) As part of its advertising-sales strategy, radio KZZD wants to stress the fact that their programming appeals to young adults between the ages of 19 and 25. The advertising salespeople need "numbers" to back up this claim.
   (b) Pulitzer Peanut Company has developed a unique couponing and television ad campaign for their 36-ounce container of Spanish peanuts. They need to know the following in order to evaluate the campaign:
      (1) Are people more likely to use the coupon when they've also seen the television ad?
      (2) What is the median size of the households using the coupon?
      (3) What is the proportion of new purchasers to past purchasers among the users of the coupon?
   (c) EMM Advertising Agency assured one of its clients that despite the $200,000 cost of placing a half-page ad in one issue of a national magazine, the actual cost per reader of the ad would be less than two cents. EMM is preparing a report to the client and needs data to back its assurance.
   (d) Eco-Soft, Inc., is introducing a software package that will make long-range forecasts of contaminant buildup levels in plants that manufacture polyester fibers. They need a current listing of potential customers, organized by plant sales volume, in order to prioritize their sales calls for the new package.
   (e) The advertising agency for a leading brand of disposable razors for men needs to choose which network television shows might be best for its ads.

2. Interview representatives of your local media outlets (e.g., radio stations, television stations, and newspapers) and determine the extent to which they utilize sources of standardized marketing information. You may wish to use the following questions as a guideline for your interviews.
   (a) Which sources do they use?
   (b) What specific types of information do they obtain from the source?
   (c) How do they use the information?
   (d) How important is the information in the conduct of their business?
   (e) How do they rate the accuracy of the information?
   (f) Do they supplement the standardized information with locally collected primary data?

Suggested Additional Readings

The best source of additional readings with respect to the operation of, and possible analyses with, standardized marketing information services are the brochures describing their services put out by the companies themselves. Complimentary copies are often available for the asking. Much information can also be found on the companies' Web sites.

Collecting Primary Data

© Eyewire/Getty Images

Learning Objectives

1 List the kinds of demographic and socioeconomic characteristics that interest marketers.

2 Relate the premise on which lifestyle analysis rests.

3 Cite the three main approaches used to measure the effectiveness of magazine ads.

4 Give two reasons why researchers are interested in people's motives.

5 Describe the two basic means of obtaining primary data.

6 State the specific advantages of each method of data collection.

Recently Moen Inc. arranged for a marketing research firm to watch individuals take showers. Strange as that may sound, the observations were part of a well-planned research project.

Moen sells plumbing fixtures, and its brand of faucets is the market leader in that category. Until a few years ago, Moen sold all its faucets and sinks through plumbing supply houses. To build sales, the company decided to begin selling shower heads to consumers through hardware and home-center stores. Existing data showed that although the average price of a shower head was below $20, more than half of total sales dollars came from higher-priced models. Moen decided to enter the market at the high end by developing a superior product. For this, it would need to know what consumers value in a shower.

Moen's marketing research director, Jack Suvak, hired QualiData Research to help Moen answer some very basic questions: What do consumers do in the shower? What benefits do they associate with taking a shower? How do they go about buying a new shower head? How can a shower head deliver the qualities that consumers value most?

As Suvak and QualiData founder Hy Mariampolski discussed these issues, it became apparent they would need to combine several forms of research. They could get some basic data by asking consumers to provide information about their behavior and attitudes. Consumers could record their time in the shower and their opinions about showering and shower heads. But Mariampolski's background as a sociologist told him that people often have difficulty putting into words their thoughts about everyday activities like showering. They may be so used to the pleasures and irritations of their morning or evening shower that they don't consciously notice those experiences anymore. As Suvak later explained to a newspaper reporter, "The obvious things don't bubble to the surface all the time." To find the issues that don't "bubble to the surface," the researchers would need to watch what consumers actually do.

The decision to use observation gave rise to another set of challenges. To learn about consumers' purchasing behavior, the researchers could observe consumers as they shopped in a store's plumbing aisle. But how could they observe consumers in the shower without offending them? The solution would require a combination of technology to carry out the observations and careful recruiting to find people who were not too self-conscious yet appropriately motivated. Moen also wanted subjects to be a diverse slice of American consumers.

Suvak and Mariampolski discussed these issues for several weeks. At the end of that time, QualiData presented Suvak with a plan weaving together questioning and observation of consumers, a combination that produced a wealth of useful data.

Discussion Issues

1. For Moen to introduce a new product to a new customer segment (consumers rather than plumbers), what information does the company need most?

2. Why should Moen use a research design that includes both observing consumers and questioning them? How can these methods work together?

3. How could the researchers observe consumers' use of showers without invading their privacy? ■

In Chapter 7 we emphasized the advantages of using secondary data. Such research information is usually fast, inexpensive, and fairly easy to obtain. We also noted that researchers who give secondary data only a casual look are being reckless. However, as we have seen, such data also have certain shortcomings and rarely will provide a complete solution to a research problem. The units of measurement or classes used to report the data may be wrong; the data may be nearly obsolete by the time of their publication; the data may be incomplete; and so on. When these conditions occur, the researcher logically turns to primary data.

This chapter is the first of three dealing with primary data, and it serves as an introduction to the subject. In this chapter we will discuss the various types of primary data researchers collect from and about subjects.

The information of interest that marketing researchers collect falls into one of the following categories: (1) demographic/socioeconomic characteristics, (2) psychological/lifestyle characteristics, (3) attitudes/opinions, (4) awareness/knowledge, (5) intentions, (6) motivation, and (7) behavior, and it is important to understand each type and the issues involved in collecting it. We also examine the two main methods that are used to collect these types of information: communication and observation. In subsequent chapters we explore each of these methods in more detail.

Types of Primary Data

Demographic/Socioeconomic Characteristics

One type of primary data of great interest to marketers is the subject's demographic and socioeconomic characteristics, such as age, education, occupation, marital status, sex, income, and social class. These variables are used to cross-classify the collected data to help interpret the consumers' responses. Suppose we are interested in people's attitudes toward ecology and pollution. We might suspect, test, and find that attitudes toward green marketing are related to the respondents' level of education. Similarly, marketers frequently ask whether the consumption of particular products (for example, SUVs, disposable diapers, vacation golf packages) are related to a person's (or family's) age, education, income, and so on. Demographic variables may seem simple (that is, that they would not capture nuances of consumer preferences), so it may seem risky to make such generalizations about people. However, consider two stable examples of the usefulness of demographics in predicting consumer preferences and behaviors: (1) 18- to 49-year-old men tend to be interested in sports, and it is this segment that makes sports TV programming highly profitable; (2) most of the disposable income in the U.S. comes from people 40 years old and older.[1] Such demographic information (for example, age and gender) and socioeconomic characteristics (such as wealth and discretionary funds) are often used to delineate market segments.[2]

Demographic and socioeconomic characteristics are sometimes called "states of being," in that they represent attributes of people. Some of these states of being, such as a respondent's age, sex, and level of formal education, can be readily verified. Some, such as social class, cannot be verified except very crudely, since they are relative and not absolute measures of a person's standing in society. A person's income can also be a fairly difficult piece of information to verify. Although the amount a person earns in a given year is an absolute, not a relative, quantity, in our society, money is such a sensitive topic that exact numbers may be hard to determine.

Psychological/Lifestyle Characteristics

Another type of primary data of interest to marketers is the subject's psychological and lifestyle characteristics in the form of personality traits, activities, interests, and values. **Personality** refers to the normal patterns of behavior exhibited by an individual—the attributes, traits, and mannerisms that distinguish one individual from another. We often characterize people

List the kinds of demographic and socioeconomic characteristics that interest marketers.

personality
Normal patterns of behavior exhibited by an individual; the attributes, traits, and mannerisms that distinguish one individual from another.

by the personality traits—aggressiveness, dominance, friendliness, sociability—they display. Marketers are interested in personality because it seems as if it would affect the way consumers and others in the marketing process behave. Many marketers maintain, for example, that personality can affect a consumer's choice of stores or products, or an individual's response to an advertisement or point-of-purchase display. Similarly, they believe that successful salespeople are more likely to be extroverted and understanding of other people's feelings than are unsuccessful salespeople. Although the empirical evidence regarding the ability of personality to predict consumption behavior or salesperson success is weak, personality remains a very popular variable with marketing researchers. Typically, it is measured by one of the standard personality inventories that have been developed by psychologists.[3]

Lifestyle analysis rests on the premise that a company can plan more effective strategies to reach its target market if it knows more about its customers in terms of how they live, what interests them, and what they like. For example, Frito-Lay conducted research that identified two broad categories of snackers, which it called Compromisers and Indulgers. The Compromisers are typically female and are more likely to exercise, read health and fitness magazines, be concerned about nutrition, and read product labels. Frito-Lay appeals to this group with its Baked Lay's potato chip, a reduced fat snack. Frito-Lay's traditional potato chips are targeted to the other psychographic category, the Indulgers, who are mostly male, in their late teens and early twenties, snack heavily, feel unconcerned about what they eat, and hesitate to sacrifice taste for a reduction in fat.[4]

The general thrust of such research, which is often called **psychographic analysis,** has been to develop statements that reflect a person's AIO—activities (A), interests (I), and opinions (O)—and consumption behavior. The statements might include such things as "I like to watch football games on television," "I like stamp collecting," "I am interested in national politics." Such a psychographic test would typically contain a great many such statements for respondents to choose from and would be administered to a large sample of respondents.[5]

For example, the NPD Group taps its ongoing panel of 65,000 to 250,000 consumers monthly with multipage surveys of their lifestyles as well as their category-specific (e.g., apparel, food, sporting goods) purchase behaviors. Exhibit 9.1 contains the list of characteristics that are usually assessed with AIO inventories. The analysis attempts to identify groups of consumers who are likely to behave similarly toward a product, and who have similar lifestyle profiles. Research Window 9.1 provides lifestyle descriptions of the five most common gasoline buyers identified by Mobil's marketing research. Finding that the Price Shopper spends no more than $700 annually, while the biggest spenders, the Road Warriors and True Blues, average at least $1,200 a year, Mobil decided to refocus its strategy to emphasize exceptional service over low prices.[6]

One problem marketers experienced when using psychographics or AIO inventories was that the categories of users distinguished in one study focusing on one type of product would be very different from the categories of individuals identified in another study examining a different product. This meant that each product required a new data collection and analysis exercise. Because the profiles across products were so unstable, it was impossible to develop demographic descriptions of the various groups that would be useful in planning marketing strategies for new products or brands.

The purpose of value and lifestyle (VALS) research is to avoid these problems by creating a standard psychographic framework that can be used for a variety of products. Exhibit 9.2, for

2 *Relate the premise on which lifestyle analysis rests.*

psychographic analysis
A technique that investigates how people live, what interests them, and what they like; it is also called *lifestyle analysis,* since it relies on a number of statements about a person's AIO—activities (A), interests (I), and opinions (O).

Frito-Lay used lifestyle analysis to identify a target market for its Baked Lay's potato chips.

PART 3:
Data Collection Methods

Exhibit 9.1

Lifestyle Dimensions

Activities	Interests	Opinions
Work	Family	Themselves
Hobbies	Home	Social issues
Social events	Job	Politics
Vacation	Community	Business
Entertainment	Recreation	Economics
Club membership	Fashion	Education
Community	Food	Products
Shopping	Media	Future
Sports	Achievements	Culture

Source: Adapted from Joseph T. Plummer, "The Concept and Application of Life Style Segmentation," *Journal of Marketing* 38 (January 1974), p. 34. Published by the American Marketing Association. See also Ronald D. Michman, *Lifestyle Market Segmentation* (New York: Praeger Publishers, 1991).

example, shows six international segments that have been identified from applying values surveys to teenagers.[7]

Attitudes/Opinions

Some authors distinguish between attitudes and opinions, while others use the terms interchangeably. Most typically **attitude** is used to refer to an individual's "preference, inclination, views, or feelings toward some phenomenon," while **opinions** are "verbal expressions of attitudes." We shall not make the distinction between the terms in this text but will treat attitudes and opinions interchangeably as representing a person's ideas, convictions, or liking with respect to a specific object or idea.

Attitude is one of the more important notions in the marketing literature, since it is generally thought that attitudes are related to behavior.[8] In general, if a person has a positive attitude toward a product or brand, the person is more likely to buy that product or to choose

attitude
An individual's preference, inclination, views, or feelings toward some phenomenon.

opinion
Verbal expression of an attitude.

RESEARCH *Window*

9.1

Lifestyle Descriptions of the Five Most Common Types of Gasoline Buyers

Road Warriors (16%) Generally higher income, middle-aged men who drive 25,000 to 50,000 miles a year . . . buy premium with a credit card . . . purchase sandwiches and drinks from the convenience store . . . will sometimes wash their cars at the car wash.

True Blues (16%) Usually men and women with moderate to high incomes who are loyal to a brand and sometimes to a particular station . . . frequently buy premium gasoline and pay in cash.

Generation F3 (for fuel, food and fast) (27%) Upwardly mobile men and women—half under 25 years of age—who are constantly on the go . . . drive a lot and snack heavily from the convenience store.

Homebodies (21%) Usually housewives who shuttle their children around during the day and use whatever gasoline station is based in town or along their route of travel.

Price Shoppers (20%) Generally aren't loyal to either a brand or a particular station, and rarely buy the premium line . . . frequently on tight budgets . . . efforts to woo them have been the basis of marketing strategies for years. ■

Source: Allanna Sullivan, "Mobil Bets Drivers Pick Cappuccino over Low Prices," *The Wall Street Journal* (January 30, 1995), pp. B1, B4.

Segments Identified Using Values Surveys among Teens Worldwide

Exhibit 9.2

Segment	%	Key Countries	Enjoy	Worry About	Own/Wear/Do
Thrills & chills (sensations)	18	Germany, U.K., Lithuania, Greece, Netherlands, South Africa, U.S.	going out to eat, going to a bar, drinking, smoking cigarettes, going to a party, going on a date, dancing; have most online access	finding love, unplanned pregnancy, own attractiveness	fast food, acne medication, perfume, would dye hair, would like tattoo or nose ring, do NOT have a job or attend church
Upholders (family, tradition)	16	Vietnam, Indonesia, Taiwan, China, Italy, Peru, Venezuela, Puerto Rico, India, Philippines, Singapore	reading books, spending time with family and visiting relatives; have least online access	not living up to others' expectations; believe the world will improve in their lifetime	do NOT have jobs to earn money, eat fast food, wear deodorant, wear tattoos or nose rings, carry guns; girls do NOT wear makeup
Quiet achievers (success, anonymity)	15	Thailand, China, Hong Kong, Ukraine, Korea, Lithuania, Russia, Peru	studying, listening to music, visiting museums; do NOT enjoy going to parties or drinking wine/beer	not living up to others' expectations; believe the world will improve in their lifetime; do NOT worry about finishing education, pregnancy, AIDS, or drugs	do NOT have jobs, or backpacks, blue jeans, or athletic shoes; girls do NOT wear makeup
Resigned (low expectations)	14	Denmark, Sweden, Korea, Japan, U.K., Norway, Germany, Belgium, France, Netherlands, Spain, Argentina, Canada, Turkey, Taiwan	do NOT enjoy doing something artistic/creative, attending opera, play or ballet, or visiting relatives	do NOT worry about going to college, the economy, rain forest, global warming, living up to others' expectations	have or would dye hair; do NOT care about access to new technology
Boot-strappers (achievement, individualism)	14	Nigeria, Mexico, U.S., India, Chile, Puerto Rico, South Africa, Venezuela, Colombia	spending time with family and visiting relatives	do NOT worry about not having friends or being lonely; believe education is good preparation for future and that they will have a good life	attend religious services; do NOT receive allowances
World savers (environment)	12	Hungary, Brazil, Phillippines, Venezuela, Spain, Colombia, Belgium, Argentina, Russia, Singapore, France, Poland, Ukraine, Italy, South Africa, Mexico, U.K.	attending opera, plays, and ballet, doing something artistic/creative (such as taking photos), going camping/hiking, going to a bar, dancing	racism, poverty for others, environment, AIDS, war, terrorism, being able to have children, finding love	would NOT carry gun

For more information, see Elissa Moses, *The $100 Billion Allowance: Accessing the Global Teen Market* (New York: Wiley, 2000), pp. 80–103.

that brand. Because attitudes influence behavior in this way, marketers want to shape attitudes or target people with favorable attitudes.

Thus, marketers often want to learn people's attitudes toward product categories, brands, and features of particular products or brands. For example, Ford Motor Company learned about young adults' attitudes toward advertising and used that insight to shape its own advertising for its Focus subcompact. The company determined that its young target market has a favorable attitude toward what Ford's communications manager Jan Klug calls "taking risks and living in the moment" and that they are skeptical of polished corporate messages. The company addressed those attitudes with a series of live (rather than prerecorded) commercials featuring TV star Anabelle Gurwitch.[9] Attitude is such a pervasive notion in behavioral science, and particularly in marketing, that Chapter 14 is devoted to various types of instruments used to measure it.

Awareness/Knowledge

Awareness/knowledge as used in marketing research refers to what respondents do and do not know about some object or phenomenon. For instance, a problem of considerable importance is the effectiveness of ads in TV, radio, magazine, billboard, and Web banners. One measure of effectiveness is the product awareness generated by the ad, using one of the three approaches described in Exhibit 9.3. All three tests of memory (unaided recall, aided recall, and recognition) are aimed at assessing the respondent's awareness of and knowledge about the ad. They are assumed by advertisers to reflect differences in the extent to which consumers have cognitively processed, in depth and detail or just superficially, the ad, the brand name, the featured attributes, etc. It is thought that consumers have retained more knowledge from the ad when they state the brand in an unaided recall test (for example, "What products and brands do you remember seeing ads for?") compared to a recall test where they have been given hints (such as "Do you remember recently seeing ads for PCs?"), and that both of these show superior knowledge and retention over simple recognition ("Do you remember seeing this ad for Dell?").[10]

One of the common indices used to measure the short-term success and impact of an ad is "day-after recall" (or DAR), which is a phone survey made the day following the airing of a new ad (such as the day after the Super Bowl). The DAR scores are compared to the ad agency's databank of such indices to project sales, by using other recent ads that had achieved similar DAR scores as benchmarks.

Increasingly, psychologists and advertising researchers are exploring the idea that consumers do not have to explicitly remember an ad for that ad to nevertheless have an impact on their behavior. For example, after airing an ad for Reebok, the researcher might choose to use

3 *Cite the three main approaches used to measure the effectiveness of magazine ads.*

awareness/knowledge
Insight into, or understanding of facts about, some object or phenomenon.

Exhibit 9.3

Approaches Used to Measure Awareness

Unaided recall: Without being given any clues, consumers are asked to recall what advertising they have seen recently. Prompting is not used because, presumably, even if prompting for the general category were used (such as for soups), respondents would have a tendency to remember more advertisements in that product category.

Aided recall: Consumers are prompted, typically in the form of questions about advertisements in a specific product category. Alternatively, respondents might be given a list showing the names or trademarks of advertisers that appeared recently (in the ad format being tested, such as on radio or Web), along with names or trademarks that did not appear, and would be asked to check those to which they were exposed.

Recognition: Actual advertisements are shown or described to consumers, who are asked whether they remember seeing each one.

"implicit" or indirect tests of memory. Rather than asking, "Do you remember any recent ads for athletic shoes or Reeboks?" the researcher might instead ask consumers to list brand names of sneakers, their choice of sporting shoes, shoes affiliated with athlete spokespersons, and so on, to assess the number of times the Reebok brand name appears. Researchers have even asked such questions as, "Name all the brands of any kind of product that start with R" to see how often Reebok would appear, along with names such as Reese's, Rolex, and Ramada. The assumption in these tests is that if Reebok appears disproportionately more than it should (based on market shares), the ad was successful in bringing the Reebok brand name to mind.

In addition to ad testing, memory measures are used to assess awareness of products. Marketing researchers are often interested in determining whether the respondent is aware of the product and its features, its price and where it may be purchased, its brand name and country of origin (for example, American-made, or made in Taiwan), and whether the customer connects the brand to the competitive advantages claimed in recent advertising. In general, awareness questions help the marketer assess consumers' knowledge of any element of the consumer experience—advertisements, products, retail stores, etc.

Intentions

intentions
Anticipated or planned future behavior.

A person's **intentions** refer to the individual's anticipated or planned future behavior. Marketers are interested in people's intentions primarily with regard to purchase behavior. One of the better known studies regarding purchase intentions is that conducted by the Survey Research Center at the University of Michigan. The center regularly conducts surveys for the Federal Reserve Board to determine the general financial condition of consumers and their outlook with respect to the state of the economy in the near future. The center phones a sample of 500 households monthly, asking 50 core questions about consumer confidence and buying intentions for big-ticket items such as appliances, automobiles, and homes during the next few months. The responses are then analyzed, and used as one indicator of future economic activity. In marketing, intentions are often gathered by asking respondents to indicate which of the following best describes their plans with respect to a new product or service:

- definitely would buy
- probably would buy
- undecided
- probably would not buy
- definitely would not buy

The number of people who answer that they definitely would buy or probably would buy are often combined into a "top box" to indicate likely reaction to the new product or service.

Intentions receive less attention in marketing than do other types of primary data, largely because there is often great disparity between what people say they are going to do and what they actually do. For example, in one study, consumers were told of a new pricing option for a service to which they already subscribed. They were asked to indicate how likely they were to buy the service when it became available. Only 45 percent of those indicating that they definitely would buy the service (the "top box")

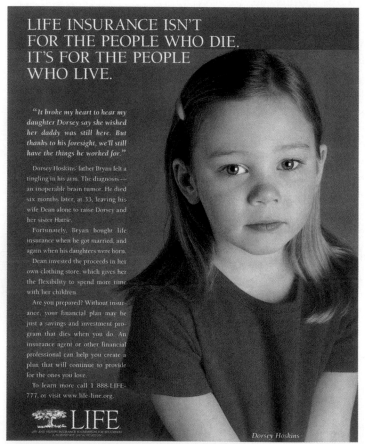

Courtesy of Life and Health Insurance Foundation for Education

The motive that this ad from LIFE, the nonprofit Life and Health Insurance Foundation for Education, is targeting is the need for parents to provide for their children even after the parents die. The ad directs consumers to a toll-free telephone number or a Web site address to learn more about reaching their financial goals through life insurance.

PART 3:
Data Collection Methods

did so within the first three months of its availability. Further, some of the respondents who indicated that they would not buy it actually did so.[11]

While the prediction of behaviors by intentions is not perfect, sometimes behavioral data are too expensive, difficult, or even impossible to obtain. For example, if Doritos were to create a new spicy salsa-flavor chip, by definition no purchase data would exist because the snack food would not have been available yet for purchase. If the marketer had data on a household's purchases of regular Doritos and salsa and spicy foods, perhaps an inference could be drawn to predict consumption of the new salsa chip (this inference requires assumptions, of course). In the absence of even these behavioral data, consumer judgments of their intentions are as close to actual behaviors as marketers can get. To help compensate for imperfect predictions, those organizations that collect purchase intentions data often adjust the data for the bias that intentions data are likely to contain (based on their past experience).

Purchase intentions are most often used when studying the purchase of commodities requiring large outlays, such as an automobile for a family, or plant and equipment for a business. The general assumption is that the larger the dollar expenditure, the more preplanning necessary and the greater the correlation between anticipated and actual behavior.

Motivation

The concept of motivation seems to contain more semantic confusion than most concepts in the behavioral sciences. Some writers insist that motives are different from drives and use the latter term primarily to characterize basic psychological needs such as hunger, thirst, shelter, and sex. Others distinguish between needs and wants, arguing that needs are the basic motivating forces, which translate into more immediate wants, which satisfy these needs (for example, hunger needs give rise to wanting a good steak dinner).

For our purposes, a **motive** may refer to a need, a want, a drive, an urge, a wish, a desire, an impulse, or any inner state that directs or channels behavior toward goals. Ensuring the financial security of one's family is the motive behind the ad shown for life and health insurance.

A marketing researcher's interest in motives typically involves determining *why* people behave as they do. There are several reasons for this interest. In the first place, researchers believe that a person's motives tend to be more stable than an individual's behavior and therefore offer a better basis for predicting future behavior than does past behavior.

The second reason researchers are interested in motives is that by understanding what drives a person's behavior, it is easier to understand the behavior itself. A desire for status may motivate one car buyer to purchase a Mercedes-Benz, while a concern for safety may send another to the local Volvo showroom. If researchers understand the forces underlying consumer behavior, they are in a better position to influence future behavior, or at least to design products consistent with what they anticipate that behavior to be.

Behavior

Behavior concerns what subjects have done or are doing. In marketing this usually means purchase and use behavior. Now, behavior is a physical activity. It takes place under specific circumstances, at a particular time, and involves one or more actors or participants. A marketing researcher investigating behavior would be interested in a description of the activity and its various components. Exhibit 9.4 is a checklist of the key elements involved in purchase behavior. Researchers can use a checklist like this one to design data collection instruments.

As a researcher fills in each category, he or she must make a decision about what information to include or omit. Consider the "where" category, for example. The "where of purchase" may be specified with respect to kind of store, the location of the store by broad geographic area or specific address, size of the store, or even the name of the store. So it is with each of the many categories. The study of behavior, then, involves the development of a description of the purchase or use activity, either past or current, with respect to some or all of the characteristics contained in Exhibit 9.4.

motive
A need, a want, a drive, a wish, a desire, an impulse, or any inner state that energizes, activates, or moves and that directs or channels behavior toward goals.

Give two reasons why researchers are interested in people's motives.

behavior
What subjects have done or are doing.

Exhibit 9.4

Behavior Checklist

	Purchase Behavior	Use Behavior
What and how much		
How		
Where		
When		
Who		

Behavior data are becoming increasingly available through various technologies (for example, scanners and the Web) and increasingly important to marketers, such as in building relationships with customers. Perhaps the most prevalent of behavioral data are scanner data—SKUs and other marketing information (such as price or coupon use) captured at purchase, stored in massive data banks, integrated with such other marketing variables as advertising exposure, to enable the marketing researcher to conduct sophisticated analyses of behavior in the marketplace. For the past 10 to 20 years, scanner data have made a great impact for consumer packaged goods marketers, but marketers responsible for pharmaceuticals, financial products, and a variety of other goods and services will also have access to these data as scanners and other technologies become more pervasive.

A different technology that yields similar behavior data is the Web and all it entails, including the production of personal profile data, click-stream trails, and records of response to Web advertising.[12] A revolution is occurring regarding data access. The marketer talented at analyzing these data sets will derive great insights.

Obtaining Primary Data

5 *Describe the two basic means of obtaining primary data.*

communication
A method of data collection involving questioning of respondents to secure the desired information, using a data collection instrument called a questionnaire.

observation
A method of data collection in which the situation of interest is watched and the relevant facts, actions, or behaviors are recorded.

6 *State the specific advantages of each method of data collection.*

The researcher attempting to collect primary data has several choices regarding the method to use (Figure 9.1). The primary decision is whether to use communication or observation. **Communication** involves questioning respondents to secure the desired information, using a data collection instrument called a questionnaire. The questions may be oral or in writing, and the responses may also be given in either form. **Observation** does not involve questioning. Rather, it means that the situation of interest is scrutinized and the relevant facts, actions, or behaviors are recorded. The observer may be one or more persons or a mechanical device. For instance, supermarket scanners may be used to determine how many boxes of a particular brand of cereal are sold in a given region in a typical week. Alternatively, a researcher interested in the brands of canned vegetables a family buys might arrange a pantry audit in which the family's shelves are checked to see which brands they have on hand.

Choosing a primary method of data collection also requires additional decisions. For example, should the questionnaires be administered by mail, over the telephone, or in person? Should the purpose of the study be disguised or remain undisguised? Should the answers be open-ended, or should the respondent be asked to choose from a limited set of alternatives? While Figure 9.1 implies that these decisions are independent, they are actually intimately related. A decision with respect to method of administration, say, has serious implications regarding the degree of structure that must be imposed on the questionnaire.

Each method of obtaining primary data has advantages and disadvantages, which are reviewed in the remainder of this chapter. In the next chapter we discuss the decisions that must be made when using the communication method, and in the following chapter, the decisions involved in the observation method. In general, the communication method of data collection has the general advantages of versatility, speed, and cost, while observational data are typically more objective and accurate.

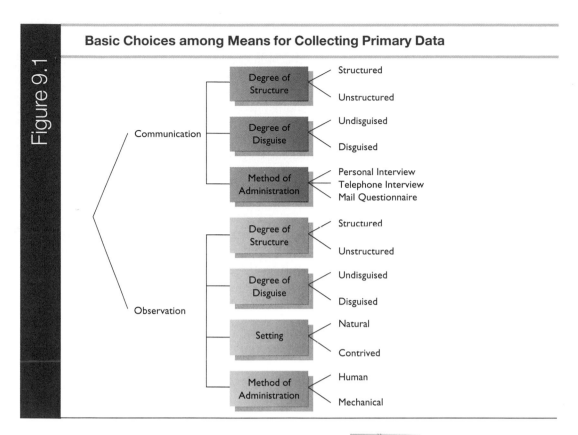

Figure 9.1

Basic Choices among Means for Collecting Primary Data

Communication
- Degree of Structure
  - Structured
  - Unstructured
- Degree of Disguise
  - Undisguised
  - Disguised
- Method of Administration
  - Personal Interview
  - Telephone Interview
  - Mail Questionnaire

Observation
- Degree of Structure
  - Structured
  - Unstructured
- Degree of Disguise
  - Undisguised
  - Disguised
- Setting
  - Natural
  - Contrived
- Method of Administration
  - Human
  - Mechanical

Versatility

Versatility is the ability of a technique to collect information on the many types of primary data of interest to marketers. A respondent's demographic/socioeconomic characteristics and lifestyle, the individual's attitudes and opinions, awareness and knowledge, intentions, the motivation underlying the individual's actions, and even the person's behavior may all be ascertained by communication. All we need to do is ask, although the replies will not necessarily be truthful.

Not so with observation. Observation techniques can provide us only with information about behavior and certain demographic/socioeconomic characteristics. Even here, our observations are limited to present behavior, for example. We cannot observe a person's past behavior. Nor can we observe the person's intentions as to future behavior. If we are interested in past behavior or intentions, we must ask.

Some demographic/socioeconomic characteristics can be readily observed. Sex is the most obvious example. Others can be observed but with less accuracy. A person's age and income, for example, might be inferred by closely examining the individual's mode of dress and purchasing behavior. Clearly, though, both of these observations may be in error, with income likely to be the furthest off. Still others, such as social class, cannot be observed with any

ETHICAL dilemma 9.1

A national department store chain with a relatively sophisticated image is planning to open a store in an area inhabited by professionals. The marketing research director of the company wants a detailed profile of the residents' characteristics and lifestyles in order to tailor the new store to the tastes of this lucrative new market. He suggests that you, a member of his staff, contribute to the research effort by spending a month observing the residents going about their daily affairs of eating in restaurants, attending church, shopping in other stores, socializing with one another, and so on. You are then to prepare a report on what expenditures support their lifestyles.

- *Are there ethical problems involved in observing people in public places? Do the ethical problems become more serious if you socialize with your subjects?*

- *Who has ethical responsibility for your behavior: the marketing research director? You? Both?*

ETHICAL dilemma 9.2

A marketing research firm was hired by a candy manufacturer to gather data on the alternatives consumers consider when deciding to buy a candy bar. Sue Samuelson, the person in charge of the research, believed that the best way to collect accurate information was through an observation study done in major supermarkets, drugstores, and discount stores in a number of large cities. Unfortunately, at that time the personnel of the firm were stretched to the limit because of a number of other assignments. The company simply did not have sufficient personnel available to do the study using personal observation and still meet the client's deadline. Samuelson consequently decided that she would propose to the client a mail study utilizing the research firm's panel of households. Not only would this place fewer demands on the research firm's personnel, but the cost to the client would be about 25 percent less than with personal observation.

- *Does Samuelson have an obligation to the client to disclose why she is recommending the mail panel?*

- *Is it ethical for a research firm to use alternative methods of gathering data because of internal constraints? What if the alternatives reduce the charges to the client?*

- *Who should make the decision as to the best way to approach the project—the client or the research supplier?*

degree of confidence about the accuracy of the recorded data.

The other basic types of primary data cannot be measured by observation at all. We simply cannot observe an attitude or opinion, a person's awareness or knowledge, or motivation. Certainly we can attempt to make some inferences about these variables on the basis of the individual's observed behavior. For instance, if a person is observed purchasing a can of a new flavor of Progresso soup, we might infer that the person has a favorable attitude toward Progresso. There is a real question, however, as to the correctness of the inference. A great deal of controversy exists over whether attitudes precede behavior or behavior precedes attitude formation. Perhaps the latter is correct, and the person, in fact, has no particular attitudes toward Progresso as a brand but just thought he or she would try it. The individual may not even have been aware of that brand previously but saw it for the first time on the shelf. Generalizing from observed behavior to states of mind is risky, and researchers need to recognize this. Questioning clearly encompasses a much broader base of primary data.

Speed and Cost

The speed and cost advantages of the communication method are closely intertwined. Assuming the data lend themselves to either, communication is often a faster means of data collection than observation, because it provides a greater degree of control over data-gathering activities. With the communication method, researchers are not forced to wait for events to occur, as they would be with the observation method. In some cases, it is impossible to predict when an event will occur precisely enough to observe it. For other behaviors, the time interval between events can be substantial. For instance, an observer seeking to determine the brand purchased most frequently in one of several appliance categories might have to wait a long time to make any observations at all. Much of the time the observer would be idle. Such idleness is expensive, as the worker will probably be compensated on an hourly, rather than a per-contact, basis. Events that last a long time can also cause difficulty. An observational approach to studying the relative influence of a husband and a wife in the purchase of an automobile would be prohibitive in terms of both time and money.

There are instances when observation is faster and costs less than communication. A primary example involves the purchase of consumer nondurables. The use of scanners, for example, allows many more purchases to be recorded and at less cost than if purchasers were questioned about what they bought.

PART 3:
Data Collection Methods

Objectivity and Accuracy

Although the observation method has some serious limitations in terms of scope, time, and cost, it does have certain advantages with regard to objectivity and accuracy. Data that can be secured by either method will typically be more accurately secured by observation. This is because the observation method is independent of the respondent's unwillingness or inability to provide the information desired. For example, respondents are often reluctant to cooperate whenever their replies might place them in an unfavorable light. Sometimes respondents conveniently forget embarrassing events, while in other cases the events are not of sufficient importance for them to remember what happened. Since observation allows the recording of behavior as it occurs, it is not dependent on the respondent's memory or mood in reporting what occurred.

Observation typically produces more objective data than does communication. The interview represents a social interaction situation. Thus, the replies of the person being questioned are conditioned by the individual's perceptions of the interviewer. The same is true of interviewers' perceptions, but their training should afford a greater degree of control over their perceptions than would be true of the interviewee. With the observation method, the subject's perceptions play less of a role than in the communication method. Sometimes people are not even aware they are being observed, so they are not tempted to tell the interviewer what they think the interviewer wants to hear or to give socially acceptable responses that are not truthful. The problems of objectivity are concentrated in the observer's methods, and this makes the task easier. The observer's selection, training, and control, and not the subject's perceptions of the field worker, become the crucial elements.

© AP/Wide World Photos

Using scanners to record consumer purchases is an efficient, cost-effective way of gathering primary data.

looking back...

To help Moen develop a shower head for which consumers would pay top dollar, QualiData Research prepared a study combining communication and observation. QualiData recruited subjects to keep diaries of their shower habits, then visit a testing facility for in-depth interviews and actual showers. At a Lowe's home center, researchers used hidden cameras to observe customers in the shower head aisle, then surveyed shoppers as they left.

Perhaps the biggest challenge was finding subjects for the in-shower observations. Brainstorming, Mariampolski and his research team identified a logical source: social nudists, whose philosophy is that nudity is natural, not embarrassing. Internet bulletin boards for such groups were one of the recruiting sources, and members of nudist groups were a sizable portion of the approximately 20 subjects. Volunteers were screened to ensure their motives were appropriate and not wholly focused on the $250 fee paid for participating. Also, researchers selected a variety of ages, body types, and ethnicities.

For the test, showers were hooked up to a computer to measure water temperature and flow. A heat- and moisture-resistant video camera was mounted next to the shower head. From these measurements, researchers identified significant patterns of behavior. For example, they determined that adjusting a shower head can be tricky, because people often have their eyes closed and are holding accessories like soap or a washcloth. The surveys told Moen that consumers want to adjust the shower head to meet the needs of different household members or to achieve different benefits (such as stress relief or an early-morning wakeup). Thus, an easily adjustable shower head would meet a need.

The research into shopping behavior also provided insights. Moen learned that most shoppers spent about five minutes looking at shower heads, then walked away without speaking to a store employee. That meant the shower head's packaging would have to catch shoppers' eyes quickly and sell them on the product. Shoppers also tested the weight of different shower heads, suggesting they use weight as an indicator of sturdy construction and high quality.

Moen's engineers used this information to develop the Revolution, a shower head that looks and feels substantial. They placed a control dial below the water stream so consumers can easily use one hand to adjust the shower's force, frequency, and coverage. To catch consumers' eyes on store shelves, package designers created holographic images on wedge-shaped boxes. Introduced in 2001, the Revolution quickly began to fly off store shelves.

Applying this research has helped Moen maintain strong performance. A subsidiary of Fortune Brands, Moen is the best-selling brand for its parent company. ∎

Sources: Dina ElBoghdady, "Naked Truth Meets Market Research: Perfecting a New Shower Head? Try Watching People Shower," *Washington Post* (February 24, 2002), downloaded from the Dow Jones Interactive Publications Library, http://nrstg2s.djnr.com; Moen, "Extensive Research by Moen Provides What Consumers Want in a Great Shower Experience," news release, July 17, 2001, downloaded from the Moen Web site, http://www.moen.com; Fortune Brands, "Home Products," Fortune Brands Web site, http://www.fortunebrands.com, downloaded February 11, 2003.

Summary

Learning Objective 1
List the kinds of demographic and socioeconomic characteristics that interest marketers.
Marketers are interested in such socioeconomic and demographic characteristics as age, education, occupation, marital status, sex, income, and social class.

Learning Objective 2
Relate the premise on which lifestyle analysis rests.
Lifestyle analysis rests on the premise that a company can plan more effective strategies to reach its target market if it knows more about its customers in terms of how they live, what interests them, and what they like.

Learning Objective 3
Cite the three main approaches used to measure the effectiveness of magazine ads.
The three main approaches used to measure awareness of magazine ads are (1) unaided recall, in which the consumer is given no clues at all; (2) aided recall, in which the consumer is given some prompting; and (3) recognition, in which the consumer is actually shown an advertisement and asked whether or not he or she remembers seeing it.

Learning Objective 4
Give two reasons why researchers are interested in people's motives.
First, researchers believe that motives tend to be more stable than behavior and therefore offer a better basis for predicting future behavior. Second, researchers believe that by understanding what drives a person's behavior, it is easier to understand the behavior itself.

Learning Objective 5
Describe the two basic means of obtaining primary data.
The two basic means of obtaining primary data are communication and observation. Communication involves questioning respondents to secure the desired information, using a data collection instrument called a questionnaire. Observation involves scrutinizing the situation of interest and recording the relevant facts, actions, or behaviors.

Learning Objective 6
State the specific advantages of each method of data collection.
In general, the communication method of data collection has the advantages of versatility, speed, and cost, while observation data are typically more objective and accurate.

Key Terms

personality (page 209)
psychographic analysis(page 210)
attitude (page 211)
opinion (page 211)
awareness/knowledge (page 213)

intentions (page 214)
motive (page 215)
behavior (page 215)
communication (page 216)
observation (page 216)

Review Questions

1. What types of primary data interest marketing researchers most? How are they distinguished?
2. What are the general advantages and disadvantages associated with obtaining information by questioning? By observation? Which method provides more control over the sample?

Discussion Questions, Problems, and Projects

Should the communication or the observation method be used in the situations described in Questions 1 and 2? Justify your choice.

1. The Metal Product Division of Miracle Ltd. devised a special metal container to store plastic garbage bags. Plastic bags pose household problems, as they give off unpleasant odors, look disorderly, and provide a breeding place for insects. The container overcomes these problems, as it has a bag-support apparatus that holds the bag open for filling and seals the bag when the lid is closed. In addition, there is enough storage area for at least four full bags. The product is priced at $53.81 and is sold through hardware stores. The company has done little advertising and relies on in-store promotion and displays. The divisional manager is wondering about the effectiveness of these displays. She has called on you to do the necessary research.

2. Friendship is a national manufacturer and distributor of greeting cards. The company has recently begun distributing a low-priced line of cards using a lower-grade paper. Quality differences between the higher- and lower-priced cards do not seem to be noticeable to consumers. The company follows a policy of printing its name and the price on the back of each card. The initial acceptance of the new line of cards has convinced the vice president of production, Sheila Howell, that the company should use this lower-grade paper for all its cards and increase its profit margin from 12.3 percent to 14.9 percent. The sales manager is strongly opposed to this move and has commented, "Sheila, consumers are concerned about the quality of greeting cards; a price difference of 5 cents on a card does not matter." The vice president has called upon you to undertake the study.

3. Stop-Buy, Inc., recently opened a new convenience store in Galveston, Texas. The store is open every day from 7:00 A.M. to 11:00 P.M. Management is interested in determining the trading area from which this store draws its customers, so that it can better plan the location of other units in the Galveston area.

   How would you determine this information by the questionnaire method? By the observation method? Which method would be preferred? Be sure to specify in your answer how you would define "trading area."

4. Following are several objectives for marketing research projects. For each objective, specify the type(s) of primary data that would be of use and a possible method of data collection.
   (a) assess "people flow" patterns inside a shopping mall
   (b) gauge the effectiveness of a new advertisement
   (c) gauge a salesperson's potential for success
   (d) segment a market
   (e) identify the shopper types that patronize a particular store
   (f) discover how people feel about a new package design

5. Lifestyle, or psychographic analysis, collects data concerning three dimensions of a respondent's lifestyle. Compare and contrast these dimensions. Are the three dimensions exhaustive, or can you suggest others that should be included?

Suggested Additional Readings

There are a number of guides to the various personality inventories. One of the better ones for marketers is Delbert C. Miller, *Handbook of Research Design and Social Measurement,* 5th ed. (Thousand Oaks, Calif.: Sage Publications, 1991).

For a general discussion of the purpose, procedures, and uses of lifestyle research, see Rebecca Piirto, *Beyond Mind Games: The Marketing Power of Psychographics* (Ithaca, N.Y.: American Demographic Books, 1991).

For a compilation of many of the most popular scales marketing researchers use to measure the traits discussed in this chapter, see William O. Bearden and Richard G. Netemeyer, *Handbook of Marketing Scales: Multi-Item Measures for Management and Consumer Behavior Research* (Thousand Oaks, CA.: Sage Publications, 1999).

Chapter 10

Collecting Information by Communication

Learning Objectives

1 *Explain the concept of* structure *as it relates to questionnaires.*

2 *Explain what is meant by* disguise *in a questionnaire.*

3 *Discuss why structured-undisguised questionnaires are the type most frequently used by marketing researchers.*

4 *Cite three drawbacks of fixed-alternative questions.*

5 *Explain why researchers use projective methods in conducting some studies.*

6 *List three common types of stimuli used in projective techniques.*

7 *Differentiate among the main methods of administering questionnaires.*

8 *Cite the points researchers generally consider when they compare the various methods of administering questionnaires.*

"**D**o you know who your customers *really* are?" asked Rick Shanahan, the domestic sales manager for Clean-Rite appliances. He was sitting in the office of Tom Karlin, a successful appliance distributor who had a nine-county Clean-Rite franchise in booming central Florida.

"What do you mean?" asked Karlin, obviously intrigued.

"I mean that demographically, I can tell you who in your region has bought a Clean-Rite appliance within the last two years. I can tell you how old they are, how much money they make, what they like to do in their free time, and why they bought Clean-Rite rather than the competition."

"That's neat," replied Karlin, "but where's the information from? I didn't think Clean-Rite did a lot of heavy demographic research, especially not anything specific to central Florida."

"Well, we don't—at least not directly. We've started using a company that specializes in providing a consumer database that it generates from the information on product registration cards."

"You mean the cards the customers fill out and send back, saying where and when they bought their dishwasher and what the serial number is?"

"Yep. Not only does the registration card help us keep track of warranty information, but we also ask the consumers to answer some quick questions about their income, education, and interests. We already know their address. Most people don't even realize they're filling out a questionnaire."

"You're right, I never thought about product registration cards as questionnaires."

"Well," continued Shanahan, warming to his subject, "we pack a postage-paid registration card in with every appliance. The buyer fills it out and sends it directly to DLD, Demographics Life-Style Data, a company in Houston. DLD uses the information from the cards to generate a demographic database similar to U.S. Census information, but much more current. In addition, DLD's database has a lot more lifestyle information about the respondents. But the real beauty of the thing isn't in national projections—any marketer can send out 2,000 questionnaires and make national projections. DLD can break out specific *geographic regions*. They can make projections down to specific postal codes or neighborhoods. Like I said, I can tell you all about the consumers in your franchise area who, over the past two years, have bought an appliance from Clean-Rite."

"That's amazing," replied Karlin, "I'd love to see the information."

When the DLD computer printouts arrived several days later, Karlin spent some time studying the data. It really was interesting to see what kind of person bought Clean-Rite over other brands. Of course, he'd already had a picture of that customer in the back of his mind, based on his experience as a dealer. Clean-Rite had a reputation as a quality manufacturer and as a rule didn't go after the low end of the market. But this information was much more specific than just a salesman's gut response.

He learned that the typical Clean-Rite purchaser in his part of Florida had an income of $40,000 or greater, a college education, and a taste for outdoor recreation like golf, tennis, and boating.

"Great," thought Karlin as he tapped his pencil against the side of his coffee cup. "Now what?"

Discussion Issues

1. What are the limitations of product registration cards used as marketing research questionnaires?

2. Should someone make any major decisions based on the product registration data alone?

3. What kinds of additional research would you recommend? ■

In Chapter 9 we discussed the types of primary data that interest marketing researchers. We also briefly examined the two methods, communication and observation, that researchers use to gather such data. In this chapter we will investigate communication techniques more closely, paying particular attention to the many types of questionnaires researchers use and the means by which they are administered.

Communication Methods

As we saw in Figure 9.1, if researchers choose to use the communication method of gathering data, they must then decide what kind of questionnaire would best serve the problem at hand. They must determine the degree of **structure,** or standardization, to be imposed on the questionnaire, and the degree of **disguise** that is appropriate to the problem they are investigating.

In a highly structured questionnaire, the questions to be asked and the responses permitted by the subjects are completely predetermined. In a highly unstructured questionnaire, the questions to be asked are only loosely predetermined, and the respondents are free to respond in their own words. A questionnaire in which the questions are fixed but the responses are open-ended would represent an intermediate degree of structure. A disguised questionnaire attempts to hide the purpose of the study, whereas an undisguised questionnaire makes the purpose of the research obvious by the questions posed. For example, if Ford wished to determine its customers' satisfaction, they might worry that a cover letter from Ford and questions all about Ford cars and trucks would bias the respondents' answers favorably toward Ford, since the survey's purpose is clear. If Ford wished for more objective data, they might forgo letterhead, or go through an outside marketing research agency, and ask their drivers about Ford, GM, and Honda cars. In this scenario, the target of the research is less clear, and it is expected that the customer would answer more truthfully.

Structured-Undisguised Questionnaires

Marketing researchers often use structured-undisguised questionnaires in which questions are presented with exactly the same wording and in exactly the same order to all respondents when collecting data. The reason for standardizing the wording is to ensure that all respondents are replying to the same questions. If one interviewer asked, "Do you drink orange juice?" and another asked, "Does your family use frozen orange juice?" the replies would not be comparable.

In the typical structured-undisguised questionnaire, the responses as well as the questions are standardized. **Fixed-alternative questions,** in which the responses are limited to the stated alternatives, are used. Consider the following question regarding the subject's attitude toward pollution and the need for more government legislation to control it.

Do you feel the United States needs more or less antipollution legislation?

■ Needs more
■ Needs less

1 Explain the concept of structure as it relates to questionnaires.

2 Explain what is meant by disguise in a questionnaire.

structure
The degree of standardization imposed on the data collection instrument.

disguise
The amount of knowledge about the purpose of a study communicated to the respondent. An undisguised questionnaire, for example, is one in which the purpose of the research is obvious.

3 Discuss why structured-undisguised questionnaires are the type most frequently used by marketing researchers.

- Neither more nor less
- No opinion

This question is a good example of a structured-undisguised question for two reasons. First, its purpose is clear: It seeks to discover the subject's attitudes toward antipollution legislation in a very straightforward manner. Second, it uses a highly structured format. Respondents are limited to only one of four stated replies.

Probably the greatest advantages of structured-undisguised questionnaires are that they are simple to administer and easy to tabulate and analyze. Subjects should be reliable in that if they were asked the question again, they would answer in a similar fashion (assuming, of course, the absence of some attitude-changing event).

Such reliability is facilitated by the consistency of fixed-alternative questions. These questions help standardize responses by providing subjects with an identical frame of reference. In contrast, consider the question, "How often do you watch television?" If no alternatives were supplied, one respondent might say "every day," another might say "regularly," and still another might respond with the number of hours per day. Responses from such an open-ended question would be far more difficult to interpret than those from a fixed-alternative question limiting replies to the categories of "every day," "at least three times a week," "at least once a week," or "less than once a week."

Providing alternative responses also often helps to make the question clear. "What is your marital status?" is less clear in its intent than "Are you married, single, widowed, or divorced?" The latter question provides the dimensions in which to frame the reply.

Although fixed-alternative questions tend to provide the most reliable responses, they may also elicit misleading answers. For example, fixed alternatives may force an answer to a question on which the respondent has no opinion. Even when a "no opinion" category is provided, interviewers often try to keep the number of "no opinions" to a minimum by pressing the respondent for a reply. The individual may agree, under pressure, to one of the other alternatives offered, but the alternative may not accurately capture the individual's true position on the issue. For example, the antipollution example presented earlier makes no allowance for those who feel that something probably should be done about pollution and that more legislation may possibly be one answer, but who fundamentally favor other approaches.

Fixed-alternative responses may also produce inaccuracies when the response categories themselves introduce bias. This is particularly true when a reasonable response is omitted because of an oversight or insufficient prior research regarding the response categories that are appropriate. The provision of an "other" category does not eliminate this bias either, since subjects are often reluctant to respond in the "other" category. In posing a fixed-alternative question, one should make sure the alternatives offered adequately cover the range of probable replies.

The fixed-alternative question is thus most productive when possible replies are well known, limited in number, and clear-cut. Thus they work well for securing factual information (age, education, home ownership, amount of rent, and so on) and for eliciting expressions of opinion about issues on which people hold clear opinions. They are not very appropriate for securing primary data on motivations, but certainly could be used to collect data on attitudes, intentions, awareness, demographic/socioeconomic characteristics, and behavior.

Unstructured-Undisguised Questionnaires

The unstructured-undisguised questionnaire is distinguished by the fact that the purpose of the study is clear but the response to the question is open-ended. Consider the following question:

"How do you feel about pollution and the need for more antipollution legislation?"

This initial question (which is often called a *stimulus* by researchers) is clear in its purpose. With it the interviewer attempts to get the subject to talk freely about his or her attitudes toward pollution. This is an **open-ended question,** and often leads to a very unstructured

might be *traffic, lakes, smokestacks,* and *city,* mixed in with words such as *margarine, blue jeans,* and *government.*

Responses to each of the key terms are recorded word-for-word and later analyzed for their meaning. The responses are usually judged in three ways: by the frequency with which any word is given as a response, by the average amount of time that elapses before a response is given, and by the number of respondents who do not respond at all to a test word after a reasonable period of time.

Any common responses that emerge are grouped to reveal patterns of interest, underlying motivations, or stereotypes. It is often possible to categorize the associations as favorable/unfavorable, pleasant/unpleasant, modern/old-fashioned, and so forth, depending upon the problem.

To determine the amount of time that elapses before a response is given to a test word, a stopwatch may be used or the interviewer may count silently while waiting for a reply. Respondents who hesitate (which is usually defined as taking longer than three seconds to reply) are judged to be sufficiently emotionally involved in the word so as to provide not their immediate reaction but rather what they consider to be an acceptable response. If they do not respond at all, their emotional involvement is judged to be so high as to block a response. An individual's pattern of responses, along with the details of the response to each question, are then used to assess the person's attitudes or feelings on the subject.

Sentence Completion The method of **sentence completion** requires that the respondent complete a number of sentences with the first thoughts that come to mind. The responses are recorded word-for-word and are later analyzed.

While the analysis of qualitative responses is subjective, sometimes the results are clear enough that there would be good agreement in their interpretation as follows:

People who are concerned about ecology *care about the future.*
A person who does not use our lakes for recreation is *being thoughtful about the ecosystem.*
When I think of living in a city, I *can't help but think of the smog over LA.*

Compare those response to these of another person:

People who are concerned about ecology *are just tree-huggers who want to run up my taxes.*
A person who does not use our lakes for recreation is *a person who doesn't enjoy water sports.*
When I think of living in a city, I *think about cruising my car downtown on Saturday night!*

Presumably, these two respondents could easily be characterized as belonging to segments of consumers who are more and less ecologically concerned.

One advantage of sentence completion over word association is that respondents can be provided with a more directed stimulus. There should be just enough direction to evoke some association with the concept of interest. The researcher needs to be careful not to convey the purpose of the study or provoke the "socially acceptable" response. Obviously, skill is needed to develop a good sentence-completion or word-association test.

Storytelling The **storytelling** approach often relies on pictorial material such as cartoons, photographs, or drawings, although other stimuli are also used. These pictorial devices are descendants of the psychologists' **Thematic Apperception Test (TAT).** The TAT consists of a copyrighted series of pictures about which the subject is asked to tell stories. Some pictures are of ordinary events and others are of unusual events; in some pictures the persons or objects are clearly represented, and in others they are relatively obscure. The way a subject responds to these events helps researchers interpret that individual's personality. For example, the nature of the response might show a subject to be impulsive or controlled, creative or unimaginative, and so on.

In a marketing situation, respondents are shown a picture and asked to tell a story about it. However, the responses are used to assess attitudes toward the phenomenon under investigation rather than to interpret the subject's personality.[4]

word association
A questionnaire containing a list of words to which respondents are instructed to reply with the first word that comes to mind.

sentence completion
A questionnaire containing a number of sentences that subjects are directed to complete with the first words that come to mind.

storytelling
A questionnaire method of data collection relying on a picture stimulus such as a cartoon, photograph, or drawing, about which the subject is asked to tell a story.

Thematic Apperception Test (TAT)
A copyrighted series of pictures about which the subject is asked to tell stories.

With respect to the pollution example, the stimulus might be a picture of a city, and the respondent might be asked to describe what it would be like to live there. The analysis of the individual's response would then focus on the emphasis given to pollution in its various forms. If no mention were made of traffic congestion, dirty air, noise, and so on, the person would be classified as displaying little concern for pollution and its control.

Each of the projective methods we have discussed differs somewhat in how structured its stimulus is. In the word-association and sentence-completion methods, researchers present each respondent with the same stimulus in the same sequence, and in this sense these methods are quite structured. However, both methods are typically categorized with storytelling as unstructured techniques, because, like the storytelling techniques, they allow very unstructured responses. Respondents are free to interpret and respond to the stimuli with their own words and in terms of their own perceptions.

Many of the same difficulties encountered with the unstructured-undisguised methods of data collection are also encountered with projective methods. Although having a standardized stimulus is a distinct advantage in interpreting the replies, the interpretation often reflects the researcher's frame of reference as much as it does the respondent's. Different researchers often reach different conclusions about the same response. This wreaks havoc with the editing, coding, and tabulating of replies and suggests that projective methods are also more suited for exploratory research than for descriptive or causal research.

Structured-Disguised Questionnaires

Structured-disguised questionnaires are seldom used in marketing research. They were developed as a way of combining the advantages of disguise in uncovering subconscious motives and attitudes with the advantages of structure in coding and tabulating replies. Those who favor the structured-disguised approach usually base their support on the importance of a person's attitudes in his or her mental and psychological makeup.

One theory holds, for example, that an individual's knowledge, perception, and memory of a subject are conditioned by his or her attitudes toward it. Thus, in order to secure information about people's attitudes when a direct question would produce a biased answer, this theory suggests we simply ask them what they know, not what their opinion is. Presumably greater knowledge reflects the strength and direction of an attitude. Democratic voters, for example, could be expected to know more about Democratic candidates and the Democratic platform than would those intending to vote Republican. This argument is consistent with what we have learned about the process that psychologists call *selective perception*. That concept holds that individuals tend to selectively expose themselves to, selectively perceive, and selectively retain ideas, arguments, events, and phenomena that are consistent with their previously held beliefs. Conversely, people tend to avoid, see differently, and forget situations and items that are inconsistent with their previously held beliefs.

This theory suggests that one way of discovering a respondent's true attitudes toward pollution and the need for antipollution legislation, for example, would be to ask the person what he or she knows about the subject. Thus, the researcher might ask, "What is the status of the antipollution legislation listed below?" and then present some actual and some hypothetical bills for the respondent to check: "In committee," "Passed by the House but not the Senate," "Vetoed by the president," etc. Respondents' attitudes toward the need for more legislation would then be assessed by the accuracy of their responses.

The main advantages of this approach emerge in analysis. Responses are easily coded and tabulated and an objective measure of knowledge quickly derived. Whether this measure of knowledge can also be interpreted as a measure of the person's attitudes, however, is another matter. Is high legislative awareness indicative of a favorable or an unfavorable attitude toward the need for more antipollution legislation? Or is it simply indicative of someone who keeps abreast of current events? In general, the evidence suggests that it is possible to obtain results with a structured-disguised approach that are at least comparable to those obtained with unstructured-disguised approaches.

Methods of Administering Questionnaires

Questionnaires can also be classified by the method that will be used to administer them. The main methods are by personal interview, telephone, mail, fax, email, and Web surveys.

A **personal interview** implies a direct face-to-face conversation between the interviewer and the respondent or interviewee. The interviewer asks the questions and records the respondent's answers, either while the interview is in progress or immediately afterward. The interview can take place in a home or an office or usually at a central location like a shopping mall, where shoppers are stopped (or intercepted, hence the term *mall intercept*) and asked to participate.

The **telephone interview** means that this conversation occurs over the phone.

The normal administration of a **mail questionnaire** involves mailing the questionnaires to designated respondents with an accompanying cover letter. The respondents complete the questionnaire at their leisure and mail their replies back to the research organization.

Faxed surveys operate just like mail questionnaires, except that they are faxed to and from the recipients. Fax surveys work much better for business-to-business research because most consumers do not have fax machines at home.

Email surveys are one of two types:

- The questions of the market research study are embedded in the text of the email itself
- The questions in the survey are in an email attachment file

Each has its pros and cons: Replying to embedded email surveys is very quick. Alternatively, the attachment is likely to look more professional than the flat embedded text, and it can allow for hyperlinking, skip-patterns, artwork, and so on. However, it is one more step to open an attachment, and any additional steps that add to the hurdle of completing a survey means that response rates will drop off. Web surveys resemble the attachment files in that hypertext and graphics can improve both the appearance and quality control of the survey, as well as enhance the inherent appeal by, for example, requesting consumer reactions to graphic depictions of an ad or product.

The preceding descriptions suggest the most common or "pure" methods of administration. A number of variations are possible. Questionnaires for a "mail" administration may simply be attached to products or printed in magazines and newspapers. Similarly, questionnaires in a personal interview may be self-administered, perhaps in the interviewer's presence, to provide an opportunity for the respondents to seek clarification on points of confusion from the interviewer. Alternatively, the respondents might complete the questionnaire in private for later pickup by a representative of the research organization, in which case the interaction would be less like a personal interview. Another possibility is for the interviewer to hand the designated respondent the questionnaire personally but then have the respondent complete it in private and mail it directly to the research organization. In this case, the personal interview is indistinguishable from the mail questionnaire method.

Each of these methods of communication possesses some advantages and disadvantages. When discussing the pros and cons, the pure cases logically serve as a frame of reference. When a modified form of administration is used, the general advantages and disadvantages may no longer hold. They may also cease to hold in specific situations, in which case a general advantage may become a disadvantage, and vice versa. The advantages and disadvantages also

7 Differentiate among the main methods of administering questionnaires.

personal interview
Direct, face-to-face conversation between a representative of the research organization, the interviewer, and a respondent, or interviewee.

telephone interview
Telephone conversation between a representative of the research organization, the interviewer, and a respondent, or interviewee.

mail questionnaire
A questionnaire administered by mail to designated respondents under an accompanying cover letter. The respondents return the questionnaire by mail to the research organization.

faxed survey
A questionnaire faxed to a respondent and, when completed, returned to the research sponsor by fax.

email survey
A questionnaire both sent and returned by email.

8 Cite the points researchers generally consider when they compare the various methods of administering questionnaires.

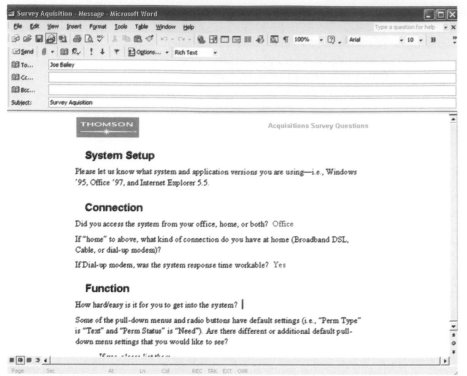

may not apply when dealing with different countries with different cultures.

For example, telephone interviews are commonly conducted in the U.S., and they are frequent also in the Netherlands, Germany, and the United Kingdom (U.K.). They are rare in Japan, where it is not culturally acceptable to answer questions from "strangers" over the telephone; for different reasons (the unreliability of the communications networks), phone surveys are exceedingly rare in Mexico, Argentina, and Hungary. Door-to-door interviewing is illegal in Saudi Arabia, legal but prohibitively expensive in the U.S., and more common in Switzerland and the U.K. Finally, good mailing lists are critical to the success and frequent use of mail surveys in the U.S. and also in Sweden, where the government routinely publishes lists of every Swedish household, making mail studies very feasible there.[5]

The specific problem and culture, then, will actually dictate the benefits and weaknesses associated with each method of communication. Nevertheless, a general discussion of advantages and disadvantages highlights the various issues that need to be considered in deciding on how the data will be collected. Sampling control, information control, and administrative control are definite points to consider when comparing the methods.

Sampling Control

Questions in an email survey can be embedded directly in the text of the email, making it quick and easy for participants to respond.

sampling control
The term applied to studies relying on questionnaires and concerning the researcher's dual abilities to direct the inquiry to a designated respondent and to secure the desired cooperation from that respondent.

sampling frame
The list of sampling units from which a sample will be drawn; the list could consist of geographic areas, institutions, individuals, or other units.

Sampling control involves the researcher's ability to direct the inquiry to a designated respondent and to get the desired cooperation from that respondent. The direction of the inquiry is guided by the **sampling frame**—that is, by the list of population elements from which the sample will be drawn. With the telephone method, for example, one or more phone books typically serve as the sampling frame. Respondents are selected by some random method from phone books serving the areas in which the study is to be done. Phone book sampling frames are inadequate because they do not include those without phones or those who have unlisted numbers.

Of course, a large percentage of the U.S. population has phones—almost 95 percent of all households. Yet there is some variation by region and by other demographic factors. In other countries, such as the U.K., phone penetration nearly resembles that in the U.S., but worldwide phone access is generally lower (for example, it is 20 percent in Russia).[6] Exhibit 10.1 summarizes the evidence regarding the demographic factors affecting phone ownership. The differences in phone ownership by various demographic factors can bias the results of a telephone survey.

The proportion of households with telephones increases each year, however; thus the problem of bias resulting from the exclusion of nontelephone households should diminish in the future. For example, differences between rural and urban penetration rates are likely to diminish with satellite services and mobile or cellular phones, since these technologies do not require infrastructures that may not exist in some rural locations.

Studies that rely on phone book sampling frames underrepresent transient households. Anywhere from 12 percent to 15 percent of the residential numbers in a typical telephone directory are disconnected when called. Phone book sampling frames also do not include numbers that were assigned after the current directory was published, or the segment of the

PART 3:
Data Collection Methods

population that has requested an unlisted telephone number. The voluntary unlisted segment has been growing steadily and now represents approximately one third of the 87.1 million U.S. telephone households. The problem is particularly acute in urban areas in general, and some urban areas in particular. Figure 10.1 for example, shows the ten metropolitan areas in the United States with the highest population of unlisted numbers.

Exhibit 10.1

Summary of Studies of Demographic Factors Related to Telephone Ownership

1. Telephone coverage is greater in urban areas than in rural areas, although in countries with very high overall telephone penetration (e.g., Canada, France, Denmark, and Norway) the difference is rather small.
2. In the United States, coverage is lower in the South. Similar regional differences prevail in at least some other countries (e.g., Ireland and Israel), but regional categorizations are country specific and are hard to compare cross-nationally.
3. In the United States, coverage is lower among nonwhites. No racial information was available from other countries.
4. Telephone coverage is always lower among those with lower incomes, the unemployed, those in manual or low-prestige occupations, and the less educated.
5. Telephone coverage is consistently lower for renters and people who live in apartments or trailers rather than in single-family homes. Only the relationship with renting has data from both the United States and other countries.
6. Households without telephones tend to be headed by younger people, unmarried people, and perhaps males (data exists only for the United States, and even in the United States, the relationship is uncertain).
7. Nontelephone households tend to be either smaller than average or larger than average.

Source: Tom W. Smith, "Phone Home? An Analysis of Household Telephone Ownership," *International Journal of Public Opinion Research* 2 (Winter 1990), p. 386.

Figure 10.1

Ten Metropolitan Areas with the Highest Proportion of Unlisted Telephone Numbers

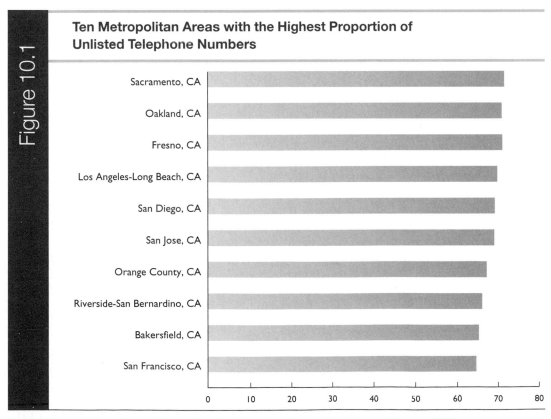

Source: For more information, see *Survey Sampling, Inc.* at http://www.ssisamples.com (Summer 2000).

random-digit dialing
A technique used in studies using telephone interviews, in which the numbers to be called are randomly generated.

A comparison of unlisted versus listed households indicates that unlisted households are younger than listed households, more likely to live in urban areas, nonwhite, more mobile, and with either very high or very low income.

Some researchers attempt to overcome the sampling bias of unlisted numbers by using **random-digit dialing (RDD).** This approach entails the random generation of numbers to be called, and often the automatic dialing of these calls as well. The calls are typically handled through one central interviewing facility. This procedure allows geographically wide distribution or coverage.

One problem with the random generation of phone numbers is that it can increase survey costs, because approximately 34,000 area-code-prefix combinations are in use in the continental United States. When the last four digits are generated randomly, approximately 340 million possible phone numbers can be called. However, there are fewer working residential telephone numbers in the United States; calling random telephone numbers will result in residential contacts only about one-fourth of the time. An alternative scheme to random digit dialing is **plus-one sampling,** in which a probability sample of phone numbers is selected from the telephone directory and a single, randomly determined digit is added to each selected number. Tests comparing RDD to the white pages of telephone listings found slightly better response rates for white-page calls, but no significant differences in demographic or other self-reported profile data between the RDD and white-page samples.[7]

One or more mailing lists typically serve as the sampling frame in mail questionnaires. The quality of these lists determines the sampling biases. If the list is a reasonably good one, the bias may be small. For example, some firms have established panels, which can be used to answer mail questionnaires and which are representative of the population in many important respects. Further, some mailing lists that may be ideally suited for certain types of studies can be purchased. Business-to-business marketing research is usually easier in this regard—the mailing list and lists of phone and fax numbers are more stable than those for consumers, and businesses are fewer in number.

Suppose you run a direct-mail business that specializes in selling monogrammed baby bibs. At any given time, for a fee, you can obtain a mailing list containing the names and addresses of up to one million pregnant women. And, if it should suit your purposes, the list can be limited to women whose babies are expected in a certain month or who are expecting their first child. Mothers-to-be are a prime potential for relationship marketing, because "not only is she likely to buy, but she must buy" maternity clothes and skin creams during pregnancy, and baby

ETHICAL**dilemma** 10.1

Pharmaceutical Supply Company derived its major source of revenue from physician-prescribed drugs. For quite some time, Pharmaceutical Supply had maintained a dominant position in the market. A new competitor had entered the market, however, and was quickly gaining market share.

In response to competitive pressure, Pharmaceutical Supply's management decided that it needed to conduct an extensive study concerning physician decision making with regard to selection of drugs. Janice Rowland, the marketing research director, decided that the best way to gather this information would be through the use of personal and telephone interviews. Rowland directed the interviewers to represent themselves as employees of a fictitious marketing research agency, as she believed that a biased response would result if the physicians were aware that Pharmaceutical Supply was conducting the study. In addition, the interviewers were instructed to tell the physicians that the research was being conducted for the research agency's own purpose and not for a particular client.

- *Was Rowland's decision to withhold the sponsor's true name and purpose a good one?*
- *Did the physicians have a right to know who was conducting the research?*
- *It has been argued that use of such deception prevents a respondent from making a rational choice about whether or not to participate in a study. Comment on this.*
- *What kind of results might have been obtained if the physicians had known the true sponsor of the study?*
- *What are the consequences for the research profession of using this form of deception?*

clothes, toys, formula, etc., upon arrival of the newborn. Lists are ultimately derived from hospital records and therefore are highly reliable. In addition, many firms continue to develop the marketing relationship by sending their representatives to deliver bedside drop-offs of gift packs, trial sizes of relevant products, and redeemable coupons at stores such as Mothercare.[8]

Sometimes the list is internally generated. Spurred on by technical advances, a number of firms are developing greater capabilities to target questionnaires or other mailings to specific households. For example, American Express, with its image-processing technology, now is able to select all its cardholders who made purchases from golf pro-shops, who traveled more than once to Europe, who attended symphony concerts, or who made some other specific purchase using their American Express card. Relationship and database marketing are giving marketers many opportunities to cross-sell to customers. These databases are continually updated, so they also serve as an excellent sampling frame to survey current customers.

The quality of the mailing list determines the sampling control in a mail study. If there is an accurate, applicable, and readily available list of population elements, the mail questionnaire allows a wide and representative sample, since it costs no more to send a questionnaire across the country than it does to send one across town. Even ignoring costs, it is sometimes the only way of contacting the relevant population, such as busy executives who will not participate in an arranged personal or telephone interview but may respond to a mail questionnaire. The key is addressing the questionnaire to a specific respondent rather than to a title or position.

It is also critical to target well—response rates will be greater for surveys on topics that the recipient cares about. Targeting is more efficient, as simply increasing the sample size increases mailing costs, and fewer complete surveys will be obtained from a mass, uncustomized effort. It is estimated that the average U.S. consumer receives some 543 unsolicited mailings per year (compared with 83, 41, and 63 for Germany, the U.K., and France, respectively); direct mailing is a $1.5 trillion market in the U.S., employing 8.7 million people.[9]

Regarding newer technologies, fax surveys operate like phone surveys in their sampling frames. Either phone or fax may be used for research on businesses, but phones are much more successful than faxes for consumer research. Email-administered questionnaires are similar to mail questionnaires when it comes to sampling control. The sample, of course, is limited to those who own or have access to a computer and an email account. However, if an accurate, applicable, and readily available list of email addresses exists, email allows a geographically dispersed sample to be used. For many populations of interest, however, generating a list of relevant email addresses is difficult. While the gap is closing, people who use email and the Internet are still more affluent and better educated than the general population, and most marketers are in the business of selling their wares to the general population.

It is conceptually difficult, but possible to achieve sampling control for the administration of questions using personal interviews. For some select populations (for example, doctors, architects, or businesses), a list of population elements from which a sample can be drawn may be readily available in association or trade directories. For studies focused on consumers in which in-house interviews are to be conducted, however, few lists are available, and those available are typically badly out of date. What is often done for consumer research sampling households is to use area sampling procedures. (The general approach is discussed in a later chapter devoted to sampling issues.) For now, simply be aware that it involves the substitution of areas (for example, zip codes) and dwelling units (apartment buildings) instead of people as the sampling units. The substitution offers the advantage of accurate, current lists of sampling units, in the form of maps, over the generally inaccurate or unavailable lists of people.

Although there is still the problem of ensuring that the field interviewer will contact the right household and person, the personal interview does provide some sampling control in directing the questionnaire to specific sampling units.

A popular alternative for conducting personal interviews among consumers is the use of **mall intercepts.** The technique involves exactly what the name implies.[10] Interviewers intercept, or stop, those passing by and ask if they would be willing to participate in a research

plus-one sampling
A technique used in studies employing telephone interviews, in which a single, randomly determined digit is added to numbers selected from the telephone directory.

mall intercept
A method of data collection in which interviewers in a shopping mall stop or interrupt a sample of those passing by to ask them if they would be willing to participate in a research study; those who agree are typically taken to an interviewing facility that has been set up in the mall, where the interview is conducted.

study. Those who agree are typically taken to the firm's interviewing facility that has been set up in the mall, where the interview is then conducted. With shopping mall intercepts, there are two issues affecting the ability to direct the inquiry to a randomly determined respondent. First, although a great many people do shop at malls, almost one in four people do not. Moreover, only those who visit the particular mall in question have a chance of being included in the study. Second, a person's chances of being asked to participate depend on the likelihood of their being in the mall. That, in turn, depends on the frequency with which they shop there. One thing that is commonly done with respect to this second source of variation in the selection probabilities is to weight the replies of the respondent by the reciprocal of the number of visits made to the mall in a set amount of time.[11]

The experience of mall intercept researchers at the Hawthorn Center shopping mall illustrates some limitations of this type of personal interview. Quick Test, Inc., a marketing research firm based in Florida, conducts research at Hawthorn Center because the Chicago-area shopping mall primarily serves shoppers who have families and are in the 25-to-49 age group—demographics that interest many marketers. At the same time, choosing a particular mall also limits the population from which the sample will be drawn. In addition, the practice of asking people to participate is not entirely random. Recruiters know that many of the shoppers they invite to participate will decline—sometimes rudely—so they develop skill in identifying who to ask. For example, experience shows that they have a better chance with a shopper who maintains eye contact with them.[12] Because it is up to the recruiters to initiate contact personally, the process is very difficult to control, even through a rigid sampling design.

It is one thing to figure out whom to contact in a study; it is quite another to get that person to agree to participate. In this respect, the personal interview affords the most sample control. With a personal interview, the respondent's identity is known, thus there is little opportunity for anyone else to reply. The problem of nonresponse as a result of refusals to participate is also typically lower with personal interviews than with either telephone interviews or mail-administered questionnaires. Sometimes a problem occurs with potential respondents not being at home but this can often be handled by coming back at more appropriate times. Usually the principle holds that the more personal the appeal, the more difficult it is for a respondent to say no: malls are face-to-face and phone solicitations are person-to-person. Mail is the least personal, most anonymous channel, and many mail surveys end up in recycling bins, unless the topic is inherently interesting to the consumer, or if some incentive is offered to complete the survey. We say more about these factors later.

Telephone methods suffer from "not-at-homes" or "no-answers." In one very large study involving more than 259,000 telephone calls, over 34 percent of the calls resulted in a no-answer, a situation that may get worse with the increased popularity of such telephone devices as the answering machine and caller ID. However, call screening (that is, through answering machines or caller ID services) has not disabled telephone interviewing as much as one might expect. While approximately 25 percent of U.S. households have caller ID and 65 percent own answering machines, research firms generally can still get through to talk to a live consumer. Doing so simply requires persistence; more contact must be attempted.[13] Fortunately, calling back is much simpler and more economical than following up personal interviews. The relatively low expense of a telephone contact allows a number of follow-up calls to secure a needed response, whereas the high cost of field contact restricts the number of follow-ups that can be made in studies using personal interviews.

As Exhibit 10.2 indicates, the probability of making contact with an eligible respondent on the first call is less than one in ten. In phone surveys, there are also known biases in the over-representation of larger households; that is, with more people in the house, there is a greater chance that someone will be home to pick up the phone and answer the survey.[14] Making sure the intended respondent replies is somewhat more difficult with telephone interviews than with personal interviews; often, researchers want the "male or female head of the household" to answer the questions, and not just any household member.

Results of First Dialing Attempts

Result	Number of Dialings	Probability of Occurrence
No answer	89,829	.347
Busy	5,299	.020
Out-of-service	52,632	.203
No eligible person	75,285	.291
Business	10,578	.041
At home	25,465	.098
Refusal	3,707	.014 (.146)[a]
Completion	21,758	.084 (.954)
Total	259,088	1.000

[a]Probability of occurrence given eligible individual is at home.

Source: Roger A. Kerin and Robert A. Peterson, "Scheduling Telephone Interviews," *Journal of Advertising Research* 23 (April/May 1983), p. 44. See also Peter Tuckel and Harry W. O'Neill, "Screened Out," *Marketing Research: A Magazine of Management & Applications* 8 (Fall 1996), pp. 34–42.

Mail questionnaires afford the researcher little control in securing a response from the intended respondent. The researcher can direct the questionnaire to the designated respondent and offer the individual some incentive for cooperating.[15] However, the researcher cannot control that cooperation. Many persons refuse to respond. Often only those most interested in the survey topic will respond. Some people are incapable of responding because they are illiterate; it is hardly any wonder that people who have difficulty with everyday tasks such as reading job notices or getting a driver's license would not respond to a mail questionnaire. Whatever the reason, the nonresponse may cause a bias of indeterminate direction and magnitude.

Email- or Web-administered questionnaires are somewhat better in these respects. For one thing, literacy is not a problem because those owning and using computers are typically better educated. Moreover, there is much less likelihood that someone other than the intended respondents will reply, given that the questionnaires reside in personal email accounts. Although fax surveys provide less control in terms of who responds, they too are less subject to literacy problems because those who have access to and use fax machines are typically better educated.

Generally, regardless of the method of survey administration, marketing researchers have noted the steady decline in sample cooperation. It has been suggested that higher compensation may be required to obtain responses. Greater incentives would drive up costs of research or tempt researchers to be frugal on sample size. Yet one consistent finding is that potential respondents are more likely to participate in the study if the research topic is inherently interesting to them. Enhanced databases may enable greater tailoring so that consumers are contacted only on topics relevant to them, and not en masse. Other solutions will continue to evolve. For example, it has been suggested that for e-commerce, filling out a survey may become part of the cost of an online service provider. Even so, the captured audience is self-selected on intrinsic interests (in venturing to the particular Web site), so they might not perceive the cost of filling out a survey as particularly high. Other implications may be that more contact attempts may be required before locating willing respondents. Finally, statistical solutions are also evolving; it has been suggested that to compensate for nonrespondents, post-survey adjustments of the data may be required.[16]

Information Control

information control
A term applied to studies using questionnaires and concerning the amount and accuracy of the information that can be obtained from respondents.

Information control, which involves the kinds of questions that can be asked and the amount and accuracy of the information that can be obtained from respondents, varies according to the method of data collection that is used. The personal interview, for example, can be conducted using almost any form of questionnaire, from structured-undisguised through unstructured-disguised. The personal nature of the interaction allows the interviewer to show the respondent pictures, examples of advertisements, lists of words, scales, and so on, as stimuli. In contrast, the telephone interview rules out most aids while the mail questionnaire allows the use of some of them.

Personal interviews also allow the automatic sequencing of questions; for example if the answer to question 4 is positive, ask questions 5 and 6, whereas if it is negative, ask questions 7 and 8. Automatic sequencing is also possible with telephone interviews, especially when the interviewer is reading from a computer screen and the question skipping is programmed. Skipping questions is not advised for mail, email, or faxed questionnaires because it is easy for respondents to become confused and make errors.

There is a greater danger of *sequence bias* with mail, email, and faxed questionnaires than with questionnaires administered in person or over the phone. Respondents can see the whole questionnaire; thus their replies to any single question may not be independently arrived at but more likely to be conditioned by their responses to other questions than if either personal interviews or telephone interviews were used.

Mail, email, and faxed questionnaires allow respondents to work at their own pace. This may produce more thoughtful responses than would be obtained in personal or telephone interviews, where there is a certain urgency associated with responding. A thought-out response, however, is no guarantee of an appropriate reply. If the question is ambiguous, these self-administered surveys offer no opportunity for clarification. Each question must succeed or fail on its own merits. Because researchers cannot decipher differences in interpretation among respondents, they cannot impose a consistent frame of reference on the replies. Thus the responses to an open-ended question in a mail, email or faxed questionnaire may be excessive or inadequate. With structured questions, the answers may simply reflect differences in the frame of reference being used rather than any subject-to-subject variation in the particular characteristic being measured.

The anonymity sometimes associated with a mail questionnaire does afford people an opportunity to be more frank on certain sensitive issues (for example, sexual behavior). Since replies to email can often be traced to the sender, there is less anonymity with email than with mail or faxed questionnaires.

Both personal and telephone interviews can cause interviewer bias because of the respondents' perception of the interviewer or because different interviewers ask questions and probe in different ways. These kinds of biases do not occur for mail, email, or faxed questionnaires. Both of these biases also can be more easily controlled in telephone surveys. There are fewer interviewer actions to which the respondent can react, and a supervisor can be present during telephone interviews to ensure that they are being conducted consistently. It is typically more difficult, however, to establish rapport over the phone than in person. The respondent in a telephone interview often demands more information about the purposes of the study, the credentials of the interviewer and research organization, and so on.

With regard to the length of the questionnaire or the amount of information to be collected, the general rule of thumb is that long questionnaires can be handled best by personal interview, next best by written formats (mail, email, fax), and least well by telephone interview. So much depends on the subject of inquiry, the form of the questionnaire, and the approach used to secure cooperation, however, that a rigid interpretation of this advice would be unwarranted and hazardous.

As with so many things, computers have changed the way surveys are conducted. Computers were first used in the early 1970s to assist with telephone interviews. Interviewers would read the questions displayed on the computer screen, then key in the answers to a file that was sent to a mainframe computer. The early systems saved so much time and money that they spawned a virtual revolution in data collection. Partly because of the advantages gained with computer administration of questionnaires, telephone interviews have become the most popular data collection technique.

Currently, there are two essential applications of **computer-assisted interviewing (CAI)** software:

1. Telephone surveys in which each interviewer has a personal computer from which to ask questions.
2. In-person interviews in which the interviewer transports a laptop computer to the interview site and uses it to interview the respondent, or places the computer in front of the respondent and lets the respondent answer questions as they appear on the screen.

One of the most important advantages of computer-assisted interviewing is the information control it allows. First, the computer displays each question exactly as the researcher intended. It will show only the questions and information that the respondent needs to, or should, see. Further, it will display the next question only when an acceptable answer to the current one is entered on the keyboard. If a respondent says that she or he bought a brand that is not available in that particular locale, for example, the computer can be programmed to reject the answer. This greatly simplifies skipping or branching procedures. The interviewer does not have to select the next question based on the response to the current one; the computer does this automatically. This saves considerable time and confusion in administering the questionnaire and permits a more natural flow of the interview. It also ensures that there will be no variation in the sequence in which the questions are asked. Information control also manifests itself in the following:

1. *Personalization of the questions.* During the course of the interview, the computer tracks all previous responses (such as name of spouse, cars owned, supermarket patronized) and can customize the wording of subsequent questions on the basis of earlier answers—for example, "When your wife, Ann, shops at the Acme, does she usually use the Toyota or the Buick?" Such personalized questions can enhance rapport and thus provide for higher-quality interviews.
2. *Customized questionnaires.* Key information elicited early in the interview can be used to customize the questionnaire for each respondent. For example, only product attributes previously acknowledged by respondents as determinants of their decisions would be used to measure their brand perceptions, rather than using a list of attributes common to all respondents.

In addition to the enhanced branching abilities and personalization of the questionnaires that they allow, computer-assisted interviews often produce increased accuracy in the results. There is evidence to suggest that people are more truthful when responding to a computer than to an interviewer or even when completing a self-administered, paper-and-pencil questionnaire. They seem to think that the computer is less judgmental and provides them greater anonymity.[17]

Computer-assisted interviewing certainly speeds the data collection and processing tasks. The preliminary tabulations of the answers are available at a moment's notice, because the replies are already stored in memory. One does not have the typical two-to-three-week delay caused by coding and data entry that is necessary when questionnaires are completed by hand.

Respondents also seem to enjoy the interviewing experience more when the questionnaire is administered by computer. That, in turn, seems to help response rates. Further, the whole notion of involving computers in the interviewing process has opened up some other capabilities with respect to managing the interviewing process, including making it easier to write the questionnaire, schedule the people to be contacted, monitor what happens to each attempted call, and prepare the research report.[18]

computer-assisted interviewing (CAI)
The conduct of surveys using computers to manage the sequence of questions and where the answers are recorded electronically through the use of a keyboard.

Even though computers have had a profound effect on interviewing techniques, there are limits to what the machines can do. They cannot win over respondents with social chitchat or explain questions that are misunderstood. Unless the interviewees are good typists, the computers can't elicit lengthy responses. Computers are incapable of recognizing fuzzy or superficial answers and they cannot prod respondents to elaborate or answer other follow-up questions. The computer systems that ask questions by phone with mechanical voices have raised the ire of some people who consider unsolicited, randomly dialed calls an invasion of privacy; luckily these surveys seem to have declined in usage. Email or Web administration can be used only among those likely to own or have access to a computer. These techniques can be quite useful in industrial marketing surveys, because most business people have access to computers and faxes, but they are more limited in general consumer surveys unless the product or service at issue involves a population likely to own such technologies (for example, consumer reaction to a new software program, or fax feature).

Administrative Control

Administrative control involves the time and cost of administering the questionnaire, as well as the control of the replies afforded by the administrative method chosen. One of the greatest advantages of Internet surveys is that they provide the marketing researcher the quickest turnaround. One half of email surveys are typically completed and returned the same day they are sent. The telephone survey is also a quick way of obtaining information. A number of calls can be made from a central exchange in a short period, perhaps as many as 15 or 20 per hour per interviewer if the questionnaire is short. An in-home personal interview affords no such time economies, since there is unproductive time between each interview in which the interviewer travels to the next respondent. If the researcher wishes to speed up the replies secured with in-home personal interviews, the size of the field force must be increased. However, as the number of interviewers increases, so do problems of interviewer-related variations in responses. By properly selecting and training interviewers, researchers can minimize some of the differences in approach that lead to variations, but personal interviews still present more problems of control than telephone interviews.

While the mail questionnaire represents a standardized stimulus, and thus allows little variation in administration, it also affords little speed control. It often takes several weeks to secure the bulk of the replies, at which time a follow-up mailing is often begun. It, too, will involve a time lapse of several weeks for the questionnaires to reach the respondents, be completed, and find their way back. Depending on the number of follow-up mailings required, the total time needed to conduct a good mail study can often be substantial. With a mail study it also takes as long to get replies from a small sample as it does from a large sample. This is not so with personal and telephone interviews, where there is a direct relationship between the number of interviews and the time required to complete them.

© Digital Vision/Getty Images

Telephone surveys provide a quick way of obtaining research data.

In general, in-home personal interviews tend to be the most expensive per completed contact; telephone surveys less costly; and mail, email and fax questionnaires least expensive. However, many factors can change the cost dramatically. For example, it costs relatively little per contact to mail a questionnaire; but if the response rate is very low, the cost per return may actually be quite high. Faxing can be expensive if many of the destination recipients are long distance. For the most part, however, the telephone, mall, and in-home personal interview methods require progressively larger field staffs. The larger the field staff, the greater the problems of control. Good quality control costs money, and that is why the personal interview in the home is typically the most expensive data collection method.

Research Window 10.1 shows how the various data collection methods compare with respect to administrative control.

Combining Administration Methods

Each method of data collection has advantages and disadvantages, which are summarized in Exhibit 10.3. While none is superior in all situations, the research problem itself will often suggest one approach over the others. However, the researcher should also recognize that a combination of approaches may be more productive. For example, a business manager could receive a letter, email, or phone call asking for his or her help in a study, and after this notification the survey could be faxed to his or her place of business. Web surveys can be initiated either by sending an email to the sample of potential respondents that asks them to visit a certain World Wide Web address to complete the survey form, or by a cooperative relationship with another Internet vendor by placing a banner at its site. The respondent then just clicks through the survey. Self-administered questionnaires can be hand-delivered to respondents along with product samples, and telephone interviews can be used for follow-up.

RESEARCH *Window*

10.1

Comparison of Data Collection Methods on Administrative Control

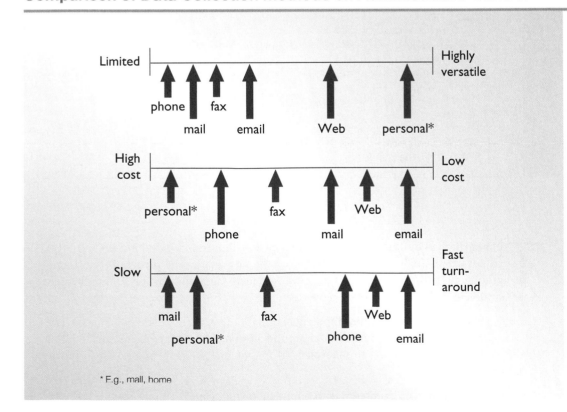

* E.g., mall, home

Exhibit 10.3

Primary Communication Methods of Data Collection: Advantages (+) and Disadvantages (–)

Personal Interview (At Home or Mall)

Sampling control

+ High response rates; best for getting response from specific, identified person
– Generally narrow distribution, difficult to identify sampling frame

Information control

+ Allows use of any type of question; sequencing of questions is easily changed; allows probing using open-ended questions; allows clarification of ambiguous questions; permits easy use of visuals and other sensory stimuli; mall interview needs to be shorter than at-home interview
– Subject to interviewer bias; interviewer supervision difficult to maintain (although easier in mall than at home)

Administrative control

– Generally most expensive method (at home even more than at mall); relatively slow (although mall is quicker)

Written Formats (Mail, Fax, Web, Email)

Sampling control

+ May be only method able to reach certain respondents; sampling frame easily developed when mailing lists are available; wide distribution possible
– Low response rates; little control in securing response from specific individual; cannot control respondent's speed of survey completion

Information control

+ Not subject to interviewer bias; respondents work at their own pace; ensures anonymity; best for personal, sensitive questions
– Researcher cannot explain ambiguous questions; does not allow probing; difficult to change sequence of questions; respondents can view entire questionnaire as they respond

Administrative control

+ Generally least expensive; very short response time for email
– Long response time for mail

Telephone

Sampling control

+ Relatively strong response rates; wide distribution possible
– Difficult to establish representative sampling frame due to unlisted numbers

Information control

+ Less interviewer bias than in person, and interviewer supervision is stronger; sequence of questions is easily changed
– Cannot use visual aids; more difficult to establish rapport over the phone than in person

Administrative control

+ Relatively low cost; quick turnaround; little difficulty and cost in handling call-backs; allows easy use of computer support
– Interview must be brief

looking back...

Tom Karlin had built a successful appliance distributorship by taking the initiative, so not surprisingly, it wasn't long before the information he received from Demographics Life-Style Data (DLD) gave him an idea. He made an appointment to see Peter Haraldsen, a Tampa real estate developer.

Haraldsen specialized in luxury developments built around golf courses. The homes in Haraldsen's latest development would start at around $200,000 when they were finished. Haraldsen had set up the meeting to take place at one of the finished model homes in that development.

"It really is beautiful," commented Karlin after he'd been given the tour.

"Thank you," replied Haraldsen, "but you know this is our fifth development, and I think we've really gotten the hang of what our clientele wants."

"What are your customers like?" asked Karlin.

"Successful businesspeople in their late 50s, early 60s. They're still active, still working. Often they buy a second home in Florida with the idea that within the next ten years they'll move down here permanently. These are active people, mind you. They could go anywhere. They come here for the golf and the tennis, the year-round good weather."

"Well," replied Karlin, launching into his pitch, "the reason I wanted to meet with you today was to have a chance to share some data with you. My data show that the profile of the high-end Clean-Rite appliances purchaser matches the profile of your potential customers perfectly."

Karlin and Haraldsen spent an hour going over the data, but in the end Haraldsen remained unconvinced. He'd had few complaints about the WasherMaid appliances he'd used in his previous developments, so even the sweet prices that Karlin was offering him didn't seem reason enough to change.

"I'll tell you what," Haraldsen concluded, "leave the data with me. I'll send the information over to my marketing director and let him take a look at it, and we'll get back to you."

Three weeks later, Karlin received a call from Haraldsen. "Tom, I've got to tell you—when I showed my marketing director that appliance-sale demographic data, he was a bit skeptical. So he asked 100 potential home buyers who came to one of our open houses to fill out a questionnaire about their appliance preferences. And you know what? Most of them preferred Clean-Rite. Let's set up a time this week to get together and talk dollars and cents." ■

Summary

Learning Objective 1

Explain the concept of **structure** *as it relates to questionnaires.*

The degree of structure in a questionnaire is the degree of standardization imposed on it. In a highly structured questionnaire the questions to be asked and the responses permitted by the subjects are completely predetermined. In a highly unstructured questionnaire, the questions to be asked are only loosely predetermined, and the respondents are free to respond in their own words. A questionnaire in which the questions are fixed but the responses are open-ended would represent an intermediate degree of structure.

Learning Objective 2

Explain what is meant by **disguise** *in a questionnaire.*

The amount of disguise in a questionnaire is the amount of knowledge hidden from the respondent as to the purpose of the study. An undis-

guised questionnaire makes the purpose of the research obvious by the questions posed, while a disguised questionnaire attempts to hide the purpose of the study.

Learning Objective 3

Discuss why structured-undisguised questionnaires are the type most frequently used by marketing researchers.

Structured-undisguised questionnaires are the most popular type of data collection because they are simple to administer and easy to tabulate and analyze. They are also relatively reliable, since they typically use fixed-alternative questions.

Learning Objective 4

Cite three drawbacks of fixed-alternative questions.

Fixed-alternative questions may force a subject to respond to a question on which he or she does not really have an opinion. They may also prove inaccurate if none of the response categories allows the accurate expression of the respondent's opinion. The response categories themselves may introduce bias if one of the probable responses is omitted because of an oversight or insufficient prior research.

Learning Objective 5
Explain why researchers use projective methods in conducting some studies.

Researchers use projective techniques as a way of overcoming subjects' reluctance to discuss their feelings. The main thrust of these techniques has been to conceal the true subject of the study by using a disguised stimulus. The basic assumption in projective methods is that the way an individual responds to a relatively unstructured stimulus provides clues as to how that person really perceives the subject under investigation and what his or her reactions are to it.

Learning Objective 6
List three common types of stimuli used in projective techniques.

Three common types of stimuli used in projective techniques are word association, sentence completion, and storytelling.

Learning Objective 7
Differentiate among the main methods of administering questionnaires.

Personal interviews imply a direct face-to-face conversation between the interviewer and the respondent, as opposed to *telephone interview*. In both types, the interviewer asks the questions and records the respondents' answers, either while the interview is in progress or immediately afterward. *Mail questionnaires* are sent to designated respondents with an accompanying cover letter. The respondents complete the questionnaire at their leisure and mail their replies back to the research organization. *Faxed surveys* operate like mail questionnaires except that the transmission of the questionnaire to the respondent and its return is by fax. *Email surveys* are both sent and returned by email.

Learning Objective 8
Cite the points researchers generally consider when they compare the various methods of administering questionnaires.

Sampling control, information control, and administrative control are the points researchers generally consider when comparing the various methods of collecting data. Sampling control concerns the researcher's ability to direct the inquiry to a designated respondent and to get the desired cooperation from that respondent. Information control addresses the type of questions that may be asked, and the amount and accuracy of the information that can be obtained from respondents. Administrative control involves the time and cost of administering the questionnaires as well as the control of the replies afforded by the administration method chosen.

Key Terms

structure (page 225)
disguise (page 225)
fixed-alternative questions (page 226)
open-ended question (page 226)
depth interview (page 227)
projective method (page 228)
word association (page 229)
sentence completion (page 229)
storytelling (page 229)
Thematic Apperception Test (TAT) (page 229)
personal interview (page 231)
telephone interview (page 231)

mail questionnaire (page 231)
faxed survey (page 231)
email survey (page 231)
sampling control (page 232)
sampling frame (page 232)
random-digit dialing (page 234)
plus-one sampling (page 235)
mall intercept (page 235)
information control (page 238)
computer-assisted interviewing (CAI) (page 239)
administrative control (pgae 240)

Review Questions

1. What is a disguised questionnaire? What is a structured questionnaire?
2. What are the advantages and disadvantages of structured-undisguised questionnaires? Of unstructured-undisguised questionnaires?
3. What is the rationale for using unstructured-disguised stimuli? What is a word association test? A sentence completion test? A storytelling test?
4. What operating principle or assumption underlies the use of structured-disguised questionnaires? What are the advantages and disadvantages associated with structured-disguised questionnaires?
5. How do mail, telephone, and personally administered questionnaires differ with respect to the following:
   (a) sampling control
   (b) information control
   (c) administrative control

Discussion Questions, Problems, and Projects

1. Pick three of your friends and conduct a depth interview with each of them to determine their feelings toward purchasing designer jeans.
   (a) What factors were mentioned in the first interview?
   (b) What factors were mentioned in the second interview?
   (c) What factors were mentioned in the third interview?
   (d) Based on the findings for Questions a, b, and c, what specific hypotheses would you suggest?
   (e) Briefly discuss the strengths and weaknesses of depth interviews.

2. Design and administer a word-association test to determine a student's feelings toward eating out.
   (a) List ten stimuli and the subject's responses and the amount of time that elapsed before the subject reacted to each stimulus.

Stimulus	Response	Time
1.		
2.		
3.		
4.		
5.		
6.		
7.		
8.		
9.		
10.		

   (b) On the basis of your mini-survey, what tentative conclusions can you infer regarding the person's feelings toward eating out?
   (c) Briefly discuss the strengths and weaknesses of this technique.

3. Design and administer a sentence-completion test to determine a student's feelings toward coffee consumption.
   (a) List at least eight sentences that are to be used in the sentence-completion exercise.
   1.
   2.
   3.
   4.
   5.
   6.
   7.
   8.

(b) On the basis of the respondent's reactions, how would you describe the respondent's attitudes toward drinking coffee?

(c) How would a researcher analyze the responses?

4. Design and administer a storytelling test to determine a student's reasons for not living in a residence hall, or dormitory.

(a) Develop a stimulus (verbal or pictorial) for the story-completion exercise. (Hint: It might be easier to use a verbal stimulus.)

(b) Based on this exercise, what are your findings as to the person's reasons for not living in a residence hall?

5. Suppose you were asked to design an appropriate communication method to find out students' feelings and opinions about the various food services available on campus.

(a) What degree of structure would be appropriate? Justify your choice.

(b) What degree of disguise would be appropriate? Justify your choice.

(c) What method of administration would be appropriate? Justify your choice.

6. Which survey method (mail, telephone, or personal) would you use for the following situations? Justify your choice.

(a) Administration of a questionnaire to determine the number of people who listened to the "100 Top Country Tunes in 2002," a program that aired on December 31, 2002.

(b) Administration of a questionnaire to determine the number of households having a mentally ill individual in the household and the history of mental illness in the family.

(c) Administration of a questionnaire by a national manufacturer of microwave ovens in order to test people's attitudes toward a new model.

(d) Administration of a questionnaire by a local dry cleaner who wants to determine customers' satisfaction with a recent discount promotion.

(e) Administration of a questionnaire by the management of a small local hotel that wants to assess customers' opinions of its service.

7. Arrange an interview with a professional researcher engaged in commercial marketing research. Discuss the objectives of the researcher's current project and what type of method(s) she or he is using to collect primary data. Report on the advantages and disadvantages of the data collection method(s) used in relation to the research objective. Try to determine if trade-offs have been necessary (e.g., cost against speed; structure against disguise) in order to collect the data, and if so, the reasons for those trade-offs. Be sure to address the broad issues of structure, disguise, sampling control, information control, and administrative control in your report.

8. Arrange an interview with a member of the marketing faculty at your school (other than your instructor in this course) who is actively engaged in academic marketing research. Discuss the objectives of the faculty member's research and what type of method(s) she or he uses to collect primary data. Report on the advantages and disadvantages of the data collection method(s) used in relation to the research objective. Try to determine if trade-offs have been necessary (e.g., cost against speed; structure against disguise) in order to collect the data, and if so, the reasons for those trade-offs. Be sure to address the broad issues of structure, disguise, sampling control, information control, and administrative control in your report.

Suggested Additional Readings

For specific suggestions as to how to conduct the various types of surveys, see James H. Frey and Sabine Martens Oishi, *How to Conduct Interviews by Telephone and in Person* (Thousand Oaks, Calif.: Sage Publications, 1995).

Paul J. Lavrakas, *Telephone Survey Methods* (Thousand Oaks, Calif.: Sage Publications, 1993).

Thomas W. Mangione, *Mail Surveys* (Thousand Oaks, Calif.: Sage Publications, 1995).

David de Vaus, *Conducting Surveys Using the Internet* (Thousand Oaks, Calif.: Sage Publications, 2003).

Floyd J. Fowler, Jr., *Survey Research Methods,* 3rd ed. (Thousand Oaks, Calif.: Sage Publications, 2001).

Chapter 11

Collecting Information by Observation

© Eyewire/Getty Images

Learning Objectives

1   *List the different methods by which observational data can be gathered.*

2   *Cite the main reason researchers may choose to disguise the presence of an observer in a study.*

3   *Explain the advantages and disadvantages of conducting an observational experiment in a laboratory setting.*

4   *Discuss the principle that underlies the use of a galvanometer.*

5   *Explain how researchers use eye cameras.*

6   *Define* response latency *and explain what it measures.*

7   *Define* voice-pitch analysis *and explain what it measures.*

Tom Stemberg, founder and chairman of the Staples office supply retailer, likes to tell a story about the late Sam Walton, founder of Wal-Mart. Walton, according to Stemberg, believed he could visit any competitor and learn something that competitor did better than Wal-Mart. Stemberg says Walton visited a dismal store in Tennessee. "The produce smelled, and it was just a disaster. And his associates were kidding each other, saying, 'I wonder what Sam is going to say now.' And Sam looked at the back of the store and saw this cigarette rack and said, 'You know, that's the finest cigarette merchandising I've seen in a year.'"

For Stemberg, the principle behind this story is that a company can generate an endless stream of inspiration by observing the competition. Stemberg made a practice of following Walton's lead. In his years as chief executive of Staples (he retired from that position in 2002), Stemberg would visit at least one of his stores and another company's store every week. Like Walton, Stemberg insisted he always learned something. These lessons helped him transform an innovative idea (selling office supplies at superstores) into an $11 billion retailing enterprise.

Stemberg settled on a methodology for this research. He would take note of how easy the store was to find. Then he would walk in unannounced, carrying a small notebook in which to record his observations. He would observe how much time passed before an employee offered to help him. He would look for specific problem areas, such as out-of-stock merchandise or incorrect price tickets. He would ask an employee a question, such as where to find a particular item, and note whether the employee rattled off an aisle number of walked along to help him. He would record subjective data as well—his impressions of the shopping experience, including whether prices seemed high or low, whether items were easy to find, and whether it was easy to get questions answered.

Stemberg didn't do all his own research; his mother-in-law helped. He would ask her to shop the competition, the Office Depot store near her home. Stemberg's mother-in-law bought products there and then returned some of them. Stemberg took note of the whole experience, including delivery, billing, and pickup of the returned items. His mother-in-law even chatted with the truck driver to learn how many orders were in the truck.

Over the years, Stemberg visited most of the Staples stores. And his research went beyond Staples and Office Depot to any retailer he thought might have lessons for him. He visited—and learned from—Price Club, Costco, Toys "R" Us, and even ExxonMobil gas stations.

Discussion Issues

1. What kinds of information can a retailer's employees learn by observing their stores and competitors?

2. What observational research would you recommend for a company like Staples? How would you add to or revise Stemberg's research methods?

3. How can an organization benefit from using a team of researchers with a formal research design, rather than the executives gathering information? Are there any benefits from executives' involvement in data gathering? ■

In Chapter 10 we examined how researchers use communication techniques to collect data, specifically by questioning respondents. In this chapter we will look at another method by which researchers gather information—observation.

PART 3:
Data Collection Methods

Methods of Observation

Observation is a fact of everyday life. We are constantly observing other people and events as a means of securing information about the world around us.

Observation is also a tool of scientific inquiry. When used for that purpose, the observations are systematically planned and recorded to relate to the specific phenomenon of interest. For example, researchers watched consumers buy dog food. They found that adults bought the dog food, but that senior citizens and children bought dog treats. Unfortunately for these no-longer-flexible adults and small children, the treats were usually stocked on the top shelf. These researchers' cameras "witnessed one elderly woman using a box of aluminum foil to knock down her brand of dog biscuits." When the retail grocer moved the treats to where children and older people could reach them more easily, sales soared.[1]

Although planned, observation as a means of collecting data does not have to be sophisticated to be effective. It can be as basic as United Airlines' study of the garbage gathered from its various flights, which prompted the airline to discontinue serving butter on many of its short-range flights because few people were eating it. Or take the method used by the retailer who used a different color of promotional flyer for each zip code to which he mailed. When customers came into the store with the flyers, he could identify which trading areas the store was serving.

A more sophisticated scheme is used by many malls to determine their trading areas. People are hired to walk the parking lot of the mall and record every license number they find. A typical day yields 2,500 different numbers. The data are then fed into computers at R. L. Polk & Company of Detroit, specialists in auto industry statistics. Polk matches the license plates to zip code areas or census tracts and prepares a color-coded map showing customer density from the various areas. At a cost of $5,000 to $25,000, these studies are not only less expensive, but quicker and more reliable than store interviews or examinations of credit card records.

Like communication methods, observation methods may be structured or unstructured, disguised or undisguised. Further, as Figure 11.1 shows, the observations may be made in a contrived or a natural setting and may be secured by a human or a mechanical observer.

1 *List the different methods by which observational data can be gathered.*

Structured versus Unstructured Observation

The distinction between structured and unstructured observation is similar to that between structured and unstructured communication methods. **Structured observation** applies when the problem has been defined precisely enough so that the behaviors that will be observed

structured observation
The problem has been defined precisely enough so that the behaviors that will be observed can be specified beforehand, as can the categories that will be used to record and analyze the situation.

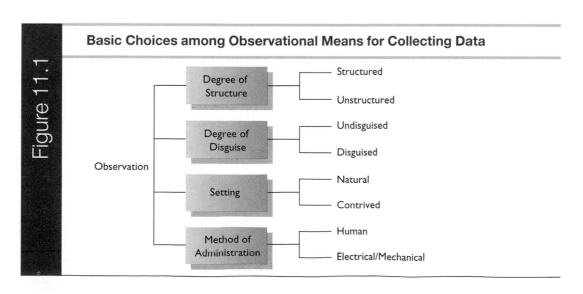

Figure 11.1

Basic Choices among Observational Means for Collecting Data

Observation
- Degree of Structure
  - Structured
  - Unstructured
- Degree of Disguise
  - Undisguised
  - Disguised
- Setting
  - Natural
  - Contrived
- Method of Administration
  - Human
  - Electrical/Mechanical

unstructured observation

The problem has not been specifically defined, so a great deal of flexibility is allowed the observers in terms of what they note and record.

can be specified beforehand, as can the categories that will be used to record and analyze the situation. **Unstructured observation** is used for studies in which the problem has not been so specifically defined, so that a great deal of flexibility is allowed the observers in terms of what they note and record. For example, by peering from the catwalks, researchers for Marsh Supermarkets discovered to their dismay that people shopped heavily the periphery of the store—the produce, dairy, and meat sections—but often bypassed the dry-goods section that accounted for the bulk of the store space.[2]

To distinguish between structured and unstructured observation, consider a study designed to investigate the amount of search and deliberation that a consumer goes through in buying soup. On the one hand, the observers could be told to stand at one end of a supermarket aisle and record whatever behavior they think is appropriate with respect to each sample customer's deliberation and search. This might produce the following record: "Purchaser first paused in front of the Campbell's brand. He glanced at the price on the shelf, picked up a can of Campbell's, glanced at its picture and list of ingredients, and set it back down. He then checked the label and price for Progresso. He set that back down and after a slight pause, picked up a different flavor can of Campbell's than he originally looked at, placed it in his cart, and moved down the aisle." Alternatively, observers might simply be told to record the first soup can examined, the total number of cans picked up by any customer, and the time in seconds that the customer spent in front of the soup shelves—and to record these observations by checking the appropriate boxes on the observation form. The last situation represents a good deal more structure than the first.

© Myrleen Cate/Index Stock Imagery

To use the more structured approach, researchers must decide precisely which behaviors are to be observed and which specific categories and units will be used to record the observations. In order to make such decisions, researchers must have specific hypotheses in mind. Thus, the structured approach is again more appropriate for descriptive and causal studies than for exploratory research. The unstructured approach would be useful in generating insights about the various aspects of the search and deliberation behavior in the preceding example. But it is less appropriate for testing hypotheses about it. Since so many different kinds of behaviors could be recorded, it would be difficult for researchers to code and quantify the data in a consistent manner.

In-store observations can be unstructured, in which any and all behaviors are noted, or structured, in which specific actions are recorded. Which method researchers use often depends on whether hypotheses have been clearly defined prior to the observations.

One way to develop consistency in coding unstructured observations is to use multiple coders who are extremely well trained. This technique is used, for example, in observational studies examining the patterns of interactions between married couples in making selections of large household expenditures at electronics and appliances stores, such as the purchase of a large-screen TV or a washer and dryer. The observers record verbatim the verbal exchanges between the couple when making the choice. The coders then assess which party initiated the selection, the response of the other party, and the content and tone of the communication, including the occurrence of any unpleasant consequences, such as arguments. The aim of such studies is to determine which party dominates the purchase choice in a given category and whether both parties appear to be satisfied.

The advantages and disadvantages of structure in observation are very similar to those in communication. Structuring the observation reduces the potential for bias and increases the

PART 3:

Data Collection Methods

reliability of observations. However, the reduction in bias may be accompanied by a loss of validity, since the number of seconds spent in deliberation or the number of cans of soup picked up and examined may not represent the complete story of deliberation and search. What about the effort spent in simply looking at what is available but not picking them up, or the discussion between husband and wife as to which brand to buy. A well-trained, highly qualified observer might be able to interpret these kinds of behaviors and relate them in a meaningful way to search and deliberation.

As suggested earlier, unstructured observation is well-suited for exploratory research where the emphasis is on developing insights into a phenomenon. For example, researchers wanted to see how women used body lotion. They thought direct observation might be too intrusive, so they videotaped the product in use. They found two groups of women: one group "slapped on the lotion, rubbing it briskly into their skin." The other group "caressed their skin as they applied it." Querying the women, the researchers found that the first group saw the lotion as a restorative for dry skin. The second group sought the benefit of imparting softness and moisture to their skin.[3]

Structured observation can be quite precise as a follow-up method of inquiry. For example, State Farm Insurance began with secondary data and its compilation of accident reports, and created the list of the "10 Most Dangerous Intersections." They then sent researchers to those sites to try to piece together possible suggestions and solutions to the troublesome spots. Their work helped promote road safety and contributed to enhancing State Farm's perception in consumers' eyes that it is a premier automobile insurer.[4]

Disguised versus Undisguised Observation

In **undisguised observation,** the subjects know they are being observed; in **disguised observation,** they do not. In the search and deliberation study described earlier, observers could assume a position well out of the way of shoppers' notice. Or the disguise could be accomplished by observers' becoming part of the shopping scene. For example, some firms use paid observers disguised as shoppers, or mystery shoppers as they are often called, to evaluate sales service and the attitudes and courtesy of the employees. Hilton Hotels supplement guest and employee surveys with reports from secret shoppers to diagnose which features of the customer experience at the hotel (for example, the check-in process or the cleanliness of the bathrooms) should be high priority for redesign and improvement.[5]

The reason the observer's presence is disguised, of course, is to control the tendency for people to behave differently when they know their actions are being watched. Several issues can be raised about the disguised observation, however. First, it is often very difficult to disguise an observation completely, and second, one cannot obtain other relevant information, such as background data, that can often be obtained by identifying oneself as a researcher. Third, under what circumstances is disguised observation ethical?

Disguised observations may be *direct* or *indirect*. A direct observation, for example, might be a person at the checkout counter counting the number of cans of each brand of soup being purchased. An indirect observation might involve counting the inventory on hand by brand at the end of each day and adjusting the results for shipments received to determine how much of each brand was sold. The key difference is that the behavior itself is observed in direct observation, whereas the *effects* or *results* of that behavior are observed in indirect observation.

There are many types of indirect observation.[6] One could, for example, determine the market share held by each brand of soup by conducting pantry audits. In a pantry audit, researchers would visit respondents' homes and ask permission to examine the "pantry inventory." Their goal would be to determine what brands of soup the family had on hand and the amount of each. While it is rare that researchers would go to the expense of a pantry audit for one product, they might use this method if they wanted to determine consumption of a number of products at once.

Pantries are not the only focus for an audit: researchers have inventoried or photographed the contents of consumers' refrigerators, their medicine cabinets, their closets, and their

undisguised observation
The subjects are aware that they are being observed.

disguised observation
The subjects are not aware that they are being observed.

2 *Cite the main reason researchers may choose to disguise the presence of an observer in a study.*

ACNielsen SCANTRACK®
In-Store Conditions
Service, a division of the
ACNielsen Corporation,
offers structured obser-
vation services to clients. It
can help marketers by
tracking sales movement,
"accurately demonstrating
cause and effect." The
service is described at
ACNielsen.com.

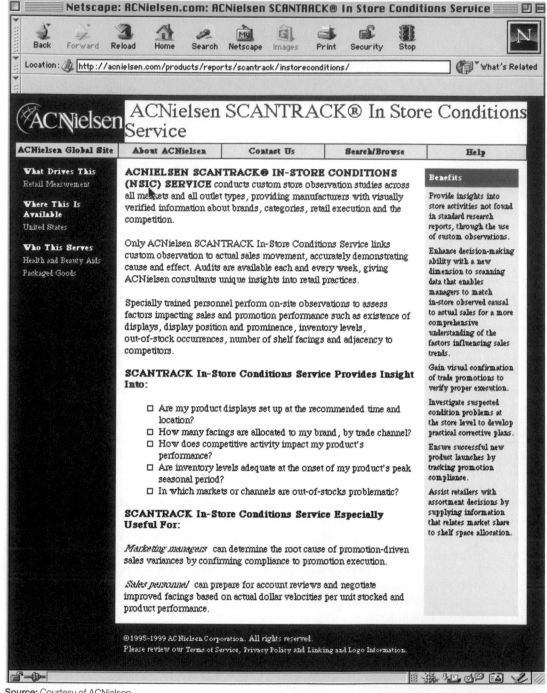

Source: Courtesy of ACNielsen

garages. Photos of a medicine cabinet will indicate not only what products it contains, and what brands and sizes, but also their arrangement—that which is stored front and center is probably used most frequently.

Researchers for *Gourmet* magazine have moved right into their readers' homes to "look into their cabinets," "pore over their Visa bills," or "snip labels out of their clothes." *Gourmet* is especially trying to understand its younger readers—readers who are affluent, knowledgeable about food trends, and know hot restaurants and fine wines. A sample of readers were given disposable cameras and asked to take photos of cherished household belongings. Knowing what customers treasure can yield insight into cross-selling opportunities, or even subtle messages in ads to appeal to this target group's values.[7]

PART 3:
Data Collection Methods

Observation methods are proving to be especially useful for marketers to learn about tastes and preferences of different ethnic groups. Rather than creating a survey that might not be in the respondent's first language, or worrying about translations and back-translations, researchers can simply watch what these consumers do, or they can go to their homes and inventory their kitchens (with permission, of course!). For example, consumer packaged goods manufacturers such as General Mills and Procter & Gamble are testing bilingual packaging and are asking Hispanic and Asian women what they serve their families. These inquiries are highly motivating because these segments of the population are under-served, and any relevant product offerings are hugely successful; for example, when Frito-Lay extended its Doritos snack chip line to include Salsa Verde and Flamin' Hot Sabrositos, targeting Hispanic consumers, sales were extremely successful, topping $100 million within one year after the new flavor introductions. In a pantry audit of Hispanic households, one is more likely to find eggs, fish and other seafood, and beef than in non-Hispanic households, and less likely to find sugars and sweets. They also inventory more because Hispanic families do not eat out as frequently as non-Hispanic households.[8]

Over the years, many innovative, indirect measures of behavior have been used:

- A car dealer in Chicago checked the position of the radio dial of each car brought in for service. The dealer then used this information to decide on which stations to advertise.
- The number of different fingerprints on a page has been used to assess the readership of various ads in a magazine, and the age and condition of cars in a parking lot has been used to gauge the affluence of those patronizing a particular store.
- Scuff marks on museum floor tile have long been used as a means of measuring the popularity of a display.
- Consumers have been watched through one-way mirrors trying to assemble a computer from right out of the box to surfing on the Internet.

For more examples of observational techniques in marketing research, see Research Window 11.1.

Observation is often more useful than surveys in sorting fact from fiction with respect to behaviors, particularly "desirable" behaviors. For example, most people would not want to acknowledge that they spend more on cat food than on baby food, but consumers can be observed doing so. In another study, asking parents whether the color of a new toy would matter, the parents uniformly said no. At the end of the study, as a token of their participation, the parents were offered a toy to take home to their child, and all the parents clamored for the purple and blue toys.

Observation can be helpful in designing store layout and operations. For example, to try to understand why a new frozen baby food was underperforming relative to expectations, a researcher positioned himself where that product was sold and noticed that children got finicky in the frozen-food sections because they were cold, so mothers would rush down that aisle. The researcher was able to persuade managers to place smaller freezer units in the regular baby-food aisles. Sales were then quite successful. Or consider that over 90 percent of furniture shoppers are couples, and potential purchases are most likely if one of the parties is in the store at least ten minutes. The woman may be looking over the fluffed pillows and floral duvets, but if the spouse pulls her away, the sale is lost. As a result, some furniture stores are being retrofit with entertainment centers where sports fans can watch live events via cable.[9]

Videotaping is an especially useful technology for marketing research observations. Sometimes it is used in conjunction with mall intercept interviews by the marketing researcher conducting the ethnography. For example, grocery shoppers videotaped purchasing beef have been engaged in conversation to see whether they comment on the product's fat content, or to determine their knowledge of how to prepare a particular cut.

Observation can be a useful tool in redesigning and selling hi-tech products to business customers also. For example, Hewlett-Packard's medical products division sent their researchers to watch surgeons operate. They noticed that monitors portraying electronic

RESEARCH *Window*

11.1

Additional Examples of Observational and Ethnographic Marketing Research

1. Researchers can evaluate the "service-scape," the atmosphere and "feeling" a store radiates. Such qualitative observations can be informative to management about the image that is portrayed in preparation for repositioning a chain or a local provider. In a complementary manner, researchers can assess customers' expectations and desires using interviews and then use observational techniques to see if any retailers are currently providing the service sought. For example, in a study of women shopping for bridal gowns and related accessories, researchers found that some women expected to use the bridal salon retailers as "clearinghouses." In interviews, such customers would say, "I like brides' magazines . . . What I did is look in there and got a good idea of what I wanted and went from there . . . I would look at the magazine and pick out what I wanted and then take it to the stores and say, 'I want this right here.'" For this segment, a bridal salon that had good channel access to dress lines and offered a business-like, efficient setting would be optimal.

   Other brides sought other attributes, such as convenience. For them, they hoped the bridal salon would be a "one-stop shop" where they could also purchase tuxedos, bridal party dresses, flowers, and other accoutrements. Bridal salons may position themselves differently to these segments, some emphasizing quality, and others value, each seeking the satisfaction of their targeted segments.

2. Other qualitative researchers have conducted content analysis of ads running during actual televised shows to determine whether they were story-like in structure or had some other format; for example, did they provide information to the viewer on the product benefits in more of a lecture, or a cognitive ar-

gument form? Story elements include scenes, actors, goals, outcomes, and a temporal dimension (beginning, middle, and end). The idea is that a story is engaging. Thus, a viewer might relate better to its richness, find it memorable and more persuasive, and in turn like the brand more. For example, an AT&T ad depicts a businessman traveling alone who feels better after he calls his wife from the airfone while on board. Presumably this vignette enhances a consumer's positive feeling toward airfones; the moral of the ad's story was that using an airfone could help the traveler achieve the goal of staying in touch with his family and overcoming homesickness. If the story engaged viewers, they might "relate" to the story and be persuaded that the phone could be beneficial to them as well.

3. Qualitative data (interviews, focus groups, and observations) have also been instrumental to marketers interested in enhancing consumers' perceptions of destinations and the brand equity of locations, for example, for consumer tourism or to attract businesses. Researchers studying perceptions of Scotland found that the country's core industries were incorrectly perceived to be whisky, wool, and salmon, when in fact, information technology (IT) is its greatest export. Ad copies were tested for consumer reaction: themes of tenacity played well (especially to the Japanese consumers), and an ad that emphasized Scotland's spirit with bright and dramatic tartan colors played especially well to younger, rebellious consumers. (The author notes that the project's name, "Galore," comes from the fact that *galore* is supposedly one of only two words to come out of Gaelic to enter into the English language. She notes the other word is *whisky*.) ∎

Sources: Cele Otnes, "Friend of the Bride," in John F. Sherry Jr., ed., *Servicescapes: The Concept of Place in Contemporary Markets* (Chicago: AMA, 1998), pp. 229–257; Jennifer Edson Escalas, "Advertising Narratives," in Barbara B. Stern, ed., *Representing Consumers: Voices, Views and Visions* (New York: Routledge, 1998), pp. 267–289; Kate Hamilton, "Project Galore: Qualitative Research and Leveraging Scotland's Brand Equity," *Journal of Advertising Research* 40 (April 2000), pp. 107–111.

video of scalpel movement were often blocked by other staff members walking between the physician and the monitor, so HP created a surgical helmet that casts images nearly holographically, in front of a surgeon's eyes.[10]

Natural versus Contrived Setting for Observation

Observations may be obtained in either **natural** or **contrived settings.** Sometimes the natural setting is altered to some degree for experimental purposes. In the search and deliberation study mentioned earlier, for example, researchers may choose to keep the setting completely natural and study only the extent of the activities that normally go into the purchase of soup. Alternatively, they may wish to introduce some point-of-purchase display materials and measure their effectiveness. One measure of effectiveness might be the amount of search and deliberation the materials stimulate for the particular brand being promoted.

If a contrived setting is desired, the researcher could bring a group of people into a very controlled environment such as a multiproduct display in a laboratory and ask them to engage in some simulated shopping behavior. This controlled environment might contain, for example, a soup display that would enable researchers to study the degree of search and deliberation each participant goes through as he or she decides what to buy.

An increasingly popular method for assessing customer reactions in a controlled environment is computer simulations, even virtual reality, which enables marketers to display potential new products or product displays without going to the expense of physically building them. The technology originally relied on users wearing special goggles and gloves to see and manipulate objects. The advantage was that the objects appeared in three dimensions, as if they were actually there. For example, General Motors used virtual reality technology to test consumers' reactions to the view from the front seat of a new car.[11] The technology has also been used in consumer shopping experiments.[12]

The advantage of the laboratory environment is that researchers are better able to control outside influences that might affect the interpretation of what happened. For example, a shopper in a natural setting might pause to chat with a friend while deciding what soup to buy. If researchers were measuring the time spent in deliberation, this interruption could distort the accuracy of the measurement. The disadvantage of the laboratory setting is that it may cause differences in behavior and thus raise real questions about the external validity (generalizability) of the findings.

A contrived setting also tends to speed the data collection process, results in lower-cost research, and allows the use of more objective measurements. Hilton's "Vacation Stations" lend age-appropriate toys to children and families staying at the participating hotels in North and South America. Toy Tips and the Toy Research Institute can observe the children to obtain information on which toys will be most popular during upcoming holiday seasons.[13]

Another advantage of the contrived setting is that the researcher does not need to wait for events to occur but can instruct the participants to engage in the needed kind of behavior. This means that a great many observations can be made in a short period of time; perhaps an entire study can be completed in a couple of days or a week, which can substantially reduce costs. As the Hilton toys example illustrates, observational techniques can be especially useful in studying consumer behavior in children. For more examples, see Research Window 11.2.

natural setting
Subjects are observed in the environment where the behavior normally takes place.

contrived setting
Subjects are observed in an environment that has been specially designed for recording their behavior.

3 *Explain the advantages and disadvantages of conducting an observational experiment in a laboratory setting.*

© Tomas del Amo/Index Stock Imagery

Operating in natural settings, researchers can record observations on laptops.

Using Observational Techniques to Study Children as Consumers

1. Ethnography involves observation techniques, depth interviews, and perhaps audio- and videotaping technology to record people, typically in their natural settings. It is a technique that is gaining ground and credibility in marketing research. For example, General Mills has researchers watching children and their eating habits. To allow children to eat on the run, while simultaneously assuring mothers that they were providing healthy food snacks, General Mills created "Go-Gurt," a yogurt packaged in a tube, so that it could be eaten "on the go," without a spoon.

2. Researchers find that, like adults, children have less free playtime—toy manufacturers find themselves competing with the Internet, children's time with their friends, TV shows, and soccer practice. Today's kids are sophisticated, having outgrown dolls and action figures by age 8, instead preferring complex software. It is simply difficult to capture their attention and advertise toys to them. Marketing researchers have found it to be much more effective to get children to try toys (and then parents to buy toys) through demo testing and sampling the products

and brands. Researchers then observe the children in play, noting what toys are popular, what features might be troublesome, and so forth. Observational research provides feedback about the products, which the researchers expected, but it also functions as a sales vehicle because these play sessions generate word-of-mouth acceptance/advertising among the pint-size consumers.

3. Observational techniques can be used on older children also. For example, MTV tries to understand the youth market, to be on the leading edge in trendsetting. It's easier to project an image of "cool" if the music station knows what teens care about. MTV researchers regularly reconnaissance young teen consumers' CD collections, their closets, and the music clubs they frequent. All these venues give the adult researchers insights into youth values, enabling them to design more relevant programming and to advertise in a way that communicates more authentically to these rather affluent young people. Teens are a substantial segment of the population, spending a good $150 billion. ■

Source: Michelle Wirth Fellman, "Breaking Tradition," *Marketing Research* 11 (Fall 1999), pp. 20–24; T. L. Stanley and Becky Ebenkamp, "In Search of the Magic Formula," *Brandweek* 41 (February 14, 2000), pp. 28–34; Margaret Littman, "How Marketers Track Underage Consumers," *Marketing News* 34 (May 8, 2000), pp. 4, 7; Lisa Holton, "The Surfer in the Family," *American Demographics* 22 (April 2000), pp. 34–36; Sally Beatty and Carol Hymowitz, "How MTV Stays Tuned in to Teens," *The Wall Street Journal* (March 21, 2000), pp. B1, B4; Denise Lavoie, "Agency Aims to Get Inside Teenagers' Minds," *Marketing News* 33 (September 27, 1999), p. 8.

Human versus Mechanical Observation

human observation
Individuals are trained to systematically observe a phenomenon and to record on the observational form the specific events that take place.

electrical/mechanical observation
An electrical or mechanical device observes a phenomenon and records the events that take place.

Much scientific observation is in the field, with researchers taking notes on the observations they make. With **human observation**, one or more individuals are trained to systematically observe a phenomenon and to record on the observational form the specific events that took place. Researchers commonly use tools such as written field notes, first making their impressions on-site, and later reflecting their theoretical and summary thoughts off-site. While much field research is still of this pencil-and-paper variety, **electrical or mechanical observation** also has its place in marketing research. While some technologies (such as tape recorders) have been used for a long time, the development of new and less-expensive technologies is expanding the role and importance of electrical/mechanical observation. Increasingly, ethnographic researchers rely on technology to assist them, particularly as various tools—such as tape and video recorders—get smaller in size, which means they are lighter in weight and less intrusive. Field researchers also bring laptops with them and rely later on computer transcriptions. Researchers who want to understand the fuller lives and contexts of consumers and their uses of brands sometimes ask those consumers to choose representative artifacts or photographs to express their individualities (for example, "This tie is special to me because I wore it at my first job interview," or "I know this vase is chipped, but it was my grandmother's, from the old country, and it always adds warmth to the flowers I pick up at the market," or "This picture shows me and my kid brother on our trip to Vegas—our first trip without our parents—it was cool that the hotel treated us like adults").[14]

Some of the earliest uses of electrical/mechanical observation focused on copy research and involved the galvanometer and eye camera. The **galvanometer** is used to measure the emotional arousal induced by an exposure to specific advertising copy. It belongs to the class of instruments that measure autonomic reactions, or reactions that are not under an individual's voluntary control. Because these responses are not controlled, it is not possible for individuals to mask or hide their true reactions to a stimulus. The galvanometer records changes in the electrical resistance of the skin associated with the minute degree of sweating that accompanies emotional arousal. For example, a person could be fitted with small electrodes to monitor electrical resistance and then shown different advertising copy. The strength of the current induced would then be used to infer the subject's interest or attitude toward the copy.[15]

The **eye camera** is used to study eye movements while a respondent reads advertising copy. Eye cameras are positioned to strike the cornea of the subject's eye, and eye movements are traced on videotape and analyzed by computer. Alternatively, tiny video cameras can be clipped to a respondent's eyeglasses to yield a visual record as that person reads an advertisement. Watching where people look allows the marketer detailed study of consumer behavior, answering questions such as: Where did the individual look first? How long did the person linger on any particular place? Did the consumer read the whole ad or just part of it? Following eye paths has also been used to analyze package designs, billboards, and displays in the aisles of supermarkets.[16] Similar technology can also measure pupil dilation, which is assumed to indicate a person's interest in the stimulus being viewed. Pupilmetrics have been used to evaluate color schemes in packaging and optimal advertisement placement in magazines.

Two methods of mechanical observation that are used to provide useful supplementary information in telephone interviews—response latency and voice-pitch analysis—owe their current popularity to mechanical/electronic recorders and the computer's ability to diagnose what is recorded. **Response latency** is the amount of time a respondent deliberates before answering a question. Since response time seems to be directly related to the respondent's uncertainty in the answer, it assists in assessing the individual's strength of preference when choosing among alternatives. Thus, it provides an unobtrusive measure of, for example, brand preference or ambiguity experienced by a respondent in answering a particular question. Once a survey question appears on the computer screen, two methods are used to measure response time: (1) a stopwatch function internal to the computer gets reset to zero and counts time until the respondent enters a response into the keyboard; or (2) a voice-activated electronic function in the computer is automatically triggered at the onset of the respondent's voice and stopped when the voice stops. A digital readout indicates response latency to the interviewer for each consumer and each question. Such a system has several advantages. First, the method provides an accurate response latency measure without respondents being aware that this dimension of behavior is being recorded. Second, because the time is measured by an automatic device, the technique does not make the interviewer's task any more difficult, nor does it appreciably lengthen the interview.[17]

Voice-pitch analysis relies on the same basic premise as the galvanometer: participants experience a number of involuntary physiological reactions, such as changes in blood pressure, rate of perspiration, or heart rate, when emotionally aroused by external or internal stimuli. Voice pitch analysis examines changes in the relative vibration frequency of the human voice that accompany emotional arousal. All individuals function at a certain physiological pace, called the baseline. The baseline in voice analysis is established by engaging the respondent in unemotional conversation, which is recorded. Deviations from the baseline level indicate that the respondent has reacted to the stimulus question. These deviations can be assessed by special audio-adapted computer equipment that can measure the abnormal frequencies in the voice caused by changes in the nervous system, changes that may not be discernible to the human ear. A net reaction score can be generated by comparing the abnormal frequency produced by the stimulus to the person's normal frequency. The greater the difference, the greater the emotional intensity of the consumer's reaction is said to be.

4 *Discuss the principle that underlies the use of a galvanometer.*

5 *Explain how researchers use eye cameras.*

galvanometer
A device used to measure the emotion induced by exposure to a particular stimulus by recording changes in the electrical resistance of the skin associated with the minute degree of sweating that accompanies emotional arousal; in marketing research, the stimulus is often specific advertising copy.

6 *Define response latency and explain what it measures.*

eye camera
A device used by researchers to study a subject's eye movements while he or she is reading advertising copy.

response latency
The amount of time a respondent deliberates before answering a question.

7 *Define voice-pitch analysis and explain what it measures.*

voice-pitch analysis
Analysis that examines changes in the relative frequency of the human voice that accompany emotional arousal.

Voice-pitch analysis has at least two advantages over other physiological-reaction techniques. First, these techniques measure the intensity but not the direction of feeling. With voice pitch analysis, the "recording of the physical phenomenon (voice pitch) occurs simultaneously with the subject's conscious interpretation of the attitude (verbal response); the direction (positive or negative) of the attitude is ascertained from the subject's self-report, while the intensity of the emotion is measured at the same time by mechanical means."[18] Second, whereas the measurement of blood pressure, pulse rate, psychogalvanic response, or other physiological reactions requires subjects to be connected to the equipment, voice pitch analysis allows a much more natural interaction between researcher and participant. This tends to make it less time consuming and less expensive to use.

As mentioned, electrical/mechanical equipment frees the observation from the observer's selective process. This is both its major strength and its major weakness. Certainly recording when a television set is turned on, to what channel it is tuned, and who is "watching" can be accomplished much more accurately by a people meter than by some other means. The fact that the set is tuned to a particular channel and that someone pushed the button indicating that he or she was in the room does not say anything about the person's level of interest, however. A trained human observer's record might be more difficult to analyze, and it might be less objective, but his or her powers of integration could certainly produce a more valid assessment of what occurred. The essential point is that marketing researchers need to be aware of the electrical/mechanical equipment that is available so they can make an informed choice as to the best technique for a particular study. Would a piece of equipment make a better observer than a human in a given instance, or vice versa? Or would a combination approach be more productive? These are difficult decisions that can greatly affect the quality of a study. A researcher who keeps abreast of the developments in the field is in the best position to make those decisions.

looking back...

Tom Stemberg says visiting his stores helped him correct misperceptions. To an executive studying reports, customer complaints can seem isolated and minor. Walking around the aisles and talking to people gave Stemberg a customer's eye view.

For example, he once concluded that credit was easy for customers. Staples' credit policy appeared liberal, and secondary data showed credit card companies handing out cards to almost everyone. But on a visit to a South Carolina store, Stemberg listened as a manager told how his church couldn't obtain credit approval. As the manager gave details, Stemberg saw the issue of credit from the customer's view. Stemberg had focused on the credit terms, but this customer struggled with the approval process. For some customers, the process was so arduous they didn't even bother to try.

In spite of such insights, Stemberg has acknowledged that research by walking around has limits. For one thing, shopping the competition to gather data narrows the problem definition. Visiting stores focuses on existing competitors and retail channels, possibly overlooking customer attitudes and new competitors. In the early days of the World Wide Web, Stemberg thought Borders and Barnes and Noble compared themselves to one another so much that they were slow to address competition online from Amazon.com. (Ironically, Staples lagged rival Office Depot in launching its Web business in 1998, and Office Depot's site was recently named the second-largest Internet retailer, after Amazon.com.) Another issue is that marketing research offers many techniques to deliver in-depth information not available from observing a store.

Stemberg also noted that his role as CEO limited his effectiveness as a researcher. Although he tried to make surprise visits, his managers kept an eye out for him. This problem emerged on a visit to Pennsylvania and Ohio. After visiting stores in Pittsburgh and Youngstown, Stemberg traveled to New Kensington, Pennsylvania, where he was amazed by the excellent service. Three different employees approached him and offered to help. He commented, "I've got a funny feeling you were waiting for me." Indeed, they had been. The Youngstown manager had called the New Kensington manager to tip him off. Besides this bias came the challenge of visiting stores as the start-up company grew into an international chain. Staples now has over 1,400 stores in the United States, Canada, the United Kingdom, Germany, the Netherlands, and Portugal.

Certainly, a professional research team could devise many ways to record and observe the behavior of shoppers and employees at Staples. The team could also tabulate and analyze the data. Even so, firsthand visits were an invaluable tool that let Tom Stemberg build an idea into a retailing story anyone would file under *S* for Success. ■

Sources: Stephanie Gruner, "Face-to-Face: Spies Like Us," *Inc.*, August 1998, pp. 45, 47, 49; Staples, "Corporate Overview," Staples Web site, http://investor.staples.com, accessed January 21, 2003; Geoffrey Colvin, "Staples and the Internet: Here's How Staples Got into Trouble on the Internet," *Fortune*, July 7, 2000, http://www.fortune.com; Tom Stemberg, "How We Got Started," *Fortune*, August 1, 2002, http://www.fortune.com; David Stires, "Office Depot Finds an E-Business That Works," *Fortune*, February 8, 2001, http://www.fortune.com.

ETHICAL dilemma 11.2

You are running a laboratory experiment for the promotion manager of a soft drink company. The promotion manager has read a journal article indicating that viewers' responses to upbeat commercials are more favorable if the commercials follow very arousing film clips, and he is interested in testing this proposition with respect to his firm's commercials. To establish whether film clips that induce high levels of arousal result in more extreme evaluations of ensuing commercials than film clips that induce low levels of arousal, you are pretesting film clips for their arousing capacity. To do this, you are recording subjects' blood pressure levels as they watch various film clips. The equipment is not very intrusive, consisting of a finger cuff attached to a recording device. You are satisfied that the procedure does not threaten the subject's physical safety in any way. In addition, you have made the subjects familiar with the equipment, with the result that they are relaxed and comfortable and absorbed in the film clips. On getting up to leave at the end of the session, one subject turns to you and asks, "Is my blood pressure normal, then?"

- *Is it ethical to give respondents information about their physiological responses that they can interpret as an informed comment on the state of their health?*
- *What might be the result if you do not tell the subject the function of the equipment?*

Summary

Learning Objective 1
List the different methods by which observational data can be gathered.
Observational data may be gathered using structured or unstructured methods that are either disguised or undisguised. The observations may be made in a contrived or a natural setting and may be secured by a human or an electrical/mechanical observer.

Learning Objective 2
Cite the main reason researchers may choose to disguise the presence of an observer in a study.
Most often an observer's presence is disguised in order to control the tendency of people to behave differently when they know their actions are being watched.

Learning Objective 3
Explain the advantages and disadvantages of conducting an observational experiment in a laboratory setting.
The advantage of a laboratory environment is that researchers are better able to control outside influences that might affect the interpretation of what happened. The disadvantage of the laboratory setting is that the contrived setting itself may cause differences in behavior and thus threaten the external validity of the findings. A contrived setting, however, usually speeds the data collection process, results in lower-cost research, and allows the use of more objective measurements.

Learning Objective 4
Discuss the principle that underlies the use of a galvanometer.
The galvanometer records changes in the electrical resistance of the skin associated with the minute degree of sweating that accompanies emotional arousal. When the subject is shown different advertising copy, the strength of the current that results is used to gauge his or her attitude toward the copy.

Learning Objective 5
Explain how researchers use eye cameras.
Eye cameras are used by researchers to study a subject's eye movements while he or she is reading advertising copy. The visual record produced can allow researchers to determine the part of the ad the subject noticed first, how long his or her eyes lingered on a particular item, and whether the subject read all the copy or only part of it.

Learning Objective 6
Define response latency *and explain what it measures.*
Response latency is the amount of time a respondent deliberates before answering a question. Since response time seems to be directly related to the respondent's uncertainty in the answer, it assists in assessing the individual's strength of preference when choosing among alternatives.

Learning Objective 7
Define voice-pitch analysis *and explain what it measures.*
Voice-pitch analysis examines changes in the relative vibration frequency of the human voice that accompany emotional arousal. The amount an individual is affected by a stimulus question can be measured by comparing the person's abnormal frequency to his or her normal frequency. The greater the difference, the greater the emotional intensity of the subject's reaction is said to be.

Key Terms

structured observation (page 249)
unstructured observation (page 250)
undisguised observation (page 251)
disguised observation (page 251)
natural setting (page 255)
contrived setting (page 255)

human observation (page 256)
electrical/mechanical observation (page 256)
galvanometer (page 257)
eye camera (page 257)
response latency (page 257)
voice-pitch analysis (page 257)

Review Questions

1. How can observational methods be classified? What are the key distinctions among the various types?
2. What principle underlies the use of a galvanometer?
3. What is an eye camera?
4. What does response latency assess? How is it measured?
5. What is voice-pitch analysis? What does it measure?

Discussion Questions, Problems, and Projects

1. Next time you go shopping (grocery or otherwise) do the following disguised observation study with a fellow student. The objective is to assess the service provided to customers while checking out purchases. One of you should complete the following structured observation table. The other should conduct an unstructured observation study by observing and recording all that seems relevant to the objective.

   (a) Store _____   Date _____
       Location _____   Time _____

Too few checkout counters	Yes	No
Long wait in line	Yes	No
Cashier: Quick and efficient	Yes	No
Cashier: Prices well recorded	Yes	No
Cashier: Friendly and pleasant	Yes	No
Purchases packed quickly	Yes	No
Purchases packed poorly	Yes	No
Bags carried to car	Yes	No
Bags provided were flimsy	Yes	No
Bags provided were attractive	Yes	No

   Other facts _____
   _____
   _____

   (b) Compare the two sets of results and discuss the strengths and weaknesses of structured versus unstructured observation.

2. Discuss the ethical ramifications of disguised observation versus undisguised observation.

3. Discuss the strengths and weaknesses of a natural setting versus a contrived setting.

4. Describe how each of the following instruments work and in what area of marketing they are most useful.
   (a) galvanometer
   (b) eye camera

5. If you were the product manager of a leading brand of toothpaste, how would observational studies in a retail store help you do your job.

6. The Better Business Bureau (BBB) has received several complaints over the past six months that certain local automobile dealers are engaging in subtle forms of racial discrimination. The alleged discrimination concerns such things as overly restrictive credit terms, lack of salesperson assistance, and refusals to perform routine maintenance services in a timely manner. The BBB has surveyed the firms in question and found no evidence of discriminatory practices, yet complaints continue to be received. The BBB decided to call in professional researchers and has contracted with your marketing research firm to collect data for use in their investigation of these allegations.
   (a) Briefly outline the manner in which you would collect information for the BBB using observation techniques. Be sure to address the issues of structure, disguise, setting, and mechanical versus

human observers in your answer. Do you think an observational study will yield information as good as, better than, or worse than, the survey?

(b) Is it ethical and/or proper for a marketing research firm to conduct this type of research project? Why or why not?

7. Discuss the advantages and disadvantages of using electrical/mechanical methods of data collection versus using human observers. What criteria should the researcher consider when deciding which method to use for a particular project?

Suggested Additional Readings

For discussion of the strengths and weaknesses of observation as a data collection method, see Fred N. Kerlinger, *Foundations of Behavioral Research,* 4th ed. (New York: Holt, Rinehart and Winston, 1999).

For general discussions of observational techniques in marketing research, see Bill Abrams, *The Observational Research Handbook: Understanding How Consumers Live with Your Product* (Chicago: AMA and NTC, 2000).

Patricia A. Adler and Peter Adler, "Observational Techniques," in Norman K. Denzin and Yvonna S. Lincoln, eds., *Collecting and Interpreting Qualitative Materials* (Thousand Oaks, Calif.: Sage Publications, 1998), pp. 79–109.

For discussion and examples of some of the many ingeneous ways to make indirect observations, see Eugene J. Webb, Donald T. Campbell, Richard D. Schwartz, and Lee Sechrest, *Unobtrusive Measures* (Thousand Oaks, Calif.: Sage Publications, 1999).

The third stage in the research process is to determine the data collection method. As we have seen from the chapters in this section, two types of data may be useful in addressing the research problem: secondary data and primary data. While a beginning researcher's initial impulse may be to advocate a survey among respondent groups, the prudent and experienced researcher will always begin the study by investigating available secondary data first. Only if the answer the decision maker is seeking is unavailable in the secondary data should the researcher consider gathering primary data.

If a research study seems to be warranted, many other decisions must be made. In the data collection stage, one of the primary decisions is whether to collect information by questionnaire or by observation.

Researchers for CARA sought to determine whether differences existed in the attitudes of local businesspeople toward the advertising media or television, radio, and newspaper, and toward the sales representatives of those media. They also wanted to test the hypothesis that differences in attitudes were associated with differences in annual advertising budgets.

As the researchers told their clients, when the purpose of a study is to determine the association between variables, the most common research design is descriptive. Descriptive designs presuppose a good deal of knowledge about the phenomenon to be studied, and they are guided by one or more hypotheses. Knowledge about the phenomenon under investigation was gleaned from the exploratory research phase of the study. The hypotheses mentioned here and discussed in earlier parts of this textbook guided the descriptive design.

Researchers used secondary data—existing data gathered for some purpose other than the study at hand—during the exploratory research phase to help in understanding the topic of advertising and its perceived strengths and weaknesses.

The information gained from the descriptive phase of the study, however, was based on primary data (data collected to solve the particular problem under investigation)

and was secured with a structured-undisguised questionnaire. This type of data collection instrument is characterized by standardized questions and responses, which simplify administration, make the purpose of the study clear, facilitate easy tabulation and analysis of the data, and provide reliable responses.

The researchers chose to administer the questionnaire by mail. This method was chosen partly to avoid the disadvantages posed by telephone and personal interviews and also because researchers wanted a tangible form that would allow a respondent to view all the alternative responses. The mail questionnaire's format was designed with standardized questions and responses for reporting attitudes.

While the mail questionnaire format had many advantages, researchers were also aware of its possible drawbacks. For one, researchers often find it difficult to get individuals to respond to this type of questionnaire. In many studies researchers find that offering respondents an incentive of some sort may help to increase the response rate. Nonetheless, the problem of determining how those who do respond differ from those who do not remains.

Despite these problems, mail questionnaires are often the least expensive method of administration per completed contact. Researchers for CARA estimated that the cost per contact for personal interviews would be about $25; the cost per contact for mail questionnaires was $1.70. When the cost of an incentive for return was added in, the cost jumped to between $4.50 and $5.50. While substantially higher than the base cost per contact, this cost was still much lower than the cost of a personal interview.

Discussion Issue:

1. Besides lower cost and the opportunity for the respondent to mull over a list of possible alternative answers, what other advantages might the mail questionnaire have had over personal or telephone interviews in this study?

Case • 3.1

Suchomel Chemical Company

Suchomel Chemical Company was an old-line chemical company that was still managed and directed by its founder, Jeff Suchomel, and his wife, Carol. Jeff served as president and Carol as chief research chemist. The company, which was located in Savannah, Georgia, manufactured a number of products that were used by consumers in and around their homes. The products included waxes, polishes, tile grout, tile cement, spray cleaners for windows and other surfaces, aerosol room sprays, and insecticides. The company distributed its products regionally. It had a particularly strong consumer following in the northern Florida and southern Georgia areas.

The company had not only managed to maintain but had increased its market share in several of its key lines in the past half dozen years in spite of increased competition from the national brands. Suchomel Chemical had done this largely through product innovation, particularly innovation that emphasized modest product alterations rather than new technologies or dramatically new products. Jeff and Carol both believed that the company should stick to the things it knew best rather than try to be all things to all people and in the process spread the company's resources too thin, particularly given its regional nature. One innovation the company was now considering was a new scent for its insect spray, which was rubbed or sprayed onto a person's body. The new scent had undergone extensive testing both in the laboratory and in the field. The tests indicated that it repelled insects, particularly mosquitoes, as well as or even better than the two leading national brands. One thing that the company was particularly concerned about as it considered the introduction of the new brand was what to call it.

The Insecticide Market

The insecticide market had become a somewhat tricky one to figure out over the past several years. Although there had been growth in the purchase of insecticides in general, much of this growth had occurred in the tank liquid market. The household spray market had decreased slightly during the same time span. Suchomel Chemical had not suffered from the general sales decline, however, but had managed to increase its sales of spray insecticides slightly over the past three years. The company was hoping that the new scent formulation might allow it to make even greater market share gains.

The company's past experience in the industry led it to believe that the name that was given to the new product would be a very important element in the product's suc-cess, because there seemed to be some complex interactions between purchase and usage characteristics among repellent users. Most purchases were made by married women for their families. Yet repeat purchase was dependent on support by the husband that the product worked well. Therefore, the name must appeal to both the buyer and the end user, but the two people are not typically together at the time of purchase. To complicate matters further, past research indicated that a product with a name that appeals to both purchaser and end user would be rejected if the product's name and scent do not match. In sum, naming a product that is used on a person's body is a complex task.

Research Alternatives

The company followed its typical procedures in developing possible names for the new product. First, it asked those who had been involved in the product's development to suggest names. It also scheduled some informal brainstorming sessions among potential customers. Subjects in the brainstorming sessions were simply asked to throw out all the names they could possibly think of with respect to what a spray insecticide could or should be called. A panel of executives, mostly those from the product group but a few from corporate management as well, then went through the names and reduced the large list down to a more manageable subset based on their personal reactions to the names and subsequent discussion about what the names connoted to them. The subset of names was then submitted to the corporate legal staff, who checked them for possible copyright infringement. Those that survived this check were discussed again by the panel, and a list of 20 possibilities was generated. Those in the product group were charged with the responsibility of developing a research design by which the final name could be chosen.

The people charged with the name test were considering two different alternatives for finding out which name was preferred. Both alternatives involved personal interviews at shopping malls. More specifically, the group was planning to conduct a set of interviews at one randomly determined mall in Atlanta, Savannah, Tallahassee, and Orlando. Each set of interviews would involve 100 respondents. The target respondents were married females, ages 21 to 54, who purchased the product category during the past year. Likely-looking respondents would be approached at random and asked if they had used any insect spray at all over the past year and then asked their age. Those who qualified would be asked to complete the insecticide-naming exercise using one of the two alternatives being considered.

Alternative 1 involved a sort of the 20 tentative names by the respondents. The sort would be conducted in the following way. First, respondents would be asked to sort the 20 names into two groups based on their appropriateness for an insect repellent. Group 1 was to consist of the 10 best names and Group 2 the 10 worst. Next, respondents would be asked to select the four best from Group 1 and the four worst from Group 2. Then they would be asked to pick the one best from the subset of the four best and the one worst from the subset of the four worst. Finally, all respondents would be asked why they picked the specific names they did as the best and the worst.

Alternative 2 also had several stages. All respondents would first be asked to rate each of the 20 names on a seven-point semantic differential scale with end anchors "Extremely inappropriate name for an insect repellent" and "Extremely appropriate name for an insect repellent." After completing this rating task, they would be asked to spray the back of their hands or arm with the product.

They would then be asked to repeat the rating task using a similar scale, but this time it was one in which the polar descriptors referred to the appropriateness of the name with respect to the specific scent. Next they would be asked to indicate their interest in buying the product by again checking one of the seven positions on a scale that ranged from "Definitely would not buy it" to "Definitely would buy it." Finally, each respondent would be asked why she selected each of the names she did as being most appropriate for insect repellents in general and the specific scent in particular.

Questions

1. Evaluate each of the two methods being considered for collecting the data. Which would you recommend and why?
2. How would you use the data from each method to decide what the brand name should be?
3. Do you think that personal interviews in shopping malls are a useful way to collect these data? If not, what would you recommend as an alternative?

Case • 3.2

Wisconsin Power & Light (B)[1]

In response to the current consumer trend towards increased environmental sensitivity, Wisconsin Power & Light (WP&L) adopted several high-visibility environmental initiatives. These environmental programs fell under the BuySmart umbrella of WP&L's Demand-Side Management Programs and were intended to foster the conservation of energy among WP&L's residential, commercial, and industrial customers. Examples of specific programs include: Appliance Rebates, Energy Analysis, Weatherization Help, and the Home Energy Improvement Loan (HEIL) program. All previous marketing research and information gathering focused primarily on issues from the customers' perspective, such as an evaluation of net program impacts in terms of energy and demand savings, and an estimation of the levels of free ridership (individuals who would have undertaken the conservation actions promoted by the program, even if there was no program in place). In addition, a study has been designed and is currently being conducted to evaluate and identify customer attitudes and opinions concerning the design, implementation, features, and delivery of the residential programs. Having examined the consumer perspective, WP&L's next objective is to focus on obtaining information from other participants in the programs, namely employees and lenders.

WP&L's first step in shifting the focus of its research is to undertake a study of the Home Energy Improvement Loan (HEIL) program of the BuySmart umbrella. The HEIL program had been introduced four years ago. It was designed to make low-interest-rate financing available to residential gas and electric WP&L customers for conservation and weatherization measures. The low-interest guaranteed loans are delivered through WP&L account representatives in conjunction with participating financial institutions and trade allies. The procedures for obtaining a loan begin with an energy "audit" of the interested customer's residence to determine the appropriate conservation measures. Once the customer decides on which measures to have installed, the WP&L representative assists in arranging low-interest-rate financing through one of the participating local banking institutions. At the completion of the projects, WP&L representatives conduct an inspection of the work by checking a random sample of participants. Conservation measures eligible under the HEIL program include the installation of natural gas furnaces/boilers, automatic vent dampers, intermittent ignition devices, heat pumps, and heat pump water heaters.

Eligible structural improvements include the addition of attic/wall/basement insulation, storm windows and doors, sillbox insulation, window weather-stripping, and caulking.

Purpose

The primary goal of the current study is to identify ways of improving the HEIL program from the lenders' point of view. Specifically, the following issues need to be addressed:

- Identify the lenders' motivation for participating in the program.
- Determine how lenders get their information regarding various changes/updates in the program.
- Identify how lenders promote the program.
- Assess the current program with respect to administrative and program features.
- Determine the type of credit analysis conducted by the lenders.
- Identify ways of minimizing the default rate from the lenders' point of view.
- Assess the lenders' commitment to the program.
- Identify lenders' opinions of the overall program.
- Identify if the reason for loan inactivity in some lending institutions is due to lack of a customer base.

Methodology

WP&L decided to use a telephone survey of participating lending institutions to collect the data for its study. WP&L referenced two lists of lending institutions, which were supplied by its resident marketing staff, in order to select the sample for the survey. A total of 124 participating lending institutions were identified. However, it was found that one of the lists was shorter than the other by 15 names. Specifically, the names of some of the branches of major banks were not enumerated on one of the lists. Nevertheless, all 124 institutions, including the 15 discrepant ones, were included in the pool of names from which the sample was drawn.

The sample pool was classified into three groups based on loan activity in the 1998 calendar year. The groups were as follows:

Group	Number of Lenders	Loan Activity, 1998
1	44	0 loans
2	40	1 to 7 loans
3	40	8 to 54 loans

[1]The contributions of Kavita Maini and Paul Metz to the development of this case are gratefully acknowledged, as is the permission of Wisconsin Power & Light to use the material included.

The rationale for the classification strategy was to allow analysis of key variables by three key groups: no loan activity, "light" loan activity, and "heavy" loan activity. The delineation between "light" and "heavy" activity was determined by the median number of loans issued by "active" participants.

The final sample for the survey consisted of 20 randomly chosen institutions from Groups 2 and 3, and 10 from Group 1. The samples of 20 lenders from both Groups 2 and 3 were identified by selecting every other listed respondent after a randomly determined starting point in each list. The 40 institutions selected from among Groups 2 and 3 formed the sample base in which WP&L was most interested (this was because each of these 40 institutions demonstrated loan activity in the past year). The sample size (n = 40) was based on judgment. The 10 randomly selected institutions from Group 1 were chosen primarily to explore the hypothesized reasons for zero-loan activity. These 10 zero-loan lenders received a shortened version of the telephone survey that focused only on their lack of activity.

All of the districts within WP&L's service territory were notified two weeks in advance that a survey was going to be conducted. The survey was pretested and modified prior to final administration. All interviewing was conducted over a one-week period by a project manager and a research assistant, both employees of WP&L's marketing department.

Questions

1. Given the project's objectives, describe the best way to proceed in terms of data collection. Provide support for your conclusion.
2. What kind of sample was used by Wisconsin Power & Light in their research effort? What advantages did WP&L gain by using the sampling method they used? What were the disadvantages? Suggest possible sampling alternatives that WP&L could have used.

Case • 3.3

Office of Student Financial Services (A)[1]

Background

Magnus Pym, dean of Student Affairs at a midwestern university, developed a campuswide service quality initiative program that he was interested in implementing. As an initial measure, he fielded a quality service initiative (QSI) campuswide survey designed to ascertain the level of satisfaction undergraduate students had with the various student services provided on campus. After analyzing the results of the survey instrument, he noticed that the Office of Student Financial Services (OSFS) received one of the lowest rankings among all the departments. Because the financing of a college education is a high-involvement issue for most students, Magnus felt that he needed to examine this area more closely.

Magnus contacted Susan Solacy, director of the OSFS for the past 10 years, to discuss his preliminary concerns. After examining the QSI survey instrument, she defended the performance of her department by raising three issues:

- The campuswide QSI survey had only one question that pertained directly to satisfaction with the OSFS, and thus it may have provided a distorted view of what students were actually feeling.
- All the questions in the QSI survey were structured (closed-ended). This may have caused respondents to feel that they needed to provide an answer even when they did not have an opinion on the issue. This may be the case in this instance, as historically, only about 30 percent of the student body applies for financial aid through the OSFS. However, almost all the students completing the QSI survey had responded to the question regarding satisfaction with the OSFS.
- The majority of the funding guidelines regarding scholarships, grants, and loans are established by the federal government. Given that the role of the OSFS is simply to execute the procedures set forth at the national level, it has no control over the final allocation decision. In sum, students might be dissatisfied with issues over which the OSFS has no control.

Research Method

To address these concerns, Susan recommended that the university commission a more focused study to better understand the factors contributing to the low satisfaction with the OSFS. Based upon her personal experience, she felt that a survey would be the best method for gathering this descriptive information. In fact, she recently came across a financial aid survey used at Bond University that examined many of the same issues that applied to the OSFS. It contained 40 five-point Likert scale items pertaining to the application process (speed in receiving checks/awards, satisfaction with work study/scholarship/loan process, and so on), the helpfulness of the staff/counselors, and demographic information of the respondents.

Susan hired three undergraduate students from a marketing research class to develop an instrument that addressed potential areas of dissatisfaction with the OSFS. In addition to the structured questions appearing in the Bond survey, Susan wanted the questionnaire to include open-ended questions that tapped into students' concerns associated with picking up the checks/awards, the services provided by the OSFS students felt were the most important, and suggestions/areas for improvement. Prior to letting the student research team begin developing the questionnaire, Susan identified several other issues that would influence the study:

- She highlighted the accessibility to the OSFS database, which consists of 13,000 students who had applied for financial aid within the last 12 months.
- She mentioned that she had a very limited budget.
- She wants to ensure that enough information is generated for each cell so that the results are statistically significant. This is key, as she had seen previous surveys that had drawn conclusions from what she felt was insufficient data. Therefore, for the approximately 40 to 45 five-point Likert scale items that she envisions for the OSFS instrument, she feels that it is necessary to receive 1,000 completed surveys.
- She wants the completed research report citing results/recommended actions within four months, as she is up for a promotion next year.

Questions

1. In light of the parameters mentioned by Susan, what method of administration (personal interview, telephone interview, or mail questionnaire) would you recommend to her if you were part of the student team?
2. Given the method you prescribed in Question 1, what could be done to increase the response rate?

---

[1]The contributions of Neeraj Bharadwaj to the development of this case are gratefully acknowledged.

Case • 3.4

Premium Pizza Inc.[1]

The 1980s saw a sharp increase in the use of promotions (coupons, cents-off deals marked on the package, free gifts, etc.) because of their manifest success at increasing short-term purchase behavior. In fact, sales promotion is now estimated to account for over one-half of the typical promotion budget while advertising accounts for less than half. In many industries, however, the initial benefit of increased sales has resulted in long-term escalation of competition. As firms are forced to "fight fire with fire," special offer follows special offer in a never-ending spiral of promotional deals.

The fast-food industry has been one of the most strongly affected by this trend. Pizzas come two for the price of one; burgers are promoted in the context of a double-deal involving cuddly toys for the kids; tacos are reduced in price on some days, but not on others. It is within this fiercely competitive, erratic environment that Premium Pizza Corporation has grown from a small local chain into an extensive midwestern network with national aspirations. Over the past few years, Jim Battaglia, vice president of marketing, has introduced a number of promotional offers, and Premium Pizza parlors have continued to flourish. Nevertheless, as the company contemplates further expansion, Jim is concerned that he knows very little about how his customers respond to his promotional deals. He believes that he needs a long-term strategy aimed at maximizing the effectiveness of dollars spent on promotions. And, as a first step, he thinks it is important to assess the effectiveness of his existing offers.

Specific Objectives
In the past, Jim has favored the use of five types of coupons, and he now wants to determine their independent appeal, together with their relation to several identifiable characteristics of fast-food consumers. The five promotional concepts are listed in Exhibit 1. The consumer characteristics that Jim's experience tells him warrant investigation include number of children living at home, age of youngest child, propensity to eat fast food, propensity to eat Premium Pizza in particular, preference for slices over pies, propensity to use coupons, and occupation.

The specific objectives of the research study can be summarized as follows:

■ To evaluate the independent appeal of the five promotional deals to determine which deals are most preferred;
■ To gain insight into the reasons certain deals are preferred; and
■ To examine the relationships between the appeal of each promotional concept and various consumer characteristics.

Proposed Methodology
After much discussion, Jim's research team finally decided that the desired information could best be gathered by means of personal interviews, using a combination of open-ended and closed-ended questions. A medium-sized shopping mall on the outskirts of a metropolitan area in the Midwest was selected as the research site. Shoppers were intercepted by professional interviewers while walking in the mall and asked to participate in a survey requiring five minutes of their time.

The sampling procedure used a convenience sample in which interviewers were instructed to approach anyone passing by, provided that they met certain criteria

---

Exhibit 1

Five Promotional Concepts

Coupon A: Get a medium soft drink for 5 cents with the purchase of any slice.
Coupon B: Buy a slice and get a second slice of comparable value free.
Coupon C: Save 50 cents on the purchase of any slice and receive one free trip to the salad bar.
Coupon D: Buy a slice and a large soft drink and get a second slice free.
Coupon E: Get a single-topping slice for only 99 cents.

---

[1]The contributions of Jacqueline C. Hitchon to this case are gratefully acknowledged.

Exhibit 2

Interviewer Instructions

Below are suggestions for addressing each question. Please read all of the instructions before you begin questioning people.

Interviewer Instructions

Approach shoppers who appear to be between 18 and 49 years of age. Since we would like equal numbers of respondents in each age category and a 50 percent male-female ratio, please do not select respondents based on their appeal to you. The interview should take approximately five minutes. When reading questions, read answer choices *if indicated.*

Question 1: Terminate any respondent who has not eaten lunch or dinner from any fast-food restaurant in the last seven days.

Question 2: Terminate any respondent who has not eaten pizza within the last 30 days. This includes carry-out, drive-thru, or dining in.

Question 3: Terminate respondent if not between 18 and 49 years of age. If between 18 and 49, circle the appropriate number answer. For this question, please read the question and the answer choices.

After completing questions 1 through 3, hand respondent the coupon booklet. *Make sure that the booklet and the response sheets are the same color.* Also check to see that the coupon booklet number indicated on the upper right-hand corner of the response sheet matches the coupon book number.

Question 4: Ask the respondent to open the coupon booklet and read the first coupon concept. Read the first section of Question 4 showing the respondent that the scales are provided on the page above the coupon concept. Enter his or her answer in the box provided.

    Read the second section of the question and enter respondent's answer in the second box provided.

    When asking the respondent, "Why did you respond as you did for use," please record the first reason mentioned and use the lines provided to probe and clarify the reasons.

This set of instructions applies to Questions 5 through 8. Periodically remind the respondent to look at the scales provided on the page above the coupon concept that he or she is looking at.

Question 9: Enter number of children living at home. If none, enter the number zero and proceed to Question 11.

Question 10: Enter age of *youngest* child living at home in the box provided.

Question 11: Read the question and each answer slowly. Circle the number corresponding to the appropriate answer.

Question 12: Read the question and each answer slowly. Circle the number corresponding to the appropriate answer. If answer is never, proceed to Question 14. Otherwise, continue to Question 13.

Question 13: Circle the number corresponding to the appropriate answer. Do not read answer choices.

Question 14: Circle the number corresponding to the appropriate answer. Do not read answer choices.

Question 15: Read the question and each answer slowly. Circle the number corresponding to the appropriate answer.

Question 16: Read the question and each answer slowly. Circle the number corresponding to the appropriate answer.

Question 17: If an explanation is requested for occupation, please tell respondent that we are looking for a broad category or title. "No occupation" is not an acceptable answer. If this should happen, please probe to see if the person is a student, homemaker, retired, unemployed, etc.

At the end of the questionnaire, you are asked to indicate whether the respondent was male or female. Please circle the appropriate answer. This is not a question for the respondent.

(see Exhibit 2). In sum, the sample of respondents was restricted to adult men and women between the ages of 18 and 49 who had both purchased lunch, dinner, or carry-out food at a fast-food restaurant in the past seven days and had eaten restaurant pizza within the last 30 days, either at a restaurant or delivered to the home. In addition, interviewers were warned not to exercise any bias during the selection process, as they would do, for example, if they approached only those people who looked particularly agreeable or attractive. Finally, interviewers were asked to obtain as close as possible to a 50–50 split of male and female participants.

The questionnaire was organized into three sections (Exhibit 3). The first section contained the screening questions aimed at ensuring that respondents qualified for the sample. In the second section, respondents were asked to evaluate on 10-point scales the appeal of each of the five promotional concepts based on two factors: perceived value and likelihood of use. After they had evaluated a concept, interviewees were asked to give reasons for their likelihood-of-use rating. The third and final section consisted of the questions on consumer characteristics that Jim believed to be pertinent.

Exhibit 3

Questionnaire

Response Number _____
Coupon Book _____

(Approach shoppers who appear to be between the ages of 18 and 49 and say . . .)

Hi, I'm _____ from Midwest Research Services. Many companies like to know your preferences and opinions about new products and promotions. If you have about 5 minutes, I'd like to have your opinions in this marketing research study.

(If refused, terminate)

1. *Have you eaten lunch or dinner in, or carried food away from, a fast-food restaurant in the last seven days? . . . (must answer yes to continue)*

2. *Have you eaten restaurant pizza within the last thirty days, either at the restaurant or by having it delivered? . . . (must answer yes to continue)*

3. *Which age group are you in? (read answers, circle number)*

    1 18–24 2 25–34 3 35–49 4 Other—Terminate interview

I am now going to show you five different coupon concepts and ask you three questions for each. Please respond to each coupon independently of the others. Look at the next coupon only when I ask you to.

4. *Please read the first coupon concept. Using a ten-point scale, how would you rate rate this concept if one represents very poor value and ten represents very good value? _____*

    Looking at the second scale, how would you rate this concept if one represents definitely would not use and ten represents definitely would use? _____

    Why did you respond as you did for use? _____
    _____
    _____

5. *Please turn the page and read the next coupon concept. Ignoring the last coupon and using the same scale, how would you rate this concept in terms of value?*

    Referring to the second scale, how would you rate this concept in terms of your likeliness to use? _____

    Why did you respond as you did for use? _____
    _____
    _____

6. *Please turn the page and read the next coupon concept. Ignoring the last coupon and using the same scale, how would you rate this concept in terms of value?*

    Referring to the second scale, how would you rate this concept in terms of your likeliness to use? _____

    Why did you respond as you did for use? _____
    _____
    _____

7. *Please turn the page and read the next coupon concept. Ignoring the last coupon and using the same scale, how would you rate this concept in terms of value?*

    Referring to the second scale, how would you rate this concept in terms of your likeliness to use? _____

    Why did you respond as you did for use? _____
    _____
    _____

8. *Please turn the page and read the next coupon concept. Ignoring the last coupon and using the same scale, how would you rate this concept in terms of value?*

    Referring to the second scale, how would you rate this concept in terms of your likeliness to use? _____

    Why did you respond as you did for use? _____
    _____
    _____

continued

Exhibit 3

Questionnaire (continued)

Thank you. The following questions will help us classify the preceding information.

9. *How many children do you have living at home?* _____
   If answer is none, proceed to question 11.

10. *What is the age of your youngest child?* _____

11. *How often do you eat fast food for lunch or dinner?* _____
    (read answers, circle number) 1 Once per month or less
                                    2 Two to three times per month
                                    3 Once or twice a week
                                    4 More than twice a week

12. *How often do you eat at Premium Pizza?* _____
    (read answers, circle number) 1 Never visited Premium Pizza
                                    2 Once per month or less
                                    3 Two to three times per month
                                    4 Once a week or more
    If answer is never, proceed to question 14.

13. *Do you yourself usually buy whole pies or slices at Premium Pizza?*
                                    1 whole pies
                                    2 slices
                                    (circle one)

14. *Have you used fast-food or restaurant coupons in the last 30 days?*
                                    1 yes
                                    2 no
                                    (circle one)

15. *Have you ever used coupons for Premium Pizza?*
    (read answers, circle number) 1 Never
                                    2 I sometimes use them when I have them.
                                    3 I always use them when I have them.

16. *What is your marital status:*
    (read answers, circle number) 1 Single
                                    2 Married
                                    3 Divorced, separated, widowed

17. *What is your occupation?* _____

   This is *not* a question for the respondent.
   Please circle appropriate answer—respondent was: 1 male
                                                      2 female
                                                      (circle number)

Thank you for your participation—Terminate interview at this time.

The questionnaire was to be completed by the interviewer based on the respondent's comments. In other words, the interviewer read the questions aloud and wrote down the answer given in each case by the interviewee. It was decided to show respondents an example of each coupon before they rated it. For this purpose, enlarged photographs of each coupon were produced. It was also thought necessary to depict the 10-point scales that consumers would use to evaluate the promotional offer. Coupons and scales were therefore assembled in a booklet so that, as the interviewer showed each double-page spread, the respon-

dent would see the scales on the top page and the coupon in question on the bottom page (see Exhibit 4).

Because the researcher wished to counterbalance the order in which the coupons were viewed and rated, the five coupons were organized into booklets of six different sequences. Each sequence was subsequently bound in one of six distinctly colored binders. A total of 96 questionnaires were then printed in six different colors to match the binder. In this way, there were 16 questionnaires of each color, and the color of the respondent's questionnaire indicated the sequence that he or she had seen.

Exhibit 4

Stimuli

	1	2	3	4	5	6	7	8	9	10	
Very Poor Value											Very Good Value
Definitely Would Not Use											Definitely Would Use

The questionnaire and procedure were pretested at a mall similar to the target mall and were found to be satisfactory.

Questions

1. Is the choice of mall intercept interviews an appropriate data collection method given the research objectives?
2. Do you think that there are any specific criteria that the choice of shopping mall should satisfy?
3. Evaluate the instructions to interviewers.
4. Evaluate the questionnaire.
5. Do you think that it is worthwhile to present the coupons in a binder, separate from the questionnaire? Why or why not?
6. Do you consider it advisable to rotate the order of presentation of coupons? Why or why not?

Case • 3.5

International Differences in the Cost of Data

A multinational bank, MNB, was interested in measuring customer satisfaction with its consumer banking services and financial products. The managers at MNB Corporate differed in their opinions regarding the form of the optimal customer satisfaction study, for example, survey, focus group, interview, and so on. So as a starting point, MNB commissioned bids from marketing research firms in the United States to describe how they would approach studying their U.S. banking customers. In particular, they asked the bidding firms to offer cost estimates; that is, how many customers could be sampled given the proposed budget of $15,000 for this research project using different techniques.

The bids covered a variety of research methods, which differed in their costs. They considered a personal interview method in which the customer would be intercepted in the bank and asked several questions regarding service and satisfaction. They compared that method to the cost of sending out mail surveys to current customers. Finally, they explored the efficiency of placing small, postcard-sized surveys at each teller station that the banking customer might pick up and complete and return at their leisure.

MNB gathered the marketing research firms' proposals to begin to make a decision of how the bank should approach its customers. In terms of outlay expenses, more postcards could be printed less expensively than surveys sent or interviewers staffing each of the local bank branches. However, in terms of response rates, somewhat fewer people turned down the personal interview than returned the mail survey or postcard survey. Exhibit 1 presents the comparative estimates for the three different techniques. Clearly the table shows that in the U.S., the postcard technique appears to be the most cost effective. Thus, the bank managers are considering implementing this research tool.

MNB Corporate's second concern is with a few of its satellite locations; in particular, the news from abroad is that the Indonesian banking customers are not happy, and MNB wants to understand what is going on. Its first assumption was that the bank should proceed with the postcard methodology to be able to compare the results in Indonesia to those from the U.S. However, they conducted some preliminary investigations and found the costs of the methods to be quite different. The bank plans to proceed with personal interviews in Indonesia. Consider Exhibits 1 and 2 and answer the questions that follow.

Questions

1. Under what conditions might it matter that one method is used in one country and another method is used in another?
2. What is the target population under investigation, both in the U.S. and in Indonesia? What are the differences between the sampling frames of each of the three techniques? What customers will each technique miss?
3. What other issues must the bank managers consider in addition to the cost efficiencies of the three methods?

Exhibit 1

The Estimates for the U.S. Samples

	Interview	Mail Survey	Postcards
a. research budget	$15,000	$15,000	$15,000
b. cost per contact	$25	$2.50	$.25
c. prospects reached*	2400	6000	60,000
d. response rate	5%	3%	1.5%
e. estimated net sample size (c x d)	120	180	900
f. effective cost per capita (a/e)	$125.00	$83.33	$16.67

*For mail and postcards, c = a/b; for interviews, cost is $25 per hour, times a five-hour day = $125 per day, for each interviewer. Each of 12 interviewers (spread across the area local bank branches) would spend two weeks (10 bank days) approaching and interviewing customers. Each interviewer on each day would target 20 bank customers, on average.

PART 3:
Data Collection Methods

Exhibit 2

The Projections for Indonesia

	Interview	Mail Survey	Postcards
a. research budget	$15,000	$15,000	$15,000
b. cost per contact	$12*	$2.50	$.25
c. prospects reached*	5000	6000	60,000
d. response rate	20%	1.5%	.5%
e. estimated net sample size (c x d)	1000	90	300
f. effective cost per capita (a/e)	$15.00	$166.67	$50.00

*These estimates differ from those for conducting the research in the U.S. Labor costs for interviewing are much less, propensities for customers to acquiesce and be interviewed are much greater, mail surveys are somewhat less efficient because CD-ROM databases on addresses are less accurate, and postcards are an unfamiliar format and are therefore rarely filled out. Given the changes in the interviewing parameters, if the project duration is still two weeks, 25 interviewers can be deployed, so 5,000 customers would be approached.

Case • 3.6

Digital Euro Music[1]

The music industry is nearing a revolution as consumers are pulling digital recordings off the Internet. Music is available online through a variety of portals, most of which use a compression software like MP3 to file music in portable sizes to download and play. A handheld device can contain hours of personally selected favorite tunes.

A variety of devices are available for purchase to store and play back the digital, compressed music files. These handheld jukeboxes differ on a number of attributes: price, memory storage, batteries required, whether the LCD provides information on the album title and artist, remaining battery life and storage space, and so forth. Music industry experts claim the sound is not as good as CD-quality sound, but "blind" hearing tests suggest consumers cannot distinguish between a song played directly from a CD versus one that had been compressed, stored, and replayed.

Downloading music is becoming an increasingly popular phenomenon. Currently, approximately one-third to one-half of Internet users have or shortly expect to download music. The confluence of the product sought (that is, music) and the technology by which it is obtained (the Internet) suggests that digital music players would be more popular with younger people, and indeed, teenagers are more likely to be visitors of online music sites than are older people.

Internet music sites are hitting heads with traditional music providers (for example, Sony Music Entertainment) over copyrights and issues of piracy. However, even the big, established music companies acknowledge the digital music future, as all the industry players struggle to sort out what form it will take that will be attractive to consumers and yet protect the current copyrights.

A new wrinkle is that the software and playback devices are entering other markets. The handheld devices are being "pulled" through channels by international customers who have Internet access, and therefore access to the compressed music files, but no devices for playback. Some music industry analysts think the European market will not be a large one for these portable MP3 players because Internet penetration in Europe still somewhat lags that in the U.S. Others worry that it might become even more popular to circumvent the European taxes. Specifically, Exhibit 1 contains the Value Added Tax (VAT) for CDs in most European countries; the VATs for books are given for comparison. (The VATs for books are lower than those for CDs because a book is considered a purchase of greater cultural status.) Consider these figures and answer the questions that follow.

Exhibit 1

Country	Population (millions)	Expenditure per Capita (ECU)	Album Units per Capita	VAT on CDs (%)	VAT on Books (%)
Austria	8.1	38.9	2.7	20	10
Belgium	10.2	30.0	2.0	21	6
Denmark	5.3	45.5	3.4	25	25
Finland	5.1	22.0	2.1	22	0
France	58.6	33.1	2.1	21	6
Germany	81.7	30.6	2.7	16	7
Greece	10.5	9.8	0.8	18	4
Ireland	3.6	26.7	1.8	21	0
Italy	57.6	9.1	1.0	20	4
Netherlands	15.6	34.3	2.4	18	6
Norway	4.4	52.3	3.0	23	0
Portugal	9.9	14.5	1.4	17	5
Spain	39.4	13.4	1.4	16	4
Sweden	8.9	36.8	2.5	25	25
Switzerland	7.1	38.4	3.1	7	0
U.K.	60.0	40.1	3.3	18	0

[1]Information based on euromusic.com, Matthew Graven and Jeremy A. Kaplan, "MP3 to Go," *PC Magazine* (February 8, 2000), pp. 220–221; Martin Peers, "Sony Music," *Wall Street Journal* (April 7, 2000), p. B3.

PART 3:
Data Collection Methods

Questions

1. If you were determining which European countries to target first, what information would be most useful to you in the table? What information is lacking?

2. How would you sample potential customers from more than one country?

3. If the MP3 music format is newer to Europeans, what kinds of questions would you ask in those countries compared to the questions you would ask of U.S. consumers?

4. How would you determine whether there might be market potential in Australia, Japan, or Hong Kong?

© PhotoDisc/Getty Images

Part 4

Data Collection Forms

Once the data collection method has been decided, the researcher needs to design the data collection forms that will be used. Chapter 12 discusses the construction of questionnaires and observation forms. Chapter 13 provides some measurement basics that researchers need to be aware of so that they don't mislead others. Chapter 14 then discusses the measurement of attitudes, perceptions, and preferences.

Chapter 12

Designing the Questionnaire or Observation Form

© PhotoDisc/Getty Images

Learning Objectives

1. *Explain the role of research hypotheses in developing a questionnaire.*

2. *Define* telescoping *error and* recall loss *and explain how they affect a respondent's ability to answer questions accurately.*

3. *Cite some of the techniques researchers use to secure respondents' cooperation in answering sensitive questions.*

4. *Explain what an open-ended question is.*

5. *Name two kinds of fixed-alternative questions and tell the difference between them.*

6. *List some of the primary rules researchers should keep in mind in trying to develop bias-free questions.*

7. *Explain what the funnel approach to question sequencing is.*

8. *Explain what a branching question is and discuss when it is used.*

9. *Explain the difference between basic information and classification information and tell which should be asked first in a questionnaire.*

B ill Hershey, a young staffer at Wright Communications Research, was leafing through the first batch of questionnaires that had been returned on the MedAccounts study. To anyone passing his desk, he presented a picture of frustration and bewilderment. This was supposed to be a very straightforward survey, and Hershey didn't understand what could have gone wrong.

MedAccounts was a company that provided specialized computer systems for doctors' offices. Its systems centralized all record-keeping and billing functions, which cut down on the cost and time devoted to updating charts and sending bills. However, when there was a service problem with the MedAccounts system, a doctor's office could be paralyzed. That was why the people at MedAccounts had hired Wright Communications Research to find out how quickly and effectively their service department was handling service calls.

It had been decided that the most cost-efficient method for the study would be to send out a questionnaire. Hershey had been picked to help draft it. He had taken the questionnaire through several versions and had fine-tuned it with more experienced staffers. Then the final version had been printed and mailed to the sample of 900 physicians listed by MedAccounts as using its system.

Hershey had thought that the hard part was over; all that remained was to tabulate the responses from the completed questionnaires. The stack of completed forms on his desk, however, constituted a rude surprise.

For one thing, it represented a much lower response rate than he'd counted on. He had expected that many of the physicians surveyed would be too busy to reply to the questionnaire, but he'd expected more responses than this.

Even more perplexing was the Jekyll and Hyde quality of the replies. About half of the questionnaires were intelligently completed. The other half were full of sketchy answers and questions left blank.

Hershey had no idea what was going on, but he was determined to find out. He picked up the phone and began dialing the number of one of the physicians whose half-filled-out questionnaire sat on the desk in front of him.

Discussion Issues

1. Do you think that a mail questionnaire was a good choice for the MedAccounts study? Why or why not?

2. Do you think that Hershey might have avoided some of the problems with a pretest of his questionnaire?

3. What are some of the possible explanations for the kinds of initial results Hershey received? ■

In the previous chapters we discussed the various types of questionnaires and observation forms researchers use and how they are administered, as well as the pros and cons of the specific types of questionnaires and observation methods. We also examined the various advantages and disadvantages of using communication and observation research techniques.

In this chapter we will build on that discussion by reviewing the procedures researchers can follow in developing a questionnaire or observation data collection form.

Questionnaire Design

Although much progress has been made, designing questionnaires is still an art and not a science. Much of the progress has been simply an awareness of what to avoid, such as leading questions and ambiguous questions. Few guidelines exist, however, on how to develop questions that are not leading or ambiguous.

Figure 12.1 offers a method the beginning researcher might find helpful to develop questionnaires.[1] More experienced researchers would be expected to develop their own patterns, although the steps listed in Figure 12.1 would certainly be part of that pattern.

Although the stages of development are presented in the figure in sequence, researchers will rarely be able to develop a questionnaire in that step-by-step fashion. A more typical development will involve circling back to clarify some aspects of earlier steps after they have been found to be faulty later on in the questionnaire's design. The researcher may find, for example, that the way a question is worded tends to elicit unhelpful responses. Researchers should not be surprised if they find themselves working back and forth among some of the stages. That is natural.

Researchers should also be warned to not take the stages too literally. They are presented as a guide or a checklist. With questionnaires, the proof of the pudding is very much in the eating. Does the questionnaire produce accurate data of the kind needed? Blind adherence to procedure is no substitute for creativity in approach, nor is it any substitute for a pretest (Step 9 of Figure 12.1), with which one can discover if the typical respondent indeed understands each question and is able and willing to supply the information sought.

Step 1: Specify What Information Will Be Sought

The first step in questionnaire design, deciding what information will be sought, is easy, provided that researchers have been meticulous and precise at earlier stages in the research process. Careless earlier work will make this decision difficult.

Both descriptive and causal research require that researchers have enough knowledge about the problem to frame some specific hypotheses to guide the research. The hypotheses also guide the questionnaire. They determine what information will be sought, and from whom, because they specify what relationships will be investigated. If researchers have already

Explain the role of research hypotheses in developing a questionnaire.

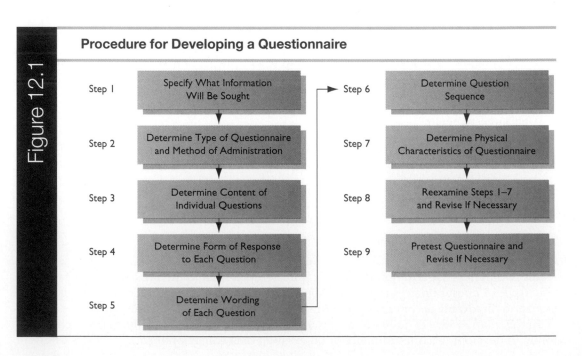

Figure 12.1

Procedure for Developing a Questionnaire

Step 1	Specify What Information Will Be Sought
Step 2	Determine Type of Questionnaire and Method of Administration
Step 3	Determine Content of Individual Questions
Step 4	Determine Form of Response to Each Question
Step 5	Determine Wording of Each Question
Step 6	Determine Question Sequence
Step 7	Determine Physical Characteristics of Questionnaire
Step 8	Reexamine Steps 1–7 and Revise If Necessary
Step 9	Pretest Questionnaire and Revise If Necessary

PART 4:
Data Collection Forms

established dummy tables to structure the data analysis, their job of determining what information is to be collected is essentially complete. You may remember that a dummy table is a table designed to catalog the data that will be collected. It is identical to the one that will be used in the actual research, but in this early stage it has no numbers.

Researchers must collect information on the variables specified in the dummy tables in order to investigate the hypotheses. Further, researchers must collect this information from the right people and in the right units. Hence, it is clear that hypotheses are not only guides to what information will be sought, but will also affect the type of question and form of response used to collect it.

Of course, the preparation of the questionnaire may itself suggest further hypotheses and other relationships that might be investigated at slight additional effort and cost. A most important warning is in order here: If the new hypothesis is indeed vital to understanding the phenomenon, by all means include it and use it to advantage when designing the questionnaire. On the other hand, and we are repeating ourselves, if it simply represents one of those potentially "interesting findings" but is not vital to the research effort, forget it. The inclusion of interesting but not vital items simply lengthens the questionnaire, causes problems in administration and analysis, and often increases nonresponse.

The exploratory research effort is, of course, aimed at the discovery of ideas and insights and not at their systematic investigation. The questionnaire for an exploratory study is therefore loosely structured, with only a rough idea of the kind of information that might be sought. This is particularly true at the earliest stages of exploratory research. It is also true, but to a lesser extent, at the later stages of exploratory research, when the emphasis is on determining the priorities that should be given to various hypotheses in guiding future research.

When Murray Simon was conducting exploratory research about a new medication for a pharmaceutical company, he found that the doctors he interviewed were unwilling to speculate about how they would use the medication. Thus, asking, "Would you write a prescription for this medicine?" was unproductive. The doctor would say, "I can't make a judgment until I see the clinical trials," or, "Send your rep around with samples. After I have some experience with it, we can talk about it." So Simon tried a less structured type of question in his one-on-one interviews. He asked the doctor to imagine he or she was playing the role of the salesperson calling on a doctor, and Simon would play the role of the doctor. Most of the doctors willingly participated, and Simon's client learned a great deal by evaluating what selling points the doctors-as-sales-reps incorporated into their sales pitches. For example, they indicated that a sizable share of patients were unhappy with the new drug's primary competitor. The drug company also learned that some of the claims it planned to make

ETHICAL dilemma 12.1

A financial institution has developed a new type of savings bond. The marketing director of this institution has requested that a local research supply company design a questionnaire that will help quantify target consumers' interest in this new bond. However, the marketing director is concerned about the possibility of competitors hearing about the new product concept because of the survey. She requests that the questionnaire be written in such a way as to mask the true purpose of the study.

To mask the actual purpose of the study, the questionnaire primarily asks respondents for details of their holiday plans and budgets. Because respondents are asked questions about their finances only after multiple vacation-related questions, it is hoped that the respondents will assume the information is for a travel company. Moreover, the marketing director of the financial institution asks that interviewers tell respondents that the information is being gathered for a travel-related company.

- *Discuss the implications of deceiving respondents on a questionnaire in this way.*

- *If the interviewers had not been told to explicitly tell respondents that the information was for a travel-related corporation, would the deception be acceptable?*

- *Are there ways of gaining this type of information without resorting to deception while still protecting the institution's new product idea?*

- *Discuss the validity issues associated with respondents knowing the purpose of the survey as they are completing it.*

about the new drug were difficult to defend, so it modified those statements before launching the product.[2]

Step 2: Determine Type of Questionnaire and Method of Administration

After specifying the basic information that will be sought, the researcher needs to specify how it will be gathered. Decisions on the type of questionnaire and method of administering it constitute the second step. Such decisions center on the structure and disguise to be used in the questionnaire and whether it will be administered by mail, fax, email, telephone, or personal interviews. We saw previously that these decisions are not independent of one another. If the researcher decides on a disguised-unstructured questionnaire in which subjects will be shown a picture and asked to tell a story about it, a telephone interview would be out of the question, and even mail, fax, and email surveys might pose serious problems. Similarly, it is probably not a good idea to use these types of surveys for an unstructured-undisguised questionnaire that asks open-ended questions.

The type of data to be collected will have an important effect, of course, on the method of data collection. For example, the San Francisco research firm King, Brown & Partners had a client that wanted to know what proportion of Internet users had various multimedia plug-ins for downloading and playing multimedia files). From experience, King, Brown knew that one-third or more users don't accurately know which plug-ins they have, especially when it comes to such detailed information as which version of the plug-in. It would have been a waste of time to call or write to computer users and pose such questions. Rather, the researchers set up an online survey that was structured to help the users answer accurately. They created a kind of multimedia test, in which they used a variety of plug-in file formats to display images. For each image, users who downloaded the survey were asked whether they could see the image. If they clicked "yes," the researchers knew, by the format used to create the image, precisely what plug-in they were using. This methodology let respondents provide data without knowing the technical details.[3]

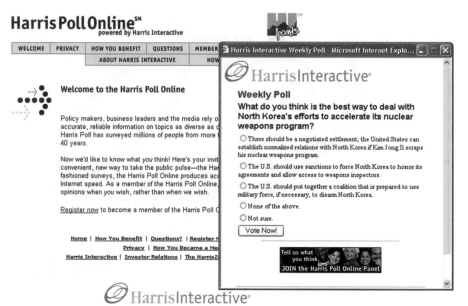

Courtesy of Harris Interactive

Harris Interactive conducts online polls to gauge public attitudes and opinions. This type of study often yields better results than might be obtained by other methods—phone interviews, for example—because people can be more comfortable revealing their true opinions in the relative anonymity an online method provides.

Another influence on the data collection method is the culture of the country where the study is being done (see Research Window 12.1). A researcher investigating the relationship between some behavior and a series of demographic characteristics in the United States (for example, How is dishwasher ownership related to income, age, family size, and so on?) might use mail, fax, email, telephone, or in-home or mall personal interviews to gather the data. The methods would not be equally attractive because of cost and other considerations, but they all could be used. On the other hand, a researcher interested in measuring attitudes could not use all of the methods. The method that would be most appropriate would be largely determined by decisions made earlier about structure and disguise. If researchers decided to use a lengthy attitude scale, for example, they would probably have to rule out telephone interviews. Such data could be gathered best either by mail, email, or in personal interviews. Likewise, an open-ended questionnaire on attitudes might be unsuitable for mail or email administration. Thus, the researcher must specify precisely what primary data are needed, how these data might be collected, what degree of structure and disguise will be used, and then how the questionnaire will be administered.

Willingness to Cooperate

Compared with people around the world, Americans tend to be unusually helpful and friendly, which is reflected in their general willingness to cooperate in marketing research surveys. Quite often, Americans will answer the questions of a total stranger (in the research industry we call them "interviewers") about almost any subject—up to and including one's sex life. And Americans will agree to be interviewed anywhere: over the telephone, in a shopping mall, or at their place of business.

This climate of assumed cooperation can spoil Americans for doing research elsewhere in the world. Individual consumers in many other countries are less ready to answer any questions from an interviewer, let alone delicate or personal ones. Businesspeople in many parts of the world have a more closed attitude than Americans about taking part in surveys.

In Korea, for example, businesspeople are reluctant to answer any survey questions about their company—it is considered disloyal to divulge any type of information to "outsiders." And most Japanese businesspeople are hesitant to take part in surveys during business hours—taking time away from your work for a survey is like "stealing" from your employer.

Differences in Research Costs

The cost of doing exactly the same research can vary dramatically from country to country. Japan is generally regarded as the most expensive research market in the world; projects there usually cost several times what the same study would cost in the United States.

But even within a single region, such as the European community, costs can vary dramatically from country to country. ESOMAR, the European Society for Opinion and Marketing Research (the European equivalent of a combined American Marketing Association and Advertising Research Foundation), periodically studies differences in research costs from country to country within Europe. Here are examples of some of the cost differences ESOMAR found in its most recent study:

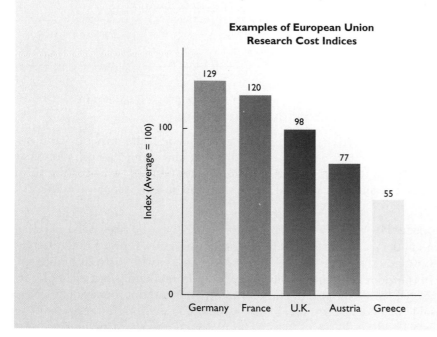

Examples of European Union Research Cost Indices

Source: Jeffrey Pope, *How Cultural Differences Affect Multi-Country Research* (Minneapolis, Minn.: GfK Custom Research Inc., 1991).

Figure 12.2 offers an example of a questionnaire. The primary data at issue are the use of caffeinated ground coffee and attitudes toward various brands. The questions are all very structured and undisguised. The questionnaire is to be administered by mail, using part of the National Family Opinion panel. Note the ease with which the responses could be tabulated.

Figure 12.2

Mail Questionnaire for Caffeinated Ground Coffee Study

1. What type of coffeemaker do you usually use to prepare your ground coffee at home? (CHECK *ONE* BOX)

   1 ☐ Automatic drip
   2 ☐ Electric percolator
   3 ☐ Stove top percolator
   4 ☐ Stove top dripolator
   ☐ Other (Specify): _____

2. a. Check all the brands of regular ground coffee that you have **ever used** at home. (CHECK *ALL* THAT APPLY)

   b. Check the **one** brand you **use most often**. (CHECK *ONE* BOX)

   c. Check all the brands you currently **have on hand**. (CHECK *ALL* THAT APPLY)

   d. Check the **one** brand you will probably **buy next**. (CHECK *ONE* BOX)

   e. For each brand please indicate how much you like the brand overall on a scale of **1** to **10** with "**1**" meaning **dislike it extremely** and "**10**" meaning **like it extremely**. Rate each brand, whether you have used the brand or not.

	"A" Ever Used	"B" Use Most Often	"C" Have On Hand	"D" Will Buy Next	Brand Rating "1" Dislike It Extremely ◄----------------► "10" Like It Extremely
Folgers	1☐	1☐	1☐	1☐	01☐ 02☐ 03☐ 04☐ 05☐ 06☐ 07☐ 08☐ 09☐ 10☐
Hills Brothers	2☐	2☐	2☐	2☐	01☐ 02☐ 03☐ 04☐ 05☐ 06☐ 07☐ 08☐ 09☐ 10☐
Maxwell House Regular	3☐	3☐	3☐	3☐	01☐ 02☐ 03☐ 04☐ 05☐ 06☐ 07☐ 08☐ 09☐ 10☐
Maxwell House Master Blend	4☐	4☐	4☐	4☐	01☐ 02☐ 03☐ 04☐ 05☐ 06☐ 07☐ 08☐ 09☐ 10☐
Yuban	5☐	5☐	5☐	5☐	01☐ 02☐ 03☐ 04☐ 05☐ 06☐ 07☐ 08☐ 09☐ 10☐
Other (Specify): _____	6☐	6☐	6☐	6☐	01☐ 02☐ 03☐ 04☐ 05☐ 06☐ 07☐ 08☐ 09☐ 10☐

3. What do you usually add to the coffee you drink? (CHECK *ALL* THAT APPLY)

   1 ☐ Nothing (I drink it black)
   2 ☐ A dairy creamer, like milk, cream, or Half and Half
   3 ☐ A non–dairy creamer, powdered or liquid
   4 ☐ Sugar
   5 ☐ Artificial sweetener
   ☐ Something else (Specify): _____

4. Are you the principal coffee **purchaser** for your household?

   1 ☐ Yes
   2 ☐ No

Step 3: Determine Content of Individual Questions

The researcher's previous decisions regarding information needed, the structure and disguise to be imposed on its collection, and the method for administering the questionnaire will largely control the decisions regarding individual question content, which is the third step in designing a questionnaire. But the researcher can and should ask some additional questions.[4]

Is the Question Necessary? Suppose an issue is important. Then the researcher needs to ask whether the point has been adequately covered by other questions. If not, a new question is in order. The question should then be framed to secure an answer with the required detail, but not an answer with more detail than needed. Very often in marketing, for example, we employ the concept of *stage in the life cycle* to explore family consumption behavior. Stage in the life cycle is a variable made up of several elements, including marital status, presence of children, and the ages of children. The presence of children is an important factor, because it most often indicates a dependency relationship. This is especially true if the youngest child is under 6 years old and thus represents one type of responsibility for the parents, whereas children over 6 but under 17 represent another type of responsibility. In a study using stage in the life cycle as a variable, there is no need to ask the age of each child. Rather, all that is needed is one question aimed at securing the age of the youngest child if there are any children.

PART 4:
Data Collection Forms

Figure 12.2

Mail Questionnaire for Caffeinated Ground Coffee Study *(continued)*

5. Please indicate how important it is to you that a ground coffee have each of the following characteristics. (CHECK *ONE* BOX FOR *EACH* CHARACTERISTIC)

	Not At All Important									Extremely Important
	01	02	03	04	05	06	07	08	09	10
Rich taste	☐	☐	☐	☐	☐	☐	☐	☐	☐	☐
Always fresh	☐	☐	☐	☐	☐	☐	☐	☐	☐	☐
Gets the day off to a good start	☐	☐	☐	☐	☐	☐	☐	☐	☐	☐
Full-bodied taste	☐	☐	☐	☐	☐	☐	☐	☐	☐	☐
Rich aroma in the cup	☐	☐	☐	☐	☐	☐	☐	☐	☐	☐

	Not At All Important									Extremely Important
	01	02	03	04	05	06	07	08	09	10
Good value for the money	☐	☐	☐	☐	☐	☐	☐	☐	☐	☐
The best coffee to drink in the morning	☐	☐	☐	☐	☐	☐	☐	☐	☐	☐
Rich aroma in the can/bag	☐	☐	☐	☐	☐	☐	☐	☐	☐	☐
Smooth taste	☐	☐	☐	☐	☐	☐	☐	☐	☐	☐
Highest quality coffee	☐	☐	☐	☐	☐	☐	☐	☐	☐	☐

	Not At All Important									Extremely Important
	01	02	03	04	05	06	07	08	09	10
Premium brand	☐	☐	☐	☐	☐	☐	☐	☐	☐	☐
Not bitter	☐	☐	☐	☐	☐	☐	☐	☐	☐	☐
The coffee that brightens my day the most	☐	☐	☐	☐	☐	☐	☐	☐	☐	☐
Costs more than the other brands	☐	☐	☐	☐	☐	☐	☐	☐	☐	☐
Strong taste	☐	☐	☐	☐	☐	☐	☐	☐	☐	☐

	Not At All Important									Extremely Important
	01	02	03	04	05	06	07	08	09	10
Has no aftertaste	☐	☐	☐	☐	☐	☐	☐	☐	☐	☐
Economy brand	☐	☐	☐	☐	☐	☐	☐	☐	☐	☐
Rich aroma while brewing	☐	☐	☐	☐	☐	☐	☐	☐	☐	☐
The best ground coffee available	☐	☐	☐	☐	☐	☐	☐	☐	☐	☐
Enjoy drinking with a meal	☐	☐	☐	☐	☐	☐	☐	☐	☐	☐
Costs less than other brands	☐	☐	☐	☐	☐	☐	☐	☐	☐	☐

continued

Once again, the roles of the hypotheses and dummy tables are obvious when designing the questionnaire.

Are Several Questions Needed Instead of One? There will often be situations in which several questions are needed instead of one. Consider the question, "Why do you use Crest?" One respondent may reply, "To reduce cavities," while another may reply, "Because our dentist recommended it." Obviously two different frames of reference are being used to answer this question. The first respondent is replying in terms of why he is using it now, while the second is replying in terms of how she started using it. It would be better to break this one question down into separate questions that reflect the possible frames of reference that could be used. For example:

How did you first happen to use Crest? _____
What is your primary reason for using it? _____

Do Respondents Have the Necessary Information? The researcher should carefully examine each issue to determine whether the typical respondent can be expected to have the information sought. Respondents will give answers; whether the answers mean anything, however, is another matter. In one public opinion survey, the following question was asked:[5]

Figure 12.2

Mail Questionnaire for Caffeinated Ground Coffee Study *(continued)*

6. On a scale of **0 to 10** with **"0"** meaning **does not describe at all** and **"10"** meaning **describes completely**, please indicate how well the following statements describe **each** of the coffee brands listed below. Rate each brand, whether you have used the brand or not. Please write in the number which indicates your answer on the lines provided.

	Folgers	Hills Brothers	Maxwell House Regular	Maxwell House Master Blend	Yuban
Rich taste	____	____	____	____	____
Always fresh	____	____	____	____	____
Gets the day off to a good start	____	____	____	____	____
Full-bodied taste	____	____	____	____	____
Rich aroma in the cup	____	____	____	____	____

	Folgers	Hills Brothers	Maxwell House Regular	Maxwell House Master Blend	Yuban
Good value for the money	____	____	____	____	____
The best coffee to drink in the morning	____	____	____	____	____
Rich aroma in the can/bag	____	____	____	____	____
Smooth taste	____	____	____	____	____
Highest quality coffee	____	____	____	____	____

	Folgers	Hills Brothers	Maxwell House Regular	Maxwell House Master Blend	Yuban
Premium brand	____	____	____	____	____
Not bitter	____	____	____	____	____
The coffee that brightens my day the most	____	____	____	____	____
Costs more than the other brands	____	____	____	____	____
Strong taste	____	____	____	____	____

	Folgers	Hills Brothers	Maxwell House Regular	Maxwell House Master Blend	Yuban
Has no aftertaste	____	____	____	____	____
Economy brand	____	____	____	____	____
Rich aroma while brewing	____	____	____	____	____
The best ground coffee available	____	____	____	____	____
Enjoy drinking with a meal	____	____	____	____	____
Costs less than other brands	____	____	____	____	____

7. Please indicate your **sex** and **age**.

   1 ☐ Male
   2 ☐ Female   Age: _____

Source: Contributed by NFO Research, Inc.

Which of the following statements most closely coincides with your opinion of the Metallic Metals Act?

- It would be a good move on the part of the United States.
- It would be a good thing, but it should be left to the individual states.
- It is all right for foreign countries, but it should not be required here.
- It is of no value at all.
- No opinion.

The proportion of respondents checking each alternative was, respectively, 21.4 percent, 58.6 percent, 15.7 percent, 4.3 percent, and 0.3 percent. The second alternative captures the prevailing sentiment, right? Wrong! There was no Metallic Metals Act, and the point of the example is that *most questions will get answers, but the real concern is whether the answers mean anything*.[6] For the answers to mean anything, the questions need to mean something to the respondent. This means that, first, the respondent needs to be informed with respect to the issue addressed by the question, and, second, the respondent must remember the information.

Consider the question, "How much does your family spend on groceries in a typical week?" Unless the respondent does the grocery shopping or the family operates with a fairly strict budget, he or she is unlikely to know. In a situation like this, it might be helpful to ask "filter questions" before this question to determine if the individual is indeed likely to have this information. A filter question might be, "Who does the grocery shopping in your family?" It is not unusual, for example, to use filter questions such as, "Do you have an opinion on . . . ?" before asking about the specific issue in question. The empirical evidence indicates that providing a filter will typically increase the proportion responding "no opinion" by 20 to 25 percentage points.[7]

Not only should the individual have the information sought, but he or she should remember it. Our ability to remember various events is influenced by the event itself and its importance, the length of time since the event, and the presence or absence of stimuli that assist in recalling it. Important events are more easily remembered than unimportant events. While many older adults might be able to remember who shot President John F. Kennedy or the make of the first car they ever owned, many of them will be unable to recall the particular television shows they watched last Wednesday evening. Returning to our toothpaste example, many people will be unable to recall the first brand they ever used, when they switched to their current brand, or why they switched. While the switching and use information might be very important to a brand manager for toothpastes, it is unimportant to most individuals, a condition we have to keep in mind continually when designing questionnaires. We need to put ourselves in the shoes of the respondent, not those of the product manager, when deciding whether the information is important enough for the individual to remember.

We also need to recognize that an individual's ability to remember an event is influenced by how long ago it happened. While we might recall the television programs we watched last evening, we might have much greater difficulty remembering those we watched last week on the same evening, and might find it all but impossible to recall our viewing pattern of a month ago. The moral of this is that if the event could be considered relatively unimportant to most individuals, we should ask about very recent occurrences of it.[8] For more important events, there are two forces, operating in opposite directions, that affect a respondent's ability to provide accurate answers to questions referring to some specified time period: **Telescoping error** is the tendency to remember an event as having occurred more recently than it did. **Recall loss** is the tendency to forget the relatively important event entirely. The degree to which the two sources of error affect the accuracy of the reported information depends on the length of the period in question. For long periods, the telescoping effect is smaller, while the recall loss is greater. For short periods, the reverse is true: "Thus, for short reference periods, the telescoping error may outweigh the recall loss, while for long periods the reverse will apply; in between there will be a length of reference periods at which the two effects counterbalance each other."[9] Unfortunately, there is no single reference period that can be used to frame questions for all events, because what is optimal depends on the importance of the event to those involved.

Will Respondents Give the Information?

Even though respondents have the information, there is always a question of whether they will share it. Eastern Europeans are wonderful in this regard.

> [U]nlike blasé Western consumers, people in Eastern Europe are more than willing to answer questions. After years of directives from the top, people are flattered to be asked their opinions, even if they're just being asked about the taste of a toothpaste or the feel of a shaving cream. Gallup's Mr. Manchin [a regional vice president] recounts how an old lady in Hungary thanked the interviewer at the end of an hour-long session. "It was such a wonderful experience to have a chance to talk to you for so long," she said. "How much do I pay you?"[10]

Researchers in many other parts of the world are not as fortunate and sometimes encounter situations in which respondents have the necessary information, but they will not give

2 *Define* telescoping error *and* recall loss *and explain how they affect a respondent's ability to answer questions accurately.*

telescoping error
A type of error resulting from the fact that most people remember an event as having occurred more recently than it did.

recall loss
A type of error caused by a respondent's forgetting that an event happened at all.

it. Their unwillingness may be a function of the amount of work involved in producing an answer, their ability to articulate an answer, or the sensitivity of the issue.

Although a purchasing agent may be able to determine to the penny how much the company spent on cleaning compound last year, or the relative amount spent on each brand bought, the agent is unlikely to take the time to look up these data to reply to an unsolicited questionnaire. Questionnaire developers need to be constantly mindful of the amount of effort it might take respondents to give the information sought. When the effort is excessive, the respondent may either ignore the question or give only an approximate answer. It may be wiser to omit these types of questions, since they tend to irritate respondents and lessen their cooperation in responding to the rest of the survey.

Otherwise, the researcher needs to use a good deal of creative energy designing a mechanism that allows respondents to articulate their views. Although respondents might not be able to express their preferences in furniture styles, for example, they should be able to indicate the style they like best when shown pictures, prototypes, hardware samples, and fabric swatches. La-Z-Boy used this approach when it invited a panel of consumers to evaluate a line of new products, including fabrics and styles. The consumers liked all the fabrics except for two plaid designs, which they rated as not soft enough. La-Z-Boy dropped one of the patterns and asked the manufacturer to modify the other one to make it softer.[11]

When an issue is embarrassing or otherwise threatening to respondents, they are also apt to refuse to cooperate. Such issues should be avoided whenever possible. If that is impossible because the issue is very significant to the study, then the researcher needs to pay close attention to how the issue is addressed, particularly with respect to question location and question phrasing.

In general, it is better to address sensitive issues later, rather than earlier, in the survey. Most surveys will produce some initial mistrust in respondents. One has to overcome this skepticism and establish rapport. This is made easier when respondents have the opportunity to warm to the task by answering nonthreatening questions early in the interview, particularly questions that establish the legitimacy of the project.

When sensitive questions must be asked, it helps to consider ways to make them less threatening. Some helpful techniques in this regard follow:[12]

3 *Cite some of the techniques researchers use to secure respondents' cooperation in answering sensitive questions.*

1. Hide the question in a group of other, more innocuous questions.
2. Before asking the specific question, state that the behavior or attitude is not unusual; for example, "Recent studies show that one of every four households has trouble meeting its monthly financial obligations." This technique, known as the use of counterbiasing statements, makes it easier for the respondent to admit the potentially embarrassing behavior.
3. Phrase the question in terms of other people and how they might feel or act; for example, "Do you think most people cheat on their income taxes? Why?" While respondents might readily reveal their attitudes toward cheating on income tax forms when asked about other people, they might be very reluctant to do so if *they* were asked outright if they ever cheat on their taxes and why.
4. State the response in terms of a number of categories that the respondent may simply check. Instead of asking respondents for their age, for example, one could simply hand them a card with the age categories,

   A: 20–29   D: 50–59
   B: 30–39   E: 60+
   C: 40–49

   and ask them to respond with the appropriate letter.
5. Use the **randomized-response model,** in which the respondent answers one of several paired questions at random.[13] For example, the respondent may draw colored balls from an urn, being instructed to answer Question A if the ball is blue and Question B if the ball is red. The interviewer is unaware of the question being answered by the respondent, be-

randomized-response model
An interviewing technique in which potentially embarrassing and relatively innocuous questions are paired, and the question the respondent answers is randomly determined but is unknown to the interviewer.

PART 4:
Data Collection Forms

cause he or she never sees the color of the ball drawn. Under these conditions the respondent is less likely to refuse to answer or to answer untruthfully. A study to investigate the incidence of shoplifting might pair the sensitive question, "Have you ever shoplifted?" with the innocuous question, "Is your birthday in January?" The incidence of shoplifting can still be estimated by using an appropriate statistical model, since the percentage of respondents answering each question is controlled by the proportion of red and blue balls in the urn. See Technically Speaking 12.1 for details of how the randomized-response model works. Since the researcher cannot determine specifically which respondents have admitted to shoplifting by this technique, however, there is no opportunity to examine if shoplifting behavior was associated with any particular demographic characteristics.

© PhotoDisc/Getty Images

Step 4: Determine Form of Response to Each Question

Once the content of the individual questions is determined, researchers must decide whether to use questions that are open-ended or that have multiple choices, two choices, or perhaps represent a scale.

Open-Ended Questions   Respondents are free to reply to **open-ended questions** in their own words rather than being limited to choosing from a set of alternatives. The following are examples:

> **How old are you?** _____
>
> **Do you think laws requiring passengers in motor vehicles to wear seat belts are needed?** _____
>
> **Can you name three sponsors of the Monday-night football games?** _____
>
> **Do you intend to purchase an automobile this year?** _____
>
> **Why did you purchase a Zenith brand color television set?** _____
> **Do you own a VCR?** _____

These questions span the gamut of the types of primary data that could be collected—from demographic characteristics, through attitudes and intentions, to behavior. The open-ended question is indeed a versatile device.

Open-ended questions are often used to begin a questionnaire. The general feeling is that it is best to proceed from the general to the specific in constructing questionnaires. So an opening question like, "When you think of television sets, which brands come to mind?" gives some insight into the respondent's frame of reference and could be most helpful in interpreting the individual's replies to later questions. The open-ended question is also often used to probe for additional information. The probes "Why do you feel that way?" and "Please explain" are often used to seek elaboration of a respondent's reply.

In a fixed-alternative format, respondents choose their answer from a predetermined number of responses. Researchers generally use one of three types of fixed-alternative formats.

Multichotomous Questions   Despite the daunting name, every college student is probably familiar with the **multichotomous question.** From grade school to graduate school, students

It can be easier to elicit responses to some types of questions when the respondent has something concrete—such as fabric swatches—to evaluate.

4 Explain what an open-ended question is.

open-ended question
A question that respondents are free to answer in their own words rather than being limited to choosing from among a set of alternatives.

5 Name two kinds of fixed-alternative questions and tell the difference between them.

Operation of the Randomized-Response Model

Question A: Have you ever shoplifted?
☐ Yes   ☐ No

Question B: Is your birthday in January?
☐ Yes   ☐ No
Probability of a person's birthday being in January is known from census data. Suppose it is .05.

Contents of urn: 10 balls; 5 red and 5 blue.
Instruction to respondent: Pick a ball from the urn but do not show it to me (the interviewer). If it is red, please answer question A, if it is blue, please answer question B.

Suppose the proportion of all respondents who answered "yes" is 20, although the researcher does not know to which question each respondent was replying.

Let

λ = the total proportion of "yes" responses = .20
p = probability that the sensitive question was asked = .5 since half of the balls are red
$1-p$ = probability that the innocuous question was asked = .5 since half of the balls are blue
π_s = the proportion of "yes" responses to the sensitive question
π_I = the proportion of "yes" responses to the innocuous question = .05

Now $\lambda = p\pi_s + (1-p)\pi_I$
or $.20 = (.50)\pi_s + (.50).05$
and $\pi_s = .35$

Thus, 35 percent of the respondents had shoplifted. ■

multichotomous question

A fixed-alternative question in which respondents are asked to choose the alternative that most closely corresponds to their position on the subject.

answer questions in the same format on multiple-choice exams. In a multichotomous question, respondents are asked to choose the one alternative from several choices that most closely reflects their position on the subject. Exhibit 12.1 presents some of the open-ended questions from the preceding list as multichotomous questions. Respondents would be instructed to check the box or boxes that apply.

The examples in Exhibit 12.1 illustrate some of the difficulties encountered in using multiple-choice questions. None of the alternatives in the seat belt question, for example, may correctly capture the respondent's true feeling on the issue. The individual's opinion may be more complex. He may feel that seat belts should be required on school buses but not in private vehicles. Or she may think that seat belts should be required but that tickets for noncompliance should be issued only in conjunction with another traffic violation. The multiple-choice question does not permit individuals to elaborate on their true position but requires them to condense their complex attitude into a single statement. Of course, a well-designed series of multiple-choice questions could allow for such elaborations. Researchers must be careful, however, not to allow so many possible choices that the questionnaire becomes too long to be used effectively.

The seat belt question also illustrates a general problem in question design: Should respondents be provided with a "don't know" or "no opinion" option? If a respondent truly does not know an answer, or has no opinion on an issue, he or she should obviously be allowed to say so. But should the option be explicitly provided to the respondent in the form of a "don't know" or "no opinion" category or by asking a filter question like, "Do you have an opinion . . . "? The arguments about the desirability of a neutral point or "no opinion" cate-

Exhibit 12.1

Examples of Multichotomous Questions

Age	Television Purchase
How old are you?	**Why did you purchase a Zenith brand color TV?**
☐ Less than 20	☐ Price was lower than other alternatives
☐ 20–29	☐ Feel it represents the highest quality
☐ 30–39	☐ Availability of local service
☐ 40–49	☐ Availability of a service contract
☐ 50–59	☐ Picture is better
☐ 60 or over	☐ Warranty is better
	☐ Other

Seat Belt Legislation	Telephone Use
Do you think laws requiring passengers in motor vehicles to wear seat belts are needed?	**How many long-distance telephone calls do you make in a typical week?**
☐ Definitely needed	☐ Less than 5
☐ Probably needed	☐ 5–10
☐ Probably not needed	☐ More than 10
☐ Definitely not needed	
☐ No opinion	

gory center on the need for data accuracy versus the desire to have as many respondents as possible answer the question at issue.

Those opposed to including a "no opinion" answer argue that most respondents are unlikely to be truly neutral on an issue. Instead of providing them an easy way out, critics say, it is much better to have them think about the issues so that they can frame their preference, however slight it may be. That is much better than allowing the researcher to infer the majority opinion from the responses of those taking a stand on the issue. The argument for including a neutral or "no opinion" category among the responses claims that forcing a respondent to make a choice when his or her preference is fuzzy or nonexistent simply introduces response error into the results. Further, it makes it harder for respondents to answer, and it may turn them against the whole survey. The jury is still out with respect to which form better captures respondents' true position on an issue.

There is no question, however, that the two alternatives can produce widely differing proportions regarding the number holding a neutral view, potentially in the range of 10 to 50 percent.[14] For example, in a national telephone survey of 1,422 adults, results differed according to whether respondents were given a "don't know" option. The poll, jointly sponsored by the Kaiser Family Foundation, National Public Radio, and Harvard's Kennedy School of Government, asked a variety of questions to gauge public opinion about education issues.[15] Two questions asked about attitudes toward issues that have lately received media attention: school vouchers and charter schools. Half of the respondents were given two choices: whether they favor or oppose these programs. The other half of the respondents were given three choices: whether they favor or oppose the programs or haven't heard enough about the issue to have an opinion. As Figure 12.3 shows, people who heard this third choice were much more likely to say they didn't know enough to have an opinion.

The television set purchase question in Exhibit 12.1 illustrates a number of problems associated with multiple-choice questions. First, the list of reasons cited for purchasing a Zenith color television may not exhaust the reasons that could have been used by the respondent. The person may have purchased a Zenith out of loyalty to a friend who owns the local distributorship or because she really supports the "buy locally" plea advanced by many small-town chambers of commerce. The "other" response category attempts to solve this problem. If a great many respondents check the "other" category, however, they could render the study useless. Thus, the burden is on the researcher to make the list of alternatives in a multiple-choice question exhaustive. This may entail a good deal of prior research into the phenomenon that is to serve as the subject of a multiple-choice question.

Unless the respondent is instructed to check all alternatives that apply, or is to rank the alternatives in order of importance, the multiple-choice question also demands that the alternatives be mutually exclusive. The income categories of $10,000–$20,000 and $20,000–$30,000 violate this principle. A respondent with an income of $20,000 would not know which alternative to check. A legitimate response with respect to the color television purchase question might include several of the alternatives listed. The respondent thought the picture, warranty, and price were all more attractive on the Zenith than they were on other makes. Thus, the instructions would necessarily have to be "Check the most important reason," "Check all reasons that apply," or "Rank all the reasons that apply from most important to least important."

A third difficulty with the television purchase question is its great number of alternative responses. The list should be exhaustive. Yet the number of alternative statements an individual can process simultaneously appears to be limited. In one early study, the researchers presented each respondent with a card with six alternative statements. After each respondent had

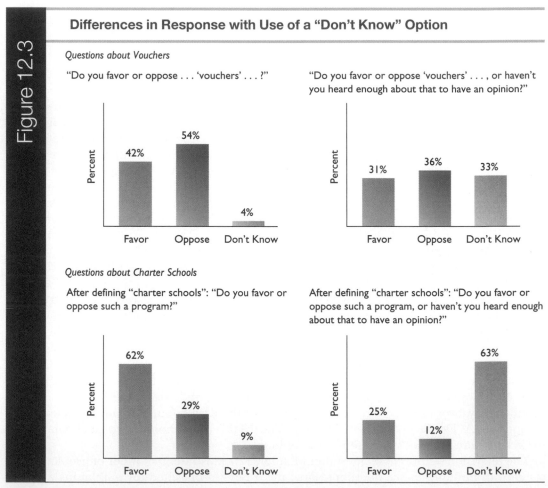

Figure 12.3

Differences in Response with Use of a "Don't Know" Option

Questions about Vouchers

"Do you favor or oppose . . . 'vouchers' . . . ?"

| Favor | Oppose | Don't Know |
| 42% | 54% | 4% |

"Do you favor or oppose 'vouchers' . . . , or haven't you heard enough about that to have an opinion?"

| Favor | Oppose | Don't Know |
| 31% | 36% | 33% |

Questions about Charter Schools

After defining "charter schools": "Do you favor or oppose such a program?"

| Favor | Oppose | Don't Know |
| 62% | 29% | 9% |

After defining "charter schools": "Do you favor or oppose such a program, or haven't you heard enough about that to have an opinion?"

| Favor | Oppose | Don't Know |
| 25% | 12% | 63% |

Note: The results are from a random telephone survey of 1,422 adults (18 and over) nationwide, developed jointly by National Public Radio, the Henry J. Kaiser Family Foundation, and Harvard University's Kennedy School of Government and administered by ICR/International Communications Research in June and July 1999.
Source: "NPR/Kaiser/Kennedy School Education Survey," National Public Radio Web site (http://www.npr.org, downloaded September 9, 1999).

PART 4:
Data Collection Forms

made his or her choice, the card was immediately replaced with another. On the second card, two of the six statements had been changed, and one statement from the original list was omitted. Yet only one-half of the respondents "could identify the changes, and a mere handful located the omission."[16] The meaning of all this is that in designing multiple-choice questions, the researcher should remain aware of human beings' limited data-processing capabilities. Perhaps a series of questions is more appropriate than one question. If there are a great many alternatives to a single question, then they should be shown to respondents using cards, and not simply read to them.

The fourth weakness of the television purchase question in Exhibit 12.1 is that it is susceptible to order bias. That is, the responses are likely to be affected by the order in which the alternatives are presented. Research Window 12.2 shows how the distribution of responses to the same questions was affected by the order in which the alternatives were listed on two versions of a mail questionnaire. That the three questions produced statistically significant different distributions of replies is especially noteworthy because order bias is least likely to occur in mail questionnaires, because respondents can see all the response categories. In fact, response order bias is typically much greater in telephone surveys or interviews in which the structured responses are read to the respondents. The recommended procedure for combating this order, or position, bias is to prepare several forms of the questionnaire, or several cards, if cards are used to list the alternatives. The order in which the alternatives are listed is then altered from form to form. If each alternative appears once at the extremes of the list, once in the middle, and once somewhere in between, the researcher can feel reasonably comfortable that the possible effects of position bias have been neutralized.

The long-distance telephone call example in Exhibit 12.1 illustrates another problem with multiple-choice questions when they are used to determine the frequency of various behaviors. The range of the categories used in the question seems to cue respondents about how they should reply. That is, the response scale categories themselves affect subjects' reports of the frequency with which they engage in the behavior. A scale with the three categories

- Less than 10
- 10–20
- More than 20

would likely produce a different picture of the frequency with which these same respondents make long-distance telephone calls. It seems that respondents make judgments about the researcher's knowledge or expectations from the categories and then respond accordingly. Specifically, they seem reluctant to report behaviors that are unusual in the context of the response scale—namely, those that constitute the extreme categories.[17] A general strategy for combating this tendency is to use open-ended answer formats when obtaining data on behavioral frequencies.

Dichotomous Questions Also a fixed-alternative question, the **dichotomous question** is one in which there are only two alternatives listed, as in the following examples:

Do you think laws requiring passengers in motor vehicles to wear seat belts are needed?

☐ Yes

☐ No

Do you intend to purchase an automobile this year?

☐ Yes

☐ No

We have already seen how the first of these questions could also be handled as a multiple-choice question. The second could also be given a multichotomous structure. Instead of simply presenting the yes-no alternatives, the list could be framed as "Definitely intend to buy,"

dichotomous question
A fixed-alternative question in which respondents are asked to indicate which of two alternative responses most closely corresponds to their position on a subject.

RESEARCH *Window*

12.2

How the Order in Which the Alternatives Are Listed Affects the Distribution of Replies

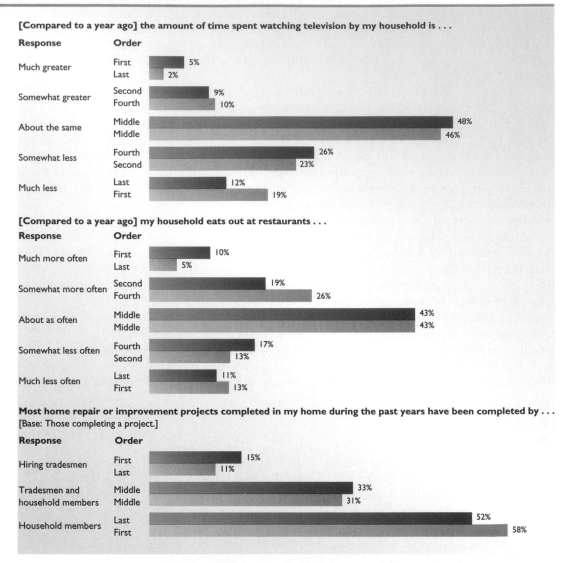

[Compared to a year ago] the amount of time spent watching television by my household is . . .

Response	Order	%
Much greater	First	5%
	Last	2%
Somewhat greater	Second	9%
	Fourth	10%
About the same	Middle	48%
	Middle	46%
Somewhat less	Fourth	26%
	Second	23%
Much less	Last	12%
	First	19%

[Compared to a year ago] my household eats out at restaurants . . .

Response	Order	%
Much more often	First	10%
	Last	5%
Somewhat more often	Second	19%
	Fourth	26%
About as often	Middle	43%
	Middle	43%
Somewhat less often	Fourth	17%
	Second	13%
Much less often	Last	11%
	First	13%

Most home repair or improvement projects completed in my home during the past years have been completed by . . .
[Base: Those completing a project.]

Response	Order	%
Hiring tradesmen	First	15%
	Last	11%
Tradesmen and household members	Middle	33%
	Middle	31%
Household members	Last	52%
	First	58%

Source: "An Examination of Order Bias," *Research on Research* No. 1 (Chicago: Market Facts, Inc., undated). Reprinted with permission.

"Probably will buy," "Probably will not buy," "Definitely intend not to buy," and "Undecided." Dichotomous questions can often be framed as multichotomous questions, and vice versa. (The two possess similar advantages and disadvantages, which were reviewed earlier when discussing structured questions. The advantages and disadvantages will not be repeated here.) The dichotomous question offers the ultimate in ease of coding and tabulation, and this probably accounts for its being the most commonly used type of question in communication studies.

One special problem with the dichotomous question is that the response can well depend on how the question is framed. This is true, of course, of all questions, but with the dichotomous question it represents a special problem. Consider two alternative questions:

Do you think that gasoline will be more expensive or less expensive next year than it is now?

☐ More expensive

☐ Less expensive

Do you think that gasoline will be less expensive or more expensive next year than it is now?

☐ Less expensive

☐ More expensive

Now the questions appear identical, and certainly we might want to expand each to include categories for "no opinion" and "about the same." The fact remains, though, that the two questions will elicit different responses.[18] The simple switching of the positions of "More expensive" and "Less expensive" can affect the response an individual gives. Which, then, is the correct wording?

As mentioned earlier, one generally accepted procedure for combating this order bias is to use a **split ballot.** One phrasing is used on one half of the questionnaires, and the alternative phrasing on the other half of the questionnaires. The averaged percentages from the two forms should then cancel out any biases.

Scales Another type of fixed-alternative question is the question that uses a scale to capture the response. For instance, when inquiring about VCR use, the following question might be asked:

How often do you tape programs for later viewing with your VCR?

☐ Never

☐ Occasionally

☐ Sometimes

☐ Often

In this form, the question is a multichotomous question. However, the responses also represent a scale of use. The scale nature of the question would be more obvious, perhaps, if the following form were used to secure the replies:

Never	Occasionally	Sometimes	Often

The advantage of this scheme is that the descriptors or categories could be presented at the top of the page, and types of programs could be listed along the left margin—for example, films, sporting events, and network specials. The respondent would then be instructed to designate the frequency with which the VCR is used to record each type. The instruction would need to be given only once, at the beginning, and thus a great deal of information could be secured from the respondent in a short time.

Step 5: Determine Wording of Each Question

Step 5 in the questionnaire development process involves the phrasing of each question. This is a critical task, in that poor phrasing of a question can cause respondents to refuse to answer it even though they agreed to cooperate in the study. Poor phrasing may also cause respondents to answer a question incorrectly, either on purpose or because of misunderstanding. The first condition, known as **item nonresponse,** can create a great many problems in analyzing the data. The second condition produces measurement error in that the recorded or obtained score does not equal the respondent's true score on the issue.[19]

Experienced researchers know that the phrasing of a question can directly affect the responses to it. One humorous anecdote in this regard involves two priests, a Dominican and a Jesuit, who are discussing whether it is a sin to smoke and pray at the same time. "After failing to reach a conclusion, each goes off to consult his respective superior. The next week they meet again. The Dominican says, 'Well, what did your superior say?' The Jesuit responds, 'He

split ballot
A technique used to combat response bias in which one phrasing is used for a question in one half of the questionnaires while an alternative phrasing is used in the other one half of the questionnaires.

item nonresponse
A source of nonsampling error that arises when a respondent agrees to an interview but refuses, or is unable, to answer specific questions.

said it was all right.' 'That's funny,' the Dominican replies, 'my superior said it was a sin.' Jesuit: 'What did you ask him?' Reply: 'I asked him if it was all right to smoke while praying,' 'Oh,' says the Jesuit, 'I asked my superior if it was all right to pray while smoking.'"[20]

Although researchers recognize that question wording can affect the answers obtained, there are, unfortunately, few basic principles researchers can rely upon to develop bias-free ways of framing a question. Instead, the literature is replete with rules of thumb. Although these rules of thumb are often easier to state than to practice, researchers need to be aware of them.

6 *List some of the primary rules researchers should keep in mind in trying to develop bias-free questions.*

Use Simple Words Most researchers are more highly educated than the typical questionnaire respondent, thus they tend to use words they are familiar with but that are not understood by many respondents. This is a difficult problem because it is not easy to dismiss what one knows and put oneself instead in the respondent's shoes when trying to determine appropriate vocabulary. A significant proportion of the population, for example, does not understand the word *Caucasian,* although most researchers do, and a very serious problem in designing questionnaires to survey Hispanics is in developing an unambiguous ethnic identifier.[21] The researcher needs to be constantly aware that the average person in the United States has a high school, not a college, education and that many people have difficulty coping with such routine tasks as making change, reading job notices, or completing a driver's license application. Even common words can cause difficulty on questionnaires as Research Window 12.3 indicates. The best advice is to keep the words simple.

Avoid Ambiguous Words and Questions Not only should the words and questions be simple, they should also be unambiguous. Consider again the multichotomous question:

How often do you tape programs for later viewing with your VCR?

☐ Never

☐ Occasionally

☐ Sometimes

☐ Often

RESEARCH *Window* **12.3**

A Rogues' Gallery of Problem Words

"Use Simple Words!" "Use unambiguous words!" Students of questionnaire design are accustomed to hearing those rules cited loudly and often. But, unfortunately, some of the simplest words may still be ambiguous in meaning. Here's a short list of words that may cause trouble if you're not sensitive to their possibilities for misinterpretation.

You

"You" is extremely popular with question worders, since it is implicated in every question they ask. In most cases "you" gives no trouble, since it is clear that it refers to the second person singular. However, and here is

the problem, the word sometimes may have a collective meaning. Consider the question:

How many television sets did you repair last month?

The question seems to be straightforward, until it is asked of a repairman in a large shop, who counters with, "Who do you mean, me or the whole shop?"

Sometimes "you" needs the emphasis of "you yourself," and sometimes it just isn't the word to use, as in the above situation, where the entire shop is meant.

All

"All" is one of those dead-giveaway words. From your own experience with true-false exams, you probably know that it is safe to count almost every all-inclusive statement as false. That is, you have learned that in such tests it is safe to follow the idea that all statements containing "all" are false, including this one. Some people have the same negative reaction to opinion questions that hinge upon all-inclusive or all-exclusive words. They may be generally in agreement with a proposition, but nevertheless hesitate to accept the extreme idea of *all, always, each, every, never, nobody, only, none,* or *sure.*

Bad

In itself the word "bad" is not at all bad for question wording. It conveys the meaning desired and is satisfactory as an alternative in a "good or bad" two-way question. Experience seems to indicate, however, that people are generally less willing to criticize than they are to praise. Since it is difficult to get them to state their negative views, sometimes the critical side needs to be softened. For example, after asking, "What things are good about your job?" it might seem perfectly natural to ask, "What things are bad about it?" But if we want to lean over backwards to get as many criticisms as we can, we may be wise not to apply the "bad" stigma, but to ask, "What things are not so good about it?"

Dinner

"Dinner," the main meal of the day, comes at noon with some families and in some areas. Elsewhere it is the evening meal. The question should not assume that it is either one or the other.

Government

"Government" is one of those words heavily loaded with emotional concepts. It is sometimes used as a definite word meaning the federal government, sometimes as an inclusive term for federal, state, and local government, sometimes as an abstract idea, and sometimes as the party in power as distinct from the opposition party. The trouble is that the respondent does not always know which "government" is meant. One person may have a different idea from another. It is best to specify if we want all respondents to answer with the same government in mind.

Like

"Like" is on the problem list only because it is sometimes used to introduce an example. The problem with bringing an example into a question is that the respondent's attention may be directed toward the particular example and away from the general issue which it is meant only to illustrate. The use of examples may sometimes be necessary, but the possible hazard should always be kept in mind. The choice of an example can affect the answers to the question—in fact, it may materially change the question, as in these two examples:

Do you think that leafy vegetables like spinach should be in the daily diet?
Do you think that leafy vegetables like lettuce should be in the daily diet?

Where

The frames of reference in answers to a "where" question may vary greatly. Consider the possible answers from this simple question:

Where did you read that?

Three of the many possible answers are,

In the New York Times.
At home in front of the fire.
In an advertisement.

Despite the seemingly wide variety of these three answers, some respondents could probably have stated them all: "In an ad in the *New York Times* while I was at home sitting in front of the fire." ∎

Source: Stanley L. Payne, *The Art of Asking Questions* (Princeton: Princeton University Press, 1979), pp. 158–176.

For all practical purposes, the replies to this question would be worthless. The words *occasionally, sometimes,* and *often* are ambiguous. For example, to one respondent, the word "often" might mean "almost everyday." To another it might mean, "Yes, I use it when I have the specific need. This happens about once a week." The words *occasionally* and *sometimes* could also be interpreted differently by different respondents. Thus, although the question would get answers, it would generate little real understanding of the frequency of use of the VCR to tape programs. A much better strategy would be to provide concrete alternatives for the respondent, such as the following:

☐ Never use

☐ Use approximately once a month

☐ Use approximately once a week

☐ Use almost every day

Another way to avoid ambiguity in asking about the frequency of behavior is to ask when the behavior last occurred. Our earlier question might be framed in the following way:

Did you tape any programs with your VCR in the last two days?

☐ Yes

☐ No

☐ Can't recall

The proportion responding yes would then be used to infer the frequency with which the VCR was used, while the follow-up question among all those responding yes—"For what purpose?"—would give insight as to how respondents are using it. Among the people responding, there will be some who normally use their VCR but did not use it in the last two days. There will be others who do not normally use it but did use it within the last two days. These variations should cancel each other out if a large enough sample of respondents is used.

The total sample should provide a good indication of the proportion of times the VCR is used, and the proportion of times it is used to tape various types of programs. The researcher, in effect, relies on the sample to provide insight into how frequently the phenomenon occurs, rather than relying on a specific question that may contain ambiguous alternatives. In such cases it is important that the sample be large enough so that the proportions can be estimated with the appropriate degree of confidence.

Avoid Leading Questions   A question framed so as to give the respondent a clue as to how he or she should answer is a **leading question.** Consider this question:

Do you feel that limiting taxes by law is an effective way to stop the government from picking your pocket every payday?

☐ Yes

☐ No

☐ Undecided

This was one of three questions in an unsolicited questionnaire that the author received as part of a study sponsored by the National Tax Limitation Committee. The committee intended to make the results of the poll available to Congress and to state legislators. Given the implied purpose, it is probably not surprising to see the leading words "picking your pocket" being used in this question, or the leading word "gouge" being used in another question. What is especially unfortunate is that it is unlikely that the questions themselves accompanied the report to Congress. Rather, it is more likely that the report suggested that some high percentage (e.g., 90 percent of those surveyed) favored laws limiting taxes. Conclusion: Congress should pay attention to the wishes of the people and pass such laws.

One sees instances of this phenomenon every day in the newspaper. The public is treated to a discussion of the results of this or that study with respect to how the American people feel on issues, but the questionnaire is not shown. Yet question wording makes a difference, and it is important for researchers to realize that if one truly wants an accurate picture of the situation, one needs to avoid leading the respondent as to how he or she should answer.

Avoid Implicit Alternatives   An alternative that is not expressed in the options is an **implicit alternative.** In one study, researchers wanted to know the attitudes of full-time homemakers toward the idea of having a job outside the home. They asked two random samples of homemakers the following two questions:[22]

> **Would you like to have a job, if this were possible?** _____
> **Would you prefer to have a job, or do you prefer to do just your housework?** _____

While the two questions appear very similar, they produced dramatically different responses. In the first version, 19 percent of the homemakers said they would not like to have a job. In the second version, 68 percent said they would prefer not to have one—over three and one-half times as many as in the first version. The difference in the two questions is that the second version makes explicit the alternative only implied in the first version. As a general rule, one should avoid implicit alternatives unless there is a special reason for including them. Thus, the second version is better than the first. Further, because the order in which the alternatives appear can affect the responses, one should rotate the order of the options in samples of questionnaires.

Avoid Implicit Assumptions   Questions are frequently framed so that there is an **implicit assumption** as to what will happen as a consequence. The question "Are you in favor of placing price controls on crude oil?" will elicit different responses from individuals, depending on whether they think price controls will result in rationing, long lines at the pump, or lower prices. A better way of stating this question is to make explicit the possible consequence(s). For example, the question could be altered to ask, "Are you in favor of placing price controls on crude oil if it would produce gas rationing?"

Figure 12.4 shows what can happen when the consequences are explicitly stated in a question. Version B makes the implied consequence in Version A explicit; the only way the seat belt law could be effective would be if there were some penalty for not complying with it. Yet, when there was no explicit statement about what would happen if a person did not comply with the proposed law, 73 percent were in favor of it. When people faced the prospect of a fine for noncompliance, only 50 percent favored a mandatory seat belt law.

Avoid Generalizations and Estimates   Questions should always be asked in specific, rather than general, terms. Consider the question "How many salespeople did you see last year?" which might be asked of a purchasing agent. To answer the question, the agent would probably estimate how many salespeople call in a typical week and would multiply this estimate by 52. This burden should not be placed on the agent. Rather, a more accurate estimate would be obtained if the purchasing agent were asked "How many representatives called last week?" and the researcher multiplied the answer by 52.

Avoid Double-Barreled Questions   A question that calls for two responses and thereby creates confusion for the respondent is a **double-barreled question.** The question "What is your evaluation of the price and convenience offered by XYZ's catalog showroom?" is asking respondents to react to two separate attributes by which the showroom could be described. The respondent might feel the prices are attractive but the location is not, for example, and thereby is placed in a dilemma as to how to respond. The problem is particularly acute if the

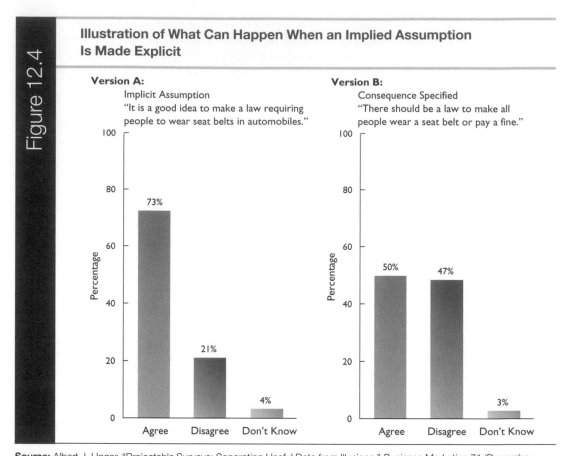

Figure 12.4

Illustration of What Can Happen When an Implied Assumption Is Made Explicit

Version A:
Implicit Assumption
"It is a good idea to make a law requiring people to wear seat belts in automobiles."

(Percentage chart) Agree 73%, Disagree 21%, Don't Know 4%

Version B:
Consequence Specified
"There should be a law to make all people wear a seat belt or pay a fine."

(Percentage chart) Agree 50%, Disagree 47%, Don't Know 3%

Source: Albert J. Ungar, "Projectable Surveys: Separating Useful Data from Illusions," *Business Marketing* 71 (December 1986), p. 90. Reprinted with permission from the December 1986 issue of *Business Marketing.* Copyright, Crain Communications, Inc.

individual must choose an answer from a fixed set of alternatives. One can and should avoid double-barreled questions by splitting the initial question into two separate questions. A useful indicator that two questions might be needed is the use of the word *and* in the initial wording of the question.

Step 6: Determine Question Sequence

Once the form of response and specific wording for each question have been decided, the researcher is ready to begin putting them together into a questionnaire. The researcher needs to recognize immediately that the order in which the questions are presented can be crucial to the success of the research effort. Again, there are no hard-and-fast principles but only rules of thumb to guide the researcher in this activity.

Use Simple and Interesting Opening Questions The first questions asked are crucial. If respondents cannot answer them easily or if they find them uninteresting or threatening in any way, they may refuse to complete the remainder of the questionnaire. Thus, it is essential that the first few questions be simple, interesting, and in no way threatening to respondents. Questions that ask respondents for their opinion on some issue are often good openers, as most people like to feel their opinion is important. Sometimes it is helpful to use such an opener even when responses to it will not be analyzed, since opinion questions are often effective in relaxing respondents and securing their cooperation.

Use the Funnel Approach One approach to question sequencing is the **funnel approach,** which gets its name from its shape, starting with broad questions and progressively narrowing

7 Explain what the funnel approach to question sequencing is.

down the scope. If respondents are to be asked, "What improvements are needed in the company's service policy?" and also, "How do you like the quality of service?" the first question needs to be asked before the second. Otherwise, quality of service will be emphasized disproportionately in the responses simply because it is fresh in the respondents' minds.

There should also be some logical order to the questions. This means that sudden changes in topics and jumping around from topic to topic should be avoided. Transitional devices are sometimes necessary to smooth the flow when a change in subject matter occurs. Sometimes researchers will insert filter questions as a way to change the direction of the questioning. Most often, however, researchers will insert a brief explanation as a way of bridging a change in subject matter.

Design Branching Questions with Care A direction as to where to go next in the questionnaire based on the answer to a preceding question is called a **branching question.** For example, the initial question might be, "Have you bought a car within the last six months?" If the respondent answers yes, he or she is then instructed to go to another place in the questionnaire, where questions are asked about specific details of the purchase. Someone replying no to the same question would be directed to skip the questions relating to the details of the purchase. The advantage to branching questions is that they reduce the number of alternatives that are needed in individual questions, while ensuring that those respondents capable of supplying the needed information still have an opportunity to do so. Those for whom a question is irrelevant are simply directed around it.

Branching questions and directions are much easier to develop for telephone or personal interviews, especially for those administered through computer-assisted interviewing than for mail or email surveys. With mail or email questionnaires the number of branching questions needs to be kept to an absolute minimum so that respondents do not become confused when responding, or refuse to cooperate because the task becomes too difficult. While they can be used more liberally with telephone and personal interview surveys, branching questions still need to be designed with care, since the evidence indicates that branching instructions increase the rate of item nonresponse for items immediately following the branch.[23] When using branching questions, it is generally good practice to (1) develop a flow chart of the logical possibilities and then prepare the branching questions and instructions to follow the flow chart, (2) place the question that follows the branch as close as possible to the original question, so as to minimize the amount of page-flipping that is necessary, and (3) order the branching questions so that respondents cannot anticipate what additional information is required.[24]

The last point can be illustrated by a questionnaire seeking information about small appliance ownership. A skillfully designed questionnaire might begin by asking if a respondent owns any of a certain list of small appliances. If she answers yes to any, the researcher may then go on to ask the brand name, the store where purchased, and so on, for each. If instead the researcher had begun by asking, "Do you own a food processor?" and followed up with questions about brand, price, and so on, the respondent would soon recognize that "yes" answers to subsequent questions about the ownership of other appliances would inevitably lead to many other questions, and she may decide it is less taxing to say no in the first place.

Ask for Classification Information Last The typical questionnaire contains two types of information: basic information and classification information. *Basic information* refers to the subject of the study, for example, intentions or attitudes of respondents. *Classification information* refers to the other data we collect to classify respondents so as to extract more information about the phenomenon of interest. For instance, we might be interested in determining if a respondent's attitudes toward the need for seat belt legislation are in any way affected by the person's income. Income here would be a classification variable. Demographic/socioeconomic characteristics of respondents are often used as classification variables for understanding the results.

The proper questionnaire sequence is to present questions securing basic information first and those seeking classification information last. There is a logical reason for this. The basic information is

funnel approach
An approach to question sequencing that gets its name from its shape, starting with broad questions and progressively narrowing down the scope.

8 *Explain what a branching question is and discuss when it is used.*

branching question
A technique used to direct respondents to different places in a questionnaire, based on their response to the question at hand.

9 *Explain the difference between basic information and classification information and tell which should be asked first in a questionnaire.*

most critical. Without it, there is no study. Thus, the researcher should not risk alienating the respondent by asking a number of personal questions before getting to the heart of the study, since it is not unusual for personal questions to alienate respondents most. Respondents who readily offer their opinions about television programming may balk when asked about their income. An early question aimed at determining their income may affect the whole tone of the interview or other communication. It is best to avoid this possibility by placing the classification information at the end.

Place Difficult or Sensitive Questions Late in the Questionnaire   The basic information itself can also present some sequence problems. Some of the questions may be sensitive. Early questions should not be, for the reasons we mentioned earlier. If respondents feel threatened, they may refuse to participate in the study. Thus, sensitive questions should be placed in the body of the questionnaire and intertwined and hidden among some not-so-sensitive ones. Once respondents have become involved in the study, they are less likely to react negatively or refuse to answer when delicate questions are posed.

© Alyx Kellington/Index Stock Imagery

The importance of a well-designed questionnaire was illuminated by the 2000 presidential election in the United States in which confusing ballots in Florida led to a legal battle over the election results.

Step 7: Determine Physical Characteristics of Questionnaire

The physical characteristics of the questionnaire can affect the accuracy of the replies that are obtained.[25] The Florida ballots in the 2000 presidential election and the controversy surrounding who actually won the electoral vote, Bush or Gore, provides a vivid example. Put simply, the physical characteristics of a questionnaire can affect how respondents react to it and the ease with which the replies can be processed. In determining the physical format of the questionnaire, a researcher wants to do those things that help get the respondent to accept the questionnaire, and facilitate handling and control by the researcher.

Securing Acceptance of the Questionnaire   The physical appearance of the questionnaire can influence respondents' cooperation. This is particularly true with mail questionnaires, but it applies as well to questionnaires used in personal interviews. If the questionnaire looks sloppy, respondents are likely to feel the study is unimportant and hence refuse to cooperate despite researchers' assurance that it is important. If the study is important, and there is no reason to conduct it if it is not, make the questionnaire reflect that importance. This means that good-quality paper should be used for the questionnaires. It also means that the questionnaires should be printed, not photocopied.

The introduction to the research can also affect acceptance of the questionnaire. With mail questionnaires, the cover letter serves to introduce the study. It is very important the cover letter convince the designated respondent to cooperate. Good cover letters are rarely written in a hurry; rather, they usually require a series of painstaking rewrites to get the wording just so. Research Window 12.4 lists important content considerations in the construction of cover letters.[26] With personal and telephone interviews, the introduction to the research is necessarily shorter. Nonetheless, the introduction needs to convince respondents about the importance of the research and the importance of their participation. Typically, this means

Contents of and Sample Cover Letter for a Mail Questionnaire

Panel A: Contents

1. Personal communication
2. Asking a favor
3. Importance of the research project and its purpose.
4. Importance of the recipient.
5. Importance of the replies in general.
6. Importance of the replies when the reader is not qualified to answer most questions.
7. How the recipient may benefit from this research.
8. Completing the questionnaire will take only a short time.
9. The questionnaire can be answered easily.
10. A stamped reply envelope is enclosed.
11. How recipient was selected.
12. Answers are anonymous or confidential.
13. Offer to send report on results of survey.
14. Note of urgency.
15. Appreciation of sender.
16. Importance of sender.
17. Importance of the sender's organization.
18. Description and purpose of incentive.
19. Avoiding bias.
20. Style
21. Format and appearance.
22. Brevity.

The numbers refer to the corresponding items in Panel A.

Panel B: Sample

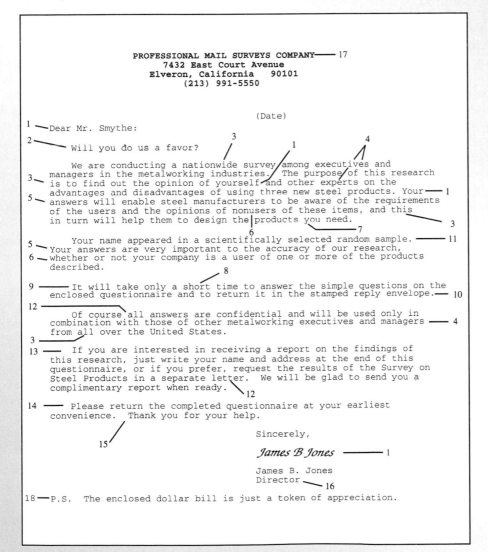

Source: Paul L. Erdos, *Professional Mail Surveys* (Melbourne, Fla.: Robert E. Krieger Publishing Co., Inc., 1983), pp. 102–103. Reprinted with permission.

describing how they can benefit from it, the fact that their replies will be confidential, and the incentive, if any, that they will receive for participating.

It is also a good idea to include the name of the sponsoring organization and the name of the project on the first page or on the cover if the questionnaire is in book form. Both of these lend credibility to the study. However, since awareness of the sponsoring firm may bias respondents' answers, many firms use fictitious names for the sponsoring organization. This practice also helps eliminate phone calls or other inquiries from respondents asking for the results of the study.

Facilitate Handling and Control   Several steps that facilitate handling and control by the researcher also contribute to acceptance of the questionnaire by respondents. These include questionnaire size and layout and question sequencing.

Questionnaire size is important.[27] Smaller questionnaires are better than larger ones if— and this is a big if—they do not appear crowded. Smaller questionnaires seem easier to complete; they appear to take less time and are less likely to cause respondents to refuse to participate. They are easier to carry in the field and are easier to sort, count, and file in the office than are larger questionnaires.

If, on the other hand, smaller size is gained at the expense of an uncluttered appearance, these advantages are lost. A crowded questionnaire has a bad appearance, leads to errors in data collection, and results in shorter and less informative replies for both self-administered and interviewer-administered questionnaires. Researchers have found, for example, that the more lines or space left for recording the response to open-ended questions, the more extensive the reply will be. Similarly, the more information a respondent is given about the kind of information being sought, the better the reply is apt to be. Both of these techniques, however, increase the physical size of the questionnaire needed for the study.

While post-card size probably represents the lower limit, letter size probably represents the upper limit to the size of an individual page in a questionnaire. When the questions will not all fit on the front and back of one sheet, multiple sheets need to be used. When this happens, one should make the questionnaire into a booklet rather than staple or paper-clip the pages together. The method of binding not only facilitates handling but also reinforces an image of quality. So does numbering the questions, which also promotes respondent cooperation, particularly when branching questions are used. Without numbered questions, instructions as to how to proceed (e.g., "If the answer to Question 2 is yes, please go to Question 5") cannot be used. Even with numbered questions, however, it is helpful if the respondent can be directed by arrows to the appropriate next question after a branching question. Another technique researchers have found useful with branch-type questions is the use of color coding on the questionnaire, where the next question to which the respondent is directed matches the color of the space in which the answer to the branching or filter question was recorded.

Numbering the questions also makes it easier to edit, code, and tabulate the responses.[28] It also helps if the questionnaires themselves are numbered. This makes it easier to keep track of the questionnaires and to determine which ones, if any, are lost. It also makes it easier to monitor interviewer performance and to detect interviewer biases, if any. The research director will be able to develop a log listing which questionnaires were assigned to which interviewers. Mail questionnaires are an exception to the principle that the questionnaires themselves be numbered. Respondents often interpret an assigned number on a mail questionnaire as a mechanism by which their responses can be identified as theirs. The possible loss in anonymity is threatening to many of them, and they may refuse to cooperate or may even distort their answers.

Step 8: Reexamine Steps 1 through 7 and Revise If Necessary

A researcher should not expect that the first draft will result in a usable questionnaire. Rather, reexamination and revision are staples in questionnaire construction. Each question should be reviewed to ensure that the question is easy to answer and not confusing, ambiguous, or potentially offensive to the respondent. Neither should any question be leading or bias-inducing. How can one tell? An extremely critical attitude and good common sense should help. The researcher should examine each word in each question. The literature on question phrasing is full of examples of how some seemingly innocuous questions produced response problems.[29] When a potential problem is discovered, the question should be revised. After examining each question, and each word in each question, for its potential meanings and implications, the researcher might test the questionnaire in some role-playing situations, using others working on the project as subjects. This role playing should reveal some of the most serious shortcomings and should lead to further revision of the questionnaire.

Step 9: Pretest Questionnaire and Revise If Necessary

The real test of a questionnaire is how it performs under actual conditions of data collection. For this assessment, the questionnaire **pretest** is vital. The questionnaire pretest serves the same role in questionnaire design that test-marketing serves in new product development. While the product concept, different advertising appeals, alternative packages, and so on, may all have been tested previously in the product development process, test-marketing is the first place where they all come together. Thus, test-marketing provides the real test of customer reactions to the product and the accompanying marketing program. Similarly, the pretest provides the real test of the questionnaire and the mode of administration.

pretest
Use of a questionnaire (or observation form) on a trial basis in a small pilot study to determine how well the questionnaire (or observation form) works.

There are a number of interesting examples in the literature of questions with unintended implications that could have been avoided with an adequate pretest of the questionnaire. In one lifestyle study, for example, the following question was asked: "How would you like to be living two years from now?" While the question was intended to get at hoped-for lifestyles, a large group of the respondents simply replied "yes."[30]

Data collection should never begin without an adequate pretest of the questionnaire. The pretest can be used to assess both individual questions and their sequence.[31] It is best if there are two pretests. The first should be done by personal interview, regardless of the actual mode of administration that will eventually be used. An interviewer can watch to see if people actually remember data requested of them, or if some questions seem confusing or produce resistance or hesitancy among respondents for one reason or another. The pretest interviews should be conducted among respondents similar to those who will be used in the actual study, by the firm's most experienced interviewers.

The personal interview pretest should reveal some questions in which the wording could be improved or the sequence changed. If the changes are major, the revised questionnaire should again be pretested in personal interviews. If the changes are minor, the questionnaire can be pretested a second time using mail, telephone, fax, email, Internet, or personal interviews, whichever is going to be used for the full-scale study. This time, however, less experienced interviewers should also be used in order to determine if typical interviewers will have any special problems with the questionnaire. The purpose of the second pretest is to uncover problems unique to the mode of administration.

Finally, the responses that result from the pretest should be coded and tabulated. We have previously discussed the need for the preparation of dummy tables prior to the development of the questionnaire. The tabulation of pretest responses can check on the researcher's conceptualization of the problem and the data and method of analysis necessary to answer it. If there is no place in one of the dummy tables to put the responses to a question, the question is either not needed or the researcher has omitted some contemplated analysis. Moreover, if some part of a dummy table remains empty, a necessary question may have been omitted. Trial tabulations reveal better than any alternative whether all the data collected will be put to use and that all needed data will be collected.

The researcher who avoids a questionnaire pretest and tabulation of replies is either naive or a fool. The pretest is the most inexpensive insurance the researcher can buy to ensure the success of the questionnaire and the research project. A careful pretest along with proper attention to the dos and don'ts presented in this chapter and summarized in Exhibit 12.2 should make the questionnaire development process successful.

Exhibit 12.2

Some Dos and Don'ts When Preparing Questionnaires

Step 1: Specify What Information Will Be Sought
1. Make sure that you have a clear understanding of the issue and what it is that you want to know (expect to learn). Frame your research questions, but refrain from writing questions for the questionnaire at this time.
2. Make a list of your research questions. Review them periodically as you are working on the questionnaire.
3. Use the dummy tables that were set up to guide the data analysis to suggest questions for the questionnaire.
4. Conduct a search for existing questions on the issue.
5. Revise existing questions on the issue, and prepare new questions that address the issues you plan to research.

Step 2: Determine Type of Questionnaire and Method of Administration
1. Use the type of data to be collected as a basis for deciding on the type of questionnaire.
2. Use the degree of structure and disguise as well as cost factors to determine the method of administration.
3. Compare the special capabilities and limitations of each method of administration and the value of the data collected from each with the needs of the survey.

Step 3: Determine Content of Individual Questions
1. For each research question ask yourself, "Why do I want to know this?" Answer it in terms of how it will help your research. "It would be interesting to know" is not an acceptable answer.
2. Make sure each question is specific and addresses only one important issue.
3. Ask yourself whether the question applies to all respondents; it should, or provision should be made for skipping it.
4. Split questions that can be answered from different frames of reference into multiple questions, one corresponding to each frame of reference.
5. Ask yourself whether respondents will be informed about, and can remember, the issue that the question is dealing with.
6. Make sure the time period of the question is related to the importance of the topic. Consider using aided-recall techniques like diaries or written records.
7. Avoid questions that require excessive effort, that have hard-to-articulate answers, and that deal with embarrassing or threatening issues.
8. If threatening questions are necessary,
   (a) hide the questions among more innocuous ones.
   (b) make use of a counterbiasing statement.
   (c) phrase the question in terms of others and how they might feel or act.
   (d) ask respondents if they have ever engaged in the undesirable activity, and then ask if they are presently engaging in such an activity.
   (e) use categories or ranges rather than specific numbers.
   (f) use the randomized-response model.

Step 4: Determine Form of Response to Each Question
1. Determine which type of question—open-ended, dichotomous, or multichotomous—provides data that fit the information needs of the project.
2. Use structured questions whenever possible.
3. Use open-ended questions that require short answers to begin a questionnaire.
4. Try to convert open-ended questions to fixed-response questions to reduce respondent work load and coding effort for descriptive and causal studies.
5. If open-ended questions are necessary, make the questions sufficiently directed to give respondents a frame of reference when answering.
6. When using dichotomous questions, state the negative or alternative side in detail.
7. Provide for "don't know," "no opinion," and "both" answers.

Exhibit 12.2

Some Dos and Don'ts When Preparing Questionnaires *(continued)*

8. Be aware that there may be a middle ground.
9. Be sensitive to the mildness or harshness of the alternatives.
10. When using multichotomous questions, be sure the choices are exhaustive and mutually exclusive, and if combinations are possible, include them.
11. Be sure the range of alternatives is clear and that all reasonable alternative answers are included.
12. If the possible responses are numerous, consider using more than one question to reduce the potential for information overload.
13. When using dichotomous or multichotomous questions, consider the use of a split-ballot procedure to reduce order bias.
14. Clearly indicate if items are to be ranked or if only one item on the list is to be chosen.

Step 5: Determine Wording of Each Question

1. Use simple words.
2. Avoid ambiguous words and questions.
3. Avoid leading questions.
4. Avoid implicit alternatives.
5. Avoid implicit assumptions.
6. Avoid generalizations and estimates.
7. Use simple sentences and avoid compound sentences.
8. Change long, dependent clauses to words or short phrases.
9. Avoid double-barreled questions.
10. Make sure each question is as specific as possible.

Step 6: Determine Question Sequence

1. Use simple, interesting questions for openers.
2. Use the funnel approach, first asking broad questions and then narrowing them down.
3. Ask difficult or sensitive questions late in the questionnaire, when rapport is better.
4. Follow chronological order when collecting historical information.
5. Complete questions about one topic before moving on to the next.
6. Prepare a flow chart whenever branching questions are being considered.
7. Ask filter questions before asking detailed questions.
8. Ask demographic questions last so that if respondent refuses, the other data are still usable.

Step 7: Determine Physical Characteristics of Questionnaire

1. Make sure the questionnaire looks professional and is relatively easy to answer.
2. Use quality paper and print; do not photocopy the questionnaire.
3. Attempt to make the questionnaire as short as possible while avoiding a crowded appearance.
4. Use a booklet format for ease of analysis and to prevent lost pages.
5. List the name of the organization conducting the survey on the first page.
6. Number the questions to ease data processing.
7. If the respondent must skip more than one question, use a "go to."
8. If the respondent must skip an entire section, consider color coding the sections.
9. State how the responses are to be reported, such as a check mark, number, circle, etc.

Step 8: Reexamine Steps 1–7 and Revise If Necessary

1. Examine each word of every question to ensure that the question is not confusing, ambiguous, offensive, or leading.
2. Get peer evaluations of the draft questionnaire.

Step 9: Pretest Questionnaire and Revise If Necessary

1. Pretest the questionnaire first by personal interviews among respondents similar to those to be used in the actual study.
2. Obtain comments from the interviewers and respondents to discover any problems with the questionnaire, and revise it if necessary. When the revisions are substantial, repeat Steps 1 and 2 of Step 9.
3. Pretest the questionnaire by mail or telephone to uncover problems unique to the mode of administration.
4. Code and tabulate the pretest responses in dummy tables to determine if questions are providing adequate information.
5. Eliminate questions that do not provide adequate information, and revise questions that cause problems.

ETHICAL dilemma 12.2

A candy manufacturer tells you that he wants to raise the price of his gourmet chocolates and he needs you to establish the greatest price increase that shoppers will stand. He suggests that you interview patrons of gourmet candy shops without informing them of the sponsor or purpose of the research, describe the candy to them in general terms, and suggest prices that they might find acceptable, starting with the highest price.

- *Is it ethical to ask people questions when their answer may be detrimental to their self-interest?*

- *Is it ethical not to reveal the purpose or sponsor of the research? If you did reveal the purpose of the research, would survey respondents give the same answers as otherwise?*

ETHICAL dilemma 12.3

As you supervise the sending out of a mail survey from a client's place of business, you notice some numbers printed on the inside of the return envelopes. You point out to the client that the cover letter promises survey respondents anonymity, which is not consistent with a policy of coding the return envelopes. She replies that she needs to identify those respondents who have not replied so that she can send a follow-up mailing. She also suggests the information might be useful in the future in identifying those who might react favorably to a sales call for the product.

- *Is it ethical to promise anonymity and then not adhere to your promise?*

- *Is it healthy for the marketing research profession if legitimate research becomes associated with subsequent sales tactics?*

There are generally fewer problems in constructing observation forms than in constructing questionnaires, because the researcher is no longer concerned with the fact that the question and the way it is asked will affect the response. Through proper training of observers, the researcher can create the necessary expertise so that the data collection instrument is handled consistently. Alternatively, the researcher may simply use a mechanical device to measure the behavior of interest and secure complete consistency in measurement. This is not to imply that observation forms offer no problems of construction. Rather, the researcher needs to make very explicit decisions about what is to be observed and the categories and units that will be used to record this behavior. Figure 12.5, which is the observation form used by a bank to evaluate the service provided by its employees having extensive customer contact, shows how detailed some of these decisions can be. In this case the observers posed as shoppers.

The statement that "one needs to determine what is to be observed before one can make a scientific observation" seems trite. Yet this is exactly the case. Almost any event can be described in a number of ways. When we watch someone making a cigarette purchase, we might report that (1) the person purchased one package of cigarettes; (2) the woman purchased one package of cigarettes; (3) the woman purchased a package of Tareyton cigarettes; (4) the woman purchased a package of Tareyton 100s; (5) the woman, after asking for and finding that the store was out of Virginia Slims, purchased a package of Tareyton 100s; and so on.

A great many additional variations are possible, such as adding the type, name, or location of the store where this behavior occurred. In order for this observation to be productive for scientific inquiry, we must predetermine which aspects of this behavior are relevant. In this particular example, the decision as to what to observe requires that the researcher specify the following:

- Who should be observed? Anyone entering the store? Anyone making a purchase? Anyone making a cigarette purchase?
- What aspects of the purchase should be reported? Which brand they purchased? Which brand they asked for first? Whether the purchase was of king-size or regular cigarettes? What about the purchaser? Is the person's sex to be recorded? Is the individual's age to be estimated? Does it make any difference if the person was alone or in a group?

- When should the observation be made? On what day of the week? At what time of the day? Should day and time be reported? Should the observation be recorded only after a purchase occurs, or should an approach by a customer to a salesclerk also be recorded even if it does not result in a sale?
- Where should the observation be made? In what kind of store? How should the store be selected? How should it be noted on the observation form—by type, by location, by name? Should vending-machine purchases also be noted?

The careful reader will note that these are the same kinds of who, what, when, and where decisions that need to be made in selecting the research design. The why and how are also implicit. The research problem should dictate the why of the observation, while the how involves choosing the observation device or form that will be used. A paper-and-pencil form should be very simple to use. It should parallel the logical sequence of the purchase act (for example, a male approaches the clerk, asks for a package of cigarettes, and so on, if these behaviors are relevant) and should permit the recording of observations by a simple check mark if possible. Again, careful attention to detail, exacting examination of the preliminary form, and an adequate pretest should return handsome dividends with respect to the quality of the observations made.

Figure 12.5

Form Used by Observer Acting as Shopper to Evaluate Service Provided by Bank Employees

Bank _____

Date _____   Time _____   Shopper's Name _____

Nature of Transaction: ☐ Personal   ☐ Telephone

Details _____

_____

_____

A. FOR PERSONAL TRANSACTIONS

Bank Employee's Name _____

1. How was name obtained?
- ☐ Employee had name tag
- ☐ Nameplate on counter or desk
- ☐ Employee gave name
- ☐ Shopper had to ask for name
- ☐ Name provided by other employee
- ☐ Other _____

B. FOR TELEPHONE TRANSACTIONS

Bank Employee's Name _____

1. How was name obtained?
- ☐ Employee gave name upon answering the telephone
- ☐ Name provided by other employee
- ☐ Shopper had to ask for name
- ☐ Employee gave name during conversation
- ☐ Other _____

continued

Figure 12.5

Form Used by Observer Acting as Shopper to Evaluate Service Provided by Bank Employees *(continued)*

C. CUSTOMER RELATIONS SKILLS	YES	NO	DOES NOT APPLY
1. Did the employee notice and greet you immediately?	☐	☐	☐
2. Did the employee speak pleasantly and smile?	☐	☐	☐
3. Did the employee answer the telephone promptly?	☐	☐	☐
4. Did the employee find out your name?	☐	☐	☐
5. Did the employee use your name during the transaction?	☐	☐	☐
6. Did the employee ask you to be seated?	☐	☐	☐
7. Was the employee helpful?	☐	☐	☐
8. Was the employee's desk or work area neat and uncluttered?	☐	☐	☐
9. Did the employee show a genuine interest in you as a customer?	☐	☐	☐
10. Did the employee thank you for coming in?	☐	☐	☐
11. Did the employee enthusiastically support the bank and its services?	☐	☐	☐
12. Did the employee handle any interruptions (phone calls, etc.) effectively?	☐	☐	☐

Comment on any positive or negative details of the transaction that you found particularly noticeable.

_____

_____

_____

_____

_____

D. SALES SKILLS	YES	NO	DOES NOT APPLY
1. Did the employee determine if you had any accounts with this bank?	☐	☐	☐
2. Did the employee use "open-ended" questions in obtaining information about you?	☐	☐	☐
3. Did the employee listen to what you had to say?	☐	☐	☐

continued

Figure 12.5

Form Used by Observer Acting as Shopper to Evaluate Service Provided by Bank Employees *(continued)*

4. Did the employee sell you on the bank service by showing you what the service could do for you? ☐ ☐ ☐

5. Did the employee ask you to open the service which you inquired about? ☐ ☐ ☐

6. Did the employee ask you to bank with this particular bank? ☐ ☐ ☐

7. Did the employee ask you to contact him/her when visiting the bank? ☐ ☐ ☐

8. Did the employee ask you if you had any questions or if you understood the service at the end of the transaction? ☐ ☐ ☐

9. Did the employee give you brochures about other services? ☐ ☐ ☐

10. Did the employee give you his/her calling card? ☐ ☐ ☐

11. Did the employee indicate that you might be contacted by telephone, engraved card, or letter as a means of follow-up? ☐ ☐ ☐

12. Did the employee ask you to open or use other services? Check the following if they were mentioned. ☐ ☐ ☐

☐ savings account

☐ checking account

☐ automatic savings

☐ Mastercharge

☐ Master Checking

☐ safe-deposit box

☐ loan services

☐ trust services

☐ automatic payroll deposit

☐ bank-by-mail

☐ automatic loan payment

☐ bank hours

☐ other _____

Comment on the overall effectiveness of the employee's sales skills.

_____

_____

_____

_____

_____

Source: Courtesy of Neil M. Ford.

I t wasn't really funny, but Bill Hershey had to laugh. He had spent the afternoon on the phone with a random sample of the physicians that MedAccounts had earmarked to reply to its service questionnaire. The poor overall response to the questionnaire now made perfect sense. And while the whole situation was quite a screwup, he could laugh about it because his boss had taken it philosophically, and it was at least as much the client's fault as it was Hershey's.

In a nutshell, the problem was that MedAccounts didn't have a clear idea of who its customers were, at least in terms of service. True, its sales reps called on the physicians in a practice, and some physicians purchased the MedAccounts billing system. But in reality, the doctors spent their days treating patients, not billing them. While the doctors might have been the purchasers of the system, they were certainly not the users. Most of the doctors who purchased the MedAccounts system didn't even know where it was located in their office. They weren't the ones who called the service department: they had no idea of whether the service rep was punctual, polite, or quick to spot the problem.

It was the office manager who called MedAccounts when there was a problem, who knew the service rep's name and whether his or her appearance was neat and demeanor professional. Hershey's informal phone research explained a lot. Many of the doctors to whom the questionnaire had been sent had just thrown it away. Some of the doctors had given the questionnaire to their office manager or had filled it out with the office manager's assistance. Other doctors had taken a couple of minutes and filled it out as best as they could with their limited knowledge and had sent it off half finished.

In school Hershey had been taught the importance of checking one's hypothesis when formulating a questionnaire. Still, it had never occurred to him to question whether a client knew who its own customers were. As a result, the research firm and the client had wasted some money, and they'd wasted some time. Hershey was more than a little embarrassed, but he recognized that he'd learned an important lesson, albeit the hard way. ■

Summary

Learning Objective 1
Explain the role of research hypotheses in developing a questionnaire.
Research hypotheses guide the questionnaire by determining what information will be sought and from whom (since the hypotheses specify what relationships will be investigated). Hence, research hypotheses also affect the type of question and the form of response used to collect it.

Learning Objective 2
Define telescoping error *and* recall loss *and explain how they affect a respondent's ability to answer questions accurately.*
Telescoping error refers to people's tendency to remember an event as having occurred more recently than it did. *Recall loss* means they forget it

happened at all. The degree to which the two types of error affect the accuracy of the reported information depends on the length of the period in question. For long periods, the telescoping effect is smaller, while the recall loss is larger. For short periods, the reverse is true.

Learning Objective 3
Cite some of the techniques researchers use to secure respondents' cooperation in answering sensitive questions.
When asking sensitive questions, researchers may find it helpful to (1) hide the question in a group of other, more innocuous, questions; (2) state that the behavior or attitude is not unusual before asking the specific question of the respondent; (3) phrase the question in terms of other people and

how they might feel or act; (4) state the response in terms of a number of categories that the respondent may simply check; (5) use the randomized-response model.

Learning Objective 4
Explain what an open-ended question is.
An open-ended question is one in which respondents are free to reply in their own words rather than being limited to choosing from a set of alternatives.

Learning Objective 5
Name two kinds of fixed-alternative questions and tell the difference between them.
Two types of fixed-alternative questions are multichotomous and dichotomous questions. In a multichotomous question respondents are asked to choose from a list of alternatives the one that most closely reflects their position on the subject. In a dichotomous question, only two alternatives are listed.

Learning Objective 6
List some of the primary rules researchers should keep in mind in trying to develop bias-free questions.
Among the rules of thumb that researchers should keep in mind in developing bias-free questions are (1) use simple words, (2) avoid ambiguous words and questions, (3) avoid leading questions, (4) avoid implicit alternatives, (5) avoid implicit assumptions, (6) avoid generalizations and estimates, and (7) avoid double-barreled questions.

Learning Objective 7
Explain what the funnel approach to question sequencing is.
The funnel approach to question sequencing gets its name from its shape, starting with broad questions and progressively narrowing down the scope.

Learning Objective 8
Explain what a branching question is and discuss when it is used.
A branching question is one that contains a direction as to where to go next on the questionnaire based on the answer given. Branching questions are used to reduce the number of alternatives that are needed in individual questions, while ensuring that those respondents capable of supplying the needed information still have an opportunity to do so.

Learning Objective 9
Explain the difference between basic information and classification information and tell which should be asked first in a questionnaire.
Basic information refers to the subject of the study; classification information refers to the other data we collect to classify respondents so as to extract more information about the phenomenon of interest. The proper questionnaire sequence is to present questions securing basic information first and those seeking classification information last.

Key Terms

telescoping error (page 289)
recall loss (page 289)
randomized-response model (page 290)
open-ended question (page 291)
multichotomous question (page 292)
dichotomous question (page 295)
split ballot (page 297)
item nonresponse (page 297)

leading question (page 300)
implicit alternative (page 301)
implicit assumption (page 301)
double-barreled question (page 301)
funnel approach (page 303)
branching question (page 303)
pretest (page 307)

Review Questions

1. What role do the research hypotheses play in determining the information that will be sought?
2. Suppose you wanted to determine the proportion of men in a geographic area who use hair sprays. How could the information be obtained by open-ended question, by multiple-choice question, and by dichotomous question? Which would be preferable?
3. How does the method of administration of a questionnaire affect the type of question to be used?
4. What criteria can a researcher use to determine whether a specific question should be included in a questionnaire?
5. What is telescoping error? What does it suggest about the period to be used when asking respondents to recall past experiences?
6. What are some recommended ways by which one can ask for sensitive information?
7. What is an open-ended question? A multichotomous question? A dichotomous question? What are some of the key things researchers must be careful to avoid in framing multichotomous and dichotomous questions?
8. What is a split ballot, and why is it used?
9. What is an ambiguous question? A leading question? A question with implicit alternatives? A question with implied assumptions? A double-barreled question?
10. What is the proper sequence when asking for basic information and classification information?
11. What is the funnel approach to question sequencing?
12. What is a branching question? Why are such questions used?
13. Where should one ask for sensitive information in the questionnaire?
14. How can the physical features of a questionnaire affect its acceptance by respondents? Its handling and control by the researcher?
15. What is the overriding principle guiding questionnaire construction?
16. What decisions must the researcher make when developing an observational form for data collection?

Discussion Questions, Problems, and Projects

1. Evaluate the following questions.
   (a) **Which of the following magazines do you read regularly?**
   _____ *Time*
   _____ *Newsweek*
   _____ *Business Week*
   (b) **Are you a frequent purchaser of Birds Eye Frozen vegetables?**
   _____ Yes   _____ No
   (c) **Do you agree that the government should impose import restrictions?**
   _____ Strongly agree
   _____ Agree
   _____ Neither agree nor disagree
   _____ Disagree
   _____ Strongly disagree
   (d) **How often do you buy detergent?**
   _____ Once a week
   _____ Once in two weeks
   _____ Once in three weeks
   _____ Once a month
   (e) **Rank the following in order of preference:**
   _____ Kellogg's Corn Flakes
   _____ Quaker's Life
   _____ Post Bran Flakes
   _____ Kellogg's Bran Flakes

_____ Instant Quaker Oatmeal
_____ Post Rice Krinkles
(f) **Where do you usually purchase your school supplies?**
(g) **When you are watching television, do you also watch most of the advertisements?**
(h) **Which of the following brands of tea are most similar?**
_____ Lipton's Orange Pekoe
_____ Twinings Orange Pekoe
_____ Bigelow Orange Pekoe
_____ Salada Orange Pekoe
(i) **Do you think that the present policy of cutting taxes and reducing government spending should be continued?**
_____ Yes   _____ No
(j) **In a seven-day week, how often do you eat breakfast?**
_____ Every day of the week
_____ 5–6 times a week
_____ 2–4 times a week
_____ Once a week
_____ Never

2. Make the necessary corrections to the above questions.

3. Evaluate the following multichotomous questions. Rephrase them as dichotomous or open-ended questions if you think it would be more appropriate.
(a) **Which one of the following reasons is most important in your choice of stereo equipment?**
_____ Price
_____ In-store service
_____ Brand name
_____ Level of distortion
_____ Guarantee/warranty
(b) **Please indicate your education level.**
_____ Less than high school
_____ Some high school
_____ High school graduate
_____ Technical or vocational school
_____ Some college
_____ College graduate
_____ Some graduate or professional school
(c) **Which of the following reflects your views toward the issues raised by ecologists?**
_____ Have received attention
_____ Have not received attention
_____ Should receive more attention
_____ Should receive less attention
(d) **With which of the following statements do you most strongly agree?**
_____ Delta Airlines has better service than Northwest Airlines.
_____ Northwest Airlines has better service than United Airlines.
_____ United Airlines has better service than Delta Airlines.
_____ United Airlines has better service than Northwest Airlines.
_____ Northwest Airlines has better service than Delta Airlines.
_____ Delta Airlines has better service than United Airlines.

4. Evaluate the following open-ended questions. Rephrase them as multichotomous or dichotomous questions if you think it would be more appropriate.
(a) **Do you go to the movies often?**
(b) **Approximately how much do you spend per week on groceries?**
(c) **What brands of cheese did you purchase during the last week?**

5. Assume you are doing exploratory research to find out people's opinions about television advertising.
(a) Specify the necessary information to be sought.

You have decided to design a structured-undisguised questionnaire and to use the personal interview method.

(b) List the individual questions on a separate sheet of paper.

(c) Specify the form of the response for each question (i.e., open-ended, multichotomous, dichotomous, scale). Provide justification for selecting a particular form of response.

(d) Determine the sequence of the questions. Reexamine and revise the questions.

(e) Attach the final version of the questionnaire.

(f) Pretest the questionnaire on a convenience sample of five students, and report the results of your pretest.

6. The objective of this study is to determine whether brand names are important for mothers purchasing children's clothing.

(a) Specify the necessary information that is to be sought.

You have decided to use a structured-undisguised questionnaire and to use the telephone interview method.

(b) List the individual questions on a separate sheet of paper.

(c) Specify the form of the response for each question. Provide justification for selecting a particular form of response.

(d) Determine the sequence of the questions. Reexamine and revise the questions.

(e) Attach the final version of the questionnaire.

(f) Using the phone book as a sampling frame, pretest the questionnaire on a sample of five respondents, and report the results of your pretest.

7. A small brokerage firm was concerned with its declining number of customers and decided to do a quick survey. The major objective was to find out the reasons for patronizing a particular brokerage firm and to find out the importance of customer service. The following questionnaire was to be administered by telephone.

Good Afternoon, Sir/Madam:

We are doing a survey on attitudes toward brokerage firms. Could you please answer the following questions? Thank you.

1. Have you invested any money in the stock market?

_____ Yes   _____ No

If respondent replies "yes" continue; otherwise terminate interview.

2. Do you manage your own investments, or do you go to a brokerage firm?

_____ Manage own investments   _____ Go to brokerage firm

If respondent replies "go to a brokerage firm," continue; otherwise terminate interview.

3. How satisfied are you with your brokerage firm?

Very Satisfied	Satisfied	Neither Satisfied nor Dissatisfied	Dissatisfied	Very Dissatisfied
___	___	___	___	___

4. How important is personal service to you?

Very Important	Important	Not Particularly Important	Not at All Important
___	___	___	___

5. Which of the following reasons is the most important in patronizing a particular firm?

_____ The commission charged by the firm
_____ The personal service
_____ The return on investment
_____ The investment counseling

6. Approximately how long have you been investing through the brokerage firm you are currently using?

_____ about 3 months   _____ about 9 months
_____ about 6 months   _____ about 1 year or more

7. How much capital do you have invested?

_____ $500–$750   _____ $1,000–$1,500
_____ $750–$1,000   _____ $1,500 or more

Good-bye, and thank you for your cooperation.

Evaluate the above questionnaire.

8. Assume that a medium-sized manufacturer of candy employs you to conduct an observation study in determining children's influence on adults in the purchase of candy.
   (a) List the variables that are relevant in determining this influence.
   (b) List the "observations" that might reflect each of these variables.
   (c) Develop an observation form that will enable you to collect the needed information.
   (d) Observe three such purchases in a store/supermarket or the location that you specified above.
   (e) Report your findings.

9. This observation task can be conducted near the vending machines in the cafeteria, library, or business school: The objective is to observe the deliberation time taken at the various machines and determine the factors that influence the deliberation time.
   (a) List the variables that would be relevant in achieving the above objective.
   (b) List the "observations" that would reflect each of these variables.
   (c) Develop an observation form that will enable you to collect the needed information.
   (d) Do five such observations and report your findings.

10. Your employer, a commercial marketing research firm, has contracted to perform a study whose objective is the investigation of usage patterns and brand preferences for premixed infant formula among migrant farm workers in the southeastern United States. You have been assigned to develop a suitable questionnaire and method of administration to collect the desired information. What potential problems might arise in design and administration due to the unique nature of the population in question? List these problems and provide solutions. What method of administration will you recommend?

11. Discuss various reasons a researcher might have for using an observation form as opposed to a questionnaire.

Suggested Additional Readings

For more elaborate treatments of how to go about constructing questionnaires, see A. N. Oppenheim, *Questionnaire Design, Interviewing and Attitude Measurement* (New York: St. Martin's Press, 1992).

Floyd J. Fowler, Jr., *Improving Survey Questions: Design and Evaluation* (Thousand Oaks, Calif.: Sage Publications, 1995).

Howard Schuman and Stanley Presser, *Questions and Answers in Attitude Surveys: Experiments on Question Form, Wording and Context* (Thousand Oaks, Calif.: Sage Publications, 1996).

Robert A. Peterson, *Constructing Effective Questionnaires* (Thousand Oaks, Calif.: Sage Publications, 1999).

Measurement Basics

Learning Objectives

1 Define the term measurement *as it is used in marketing research.*

2 *List the four types of scales that can be used to measure an attribute.*

3 *Explain the primary difference between a ratio scale and an interval scale.*

4 *Cite some of the factors that may cause differences in two measures of the same attribute.*

5 *Name the two types of error that may affect measurement scores and define each.*

6 *Explain the concept of validity as it relates to measuring instruments.*

7 *List three general types of validity that can be used to assess the quality of a measure.*

8 *Outline the sequence of steps to follow in developing valid measures of marketing constructs.*

Project manager Neil Larson strode into the conference room and took at seat at the table. With a quizzical smile, he said to Linda Witkowski, the marketing director, "So you want to discuss some problems with researching the expansion of our product line. Does that mean you don't see much potential for the International Soup brand?"

"No, that's not it at all," replied Linda hastily. "I think your idea of soup as a 'global food' sounds very exciting. Offering flavors from around the world is a wonderful concept. I would just love to find a good hot-and-sour soup at my local supermarket. What I want to talk to you about is that identifying the market segments is going to be a little harder than your proposal suggests."

"What do you mean?"

"You want to use Census Bureau data to identify areas where different ethnic groups are concentrated."

"What's wrong with that? I know very well that the 2000 census had questions about race. The data are all public, and we can sort by geographic area. We can introduce each flavor of soup in the areas where the demand will be strongest, based on what people are used to eating."

"My main concern is that the census categories don't always match the groups you've identified. For example, you have a group of recipes you're calling 'Middle Eastern.' There's no census category like that."

"No? Well, we'll have to use whatever category they have—Arab or Muslim."

"Those aren't categories either. 'Muslim' describes a religious affiliation, and the Census Bureau doesn't gather data about religions. 'Arab' would go under—let's see," Linda consulted a table she had downloaded from the Internet, "under the White category."

"That doesn't tell us anything!" exclaimed Neil.

"Exactly. If you want to use Census Bureau data, we'll have to spend some time looking at these categories to be sure the data are valid for our purposes. We may need to go elsewhere or develop our own survey to uncover some of the data."

"OK, where do we start?"

"I've printed out the questions the Census Bureau used on the 2000 census to ask about race and Hispanic origin. Also, because you want to look at population trends, I have some information on how those questions changed between 1990 and 2000. Changing the questions can remove sources of error or introduce new errors, so we have to consider that when we make comparisons. Keep in mind that asking people to categorize themselves is not always as straightforward as quantitative measures like recording weight or asking for a birth date."

"Linda, I think you're saying we can't use any data until we've looked at all the sources of error, not to mention whether the numbers are valid in the first place."

"That's right, Neil! You'd make a great researcher."

Discussion Issues

1. What sources of error would you expect the Census Bureau to encounter in gathering data about race and Hispanic origin?

2. Explain whether the Census Bureau's racial and Hispanic origin categories could be a valid measure of ethnic origin to be used for predicting food preferences.

3. What other methods might a company use for segmenting consumers by ethnicity? How do these methods compare with Census data in terms of validity and reliability? ■

Although we don't usually think about it, most of us spend the day engaging in various forms of measurement. We stagger out of bed and get onto the bathroom scale, hoping our midnight trips to the refrigerator will fail to register. We measure coffee into the coffee maker, or stir a teaspoonful of instant coffee into a cup of water. We keep an eye on the clock so that we will not miss the bus or leave too little time to negotiate traffic on our way to class. We check the sports page for the score of the previous night's game—and perhaps the business section for the closing price on a favorite investment.

Most of the things we measure are fairly concrete: pounds on a scale, teaspoons of coffee, the amount of gas in a tank. But how does one measure a person's attitude toward bubble gum? The likelihood of a teenager going to see a particular new movie? A family's social class? Marketers are interested in measuring many attributes that most people rarely think of in terms of numbers. All of the questions on a survey are attempting to measure important attributes of some group that is of interest to marketing managers. In this chapter and the next, we will discuss how marketing researchers go about assigning numbers to various objects and phenomena.

Scales of Measurement

1 *Define the term measurement as it is used in marketing research.*

measurement
Rules for assigning numbers to objects to represent quantities of attributes.

Measurement consists of "rules for assigning numbers to objects in such a way as to represent quantities of attributes."[1] Note two things about the definition. First, it indicates that we measure the attributes of objects and not the objects themselves. We do not measure a person, for example, but may choose to measure the individual's income, social class, education, height, weight, or attitudes, all of which are attributes of this person. Second, the definition is broad in that it does not specify how the numbers are to be assigned. Researchers must be careful when designing a measure because the type of measure used will dictate the kinds of analyses that will be possible with the data collected using the measure. We have to take care to not read more meaning into the numbers than they actually contain.

For example, when we see the numbers 1, 2, 3, and 4, we usually assume that the number 1 stands for one object, 2 for two objects, and so on. Usually, we will say that 2 is larger than 1, and 3 is larger than 2; that the interval between 1 and 2 is the same size as the interval between 3 and 4; and that 3 is three times greater than 1, while 4 is four times greater than 1. Unfortunately, these assumptions are often not true when it comes to measuring attributes of objects. It is important that we first determine the properties of the attribute and then assign numbers so that they accurately reflect the properties of the attribute. The numbering system is simply a tool that must be used correctly in order to avoid misleading ourselves and those who are counting on the information we are delivering.

2 *List the four types of scales that can be used to measure an attribute.*

There are four types of scales used to measure attributes of objects: nominal, ordinal, interval, and ratio.[2] Exhibit 13.1 summarizes some of the more important features of these scales. Sometimes these are referred to as four "levels" of measurement because measures at higher levels of measurement (e.g., ratio scales) have more properties and can be used for more kinds of analyses than can measures at lower levels of measurement (e.g., nominal scales). For this reason, the highest level of measurement possible should normally be used when devel-

Exhibit 13.1

Scales of Measurement

Scale	Basic Comparison[a]	Measures of Typical Examples	Average[b]
Nominal	Identity	Male/Female User/nonuser Occupations Uniform numbers	Mode
Ordinal	Order	Brand preference Social class Hardness of minerals Graded quality of lumber	Median
Interval	Comparison of intervals	Temperature scale Grade point average Attitude toward brands	Mean
Ratio	Comparison of absolute magnitudes	Units sold Number of purchases Income Age	Geometric mean Harmonic mean

[a] All the comparisons applicable to a given scale are permissible with all scales below it in the table. For example, the ratio scale allows the comparison of intervals and the investigation of order and identity, in addition to the comparison of absolute magnitudes.

[b] The measures of average applicable to a given scale are also appropriate for all scales below it in the table; e.g., the mode is also a meaningful measure of the average when measurement is on an ordinal, interval, or ratio scale.

oping a measure for some attribute. However, it is important to remember that it is the properties of the attribute itself that determine which levels of measurement are possible.

Nominal Scale

One of the most basic uses of numbers is to *identify* particular objects. A person's social security number is a **nominal scale,** as are the numbers on football jerseys, lockers, and so on. These numbers simply identify the individual assigned the number. Nominal scales also allow us to categorize objects into groups based on their attributes. For example, if we assign the number 1 to represent male respondents to a survey and the number 2 to represent female respondents, we have used a nominal scale that allows us to identify the gender of a particular respondent and to determine the relative proportions of males vs. females in our sample.

With nominal scales, there is nothing implied by the assigned numbers other than identification. A football player wearing uniform number 52 isn't necessarily faster, bigger or stronger than a player with the number 51; we must use other measures with different scale properties to make those kinds of assessments. Similarly, the fact that females have been identified as 2 and males as 1 in our measurement system doesn't imply anything at all about females vs. males on any attribute other than identification. Females are not necessarily "superior" to males, or "more" than males or twice as many as males—as the numbers 2 and 1 might indicate. We can just as easily reverse our coding procedure so that each female is a 1 and each male a 2.

The reason we can reverse our codes is that the only property conveyed by the numbers is identity. With a nominal scale, the only permissible operation is counting. Thus, the mode (the most frequently occurring category) is the only legitimate measure of central tendency or average. It does not make sense in a sample consisting of 60 men and 40 women to say that the average sex is 1.4, given that males were coded 1 and females 2, even though the computer will calculate the mean *if you tell it to do so.* This is an incredibly important point: the numbers have been assigned by the researcher and the researcher must be aware of what kinds of analyses are possible with different scales of measurement. In this example, all we can say is that there were more males in the sample than females, or that 60 percent of the sample was male. If we want to say more than that, we'll need to take additional measures.

nominal scale
Measurement in which numbers are assigned to objects or classes of objects solely for the purpose of identification.

Ordinal Scale

ordinal scale
Measurement in which numbers are assigned to data on the basis of some order (for example, more than, greater than) of the objects.

A useful property of all scales beyond the nominal level of measurement is that of *order*. Thus, with an **ordinal scale** we could say that the number 2 is greater than the number 1, that 3 is greater than both 2 and 1, and that 4 is greater than all three of these numbers. The numbers 1, 2, 3, and 4 are ordered, and the larger the number, the greater the property. Note that the ordinal scale implies identity, since the same number would be used for all objects that are the same. An example would be the assignment of the number 1 to identify freshmen, 2 to identify sophomores, 3, juniors, and 4, seniors. We could just as well use the numbers 10 for freshmen, 20 for sophomores, 25 for juniors, and 30 for seniors. This assignment would still indicate the class level of each person and the *relative standing* of two persons when compared in terms of who is further along in the academic program. Note that this is all that is conveyed by an ordinal scale. For example, the difference in ranks says nothing about the difference in academic achievement between two ranks.

Suppose that there were three new restaurants located in a mid-sized college town and that the general manager of one of the restaurants wanted to know where her restaurant ranks with college students relative to the others. A team of student researchers worked with the manager to develop a telephone survey that asked a sample of students to rank-order their preferences among the new restaurants, with 1 assigned to the first choice, 2 to the second choice, and 3 to the third choice. The manager was encouraged when she reviewed the results: 52% of respondents ranked her restaurant as their first choice, 40% ranked it as their second choice, and 8% ranked it as their third choice. Thus, the modal ranking for the restaurant was "first choice" because that is the largest category of respondents. Because there is an order for the responses (that is, first choice is better than second choice, and so on), however, we can also calculate an additional measure of central tendency: the median. If there were 100 students in our sample, imagine lining them up according to their ranking of the restaurant. First might come the 8 who ranked it as third choice, then would come the 40 who ranked it as second choice, followed by the 52 who ranked it as first choice. The median ranking for the restaurant would be the ranking provided by the person in the center of our line-up (with an even number of respondents, we would consider the scores of the two people in the center). In our example, the median ranking would thus be "first choice."

Whether or not we can use the ordinal scale to assign numbers to objects depends on the attribute in question. The attribute itself must possess the ordinal property to allow ordinal scaling that is meaningful. Further, we can transform an ordinal scale in any way we wish as long as we maintain the basic ordering of the objects, because the order of the objects is all that we know with an ordinal scale. It is impossible to say how much someone preferred one object to another; we can only say that one is preferred over the other. In our restaurant example, one respondent may really like all three restaurants, ranking them in the following order: first-restaurant A, second-restaurant B, third-restaurant C. Another respondent may really dislike all three restaurants, yet still rank them in the same order. Still another student may like A and B and dislike C, and still rank them in the same order. In each case, rank order is the same, while the underlying feelings about the restaurants are quite different. Representing those feelings requires a higher level of measurement.

Interval Scale

interval scale
Measurement in which the assigned numbers legitimately allow the comparison of the size of the differences among and between members.

Some scales possess the following useful property: the *intervals* between the numbers are meaningful in the sense that the numbers tell us how far apart the objects are with respect to the attribute. This means that the differences can be compared. The difference between 1 and 2 is equal to the difference between 2 and 3.

Rating scales for measuring consumer attitudes are commonly used in marketing research and are great examples of **interval scales.** Consider the restaurant example again. Suppose that respondents were asked to rate their attitudes toward the three restaurants using 1–7 scales, where 1 = "extremely unfavorable" and 7 = "extremely favorable." Such an approach allows us to see the relative strength of a respondent's feelings toward each of the restaurants.

A respondent who really likes all three restaurants might assign each of them high scores, such as 6 or 7. Similarly, someone who dislikes each restaurant might assign low scores to each. Respondents can indicate the full range of possible attitudes (extremely unfavorable to extremely favorable) toward each restaurant, a large step forward from simply knowing the order of preference.

Thus, with an interval scale we can say that one restaurant is generally liked or disliked by its score on the scale and, even better, whether or not it is preferred over another restaurant by comparing scores. Further, if we have measures on at least three restaurants we can compare the intervals. That is, we can say that the difference in attitude between a restaurant with a score of 6 and a restaurant with a score of 4 is the same as the difference in attitude between a restaurant with a score of 3 and a restaurant with a score of 1. Or we could say that the difference between scores of 2 and 6 is twice as great as the difference between scores of 3 and 5. The comparison of intervals is legitimate with an interval scale because the relationships among the differences hold regardless of the particular numbers used on the scale. (Try this: see what happens if the rating scale ranged from 201 through 207 instead of 1–7. Determine if each of the properties described in this paragraph still hold.)

Suppose, however, that one respondent rates a particular restaurant as a 6 on the 1–7 favorability scale, and a second respondent rates the same restaurant as a 3. Can we say that the first respondent's attitude is twice as favorable as that held by the second respondent? The answer is no. We cannot compare the absolute magnitude of numbers when measurement is made on the basis of an interval scale. The reason is that on an interval scale, the zero point is established arbitrarily. Is there such a thing as having zero attitude toward some object? Attitudes may be negative or positive (or nonexistent for unknown objects), but there is no obvious point at which attitude is equal to zero. Even if we assign the number zero to a scale position, the assignment is completely arbitrary because there is no naturally occurring zero point for attitudes or other concepts measured using interval scales.

With an interval scale, the researcher can determine mean scores on measures in addition to median and modal scores. The mean is "meaningful" for interval scales because of the equal intervals between scale positions. Thus, if restaurant A achieves a mean score of 6.5 on the 1–7 favorability scale, compared with mean scores of 4.7 and 3.4 for restaurants B and C, respectively, we have much stronger information about the relative popularity of the restaurant compared with what was available using only an ordinal measurement scale.

Ratio Scale

The **ratio scale** differs from an interval scale in that it possesses a *natural,* or *absolute,* zero, one for which there is universal agreement as to its location. Height and weight are obvious examples. Because there is an absolute zero, comparison of the *absolute magnitude* of the numbers is legitimate. Thus, a person weighing 200 pounds is twice as heavy as one weighing 100 pounds, and a person weighing 300 pounds is three times as heavy.

In a ratio scale, zero has an absolute meaning—that is, that none of the property being measured exists. Further, we have already seen that the more powerful scales include the properties possessed by the less powerful ones. This means that with a ratio scale we can compare intervals, rank objects according to magnitude, or use the numbers to identify the objects (everything that interval, ordinal, and nominal scales do). And the geometric mean, as well as the more usual arithmetic mean, median, and mode, is a meaningful measure of average when attributes are measured on a ratio scale.

There are a number of attributes of consumers that can be measured using ratio scales, including age in years, income in dollars (or other monetary unit), probability of product purchase, units purchased or consumed, frequency of shopping behavior, and so on. Researchers should use ratio scales for measuring these sorts of attributes whenever possible, unless there is a compelling reason not to do so. For instance, consider the measurement of respondent age. One way to assess age is to use an open-ended item that asks for the age of the respondent in years (a ratio scale). A second approach is to ask the respondent to check the

3 Explain the primary difference between a ratio scale and an interval scale.

ratio scale
Measurement that has a natural, or absolute, zero and therefore allows the comparison of absolute magnitudes of the numbers.

appropriate age category, with categories such as "less than 20," "21 to 30," and so on (an ordinal scale). As we will see later in the chapters on data analysis, using the ratio scale will allow us to compute a mean age across a sample of respondents; compute correlations between age and other variables such as product ratings, satisfaction scores, etc.; and perform other statistical techniques. Although there are analyses that can be performed with ordinal measures, they are less powerful. A researcher might make a valid argument, however, that asking respondents for their ages in broad categories is less intimidating for those sensitive about age and might get some consumers to accurately respond to the question instead of skipping it, throwing the questionnaire away, or fudging the answer. Thus, while the higher level of measurement is usually preferred, the researcher must consider other factors as well.

Figure 13.1 uses the issue of a respondent's preferences for six different soft drinks to illustrate how questions about this issue might be framed to secure reactions on a nominal, an ordinal, an interval, and a ratio scale. How would you respond to the items? Do you find it more difficult to complete some types of scales than others?

The Measurement Problem

AP/Wide World Photos

Craig Bacon, a director of research and development at Tyson Foods, Inc., shows several products that have been developed and marketed by Tyson. The process of developing new products often includes the measurement of a product's popularity, a hypothetical construct.

A problem that marketing researchers have in common with other scientists is how to go about measuring the variables that interest them. For example, marketers are well aware that consumers' spending can be affected by their general feelings as to "how good things are." But how do you measure such a concept? This isn't something you can touch or see, so tape measures, scales, and rulers won't work. In developing its "Well-Being Index," which is used for comparing areas and preparing forecasts, *American Demographics* considered measures of productivity and technology, leisure, consumer attitudes, social and physical environment, income, and employment opportunities.[3] While none of these measures provides a direct measure of well-being, they each represent something that should provide some indication of "how good things are."

Scientists and other researchers use theories in an attempt to understand and explain how things work in their areas of interest. These theories or models consist of relationships between concepts. In the social sciences (which includes marketing research), many of the concepts in our theories cannot be directly observed (e.g., attitudes, intentions). For that matter, there is no objective way to prove that many of these concepts really exist at all. For example, who can prove that attitudes really exist? No human can, yet psychologists have relied on the concept of attitudes to explain phenomena for decades. An attitude, like many other concepts we use and attempt to measure in marketing research, is a **hypothetical construct,** a concept that has been developed by researchers for use in theoretical models to explain how things work.

Of course, some of the concepts we measure in marketing research aren't hypothetical at all. For instance, the fact that a company sold a certain number of units of a new product in a particular store in a test market city can be confirmed relatively easily. The age, gender, ethnic background, zip code, and so on for a particular consumer isn't hypothetical, either, although we often have to depend on the consumer to provide accurate responses to our measures. The point is that some of the things that we want to measure are straightforward, while other concepts are much more difficult to conceptualize and measure.

Figure 13.1

Assessing a Respondent's Preference for Soft Drinks with Nominal, Ordinal, Interval, and Ratio Scales

NOMINAL SCALE

Which of the soft drinks on the following list do you like? Check all that apply.

_____ Coke
_____ Dr Pepper
_____ Mountain Dew
_____ Pepsi
_____ Seven Up
_____ Sprite

ORDINAL SCALE

Please rank the soft drinks on the following list according to your degree of liking for each, assigning your most preferred drink rank = 1 and your least preferred drink rank = 6.

_____ Coke
_____ Dr Pepper
_____ Mountain Dew
_____ Pepsi
_____ Seven Up
_____ Sprite

INTERVAL SCALE

Please indicate your degree of liking each of the soft drinks on the following list by checking the appropriate position on the scale.

	DISLIKE A LOT	DISLIKE	LIKE	LIKE A LOT
Coke	_____	_____	_____	_____
Dr Pepper	_____	_____	_____	_____
Mountain Dew	_____	_____	_____	_____
Pepsi	_____	_____	_____	_____
Seven Up	_____	_____	_____	_____
Sprite	_____	_____	_____	_____

RATIO SCALE

Please divide 100 points among each of the following soft drinks according to your degree of liking for each.

_____ Coke
_____ Dr Pepper
_____ Mountain Dew
_____ Pepsi
_____ Seven Up
_____ Sprite
100

The essence of the measurement problem is presented in Figure 13.2. This diagram illustrates constructs (circles with *C's* in them), linkages among and between the constructs (single lines connecting the constructs), and data that connect the constructs with the observable world (double lines). The relationships among the constructs represent a theory about how things work. For example, recent research has proposed that certain basic personality traits like emotional stability and agreeability help produce customer orientation (the desire to satisfy customer needs) among service workers.[4] Each of these concepts might be represented by circles in a diagram similar to that in Figure 13.2. Single lines could be drawn between the basic personality trait variables and customer orientation to represent the proposed theoretical relationships. These linkages represent **conceptual definitions,** in that a given construct is defined

hypothetical construct
A concept used in theoretical models to explain how things work. Hypothetical constructs include such things as attitudes, personality, and intentions—things that cannot be seen but that are useful in theoretical explanations.

conceptual definition
A definition in which a given construct is defined in terms of other constructs in the set, sometimes in the form of an equation that expresses the relationship among them.

operational definition
A definition of a construct that describes the operations to be carried out in order for the construct to be measured empirically.

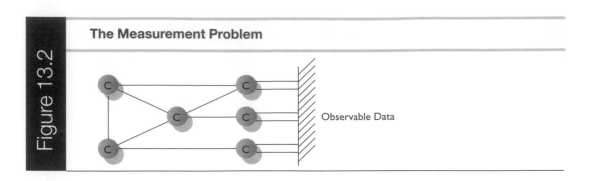

Figure 13.2

The Measurement Problem

Observable Data

in terms of other constructs in the set. The definition may take the form of an equation that precisely expresses the interrelationship of the construct to the other constructs, such as the equation in mechanics that suggests that force equals mass times acceleration. Alternatively, the relationship may be only imprecisely stated, which is typically the case in the social sciences.

Theory and hypothetical constructs are fine, but how are they useful to a marketing researcher? They really aren't of much practical use—until they are tested using empirical research. Testing the relationships, however, requires specifying how each of the constructs is to be measured. An **operational definition** describes how a construct is to be measured and is represented in Figure 13.2 by double lines. The operational definition tells the investigator what measures to use and how to use them. Exhibit 13.2, for example, shows measures that were used to assess customer orientation in the project discussed above. Conceptual definitions logically precede operational definitions and guide their development, for we must specify what a construct is before we can develop rules for assessing its magnitude.

How can we tell whether a measure is valid or not? We cannot see an attitude, a personality characteristic, a person's knowledge about or awareness of a particular product, or other psychological characteristics such as intelligence, mental anxiety, etc. Since we cannot visually check on the accuracy of our measures (if the issue were which of two women were taller, we could simply stand them side-by-side to see if our measures were accurate), we must rely on evaluating the procedures we used to determine the measure. A manufacturer, for example, interested in assessing customer reactions to a new product needs to know that the research is actually measuring consumers' attitudes toward the new product and that the accuracy of the data is not being influenced by the interviewers asking the questions or by one of the many other factors with which research must contend. The ability to make these assessments relies heavily on an understanding of measurement, measurement error, and the concepts of reliability and validity, the task to which we now turn.

ETHICAL dilemma 13.1

José Cardenas, a research analyst for Quality Surveys, was working on a study attempting to assess the image of the various automobile dealers in a metropolitan area. The survey instrument asked about such things as the quality and promptness of the dealer's repair service; the courteousness, knowledge, and helpfulness of its salespeople; how competitive the dealer was with respect to its automobile assortment and prices; and so on. Altogether there were 35 items that addressed the various attributes by which customers might evaluate automobile dealers. Respondents were asked to evaluate the dealer with whom they were most familiar on each attribute using one of four categories: poor (1), fair (2), good (3), or excellent (4). Thus, the range of scores could run from 35 to 140. In presenting the results to the client, a Ford dealership, Cardenas stated that, on average, people in town had twice as favorable an attitude toward the Ford dealer as toward its nearest Chevrolet dealer. This was based on the average scores of 120 for the Ford dealership and 60 for the Chevrolet dealership.

- *Could Cardenas rightly make such a claim? If not, what could he say?*

- *What were Cardenas' responsibilities to the client with respect to understanding measurement-scale issues?*

- *Did Cardenas' superiors have any responsibility in this regard?*

Exhibit 13.2

Illustration of Operational Definitions: Assessing Two Dimensions of Customer Orientation

Dimension	Measurements
	Average of responses to the following items, each measured on a nine-point strongly disagree–strongly agree scale.
Enjoyment	I find it easy to smile at each of my customers.
	I enjoy remembering my customers' names.
	It comes naturally to have empathy for my customers.
	I enjoy responding quickly to my customers' requests.
	I get satisfaction from making my customers happy.
	I really enjoy serving my customers.
Needs	I try to help customers achieve their goals.
	I achieve my own goals by satisfying customers.
	I get customers to talk about their service needs with me.
	I take a problem-solving approach with my customers.
	I keep the best interests of the customer in mind.
	I am able to answer a customer's questions correctly.

Source: Tom J. Brown, John C. Mowen, D. Todd Donavan, and Jane Licata, "The Customer Orientation of Service Workers: Personality Trait Effects on Self- and Supervisor Performance Ratings," *Journal of Marketing Research* 39 (February 2002), pp. 110–119. The "needs" dimension is adapted from Robert Saxe and Barton A. Weitz, "The SOCO Scale: A Measure of the Customer Orientation of Salespeople," *Journal of Marketing Research* 19 (August 1982), pp. 343–351.

Variations in Measured Scores

Most measurement tasks present problems, but psychological measurement is particularly difficult because there are many factors that can cause our measurements of attributes to contain error, including the measurement process itself. For example, assume that a tobacco company is interested in measuring people's attitudes toward smoking in public places such as restaurants and office buildings. An attitude scale to measure these feelings has been administered to a sample of respondents. A high score (maximum: 100) means that the respondent has a strong objection to smoking in public areas, while a low score (minimum: 25) indicates the opposite. If Mary scored 75 and Jane scored 40, we would say that Mary has a much more negative attitude toward smoking in public places than does Jane. But the validity of that conclusion would depend on the quality of the measurement. Here are some possible causes for the difference in the two scores:[5]

Cite some of the factors that may cause differences in two measures of the same attribute.

1. *A true difference in the characteristic we are measuring.* In an ideal situation, the difference in scores would reflect true differences in the attitudes of Mary and Jane and nothing else. This situation will rarely, if ever, occur. More likely, the different scores will also reflect some of the intruding factors that follow.

2. *Differences in other relatively stable characteristics of the individual.* Not only does a person's position on an issue affect his or her score, but other characteristics can also be expected to have an effect. For example, Research Window 13.1 illustrates the impact culture has on people's response styles. Perhaps the difference between Mary's and Jane's scores is simply due to the greater willingness of Mary to express negative feel-

© Eyewire/Getty Images

Self-administered multiple-choice questionnaires can eliminate variation that may occur due to the presence of the interviewer.

Impact of Culture on Response Styles

One of the most important and dramatic ways culture impacts multicountry research is in the different ways people in various countries respond to survey questions and use questionnaire scales. In a carefully controlled experiment, GfK Custom Research Inc. (CRI) explored the use of different kinds of scales in new product research. The result: *We found extraordinary differences from country to country in the way respondents use common survey scales.* For example: Survey respondents in the Philippines and Italy are four times more likely than respondents in Hong Kong or Japan to use the "top box" of a buying intent scale.

And these differences are clearly the result of culture, not economic levels. Japan and the United States, two of the most affluent countries in the world, are dramatically different on these measures. These differences must be understood and taken into account in analyzing multicountry studies. In the CRI experiment across 18 countries, here are a few of the differences we found on use of the buying intent scale:

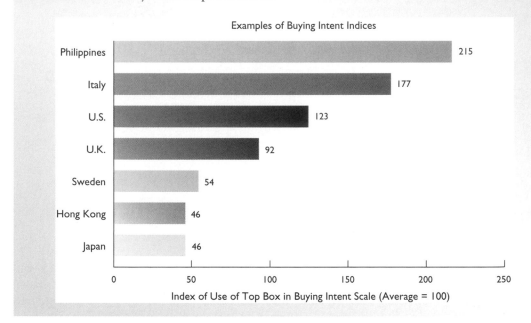

Examples of Buying Intent Indices

Country	Index
Philippines	215
Italy	177
U.S.	123
U.K.	92
Sweden	54
Hong Kong	46
Japan	46

Index of Use of Top Box in Buying Intent Scale (Average = 100)

ings. Jane, by contrast, follows the adage, "If you can't say something nice, don't say anything at all." Her cooperation in the study has been requested, so she responds, but not completely truthfully.

In general, peoples' responses to survey questions can be affected by a host of individual characteristics that push responses away from the true score. As an example, research has demonstrated that consumers sometimes have a hard time accurately reporting how frequently they perform behaviors. Those that perform behaviors frequently tend to underreport the level of behavior and those that perform those behaviors less frequently tend to overreport the level of behavior. In a clever study, researchers demonstrated that consumers who make a lot of long distance telephone calls report making fewer calls than they actually do, while the reverse is true for consumers who make few long distance calls. The same effect applied to estimates of how long the calls lasted.[6]

3. *Differences due to temporary personal factors.* A person's mood, state of health, fatigue, etc., may all affect his or her responses, yet these factors are temporary and can vary. Thus, if Mary, a nonsmoker, has just returned from lunch in a smoke-filled cafe, her responses may be different than if she had been interviewed several days earlier.

But the effect of cultural differences on scale use is even more complex: Differences even exist within the same country from one scale to another.

That is illustrated by comparing the example below, showing use of the uniqueness scale, with the previous example on buying intent. Italians are less bullish in their use of the uniqueness scale, while respondents in the United Kingdom are more aggressive in using the uniqueness scale than in stating buying intent.

This means there is no single, simple way to adjust for country-to-country differences. It requires experience across countries and a thorough understanding of how each scale is used differently country by country.

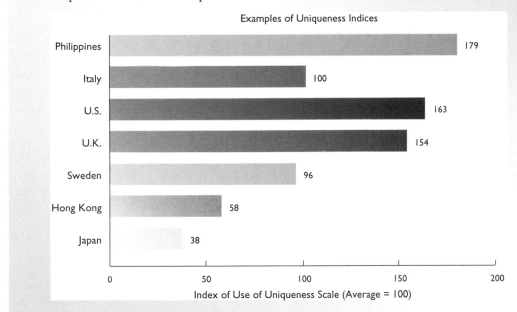

Examples of Uniqueness Indices

Source: Jeffrey Pope, *How Cultural Differences Affect Multi-Country Research* (Minneapolis, Minn.: GfK Custom Research Inc., 1991). See also Irvine Clarke III, "Global Marketing Research: Is Extreme Response Style Influencing Your Results?" *Journal of International Consumer Marketing* 12 (4, 2000), pp. 91–111.

4. *Differences due to situational factors.* The situation surrounding the measurement also can affect the score. Mary's score might be different if her husband were there while the scale was being administered. Incidentally, this is a frequent problem for researchers studying the decision-making process of married couples. When the husband is asked for the respective roles of husband and wife in purchasing a new automobile, for instance, one set of responses is secured; when the wife is asked, the responses are different; when the two are asked together, still a third set is obtained. Which is correct? It is hard to say, since the fact remains that the situation surrounding a measurement can affect the scores that are obtained.

5. *Differences due to variations in administration.* Much measurement in marketing involves the use of questionnaires administered by phone or in person. Since interviewers can vary in the way they ask questions, the responses also may vary as a function of the interviewer. The same interviewer may even handle two interviews differently enough to trigger a variance in recorded answers, although the respondents do not really differ on the characteristic.

Differences in method of administration can also make a difference in how people respond to survey items. Researchers at Silver Dollar City, a theme park located near Branson, Missouri, regularly assess visitors' satisfaction with the park a few days after they visit. While examining responses to telephone surveys vs. email surveys, they discovered that responses to the same satisfaction question were consistently higher when obtained via telephone compared with email. Because there were no differences in answers for virtually all other questions, the researchers concluded that the telephone survey respondents were likely inflating satisfaction scores because of the social context: they were talking directly to someone else. There was apparently less social stigma associated with less flattering answers when delivered by electronic means.

6. *Differences due to the sampling of items.* As we attempt to measure any construct, we typically tap only a small number of the items relevant to the characteristic being measured. Thus, our attitude scale for the tobacco companies will contain only a sample of all the items or statements we could possibly have included. In fact, often we will not even know what all the relevant items are. If we added, deleted, or changed the wording of some items, we would undoubtedly change the outcome with respect to the scores of Mary and Jane. We must constantly be aware that our instrument reflects our interpretation of the construct and the items we use to measure it and that the resulting scores will vary according to the way in which items are chosen and the way those items are expressed.

Our final score is also influenced by the number of items presented. A man's height can serve as an indicator of his "size," but so can his weight, the size of his waistline, chest, and so on. We certainly could expect to have a better measure of a man's size if we included all these items. So it is with psychological measurements. Other things being equal, a one-item scale is less adequate than is a 25-item scale.

7. *Differences due to lack of clarity of the measuring instrument.* Sometimes a difference in response to a questionnaire or an item on a scale may represent differences in interpretation of an ambiguous or complex question rather than any fundamental differences in the characteristic we are attempting to measure. We saw in the last chapter how even simple words can be open to misinterpretation. In measuring complex concepts such as attitudes, the possibilities for misunderstanding increase greatly. One of the researcher's main tasks is to generate items or questions that mean the same thing to all respondents, so that the observed differences in scores are not caused by differences in interpretation.

8. *Differences due to mechanical factors.* Mechanical factors can also affect obtained scores. Such things as a lack of space to record the responses, inadvertent check marks in the wrong box, and improper interpretation of a hard-to-read answer can all affect the scores that are assigned.

Classification and Assessment of Error

5 *Name the two types of error that may affect measurement scores and define each.*

systematic error
Error in measurement that is also known as constant error since it affects the measurement in a constant way.

The goal of any question that we might ask on a survey is to accurately measure some characteristic, without interference from irrelevant factors. Usually this goal is impossible to achieve, because of two general categories of error: systematic error and random error.

One type of error that may appear in our scores is **systematic error,** which is also called constant error since it affects the measurement in a constant way. An example would be the measurement of a man's height with a poorly calibrated wooden yardstick. No matter how many men are measured with the yardstick or how many times they are measured, the measures will be in error in a systematic way. Another example involves the federal government's collection of data about economic activity. The Department of Commerce routinely measures annual domestic growth by tallying the amount of goods and services sold in the United States, finding the difference from the previous year, and subtracting the amount contributed by inflation. However, until recent years, the government did not include Internet commerce in its sales data. For instance, it would have counted Dell Computer's sales to retailers but not its online sales, thus understating each year's economic activity.[7]

The other general type of error, **random error,** is not constant but is due to temporary aspects of the person or measurement situation, and which affects the measurement in irregular ways. A random error is present when we repeat a measurement on an individual or

PART 4:
Data Collection Forms

group of individuals and do not get the same scores as the first time we did the measurement, even though the characteristic being measured has not changed. For instance, if a man who was measured once changes his shoes before being measured again, the two measures may not agree even though the man's actual height has not changed.

The distinction between systematic error and random error is important because of the way the **validity,** or correctness, of a measure is assessed. Any scale or other measurement instrument that accurately measures what it was intended to measure is said to have validity. The validity of a measuring instrument is defined as "the extent to which differences in scores on it reflect true differences among individuals on the characteristic we seek to measure, rather than constant or random errors."[8] While both types of error compromise a measure's validity, in some ways systematic error is less troublesome than random error. For example, even though measurements of height using a poorly calibrated yardstick will be in error, comparisons between objects measured with the yardstick may be useful if the error is constant across all objects.

Building valid measures is a very difficult task. It is not accomplished by simply sitting down for ten minutes and making up a set of questions to measure a person's attitude toward smoking in public places, for example. The researcher must take the necessary steps to ensure that the questionnaire does actually measure a person's attitude on this subject, although we can never know this with certainty.[9]

The Assessment of Validity and Reliability

There are three types of techniques we can use to assess the validity of a measure. We can look for evidence of its predictive validity, content validity, and construct validity. We also must check for the reliability of the measure.

Predictive Validity How well the measure actually predicts some characteristic or specific behavior of the individual, an organization, the marketplace, etc., is its predictive validity. An example would be the Graduate Management Admissions Test (GMAT). The fact that this test is required by most of the major schools of business attests to its **predictive validity;** it has proven to be useful in predicting how well a student with a particular score on the exam will do in an accredited M.B.A. program. The test score is used to predict the criterion of performance. If a measure of salesperson job satisfaction does a good job of forecasting which salespeople actually quit over some time frame, then the job satisfaction measure is said to have predictive validity. Both of these examples illustrate predictive validity in the true sense of the word—that is, the use of the score to predict some future occurrence. Another type of predictive validity, known as concurrent validity, is concerned with the relationship between the predictor variable and the criterion variable when both occur at the same time. For example, most medical tests are meant to predict whether or not a person has specific medical problems at the present time, rather than at some point in the future.

Predictive validity is determined strictly by the correlation between the measuring instrument and the characteristic or behavior being measured. If the correlation is high, the measure is said to have predictive validity. Thus, if the number of birds sitting on a fence in your backyard is highly correlated with the average price of a company's shares on the New York Stock Exchange, then the number of birds is said to have predictive validity with respect to that company's stock price. It is completely irrelevant whether or not that relationship makes sense or can be explained. While easy to assess, predictive validity is rarely the most important kind of validity. We are often concerned with "what the measure in fact measures" rather than simply whether it predicts accurately or not.

Content Validity If the measurement instrument adequately covers the most important aspects of the construct that is being measured, it has **content validity,** which is sometimes called face validity. Consider, for example, the characteristic of "spelling ability," and suppose that the following list of words was used to assess an individual's general spelling ability: *catcher, shortstop, foul, strike, walk, pitcher, umpire, outfield*. Now, you might object to this spelling test on the grounds that all the words relate to the sport of baseball and nothing else. A person who is basically a very poor speller could do well on this test simply because he or she is a baseball fan. A person with a good basic ability for spelling but little interest in baseball might, in fact, do very poorly. This test appears to lack content validity, since it does not properly sample the range of all possible words that could be used to assess general spelling ability.

Theoretically, to capture a person's general spelling ability (in English) most accurately, we would have to build a test that includes all the words in the English language. Since we can't really do this, we construct tests consisting of much smaller samples of words. The goal is simply to come up with a set of items that adequately represents the full range of words that could be included on the spelling test. Whether we have assessed the true characteristic depends on how well we have sampled the range of the characteristic. This is true not only for spelling ability, but also holds for psychological characteristics.

How can we ensure that our measure will possess content validity? We can never guarantee it, because it is partly a matter of judgment. What we can do, however, is to be systematic in how we develop the items to be used as a measure of some construct. A systematic process usually starts with a review of any relevant literature to see how other people have measured the concept in the past. Then a large number of possible items can be developed, with the goal of covering the entire range of the characteristic being measured. For example, a measure of a sales representative's job satisfaction might include items about each of the components of the job (duties, fellow workers, top management, sales supervisor, customers, pay, and promotion opportunities). The initial set of items must be large, so that after refinement the measure still contains enough items to adequately sample the entire range of the variable. The set of items can then be "purified" to a smaller set of items through discussion with experts in the area and/or through data collection and analysis. Again, the goal is to end up with a set of items that appear to adequately represent the construct being assessed.

Construct Validity   Construct validity is the most difficult type of validity to establish.[10] With predictive validity, the only concern was whether or not the measure was useful for predicting some phenomenon, and content validity involved an assessment of the degree to which the measure appeared to be measuring the full range of the construct. A measure is said to have **construct validity** if it actually measures the construct, concept, or trait it is supposed to be measuring. That is, each item in the instrument must reflect the construct and must also show a correlation with other items in the instrument.

Thus, a scale designed to measure attitude would have construct validity if it measured the attitude in question and not some other underlying characteristic of the individual that affects his or her score. Construct validity lies at the heart of scientific progress. Scientists need constructs with which to communicate their theories, and they need to know that their measures actually measure what they intend them to measure and not something else.

But how is construct validity established? The process is not a simple one and involves consideration of several factors. In general terms, the measure must be reliable, or consistent (see below), and must be related to other measures in appropriate ways. For example, consider our earlier example relating job satisfaction to job turnover among sales representatives. Suppose we had developed a new measure of job satisfaction and the task is to determine its degree of construct validity. Assuming that the measure has content validity (that is, it appears to measure the full range of the job satisfaction construct as we have defined it), the next step would be to collect data from salespeople in order to determine the statistical relationships between the new measure and other measures.

If our new measure is really assessing job satisfaction, it is reasonable to expect the measure to be highly correlated with other existing measures of job satisfaction, particularly ones that have been validated in previous research. After all, two measures of the same thing ought to

construct validity
Assessment of how well the instrument captures the construct, concept, or trait it is supposed to be measuring.

be highly related to one another. Establishing that the new measure is highly correlated with other measures of the same construct (ideally assessed using independent measurement procedures) provides evidence of *convergent validity*.

At the same time, it is entirely reasonable to expect that measures of different constructs should not be too highly correlated with one another. Demonstrating that our new measure of job satisfaction has small correlations with measures of other constructs provides evidence of *discriminant validity*.[11] For such validity tests to be useful, however, the other constructs selected should be at least marginally relevant to the situation. For example, demonstrating that the new job satisfaction scale is unrelated to respondents' shoe size provides some evidence of discriminant validity, but offers little confidence about the construct validity of the new measure. On the other hand, showing that the measure of job satisfaction discriminates from measures of role conflict, organizational commitment, or other job-related constructs would provide much stronger evidence.

If a measure is to have construct validity, it must also possess another kind of validity known as *nomological validity*. As we've noted, researchers often develop theories or models about how constructs are related to one another. Nomological validity is concerned with the degree to which a measure behaves as it should in relation to measures of theoretically related constructs. Thus, we would expect our measure of salesperson job satisfaction to predict salesperson intentions to quit (similar to the notion of predictive validity discussed above). The problem, of course, is that failure to support any particular hypothesized relationship may be due either to a lack of construct validity of our measure or to incorrect theory. We often try to establish the nomological validity of a measure, therefore, by relating it to a number of other constructs rather than only one. For example, our theory might also suggest that compensation, attitude toward the sales manager, degree of organizational support, etc. might influence job satisfaction. Accordingly, if we find that measures for these constructs are positively related to our new measure of job satisfaction in the manner proposed by theory, we have provided evidence of nomological validity. It is also quite helpful to use theories and hypotheses that have been tested by others and found to be sound.

Finally, measures that possess construct validity must also be stable and consistent. Otherwise, we could never have confidence in any particular score obtained using the measure. The notion of reliability is discussed next.

Reliability **Reliability** refers to the ability of a measure to obtain similar scores for the same object, trait, or construct across time, across different evaluators, or across the items forming the measure.[12] For example, if we measured job satisfaction among a group of salespeople at the first of the month and then measured it again two weeks later we would expect the job satisfaction scores to be highly correlated. If they are not, the measure is unstable and its reliability must be questioned. Similarly, if we asked a group of salespeople to evaluate the quality of a new competing product that has just entered the market, we would anticipate that the product quality measures would be highly correlated across the group of salespeople. If so, the measure has demonstrated reliability through equivalence across different evaluators. This latter form of reliability might be called interjudge reliability and is relevant to any situation in which multiple judges evaluate a single object. Common examples include talent and beauty contests and Olympic competitions such as diving and figure skating. Figure 13.3 depicts a situation in which the judgments of two different observers do not agree. This type of equivalence is the basis of convergent validation when the measures are independent.[13]

The reliability of a measure can also be established through equivalence in other ways. For example, every item in our job satisfaction scale can theoretically be considered a separate measure of the construct, and a respondent's score on one part of the scale should correlate with his or her score on other parts of the scale. This kind of reliability focuses on the internal consistency of the set of items forming the scale. One popular means of assessing the internal consistency reliability of a measure is coefficient alpha, which provides a summary measure of the intercorrelations that exist among the set of items in a measure of a construct. Technically

reliability
Ability of a measure to obtain similar scores for the same object, trait, or construct across time, across different evaluators, or across the items forming the measure.

A Situation in Which the Judgments of Two Observers Do Not Agree

Speaking 13.1 provides a more detailed treatment of the philosophy and techniques underlying this popular method of assessing internal consistency reliability.

Evaluating the reliability of any measuring instrument consists of determining how much of the variation in scores is due to inconsistencies in measurement. If a measure is reliable, it is not heavily influenced by transitory factors that cause random errors. However, a measure could be reliable but not necessarily valid because of systematic error. Suppose that a sportsman were comparing three different rifles—an old rifle and two new ones. Further suppose that he fires each of the rifles a number of times and that each time he lines up the sights on the gun perfectly with the center of the target.

Figure 13.4 illustrates the results for the three different rifles. The old rifle is unreliable; despite the fact that the sights are set on the center of the target, the shots go off in random directions. The first new rifle is relatively reliable—it hits about the same spot on the target each time—but its sights are set incorrectly in the center diagram. The error is systematic and not random, but the rifle still misses the mark. The right-hand diagram shows a new rifle with its sights set correctly. Only in the right-hand diagram could a user of any of the rifles be expected to hit the center of the target with regularity.

As a research example, the Food Marketing Institute (FMI) annually conducts a survey of its member companies to estimate the causes of merchandise loss by supermarkets. It measures the extent of shoplifting by asking the stores how many shoplifters they caught and how much the merchandise they recovered was worth. Assuming stores keep records of such incidents, the data may be quite reliable. However, just like a reliable new rifle that still misses the target, this method may not be a valid measure of the extent of shoplifting, because it does

Illustration of Difference Between Random and Systematic Error

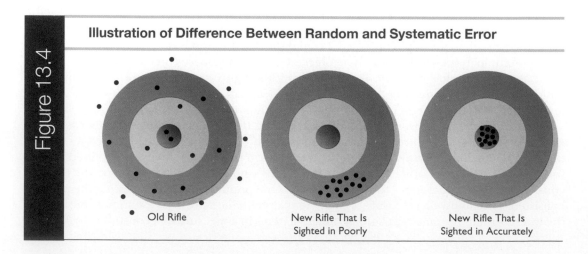

Old Rifle

New Rifle That Is Sighted in Poorly

New Rifle That Is Sighted in Accurately

Estimating Reliability with Coefficient Alpha

A VERY POPULAR WAY TO ASSESS THE INTERNAL CONSISTENCY RELIABILITY OF A set of items is to estimate coefficient alpha. Coefficient alpha has a direct relationship to the most accepted and conceptually appealing measurement model, the domain sampling model. This model holds that the purpose of any particular measurement is to estimate the score that would be obtained if *all* the items in the domain were used. The score that any subject would obtain over the whole sample domain is the person's true score, X_T.

In practice, one typically does not use all of the items that could be used, but only a sample of them. To the extent that the sample of items correlates with true scores, it is good. According to the domain sampling model, then, a primary source of measurement error is the inadequate sampling of the domain of relevant items.

Basic to the domain sampling model is the concept of a very large correlation matrix showing all correlations among the items in the domain. No single item is likely to provide a perfect representation of the concept, just as no single word can be used to test for difference in subjects' spelling abilities and no single question can measure a person's intelligence.

The average correlation among the items in this large matrix, $\bar{r}$, indicates the extent to which some common core is present in the items. The dispersion of correlations about the average indicates the extent to which items vary in sharing the common core. The key assumption in the domain sampling model is that all items, *if they belong to the domain of the concept,* have an equal amount of common core. This statement implies that the average correlation in each column of the hypothetical matrix is the same, and in turn equals the average correlation in the whole matrix. That is, if all the items in a measure are drawn from the domain of a single construct, responses to those items should be highly intercorrelated. Low inter-item correlations, in contrast, indicate that some items are not drawn from the appropriate domain and are producing error and unreliability.

Coefficient alpha provides a summary measure of the intercorrelations that exist among a set of items. Alpha is calculated as [a]

$$\alpha = \left(\frac{k}{k-1} \right) \left(1 - \frac{\sum\limits_{i=1}^{k} \sigma_i^2}{\sigma_t^2} \right)$$

where

$k =$ number of items in the scale,

$\sigma_i^2 =$ variance of scores on item i across subjects, and

$\sigma_t^2 =$ variance of total scores across subjects where the total score for each respondent represents the sum of the individual item scores.

Coefficient alpha routinely should be calculated to assess the quality of a measure. It is especially meaningful because the *square root* of coefficient alpha is the *estimated correlation of the k-item test with errorless true scores.*

If alpha is low, what should the analyst do? If the item pool is sufficiently large, this outcome suggests that some items do not share equally in the common core and possibly should be eliminated. The easiest way to find them is to calculate the correlation of each item with the total score and to plot these correlations by decreasing order of magnitude. Items with correlations near zero would be eliminated. Further, items that produce a substantial or sudden drop in the item-to-total correlations would also be considered candidates for deletion.

If the construct had, say, five identifiable dimensions or components, coefficient alpha would be calculated for each dimension. The item-to-total correlations used to delete items would also be based on the items in the component and the total score for that dimension. ■

Technically SPEAKING

13.1

[a]See Jum C. Nunnally and Ira H. Bernstein, *Psychometric Theory, Third Edition,* Chapters 6 and 7, pp. 209–292, for the rationale behind coefficient alpha and more detailed discussion of the formula for computing it. For discussion of its use in marketing and psychology, see Robert A. Peterson, "A Meta-Analysis of Cronbach's Coefficient Alpha," *Journal of Consumer Research* 21 (September 1994), pp. 381–391.

not count the number of shoplifters who were not caught or the value of merchandise not recovered.[14]

Although a measure that is reliable may or may not be valid, if it is not reliable, it is surely not valid. Thus, reliability is necessary, but not sufficient, for establishing the validity of a measure. Reliability is more easily determined than validity, however, so there has been a greater emphasis on it historically for inferring the quality of measures.

Developing Measures

Outline the sequence of steps to follow in developing valid measures of marketing constructs.

For a beginning researcher, it is easy to get confused about the process of developing measures of marketing constructs. How should a measure be developed, and how should you deal with the basic issues of reliability and validity? Figure 13.5 diagrams a sequence of steps that can be followed to develop valid measures of marketing constructs.[15]

Step 1 in the process involves defining the construct that is to be measured. Researchers need to be careful in specifying what is included in the domain of the construct and what is excluded. Consider measuring customer satisfaction with a new space heater the family recently purchased. What attributes of the product and the purchase should be measured to assess accurately the family's satisfaction? Certainly we would want to be reasonably exhaustive in the list of product features to be included, incorporating such things as cost, durability, quality, operating performance, and style. But what about the purchaser's reaction to the sales assistance received? What about the family members' reactions to subsequent advertising for a competitor's product offering the same features at lower cost? Or what about the family's reactions to news of some negative environmental effects of using the product? To detail which of these factors should be included or how customer satisfaction should be operationalized is beyond the scope of this book. But, obviously, researchers need to be very careful in specifying what is to be included in the domain of the construct being measured and what is to be excluded.

Step 2 in the process is to generate items that capture the domain as specified. Techniques that are typically productive in exploratory research, including literature searches, experience surveys, and insight-stimulating examples, are generally productive here. The literature should indicate how the variable has been defined previously and how many dimensions or components it has. The search for ways to measure customer satisfaction would include product brochures, articles in trade magazines and newspapers, or results of product tests such as those published by *Consumer Reports*. The experience survey might include discussions with people in the product group responsible for the product, sales representatives, dealers, per-

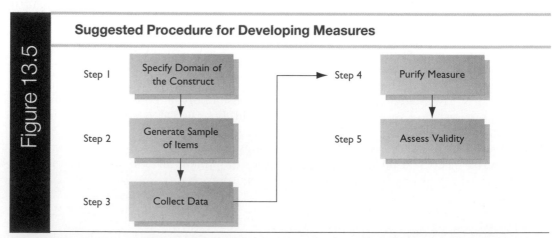

Figure 13.5

Suggested Procedure for Developing Measures

Step 1 — Specify Domain of the Construct
Step 2 — Generate Sample of Items
Step 3 — Collect Data
Step 4 — Purify Measure
Step 5 — Assess Validity

Source: Adapted from the procedure suggested by Gilbert A. Churchill, Jr., "A Paradigm for Developing Better Measures of Marketing Constructs," *Journal of Marketing Research* 16 (February 1979), p. 66. American Marketing Association.

PART 4:
Data Collection Forms

sons in marketing research, consumers, and outsiders who have a special expertise in heating equipment. The insight-stimulating examples could involve a comparison of competitors' products or a detailed examination of some particularly vehement complaints in unsolicited letters about the performance of the product. Examples that reveal sharp contrasts or have striking features would be most productive. Focus groups could also be used at the item-generation stage.

Another potential source of items involves having respondents focus on interactions that were crucial or critical in shaping their reactions to phenomenon. For example, the following questions were asked of all respondents in an attempt to identify the features of service encounters that make them satisfactory or unsatisfactory.[16]

- Think of a time when, as a customer, you had a particularly *satisfying (dissatisfying)* interaction with an employee of an airline, hotel, or restaurant.
- When did the incident happen?
- What specific circumstances led up to this situation?
- Exactly what did the employee say or do?
- What resulted that made you feel the interaction was *satisfying (dissatisfying)*?

Note the emphasis on having respondents describe a specific instance in which a good or poor service interaction occurred. A similar procedure could be used among a sample of purchasers of the space heater to generate items.

Step 3 involves collecting data about the concept from a relevant sample of the target population—for example, all those who have purchased a space heater within the last six months.

Step 4 uses the data collected in Step 3 to purify the original set of items. The purification involves eliminating items that seemed to create confusion among respondents and items that did not discriminate between subjects with fundamentally different positions on the construct. The fundamental criterion used to eliminate items is how each item goes together with the other items. If all the items in a measure are drawn from the domain of a single construct, responses to those items should be highly correlated. If they are not, that is an indication that some of the items are not drawn from the appropriate domain and are producing error and unreliability, and those items should be eliminated. Coefficient alpha can be used to make this assessment, as can other statistical techniques.[17]

Step 5 in the process is to determine the validity of the purified measure. This involves assessing primarily its construct validity, since its content validity will have largely been addressed in Steps 1 through 4.

L inda spread out her printouts of Census Bureau reports. "Let's start by looking at what the Census Bureau was trying to do," she said to Neil. "The Office of Management and Budget, or OMB, requires federal agencies to provide data on five categories: white, black or African American, American Indian or Alaska Native, Asian, and Native Hawaiian or other Pacific Islander. To meet the OMB's requirements, the Census

looking back...

Bureau used those categories on the 2000 census questionnaire. Also, the OMB wants data on Hispanic origin, but that's a separate concept from race, so it's a separate question on the census."

"Even with all those categories, I think some people would have a hard time deciding where they fit."

"You're right. That's an ongoing challenge. The Census Bureau tries to word the questions in ways that reduce confusion and mistakes. For example, instead of just asking Asian Americans to check a box labeled 'Asian,' the questionnaire gave them a series of boxes for Asian Indian, Chinese, Filipino, and so on. Also, there's a sixth choice of categories called 'Some other race.'"

"So if your grandparents came from India, you'd be classified as Asian, and if they came from Lebanon or Saudi Arabia, you'd be—uh, I'm not sure. Help me here."

"According to the Census Bureau definitions, you're supposed to check 'White,' which refers to people whose origin is Europe, the Middle East, or North Africa."

"That's a pretty broad category."

"For our purposes, yes. Families from Egypt might be eating different foods than families from Germany."

"Who's in the 'Some other race' category then?"

"According to the Census Bureau, most of the people who checked 'Some other race' also checked a box indicating they are Hispanic. And over 40 percent of those who called themselves Hispanic checked 'Some other race.'"

"You mean they don't think of themselves as white or black or American Indian?"

"We don't know for sure what they were thinking, but it does look like a sizable share of U.S. Hispanics didn't identify with the categories offered by the Census Bureau, even though they could check as many of those categories as they felt were true. That's something else for us to think about when we consider whether these data apply to our research goals."

"Does this mean the Census Bureau data aren't valid?"

"Well, the questions were designed to count people in categories defined by the OMB, not to segment consumers by their taste in soup."

"You mean we may have to supplement this information with some research of our own."

"Precisely." ■

Sources: Nicholas Kulish, "Why the Census of 2000 Failed to Count Arabs," *The Wall Street Journal* (September 26, 2001), pp. B1, B4; U.S. Census Bureau, *Overview of Race and Hispanic Origin*, Census 2000 Brief, Washington, D.C.: U.S. Department of Commerce, March 2001; U.S. Census Bureau, "Major Differences in Subject-Matter Content between the 1990 and 2000 Census Questionnaires," March 15, 2002, Census Bureau Web site, http://www.census.gov, accessed February 13, 2003; Bob Edwards, "Analysis: Businesses Eagerly Anticipating the Release of U.S. Census Numbers," *Morning Edition*, National Public Radio, March 7, 2001, downloaded from EBSCOhost, May 2, 2002.

PART 4:

Data Collection Forms

Summary

Learning Objective 1
Define the term measurement as it is used in marketing research.
Measurement consists of rules for assigning numbers to objects in such a way as to represent quantities of attributes.

Learning Objective 2
List the four types of scales that can be used to measure an attribute.
The four types of scales on which an attribute can be measured are nominal, ordinal, interval, and ratio scales.

Learning Objective 3
Explain the primary difference between a ratio scale and an interval scale.
In an interval scale, the zero point is established arbitrarily. The ratio scale possesses a natural, or absolute, zero—one for which there is universal agreement as to its location.

Learning Objective 4
Cite some of the factors that may cause differences in two measures of the same attribute.
Some of the factors that may cause differences in two measures of the same attribute are (1) true differences in the characteristic being measured, (2) true differences in other relatively stable characteristics of the individual that affect the score, (3) differences due to transient personal factors, (4) differences due to situational factors, (5) differences due to variations in administration, (6) differences due to the sampling of items, (7) differences due to lack of clarity of the measuring instrument, and (8) differences due to mechanical factors.

Learning Objective 5
Name the two types of error that may affect measurement scores and define each.
Two types of error may affect scores. The first type is systematic error, which affects the measurement in a constant way. The second type is random error, which is due to transient aspects of the person or measurement situation, and which affects the measurement in irregular ways.

Learning Objective 6
Explain the concept of validity as it relates to measuring instruments.
Any scale or other measurement instrument that actually measures what it was intended to measure is said to have validity. The validity of a measuring instrument is defined as "the extent to which differences in scores on it reflect true differences among individuals on the characteristic we seek to measure, rather than constant or random errors."

Learning Objective 7
List three general types of validity that can be used to assess the quality of a measure.
The three types of validity are predictive validity, content validity, and construct validity.

Learning Objective 8
Outline the sequence of steps to follow in developing valid measures of marketing research.
The following sequence of steps is helpful in developing better measures of marketing constructs: (1) specify the domain of the construct, (2) generate a sample of items, (3) collect data, (4) purify the measure, and (5) assess validity.

Key Terms

measurement (page 322)
nominal scale (page 323)
ordinal scale (page 324)
interval scale (page 324)
ratio scale (page 325)
hypothetical construct (page 327)
conceptual definition (page 328)
operational definition (page 328)

systematic error (page 332)
random error (page 333)
validity (page 333)
predictive validity (page 333)
content validity (page 333)
construct validity (page 334)
reliability (page 335)

Review Questions

1. What is measurement?
2. What are the scales of measurement? What comparisons among scores can be made with each?
3. What are the factors that may produce differences in the scores held by two individuals with respect to measurement of the same trait?
4. What is reliability? What information does it contribute to determining if a measure is accurate?
5. What is coefficient alpha? How is it calculated?
6. What is validity?
7. What are the various types of validity?

Discussion Questions, Problems, and Projects

1. Identify the type of scale (nominal, ordinal, interval, ratio) being used in each of the following questions. Justify your answer.
   (a) *During which season of the year were you born?*
      _____ winter _____ spring _____ summer _____ fall
   (b) *What is your total household income?* _____
   (c) *Which are your three most preferred brands of cigarettes? Rank them from 1 to 3 according to your preference, with 1 as most preferred.*

_____ Marlboro	_____ Salem
_____ Kent	_____ Kool
_____ Benson and Hedges	_____ Vantage

   (d) *How much time do you spend traveling to school every day?*

_____ under 5 minutes	_____ 16–20 minutes
_____ 5–10 minutes	_____ 30 minutes and over
_____ 11–15 minutes	

   (e) *How satisfied are you with* Newsweek *magazine?*

_____ very satisfied	_____ dissatisfied
_____ satisfied	_____ very dissatisfied
_____ neither satisfied nor dissatisfied	

   (f) *On average, how many cigarettes do you smoke in a day?*

_____ over 1 pack	_____ less than ½ pack
_____ ½ to 1 pack	

   (g) *Which of the following courses have you taken?*

_____ marketing research	_____ sales management
_____ advertising management	_____ consumer behavior

   (h) *What is the level of education for the head of household?*

_____ some high school	_____ some college
_____ high school graduate	_____ college graduate and/or graduate work

2. The analysis for each of the preceding questions follows. Is the analysis appropriate for the scale used?
   (a) About 50 percent of the sample was born in the fall, while 25 percent of the sample was born in the spring, and the remaining 25 percent was born in the winter. It can be concluded that the fall is twice as popular as the spring and the winter seasons.
   (b) The average income is $25,000. There are twice as many individuals with an income of less than $9,999 than individuals with an income of $40,000 and over.
   (c) Marlboro is the most preferred brand. The mean preference is 3.52.
   (d) The median time spent on traveling to school is 8.5 minutes. There are three times as many respondents traveling less than 5 minutes as respondents traveling 16–20 minutes.
   (e) The average satisfaction score is 4.5, which seems to indicate a high level of satisfaction with *Newsweek* magazine.

(f) Ten percent of the respondents smoke less than one-half pack of cigarettes a day, while three times as many respondents smoke more than one pack a day.

(g) Sales management is the most frequently taken course, since the median is 3.2.

(h) The responses indicate that 40 percent of the sample have some high school education, 25 percent of the sample are high school graduates, 20 percent have some college education, and 10 percent are college graduates. The mean education level is 2.6.

3. You have developed a questionnaire designed to measure attitudes toward a set of television ads for a new snack food product. The respondents, as a group, will view the ads on a television set and then complete the questionnaire. Due to logistical circumstances beyond your control, you must split your sample of respondents into three groups and collect data on three separate days. What steps might you take in an effort to minimize possible variance in scores caused by the three separate administrations?

4. Many areas of marketing research rely heavily on measures of psychological constructs. What characteristics inherent in these constructs make them so difficult to measure? What tools can the marketing researcher use when evaluating the "correctness" of his or her measure? In other words, what can we do that allows us to state with some degree of confidence that we are indeed measuring the construct of interest?

5. Discuss the notion that a particular measure could be reliable and still not be valid. In your discussion, distinguish between reliability and validity.

6. Feather-Tote Luggage is a producer of cloth-covered luggage, one of the primary advantages of which is its light weight. The company distributes its luggage through major department stores, mail-order houses, clothing retailers, and other retail outlets such as stationery stores, leather good stores, and so on. The company advertises rather heavily, but it also supplements this promotional effort with a large field staff of sales representatives, numbering around 400. The number of sales representatives varies, and one of the historical problems confronting Feather-Tote Luggage has been the large number of sales representatives' resignations. It is not unusual for 10 to 20 percent of the sales force to turn over every year. Since the cost of training a new sales representative is estimated at $15,000 to $20,000, not including the lost sales that might result because of a personnel switch, Mr. Harvey, the sales manager, is concerned. He has been concerned for some time, and thus has been conducting exit interviews with each departing sales representative. On the basis of these interviews, he has formulated the opinion that the major reason for this high turnover is general sales representatives' dissatisfaction with company policies, promotional opportunities, and pay. But top management has not been sympathetic to Harvey's pleas regarding the changes needed in these areas of corporate policy. Rather, it has tended to counter Harvey's pleas with arguments that too much of what he is suggesting is based on his gut reactions and little hard data. Before it would be willing to change things, top management desires more systematic evidence that job satisfaction, in general, and these dimensions of job satisfaction, in particular, are the real reasons for the high turnover.

Describe the procedures you would use in developing a measure by which the job satisfaction of Feather-Tote Luggage sales representatives could be assessed. Indicate the type of scale you would use and why, and detail the specific steps you would undertake to assure the validity and reliability of this measure.

Suggested Additional Readings

For a procedure that can be used to construct scales having construct validity, see Gilbert A. Churchill, Jr., "A Paradigm for Developing Better Measures of Marketing Constructs," *Journal of Marketing Research* 16 (February 1979), pp. 64–73.

For a treatment of the various types of reliability and the role of reliability in measurement, see Gilbert A. Churchill, Jr., and J. Paul Peter, "Research Design Effects on the Reliability of Rating Scales: A Meta-Analysis," *Journal of Marketing Research* 21 (February 1984), pp. 360–375.

Jum C. Nunnally and Ira H. Bernstein, *Psychometric Theory,* 3rd ed. (New York: McGraw-Hill, 1994).

J. Paul Peter, "Reliability: A Review of Psychometric Basics and Recent Marketing Practices," *Journal of Marketing Research* 16 (February 1979), pp. 6–17.

For in-depth discussions of the notions of validity, see Mark S. Litwin, *How to Measure Survey Reliability and Validity* (Thousand Oaks, Calif.: Sage Publications, 1995).

J. Paul Peter, "Construct Validity: A Review of Basic Issues and Marketing Practices," *Journal of Marketing Research* 18 (May 1981), pp. 133–145.

J. Paul Peter and Gilbert A. Churchill, Jr., "The Relationship among Research Design Choices and Psychometric Properties of Rating Scales: A Meta-Analysis," *Journal of Marketing Research* 23 (February 1986), pp. 1–10.

Chapter 14

Measuring Attitudes, Perceptions, and Preferences

© PhotoDisc/Getty Images

Learning Objectives

1   *List the various ways by which attitudes can be measured.*

2   *Name the most widely used attitude scaling techniques in marketing research and explain why researchers prefer them.*

3   *Explain how a Stapel scale differs from a semantic-differential scale.*

4   *List three general categories of ratings scales.*

5   *Explain the difference between a graphic-ratings scale and an itemized-ratings scale.*

6   *Explain how the constant-sum scaling method works.*

7   *Explain how norms are useful for interpreting rating scale results.*

8   *Explain the basic purpose of multidimensional scaling and conjoint analysis.*

I t's four o'clock in the afternoon of a typical working mother. What's that little rumble in her stomach? Well, she barely had time to heat up her soup in the microwave for lunch, and now she's getting hungry. Better think about dinner.

This scene happens across America every workday, according to Angelo Iantosca, vice president of marketing for Nestlé Frozen Food. His company has asked working mothers how they handle meal planning and preparation. The research found that almost half plan dinner after 4 P.M. each workday.

By that time, the prospect of making dinner can be exhausting even to contemplate. What to prepare? Do we have the ingredients? Do we have the time, between runs to day care and soccer and homework, to shop for and prepare a meal?

Iantosca and his colleagues at Nestlé have their own questions. Nestlé, whose brands include Stouffer's and Lean Cuisine, wants consumers to choose these frozen-dinner lines when it is time to shop for a meal. Industry data show that dollar sales of frozen food have been on the rise, but the unit volume has not. How can the company persuade consumers to look for their dinner in the frozen-food aisle of the supermarket? When do consumers even consider this as an option? And when they do, how do they decide which product to buy?

At Nestlé's rival, Vlasic Foods, marketing researchers are asking similar questions about their line of Swanson frozen foods. According to Vlasic Foods vice president Kevin Lowery, the company has established a focus: "to go after a significant segment of the [frozen dinner] business by improving our quality and advertising those improvements nationally." To do this effectively, Vlasic, too, seeks to know the mind of its consumers.

Knowing what's inside another person's head is never easy. Companies like Vlasic and Nestlé conduct their own research and join trade groups that sponsor research. For example, the National Frozen Food Institute sponsored a study called "Understanding the Frozen Food Consumer," conducted by The Alcott Group, Chicago. The study explored the reasons behind soft sales of frozen food. Researchers asked whether consumers were intentionally avoiding frozen foods and, when they did buy, what benefits they were seeking in frozen foods. In addition, the companies study consumers' attitudes toward their own brands and products.

Discussion Issues

1. How can marketers like Nestlé Frozen Food and Vlasic Foods benefit from gathering data about attitudes and preferences, as opposed to data about purchasing behavior?

2. What problems would you expect them to encounter in measuring attitudes and preferences?

3. How might the companies apply this information to their decisions about frozen dinners? ■

Marketers are necessarily interested in people's attitudes towards their products and services. Nisson Motor Co. has spent hundreds of millions of dollars redesigning its classic line of Z cars and is betting that consumer attitudes will be positive toward its new 350Z sports car.[1] Levi Strauss & Co. is struggling to overcome negative attitudes towards its jeans among younger shoppers who tend to view them as jeans for middle-aged people. A popular brand for decades, Levi's experienced large decreases in market share between 1997 and 2002. The ultimate success of the brand will depend upon the ability of the company to design products that consumers will like and start buying again.[2] Research Window 14.1 demonstrates that filmmakers are keenly interested in consumer attitudes toward their movies and often use these attitudes to guide the final edit of a movie.

Marketers are worried about more than just consumer attitudes. Consider the following: (1) The appliance manufacturer's interest in dealer attitudes toward the company's warranty policy. If the dealers support the policy, the company feels they are more likely to give adequate, courteous service and, in the process, produce more satisfied customers. (2) The industrial marketer's interest in the general job satisfaction of its highly trained, highly skilled field staff of sales representatives.

These examples indicate some of the many groups of people in whose attitudes the marketer is interested: the company's employees, its intermediaries, and its customers. Their attitudes can be an important determinant of the company's success, and the marketer needs a way to measure these attitudes. This chapter reviews several methods used to measure attitudes.

Although the attitude concept is one of the most widely used in psychology, it is used inconsistently. Both researchers and practitioners have trouble agreeing on interpretations of its various aspects. However, most theorists agree that (1) an attitude is an evaluation of an idea or object that can range from very negative to very positive; (2) an attitude that is strongly held is difficult to change; and (3) there is usually a consistency between attitudes and behavior. These ideas led to our definition of attitude as representing a person's ideas, convictions, or liking with regard to a specific object or idea, presented in Chapter 9.

In addition to attitudes, marketers also have a keen interest in perceptions and preferences. In this chapter we will examine some of the techniques researchers use to measure attitudes, perceptions, and preferences.

Consumers and businesses alike have benefited from customer ratings of online businesses. Reviews on BizRate.com are compiled from self-report ratings of customer experiences.

Putting Hollywood to the Test

RESEARCH *Window*

14.1

In *The Perfect Storm,* moviegoers are spared a litany of the fishermen's final maudlin thoughts. In *The Patriot,* Mel Gibson shares a kiss with his sister-in-law, but their passion stops there. And in *Scary Movie,* potshots are aimed at a previous summer hit, *Big Momma's House.*

These changes were made because Hollywood listened to people like Peter Larkey, a veteran of test screenings, one of the most important and secretive processes shaping today's movies.

"I get to say, 'This movie is awful,' 'This character has to go,'" says Larkey, a 27-year-old computer graphics designer who lives in Northridge, Calif. "It's kind of changed the way I look at films. I'm always thinking, 'What could they have cut out?'"

Filmmakers may bristle at the presumptuousness of these armchair critics, but test-screening feedback—be it visceral, written or conversational—now holds lots of clout in Hollywood. And studios, especially with big-budget summer fare, demand the insurance.

"We all have to go through it because there's so much riding on the movie," *The Perfect Storm* director Wolfgang Petersen says.

Months before a movie's opening, studios hire market researchers to see how a film plays to an audience. For $9,000 to $12,000 per screening, researchers recruit an audience, usually at malls or multiplexes. Fliers with a brief description of the movie and its stars are passed out, often to a specific demographic. The actual screening usually takes place a few days later, and those who make it in sign a statement promising not to disclose anything about the film.

During the movie, researchers (and often filmmakers and studio execs, sitting anonymously in the darkened theater) scrutinize the audience members, watching to see whether they laugh, tense up or snooze. If people get up to use the bathroom, testers check to see whether they hurry back to their seats.

After the movie, audience members fill out questionnaires, answering queries such as "What would you tell your friends about this movie?" Or "Please list what scenes you liked most and least" and "What are your feelings about the way the movie ended?" They also are asked about pacing, plot, and performances and are given a place for less-structured commentary.

Afterward, 12 to 20 audience members often are asked to stay for additional discussions.

The typical film is test-screened three times, but for some, the process is repeated as many as 10 times. Testing is considered especially useful for comedies, action flicks, and thrillers.

"Test screenings help the artist and studio fine-tune the material and refine their intentions," says Marc Shmuger, president of marketing at Universal Pictures. "The research process rests squarely in that awkward intersection between art and commerce."

The belief that test screenings can predict commercial success became widespread with 1987's *Fatal Attraction*. Test audiences balked at the original version, in which Glenn Close's character committed suicide to a *Madame Butterfly* aria. So the ending was made more sensational, with a slasher-movie-style battle between Close and the family she has been terrorizing.

The movie was a hit, grossing $156.6 million, and test screening was credited with the victory.

Insurance for Studios

Now, most studio movies—especially would-be summer blockbusters—are tested, and the process has become more common and elaborate as moviemaking costs have increased.

Attitude-Scaling Procedures

1 *List the various ways by which attitudes can be measured.*

self-report
A method of assessing attitudes in which individuals are asked directly for their beliefs about or feelings toward an object or class of objects.

There are a number of ways in which attitudes have been measured, including self-reports, observation of behavior, indirect techniques, performance of objective tasks, and physiological reactions.[3] By far the most common approach has been **self-reports,** in which people are asked directly for their beliefs or feelings toward an object or class of objects. Exhibit 14.1 depicts consumers' self-report ratings of their purchase experience with several online sources for musical instruments. The online business rating service BizRate.com has developed these ratings so that both online businesses and prospective customers can gauge customer attitudes toward stores across many product categories. A number of scales and scaling methods using self-reports have been devised to measure self-report attitudes. The main types will be reviewed here, but first let us briefly review the other approaches to attitude determination.

Observation of Behavior

The observation approach rests on the assumption that a subject's behavior is caused by his or her attitudes, and that we can therefore use the observed behavior to infer these attitudes. Several years ago McDonald's introduced the McLean Deluxe hamburger, designed to appeal

PART 4:
Data Collection Forms

"Methods employed have become ever-more scientific," says Janet Dubin, whose Dubin Market Research is one of the two main test-screening firms. "Now everything is about mathematical models for projections."

But no accurate formula has surfaced. "It certainly does not work that you can ever say, 'If X movie passes at Y level, then you can put an equal sign and come up with a box office figure on the other side of the equation,'" Shmuger says.

The screening information that testing organizations provide includes numerical ratings. Films that get at least an 80% rating (meaning 80% of the audience rated the movie very good or excellent) are considered potential hits; 55% is the norm.

More extensive comments also are available. And while some filmmakers say they don't even read them, studio execs have been known to use them to bolster their own opinions and demand changes.

Often, the information does not spell out a clear course of action, as was the case with *Shakespeare in Love.*

The audience seemed to like the movie, even applauded at the end, says co-screenwriter Marc Norman. "The next day we were told there was a strange anomaly on the Q-and-A cards. They were asked, 'Would you recommend it to a friend?' And that number was somewhat less than the figure for 'Did you enjoy the movie?'"

Usually, those figures are about equal.

"We couldn't understand the disparity," Norman says. "You're given this raw data, and it's up to you to figure out what it means. There's no book of interpretation."

Eventually, he says, "the consensus arrived at was that the movie was satisfying people all the way through until the last five minutes, and then it was kind of letting them down."

So Tom Stoppard rewrote the scene in which Shakespeare (Joseph Fiennes) says goodbye to Viola (Gwyneth Paltrow) with more passion, and the scene was reshot, even though both actors had moved on to other projects and had to be flown back to England, sets had to be rebuilt, costumes dusted off, and a film crew put together.

"We had no idea if this was the answer to the testing problem, and it cost Miramax quite a lot of money," Norman says.

But when the movie was put to the screening test again, the two figures were in sync, and the movie not only was a box office success, but also won seven Oscars, including Best Picture. ∎

to consumers looking for a low-fat alternative to its other hamburger options. The fact that the product failed allows us to infer that consumer attitudes were negative toward the product. Since the company spent $50 million to launch the product, consumers must have

Exhibit 14.1

Self-Report Attitude Ratings for Online Musical Instrument Suppliers

Online Store	Would Shop Here Again	On Time Delivery	Customer Support	Products Met Expectations	Overall Rating
zZounds	9.1	9.2	8.8	9.2	9.2
Apollo's Axes	9.0	9.0	9.0	8.8	9.2
GuitarTrader.com	9.3	9.3	8.6	8.8	9.0
American Musical Supply	9.0	9.0	8.9	9.1	8.9
Mars Music	8.9	9.2	8.4	9.2	8.9
J&R Music and Computer World	8.8	8.7	8.6	9.0	8.8
MandalayMusic.com	8.7	8.5	8.4	8.9	8.8
8th Street Music, Inc.	8.4	8.6	8.6	9.3	8.6
Musician's Friend	8.6	8.1	8.1	8.8	8.4
Music 123	8.3	8.3	7.9	8.6	8.2

All ratings taken on 1–10 rating scales, where 10 is most positive, from online customers of the stores.
Source: Ratings downloaded from the BizRate.com Web site (http://www.bizrate.com) on August 10, 2002.

responded differently in concept tests when asked to directly state their attitudes toward a low-fat hamburger.[4]

The behavior that the researcher wishes to observe is often elicited by creating an artificial situation. For example, to assess a person's attitude toward a proposed law to require motorcycle riders to wear helmets, the subject might be asked to sign a strongly worded petition in favor of the proposed law. The individual's attitude toward helmets would be inferred based on whether or not he or she signed. Alternatively, subjects might be asked to participate in a group discussion of the helmet issue, and the researcher would note whether the individuals supported or opposed helmet legislation in the discussion.

Indirect Techniques

The **indirect techniques** of attitude assessment use some unstructured or partially constructed stimuli such as word-association tests, sentence-completion tests, and storytelling. We discussed these approaches in detail in Chapter 10, and encourage you to review that material for more information.

Performance of Objective Tasks

On the theory that people's **performance of objective tasks** will reflect their attitudes, one might ask a person to memorize a number of facts about an issue and then assess his or her attitude toward that issue from the facts that were successfully memorized. Thus, to assess a person's attitude toward helmet use legislation, one might ask him or her to memorize such facts as (1) the number of lives saved by helmet usage, (2) the average cost of helmets, and (3) the number of states that have adopted a mandatory helmet law. The material should reflect both sides of the issue. The researcher then would determine what facts the person remembered. The assumption is that subjects would be more likely to remember those arguments that are most consistent with their own position.

Physiological Reaction

Another approach to attitude measurement involves **physiological reaction,** which we discussed in Chapter 11. Here, through electrical or mechanical means, such as the galvanic skin response technique, the researcher monitors the subject's response to the controlled introduction of some stimuli. One problem that arises in using these measures to assess attitude is that, with the exception of voice-pitch analysis, the individual's physiological response indicates only the intensity of the individual's feelings and not whether they are negative or positive.

Although self-report techniques for attitude assessment are the most widely used in marketing research studies because they are easy to administer, one should be aware of these other approaches, particularly when attempting to establish the validity of a self-report measure. They can provide useful insight into how the method of measurement, rather than differences in the basic attitudes of subjects, caused the scores to vary. This is consistent with the notion of using multiple indicators to establish the convergent and discriminant validity of a measure.

Self-Report Attitude Scales

Since attitude is such an important concept, it isn't surprising that researchers have developed a number of methods to measure it. Although many of the methods use self-reports, each method uses them in different ways. In this section, we review some of these self-report scales, particularly those that have novel features or have been used extensively in marketing studies.

PART 4:
Data Collection Forms

Summated-Ratings (Likert) Scale

The *Likert scale,* also called a **summated-ratings scale,** is one of the most widely used attitude-scaling techniques in marketing research. It is particularly useful since it allows respondents to express the intensity of their feelings.[5]

With the summated-ratings scale, researchers write a number of statements that relate to the issue or object in question. Figure 14.1 is an example of a scale that might be used by a bank interested in comparing its image with that of its competitors. Subjects are asked to indicate their degree of agreement or disagreement with each statement in the series. The response categories represent various degrees of agreement and are assigned scale values. Let's assume the values 1, 2, 3, 4, and 5 are assigned to the respective response categories shown in Figure 14.1. A total score can then be calculated for each subject by adding (thus the name "summated-ratings") or averaging the scores across items.

Suppose that one customer of the bank checked "agree" on items 1 and 4 and "strongly agree" on items 2 and 3. This customer's total attitude score toward the bank would thus be 18 if we add the scores, or 4.5 if we average the scores.

Researchers often use variations of the scale we've shown in Figure 14.1. For example, the version shown includes verbal descriptors, or *anchors,* for each scale position (i.e., "strongly disagree," "disagree," and so on). Some researchers will anchor only the endpoints of the scale, letting respondents infer the meaning of the internal scale positions. On the one hand, this introduces error to the degree that respondents interpret the non-anchored positions differently. On the other hand, such an approach may come closer to producing equal scale intervals if people are likely to interpret the verbal anchors differently.[6]

Another variation of the summated-ratings scale asks respondents to circle a number representing the level of agreement rather than check the appropriate category. Further, some researchers offer more response categories than the traditional five categories shown in Figure 14.1. Regardless of how the particular scale is designed, the key features of the summated-ratings scale remain the same: a set of statements with which respondents indicate level of agreement.

Semantic-Differential Scale

One of the most popular techniques for measuring attitudes in marketing research is the **semantic-differential scale.** It has been found to be particularly useful in corporate, brand, and product-image studies. The scale grew out of research concerning the underlying structure of words, but has since been adapted to make it suitable for measuring attitudes.[7]

Semantic-differential scales consist of pairs of bipolar words or phrases that can be used to describe the attitude object. Let's look again at measuring attitude toward a bank. Using the semantic-differential approach, the researcher would first generate a list of bipolar adjectives

summated-ratings scale
A self-report technique for attitude measurement in which respondents are asked to indicate their degree of agreement or disagreement with each of a number of statements; a subject's attitude score is the total obtained by summing over the items in the scale.

2 *Name the most widely used attitude scaling techniques in marketing research and explain why researchers prefer them.*

semantic-differential scale
A self-report technique for attitude measurement in which the subjects are asked to check which cell between a set of bipolar adjectives or phrases best describes their feelings toward the object.

Figure 14.1

Example of Likert Summated-Ratings Scale

	Strongly Disagree	Disagree	Neither Agree nor Disagree	Agree	Strongly Agree
1. The bank offers courteous service.	____	____	____	____	____
2. The bank has a convenient location.	____	____	____	____	____
3. The bank has convenient hours.	____	____	____	____	____
4. The bank offers low-interest-rate loans.	____	____	____	____	____

Figure 14.2

Example of Semantic-Differential Scaling Form

Service is discourteous.	:___:___:___:___:___:___:___:	Service is courteous.
Location is inconvenient.	:___:___:___:___:___:___:___:	Location is convenient.
Hours are inconvenient.	:___:___:___:___:___:___:___:	Hours are convenient.
Loan interest rates are high.	:___:___:___:___:___:___:___:	Loan interest rates are low.

or phrases. Figure 14.2 parallels Figure 14.1 in terms of the attributes used to describe the bank, but it is arranged in semantic-differential format. All we have done in Figure 14.2 is to try to express the things that could be used to describe a bank, and thus serve as a basis for attitude formation, in terms of positive and negative statements. Respondents are instructed to read each set of bipolar phrases and to check the space that best represents their opinions for each set of phrases. A respondent who believed that the hours were terribly inconvenient might check the space closest to the phrase "Hours are inconvenient;" someone who was about neutral on this issue would select the middle position on the scale.

Semantic-differential scales are popular in marketing for several reasons. They are quite flexible and easy to administer from the researcher's perspective. Importantly, they are easy for study respondents to understand and complete. They are also quite good when it comes to presenting the results of a study. For example, suppose that respondents were asked to evaluate two or more banks using the same scale. When several banks are rated, the different bank profiles can be compared. Figure 14.3 (which is sometimes referred to as a **snake diagram** because of its shape), illustrates that Bank A is perceived as having more courteous service and a more convenient location and as offering lower interest rates on loans, but as having less convenient hours than Bank B. The plotted values represent the average score of all subjects on each descriptor. The profile that emerges gives a clear indication of how respondents perceive the differences between the two banks.

Rather than developing a profile, one can also total the scores on a semantic-differential scale in order to compare attitudes toward different objects (for example, alternative package designs). This score is computed by totaling or averaging the scores for the individual descriptors. Further, as was true for summated-rating scales, variations in scale design are common. Numbers are sometimes substituted for blanks, and different numbers of scale positions can be used.

snake diagram
A diagram that connects the average responses to a series of semantic-differential statements, thereby depicting the profile of the object or objects being evaluated.

Figure 14.3

Snake Diagram Showing Contrasting Profiles of Banks A and B

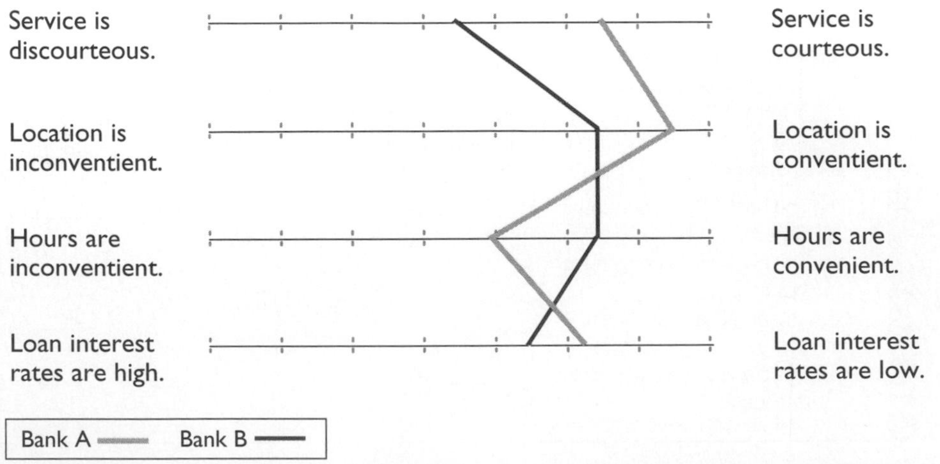

Bank A ——— Bank B ———

Example of Stapel Scale

	−5	−4	−3	−2	−1	+1	+2	+3	+4	+5
Service is courteous.	☐	☐	☐	☐	☐	☐	☐	☐	☐	☐
Location is convenient.	☐	☐	☐	☐	☐	☐	☐	☐	☐	☐
Hours are convenient.	☐	☐	☐	☐	☐	☐	☐	☐	☐	☐
Loan interest rates are high.	☐	☐	☐	☐	☐	☐	☐	☐	☐	☐

Stapel Scale

A modification of the semantic-differential scale that has received some attention is the **Stapel scale.** It differs from the semantic-differential scale in that (1) adjectives or descriptive phrases are tested separately instead of simultaneously as bipolar pairs, (2) points on the scale are identified by number, and (3) there are ten scale positions rather than seven. Figure 14.4 presents the same four attributes previously used to measure attitudes toward banks in a Stapel scale format. Respondents would be told to rate how accurately each of a number of statements describes the object of interest, Bank A.

Researchers who regularly use the Stapel scale point out that this method not only frees the researcher from the sometimes difficult task of developing bipolar adjectives for each of the items on the test, but also permits finer discriminations in measuring attitudes. Despite these advantages, the Stapel scale has not been as warmly embraced as the semantic-differential scale, judging by the number of published marketing studies using each.[8] One problem with the Stapel scale is that many of the descriptors used to evaluate an object can be phrased one of three ways—positively, negatively, or neutrally—and the particular choice of phrasing seems to affect the results as well as subjects' ability to respond. Nevertheless, it is potentially useful for the researcher, especially since it can be administered over the telephone.[9]

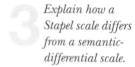

Explain how a Stapel scale differs from a semantic-differential scale.

Stapel scale
A self-report technique for attitude measurement in which respondents are asked to indicate how accurately each of a number of statements describes the object of interest.

Other Ratings Scales

The previous section presented some of the main self-report scaling methods that have been used to measure attitudes. In this section we'll demonstrate some other types of ratings scales, while we focus on the issue of how to measure the importance of various attributes to the individual. That is, in the bank example, even though the individual believes the bank has convenient hours, the person may not value this attribute, and, therefore, it may not affect his or her attitude toward the bank. On the other hand, if the individual places a strong emphasis on the convenience of a bank's location, and if he or she perceives the bank as being inconveniently located, this will have a negative impact on his or her feelings toward the bank. As a result, researchers often try to measure the importance of various attributes of products, services, stores, etc. Research Window 14.2 depicts the importance of various attributes of religious services for a sample of United Kingdom residents.

There is a good deal of controversy about how importance of various attributes should be incorporated in determining a person's attitude toward an object. We will not go over this, however, because it involves some very complex arguments as to how one

© James Nelson/Stone/Getty Images

Importance of Selected Service Quality Dimensions as Applied to Religious Services

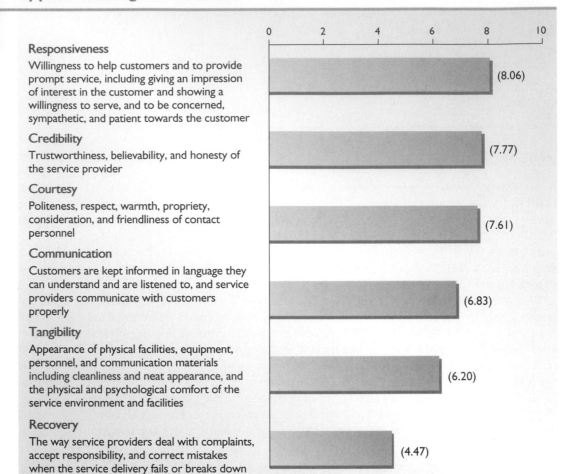

Responsiveness

Willingness to help customers and to provide prompt service, including giving an impression of interest in the customer and showing a willingness to serve, and to be concerned, sympathetic, and patient towards the customer

(8.06)

Credibility

Trustworthiness, believability, and honesty of the service provider

(7.77)

Courtesy

Politeness, respect, warmth, propriety, consideration, and friendliness of contact personnel

(7.61)

Communication

Customers are kept informed in language they can understand and are listened to, and service providers communicate with customers properly

(6.83)

Tangibility

Appearance of physical facilities, equipment, personnel, and communication materials including cleanliness and neat appearance, and the physical and psychological comfort of the service environment and facilities

(6.20)

Recovery

The way service providers deal with complaints, accept responsibility, and correct mistakes when the service delivery fails or breaks down

(4.47)

Note: Higher scores reflect higher levels of importance to respondents.
Source: Adapted from Jessica Santos and Brian P. Mathews, "Quality in Religious Services," *International Journal of Nonprofit and Voluntary Sector Marketing* 6 (3, 2001), pp. 278–288.

determines which attributes are salient (that is, used in forming an attitude) and how they should be measured. Instead, we will simply use importance values as a way of focusing on the differences in the general types of ratings scales. Knowledge of the basic types should help in developing special scales for particular purposes. Three general categories of ratings scales are the graphic, the itemized, and the comparative.

Graphic-Ratings Scale

4 *List three general categories of ratings scales.*

graphic-ratings scale
A scale in which individuals indicate their ratings of an attribute by placing a check at the appropriate point on a line that runs from one extreme of the attribute to the other.

When using **graphic-ratings scales** individuals indicate their rating by placing a check at the appropriate point on a line that runs from one extreme of the attribute to the other. Many variations are possible. The line may be vertical or horizontal; it may be unmarked or marked; if marked, the divisions may be few or many as in the case of a *thermometer scale,* so called because it looks like a thermometer. Figure 14.5 is an example of a horizontal, end-anchored only, graphic-ratings scale. Each individual would be instructed to indicate the importance of the attribute by checking the appropriate position on the scale. The importance value would then be inferred by measuring the length of the line from the left origin to the marked position.

One of the great advantages of graphic-ratings scales is the ease with which they can be constructed and used. As with all scales, however, the endpoints should not be too extreme, since extreme endpoints tend to force respondents into the center of the scale, resulting in less useful information.

Figure 14.5

Graphic-Ratings Scale

Please evaluate each attribute, in terms of how important the attribute is to you personally, by placing an "X" at the position on the horizontal line that most reflects your feelings.

ATTRIBUTE   NOT IMPORTANT   VERY IMPORTANT

Courteous service
Convenient location
Convenient hours
Low-interest-rate loans

Itemized-Ratings Scale

The **itemized-ratings scale** is similar to the graphic-ratings scale except that the rater must select from a limited number of categories instead of placing a mark on a continuous scale. In general, five to nine categories work best; they permit fine distinctions and yet seem to be readily understood by respondents. More categories can be used, of course.[10]

There are lots of possible variations of itemized-ratings scales. Figure 14.6 depicts three different forms of itemized-ratings scales that have been used to measure customer satisfaction. The categories are ordered in terms of their scale positions; in some cases the categories have verbal descriptions attached and in other cases they do not. The distinguishing feature of an itemized scale is that the possible response categories are limited in number. Thus, a set of faces varying systematically in terms of whether they are frowning or smiling used to capture a person's satisfaction or preference (appropriately called a *faces scale*) would be considered an

5 Explain the difference between a graphic-ratings scale and an itemized-ratings scale.

itemized-ratings scale
A scale distinguished by the fact that individuals must indicate their ratings of an attribute or object by selecting the response category that best describes their position on the attribute or object.

Figure 14.6

Three Forms of Itemized-Ratings Scales Used to Measure Satisfaction

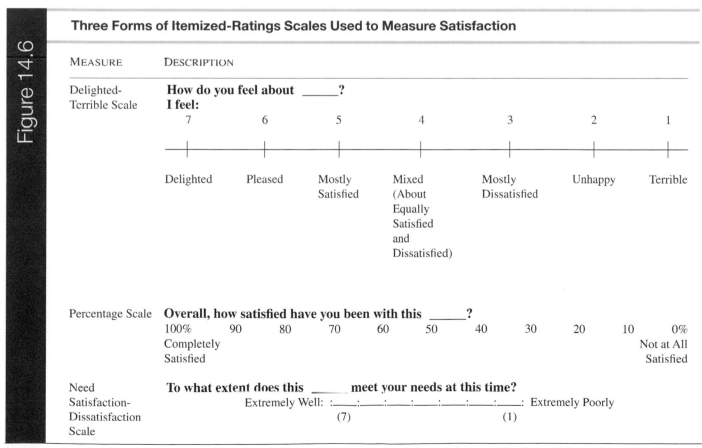

MEASURE	DESCRIPTION

Delighted-Terrible Scale

How do you feel about _____?
I feel:

7	6	5	4	3	2	1
Delighted	Pleased	Mostly Satisfied	Mixed (About Equally Satisfied and Dissatisfied)	Mostly Dissatisfied	Unhappy	Terrible

Percentage Scale

Overall, how satisfied have you been with this _____?

100%	90	80	70	60	50	40	30	20	10	0%
Completely Satisfied										Not at All Satisfied

Need Satisfaction-Dissatisfaction Scale

To what extent does this _____ meet your needs at this time?

Extremely Well: :___:___:___:___:___:___: Extremely Poorly
        (7)   (1)

Source: Adapted from Robert A. Westbrook, "A Rating Scale for Measuring Product/Service Satisfaction," *Journal of Marketing* 44 (Fall 1980), p. 69. Published by the American Marketing Association, Chicago, Ill.

comparative-ratings scale
A scale requiring subjects to make their ratings as a series of relative judgments or comparisons rather than as independent assessments.

Figure 14.7

Itemized-Ratings Scale Used to Measure Importance Values

Please evaluate each attribute, in terms of how important the attribute is to you personally, by placing an "X" in the appropriate box.

ATTRIBUTE	NOT IMPORTANT			VERY IMPORTANT
Courteous service	☐	☐	☐	☐
Convenient location	☐	☐	☐	☐
Convenient hours	☐	☐	☐	☐
Low-interest-rate loans	☐	☐	☐	☐

ETHICAL dilemma 14.1

An independent researcher was hired by a national chain of department stores to develop a scale by which the chain could measure the image of each of its stores. The researcher thought that the best way to do this was through a semantic-differential scale. Since she was interested in establishing her credentials as an expert on store-image research, however, she decided to also develop items for a Likert scale and to administer both of the scales to designated participants. She realized that this might induce greater respondent fatigue and perhaps lower-quality responses, but she was willing to take the chance because she knew that the client would not sanction nor pay for administering the second survey to an independent sample of respondents.

- *Was it ethical for the researcher to accept the risk of lowering the quality of the data addressing the client's issue so that she could further her own goals and career?*

- *What if the data collected by the two instruments provided stronger evidence that store image had indeed been measured even more adequately than if data had been collected through the sole use of the semantic-differential scale?*

- *Would it make any difference if there had been a reasonable chance that the Likert format would produce a better instrument for measuring retail image than a semantic-differential format?*

itemized scale. A summated-ratings statement is an example of an itemized-ratings scale, as is a semantic-differential scale. Figure 14.7 is an itemized-ratings scale used to measure importance values; this four-point scale has the descriptor labels attached to the end scale positions only.

Comparative-Ratings Scale

In graphic and itemized scales, respondents are asked to consider attributes of an entity independently. For example, respondents may be asked to indicate how important convenient location is to them in choosing a bank, but not if convenient location is more or less important than convenient hours. In **comparative-ratings scales,** however, respondents are asked to judge each attribute with direct reference to the other attributes being evaluated.

The constant-sum scaling method is an example of a comparative-ratings scale that can be used to measure importance values. In the **constant-sum method,** the individual is instructed to divide some given sum among two or more attributes on some basis such as importance or favorability. Thus, in Figure 14.8, if the subject assigned 50 points to courteous service and 50 points to convenient location, the attributes would be judged to be equally important; if the individual assigned 80 to courteous service and 20 to convenient location, courteous service would be considered to be four times as important. Note the difference in emphasis with this method. All judgments are now made in comparison to some other alternative.

Respondents are generally asked to compare two attributes in this method, although it is possible to compare more. For example, the individual could be asked to divide 100 points among three or more attributes.

Although comparative scales require more judgments from the individual than either graphic or

Figure 14.8

Constant-Sum Comparative-Ratings Scale

Please divide 100 points between the following two attributes in terms of the relative importance of each attribute to you.

Courteous service   _____

Convenient location   _____

constant-sum method
A type of comparative-ratings scale in which an individual is instructed to divide some given sum among two or more attributes on some basis such as importance or favorability.

itemized scales, they do tend to eliminate the **halo effect** that is common in scaling. A halo effect occurs when there is carryover from one judgment to another. For example, suppose we are conducting a satisfaction study among recent shoppers of a department store and we are concerned about two key issues: satisfaction with service provided at the check-out counter and satisfaction with store location. If questions about these issues are asked back-to-back on the survey, a respondent with strong positive feelings about the service provided is likely to provide more positive assessments of store location than s/he might normally provide. In this case, the positive response to location may be due more to halo effects from the preceding question than to true feelings about the location. Comparative rating scales help control this problem by requiring respondents to consider two or more attributes in combination.

Another problem that researchers may encounter when using graphic or itemized scales to measure importance values is that respondents may be inclined to indicate that all, or nearly all, of the attributes are important. The comparative scaling methods usually allow more insight into the relative ranking, if not the absolute importance, of the attributes to each individual.

halo effect
A problem that arises in data collection when there is carryover from one judgment to another.

Other Considerations in Designing Scales

There are a number of issues that must also be considered when designing scales for measuring concepts like attitudes. In this section, we'll deal with some of these issues.

Reverse Scaling

One of the problems that researchers often encounter, particularly when using multiple-item scales for measuring constructs, is that respondents sometimes fall victim to response set bias. **Response set bias** refers to error that enters into our measures when respondents begin to answer all the questions in a similar way, often due to boredom or lack of attention (possibly caused by poor questionnaire design). Such respondents are "set" in their responses. Indeed, we have had whole sections of surveys returned in which respondents circled exactly the same response for every item (for example, circling the 6 on a 1–7 itemized-ratings scale for 20 questions in a row).

Response set bias clearly creates error in our attempts to accurately measure things. One technique designed to deal with this issue is **reverse scaling,** in which some of the items in a multi-item scale for measuring a construct are written in the negative form so that the most positive responses to the item are actually at the opposite end of the scale from where they would normally be. This technique is designed to encourage respondents to pay greater attention to the items and to help identify cases where response set bias has likely become a problem. For example, look back at Figure 14.1 and the example of the Likert, or summated-ratings, scale. Suppose that the second item were worded as follows: "The bank has an inconvenient location." From the bank's perspective, what would be the most positive response to this item?

response set bias
A problem that arises when respondents answer questionnaire items in a similar way without thinking about the items.

reverse scaling
A technique in which some of the items on a multi-item scale are written so that the most positive responses are at the opposite end of the scale from where they would normally appear.

That's right, the most positive response would be "strongly disagree." Here's the important part: a respondent who checked "strongly agree" on all four items may well have been responding more to response set than to the actual items. The usual recommendation is to reverse scale half of the items in a multiple-item measure. Then, if a respondent provides the same response to all the items, we can be fairly certain that response set bias is present, and researchers must decide whether to eliminate the questionnaire completely or to discard responses only in that section.

Before we rush off and reformat half of the items on our scales, however, we want you to consider the other side of the story. While it is true that response set bias is a problem, there is some evidence that the cure (reverse scaling) may be worse than the disease. In short, the practice of negatively wording some of the items often seems to introduce a sort of negativity bias that may distort responses even more than does response set bias. In some cases, respondents seem to react more to the negative wording than to the actual content of the question.[11] As a result, reverse scaling should be used only sparingly. Instead, researchers should rely upon the physical inspection of questionnaires to identify obvious response set bias. Another option is to include a number of items that are designed to generate negative responses but that are unrelated to any of the other scales in the questionnaire. Unfortunately, space on a questionnaire is usually limited, and adding items solely for the detection of response set bias may not always be justified.

Number of Items in a Scale

global measure
A measure designed to provide an overall assessment of an object or phenomenon, typically using one or two items.

composite measure
A measure designed to provide a comprehensive assessment of an object or phenomenon, with items to assess all relevant aspects or dimensions.

Another consideration involves exactly how many items are needed to measure the construct. Should attitude toward a company be assessed using a single item, 3 items, 10 items, or 35 items? The answer depends upon the purpose of the measure. If an overall summary judgment of how consumers feel about the company is needed, then a single-item **global measure** of attitude on a "very unfavorable—very favorable" may be enough. The goal of a global measure is to provide a succinct assessment of some attitude object.

Sometimes, however, we need to develop a more comprehensive measure of a construct that will provide more information about how respondents view various aspects of the phenomenon being studied. These types of measures, often called **composite measures,** are more diagnostic in the sense that they provide more information for identifying strong or weak areas, particularly when aspects can be compared with one another or with measures for other entities. For example, suppose that marketing managers for a major discount chain are concerned about customer satisfaction. A global measure of satisfaction would provide an overall indication of how things are going, but a composite measure, consisting of measures of satisfaction with the location, product selection, prices, employees, and so on, would allow the managers to more easily diagnose any problem areas. The managers would benefit even more if they had similar satisfaction ratings for competing discount stores (see "Interpreting Rating Scales: Raw Scores vs. Norms" on page 363).

How many items should be used with a composite measure? As many as it takes to fully capture the phenomenon being measured. Recall from the previous chapter that for a measure to have content validity it must adequately represent the domain of the concept. That may mean 3 or 4 items, or it may require 50 or more. An extensive study of the marketing literature over a 20-year period confirmed that the reliability of a measure increases with an increasing number of items, suggesting that more items are better than fewer items.[12] This advice must be balanced, however, with concerns about questionnaire length. Researchers must use their judgment to ensure that the construct is adequately represented and reliable, yet is not so long as to create unnecessary burdens for respondents.

Number of Scale Positions

Researchers must also decide how many scale positions to include when designing measures. For most purposes, a minimum of 5 response categories should be included. Research has demonstrated that extreme response style effects become problematic with fewer than 5 positions.[13] Moreover, measure reliability seems to increase as the number of scale positions increases.[14]

What is the upper limit on number of scale positions? Theoretically, there is no limit. For example, with a graphic-ratings scale there are an infinite number of positions along the line between, say, "not important" and "very important" (see Figure 14.5), although a finite scale will be imposed when measuring the distance from the start of the line to the point at which the respondent indicated his or her response. With itemized-ratings scales, there seems to be a general consensus that 10 or 11 items are more than sufficient for capturing the variation on an item among a group of respondents. In fact, scales with 5–9 positions work quite well and are used routinely in marketing research. As a practical matter, going beyond 5–9 scale positions becomes quite difficult for researchers who have chosen to anchor, or attach descriptive labels to, each scale position, although this is less of a problem for those who anchor only the end scale positions.

The researcher must also make an important decision with respect to whether to have an even or odd number of scale positions. An odd number allows for a center position, usually interpreted as "neutral" by respondents. Sometimes it is easier for a respondent to choose the center position than to actually think carefully about an item, so some researchers use an even number of scale positions to ensure that the respondent won't just opt for the middle position and go on. On the other hand, there are plenty of issues on which a perfectly well-thought-out answer may be "neutral." As a result, some researchers routinely use an odd number of scale positions. Both even and odd numbers are used regularly in practice.

Including a "Don't Know" Response Category

Sometimes researchers choose to include a "don't know" option along with the regular scale positions for an item. This is probably a good idea if a fairly sizable percentage of respondents are likely not to have encountered or thought about the object or issue being addressed in the study. Otherwise, any answers that they provide will probably have little meaning and as a result will simply add error to the study. Exploratory research and pilot studies can be used to shed light on the issue.

If it is clear that most of the respondents have come in contact with the store, brand, etc., that is being studied, we advise against including a "don't know" category. For example, consider a retailer who regularly conducts satisfaction research among recent customers of the store whose names have been randomly selected from the store's database. It is quite reasonable to expect the respondents to be able to answer questions about satisfaction with the store, products purchased, and so on, because we know that they are recent customers of the store. If the store conducted the research by randomly selecting names from the local telephone directory, a don't know option would be quite appropriate. A word of caution: If you include the don't know option, you can be assured that some respondents will choose it—including some who simply are looking for the easiest way to complete the survey.

Determining Which Type of Scale to Use

Many beginning researchers are baffled by the choices that confront them when it comes to designing the questionnaire. Should they use summated-ratings scales, semantic differential scales, other forms of itemized-ratings scales, or constant sum scales, to measure the concepts they need to assess? Many times several approaches might work equally well, and researchers should let common sense guide their choices. All the scales have proven useful at one time or another. All rightly belong in the researcher's measurement tool kit.

The nature of the problem and the planned mode of administration will affect the final choice. So will the characteristics of the respondents, their commitment to the task, and their experience and ability to respond. In some cultures, graphic-ratings scales may be unknown, and respondents with low levels of education may not even be able to conceptualize a continuous scale from extreme dissatisfaction to extreme satisfaction, say, that is divided into equal increments of satisfaction. In other cultures the use of these scales may be a very new experience for most research participants, and interviewers may need to spend considerable time explaining the scale. In still other situations, it might be necessary to develop new scales. For example, the "sad-to-happy faces" scale that works in the United States does not work well in Africa, where culture requires some different-looking faces to depict the various stages of happiness (Figure 14.9).

Figure 14.9

Examples of "Sad-to-Happy Faces" Scales That Work in the United States versus Those That Work in Africa

Source: The African faces can be found in C. K. Corder, "Problems and Pitfalls in Conducting Marketing Research in Africa," in Betsy Gelb, ed., *Marketing Expansion in a Shrinking World,* Proceedings of American Marketing Association Business Conference (Chicago: American Marketing Association, 1978), pp. 86–90. Reprinted with permission of American Marketing Association.

PART 4:
Data Collection Forms

Interpreting Rating Scales: Raw Scores vs. Norms

One of the biggest difficulties with rating scales is trying to interpret what the scores obtained using the scales actually mean. Some time ago we were asked to develop a scale for measuring patients' perceptions of the quality of service they received from endodontists, who provide specialized dental services such as root canals and oral surgery. We developed a composite scale consisting of 23 items covering two primary dimensions, (a) the procedure and service provided by the endodontist and (b) the service provided by the endodontist's staff. Each of the items described an aspect of the service and asked patients how performance on each aspect compared with their expectations using a 7-point scale anchored by "much less than I expected" and "much more than I expected" (the center position was anchored by "about what I expected"). Scores were averaged across the items in each dimension to get a composite rating for each dimension, and the composite scores for the two dimensions were averaged to get an overall service quality score. A total of 95 endodontists and 7,479 of their patients participated in the project.

One endodontist earned an overall service quality score of 5.13. How would you interpret his performance? Is this good, average, or poor performance? The score is well above the middle position on the 1–7 scale, so most people would probably conclude that his performance was above average based only on the raw score. To do so without a point of comparison, however, would be a mistake. What if 5.40 were the lowest score achieved by any of the other 94 endodontists? If that were the case, his performance was nothing short of awful. What if the highest score achieved by other endodontists was a 4.88? In this case, a score of 5.13 would represent an outstanding achievement. Here's the point: *it is very difficult to interpret a rating scale score using only the score itself and the scale on which it was obtained to provide meaning.*

When we compare the one endodontist's score against those of the others in the study, it turns out that 75% of the endodontists posted higher scores than he did. Armed with this knowledge, we can say with more confidence that this level of performance was relatively poor, even though the raw score suggested otherwise. In psychological scaling, researchers need to develop **normative standards,** or norms, for use in interpreting raw scores. In this case, norms also come in handy for diagnosing the likely causes of the poor performance. While the overall score was 5.13, the average score for the first dimension (covering aspects of the procedure and the endodontist) was 5.26 and that for the second dimension (covering the staff) was 5.00, suggesting that the endodontist should focus his attention on improving the quality of service provided by the staff. Right? Unfortunately for the endodontist, the comparison of raw scores against norms again points to another conclusion. The staff score was actually

> **7** *Explain how norms are useful for interpreting rating scale results.*

ETHICAL dilemma 14.2

The Samuelson Research Firm was contacted by Larkin Electronics, a manufacturer of small electronic radio parts, to conduct a survey of Larkin's employees. The purpose of the research was to determine the state of worker morale and the importance of certain employee grievances so that Larkin's management could gauge the strength of its position in collective bargaining with the employee union. Samuelson Research agreed to conduct the study.

- *What are the consequences for employees who participate in such a survey?*

- *Would cooperating in this research be detrimental to the employees' immediate self-interest?*

- *Do researchers have the right to ask questions concerning this issue?*

- *Does this research undercut the position of labor's representatives since they have no corresponding way of gauging the intensity of management's opinions?*

- *If you had been director of the research, what kind of questions might you have asked of Larkin's management?*

- *Would you have agreed to conduct such a survey?*

- *In general, should a researcher be concerned with the uses of the research that he or she conducts or its effects on the research participants?*

normative standard
A comparative standard used to provide meaning to raw scale scores.

much stronger, ranking at the 42nd percentile (meaning that this staff outperformed 41% of the others in the study). The endodontist's score, even though it was higher, placed him only at the 17th percentile when compared to scores for other endodontists on this dimension.[15]

There are two general kinds of norms that can be used, population-based and time-based. Population-based norms, such as the example we've been using, give meaning to scores by comparing them to scores obtained by similar entities. For example, a department store chain might choose to compare the satisfaction score for a particular store with those of all other stores in the chain. Similarly, a researcher investigating consumer perceptions of a particular producer, service provider, product, or brand, should also measure consumer perceptions of competing producers, service providers, etc., in order to gain a better understanding of what the raw scores mean.

Time-based norms track scores for an entity over time. For example, suppose that the endodontist in our example decided to implement changes in the way service was delivered. To monitor the effectiveness of the changes, he decided to collect service quality information from patients on an annual basis. The ratings from earlier time periods serve as norms for ratings in future time periods. Although time-based norms are less informative than population-based norms (because there is no way to tell how scores at any given time compare against similar entities), they are still very useful for tracking progress and identifying problem areas. And they are certainly better than relying on raw scores alone for meaning.

Sometimes it is possible to utilize both kinds of norms. This is the approach taken with the American Customer Satisfaction Index (ACSI) in measuring customer satisfaction with products and services. To compute the ACSI, researchers conduct telephone interviews of people who have recently bought or used a company's product or service, asking them about three determinants of satisfaction: their expectations, perception of quality, and perception of value. Using a sophisticated model, ACSI researchers use their responses to rate organizations and industries on a 1–100 scale of satisfaction, as well as to produce a national customer satisfaction score. An organization can track its own performance since the baseline measure was made in 1994, or it can compare its performance to industrywide numbers, or its industry to overall customer satisfaction. For example, customer satisfaction with the U.S. Postal Service had risen from a low of 61 in 1994 to 73 by the first quarter of 2002. In contrast, customer satisfaction with AT&T Corporation had fallen from a high of 85 to a low of 73 over the same time frame.[16]

Perceptual Scaling

Thus far in this chapter, we have emphasized the measurement of people's attitudes toward objects. Marketing managers are also interested in determining how people perceive various objects, such as products, companies, or brands. In its quest for a differential advantage, a firm needs to correctly position its products against competitive offerings. To do this, the product manager needs to identify the following:[17]

1. The number of dimensions consumers use to distinguish products
2. The names of these dimensions
3. The positioning of existing products along these dimensions
4. Where consumers prefer a product to be on the dimensions

One way in which managers can grasp the positioning of their brand (or product or company) versus competing brands is through the study of perceptual maps. In a perceptual map, each product or brand occupies a specific point. Products or brands that are similar lie close together, and those that are different lie far apart. Perceptual maps provide managers with meaningful pictures of how their products and brands compare with other products and brands.

PART 4:
Data Collection Forms

There are several ways to create perceptual maps. One approach is to ask respondents to judge how similar the objects are to one another on a number of characteristics (such as convenience, friendliness, or value for the money), using summated-ratings or semantic-differential scales. The ratings of the objects on each of the items are subsequently analyzed using various statistical techniques to identify the key dimensions or attributes consumers use to distinguish the objects. Another approach is to ask respondents to make overall judgments about the objects. Then the researcher attempts to infer which characteristics were used to form those judgments. This indirect approach is sometimes used because in many cases the attributes may be unknown and the respondents unable or unwilling to represent their judgments accurately.

Typically, participants are asked for their *perceptions of the similarity* between various objects and their *preferences* among these objects. An attempt is then made to place the objects in a multidimensional space where the number of dimensions corresponds to the number of characteristics the individual used in forming the judgments. **Multidimensional-scaling** analysis is the label used to describe the similarity- and preference-based approaches.

Regardless of the approach taken, the appeal of multidimensional scaling lies in the maps produced by the technique. These maps can be used to provide insight into some very basic questions about markets. For example, researchers can determine the salient product attributes perceived by buyers in the market; the combination of attributes buyers most prefer; the products that are viewed as substitutes and those that are differentiated from one another; the viable segments that exist in a market; the "holes" in a market that can support a new product venture.

Figure 14.10 presents a two-dimensional perceptual map for seven brands of prescription drugs (labeled Brands A through G) based on preferences provided by a large sample of physicians. The horizontal dimension appears to reflect how long the chemical compound

8 *Explain the basic purpose of multidimensional scaling and conjoint analysis.*

multidimensional scaling
An approach to measurement in which people's perceptions of the similarity of objects and their preferences among the objects are measured, and these relationships are plotted in a multidimensional space.

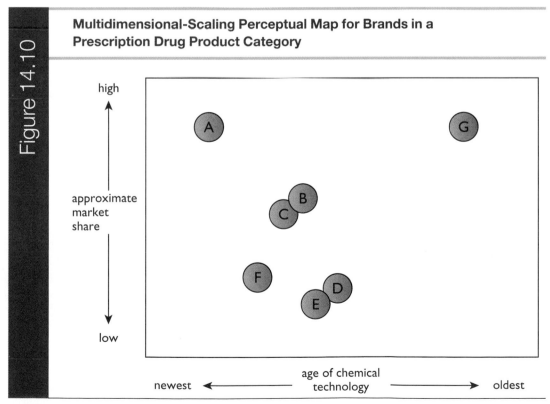

Figure 14.10

Multidimensional-Scaling Perceptual Map for Brands in a Prescription Drug Product Category

Source: Adapted from Wayne S. DeSarbo, Juyoung Kim, S. Chan Choi, and Melinda Spaulding, "A Gravity-Based Multidimensional Scaling Model for Deriving Spatial Structures Underlying Consumer Preference/Choice Judgments," *Journal of Consumer Research* 29 (June 2002), pp. 91–100.

used in the drugs has been available, with Brand G using the oldest compound and Brands A and F representing a newer chemical. The vertical dimension reflects the market share of the drugs, with Brands A and G holding the largest shares. Note that the analysis itself produced these dimensions based on the preference data provided by the physicians.

Conjoint Analysis

conjoint analysis
A technique in which respondents' utilities or valuations of attributes are inferred from the preference they express for various combinations of these attributes.

Like multidimensional-scaling analysis, **conjoint analysis** relies on the ability of respondents to make judgments about stimuli. In multidimensional-scaling analysis, the stimuli are existing products or brands, and respondents are asked to make judgments about their relative *similarity*. In conjoint analysis, the stimuli represent some *predetermined combinations of features, benefits, and attributes* offered by a product, and respondents are asked to make judgments about their *preference* for these various combinations. In essence, conjoint analysis seeks to determine which benefit or attributes buyers are willing to trade off to retain others. The basic aim is to determine which combinations of features respondents prefer most.

Respondents might use, for example, such attributes as miles per gallon, seating capacity, price, length of warranty, and so on, in making judgments about which automobile they prefer. Yet, if asked to do so directly, many respondents might find it very difficult to state which attributes they were using and how they were combining them to form overall judgments.

Conjoint analysis attempts to handle this problem by estimating how much each of the attributes are valued on the basis of the choices respondents make among product concepts that are varied in systematic ways. In this type of analysis, researchers attempt to infer respondents' value systems based on their choices rather than on the respondents' own estimations.

Suppose that a manufacturer of small appliances planned to develop and market a new coffeemaker and wished to assess how consumers evaluated the following levels of each of these product attributes:

© PhotoDisc/Getty Images

Researchers trying to discover which combination of features consumers prefer in a coffeemaker or other new product might use conjoint analysis.

- Capacity—4, 8, and 10 cups
- Price—$28, $32, and $38
- Brewing time—3, 6, 9, and 12 minutes

All three of these attributes are *motherhood* attributes, meaning that, other things being equal, most consumers would prefer either the most or least of each property—in this instance, the largest-capacity maker with the shortest brewing time and the lowest price. Unfortunately, life is not that simple. The larger coffeemaker will cost more; faster brewing means a larger heating element for the same pot capacity, which also raises the cost. And a larger-capacity maker with no change in the heating element will require increased brewing time. In sum, a consumer is going to have to trade off one property to secure more of another. The manufacturer is interested in determining how consumers value these specific attributes. Is low price most valued, or are consumers willing to pay a higher price to secure some of the other properties? Which price? Which properties? Conjoint analysis is an ideal technique for determining the answers to these questions.

One simple method of implementing conjoint analysis in this situation is to develop a set of index cards containing all possible combinations of these product attributes. If each card contained a combination of one possible aspect of each category (e.g., 4-cup capacity, $32 price, 6-minute brewing time), there would be 36 possible combinations. Respondents might then rank the various combinations in order of preference. Although we will spare you the statistical details, conjoint analysis will provide an estimate of how much respondents value each product attribute, which will aid the manufacturer in the design of the new coffee maker.

Conjoint analysis has been most often used to make product design decisions. Researchers have used it on projects ranging from determining the best way to package olive oil for consumers in Great Britain to designing the Courtyard by Marriott hotel chain.[18]

looking back...

If Vlasic Foods and Nestlé Frozen Food made their marketing decisions based strictly on observable behavior, they couldn't be responsive to consumers. They might spend many years and millions of dollars tinkering with a product until they stumbled on the combination that would increase sales. Therefore, despite the limitations of measuring attitudes and preferences, the companies use research that asks consumers' opinions, and they apply the response data to their marketing decisions.

Either company might start with existing data such as the National Frozen Food Association's "Understanding the Frozen Food Consumer" study, which found some general patterns in consumers' attitudes toward frozen food. Consumers are well aware that frozen food provides convenience, but they are less apt to think of frozen food as offering "peak taste and nutrition." Nevertheless, consumers tend to have a higher opinion of frozen food than boxed or canned alternatives. The study also grouped frozen-food buyers into five categories, based on their attitudes and buying behavior:

1. Good Meal Makers (26 percent of the sample): These confident cooks use frozen food as a meal component. They turn to frozen food for side dishes, vegetables, or selected cuts of meat and poultry.

2. Hectic Have To's (24 percent): Very busy and very pressed for time, they buy whatever will save the most time. This segment purchases the most frozen food.

3. Simply Content (19 percent): These less-than-competent cooks are looking for simple meals. They are very satisfied with frozen food.

4. Basic Cooks (19 percent): These cooks are practical and economical. They tend to prefer canned or boxed foods over frozen foods, which they view as being of lower quality.

5. Frozen Rejecters (12 percent): They don't care about convenience and don't like frozen food. They use it only as a backup in a pinch.

These descriptions can help each company define market segments and create questions to ask when they conduct their own research.

Vlasic talked to consumers about their associations with the Swanson brand. They found that consumers in the 25–54 age bracket had strong memories of Swanson TV dinners. When these consumers were children, their parents would let them pick out a Swanson dinner to eat while the parents went out for an evening. This was a pleasant memory for these consumers, and Vlasic decided to capitalize on that positive relationship with the brand. it launched an advertising campaign with the theme "Make New Memories with Swanson." The advertising supports an improved fried chicken dinner—the perennial favorite.

Nestlé's Lean Cuisine brand, a later entry to the frozen-food aisle, does not have the same appeal to nostalgia. That company has used consumer data to find its own niche. Nestlé talked to its target market, working mothers, and learned that almost half of them plan dinner after 4 P.M. and about the same number believe that 6 P.M. is too late to start preparing a meal with fresh ingredients. For these consumers, Nestlé developed Lean Cuisine

Skillet Sensations, which combines frozen meat and frozen vegetables in a single bag. Consumers can pick up the whole meal without making trips to the meat counter and the frozen-vegetable case, yet they still can prepare fresh-tasting food.

Why not simply put everything on a tray and sell TV dinners as Swanson does? Then consumers wouldn't have to bother with a skillet on a stove. Nestlé positioned this offering based on its own research. The company talked to the household members who made decisions about dinner, asking them about the timing and factors considered in these decisions. Nestlé learned that most working mothers would be happy to cook but believe they don't have enough time. According to Nestlé's Angelo Iantosca, "Skillet Sensations is designed for . . . consumers who need a balance between convenience and fresh taste." Packaging indicates that preparation time is just 15 minutes. ■

Sources: David Wellman, "New Life in the Freezer Case," *Supermarket Business* (February 1999), pp. 34–36; Maryellen Lo Bosco, "NFFA Study: Target the Right Consumer," *Supermarket News* (November 2, 1998), p. 47.

Summary

Learning Objective 1
List the various ways by which attitudes can be measured.

Attitudes can be measured by self-reports, observation of overt behavior, indirect techniques, performance of objective tasks, and physiological reactions.

Learning Objective 2
Name the most widely used attitude scaling techniques in marketing research and explain why researchers prefer them.

The Likert scale, or summated-ratings scale, and the semantic-differential scale are the most widely used attitude scaling techniques in marketing research. Both are particularly useful because they allow respondents to express the intensity of their feelings.

Learning Objective 3
Explain how a Stapel scale differs from a semantic-differential scale.

A Stapel scale differs from a semantic-differential scale in that (1) adjectives or descriptive phrases are tested separately instead of simultaneously as bipolar pairs, (2) points on the scale are identified by number, and (3) there are ten scale positions rather than seven. Respondents are told to rate how accurately each of a number of statements describes the object of interest.

Learning Objective 4
List three general categories of ratings scales.

Three general categories of rating scales are the graphic, the itemized, and the comparative scales.

Summated-ratings, semantic differential, and Stapel scales are all examples of itemized rating scales.

Learning Objective 5
Explain the difference between a graphic-ratings scale and an itemized-ratings scale.

The itemized-ratings scale is similar to the graphic-ratings scale except that the rater must select from a limited number of categories instead of placing a mark on a continuous scale. In general, five to nine categories work well.

Learning Objective 6
Explain how the constant-sum scaling method works.

In the constant-sum method of comparative rating, the individual is instructed to divide some given sum among two or more attributes on the basis of their importance to him or her. Respondents are generally asked to compare two attributes in this method, although it is possible to compare more.

Learning Objective 7
Explain how norms are useful for interpreting rating scale results.

A rating scale score, interpreted in isolation, can provide misleading information. Whenever possible, a rating scale score should be compared against scores obtained for similar entities (i.e., population-based norms) or for the same entity in prior time periods (i.e., time-based norms) to gain a better understanding of what the score really means.

Learning Objective 8

Explain the basic purpose of multidimensional scaling and conjoint analysis.

Multidimensional scaling is used to develop a perceptual map of the relative standing of multiple products, brands, companies, etc., along key dimensions. Conjoint analysis is used to discover which attributes of products and services people are willing to trade-off for other attributes, with a goal of determining which combination of attributes respondents prefer the most.

Key Terms

self-report (page 348)
indirect techniques (page 350)
performance of objective tasks (page 350)
physiological reaction (page 350)
summated-ratings scale (page 351)
semantic-differential scale (page 351)
snake diagram (page 352)
Stapel scale (page 353)
graphic-ratings scale (page 354)
itemized-ratings scale (page 355)

comparative-ratings scale (page 356)
constant-sum method (page 357)
halo effect (page 357)
response set bias (page 357)
reverse scaling (page 357)
global measure (page 358)
composite measure (page 358)
normative standard (page 361)
multidimensional scaling (page 363)
conjoint analysis (page 364)

Review Questions

1. What are the major ways that have been used to measure attitudes?
2. How does one construct a Likert summated-ratings scale? How are subjects scaled with a Likert scale?
3. What is a semantic-differential scale? How is a person's overall attitude assessed with a semantic-differential scale?
4. How does a Stapel scale differ from a semantic-differential scale?
5. What is a graphic-ratings scale? An itemized scale? A constant-sum scale?
6. What is reverse scaling? Why is it used? What is a potential problem with its use?
7. What is the difference between a global measure and a composite measure? When might each be used effectively?
8. What is the key issue involved in the decision to use an even or an odd number of scale positions?
9. How can norms be developed? Why are they important?
10. What is a perceptual map? What can a perceptual map tell a researcher?
11. What is the purpose of conjoint analysis?

Discussion Questions, Problems, and Projects

1. (a) List at least eight attributes that students might use in evaluating bookstores.
   (b) Using these attributes, develop eight summated-ratings items and eight semantic-differential items by which attitudes toward (i) the university bookstore and (ii) some other bookstore can be evaluated.
   (c) Administer each of the scales to ten students.
   (d) What are the average sample scores for the two bookstores using the scale of summated ratings? What can be said about students' attitudes toward the two bookstores?
   (e) Develop a profile analysis or snake diagram for the semantic-differential scale.

(f) Based on the semantic-differential scale, what can be said about students' attitudes toward the two bookstores?

2. (a) Assume that a manufacturer of a line of cheese products wanted to evaluate customer attitudes toward the brand. A panel of 500 regular consumers of the brand responded to a questionnaire that was sent to them and that included several attitude scales, which produced the following results:

(i) The average score for the sample on a 25-item summated-ratings scale was 105.
(ii) The average score for the sample on a 20-item semantic-differential scale was 106.
(iii) The average score for the sample on a 15-item Stapel scale was 52.

The vice-president has asked you to indicate whether his customers have a favorable or unfavorable attitude toward the brand. What will you tell him? Please be specific.

(b) Following your initial report, the vice-president has provided you with more information. The following memo has been given to you: "The company has been using the same attitude measures over the past eight years. The results of the previous studies are as follows:

Year	Summated Ratings	Semantic-Differential	Stapel
1	86	95	43
2	93	95	48
3	97	98	51
4	104	101	55
5	110	122	62
6	106	112	57
7	104	106	53
8	105	106	52

We realize there may not be any connection between attitude and behavior, but it must be pointed out that sales peaked in year 5 and since then have been gradually declining." With this information, do your conclusions change? Can anything more be said about customer attitudes?

3. Generate five attributes that assess students' attitudes toward "take-home exams." Use (i) graphic-ratings scales, (ii) itemized-ratings scales, and (iii) comparative-ratings scales to determine the importance of each of these attributes in students' evaluation of take-home exams. Administer each of these scales to separate samples of five students.
(a) What are your findings with the graphic-ratings scale? Which attributes are important?
(b) What are your findings with the itemized-ratings scale? Which attributes are important?
(c) What are your findings with the comparative-ratings scale? Which attributes are important?

4. Assume that you are a staff researcher for a manufacturer of three nationally branded laundry detergents. The research and development department has formulated a new type of detergent that the company has decided to introduce under a new brand name. The product manager for the laundry detergent line has expressed concern that the new brand, unless it is carefully positioned, may cannibalize sales of the firm's current brands. You have been assigned to provide research-based information that will assist management in properly positioning the new brand in order to minimize the possibility of cannibalization. What method of analysis should you use and why? Given your choice of method, what are some fundamental decisions that you must make?

5. Questionnaire design is, at best, guided by only generalized rules and procedures. As a result, two researchers with the same objective may design very different questionnaires. With this in mind, critically review the CARA questionnaire presented in the Part Four Research Project, on the following pages. What are its good points? What features would you change? Provide specific examples and justify them if you feel an alternative technique would provide more useful information.

Suggested Additional Readings

For a general discussion of how to ask questions in attitude surveys, see Howard Schuman and Stanley Presser, *Questions and Answers in Attitude Surveys* (Orlando, Fla.: Academic Press, 1981).

For discussion of a general procedure that can be followed to develop attitude scales having desirable qualities, see Gilbert A. Churchill, Jr., "A Paradigm for Developing Better Measures of Marketing Constructs," *Journal of Marketing Research* 16 (February 1979), pp. 64–73.

For discussion of the various alternatives for perceptual mapping, see Glen L. Urban and John R. Hauser, *Design and Marketing of New Products,* 2nd ed. (Englewood Cliffs, N.J.: Prentice-Hall, 1993).

For discussion of the various issues surrounding conjoint analysis, see J. Douglas Carroll and Paul E. Green, "Psychometric Methods in Marketing Research: Part I, Conjoint Analysis," *Journal of Marketing Research* 32 (November 1995), pp. 385–391.

Paul E. Green and V. Srinivasan, "Conjoint Analysis in Marketing: New Developments with Implications for Research and Practice," *Journal of Marketing* 54 (October 1990), pp. 3–19.

The fourth stage in the research process is to design the data-collection form. As we learned from the chapters in this part, designing a questionnaire is still an art, not a science. Nonetheless, as we saw in Chapter 12, there is a pattern of steps that beginning researchers often find useful in developing questionnaires. The method outlined begins with specifying what information will be sought, and it ends with pretesting the questionnaire and revising it if necessary. As seen, however, only rarely will actual questionnaire development be so orderly. More often, researchers will find themselves circling back to revise an earlier part of the questionnaire after subsequent development has proven it to be faulty in some respect.

We also learned in these chapters that the typical questionnaire contains two types of information: basic and classification. Basic information refers to the subject of the study, while classification information refers to the data collected about respondents, such as demographic and socioeconomic characteristics, that help in understanding the results. As we saw, the proper questionnaire sequence is to secure basic information first and classification information last, since without the basic information, there is no study.

Researchers for CARA decided to use a self-report attitude scale to measure local businesspeople's feelings toward various advertising media and their sales representatives. In the chosen format, respondents were asked to indicate the extent to which they agreed or disagreed with statements about sales representatives and advertising media by checking one of the blanks ranging from strong agreement to strong disagreement. This format allowed the researchers two advantages: they could measure a respondent's intensity of feeling, and responses could be easily scored.

In the CARA study, the degrees of agreement were assigned the values of 5, 4, 3, 2, and 1, with "strongly agree" representing the value of 5 and "strongly disagree" representing the value of 1. A total attitude score for each respondent could thereby be calculated by summing the ratings of the individual items.

Respondents were asked to rate the importance of the attributes and characteristics used to describe sales representatives and advertising media by checking the three most important items in each category. Researchers thought this was important because an individual may strongly agree or disagree with an item but may not value that characteristic or attribute.

Each of the three categories of sales representatives contained 12 descriptive attributes. The attributes were ordered randomly, and the identical order was then used in each category. By using identical items in identical order, researchers could compare total attitude scores between the sales representative categories. If different items, or a different ordering of items, within each category had been used, variation in the testing instrument might have been responsible for differences in resulting scores.

Respondents were also asked to indicate which 3 of the 12 attributes they felt were the most important. These attributes were listed in the same order as the items in the sales representatives' scales.

The advertising media of television, radio, and newspaper were also described by 12 characteristics. These characteristics were randomly ordered, and each category used the identical order of items for the reason just cited. The 12 attributes were also listed in an importance scale in the same order as the items in the media categories, and respondents were asked to select the 3 attributes they believed to be most important.

Questions regarding the sales representatives were asked first so as to generate interest in the questionnaire. This section was followed by questions about attitudes toward the various media. Finally, researchers added a section requesting classification information. This section was last because, while important, it was the least critical to the study.

Researchers chose the 12 specific attributes used to describe the sales representatives and the advertising media based on their review of the literature, discussions with CARA members, and experience surveys with local retailers.

CARA Questionnaire

Section 1

Please indicate your opinion as to the extent to which you agree or disagree with the following statements for your television, radio, and newspaper sales representatives by placing an "X" in the appropriate blank. If you have more than one sales representative in any of these media, your opinions should include your general impressions of the sales representatives calling on you. If you have never been in contact with a sales representative in one or more of these media, please omit that section (or those sections) and proceed to the next. Don't worry over individual responses. It is your first impression on each item that is important.

TELEVISION SALES REPRESENTATIVE

The television sales representatives calling on me are	Strongly Agree	Agree	Neither Agree nor Disagree	Disagree	Strongly Disagree
1. Creative	___	___	___	___	___
2. Reliable	___	___	___	___	___
3. Sincere	___	___	___	___	___
4. Results oriented	___	___	___	___	___
5. Knowledgeable about my business	___	___	___	___	___
6. Cooperative	___	___	___	___	___
7. Available when needed	___	___	___	___	___
8. Hardworking	___	___	___	___	___
9. Concerned about my particular advertising needs	___	___	___	___	___
10. Able to get my ads placed quickly	___	___	___	___	___
11. Aware of who my customers are	___	___	___	___	___
12. Concerned about follow-through after the service	___	___	___	___	___

RADIO SALES REPRESENTATIVE

The radio sales representatives calling on me are	Strongly Agree	Agree	Neither Agree nor Disagree	Disagree	Strongly Disagree
1. Creative	___	___	___	___	___
2. Reliable	___	___	___	___	___
3. Sincere	___	___	___	___	___
4. Results oriented	___	___	___	___	___
5. Knowledgeable about my business	___	___	___	___	___
6. Cooperative	___	___	___	___	___
7. Available when needed	___	___	___	___	___
8. Hardworking	___	___	___	___	___
9. Concerned about my particular advertising needs	___	___	___	___	___
10. Able to get my ads placed quickly	___	___	___	___	___
11. Aware of who my customers are	___	___	___	___	___
12. Concerned about follow-through after the service	___	___	___	___	___

NEWSPAPER SALES REPRESENTATIVE

The newspaper sales representatives calling on me are	Strongly Agree	Agree	Neither Agree nor Disagree	Disagree	Strongly Disagree
1. Creative	___	___	___	___	___
2. Reliable	___	___	___	___	___
3. Sincere	___	___	___	___	___
4. Results oriented	___	___	___	___	___
5. Knowledgeable about my business	___	___	___	___	___
6. Cooperative	___	___	___	___	___
7. Available when needed	___	___	___	___	___
8. Hardworking	___	___	___	___	___
9. Concerned about my particular advertising needs	___	___	___	___	___
10. Able to get my ads placed quickly	___	___	___	___	___
11. Aware of who my customers are	___	___	___	___	___
12. Concerned about follow-through after the service	___	___	___	___	___

part 4 research project

Please indicate what you believe are the three most important characteristics of a sales representative by placing an "X" in the appropriate blank. For example, if you feel Items 4, 8, and 10 are the most important characteristics, you would place an "X" in the blank next to each of these items.

The three most important characteristics of a media sales representative are

1. Creativity _____
2. Reliability _____
3. Sincerity _____
4. An orientation toward results _____
5. A knowledge about my business _____
6. Cooperation _____
7. Availability when needed _____
8. A willingness to work hard _____
9. A concern about my particular advertising needs _____
10. The ability to quickly place my ads _____
11. Awareness of who my customers are _____
12. Concern about follow-through after the service _____

Section 2

Please indicate your opinion as to the extent to which you agree or disagree with the following statements about television, radio, and newspaper advertising, regardless of whether you use that form of advertising or not. Place an "X" in the appropriate blank. Again, don't worry about individual responses, since it is your first impression on each item that is important.

Television Advertising	Strongly Agree	Agree	Neither Agree nor Disagree	Disagree	Strongly Disagree
1. People pay attention to the ads.	_____	_____	_____	_____	_____
2. The ads reach my target market.	_____	_____	_____	_____	_____
3. The ads do not cost too much.	_____	_____	_____	_____	_____
4. The ads improve my sales volume.	_____	_____	_____	_____	_____
5. The ads are creative.	_____	_____	_____	_____	_____
6. The ads do not have to be repeated frequently to be effective.	_____	_____	_____	_____	_____
7. The ads reach a large number of people.	_____	_____	_____	_____	_____
8. The ads build up recognition of my business.	_____	_____	_____	_____	_____
9. There is evidence that ads reach a known market.	_____	_____	_____	_____	_____
10. Buying the ads is not a difficult process.	_____	_____	_____	_____	_____
11. It is easy to monitor when the ads are being run.	_____	_____	_____	_____	_____
12. The quality of the ads is high (good).	_____	_____	_____	_____	_____

Radio Advertising	Strongly Agree	Agree	Neither Agree nor Disagree	Disagree	Strongly Disagree
1. People pay attention to the ads.	_____	_____	_____	_____	_____
2. The ads reach my target market.	_____	_____	_____	_____	_____
3. The ads do not cost too much.	_____	_____	_____	_____	_____
4. The ads improve my sales volume.	_____	_____	_____	_____	_____
5. The ads are creative.	_____	_____	_____	_____	_____
6. The ads do not have to be repeated frequently to be effective.	_____	_____	_____	_____	_____
7. The ads reach a large number of people.	_____	_____	_____	_____	_____
8. The ads build up recognition of my business.	_____	_____	_____	_____	_____
9. There is evidence that ads reach a known market.	_____	_____	_____	_____	_____
10. Buying the ads is not a difficult process.	_____	_____	_____	_____	_____
11. It is easy to monitor when the ads are being run.	_____	_____	_____	_____	_____
12. The quality of the ads is high (good).	_____	_____	_____	_____	_____

PART 4:
Data Collection Forms

Newspaper Advertising	Strongly Agree	Agree	Neither Agree nor Disagree	Disagree	Strongly Disagree
1. People pay attention to the ads.	_____	_____	_____	_____	_____
2. The ads reach my target market.	_____	_____	_____	_____	_____
3. The ads do not cost too much.	_____	_____	_____	_____	_____
4. The ads improve my sales volume.	_____	_____	_____	_____	_____
5. The ads are creative.	_____	_____	_____	_____	_____
6. The ads do not have to be repeated frequently to be effective.	_____	_____	_____	_____	_____
7. The ads reach a large number of people.	_____	_____	_____	_____	_____
8. The ads build up recognition of my business.	_____	_____	_____	_____	_____
9. There is evidence that ads reach a known market.	_____	_____	_____	_____	_____
10. Buying the ads is not a difficult process.	_____	_____	_____	_____	_____
11. It is easy to monitor when the ads are being run.	_____	_____	_____	_____	_____
12. The quality of the ads is high (good).	_____	_____	_____	_____	_____

Please indicate what you believe are the three most important attributes of advertising by placing an "X" in the appropriate blank. For example, if you feel Items 4, 8, and 10 are the most important attributes, you would place an "X" in the blank next to each of these items.

The three most important attributes of advertising are that

1. People pay attention to the ads. _____
2. The ads reach my target market. _____
3. The ads do not cost too much. _____
4. The ads improve my sales volume. _____
5. The ads are creative. _____
6. The ads do not have to be repeated frequently to be effective. _____
7. The ads reach a large number of people. _____
8. The ads build up recognition of my business. _____
9. There is evidence that ads reach a known market. _____
10. Buying the ads is not a difficult process. _____
11. It is easy to monitor when the ads are being run. _____
12. The quality of the ads is high (good). _____

Section 3: Classification Data

1. **What types of advertising have you used over the last 12 months?**

Outdoor	_____
Radio	_____
Television	_____
Newspaper	_____
Magazine	_____
Yellow Pages	_____
Direct Mail	_____
Shoppers	_____
Other	_____

2. **Approximately what proportion of your total yearly advertising budget is spent on each of the following types of advertising?**

Outdoor	_____
Radio	_____
Television	_____
Newspaper	_____
Magazine	_____
Yellow Pages	_____
Direct Mail	_____
Shoppers	_____
Other	_____
Total =	100%

3. **How much do you spend annually on advertising?**

   0–$9,999 _____

   $10,000–$24,999 _____

   $25,000–$49,999 _____

   $50,000 and over _____

4. **Which category best descibes your position?**

   Manager _____

   Owner/Manager _____

   Secretary _____

   Clerk _____

   Other _____

5. **Do you make decisions regarding advertising expenditures?**

   Yes _____

   No _____

6. **Do you use an advertising agency?**

   Yes _____

   No _____

Case • 4.1

Rumstad Decorating Centers (B)

Rumstad Decorating Centers was an old-line Rockford, Illinois, business. The company was originally founded as a small paint and wallpaper supply store in 1929 by Joseph Rumstad, who managed the store until his retirement in 1970, at which time Jack Rumstad, his son, took over. In 1974, the original downtown store was closed and a new outlet was opened on the city's rapidly expanding west side. In 1999, a second store was opened on the east side of the city, and the name of the business was changed to Rumstad Decorating Centers.

Jack Rumstad's review of 2002 operations proved disconcerting. Both stores had suffered losses for the year [see Case 2.1, Rumstad Decorating Centers (A)]. The picture was far more dismal at the west side store. Losses at the east side store were 80 percent less than the previous year's, which was partially due to some major organizational changes. Further, the east side store had experienced a 25 percent increase in net sales and a 25 percent increase in gross profits over 2001. The west side store, in contrast, had shown a 21 percent decrease in net sales and a 31 percent decrease in gross profit.

Some preliminary research by Rumstad suggested that the problem at the west side store might be traced to the store's location or its advertising. Was the location perceived as convenient? Were potential customers aware of Rumstad Decorating Centers, the products they carried, and where they were located? Did people have favorable impressions of Rumstad? How did attitudes toward Rumstad compare with those toward Rumstad's major competitors?

Rumstad realized that he did not have the expertise to answer these questions. Consequently, he called in Sandra Parrett, who owned and managed her own marketing research service in the Rockford area. Parrett handled all liaison work with the client and assisted in the research design. In addition to Parrett, Lisa Parrett, her daughter, supervised the field staff of four, analyzed data, and prepared research reports. Although the company was small, it had an excellent reputation within the business community.

Research Design

Rumstad agreed with Sandra Parrett's suggestion that the best way to investigate Rumstad's concerns would be to use a structured, somewhat disguised questionnaire (Exhibit 1). The sponsor of the research was to be hidden from the respondents to prevent them from answering "correctly" instead of honestly, so questions about two of Rumstad's main competitors, the Nina Emerson Decorating Center and the Wallpaper Shop, were introduced. Both of these stores offered products and services similar to those carried by Rumstad, and they were located in the same area as Rumstad's west side store. The study was to be confined to the west side store because of cost; loss of profits for the last several years had severely constrained Rumstad's ability to engage in research of this sort. However, the west side store was so critical to the very survival of Rumstad Decorating Centers that Rumstad was willing to commit funds to this investigation, although he repeatedly stressed to Parrett the need to keep the cost as low as possible.

Even though the Emerson Decorating Center and the Wallpaper Shop were similar to Rumstad, there were differences in their marketing strategies. Both stores seemed to advertise more than Rumstad, for example, although the exact amounts of their advertising budgets were not available. Emerson advertised in the *Shopper's World* (a weekly paper devoted exclusively to advertising that is distributed free), ran ads four times a year in the *Rockford Morning Star*, and did a small amount of radio and outdoor advertising. The Wallpaper Shop also advertised regularly in the *Shopper's World*, but ran small ads daily in the *Morning Star* and had daily radio commercials as well. Rumstad had formerly advertised in the *Morning Star* but now relied exclusively on the *Shopper's World*.

Sample

Because of the financial constraints imposed on the study by Jack Rumstad, it was decided to limit the study to households within a two-mile radius of Rumstad, Emerson, and the Wallpaper Shop. Aldermanic districts within the two-mile radius were identified; there were four in all, and the wards within each district were listed. Two of the 12 wards were then excluded because they were outside the specified area. Blocks within each of the 10 remaining wards were enumerated, and 5 blocks were randomly selected from each ward. An initial starting point for each block was determined, and the questionnaires were then administered by the Parrett field staff at every sixth house on the block. All interviews were conducted on Saturday and Sunday. If there was no one at home or if the respondent refused to cooperate, the next house on the block was substituted; there was no one at home at 39 households, and 18 others refused to participate. The field work was completed within one weekend and produced a total sample of 123 responses.

Exhibit 1

Sample Questionnaire—Rumstad Decorating Centers

Section I

For Questions 1–8, please indicate your opinion about the importance of the following factors in choosing a decorating center. Place an X in the appropriate blank.

	Not Important	Slightly Important	Fairly Important	Very Important
1. Saw or heard an advertisement	_____	_____	_____	_____
2. Special sale	_____	_____	_____	_____
3. Convenient location	_____	_____	_____	_____
4. Convenient hours	_____	_____	_____	_____
5. Knowledgeable sales personnel	_____	_____	_____	_____
6. Good quality products	_____	_____	_____	_____
7. Additional services (e.g., matching paints, decorator services, etc.)	_____	_____	_____	_____
8. Reasonable prices in relation to quality	_____	_____	_____	_____

Below is a list of abbreviations for the three west side stores that will be referred to throughout the questionnaire:

Emerson Decorating Center—"Emerson"
Rumstad Decorating Center—"Rumstad"
Wallpaper Shop—"Wallpaper Shop"

Please indicate your response with an X in the appropriate blank.

9. Do you know where any of the following west side stores are located? (i.e., could you find any of these stores without referring to another source?)

	Yes	No
Emerson	____	____
Rumstad	____	____
Wallpaper Shop	____	____

10. When was the last time you heard or saw any advertisements for the following stores?

	Never	Within the Last Month	1–6 Months	More than 6 Months
Emerson	____	____	____	____
Rumstad	____	____	____	____
Wallpaper Shop	____	____	____	____

11. Please indicate the source(s) of any advertisements you have seen or heard.

	Have Not Seen/Heard	*Shopper's World*	*Rockford Morning Star*	Radio	TV	Other	Don't Recall
Emerson	____	____	____	____	____	____	____
Rumstad	____	____	____	____	____	____	____
Wallpaper Shop	____	____	____	____	____	____	____

12. Do you know which of the following items are available in these stores? If so, check the item(s) that apply.

	Don't Know	Paint	Paneling	Carpeting	Draperies	Other
Emerson	____	____	____	____	____	____
Rumstad	____	____	____	____	____	____
Wallpaper Shop	____	____	____	____	____	____

Exhibit 1

Sample Questionnaire—Rumstad Decorating Centers (*continued*)

13. Which name brands of paint, if any, do you associate with the following stores?

	Benjamin Moore	Dutch Boy	Glidden	Pittsburgh	Do Not Associate Any Listed
Emerson	_____	_____	_____	_____	_____
Rumstad	_____	_____	_____	_____	_____
Wallpaper Shop	_____	_____	_____	_____	_____

14. Have you ever visited any of these west side stores?

	Never	Within Last Year	1–5 Yrs. Ago	More than 5 Yrs. Ago
Emerson	_____	_____	_____	_____
Rumstad	_____	_____	_____	_____
Wallpaper Shop	_____	_____	_____	_____

Section II

If you have visited or have knowledge of one or more of the stores listed below, please indicate the extent to which you agree or disagree with the following statements for each store(s). For instance, if you have knowledge of only one store, please answer each question for that particular store. If you have not visited or have no knowledge of any of these stores, omit this section and proceed to Section III.

	Strongly Agree	Agree	Neither Agree nor Disagree	Strongly Disagree	Disagree
15. The location of the store is convenient.					
Emerson	_____	_____	_____	_____	_____
Rumstad	_____	_____	_____	_____	_____
Wallpaper Store	_____	_____	_____	_____	_____
16. The sales personnel are knowledgeable.					
Emerson	_____	_____	_____	_____	_____
Rumstad	_____	_____	_____	_____	_____
Wallpaper Store	_____	_____	_____	_____	_____
17. The store lacks additional services (e.g., matching paint, decorator services, etc.).					
Emerson	_____	_____	_____	_____	_____
Rumstad	_____	_____	_____	_____	_____
Wallpaper Store	_____	_____	_____	_____	_____
18. The store carries good-quality products.					
Emerson	_____	_____	_____	_____	_____
Rumstad	_____	_____	_____	_____	_____
Wallpaper Store	_____	_____	_____	_____	_____
19. The prices are reasonable in relation to the quality of the products.					
Emerson	_____	_____	_____	_____	_____
Rumstad	_____	_____	_____	_____	_____
Wallpaper Store	_____	_____	_____	_____	_____
20. The store hours are inconvenient.					
Emerson	_____	_____	_____	_____	_____
Rumstad	_____	_____	_____	_____	_____
Wallpaper Store	_____	_____	_____	_____	_____

continued

Exhibit 1

Sample Questionnaire—Rumstad Decorating Centers (*continued*)

Section III

1. Your sex: _____ Male   _____ Female

2. Your age: _____ Under 25   _____ 25–29 years   _____ 30–39 years
            _____ 40–54 years   _____ 55 or over

3. How long have you lived in Rockford?
   _____ Less than 1 year   _____ 1–3 years   _____ 4 or more years

4. Do you: _____ Own a home or condominium _____ Rent a house
           _____ Rent an apartment   _____ Other

5. When was the last time you painted or remodeled your residence?
   _____ Never   _____ Within past year   _____ 1–5 years ago   _____ More than 5 years ago

6. Approximately how many times have you received the weekly *Shopper's World* in the past 3 months?
   _____ Never   _____ 1–5 times   _____ 6–12 times

7. Do you read or page through the *Shopper's World*?
   _____ Do not receive it   _____ Never   _____ Less than ½ the time
   _____ About ½ the time   _____ More than ½ the time

Questions

1. Evaluate the questionnaire. Do you think the questionnaire adequately addresses the concerns raised by Rumstad?
2. How would you suggest the data collected be analyzed to best solve Rumstad's problem?
3. Do you think personal administration of the questionnaires was called for in this study, or would you suggest an alternative scheme? Why or why not?

Case • 4.2

School of Business (A)[1]

The School of Business, one unit in a public university enrolling over 40,000 students, has approximately 2,100 students in its bachelor's, master's, and doctorate programs emphasizing such areas of business as accounting, finance, information and operations management, marketing, management, and others. Because the School of Business must serve a diverse student population on limited resources, it feels it is important to accurately measure students' satisfaction with the school's programs and services.

Accurate measurement of student satisfaction will enable the school to target improvement efforts to those areas of greatest concern to students, whether that be by major, support services, or some other aspect of their educational experience. The school feels that improving its service to its customers (students) will result in more satisfied alumni, better community relations, additional applicants, and increased corporate involvement. Because graduate and undergraduate students are believed to have different expectations and needs, the school plans to investigate the satisfaction of these two groups separately.

In a previous survey of graduating seniors using open-ended questions, three primary areas of concern were identified: the faculty, classes/curriculum, and resources. Resources consisted of five specific areas: Undergraduate Advising Services, the Learning Center, Computer Facilities, the Library, and the Career Services Office. The research team for this project developed five-point Likert scale questions to measure students' satisfaction in each of these areas. In addition, demographic questions were included to determine whether satisfaction with the school was a function of a student's grade point average, major, job status upon graduation, or gender. Previous surveys used by the School of Business and other published satisfaction scales provided examples of questions and question formats. Exhibit 1 shows the questionnaire that was used.

Although the survey contained primarily Likert-scale questions, a few open-ended questions were also asked. Specifically, respondents were asked to list the Business School's strengths and weaknesses as well as their reasons for not using the various resource areas. The responses obtained to the question seeking the school's strengths and weaknesses were classified into four major subgroups: classes, reputation, resources, and professors. A sample of the actual verbatims are provided in Exhibit 2.

Questions

1. Considering customer satisfaction as it applies to a university setting, what are some other areas in addition to those identified for the project that may contribute to students' satisfaction/dissatisfaction with their education experience?
2. Does the current questionnaire provide information on students' overall satisfaction with their undergraduate degree program? Explain. What revisions are necessary to this questionnaire to obtain an overall satisfaction rating?
3. Can the School of Business use the results of this study to target the most important areas for improvement? Explain. Identify changes to the questionnaire that would allow the school to target areas based on importance.
4. What are the advantages and disadvantages of using open-ended questions to identify the school's strengths and weaknesses? Taking the responses in Exhibit 2, what system would you use for coding these responses?

[1]The contributions of Sara Pitterle to the development of this case are gratefully acknowledged.

Survey of Graduating Business Students

In your opinion, what are the greatest strengths and weaknesses of the Business School?

Strengths

_____
_____
_____
_____

Weaknesses

_____
_____
_____
_____

CLASSES/CURRICULUM

Please indicate the extent to which you agree with the following statements.

	Strongly Agree	Agree	Neither Agree/Disagree	Disagree	Strongly Disagree
I was satisfied with the quality of classes I took within my major.	(1) ___	(2) ___	(3) ___	(4) ___	(5) ___
I was able to take enough electives within my major.	(1) ___	(2) ___	(3) ___	(4) ___	(5) ___
"Lecture-Driven" vs. "Project" or "Group" class formats are most useful for learning.	(1) ___	(2) ___	(3) ___	(4) ___	(5) ___
The business school taught too much theory and not enough about real-life applications.	(1) ___	(2) ___	(3) ___	(4) ___	(5) ___
Creative problem solving was encouraged in my classes.	(1) ___	(2) ___	(3) ___	(4) ___	(5) ___
My classes were too large.	(1) ___	(2) ___	(3) ___	(4) ___	(5) ___
I was challenged by my coursework.	(1) ___	(2) ___	(3) ___	(4) ___	(5) ___
There were not enough group projects in my classes.	(1) ___	(2) ___	(3) ___	(4) ___	(5) ___
More night courses should be offered.	(1) ___	(2) ___	(3) ___	(4) ___	(5) ___
Overall, the material presented in my classes was current.	(1) ___	(2) ___	(3) ___	(4) ___	(5) ___

FACULTY

	Strongly Agree	Agree	Neither Agree/Disagree	Disagree	Strongly Disagree
My professors are concerned about my future success.	(1) ___	(2) ___	(3) ___	(4) ___	(5) ___
Overall, the Business School professors are good teachers.	(1) ___	(2) ___	(3) ___	(4) ___	(5) ___
The Business School places too much emphasis on research and not enough on teaching.	(1) ___	(2) ___	(3) ___	(4) ___	(5) ___
Overall, my professors were accessible outside of class.	(1) ___	(2) ___	(3) ___	(4) ___	(5) ___
The Business School takes my comments on professor evaluation forms seriously.	(1) ___	(2) ___	(3) ___	(4) ___	(5) ___
Overall, my professors provided adequate office hours during the semester.	(1) ___	(2) ___	(3) ___	(4) ___	(5) ___

Exhibit 1

Survey of Graduating Business Students (*continued*)

Overall, my professors encouraged students to raise relevant questions during class.

(1) ____   (2) ____   (3) ____   (4) ____   (5) ____

My professors tested memorization skills on exams more than my ability to apply concepts.

(1) ____   (2) ____   (3) ____   (4) ____   (5) ____

Overall, the Business School professors interacted well with students.

(1) ____   (2) ____   (3) ____   (4) ____   (5) ____

My professors showed creativity in their teaching methods.

(1) ____   (2) ____   (3) ____   (4) ____   (5) ____

My professors are at the leading edge of knowledge in their fields.

(1) ____   (2) ____   (3) ____   (4) ____   (5) ____

I approve of TA's teaching foundation courses.

(1) ____   (2) ____   (3) ____   (4) ____   (5) ____

My professors were stimulating.

(1) ____   (2) ____   (3) ____   (4) ____   (5) ____

RESOURCES
Advising

Did you ever use the undergraduate advising office?

(1) ____ Yes   (2) ____ No

If not, why not?

_____

_____

_____

_____

If you answered yes to the question above, please complete the remainder of the questions regarding Advising. If you answered no, please proceed to the following section—Learning Center.

Strongly Agree	Agree	Neither Agree/Disagree	Disagree	Strongly Disagree

The undergraduate advising office played a big role in helping me plan my business curriculum.

(1) ____   (2) ____   (3) ____   (4) ____   (5) ____

The undergraduate advising office should have more advisors.

(1) ____   (2) ____   (3) ____   (4) ____   (5) ____

The advisor(s) in the undergraduate advising office was (were) helpful.

(1) ____   (2) ____   (3) ____   (4) ____   (5) ____

The staff in the advising office was helpful.

(1) ____   (2) ____   (3) ____   (4) ____   (5) ____

I felt like I was bothering the advisor(s) in the undergraduate advising office if I asked him/her a question.

(1) ____   (2) ____   (3) ____   (4) ____   (5) ____

The advisor(s) in the undergraduate advising office was (were) concerned about my needs.

(1) ____   (2) ____   (3) ____   (4) ____   (5) ____

If there were more undergraduate advisors, I would have utilized the advising services more often.

(1) ____   (2) ____   (3) ____   (4) ____   (5) ____

Advice offered by the advising office was not helpful to me.

(1) ____   (2) ____   (3) ____   (4) ____   (5) ____

continued

Exhibit 1

Survey of Graduating Business Students (*continued*)

Learning Center

Did you ever use The Learning Center?

     (1) _____ Yes   (2) _____ No

If not, why not?

_____
_____
_____
_____

If you answered yes to the question above, please complete the remainder of the questions regarding The Learning Center. If you answered no, please proceed to the following section—Career-Services Facilities/Staff.

		Strongly Agree	Agree	Neither Agree/Disagree	Disagree	Strongly Disagree

The Learning Center was useful to me.

    (1) _____   (2) _____   (3) _____   (4) _____   (5) _____

The staff at the Learning Center are helpful.

    (1) _____   (2) _____   (3) _____   (4) _____   (5) _____

The Learning Center needs to extend its hours.

    (1) _____   (2) _____   (3) _____   (4) _____   (5) _____

Career-Services Facilities/Staff

Did you ever use the Career-Services office as a resource in your search for full- or part-time employment?

     (1) _____ Yes   (2) _____ No

If not, why not?

_____
_____
_____
_____

If you answered yes to the question above, please complete the remainder of the questions regarding Career-Services Facilities/Staff. If you answered no, please proceed to the following section—Computer Facilities/Staff.

		Strongly Agree	Agree	Neither Agree/Disagree	Disagree	Strongly Disagree

Overall, the Career-Services office has been a valuable resource in my job search.

    (1) _____   (2) _____   (3) _____   (4) _____   (5) _____

The staff in the Career-Services office are helpful.

    (1) _____   (2) _____   (3) _____   (4) _____   (5) _____

The Career-Services office is/was my main resource used in my search for my job.

    (1) _____   (2) _____   (3) _____   (4) _____   (5) _____

In my opinion, the Career-Services office is understaffed.

    (1) _____   (2) _____   (3) _____   (4) _____   (5) _____

I was pleased with the number of companies interviewing at the Career-Services office within my major.

    (1) _____   (2) _____   (3) _____   (4) _____   (5) _____

The Career-Services office is successful at attracting desirable employers to interview on campus.

    (1) _____   (2) _____   (3) _____   (4) _____   (5) _____

The sign-up process for interviews at the Career-Services office is fair.

    (1) _____   (2) _____   (3) _____   (4) _____   (5) _____

The Career-Services office provides enough information on how to use the Resume Expert software.

    (1) _____   (2) _____   (3) _____   (4) _____   (5) _____

The Career-Services office offers adequate interview training.

    (1) _____   (2) _____   (3) _____   (4) _____   (5) _____

Exhibit 1

Survey of Graduating Business Students (*continued*)

Computer Facilities/Staff

Did you ever use the Business School's computer facilities?

(1) _____ Yes   (2) _____ No

If not, why not?

_____
_____
_____
_____

If you answered yes to the question above, please complete the remainder of the questions regarding Computer Facilities/Staff. If you answered no, please proceed to the following section—Library Facilities/Staff.

	Strongly Agree	Agree	Neither Agree/Disagree	Disagree	Strongly Disagree
The computer room needs to extend its weekend hours.	(1) ____	(2) ____	(3) ____	(4) ____	(5) ____
The computer room needs to extend its night hours.	(1) ____	(2) ____	(3) ____	(4) ____	(5) ____
More computers are needed in the computer room.	(1) ____	(2) ____	(3) ____	(4) ____	(5) ____
More printers are needed in the computer facilities.	(1) ____	(2) ____	(3) ____	(4) ____	(5) ____
The computer-room staff is helpful.	(1) ____	(2) ____	(3) ____	(4) ____	(5) ____
A computer was available when I needed to use one.	(1) ____	(2) ____	(3) ____	(4) ____	(5) ____

Library Facilities/Staff

Did you use the Business School's library facilities?

(1) _____ Yes   (2) _____ No

If not, why not?

_____
_____
_____
_____

If you answered yes to the question above, please complete the remainder of the questions regarding Library Facilities/Staff. If you answered no, please proceed to the following section—Student Organizations.

	Strongly Agree	Agree	Neither Agree/Disagree	Disagree	Strongly Disagree
The Library staff is helpful.	(1) ____	(2) ____	(3) ____	(4) ____	(5) ____
The Library has adequate study space.	(1) ____	(2) ____	(3) ____	(4) ____	(5) ____

continued

Exhibit 1

Survey of Graduating Business Students (*continued*)

Student Organizations

Were you a member of any Business School student organizations?

(1) _____ Yes   (2) _____ No

If not, why not?

_____
_____
_____
_____

If you answered yes to the question above, please complete the remainder of the questions regarding Student Organizations. If you answered no, please proceed to the following section—GENERAL.

How many organizations were you a member of?

(1) _____ 1
(2) _____ 2
(3) _____ 3
(4) _____ 4

Did you hold an office?   (1) _____ Yes   (2) _____ No

Do you believe the faculty and staff were supportive of the student organizations?

(1) _____ Yes   (2) _____ No   (3) _____ Don't know

What were your reasons for joining?

_____
_____
_____
_____

GENERAL

	Strongly Agree	Agree	Neither Agree/Disagree	Disagree	Strongly Disagree
My Business School education has given me a sense of accomplishment.	(1) ____	(2) ____	(3) ____	(4) ____	(5) ____
The Business School is well respected nationally.	(1) ____	(2) ____	(3) ____	(4) ____	(5) ____
My undergraduate degree has prepared me well for a successful career in business.	(1) ____	(2) ____	(3) ____	(4) ____	(5) ____
The caliber of my classmates enhanced my learning.	(1) ____	(2) ____	(3) ____	(4) ____	(5) ____
The Business School should require more computer courses.	(1) ____	(2) ____	(3) ____	(4) ____	(5) ____
The copying facilities at the Business School are inadequate.	(1) ____	(2) ____	(3) ____	(4) ____	(5) ____
My undergraduate experience was disappointing.	(1) ____	(2) ____	(3) ____	(4) ____	(5) ____
The Business School placed too much emphasis on a high GPA and not enough on learning.	(1) ____	(2) ____	(3) ____	(4) ____	(5) ____
I felt like a number here at the Business School.	(1) ____	(2) ____	(3) ____	(4) ____	(5) ____
The Business School should have a mandatory class on ethics for undergraduates.	(1) ____	(2) ____	(3) ____	(4) ____	(5) ____

Exhibit 1

Survey of Graduating Business Students (*continued*)

Please indicate the extent to which you agree that each of the following factors POSITIVELY CONTRIBUTED to the quality of your overall undergraduate business education:

	Strongly Agree	Agree	Neither Agree/Disagree	Disagree	Strongly Disagree
Class size in major classes:	(1) ____	(2) ____	(3) ____	(4) ____	(5) ____
Class size in required courses:	(1) ____	(2) ____	(3) ____	(4) ____	(5) ____
Group projects:	(1) ____	(2) ____	(3) ____	(4) ____	(5) ____
Case studies:	(1) ____	(?) ____	(3) ____	(4) ____	(5) ____
Multiple-choice exams:	(1) ____	(2) ____	(3) ____	(4) ____	(5) ____
Use of creative thought:	(1) ____	(2) ____	(3) ____	(4) ____	(5) ____
Guest lecturers:	(1) ____	(2) ____	(3) ____	(4) ____	(5) ____
Required classes:	(1) ____	(2) ____	(3) ____	(4) ____	(5) ____
Number of electives you can take:	(1) ____	(2) ____	(3) ____	(4) ____	(5) ____
Number of required computer courses:	(1) ____	(2) ____	(3) ____	(4) ____	(5) ____

Please indicate the extent to which you agree that each of the following core classes POSITIVELY CONTRIBUTED to the quality of your overall undergraduate business education:

Comp Sci	(1) ____	(2) ____	(3) ____	(4) ____	(5) ____
Managerial Acctg 302	(1) ____	(2) ____	(3) ____	(4) ____	(5) ____
Financial Acctg 200	(1) ____	(2) ____	(3) ____	(4) ____	(5) ____
Communications 320	(1) ____	(2) ____	(3) ____	(4) ____	(5) ____
Business Law 330	(1) ____	(2) ____	(3) ____	(4) ____	(5) ____
Corporate Finance 510	(1) ____	(2) ____	(3) ____	(4) ____	(5) ____
Marketing 520	(1) ____	(2) ____	(3) ____	(4) ____	(5) ____
Org. Behavior 530	(1) ____	(2) ____	(3) ____	(4) ____	(5) ____
Business Statistics 570	(1) ____	(2) ____	(3) ____	(4) ____	(5) ____
Mgt of Serv-Mfg Op 574	(1) ____	(2) ____	(3) ____	(4) ____	(5) ____
OVERALL	(1) ____	(2) ____	(3) ____	(4) ____	(5) ____

GENERAL INFORMATION

Please mark the number corresponding to your gender:

(1) ____ Female   (2) ____ Male

Are you a state resident?

(1) ____ Yes   (2) ____ No

Please mark the number(s) corresponding to your major(s).

(1) ____ Accounting   (7) ____ Marketing
(2) ____ Actuarial Science   (8) ____ Quantitative Analysis
(3) ____ Diversified   (9) ____ Real Estate
(4) ____ Finance   (10) ____ Risk Management
(5) ____ Information Systems   (11) ____ Transportation and Public Utilities
(6) ____ Management and Human Resources

continued

Exhibit 1

Survey of Graduating Business Students (*continued*)

Please mark the number corresponding to your GPA.
    (1) ____3.5–4.0   (2) ____3.0–3.49   (3) ____2.5–2.99   (4) ____2.0–2.49

Please mark the number of years it will take you to graduate.
    (1) ____3½   (2) ____4   (3) ____4½   (4) ____5   (5) ____>5½

During the program (excluding summers), have you been employed?
    (1) ____Employed full time   (2) ____Employed part-time   (3) ____Not employed

What do you plan to do upon graduation?
    (1) ____full-time employment
    (2) ____part-time employment
    (3) ____graduate school
    (4) ____other, please specify

If you intend to work full time, please specify if you:
    (1) ____have already accepted a position
    (2) ____are still in the process of interviewing
    (3) ____other, please specify

THANK YOU FOR COMPLETING THE SURVEY OF GRADUATING BUSINESS STUDENTS

Exhibit 2

A Sample of the Survey Responses to Question 1 Regarding Strengths and Weaknesses

Strengths	Weaknesses
Breadth of courses and disciplines.	Not enough real-life applications
The increase in group projects was also helpful.	Core classes tedious.
Classes in your major are relatively small.	Too much emphasis on GPA.
Excellent faculty advising (not undergrad advising).	Lack of advisors.
Good Faculty. Excellent Profs	Lack of support facilities.
Has a good reputation.	Awful Undergraduate advising.
Required some thought-provoking classes (literature, philosophy).	Classes are too much on theory.
Free laser printing in the computer lab.	The computer classes are a waste of time.
The resources for information gathering are great.	Too many unnecessary core requirements that could be used for another class or elective.
The options of resources available are great.	Too many exams scheduled in the 6th and 12th weeks.
The competitiveness, quality of students.	Too many required group projects.
Nice that classes aren't greatly dependent on Fridays (open to work or volunteering).	Can't get classes when needed.
Clear curriculum of what classes are needed if in Pre-Business or Business—although there are a lot of them, the core classes allow you to touch all majors.	Too few resources for the number of students.
	Students not treated as individuals.
	Not enough computers.
A well-respected and less costly route to a business under-grad degree than other alternatives available.	Makes students take core classes in each function of business.
National Reputation.	Need more case studies and seminar type classes with fewer students.
A few good professors that make up for all the bad ones.	There is too much memorization and not enough practical application of knowledge.
Some of the professors are terrific and really care about the students.	Making appointments to see advisors.
	Professors expect too much.
	Computer courses are too technical.

Case • 4.3

Young Ideas Publishing Company (A)

How does a company go about marketing products to a specific niche of the teenage market? That is the question confronting Linda Halley, co-owner of Young Ideas Publishing Company. Halley is convinced that her unconventional novels for young people would be very attractive to at least a segment of the teenaged market. She is unsure, however, about how to reach this "nonconformist" segment of the market.

Background

Three years ago, Halley wrote her first novel, a youth-oriented book (ages 15–18) entitled *Illusions of Summer.* None of the major publishers would publish the book, however, primarily because it dealt with several controversial social and political concerns. Most publishers simply felt that such topics would not be of interest to enough high school teenagers to justify publication, although many agreed that the novel was of publication quality in other respects.

Frustrated in her efforts to publish her novel, Halley and a business partner, Teresa Martinez, decided to form their own publishing company and publish the book themselves. Both believed that teenagers would be interested in social and political topics and would buy the book. Thus, Young Ideas Publishing Company was born. Halley hoped that effective marketing of the book on a local basis by the company might encourage national distributors to alter their positions toward the novel.

When *Illusions of Summer* was released, it was very well received by several literary critics, winning promising reviews and awards. Despite its critical success, however, commercial acceptance has been much harder to find. During the first 24 months after publication, only about 1,500 copies of the book have been sold, mostly through local bookstores, mail orders, and the company's Web site. Most distributors were unwilling to handle the book because it was not from an established publisher. With few channels through which to market the product, it remains virtually unknown outside of a limited local market.

Even with this poor showing from a commercial standpoint, Halley continued to believe that so-called "nonconformist" teenagers would be willing to buy books of this nature. Accordingly, she wrote and published a second novel, *Ultimate Choices.* Once again, the novel dealt with several controversial issues for teens and social and political concerns; once again, the critics reacted favorably. Initial sales for *Ultimate Choices* have been better than they were for *Illusions of Summer;* currently (two months after publication), about 250 copies have been sold. By talking to clerks in local bookstores, Halley has learned that most of the books are being sold to teenagers.

Nature of the Problem

Although encouraged by the good reviews and increased sales of the second book, Halley and Martinez are concerned about the future of Young Ideas Publishing Company. The company has struggled to break even so far, and Martinez has indicated that the survival of the company may well depend on the success of the new novel.

Both partners are still convinced that a market exists for the novels. They now recognize, however, that they may not know enough about the teenage market to effectively market the novels. For example, they believe that insights are needed in the following areas:

- Will high school teenagers specifically select young adult novels, or do they think that these are written for younger teens?
- Are teenagers interested in social and political issues?
- Where do high school teenagers usually obtain books for pleasure reading?
- Do teens purchase books for themselves, or do parents purchase books for them?
- What types of promotional items do high school teens enjoy most?
- What advertising media are most effective in reaching teens?
- How do "nonconformist" teens differ on these issues from other teens?

You have been hired by Young Ideas Publishing Company to develop and implement a research project to investigate these ideas. Resources are limited; Halley would like the results of the research within 60 days.

Questions

1. Based on the information provided and your knowledge of marketing and marketing research, define the research problem.
2. How would you propose to measure the degree of nonconformity? Develop a set of items intended to assess this construct.
3. What is the target population for your study?
4. Discuss your proposed sampling plan, including the implications for the implementation of the project.

Case • 4.4

CTM Productions[1]

CTM Productions, formerly Children's Theatre of Madison, was formed in 1965 to "produce theater of the highest quality." CTM's mission is to "ensure that our [CTM's] efforts are inclusive of all the human family, rather than parts of it." In order to measure its present and future achievement of this goal, CTM must learn who its audience actually is.

CTM's research team decided to study the audience of CTM's production *To Kill a Mockingbird*. The study had three major objectives: (1) to develop an audience profile including demographic and media exposure data; (2) to provide a framework and data collection instrument for future marketing research; and (3) to supply a list of potential season subscribers. Since CTM had never undertaken any marketing research prior to this study, internal secondary information did not exist. External secondary information provided guidance as to the types of questions to be asked on this type of questionnaire and the appropriate phrasing for such questions. The questionnaire is shown in Exhibit 1.

CTM's volunteer ushers distributed the survey at each of the 15 performances of *To Kill a Mockingbird*. The number of completed surveys for each show varied with the size of the audience for that show.

Questions

1. The CTM research team used secondary data for question types and wording of specific questions. Did the research team utilize secondary information effectively in this study?
2. Read through the questionnaire shown in Exhibit 1. Does the questionnaire provide CTM with the information necessary to meet the stated objectives? Explain. Revise the survey instrument as necessary.
3. Considering CTM's objectives, does the sampling plan used for the study provide the necessary information? Does the sampling plan bias the results?

Exhibit 1

CTM Questionnaire

Introduce Yourself to CTM

Welcome to CTM's production of *To Kill a Mockingbird*. CTM Productions has been around for a long time—since 1965. And in this time we have had over 33,000 people in our audience. People to whom we have never been introduced. Real people like you that presently exist as numbers in our records. Now you have a chance to change your status. Introduce yourself to us by taking two minutes to answer the following questions to help us understand who you really are.

Let's start out with the basics. Your name is _____
and you live at (please include mailing address with zip code) _____

How many CTM productions have you attended?[ ] this is my first CTM production

1999–2000 Season	**1998–1999 Season**	**1997–1998 Season**
[ ] season subscriber	[ ] season subscriber	[ ] season subscriber
[ ] *Wind in the Willows*	[ ] *Red Shoes*	[ ] *Beauty and the Beast*
[ ] *A Christmas Carol*	[ ] *A Christmas Carol*	[ ] *A Christmas Carol*
[X] *To Kill a Mockingbird*	[ ] *Anne of Green Gables*	[ ] *I Remember Mama*
[ ] *Babar II* (plan to attend)	[ ] *Narnia*	[ ] *Babar the Elephant*

Who is with you today? (check all that apply)
[ ] myself		
[ ] adult friend(s)	[ ] my spouse/partner	[ ] my kids
	[ ] unrelated kids	[ ] other families

---

[1]The contribution of Sara L. Pitterle to this case are gratefully acknowledged.

Exhibit 1

CTM Questionnaire (*continued*)

Who have you attended with in the past? (again, check all that apply)

[ ] myself [ ] my spouse/partner [ ] my kids
[ ] adult friend(s) [ ] unrelated kids [ ] other families

Have you or any of your family participated in any of these CTM activities? (check all that apply)

[ ] after-school drama classes [ ] auditions [ ] have not participated
[ ] summer school [ ] performances [ ] did not know I could

How did you find out about our production of *To Kill a Mockingbird?* (check all that apply)

[ ] season brochure [ ] poster

Read story in:

[ ] *State Journal* [ ] *Capitol Times* [ ] *Isthmus* [ ] other

Saw ad in:

[ ] *State Journal* [ ] *Capitol Times* [ ] *Isthmus* [ ] other
[ ] radio (which station)
[ ] television (which station)
[ ] magazine (which one)
[ ] word of mouth
[ ] other

Did you come to this performance because you knew someone in the cast? [ ] yes [ ] no

What other events have you attended in the last six months? (check all that apply)

With your family or friends:

[ ] sports [ ] movies [ ] live musical performances
[ ] museums [ ] lectures [ ] other live theatrical performances

Alone:

[ ] sports [ ] movies [ ] live musical performances
[ ] museums [ ] lectures [ ] other live theatrical performances

Your answers to the following demographic questions will help us understand who you are.

Are you a female or male? [ ] female [ ] male

Which age category do you belong to?

[ ] 16–20 [ ] 31–40 [ ] 51–60 [ ] 71–80
[ ] 21–30 [ ] 41–50 [ ] 61–70 [ ] 81–100

How did you get here today?

[ ] walked [ ] car [ ] bus [ ] other

From how far away did you come?

[ ] within Madison [ ] less than 5 miles [ ] 6–10 miles [ ] over 10 miles

How long have you lived in the Madison/south-central Wisconsin area?

[ ] do not live here [ ] just arrived [ ] 1–3 years [ ] 4–7 years [ ] more

What is your highest level of education?

[ ] some high school [ ] some college [ ] some graduate school [ ] more
[ ] high school graduate [ ] college graduate [ ] graduate school graduate

What is your annual household income?

[ ] below $20,000 [ ] $31–40,000 [ ] more than $50,000 [ ] do not wish to reply
[ ] $21–30,000 [ ] $41–50,000 [ ] not sure

Does this represent a dual income household? [ ] yes [ ] no

How many people live in your household? (circle only one, include yourself)

1 2 3 4 5 6 more

If you have children, how many are in each grade category?

[ ] not in school yet [ ] 4th–5th grade [ ] high school [ ] other
[ ] kindergarten–3rd grade [ ] 6th–8th grade [ ] college

Would you like to be on our mailing list to keep informed of CTM activities? [ ] yes [ ] no

Case • 4.5
Caldera Industries[1]

Chris Totten has just begun a summer internship at Caldera Industries, a national supplier of electronics components. Caldera's clients include OEM (original equipment manufacturers) firms that market televisions, home stereo and audio, and computer products to the general public. Returning from lunch, Chris finds a memo and questionnaire in her mailbox (see Exhibits 1 and 2).

Questions

1. Evaluate the questionnaire in relation to the issues raised by Manuel Ortega.
2. How would you recommend the instrument be pretested?

Caldera Industries

Serving our Customers' Electronics Needs For Over 15 Years

CI

Internal Memorandum

TO: Chris Totten
Marketing Analyst Intern

cc: Caren Menlo
Marketing Manager

From: Manuel Ortega
Vice President for Sales and Marketing

Date: May 23, 2003

Regarding: Evaluation of Market Research Questionnaire

In three weeks I will be meeting with executives from a number of our client companies. One of the items on the agenda is the research project our company has agreed to undertake on their behalf. At that meeting, the final version of our questionnaire will be distributed and approved.

On the attached pages is an initial draft of the Consumer Electronics Questionnaire we plan on using for the study. As the newly hired Marketing Intern, and because of your marketing research coursework experience, I suggested to our Marketing Manager, Caren Menlo, that reviewing the questionnaire would make an ideal first assignment for you. She agreed.

Please examine the attached questionnaire and provide me with a written memo of your analysis, comments, and suggestions for improvement (if you believe any are warranted) within two (2) weeks. More specifically, I am interested in your comments on the following issues:

■ the type and amount of information being sought
■ appropriateness of the type of questionnaire designed and its method of administration
■ the content of questions in the draft document
■ response formats used for the various questions
■ question wording
■ question sequencing
■ physical characteristics and layout of the instrument

I am also interested in any comments or suggestions you have on pretesting the questionnaire. I look forward to reading your memo.

[1]This case was prepared by Michael R. Luthy, Ph.D., Associate Professor of Marketing, W. Fielding Rubel School of Business, Bellarmine College, 2001 Newburg Road, Louisville, KY 40205. Reprinted with permission.

Exhibit 2

Consumer Electronics Research Questionnaire

Directions: This questionnaire has been developed for a consortium of computer and home entertainment companies (who wish to remain anonymous). Complete all questions and mail this questionnaire to us today.

Quality Research Associates
5716 N. Woodlawn Court
Champaign, IL 61820

1. Name: _____ ____ Mr. ____ Mrs.
2. Sex: _____
3. How old are you: _____
4. Intelligence: ____ Only completed college degree (Bachelor's)
____ Completed some graduate work
____ Completed graduate degree
____ Completed graduate degree beyond masters
5. Ethnic Status: ____ White ____ Asian
____ Black ____ Indian
____ Asian ____ Other   What? _____
6. Political Party Support: ____ Democrat
____ Republican
____ Independent
____ Other
7. Your Occupation: _____
8. Spouse's Name and Age: _____
9. Number of Children: _____ (if children, go to question 41)
10. Your Company: _____
11. Your Work Fax Number: (__ __ __) __ __ __ - __ __ __ __
12. How Long Have You Been Married: ____ Never married
____ Less than a year
____ Between 1 and 5 years
____ Over 5 but less than 10 years
____ Over 15 years but less than 20 years
____ More than 20 years
13. Your Annual Income: $ _____
14. Social Security Number: __ __ __ - __ __ - __ __ __ __
15. The sponsors of this research are constantly introducing new products that they believe you (and your loved one, if any) will be interested in. In order to better make you aware of these offerings, please provide your telephone number below.
(__ __ __) __ __ __ - __ __ __ __
16. Do you own a computer at home or at work?
____ Yes ____ No
17. During an average week, how much time do you spend on it?
_____ Hours _____ Minutes
18. Doing what mostly?

_____

For each of the products listed below, please indicate the extent of your satisfaction with it, ceteris paribus, by either circling or placing an "X" on the line to the right of each statement.

	Mild Satisfaction	**Extremely Satisfied**

19. Apple Computers and Peripherals.
20. Gateway Computers and Peripherals.
21. Dell Computers and Peripherals.
22. IBM Computers and Peripherals.
23. Samsung Computers and Peripherals.
24. Hewlett-Packard Computers and Peripherals.
25. MacIntosh Computers and Peripherals.
26. Hitachi, Ltd. Computers and Peripherals.
27. Unisys Computers and Peripherals.
28. Tandy Computers and Peripherals.

continued

Exhibit 2

Consumer Electronics Research Questionnaire (*continued*)

29. Without being too loquacious, what emerging trends or technologies do you see as important to you that computer manufacturers (both hardware and software) should consider in developing new products?

_____

_____

30. How many different computer chatrooms have you visited in the last month?

____ 1–2

____ 2–3

____ 3–4

____ more than four

Below is a listing of ways in which people interact with consumer electronics on a quasi regular basis. What percentage of your time do you typically spend with each?

Check Below If You Do Not Use	Do Use		On Average, Number of "Others" Present During Your Usage
31. ____	_____ %	Work related computer activities	____
32. ____	_____ %	Entertainment related computer activities	____
33. ____	_____ %	Watching Network Television	____
34. ____	_____ %	Watching Cable Television	____
35. ____	_____ %	Watching Premium Cable Services	____
36. ____	_____ %	Watching Rented Movies on VCR	____
37. ____	_____ %	Watching Rented Movies on DVD	____
38. ____	_____ %	Listening to Music on Radio or on CD's	____
39. ____	_____ %	Other (specify)	____

Referencing the music you listen to, vis à vis your response to question 38 above (see question 38 if needed), which are your favorite musical periods or types? Please indicate your first 10 choices in numerical order.

40. Earlier than Renaissance ____

41. Renaissance ____

42. Baroque ____

43. Classical ____

44. Romantic ____

45. Impressionistic ____

46. Neo-Classical ____

47. Contemporary ____

48. Contemporary Christian ____

49. Rock ____

50. Hard Rock ____

51. Grunge Rock ____

52. Jazz ____

53. Easy Listening ____

54. Jazz/Rock Fusion ____

55. Bluegrass ____

56. Contemporary ____

57. Folk Music ____

58. Country ____

59. Western ____

60. Other ____

continued

PART 4:

Data Collection Forms

Exhibit 2

Consumer Electronics Research Questionnaire (*continued*)

61. Chart your child's usage of the following computer-related activities in 2002: (A = never, B = once to twice a per month, C = once to twice a week, D = every week, E = twice or more per week, F = daily, G = multiple times a day). If you have more than one child, use the computer usage of the oldest.

	Word Processing	EXCEL	Database Programs	E-Mail	Internet "Surfing"	Internet Chatrooms	Games
Jan 1–Jan 15	_____	_____	_____	_____	_____	_____	_____
Jan 16–Jan 31	_____	_____	_____	_____	_____	_____	_____
Feb 1–Feb 15	_____	_____	_____	_____	_____	_____	_____
Feb 16–Feb 28	_____	_____	_____	_____	_____	_____	_____
Mar 1–Mar 15	_____	_____	_____	_____	_____	_____	_____
Mar 16–Mar 30	_____	_____	_____	_____	_____	_____	_____
Apr 1–Apr 15	_____	_____	_____	_____	_____	_____	_____
Apr 16–Apr 30	_____	_____	_____	_____	_____	_____	_____
May 1–May 15	_____	_____	_____	_____	_____	_____	_____
May 16–May 30	_____	_____	_____	_____	_____	_____	_____
Jun 1–Jun 15	_____	_____	_____	_____	_____	_____	_____
Jun 16–Jun 30	_____	_____	_____	_____	_____	_____	_____
Jul 1–Jul 15	_____	_____	_____	_____	_____	_____	_____
Jul 16–Jul 31	_____	_____	_____	_____	_____	_____	_____
Aug 1–Aug 15	_____	_____	_____	_____	_____	_____	_____
Aug 16–Aug 31	_____	_____	_____	_____	_____	_____	_____
Sep 1–Sep 15	_____	_____	_____	_____	_____	_____	_____
Sep 16–Sep 30	_____	_____	_____	_____	_____	_____	_____
Oct 1-Oct 15	_____	_____	_____	_____	_____	_____	_____
Oct 16–Oct 31	_____	_____	_____	_____	_____	_____	_____
Nov 1–Nov 15	_____	_____	_____	_____	_____	_____	_____
Nov 16–Nov 30	_____	_____	_____	_____	_____	_____	_____

After completing, return to question 23

What is the *most* you would be willing to spend to purchase the following consumer electronic products if you were going to purchase them within the next year? and why?

Why?

62. $ _____ DVD player _____

63. $ _____ External Zip drive _____

64. $ _____ Big Screen Television _____

65. $ _____ Portable Stereo or Television _____

66. $ _____ Digital Camera _____

67. To what degree do you believe that access to the Internet is important to your family's entertainment needs?   A ⬅————————➡ E

68. What emerging trends or technologies do you see as important to you that computer manufacturers (both hardware and software) should consider in developing new products?

_____

_____

69. On a separate sheet of paper, please provide the names and addresses of at least three (3) friends or relatives that have recently (within the last two years) purchased an advanced consumer electronics product so that we may contact them.

Mail your completed questionnaire in a standard business size envelope to:

Quality Research Associates
4518 North Trails End
Cleveland, OH 34454
(a first-class stamp will be needed)

Case • 4.6

Calamity-Casualty Insurance Company[1]

Calamity-Casualty is an insurance company located in Dallas, Texas, that deals exclusively with automobile coverage. Its policy offerings include the standard features offered by most insurers, such as collision, comprehensive, emergency road service, medical, and uninsured motorist. The unique aspect of Calamity-Casualty Insurance is that all policies are sold through the mail. Agents do not make personal calls on clients, and the company does not operate district offices. As a result, Calamity-Casualty's capital/labor requirements are greatly reduced, at a substantial cost savings to the company. A great portion of these savings are passed on to the consumer in the form of lower prices. The data indicate that Calamity-Casualty offers its policies at 20 to 25 percent below the average market rate.

The company's strategy of selling automobile insurance by mail at low prices has been very successful. Calamity-Casualty has traditionally been the third largest seller of automobile insurance in the Southwest. During the past five years, it has consistently achieved an average market share of 14 percent in the four states it serves—Arizona, New Mexico, Nevada, and Texas. This compares favorably with the 19 percent and 17 percent market shares realized by the two leading firms in the region. However, Calamity-Casualty has never been highly successful in Arizona. The largest market share gained by Calamity-Casualty in Arizona for any one year was 4 percent, which placed the company seventh among firms competing in that state.

The company's poor performance in Arizona greatly concerns Calamity-Casualty's board of executives. Demographic experts estimate that during the next six to ten years, the population in Arizona will increase some 10 to 15 percent, the largest projected growth rate of any state in the Southwest. Thus, for Calamity-Casualty to remain a major market force in the area, the company needs to improve its sales performance in Arizona.

In response to this matter, Calamity-Casualty sponsored a study that was conducted by the Automobile Insurance Association of America (AIAA), the national association of automobile insurance executives, to determine Arizona residents' attitudes toward and perceptions of the various insurance companies selling policies in that state. The results of the AIAA research showed that Calamity-Casualty was favorably perceived across most categories measured. Calamity-Casualty received the highest ratings with respect to service, pricing, policy offering, and image. Although these findings were well received by the company's board of executives, they provided little strategic insight into how Calamity-Casualty might increase sales in Arizona.

Since the company was committed to obtaining information useful for developing a more effective Arizona sales campaign, the executive board sought the services of Aminbane, Pedrone, and Associates, a marketing research firm specializing in insurance consulting. After many discussions between members of the research team and executives at Calamity-Casualty, it was decided that the most beneficial approach toward designing a more appropriate sales campaign would be to ascertain the psychographic profiles of nonpurchasers and direct mail purchasers of Calamity-Casualty insurance. This would help the company better understand the personal factors influencing people's decision to respond or not respond to direct mail solicitation.

Research Design

To learn more about which psychographic factors are important in describing purchasers of automobile insurance, some exploratory research was undertaken. In-depth interviews were held with two insurance salespersons, who offered various insights on the subject. These experience interviews were followed by a focus-group meeting with Arizona residents who had received a direct mail offer from Calamity-Casualty. Finally, the research team consulted university professors in both psychology and mass communications to uncover other determinants of buyer behavior. Output from these procedures revealed three primary factors that could be used to describe purchasers of insurance by mail—risk aversion, powerlessness, and convenience orientation. It was believed that people who were risk averse, had a sense of powerlessness, and were convenience oriented would be more favorably disposed toward direct mail marketing efforts and thus would be more likely to purchase Calamity-Casualty automobile insurance.

Method of Data Collection

Given these factors of interest, the list of items contained in Exhibit 1 was generated to form the basis of a questionnaire to be administered to Arizona residents. Two samples of subjects were to be used—one of direct mail buyers and one of nonbuyers. The research team estimated that 175 subjects would be required from both samples to adequately assess the three constructs. Because a mail questionnaire dealing with psychographic subject

[1]The contributions of David M. Szymanski to the development of this case are gratefully acknowledged.

Exhibit 1

Calamity-Casualty Marketing Research Questionnaire Items

Note: Each item requires one of the following responses:

Responses	Code
S.A.—Strongly Agree	5
A.—Agree	4
N.—Neither Agree nor Disagree	3
D.—Disagree	2
S.D.—Strongly Disagree	1

Risk Aversion

1. It is always better to buy a used car from a dealer than from an individual.
2. Generally speaking, I avoid buying generic drugs at the drugstore.
3. It would be a disaster to be stranded on the road due to a breakdown.
4. It would be important to me to plan a long road trip very carefully and in great detail.
5. I would like to try parachute jumping sometime.
6. Before buying a new product, I would first discuss it with someone who had already used it.
7. Before deciding to see a new movie in a theater, it is important to read the critical reviews.
8. If my car needed even a minor repair, I would first get cost estimates from several garages.

Powerlessness

1. Persons like myself have little chance of protecting our personal interests when they conflict with those of strong pressure groups.
2. A lasting world peace can be achieved by those of us who work toward it.
3. I think each of us can do a great deal to improve world opinion of the United States.
4. This world is run by the few people in power, and there is not much the little guy can do about it.
5. People like me can change the course of world events if we make ourselves heard.
6. More and more, I feel helpless in the face of what's happening in the world today.

Convenience Orientation

1. I like to buy things by mail or catalog because it saves time.
2. I think that it is not worth the extra effort to clip coupons for groceries.
3. I would rather wash my own car than pay to have it washed at a car wash.
4. I would prefer to have an automatic transmission rather than a stick shift in my car.
5. When choosing a bank, I believe that location is the most important factor.
6. When shopping for groceries, I would be willing to drive a longer distance in order to buy at lower prices.

matter might have a very low response rate, and because attitude toward direct mail was one of the attributes being measured, a telephone interview was believed to be best suited to the needs at hand.

Questions

1. Conceptually, what are the constructs risk aversion, convenience, and powerlessness?

2. Do you think that the sample of items adequately assesses each construct? Can you think of any additional items that could or should be used?

© PhotoDisc/Getty Images

Part 5

Sampling and Data Collection

Part 5 focuses on the collection of data needed to answer a problem. Chapter 15 overviews the various types of sampling plans that can be used to determine the population elements from which data should be collected. It also describes nonprobability sampling and simple random sampling, one of the probability sampling plans. Chapter 16 then discusses two popular, but more complex, probability sampling schemes— stratified and cluster sampling. Chapter 17 treats the question of how many of the population elements are needed to answer the problem with precision and confidence in the results. Chapter 18 discusses the many nonsampling errors that can arise in completing the data collection task and what researchers might do to reduce them.

Chapter 15

Sampling Basics, Nonprobability, and Simple Random Samples

© PhotoDisc/Getty Images

Learning Objectives

1   *Distinguish between a census and a sample.*

2   *List the six steps researchers use to draw a sample of a population.*

3   *Define sampling frame.*

4   *Explain the difference between a probability sample and a nonprobability sample.*

5   *Distinguish between a fixed and a sequential sample.*

6   *Explain what a judgment sample is and describe its best use and its hazards.*

7   *Define quota sample.*

8   *Explain what a parameter in a sampling procedure is.*

9   *Explain what the derived population is.*

10   *Explain why the concept of sampling distribution is the most important concept in statistics.*

Jill Zimmerman was preparing for the next meeting of her cross-functional team. The team of designers, engineers, production, and financial people would rely on her marketing expertise as they planned the company's next generation of cell phones. Everyone agreed that future products would require further development of multimedia capabilities. Questions remained about who would be the new product line's early adopters and what features they would embrace. Jill had been working with a marketing research firm to create a research design that would answer those questions.

According to Tomás Mendoza, the representative from the research firm Jill was using, the group of buyers doing the most to drive innovation in electronics was not business users, as Jill had expected. Rather, Tomás recommended focusing on teenagers. "You'd be surprised," he told Jill. "A lot of the big companies—Microsoft, Nokia, AOL Time Warner—have been devoting research dollars to the teen market. Kids have their own ways of using technology. They've grown up with it. It's so much a part of their life that they don't even give it much thought. They expect cell phones to be at the heart of their lives—the way they keep in touch. It's the same with the Internet. Technology is how they stay connected with each other. For example, teens paved the way for instant messaging. They showed the business world how to use it to collaborate on a project. So if you want to keep in the forefront, teens are the customers you need to be watching."

"OK," agreed Jill as she reviewed the tables Tomás spread out on the conference table. "You make a good case for why we should target teens as the population to study. And we already know they are an important group of customers for us. The majority of teens have cell phones now, and we're forecasting our sales based on industry trends that project teen usage at 75 percent in a couple more years. Where do we find them so we can do a survey, and how do we figure out if we have a good sample? We can't afford to talk to every teen."

"I propose we do an online survey. A relatively inexpensive way to get some basic data would be to participate in one of the online panels that already exist. For example, a company called Teenage Research Unlimited does a monthly survey of 600 teens and 250 'tweens.'"

"Tweens?"

"Kids between the ages of 8 and 12."

"Is that sample big enough for our purposes?"

"The size of the sample is just one of the factors we should consider. Let's look at some general information about this survey sample, and you can decide if it's what you want."

Discussion Issues

1. How can researchers obtain a sample of teenagers that represents the buying behavior of all teens?

2. What challenges would you expect in putting together a representative sample of teens on the Internet? In what ways would this be different from recruiting a sample offline?

3. What other criteria should Jill and Tomás consider in evaluating the usefulness of the Teenage Research Unlimited online survey sample? ■

1 *Distinguish between a census and a sample.*

census
A complete canvass of a population.

sample
Selection of a subset of elements from a larger group of objects.

population
The totality of cases that conform to some designated specifications.

sampling frame
The list of sampling units from which a sample will be drawn; the list could consist of geographic areas, institutions, individuals, or other units.

Once the researcher has clearly specified the problem and developed an appropriate research design and data collection instruments, the next step in the research process is to select those elements from which the information will be collected. One way to do this is to collect information from each member of the population of interest by completely canvassing this population. A complete canvass of a population is called a **census**. Another way would be to collect information from a portion of the population by taking a **sample** of elements from the larger group and, on the basis of the information collected from the subset, to infer something about the larger group. One's ability to make this inference from subset to larger group depends on the method by which the sample of elements was chosen. A major part of this chapter is devoted to the "why" and "how" of taking a sample.

Incidentally, **population** refers here not only to people but also to manufacturing firms, retail or wholesale institutions, or even inanimate objects such as parts produced in a manufacturing plant; it is defined as the totality of cases that conform to some designated specifications. The specifications define the elements that belong to the target group and those that are to be excluded. A study aimed at establishing a demographic profile of frozen-pizza eaters requires specifying who is to be considered a frozen-pizza eater. Anyone who has ever eaten a frozen pizza? Those who eat at least one such pizza a month? A week? Those who eat a certain minimum number of frozen pizzas per month? Researchers need to be very explicit in defining the target group of interest. They also need to be very careful that they have actually sampled the target population and not some other population due to an inappropriate or incomplete **sampling frame**, which is the listing of the elements from which the actual sample will be drawn.

One might choose to sample rather than to canvass a whole population for several reasons. First, complete counts on populations of even moderate size are very costly and time-consuming. Often the information will be obsolete by the time the census is completed and the information processed. In some cases, a census is impossible. If, for example, researchers sought to test the life of a company's electric light bulbs by leaving all its inventory of bulbs on until they burned out, they would have reliable data, but no product to sell.

Finally—and to novice researchers, surprisingly—one might choose a sample over a census for purposes of accuracy. Censuses involve larger field staffs, which in turn introduce greater potential for nonsampling error. This is one reason the U.S. Bureau of the Census uses sample surveys to check the accuracy of various censuses. That is correct; samples are used to infer the accuracy of the census.[1]

© Tom Vano/Index Stock Imagery

Researchers must carefully define a population in order to get accurate results. Should anyone who has ever eaten a frozen pizza be included when determining the demographics of frozen pizza eaters?

Required Steps in Sampling

2 *List the six steps researchers use to draw a sample of a population.*

Figure 15.1 outlines a useful six-step procedure that researchers can follow when drawing a sample of a population. Note that it is first necessary to define the target population, or the collection of elements, about which the researcher wishes to make an inference. For example, when the preferences of children are involved, researchers have to decide whether the target population to be measured is the kids, their parents, or both.

> One company tested its slotless road racing sets only with children. Kids loved them. But moms said they didn't like the sets because they were teaching children to crash cars, and dads didn't like the fact that the product was made into a toy.

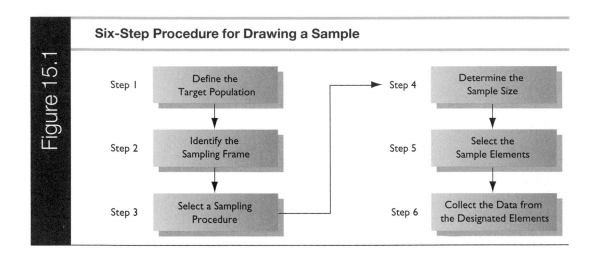

Figure 15.1

Six-Step Procedure for Drawing a Sample

Step 1 → Define the Target Population
Step 2 → Identify the Sampling Frame
Step 3 → Select a Sampling Procedure
Step 4 → Determine the Sample Size
Step 5 → Select the Sample Elements
Step 6 → Collect the Data from the Designated Elements

It can work the other way, too. One company introduced a food product with a national ad campaign that starred a rather precocious child. The company tested the campaign only with mothers, who thought it was great. Kids thought the precocious child was obnoxious—and the product, too. End of product.[2]

The researcher must decide if the relevant target population consists of individuals, households, business firms, other institutions, or credit card transactions, for example. In making these decisions, the researcher also has to be careful to specify what units are to be excluded. Geographic boundaries and a time period for the study must always be specified, although additional restrictions are often placed on the elements. When the elements are individuals, for example, the relevant target population may be defined as all those over 18 years of age, or females only, or those with a high school education only.

The problem of specifying the geographic boundaries for the target population is sometimes more difficult in international marketing research studies because of the additional complexity an international perspective introduces. For example, urban versus rural areas may be significantly different from each other in various countries. Also, the composition of the population can vary depending on the location within the country. In Chile, for example, the north has a highly centralized Indian population, whereas the south has high concentrations of persons of European descent.

In general, the simpler the definition of the target population, the higher the incidence and the easier and less costly it is to find the sample.[3] **Incidence** refers to the percent of the *general population or group* that qualifies for inclusion in the sample using some criteria. Incidence has a direct bearing on the time and cost it takes to complete studies. When incidence is high (i.e., most elements in the general population qualify for the study because only one or very few easily satisfied criteria are used to screen potential respondents), the cost and time to collect data are minimized. Alternatively, as the number of criteria used to describe what constitutes eligible respondents for the study increases, so do the cost and time necessary to find them.

Figure 15.2 shows the percentage of adults who are estimated to participate in various sports. The data in Figure 15.2 suggest that it would be more difficult and costly to focus a study on people who motorcycle, only 3.6 percent of all adults, than people who walk for health, 27.4 percent of all adults. The most important thing is that the researcher be precise in specifying exactly what elements are of interest and what elements are to be excluded. A clear statement of research purpose helps immeasurably in determining the appropriate elements of interest.

The second step in the sample-selection process is identifying the sampling frame, the listing of elements from which the actual sample will be drawn. Say that the target population for a particular study is all the households in the metropolitan Dallas area. At first glance, the Dallas phone book would seem an easy and good example of a sampling frame. However, upon

incidence
The percent of the general population or group that qualifies for inclusion in the sample using some criteria.

Define sampling frame.

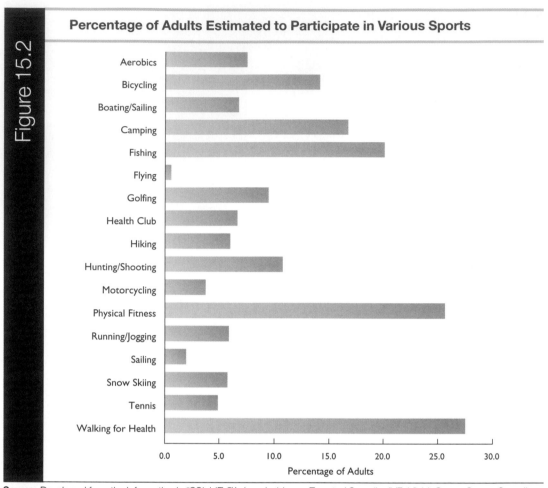

Figure 15.2

Percentage of Adults Estimated to Participate in Various Sports

Aerobics
Bicycling
Boating/Sailing
Camping
Fishing
Flying
Golfing
Health Club
Hiking
Hunting/Shooting
Motorcycling
Physical Fitness
Running/Jogging
Sailing
Snow Skiing
Tennis
Walking for Health

0.0 5.0 10.0 15.0 20.0 25.0 30.0

Percentage of Adults

Source: Developed from the information in "SSI-*LITe*™: *Low Incidence Targeted Sampling*" (Fairfield, Conn.: Survey Sampling, Inc., 1994).

closer examination it becomes clear that the telephone directory provides an inaccurate listing of Dallas households, omitting those with unlisted numbers (and, of course, those without phones) and double-counting those with multiple listings. People who have recently moved and thus received new phones not yet listed are also omitted.

Experienced researchers have found that only rarely is there a perfect correspondence between the sampling frame and the target population in which they are interested. One of the researcher's more creative tasks in sampling is developing an appropriate sampling frame when the list of population elements is not readily available. This may require sampling working blocks of numbers and exchanges, as when random digit dialing is used with telephone surveys because of the inadequacies of directory samples. However, the dramatic increase in the number of working blocks over the last 10 years has made this task more difficult (see Research Window 15.1). Or it sometimes means sampling geographic areas or institutions and then subsampling within these units when, say, the target population is individuals but a current, accurate list of appropriate individuals is not available.

The third step in the procedure for drawing a sample is closely linked with the identification of the sampling frame. Choosing a sampling method or procedure depends largely on what the researcher can develop for a sampling frame. Different types of samples require different types of sampling frames. This chapter and the next review the main types of samples used in marketing research. The connection between sampling frame and sampling method should become obvious from these discussions.

The fourth step in the sample-selection process is to determine sample size. Chapter 17 dis-

PART 5:
Sampling and Data Collection

Changes in the Structure of Telephone Numbers

Since 1986, the estimated number of telephone households in the United States has increased by 14.2 percent, while the number of working residential exchanges has increased by 27.1 percent and the number of working blocks by 182.4 percent. During the same time period, the number of directory-listed households has increased by only 10.4 percent, causing the continuing decline in listed rates.

	1986	2003	Growth
Telephone households	80,900,000	105,550,599	30.5%
Directory-listed households	59,788,590	72,227,986	20.8%
Working residential exchanges	31,530	52,617	66.9%
Working blocks	1,391,237	2,587,002	85.9%
Average Block Size	44	28	
Median Block Size	53	35	

Definitions

Block or bank: the first two digits of the last four digits of the telephone number

Working block: any block with at least one listed number

Exchange/ prefix: "Exchange" designates the city, town, or community in which the number originates. "Prefix" is the 3-digit number assigned to an exchange area. The terms are often used interchangeably.

Technological changes, particularly the explosive growth of cellular and mobile phones, paging equipment modems, and fax machines, have dramatically increased the demand for telephone numbers. This has not only spurred the introduction of new area codes, but has also reduced the density of listed numbers in the working blocks because some of the numbers are dedicated to modems and fax machines.

The new competitive telephone market is also contributing to the declining working block density. Multiple telephone companies are serving smaller markets and are assigned exclusive exchanges. More exchanges are being assigned to more telephone companies, but the working blocks are not being filled out as completely.

What's the significance for sampling? The most obvious change concerns the working phone rate (WPR) of a random digit (RDD) sample. As the number of listed phones per working block decreases, the probability of selecting a listed number in an RDD sample decreases, which may decrease the WPR. Samples that include metropolitan areas are more likely to be affected by this trend. ■

Source: "Working Block Density Declines" (Fairfield, Conn.: Survey Sampling, Inc., 1996).

---

cusses this question. The fifth step indicates that the researcher needs to actually pick the elements that will be included in the study. How this is done depends upon the type of sample being used. We will explore the topic of sample selection when we discuss sampling methods. Finally, the researcher needs to actually collect data from the designated respondents. A great many things can go wrong with this task. These problems are reviewed, and some methods for handling them are discussed, in Chapter 18.

4 *Explain the difference between a probability sample and a nonprobability sample.*

Types of Sampling Plans

Sampling techniques can be divided into the two broad categories of **probability** and **nonprobability samples**. In a probability sample, each member of the target population has a *known, nonzero* chance of being included in the sample. The chances of each member of the target population being included in the sample may not be equal, but everyone has a known probability of inclusion. That probability is determined by the specific mechanical procedure that is used to select sample elements.

With nonprobability samples, on the other hand, there is no way of estimating the probability that any target population element will be included in the sample. Thus, there is no way of ensuring that the sample is representative of the population. For example, Allstate Corporation has been developing a system for mining the claims data of its 14 million customer households. The company plans to use the data to identify patterns in the demand for its products—say, the likelihood that a household with a Mercedes Benz would own a vacation home (which would require insurance). Although the database is huge, the company has

probability sample
A sample in which each target population element has a known, nonzero chance of being included in the sample.

nonprobability sample
A sample that relies on personal judgment in the element selection process and therefore prohibits estimating the probability that any population element will be included in the sample.

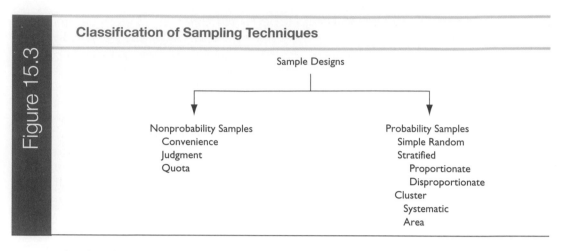

Figure 15.3

Classification of Sampling Techniques

Sample Designs

Nonprobability Samples
Convenience
Judgment
Quota

Probability Samples
Simple Random
Stratified
Proportionate
Disproportionate
Cluster
Systematic
Area

no way of estimating the probability of any individual customer making a claim. It therefore cannot be positive that data about customers who file claims are representative of all its customers, much less its potential customers.[4]

All nonprobability samples rely on personal judgment somewhere in the sample-selection process rather than on a mechanical procedure to select sample members. While these judgments may sometimes yield good estimates of a population characteristic, there is no way of determining objectively if the sample is adequate. It is only when the target population elements have been selected with known probabilities that one is able to evaluate the precision of a sample result. For this reason, probability sampling is usually considered to be the superior method, in terms of being able to estimate the amount of sampling error present.

Samples can also be categorized by whether they are **fixed** or **sequential samples**. In fixed samples, the sample size is decided before the study begins, and all the necessary information is collected before the results are analyzed. In our discussion we shall emphasize fixed samples since they are the type most commonly used in marketing research. Nevertheless, you should be aware that sequential samples can also be taken, and they can be used with each of the basic sampling plans we will discuss.

In a sequential sample, the number of elements to be sampled is not decided in advance but is determined by a series of decisions as the data are collected. For example, if, after a small sample is taken, the evidence is not conclusive, more observations will be made. If the results are still inconclusive, the size of the sample will be expanded further. At each stage, a decision is made as to whether more information should be collected or whether the evidence is now sufficient to permit a conclusion. The sequential sample allows trends in the data to be evaluated as the data are being collected, and this affords an opportunity to reduce costs when additional observations show diminishing usefulness.

Both probability and nonprobability sampling plans can be further divided by type. Nonprobability samples, for instance, can be classified as *convenience, judgment,* or *quota,* while probability samples can be *simple random, stratified,* or *cluster,* and some of these can be further divided. Figure 15.3 shows the types of samples we shall discuss in this chapter and the next. You should be aware that the basic sample types can be combined into more complex sampling plans. If you understand the basic types, though, you should be able to understand the more complex designs.

5 *Distinguish between a fixed and a sequential sample.*

fixed sample
A sample for which size is determined *a priori* and needed information is collected from the designated elements.

sequential sample
A sample formed on the basis of a series of successive decisions. If the evidence is not conclusive after a small sample is taken, more observations are taken; if it is still inconclusive after these additional observations, still more observations are taken. At each stage a decision is made as to whether more information should be collected or whether the evidence is sufficient to draw a conclusion.

Nonprobability Samples

As we stated earlier, nonprobability samples involve personal judgment somewhere in the selection process. Sometimes this judgment is imposed by the researcher, while in other cases the selection of population elements to be included is left to individual field-workers. Since the elements are not selected by a mechanical procedure, it is impossible to assess the probability of any population member being included and, thus, the degree of sampling error involved. Without knowing how much error results from a particular sampling procedure, researchers cannot gauge the accuracy of their estimates with any precision.

Convenience Samples

Convenience samples are sometimes called *accidental samples* because those composing the sample enter by "accident"—they just happen to be where the information for the study is being collected. Examples of convenience samples abound in our everyday lives. We talk to a few friends, and on the basis of their reactions, we infer the political sentiment of the country; our local radio station asks people to call in and express their reactions to some controversial issue, and the opinions expressed are interpreted as prevailing sentiment; we ask for volunteers in a research study and use those who come forward.

The problem with convenience samples, of course, is that we have no way of knowing if those included are representative of the target population. And while we might hesitate to infer that the reactions of a few friends indicate prevailing political sentiment, we are often tempted to conclude that large samples, even though selected conveniently, are representative. The fallacy of this assumption is illustrated by a personal incident.

One of the local television stations in the city where one of the authors resides conducted a daily public opinion poll several years ago on topics of interest to the local community. The polls were labeled the "Pulse of Madison" and were conducted in the following way. During the six o'clock news every evening, the station would ask a question about some controversial issue to which people could reply with a yes or no. Persons in favor would call one number; persons opposed would call another. The number of viewers calling each number was recorded electronically. Percentages of those in favor and opposed would then be reported on the ten o'clock news. With some 500 to 1,000 people calling in their opinions each night, the local television commentator seemed to interpret these results as reflecting the true state of opinion in the community.

On one six o'clock broadcast, the following question was posed: "Do you think the drinking age in Madison should be lowered to 18?" The existing legal limit was 21. Would you believe that almost 4,000 people called in that night and that 78 percent were in favor of lowering the drinking age requirement? Clearly, 4,000 responses in a community of 180,000 people "must be representative"! Wrong. As you may have suspected, certain segments of the population were more interested in the issue than others. Thus, it was no surprise, when discussing the issue in class a few weeks later, to find that students had taken half-hour phone shifts on an arranged basis. Each person would call the yes number, hang up, call again, hang up, and so on, until it was the next person's turn. Thus, neither the size of the sample nor the proportion favoring the age change was surprising. The sample was simply not representative.

Further, increasing a sample's size does not make it representative. The representativeness of a sample must be ensured by the sampling procedure. When participation is voluntary, or sample elements are selected because they are convenient, the sampling plan provides no assurance that the sample is representative. Empirical evidence, as a matter of fact, is much to the contrary. Rarely do samples selected on a convenient basis, regardless of size, prove representative. Telephone polls using 800 and 900 numbers represent a particularly common example of large but unrepresentative samples. What is especially unfortunate is that a great many people believe the results of these polls are accurate.

An all too common use of convenience samples in international marketing research is to use foreigners from the countries being studied who are currently residing in the country where the study is being conducted (e.g., Scandinavians currently residing in the United States). Even though such convenience samples can shed some light on certain country conditions, it must be recognized that these individuals typically represent the elite class, often are already "westernized," and may not be in touch with current developments in their own country. Convenience samples are not recommended for descriptive or causal research. They

convenience sample
A nonprobability sample that is sometimes called an *accidental sample* because those included in the sample enter by accident, in that they just happen to be where the study is being conducted when it is being conducted.

may be used with exploratory designs in which the emphasis is on generating ideas and insights, but even here the judgment sample seems superior.

Judgment Samples

6 *Explain what a judgment sample is and describe its best use and its hazards.*

judgment sample
A nonprobability sample that is often called a *purposive sample;* the sample elements are handpicked because they are expected to serve the research purpose.

snowball sample
A judgment sample that relies on the researcher's ability to locate an initial set of respondents with the desired characteristics; these individuals are then used as informants to identify still others with the desired characteristics.

7 *Define* quota sample.

quota sample
A nonprobability sample chosen in such a way that the proportion of sample elements possessing certain characteristics is approximately the same as the proportion of the elements with the characteristics in the target population; each field-worker is assigned a quota that specifies the characteristics of the people he or she is to contact.

Judgment samples are often called *purposive samples;* the sample elements are handpicked because it is expected that they can serve the research purpose. Procter & Gamble used this method when it advertised for "interns" aged 13 to 17 from the area around its Cincinnati headquarters. The company's food and beverage division hired this group of teenagers to serve as a kind of consumer panel. Working 10 hours a week in exchange for $1,000 and a trip to a concert, they reviewed television commercials, visited the mall with P&G managers to study retail displays, tested new products, and discussed their purchasing behavior. By selecting the panel members through a "hiring" process rather than randomly, the company could focus on traits it considered helpful—for example, the teenagers' ability to articulate their views clearly—at the risk that their views might not be representative of their age group.[5]

As mentioned, the key feature of judgment samples is that population elements are purposively selected. In some cases, sample elements are chosen not because they are representative but rather because they can offer researchers the information they need. When the courts rely on expert testimony, they are in a sense using judgment samples. The same kind of philosophy may prevail in creating exploratory designs. When searching for ideas and insights, the researcher is not interested in sampling a cross section of opinion but rather in sampling those who can offer some perspective on the research question.

The **snowball sample** is a judgment sample that is sometimes used to sample special populations.[6] This sample relies on the researcher's ability to locate an initial set of respondents with the desired characteristics. These individuals are then used as informants to identify others with the desired characteristics.

Imagine, for example, that a company wanted to determine the desirability of a certain product that would enable deaf people to communicate over telephone lines. Researchers might begin by identifying some key people in the deaf community and asking them for names of other deaf people who might be used in the study. Those asked to participate would also be asked for names of others who might cooperate. In this way the sample "snowballs" by getting larger as participants identify still other possible respondents.

As long as the researcher is at the early stages of research when ideas or insights are being sought—and when the researcher realizes its limitations—the judgment sample can be used productively. It becomes dangerous, however, when it is used in descriptive or causal studies and its weaknesses are conveniently forgotten. The Consumer Price Index (CPI) provides a classic example of this. As Sudman points out, "the CPI is in only fifty-six cities and metropolitan areas selected judgmentally and to some extent on the basis of political pressure. In reality, these cities represent *only themselves,* although the index is called the *Consumer Price Index for Urban Wage Earners and Clerical Workers,* and most people believe the index reflects prices everywhere in the United States. Within cities, the selection of retail outlets is done judgmentally, so that the *possible size of sample bias is unknown*" (emphasis added).[7]

Quota Samples

A third type of nonprobability sample, the **quota sample**, attempts to be representative of the population by including the same proportion of elements possessing certain characteristics as is found in the target population (see Research Window 15.2). Consider, for example, an attempt to select a representative sample of undergraduate students on a college campus. If the eventual sample of 500 contained no seniors, one would have serious reservations about the representativeness of the sample and the generalizability of the conclusions beyond the immediate sample group. With a quota sample, the researcher could ensure that seniors would be included and in the same proportion as they occur in the entire undergraduate student body.

PART 5:
Sampling and Data Collection

The Ad Is Slick, Clever, Expensive—But Is Anybody Reading It?

Every year advertisers spend millions of dollars producing the ads that appear in publications ranging from *Advertising Age* to *Yankee* magazine. While a certain amount of copy and art testing can be done in-house at the agency before the ad is published, the real test of its success is when it appears in a publication, alongside dozens of other ads designed equally carefully, and vies for a reader's attention.

RoperASW is a company that measures advertising readership in consumer, business, trade, and professional magazines and newspapers and reports its findings to advertisers and agencies—for a fee, of course. Since large sums are being gambled daily by advertisers seeking to get their message across to consumers, the Starch Communications division of RoperASW has been careful to design a sample for its research that can give subscribers fast—and accurate—information about the success of its advertising. Each year Starch interviews more than 50,000 people on their reading of over 20,000 advertisements. Approximately 500 individual issues are studied annually.

Starch uses a quota sample comprised of a minimum of 100 readers per sex. Starch has determined that at this sample size, major fluctuations in readership levels stabilize. Adults, eighteen years and older, are personally interviewed face-to-face for all publications except those that are directed exclusively to special groups (e.g., for *Seventeen* magazine they would interview only teenaged girls).

Interviews are arranged to parallel the publication's geographic circulation. For *Los Angeles* magazine, for example, the study would focus on readers in southern California. A study of *Time* magazine would parallel its national circulation. Interviews are conducted in 20 to 30 cities for each issue under study. Each interviewer is assigned only a small quota of interviews in order to minimize interviewer bias. Interviews are distributed among people of varied ages, income levels, and occupations so that collectively each study is broadly representative of the publication's audience. For certain business, trade, and professional publications, interviewing assignments are also designed to parallel the circulation by field of industry and job responsibility. For publications with small circulations, subscriber lists are used to help locate eligible respondents.

In each interview, interviewers ask respondents, who are permitted to look through the publication at the time of the interview, if they have seen or read any part of a particular advertisement. If the respondent answers yes, the interviewer follows up with more questions to determine the extent to which the respondent has read the ad.

Three degrees of readership are measured:

- *Noted:* The percent who remember having previously seen the ad in the issue.
- *Associated:* The percent who saw any part of the ad and clearly indicated the brand or advertiser.
- *Read Most:* The percent who read 50% or more of the written material in the ad.

After all the ads are asked about, interviewers record basic classification data on sex, age, occupation, marital status, race, income, family size and composition, so that sampling can be checked and cross tabulations of readership can be made.

Properly used, Starch data help advertisers and agencies identify the types of advertisement layouts that attract and retain the highest readership and those that result in average or poor readership. For advertisers, this kind of information can be invaluable in designing an effective campaign for their products. ■

Source: RoperASW.

Assume that a researcher was interested in sampling the undergraduate student body in such a way that the sample would reflect the composition of the student body by class and sex. Suppose further that there were 10,000 undergraduate students in total and that there were 3,200 freshmen, 2,600 sophomores, 2,200 juniors, and 2,000 seniors, and further that 7,000 were males and 3,000 were females. In a sample of 1,000, the quota sampling plan would require that 320 sample elements be freshmen, 260 sophomores, 220 juniors, and 200 seniors, and further that 700 of the sample elements be male and 300 female. The researcher would

ETHICAL dilemma 15.1

You are designing an experiment to compare the effectiveness of different types of commercials and need to recruit a large group of subjects of varying ages to watch television for an hour every night for a week. You approach your local church minister and tell her that you will make a donation to the church restoration fund for every member of the congregation who agrees to participate.

• *When might incentives be coercive?*

• *Is it ethical to coerce people to participate in research?*

• *Will the quality of the data suffer from the coercive recruitment of participants?*

© Michael Newman/Photo Edit

Field-workers can inadvertently introduce bias into the quota sample by, for example, only interviewing respondents who are home during the day—perhaps yielding responses skewed toward families with young children, or people who do not work outside the home.

accomplish this by giving each field-worker a quota—thus the name *quota sample*—specifying the types of undergraduates he or she is to contact. Thus, one field-worker assigned 20 interviews might be instructed to find and collect data from

■ Six freshmen—five male and one female
■ Six sophomores—four male and two female
■ Four juniors—three male and one female
■ Four seniors—two male and two female

Note that the specific sample elements (i.e., students) to be used would not be specified by the research plan, but would be left to the discretion of the individual field-worker. The field-worker's personal judgment would govern the choice of specific students to be interviewed. The only requirement would be that the interviewer diligently follow the established quota and interview five male freshmen, one female freshman, and so on.

Note further that the quota for this field-worker accurately reflects the sex composition of the student population, but does not completely parallel the class composition; 70 percent (14 of 20) of the field-worker's interviews are with males but only 30 percent (6 of 20) are with freshmen, whereas freshmen represent 32 percent of the undergraduate student body. It is not necessary or even usual with a quota sample that the quotas per field-worker accurately mirror the distribution of the control characteristics in the target population; usually only the total sample has the same proportions as the population.

Note finally that quota samples still rely on personal, subjective judgment rather than objective procedures for the selection of sample elements. Here the personal judgment is that of the field-worker rather than the designer of the research, as it might be in the case of a judgment sample. This raises the question of whether quota samples can indeed be considered representative even though they accurately reflect the target population with respect to the proportion of the sample possessing each control characteristic. Three points need to be made in this regard.

First, the sample could be very far off with respect to some other important characteristic likely to influence the result. Thus, if the campus study is concerned with racial prejudice existing on campus, it may very well make a difference whether field-workers interview students from urban or rural areas. Since a quota for the urban-rural characteristic was not specified, it is unlikely that those participating will accurately reflect this characteristic. The alternative, of course, is to specify quotas for all potentially important characteristics. The problem is that increasing the number of control characteristics makes specifications more complex. This in turn makes the location of sample elements more difficult—perhaps even impossible—and certainly more expensive. If, for example, geographic origin and socioeconomic status were also important characteristics in the study, the field-worker might be assigned to find an upper-middle-class male freshman from an urban area. This is obviously a much more difficult task than simply locating a male freshman.

Also, it is difficult to verify whether a quota sample is representative. Certainly one can check the distribution of characteristics in the sample not used as controls to determine whether the distribution parallels that of the target population. However, this type of comparison provides only negative evidence. It can indicate that the sample does not reflect the target population if the distributions on some characteristics are different. If the sample and target population distributions are similar for each of these characteristics, it is still possible for the sample to be vastly different from the target population on some characteristic not explicitly compared.

Finally, interviewers left to their own devices are prone to follow certain practices. They tend to interview their friends in excessive proportion. Since their friends are often similar to themselves, this can introduce bias. The empirical evidence from England, for example, indicates that quota samples are biased (1) toward the accessible, (2) against small households, (3) toward households with children, (4) against workers in manufacturing, (5) against extremes of income, (6) against the less educated, and (7) against low-status individuals.[8] Interviewers who fill their quotas by stopping passersby are likely to concentrate on areas where there are large numbers of potential respondents, such as business districts, railway and airline terminals, and the entrances to large department stores. This practice tends to overrepresent the kinds of people who frequent these areas. When home visits are required, interviewers often succumb to the lures of convenience and appearance. They may conduct interviews only during the day, for example, resulting in an underrepresentation of working people. They often avoid dilapidated buildings and the upper stories of buildings without elevators.

Depending on the subject of the study, all these tendencies have the potential for bias. They may or may not in fact actually bias the result, but it is difficult to correct them when analyzing the data. When the sample elements are selected objectively, on the other hand, researchers have certain tools they can rely on to make the question of whether a particular sample is representative less difficult. In these probability samples, one relies on the sampling procedure and not on the composition of the specific sample to solve the problem of representation.

Probability Samples

In a probability sample, researchers can calculate the likelihood that any given population element will be included, because the final sample elements are selected objectively by a specific process and not according to the whims of the researcher or field-worker. Since the elements are selected objectively, researchers are able to assess the reliability of the sample results, something not possible with nonprobability samples regardless of the careful judgment exercised in selecting individuals.

This is not to say that probability samples will always be more representative than nonprobability samples. Indeed, a nonprobability sample may be more representative. The advantage of probability samples is that they allow an assessment of the amount of sampling error likely to occur, because a sample rather than a census was used when gathering the data. Nonprobability samples, on the other hand, allow the investigator no objective method for evaluating the adequacy of the sample.

Simple Random Sampling

Most people have had experience with simple random samples either in beginning statistics courses or in reading about the results of such samples in newspapers or magazines. In a simple random sample, each unit included in the sample has a known and equal chance of being selected for study, and every combination of population elements is a sample possibility. For example, if we wanted a simple random sample of all students enrolled in a particular college, we might assign a number to each student on a comprehensive list of all those enrolled and then have a computer pick a sample randomly.

Hypothetical Population

Element	Income (Dollars)	Education (Years)	Newspaper Subscription	Element	Income (Dollars)	Education (Years)	Newspaper Subscription
1 A	5,600	8	X	11 K	9,600	13	X
2 B	6,000	9	Y	12 L	10,000	13	Y
3 C	6,400	11	X	13 M	10,400	14	X
4 D	6,800	11	Y	14 N	10,800	14	Y
5 E	7,200	11	X	15 O	11,200	15	X
6 F	7,600	12	Y	16 P	11,600	16	Y
7 G	8,000	12	X	17 Q	12,000	16	X
8 H	8,400	12	Y	18 R	12,400	17	Y
9 I	8,800	12	X	19 S	12,800	18	X
10 J	9,200	12	Y	20 T	13,200	18	Y

Parent Population

8 *Explain what a parameter in a sampling procedure is.*

parent population
The totality of cases that conform to some designated specifications; also called a *target population.*

parameter
A fixed characteristic or measure of a parent, or target, population.

The **parent population**, or *target population,* is the population from which the simple random sample will be drawn. This population can be described by certain **parameters**, which are characteristics of the parent population, each representing a fixed quantity that distinguishes one population from another. For example, suppose the parent population for a study were all adults in Cincinnati. A number of parameters could be used to describe this population: the average age, the proportion with a college education, the range of incomes, and so on. Note that these quantities are fixed in value. Given a census of this population, we can readily calculate them. Rather than relying on a census, we usually select a sample and use the values calculated from the sample observations to estimate the required population values.

To see how this is done, consider the hypothetical population of 20 individuals shown in Exhibit 15.1. There are several advantages in working with a small hypothetical population like this. First, the population's small size makes it easy to calculate the parameters that might be used to describe it. For example, we could readily calculate the mean income in dollars, the median education in years, the proportion of people subscribing to newspaper X, and a number of other parameters such as the range in incomes that might be used to describe this population. Second, its size makes it relatively easy to see what might happen under a particular sampling plan. Both of these features make it easier to compare the sample results to the "true," but now known, population value than would be the case in the typical situation where the actual population value is unknown. The comparison of the estimate with the "true" value is thus more vivid than it otherwise would be.

Consider, for example, the *population mean income,* which is a parameter in that it is a fixed quantity that can be used to describe this population. To estimate a population mean, denoted by μ, we would divide the sum of all the values by the number of values making up the sum. That is,

$$\text{population mean } \mu = \frac{\text{sum of population elements}}{\text{number of population elements}}$$

In this case the calculation yields

$$\frac{5,600 + 6,000 + \ldots + 13,200}{20} = 9,400$$

Derived Population

9 *Explain what the derived population is.*

The **derived population** consists of all the possible samples that can be drawn from the parent population under a given sampling plan. A **statistic** is a characteristic or measure of a sample. The value of a statistic used to estimate a particular parameter depends on the particular sample selected from the parent population under the sampling plan specified. Different samples yield different statistics and different estimates of the same population parameter.

Consider the derived population of *all* the possible samples that could be drawn from our hypothetical parent population of 20 individuals, under a sampling plan that specifies that a sample size of $n = 2$ be drawn by simple random sampling without replacement.

Let us assume, for the time being, that the information for each population element—in this case, the person's name and income—is written on a disk, placed in a jar, and shaken thoroughly. The researcher then reaches into the jar, pulls out one disk, records the information on it, and puts it aside. She does the same with a second disk. Then she places both disks back in the jar and repeats the process. Exhibit 15.2 shows the many possible results of following this procedure. There are 190 possible combinations of the 20 disks.

For each combination, one could calculate the sample mean income. Thus, for the sample AB, $(k = 1)$,

$$k\text{th sample mean} = \frac{\text{sum of sample elements}}{\text{number of elements in sample}} = \frac{5,600 + 6,000}{2} = 5,800$$

Figure 15.4 displays the estimates of population mean income and the amount of error in each estimate when samples $k = 25, 62, 108, 147,$ and 189 are drawn.

derived population
A population of all possible distinguishable samples that could be drawn from a parent population under a specific sampling plan.

statistic
A characteristic or measure of a sample.

Figure 15.4

Several Possible Samples and Their Respective Errors When Estimating the Population Mean

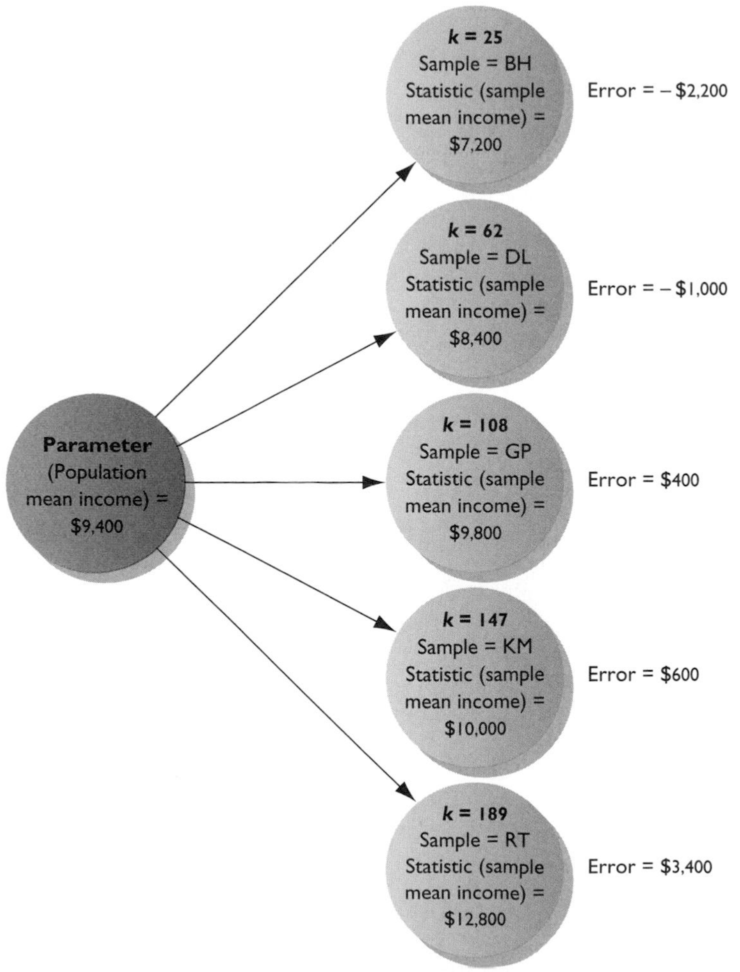

Parameter (Population mean income) = $9,400

k = 25
Sample = BH
Statistic (sample mean income) = $7,200
Error = – $2,200

k = 62
Sample = DL
Statistic (sample mean income) = $8,400
Error = – $1,000

k = 108
Sample = GP
Statistic (sample mean income) = $9,800
Error = $400

k = 147
Sample = KM
Statistic (sample mean income) = $10,000
Error = $600

k = 189
Sample = RT
Statistic (sample mean income) = $12,800
Error = $3,400

Exhibit 15.2

Derived Population of All Possible Samples of Size *n* = 2 with Simple Random Selection

K	Sample Identity	Mean	K	Sample Identity	Mean	K	Sample Identity	Mean	K	Sample Identity	Mean
1	AB	5,800	51	CQ	9,200	101	GI	8,400	151	KQ	10,800
2	AC	6,000	52	CR	9,400	102	GJ	8,600	152	KR	11,000
3	AD	6,200	53	CS	9,600	103	GK	8,800	153	KS	11,200
4	AE	6,400	54	CT	9,800	104	GL	9,000	154	KT	11,400
5	AF	6,600	55	DE	7,000	105	GM	9,200	155	LM	10,200
6	AG	6,800	56	DF	7,200	106	GN	9,400	156	LN	10,400
7	AH	7,000	57	DG	7,400	107	GO	9,600	157	LO	10,600
8	AI	7,200	58	DH	7,600	108	GP	9,800	158	LP	10,800
9	AJ	7,400	59	DI	7,800	109	GQ	10,000	159	LQ	11,000
10	AK	7,600	60	DJ	8,000	110	GR	10,200	160	LR	11,200
11	AL	7,800	61	DK	8,200	111	GS	10,400	161	LS	11,400
12	AM	8,000	62	DL	8,400	112	GT	10,600	162	LT	11,600
13	AN	8,200	63	DM	8,600	113	HI	8,600	163	MN	10,600
14	AO	8,400	64	DN	8,800	114	HJ	8,800	164	MO	10,800
15	AP	8,600	65	DO	9,000	115	HK	9,000	165	MP	11,000
16	AQ	8,800	66	DP	9,200	116	HL	9,200	166	MQ	11,200
17	AR	9,000	67	DQ	9,400	117	HM	9,400	167	MR	11,400
18	AS	9,200	68	DR	9,600	118	HN	9,600	168	MS	11,600
19	AT	9,400	69	DS	9,800	119	HO	9,800	169	MT	11,800
20	BC	6,200	70	DT	10,000	120	HP	10,000	170	NO	11,000
21	BD	6,400	71	EF	7,400	121	HQ	10,200	171	NP	11,200
22	BE	6,600	72	EG	7,600	122	HR	10,400	172	NQ	11,400
23	BF	6,800	73	EH	7,800	123	HS	10,600	173	NR	11,600
24	BG	7,000	74	EI	8,000	124	HT	10,800	174	NS	11,800
25	BH	7,200	75	EJ	8,200	125	IJ	9,000	175	NT	12,200
26	BI	7,400	76	EK	8,400	126	IK	9,200	176	OP	11,400
27	BJ	7,600	77	EL	8,600	127	IL	9,400	177	OQ	11,600
28	BK	7,800	78	EM	8,800	128	IM	9,600	178	OR	11,800
29	BL	8,000	79	EN	9,000	129	IN	9,800	179	OS	12,000
30	BM	8,200	80	EO	9,200	130	IO	10,000	180	OT	12,200
31	BN	8,400	81	EP	9,400	131	IP	10,200	181	PQ	11,800
32	BO	8,600	82	EQ	9,600	132	IQ	10,400	182	PR	12,000
33	BP	8,800	83	ER	9,800	133	IR	10,600	183	PS	12,200
34	BQ	9,000	84	ES	10,000	134	IS	10,800	184	PT	12,400
35	BR	9,200	85	ET	10,200	135	IT	11,000	185	QR	12,200
36	BS	9,400	86	FG	7,800	136	JK	9,400	186	QS	12,400
37	BT	9,600	87	FH	8,000	137	JL	9,600	187	QT	12,600
38	CD	6,600	88	FI	8,200	138	JM	9,800	188	RS	12,600
39	CE	6,800	89	FJ	8,400	139	JN	10,000	189	RT	12,800
40	CF	7,000	90	FK	8,600	140	JO	10,200	190	ST	13,000
41	CG	7,200	91	FL	8,800	141	JP	10,400			
42	CH	7,400	92	FM	9,000	142	JQ	10,600			
43	CI	7,600	93	FN	9,200	143	JR	10,800			
44	CJ	7,800	94	FO	9,400	144	JS	11,000			
45	CK	8,000	95	FP	9,600	145	JT	11,200			
46	CL	8,200	96	FQ	9,800	146	KL	9,800			
47	CM	8,400	97	FR	10,000	147	KM	10,000			
48	CN	8,600	98	FS	10,200	148	KN	10,200			
49	CO	8,800	99	FT	10,400	149	KO	10,400			
50	CP	9,000	100	GH	8,200	150	KP	10,600			

Before discussing the relationship between the sample mean income (a statistic) and the population mean income (the parameter to be estimated), a few words are in order regarding the notion of derived population. First, in practice, we do not actually generate the derived population. This would be extremely wasteful of time and data. Rather, the practitioner merely generates one sample of the needed size. But the researcher will make use of the *concept* of a derived population and the associated notion of sampling distribution in making inferences. We shall see how in just a moment.

Second, the derived population is defined as the population of all possible distinguishable samples that can be drawn under a *given sampling plan*. Change any part of the sampling plan, and the derived population will also change. Thus, when selecting disks, if the researcher is to replace the first disk drawn, the derived population will include the sample possibilities *AA, BB,* and so on. With samples of Size 3 instead of 2, drawn without replacement, *ABC* is a sample possibility, and there are a number of additional possibilities as well—1,140 versus the 190 with samples of Size 2. Change the method of selecting elements by using something other than simple random sampling, and the derived population will also change.

Finally, picking a sample of a given size from a parent population is equivalent to picking 1 of the 190 possible combinations out of the derived population. This fact is basic in making statistical inferences.

Sample Mean versus Population Mean

If we want to evaluate the income of those in a simple random sample, can we assume that the sample mean will equal the parent population mean? To a large extent we generally assume there is a relationship. Sometimes we know *a priori* that the estimate could be in error. We might expect information gathered from a sample of Internet users, for example, to vary greatly from the population as a whole (see the e-centives ad). In other cases, we think the sample mean should fairly accurately estimate the population mean; otherwise, it would be senseless to use the sample value to estimate the population value. But how much error is there likely to be?

Suppose we added up all the sample means in Exhibit 15.2 and divided by the number of samples; that is, suppose we were to average the averages. By doing this, we would get the following:

$$\frac{5,800 + 6,000 + \ldots + 13,000}{190} = 9,400$$

This is the mean of the parent population also. And this is what is meant by an *unbiased statistic*.

A statistic is unbiased when its average value across all possible samples equals the population parameter that it is supposed to estimate. Note that the fact that it is unbiased says nothing about any particular value of the statistic. Even though unbiased, a particular estimate may be very far from the true population value—for example, the sample means with sample AB or sample ST provide very poor estimates of the population mean. In some cases, the true population value may even be impossible to achieve with any possible sample even though the statistic is unbiased; this is not true in the example, however, since a number of sample possibilities—for example, *AT*—yield a sample mean that equals the population average.

Next, it is useful to look at the spread of these sample estimates, and particularly the relationship between this spread of estimates and the dispersion of incomes in the population. A very useful measure of spread is the population variance. To compute the population variance, we calculate the deviation of

Courtesy of E-centives, Inc.

The Internet is a source of information for marketers, who can track people's browsing and purchasing habits. Programs such as e-centives reward browsers with online coupons and other offers for filling out personal profiles.

each value from the mean, square these deviations, sum them, and divide by the number of values making up the sum. Letting σ^2 denote the population variance, the calculation yields

$$\text{population variance } \sigma^2 = \frac{\text{sum of squared differences of each}}{\text{population element from the population mean}}$$
$$\frac{}{\text{number of population elements}}$$

$$= \frac{(5,600 - 9,400)^2 + (6,000 - 9,400)^2 + \ldots + (13,200 - 9,400)^2}{20}$$

$$= 5,320,000$$

The variance of *mean incomes* could be calculated similarly. That is, we could calculate the variance of mean incomes by taking the deviation of each mean around its overall mean, squaring and summing these deviations, and then dividing by the number of cases.

Alternatively, we could determine the variance of mean incomes indirectly by using the variance of incomes in the parent population, since there is a direct relationship between the two quantities. More specifically, it turns out that when the sample is only a small part of the parent population, the variance of sample mean incomes is equal to the parent population variance divided by the sample size. In symbols, this means that

$$\sigma_{\bar{x}}^2 = \frac{\sigma^2}{n}$$

where $\sigma_{\bar{x}}^2$ is the variance of sample mean incomes, while σ^2 is the variance of incomes in the population, and n is the sample size.[9]

10 *Explain why the concept of sampling distribution is the most important concept in statistics.*

sampling distribution
The distribution of values of some statistic calculated for each possible distinguishable sample that could be drawn from a parent population under a specific sampling plan.

central-limit theorem
A theorem that holds that if simple random samples of size n are drawn from a parent population with mean μ and variance σ^2, then when n is large, the sample mean $\bar{x}$ will be approximately normally distributed with mean equal to μ and variance equal to σ^2/n. The approximation will become more and more accurate as n becomes larger.

Third, consider the distribution of the estimates in contrast to the distribution of the variable in the parent population. Figure 15.5 indicates that the parent population distribution, depicted by Panel A, is spiked—each of the 20 values occurs once—and is symmetrical about the population mean value of 9,400. The distribution of estimates, displayed in Panel B, was constructed from Exhibit 15.3, which in turn was generated by placing each of the estimates in Exhibit 15.2 in categories according to size and then counting the number contained in each category. Panel B is the traditional histogram discussed in beginning statistics courses and represents the **sampling distribution** of the statistic. Note this: The notion of sampling distribution is the single most important notion in statistics; it is the cornerstone of statistical inference procedures. If one knows the sampling distribution for the statistic in question, one is in a position to make an inference about the corresponding population parameter. If, on the other hand, one knows only that a particular sample estimate will vary with repeated sampling and has no information as to *how* it will vary, then it will be impossible to devise a measure of the sampling error associated with that estimate. Since the sampling distribution of an estimate describes how that estimate will vary with repeated sampling, it provides a basis for determining the reliability of the sample estimate. This is why probability sampling plans are so important to statistical inference. With known probabilities of inclusion of any population element in the sample, statisticians are able to derive the sampling distribution of various statistics. Researchers then rely on these distributions—be they for a sample mean, sample proportion, sample variance, or some other statistic—in making their inferences from single samples to population values. Note also that the distribution of sample means is mound-shaped and symmetrical about the population mean with samples of Size 2.

Recapitulating, we have shown that

1. The mean of all possible sample means is equal to the population mean.
2. The variance of sample means is related to the population variance.
3. The distribution of sample means is mound-shaped, whereas the population distribution is spiked.

Central-Limit Theorem The mound-shaped distribution of estimates provides preliminary evidence of the operation of the **central-limit theorem**, which holds that if simple random

Figure 15.5

Distribution of Variable in Parent Population and Distribution of Estimates in Derived Population

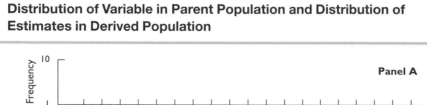

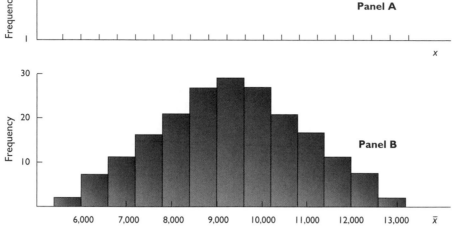

Exhibit 15.3

Classification of Estimates by Size

Sample Mean	Number of Samples
$6,000 or less	2
$6,100 to 6,600	7
$6,700 to 7,200	11
$7,300 to 7,800	16
$7,900 to 8,400	20
$8,500 to 9,000	25
$9,100 to 9,600	28
$9,700 to 10,200	25
$10,300 to 10,800	20
$10,900 to 11,400	16
$11,500 to 12,000	11
$12,100 to 12,600	7
$12,700 or more	2

samples of a given size n are drawn from a parent population with mean equal to μ, and variance equal to σ^2, then when the sample size n is large, the *distribution of sample means* will be approximately normally distributed with its mean equal to the population mean and its variance equal to the parent population variance divided by the sample size; that is,

$$\sigma_{\bar{x}}^{2} = \frac{\sigma^{2}}{n}$$

The approximation will become more and more accurate as n becomes larger. Note the impact of this. It means that regardless of the shape of the parent population, the distribution of *sample means will be normal* if the sample is large enough. How large is large enough? If the distribution of the variable in the parent population is normal, then the distribution of means of samples of size $n = 1$ will be normal. If the distribution of the variable is symmetrical but not normal, then samples of very small size will produce a distribution in which the means are normally distributed. If the distribution of the variable is highly skewed in the parent population, then samples of a larger size will be needed.

The fact remains that the distribution of the statistic, sample mean, can be assumed normal if only we work with a sample of sufficient size. We do not need to rely on the assumption that the variable is normally distributed in the parent population in order to make inferences using the normal curve. Rather, we rely on the central-limit theorem and adjust the sample size according to the population distribution so that the normal curve can be assumed to hold. Fortunately, the normal distribution of the statistic occurs with samples of relatively small size, as Figure 15.6 indicates.

Confidence Interval Estimates   How does all of the preceding help us make inferences about the parent population mean? After all, in practice we do not draw all possible samples

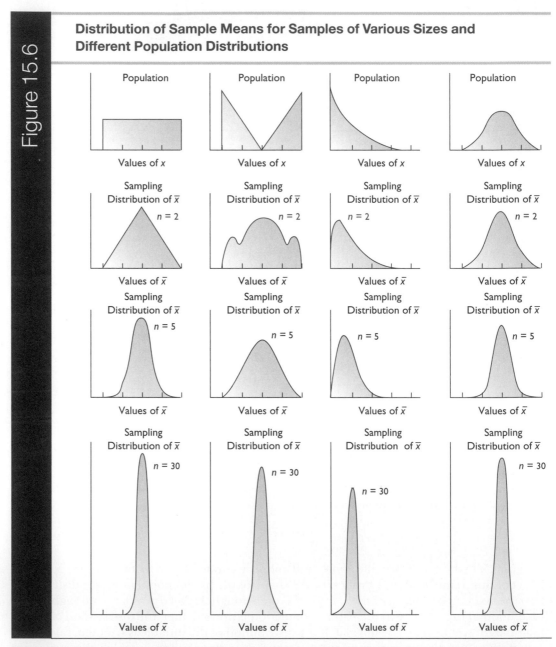

Figure 15.6

Distribution of Sample Means for Samples of Various Sizes and Different Population Distributions

Source: Ernest Kurnow, Gerald J. Glasser, and Frederick R. Ottman, *Statistics for Business Decisions* (Homewood, Ill.: Richard D. Irwin, Inc., © 1959), pp. 182–183. Used with permission.

PART 5:
Sampling and Data Collection

of a given size, but only one, and we use the results obtained in it to infer something about the target group. It all ties together in the following way.

It is known that with any normal distribution, a specific percentage of all observations is within a certain number of standard deviations of the mean; for example, 95 percent of the values are within ±1.96 standard deviations of the mean. The distribution of sample means is normal if the central-limit theorem holds and thus is no exception. Now, the mean of this sampling distribution is equal to the population mean μ, and its standard deviation is given by the square root of the variance of means, which is called the standard error of the mean, specifically $\sigma_{\bar{x}} = \sigma/\sqrt{n}$. Therefore, it is true that

- 68.26 percent of the sample means will be within ± 1 $\sigma_{\bar{x}}$ of the population mean
- 95.45 percent of the sample means will be within ± 2 $\sigma_{\bar{x}}$ of the population mean
- 99.73 percent of the sample means will be within ± 3 $\sigma_{\bar{x}}$ of the population mean

and in general, that $\mu \pm z\sigma_{\bar{x}}$ will contain some certain proportion of all sample means depending on the selected value of z. This expression can be rewritten as an inequality relation that

$$\begin{array}{c}\text{population}\\\text{mean}\end{array} - z \left(\begin{array}{c}\text{standard error}\\\text{of the mean}\end{array}\right) \le \begin{array}{c}\text{sample}\\\text{mean}\end{array} \le \begin{array}{c}\text{population}\\\text{mean}\end{array} + z \left(\begin{array}{c}\text{standard error}\\\text{of the mean}\end{array}\right)$$

or

$$\mu - z\sigma_{\bar{x}} \le \bar{x} \le \mu + z\sigma_{\bar{x}} \tag{15.1}$$

which is held to be true a certain percentage of the time, and which implies that the sample mean will be in the interval formed by adding and subtracting a certain number of standard deviations to the mean value of the distribution. This inequality can be transferred to the equivalent inequality:

$$\begin{array}{c}\text{sample}\\\text{mean}\end{array} - z \left(\begin{array}{c}\text{standard error}\\\text{of the mean}\end{array}\right) \le \begin{array}{c}\text{population}\\\text{mean}\end{array} \le \begin{array}{c}\text{sample}\\\text{mean}\end{array} + z \left(\begin{array}{c}\text{standard error}\\\text{of the mean}\end{array}\right)$$

or

$$\bar{x} - z\sigma_{\bar{x}} \le \mu \le \bar{x} + z\sigma_{\bar{x}} \tag{15.2}$$

And, if Equation 15.1 is true, say, 95 percent of the time ($z = 1.96$), then Equation 15.2 is also true 95 percent of the time. *When we make an inference on the basis of a single sample mean, we make use of Equation 15.2.*

It is important to note that Equation 15.2 says *nothing about the interval constructed from a particular sample as including the population mean.* Rather, the interval addresses the *sampling procedure.* The interval around a single mean may or may not contain the true population mean. Our confidence in our inference rests on the property that 95 percent of all the intervals we could construct under that sampling plan would contain the true value. We trust or hope that our sample is one of those 95 out of 100 that does (when we are 95 percent confident) include the true value.

To illustrate this important point, suppose for the moment that the distribution of sample means of size $n = 2$ for our hypothetical example was normal. Exhibit 15.4 illustrates the outcome pictorially for the first 10 out of the possible 190 samples that could be drawn under the specified sampling plan. Note that only 7 of the 10 intervals contain the true population mean. Confidence in the estimate arises because of the *procedure*, therefore, and not because of a particular estimate. The procedure suggests that with, say, a 95 percent confidence interval, if 100 samples were to be drawn and the sample mean and the confidence interval computed

Exhibit 15.4

Confidence Intervals for First Ten Samples Assuming the Distribution of Sample Means Was Normal

			Confidence Interval		
Sample Number	Sample Identity	Mean	Lower Limit	Upper Limit	Pictorial True $\mu = 9,400$ (represented by vertical line)
1	AB	5,800	2,689	8,911	
2	AC	6,000	2,889	9,111	
3	AD	6,200	3,089	9,311	
4	AE	6,400	3,289	9,511	
5	AF	6,600	3,489	9,711	
6	AG	6,800	3,689	9,911	
7	AH	7,000	3,889	10,111	
8	AI	7,200	4,089	10,311	
9	AJ	7,400	4,289	10,511	
10	AK	7,600	4,489	10,711	

for each, 95 of the constructed intervals would include the true population value. The accuracy of a specific sample is evaluated only by reference to the procedure by which the sample was obtained. A sampling plan that is representative does not guarantee that a particular sample is representative. Statistical inference procedures rest on the representativeness of the sampling plan, and this is why probability samples are so critical to those procedures. Probability samples allow an estimate of the *precision* of the results in terms of how closely the estimates will tend to cluster about the true value. The greater the standard error of the statistic, the more variable the estimates and the less precise the procedure.

If it disturbs you that the confidence level applies to the procedure and not a particular sample result, you can take comfort in the fact that you can control the level of confidence with which the population value is estimated. Thus, if you do not wish to take the risk that you might have 1 of the 5 sample intervals in 100 that does not contain the population value, you might use a 99 percent confidence interval, in which the risk is that only 1 in 100 sample intervals will not contain the population mean. Further, if you are willing to increase the size of the sample, you can increase your confidence and at the same time maintain the precision with which the population value is estimated. This will be explored more fully in Chapter 17.

There is one other perhaps disturbing ingredient in our procedure: The confidence interval estimate made use of three values: $\bar{x}$, z, and $\sigma_{\bar{x}}$. Now the sample mean $\bar{x}$ is computed from the selected sample, and z is specified to produce the desired level of confidence. But what about the standard error of the mean, $\sigma_{\bar{x}}$? It is equal to $\sigma_{\bar{x}} = \sigma/\sqrt{n}$, and thus, in order to calculate it, we need to know the standard deviation of the variable in the population—that is, σ. What do we do if the population standard deviation, σ, is unknown? There is no problem, for two reasons. First, variation typically changes much more slowly than level for most variables of interest in marketing. Thus if the study is a repeat, we can use the previously discovered value for σ. Second, once the sample is selected and the information gathered, we can calculate the sample variance to estimate the population variance. The unbiased sample variance $\hat{s}^2$ is calculated as

$$\text{sample variance } \hat{s}^2 = \frac{\text{sum of deviations around sample mean squared}}{\text{sample size} - 1}$$

To compute the sample variance then, we first calculate the sample mean. We then calculate the difference between each of our sample values and the sample mean, square these differences, sum them, and divide the sum by one less than the number of sample observations. The sample variance not only provides an estimate of the population variance, but it can also be used to secure an estimate of the standard error of the mean. When the population variance, σ^2, is known, the standard error of the mean, $\sigma_{\bar{x}}$, is also known, since $\sigma_{\bar{x}} = \sigma/\sqrt{n}$. When the population variance is unknown, the standard error of the mean can only be estimated. The estimate is given by $s_{\bar{x}}$, which equals the sample standard deviation divided by the square root of the sample size—that is, $\hat{s}/\sqrt{n}$. The estimate calculation parallels that for the true value with the sample standard deviation substituted for the population standard deviation. Thus, if we draw sample AB, with a mean of 5,800,

$$\hat{s} = \frac{(5,600-5,800)^2 + (6,000-5,800)^2}{1} = 80,000$$

and thus $\hat{s} = 283$ and $s_{\bar{x}} = \hat{s}/\sqrt{n} = 283/\sqrt{2} = 200$, and the 95 percent confidence interval is now

$$5,800 - 1.96(200) \le \mu \le 5,800 + 1.96(200) = 5,408 \le \mu \le 6,192$$

which is somewhat smaller than before.

Exhibit 15.5 summarizes the computational formulas for the various means and variances used in this chapter.

Drawing the Simple Random Sample   Although it was useful for illustrating the concepts of derived population and sampling distribution, the selection of sample elements from a jar containing all the population elements is not particularly recommended because of its great potential for bias. It is unlikely that the disks would be exactly uniform in size or feel, and slight differences could affect the likelihood that any single element would be drawn. The national draft during the Vietnam War using a lottery serves as an example. Draft priorities were determined by drawing disks with birth dates stamped on them from a large container in full view of a television audience. Unfortunately, the dates of the year had initially been poured into the bowl systematically, January first and December last. Although the bowl was then stirred vigorously, December dates tended to be chosen first and January dates last. The procedure was later revised to produce a more random selection process.

Exhibit 15.5

Symbols and Formulas Used for Means and Variances with Simple Random Samples

	Mean	Variance
Population	$\mu = \dfrac{\text{sum of population elements}}{\text{number of population elements}}$	$\sigma^2 = \dfrac{\text{sum of squared differences of each population element from the population mean}}{\text{number of population elements}}$
Sample	$\bar{x} = \dfrac{\text{sum of sample elements}}{\text{number of sample elements}}$	$\hat{s}^2 = \dfrac{\text{sum of squared differences of each sample element from the sample mean}}{\text{number of sample elements}-1}$
Derived Population of Sample Means	average = unknown population mean	$\sigma_{\bar{x}}^2 = \dfrac{\sigma^2}{n}$ (when population variance is known) $s_{\bar{x}}^2 = \dfrac{\hat{s}^2}{n}$ (when population variance is unknown)

The preferred way of drawing a simple random sample is through the use of a table of random numbers. Using a random-number table involves the following steps: First, the elements of the parent population are numbered serially from 1 to N; for the hypothetical population, the element A would be numbered 1, B as 2, and so on. Next, the numbers in the table are treated so as to have the same number of digits as N. With $N = 20$, two-digit numbers would be used; if N were between 100 and 999, three-digit numbers would be required, and so on. Third, a starting point is determined randomly. We might simply open the table to some arbitrary place and point to a position on the page with our eyes closed. Since the numbers in a random-number table are in fact random—that is, without order—it makes little difference where we begin.[10] Finally, we proceed in some arbitrary direction, for example, up, down, or across, and select those elements for the sample for which there is a match of serial number and random number.

To illustrate, consider the partial list of random numbers contained in Exhibit 15.6. Since $N = 20$, we need work with only two digits, and therefore we can use the entries in Exhibit 15.6 as is, instead of having to combine columns to produce numbers covering the range of serial numbers. Suppose we had previously decided to read down and that our arbitrary start indicated the eleventh row, fourth column, specifically the number 77. This number is too high and would be discarded. The next two numbers would also be discarded, but the fourth entry, 02, would be used, since 2 corresponds to one of the serial numbers in the list, Element B. The next five numbers would also be passed over as too large, whereas the number 05 would designate the inclusion of Element E. Elements B and E would thus represent the sample of two from whom we would seek information on income.

An alternative strategy would be to use a computer program to generate the random numbers. Although there is some evidence that suggests the numbers generated by computer programs are not as random as is commonly believed, their accuracy is sufficient for most applied marketing research studies, although perhaps not for complex mathematical model building.[11]

You should note that a simple random sample requires a serial numbered list of population elements. This means that the identity of each member of the target population must be known. For some populations this is no problem—for example, if the study is to be conducted among *Fortune* magazine's list of the 500 largest corporations in the United States. The list is readily available, and a simple random sample of these firms could be easily selected. For many other target populations of interest (for example, all families living in a particular city), the list of universe elements is much harder to come by, and applied researchers often resort to other sampling schemes.

Exhibit 15.6

Abridged List of Random Numbers

10 09 73 25 33	76 52 01 35 86	34 67 35 48 76	80 95 90 91 17	39 29 27 49 45
37 54 20 48 05	64 89 47 42 96	24 80 52 40 37	20 63 61 04 02	00 82 29 16 65
08 42 26 89 53	19 64 50 93 03	23 20 90 25 60	15 95 33 47 64	35 08 03 36 06
99 01 90 25 29	09 37 67 07 15	38 31 13 11 65	88 67 67 43 97	04 43 62 76 59
12 80 79 99 70	80 15 73 61 47	64 03 23 66 53	98 95 11 68 77	12 17 17 68 33
66 06 57 47 17	34 07 27 68 50	36 69 73 61 70	65 81 33 98 85	11 19 92 91 70
31 06 01 08 05	45 57 18 24 06	35 30 34 26 14	86 79 90 74 39	23 40 30 97 32
85 26 97 76 02	02 05 16 56 92	68 66 57 48 18	73 05 38 52 47	18 62 38 85 79
63 57 33 21 35	05 32 54 70 48	90 55 35 75 48	28 46 82 87 09	83 49 12 56 24
73 79 64 57 53	03 52 96 47 78	35 80 83 42 82	60 93 52 03 44	35 27 38 84 35
98 52 01 77 67	14 90 56 86 07	22 10 94 05 58	60 97 09 34 33	50 50 07 39 98
11 80 50 54 31	39 80 82 77 32	50 72 56 82 48	29 40 52 42 01	52 77 56 78 51
83 45 29 96 34	06 28 89 80 83	13 74 67 00 78	18 47 54 06 10	68 71 17 78 17
88 68 54 02 00	86 50 75 84 01	36 76 66 79 51	90 36 47 64 93	29 60 91 10 62
99 59 46 73 48	87 51 76 49 69	91 82 60 89 28	93 78 56 13 68	23 47 83 41 13
65 48 11 76 74	17 46 85 09 50	58 04 77 69 74	73 03 95 71 86	40 21 81 65 44
80 12 43 56 35	17 72 70 80 15	45 31 82 23 74	21 11 57 82 53	14 38 55 37 63
74 35 09 98 17	77 40 27 72 14	43 23 60 02 10	45 52 16 42 37	96 28 60 26 55
69 91 62 68 03	66 25 22 91 48	36 93 68 72 03	76 62 11 39 90	94 40 05 64 18
09 89 32 05 05	14 22 56 85 14	46 42 75 67 88	96 29 77 88 22	54 38 21 45 98
91 49 91 45 23	68 47 92 76 86	46 16 28 35 54	94 75 08 99 23	37 08 92 00 48
80 33 69 45 98	26 94 03 68 58	70 29 73 41 35	53 14 03 33 40	42 05 08 23 41
44 10 48 19 49	85 15 74 79 54	32 97 92 65 75	57 60 04 08 81	22 22 20 64 13
12 55 07 37 42	11 10 00 20 40	12 86 07 46 97	96 64 48 94 39	28 70 72 58 15
63 60 64 93 29	16 50 53 44 84	40 21 95 25 63	43 65 17 70 82	07 20 73 17 90
61 19 69 04 46	26 45 74 77 74	51 92 43 37 29	65 39 45 95 93	42 58 26 05 27
15 47 44 52 66	95 27 07 99 53	59 36 78 38 48	82 39 61 01 18	33 21 15 94 66
94 55 72 85 73	67 89 75 43 87	54 62 24 44 31	91 19 04 25 92	92 92 74 59 73
42 48 11 62 13	97 34 40 87 21	16 86 84 87 67	03 07 11 20 59	25 70 14 66 70
23 52 37 83 17	73 20 88 98 37	68 93 59 14 16	26 25 22 96 63	05 52 28 25 62
04 49 35 24 94	75 24 63 38 24	45 86 25 10 25	61 96 27 93 35	65 33 71 24 72
00 54 99 76 54	64 05 18 81 59	96 11 96 38 96	54 69 28 23 91	23 28 72 95 29
35 96 31 53 07	26 89 80 93 54	33 35 13 54 62	77 97 54 00 24	90 10 33 93 33
59 80 80 83 91	45 42 72 68 42	83 60 94 97 00	13 02 12 48 92	78 56 52 01 06
46 05 88 52 36	01 39 09 22 86	77 28 14 40 77	93 91 08 36 47	70 61 74 29 41
32 17 90 05 97	87 37 92 52 41	05 56 70 70 07	86 74 31 71 57	85 39 41 18 38
69 23 46 14 06	20 11 74 52 04	15 95 66 00 00	18 74 39 24 23	97 11 89 63 38
19 56 54 14 30	01 75 87 53 79	40 41 92 15 85	66 67 43 68 06	84 96 28 52 07
45 15 51 49 38	19 47 60 72 46	43 66 79 45 43	59 04 79 00 33	20 82 66 95 41
94 86 43 19 94	36 16 81 08 51	34 88 88 15 53	01 54 03 54 56	05 01 45 11 76
98 08 62 48 26	45 24 02 84 04	44 99 90 88 96	39 09 47 34 07	35 44 13 18 80
33 18 51 62 32	41 94 15 09 49	89 43 54 85 81	88 69 54 19 94	37 54 87 30 43
80 95 10 04 06	96 38 27 07 74	20 15 12 33 87	25 01 62 52 98	94 62 46 11 71
79 75 24 91 40	71 96 12 82 96	69 86 10 25 91	74 85 22 05 39	00 38 75 95 79
18 63 33 25 37	98 14 50 65 71	31 01 02 46 74	05 45 56 14 27	77 93 89 19 36
74 02 94 39 02	77 55 73 22 70	97 79 01 71 19	52 52 75 80 21	80 81 45 17 48
54 17 84 56 11	80 99 33 71 43	05 33 51 29 69	56 12 71 92 55	36 04 09 03 24
11 66 44 98 83	52 07 98 48 27	59 38 17 15 39	09 97 33 34 40	88 46 12 33 56
48 32 47 79 28	31 24 96 47 10	02 29 53 68 70	32 30 75 75 46	15 02 00 99 94
69 07 49 41 38	87 63 79 19 76	35 58 40 44 01	10 51 82 16 15	01 84 87 69 38

Source: This table is reproduced from page 1 of The Rand Corporation, *A Million Random Digits with 100,000 Normal Deviates* (New York: The Free Press, 1955). Copyright © 1955 and 1983 by The Rand Corporation. Used by permission.

"Let's look at this background information from Teenage Research Unlimited," Tomás Mendoza said to his research client, Jill Zimmerman. "TRU calls its online survey Omnibuzz. The 850 Omnibuzz subjects are not strictly a random sample. Every month TRU draws a sample from its teen panelists. They have about 500,000 panelists."

"Where do those panelists come from?" asked Jill.

"TRU puts ads on youth-oriented Web sites. Teens who respond can choose to participate in the panel, and the company takes a sample from the panel. They send an email to the kids in the sample, directing them to a site where the survey is posted."

"And if some kids don't answer?"

"TRU sends one follow-up email. Also, they give an incentive to participate—points for completing a survey. Kids can redeem their points for prizes."

"What else do we know about the participants?"

"The company takes what we call a quota sample to ensure all ages are represented. They select 100 kids of each age from 13 to 18, and they select 50 each of kids aged 8 to 12. That assures us you're not making decisions based only on a sample of 12- and 13-year-olds."

"Do we know anything about them except their age and that they're using the Internet?"

"The survey includes questions on gender, ethnicity, and geographic region. Omnibuzz uses the data to weight the sample to match Census Bureau demographics."

"Might kids in an Internet sample be different from the whole target population?"

"The issue of Internet users versus nonusers is less important than it once was, as more people go online. Also, I'd expect a lot of overlap between Internet users and cell phone users. The difference tends to be that Internet users are younger, more affluent, and better educated than nonusers. For the target population you have in mind, this may not be a problem. Internet users may not represent the whole population, but they may represent your best customers."

"Still, I'm concerned about the sample not being random."

"That's reasonable. If you took a random sample, you could run a lot of statistics to test for reliability. But it could be very expensive to survey enough teens with confidence that we were getting the whole spectrum of ages and geographic regions. In a fast-moving market like yours, an extensive survey might also be too time-consuming. The Omnibuzz data could be available to you in a few weeks."

"From a practical standpoint, we might want to accept some uncertainty if the panel members are enthusiastic enough about our ideas."

"Of course, if you want to adjust your budget, we'd be happy to put together a rigorous study with a large random sample."

"It would be an excellent study, I know! Let me run some more numbers, and I'll get back to you, Tomás. Thanks for your input." ■

Sources: Based on ideas and data in "Tech Firms Look to Young for Tomorrow's Gadgets," *Dallas Morning News* (December 1, 2002), downloaded from Dow Jones Interactive Publications Library, http://nrstg2s.djnr.com; Cheryl Wetzstein, "Family Life at Hand," *Washington Times* (February 7, 2003), downloaded from the Teen Research Unlimited (TRU) Web site, http://www.teenresearch.com; "TRU Announces Launch of First Teen Online Offering," Teen Research Unlimited news release, April 19, 2001, http://www.teenresearch.com; TRU, "Overview" and "Methodology," from Omnibuzz section of TRU Web site, http://www.teenresearch.com, downloaded February 17, 2003; Matt Michel, "The Internet as a Market Research Tool," *Public Relations Tactics*, March 2002, downloaded from Pro-Quest, http://proquest.umi.com/pqdweb.

Summary

Learning Objective 1

Distinguish between a census and a sample.
A complete canvass of a target population is called a census. A *sample* is a portion of the population taken from the larger group.

Learning Objective 2

List the six steps researchers use to draw a sample of a population.
The six steps researchers use in drawing a sample are (1) define the target population, (2) identify the sampling frame, (3) select a sampling procedure, (4) determine the sample size, (5) select the sample elements, and (6) collect the data from the designated elements.

Learning Objective 3

Define sampling frame.
A sampling frame is the listing of the elements from which the actual sample will be drawn.

Learning Objective 4

Explain the difference between a probability sample and a nonprobability sample.
In a probability sample, each member of the target population has a known, nonzero chance of being included in the sample. The chances of each member of the target population being included in the sample may not be equal, but everyone has a known probability of inclusion.

With nonprobability samples, on the other hand, there is no way of estimating the probability that any population element will be included in the sample. Thus, there is no way of ensuring that the sample is representative of the target population. All nonprobability samples rely on personal judgment at some point in the sample-selection process. While these judgments may yield good estimates of a population characteristic, there is no way of determining objectively if the sample is adequate.

Learning Objective 5

Distinguish between a fixed and a sequential sample.
In a fixed sample, the sample size is decided before the study begins, and all the needed information is collected before the results are analyzed. In a sequential sample, the number of elements to be sampled is not decided in advance but is determined by a series of decisions as the data are collected.

Learning Objective 6

Explain what a judgment sample is and describe its best use and its hazards.
A judgment sample is that in which sample elements are handpicked because it is expected that they can serve the research purpose. Sometimes the sample elements are selected because it is believed that they are representative of the population of interest.

As long as the researcher is at the early stages of research, when ideas or insights are being sought—or when the researcher realizes its limitations—the judgment sample can be used productively. It becomes dangerous, however, when it is used in descriptive or causal studies and its weaknesses are conveniently forgotten.

Learning Objective 7

Define quota sample.
The quota sampling technique attempts to ensure that the sample is representative of the population by selecting sample elements in such a way that the proportion of the sample elements possessing a certain characteristic is approximately the same as the proportion of the elements with the characteristic in the target population. This is accomplished by assigning each field-worker a quota that specifies the characteristics of the people the interviewer is to contact.

Learning Objective 8

Explain what a parameter in a sample procedure is.
A parameter is a characteristic of the parent population; it is a fixed quantity that distinguishes one target population from another.

Learning Objective 9

Explain what the derived population is.
The derived population consists of all the possible samples that can be drawn from the parent population under a given sampling plan.

Learning Objective 10

Explain why the concept of sampling distribution is the most important concept in statistics.
The notion of the sampling distribution of the statistic is the cornerstone of statistical inference procedures. If one knows the sampling distribution for the statistic in question, one is in a position to make an inference about the corresponding population parameter. If, on the other hand, one knows only that a particular sample estimate will vary with repeated sampling and has no information as to how it will vary, then it will be impossible to devise a measure of the sampling error associated with that estimate. Since the sampling distribution of an estimate describes how that estimate will vary with repeated sampling, it provides a basis for determining the reliability of the sample estimate.

Key Terms

census (page 400)
sample (page 400)
population (page 400)
sampling frame (page 400)
incidence (page 401)
probability sample (page 403)
nonprobability sample (page 403)
fixed sample (page 404)
sequential sample (page 404)
convenience sample (page 405)

judgment sample (page 406)
snowball sample (page 406)
quota sample (page 406)
parent population (page 410)
parameter (page 410)
derived population (page 411)
statistic (page 411)
sampling distribution (page 414)
central-limit theorem (page 414)

Review Questions

1. What is a census? What is a sample?
2. Is a sample ever preferred to a census? Why?
3. What distinguishes a probability sample from a nonprobability sample?
4. What is a convenience sample?
5. What is a judgment sample?
6. Explain the operation of a quota sample. Why is a quota sample a nonprobability sample? What kinds of comparisons should one make with the data from quota samples to check their representativeness, and what kinds of conclusions can one legitimately draw?
7. What are the distinguishing features of a simple random sample?
8. What is a derived population? How is it distinguished from a parent population?
9. Consider the estimation of a population mean. What is the relation between the mean of the parent population and the mean of the derived population? Between the variance of the parent population and the variance of the derived population?
10. What is the central-limit theorem? What roles does it play in making inferences about a population mean?
11. What procedure is followed in constructing a confidence interval for a population mean when the population variance is known? When the population variance is unknown? What does such an interval mean?
12. How should a simple random sample be selected? Describe the procedure.

Discussion Questions, Problems, and Projects

1. For each of the following situations identify the appropriate target population and sampling frame.
   (a) A local chapter of the American Lung Association wants to test the effectiveness of a brochure titled "12 Reasons for Not Smoking" in the city of St. Paul, Minnesota.
   (b) A medium-sized manufacturer of cat food wants to conduct an in-home usage test of a new type of cat food in Sacramento, California.
   (c) A large wholesaler dealing in household appliances in the city of New York wants to evaluate dealer reaction to a new discount policy.
   (d) A local department store wants to assess the satisfaction with a new credit policy offered to charge account customers.
   (e) A national manufacturer wants to assess whether adequate inventories are being held by wholesalers in order to prevent shortages by retailers.
   (f) Your school cafeteria wants to test a new soft drink manufactured and sold by the staff of the cafeteria.
   (g) A manufacturer of cake mixes selling primarily in the Midwest wants to test-market a new brand of cake mix.

2. The management of a popular tourist resort on the West Coast had noticed a decline in the number of tourists and length of stay over the past three years. An overview of industry trends indicated that the overall tourist trade was expanding and growing rapidly. Management decided to conduct a study to determine people's attitudes toward the particular activities that were available at the resort. It wanted to cause the minimum amount of inconvenience to its customers and hence adopted the following plan: A request was deposited in each hotel room of the two major hotels in the resort, indicating the nature of the study and encouraging customers to participate. The customers were requested to report to a separate desk located in the lobby of the hotels. Personal interviews, lasting 20 minutes, were conducted at this desk.
   (a) What type of sampling method was used?
   (b) Critically evaluate the method used.
3. A national manufacturer of baby food was planning to enter the Canadian market. The initial thrust was to be in the provinces of Ontario and Quebec. Prior to the final decisions of launching the product, management decided to test-market the products in two cities. After reviewing the various cities in terms of such external criteria as demographics, shopping characteristics, and so on, the research department settled on the cities of Hamilton, Ontario, and Sherbrooke, Quebec.
   (a) What type of sampling method was used?
   (b) Critically evaluate the method used.
4. The Juno Company, a manufacturer of clothing for large-size consumers, was in the process of evaluating its product and advertising strategy. Initial efforts consisted of a number of focus-group interviews. The focus groups consisted of 10 to 12 large men and women of different demographic characteristics who were selected by the company's research department using on-the-street observations of physical characteristics.
   (a) What type of sampling method was used?
   (b) Critically evaluate the method used.
5. The Hi-Style Company is a chain of beauty salons in San Diego, California. During the past five years the company has seen a sharp increase in the number of shops it operates and in the company's gross sales and net profit margin. The owner plans to offer a free service of hair analysis and consultation, a service for which competing salons charge a substantial price. In order to offset the increase in operating expenses, the owner plans to raise the rates on other services by five percent. Prior to introducing this new service and increasing rates, the owner wants to do a survey using her customers as a sample and employing the method of quota sampling. Your assistance is required in planning the study.
   (a) On what variables will you suggest the quotas be based? Why? List the variables with their respective levels.
   (b) The owner has kept close track of the demographic characteristics of her customers over a five-year period and decides that these would be most relevant in identifying the sample elements to be used.

Variable	Level	Percent of Customers
Age	0–15 years	5
	16–30 years	30
	31–45 years	30
	46–60 years	15
	61–75 years	15
	76 years and over	5
Sex	Male	24
	Female	76
Income	$0–$9,999	10
	$10,000–$19,999	20
	$20,000–$29,999	30
	$30,000–$39,999	20
	$40,000 and over	20

   Based on these three quota variables, indicate the characteristics of a sample of 200 subjects.
   (c) Discuss the possible sources of bias with the sampling method.

Suggested Additional Readings

For a more in-depth discussion of some of the more fundamental issues in sampling, see Martin Frankel, "Sampling Theory," in Peter H. Rossi, James D. Wright, and Andy B. Anderson, eds., *Handbook of Survey Research* (Orlando: Academic Press, 1983), pp. 21–67.

Gary T. Henry, *Practical Sampling* (Thousand Oaks, Calif.: Sage Publications, 1990).

Richard L. Schaeffer and William Mendenhall, *Elementary Survey Sampling*, 5th ed. (Belmont, Calif.: Wadsworth Publishing, 1996).

Chapter 16

Stratified and Cluster Sampling

© ProtoDisc/Getty Images

Learning Objectives

1   *Specify the two procedures that distinguish a stratified sample.*

2   *Cite two reasons researchers might opt to use a stratified sample rather than a simple random sample.*

3   *Note what points investigators should keep in mind when dividing a population into strata for a stratified sample.*

4   *Explain what a proportionate stratified sample is.*

5   *Explain what a disproportionate stratified sample is.*

6   *List the steps followed in drawing a cluster sample.*

7   *Explain the difference between a one-stage cluster sample and a two-stage cluster sample.*

8   *Explain why cluster sampling, though far less statistically efficient than comparable stratified samples, is the sampling procedure used most in large-scale field surveys using personal interviews.*

9   *Distinguish between one-stage area sampling and simple two-stage area sampling.*

10   *Note the quality that distinguishes probability-proportional-to-size sampling and explain when it is used.*

Pam Heisler looked across the table at the two advisers whose efforts had allowed her to keep a pulse on the mood of the electorate during the early months of her campaign for state senator. She had the highest respect for their judgment. They had helped her keep the Heisler for Senate campaign focused on issues that mattered most to her constituents. The only problem was that right now, they were giving her conflicting advice.

"We know your ideas for school finance reform are solid," said one adviser, Terry Shapiro. "But the polls show voters are divided. Almost everyone says they want reform. It's just the details of the plan that they're split on. That tells me we need to focus on educating the voters because they're uncertain."

"Why do you think the split in opinions means they're uncertain?" Pam asked Terry.

"First, your ideas are new, so voters are on a learning curve. Second, your opponent says your plan is a tax increase in disguise. The voters are hearing different viewpoints, and they need time to sort the issue through and make up their minds. It reminds me of a big issue in 2002—whether to go to war against Iraq. The population was split. A poll in which researchers read people arguments for war and for continued inspections found that a majority of people agreed with *both* sets of arguments. They could see both sides of the issue. I think it's the same for you now with school finance reform."

"So what do we do?"

"Keep educating the voters, keep doing the statewide surveys, and ask questions that get at the reasons behind the voters' attitudes."

"OK, Jim, let's get your opinion," Pam addressed Jim Lovesay, the other adviser. "You said you would approach this issue differently."

"That's right, Pam. When we polled voters, we asked if they 'strongly favor, favor, oppose, or strongly oppose' your school finance plan. Most chose 'strongly favor' or 'strongly oppose.' That means they already know what they think. They aren't undecided. But they *are* split. We need to adjust our sampling technique to see where that split is occurring."

"Adjust our technique how?"

"My hunch is that there's a split based on age. Retirees don't want to abandon the current system; younger folks, the ones with kids in the schools, are more interested in change. So we need to sample every age group."

"Wouldn't our existing polls already include different age groups?"

"Sure, but it's a random sample of the whole population. Sometimes we might happen to get a lot of older people or young adults. To avoid that, we can ask the researchers to get 100 people in their twenties, 100 in their thirties, and so on."

"But that won't necessarily be a more representative sample," objected Terry. "I think we need to stick with the simple random sample and ask more detailed questions."

Discussion Issues

1. If you were Pam Heisler, what additional information would you want to know concerning voters' attitudes toward your reform plan?

2. How might sampling strata (samples from each age group) help Pam understand voter attitudes?

3. What pitfalls should the researchers avoid if they take samples from the different age groups? ∎

PART 5:
Sampling and Data Collection

In the preceding chapter we discussed the basic types of samples and how they are drawn. Simple random samples were used to illustrate the basis of statistical inference in which a parameter is estimated from a statistic. In this chapter we will take these concepts a bit further to explore two other types of probability samples: stratified samples and cluster samples.

Stratified Sample

Sometimes a simple random sample is not the most useful way to answer a research question. A Westport, Connecticut, retail marketing agency called TradeZone, for example, wanted to compare different kinds of retailers' experiences with promotions. Specifically, TradeZone wanted to compare the opinions of supermarkets, drugstores, and mass merchandisers regarding the success of various promotional activities, from frequent-shopper programs to in-store demonstrations. The agency wondered if some promotional activities were more appropriate for one category of retailers than for the others.[1] A simple random sample would not ensure that each category of retailer was well represented. A more targeted approach would be to use some form of stratified sample. A **stratified sample** is a probability sample that is distinguished by the following two-step procedure:

1. The parent population is divided into mutually exclusive and exhaustive subsets.
2. A simple random sample of elements is chosen independently from each group or subset.

In the case of the TradeZone study, the parent population would be retailers, and the subsets would be supermarkets, drugstores, and mass merchandisers.

Note that the definition says nothing about what criteria are used to separate the universe elements into subsets. That is because it is not the criteria that determine whether a stratified sample has been drawn. Admittedly, those criteria will make a difference as to the ultimate usefulness of the particular sample in question. But as long as the sample reflects the two-stage process, it is a stratified sample. Keep this distinction in mind. It will be useful later when distinguishing cluster samples from stratified samples.

The subsets into which the universe elements are divided are called *strata* or *subpopulations*. Note that our definition specified that this division be mutually exclusive and exhaustive. This means that every population element must be assigned to one, and only one, stratum and that no population elements are omitted in the assignment procedure.

To illustrate the process, suppose we again use the hypothetical population of 20 people used in the preceding chapter and shown again in Exhibit 16.1. That population could be described by several parameters, such as the average income, the range in education, and the proportion subscribing to various newspapers. Now assume we divide the group into two

Specify the two procedures that distinguish a stratified sample.

stratified sample
A probability sample that is distinguished by a two-step procedure in which (1) the parent population is divided into mutually exclusive and exhaustive subsets, and (2) a simple random sample of elements is chosen independently from each group or subset.

	Hypothetical Population						
Element	**Income (Dollars)**	**Education (Years)**	**Newspaper Subscription**	**Element**	**Income (Dollars)**	**Education (Years)**	**Newspaper Subscription**
1 A	5,600	8	X	11 K	9,600	13	X
2 B	6,000	9	Y	12 L	10,000	13	Y
3 C	6,400	11	X	13 M	10,400	14	X
4 D	6,800	11	Y	14 N	10,800	14	Y
5 E	7,200	11	X	15 O	11,200	15	X
6 F	7,600	12	Y	16 P	11,600	16	Y
7 G	8,000	12	X	17 Q	12,000	16	X
8 H	8,400	12	Y	18 R	12,400	17	Y
9 I	8,800	12	X	19 S	12,800	18	X
10 J	9,200	12	Y	20 T	13,200	18	Y

Exhibit 16.1

Exhibit 16.2

Stratification of Hypothetical Population by Education

Stratum I Elements		Stratum II Elements	
A	F	K	P
B	G	L	Q
C	H	M	R
D	I	N	S
E	J	O	T

strata on the basis of educational level. Exhibit 16.2 shows the results of this stratification procedure. Elements A though J form the *first stratum* (education of 12 years or less) and Elements K through T form the *second stratum* (education of more than 12 years). There is no particular reason to choose two strata. The parent population can be divided into any number of strata. We chose two as a convenient way of illustrating the technique.

The second step in the process requires that a simple random sample be drawn independently from *each* stratum. Let us again work with samples of Size 2, formed in this case by selecting one element from each stratum. (The number of elements from each stratum does not have to be equal, however.)

The procedure that would be used to select the two elements for the stratified sample would be the same as that used in drawing a simple random sample. Within each stratum, the population elements would be serially numbered from 1 to 10. A table of random numbers would be consulted. The first number encountered between 1 and 10 would designate the element from the first stratum. The element from the second stratum could be selected from another independent start or by continuing from the first randomly determined start. In either case, it would again be designated by the first encounter with a number between 1 and 10.

Derived Population

Although only one sample of Size 2 will in fact be selected, let us look briefly at the derived population of all possible samples of Size 2 that could be selected under this sampling plan. This derived population along with the mean of each sample is displayed in Exhibit 16.3.

Note that in this sampling plan there are only 100 possible sample combinations of elements, whereas with simple random sampling there were 190 possible combinations. That is because this type of sampling specified that one element be drawn from each stratum. In simple random sampling, you will recall, any two elements could be drawn from the population of items. In this sense, stratified sampling is always more restrictive than simple random sampling. Note further that every element has an equal chance of being included in the sample—1 in 10—since each can be the single element selected from the stratum that it is in. This explains why we specified an additional requirement to define a simple random sample. Although simple random samples provide each element an equal chance of selection, other techniques can also. Thus, equal probability of selection is a necessary but not sufficient condition for simple random sampling; in addition, each combination of n elements must be a sample possibility and as likely to occur as any other combination of n elements.

Sampling Distribution

2 *Cite two reasons researchers might opt to use a stratified sample rather than a simple random sample.*

Exhibit 16.4 contains the classification of sample means by size, and Figure 16.1 displays the plot of this sample statistic. Note that in relation to Figure 15.4, for simple random sampling, stratified sampling can produce a more concentrated distribution of estimates. This suggests one reason why we might choose a stratified sample; stratified samples can produce sample statistics that are more precise, or that have smaller error due to sampling, than simple random samples. With education as a stratification variable, there is a marked reduction in the number of sample means that deviate widely from the population mean.

Derived Population of All Possible Samples of Size 2 with Stratified Sampling

k	Sample Identity	Mean	k	Sample Identity	Mean	k	Sample Identity	Mean	k	Sample Identity	Mean
1	AK	7,600	26	CP	9,000	51	FK	8,600	76	HP	10,000
2	AL	7,800	27	CQ	9,200	52	FL	8,800	77	HQ	10,200
3	AM	8,000	28	CR	9,400	53	FM	9,000	78	HR	10,400
4	AN	8,200	29	CS	9,600	54	FN	9,200	79	HS	10,600
5	AO	8,400	30	CT	9,800	55	FO	9,400	80	HT	10,800
6	AP	8,600	31	DK	8,200	56	FP	9,600	81	IK	9,200
7	AQ	8,800	32	DL	8,400	57	FQ	9,800	82	IL	9,400
8	AR	9,000	33	DM	8,600	58	FR	10,000	83	IM	9,600
9	AS	9,200	34	DN	8,800	59	FS	10,200	84	IN	9,800
10	AT	9,400	35	DO	9,000	60	FT	10,400	85	IO	10,000
11	BK	7,800	36	DP	9,200	61	GK	8,800	86	IP	10,200
12	BL	8,000	37	DQ	9,400	62	GL	9,000	87	IQ	10,400
13	BM	8,200	38	DR	9,600	63	GM	9,200	88	IR	10,600
14	BN	8,400	39	DS	9,800	64	GN	9,400	89	IS	10,800
15	BO	8,600	40	DT	10,000	65	GO	9,600	90	IT	11,000
16	BP	8,800	41	EK	8,400	66	GP	9,800	91	JK	9,400
17	BQ	9,000	42	EL	8,600	67	GQ	10,000	92	JL	9,600
18	BR	9,200	43	EM	8,800	68	GR	10,200	93	JM	9,800
19	BS	9,400	44	EN	9,000	69	GS	10,400	94	JN	10,000
20	BT	9,600	45	EO	9,200	70	GT	10,600	95	JO	10,200
21	CK	8,000	46	EP	9,400	71	HK	9,000	96	JP	10,400
22	CL	8,200	47	EQ	9,600	72	HL	9,200	97	JQ	10,600
23	CM	8,400	48	ER	9,800	73	HM	9,400	98	JR	10,800
24	CN	8,600	49	ES	10,000	74	HN	9,600	99	JS	11,000
25	CO	8,800	50	ET	10,200	75	HO	9,800	100	JT	11,200

Classification of Sample Means by Size with Stratified Sampling

Sample Mean	Number of Samples
7,300 to 7,800	3
7,900 to 8,400	12
8,500 to 9,000	21
9,100 to 9,600	28
9,700 to 10,200	21
10,300 to 10,800	12
10,900 to 11,400	3

A second reason for drawing a stratified sample is that stratification allows the investigation of the characteristic of interest for particular subgroups. Thus, by stratifying, one is able to guarantee representation of those with a high school education or less, and those with more than a high school education. This can be extremely important when sampling from populations with rare segments. Suppose, for example, that a manufacturer of diamond rings wants to conduct a study of sales of the product by social class. Unless special precautions are taken, it is likely that the upper class—which represents only 3 percent of the total population—will not be represented at all, or will be represented by too few cases. Yet this may be an extremely important segment to the ring manufacturer. It is often true in marketing that a small subset of the population of interest will account for a large proportion of the behavior of interest—for example, consumption of the product. It then becomes critical that this subgroup be adequately represented in the sample. Stratified sampling is one way of ensuring adequate representation from each subgroup of interest.

Figure 16.1

Distribution of Sample Means with Stratified Sampling

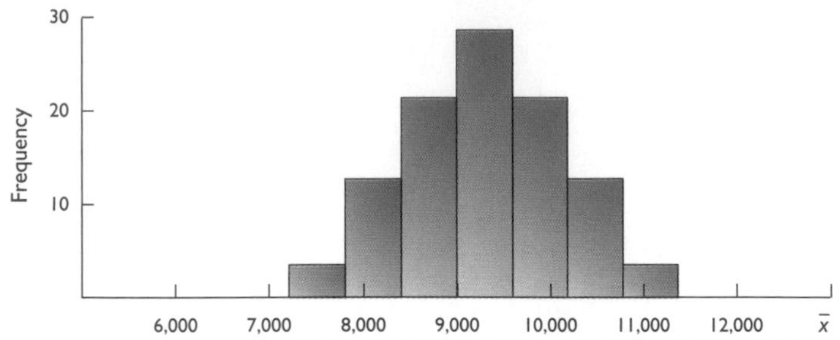

Increased Precision of Stratified Samples We mentioned previously that one might choose a stratified sample because such samples offer an opportunity for reducing sampling error or increasing precision. When estimating a mean, sampling error is given by the size of the standard error of the mean, $s_{\bar{x}}$; the smaller $s_{\bar{x}}$ is, the less the sampling error and the more precise the estimate will be, as indicated by the narrower confidence interval associated with a specified degree of confidence. (See Technically Speaking 16.1 for the procedure for developing confidence intervals with stratified samples.)

"Technically SPEAKING" 16.1

Confidence Interval Estimates with Stratified Samples

IN ESTABLISHING A CONFIDENCE INTERVAL WITH A SIMPLE RANDOM SAMPLE, WE SAW THAT WE need three things to complete the confidence interval specifications given by

$$\bar{x} - zs_{\bar{x}} \leq \mu \leq \bar{x} + zs_{\bar{x}}$$

1. The degree of confidence desired so that a z value can be selected.
2. A point estimate of the population mean given by the sample mean $\bar{x}$.
3. An estimate of the amount of sampling error associated with the sample mean, which was given by the standard error of the mean, $s_{\bar{x}} = \hat{s}\sqrt{n}$, when the population variance was unknown.

The same three quantities are required for making inferences with a stratified sample. The only difference in the procedure occurs in the way Items 2 and 3 are generated. With stratified sampling, the sample estimate of the population mean and the standard error of estimate associated with this statistic are determined by weighting the individual strata results.

More specifically, the analyst needs to compute the sample mean and the sample variance for each stratum. These would be calculated exactly as before, since a simple random sample is being taken from each stratum. The mean for the sample as a whole is then determined by weighting each of the respective strata means by the relative proportion of elements in the population that belong to the stratum. For example, if the population is divided into groups in such a way that one stratum contains one-fourth of all the population members, the sample mean for that stratum receives a weight of .25 when one is determining the mean for the total sample. Similarly, the sample mean for a stratum that contains 10 percent of the population elements is weighted .10 when one is estimating the overall sample mean.

The process to get the overall standard error of the mean is slightly more complex. The relative sizes of the respective strata are again used but the ratios are squared; for example, a stratum containing 10 percent of the population members would be weighted $(.10)^2 = .01$. Further, one needs to weight the variances of means by strata to get the overall variance of the mean. Then one takes the square root of the overall result to get the standard error of the mean for the overall sample. The variance of means for each stratum is obtained just as it was for a simple random sample—that is, by dividing the sample variance for the stratum by the sample size from that stratum.

Consider the example in Exhibit 16.1 again. The total size of the population and the population within each stratum are fixed. The only way, therefore, for total sampling error to be reduced is for the variance of the estimate within each stratum to be made smaller. Now the variance of the estimate by strata in turn depends on the variability of the characteristic within the strata. Thus, the estimate of the mean can be made more precise to the extent that the population can be partitioned so that there is little variability within each stratum—that is, to the extent the strata can be made internally homogeneous.

A characteristic of interest will display a certain amount of variation in the population. The investigator can do nothing about this total variation because it is a fixed characteristic of the population. In the population in Exhibit 16.1, for example, there is variation in incomes which the investigator can do nothing about. But the analyst can do something when dividing the elements of the population into strata so as to increase the precision with which the average value of the characteristic (i.e., average income) can be estimated. Specifically, the goal is to divide the population into strata so that the elements within any given stratum are as similar in value as possible and the values between any two strata are as disparate as possible. In this case, the

Note what points investigators should keep in mind when dividing a population into strata for a stratified sample.

Exhibit A below illustrates the procedure assuming Elements B and E were randomly selected from the first stratum and Elements N and S from the second stratum. Since each stratum contains 10 of the 20 population elements, the sample mean for each stratum is weighted by one-half ($10 \div 20$) when one is determining the overall sample mean, while each variance of estimate is weighted .25. With the overall sample mean of 9,200 and standard error of estimate of 583, the 95 percent confidence interval ($z = 1.96$) is $9,200 \pm (1.96)583$ or $8,057 \leq \mu \leq 10,343$. This interval is interpreted as before. The true mean may or may not be in the interval, but since 95 of 100 intervals constructed by this process will contain the true mean, we are 95 percent confident that the true population mean income is between \$8,057 and \$10,343. ∎

Exhibit A

Computation of Mean and Standard Error of Estimate for Stratified Sample

STRATUM 1		STRATUM 2	
Element	Income	Element	Income
B	6,000	N	10,800
E	7,200	S	12,800

Mean: $\bar{x}_1 = \dfrac{6,600 + 7,200}{2} = 6,600$ $\qquad$ $\bar{x}_2 = \dfrac{10,800 + 12,800}{2} = 11,800$

Variance: $\hat{s}_1^2 = \dfrac{(6,000 - 6,600)^2 + (7,200 - 6,600)^2}{2 - 1}$ $\qquad$ $\hat{s}_2^2 = \dfrac{(10,800 - 11,800)^2 + (12,800 - 11,800)^2}{2 - 1}$

$\qquad = 720,000$ $\qquad\qquad = 2,000,000$

Variance of estimate: $s_{\bar{x}_1}^2 = \dfrac{\hat{s}_1^2}{n_1} = \dfrac{720,000}{2} = 360,000$ $\qquad$ $s_{\bar{x}_2}^2 = \dfrac{\hat{s}_2^2}{n_2} = \dfrac{2,000,000}{2} = 1,000,000$

Overall Sample

Mean: $\bar{x} = \dfrac{10}{20}(6,600) + \dfrac{10}{20}(11,800) = 9,200$

Variance of estimate: $s_{\bar{x}}^2 = \left(\dfrac{10}{20}\right)^2 (360,000) + \left(\dfrac{10}{20}\right)^2 (1,000,000) = 340,000$

Standard error of estimate: $s_{\bar{x}} = \sqrt{s_{\bar{x}}^2} = 583$

division of the population between those who have more than a high school education and those who do not was a good way of separating the population into two strata since the elements within each stratum have similar incomes.

In the limit, if the investigator is successful in partitioning the population so that the elements in each stratum are exactly equal, there will be no error associated with the estimate of the population mean. That is right! The population mean could then be estimated without error because *the variability that exists between strata does not enter into the calculation of the standard error of estimate with stratified sampling.*

One can see this readily in a simple case with a limited number of values. Suppose that in a population of 1,000 elements, 200 had the value 5; 300 had the value 10; and 500 had the value 20. Now the mean of this population is $\mu = 14$, and the variance is $\sigma^2 = 39$. If a simple random sample of size $n = 3$ is used to estimate this mean, then the standard error of estimate is

$$\sigma_{\bar{x}} = \frac{\sigma}{\sqrt{n}} = \frac{\sqrt{39}}{\sqrt{3}} = 3.61$$

and the width of confidence interval would be $\pm z$ times this value, 3.61. Suppose, on the other hand, a researcher used a stratified sample and was successful in partitioning the total population so that all the elements with a value of 5 on the characteristic were in one stratum, those with the value 10 in the second stratum, and those with the value 20 in the third stratum. To generate a completely precise description of the mean of each stratum, the researcher would then need only to take a sample of one from each stratum. Further, when the investigator combined these individual results into a global estimate of the overall mean, the standard error of the estimate is zero. The population mean value would be determined exactly.

Bases for Stratification   The fact that variation among strata does not enter into the calculation of the standard error of estimate suggests the kinds of criteria that should be used to partition the population. The values assumed by the characteristic will be unknown, for if they were known, there would be no need to take a sample to estimate their mean level. What the investigator attempts to do, therefore, is to partition the population according to one or more criteria that are expected to be related to the characteristic of interest. It was no accident, therefore, that in our hypothetical example, education was used to divide the population elements into strata. As Exhibit 16.1 indicates, there is a relationship between educational level and income level: the more years of school, the higher the income tends to be. Newspaper subscriptions, on the other hand, would have made a poor variable for partitioning the population into segments, since there is almost no relation between the paper to which a person subscribes and the individual's income. Whether one selects a "good" or a "bad" variable to partition the population does not affect whether a stratified sample is selected or not. It is significant in determining whether a good or poor sample is selected, but the two features defining a stratified sample are still (1) the partitioning of the population into subgroups and (2) the random selection of elements from each subgroup.

The calculation of the standard error of estimate provides some clue as to the number of strata that should be used. Since the standard error of estimate depends only on variability within strata, the various strata should be made as homogeneous as possible. One way of doing this is to use many, very small strata. In our education example, for instance, additional strata could be grade school education or less, some high school education, some college education, and graduate school education. Or even finer distinctions could be made. There are practical limits, however, to the number of strata that should be and are used in actual research studies. First, the creation of additional strata is often expensive in terms of sample design, data collection, and analysis. Second, there is an upper limit to the amount of variation that can be accounted for by any practical stratification. Regardless of the criteria by which the population is partitioned, a certain amount of variation is likely to remain unaccounted for, and thus the additional strata will serve no productive purpose.

© Derek Gardner: Courtesy of Toyota Motor Sales U.S.A., Inc.   Courtesy of Land Rover, Photographer: RJ Muna

These two magazine ads are both for four-wheel-drive vehicles. One would expect greater variability among the income levels of consumers purchasing a Toyota 4Runner, which advertises the potential to save money, and lesser income level variability for those interested in the Range Rover, whose ad is written to appeal to those consumers interested in a luxury vehicle.

Proportionate and Disproportionate Stratified Samples

Whether one chooses a stratified sample over a simple random sample depends in part on the trade-off between cost and precision. Although stratified samples typically produce more precise estimates, they also usually cost more than simple random samples. If the decision is made in favor of a stratified sample, the researcher must still decide whether to select a proportionate or disproportionate one.

With a **proportionate stratified sample,** the number of observations in the total sample is allocated among the strata in proportion to the *relative* number of elements in each stratum in the population. A stratum containing one-fifth of all the population elements would account for one-fifth of the total sample observations, and so on. Proportionate sampling was used in our education example, since each stratum contained one-half of the population and they were sampled equally.

Explain what a proportionate stratified sample is.

One advantage of proportionate allocation is that the investigator needs to know only the relative sizes of each stratum in order to determine the number of sample observations to select from each stratum with a given sample size. A **disproportionate stratified sample,** however, can produce still more efficient estimates. It involves balancing the two criteria of strata size and strata variability. With a fixed sample size, strata exhibiting more variability are sampled more than proportionately to their relative size. Conversely, those strata that are very homogeneous are sampled less than proportionately. Research Window 16.1 describes the disproportionate stratified sampling scheme used by Nielsen in developing its SCANTRAK® service, described in Chapter 8.

Explain what a disproportionate stratified sample is.

Disproportionate Stratified Sampling Scheme Used by Nielsen

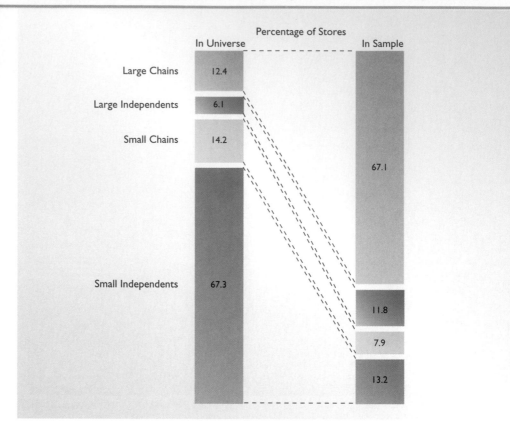

Source: Developed from information supplied by ACNielsen.

proportionate stratified sample

A stratified sample in which the number of observations in the total sample is allocated among the strata in proportion to the relative number of elements in each stratum in the population.

disproportionate stratified sample

A stratified sample in which the individual strata or subsets are sampled in relation to both their size and their variability; strata exhibiting more variability are sampled more than proportionately to their relative size, while those that are very homogeneous are sampled less than proportionately.

While a full discussion of how the sample size for each stratum should be determined would take us too far afield and would be much too technical for our purpose, some discussion for the rationale behind disproportionate sampling is useful. Consider at the extreme, a stratum with zero variability. Since all the elements are identical in value, a single observation tells all. On the other hand, a stratum characterized by great variability will require a large number of observations to produce a precise estimate of the stratum mean. One would expect, for example, great variability among income levels of those people subscribing to *Newsweek* but much less among people subscribing to the glossy society magazine *Town and Country* (see another example in the ads for sport-utility vehicles). One can expect greater precision when the various strata are sampled proportionate to the relative variability of the characteristic under study rather than proportionate to their relative size in the population.

A disproportionate stratified sample requires more knowledge about the population of interest than does a proportionate stratified sample. To sample the strata in relation to their variability, one needs knowledge of relative variability. Sampling theory is a peculiar phenomenon in that knowledge begets more knowledge. Disproportionate sampling can produce more efficient estimates than proportionate sampling, but the former method also requires that some estimate of the relative variation within strata be known. One can sometimes anticipate the relative homogeneity likely to exist within a stratum on the basis of past studies and experience. Sometimes the investigator may have to rely on logic and intuition in establishing sample sizes for each stratum. For example, one might expect that large retail stores would show greater variation than small stores in sales of some products. That is one reason why the large stores are sampled more heavily in the Nielsen's SCANTRAK® service.

Stratified versus Quota Samples

Inexperienced researchers sometimes confuse stratified samples with quota samples. There are similarities. In each case, the population is divided into segments, and elements are selected from each segment. There is one key difference, however. In stratified samples, sample elements are selected by probability methods; in quota samples, elements are chosen based on a researcher's judgment. This difference has important implications. Since elements in a stratified sample are selected probabilistically, researchers can establish the sampling distribution of the statistic in question, and hence a confidence interval judgment. In a quota sample there is no objective way to assess the degree of sampling error. Therefore there is also no way to arrive at confidence interval estimates and statistical tests of significance.

Cluster Sample

Cluster samples are another probability sampling technique often used by researchers. Cluster sampling shares some similarities with stratified sampling, but also has some key differences. Cluster sampling involves the following steps:

1. The parent population is divided into mutually exclusive and exhaustive subsets.
2. A random sample of the subsets is selected.

6 List the steps followed in drawing a cluster sample.

If the investigator then uses all the population elements in the selected subsets for the sample, the procedure is one-stage cluster sampling. If, on the other hand, a sample of elements is selected probabilistically from the selected subsets, the procedure is known as two-stage cluster sampling.

Note the similarities and differences between cluster sampling and stratified sampling. Although in each case the population is divided into mutually exclusive and exhaustive subgroups, in stratified sampling a sample of elements is selected *from each subgroup*. With cluster sampling, one chooses a *sample of subgroups*.

7 Explain the difference between a one-stage cluster sample and a two-stage cluster sample.

Remember that in stratified sampling, the goal is to separate the population into strata that are fairly homogeneous for a certain characteristic. In cluster sampling, the goal is to form subgroups that are similar to each other and are each small-scale models of the population. Each cluster should reflect the diversity of the whole population.

In our earlier example relating income to level of education, we noted that dividing the population into subgroups based on newspaper subscriptions was probably not a good idea for stratified sampling because that characteristic is not a good predictor of income. However, since the goal in cluster sampling is to form subgroups that are as heterogeneous as possible, newspaper subscriptions might be a good basis for dividing the population for this form of sample.

If all those subscribing to Paper X were considered to form one subgroup and all those subscribing to Paper Y a second subgroup, then one could be relatively safe in randomly selecting either subgroup to estimate the mean income in the population. While the distribution of incomes within each subgroup is not exactly the same as it is in the population, the range of incomes is such that there would be only a slight error if one were to estimate the mean income and variance of incomes of the population with the elements from either subset.

Admittedly, in practice clusters are not always formed to be as heterogeneous as possible. Because of the way cluster samples are often drawn, the defined clusters often turn out to be homogeneous rather than heterogeneous in regard to the characteristic of interest. Beginning researchers often mistakenly then call the procedure *stratified sampling*, since it involves the construction of homogeneous subgroups of population elements. But as long as subgroups are subsequently selected for investigation randomly, the procedure is *cluster sampling* regardless of how the subgroups are formed. Admittedly, however, homogeneous subgroups produce less ideal cluster samples from a statistical efficiency viewpoint than do heterogeneous subgroups.

cluster sample
A probability sample distinguished by a two-step procedure in which (1) the parent population is divided into mutually exclusive and exhaustive subsets, and (2) a random sample of subsets is selected. If the investigator then uses all the population elements in the selected subsets for the sample, the procedure is one-stage cluster sampling; if a sample of elements is selected probabilistically from the subsets, the procedure is two-stage cluster sampling.

8 *Explain why cluster sampling, though far less statistically efficient than comparable stratified samples, is the sampling procedure used most in large-scale field surveys using personal interviews.*

Statistical efficiency is a relative notion by which sampling plans can be compared. One sampling plan is said to be more statistically efficient than another if, for the same size sample, it produces a smaller standard error of estimate. When the characteristic of interest is the mean, for example, the sampling plan that produces the smallest value of the standard error of the mean, $s_{\bar{x}}$, for a given-size sample is most statistically efficient. Cluster samples are typically much less statistically efficient than comparable stratified samples or even simple random samples because the probable margin of error with a fixed-size sample is often greatest with cluster sampling.

Even with its typically lower statistical efficiency, cluster sampling is probably the sampling procedure used most in large-scale field surveys using personal interviews, particularly those involving in-home personal interviews. Why? Simply because cluster sampling is often more *economically efficient* in that the cost per observation is less. The economies permit the selection of a larger sample at a smaller cost. Since cluster sampling allows researchers to secure so many more observations for a given cost than they would be able to secure with stratified sampling, the margin of error associated with the estimate may actually be smaller for cluster sampling. That is, cluster sampling is often more *efficient overall* than the other forms of sampling. Although it requires a larger sample for the same degree of precision, and is thus less statistically efficient, the smaller cost per observation allows samples so much larger that estimates with a smaller standard error can be produced for the same cost.

Systematic Sample

The **systematic sample** is a form of cluster sampling that offers one of the easiest ways of sampling many populations of interest. It involves selecting every *k*th element after a random start. For example, a database technology firm called Informix wanted to gather basic data about the preferences of visitors to its Web site, including what they were looking for at the site and what they liked or disliked about the site. To gather this information, Informix set up its software to count visitors to the site and invited every fourth visitor to take a survey. Although the company was well aware that this method would not generate a random sample of all potential customers, the survey was a low-cost way to identify areas in which the Web site could be improved.[2]

To see how to draw a systematic sample, consider again the hypothetical population of 20 individuals in Exhibit 16.1, and suppose a sample of 5 is to be selected from this population. Number the elements from 1 to 10. With 20 population elements and a sample size of 5, we will need to select 1/4 of all the population elements; more formally, the sampling fraction f is 1/4 where $f = \dfrac{n}{N} = \dfrac{5}{20} = \dfrac{1}{4}$. The sampling interval i which is the reciprocal of the sampling fraction is thus 4 since $i = 1/f = 4$. This means that, after a random start, every fourth element will be chosen. The random start, which must be some number between 1 and 4—1 and i in general—is determined from a random-number table. Thus if the random start were 1, the first, fifth, ninth, thirteenth, and seventeenth items would be the sample. If it were 2, the second, sixth, tenth, fourteenth, and eighteenth items would be the sample, and so on.

Systematic sampling is one-stage cluster sampling since the subgroups are not subsampled, but rather all the elements in the selected clusters are used. The subgroups or clusters in this case are

- Cluster I: A, E, I, M, Q
- Cluster II: B, F, J, N, R
- Cluster III: C, G, K, O, S
- Cluster IV: D, H, L, P, T

and one of these clusters is selected randomly for investigation. The random start, of course, determines the cluster that is to be used.

In our simplified example, the sampling interval i conveniently came out to be a whole number 4. What should an analyst do though in the more usual case when the sampling interval is not a whole number? The easiest solution is to use as the interval the whole number just below or above i. Thus, if the calculated interval i turned out to be 16.2, say, we would select every sixteenth element after a randomly determined start between 1 and 16, whereas if it turned out to be 16.8, we would select every seventeenth element after a randomly determined start between 1 and 17. Using such a rounding procedure will generally result in a sample that is only slightly larger or smaller than the sample required. The exception is when i is small, say 10 or less. In situations like this, it is generally better to always round down, which produces a sample that is larger than needed. If this is an intolerable situation, some of the elements initially selected can be deleted using another systematic sample.

One can readily see the ease with which a systematic sample can be drawn. It is much easier to draw a systematic sample than it is to select a simple random sample of the same size. With a systematic sample one needs to enter the random-number table only once. The problem of checking for the duplication of elements, which is cumbersome with simple random samples, does not occur with systematic samples. All the elements are uniquely determined by the selection of the random start.

A systematic sample can often be made more representative than a simple random sample. With our hypothetical population, for example, we are guaranteed representation from the low-income segment and the high-income segment with our systematic sampling plan. Regardless of which of the four clusters is chosen, one element must have an income of $6,800 or less; another must have an income of $12,000 or more; and the remaining three elements must have incomes between these two values. A simple random sample of Size 5 might or might not include low-income or high-income people.

The same is true when sampling from other populations. Thus, if we are sampling retail stores, we can guarantee representation of both small and large stores by using a systematic sample, if the stores can be arrayed from smallest to largest according to some criteria such as annual sales or square footage. The ability to guarantee representation from each size segment depends on the availability of knowledge about the size of each store so that the stores can be arrayed from smallest to largest and numbered serially. A simple random sample of stores would be apt to represent large stores inadequately since there are fewer large stores than small stores. Yet the fewer large stores account for a great proportion of all sales.

The degree to which the systematic sample will be more representative than a simple random sample thus depends on the clustering of objects within the list from which the sample will be drawn. The ideal list for a systematic sample will have elements similar in value on the characteristic (for example, similar levels of income, sales, education) close together and elements diverse in value spread apart.

At least one danger with systematic samples is that if there is a natural periodicity in the list of elements, the systematic sample can produce estimates with serious errors. For example, suppose we have the annual ticket sales of an airline by day and wish to analyze these sales in terms of length of trip. To analyze all 365 days may be prohibitively costly, but suppose the research budget does allow the investigation of 52 days of sales. A systematic sample of days using a sampling interval of 7 (365 ÷ 52) would obviously produce some misleading conclusions, since the day's sales would reflect all Monday trips, Friday trips, or Sunday trips, for example. Of course, any other sampling interval would be acceptable, and in general, an enlightened choice of the sampling interval can do much to eliminate the problems associated with natural periodicities in the data. An appropriate choice of sampling interval, of course, depends on knowledge of the phenomenon and the nature of the periodicity.

Area Sample

In every probability sampling plan discussed so far, the investigator needs a list of population elements in order to draw the sample. A list identifying each population element is a necessary requirement for simple random samples, stratified samples, and systematic samples. The latter two procedures also require knowledge about some other characteristic of the population if they are to be designed optimally. For many populations of interest, however, such detailed lists are unavailable. Further, it will often prove prohibitively costly to construct them. When this condition arises, the cluster sample offers the researcher another distinct benefit— he or she needs only the list of population elements for the selected clusters.

9 *Distinguish between one-stage area sampling and simple two-stage area sampling.*

Suppose, for example, that an investigator wishes to measure certain characteristics of industrial sales representatives, such as their earnings, attitudes toward the job, hours worked, and so on. It would be extremely difficult, if not impossible, and certainly costly to develop an up-to-date roster listing each industrial sales representative. Yet such a list would be required for a simple random sample. A stratified sample would further require that the investigator possess knowledge about some additional characteristics of each sales representative (for example, education or age) so that the population could be divided into mutually exclusive and exhaustive subsets. With a cluster sample, on the other hand, one could use the companies as sampling units. The investigator would generate a sample of business firms from the population of firms of interest. The business firms would be primary **sampling units** where a sampling unit is defined as that element or set of elements considered for selection in some stage of sampling.[3] The investigator could then compile a list of sales representatives working for each of the selected firms, a much more realistic assignment. If the investigator then studied each of the sales representatives in each of the selected firms, it would be one-stage cluster sampling. If the researcher subsampled sales representatives from each company's list, it would be two-stage cluster sampling. Exhibit 16.5 lists some other possible clusters that could be used to sample various types of population elements.

The same principle underlies **area sampling**. Current, accurate lists of population elements are rarely available. Directories of all those living in a city at a particular moment simply do not exist for many cities, and when they do exist, they are obsolete when published: people move, others die, new households are constantly being formed.[4] Although lists of families are nonexistent, relatively accurate lists of primary sampling units are available in the form of city maps, if the area divisions of the city serve as the primary sampling units. Although the complex details of area sampling are not relevant here, an appreciation for the rationale underlying the various approaches is.

One-Stage Area Sample Suppose the investigator is interested in estimating the amount of wine consumed per household in the city of Chicago, and how consumption is related to family income. An accurate listing of all households is unavailable for the Chicago area. A phone book when published is already somewhat obsolete, in addition to having the other inadequacies previously mentioned. One approach to this problem would be to

1. Choose a simple random sample of n city blocks from the population of N blocks.
2. Determine wine consumption and income for all households in the selected blocks and generalize the sample relationships to the larger population.

The probability of any household being included in the sample can be calculated. It is given simply as $\dfrac{n}{N}$ since it equals the probability that the block on which it is located will be selected. Since the probabilities are known, the procedure is indeed probability sampling. Here, how-

---

Exhibit 16.5

Possible Clusters to Use to Sample Various Types of Population Elements

Population Elements	Possible Clusters
College students	Colleges
Elementary school students	Schools
Manufacturing firms	Counties
	Localities
Airline travelers	Airports
	Planes
Hospital patients	Hospitals
Government workers	Government buildings

PART 5:
Sampling and Data Collection

ever, blocks have been substituted for households when selecting primary sampling units. The substitution is made because the list of blocks in the Chicago area can be developed from city maps. Each block can be identified, and the existence of this universe of blocks permits the calculation of the necessary probabilities.

Since each household on the selected blocks is included in the sample, the procedure is one-stage area sampling. Note that the blocks serve to divide the parent population into mutually exclusive and exhaustive subsets. Note further that the blocks do not serve very well as ideal subsets statistically for cluster samples; households on a given block can be expected to be somewhat similar with respect to income and wine consumption rather than heterogeneous as desired. On the other hand, the data collection costs will be very low because of the concentration of households on each block.

Two-Stage Area Sample The distinguishing feature of the one-stage area sample is that all the households on the selected blocks (or other areas) are enumerated and studied. It is not necessary to use all items in a selected cluster; the selected areas themselves can be subsampled, and it is often quite advantageous to do so. Two types of two-stage sampling need to be distinguished:

1. Simple, two-stage area sampling.
2. Probability-proportional-to-size area sampling.

With **simple two-stage area sampling**, a certain proportion of second-stage sampling units (e.g., households) is selected from each first-stage unit (e.g., a block). Consider a universe of 100 blocks; suppose there are 20 households per block; assume that a sample of 80 households is required from this total population of 2,000 households. The overall sampling fraction is thus $\frac{80}{2000} = \frac{1}{25}$. There are a number of ways by which the sample can be completed, such as by (1) selecting 10 blocks and 8 households per block, (2) selecting 8 blocks and 10 households per block, (3) selecting 20 blocks and 4 households per block, or (4) selecting 4 blocks and 20 households per block. The last alternative would, of course, be one-stage area sampling, while the first three would all be two-stage area sampling.

The probability with which the blocks are selected is called the *block*, or *first-stage*, *sampling fraction* and is given as the ratio of n/N_B, where n_B and N_B are the number of blocks in the sample and in the population, respectively. For the first three schemes illustrated above, the first-stage sampling fractions would be, in order, 1 in 10, 1 in 12.5, and 1 in 5.

The probability with which the households are selected is called the *household*, or *second-stage*, *sampling fraction*. Since there must be a total of 80 households in the sample, the second-stage sampling fraction differs for each alternative. The second-stage sampling fraction is given as

© Jim Wark/Index Stock Imagery

Researchers could use simple two-stage area sampling to select a certain proportion of households from a larger unit, such as a block.

simple two-stage area sampling
A form of cluster sampling in which a certain proportion of second-stage sampling units (e.g., households) is selected from each first-stage unit (e.g., blocks).

$n_{H/B}/N_{H/B}$, where $n_{H/B}$ and $N_{H/B}$ are the number of households per block in the sample and in the population. For the first sampling scheme, the household sampling fraction is calculated to be $\frac{8}{20} = \frac{2}{5}$, while for the second scheme, it is $\frac{10}{20} = \frac{1}{2}$, and for the third scheme, $\frac{4}{20} = \frac{1}{5}$ Note that the product of the first-stage and second-stage sampling fractions in each case equals the overall sampling fraction of $\frac{1}{25}$.

Which scheme would be preferable? Although it is beyond the scope of this text to present the detailed calculation for determining this, we will illustrate the general principle. Economies of data collection would dictate that the second-stage sampling fraction be high. This means that a great many households would be selected from each designated block, as with the second scheme. Statistical efficiency would dictate a small second-stage sampling fraction, since it can be expected that the blocks would be relatively homogeneous and thus it would be desirable to have only a few households from any one block. The third scheme would be preferred on statistical grounds. Statistical sampling theory would suggest the balancing of these two criteria. There are formulas for this purpose that essentially reflect the cost of data collection and the variability of the characteristic within and between clusters, although a useful rule of thumb is that clusters of three to eight households per block or segment are near optimum for most social science variables.

Simple two-stage area sampling is quite effective when there is approximately the same number of second-stage units (e.g., households) per first-stage unit (e.g., a block). When the second-stage units are decidedly unequal, simple two-stage area sampling can cause bias in the estimate. To pursue our hypothetical example, some blocks in Chicago may contain multi-storied low-income housing. Blocks in more affluent parts of the city may contain relatively few, single-family houses. In such a case, the number of second-stage units per first-stage unit would be vastly different. Sometimes this problem can be overcome by combining areas. When this option is not available or is cumbersome to implement, **probability-proportional-**

probability-proportional-to-size sampling
A form of cluster sampling in which a fixed number of second-stage units is selected from each first-stage unit. The probabilities associated with the selection of each first-stage unit are in turn variable because they are directly related to the relative sizes of the first-stage units.

Technically SPEAKING 16.2

The Counterbalancing of Probabilities in Probability-Proportion-to-Size Sampling

TO ILLUSTRATE THE COUNTERBALANCING OF PROBABILITIES WITH PROBABILITY-proportional-to-size sampling, consider the data below and suppose a sample of 20 elements is to be selected from this population of 2,000 households. Suppose after balancing economic and statistical considerations, that the number of second-stage units per first-stage unit is determined to be 10. Two first-stage units must be selected to produce a total sample of 20. As mentioned, the procedure gets its name from the way these first-stage units are selected in that the probability of selection is variable—it depends on the size of the first-stage unit. In this particular case, a table of four-digit random numbers will be consulted. The first two numbers encountered between 1 and 2,000 will be used to indicate the blocks that will be used.

All numbers between 1 and 800 will indicate the inclusion of Block 1; those from 801 to 1,200, Block 2; from 1,201 to 1,400, Block 3; and so on.

The probability that any particular household is included in the sample is equal, since the unequal first-stage selection probabilities are balanced by unequal second-stage selection probabilities. Consider, for example, Blocks 1 and 10, the two extremes. The first-stage selection probability for Block 1 is $\frac{800}{2000} = \frac{1}{2.5}$, since 800 of the permissible 2,000 random numbers correspond to Block 1. Only 25 of the permissible random numbers (1,976 to 2,000) correspond to Block 10, on the other hand, and thus the first-stage sampling fraction for Block 10 is $\frac{25}{2000} = \frac{1}{80}$. Since 10 households are to be selected from each block, the second-stage sampling fraction to-size sampling can be used, in which a fixed number of second-stage units is selected from each first-stage unit, and where the probability of a first-stage unit being selected depends on its relative size. Thus, while larger first-stage units have a greater probability of being chosen, the individual elements within them have a smaller chance since the same number of second-stage units are selected from each first-stage unit regardless of their sizes. As a matter of fact, the probabilities exactly counterbalance each other so that every element turns out to have an equal chance of being included in the study. (See Technically Speaking 16.2 for an illustration of how the probabilities counterbalance each other.)

Probability-proportional-to-size sampling is another illustration of how information begets information with applied sampling problems. One can avoid the bias of simple two-stage area sampling and can also produce estimates that are more precise when there is great variation in the number of second-stage units per first-stage unit. The price one pays, of course, is that probability-proportional-to-size sampling requires that one have detailed knowledge about the size of each first-stage unit. This is not quite as high a price as it might be, since the Census Bureau has reported the number of households per block for all cities of over 50,000 in population as well as for a number of other urbanized areas.[5] Maps are included in each report. Although somewhat obsolete when published, these map and block statistics can be updated. The local electric utility will have records of connections current to the day, and so will the telephone company. In many cases, these statistics will be broken down by blocks.

Combining Sample Types

As you can probably begin to appreciate, sample design is a very detailed subject. Our discussion has concentrated on only a few of the fundamentals and, in particular, the basic types of probability samples. You should be aware that the basic types can be, and are, combined in large-scale field studies to produce some very complex designs.

The Gallup Poll, for example, is probably one of the best known of all the polls. The sample for the Gallup Poll for each survey consists of adults selected from locations using area sampling methods. At each location the interviewer is given a map with an indicated starting point and is required to follow a specified direction. At each occupied dwelling unit, the interviewer must attempt to meet sex quotas. In sum, the Gallup Poll uses a combination of area

for Block 1 is $\frac{10}{800} = \frac{1}{80}$, while for Block 10 it is $\frac{10}{25} = \frac{1}{25}$. The products of the first-

and second-stage sampling thus compensate, since

$$\frac{800}{2,000} \times \frac{10}{800} = \frac{25}{2,000} \times \frac{10}{25}$$

which is also true for the remaining blocks.

Illustration of Probability-Proportional-to-Size Sampling

Block	Households	Cumulative Number of Households
1	800	800
2	400	1,200
3	200	1,400
4	200	1,600
5	100	1,700
6	100	1,800
7	100	1,900
8	50	1,950
9	25	1,975
10	25	2,000

and quota sampling. Further, it is not uncommon to have several levels of stratification—such as by geographic area and density of population—precede several stages of cluster sampling. Thus, you cannot expect to be a sampling expert with the brief exposure to the subject contained here.[6] But you should be able to communicate effectively about the sample design and use effectively the available computer software for selecting samples. Further, although you may not understand completely, say, why n_1 observations were taken from one stratum and n_2 from another, you should appreciate the basic considerations determining the choice.

<h1>looking back...</h1>

Pam Heisler was determined to end the meeting with her advisers only when they had a plan. "Even though you two have different ideas about the split in voters' opinions," she said to Terry Shapiro and Jim Lovesay, "I think we can agree that we need to learn more to interpret the split." Seeing agreement, Pam continued, "Terry, you think voters are giving conflicting answers because they're still sorting through the pros and cons of school financing. How can we test that idea?"

"We need a representative sample of voters and questions that probe what they are thinking. Remember that poll of the U.S. public's opinions about war in Iraq? It sticks in my mind because it was such an interesting type of poll. They read statements supporting arguments that the UN should strengthen inspections of Iraq and that the United States should proceed with military action. A majority of respondents agreed with statements for both sides. You're not talking about war, but you are talking about the public trying to make up its mind. We need to present the arguments for and against your school financing plan and see what people think."

"It sounds expensive."

"It sure does," exclaimed Jim. "And that poll Terry likes so much was an online poll. How random is that—interviewing people with Internet access?"

"The sample was random. The research firm recruited participants by phoning them and offering to set them up with WebTV if they would participate in a panel. So they didn't start with a sample of people online; they started with a sample of people with phones."

"Still," Jim persisted, "Pam can make a strong case for her plan, and she can persuade the voters. We need more information about who still needs to be persuaded."

"You want to look at groups of voters?" asked Pam.

"That's right. If my memory serves me correctly, we'd do what our researchers told me is called stratified sampling. We could look for patterns in how different age groups view your plan. We don't have to get into the details of the arguments—just ask for their opinions and see if there's a big difference between age groups."

"But how could you rely on the data when your sample isn't random?" asked Terry.

"I checked with our research staff. We can still run statistics on confidence, and the results for the different strata—the different age groups—can be more precise than for a simple random sample."

"Well, that clinches it," said Pam. "We have a limited budget, and getting data for each age group sounds like the most efficient approach overall. But I don't want to forget Terry's idea. Let's pay extra attention to the kinds of questions we get about school financing when I'm meeting the voters this week. My plan is good for the community, so I can't let it die."

Sources: The online polling issue is discussed in Farhad Manjoo, "Online Polls: Can We Trust 'Em?" *Wired News*, October 16, 2000, http://www.wired.com. The national poll about Iraq is discussed at Program on International Policy Attitudes (PIPA), University of Maryland, "Public Conflicted Whether UN Should Strengthen Inspections or Authorize Invasion," news release, February 20, 2003, PIPA Web site, http://pipa.org; and National Public Radio, "Poll Reveals Deep Conflicts on Iraq Policy," *Morning Edition*, February 20, 2003, the NPR Web site, http://www.npr.org.

Summary

Learning Objective 1
Specify the two procedures that distinguish a stratified sample.

A stratified sample is a probability sample that is distinguished by the following two-step procedure: (1) the parent population is divided into mutually exclusive and exhaustive subsets, and (2) a simple random sample of elements is chosen independently from each group or subset.

Learning Objective 2
Cite two reasons researchers might opt to use a stratified sample rather than a simple random sample.

Stratified samples can produce sample statistics that are more precise, meaning they have smaller error due to sampling, than simple random samples. Stratification also allows the investigation of the characteristics of interest for particular subgroups.

Learning Objective 3
Note what points investigators should keep in mind when dividing a population into strata for a stratified sample.

Investigators should divide the population into strata so that the elements within any given stratum are as similar in value as possible, and so that the values between any two strata are as disparate as possible.

Learning Objective 4
Explain what a proportionate stratified sample is.

With a proportionate stratified sample, the number of observations in the total sample is allocated among the strata in proportion to the relative number of elements in each stratum in the population.

Learning Objective 5
Explain what a disproportionate stratified sample is.

Disproportionate stratified sampling involves balancing the two criteria of strata size and variability. With a fixed sample size, strata exhibiting more variability are sampled more than proportionately to their relative size. Conversely, those strata that are very homogeneous are sampled less than proportionately.

Learning Objective 6
List the steps followed in drawing a cluster sample.

Cluster sampling involves the following steps: (1) the parent population is divided into mutually exclusive and exhaustive subsets, and (2) a random sample of the subsets is selected.

Learning Objective 7
Explain the difference between a one-stage cluster sample and a two-stage cluster sample.

If an investigator uses all the population elements in the selected subsets for the sample, the procedure is one-stage cluster sampling. If, on the other hand, a sample of elements is selected probabilistically from the selected subsets, the procedure is known as two-stage cluster sampling.

Learning Objective 8
Explain why cluster sampling, though far less statistically efficient than comparable stratified samples, is the sampling procedure used most in large-scale field surveys using personal interviews.

Cluster sampling is the sampling procedure used most in large-scale field surveys using personal interviews because it is often more economically efficient in that the cost per observation is less. The economies permit the selection of a larger sample at a smaller cost. Although cluster sampling requires a larger sample for the same degree of precision, and is thus less statistically efficient, the smaller cost per observation allows samples so much larger that estimates with a smaller standard error can be produced for the same cost.

Learning Objective 9
Distinguish between one-stage area sampling and simple two-stage area sampling.

The distinguishing feature of the one-stage area sample is that all of the households in the selected blocks (or other areas) are enumerated and studied. With simple two-stage area sampling, a certain proportion of second-stage sampling units is selected from each first-stage unit.

Learning Objective 10
Note the quality that distinguishes probability-proportional-to-size sampling and explain when it is used.

With probability-proportional-to-size sampling, a fixed number of second-stage units is selected from each first-stage unit. This type of sampling is particularly useful when the number of second-stage units is unequal and simple two-stage area sampling could cause bias in the estimate.

Key Terms

stratified sample (page 429)
proportionate stratified sample (page 436)
disproportionate stratified sample (page 436)
cluster sample (page 437)
statistical efficiency (page 438)
systematic sample (page 438)

sampling units (page 440)
area sampling (page 440)
simple two-stage area sampling (page 442)
probability-proportional-to-size sampling
(page 442)

Review Questions

1. What is a stratified sample? How is a stratified sample selected?
2. Is a stratified sample a probability or nonprobability sample? Why?
3. What principle should be followed in establishing the strata for a stratified sample? Why? How can this principle be implemented in practice?
4. Describe the procedure that is followed in developing a confidence interval estimate for a population mean with a stratified sample. Be specific.
5. Which sampling method typically produces more precise estimates of a population mean—simple random sampling or stratified sampling? Why?
6. What is a proportionate stratified sample? What is a disproportionate stratified sample? What must be known about the parent population to select each?
7. What is a cluster sample? How is a cluster sample selected?
8. What are the similarities and differences between a cluster sample and a stratified sample?
9. What is a systematic sample? How are the random start and sampling interval determined with a systematic sample?
10. What are the advantages and disadvantages associated with systematic samples?
11. What is an area sample? Why are area samples used?
12. How does a two-stage area sample differ from a one-stage area sample?

Discussion Questions, Problems, and Projects

1. The Minnesota National Bank, headquartered in Minneapolis, Minnesota, has some 400,000 users of its credit card scattered throughout the state of Minnesota. The application forms for the credit card asked for the usual information on name, address, phone, income, education, and so on, that is typical of such applications. The bank is now very much interested in determining if there is any relationship between the uses to which the card is put and the socioeconomic characteristics of the using party; for example, is there a difference in the characteristics of those people who use the credit card for major purchases only, such as appliances, and those who use it for minor as well as major purchases?
   (a) Identify the population and sampling frame that would be used by Minnesota National Bank.
   (b) Indicate how you would draw a simple random sample from the above sampling frame.
   (c) Indicate how you would draw a stratified sample from the above sampling frame.
   (d) Indicate how you would draw a cluster random sample from the above sampling frame.
   (e) Which method would be preferred? Why?
2. Exclusive Supermarkets is considering entering the Boston market. Before doing so, however, management wishes to estimate the average square feet of selling space among potential competitors, in order to plan the size of the proposed new store. A stratified sample of supermarkets in Boston produced the following results:

Size	Total Number in City	Number of This Size in Sample	Mean Size of Stores in Sample	Standard Deviation of Stores in Sample
Small supermarkets	1,000	20	4,000 sq. ft.	2,000 sq. ft.
Medium supermarkets	600	12	10,000 sq. ft.	1,000 sq. ft.
Large supermarkets	400	8	60,000 sq. ft.	3,000 sq. ft.

(a) Estimate the average-sized supermarket in Boston. Show your calculations.

(b) Develop a 95 percent confidence interval around this estimate. Show your calculations.

(c) Was a proportionate or disproportionate stratified sample design used in determining the number of sample observations for each stratum? Explain.

3. Store-More is a large department store located in Lansing, Michigan. The manager is worried about the constant overstocking of a number of items in the various departments. Approximately 3,000 items ranging from small multipurpose wrenches to lawn mowers are overstocked every month. The manager is uncertain whether the surpluses are primarily due to poor purchasing policies or poor store layout and shelving practices. The manager realizes the difficulty of scrutinizing the purchase orders, invoices, and inventory cards for all the items that are overstocked. She decides on choosing a sample of items but does not know how to proceed.

(a) Identify the population elements and sampling frame.

(b) What sampling method would you recommend? Why? Be specific.

(c) How would you draw the sample based on this sampling method?

4. The university housing office has decided to conduct a study to determine what influence living in dormitories versus off-campus housing has on the academic performance of the students. You are required to assist the housing office.

(a) What sampling method will you recommend? Why? Be specific.

(b) How would you draw the sample based on this sampling method?

5. Maxwell Federated operates a chain of department stores in the greater Chicago metropolitan area. The management of Maxwell Federated has been concerned of late with tight money conditions and the associated deterioration of the company's accounts receivable. It appears on the surface that more and more customers are becoming delinquent each month. Management wishes to assess the current state of delinquencies, to determine if they are concentrated in particular stores, and to determine if they are concentrated among any particular types of purchases or purchasers.

(a) What sampling method would you recommend? Why? Be specific.

(b) How would you draw the sample based on this sampling method?

6. A retailer of household appliances is planning to introduce a new brand of dishwashers to the local market and wishes to estimate demand for the product. He has decided to use two-stage area sampling and has secured an up-to-date map of your area, but he does not know how to proceed and requires your assistance. Outline a step-by-step approach you will recommend for conducting the study.

7. In February, a midwestern city instituted a mandatory recycling plan for certain types of household waste. A marketing research firm was hired to evaluate the progress of the plan in July. Among several measures of effectiveness to be used, the researchers wished to compare the weight of recyclables collected per household per week with a pre-implementation estimate of ten pounds per week. In order to do this, the following sampling procedure was used. First, the city was divided into 840 blocks. The blocks were then arrayed from largest to smallest based on the estimated number of households they contained and, based on the selection of a random number, every twelfth block was selected. Researchers then accompanied collectors on their weekly rounds and weighed each bag of recyclables collected on the specified blocks. (Assume each household puts out one bag per week.)

(a) What are the population elements and the sampling frame?

(b) What are the primary sampling units?

(c) Describe the sampling plan used by the researchers?

(d) What is the approximate probability that a household will be included in the sample?

8. A researcher is interested in studying the job satisfaction of salespeople in the automatic milking machine industry. She has decided to use probability-proportional-to-size sampling to select a

sample. Preliminary work has identified only eight companies that manufacture automatic milkers. Each company is considered to be one first-stage unit. The researcher has determined that she wants to draw four second-stage units per first-stage unit. The total sample size desired is 16. The following table has been generated:

Unit	Salespeople	Cumulative Salespeople
1	6	6
2	10	16
3	7	23
4	12	35
5	8	43
6	8	51
7	14	65
8	9	74

(a) How many first-stage units must be selected?
(b) Refer to Exhibit 15.6, "Abridged List of Random Numbers," in the preceding chapter. Entering at the first column, first row and moving downward, which first-stage units will be selected for second-stage sampling?
(c) Demonstrate that the probability of any salesperson's being included in the sample is equal.

Suggested Additional Readings

There are a number of excellent books that discuss in more detail than here the rationale for and various types of stratified and cluster samples. Three of the better and more extensive treatments are Morris H. Hansen, William N. Hurwitz, and William G. Madow, *Sample Survey Methods and Theory, Vol. 1, Methods and Applications* (New York: John Wiley, 1993).

Leslie Kish, *Survey Sampling* (New York: John Wiley, 1995).

Paul S. Levy and Stanley Lemeshow, *Sampling of Populations: Methods and Applications,* 3rd ed. (New York: John Wiley and Sons, Inc., 1999).

For more abbreviated but still useful treatments of the principles underlying survey sampling, see Richard L. Schaeffer and William Mendenhall, *Elementary Survey Sampling,* 5th ed. (Belmont, Calif.: Wadsworth Publishing Company, 1996).

Gary T. Henry, *Practical Sampling* (Thousand Oaks, Calif.: Sage Publications, 1990).

Chapter 17

Sample Size

© PhotoDisc/Getty Images

Learning Objectives

1. Specify the key factor a researcher must consider in estimating sample size using statistical principles.

2. Cite two other factors researchers must also take into account when estimating a sample size and explain their relationship.

3. Explain in what way the size of the population influences the size of the sample.

4. Specify the circumstances under which the finite population correction factor should be used.

5. Explain the impact that cost has on sample size in stratified or cluster samples.

6. Cite the general rule of thumb for calculating sample size when cross-classification tables are used.

"H ow was your dinner this evening?" inquired Rosemary Malgieri of William and Emily Bader as they finished their veal picata.

"It was wonderful, as always," answered Emily. Her husband, still chewing, nodded appreciatively.

"I've asked Vincent to bring you some cannoli and cappuccino for dessert, with my compliments."

"How lovely, thank you," replied Emily.

"I feel a little bit awkward intruding on your dinner," began Rosemary, "but I remember Mr. Bader telling me one evening that he works for a marketing research company. I was wondering if there might be a time that I could discuss a little idea of mine. . . ."

"No time like the present," replied William, wiping his mouth and motioning to the empty chair next to him. "That is, if you can manage to leave your duties in the restaurant for a few minutes."

Rosemary motioned to the busboys to clear the Baders' table as she sat down. Vincent appeared at double speed with frothing cups of hot cappuccino and crisp tubes of pastry filled with ricotta cream.

"As I'm sure you know, the restaurant business is a very competitive one. Customer satisfaction is everything. Careless service, a change in the kitchen, can spell death for a restaurant. We have been very lucky here at Malgieri's. We have done very well since we opened three years ago. We've had very little turnover in our wait staff, and our chef, while temperamental, has been very loyal to us."

"So what is it you want my help with?" asked William.

"You know that my husband, Michael, and I are partners in this restaurant. I manage the dining room and oversee the kitchen. He handles the financial end. We both agree that it is time to expand. He would like to see us open a second location. He has his eye on a restored storefront in Bentleyville."

"On the west side?" asked Emily. "Where they're doing all the renovations in the old warehouse district?"

"Exactly. Michael feels that the area has a big potential for attracting the after-work crowd from downtown. He's probably right. On the other hand, I'm not convinced that another location is the right way to expand. I feel that Michael and I are the reason Malgieri's is a success. One of us is in the restaurant at all times. With two locations some distance apart, we will have to hire a manager, which will dilute our level of personal control."

"So how would you like to expand?" inquired Emily. "Do you want to increase the size of the existing restaurant?"

"No. I'd like to start a take-out and delivery service. When I was in Chicago for the restaurant show, I noticed that there is a big trend toward restaurant meals at home. I'd like to see us tap into that market. The problem is, I don't know whether to gear the service toward young professionals who don't have time to cook and want an elegant, restaurant-style meal at home or toward busy families who would see our take-out and delivery service as an alternative to a home-cooked meal."

"Well, one way to find out what people want and are willing to pay is to do a survey. A good start would be to survey people who've dined at Malgieri's during the past six months," William replied.

"But how many people would you want to survey?" asked the restaurateur. "I can't afford to spend a lot of money on marketing research. Restaurants operate on a very slim margin. Besides, my husband is determined to open a second restaurant. While solid marketing research might convince him that my plan is the better one, he's not going to agree to invest a lot of money in studying an option he's not particularly interested in."

Discussion Issues

1. What factors might influence sample size for a study that William Bader would do for Malgieri's Restaurant?

2. If you were William Bader, what information might you want to have about the patrons of Malgieri's Restaurant? ■

Thus far, our discussion of sampling has concentrated on sample type. Another important consideration is sample size. Unless the researcher is going to use a sequential sample, he or she needs some means of determining the necessary size of the sample before beginning data collection.

Beginning researchers might suppose that the sample should be as large as the client can afford, but the question of sample size is complex. It depends on, among other things, the type of sample, the statistic in question, the homogeneity of the population, and the time, money, and personnel available for the study. We cannot discuss all of these issues adequately in one chapter, but we will present the important statistical principles that determine sample size, using only simple random samples and a few of the more popular statistics. Readers interested in how sample size is determined for stratified or cluster samples should consult one of the standard references on sampling theory. Readers who would like to be able to use a simple random sample to estimate such things as population variance, which is beyond the scope of this chapter, will find help in a good intermediate-level statistics text. The principles are the same in each case, but the formulas differ since they depend on the sampling plan and the statistic in question.

Basic Considerations in Determining Sample Size

Not surprisingly, the sampling distribution of the statistic is the key to determining sample size. You will recall that the sampling distribution of the statistic indicates how the sample estimates vary as a function of the particular sample selected. If a researcher knows the spread of the sampling distribution, he or she can then determine the amount of error that can be associated with any estimate. For instance, in Chapter 15, we saw that the error associated with the estimation of a population mean by a sample mean was given by the standard error of the mean $\sigma_{\bar{x}} = \sigma/\sqrt{n}$, or the population standard deviation divided by the square root of the sample size when the population variance was known, and $\hat{s}_{\bar{x}} = \hat{s}\sqrt{n}$, or the sample standard deviation divided by the square root of the sample size when the population variance was unknown. The first factor one must consider in estimating sample size is the standard error of the estimate obtained from the known sampling distribution of the statistic.

A second consideration is how precise the estimate must be. For example, a researcher investigating mean income might want the sample estimate to be within ±$100 of the true population value. Or a less precise estimate might be required—say, one within ±$500 of the true value. When the problem involves estimating a population parameter, **precision** can be said to be measured by the magnitude of error, or the size of the estimating interval. The degree of precision required will be greatly influenced by the importance of the decision

1 Specify the key factor a researcher must consider in estimating sample size using statistical principles.

2 Cite two other factors researchers must also take into account when estimating a sample size and explain their relationship.

© Peter Beck/Corbis

involved in the study from a managerial perspective. If millions of dollars and hundreds of employees' jobs ride on the results of the study, the acceptable range of error is likely to be small.

Another factor that affects sample size is the degree of **confidence** the researcher requires in the estimate. With a sample of fixed size, there is a trade-off between degree of confidence and degree of precision. One can specify either the degree of precision or the degree of confidence, but not both. It is only when sample size is allowed to vary that one can achieve both a specified precision and a specified degree of confidence in the result. Actually, the determination of sample size using statistical principles involves balancing the two considerations against each other.

Suppose that one wished to estimate the mean annual expenditure by fishers in a certain state. The central-limit theorem suggests that the distribution of sample means will be normal for samples of reasonable size regardless of the distribution of expenditures in the population of fishers.

To understand the distinction between confidence and precision, suppose that we need to know the mean income of a certain population. The most precise measure of that particular parameter would be a point estimate of the mean, which is an estimate that involves a single value with no associated bounds of error. In the case of our study, calculations may show that the population mean income as estimated by the sample mean is $19,243. This point estimate is most assuredly wrong, and thus we can have no confidence in it despite its preciseness. On the other hand, we can have complete confidence in an estimate that the population mean income is between zero and $1 million, but that estimate is too imprecise to be of value.

To further illustrate the distinction between confidence and precision, suppose instead we want to estimate the proportion of people who have an annual income greater than $50,000 and 37 percent of the people within our sample did so. We would probably be hesitant to conclude (i.e., we would have virtually no confidence) that exactly 37 percent of the population had an income greater than $50,000. On the other hand, we might feel quite confident in the less precise estimate that the true proportion lies somewhere between 33 and 41 percent.

Sample Size Determination When Estimating Means

precision
The degree of error in a study, or the size of the estimating interval.

confidence
The degree to which one can feel confident that an estimate approximates the true value.

We can best see the interrelationship of the basic factors affecting the determination of sample size by looking at an example. Imagine that the Division of Tourism in a certain state wants to know the average amount that fishermen spend each year on food and lodging while on fishing trips within the state. Our job as researchers is to use a simple random sample to estimate the mean annual expenditure of those fishermen, using a list of all those who applied for fishing licenses within the year.[1]

Since we are interested in estimating a population mean, the sampling distribution of interest is the distribution of sample means. Now, the central-limit theorem suggests that the distribution of sample means will be normal for samples of reasonable size regardless of the distribution of expenditures in the population of fishermen. Moreover, the mean of all possible sample means will be equal to the population mean, and the variance of means will be equal to the population variance divided by the sample size, i.e. $\sigma_{\bar{x}}^2 = \frac{\sigma^2}{n}$ (Figure 17.1). We thus have the first of the three factors we need in order to estimate sample size.

The second factor is the degree of precision needed in the estimate. Let the needed precision be denoted by H. Suppose the director of tourism wanted the estimate to be within ±$25 of the true population value, or $H = 25$.

The remaining item that needs to be specified is the degree of confidence desired in the result. Suppose the director of tourism wants to be 95 percent confident that the interval the researcher constructs will contain the true population mean. Since we are working with a normal curve, this implies that z is approximately equal to 2.[2]

Given the three quantities: (1) the sampling distribution of the statistic, (2) the degree of precision, and (3) the degree of confidence, the needed sample size can be determined using the formula

$$n = \frac{z^2}{H^2}\left(\text{est } \sigma\right)^2 \qquad \textbf{(17.1)}$$

or in words,

$$\text{sample size} = \frac{z\,(\text{corresponding to desired degree of confidence}) \text{ squared} \times \text{population variance}}{\text{desired level of precision squared}}$$

While z and H have both been specified by the problem requirements, we need to estimate the population standard deviation to determine the sample size.

But how does one generate an estimate of the population standard deviation? One could do a pilot study.[3] Alternatively, sometimes the variance can be estimated from the conditions surrounding the approach to the problem. Research Window 17.1, for example, discusses the estimation of the variance when rating scales are used to measure the important variables. A third possibility is to take into account the fact that for a normally distributed variable, the range of the variable is approximately equal to plus or minus three standard deviations. Thus, if one can estimate the range of variation, one can estimate the standard deviation by dividing by 6. A little a priori knowledge of the phenomenon is often enough to estimate the range. If the estimate is in error, the consequence is a confidence interval more or less precise than desired. Let us illustrate.

Certainly there would be some licensed fishermen who would spend zero dollars on food and lodging while on fishing trips, since they would only be making one-day trips. Some might also be expected to go on several one-week trips a year. Suppose that 15 days a year were considered typical of the upper limit, and food and lodging expenses were calculated at $30 per day; the total dollar upper limit would be $450. The range would also be 450 (since they could not spend less than zero); and the estimated standard deviation would then be $\frac{450}{6} = 75$.

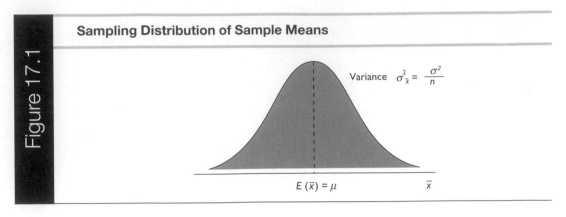

Figure 17.1

Sampling Distribution of Sample Means

Variance $\sigma_{\bar{x}}^2 = \dfrac{\sigma^2}{n}$

$E(\bar{x}) = \mu$ $\quad\quad \bar{x}$

With desired precision of ±$25 and a 95 percent confidence interval, the calculation of sample size is now

$$n = \frac{z^2}{H^2}\left(\text{est. } \sigma\right)^2$$

$$= \frac{(2)^2}{(25)^2}(75)^2$$

and $n = 36$.

RESEARCH *Window*

17.1

Guidelines for Estimating Variance for Data Obtained Using Rating Scales

Rating scales are doubly bounded: on a 5-point scale, for instance, responses cannot be less than 1 or greater than 5. This constraint leads to a relationship between the mean and the variance. For example, if a sample mean is 4.6 on a 5-point scale, there must be a large proportion of responses of 5, and it follows that the variance must be relatively small. On the other hand, if the mean is near 3.0, the variance can be potentially much greater. The nature of the relationship between the mean and the variance depends on the number of scale points and on the "shape" of the distribution of responses (e.g., approximately normal or symmetrically clustered around some central scale value, or skewed, or uniformly spread among the scale values). By considering the types of distribution shapes typically encountered in practice, it is possible to estimate variances for use in calculating sample size requirements for a given number of scale points.

The table lists ranges of variances likely to be encountered for various numbers of scale points. The low end of the range is the approximate variance when data values tend to

be concentrated around some middle point of the scale, as in a normal distribution. The high end of the range is the variance that would be obtained if responses were uniformly spread across the scale points. Although it is possible to encounter distributions with larger variances than those listed (such as distributions with modes at both ends of the scale), such data are rare.

In most cases, data obtained using rating scales tend to be more uniformly spread out than in a normal distribution. Hence, to arrive at conservative sample size estimates (i.e., sample sizes that are *at least* large enough to accomplish the stated objectives), it is advisable to use a variance estimate at or near the high end of the range listed. ■

Number of Scale Points	Typical Range of Variances
4	0.7–1.3
5	1.2–2.0
6	2.0–3.0
7	2.5–4.0
10	3.0–7.0

Source: *Research on Research,* No. 37 (Chicago: Market Facts, Inc., undated).

PART 5:
Sampling and Data Collection

A sample of size 36 would then be selected and the information collected. Suppose these observations generated a sample mean, $\bar{x} = 35$, and a sample standard deviation, $\hat{s} = 60$. The confidence interval is calculated as before, using the expression sample mean $\pm z$ (standard error of the mean), where now the standard error of the mean is estimated using the sample standard deviation, where $s_{\bar{x}} = \hat{s}\sqrt{n}$, or in symbols, $\bar{x} \pm z s_{\bar{x}}$, or

$$35 \pm 2 \frac{\hat{s}}{\sqrt{n}} = 35 \pm 2 \frac{60}{\sqrt{36}} = 35 \pm 20$$

or

$$15 \leq \mu \leq 55$$

Note what has happened. The desired precision was $\pm\$25$; the obtained precision is $\pm\$20$. The interval is narrower than planned (a bonus) because we overestimated the population standard deviation as judged by the sample standard deviation. If we had underestimated the standard deviation, the situation would have been reversed, and we would have ended up with a wider confidence interval than desired.

Case of Multiple Objectives

Researchers rarely conduct a study to determine only one parameter. It is much more typical for a study to involve multiple objectives. Because multiple objectives are typical, let us return to our previous example of fishermen and assume more realistically that the researcher has also been asked to estimate the annual mean level of expenditures on tackle and equipment by licensed fishermen, and the number of miles traveled on fishing trips in a year. There are now three means to be estimated. Suppose each is to be estimated with 95 percent confidence, and the desired precision and estimated standard deviation are as given in Exhibit 17.1. Exhibit 17.1 also contains the sample sizes needed to estimate each variable, which were calculated using Equation 17.1.

The three requirements produce conflicting sample sizes. Depending on the variable being estimated, n should equal 36, 16, or 100. The researcher must somehow reconcile these values to come up with a sample size suitable for the study as a whole. The most conservative approach would be to choose $n = 100$, the largest value. This would ensure that each variable would be estimated with the required precision, assuming that the estimates of the standard deviations were accurate.

However, let us assume that of the three means to be determined, the estimate of miles traveled is the least critical. In such a case, it would be wasteful of resources to use a sample size of 100. A better approach would be to focus on those variables that are most critical and to select a sample sufficient in size to estimate them with the required precision and confidence. The variables for which a larger sample size is needed would then be estimated with

Exhibit 17.1

Sample Size Needed to Estimate Each of Three Means

	VARIABLE		
	Expenditures on Food and Lodging	Expenditures on Tackle and Equipment	Miles Traveled
Confidence level	95 percent ($z = 2$)	95 percent ($z = 2$)	95 percent ($z = 2$)
Desired precision	$\pm\$25$	$\pm\$10$	±100 miles
Estimated standard deviation	$\pm\$75$	$\pm\$20$	±500 miles
Required sample size	36	16	100

either a lower degree of confidence or less precision than planned. Suppose in this case that the expenditure data are most critical and that the analyst, therefore, decides on a sample size of 36. Suppose also that the information from this sample of 36 fishermen produced a sample mean of $\bar{x} = 300$ and a sample deviation of $\hat{s} = 500$ miles traveled. The sample result is thus seen to agree with the original estimate of the population standard deviation, and so the confidence interval estimate will not be affected by inaccuracies here.

Using the standard expression, sample mean $\pm z$ (standard error of the mean), the confidence interval for miles traveled is calculated as

$$\bar{x} \pm z s_{\bar{x}} = \bar{x} \pm \frac{z\hat{s}}{\sqrt{n}} = 300 \pm 2\frac{500}{\sqrt{36}}$$

or $133.3 \leq \mu \leq 466.7$. Whereas the desired precision was ± 100 miles, the obtained precision is ≤ 166.7 miles. In order to produce an estimate with the desired precision, the degree of confidence would have to be lowered from its present 95 percent level.

Sample Size Determination When Estimating Proportions

The preceding examples all concern mean values. Marketers are also often interested in estimating other parameters, such as the population proportion, π. In our example, the researcher might be interested in determining the proportion of licensed fishermen who are from out of state, or from rural areas, or who took at least one overnight trip.

© George Cassidy/Index Stock Imagery

In order to determine the sample size for a study of the proportion of fishers who make overnight trips, a researcher would first have to estimate the number of fishers who do so. To make that estimate, the researcher might need to begin by conducting a pilot study, or could use previously published data.

At the beginning of this chapter we suggested that three things were needed to determine sample size: a specified degree of confidence, specified precision, and knowledge of the sampling distribution of the statistic. As noted earlier, the specific requirements of the research problem determine how the first two items will be specified. With percentages, however, precision means that the estimate will be within plus or minus so many percentage points of the true value, as, for example, within ± 5 percentage points of the true value. For example, when the *Chicago Tribune* conducted a poll of local suburbanites to learn their sense of economic well-being, it sampled 930 residents of the counties surrounding Chicago. The newspaper reported that the degree of precision was plus or minus 3 percentage points. Thus, whereas the paper said 50 percent of residents of the Chicago suburbs believed they will be better off in five years, the true percentage could be anywhere between 47 and 53 percent.[4]

The remaining consideration then is the sampling distribution of the sample proportion. If the sample elements are selected independently, as can reasonably be assumed if the sample size is small relative to the population size, then the theoretically correct distribution of the sample proportion is the binomial. But the binomial becomes indistinguishable from the normal with large samples or when the population proportion is close to one-half.[5] It is convenient to use the normal approximation when estimating sample size. After the sample is drawn and the sample proportion determined, the researcher can always fall back on the binomial distribution to determine the confidence interval if the normal approximation proves to be in error.

The distribution of sample proportions is centered about the population proportion (Figure 17.2). The sample proportion is an unbiased estimate of the population proportion. The

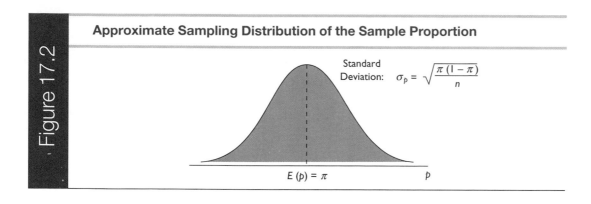

Figure 17.2

Approximate Sampling Distribution of the Sample Proportion

Standard Deviation: $\sigma_p = \sqrt{\dfrac{\pi(1-\pi)}{n}}$

$E(p) = \pi$

p

standard deviation of the normal distribution of sample proportions, that is, the standard error of the proportion, denoted by σ_p, is equal to $\sqrt{\pi(1-\pi)/n}$.

Sample size is given by the formula

$$n = \frac{z^2}{H^2}\pi(1-\pi) \qquad\qquad (17.2)$$

or, in words,

$$\text{sample size} = \frac{\begin{array}{c} z\ (\text{corresponding to desired} \qquad \text{population} \qquad (1-\text{population} \\ \text{degree of confidence) squared} \times \text{proportion} \times \text{proportion)} \end{array}}{\text{desired level of precision squared}}$$

Suppose, for example, the Division of Tourism is interested in knowing the proportion of all fishermen who took at least one overnight fishing trip in the past year. Suppose also that they wanted this estimate within ±2 percentage points, and they wanted to be 95 percent confident ($z = 2$) in the result. Substituting these values in the formula yields

$$n = \frac{(2)^2}{(.02)^2}\pi(1-\pi)$$

This equation contains two unknowns: the population proportion being estimated and the sample size. Thus, it is not solvable as it stands. In order to determine sample size, the researcher needs to estimate the population proportion. That is right! *The researcher must estimate the very quantity the study is being designed to discover in order to determine sample size.*

This fact is often bewildering, and certainly disconcerting, to decision makers and beginning researchers alike. Nevertheless, it is true that with proportions one is forced to make some judgment about the approximate value of the parameter in order to determine sample size. This is another example of how information begets information in sample design. To arrive at an initial estimate, researchers might consult past studies or other published data. Alternatively, they might conduct a pilot study. If neither of these options is available, they might simply use informed judgment—a best guess—as to the approximate likely value of the parameter.

A poor estimate will make the confidence interval more or less precise than desired. Suppose, for example, that the best considered judgment was that 20 percent of all licensed fishermen could be expected to take an overnight fishing trip during the year. Sample size is then calculated to be

$$n = \frac{(2)^2}{(.02)^2}(.20)(1-.20)$$

and $n = 1,600$. After data are collected from the designated 1,600 fishermen, suppose that the sample proportion, p, actually turns out to be equal to 0.40. The confidence interval is then established, using the sample standard error of the proportion, s_p, to estimate the unknown population standard error of the proportion, σ_p, where

$$s_p = \sqrt{\frac{pq}{n}}$$

where p is the proportion engaging in the behavior in the particular sample selected, and $q = 1 - p$. In the example,

$$s_p = \sqrt{\frac{0.40\,(0.60)}{1,600}} = \sqrt{\frac{0.24}{1,600}} = 0.012$$

The confidence interval for the population proportion is given by the expression, sample proportion $\pm$ (z) (standard error of the proportion), or

$$p \pm zs_p = 0.40 \pm 2(0.012)$$

or

$$0.376 \leq \pi \leq 0.424$$

Note that the interval is wider than desired. This is because the sample proportion turned out to be larger than the *estimated* population proportion.

Suppose a wider interval than planned was unacceptable. One way of preventing it is to choose the sample size so as to reflect the "worst of worlds." Note from the formula that the largest sample size will be obtained when the product $\pi(1 - \pi)$ is greatest, since sample size is directly proportional to this quantity. This product is in turn greatest when the population proportion $\pi = 0.5$, as might be intuitively expected, since, if one-half the population behaves one way and the other half the other way, then one would require more evidence for a valid inference than if a substantial proportion all behaved in the same way.

In the absence of any other information about the population proportion, then, one can always conservatively assume that π is equal to 0.5. The established confidence interval will simply be more precise to the extent that the sample estimate deviates from the assumed 0.5 value.

Population Size and Sample Size

3 *Explain in what way the size of the population influences the size of the sample.*

Although you may not have noticed it before, note it now: *The size of the population does not enter into the calculation of the size of the sample.* Except for one slight modification that we will discuss shortly, the size of the population has *no direct effect* on the size of the sample.

Although this statement may initially seem strange, consider it carefully and you will see why it is true. When estimating a mean, if all population elements have exactly the same value of the characteristic (for example, if each of our fishermen spent exactly $74 per year on food and lodging), then a sample of one is all that is needed to determine the mean. This is true whether there are 1,000, 10,000, or 100,000 elements in the population. What directly affects the size of the sample is the variability of the characteristic in the population.

Suppose that our example state offered some of the best fishing in the country and drew fishermen from across the nation as well as locally. If the parameter we sought to measure was mean number of miles traveled annually on fishing trips, there would be great variation in the characteristic. The more variable the characteristic, the larger the sample needed to estimate it with some specified level of precision. This idea not only makes intuitive sense, but we can see it directly expressed in the formulas for determining sample size to estimate a population mean. (See Equation 17.1.) Thus, population size affects sample size only indirectly through variability. In most cases, the larger the population, the greater the *potential* for variation of the characteristic.

It is also true that population size does not affect sample size when estimating a proportion. (See Equation 17.2.) With a proportion, the determining factor is the estimated proportion of the population possessing the characteristic; the closer the proportion is to 0.5, the larger the sample that will be needed, regardless of the size of the population. A value of 0.5 signifies greatest variability because one-half of the population possesses the characteristic and one-half does not.

The procedures we have discussed so far apply to situations where the target population is essentially infinite. This is the case in most consumer goods studies. However, when we first began our discussion, we mentioned that there was one modification to the general rule that population size has no direct effect on sample size. In cases where the sample represents a large portion of the population, the formulas must be altered or they will overestimate the required sample. Since the larger the sample, the more expensive the study, the finite population correction factor should be used.

As we have seen previously, the formula for the standard error of the mean is $\sigma_{\bar{x}} = \sigma/\sqrt{n}$ for most sampling problems. When the finite population correction factor is required, the formula becomes

$$\sigma_{\bar{x}} = \frac{\sigma}{\sqrt{n}} \sqrt{\frac{N-n}{N-1}}$$

where N denotes the size of the population and n denotes the size of the sample. The factor $(N-n)/(N-1)$ is the finite population correction factor.

When the estimated sample represents more than 5 percent of the population, the calculated size should be reduced by the finite population correction factor.[6] If, for example, the population contained 100 elements and the calculation of sample size indicated that a sample of 20 was needed, fewer than 20 observations would, in fact, be taken if the finite population correction factor were used.

The required sample would be given as $n' = n[N/(N+n-1)]$, where n was the originally determined size and n' was the revised size. Thus, with $N = 100$ and $n = 20$, only 17 sample elements would, in fact, be used.

4 Specify the circumstances under which the finite population correction factor should be used.

Other Probability Sampling Plans

So far, the discussions of sample size have been based on simple random samples. You should be aware that there are also formulas for determining sample size when other probability sampling plans are used. The formulas are more complex, to be sure, but the same underlying principles apply. One still needs a knowledge of the sampling distribution of the statistic in addition to the research specifications regarding level of precision and degree of confidence.

The issue of sample size is compounded by the fact that one now has a number of strata or a number of clusters with which to work. This means that one must deal with within-strata variability and within- and between-cluster variability in calculating sample size, whereas with simple random sampling only total population variability entered the picture. As before, the more variable the stratum or cluster, the larger the sample that needs to be taken from it, other things being equal. This is precisely the basis for disproportionate stratified sampling discussed in Chapter 16.

Something else that must be equal, however, is cost. Cost did not enter directly into the calculation of sample size with simple random sampling, although it often does affect sample size. If the cost of data collection with a sample of the calculated size would exceed the research budget, the cost could be the factor keeping the sample size below what was indicated by the formulas. In fact, it is not unusual for the size of a simple random sample to be determined by dividing the data collection budget by the estimated cost per observation. From a strictly statistical viewpoint, however, cost per observation does not enter into the formulas for calculating sample size with simple random samples.

5 Explain the impact that cost has on sample size in stratified or cluster samples.

With stratified or cluster samples, cost exerts a direct impact. In calculating sample size, one has to allow for unequal costs per observation by strata or by cluster, and in implementing the sample size calculation, one has to have some initial estimate of these costs. The task then becomes one of balancing variability against costs and assessing the trade-off function relating the two. With a stratified sample, for example, if cost were the same by strata, one would want to sample most heavily the stratum that was most variable. On the other hand, if there were little variation within strata, one might choose to sample more heavily those strata in which the cost per observation was less. Since it is unlikely that the cost per observation or variability will be the same for each stratum, the challenge becomes one of determining sample size by considering the precision likely to result from sampling each stratum at a given rate. Formulas are available for this purpose, as for cluster samples. We shall not go into these formulas here, as they are readily available in the standard works on sampling theory and fall largely in the domain of the sampling specialist.[7] You should be aware, though, that when dealing with stratified or cluster samples, cost per observation by subgroup enters directly into the calculation of sample size.

You should also be aware that there are formulas for determining sample size when the problem is one of hypothesis testing and not confidence interval estimation. Once again, the principles are the same, although there are some additional considerations such as the levels of Type I and Type II errors to be tolerated and the issue of whether it is necessary to detect subtle differences or only obvious differences. We shall not deal with these formulas, since they are also readily available in standard statistical works and their discussion would take us too far afield.[8]

Sample Size Determination Using Anticipated Cross Classifications

Thus far, our discussion of how sample size is determined has been based primarily on the use of statistical principles, with a particular focus on the sampling error involved and the trade-off between degree of confidence and degree of precision. We limited ourselves to a discussion of these considerations because they are the most important ones theoretically. But in applied problems, the size of the sample is also going to be affected by certain practical considerations. In our discussion of stratified and cluster samples we already mentioned that the size of the budget for the study and the anticipated cost per observation would affect sample size. In addition to that, the size of the sample may also be affected by other, quite subjective factors. For example, researchers may find themselves increasing the size of the sample beyond what is required statistically in order to convince skeptical executives, who have little understanding of sampling theory, that they can have confidence in the results of the study.

One of the more important practical bases for determining the size of sample that will be needed is the cross classifications to which researchers plan to subject the data. Suppose that in our task of estimating the proportion of all fishermen who took at least one overnight fishing trip in the past year, we also proposed to determine whether this pattern of behavior was somehow related to an individual's age and income. Assume that the age categories of interest were as follows: younger than 20, 20–29, 30–39, 40–49, and 50 and older. Assume the income categories of interest were as follows: less than $10,000, $10,000–$19,999, $20,000–$29,999, $30,000–$39,999, and $40,000 and over. There are thus five age categories and five income categories for which the proportion of fishermen taking an overnight trip would be estimated.

While we could estimate proportions for each of these variables separately, we should also recognize that the two variables are interrelated in that increases in incomes are typically related to increases in age. To allow for this interdepen-

© Eyewire/Getty Images

Each stage of the research process is interrelated and research teams should consider the entire process before undertaking any data collection.

PART 5:
Sampling and Data Collection

460

dence, we need to consider the impact of the two variables simultaneously. The way to do this is through a cross-classification table in which age and income jointly define the cells or categories in the table.[9]

Exhibit 17.2 is a cross-classification table that could be used for the example at hand. Note that this dummy table is complete in all respects except for the numbers that actually go in each of the cells. These would, of course, be determined by the data actually collected on the number and proportion of all those sampled who actually made at least one overnight trip. In the table there are 25 cells that need estimation. It is unlikely, however, that the decision maker for whom our study is designed is going to be comfortable with an estimate based on only a few cases of the phenomenon. Yet even with a sample of, say, 500 fishermen, there is only a potential of 20 cases per cell (i.e., 500 cases divided by 25 cells) if the sample is evenly divided with respect to the age and income levels considered. Further, it is very unlikely that the sample would split this way, which would put the researcher in the awkward position of estimating the proportion in a cell engaging in this behavior on the basis of fewer than 20 cases.

One can reverse this argument to estimate how large a sample should be taken. First, the researcher would calculate the number of cells in the intended cross classifications. That number can be found by multiplying the number of levels of the characteristics forming each of the cross classifications. In our study, researchers would multiply five levels of income by five levels of age to get 25 cells. If it was felt that the decision maker might need at least 30 observations per cell in order to feel comfortable with the cell's estimate, that would mean a sample of 750 subjects would be needed. However, the sample of 750 is unlikely to be evenly distributed across the cells of the table, so the researchers would need to determine how the variables are likely to be distributed. Once the most important cells have been identified, the researcher can compute a sample size large enough to satisfy concerns about sufficient sampling. One general rule of thumb is that "the sample should be large enough so that there are 100 or more units in each category of the major breakdowns and a minimum of 20 to 50 in the minor breakdowns."[10] Major breakdowns refer to the cells in the most critical cross tabulations for the study, and minor breakdowns refer to the cells in the less important cross classifications.

Through all of this one has to make allowances

ETHICAL dilemma 17.2

A recent discussion between the account manager for an independent research agency and the marketing people for the client left the account manager feeling perplexed. After numerous discussions, the account manager believed that she had a good handle on the client's problem and major concerns. On the basis of this understanding, she had developed a set of dummy tables by which the client's concerns could be investigated. During the most recent meeting, she had presented these to the client. The client had completely accepted the account manager's recommendation about how the data would be viewed, and closed the meeting by asking how large a sample the account manager would recommend and how much the study would cost. The account manager's anxiety was caused by the fact that she believed from the earlier discussions and some preliminary investigation that two of the seven hypotheses were especially promising. The sample size that was needed to investigate these two hypotheses was almost 60 percent smaller than that needed to address some of the other hypotheses because of the fewer cells in the cross-classification table. The account manager was in a dilemma about whether she should take the safe route and recommend the larger sample size to the client and thereby assure that all the planned cross-classifications could be completed or whether she should go with her instinct and recommend the smaller sample size and save the client some money.

- *What would you recommend that the account manager do?*

- *Is it ethical for the account manager to recommend the larger sample size when she is fairly certain that the smaller one will provide the answers the client needs? Is it ethical to do the reverse and recommend the smaller sample when there is some risk that the smaller sample will not adequately answer the problem that the firm was hired to solve?*

- *What are the account manager's responsibilities to the client in a case like this?*

Exhibit 17.2

Number and Proportion of Fishermen Staying Overnight as a Function of Age and Income

Income	AGE				
	Younger than 20	20–29	30–39	40–49	50 and older
Less than $10,000					
$10,000–$19,999					
$20,000–$29,999					
$30,000–$39,999					
$40,000 and over					

for nonresponses, since some individuals designated for inclusion in the sample will be unavailable and others will refuse to participate. The researcher "builds up" the sample, so to speak, from the size of the cross-classification table with due allowance for these considerations.

Perhaps cross classification will not be the basic method used to analyze the data. Perhaps, instead, other statistical techniques will be used. If so, the same arguments for determining sample size apply. That is, one needs a sufficient number of cases to satisfy the requirements of the technique, so as to inspire confidence in the results. Different techniques have different sample size requirements, often expressed by the degrees of freedom required for the analysis. Readers interested in using a particular statistical technique for analysis should pay close attention to the sample size requirements for the technique to be used safely. For now, we merely wish to reiterate the important point made earlier when introducing the research process—that the stages are very much related, and a decision with respect to one stage can affect all the other stages. In this case a decision with respect to Stage 6 regarding the method of analysis can have an important impact on Stage 5, which precedes it, with respect to the size of the sample that should be selected. Therefore, the researcher needs to think through the entire research problem, including how the data will be analyzed, before beginning the data collection process.

6 *Cite the general rule of thumb for calculating sample size when cross-classification tables are used.*

Determining Sample Size Using Historical Evidence

A final method by which an analyst can determine the size of the sample to use is to use the size that others have used for similar studies in the past. Although this may be different from the ideal size in a given problem, the fact that the contemplated sample size is in line with that used for similar studies is psychologically comforting, particularly to inexperienced researchers. Exhibit 17.3, which summarizes the evidence, provides a crude yardstick in this respect. Note that national studies typically involve larger samples than regional or special studies. Note further that the number of subgroup analyses has a direct impact on sample size.

Exhibit 17.3

Typical Sample Sizes for Studies of Human and Institutional Populations

Number of Subgroup Analyses	PEOPLE OR HOUSEHOLDS		INSTITUTIONS	
	National	Regional or Special	National	Regional or Special
None or few	1,000–1,500	200–500	200–500	50–200
Average	1,500–2,500	500–1,000	500–1,000	200–500
Many	2,500+	1,000+	1,000+	500+

PART 5:
Sampling and Data Collection

At three o'clock in the afternoon Malgieri's Restaurant looked very different than it did at night when it was filled with people. Without tablecloths, the tables were revealed to be pitted and worn. In one corner, busboys in shirtsleeves sat folding napkins while they watched soap operas on a small black-and-white television.

Michael and Rosemary Malgieri were seated at another table going over what looked like receipts. They greeted William Bader warmly, and if Michael objected to his wife's exploring a business alternative that he didn't support, he certainly didn't show it.

"I've been giving Rosemary's idea of a take-out and delivery service a good deal of thought," began William. "In order to know whether it would be a profit-making venture for you, I think the single most important thing to find out is where your customers live relative to the restaurant. People won't go too far to pick up food, for fear that it'll be cold when they get home and because the whole idea of takeout is convenience. And if you're going to add a delivery service, you'll have the same concerns about hot food, as well as time and fuel costs for deliveries far away."

"So how about if tonight we instruct the wait staff to ask all patrons where they live and how far it is from the restaurant? They can ask when the patrons pay their check. We'll serve at least a hundred people tonight: that should give us a pretty good idea," suggested Michael.

"It would be a start, but not a particularly accurate one. I'd feel more comfortable if you would let me write out a little question-and-answer sheet for each waiter to read to the patrons on a given night. That way we'd be sure that everyone was responding to the same questions, and I'd be able to tabulate the results with some confidence. Also, I know that a hundred people sounds like a lot, but I'm not sure of how reliable an estimate of average miles traveled would be, based on that number of respondents. I'd feel much more comfortable if you'd be willing to repeat the survey on one or two more nights if it turned out to be necessary."

"That seems reasonable," replied Rosemary.

"Then, I propose that if the simple location survey shows enough patrons clustered within a comfortable radius of the restaurant, we do another patron survey. The focus of this one would be to explore age, income, and interest in a take-out and delivery service. That way we'd be able to see whether it would be better to gear your out-of-restaurant menu toward people wanting restaurant meals or those wanting family-style meals."

"How many people would you like to survey in the second stage?" asked Michael.

"Again, I'd like to keep that open-ended," replied William. "In any sample there's a trade-off between degree of confidence and degree of precision. If we allow ourselves to vary the sample size to produce an estimate with precision and confidence levels that we want, then you're going to feel confident putting your time and dollars behind the decision you make." ∎

Summary

Learning Objective 1
Specify the key factor a researcher must consider in estimating sample size using statistical principles.
The key factor a researcher must consider in estimating sample size is the standard error of the estimate obtained from the known sampling distribution of the statistic.

Learning Objective 2
Cite two other factors researchers must also take into account when estimating a sample size and explain their relationship.
When estimating a sample size, researchers must consider both how precise the estimate must be and the degree of confidence that is required in the estimate. With a sample of fixed size, there is a trade-off between degree of confidence and degree of precision. One can specify either the degree of precision or the degree of confidence, but not both. It is only when sample size is allowed to vary that one can achieve both a specified precision and a specified degree of confidence in the result. The determination of sample size involves balancing the two considerations against each other.

Learning Objective 3
Explain in what way the size of the population influences the size of the sample.
In most instances, the size of the population has no direct effect on the size of the sample but only affects it indirectly through the variability of the characteristic; and sample size is directly proportional to variability.

Learning Objective 4
Specify the circumstances under which the finite population correction factor should be used.
In general, when the estimated sample represents more than 5 percent of the population, the calculated sample size should be reduced by the finite population correction factor.

Learning Objective 5
Explain the impact that cost has on sample size in stratified or cluster samples.
With stratified or cluster samples, cost exerts a direct impact. In calculating sample size, one has to allow for unequal costs per observation by strata or by cluster; and in implementing the sample size calculation, one has to have some initial estimate of these costs. The task, then, becomes one of balancing variability against costs and assessing the trade-off function relating the two.

Learning Objective 6
Cite the rule of thumb for calculating sample size when cross-classification tables are used.
When calculating sample size by using cross-classification tables, the rule of thumb is that the sample should be large enough so that there are 100 or more units in each category of the major breakdowns and a minimum of 20 to 50 in the minor breakdowns.

Key Terms

precision (page 452)

confidence (page 452)

Review Questions

1. In determining sample size, what factors must an analyst consider?
2. What is the difference between degree of confidence and degree of precision?
3. How do you determine the sample size necessary to estimate a population mean with some desired degree of precision and confidence? Given that the sample has been selected, how do you generate the desired confidence interval?
4. What effect would relaxing by 25 percent the absolute precision with which a population mean is estimated have on sample size? Decreasing the degree of confidence from 95 percent to 90 percent? ($z = 1.64$)

5. Suppose that you wanted to estimate a population proportion within ±3 percentage points at the 95 percent level of confidence. How would you proceed and what quantities would you need to estimate?

6. What happens if the sample proportion is larger than the estimated population proportion used to determine sample size? If it is smaller? What value of the population proportion should be assumed if you wish to take no chance that the generated interval will be larger than the desired interval?

7. What is the correct procedure for treating multiple study objectives when calculating sample size?

8. How is sample size determined based on anticipated cross classifications of the data?

Discussion Questions, Problems, and Projects

1. A survey was being designed by the marketing research department of a medium-sized manufacturer of household appliances. The general aim was to assess customer satisfaction with the company's dishwashers. As part of this general objective, management wished to measure the average maintenance expenditure per year per household, the average number of malfunctions or breakdowns per year, and the number of times a dishwasher is cleaned within a year. Management wished to be 95 percent confident in the results. Further, the magnitude of the error was not to exceed ±$4 for maintenance expenditures, ±1 for malfunctions, and ±4 for cleanings. The research department noted that while some households would spend nothing on maintenance expenditures per year, others might spend as much as $120. Also, while some dishwashers would experience no breakdowns within a year, the maximum expected would be no more than three. Finally, while some dishwashers might not be cleaned at all during the year, others might be cleaned as frequently as once a month.

(a) How large a sample would you recommend if each of the three variables were considered separately? Show all your calculations.

(b) What size sample would you recommend *overall* given that management felt that the expenditure on repairs was most important and the number of cleanings least important to know accurately?

(c) The survey indicated that the average maintenance expenditure was $30, and the standard deviation was $15. Estimate the confidence interval for the population parameter μ. What can you say about the degree of precision?

2. The management of a major dairy wanted to determine the average ounces of milk consumed per resident in the state of Montana. Past trends indicated that the variation in milk consumption (s) was 4 ounces. A 95 percent confidence level is required and the error is not to exceed ±½ ounce.

(a) What sample size would you recommend? Show your calculations.

(b) Management wanted to double the level of precision and increase the level of confidence to 99 percent. What sample size would you recommend? Show your calculations. Comment on your results.

3. The manager of a local recreational center wanted to determine the average amount each customer spent on traveling to and from the center. On the basis of the findings, the manager was planning on raising the entrance fee. The manager noted that customers living near the center would spend nothing on traveling. On the other hand, customers living at the other side of town had to travel about 15 miles and spent about 20 cents per mile. The manager wanted to be 95 percent confident of the findings and did not want the error to exceed ±10 cents.

(a) What sample size should the manager use to determine the average travel expenditure? Show your calculations.

(b) After the survey was conducted, the manager found the average expenditure to be $1.00, and the standard deviation was $0.60. Construct a 95 percent confidence interval. What can you say about the level of precision?

4. A large manufacturer of chemicals recently came under severe criticism from various environmentalists for its disposal of industrial effluent and waste. In response, management launched a campaign to counter the bad publicity it was receiving. A study of the effectiveness of the campaign indicated that about 20 percent of the residents of the city were aware of the campaign and the company's position. In conducting the study, a sample of 400 was used and a 95 percent confidence interval was specified. Three months later, it was believed that 30 percent of the residents were aware of the campaign. However, management decided to do another survey and specified a 99 percent confidence level and a margin error of ±2 percentage points.

    (a) What sample size would you recommend for this study? Show all your calculations.

    (b) After doing the survey it was found that 50 percent of the population was aware of the campaign. Construct a 99 percent confidence interval for the population parameter.

5. Score-It, Inc., is a large manufacturer of video games. The marketing research department is designing a survey to determine attitudes toward the products. Additionally, the percentage of households owning video games and the average usage rate per week are to be determined. The department wants to be 95 percent confident of the results and does not want the error to exceed ±3 percentage points for video game ownership and ±1 hour for average usage rate. Previous reports indicate that about 20 percent of the households own video games and the average usage rate is 15 hours with a standard deviation of 5 hours.

    (a) What sample size would you recommend, assuming only the percentage of households owning video games is to be determined? Show all your calculations.

    (b) What sample size would you recommend, assuming only the average usage rate per week is to be determined? Show all your calculations.

    (c) What sample size would you recommend, assuming both the above variables are to be determined? Why?

After the survey was conducted, the results indicated that 30 percent of the households owned video games and the average usage rate was 13 hours with a standard deviation of 4 hours.

    (d) Compute the 95 percent confidence interval for the percentage of individuals owning video games. Comment on the degree of precision.

    (e) Compute the 95 percent confidence interval for the average usage rate. Comment on the degree of precision.

6. The local gas and electric company in a city in the northeast United States recently started a campaign to encourage people to reduce unnecessary use of gas and electricity. To assess the effectiveness of the campaign, management wanted to do a survey to determine the proportion of people that had adopted the recommended energy-saving measures.

    (a) What sample size would you recommend if the error was not to exceed ±0.025 percentage points and the confidence level was to be 90 percent? Show your calculations.

    (b) The survey indicated that the proportion adopting the measures was 40 percent. Estimate the 90 percent confidence interval. Comment on the level of precision. Show your calculations.

7. Assume you are a marketing researcher analyst for TV Institute, and you have just been given the assignment of estimating the percentage of all American households that watched the ABC movie last Sunday night. You have been told that your estimate should have a precision ±1 percentage point and that there should be a 95 percent "probability" of your being "correct" in your estimate. Your first task is to choose a sample of the appropriate size. Make any assumptions that are necessary.

    (a) Recast the problem in a statistical format.

    (b) Compute the sample size that will satisfy the required specifications.

    (c) What is the required sample size if the precision is specified as ±2 percentage points?

    (d) What would be the sample size if the probability of being "correct" were decreased to 90 percent, keeping the precision at ±1 percentage points?

    (e) If you had only enough time to take a sample of Size 100, what precision could you expect from your estimate? (Assume a 95 percent confidence interval.)

    (f) Assume that instead of taking a sample from the entire country (60 million households), you would like to restrict yourself to one state with one million households. Would the sample size computed in (b) be too large? Too small? Explain.

8. Assume TV Institute has hired you to do another study, this time estimating the average number of hours of television viewing per week per family in the United States. You are asked to generate an estimate within ±5 hours. Further, there should be 95 percent confidence that the estimate is correct. Make any assumptions that are necessary.

(a) Compute the sample size that will satisfy the required specifications.

(b) What would be the required sample size if the precision were changed to ±10 hours?

9. The manager of a local bakery wants to determine the average expenditure per household on bakery products. Past research indicates that the standard deviation is $10.

(a) Calculate the sample size for the various levels of precision and confidence. Show your calculations:

	Desired Precision (±)	Desired Confidence	Estimated Sample Size
1	0.50	0.95	
2	1.00	0.99	
3	0.50	0.90	
4	0.25	0.90	
5	0.50	0.99	
6	0.25	0.95	
7	1.00	0.90	
8	1.00	0.95	
9	0.25	0.99	

(b) Which alternative gives the largest estimate for sample size? Explain.

10. A manufacturer of liquid soaps wishes to estimate the proportion of individuals using liquid soaps as opposed to bar soaps. Prior estimates of the proportions are listed below.

(a) For the various levels of precision and confidence indicated, calculate the needed size of the sample.

	Desired Precision in Percentage Points (±)	Desired Confidence	(%) Estimated Proportion	Estimated Sample Size
1	6	0.99	20	
2	2	0.90	10	
3	6	0.99	10	
4	4	0.95	30	
5	2	0.90	20	
6	2	0.99	30	
7	6	0.90	30	
8	4	0.95	10	
9	4	0.95	20	

(b) Which alternative gives the largest estimate of the sample size? Explain.

11. Your World, Inc., is a large travel agency located in Cincinnati, Ohio. Management is concerned about its declining leisure travel-tour business. It believes that the profile of those engaging in leisure travel has changed in the past few years. To determine if that is indeed the case, management decides to conduct a survey to determine the profile of the current leisure travel-tour customer. Three variables are identified that require particular attention. Prior to conducting the survey, the following three dummy tables are developed.

	Age			
Income	18–24	25–34	35–54	55+
0–$9,999				
$10,000–$19,999				
$20,000–$29,999				
$30,000–$39,999				
$40,000 and over				

Age	Education			
	Some High School	High School Graduate	Some College	College Graduate
18–24				
25–34				
35–54				
55+				

Income	Education			
	Some High School	High School Graduate	Some College	College Graduate
0–$9,999				
$10,000–$19,999				
$20,000–$29,999				
$30,000–$39,999				
$40,000 and over				

(a) How large a sample would you recommend be taken? Justify your answer.

(b) The survey produced the following incomplete table for the variables of age and education. Complete the table on the basis of the assumption that the two characteristics are independent (even though that assumption is wrong). On the basis of the completed table, do you think an appropriate sample size was used? If yes, why? If no, why not?

Age	Education				Total
	Some High School	High School Graduate	Some College	College Graduate	
18–24					100
25–34					200
35–54					350
55+					350
Total	200	400	300	100	1,000

12. You are the assistant director of political research for the ABC television network, and two candidates, Marge Simpson and Ethan Martin, are running for president of the United States of America. You need to furnish a prediction of the percentage of the vote going to Martin, assuming the election was held today, for tomorrow's evening newscast. You want to be 95 percent confident in your prediction and desire a total precision of 6 percent.

(a) Assume that you have no reliable information concerning the percentage of the population that prefers Martin. What sample size will you use for the project?

(b) Assume that a similar poll, taken 30 days ago, revealed that 40 percent of the respondents would vote for Martin. Taking this information into account, what sample size will you use for the project?

(c) Which of the two sample sizes you have just calculated would you prefer to use for your study? Why?

(d) Most polls of this type are conducted by telephone. When a potential respondent answers the phone, what is the *first* question you should ask? Why?

13. A city is considering implementing a "pay as you throw" billing system for residential garbage pickup. Under the plan, a household would be charged by the pound for garbage removal. As part of its proposal to the city council, the sanitation department needs to calculate an average monthly bill per household under the proposed system. To do so, the sanitation department plans to weigh the garbage collected from a random sample of households over the next two months. Based on an informal poll of route drivers, the department estimates that a household throws away between 30 and 90 pounds of garbage a month. The department wants the estimate to be within ±2 pounds

of the true population average, and the city council insists that it will accept only a figure that has a 99 percent probability of being correct.

(a) What sample size would you recommend?

(b) You have just been informed that the budget has been cut and the size of the sample must be cut by 20 percent. However, a 99 percent confidence level must be maintained. What is the new sample size? What does this mean in terms of the precision of the estimate?

Suggested Additional Readings

For a more thorough discussion of the estimation of sample size for different types of samples and characteristics other than the mean and proportion, see Morris H. Hansen, William N. Hurwitz, and William G. Madow, *Sample Survey Methods and Theory, Vol. I, Methods and Applications* (New York: John Wiley, 1993).

Leslie Kish, *Survey Sampling* (New York: John Wiley, 1995).

Paul S. Levy and Stanley Lemeshow, *Sampling of Populations: Methods and Applications,* 3rd ed. (New York: John Wiley and Sons, Inc., 1999).

Richard L. Schaeffer, William Mendenhall, and Lyman Ott, *Elementary Survey Sampling,* 5th ed. (Belmont, Calif.: Wadsworth Publishing Co., 1996).

Chapter 18

Collecting the Data: Nonsampling Errors and Response Rate Calculation

© PhotoDisc/Getty Images

Learning Objectives

1. Explain what sampling error is.

2. Describe four basic types of nonsampling errors.

3. Outline several ways in which noncoverage error can be reduced.

4. Explain what nonresponse error is.

5. Identify the two main sources of nonresponse error.

6. Define response error and discuss some of its causes.

7. Discuss how interviewers can contribute to response error.

8. Cite the standard definition for response rate.

9. Discuss several ways in which response rates might be improved.

re you listening to the radio right now? Did you listen while you were getting up this morning? Last night? Last Monday at 9 A.M.? And what did you listen to the last time the radio was on? Some people have trouble remembering such details. Have you ever been tempted to fib about your listening preferences to impress someone? Not too surprisingly, some people say they listen to classical music or National Public Radio, not because they do, but because they want to signal they are cultured and intelligent.

Now imagine you work for a radio station or a business that advertises on radio stations. You need information about who is listening—and when. If you want to learn about people's attitudes toward radio stations, you might conduct a phone survey. To learn about listenership, however, the traditional method is to ask people to keep diaries of their listening behavior. You would recruit a panel and ask panel members to write down what station, if any, they were listening to at specific times.

A basic challenge of recruiting a panel is figuring out how to obtain a random sample of radio listeners. No sample can exactly mirror the total audience of listeners, so researchers also have to estimate sampling error. But even after these efforts, sources of error remain. Some people will forget what they were listening to, or they will mix up stations in their memories. They might get tired of writing in the diary, and not bother to record every 10-minute listening period. And they might "forget" to record times when they were listening to lowbrow entertainment, such as an A.M. shock jock or pop songs on a Top 40s station.

When a station's advertising sales rep sits down with the owner of the local car wash to plan an advertising campaign, the sales rep uses the diary data to justify the station's advertising rates. How can the car wash owner decide whether the advertising rates are reasonable? How can the sales rep convince her that the station is a cost-effective medium? Both may feel they are basing business decisions on a work of fiction.

Enter marketing research firm Arbitron, with a new data collection device called the Portable People Meter (PPM). The PPM is a pager-sized device that "listens" for broadcast signals. The device translates the signals into data on exposure to radio and television programming. Members of a panel wear the PPM throughout the day. At the end of the day, the panel member places the meter into a "base station," which recharges the device and transmits the day's data to Arbitron. Arbitron has been testing the PPM through spring 2003, and initial results show that the PPM records more exposure to media than consumer panels had been writing in their diaries.

Discussion Issues

1. Would you expect to have more difficulty correcting for sampling errors or for errors associated with poor memory and lack of motivation?

2. In a diary panel measuring radio listenership, what kinds of radio programming do you predict would be underreported? Overreported?

3. With Portable People Meters, what sources of error (besides sampling errors) would you expect? How might they be prevented? ◼

To most people, the words "marketing research" mean the data collection process. At this stage, data are collected either in the field or by phone, mail, email, etc. In this chapter we focus on the various things that can go wrong in conducting a study, with special emphasis on sources of error we have not discussed in earlier chapters. Understanding the possible sources of error in data collection is important for understanding how much faith to put into the results of a study. We also address the calculation of a study's response rate, an important consideration for assessing the overall quality of the data collection effort. Finally, we offer several suggestions for improving response rates.

Impact and Importance of Nonsampling Errors

Explain what sampling error is.

sampling error
The difference between the observed values of a variable and the long-run average of the observed values in repetitions of the measurement.

nonsampling error
Error that arises in research that is not due to sampling; nonsampling error can occur because of errors in conception, logic, interpretation of questions and replies, statistics, arithmetic, analyzing, coding, or reporting.

Two basic types of errors arise in research studies: *sampling errors* and *nonsampling errors*. The concept of sampling error underlies much of the discussion in Chapters 15, 16, and 17. The sampling distribution of a statistic reflects the fact that the different possible samples that could be drawn under the sampling plan will produce different estimates of the parameter. The statistic varies from sample to sample simply because we are only sampling part of the population in each case. **Sampling error** then is "the difference between the observed values of a variable and the long-run average of the observed values in repetitions of the measurement."[1] As we saw, the degree of sampling error can be estimated (assuming probability sampling procedures) and can be reduced by increasing sample size.

Nonsampling errors reflect the many other kinds of error that arise in research, even when the survey is not based on a sample. They can be *random* or *nonrandom*. Nonrandom nonsampling errors are more troublesome. Random errors produce estimates that vary from the true value; sometimes these estimates are above and sometimes below the true value, but on a random basis. As a result, random errors tend to cancel each other out. Nonrandom nonsampling errors, on the other hand, tend to produce mistakes only in one direction. They tend to bias the sample value away from the true value of the population parameter. Nonrandom errors can occur because of errors in conception, wording of questions, interpretation of replies, statistics, arithmetic, analysis, coding, or reporting.

Unfortunately, nonsampling errors are quite common because of the many ways they can creep into a project. Worse, nonsampling errors are not as manageable as sampling errors, which decrease with increases in sample size. Nonsampling errors do not necessarily decrease with increases in sample size. They may, in fact, increase. Further, it is difficult to even estimate the size and effects of nonsampling errors.

As an example of the impact of sampling vs. nonsampling error, consider how a sample of consumers might respond to the following question on a survey: "On average, how many times per week do you brush your teeth?" Suppose that data were collected from a random sample of consumers, producing a mean of 21 times per week and, further, that we could be 95% confident that had we talked with all consumers in the population the answer would fall between 19 and 23. In our analysis, we have fully accounted for possible sampling error. Accounting for sampling error, however, does not help with the fact that many people will have overstated their brushing behavior in order to be seen as socially acceptable. The appropriate allowance for sampling error provides accurate insights into how the population would have responded to the question given the data collection method, but provides very little insight into the validity of the manner in which the data were collected or the question itself.

As you can begin to see from this example, nonsampling errors are frequently the most important errors that arise in research. In special Census Bureau investigations of their size, for example, nonsampling errors have been found ten times more than sampling errors.[2] This is not an unusual finding. Nonsampling error has been consistently shown to be the major contributor to total survey error, while sampling error has minimal impact.[3] Nonsampling errors can be reduced, but reduction depends on improving the method of collection rather than increasing sample size. By understanding the sources of nonsampling errors, the analyst is in a better position to reduce them.

Types of Nonsampling Errors

There are four main types of nonsampling error: noncoverage error, nonresponse error, response error, and office error. The first two types are sometimes referred to as nonobservation errors, because they result from a failure to obtain data from parts of the survey population. These errors occur because part of the population of interest was not included, or because some respondents designated for inclusion in the sample did not participate.[4] Response errors and office errors are sometimes called observation errors. In these cases, data were obtained from the appropriate sample elements, but the data were either inaccurate or mistakes were made during the coding, analysis, or reporting stages of the research.

2 Describe four basic types of non-sampling errors.

Noncoverage Errors

Noncoverage error arises because of a failure to include some part of the defined population in the sampling frame. That is, one or more consumers, households, etc., that meet the criteria for membership in the population are not included in the list of population members and thus have no chance of being included in the sample. Noncoverage error, then, is essentially a sampling frame problem.

Researchers realize that the telephone directory, for instance, does not provide a complete sampling frame for most general surveys. Not every family has a phone, and not all people who do have their numbers listed in the directory. Further, some variation exists between those having and not having phones in terms of certain important demographic characteristics. These conditions are compounded in fax surveys of the general population. They are less of a problem, although not eliminated, in surveys of businesses or other institutions.

Noncoverage is also a problem in mail and email surveys. The mailing and email lists dictate the sampling frame. If the lists inadequately represent segments of the population, the survey will also suffer from the bias of noncoverage. Almost all mailing lists or lists of email addresses do not exactly capture the population the researcher wishes to study, even though mailing lists are available for very specific population groups, as Exhibit 18.1 indicates.

When data are to be collected by personal interview in the home, some form of area sample is typically used to pinpoint respondents. In this case, the sampling frame is one of areas, blocks, and dwelling units, rather than a list of respondents. However, this does not eliminate the incomplete frame problem. Maps of the city may not be totally current, so the newest areas may not have a proper chance of being included in the sample. The instructions to the interviewer may not be sufficiently detailed. The direction, "Start at the northwest corner of the selected blocks, generate a random start, and take every fifth dwelling unit thereafter," may be inadequate in blocks with a number of apartment units. The evidence indicates that lower-income households are avoided when the selection of households is made by the field staff rather than the home office. Further, interviewers typically select the most accessible individuals within the household, contrary to instructions for random selection. This again means that a portion of the intended population is underrepresented in the study, while the accessible segment is overrepresented.

There are also sampling frame problems when personal interviews in shopping malls are used to collect data. For one thing, there is no list of population elements. Rather, only those who shop in a particular mall have a chance of

3 Outline several ways in which non-coverage error can be reduced.

noncoverage error
Nonsampling error that arises because of a failure to include some units, or entire sections, of the defined target population in the sampling frame.

© Roy Morsch/Corbis

People may report different behaviors than they actually practice—a type of nonsampling error. In today's health-conscious society, some people might overstate their consumption of fresh fruit and vegetables or believe they are living healthier lifestyles than they actually are.

Exhibit 18.1

Some Population Groups for Which Mailing Lists Are Available

Quantity		Price
12,900	Babies' Wear Retail	$45/M
800	Bagel Shops	$85
30,200	Bakeries, Retail	$45/M
2,400	Bakery Products Mfrs	$45/M
600	Ballet/Dance Companies	$85
2,450	Balloon (Hot Air) Owners	$45/M
10,500	Band Directors, High School	$45/M
16,100	Bankers, Mortgage, Executives	$45/M
4,100	Bankers, Mortgage, Firms	$45/M

Banks

Quantity		Price
13,790	Banks, Main Offices	$45/M
324	Banks with Assets $1 Billion or more	$85
538	Banks with Assets $500 Million or more	$85
1,278	Banks with Assets $200 Million or more	$85
3,582	Banks with Assets $75 Million or more	$45/M
8,835	Banks with Assets $25 Million or more	$45/M
12,400	Banks with Assets $10 Million or more	$45/M
13,245	Banks with Assets $5 Million or more	$45/M
200	Banks with Assets less than $5 Million	$85
40,100	Banks, Branches	$45/M
20,000	Banks, Cashiers	$45/M
209,600	Banks, Executives	$45/M
66,700	Banks, Executives, Women	$45/M
3,490	Banks, Savings & Loans (HQ)	$45/M
16,800	Banks, Savings & Loans (Branches)	$45/M
6,000	Banks, Trust Officers	$45/M
11,030	Banks, Loan Offices	$45/M
243	Bankruptcy, Judges	$85
8,400	Barber & Beauty Supplies	$45/M
64,200	Barber Shops	$45/M
81,900	Bars, Taverns, Cocktail Lounges	$45/M
2,800	Beauty Schools	$45/M
200,000	Beauty Shops	$45/M
315	Beekeepers	$85
90	Beer Brewers	$85
11,900	Beer Distributors	$45/M
37,000	Behavioral Scientists	$45/M

Quantity		Price
170	Better Business Bureaus	$85
4,000	Beverage Bottlers & Distributors	$45/M
26,000	Beverage Industry Executives	$45/M
11,700	Bicycle Dealers & Repairs	$45/M
2,500	Billiard Parlors & Poolrooms	$45/M
1,380	Billion Dollar Companies	$85
5,700	Biological Chemists	$45/M
23,700	Biologists	$45/M
3,900	Birth Control Centers	$45/M
6,400,000	Black Families	Inquire
4,600	Blood Banks	$45/M
3,000,000	Blue Collar Workers	Inquire

Boats

Quantity		Price
5,250	Boat Basins (Marinas)	$45/M
12,350	Boat Dealers	$45/M
21,000	Boat & Marine Supplies	$45/M
567,400	Boat Owners (Select by Type, Length, Power)	$50/M
10,000	Boat Yards, Building & Repairing	$45/M
14,000	Boards of Education	$45/M
67,700	Body & Top Repair, Automobile	$45/M
5,000	Boiler Contractors	$45/M
135	Book Clubs	$85
6,300	Book Publishers	$45/M
1,725	Book Publishers (Major)	$85
850	Book Wholesalers	$85
24,000	Bookkeeping Services	$45/M
20,100	Bookstores	$45/M
588	Bookstores, Chains	$85
3,100	Bookstores, College	$45/M
3,300	Bookstores, Religious	$45/M
132	Botanical Gardens	$85
2,700	Botanists	$45/M
2,600	Bottlers, Soft Drink	$45/M
4,600	Boutiques	$45/M
7,500	Bowling Alleys	$45/M
6,000	Box & Container Mfrs	$45/M

Source: Zeller List Corp., 15 East 26th Street, New York, NY 10010. Reprinted with permission.

being included in the study, and their chances of being included depend on how often they shop there. That is why quota samples are often used in mall intercept studies. However, noncoverage bias is not eliminated in quota samples, whether conducted in a mall or elsewhere. Rather, the interviewers' flexibility in choosing respondents can introduce substantial noncoverage bias, as interviewers typically underselect in both the high- and low-income classes. The research director may not discover this bias, since field staffers also have a tendency to falsify characteristics so that it appears that they interviewed the appropriate number of cases per cell.

Noncoverage error is not a problem in every survey. For some studies, clear, convenient, and complete sampling frames exist. For example, a department store wishing to conduct a study among its charge-account customers should have little trouble with frame bias. The sampling frame is simply those with charge accounts. There might be some difficulty in distinguishing active accounts from inactive accounts, but this problem can be addressed during the design stage of the study. Similarly, a firm should experience little noncoverage bias in conducting a study among its employees. The population of interest here would be the firm's employees, and it could be expected that the list of employees would be current and accurate since it is needed to generate the payroll.

Given that noncoverage bias is likely, what can the researcher do to lessen its effect? The most obvious step, of course, is to improve the quality of the sampling frame. This may mean taking the time to bring available city maps up to date, or taking a sample to check the quality and representativeness of a mailing list with respect to a target population. The unlisted-number problem common to telephone surveys can be handled by random-digit or plus-one dialing, although this will not provide adequate sample representation of those without phones.

We should mention one other relatively common problem with sampling frames. Overcoverage error can arise because of duplication in the list of sampling units. Units with multiple entries in the sampling frame—for example, families with several phone listings—have a higher probability of being included in the sample than do sampling units with one listing. For most surveys, however, noncoverage is much more common and troublesome than overcoverage.

Nonresponse Errors

Nonresponse error represents a failure to obtain information from elements of the population that were selected for the sample. The first hurdle to overcome in dealing with nonresponse errors is simply anticipating everything that can go wrong with an attempt to contact a designated respondent. Figure 18.1 depicts various outcomes of an attempted telephone contact. Notice the many different reasons an interview might not be completed on a particular attempted contact. Other forms of data collection are also subject to nonresponse errors.

Suppose that five years from now your school was to conduct a mail survey among you and your classmates to update records and to determine how "successful" the school's graduates were. Included on the survey was an item assessing current salary. Who is most likely to complete and return the survey? Probably those who are pleased with their salaries. Who is least likely? Probably those who are not happy with their salaries. As a result, there is a very real

4 Explain what non-response error is.

nonresponse error
Nonsampling error that represents a failure to obtain information from some elements of the population that were selected and designated for the sample.

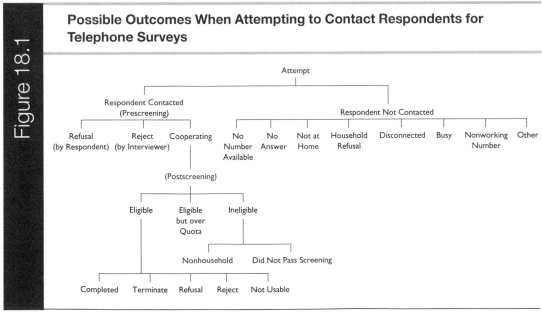

Figure 18.1

Possible Outcomes When Attempting to Contact Respondents for Telephone Surveys

Source: Frederick Wiseman and Philip McDonald, *Toward the Development of Industry Standards for Response and Nonresponse Rates* (Cambridge, Mass.: Marketing Science Institute, 1980), p. 29. Reprinted with permission. American Marketing Association.

possibility that those who respond to the survey are different from those who do not respond to the survey on a key dimension, current salary, and the results with respect to salary will be systematically biased upward. This upward bias reflects nonresponse error.

Nonresponse error is a potential problem in any project for which data are not collected from all respondents selected for the sample. It is a *potential* problem, because it only occurs when those who respond are systematically different from those who do not respond in some important way. The degree of nonresponse error, however, is difficult to assess because we obviously do not have answers from those who do not respond. Study after study, however, has indicated that the assumption that those who did not respond were in fact equal to those who did is risky. Exhibit 18.2 presents several possible methods of determining if nonresponse error is likely to be a problem in a particular study.

The two main sources of nonresponse bias are refusals, which apply to projects using all forms of data collection, and not-at-homes, which apply mainly to telephone surveys and some types of personal interviews.

refusals
Nonsampling error that arises because some designated respondents refuse to participate in the study.

Refusals In almost every study, some respondents will refuse to participate. In one of the most extensive investigations of the magnitude of this problem, 46 field research companies sponsored a study called "Your Opinion Counts," which involved almost 1.4 million phone and personal interviews. The study indicated that 38 percent of the people asked to participate declined to do so, with 86 percent of those people refusing to participate before or during the introduction. The rest of those who declined broke away before the survey was completed.[5] Research Window 18.1 depicts what is happening to refusal rates in general.

The rate of refusals depends on many factors, including the nature of the respondent, the nature of the organization sponsoring the research, the circumstances surrounding the contact, the topic of the study, and the skill of the interviewer in the case of telephone and personal interviews. Even the culture of the country can affect the refusal rate. For example, in some cultures like Saudi Arabia, it is nearly impossible to interview women.

The method used to collect the data also makes a difference. The empirical evidence indicates that personal interviews are most effective, and mail questionnaires least effective, in generating response. Telephone interviews are usually less successful than personal interviews in getting target respondents to cooperate, but they typically have higher response rates than do mail surveys. The most obvious reason for the superiority of personal interviews and telephone surveys over mail surveys is the social nature of the contact: a respondent doesn't run the risk of hurting someone's feelings by throwing a mail survey in the nearest trash can.

In general, there is a tendency for females, nonwhites, those who are less well educated, those who have lower incomes, and those who are older to be more likely to refuse to participate in a study.[6] In addition, the type of organization sponsoring the research can also make a difference in the number of refusals. As a general rule, most people are probably more inclined to "help" a not-for-profit entity than a for-profit enterprise by taking the time to respond to a survey, especially when the cause is one they support.

Sometimes the circumstances surrounding the contact can cause a refusal. A respondent may be busy, tired, or sick when contacted. And the subject of the research also affects the refusal rate. Those interested in the subject are most likely to respond. The most commonly cited reasons for refusing to participate in a survey include lack of time, approaching a potential respondent at an inappropriate time, and lack of interest in the subject matter.[7]

Finally, interviewers themselves can have a significant impact on the number of refusals they obtain. Their approach, manner, and even their own demographic characteristics can affect a respondent's willingness to participate.

not-at-homes
Nonsampling error that arises when replies are not secured from some designated sampling units because the respondents are not at home when the interviewer calls.

Not-at-Homes With refusals, we can be fairly certain that at least we contacted a potential respondent (or his/her household) and provided an opportunity to respond. We may not like the response (i.e., a refusal), but at least we received one. **Not-at-homes** present a different sort of problem. Sometimes we simply cannot reach designated sampling units at home during the data collection time frame. The empirical evidence indicates that the percentage of

Three Methods for Diagnosing Nonresponse Error

Method 1 Contact a sample of nonrespondents If a researcher can identify persons who have not responded to a survey (perhaps after several attempts), it is sometimes possible to select a sample of the nonrespondents and contact them again, typically using a different method of contact. This time, however, the goal is not to get the respondent to complete the entire survey, but instead to simply answer one or two questions that focus on the key issue in the project. The answers from this "nonrespondent" sample on these items are then compared with those from the initial sample. If the responses from the two samples are not different on the key items (see Chapter 21 for methods of testing for statistically significant differences), then nonresponse error is probably not an issue in the project. This is the preferred method of diagnosing nonresponse bias, but it is also the most difficult under normal circumstances.

Method 2 Compare respondent demographics against known demographics of population Sometimes researchers conduct sample surveys among populations for which data about the population are available from other sources. For example, suppose that you were conducting a telephone survey among the residents of a particular state in the U.S. and that when you completed the data collection process you computed the various demographic characteristics of your sample (e.g., gender, age, education). These sample statistics could then be compared to statistics from other sources such as U.S. census data to determine if certain demographic groups are over- or underrepresented in the sample, which would likely indicate the presence of nonresponse error. Note, however, that this result might also be an indication of noncoverage error if the sampling frame is less than adequate. Further, even if the sample demographic statistics match perfectly with the known population parameters, we haven't eliminated the possibility of nonresponse error, because the key issues being addressed may be completely unrelated to the demographic variables we are considering. In that case, those who respond may be systematically different from those who don't respond, yet still have the same demographic characteristics on average. Despite its shortcomings, however, this approach is much better than simply assuming that those who don't respond are no different than those who do respond.

Method 3 Conduct an analysis of late responders vs. early responders With data collection methods that allow subjects to respond at their convenience (e.g., mail, email, internet, fax), it is possible to compare the responses of those who respond early with those who respond late. The idea is that those who respond late will be more like those who don't respond at all than are those who respond early. If the analysis indicates that scores on key issues are different for, say, the first 20% of respondents versus the last 20% of respondents, then the responses of those who didn't respond at all are likely to differ from those who did respond, indicating the presence of nonresponse bias. If late responders are no different from early responders, it is less likely that nonresponse bias is a problem.

not-at-homes has been increasing for a long time. Obviously, much depends upon the nature of the designated respondent and the time of the call. Married women with young children are more apt to be home during the day on weekdays than are men, married women without children, or single women. The probability of finding someone home is also greater for low-income families and for rural families. Seasonal variations, particularly during the holidays, occur, as do weekday-to-weekend variations.[8] Further, it is much easier to find a "responsible

Trends in Refusal Rates

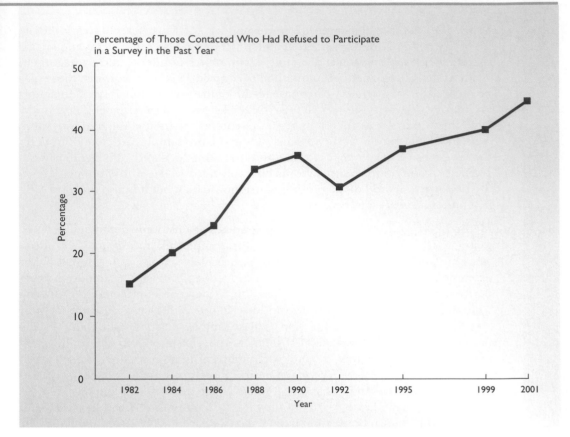

Percentage of Those Contacted Who Had Refused to Participate
in a Survey in the Past Year

Source: "2001 Respondent Cooperation and Industry Image Survey: Overview and Trends," Jane M. Sheppard, The Council for Marketing and Opinion Research, 2001.

adult" at home than a specific respondent. Thus, the choice of the basic sampling unit is important in the not-at-home problem.

Technological advancements have made the not-at-home problem even worse. As answering machines have become more prevalent in households, more and more people are using them to screen their calls. Further, a substantial portion of households now use caller ID, a technique for identifying the source of an incoming telephone call. Many people may ignore calls coming from sources they do not recognize. A recent study sponsored by the Council for Marketing and Opinion Research (CMOR) found that 75% of U.S. households report having an answering machine; 59% of those households have used their answering machines to screen calls; and 33% of households report using caller ID.[9] And these results were obtained using a telephone survey, so the results may be even more bleak than they appear because those households the researchers couldn't contact for the study may very well be screening calls via answering machine or caller ID!

Several things can be done to reduce the incidence of not-at-homes. For example, in some studies the interviewer might make an appointment in advance with the respondent. Although this approach is particularly valuable in surveys of busy executives, it may not be justifiable in an ordinary consumer survey. A commonly used technique in the latter instance is the *callback,* which is particularly effective if the callback (preferably callbacks) is made at a different time than the original call. As a matter of fact, the nonresponse problem due to not-at-homes is so acute and so important to the accuracy of most surveys that one leading expert has suggested that small samples with four to six callbacks are more efficient than large samples without callbacks, unless the percentage of initial response can be increased considerably above normal levels.[10] Panel A in Exhibit 18.3 illustrates the percentage of respondents who were contacted on the first, second, third, etc., attempted contact for a study recently conducted by one of the authors. This was a follow-up study conducted at the end of a school

Exhibit 18.3

Percentage of Respondents Reached with Each Call in a Telephone Survey

Panel A: Telephone Survey, University Seniors

Call	Number of Respondents	Percent*	Cumulative Percent*
1	35	20	20
2	31	18	38
3	34	20	58
4	14	8	66
5	40	23	89
6	17	10	99
7	1	1	100

* Percentages are based on total number of completed interviews. When refusals (4) and not-at-homes (2) are included, the overall response rate was 94%.

Panel B: Telephone Survey, Faculty Coordinators for Fire Science Training Programs

Call	Number of Respondents	Percent	Cumulative Percent
1	33	19	19
2	38	22	41
3	22	13	54
4	18	10	64
5	15	9	73
6	11	6	79
7	7	4	83
8	9	5	88
9	5	3	91
10	1	1	92
11	2	1	93
12	2	1	94
13	1	1	95
14	2	1	96
15	0	0	96
16	1	1	97
17	2	1	98
18	2	1	99
19	0	0	99
20	0	0	99
21	1	1	99
22	0	0	99
23	1	1	100

Panel B example courtesy Dr. Christine A. Johnson, Director, Oklahoma State University Bureau for Social Research.

year among students about to graduate from college. The overall response rate was very high (94%), but only because we didn't stop making callbacks after the first or second try. Panel B in Exhibit 18.3 presents similar information for a telephone survey of faculty coordinators for fire science training programs across the United States. These results are consistent with other studies that have indicated that four to five calls are often needed to reach three-fourths of the sample of households.

An alternative to the straight callback is the *modified callback*. If the initial contact attempt and first few callbacks were made by an interviewer and a contact was not established, the interviewer might simply mail a self-administered questionnaire with a stamped, self-addressed envelope (or leave one at the door of an in-person survey).

One technique that is sometimes suggested for handling the not-at-homes is to substitute the house or apartment next door or, in a telephone survey, to call the next name on the list.

ETHICAL dilemma 18.1

A well-known car agency needed to make a decision about whether to import a relatively unknown line of foreign cars to complement its domestic line. To aid in its decision making, the agency contracted a research firm to conduct a study to determine potential consumer interest and demand for this foreign car line. The results indicated that substantial awareness and interest existed, and consequently the decision was made to take on the new line.

To publicize the new line, a special preview was arranged for interested community members such as local newspaper and radio people, executives in related automotive industries, filling station and repair shop owners, and leaders of men's and women's clubs. The agency's owners also wanted to invite the survey participants who had expressed an interest in the car, and consequently asked the research firm to provide them with the respondents' names. The research firm refused to comply with this request, arguing that to do so would be a violation of the respondents' promised anonymity.

- *Should the research firm have complied with the agency's request?*

- *Did the car agency have the right to receive the participants' names since it had paid for the research?*

- *Would it have made a difference if the study had not been one to determine sales potential?*

- *What would be some of the consequences of making the respondents' names known to the car agency?*

- *If the question had been anticipated before the survey was begun, could the interview structure have avoided the dilemma in which the research company and the agency now find themselves?*

This is a very poor way of handling the not-at-home condition. All it does is substitute more "at-homes" (who may be different from the not-at-homes in a number of important characteristics) for "not-at-homes." This increases the proportion of at-homes in the sample and makes the problem worse instead of solving it. To illustrate, imagine that you were doing a telephone survey on people's enjoyment of outdoor activities for a sporting goods company. If you routinely substitute at-homes for not-at-homes (which will certainly include people engaged in outdoor activities), nonresponse error is very likely to cause an estimate of the population's enjoyment of outdoor activities to be lower than it actually is.

The proportion of reported not-at-homes is likely to depend on the interviewer's skill and the judgment used in scheduling initial contacts and callbacks. This suggests that one way of reducing not-at-home nonresponse bias is by better interviewer training, particularly with respect to scheduling callbacks more efficiently. Research has demonstrated that the timing of callbacks has an influence on the efficiency of the project. A calling pattern refers to the sequence of days and times at which attempts are made to reach a respondent. The evidence indicates that the best calling patterns include no more than one attempted contact during weekdays between 9 AM and 3 AM and instead include more late afternoon (3 AM to 6 AM) and evening (6 AM to 9 AM) callbacks.[11] Of course, the optimal calling pattern will depend upon the nature of the study.

The fact that interviewer effectiveness affects the number of not-at-homes also suggests one measure by which interviewers themselves can be compared and evaluated: by calculating the **contact rate (C)**, which is the percentage of the eligible assignments in which the interviewer makes contact with the designated respondent:

$$C = \frac{\text{number of sample units contacted}}{\text{total number of eligible sample units approached}}$$

contact rate (C)
A measure used to evaluate and compare the effectiveness of interviewers in making contact with designated respondents; *C*-number of sample units contacted divided by total number of eligible sample units approached.

The contact rate measures the interviewer's persistence. Interviewers can be compared with respect to their contact rates, and corrective measures can often be taken on that basis. The field supervisor may want to investigate the reasons for any individual interviewer's low contact rate. Perhaps this interviewer is operating in a traditionally high not-at-home area, such as a high-income section of an urban area. Alternatively, by examining the call reports for the time of each call, the trouble may be traced to poor follow-up procedures. This condition would suggest that additional training is necessary, which might then be provided by the field supervisor while the study is still in progress. The contact rate can also be used to evaluate an entire study with respect to the potential nonresponse caused by not-at-homes.

Response Errors

Response error occurs when an individual provides a response to an item, but the response is inaccurate for some reason. There are many factors that can cause response error, ranging from poorly written items that respondents misinterpret, to characteristics of the respondent that subconsciously influence his/her responses, to researcher misinterpretation of an individual's responses. Blame for response errors, therefore, can lay with the researcher, the respondent, or both.

Define response error and discuss some of its causes.

The possible causes of response error are so broad that it is often difficult for researchers to grasp their likely effect on survey results. Ronald Weiers has offered a useful series of questions for considering the different ways response errors can affect individuals' responses.[12] These questions might also be used to anticipate possible problems when developing questionnaire items in the first place.

Does the respondent understand the question? As mentioned elsewhere in this text, questionnaire items must be written using simple, direct language, especially when a general audience is being surveyed. If respondents don't understand a question, one of two things is likely to happen: they will either skip the question, leading to potential nonresponse error, or they will answer the question based on their interpretation, which may not match your intended interpretation of the item. Neither of these outcomes is good. Pre-testing the questionnaire with members of the relevant population can usually eliminate this source of error.

Several years ago we conducted a satisfaction study among patients of a number of healthcare providers. The questionnaire included items assessing patient expectations and perceptions of service provider performance across a range of relevant dimensions. Respondents were instructed to provide answers to each item on the rating scales we provided. One respondent appeared to have read the directions and (we presume) accurately responded to the first of the items on the rating scale, then proceeded to provide open-ended responses to most of the other items. For example, in response to an item that read "How physically comfortable I was during the procedure" this respondent penciled in "very comfortable" instead of responding on the scale we provided. The respondent, a 92-year-old woman, was doing her best to answer our questions. It was clear that she understood the questions, for the most part, but she didn't understand how we wanted her to respond. Was this her fault? Not really; we had failed to anticipate that the population might include very elderly people.

Does the respondent know the answer to the question? Just because a respondent understands a question correctly doesn't mean that s/he actually knows the answer to the question. The problem is that many respondents will answer the question anyway. This is especially common with closed-ended questions for which respondents simply choose a response category. Dealing with this issue is a bit trickier. Providing a "don't know" response category is one option, but as we'll discuss in the next chapter, this strategy will often create difficulties in data analysis (i.e., lots of missing cases). People will sometimes select the "don't know" option as a way of not having to think about a particular item, even when they do know the answer to the question. A preferred strategy might be to perform sufficient exploratory research and questionnaire pre-testing to understand what population members are likely—and not likely—to know.

Is the respondent willing to provide the true answer to the question? Respondents who understand a question and know the answer don't always provide a truthful answer. There are lots of reasons for this. Respondents may consciously lie because they want to make themselves look better or to avoid appearing "dumb" when they don't really know the answer to a question. Sometimes respondents are angry or in a bad mood—perhaps caused or worsened by trying to respond to a poorly developed questionnaire—and they knowingly provide inaccurate answers. Some respondents seem to just not care about their responses, even though they could understand the questions and provide accurate responses if they wanted to. Other respondents simply don't want to say something negative about a product, store, or service provider, and will inflate their answers to service quality or satisfaction items.

James Sorensen has told about a study in which interviewers for his firm, Sorensen Associates, talked to shoppers in grocery stores. An interviewer approached a man who had finished paying for his purchases and asked him some questions. The shopper said he was using a shopping list that day and that an item the interviewer asked about was on the list. To get the wording the shopper used on the list, the interviewer asked to see it. The shopper declined to show the list. The interviewer probed for a reason, and the shopper admitted the truth: "The item I just purchased was not on the list. I lied."[13]

© MaXx Images/Index Stock Imagery

AGATE used online surveys to study aviation enthusiasts.

To study people who buy and fly airplanes, the Advanced General Aviation Transport Experiment (AGATE) conducted online surveys. The developers of the AGATE questionnaire noted that when surveys ask how much people are willing to pay for some item, respondents typically give an answer near the bottom of the true acceptable range, whereas asking a yes/no question like "Are you willing to pay $200?" generates more accurate responses but only about that particular price. So the AGATE researchers set up a questionnaire format that used random numbers to select prices to present to respondents. Thus, no respondent would have the burden of evaluating all the price points. Rather, each person answered a few dozen randomly selected questions, and the results were pooled to create graphs showing the percentages of respondents who said each choice was acceptable.[14]

Finally, we once conducted a study where one of the goals was to examine the relationship between endodontist patients' self-reported mood prior to a root canal and their perceptions of the service quality provided by their endodontists. One of our measures of mood was a global six-point semantic differential scale ranging from "bad" to "good." One elderly respondent was less than thrilled with our questionnaire, writing on the form that he was "crotchety enough without seeing questionnaires like this!" His attitude toward the questionnaire also seemed to influence his response to the global mood item: he checked the category nearest "good" and added, "I always experience absolute euphoria at the prospect of going to the endodontist. I sing the 'Ode to Joy' at the top of my lungs all the way."

What can be done about these sorts of response errors? Once again, the key is thorough exploratory research and questionnaire pre-testing. Questions that are likely to cause respondents to be even slightly defensive—especially sensitive questions—must be carefully designed and tested. When the data collection forms are designed, careful attention must be given to the questions (and the order in which they are asked) so as to hold the respondent's attention.

Is the wording of the question or the situation in which it is asked likely to bias the response? As noted, the wording of a question and its response categories has a strong influence on individuals' responses. Leading questions must obviously be avoided, and researchers must be careful not to accidentally use "loaded" words if they are to uncover the truth about an issue. Interviewers must also be trained not to let the tone of their voice or inflections in their speech vary from one interview to the next. With personal interviews, interviewer nonverbal communication also becomes a potential influence on individuals' responses.

While errors in asking questions can arise with any of the basic question types, the problem is particularly acute with open-ended questions where probing follows the initial response. No two interviewers are likely to use the same probes, creating clear situational differences between respondents. The content, as well as the timing, of the probes may differ. This raises the possibility that the differences in answers may be due to the probes that are used rather than any "true" differences in the position of the respondents.

Surprisingly, closed-ended questions also possess great potential for interviewer bias, because the interviewer may place undue emphasis on one of the alternatives in stating the question. Slight changes in emphasis or tone can change the meaning of the entire question. The prob-

PART 5:
Sampling and Data Collection

lem occurs because each interviewer brings his or her own psychological make-up to work each day. The evidence tends to support the notion that interviewers' opinions, perceptions, expectations, and attitudes affect the responses they receive,[15] which will be conditioned by their backgrounds; the only way we can control these psychological factors is through training.

Most surveys, therefore, are conducted using a rigid set of procedures that interviewers must follow. The instructions should be clear, should be written, and should clearly state the purpose of the study. They should describe the materials to be used, such as questionnaires, maps, time forms, and so on. They should describe how each question should be asked, the kinds of answers that are acceptable, and the kinds and timing of probes that are to be used, if any. Practice training sessions will often be necessary.

Even when the rules are rigid, the questionnaires are relatively simple, and the training is thorough, interviewers do not always follow the rules, thus introducing response error. In one classic study, 15 college-educated researchers interviewed the same respondent, who had previously been instructed to give identical answers to all 15 interviewers.[16] All the interviews were recorded and later analyzed for errors. One of the most startling findings of the study was the sheer number of errors: there were 66 failures to ask supplementary questions when inadequate responses were given, and the number of errors per interviewer varied from 12 to 36. In another study, it was found that "one-third of the . . . interviewers deviated frequently and markedly from their instructions, sometimes failing to explain the key terms or to repeat them as required, sometimes leaving them out altogether, shortening questions, or failing to follow up certain ambiguous answers in the manner required."[17]

There are two other sources of response error that the interviewer might cause. One of the interviewer's main tasks is to keep the respondent interested and motivated. At the same time, the interviewer must try to record what the respondent is saying by dutifully writing down the person's answers to open-ended questions or checking the appropriate box with closed-ended questions. These responsibilities are sometimes incompatible, resulting in data recording errors. Interviewers may not correctly "hear" what the respondent is actually saying, instead hearing what they want to hear and recording what they want to record. This is a common failing, and in spite of interviewer training, recording errors in the interview do occur. We must remember, however, that interviewers perform a very difficult job.

Recording errors can be forgiven; interviewer cheating is another matter. Cheating may range from the fabrication of a whole interview to the fabrication of one or two answers to make the response complete. Even the best-conducted studies typically contain some degree of fabricated responses, although the percentage of false responses is likely less than 10%.[18] Because of interviewer cheating, most commercial research firms validate 10 to 20 percent of the completed interviews through follow-up telephone calls or by sending postcards to a sample of "respondents" to verify that they have in fact been contacted.

Office Errors

Problems with nonsampling errors do not end with data collection. Errors can and do arise in the editing, coding, and analyzing of the data.[19] For the most part, these errors can be reduced, if not eliminated, by exercising proper controls in data processing. These issues are discussed in the following chapter.

Total Error Is the Key

It is critically important to understand that total error, rather than any single type of error, is the key in a research investigation. We believe that far too many researchers focus too intently on decreasing sampling error when they should be focusing more closely on potential sources of nonsampling error. Managers, students (especially those with a course in statistics behind them), and some researchers often argue for the "largest possible sample," reasoning that a large sample is much more likely to produce a "valid" result than a small sample is. What these people often fail to appreciate, however, is that the argument applies only to sampling error. Increasing the sample size does, in fact, decrease sampling error. It will very likely also increase

7 Discuss how interviewers can contribute to response error.

nonsampling error because the large sample requires more interviews, for instance, and this creates additional burdens in selection, training, and control. Further, nonsampling error is a much more insidious and troublesome error than sampling error. Sampling error can be estimated. Many forms of nonsampling error cannot, and new sources of nonsampling error are being discovered all the time. We have attempted to highlight some of the better-known sources of nonsampling error and ways of dealing with them. Thus, while addressing sampling error is important, it is nonsampling error that is usually more troublesome, and wise researchers will attempt to manage total error, not just one particular kind of error.

Exhibit 18.4 attempts to summarize nonsampling errors and how they can be reduced and controlled. The table can be used as a sort of checklist for marketing managers and other users to evaluate the quality of research prior to making substantive decisions on the basis of the research results. Although not all methods for handling nonsampling errors will be applicable in every study, a systematic analysis of the research effort, using the table guidelines, should provide the proper appreciation for the quality of research information that is obtained.

Exhibit 18.4

Overview of Nonsampling Errors and Some Methods for Handling Them

Type	Definition	Methods for Handling
Noncoverage	Failure to include some units or entire sections of the defined target population in the sampling frame.	1. Improve basic sampling frame using other sources. 2. Select sample in such a way as to reduce incidence, for example, by ignoring ineligibles on a list. 3. Adjust the results by appropriately weighting the subsample results.
Nonresponse	Failure to obtain information from some elements of the population that were selected for the sample	
Not-at-homes	Designated respondent is not home when the interviewer calls.	1. Have interviewers make advance appointments. 2. Call back at another time, preferably at a different time of day. 3. Attempt to contact the designated respondent using another approach (e.g., use a modified callback.
Refusals	Respondent refuses to cooperate in the survey.	1. Attempt to convince the respondent of the value of the research and the importance of his or her participation. 2. Provide advance notice that the survey is coming. 3. Guarantee anonymity. 4. Provide an incentive for participating. 5. Hide the identification of the sponsor by using an independent research organization. 6. Try to get a foot in the door by getting the respondent to comply with some small task before getting the survey. 7. Use personalized cover letters. 8. Use a follow-up contact at a more convenient time. 9. Avoid unnecessary questions. 10. Adust the results to account for the nonresponse.

Exhibit 18.4

Overview of Nonsampling Errors and Some Methods for Handling Them (*continued*)

Response	Although the individual participates in the study, he or she refuses to answer specific questions or provides incorrect answers to them.	1. Match the background characteristics of interviewer and respondent as closely as possible. 2. Make sure interviewer instructions are clear and written down. 3. Conduct practice training sessions with interviewers. 4. Examine the interviewers' understanding of the study's purposes and procedures. 5. Have interviewers complete the questionnaire and examine their replies to see if there is any relationship between the answers they secure and their own answers. 6. Verify a sample of each interviewer's interviews.
Office[a]	Errors that arise when coding, tabulating, or analyzing the data.	1. Use a field edit to detect the most glaring omissions and inaccuracies in the data. 2. Use a second edit in the office to decide how data collection instruments containing incomplete answers, obviously wrong answers, and answers that reflect a lack of interest are to be handled. 3. Use closed-ended questions to simplify the coding, but when open-ended questions need to be used, specify the appropriate codes that will be allowed before collecting the data. 4. When open-ended questions are being coded and multiple coders are being used, divide the task by questions and not by data collection forms. 5. Have each coder code a sample of the other's work to ensure that a consistent set of coding criteria is being used. 6. Follow established conventions; for example, use numeric codes and not letters of the alphabet when coding the data for computer analysis. 7. Prepare a codebook that lists the codes for each variable and the categories included in each code. 8. Use appropriate methods to analyze the data.

[a]Steps to reduce the incidence of office errors are discussed in more detail in the analysis chapters.

Calculating Response Rates

Once the data have been collected, the researcher must calculate the **response rate** for the project. The response rate—the number of completed interviews with responding units divided by the number of eligible responding units in the sample—serves two important functions. First, it allows an assessment of the likely influence of nonresponse error on the study's results. Although this assessment is qualitative in nature (because even if you were to obtain responses from 90% of those chosen for the sample, the other 10% could have been very different on the issue in question), higher response rates generally suggest fewer problems with nonresponse bias. Second, the response rate serves as an indicator of the overall quality of a data collection effort. For example, very low response rates may indicate poor questionnaire design, lack of interest among respondents, failure to gain the intended respondents' attention, and so on. Unless the client is willing to collect more data, however, it is too late to do

8 Cite the standard definition for response rate.

response rate
The number of completed interviews with responding units divided by the number of eligible responding units in the sample.

anything about these problems. To avoid this outcome, we again strongly urge the use of thoughtful exploratory research and questionnaire pre-testing.

The following general formula is used to calculate a project's response rate:[20]

$$\text{response rate} = \frac{\text{number of completed interviews with responding units}}{\text{number of eligible responding units in the sample}}$$

How this formula is applied depends upon the data collection method used. "Completed interviews" includes completed survey forms for methods that don't include an actual interview. We address the most common approaches in the following sections.

Mail, Email, and Fax Surveys

With these forms of data collection, response rate calculation is usually straightforward. The first step is to determine the number of usable questionnaires returned. Not every questionnaire that is returned is usable, as we'll see in the following chapter. Common reasons for excluding a questionnaire include evidence that a respondent wasn't really paying attention to the questions, or a large percentage of items were not answered by the respondent.

Once the number of usable questionnaires is known, the number of eligible response units must be determined. With these types of data collection, it is usually assumed that all elements or people in the sampling frame meet the criteria for membership in the population and sample, which makes calculating the number of eligible response units quite simple. The researcher need only take the number of response units that s/he attempted to contact and subtract the number of addresses or fax numbers that turned out to be invalid. With mail surveys, the postal service will normally return surveys that are not deliverable because of a wrong address. Similarly, email systems typically notify the sender when an email message cannot be successfully delivered. Bad fax numbers can be counted as well. The point is simply that contacts that could not be made should not count against the researcher in the calculation of response rates. Thus, for these methods of data collection, response rate (RR) is calculated as follows:

$$RR = \frac{\text{number of usable questionnaires returned}}{\text{number of contacts attempted } - \text{ number of bad addresses or fax numbers}}$$

In order to accurately calculate the response rate on a project, researchers must keep track of certain information. In this case, the researcher must know the number of contacts attempted, the number of wrong addresses (or fax numbers), and, of course, the number of usable questionnaires.

Suppose that an online retailer decided to conduct a survey among its past customers. A sample of 1,000 customers was randomly selected to receive an email survey. A total of 202 customers responded to the survey; 58 of the email addresses were no longer valid. The response rate on the project would be correctly calculated as

$$RR = \frac{202}{1000 - 58} = 21\%$$

Telephone Surveys (No Eligibility Requirement)

Things get a little more complicated with telephone surveys—but not much. In cases where there is no eligibility requirement (that is, all response units meet the criteria for being included in the sample), we can categorize the attempted contacts into three groups: completed interviews, refusals, and not-at-homes (which includes cases where someone answers the telephone, but the correct respondent is not available). The response rate formula looks like this:

$$RR = \frac{\text{number of completed interviews}}{\text{number of completed interviews } + \text{ number of refusals } + \text{ not-at-homes}}$$

Notice that wrong numbers or nonworking numbers are automatically excluded from the formula and thus don't lower the calculated response rate. The researcher should keep track of the number of bad telephone numbers (along with completed interviews, refusals, and not-at-homes), however, as an indication of the quality of the sampling frame.

Consider the following scenario: A researcher has designed a project using a telephone survey as the method of data collection. The respondents are current members of a health club. Using the membership roster as a sampling frame, the researcher has randomly selected 200 members. At the conclusion of the data collection phase, 112 interviews had been successfully conducted, 27 people refused to participate in the study, 57 people could not be reached after at least three tries, and 4 telephone numbers were no longer in service. What is the response rate for this project?

$$RR = \frac{112}{112 + 27 + 57} = 57\%$$

© Spencer Grant/Photo Edit

In addition, the quality of the sampling frame appeared to be very good, with only 4 nonworking numbers, or $4/200 = 2\%$.

Before moving on, there are a couple of other issues that should be addressed. It is possible, particularly with older sampling frames, that the intended respondent has moved away from the area and the telephone number has been reassigned to someone else. These cases should be categorized as nonworking numbers for research purposes. Another concern is what counts as a "completed" interview. It is not uncommon for respondents to terminate a telephone survey prior to answering all the questions. In these cases, the researcher must use good judgment. Clearly a response that is very nearly complete should be included in the data set and counted as a completed interview. At the other extreme, a respondent who hangs up after one or two questions should probably not be included. The troubling cases are those lying between these extremes. Our general recommendation is to count any interview on which answers are obtained for more than half of the survey items as a completed interview.

A telephone survey can yield a high-quality sampling frame if the researcher has a current list of telephone numbers of the population to be studied, such as members of a health club.

Telephone Surveys (With Eligibility Requirement)

Sometimes researchers are forced to work with sampling frames that include response units that are not members of the population being studied. Suppose, for example, that a major department store wanted to know shoppers' opinion of a new store layout. Store managers believe that at least half of the households in a test market city contain at least one adult who has visited the store since the new layout was introduced; these potential respondents should be in a position to offer an opinion on the layout. Even though the store has a well-developed customer database, it cannot keep records on those who have only shopped at the store. As a result, to conduct a telephone survey, researchers working with the company might choose to use the local telephone directory as a sampling frame. The trouble is that some of the households won't include anyone who has shopped at the store during the relevant time frame. The members of these households are ineligible to complete the telephone survey. To identify these households, a screening question will be included ("Has any adult in this household visited the _____ Department Store in the previous three months?"); interviews with those that have not visited the store will end at that point.

Since some households are ineligible, how should the researcher calculate response rate?

The first step is to count the number of completed interviews, refusals, not-at-homes—*and* the number of ineligible response units. Now, you may be wondering why it is necessary to keep track of the number of ineligibles since they aren't supposed to count against the researcher in the calculation of response rate. That's true; we don't include them when we calculate response rate. We need them, however, for another purpose. Look back to the response rate formula for telephone surveys with no eligibility requirement. In particular, think about the refusals and not-at-homes. With no eligibility requirements, we know that each of these response units would have been qualified to complete the telephone survey had we been able to reach them and/or convince them to participate. In the current situation, *we don't know* that they would have been eligible; in fact, we're sure that many of them would not have visited the store in the previous three months. Adjusting for this requires one simple extra step when calculating response rate. The *eligibility percentage (E%)* is computed as follows:

$$E\% = \frac{\text{number of completed interviews}}{\text{number of completed interviews} + \text{number of ineligible}}$$

The eligibility percentage is then used to adjust the number of refusals and not-at-homes to reflect the fact that many of them would not have qualified to participate in the survey even if we had successfully contacted them and gotten them to agree to participate. Response rate is calculated as

$$RR = \frac{\text{number of completed interviews}}{\text{number of completed interviews} + \text{E\% number of refusals} + \text{number of not-at-home}}$$

Imagine that researchers working with the department store had randomly selected 1000 telephone numbers from the local telephone directory and had attempted to contact each household. Here are the final results of the calls, along with the correct response rate calculation:

completed interviews	338
refusals	89
not-at-homes	169
ineligibles	292
nonworking numbers	112
	1000 telephone numbers

$$E\% = \frac{338}{338 + 292} = 54\%$$

$$RR = \frac{338}{338 + (0.54)(89 + 169)} = 71\%$$

Without adjusting for ineligibles, the response rate would have been only 57%, so it is important to keep track of the number of response units that don't qualify for the survey.

Other Methods of Data Collection

So far, we've talked about calculating response rate for most of the major types of data collection. What about other types, such as personal interviews or the residential "drop-off" surveys common with area samples? Regardless of the type of data collection, the same logic is applied: the response rate equals the number of completed interviews with responding units divided by the number of eligible responding units in the sample. If the method used allows a distinction between refusals and not-at-homes, one of the formulas shown above for telephone surveys can likely be utilized or adapted. If not, then a variation of the formula for mail surveys is likely to apply. If there is an eligibility requirement, start with the formula for telephone surveys with an eligibility requirement. Regardless of the circumstances, the researcher can usually use common sense and the basic formulas we've discussed to arrive at the appropriate response rate.

Improving Response Rates

As noted, the lower the response rate, the more likely it is that nonresponse error will affect research results. Because of this potential problem, researchers have suggested and tested numerous techniques over the years for improving response rates. Most research has been conducted in the context of mail surveys, because this method of data collection has traditionally produced the lowest response rates.

In this section, we briefly discuss some of the techniques that are thought to increase response rates. Empirical support is available for most, if not all, of these approaches in one context or another. The trick, of course, is to figure out which ones are likely to be most influential in a particular study.

Before examining these techniques we should note one factor that probably has more effect than any other on response rates but that is, for the most part, not under the control of the researcher. The topic of the research, and its ability to generate interest among potential respondents, will have a huge influence on whether or not respondents participate, regardless of the form of data collection. Some topics are inherently more interesting than other topics to particular respondents. Although we can't change the topic of research, we can consider different approaches for introducing and framing the issue under study. Exploratory research can be effectively used to gauge respondent interest in the topic and to give trial runs to different introductory scripts.

9 *Discuss several ways in which response rates might be improved.*

"Foot-in-the-Door" Technique

Although most of the techniques in this section are most applicable to mail surveys, a couple of approaches are applicable to personal interviews and telephone surveys. The foot-in-the-door technique relies on the psychological principle that people are more likely to respond positively to a request from another person if they have previously responded positively to another, typically smaller, request. In one classic study, 74% of potential respondents agreed to complete a 20-question survey after they had already completed a brief 5-question survey for the researchers. Only 58% of potential respondents agreed to complete the 20-question survey when there was no initial request.[21] The reason for this is found in social psychology: by responding positively to the initial smaller request, something of a rudimentary relationship has been established, making it harder to say "no" to the follow-up request. An alternative

ETHICAL dilemma 18.2

"These new computer-voiced telephone surveys are wonderful!" your friend enthuses over lunch. "Because we don't have to pay telephone interviewers, we can afford to have target numbers automatically redialed until someone answers. Of course, the public finds the computer's voice irritating and the whole notion of being interviewed by a machine rather humiliating. Nevertheless, we can overcome most people's reluctance to participate by repeatedly calling them until they give in and complete the questionnaire."

- *Is it ethical to contact respondents repeatedly until they agree to participate in a research study? How many contacts are legitimate?*

- *If an industry is unable to constrain its members to behave ethically, should the government step in with regulations?*

- *If the public reacts against this kind of telephone survey, what are the results likely to be for researchers using traditional, more considerate telephone surveys?*

explanation is that people simply want to maintain consistency, and "I said 'yes' before, so I'll say 'yes' again."

Interviewer Characteristics and Training

Another approach that applies to personal interviews and telephone surveys involves the selection and training of interviewers. The evidence suggests that an interviewer is likely to get better cooperation and more information from the respondent when the two share similar backgrounds. This is particularly true for characteristics such as race, age, and gender, but also applies to things such as social class and income.

Interviewers must also be trained to quickly convince potential respondents of the value of the research and the importance of their participation. Thus, the script to be used when approaching possible respondents must be carefully developed, and interviewers must be trained to follow the script. To the extent possible, the script should also communicate information about the content and purpose of the study, so that respondents may develop greater involvement and interest in the topic.

Guarantee of Confidentiality and/or Anonymity

It is routine practice to promise respondents that their answers will be held in confidence by the researcher. Such a practice is especially important when the topic or specific questions are likely to be sensitive to the respondent. With mail surveys it is also possible to guarantee that responses will be anonymous, providing an even greater sense of security to the respondent. By the way, if you promise confidentiality or anonymity, you are ethically bound to keep the promise. Sometimes managers will want access to respondent names, addresses, or telephone numbers—particularly those that have expressed some level of interest in a proposed product or service. Even if you made no promises at all, such a practice is unacceptable because it blurs the line between research and sales.

Pre-notification

One effective strategy for increasing response rates to surveys is to notify potential respondents about the survey in advance, typically by postcard, letter, or telephone. One benefit of such a practice is that the respondent may remember the prior notification, which then serves as a sort of foot-in-the-door; at the time of data collection, the respondent may subconsciously feel something like "Well, I've heard from them before, so they're a friend, not a stranger." A second benefit is that the respondent may think a little bit in advance about the issue to be addressed, potentially raising the interest level when the actual data collection takes place. Note, however, that pre-notification will likely raise the costs of the overall project.

Personalization

Anything the researcher can do to make the data collection process seem more personalized for a particular respondent should help improve response rates. For example, research has demonstrated that hand-addressed envelopes and handwritten signatures on letters can increase response. Along the same lines, data collection forms should rarely, if ever, be sent to "occupant" or by bulk mail. In addition, some respondents will be more likely to open an envelope that has been stamped rather than one that has been sent through a postage meter. It just feels more personal, as if someone has spent the time to contact them individually. Similarly, including a reply envelope that has been stamped rather than metered is normally a good idea.

An issue that the researcher must consider is whether to include a stamped reply envelope or a business-reply envelope. With business-reply postage, the researcher opens an account with the postal service and then only pays postage on the questionnaires that are actually returned. Business reply postage is more costly than regular postage, but, again, you're only paying for questionnaires actually returned. With regularly stamped reply envelopes, the researcher obviously pays postage for each questionnaire distributed, not just those returned. The stamped envelope may increase the likelihood of response a little, but if the overall rate of response isn't great enough, the use of business-reply envelopes will be less expensive. The researcher can easily determine the response rate at which it is more economical to use either business-reply or regular postage by working with the costs of regular and business-reply postage.

Sponsor Disguise

If the identification of the organization sponsoring the research is likely to increase nonresponse, researchers can overcome this bias by concealing that information or by hiring a professional research organization to conduct the field study. This is one reason companies with established, sophisticated research departments of their own sometimes employ research firms to collect data.

Response Incentives

Considerable research has shown that offering an incentive to respondents will increase response rates on a project. Response incentives can take several forms ranging from money to lotteries to donations for charity. Monetary incentives often have the greatest influence on response rates, although interestingly enough, larger amounts of money are often less effective than smaller amounts. It seems that at some point the respondent begins to feel that s/he is being paid to participate rather than given a token of appreciation. In this case, a "gift" is more psychologically motivating than are "wages." How much is too much to include with a survey? The answer likely depends upon the nature of the survey and the type of respondent, but for most purposes it probably isn't advisable to give more than $1.00.

Many researchers have effectively used lotteries as a means of generating response. By participating in the survey, the respondent is typically entered into a drawing for some desirable prize. The difficulty, if there is one, lies in the amount of trust that the respondent must place in the researcher. From the respondents' perspective, there may or may not be an actual lottery, they may or may not actually be entered in such a lottery, and their responses may not be confidential or anonymous if name, address, and telephone number are to be kept for contact purposes (in order to notify the winner). To overcome these issues, respondents to a mail survey might be allowed to send back a separate postcard along with the reply envelope; only the postcard includes contact information and is included in the actual drawing. The downside is the added cost of postcards and postage.

Some people may respond more to an offer to make a donation on their behalf to a charity. Still others may appreciate a coupon for free food and drink, or tickets to a movie. Researchers are advised to help their clients avoid the temptation to include coupons good toward purchase of their own products and services. The temptation will sometimes be great, because such coupons will likely cost the client less than other sorts of incentives and because the client may view this as an opportunity to generate a little business. Remember, research is research, and selling is selling, and the two should never be confounded with one another.

Survey Length

Although there are exceptions, respondents typically do not appreciate nor respond well to long surveys, either by telephone or mail. Thus, all else equal, short surveys are more likely to be completed than are long surveys. This is one reason for researchers to include only questions that are truly important and will be used in the analysis.

Follow-up Surveys

In some cases, the circumstances surrounding a contact are responsible for a respondent's refusal to participate. Since these circumstances may be temporary or changeable, follow-up contacts are sometimes useful for generating a response. If a respondent declined participation because he or she was busy or sick, a callback at a different time or using a different approach may be enough to secure cooperation. In a mail survey, this may mean a follow-up mailing at a more convenient time.

If a respondent has refused to participate in a personal interview or a telephone survey for reasons other than circumstances, callbacks will be less successful. This isn't the case with mail surveys. Frequently, responses are obtained with the second and third mailings from those who did not respond to the initial mailing. Of course, follow-up in a mail survey requires identification of those not responding earlier, which in turn requires identification of those who did respond, and this removes the possibility of anonymity. The alternative, which is to send each new mailing to each designated sample member without screening those who have responded previously, can be expensive for the research organization and frustrating for the respondent.

Are Some Techniques More Effective?

An obvious question at this point is which techniques are more effective at improving response rates. While dozens of studies have been conducted, most have examined the effects of one or two techniques at a time. In recent years, however, several large review studies have been conducted. The results of one of the most extensive reviews of mail-survey response inducement techniques are shown in Figure 18.2. The weighted mean correlation associated

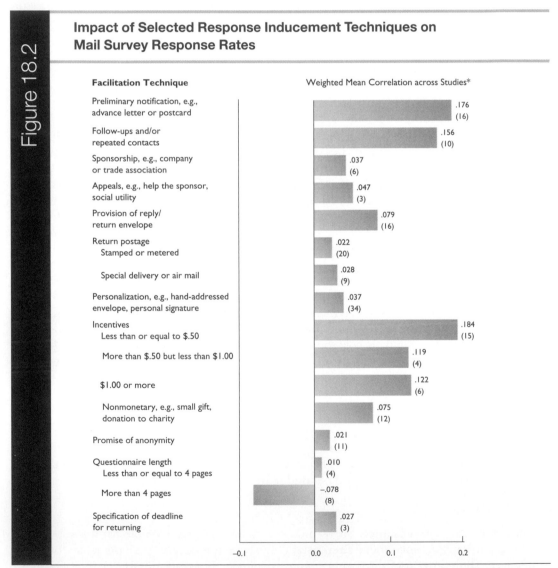

Figure 18.2

Impact of Selected Response Inducement Techniques on Mail Survey Response Rates

Facilitation Technique	Weighted Mean Correlation across Studies*
Preliminary notification, e.g., advance letter or postcard	.176 (16)
Follow-ups and/or repeated contacts	.156 (10)
Sponsorship, e.g., company or trade association	.037 (6)
Appeals, e.g., help the sponsor, social utility	.047 (3)
Provision of reply/return envelope	.079 (16)
Return postage — Stamped or metered	.022 (20)
Special delivery or air mail	.028 (9)
Personalization, e.g., hand-addressed envelope, personal signature	.037 (34)
Incentives — Less than or equal to $.50	.184 (15)
More than $.50 but less than $1.00	.119 (4)
$1.00 or more	.122 (6)
Nonmonetary, e.g., small gift, donation to charity	.075 (12)
Promise of anonymity	.021 (11)
Questionnaire length — Less than or equal to 4 pages	.010 (4)
More than 4 pages	−.078 (8)
Specification of deadline for returning	.027 (3)

*The numbers shown in brackets indicate the number of correlations on which the average correlation is based.

Source: Developed from the information in Frances J. Yammarino, Steven J. Skinner, and Terry L. Childers, "Understanding Mail Survey Response Behavior: A Meta-Analysis," *Public Opinion Quarterly* 55 (Winter 1991), pp. 613–639. Reprinted with permission, University of Chicago Press.

with each technique represents the average amount of influence that the technique has on study response rates across multiple studies. The larger the weighted mean correlation, the more impact that particular facilitation technique has. The results in Figure 18.2 indicate that, on average, the most successful response inducement techniques in mail surveys are the use of incentives, preliminary notification that the survey is coming, and follow-ups or repeated mailings.

According to media consultant Walter Sabo, Portable People Meters will prevent errors in radio listenership data. Sabo complains that more than 6 out of 10 participants in diary panels don't bother to return their diaries. Of those returned, half must be thrown away because of problems in the data, such as spelling errors. And people fill out their diaries at the beginning and end of the week, so they must try to remember the details of their midweek listening. Sabo predicts data will be more accurate because PPMs are easier to use and they don't require people to write down media choices they may not always be proud of.

Data from Arbitron's tests of the PPM in Philadelphia support Sabo's views. The data gathered during the trial included media exposure not captured by other measurement techniques. Measured in quarter-hour increments, the PPM data indicate larger audiences for broadcast and cable television and slightly larger audiences for radio stations than shown by diaries.

Of course, PPMs are vulnerable to errors, too. Panelists may not bother to wear the devices, or the devices may not work properly. Also, PPMs record only the signals they receive from the encoders Arbitron has installed at radio and television stations. If the encoders malfunction or station engineers don't operate them properly, the PPMs won't record data. In addition, if panelists don't return home some nights, they can't insert their devices into the base stations.

Arbitron has addressed these pitfalls. To encourage panelists to wear their PPMs, a message screen on the base station displays reminders, as well as congratulations to panelists for the hours they have worn the device. Also, PPMs contain motion detectors. If a motion detector indicates a PPM was lying on a dresser all day, the day's data are ignored. Arbitron considers data valid only if the PPM registers that it was in motion for at least eight hours. Arbitron offers panelists incentives, too. They earn points toward cash rewards (averaging $12 to $17 a month) and can enter a monthly sweepstakes.

Arbitron is also looking for sources of error at broadcaster sites. For example, Arbitron inspected encoders at radio stations in October 2002 and discovered that the audio input to one station's encoder was set incorrectly. For several months, data for that station may have been wrong. Such errors don't signify a problem with the panels or the PPMs, but do indicate a need for Arbitron to improve how it works with stations to be sure that engineers use the technology correctly. This change requires appropriate training, as well as checks to be sure the encoders are installed properly and are operating as intended.

Even with these drawbacks, the PPMs collect exposures that other methods miss. No wonder Walter Sabo thinks of this little device as a data-rich "friend" of the radio business. ■

Sources: Linda Moss, "A Constant Companion," *Broadcasting & Cable* (February 11, 2002), http://www.broadcastingcable.com; Arbitron, "Arbitron to Extend Portable People Meter Ratings Trial through Winter 2003 Survey," news release, December 5, 2002, Arbitron Web site, http://www.arbitron.com; Walter Sabo, "The Portable People Meter Is Your Friend," *Radio & Records* (October 18, 2002), p. 9; Arbitron, "Arbitron Releases Initial Round of Ratings Results from the Second Phase of the Portable People Meter Trial," *Business Wire* (April 15, 2002), downloaded from FindArticles.com, http://www.findarticles.com.

Summary

Learning Objective 1
Explain what sampling error is.
Sampling error is the difference between the observed values of a variable and the long-run average of the observed values in repetitions of the measurement.

Learning Objective 2
Describe four basic types of nonsampling errors.
There are four basic types of nonsampling errors: noncoverage errors, nonresponse errors, response errors, and office errors. Noncoverage errors occur because part of the population of interest was not included in the sampling frame. Nonresponse errors are possible when some elements designated for inclusion in the sample did not respond and were systematically different from those who did respond on key characteristics. Response errors occur because inaccurate information was secured from the sample elements. Office errors occur when errors are introduced in the processing of the data or in reporting the findings.

Learning Objective 3
Outline several ways in which noncoverage error can be reduced.
Noncoverage bias can be reduced, although not necessarily eliminated, by recognizing its existence and working to improve the sampling frame.

Learning Objective 4
Explain what nonresponse error is.
Error due to nonresponse represents a failure to obtain information from some elements of the population that were selected and designated for the sample. It is a problem because those who provide responses are often systematically different from those who do not provide responses.

Learning Objective 5
Identify the two main sources of nonresponse error.
The two main sources of nonresponse error are not-at-homes and refusals.

Learning Objective 6
Define response error and discuss some of its causes.
Response error reflects bias due to securing inaccurate information from a respondent. Many factors can lead to response error, including (1) respondent failure to understand, know the answer, or provide the true answer to a question; (2) the wording of questions and the situations in which the questions are asked; and (3) interviewers' failure to accurately record responses provided by respondents or fabrication of responses.

Learning Objective 7
Discuss how interviewers can contribute to response error.
There are numerous ways interviewers can increase response error during the data collection process. Some of these include the phrasing and inflection of questions, misinterpretation of respondent answers, mistakes in recording respondent answers, inconsistent follow-up questions across respondents, and the fabrication of responses.

Learning Objective 8
Cite the standard definition for response rate.
Response rate may be defined as the number of completed interviews with responding units divided by the number of eligible responding units in the sample.

Learning Objective 9
Discuss several ways in which response rates might be improved.
There are several approaches for improving response rates, including making the data collection instrument and procedure as interesting and as short as possible, carefully choosing and training interviewers, asking respondents to complete a short task before asking them to complete the longer data collection instrument (the "foot-in-the-door" technique), guaranteeing confidentiality and/or anonymity, notifying potential respondents in advance, personalizing data collection forms as much as possible, providing incentives, disguising the sponsor if necessary, and sending follow-up surveys.

PART 5:
Sampling and Data Collection

Key Terms

sampling error (page 472)
nonsampling error (page 472)
noncoverage error (page 473)
nonresponse error (page 475)

refusals (page 476)
not-at-homes (page 476)
contact rate (*C*) (page 480)
response rate (page 485)

Review Questions

1. Distinguish between sampling error and nonsampling error. Why is the distinction important?
2. What are noncoverage errors? Are they a problem with telephone surveys? How? With mail surveys? How? With personal interview studies? How?
3. How can noncoverage bias be assessed? What can be done to reduce it?
4. What is nonresponse error?
5. What are the basic types of nonresponse error? Are they equally serious for mail, telephone, or personal interview studies? Explain.
6. What can be done to reduce the incidence of not-at-homes in the final sample?
7. What is the contact rate? What role does it play in evaluating the results?
8. What are the typical reasons designated respondents refuse to participate in a study? What can be done to reduce the incidence of refusals? Do refusals generally introduce random error or systematic biases into studies?
9. What is response error?
10. What factors lead to response error? How might the respondent, the interviewer, and the situation lead to response error?
11. How might the different types of response error be reduced?
12. What is office error?
13. Explain the statement, "Total error is key."
14. What is the response rate?
15. How should response rates be calculated for (a) mail surveys, (b) telephone surveys with no eligibility requirements, and (c) telephone surveys with eligibility requirements?
16. Why does increasing response rate reduce the possibility of nonresponse error?
17. Explain how the "foot-in-the-door" technique works.
18. Why might regularly-stamped return envelopes sometimes be favored over business-reply envelopes, even if the cost is higher?
19. Explain several techniques for improving response rates.

Discussion Questions, Problems, and Projects

1. J. Hoffman was the owner of a medium-sized supermarket located in St. Cloud, Minnesota. She was considering altering the layout of the store so that the frozen food section would be near the section with fresh fruit and vegetables. These changes were designed to better accommodate customer shopping patterns and thereby increase customer patronage. Prior to making the alterations, she decided to administer a short questionnaire in the store to a random sample of customers. For a period of two weeks, three of the store cashiers were instructed to stand at the end of selected aisles and conduct personal interviews with every fifth customer. Hoffman gave specific instructions that on no account were customers to be harassed or offended. Identify the major sources of noncoverage and nonresponse errors. Explain.
2. Tough-Grip Tires was a large manufacturer of radial tires located in New Orleans, Louisiana, and it was experiencing a problem common to tire manufacturers. The poor performance of the auto

industry was having a severe negative impact on the tire industry. To try to maintain sales and competitive positions, various manufacturers were offering wholesalers additional credit and discount opportunities. Tough-Grip's management was particularly concerned about wholesaler reaction to a new discount policy it was considering. The first survey the company conducted to explore this reaction was unsatisfactory to management. Management felt it was conducted in a haphazard manner and contained numerous nonsampling errors. Tough-Grip's management decided to conduct another study, containing the following changes:

- The sampling frame was defined as a list of 1,000 of the largest wholesalers that stocked Tough-Grip tires, and the sample elements were to be randomly selected from this list.
- A callback technique was to be used, with the callbacks being made at different times than the original attempted contact.
- The sample size was to be doubled, from 200 to 400 respondents.
- The sample elements that were ineligible or refused to cooperate were to be substituted by the next element from the list.
- An incentive of $1.00 was to be offered to respondents.

Critically evaluate the steps that were being considered to prevent the occurrence of nonsampling errors. Do you think they were appropriate? Be specific.

3. The placement office at your university has asked you to assist it in determining the size of starting salaries and the range of salary offers received by graduating seniors. The placement office has always gathered some information in this regard in that historically some seniors have come in to report the name of the company for which they are going to work and the amount of their starting salary. The office feels that these statistics may be biased, and thus it wishes to approach the whole task more systematically. This is why it has hired your expertise to determine what the situation was with respect to last year's graduating seniors.

   (a) Describe how you would select a sample of respondents to answer the question of starting salaries. Why would you use this particular sample?

   (b) What types of nonsampling errors might you expect to encounter with your approach, and how would you control for them?

4. An executive recruitment firm used a lengthy mail survey to gather information on the job mobility of midlevel managers. A sample of 500 eligible middle managers was selected, using a simple random sampling procedure. The firm used three waves of mailings. Sixteen (16) of the questionnaires were returned due to bad addresses; all but two of the returned surveys were usable. After the third mailing, each of the nonresponding (N.R.) sample units was contacted by phone and asked to answer only four questions regarding variables that the recruitment firm thought were particularly important, given the objective of the study. The table below gives mean values for these variables.

Wave	Number of Responses	Age	Income ($)	Years in Current Position	Total Years of Management Experience
1	125	30	22,000	1.2	5.1
2	100	37	27,000	4.0	9.4
3	75	42	32,500	5.1	15.1
N.R.	200	50	31,250	10.2	24.2

   (a) What was the response rate for the completed questionnaire?

   (b) Which variables, if any, seem to be most affected by potential nonresponse bias? Does this tell you anything about the sample selection procedure?

5. Arrange to interview a researcher at a local marketing research firm or in-house research department. How large a problem is nonresponse for the firm? What are the typical response rates for the firm's research projects? Discuss the method(s) used to handle or estimate nonresponse error. Does the firm compensate for nonresponse in ways that are not addressed in the text? Prepare a written report of your findings.

6. Prepare a brief questionnaire (6–8 questions) regarding the television-viewing habits of adults in your city. Administer this instrument to a sample of subjects using at least ten telephone interviews and ten personal interviews. Discuss the extent of the nonresponse error with each method.

7. For this exercise you will need to use the questionnaire on television-viewing habits developed in the previous problem. Apply Weiers' four key questions to identify possible sources of response error if you were to collect data using your questionnaire.

8. A large furniture store located in a city in the Southwestern United States was interested in determining how households living in and around the city viewed the image of the store. Store managers hired a local market research company to collect data. The researchers drew a systematic sample of 2,500 names from the local telephone directory and set out to conduct telephone interviews. At the conclusion of the data collection phase of the project, the researchers recorded 1223 completed interviews, 598 not-at-homes, 427 refusals, and 252 nonworking telephone numbers. Calculate the response rate on the project.

9. Suppose that the managers in the previous question had decided prior to data collection to only include in the sample households that planned to make a furniture purchase in the next six months. A screening question was used to identify households that qualified to complete the survey. Further, the 2,500 elements drawn for the sample were accounted for as follows: 473 completed interviews, 612 not-at-homes, 431 refusals, 222 nonworking telephone numbers, and 762 ineligibles.
   (a) What was the response rate on this project?
   (b) What would the response rate have been without adjusting for ineligible households?

10. A remodeling contractor located in a small college community had developed a relatively inexpensive type of storage shed and wanted to determine the likely level of demand for the sheds among local homeowners before he began producing and marketing them. Because the population of homeowners was not easily identifiable in the telephone directory, and because it would be very inefficient to screen for homeowners due to the fact that it was a college town with the associated high proportion of renters, he couldn't use a telephone survey. Although he could purchase a mailing list of homeowners in the relevant zip code areas, the cost of mail surveys was prohibitive. Because of these constraints, the contractor decided to collect data via an area sample and residential drop-off survey. That is, for randomly selected neighborhoods, local college students working for the contractor would approach each household in the neighborhood, determine whether or not the resident was the homeowner, and if so ask him or her to complete a short written survey which the student would pick up later in the evening. If no one answered the door, the worker was to leave the survey (with instructions) at the door, and to return later to pick it up.

   At the conclusion of the project, 438 homes had been approached, with the following outcomes: 212 completed surveys, 31 refusals, 78 residents that rented the residence, and 117 not-at-homes. What was the response rate on this project?

Suggested Additional Readings

For general discussions of data quality, the differences between sampling and nonsampling error, and steps that can be taken to improve the quality of information gathered in marketing research studies, see Ronald Andersen, Judith Kasper, Martin R. Frankel, and Associates, *Total Survey Error* (San Francisco: Jossey-Bass, 1979).

Henry Assael and John Keon, "Nonsampling vs. Sampling Errors in Survey Research," *Journal of Marketing* 46 (Spring 1982), pp. 114–123.

Judith T. Lessler and William D. Kalsbeek, *Nonsampling Errors in Surveys* (New York: John Wiley and Sons, Inc., 1992).

Robert A. Peterson and Roger A. Kerin, "The Quality of Self-Report Data: Review and Synthesis," in Ben Enis and Kenneth Roering, eds., *Annual Review of Marketing 1981* (Chicago: American Marketing Association, 1981), pp. 5–20.

part 5 research project

The fifth stage in the research process is to design the sample and collect the data. As we learned from the chapters in this part, researchers generally prefer to use a sample of a population rather than a census of a population, not only because a sample is less costly to obtain, but because it is generally more accurate.

In these chapters we learned that researchers generally follow a six-step procedure for drawing a sample, which includes defining the population, identifying the sampling frame, selecting a sampling procedure, determining the sample size, selecting the sample elements, and collecting the data from the designated elements. We investigated the different types of samples that researchers use and the advantages and disadvantages of each.

In the last chapter we investigated the second type of error that affects research studies: nonsampling error. As we discussed, there are two types of nonsampling errors: those due to nonobservation and those due to observation. Nonobservation errors include coverage errors and nonresponse errors, while observation errors include response errors and office errors.

The problem with nonsampling error is that, unlike sampling error, it generally cannot be accurately estimated and corrected for. Like viruses for the common cold, new sources of nonsampling error are being discovered all the time—and, again like the common cold, are proving resistant to cure. A researcher's best tactic is to know as much as possible about the types of nonsampling errors that can occur and try to design a study that will prevent them.

Researchers for CARA were interested in assessing the attitudes of local businesspeople for their study. They decided to define the local area as the Fairview County area. Businesspeople were defined as individuals who made decisions regarding advertising expenditures for their firms. The researchers decided to exclude from the sample any firms that used an advertising agency or showed minimal interest in using any of the three major advertising media. They excluded these firms because CARA was interested in obtaining responses from firms that were likely to be targeted directly by sales representatives. Companies that use advertising agencies will normally have little direct contact with sales representatives; very small companies offer little potential for ad revenues.

The researchers decided to use the latest Centerville Telephone Directory Yellow Pages as their sampling frame. Recall that a sampling frame is the list of elements from which the sample is drawn. They identified ten major categories of business from which to select the sample: building materials and hardware; automotive sales and service; apparel; furniture and home furnishings; eating and drinking establishments; health and fitness; financial institutions; home entertainment; professional services; and a miscellaneous category including florists, jewelers, printers, book dealers, and retail photographic sales and service.

By further winnowing the list to eliminate those firms employing advertising agencies or expressing little interest in advertising, the researchers compiled a final list of 3,086 businesses.

A systematic sampling plan was chosen for this study. Recall that in this type of sampling plan each element has a known a priori chance of inclusion in the sample. Each of the 3,086 businesses identified as a part of the sampling frame was classified as a member of one of the ten categories of business and was placed in alphabetical order within that category. The ten categories were then randomly ordered, and the businesses were numbered from 1 to 3,086.

The researchers decided on a sample size of 600 and then determined two measures: the sampling interval and a random start. The sampling interval involved dividing the number of elements in the population (3,086) by the desired sample size (600). This number (5.14) was then rounded down to 5. A random-number table was used to select the initial number between 1 and 5, and every fifth element was selected thereafter until the desired sample size was achieved. This process ensured that the sample was representative of the sampling frame; the proportion of various categories of business included in the sample equaled the proportion of these types of business in the sampling frame.

The researchers then pretested the questionnaire by mailing 20 questionnaires to businesses selected by the systematic sampling plan. Half of the respondents were given a dollar for their cooperation; half were given nothing except thanks. Eight of those receiving the incentive returned the questionnaire; only one of the others complied. Since eight of the nine questionnaires that were returned were fully completed, the researchers decided that no changes needed to be made to the questionnaire. Since CARA was interested in whether offering respondents an incentive would increase response similarly in the larger group, the researchers decided to offer half the sample a dollar for responding and nothing to the other half.

A general rule for selecting sample size is that there should be 100 or more units for each category of the major breakdowns and 20 to 50 for the minor breakdowns. The researchers assumed that the section of the questionnaire requesting attitudes toward sales representatives would have the highest percentage of incomplete subsections. Based on the responses to that section in the pretest, they estimated that 150 questionnaires were necessary to fulfill the requirement for the major breakdowns. They also assumed that if the returned forms were evenly distributed among the four categories of annual advertising budgets, 25 units per minor breakdown should result, thus fulfilling the second general rule.

Since there was no assurance that an even distribution would occur, they decided to increase the number of returns to increase the probability that the desired number of units in the minor breakdowns would approach the desired level. They estimated the rates of return conservatively at 10 percent for those individuals not receiving a dollar and 50 percent for those receiving a dollar. Hence, a sample size of 300 for each group should have resulted in 30 and 150 returns for the no-dollar and dollar groups, respectively, which would be enough to satisfy the general rules mentioned.

CARA researchers recognized the sources of nonsampling error in their study. They knew, for example, that coverage errors in their sampling frame were inevitable because the Centerville Yellow Pages was not a complete list of all local businesses. Some of the businesses listed were no longer in existence, others were too new to have been listed, and others may have chosen not to be listed. Nevertheless, no alternative offered a better list of businesses at a reasonable cost.

By using only ten major categories of businesses, the researchers also recognized that they had probably included some businesses that should not have been on the list and excluded others that should have been. Errors of inclusion and exclusion were also likely in their attempts to select only businesses not employing an advertising agency and businesses that would be interested in using the three major advertising media. Because of these biases, the researchers cautioned CARA representatives about generalizing the study's results to all businesses in Fairview County.

Nonresponse errors were evident in the response rates. Of the 600 questionnaires initially mailed, a total of 212 were returned. Of these, 165 were from the 300 that received a dollar, and 47 were from the 300 that received no incentive. Thirty-four of the returned questionnaires were unusable, however, either because none of the pages were completed or because only classification data were given.

The researchers were interested in sampling from among firms that did not use an advertising agency, individuals who were involved in making advertising decisions, and individuals who held the position of manager and/or owner. The results of the study seemed to indicate that the questionnaire generally secured responses from the population of interest. Of the 178 respondents submitting usable questionnaires, 149 companies (84 percent) did not use an advertising agency, 166 respondents (93 percent) were decision makers, and 160 respondents (90 percent) were owners and/or managers.

To further ensure that the data used for analyses were representative of the desired population, mean scores on attitudes toward the various advertising media and advertising media sales representatives were compared for those companies using an advertising agency versus those not using an advertising agency, those respondents who made decisions about advertising versus those who did not, and those who were owners and/or managers versus those who were not. No significant differences (alpha = 0.05) were found, except for the attitudes of those who used an advertising agency versus those who did not. Therefore, when analyzing the attitude scores, only those scores of those companies who did not use advertising agencies were considered.

Field errors occur when an individual who has agreed to participate in a study either refuses to answer specific questions or provides untruthful answers. CARA researchers noticed several instances of probable field errors in the completed questionnaires. For example, on the scale measuring attitudes toward the advertising media of television, radio, and newspaper, 453 subsections were completed. Of this number, 133 were from the television category, 153 from the radio category, and 167 from the newspaper category. Since individuals were asked to fill out each subsection regardless of whether or not they used that type of advertising, there should not have been differences in these numbers. The researchers speculated that the respondents may have been confused as to what their task was on this section, or they may merely have decided not to complete this section.

Respondents were also asked to approximate the proportion of their yearly advertising budget spent on nine different types of advertising. The researchers took the responses and determined the mean percentage scores for each category. The percentages did not add up to 100 percent, however, which indicated that some respondents had had difficulty determining these proportions.

Discussion Issues

Besides understanding their limitations where nonsampling errors and sources were concerned, what could the CARA researchers have done to lessen the chances of not having 100 percent participation from the respondents?

Case • 5.1

St. Andrews Medical Center

The Eating Disorders Clinic of the St. Andrews Medical Center has been operating since 1985 to treat anorexia nervosa and bulimia. Anorexia nervosa, often characterized by intense obsession with dieting and weight loss, and bulimia, also known as the "binge and purge syndrome," typically afflict young women between the ages of 14 and 22 years. Both conditions can result in very serious health problems (or even death) if left untreated.

In recent years, the clinic has experienced a dramatic decline in patients, while, officials believe, a competing program offered by City Hospital has continued to grow. The programs are comparable in terms of staffing and cost of treatment. Patients are normally referred to an eating disorders program by their primary-care physician or other health-care professional.

Officials at St. Andrews were very concerned about the downward trend in the number of patients being referred to and treated at the Eating Disorders Clinic. Initially, they believed that the decrease might simply be a reflection of a decrease in the prevalence of anorexia nervosa and bulimia in the population. However, a review of the medical literature and discussions with administrators of eating disorders programs from across the country strongly suggested that this was not the case. Furthermore, conversations with the medical director at City Hospital confirmed that the number of cases of the disorders treated by the City Hospital program has continued to increase during recent years.

St. Andrews' officials next turned to the marketing department for the development and implementation of some type of research designed to uncover the reasons behind the decreasing enrollment in the eating disorders program.

Sampling Plan

Because more than 80 percent of the cases treated at the Eating Disorders Clinic are referred to the program by other health-care providers, St. Andrews' marketing staff believed that the research should be directed at these health-care providers. In particular, they wanted to obtain attitudes and opinions about the St. Andrews program specifically and about eating disorders programs in general.

The population for which a sample frame was to be developed included all health-care professionals in the market area of St. Andrews Medical Center who may treat female patients between the ages of 14 and 22 years.

A review of admittance records showed that referrals were most likely to come from primary care practitioners, including physicians in general medicine, family medicine, internal medicine, and gastroenterology. In addition, referrals have been received from pediatricians, obstetricians/gynecologists, psychiatrists, and psychologists. Although the names and addresses of physicians in these specialties were available from several sources, the marketing staff believed that the telephone directory provided the easiest and least expensive listing. The sampling frame thus included all physicians (or psychologists) from each of these specialties and was drawn from the Yellow Pages of the current telephone directory. Exhibit 1 provides the breakdown of the number of professionals of each type included in the sampling frame. All health-care providers on the list were to be contacted.

Administration

The marketing department staff decided to conduct a mail survey and constructed a three-page structured questionnaire that was sent to the 699 health-care providers on the list using the addresses obtained from the telephone directory. An appropriate cover letter was also included. Although neither the cover letter nor the questionnaire identified St. Andrews Medical Center as the sponsor of the survey, no attempt was made to disguise the purpose of the survey. In addition to questions related specifically to the St. Andrews' program, the marketing staff included questions about City Hospital's competing program and about eating disorders programs in general.

Of the 699 questionnaires distributed, 56 (8 percent) were returned as undeliverable by the postal service, while 119 were completed and returned by respondents (a 17 percent response rate). Although St. Andrews' officials were displeased with the low response rate—they had anticipated at least a 25 percent return rate—they thought that the data would provide useful information for the management of the Eating Disorders Clinic.

Questions

1. What is the appropriate target population given the hospital's interest?
2. Evaluate the sampling frame given the target population chosen by the hospital staff. What other sources might exist for use in developing the sampling frame?
3. Evaluate the use of a mail questionnaire for this research.

Exhibit 1

Sampling Frame

Specialty	Number of Practitioners
Pediatricians	63
Obstetricians/Gynecologists	63
Psychiatrists	124
Psychologists	128
Primary-Care Practitioners*	321
Total	699

*Includes specialists in family medicine, general medicine, internal medicine, and gastroenterology.

Case • 5.2

Riverside County Humane Society (B)

The demands on the Riverside County Humane Society (RCHS) had increased rather dramatically over the past several years, while the tax dollars the society received to provide services had remained relatively unchanged. In an effort to halt further decline in the quality of its services and to provide better care for the pets at the center, the Membership Committee of the board of directors began making plans for a member/contributor drive. The organized drive was to be the first of its kind for the local chapter, and the committee members wanted it to be as productive as possible.

As the plans began to evolve, the committee realized that the organization had only scattered bits and pieces of information about its current members. It did have a list of members and contributors for the last five years that had been compiled by the RCHS staff. In addition, it had access to the results of a survey that had been done by a staff member several years previous that focused on member usage of shelter facilities and their opinions of shelter services and programs. However, the organization had only sparse knowledge of the profile of its typical member and contributor, why they belonged or contributed, how long they had been associated with the humane society, how the services of the humane society could be improved, and so on. The committee members believed information on these issues was important to the conduct of a successful membership drive, and thus they commissioned some research to secure it.

Some initial contacts with other humane society chapters and interviews with some RCHS staff and board members produced a number of hypotheses regarding who is likely to become a member or contributor, why, how much people are likely to give, and so on. The researchers are interested in examining these hypotheses through a mail survey sent to current members and contributors. (See Case 2.2 Riverside County Humane Society [A] for details.)

Sampling Plan

For the last five years, the RCHS had maintained a master list of members and contributors. Contributors were those who had sent a donation to RCHS but had not opted to fill out an official form making them members, which essentially entitled them to receive RCHS's newsletter. The separate list of members contained all those who had expressed interest in membership and who were receiving the newsletter. Both lists were alphabetical. The contributor list included the amount received from each person or business, but not the number of times the person or business gave during the last five years. The member list showed the number of years each organization or person had belonged.

For purposes of the study, all names of businesses or other organizations were deleted and a separate sample was taken from each list. There were approximately 1,050 people on the member list and 300 on the contributor list. The researchers decided to take 120 names from the member list and 50 from the contributor list. They identified those to be sent questionnaires by drawing two random numbers—3 and 5—using a random number table. They then sent questionnaires to the 3rd, 11th, 19th, etc., person on the member list, and the 5th, 11th, 17th, etc., person on the contributor list.

Questions

1. What is the sampling frame and is it a good frame for the target population?
2. What type of sample is being used?
3. Can you think of some ways in which the sample could be improved?

Case • 5.3

PartyTime, Inc.

Andrew Todd, chief executive officer of PartyTime, Inc., a manufacturer of specialty paper products, is preparing to make an important decision. In the 14 years since he founded the company, sales and profits have increased over tenfold to all-time highs of $7,000,000 and $1,150,000, respectively, during the current year. Industry analysts predict continued stable growth during the upcoming year. Despite his firm belief in the adage, "If it's not broken, don't fix it," Todd thinks that it might be time for the addition of a new channel of distribution, based on information he has recently received.

About the Company

PartyTime manufactures a variety of specialty paper products that can be grouped into three basic categories: gift wrap (all types), party goods (printed plates, cups, napkins, party favors, etc.), and other paper goods (specialty advertising, calendars, etc.). When Todd founded the company, he purchased and renovated an existing paper mill located in the Pacific Northwest. Today, company headquarters and production facilities remain at the original location. During the heavy production season, the company employs approximately 200 people.

As shown in the exhibit below, gift wrap accounts for about 60 percent of revenues (50 percent of profits), and party goods amount to about 30 percent of sales (40 percent of profits). All other paper products sold by the company produce about 10 percent of revenues and an equivalent percentage of profits. Sales of gift wrap and other paper goods have been stable, increasing 3 to 4 percent per year during the previous five years. Interestingly (and as Todd is pleased to note), total sales of party goods have been increasing at about a 9 percent annual rate.

The Distribution Decision

Given the profitability of the party-goods line and its substantial sales growth in recent years, Todd is very interested in further increasing sales of specialty party goods. A recent publication of the National Association of Paper and Party Retailers (NAPPR) indicated that industrywide sales of party goods are expected to increase some 10 to 20 percent during the upcoming year. Of particular interest is the projection that sales of party goods through independent party goods (IPG) shops will increase more than 25 percent. Currently, PartyTime party goods are distributed only through mass merchandisers and chain drugstores.

Although sales have been increasing steadily using existing channels, Todd wondered if the time was right to add the IPG channel. Any decision to include the new channel would have to be made early in the year, however, before orders for the holiday season begin arriving (a large percentage of total sales of party goods at the retail level occur during the holiday season).

Independent Party Goods (IPG) Shops

IPG retailers typically operate small- to moderate-sized stores located in malls or strip shopping centers. The label "independent" indicates that the stores are not owned or franchised by major manufacturers, such as Hallmark. In recent years, the number of IPG shops has grown tremendously, to the point where it is not unusual to have 15 to 20 shops in larger cities. Growth has been particularly strong in California, Florida, the upper Midwest, and the East.

Competitive Issues

Competition within traditional channels of distribution for party goods is intense. Within these channels, PartyTime must compete against major producers, such as C.A. Reed, Beach Products, Unique, Hallmark, and Ambassador. The major competitors within the IPG channel, in contrast, are fewer in number; only AMSCAM, Contempo, and Paper Art serve as primary suppliers. Competition within the IPG channel is thought to be much less intense than that in the traditional channels.

December 13. Todd is leaning strongly toward committing the resources necessary to enter the IPG channel and has called a meeting of his managers to discuss the proposed move. He believes that there is room for at least one more supplier, because the competition is less intense than in the traditional distribution channels. In addition, he regards this as an opportunity to further expand the most profitable area of PartyTime's business.

At the meeting, most of PartyTime's managers seem to agree with Todd, although Kim Shinoda, the company's chief accountant, suggests that the company should learn more about IPG retailers before a decision is made. In a memorandum distributed at the meeting, she details the following areas in which more information is needed before a decision is reached:

- *Competitive Products* Are IPG retailers satisfied with current product offerings on the market? Do they receive a satisfactory level of service from the current suppliers?
- *Purchase Criteria* In addition to price and product considerations, what other characteristics of suppliers and product lines do retailers think are important?

■ *Supplier Loyalty*   To what extent are retailers willing to carry product lines of more than one supplier?

Todd agrees that more information would be useful in making a decision, but he realizes that time constraints will force him to make a decision within the next few weeks. Along with his managers, he decides to bring in a marketing research team.

January 16.   The marketing research team is now ready to share the results of the research project with the managers at PartyTime. To implement the research, they had developed an undisguised, semistructured telephone questionnaire designed to obtain the information that Shinoda had suggested.

Officials at PartyTime are particularly interested in the responses of retailers located in those geographic areas in which growth is expected to be strongest over the next year; therefore, a sampling frame was developed using telephone directories in the major cities within these geographic regions. Because many types of stores could conceivably be considered IPG shops, two criteria were established for inclusion in the sampling frame: (1) the

shop must devote more than 50 percent of its shelf space to paper and party goods, and (2) the shop must carry products from more than one supplier. A total of 110 shops were identified using the telephone directories. Although attempts were made to contact each of these shops during business hours, only 82 could be reached. Thirty-two of these met the two criteria, and 23 agreed to participate in the interview.

January 19.   Based on the results of the marketing research project and the input of his managers, Todd has decided to increase production of party goods and market these products through the IPG channel.

Questions

1. Evaluate the research team's development of the sample of store owners. How would you have recommended the research team develop the sampling frame?
2. Do you think that a telephone survey was the best way to collect the needed information?

Exhibit 1

Current-Year Sales and Profit Breakdown by Category

Category	Sales	Percentage	Profit	Percentage
Gift wrap	$4,302,300	61	$ 564,700	49
Party goods	2,045,500	29	472,300	41
Other paper goods	705,200	10	115,000	10
Total	$7,053,000	100	$1,152,000	100

Case • 5.4

Student Computer Lab (B)

Rod Stevenson, director of the Student Computer Center (SCC), recently opened a new computer lab in the business school at a major university. The new lab was designed to meet the needs of all business school students. It offered specialized software required by student courses, both IBM compatible and Macintosh machines, and the latest technology in hardware and software. After operating for six months, Mr. Stevenson recognized some potential problems with the new computer lab. Although the number of computers had doubled, student suggestions and complaints indicated that the demand for computers at times exceeded the available resources.

To address this problem, Mr. Stevenson established a task force to investigate the level of student satisfaction with the computer lab. The task force was made up of four business graduate students. They aimed to (1) help the computer lab identify students needs and (2) provide suggestions on how student needs could be most effectively met. After reviewing available information on the lab, the students in the task force decided to conduct some research before making recommendations on the services offered. (See Case 2.4, Student Computer Lab [A] for more information.)

Student Survey

Using the input from several focus groups, the students developed a questionnaire they felt addressed all the important computer lab issues. Before presenting this survey to Mr. Stevenson, the task force also needed to propose a method to administer the questionnaire. They defined the target population as students enrolled in the School of Business. Since there was not adequate time or funding to administer the questionnaire to all these students, the task force members all agreed they should take a sample. To achieve a 90 percent confidence level, the task force estimated that they needed to collect 100 surveys. They came up with five possible sampling plans to achieve this.

Plan 1 Since all the task force members had classes in the business school, each student in the task force could administer the survey to students before and after classes, or in the hallways of the business school. Each task force member would be responsible for completing 25 surveys.

Plan 2 The university publishes a list of courses offered in the business school. The course listing could be used as a sampling frame. A random-number table could be used to select the classes, and all students in those classrooms would be sampled. Since the average class size is about 45 students, a total of three classes would be selected for sampling.

Plan 3 A list of all business school students was available from the dean's office. This list had student names, ID numbers, and addresses. The task force could use a random-number table to pull a sample of students by their ID number, and then mail the survey including a return envelope, to the address listed. Enough surveys would be mailed to receive 100 responses.

Plan 4 Each task force member could be assigned to collect 25 surveys from either undergraduate or graduate students. Because 75 percent of the business school students are undergraduates, three task force members would collect surveys from undergraduates and one from graduate students.

Plan 5 Both the graduate and undergraduate offices have lists of students enrolled in their program. The listing includes name, ID number, address, and phone. A sample could be pulled from each list separately, using a random-number table. Because 75 percent of the business school students are undergraduates, the task force would telephone enough students to receive 75 undergraduate and 25 graduate student responses.

The SCC task force had three questions they felt were pertinent to deciding the appropriate sampling plan. First, was it necessary to take a random sample of students? Second, since both undergraduate and graduate students used the lab, did the task force need to insure responses from both groups? Third, would the method of data collection impact student responses?

Questions

1. What type of sampling plan is being proposed in each case?
2. How do you think the SCC task force should address each of the questions they listed for deciding the appropriate sampling plan?
3. What are the strengths and weaknesses of each proposed sampling plan? Which plan would you recommend and why?

[1]The contributions of Monika E. Wingate to the development of this case are gratefully acknowledged.

part 5 cases

Case • 5.5

First Federal Bank of Bakersfield

The Equal Credit Opportunity Act, which was passed in 1974, was partially designed to protect women from discriminatory banking practices. It forbade, for example, the use of credit evaluations based on gender or marital status. Although adherence to the law has changed the way many bankers do business, women's perception that there is a bias against them by a particular financial institution often remains unless some specific steps are taken by the institution to counter that perception.

Close to a dozen "women's banks"—that is, banks owned and operated by and for women—opened their doors during the 1980s with the specific purpose of targeting and promoting their services to this otherwise underdeveloped market. Although women's banks currently are evolving into full-service banks serving a wide range of clients, a number of traditional banks are moving in the other direction by attempting to develop services that are targeted specifically toward women. Many of these institutions see such a strategy as a viable way to attract valuable customers and to increase their market share in the short term while gaining a competitive advantage by which they can compete in the long term as the roles of women in the labor force gain in importance. One can find, with even the most cursory examination of the trade press, examples of credit-card advertising that depicts single, affluent, and head-of-the-household female card holders; financial seminar programs for wives of affluent professional men; informational literature that details how newly divorced and separated women can obtain credit; and entire packages of counseling, educational opportunities, and special services for women.

The First Federal Bank of Bakersfield was interested in developing its own program of this kind. The executives were curious about a number of issues. Were women's financial needs being adequately met in the Bakersfield area? What additional financial services would women especially like to have? How do Bakersfield's women feel about banks and bankers? Was First Federal in a good position to take advantage of the needs of women? What channels of communication might be best to reach women who might be interested in the services that First Federal had to offer?

The executives believed that First Federal might have some special advantages if it did try to appeal to women. For one thing, the Bakersfield community seemed to be quite sensitive to the issues being raised by the feminist movement. For another, First Federal was a small, personal bank. The executives thought that women might be more comfortable in dealing with a smaller, more personalized

institution and that the bank might not have the traditional "image problem" among women that larger banks might have.

Research Objectives

One program the bank executives were considering that they believed might be particularly attractive to women was a series of financial seminars. The seminars could cover a number of topics, including money management, wills, trusts, estate planning, taxes, insurance, investments, financial services, and establishing a credit rating. The executives were interested in determining women's reactions to each of these potential topics. They were also interested to know what the best format might be in terms of location, frequency, length of each program, and so on, if there was a high level of interest. Consequently, they decided that the bank should conduct a research study that had the assessment of the financial seminar series as its main objective, but that also shed some light on the other issues they had been debating. More specifically, the objectives of the research were as follows:

1. To determine the interest that exists among women in the Bakersfield area for seminars on financial matters.
2. To identify the reasons why Bakersfield women would change, or have changed, their banking affiliations.
3. To examine the attitudes of Bakersfield women toward financial institutions and the people who run them.
4. To determine if there was any correlation between the demographic characteristics of women in the Bakersfield area and the services they might like to have.
5. To analyze the media usage habits of Bakersfield-area women.

Method

The assignment to develop a research strategy by which these objectives could be assessed was given to the bank's internal marketing research department. The department consisted of only five members—Beth Anchurch, the research director, and four project analysts. As Anchurch pondered the assignment, she was concerned about the best way to proceed. She was particularly concerned with the relatively short amount of time she was given for the project. Top executives thought that there was promise in the seminar idea. If they were right, they wanted to get on with designing and offering the seminars before any of their competitors came up with a similar idea. Thus, they specified that they would like the results of the research department's investigation to be available within 45 to 50 days.

As Anchurch began to contemplate the data collection, she became particularly concerned with whether the study should use mail questionnaires or telephone interviews. She had tentatively ruled out personal interviews because of the short deadline that had been imposed. After several days of contemplating the alternatives, she finally decided that it would be best to collect the information by telephone. Further, she decided that it would be better to hire out the telephone interviewing than to use her four project analysts to make the calls.

Anchurch believed that the multiple objectives of the project required a reasonably large sample of women so that the various characteristics of interest would be sufficiently represented to enable some conclusions to be drawn about the population of Bakersfield as a whole. After pondering the various cross tabulations in which the bank executives would be interested, she finally decided that a sample of 500 to 600 adult women would be sufficient. The sample was to be drawn from the white pages of the Bakersfield telephone directory by the Bakersfield Interviewing Service, the firm that First Federal had hired to complete the interviews.

The sample was to be drawn using a scheme in which two names were selected from each page of the directory, first by selecting two of the four columns on the page at random and then by selecting the fifteenth name in each of the selected columns. The decision to sample names from each page was made so that each interviewer could operate with certain designated pages of the directory, since each was operating independently out of her home.

The decision to sample every fifteenth name in the selected columns was determined in the following way. First, there were 328 pages in the directory with four columns of names per page. There were 80 entries per column on average, or approximately 26,240 listings. Using Bureau of the Census data on household composition, it was estimated that 20 percent of all households would be ineligible for the study because they did not contain an adult female resident. This meant that only 20,992 (0.80 × 26,240) of the listings would probably qualify. Since 500 to 600 names were needed, it seemed easiest to select two columns on each page at random and to take the same numbered entry from each column. The interviewer could then simply count or measure down from the top of the column. The number 15 was determined randomly; thus, the fifteenth listing in the randomly selected columns on each page was called. If the household did not answer or if the women of the house refused to participate, the interviewers were instructed to select another number from that column through the use of an abbreviated table of random numbers that each was given. They were to use a similar procedure if the household that was called did not have an adult woman living there.

First Federal decided to operate without callbacks because the interviewing service charged heavily for them. Anchurch did think it would be useful to follow up with a sample of those interviewed to make sure that they indeed had been called, since the interviewers for Bakersfield Interviewing Service operated out of their own homes and it was impossible to supervise them more directly. She did this by selecting at random a handful of the surveys completed by each interviewer. She then had one of her project assistants call that respondent, verify that the interview had taken place, and check the accuracy of the responses of a few of the most important questions. This audit revealed absolutely no instances of interviewer cheating.

The completed interview forms were turned over to First Federal for its own internal analysis. As part of this analysis, the project analyst compared the demographic characteristics of those contacted to the demographic characteristics of the population in the Bakersfield area as reported in the 2000 census. The comparison is shown in Exhibit 1. The analyst also prepared a summary of the nonresponses and refusals by interviewer. This comparison is shown in Exhibit 2.

Questions

1. Compare the advantages and disadvantages of using telephone interviews rather than personal interviews or mail questionnaires to collect the needed data.
2. Compare the advantages and disadvantages of using in-house staff versus a professional interviewing service to collect the data.
3. Do you think the telephone directory provided a good sampling frame given the purposes of the study, or would you recommend an alternative sampling frame?
4. What type of sample is being used here? Still using the white pages of the telephone directory as the sampling frame, would you recommend some other sampling scheme? Why or why not?
5. If you were Anchurch, would you be happy with the performance of the Bakersfield Interviewing Service? Why or why not?

Selected Demographic Comparison of Survey Respondents with Bureau of Census Data

Characteristic/Category	PERCENTAGE OF WOMEN	
	Survey	Census
Marital Status		
Married	53	42
Single	30	40
Separated	1	2
Widowed	9	9
Divorced	7	7
Age		
18–24	23	23
25–34	30	28
35–44	16	14
45–64	18	21
65+	13	14
Income		
Less than $10,000	9	29
$10,000–$19,999	19	29
$20,000–$50,000	58	36
More than $50,000	2	6
Refused	12	

Results of Calls by Interviewer

Interviewer	NUMBER OF NOT-AT-HOMES		INELIGIBLES*	NUMBER OF REFUSALS		NUMBER OF COMPLETIONS
	Line Busy	No Answer		Initial	After Partial Completion	
1	7	101	36	15	0	30
2	2	45	13	16	0	30
3	11	71	23	17	7	30
4	14	56	47	35	6	39
5	9	93	10	23	13	30
6	5	102	28	63	14	35
7	6	36	17	16	0	18
8	7	107	23	13	0	30
9	11	106	36	47	0	30
10	10	55	6	35	9	30
11	38	83	48	92	0	30
12	5	22	3	8	0	9
13	23	453	102	65	7	99
14	12	102	27	31	0	19
15	7	173	29	66	0	34
16	2	65	9	33	0	22
Total	169	1,670	457	575	56	515
	1,839				631	

*No adult female resident.

Case • 5.6

School of Business (B)

The School of Business, one unit in a public university enrolling over 40,000 students, has approximately 2,100 students in its bachelor's, master's, and doctorate degree programs in all areas of business, including accounting, finance, operations and information management, marketing, management, and others. Because the School of Business must serve a diverse student population on limited resources, it is important to accurately measure students' satisfaction with the school's services.

Accurate measurement of student satisfaction will enable the school to target improvement efforts to those areas of greatest concern to students, whether by major, support services, or some other aspect of their educational experiences. The school feels that improving its service to its customers (students) will result in more satisfied alumni, better community relations, additional applicants, and increased corporate involvement. Since graduate and undergraduate students are believed to have different expectations and needs, the school plans to investigate the satisfaction of these two groups separately.

In a previous survey of graduating seniors using open-ended questions, three primary areas of concern were identified: the faculty, classes/curriculum, and resources. Resources consisted of five specific areas: Undergraduate Advising Services, the Learning Center, Computer Facilities, the Library, and the Career Services Office. The research team for this project developed five-point Likert scale questions to measure students' satisfaction in each of these areas. In addition, demographic questions were included to determine whether satisfaction with the school was a function of a student's grade point average, major, job status upon graduation, or gender. Previous surveys used by the School of Business and other published satisfaction scales provided examples of questions and wording for the survey.

A random sample of the 400 graduating School of Business seniors was selected to receive the questionnaire. Random sampling for this project was possible because the school maintains a computer list of all seniors graduating at the end of the current semester. The list of graduating seniors contains home phone numbers and addresses. Numbers were assigned to each student and a random number generator was used to select the respondents. Because the research team was working under a tight deadline (seniors were graduating and leaving), a modified mail format was used to increase the response rate.

Questionnaires were mailed to each of the respondents on a Friday. Over the weekend, the research team called each respondent and explained the purpose and importance of the survey. A verbal commitment to complete the survey was obtained from each respondent. One week after mailing the survey, the research team again telephoned each respondent. Those respondents who had already completed the questionnaire were thanked for their prompt response. Those who had not yet completed the questionnaire were reminded of the importance to the school of their candid responses.

In addition to the telephone calls, the team used the following strategies to increase the response rate:

- The respondents were promised anonymity.
- The questionnaire included a 10 percent off coupon from area Pizza Huts.
- Two of the respondents were randomly selected to receive a $15 cash prize.
- Convenient drop-off locations for the surveys were provided within the School of Business.

The collected information was analyzed using cross tabulations.

Questions

1. Currently, more students apply for admission to the School of Business than there are places available. Since there are more than enough applicants, is it necessary for the school to measure student satisfaction?
2. Describe how satisfaction information is useful for marketing and promoting the School of Business.
3. For the research team to determine the appropriate sample size for this research project, what other information is required?
4. The research team has put considerable effort and money into improving the response rate for this study. Discuss why it is important to obtain responses from the entire sample of respondents.
5. The School of Business has hypothesized that satisfaction levels may vary depending on certain demographic characteristics of respondents. Is simple random sampling the most appropriate sampling method to investigate these hypotheses? Explain. What are other sampling methods that may have been useful for this project?

[1]The contributions of Sara Pitterle to the development of this case are gratefully acknowledged.

Case • 5.7

Rockway Publishing Company, Inc.[1]

The Problem

Rockway Publishing Company publishes telephone directories for suburban and rural communities. Headquartered in a large midwestern metropolitan area, Rockway publishes directories for over 80 markets, mostly in the midwestern and southern parts of the United States. The telephone directories are published as an alternative to, and in competition with, directories published by the local telephone companies serving these markets. Rockway has been very successful in offering yellow-page advertisers a quality product at competitive rates. However, there have been some problems with distribution.

The distribution of the directories is handled in one of two ways. Winston Delivery Company has been under contract for the past two years to hand deliver directories in suburban areas and small cities. Winston hires college students, at minimum wage plus car expenses, to make the deliveries. Each student is given an assigned area of streets and rural routes to cover. For some locations, particularly where the households are heavily rural, the directories are sent through the mail. Recently, Rockway's salespeople have been receiving complaints from advertisers that some of their customers have not received a directory. It is believed by some of the salespeople that as much as 10 to 15 percent of households, in any given market, are not receiving a directory.

Survey Method

Faced with the prospect that not all of the directories intended for households are being delivered, Ron Combs, president of Rockway, instituted a plan for measuring the discrepancy. Approximately three weeks after a directory is delivered in an area, a sample of households is telephoned, and respondents are asked if the directory has been received. The results are tabulated according to whether the household has a city or rural address. To be counted, the respondent must be sure that the book has been received or has not been received. Respondents who are uncertain or don't know are given more information about the time of delivery, what the face of the book looks like, and how it was delivered (by mail or by hand). If they are still uncertain, they are replaced in the sample and not included in the tally. The respondent may be anyone in the household who answers the phone or is available at the time of the call. Combs wants to ensure that sampling error is not greater than plus or minus two percentage points.

The Sampling Plan

The sampling frame is an internally produced cross directory of white-page listings by street. The interviewer goes through the pages, arbitrarily pulling names from the listings. If a respondent says a directory has not been received, additional calls are made on that street to determine if the entire street was missed. However, these additional calls are not included in the survey results.

Exhibit 1 shows the results of the survey for areas distributed to in the most recent months.

The total sample size for each area was determined by taking 1.5 percent of the area population. The breakdown between city and rural sample is arbitrary and the result of actual calls completed.

Combs wants to determine three things: (1) the overall soundness of the sampling plan; (2) the amount of sampling error in the results; and (3) the amount of response error by respondents.

Questions

1. What type of sample is being taken? Are city and rural residents being represented adequately? What other approach would you recommend and why?
2. What is the range of sampling error experienced from Area 1 to Area 5? (Assume 95 percent level of confidence.) How can Combs's error goal of plus or minus two percentage points be achieved?
3. What would you recommend as a sample size for each of the five areas?
4. Does Combs have enough information to determine respondent error? What would you recommend he do to obtain this information?

[1]This case was prepared by Paul D. Boughton, Ph.D., Associate Professor of Marketing, Saint Louis University, 3674 Lindell Blvd., St. Louis, MO 63108.

Exhibit 1

Survey Results

| | HAND DELIVERED | | | MAIL DELIVERED | |
	Area 1	Area 2	Area 3	Area 4	Area 5
Total area population	35,000	50,000	69,000	85,000	155,000
City	24,000	45,700	52,000	43,000	100,000
Rural	11,000	4,300	17,000	42,000	55,000
Total Sample	525	750	1,035	1,275	2,325
City	325	650	775	685	1,325
Rural	200	100	260	590	1,000
Overall percentage receiving directory	88%	90%	95%	85%	92%

Part 6

Data Analysis

After the data have been collected, we turn our attention to analyzing the data, which is the search for meaning in the collected information. This search for meaning is usually straightforward and follows a stepwise process. Chapter 19 discusses the process of editing and coding the data, including developing the codebook, inputting data into a computer file, "cleaning" the data to correct input errors, and dealing with missing data. In Chapter 20 we present several commonly used techniques for analyzing individual variables (i.e., univariate analyses) along with the basic logic of hypothesis testing and associated tests of statistical significance. Chapter 21 presents a number of useful techniques for analyzing two or more variables at the same time (i.e., multivariate analyses), perhaps to test for differences between groups or to assess the degree of association between variables.

513

Chapter 19

Data Analysis: Preliminary Steps

© PhotoDisc/Getty Images

Learning Objectives

1. Explain the purpose of the field edit.

2. Define what coding is.

3. Discuss two types of open-ended questions.

4. List the basic steps in coding open-ended responses.

5. Describe the kinds of information contained in a codebook.

6. Describe common methods for cleaning the data file.

7. Discuss options for dealing with missing data in analyses.

Y**ou're** enjoying a night out on the town with some friends when you notice you're down to your last $5. No problem. You head for the nearest automated teller machine (ATM) and slide in your ATM card. Press a few buttons, and out slips another $40 from your checking account. As long as you have money in your account, an ATM can give you some for your wallet.

You enjoy the convenience, and the owner of that ATM is glad you do. Shared electronic services networks like PULSE EFT Association and NYCE set up networks of ATMs for banks and other depository institutions. The banks issue ATM cards to their customers and typically receive a steady stream of income from fees they charge ATM users. Naturally, they want to attract and keep more cardholders, and they encourage them to use their ATMs.

To achieve such marketing objectives, the networks commission research. For example, both PULSE and NYCE work with Richard R. Batsell's research firm, Analytica Inc., based in Houston. Analytica studies ATM usage and generates data on the demographics of ATM users.

In a study that involved interviewing 3,000 consumers nationwide, Analytica determined that almost 71 percent have an ATM card and 50 percent use it as their main way of obtaining cash. The Analytica study broke the data down according to consumers' racial and ethnic background. It found some differences in patterns of usage:

Racial/ Ethnic Group	Have an ATM Card	ATM Card Is Main Way to Get Cash
African-American	76%	58%
Native American	75%	54%
Asian-American	74%	59%
Hispanic	82%	64%
White	68%	47%

From the data, it is easy to draw some general conclusions. For instance, we can see that many Americans are aware of ATM cards (the majority already have one) and that there is room for growth in usage of the cards.

The data also raise questions. For example, why are Hispanic consumers more likely than non-Hispanic whites to own an ATM card and use it as the primary way to get cash? For the data to be useful for marketing decisions, ATM owners need to explain the difference in usage levels.

One approach would be to simply assume that something about Hispanic culture makes ATM cards more attractive. Marketers that rely on this explanation might target most marketing efforts to Hispanic consumers. However, that is the group with the least potential for growth, since almost two-thirds of Hispanics already use the cards as the main way to get cash. Some ATM owners might prefer to expand their market by broadening the appeal of cards to consumers in other groups. This requires them to study the data further and learn more about what characteristics are associated with use of ATM cards.

Discussion Issues

1. If you owned an ATM network, what else would you want to know about ATM users?

2. What other ways of segmenting the data would interest you?

3. What further research would you request? ■

Editing

The basic purpose of editing is to impose some minimum quality standards on the raw data. Editing involves the inspection and, if necessary, correction of each questionnaire or observation form. Inspection and correction are often done in two stages: the field edit and the central-office edit.

field edit
A preliminary edit, typically conducted by a field supervisor, which is designed to detect the most glaring omissions and inaccuracies in a completed data collection instrument.

central-office edit
Thorough and exacting scrutiny and correction of completed data collection forms, including a decision about what to do with the data.

Field Edit

The **field edit** is a preliminary edit designed to detect the most glaring omissions and inaccuracies in the data. It is also useful in helping to control the behavior of the field force personnel and to clear up any misunderstandings they may have about directions, procedures, specific questions, and so on. For example, in a Roper survey conducted in Ukraine, the field edit revealed that an employee had left the questionnaire with the respondents instead of interviewing them as instructed. The tip-off was the different ways the answers were circled.[1]

Ideally, the field edit is done as soon as possible after the questionnaire or other data collection form has been administered. In that way, problems can be corrected before the interviewing or observation staff is disbanded, and while the particular contacts that were the source of trouble are still fresh in the interviewer's or observer's mind. The preliminary edit is usually conducted by a field supervisor. Some of the items checked are described in Exhibit 19.1.

Central-Office Edit

The field edit is typically followed by a **central-office edit,** or "eyeball" edit, which involves the careful physical inspection of each data collection form with exacting scrutiny and the correction of mistakes where possible. For example, suppose a researcher was surveying a company's employees with respect to job satisfaction and an open-ended classification question asked respondents how long they had worked for the company in years. Further suppose that one of the respondents wrote "eleven months" in response to the item. The editor must convert this answer to the correct unit of time (i.e., years). In addition, any variables (e.g., respondent identification number) that remain to be added may be placed on the questionnaires at this point. The work calls for the keen eye of a person well versed in the objectives and procedures of the study. To ensure consistency of treatment, it is best if one individual handles all completed instruments. If the work must be divided because of length and time considerations, the division should be by parts of the data collection instruments rather than by respondents. That is, one editor would edit Part A of all questionnaires while the other would edit Part B.

Exhibit 19.1

Items Checked in the Field Edit

1. **Completeness:** The check for completeness involves scrutinizing the data form to ensure that no sections or pages were omitted, and it also involves checking individual items. A blank for a specific question could mean that the respondent refused to answer; alternatively, it may simply reflect an oversight on the respondent's part or that he or she did not know the answer. It may be very important for the purposes of the study to know which reason is correct. It is hoped that by contacting the field-worker while the interview is fresh in his or her mind, the field editor can obtain the needed clarification.

2. **Legibility:** It is impossible to code a questionnaire that cannot be deciphered because of illegible handwriting or obscure abbreviations. It is a simple matter to correct this now, whereas it is often extremely time-consuming later.

3. **Comprehensibility:** Sometimes a recorded response is incomprehensible to all but the field interviewer. By detecting this now, the field editor can obtain the necessary clarification.

4. **Consistency:** Marked inconsistencies within an interview or observation schedule typically indicate errors in collecting or recording the data and may indicate ambiguity in the instrument or carelessness in its administration. For instance, if a respondent indicated that he or she saw a particular commercial on television last night on one part of the questionnaire, and later indicated that he or she did not watch television last night, the analyst would be in a dilemma. Such inconsistencies can often be detected and corrected in the field edit.

5. **Uniformity:** It is very important that the responses be recorded in uniform units. For instance, if the study is aimed at determining the number of magazines read per week per individual, and the respondent indicates the number of magazines for which he or she has monthly subscriptions, the response base is not uniform, and the result could cause confusion in the later stages of analysis. If the problem is detected now, perhaps the interviewer can recontact the respondent and get the correct answer.

Unlike the field edit, the central-office edit depends less on follow-up procedures and more on deciding just what to do with the data. Accurate follow-up is now more difficult because of the time that has elapsed. The editor must decide how data collection instruments containing incomplete answers, obviously wrong answers, and answers that reflect a lack of interest will be handled. Because such problems are more prevalent with questionnaires than with observation forms, we will discuss these difficulties from that perspective, although our discussion applies generally to all types of data collection forms.

The study in which all the returned questionnaires are completely filled out is rare. Some will have complete sections omitted. In others, responses for one or more individual items will be missing. The editor's decision on how to handle these incomplete questionnaires depends on the severity of the omission. Questionnaires that omit complete sections are obviously suspect, yet should not be thrown out automatically. It might be, for example, that the omitted section refers to the influence of the spouse in the purchase of some durable good, and the respondent is not married. This type of reply is certainly usable in spite of the incomplete section. If there is no logical justification for the large number of unanswered questions (say, half or more of the questions on the survey), the total reply will probably be thrown out, decreasing the response rate for the study. Questionnaires containing only isolated instances of item nonresponse should be retained.

© PhotoDisc/Getty Images

After the field edit is complete, a central-office edit is performed. An experienced researcher conducts this *eyeball* edit of all questionnaires, deciding how to handle incomplete or incorrect data.

Careful editing of the questionnaire sometimes shows that an answer to a question is obviously incorrect. For example, a researcher at a consumer panel research company once reviewed data that indicated that 45 percent of the households in the panel had purchased dog food, but only 40 percent of the households reported that they owned a dog.[2] Presumably, data on some of the panel questionnaires indicated a dog food purchase but not dog ownership. One explanation for this seeming inconsistency is that some of the questionnaires contained incorrect answers. (Other possible explanations include the purchase of dog food for others, or unusual personal taste preferences.) The editor may be able to determine which of the two answers (i.e., 45% purchasing dog food vs. 40% owning a dog) is correct from other information in the questionnaire. Alternatively, the editor may need to establish policies as to which answer, if either, will be treated as correct when these inconsistencies or other types of inaccuracies arise. These policies will reflect the purposes of the study. As an example, consider the quandary of Susan Hooper, the Eastern Europe marketing director for Pepsi Cola International, who was given results of a survey conducted in Hungary that said soft drinks were sold in drugstores. Susan could not take this information at face value for she knew that drugstores didn't exist in Hungary and that the information had been forced into a structure developed in the West.[3]

Editors must also be on the alert to spot completed questionnaires that have failed to engage the respondent's interest. Evidence of this lack of interest may be obvious or quite subtle. Consider, for example, a subject who checked the "5" position on a five-point scale for each of 40 items in an attitude questionnaire, even though some items were expressed negatively and some positively. Obviously, that person did not take the study seriously, and the editor should probably throw out such a response. A discerning editor might also be able to pick up more subtle indications of disinterest, such as check marks that are not within the boxes provided, scribbles, spills on the questionnaire, and so on. An editor may not want to throw out these responses, but they should be coded so that it is later possible to run separate tabulations for the questionable instruments and the good questionnaires. Then the two groups could be compared to see whether lack of interest makes any difference in the results.

In addition to adding a code to indicate questionable surveys, it is often advisable to add any other preliminary codes to the questionnaire during the central-office edit. For example, a unique identifying number of some type should be added unless one already exists on the form. This number will be coded in the data file along with the answers provided by the respondent and will be used to look up the original questionnaire if necessary.

Coding

2 *Define what coding in the research process is.*

coding
The technical procedure by which raw data are transformed into symbols; it involves specifying the alternative categories or classes into which the responses are to be placed and assigning code numbers to the classes.

Coding is the technical procedure by which raw data are transformed into symbols. Most often the symbols are numerals, because they can be handled easily by computers. The task is to transform respondents' answers (or other information to be coded) into numbers representing the answers. Sometimes the transformation is almost automatic (e.g., when respondents have circled numbers on rating scales); sometimes, however, the coding process involves considerable effort on the part of the coder (e.g., when respondents answer certain types of open-ended questions).

Coding Closed-Ended Items

In descriptive research, most of the items included in a questionnaire are likely to be closed-ended. That is, most questions will provide a limited number of response categories and will ask the respondent to choose the best response or, sometimes, all responses that apply. These types of items are generally quite simple to code. When there is a single possible answer to a question (e.g., male or female), the researcher uses one variable for the question and simply assigns a character (almost always a number) to each possible response (e.g., 1 = female, 2 = male). The appropriate code number is then recorded in the data file. The coding process can be facilitated in advance by "precoding" the questionnaire (i.e., printing the actual code numbers beside each possible response) or by using numerical rating scales on the questionnaire, but these techniques are by no means required. If respondents have been asked to check boxes or to provide some other form of response it is usually a simple matter to assign a number to represent each particular response. For example, the following semantic differential item to measure attitude toward a service provider

unfavorable ❏ ❏ ❏ ❏ ❏ ❏ ❏ **favorable**

can easily be coded with the numbers 1–7, where 1 represents the box nearest "unfavorable" and 7 represents the box nearest "favorable." For purposes of analysis there will be a single variable representing this item with possible codes 1 through 7 representing increasing levels of favorability.

The coding process for closed-ended items becomes a bit more complex when respondents can indicate more than one answer for a given question, as with "check all that apply" types of items. For example, consider the following question:

How did you learn about Brown Furniture Company? (check all that apply)

❏ newspaper advertising
❏ radio advertising
❏ billboard advertising
❏ recommended by others
❏ drove by the store
❏ other

In this situation, using a single variable coded 1–6 representing the different options will not work; how would you code responses for someone who checked both "newspaper advertising" and "billboard advertising?" A simple solution is to create six variables to represent the six possible answers and to indicate for each whether or not the option was selected. An easy coding scheme is to record a "1" if a respondent selected a response and to record a "0" if she did not select that response. For the respondent who checked "newspaper advertising" and "billboard advertising," the variables representing these two responses would be coded "1" and each remaining variable would be coded "0."

Coding Open-Ended Items

Recall that open-ended items do not provide response categories for respondents. Instead, respondents answer open-ended questions using their own words. Coding open-ended responses is typically much more difficult than coding closed-ended responses. Before proceeding, we should distinguish between two general classes of open-ended questions. One type seeks factual information from a respondent that he or she presumably knows and can deliver. For example, consider the following open-ended questions:

Discuss two types of open-ended questions.

In what year were you born? _____
How many times have you eaten at Streeter's Grill in the last month? _____

Each of these questions seeks a factual answer from the respondent. There is a correct answer to each question and the researcher assumes that the respondent can provide that answer. This type of open-ended question is easy to code by simply coding the actual response (or, if the actual responses were not numeric, converting the responses to numbers). Numerical data should be recorded as they were reported on the data collection form, rather than be collapsed into smaller categories. For example, it is not advisable to code age as 1 = under 20 years, 2 = 20 – 29, 3 = 30 – 39, and so on, if actual ages of the people were provided. This would result in an unnecessary sacrifice of information in the original measurement and could just as easily be done at later stages in the analysis.

The other type of open-ended question is often more exploratory in nature, and consequently much more difficult and expensive to code. For many open-ended questions there are multiple legitimate responses, some of which are likely to be unanticipated by the researcher. Suppose that a researcher were interested in determining the causes of "brain drain," the migration of college and university graduates from one state to another after graduation. In response to the question, **"In your own words, give us two or three reasons why you prefer to leave the state after graduation,"** students provided answers such as "my family lives in another state," "no job opportunities here," "I don't like the people here," "want to try something different," "going to graduate school in another state," and so on. Some people provided a single reason to leave, while others provided multiple reasons to leave.

The first step in coding this type of open-ended question is to go through each questionnaire and highlight each separate response given by each individual. Some respondents can provide multiple answers in only a few words, while others can write whole paragraphs and communicate only one answer, so great care must be taken at this stage. Normally, at least two coders should review all of the responses separately and then compare results to ensure that all responses are considered.

List the basic steps in coding open-ended responses.

The next step in coding is specifying the categories or classes into which the responses are to be placed.[4] While there is no magic number of categories, the goal is to reduce the great number of individual responses into a much smaller set of general categories so that insights may be drawn from the results. The categories must be mutually exclusive and exhaustive, so that every open-ended response logically falls into one and only one category. The researcher can usually anticipate some or most of the categories in advance, but must not become "locked in" on those categories alone. A thorough review of respondents' actual answers will often reveal appropriate categories that were initially overlooked or anticipated categories that turn out to have very few responses. For example, the brain drain researcher may have expected that college graduates would leave a state for social reasons or job-related reasons but might not have anticipated negative quality of life comments about the particular state in which students went to school. To make the categories exhaustive, it is often necessary to include an "other" category for responses that simply don't fit anywhere else. However, if the number of responses in the "other" category rises to more than 5–10% of the total number of responses, the researcher should consider whether additional categories are needed.

After an appropriate set of categories is identified, the actual coding of responses into the categories begins. Each response identified during the first step must be given the code number for one and only one of the categories developed on the second step. Unless the questions (and responses) are very straightforward (rarely the case for this type of open-ended question), at least two coders who have been trained to understand the types of responses that should be placed in each category should code the responses. Multiple coders help reduce bias in the interpretation of the different responses. Each coder will individually decide which category is appropriate for a response and then assign the numerical code for the category to the response. When all responses have been coded by each coder, the coders meet to compare results, discuss differences in the codes assigned to particular responses, and assign a final code for each response. The coders must keep careful records of the number of codings for which initial disagreement existed so that a summary measure of percentage agreement can be computed. The lower the overall level of agreement, the greater the possibility that either the categories are not mutually exclusive or that one (or more) coders has not done a thorough job.

Multinational studies have their own special coding problems because the same response may mean different things in different countries. For example, take the word "conservative." A conservative in the former Soviet Union is someone who wishes to adhere to or return to the "old Communism," which in turn might be seen as very left-wing in Western countries. Liberal Russians, in turn, are the ones who wish to introduce market perspectives into economics and politics, a perspective that usually will be held by conservatives in the West.[5]

Sometimes projects are too large for a single coder (or set of coders) to handle. If there are multiple open-ended questions and so many questionnaires that several coders are needed, the general rule is that the work should be divided by task, not by dividing the questionnaires equally among the coders. By allowing coders to focus their energies on one or a few questions, researchers can ensure that a consistent set of standards is being applied to each question. When several persons do, in fact, code the same question on different batches of questionnaires, it is important that they also code a sample of the other's work to ensure that a consistent set of coding criteria is being used.[6]

© Ed Lallo/Index Stock Imagery

Data can be entered into specialized software packages, or even into word processing or spreadsheet software.

Building the Data File

In order to use a computer to analyze the data, it is necessary to enter the codes from each questionnaire into a data file that can be read by the computer. There are numerous methods of entering data including creating text data files in word processing software, using spreadsheet software, entering data directly into statistical software packages such as SPSS, or using optical scanning. Regardless of how the data input process will be handled, it is helpful to visualize the input in terms of a multiple-column record where columns represent different variables (based on items from the questionnaire) and rows represent different respondents. Our experience suggests that entering data directly in the statistical software is satisfactory when there are relatively few respondents and/or relatively few variables, but that creating a simple text file in fixed column format using a word processing package is often preferred for larger jobs.

To illustrate the process of building a data file, consider the brief questionnaire presented in Figure 19.1. Suppose that this questionnaire were sent to customers of a sporting goods retailer to determine their perceptions of buying sporting goods over the Internet through the retailer's Web page. Figure 19.2 presents the first two responses received back from customers.

Figure 19.1

SPORTING GOODS SURVEY

Please answer the following questions about purchasing sporting goods over the Internet:

1. **During the past year, what percentage of the sporting goods you purchased were ordered through the Internet?**

   _____ percent

2. **How willing are you to purchase merchandise offered through the Avery Sporting Goods Web site?**

   _____ Not at all willing
   _____ Somewhat willing
   _____ Very willing

3. **Please provide some reasons why someone might not want to purchase sporting goods over the Internet:**

   _____
   _____
   _____
   _____

4. **Have you ever ordered any merchandise from the Avery Sporting Goods Web site on the Internet?**

   _____ Never ordered
   _____ Ordered before, but not within the last year
   _____ Ordered within the last year

5. **Which of the following sporting goods are you likely to purchase over the Internet in the future? Check all that apply.**

   (a) Athletic clothing (shirts,
       warm-up suits, etc.)   _____
   (b) Athletic shoes   _____
   (c) Fishing equipment   _____
   (d) Balls (basketballs,
       footballs, etc.)   _____
   (e) Skiing equipment   _____

6. **How confident are you that the following sporting goods would be of high quality if purchased over the Internet?**

	Not at All Confident	Slightly Confident	Somewhat Confident	Confident	Very Confident
(a) Athletic clothing (shirts, warm-up suits, etc.)	_____	_____	_____	_____	_____
(b) Athletic shoes	_____	_____	_____	_____	_____
(c) Fishing equipment	_____	_____	_____	_____	_____
(d) Balls (basketballs, footballs, etc.)	_____	_____	_____	_____	_____
(e) Skiing equipment	_____	_____	_____	_____	_____

Thank You!

Figure 19.2

Initial Responses to Avery Sporting Goods Questionnaire

001

SPORTING GOODS SURVEY

Please answer the following questions about purchasing sporting goods over the Internet:

1. **During the past year, what percentage of the sporting goods you purchased were ordered through the Internet?**

   __10__ percent

2. **How willing are you to purchase merchandise offered through the Avery Sporting Goods Web site?**

   _____ Not at all willing
   __✓__ Somewhat willing
   _____ Very willing

3. **Please provide some reasons why someone might not want to purchase sporting goods over the Internet:**

   They couldn't check quality before purchasing the product. 3
   Might be afraid someone would steal their credit card number. 1

4. **Have you ever ordered any merchandise from the Avery Sporting Goods Web site on the Internet?**

   __✓__ Never ordered
   _____ Ordered before, but not within the last year
   _____ Ordered within the last year

5. **Which of the following sporting goods are you likely to purchase over the Internet in the future? Check all that apply.**

(a)	Athletic clothing (shirts, warm-up suits, etc.)	_____
(b)	Athletic shoes	_____
(c)	Fishing equipment	✓
(d)	Balls (basketballs, footballs, etc.)	✓
(e)	Skiing equipment	_____

6. **How confident are you that the following sporting goods would be of high quality if purchased over the Internet?**

		Not at All Confident	Slightly Confident	Somewhat Confident	Confident	Very Confident
(a)	Athletic clothing (shirts, warm-up suits, etc.)	_____	✓	_____	_____	_____
(b)	Athletic shoes	_____	_____	_____	✓	_____
(c)	Fishing equipment	_____	_____	✓	_____	_____
(d)	Balls (basketballs, footballs, etc.)	_____	_____	_____	✓	_____
(e)	Skiing equipment	_____	_____	_____	✓	_____

Thank You!

OO2

SPORTING GOODS SURVEY

Please answer the following questions about purchasing sporting goods over the Internet:

1. **During the past year, what percentage of the sporting goods you purchased were ordered through the Internet?**

   0 percent

2. **How willing are you to purchase merchandise offered through the Avery Sporting Goods Web site?**

   ✓ Not at all willing
   _____ Somewhat willing
   _____ Very willing

3. **Please provide some reasons why someone might not want to purchase sporting goods over the Internet:**

   I don't want the hassle of sending it back if they get it wrong.   *4*

   Who knows who might end up with your credit card number?   *1*

   If I want something, I just go to a regular store so I don't have to wait to get it.   *5*

4. **Have you ever ordered any merchandise from the Avery Sporting Goods Web site on the Internet?**

   ✓ Never ordered
   _____ Ordered before, but not within the last year
   _____ Ordered within the last year

5. **Which of the following sporting goods are you likely to purchase over the Internet in the future? Check all that apply.**

   (a) Athletic clothing (shirts, warm-up suits, etc.) _____
   (b) Athletic shoes _____
   (c) Fishing equipment _____
   (d) Balls (basketballs, footballs, etc.) _____
   (e) Skiing equipment _____

6. **How confident are you that the following sporting goods would be of high quality if purchased over the Internet?**

		Not at All Confident	Slightly Confident	Somewhat Confident	Confident	Very Confident
(a)	Athletic clothing (shirts, warm-up suits, etc.)	✓				
(b)	Athletic shoes		✓			
(c)	Fishing equipment	✓				
(d)	Balls (basketballs, footballs, etc.)		✓			
(e)	Skiing equipment	✓				

Thank You!

Figure 19.2

Figure 19.3

Codebook for Avery Sporting Goods Questionnaire

Column(s)	Variable Name	Description	
1–3	ID	Questionnaire identification number	—
4-6	PERCENT	Percentage of products purchased through Internet (open-ended)	(code actual response)
7	WILLING	Willingness to purchase merchandise from the Avery Sporting Goods Web site	1 = Not at all willing 2 = Somewhat willing 3 = Very willing
8	REASON1	First reason to not purchase sporting goods over the Internet (open-ended)	1 = security issues 2 = no Internet access 3 = can't examine goods in advance 4 = difficulty in returning merchandise 5 = don't want to wait to get merchandise 6 = prior bad experience with Internet 7 = other
9	REASON2	Second reason	SAME
10	REASON3	Third reason	SAME
11	REASON4	Fourth reason	SAME
12	REASON5	Fifth reason	SAME
13	PRIOR	Ever ordered from the Avery Sporting Goods Internet site?	1 = Never ordered 2 = Ordered before, but not within last year 3 = Ordered within the last year
14	CLOTHES	Likely to purchase athletic clothes over Internet?	0 = if not checked 1 = if checked
15	SHOES	Likely to purchase athletic shoes . . . ?	SAME
16	FISHING	Likely to purchase fishing equipment . . . ?	SAME
17	BALLS	Likely to purchase balls . . . ?	SAME
18	SKIING	Likely to purchase skiing equipment . . . ?	SAME
19	CONF1	Confidence in buying athletic clothing over the Internet	1 = Not at all confident 2 = Slightly confident 3 = Somewhat confident 4 = Confident 5 = Very confident
20	CONF2	Confidence in buying athletic shoes . . .	SAME
21	CONF3	Confidence in buying fishing equipment . . .	SAME
22	CONF4	Confidence in buying balls . . .	SAME
23	CONF5	Confidence in buying skiing equipment . . .	SAME

MISSING = BLANK

5 *Describe the kinds of information contained in a codebook.*

Note that during the editing and coding process, the researcher has added respondent identification numbers (upper left-hand corner) and code numbers for the open-ended responses. The **codebook**, presented in Figure 19.3, contains explicit directions about how raw data from the questionnaires are to be coded in the data file. At a minimum, the codebook must provide (a) the variable name to be used in statistical analyses for each variable included in the data file; (b) the column(s) in which each variable is located in the data file; (c) a description of how each variable is coded; and (d) an explanation of how missing data are treated in the data

PART 6:
Data Analysis

Figure 19.4

First Two Records in Avery Sporting Goods Data File

```
001010231    10011024344
0020001415    10000012121
```

file. In a very real sense, the codebook is a map to help the researcher navigate from completed questionnaires to the data file. Finally, Figure 19.4 presents how data from the first two respondents (Figure 19.2) would appear in the data file (text file, fixed column format).

Although there are numerous ways to code and enter data into the data file, it is advisable to use the following conventions and tips:

1. Assign column locations (i.e., fields) for particular variables; never try to locate different variables in the same field.
2. Use as many columns for the field assigned to a variable as are necessary to capture the variable. Thus, if the variable is such that the ten codes from 0 to 9 are not sufficient to exhaust the categories, then one should use two columns, providing one hundred codes from 00 through 99. Because the Avery Sporting Goods researchers only found a few general categories for why customers might not want to purchase products over the Internet, they only needed one column to code each of the possible responses. However, with many open-ended questions it will be necessary to leave two columns for each response.
3. When a question allows multiple responses, allow separate columns in the coding for each answer. Thus in the Avery Sporting Goods example, the coder has provided separate columns for each of the reasons that respondents might not prefer to buy sporting goods over the Internet. Similarly, in our earlier Brown Furniture Company example, the researcher would assign specific columns for each of the possible boxes that respondents might have checked.
4. Use only numeric codes, not letters of the alphabet or special characters, like @. Most computer statistical programs have trouble manipulating anything but numerals.
5. Use standard codes for "no information." Thus, all "don't know" responses might be coded as 8, "no answers" as 9, and "does not apply" as 0. It is best if the same code is used throughout the study for each of these types of "no information." If "don't know" and "does not apply" are not response options (and thus there is no distinction between different types of "no information"), it is often best to just leave the column(s) blank.
6. As noted, code a respondent identification number on each record. This number need not, and typically will not, identify the respondent by name. Rather, the number simply ties the questionnaire to the coded data. This is often useful information in data cleaning (discussed later). If the data from the questionnaire will not fit on one line in the data file (each line is referred to as a "record"), then code the respondent identification number and a sequence number into each record. Column 10 in the first record might then indicate how the respondent answered Question 2, while Column 10 in the second record might indicate whether the person is male or female.[7]
7. When entering data in fixed column format, use a font, such as Courier, in which all characters require equal space on the line. This practice allows easy inspection of the data file to see if all records are the same length. A record that is too long or too short indicates a mistake in the data entry process.
8. Save the data file as a text-only file, so that only the data and hard returns to start new records appear in the file. Be sure to eliminate any extra hard returns at the end of the data file before saving the file, as these will often indicate to the statistical software that more records exist, resulting in a greater number of missing cases for analyses than really exist.

codebook
A book that contains explicit directions about how data from data collection forms are to be coded in the data file.

Cleaning the Data

6 *Describe common methods for cleaning the data file.*

blunder

An error that arises during editing, coding, or data entry.

Before proceeding to data analysis, it is necessary to examine the data to ensure that they have been entered correctly into the data file. **Blunders** are errors that occur during editing, coding, or, especially, data entry. Of all possible sources of error in a marketing research project, error due to blunders is among the most frustrating because blunders are usually caused by simple carelessness and lack of attention to detail. In this section we will talk about how to identify blunders and discuss several data entry options that might limit this source of error.

There are really two kinds of blunders that can occur. The first, which is typically easy to diagnose, occurs when the mistake results in a clearly invalid response. For example, suppose that a researcher were coding a 1–5 Likert scale and accidentally entered a 7 instead of the 4 that the respondent circled on the questionnaire. This type of blunder can be seen by performing a simple univariate analysis known as a *frequency* or frequency count (which we will introduce in the next chapter). A frequency tells us all of the different responses coded for a variable along with how many cases responded in each way. In our example, the miscoded 7 will turn up as a response in the frequency, and we will immediately know that a mistake has been made (remember that only the numbers 1 through 5 are valid responses to the question). At this point, it is only a matter of identifying which questionnaire was coded 7 for that variable, pulling the actual questionnaire to find the correct response (i.e., 4), and correcting the mistake in the data file. On most projects, frequencies should initially be run on all variables to identify this kind of blunder.

The second type of blunder is more insidious. In the previous example, suppose that the researcher accidentally enters a 1 instead of the 4 circled by the respondent. Because a 1 is one of the possible valid responses to this item (i.e., a 1–5 scale), examining a frequency will not uncover this blunder; more involved types of examination are required. One possibility, analogous to quality control in manufacturing processes, is to select a sample of questionnaires that have been coded and entered and compare the data file against the original questionnaires to find discrepancies. If no blunders are found, there is less concern about data entry error. If several blunders are identified, it may be necessary to check additional records or even examine all records.

double-entry

Data entry procedure in which data are entered separately by two people in two data files and the data files are compared for discrepancies.

The preferred option, known as **double-entry** of data, requires that the data be entered by two separate people in two separate data files and then the data files compared for discrepancies. The differences are resolved by referring to the original questionnaires. Because it is unlikely that two different people would make the same blunders during data entry, this approach is likely to produce the "cleanest" data file possible with manual data entry. Using modern word processing software packages, the file comparison process is quite straightforward. Note, however, that this technique requires greater resources (i.e., time, effort, money).

Enhanced data collection technology has begun to offer solutions for greatly reducing blunders. For example, data entry software can be programmed to not allow an invalid entry in a variable field, which eliminates the first type of blunder (but does nothing to address the second type). Other options may limit data entry blunders by taking the process out of the hands of the researcher. For example, optical scanning of data collection forms takes information directly from the respondent and reads it into a data file which can then be manipulated by computer. Another option is to have respondents answer questionnaire items administered via computer, perhaps over the Internet. In effect, each respondent enters his or her replies directly into the data file, eliminating the need for a separate data entry procedure. The computer can be programmed not to accept invalid responses. Note, however, that these approaches are less useful as a means of limiting blunders when working with open-ended questions, for which categories and codes must be developed by the researcher. And they may sometimes require significant training of respondents in populations not familiar with the use of computers or optical scanning forms.

Handling Missing Data

As noted in the previous chapter, **item nonresponse** is a significant problem in most surveys. Some percentage of the survey instruments invariably suffer from it. As a matter of fact, the degree of item nonresponse often serves as a useful indicator of the quality of the research. When it is excessive, it calls the whole research effort into question and suggests that the research objectives and procedures should be examined critically. When it is in bounds, it is still necessary for the research director to make a decision regarding what should be done about the missing items before analyzing the data. There are several possible strategies:

item nonresponse
A source of nonsampling error that arises when a respondent agrees to an interview but refuses, or is unable, to answer specific questions.

7 *Discuss options for dealing with missing data in analyses.*

1. Leave the items blank, and report the number as a separate category. Although this procedure works well for some simple analyses (e.g., frequencies and cross tabulations), it does not work well for a number of other statistical techniques.

2. Eliminate the case with the missing item(s) from all further analyses. This strategy results in a "pure" data set with no missing information at all. The sample size will thus be equal for all analyses. This strategy, however, excludes data that may be perfectly useful for some analyses. In the extreme, the researcher might discard a questionnaire from which only a single piece of information was missing. Given that data are so valuable and sometimes difficult to collect, we would rarely recommend this strategy. Any case with a significant amount of missing information (say, half or more as a rule of thumb) should have been eliminated during the central office edit.

3. Eliminate the case with the missing item in analyses using the variable. When using this approach, the analyst must continually report the number of cases on which the analysis is based, since the sample size is not constant across analyses. It also ignores the fact that a significant degree of nonresponse on a particular item might be informative in that it suggests respondents do not care very deeply about the issue being addressed by the question or that they do not know the answer to the question. The obvious advantage to this strategy is that all available data are used for each analysis.

4. Substitute values for the missing items. Sometimes the analyst attempts to estimate a value for the missing item based on responses to other related items on the respondent's questionnaire, perhaps using a statistical technique known as *regression analysis,* which measures the relationship between two or more variables (see Chapter 21). Alternatively, sometimes the analyst uses the values from other respondents' questionnaires to determine the mean,

© David Young-Wolff/Photo Edit

median, or mode for the variable and substitutes that value for the missing item. The substitution of values makes maximum use of the data, since all the reasonably good cases are used. At the same time, it requires more work from the analyst, and it contains some potential for bias, because the analyst has "created" values where none previously existed. It also raises the question of which statistical technique should be used to generate the estimate.[8]

5. Eliminate the variable from a multi-item scale. Suppose that a researcher has developed a 10-item scale to measure satisfaction with a service provider and that one respondent has marked 8 of the items on her questionnaire and did not respond to the other two. Because the items are presumed to measure only slightly different aspects of the same construct (i.e., satisfaction), it is reasonable to simply compute an index score across the 8 available items. Of course, in this situation the index score must be the mean across items, not the sum of the items.

Research directors are forced to make difficult decisions about how to handle questionnaires with one or more items left blank. Often there is no one perfect solution.

6. Recontact the respondent. If the missing information is critical to the study and responses were not anonymous, it is sometimes possible to contact the respondent again to obtain the information. This approach is especially applicable if it appears that the respondent simply missed the item altogether or if the respondent tried to answer the question but didn't follow the instructions.

There is no "right" or simple answer as to how missing items should be handled. It all depends on the purposes of the study, the incidence of missing items, and the methods that will be used to analyze the data.

looking back...

Fortunately for his clients, Richard Batsell, a research pro (he is also a marketing professor at Rice University), did not stop by gathering ethnic data. He has also explored other patterns in ATM usage.

Batsell's firm, Analytica, also looked at age distributions and noted that age is associated with usage of ATM cards. In general, younger consumers are more likely to use ATMs, and younger consumers are also more heavily represented in ethnic minority groups than among non-Hispanic whites. In a study of Texas consumers, Analytica found that about 60 percent of people between the ages of 18 and 24 had an ATM card. Among those 65 and older, just 10 percent had a card.

Batsell judged that the age relationship provided a better explanation than the racial/ethnic categories. He hypothesized that older Americans had formed banking habits in the days before ATMs existed, so they were less likely to perceive a need for an ATM card.

Later, Batsell was startled by the results of a study he conducted for the Magic Line ATM network (since renamed NYCE) in the Midwest. In a single year, ATM usage among older Americans jumped from 8 percent—comparable to the findings of the Texas study—to 26 percent.

He found the likely answer to that surprise when he presented the results to a conference sponsored by Magic Line. After Batsell's presentation, the representatives of two large Michigan banks drew him aside to chat. They told him that they had tried to apply his earlier findings to their marketing programs. The banks defined the lower ATM usage rates of older customers as a signal the banks needed to learn more about these customers' banking habits and needs. They held focus groups with their older customers and discovered an unmet need. Many of their customers spent winters in the South and believed they needed separate checking accounts for their winter homes.

The Michigan banks began touting their cards as a more convenient alternative to dual checking accounts. The banks explained to their customers that they could use their Michigan ATM cards to access their funds while they were in Florida or Texas. Once the older customers realized this benefit, many started using ATM cards. The banks had used the research data to convert a marketing weakness into an opportunity.

Batsell routinely looks at a number of demographic variables when he studies ATM usage. Although other variables such as education level and income are important, age has been the most significant in predicting ATM usage. However, if more banks are as savvy as the ones in Michigan in marketing to their nonusers, that pattern may change. And Analytica will be right there measuring the new trends. ∎

Sources: "Knowledge 5 Power," ATM Magazine (September 24, 1999, downloaded from the ATM Magazine Web site, www.atmmagazine.com, October 7, 1999); "PULSE Study: Minorities Use ATM Cards More," *ATM Magazine* (May 5, 1999, downloaded from the ATM Magazine Web site, http://www.atmmagazine.com, October 7, 1999).

Summary

Learning Objective 1
Explain the purpose of the field edit.
The field edit is a preliminary edit designed to detect the most glaring omissions and inaccuracies in the data. It is also useful in helping to control the actions of the field force personnel and to clear up any misunderstanding they may have about directions, procedures, specific questions, and so on.

Learning Objective 2
Define what coding is.
Coding is the technical procedure by which data are categorized. Through coding, the raw data are transformed into symbols—usually numerals—that may be tabulated and counted. The transformation involves judgment on the part of the coder.

Learning Objective 3
Discuss two types of open-ended questions.
Some open-ended questions ask for specific information, or facts, from respondents, and are usually quite easy to code. Another type of open-ended question seeks less structured information and often allows multiple responses. This type of open-ended question is usually much more difficult to code.

Learning Objective 4
List the basic steps in coding open-ended responses.
1. Identify the separate responses given by each individual
2. Specify categories into which the responses can be placed
3. Place each response into one and only one category using multiple coders
4. Assess the degree of agreement between the multiple coders

Learning Objective 5
Describe the kinds of information contained in a codebook.
The codebook contains the general instructions indicating how each item of data was coded. It contains the variable names, location of each variable in the data file, a description of how each variable is coded, and an explanation of how missing data are treated in the data file.

Learning Objective 6
Describe common methods for cleaning the data file.
Blunders may be located by examining frequency distributions for all variables to identify obviously incorrect codings, by sampling records from the data file and comparing them with the original questionnaires, or by using double-entry of data in which data are entered into two separate data files and then compared for discrepancies.

Learning Objective 7
Discuss options for dealing with missing data in analyses.
Several options exist, including (a) reporting missing information as a separate category, (b) eliminating the case with missing information from all analyses, (c) eliminating the case with missing information from only analyses using variables with missing information, (d) substituting values for the missing items, (e) eliminating the variable (for that respondent only) from a multi-item scale, and (f) recontacting the respondent.

Key Terms

field edit (page 516)
central-office edit (page 516)
coding (page 518)
codebook (page 525)

blunder (page 526)
double-entry (page 526)
item nonresponse (page 527)

Review Questions

1. What are the differences in emphasis between a field edit and a central-office edit?
2. What should an editor do with incomplete answers? Obviously wrong answers? Answers that reflect a lack of interest?
3. How might a researcher best code "check all that apply" questions?
4. What are the two kinds of open-ended questions and why is one more difficult to code than the other?
5. What are the principles that underlie the establishment of categories so that responses to open-ended questions may be properly coded?
6. Why should multiple coders be used to establish categories and code responses for open-ended questions? Does this apply to all open-ended questions?
7. Suppose that you have a large number of very long questionnaires, making it impossible for one person to handle the entire coding task. How should the work be divided?
8. What methods are available for building a data file?
9. What is the purpose of the codebook?
10. If a respondent fails to answer a question on a survey, how should the item nonresponse be coded in the data file?
11. What is a blunder?
12. Distinguish between two types of blunders. Which is easier to spot?
13. What is double-entry of data?
14. What are the possible ways for dealing with missing data? Which strategy would you recommend?

Discussion Questions, Problems, and Projects

1. The KIST television station was conducting research in order to help develop programs that would be well received by the viewing audience and would be considered dependable sources of information. A two-part questionnaire was administered by personal interviews to a panel of 3,000 respondents residing in the city of Houston. The field and office edits were simultaneously done, so that the deadline of May 1 could be met. A senior supervisor, Marlene Howe, was placed in charge of the editing tasks and was assisted by two junior supervisors and two field-workers. The two field-workers were instructed to discard instruments that were illegible or incomplete. Each junior supervisor was instructed to scrutinize 1,500 of the instruments for incomplete answers, wrong answers, and responses that indicated a lack of interest. They were instructed to discard instruments that had more than five incomplete or wrong answers (the questionnaire contained 30 questions). In addition, they were asked to use their judgment in assessing whether the respondent showed a lack of interest and, if so, to discard the questionnaire.
   (a) Critically evaluate the above editing tasks. Please be specific.
   (b) Make specific recommendations to George Kist, the owner of the KIST television station, as to how the editing should be done.
2. (a) Establish response categories and codes for the question, "What do you like about this new brand of cereal?"
   (b) Code the following responses using your categories and codes.
       (1) "$1.50 is a reasonable price to pay for the cereal."
       (2) "The raisins and nuts add a nice flavor."
       (3) "The sizes of the packages are convenient."
       (4) "I like the sugarcoating on the cereal."
       (5) "The container does not tear and fall apart easily."
       (6) "My kids like the cartoons on the back of the packet."
       (7) "It is reasonably priced compared with other brands."
       (8) "The packet is attractive and easy to spot in the store."

PART 6:
Data Analysis

(9) "I like the price; it is not so low that I doubt the quality, and at the same time it is not so high as to be unaffordable."

(10) "The crispness and lightness of the cereal improve the taste."

3. (a) Establish response categories and codes for the following question, which was asked of a sample of business executives: "In your opinion, which types of companies have not been affected by the present economic climate?"

(b) Code the following responses using your categories and codes.

(1)	*Washington Post*	(9)	Marine Midlands Banks
(2)	Colgate Palmolive	(10)	Amana
(3)	Gillette	(11)	Holiday Inn
(4)	Hilton Hotels	(12)	The Dryden Press
(5)	Chase Manhattan	(13)	Whirlpool
(6)	Prentice-Hall	(14)	Chili's
(7)	Maytag	(15)	CitiBank
(8)	Fabergé		

4. Based on the following codebook, reconstruct the questionnaire used to gather information for a local restaurant.

Codebook for The Pasta Shop Project

Column(s)	Variable Name	Description
1–4	ID	Identification Number for respondent
5	RESID	Resident of Glendale at least 6 months per year? 1 = yes 2 = no
6	BAGES	Between ages of 18–74? 1 = yes 2 = no
7	AGEGROUP	What age group are you in? 1 = 18–24 2 = 25–44 3 = 45–74
8	SEX	Sex of respondent 1 = male 2 = female
9	DINEOUT	Number of times you dine out per 2 weeks? 1 = 1–2 times 2 = 3–4 times 3 = 5–6 times 4 = more than 6
10–11	REST1	Name your favorite restaurants? (open-ended) 01 = The Pasta Shop 02 = Applebee's 03 = El Chico 04 = Carter's 05 = Missy's Steakhouse 06 = Glendale Inn 07 = Hideaway 08 = Ko's Japanese Restaurant 09 = Pedro's 10 = Sirloin Stockade 11 = Doc's Seafood 12 = Western Sizzlin 13 = Al's Diner 14 = Denny's 15 = Pony Express

		16 = Lenny's
		17 = Red Lobster
		18 = Pizza Hut
		19 = Mom's Place
		20 = Brad's BBQ
		21 = Perkins
		22 = China Table
		23 = Bagel Shop
		24 = Pasta Palace
		25 = Dragon's Garden
12–13	REST2	Second favorite restaurant
14–15	REST3	Third favorite restaurant
16	AWARE	Have you heard of The Pasta Shop? 1 = yes 2 = no
17	NEWSPAPR	How did you hear of The Pasta Shop? By newspaper advertisement? 1 = yes 2 = no
18	RADIO	By radio advertisement? 1 = yes 2 = no
19	DRIVEBY	Did you drive by it? 1 = yes 2 = no
20	WORDOF	Word of mouth? 1 = yes 2 = no
21	DIDUEAT	Have you eaten at The Pasta Shop? 1 = yes 2 = no
22	SATISFY	Were you satisfied with overall service? (1–5, "extremely dissatisfied"–"extremely satisfied")
23	PRICE	Was the price you paid: 1 = too low 2 = about right 3 = too high

MISSING = BLANK

5. The following is a questionnaire to be completed by customers of the Hilltop Smoked Meat Co. Restaurant. Build a codebook that might be used to transfer raw answers from completed questionnaires to a data file. Be specific about locations in the data file, variable names, the codes to be used, and how missing data will be treated.

Hilltop Smoked Meat Co. Customer Survey

This survey was developed to get your opinions concerning satisfaction with your current visit to Hilltop. Please complete this survey after your meal and return it to us.

Check the boxes that most accurately reflect your candid opinion about Hilltop!
Your input and time are Greatly Appreciated!

1. Are You Currently a Customer During   Lunch ☐   Evening Meal ☐   In between ☐

2. Is this Your first visit to Hilltop?   Yes ☐   No ☐

3. If this is **not** Your first visit, approximately how many times have you eaten at Hilltop in the last 3 months? _____ times

How Would You Rate The Following:	Very Poor	Poor	Fair	Good	Very Good
4. Friendliness of the employees	☐	☐	☐	☐	☐
5. Speed of Service	☐	☐	☐	☐	☐
6. Cleanliness of the Establishment	☐	☐	☐	☐	☐
7. Price for the Quantity Received	☐	☐	☐	☐	☐
8. Price for the Quality Received	☐	☐	☐	☐	☐
9. Variety of Menu Items	☐	☐	☐	☐	☐
10. Overall Quality of the Food	☐	☐	☐	☐	☐
11. Overall Atmosphere	☐	☐	☐	☐	☐
12. How Convenient is this Location	☐	☐	☐	☐	☐
13. How would you rate Hilltop overall	☐	☐	☐	☐	☐

14. Are you aware of Hilltop's full catering menu?   Yes ☐   No ☐

15. Have you ever seen or heard an advertisement for Hilltop?   Yes ☐   No ☐

16. If you **Have, Check All that Apply:**

   Newspaper ☐   Radio ☐   Television ☐   Word of Mouth ☐

17. Do you come to Hilltop more often for:

   Dine-in Lunch ☐   Dine-in Dinner ☐   Take-out Lunch ☐   Take-out Dinner ☐

18. What, if any, items would you like to see added to the menu? _____

_____

19. What is your favorite item on the menu? _____

20. What is your zip code? _____

Thank You for your participation!

6. A research team is working on an important project and has decided to use double-entry to identify and eliminate blunders. The following are data from the first 12 respondents as they appear in the two data files constructed during the double-entry process. Enter each of the data sets into a separate file and use the "compare versions" option in a word processing software package to identify blunders.

Data Set A
00116593584585455658455689555758559
0026954582 135 65565535 55647653257
00316548857897865442554098900 43434
004142323455 514925342383694458596
00510292374764564534234234235346457
00658478319283537456758495665256475
007655445455414243 544556462345456
008948584958878485878478574 72721646
00957473135444645457513122312245465
0107346197845 58645427276469458
011738751946738549464 579454356475
01269787564615846 7647 9565749455365

Data Set B
00116593584585455658455689555758559
0026954582 135 65565535 55647653257
00316548847897865442554098900 43434
004142323455 514925342383694458596
00510292374764564534234234235346457
00658478319283537456758495665226475
007655445455414243 544556462345456
008948584958878485878478574 72721646
00957473135444645457513122312245465
0107346197845 58645427576469458
011738751946738549464 579454356475
01269787564615846 7647 9565749455365

Suggested Additional Readings

For useful discussion of the purposes and procedures to follow when editing and coding data, see John A. Sonquist and William C. Dunkelberg, *Survey and Opinion Research: Procedures for Processing and Analysis* (Englewood Cliffs, N.J.: Prentice-Hall, 1977), especially pp. 41–196.

Chapter 20

Data Analysis: Analyzing Individual Variables and Basics of Hypothesis Testing

© PhotoDisc/Getty Images

Learning Objectives

1. Distinguish between univariate and multivariate analyses.

2. Describe frequency analysis.

3. Explain the various ways in which frequency analysis can be used.

4. Discuss confidence intervals for proportions.

5. Describe commonly used descriptive statistics.

6. Discuss confidence intervals for means.

7. List the steps involved in hypothesis testing.

8. Describe the chi-square goodness-of-fit test and compare it to the Kolmogorov-Smirnov test.

9. Discuss the process for comparing a proportion against a standard.

10. Describe the appropriate tests for comparing a mean against a standard for (a) small samples and (b) large samples.

John Wanamaker made a fortune in retailing, but is better known for a statement so widely quoted that it has become a marketing cliché: "I know that half of my advertising doesn't work. The problem is, I don't know which half." Marketers still repeat his lament—which is surprising, given modern research techniques.

One company that has *not* been content to complain is Frito-Lay. Several years ago, the snack-food giant carried out a series of experiments, based on earlier work by Leonard Lodish of the University of Pennsylvania's Wharton School of Business.

Professor Lodish and his colleagues tested common assumptions about advertising. They examined historical data from Behaviorscan, a database of purchases by thousands of households, collected using store scanners. The households in the Behaviorscan panel receive all of their television programming on cable, so marketers can add or remove advertisements and identify whether their ads are associated with a change in purchases. The researchers matched advertising for certain products with sales volume and market share for those products, testing common assumptions, such as the following:

- Marketers assume that spending more than competitors on advertising leads to increased sales. But this was not necessarily the case. Some ads were effective; spending more on those ads led to a significant sales increase. Other ads were ineffective; increased spending on those ads did not make much difference in sales.
- Advertisers believe that TV ads require a long time to produce a sales increase. Again, this assumption did not hold up. The effective ads typically boosted sales within six months.

Lodish's study also looked for factors associated with advertising effectiveness. The researchers compared households exposed to the same ad, but with different frequencies and amounts of exposure. They also compared households exposed to different ads for the same product, but with the same frequencies and amounts of exposure. In all cases, they studied advertising of low-priced packaged goods purchased often.

The study found that advertising was associated with greater sales volume and market share under certain conditions. For example, increasing the amount and frequency of advertising was particularly effective for smaller, less-established brands. The common practice of scheduling advertising to run for a few weeks and then take a break for a few weeks (called "flighting") was not effective. New ad messages were associated with greater sales; old copy was less effective. Standard methods of measuring advertising "success"— recall of the ad and statements that the ad was persuasive—were not associated with sales increases.

Looking at such historical data is interesting, but Frito-Lay needed information for decisions about the future.

Discussion Issues

1. What ideas about its advertising ("hypotheses") should Frito-Lay test?

2. How could Frito-Lay measure whether its advertising is effective?

3. Why have consumer-products companies been slow to test advertising effectiveness? ■

There are some aspects of marketing research that are relatively difficult. Fortunately, data analysis is usually not one of them, despite what many students seem to believe. As we will demonstrate in the next two chapters, data analysis hinges on two key considerations about the variable(s) to be analyzed. First, will the variable be analyzed in isolation (univariate analysis) or in relationship to one or more other variables (multivariate analysis)? Second, what level of measurement (nominal, ordinal, interval, ratio) was used to measure the variable(s)? Analysis generally proceeds in a straightforward manner once these questions are answered.

In this chapter, we present a number of common types of univariate data analysis techniques and introduce the concept of hypothesis testing. A great many analyses in applied marketing research involve simple univariate analyses. For example, the publisher of a magazine might want to know the proportion of the magazine's readers that are male; a restaurant might like to know the average income of its typical diner; a service provider might need to know her customers' average level of satisfaction with the services provided. In each of these cases, a single variable is analyzed in isolation—gender, income, satisfaction.

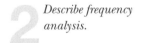

1 *Distinguish between univariate and multivariate analyses.*

Basic Univariate Statistics: Categorical Measures

Because both nominal and ordinal measures are easily used to group respondents or objects into groups or categories, researchers often refer to these types of measures as **categorical measures.** For example, suppose a researcher collected data at the household level via mail survey for a study on car ownership (Exhibit 20.1) using a probability sample and that the 100 people to whom the questionnaire was sent all replied. Among other things, the client wanted to know (1) how many families had financed their most recent car purchase and (2) the proportion of respondents who indicated that a particular model of car (Brand A) was their first choice for the next car purchase. The first measure is clearly at the nominal level of measurement: each responding family belongs to either the "did finance" group or the "did not finance" group. The second measure was assessed at the ordinal level of measurement. Respondents were told to rank order their preference for five different brands of cars. The task is to determine the proportion of responding families that fall into the "first choice" group for the particular brand. Answers to both questions are easily obtained via frequency analysis.

categorical measures
A commonly used expression for nominal and ordinal measures.

Frequency Analysis (One-Way Tabulation)

A **frequency analysis,** sometimes called a one-way tabulation because a single variable is considered, consists of counting the number of cases that fall into the various response categories. Frequencies may be repeated for each of the variables in the study, but the tabulation for each variable is independent of the tabulation for the other variables.

Although frequency tabulations can be done by hand when there are only a few variables and/or a limited number of responses to be counted, most studies rely on computer tabulation using packaged statistical programs such as SPSS (Statistical Package for the Social Sciences) and many others. Some will calculate summary statistics and plot a histogram of the values (discussed later in the chapter) in addition to reporting the number of cases in each category.

Exhibit 20.2 presents the frequency analysis for the variable representing whether or not the family had financed the most recent car purchase. The standard SPSS output for a frequency analysis includes the raw count of cases falling into each category, the percentage of total cases falling into each category, the percentage of valid (nonmissing) cases falling into each category, and the cumulative valid percentage for each category. As indicated, 30 of the 100 families in the survey financed their most recent car purchase. Because our example uses a sample size of 100 and there are no missing cases, the next two columns have identical entries as the column showing the raw count, so it makes little difference which would be included in a table presenting these results. However, this is not the normal situation. As a

2 *Describe frequency analysis.*

frequency analysis
A count of the number of cases that fall into each category when the categories are based on one variable.

general rule, when presenting frequency results the count as well as the valid percentage should be included for each category. Sometimes the percentages are presented in parentheses immediately to the right or below the actual count entry in the table. Sometimes only the percentages are presented; if so, the total number of cases on which the percentages are

Exhibit 20.1

Raw Data for Car Ownership Study

Family Ident. No.	(1) Income in Dollars	(2) Number of Members in Family	(3) Education of Household Head in Yrs.	(4) Region Where Live N = North S = South	(5) Lifestyle Orientation L = Liberal C = Conservative	(6) Number of Cars Family Owns	(7) Did Family Finance the Car Purchase?	(8) Does Family Own Station Wagon?	(9) Does Family Own Foreign Car?	(10) Does Family Own Van?	(11) Does Family Own Some Other Kind of Car?	(12) Preference Rank, Brand A (1 = First Choice)
1001	26,800	3	12	N	L	1	N	N	N	Y	N	3
1002	17,400	4	12	N	L	1	N	N	N	N	Y	2
1003	14,300	2	10	N	L	1	N	N	N	N	Y	2
1004	35,400	4	9	N	L	1	N	N	N	N	Y	5
1005	24,000	3	8	N	L	1	N	N	N	N	Y	1
1006	17,200	2	12	N	L	1	N	N	Y	N	N	1
1007	27,000	4	12	N	L	1	N	N	N	N	Y	5
1008	16,900	3	10	N	L	1	N	N	N	N	Y	2
1009	26,700	2	12	N	L	1	N	N	N	N	Y	2
1010	13,800	4	6	N	C	1	Y	N	N	N	Y	3
1011	34,100	3	8	N	C	1	N	N	N	N	Y	1
1012	16,300	3	11	N	C	1	N	N	N	N	Y	4
1013	14,700	2	12	N	C	1	N	N	N	N	Y	3
1014	25,400	4	12	N	C	1	N	N	N	N	Y	1
1015	15,400	4	12	N	C	1	N	N	N	N	Y	4
1016	25,900	3	11	N	C	1	Y	N	N	N	Y	5
1017	36,300	3	12	N	C	1	N	N	N	N	Y	2
1018	27,400	2	12	N	C	2	N	N	N	N	Y	2
1019	17,300	2	12	N	C	1	N	N	N	N	Y	3
1020	13,700	3	8	N	C	1	N	N	N	N	Y	1
1021	26,100	2	12	N	C	1	N	N	Y	N	N	2
1022	16,300	4	12	N	C	1	Y	N	N	N	Y	4
1023	33,800	3	6	N	C	1	N	N	N	N	Y	3
1024	34,400	4	8	N	C	1	N	N	N	N	Y	1
1025	15,300	2	9	N	C	1	Y	N	N	N	Y	1
1026	35,900	3	12	N	C	1	N	N	N	N	Y	5
1027	15,100	4	12	S	L	1	N	N	N	Y	N	4
1028	17,200	2	12	S	L	1	N	N	N	N	N	2
1029	35,400	4	10	S	L	1	N	N	N	N	Y	3
1030	15,600	3	12	S	L	1	N	N	N	N	Y	1
1031	24,900	3	12	S	L	1	N	N	N	N	Y	1
1032	34,800	4	11	S	C	1	N	N	N	Y	N	1
1033	14,600	4	12	S	C	1	N	N	N	N	Y	3
1034	23,100	3	9	S	C	1	N	N	N	N	Y	1
1035	15,900	3	12	S	C	1	N	N	N	Y	N	4
1036	26,700	4	12	S	C	1	N	N	N	N	Y	2
1037	17,300	4	12	S	C	1	N	N	N	Y	N	3
1038	37,100	3	12	S	C	1	N	N	N	Y	N	1
1039	14,000	3	10	S	C	1	N	N	N	N	Y	5
1040	23,600	3	10	S	C	1	N	N	N	N	Y	4
1041	16,200	3	12	S	C	1	N	N	N	N	Y	3
1042	24,100	4	10	S	C	1	N	N	N	Y	N	4
1043	12,700	2	8	S	C	1	N	N	N	N	Y	1
1044	26,000	4	13	S	L	1	N	Y	N	N	N	2
1045	15,400	3	16	N	L	2	N	Y	Y	N	N	5
1046	16,900	4	16	N	L	1	N	N	N	N	Y	4
1047	23,800	6	10	S	C	1	Y	Y	N	N	N	4
1048	37,100	8	16	N	L	2	Y	N	Y	N	Y	2
1049	16,800	5	15	S	C	2	Y	N	Y	N	Y	3
1050	22,900	5	8	N	L	1	N	Y	N	N	N	1
1051	13,700	6	8	N	L	1	Y	Y	N	N	N	1

PART 6:
Data Analysis

based must be provided. The number of missing cases (none in our example), along with percent of total cases missing, can be included as a note to the table. Alternatively, some researchers prefer to simply present missing cases (and associated percentage of total) as a

Exhibit 20.1

Raw Data for Car Ownership Study (*continued*)

Family Ident. No.	(1) Income in Dollars	(2) Number of Members in Family	(3) Education of Household Head in Yrs.	(4) Region Where Live N = North S = South	(5) Lifestyle Orientation L = Liberal C = Conservative	(6) Number of Cars Family Owns	(7) Did Family Finance the Car Purchase?	(8) Does Family Own Station Wagon?	(9) Does Family Own Foreign Car?	(10) Does Family Own Van?	(11) Does Family Own Some Other Kind of Car?	(12) Preference Rank, Brand A (1 = First Choice)
1052	26,800	8	12	S	C	2	N	Y	N	N	Y	2
1053	16,100	8	12	N	L	2	N	N	N	N	Y	4
1054	25,700	5	12	N	C	1	N	N	N	N	Y	1
1055	38,200	2	12	N	L	1	N	N	N	N	Y	5
1056	49,800	3	12	N	L	1	Y	N	N	N	Y	5
1057	60,400	4	12	N	L	1	Y	N	N	N	Y	3
1058	39,000	2	12	N	L	1	N	N	N	N	Y	2
1059	57,600	4	12	N	L	1	Y	N	N	N	Y	2
1060	42,000	3	12	N	L	1	N	N	N	N	Y	4
1061	38,600	3	12	N	L	1	N	N	N	Y	N	1
1062	66,400	4	12	N	L	2	Y	N	Y	N	Y	2
1063	71,200	2	12	N	L	1	Y	N	N	N	Y	3
1064	49,300	4	10	N	C	1	Y	N	N	N	Y	3
1065	37,700	4	10	N	C	1	Y	N	N	N	Y	4
1066	72,400	3	12	N	C	2	N	N	Y	N	Y	1
1067	88,700	3	12	N	C	1	N	N	N	Y	N	1
1068	44,200	2	12	S	L	1	Y	N	N	N	Y	3
1069	55,100	3	12	S	L	2	N	N	N	Y	Y	5
1070	73,300	4	12	S	L	1	N	N	N	Y	N	4
1071	80,200	2	12	S	L	1	Y	N	N	N	Y	2
1072	39,300	3	10	S	C	2	N	N	N	Y	Y	3
1073	48,200	4	12	S	C	1	N	N	N	N	Y	1
1074	57,800	2	12	S	C	1	Y	N	N	N	Y	2
1075	38,000	3	10	S	C	1	Y	N	N	Y	N	1
1076	81,300	4	16	N	L	1	N	Y	N	N	N	3
1077	96,900	4	16	N	L	2	N	N	N	N	Y	5
1078	44,700	3	14	N	L	1	N	N	N	N	Y	5
1079	107,300	3	17	N	L	1	N	N	N	N	Y	3
1080	38,100	2	13	N	L	2	Y	N	N	N	Y	2
1081	304,200	2	14	N	L	1	N	N	N	N	Y	4
1082	46,100	3	16	S	L	1	N	N	N	Y	N	1
1083	49,300	4	13	S	L	1	N	N	N	N	Y	1
1084	160,800	4	16	S	L	9	N	N	N	N	Y	5
1085	39,100	4	16	S	L	1	N	N	N	Y	N	3
1086	46,400	2	14	S	C	1	N	N	N	Y	N	4
1087	58,300	6	10	N	L	2	Y	N	N	N	Y	3
1088	47,800	5	10	N	L	2	Y	Y	N	N	Y	1
1089	58,000	7	8	N	L	2	Y	Y	N	N	Y	4
1090	69,600	9	12	N	L	2	Y	Y	N	N	Y	1
1091	44,200	11	12	N	L	2	N	Y	Y	N	Y	2
1092	62,100	6	10	N	L	2	Y	Y	N	N	Y	3
1093	99,000	5	12	S	L	3	Y	N	Y	Y	Y	5
1094	53,300	6	12	S	L	2	N	Y	N	N	Y	1
1095	72,200	9	10	S	C	2	N	Y	N	Y	N	3
1096	64,700	7	12	S	C	2	Y	Y	N	Y	N	3
1097	77,300	6	16	N	L	2	Y	Y	Y	N	N	3
1098	116,900	10	18	N	L	3	Y	Y	Y	N	Y	5
1099	71,200	7	15	S	L	1	N	N	N	Y	N	2
1100	103,800	5	16	S	C	2	Y	Y	Y	N	N	4

© Eyewire/Getty Images

separate category in the table. Both approaches have merit, but the former is typically easier to understand, yet still makes all pertinent information available to the reader.

Before going further, we need to mention a couple of points about the use of percentages for reporting results. It is always good practice to include percentages along with the raw count for frequency analyses because percentages are a tremendous aid to readers trying to interpret results. To illustrate, suppose that we had obtained 687 responses instead of 100 and that 206 of the responding households had financed the most recent car purchase. Without percentages, the reader is forced to estimate how small or large a portion 206 is of the 687 respondents in order to interpret the results. It is far better to simply look at the table and see that 206 represents 30% of responding households. Note that the percentages should be rounded off to whole numbers (i.e., no decimals), because whole numbers are easier to read and because decimals may convey a greater accuracy than the figures can support, especially in a small sample. While in some cases the analyst might be justified in reporting percentages to one decimal place (rarely two decimal places), the general rule in reporting percentages is that unless decimals have a special purpose, they should be omitted.[1]

Frequency analysis can be used to establish a nominal measure, such as how many new buyers finance their vehicles; or to establish an ordinal—or ranking—measure, such as preferences for different models or brands.

Exhibit 20.3 presents frequency results for the preference rankings for Brand A using an appropriate format. As seen, 26% of respondents indicated Brand A as their first choice for a new car purchase; 14% indicated that Brand A was the least preferred choice among five brands.

Other Uses for Frequencies

3 *Explain the various ways in which frequency analysis can be used.*

A frequency analysis, in addition to communicating the results of a study, can be used for several other purposes. For example, frequencies are useful for determining the degree of item nonresponse for a variable and for locating blunders. For these reasons alone, one-way tabulations should be produced for all variables included in a study before any additional data analysis is attempted. Frequencies can also be used to locate outliers and to determine the empirical distribution of the variable in question.

outlier
An observation so different in magnitude from the rest of the observations that the analyst chooses to treat it as a special case.

One use of frequency analysis is to locate **outliers,** which are not blunders but rather observations so different in magnitude from the rest of the observations that the analyst chooses to treat them as special cases. This may mean eliminating the observation from the analysis or determining the specific factors that generate this unique observation. For instance, consider

Exhibit 20.2

Did Family Finance Car Purchase?

Finance?	Number	Percent	Valid Percent	Cumulative Valid Percent
Yes	30	30	30	30
No	70	70	70	100
	100	100	100	

Exhibit 20.3

Preference Ranking for Brand A

Preference Ranking	Number	Percent
First	26	26
Second	20	20
Third	23	23
Fourth	17	17
Fifth	14	14
	100	100

(number of missing cases = 0)

Exhibit 20.4

Income Distribution of Respondents in Car Ownership Study

Income	Number of Families		Cumulative Number of Families	
Less than $15,000	8	(8)	8	(8)
$15,000 to $24,900	25	(25)	33	(33)
$25,000 to $34,900	15	(15)	48	(48)
$35,000 to $44,900	18	(18)	66	(66)
$45,000 to $54,900	8	(8)	74	(74)
$55,000 to $64,900	8	(8)	82	(82)
$65,000 to $74,900	7	(7)	89	(89)
$75,000 to $84,900	3	(3)	92	(92)
$85,000 to $94,900	1	(1)	93	(93)
$95,000 to $104,900	3	(3)	96	(96)
More than $105,000	4	(4)	100	(100)
Total number of families	100	(100)		

the tabulation of incomes contained in Exhibit 20.4. (These results were obtained after grouping respondent incomes into categories.) The frequency results indicate there are four families with incomes greater than $105,000. A review of the raw data in Exhibit 20.1 indicates that only one family had an annual income greater than $161,000, namely Number 1081 with an income of $304,200. This is clearly out of line with the rest of the sample and is properly considered an outlier. What the analyst chooses to do with this observation depends on the objectives of the study. In this case, it is not unreasonable for a family to have such an income, so the observation will be retained in the analysis for the present time.

Another use of the one-way frequency tabulation is to determine the empirical distribution of the characteristic in question, particularly for interval and ratio-level measures. Some analysts ignore the distribution of the variables, but this can be a serious mistake. It is always a good idea to get a sense of a variable's distribution before performing any analysis with it. The distribution of a variable can be visualized through a **histogram,** a form of bar chart in which successive values of the variable are placed along the abscissa, or X axis, and the absolute frequency (i.e., raw count) or relative frequency (i.e., proportion or percentage) of occurrence of the values is indicated along the ordinate, or Y axis. The histogram for the income results presented in Exhibit 20.4 appears as Figure 20.1, with the incomes over $105,000 omitted because their inclusion would have required an undue extension of the income axis. It is readily apparent that the distribution of incomes is skewed to the right. Some analysts prefer to construct the **frequency polygon,** which is obtained from the histogram by connecting the midpoints of the bars with straight lines. The frequency polygon for incomes is plotted on the histogram in Figure 20.1.

histogram
A form of bar chart on which the values of the variable are placed along the abscissa, or X axis, and the absolute frequency or relative frequency of occurrence of the values is indicated along the ordinate, or Y axis.

frequency polygon
A figure obtained from a histogram by connecting the midpoints of the bars of the histogram with straight lines.

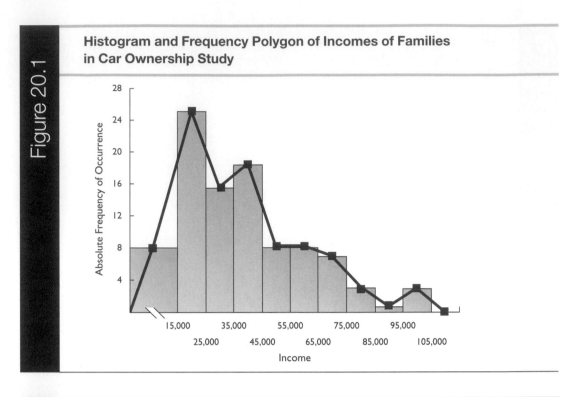

Figure 20.1

Histogram and Frequency Polygon of Incomes of Families in Car Ownership Study

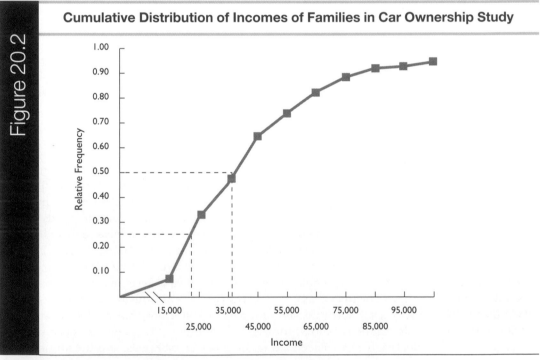

Figure 20.2

Cumulative Distribution of Incomes of Families in Car Ownership Study

cumulative distribution function

A function that shows the number of cases having a value less than or equal to a specified quantity; the function is generated by connecting points representing the given combinations of X's (values) and Y's (cumulative frequencies) with straight lines.

An alternative way of gaining insight into the empirical distribution is through the empirical **cumulative distribution function.** Once again, the frequency analysis is the source of the data. In this case, however, the percentage of observations with a value less than or equal to a specified quantity is determined; that is, the cumulative frequencies are generated. Thus, in the right-hand column of Exhibit 20.4, we see 8% of families with incomes less than $15,000, whereas 33% of families (8% + 25%) have incomes of $24,900 or less and 48% of families (8% + 25% + 15%) have incomes of $34,900 or less. Figure 20.2 presents the cumulative distribution of incomes as a graph. The empirical cumulative distribution function is generated by connecting the points representing the given combinations of X's (values) and Y's (cumulative frequencies) with straight lines.

The cumulative distribution function can be used to calculate some of the commonly used measures of location, such as the median, quartiles, and percentiles. These can simply be read from the plot once the cumulative percentages are entered. By definition, the sample median is that value for which 50 percent of the values lie below it and 50 percent above it. To read the sample median from the plot of the cumulative distribution, simply extend a horizontal line from 0.50 on the relative frequency ordinate until it intersects the graph, and then drop a vertical line from the point of intersection to the X axis. The point of intersection with the X axis is the approximate sample median. In this example, the sample median is approximately $35,700. The quality of the approximation could be checked by actually determining the median using the detailed data, perhaps by computing a cumulative distribution function for the original ratio-level measure of income in dollars rather than using the income categories created for Exhibit 20.4.

Sample quartiles could be determined in similar fashion. The first sample quartile (also known as the 25th percentile) is that value for which 25 percent of the observations are below it. The first sample quartile is determined by drawing a horizontal line from 0.25 on the relative frequency ordinate until it intersects the graph, dropping a vertical line from the point of intersection to the horizontal axis, and reading off the value of the first quartile at the point of intersection with the X axis. The first quartile is thus found to be $17,300. The procedure for the third quartile (75th percentile) or any other percentile would be the same as that for the median or first quartile. The only change would be where the horizontal line began. Again, the cumulative distribution function for the original ratio-level measure of income would be more precise.

Frequency analyses are also useful for determining the mode in a distribution. The mode, or the most frequently occurring item, can be read directly from the one-way tabulation. Thus, Exhibit 20.3 suggests that the modal preference for Brand A was first out of the five options given.

In sum, the frequency analysis is an incredible tool for communicating research results as well as the basic input to the histogram, frequency polygon, and empirical cumulative distribution function. Wise analysts quickly learn that it is worth the time to produce frequencies for all study variables and many times to plot the results in order to get a sense of how the variables are distributed.[2]

Confidence Intervals for Proportions

Consider again the initial information sought by the client in the car ownership study: How many families had financed their most recent car purchase? The frequency analysis presented in Exhibit 20.2 revealed that 30 families, or 30% of the sample, had done so. In general, however, we are less interested in what happened for a particular sample than in what would be true for the entire population. Recall that we draw a sample to represent the population. In this case, our best guess is that 30% of families in the population financed the car purchase, but because of sampling error we cannot be confident that this estimate is precisely true for the population.

Fortunately, because an appropriate sample was drawn (i.e., a probabilistic sample), we are able to make inferences about the population as a whole based on the results from the sample. The concept of a **confidence interval** was introduced in Chapter 15. A confidence interval is a projection of the range within which a population parameter will lie at a given level of confidence based on a statistic obtained from an appropriately drawn sample. To produce a confidence interval, all we need to do is calculate the degree of sampling error for the particular statistic. To calculate sampling error for a proportion, we need three pieces of information: (1) z, the z score representing the desired degree of confidence (usually 95% confidence, where $z = 1.96$); (2) n, the number of valid cases overall for the proportion; and

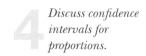
Discuss confidence intervals for proportions.

confidence interval
A projection of the range within which a population parameter will lie at a given level of confidence based on a statistic obtained from a probabilistic sample.

(3) p, the relevant proportion obtained from the sample. These pieces of information are entered into the following formula for sampling error for a proportion:

$$\text{sampling error for proportion} = z\sqrt{\frac{p(1-p)}{n}}$$

Drawing from the information presented in Exhibit 20.2, the degree of sampling error for the proportion of families who financed the most recent car purchase is thus:

$$\text{sampling error} = 1.96\sqrt{\frac{.30(1-.30)}{100}} = .09$$

The confidence interval itself is constructed around the sample statistic in the following manner:

$$(p - \text{sampling error} \leq \pi \leq p + \text{sampling error})$$
$$(0.30 - 0.09 \leq \pi \leq 0.30 + 0.09)$$
$$\text{or } (0.21, 0.39)$$

Accordingly, we can be 95% confident that the actual proportion of families who financed the car purchase *within the population* (π) lies between .21 and .39. This is a strong statement that highlights the beauty of probabilistic sampling. Even though the researchers took measures on only 100 families, they have a strong notion of what the answer would have been had they taken measures from all families within the population. As we discussed at length with respect to sample size calculation, if the analyst wants a narrower confidence interval (i.e., greater precision), she can decrease the degree of confidence desired (e.g., at 90% confidence, $z = 1.65$) or increase sample size.

A word of caution, however, before we start letting the numbers do the thinking for us. The confidence interval only takes sampling error into account. To the extent that nonsampling error has entered the study (see Chapter 18)—and you can be assured that it has to some degree—the confidence interval is less likely to have "captured" the population parameter within its bounds. Unfortunately, there is no quantitative way of adjusting the confidence interval to reflect these types of errors. Suppose that an organization promoting the lowering of taxes reported survey results indicating that 90% of U.S. citizens were in favor of lowering federal income taxes, with +/− 3% margin of sampling error at 95% confidence. Further suppose that the organization obtained this result through the use of a leading question and that the proportion representing the true sentiment of citizens is somewhat lower. The resulting confidence interval itself is probably accurate in the sense that we can be 95% confident that if all U.S. citizens were asked the same leading question, the proportion in favor of lowering income taxes would fall between .87 and .93. Obviously, however, the error introduced by the leading question makes it entirely unlikely that the actual proportion of citizens who want to lower taxes falls within this interval. As we have noted elsewhere, reducing total error is the key, and researchers must resist the temptation to focus too closely on sampling error simply because it can be readily assessed.

Basic Univariate Statistics: Continuous Measures

continuous measures
A commonly used expression for interval and ratio measures.

Because interval- and ratio-level measures are similar when it comes to analysis (the mean is the most commonly calculated statistic for both types), many researchers refer to both types as **continuous measures,** even though the label is not technically correct, especially for interval measures such as rating scales. For example, consider the household incomes reported by the

PART 6:
Data Analysis

respondents in the car ownership study in Exhibit 20.1. Suppose that the client needs this information to make an important decision.

Descriptive Statistics

For continuous measures, there are numerous types of descriptive statistics that can be calculated. **Descriptive statistics** describe the distribution of responses on a variable, including measures of central tendency (mean, median, and mode), measures of the spread, or variation, in the distribution (range, variance, standard deviation), and various measures of the shape of the distribution (e.g., skewness, kurtosis). In this section, we discuss the calculation and interpretation of two commonly used descriptive statistics, the mean and standard deviation.

The **sample mean** ($\bar{x}$) is simply the arithmetic mean value across all responses for the variable and is found using the following formula:

$$\bar{x} = \frac{\sum\limits_{i=1}^{n} X_i}{n}$$

where X_i is the value of the variable for the ith respondent and n is the total number of responses. In the car ownership study, mean household income is found by summing the income values across respondents and dividing by 100, the total number of valid cases. Fortunately, all statistics packages will easily calculate variable means. In this example, the computed mean household income turns out to be $43,773.

Although means are easy to calculate or obtain from computer output, there are several issues to keep in mind. First, while mean values can be calculated for any variable in a data set, they are only meaningful for continuous (i.e., interval, ratio) measures. Thus, knowing that the mean lifestyle orientation is 1.45 or that the mean preference rank for Brand A is 2.73 is of little value at best—and misleading at worst—because these variables are at the nominal and ordinal levels of measurement, respectively. The mean is only useful with equal-interval scales, one of the common characteristics of interval and ratio measures.

A second issue with respect to interpreting mean values concerns spurious precision. Just as we advised against the use of decimals with percentages, we must caution the analyst to carefully consider just how precise a mean value can be. The degree of precision of the outcome (the mean) depends fully upon the degree of precision of the inputs (the values in the sample to be averaged). Consider the original values of household income shown in Exhibit 20.1. Each of these values appears to have been rounded off at the hundreds level (e.g., $26,800 rather than $26,817 for Number 1001). Knowing this, is it reasonable to report that mean household income for the sample was $43,773? The appropriate value to report for mean household income would be $43,800.

The third issue about mean values concerns their use with variables with one or more extreme cases, or outliers. As noted earlier, one household reported an income of $304,200, a value far greater than any other in the data set. Although this is likely a valid response and should not be automatically excluded from all analyses, its presence has a marked effect on the resulting mean income for the sample. For variables with large outliers, the median value is often a more representative indicator of central tendency for the distribution. A frequency analysis of the income variable reveals that the median household income (i.e., the value falling at the 50th percentile) in the sample is $35,400. Because this value is substantially lower than the arithmetic mean of $43,800 the choice of mean or median to represent the distribution becomes an important issue. As a simple example, suppose that an automobile manufacturer was basing an important decision on whether or not the average income was at least $40,000. The choice of which "average" income value to consider (i.e., mean vs. median) will affect the managers' decision. As a rule, the appropriate univariate measure of central tendency for variables with extreme responses is the median because it more accurately portrays

5 *Describe commonly used descriptive statistics.*

descriptive statistics
Statistics that describe the distribution of responses on a variable. The most commonly used descriptive statistics are the mean and standard deviation.

sample mean
The arithmetic average value of the responses on a variable.

the vast majority of cases. Alternatively, the extreme cases can be temporarily ignored and the mean calculated across the remaining cases.[3]

The **sample standard deviation** (*s*) provides a convenient measure of the variation in responses for continuous measures. If there is little difference in a particular response across the sample, that is, everyone was basically the same on some characteristic or felt the same way about some topic or object, then the standard deviation will be very small. If, on the other hand, responses are different—some high, some low—then the standard deviation for the variable will be larger. Failing to take the variation of responses into account can lead to poor decisions. Consider the case of a new sauce product:

© Terri L. Miller/E-Visual Communications, Inc.

On the average, consumers wanted it neither really hot nor really mild. The mean rating of the test participants was quite close to the middle of the scale, which had "very mild" and "very hot" as its bipolar adjectives. This happened to fit the client's preconceived notion.

However, examination of the distribution of the ratings revealed the existence of a large proportion of consumers who wanted the sauce to be mild and an equally large proportion who wanted it to be hot. Relatively few wanted the in-between product, which would have been suggested by looking at the mean rating alone.[4]

Basing decisions on the mean rating alone can lead to serious blunders. The mean rating in a survey of a new salsa product suggests that consumers want medium spiciness but looking at the mean alone would miss the two large populations that want a very mild or very spicy salsa.

Imagine that a manufacturer of a new type of automobile is trying to decide how many seats an "average" family needs in a car. The data from the car ownership study suggest that the mean number of family members per household in our sample is 4.0. Should the manufacturer proceed to build only cars with four seats? Of course not; a quick review of Exhibit 20.1 reveals lots of families with less than four members and lots of families with more than four members. (In fact, a frequency analysis for the variable indicates that only 29% of families had exactly four members; 49% had less than four; and 22% had more than four.) This variation is quantified for this continuous variable using the following formula for the sample standard deviation:

$$s = \sqrt{\frac{\sum_{i=1}^{n}(x_i - \bar{x})^2}{n-1}}$$

where X_i is the value of the variable for the *i*th respondent, $\bar{x}$ is the mean value of the variable, and *n* is the total number of responses. Again, statistical software packages easily calculate descriptive statistics including the standard deviation. In this example, the sample standard deviation equals 1.9, further evidence of considerable spread in family size.

Because of the important information about variation held by the standard deviation, analysts reporting descriptive statistics for continuous measures should almost always report standard deviations along with mean values. A word of caution, however: issues related to spurious precision and the presence of outlier cases apply to standard deviations as well as to means. In addition, the standard deviation is meaningful and appropriate only for interval- and ratio-level measures.

Converting Continuous Measures to Categorical Measures

Sometimes analysts find it useful to convert interval- or ratio-level measures to categorical measures. Because higher levels of measurement have all the properties of measures lower in the hierarchy, this conversion is perfectly acceptable and in many cases advisable for aiding in interpretation of research study results. Exhibit 20.4 was created by converting open-ended responses to an income question (ratio-level measure) into 11 income categories (ordinal-level measure). Was this conversion necessary for describing the sample with respect to income? In a technical sense, no. The researchers could have simply reported descriptive statistics for the original measure ($\bar{x} = \$39,900$, $s = \$24,500$, two outliers removed; median = $\$35,400$). On the other hand, Exhibit 20.4 allows a condensed picture of the distribution that should be easy for managers or other readers to grasp, particularly when presented in combination with the descriptive statistics.

There are few rules for the actual conversion process. Normally, as with Exhibit 20.4, analysts use their own judgment to determine relevant categories. Occasionally, a client will have a predetermined structure for categories. In other cases, the data themselves determine category divisions. For example, researchers who want to convert a continuous measure into two approximately equal-sized groups often will create categories based on a **median split.** That is, the cumulative percent column of the frequency analysis output (or the corresponding cumulative distribution function plot) will identify a value at the 50th percentile, and values up to and including this value will form one group (typically the "low" group for ratio measures) and values above the median value will form the second group (the "high" group). The median-split is actually just one case of the **cumulative percentage breakdown,** a technique in which groups are created using cumulative percentages. For example, look again at Exhibit 20.4. If we wanted to further combine these data into three approximately equal-sized groups, which categories would be combined? Based on the cumulative percent breakdown, the three groups would be as follows:

Less than $24,900

$25,000 to $44,900

More than $44,900

When using statistical software for analyses—which is almost always—the recommended approach for recasting a continuous variable into categories is to create a new variable whose values are initially identical to the original continuous variable and then to recode the new variable into the desired categories using data manipulation commands. This way, both the original variable and the new categorical variable are available for analyses.

The example presented thus far involved converting a ratio-level measure to a categorical measure. It is also common to recast interval-level measures, such as rating scales, into categorical measures to aid readers in interpreting results of analyses. The **two-box technique** is sometimes used in industry to present rating scale results. A "two-box" is simply the percentage of respondents who rated some object or attribute as either of the top two positions on a rating scale. As an example, look at the questions and response frequencies (in percentages) presented in Exhibit 20.5. Two percent (2%) of respondents rated dental technicians "very poor," 6% rated them "poor," 36% rated them "neutral," 32% rated them "good," and 24% rated them "very good." Thus, 56% of the respondents rated the technicians as either "good" or "very good," resulting in a two-box of 56%. Responses for the receptionist and dentist are interpreted in the same way. The next table, Exhibit 20.6, presents two-box results and descriptive statistics for the dental technicians, the receptionist, and the dentist.

median split

A technique for converting a continuous measure into a categorical measure with two approximately equal-sized groups. The groups are formed by "splitting" the continuous measure at its median value.

cumulative percent breakdown

A technique for converting a continuous measure into a categorical measure. The categories are formed based on the cumulative percentages obtained in a frequency analysis.

two-box technique

A technique for converting an interval-level rating scale into a categorical measure usually used for presentation purposes. The percentage of respondents choosing one of the top two positions on a rating scale is reported.

Exhibit 20.5

Questionnaire Items and Response Distribution

Please rate the quality of service provided by Better Smiles Dental Office on the following scales:

	Very Poor	Poor	Neutral	Good	Very Good
dental technicians	(2)*	(6)	(36)	(32)	(24)
receptionist	(10)	(16)	(18)	(36)	(20)
dentist	(17)	(17)	(35)	(21)	(10)

*percentages in parentheses

Exhibit 20.6

Two-Box Results, with Descriptive Statistics

	Two-Box	Mean	(s.d.)
dental technicians	56%	3.70	(0.97)
receptionist	56%	3.40	(1.25)
dentist	31%	2.90	(1.21)
$n = 100$			

It is important to note that converting from continuous to categorical measures inevitably results in the loss of information about a variable. The analyst who considers only the two-box results in Exhibit 20.6 will conclude that dental technicians and the receptionist are providing about the same quality of service. The descriptive statistics calculated on the original rating scale data reveal more precise information, however; the technicians seem to be faring better, and there is considerably more variance in respondent feelings about the quality of service provided by the receptionist. Most of the time, conclusions drawn using categorical approaches will roughly parallel those drawn using the full information from the continuous measure, but as this example demonstrates, this is not necessarily so. Analyses should be performed using the highest level of measurement possible for a particular variable, but if converting the variable to a lower level of measurement makes it easier for the reader to interpret and understand the result, then we encourage the practice. A simple solution for many univariate analyses is to provide both types of results (see Exhibit 20.6).

Confidence Intervals for Means

6 *Discuss confidence intervals for means.*

The sample mean ($\bar{x}$) is an important piece of information about a variable, but as we noted earlier managers must be more concerned with the mean of the variable for the entire population (μ) than with the results for only a sample from the population. Consider again the mean number of family members across the 100 respondents to the car ownership study ($\bar{x} = 4.0$). Four (4) members per family on average is our best point estimate about the mean value of the population parameter (μ), but we have so little confidence that this point estimate is correct that we need to construct an interval that will allow us much greater confidence that we have actually "captured" the parameter within its bounds. As with proportions, to establish the confidence interval we must estimate the degree of sampling error for the sample mean. The following formula is used:

$$\text{sampling error} = z \frac{s}{\sqrt{n}}$$

where $z = z$ score associated with confidence level (for 95% confidence, $z = 1.96$), $s =$ sample standard deviation, and $n =$ total number of cases. Earlier we saw that the sample standard deviation for the number of family members was 1.9, and we know that we are working with 100 valid cases. Thus, at the 95% confidence level,

$$\text{sampling error} = 1.96 \frac{1.9}{\sqrt{100}} = 0.40$$

Thus, the degree of sampling error for this estimate is approximately 0.4. Substituting this value and the sample mean ($\bar{x} = 4.0$) into the following formula

$$(\bar{x} - \text{sampling error} \leq \mu \leq \bar{x} + \text{sampling error})$$
$$(4.0 - 0.4 \leq \mu \leq 4.0 + 0.4)$$
$$\text{or } (3.6, 4.4)$$

results in a 95% confidence interval ranging from 3.6 to 4.4. We can therefore be 95% confident that the mean number of family members *in the population* lies somewhere between 3.6 and 4.4, inclusive.

Think about what has been accomplished. On the basis of only 100 observations, we can say with 95% confidence that had we taken the measure of family size from every household in the relevant population, which might include many thousands of households, the mean number of family members would fall in the range 3.6 to 4.4. We note again, however, that the confidence interval only takes sampling error into account. To the degree that other types of error are present, our estimates may be off target.

Hypothesis Testing

The fact that marketing researchers are almost always working with a sample rather than full information from all population members creates something of a dilemma for managers who must make decisions based on research results. Simply put, *how can we tell if a particular result obtained from a sample would be true for the population as a whole and not just for the particular sample?* In truth, we can never know with complete certainty that a sample result is true for the population. However, through hypothesis testing, researchers can establish standards for making decisions about whether or not to accept sample results as valid for the overall population. We introduce hypothesis testing at this point because it applies to both univariate analyses (the remainder of this chapter) and multivariate analyses (the next chapter).

When marketers prepare to launch a research study, they generally begin with a speculation, or guess, about a phenomenon in their environment. "I'll bet," the advertising manager might say to the marketing director, "that if we hired a sultry celebrity to promote our shampoo, sales would increase." Or the sales manager might say to the company's financial officer, "If my department only had more money to spend on training, our people would be more productive." Or a product development team might predict that "At least 10% of the target market will be interested in our new product."

In marketing, as in other scientific fields, such unproven propositions are called **hypotheses.** Through the use of statistical techniques, we are often able to determine whether there is empirical evidence from a sample to confirm that such hypotheses may be true for the population. In this section we review some basic concepts that underlie hypothesis testing in classical statistical theory, such as framing the null hypothesis, setting the risk of error in making a wrong decision, and the general steps involved in testing the hypothesis.[5]

hypotheses
Unproven propositions about some phenomenon of interest.

Null and Alternative Hypotheses

Marketing research studies are unable to prove results. At best, they can indicate which of two mutually exclusive hypotheses are more likely to be true on the basis of observed results. The general forms of these two hypotheses and the symbols attached to them are as follows:

- H_0, the hypothesis that a proposed result (comparison of means or proportions to standards; differences between groups; relationships between variables) is not true for the population.
- H_a, the alternate hypothesis that a proposed result is true for the population.

The first of these hypotheses, H_0, is known as the **null hypothesis.** The typical goal is to reject the null hypothesis in favor of the **alternative hypothesis.** Note, however, that we do not "prove" that the alternative hypothesis is true even if we can reject the null; a hypothesis may be rejected but can never be accepted completely, since further evidence may prove it wrong. In other words, we either reject a hypothesis or we do not reject the hypothesis (as opposed to proving the hypothesis) on the basis of the evidence at hand.

A simple qualitative example should illustrate the issue.[6] Suppose we are testing the hypothesis that John Doe is a poor man. We observe that John dines in cheap restaurants, lives in a

null hypothesis
The hypothesis that a proposed result is not true for the population. Researchers typically attempt to reject the null hypothesis in favor of some alternative hypothesis.

alternative hypothesis
The hypothesis that a proposed result is true for the population.

run-down building, wears worn and tattered clothes, and so on. Although his behavior is certainly consistent with that of a poor man, we cannot fully accept the hypothesis that he is poor. It is possible that John may in fact be rich, but extremely frugal. We can continue gathering information about him, but for the moment we must decide not to reject the hypothesis that John is a poor man. One single observation—for example, that he has a seven-figure bank account—would allow the immediate rejection of the hypothesis and would lead to the conclusion that John Doe is rich.

Thus, researchers need to recognize that in the absence of perfect information (for example, when sampling), the best they can do is form hypotheses or conjectures about what is true. Further, their conclusions about these conjectures can be wrong, and thus there is always some probability of error in accepting any hypothesis. In statistical terms, researchers commit a Type I error when they reject a true null hypothesis and thereby tentatively accept (note that this is not the same as "proving") the alternative; they commit a Type II error when they do not reject a false null hypothesis, which they should, given that it is false. The null hypothesis is assumed to be true for the purpose of the test. The Technically Speaking box (see page 554) provides greater detail about these types of errors in hypothesis testing.

The upshot of this discussion is that the researcher needs to frame the null hypothesis in such a way that its rejection leads to the tentative acceptance of the desired conclusion, which is stated in the alternative hypothesis. For example, suppose a firm was considering introducing a new product if it could be expected to secure more than 20 percent of the market. Thus, the researchers are comparing a sample proportion against a standard. The proper way to frame the hypotheses would be

$$H_0: \pi \leq 0.20$$
$$H_a: \pi > 0.20$$

If the evidence led to the rejection of H_0, the researcher would then be able to tentatively accept the alternative that the product could be expected to secure more than 20 percent of the market, and the product would be introduced, because such a result would have been unlikely to occur if the null was indeed true. If H_0 could not be rejected, however, the product would not be introduced unless more evidence to the contrary became available. The example as framed involves the use of a one-tailed statistical test in that the alternate hypothesis is expressed directionally, that is, as being greater than 0.20. The one-tailed test is most commonly used in marketing research, although there are research problems that warrant a two-tailed test; for example, the market share achieved by the new formulation of Product X is no different from that achieved by the old formulation, which was 20 percent. A two-tailed test would be expressed as

$$H_0: \pi = 0.20$$
$$H_a: \pi \neq 0.20$$

There is no direction implied with the alternate hypothesis; the proportion is simply expressed as not being equal to 0.20.

The one-tailed test is more commonly used than the two-tailed test in marketing research for two reasons. First, there is typically some hypothesized or preferred direction to the outcome; for example, the greater the market share, the higher the product quality, or the lower the expenses, the better. The two-tailed alternative is used when there is no preferred direction in the outcome or when the research is meant to demonstrate the existence of a difference but not its direction. Second, the one-tailed test, when it is appropriate, is more powerful statistically than the two-tailed alternative.

Hypothesis Testing Procedure

List the steps involved in hypothesis testing.

Research Window 20.1 shows the typical sequence of steps that researchers follow in testing hypotheses. Suppose the problem was indeed one of investigating the potential for a new product and that the research centered around testing consumer preferences. In the judg-

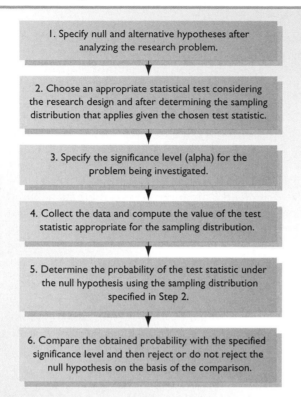

1. Specify null and alternative hypotheses after analyzing the research problem.

2. Choose an appropriate statistical test considering the research design and after determining the sampling distribution that applies given the chosen test statistic.

3. Specify the significance level (alpha) for the problem being investigated.

4. Collect the data and compute the value of the test statistic appropriate for the sampling distribution.

5. Determine the probability of the test statistic under the null hypothesis using the sampling distribution specified in Step 2.

6. Compare the obtained probability with the specified significance level and then reject or do not reject the null hypothesis on the basis of the comparison.

ment of management, the product should not be introduced unless over 20 percent of the population could be expected to prefer it, and that the research calls for 625 respondents to be interviewed for their preferences.

Step 1

The null and alternate hypotheses would be

$$H_0: \pi \le 0.20$$
$$H_a: \pi > 0.20$$

The hypotheses are framed so that if the null hypothesis is rejected, the product should be introduced.

Step 2

The appropriate sample statistic is the sample proportion, and the distribution of all possible sample proportions under the sampling plan is based on the assumption that the null hypothesis is true. Although the distribution of sample proportions is theoretically binomially distributed, the large sample size permits the use of the normal approximation.[7] The z test therefore applies. The z statistic in this case equals

$$z = \frac{p - \pi}{\sigma_p}$$

where p is the sample proportion preferring the product, σ_p is the standard error of the proportion, or the standard deviation of the distribution of sample p's. And σ_p in turn equals

$$\sigma_p = \sqrt{\frac{\pi(1-\pi)}{n}} = \sqrt{\frac{0.20\ (1-0.20)}{625}} = 0.016$$

where n is the sample size.

Step 3

The researcher selects an appropriate level of Type I error, the probability of rejecting the null hypothesis (H_0) when it is actually true for the population. The acceptable level of Type I error is usually referred to as the **significance level** or alpha level of the test and is symbolized by alpha (α). In this situation α error is the probability of rejecting H_0 and concluding that $\pi > 0.2$, when in reality $p \leq 0.2$. This conclusion will lead the company to market the new product. However, since the venture will be profitable only if $\pi > 0.2$, a wrong decision to market would be financially unprofitable, possibly disastrous. The probability of Type I error should, therefore, be minimized as much as possible. The researcher must recognize, however, that the probability of a Type II error (symbolized as β) increases as α is decreased, other things being equal. Type II error in this case implies concluding $\pi \leq 0.2$ when in fact $\pi > 0.2$, which in turn suggests that the company would table the decision to introduce the product when it could be profitable. The opportunity lost from making such an error could be quite serious. The researcher must realize that α and β are interrelated and that an extremely low value of α, say 0.01 or 0.001, would produce intolerable β errors. By convention, most social scientists have decided on an α level of 0.05 as an acceptable compromise.

Step 4

Since Step 4 involves the computation of the test statistic, it can be completed only after the sample is drawn and the information collected. Suppose 140 of the 625 sample respondents preferred the product. The sample proportion is thus $p = 140/625 = 0.224$. The basic question that needs to be answered is conceptually simple: Is this value of p too large to have occurred by chance from a population with π assumed to be less than or equal to 0.2? Or, in other words, What is the probability of getting $p = 0.224$ when $\pi \leq 0.20$? The test statistic, z, equals

$$z = \frac{p - \pi}{\sigma_p} = \frac{0.224 - 0.200}{0.016} = 1.500$$

Step 5

The probability of occurrence of a z value of 1.500 can be found from standard tabled values of areas under the normal curve. (See Table 1 in the Appendix at the end of the book.) Figure 20.3 shows the procedure. The shaded area between $-\infty$ and 1.500 equals 0.9332; this means the area to the right of $z = 1.500$ is $1.000 - 0.9332$, or 0.0668. This is the probability of securing a z value of 1.500 under a true situation of $\pi \leq 0.2$. This probability is often referred to as the **p-value.** (Some statistical software packages place p-values in a column labeled "significance.") The p-value represents the likelihood of obtaining the particular value of a test statistic if the null hypothesis were true.

Step 6

Since the calculated probability of occurrence is higher than the specified significance level of $\alpha = 0.05$, the null hypothesis is not rejected. The product would not be introduced because, while the evidence is in the right direction, it is not sufficient to conclude beyond "any rea-

significance level (α)
The acceptable level of Type I error selected by the researcher, usually set at 0.05. Type I error is the probability of rejecting the null hypothesis when it is actually true for the population.

p-value
The probability of obtaining a given result if in fact the null hypothesis were true in the population. A result is regarded as statistically significant if the p-value is less than the chosen significance level of the test.

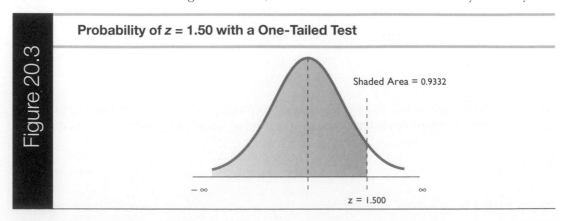

Figure 20.3

Probability of z = 1.50 with a One-Tailed Test

Shaded Area = 0.9332

$-\infty$

$z = 1.500$

∞

PART 6:
Data Analysis

sonable doubt" that $\pi > 0.20$. If the decision maker had been able to tolerate a 10 percent chance of committing a Type I error, the null hypothesis would have been rejected and the product marketed, since the probability of getting a sample $p = 0.224$ when the true $\pi \leq 0.20$ is, as we have seen, 0.0668.

Issues in Interpreting Statistical Significance

When the p-value associated with a test statistic is lower than the level of α (probability of Type I error) set by the researcher, we refer to the result as a statistically significant result. However, there are several common misinterpretations of p-values and the associated phrase "statistically significant."[8] One of the most frequent is to view a p-value as representing the probability that the results occurred because of sampling error. Thus, a p-value of .04 is taken to mean that there is a probability of only 0.04 that the results were caused by chance, and thus there must be something fundamental causing them. In actuality, a p-value of 0.04 means that if— and this is a big if—the null hypothesis is true, the odds are only 1 in 25 of getting a sample result of the magnitude that was observed. Unfortunately, there is no way in classical statistical significance testing to determine whether the null hypothesis is true.

> A p-value reached by classical methods is not a summary of the data. Nor does the p-value attached to a result tell how strong or dependable the particular result is. . . . Writers and readers are all too likely to read .05 as *p(H/E)*, "the probability that the Hypothesis is true, given the Evidence." As textbooks on statistics reiterate almost in vain, *p* is *p(E/H)*, the probability that this Evidence would arise if the (null) Hypothesis is true.[9]

Another very frequent misinterpretation is to hold that the α level set by the researcher or the p-value obtained in the analysis is in some way related to the probability that the alternative hypothesis is true. Most typically, this probability is taken as the complement of the p-value. For example, some might incorrectly interpret a p-value of .07 to mean that the probability that the research hypothesis is true is $1 - .07$, or .93. "Related to this misinterpretation is the practice of interpreting p-values as a measure of the degree of validity of research results, i.e., a p-value such as $p < .0001$ is 'highly statistically significant' or 'highly significant' and therefore much more valid than a p-value of, say, 0.05."[10] Both of these related interpretations are wrong.

A more subtle, but still too common, misinterpretation is to equate statistical significance with practical or managerial significance. Many fail to realize that a result can be of practical importance and not be statistically significant if the power of the test is weak as may occur (all too frequently) with small sample sizes. As noted in Technically Speaking 20.1, the **power** of a test is the probability of correctly rejecting a false null hypothesis. The lower the statistical power, the lower the chances of finding a statistically significant result and rejecting a false null hypothesis. Conversely, a result may be statistically significant yet be of no practical importance, particularly with large sample sizes. For example, a marketing researcher might find that attitude scores for a new product are higher for men (mean score of 6.2 on a 7-point favorability scale) than for women (mean score of 6.1 on the same scale) and that the difference is statistically significant. Does it appear that the company should forget about selling the product to women, or develop separate marketing strategies for men vs. women on the basis of this "statistically significant" result? We don't think so.

The only logical conclusion that can be drawn when a null hypothesis is rejected at some predetermined p-level is that sampling error is an unlikely explanation of the results, given that the null hypothesis is true. This really may not be saying very much, because the null hypothesis is set up to be false. The null, as typically stated, holds that there is no relationship between a certain two variables, say, or that the groups are equal with respect to some particular variable. Yet, we do not really believe that. Rather, we investigate the relationship between variables because we believe there is some association between them, and we contrast the groups because we believe they are different with respect to the variable. Further, we can control our

power
The probability of correctly rejecting a false null hypothesis.

Types of Errors in Hypothesis Testing

SINCE THE RESULT OF STATIS-
TICALLY TESTING A NULL
HYPOTHESIS IS TO REJECT IT
or not reject it, two types of errors may occur.
First, the null hypothesis may be rejected
when it is true. Second, it may not be
rejected when it is false and, therefore,
should have been rejected. These two errors
are, respectively, termed Type I error and
Type II error, or α error and β error, which
are the probabilities associated with their
occurrence. The two types of errors are not
complementary in that $\alpha + \beta \neq 1$.

To illustrate each type of error and to
demonstrate that the errors are not complementary, consider a judicial analogy. Since,
under U.S. criminal law, a person is innocent
until proven guilty, the judge and jury are
always testing the hypothesis of innocence.
The defendant may, in fact, be either innocent or guilty, but based on the evidence, the
court may reach either verdict regardless of
the true situation. Exhibit A displays the possibilities. If the defendant is innocent and

the jury finds him innocent, or if the defendant is guilty and the jury finds him guilty,
the jury has made a correct decision. If, however, the defendant truly is innocent and the
jury finds him guilty, they have made an
error, and similarly if the defendant is guilty
and they find him innocent. The jury must
find one way or the other, and thus the probabilities of the jury's decision must sum vertically to 1. Thus if we let α represent the
probability of incorrectly finding the person
guilty when he is innocent, then $1 - \alpha$ must
be the probability of correctly finding him
innocent. Similarly, β and $1 - \beta$ represent
the probabilities of findings of innocence
and guilt when he is guilty. It is intuitively
obvious that $\alpha + \beta$ is not equal to 1, although
the two types of error are related to one
another: β must increase when α is reduced
if other things remain the same. Since our
society generally holds that finding an innocent person guilty is more serious than finding a guilty person innocent, α error is
reduced as much as possible in our legal system by requiring proof of guilt "beyond any
reasonable doubt."

Exhibit A: Judicial Analogy Illustrating Decision Error

Verdict	TRUE SITUATION: DEFENDANT IS Innocent	Guilty
Innocent	Correct decision: probability = $1 - \alpha$	Error: probability = β
Guilty	Error: probability = α	Correct decision: probability = $1 - \beta$

ability to reject the null hypothesis simply by the power we build into the statistical test, primarily through the size of the sample used to test it. "Given sufficiently high statistical power,
one would expect virtually always to conclude the exact null hypothesis is false."[11]

Marketing researchers, then, need to be wary when interpreting the results of their hypothesis testing procedures so that they do not mislead themselves and others. They need to constantly keep in mind both types of errors that it is possible to make. Further, they need to
make sure they do not misinterpret what a test of significance reveals. It represents no more
than a test against the null hypothesis. One useful way of avoiding misinterpretation is to calculate confidence intervals when possible, as this gives decision makers a much better feel for
how much faith they can have in the results. A test of significance is very much a yes-no affair:
either the sample result is statistically significant or it is not. On the other hand, "the confidence interval not only gives a yes or no answer, but also, by its width, gives an indication of
whether the answer should be whispered or shouted."[12] While not every test of significance
can be put in the form of a confidence interval estimate, many of them can, and it is advisable
to put them in that form when the opportunity arises.

Exhibit B contains the corresponding research situation. Just as the defendant's true status is unknown to the jury, the true situation regarding the null hypothesis is unknown to the researcher. The researcher's dilemma parallels that of the jury in that the researcher has limited information with which to work. Suppose the null hypothesis is true. If the researcher concludes it is false, a Type I (α) error has been made. The significance level associated with a statistical test indicates the probability with which this error may be made. Since sample information will always be somewhat incomplete, there will always be some α error. The only way it can be avoided is by never rejecting the null hypothesis (never finding anyone guilty, in the judicial analogy). The confidence level of a statistical test is $1 - \alpha$, and the more confident we want to be in a statistical result, the lower we must set α error. The power associated with a statistical test is the probability of correctly rejecting a false null hypothesis. One-tailed tests are more powerful than two-tailed tests because, for the same α error, they are simply more likely to lead to a rejection of a false null hypothesis. β error represents the probability of not rejecting a false null hypothesis. There is no unique value associated with β error.

Types of Errors in Hypothesis Testing

Research Conclusion	TRUE SITUATION: NULL HYPOTHESIS IS	
	True	False
Do not reject H_0	Correct decision Confidence level Probability = $1 - \alpha$	Error: Type II Probability = β
Reject H_0	Error: Type 1 Significance level Probability = α	Correct decision Power of test Probability = $1 - \beta$

Exhibit B

Reference: The judicial analogy is based on R.W. Jastram, *Elements of Statistical Inference* (Berkeley, Calif: Book Company, 1947), p. 44.

Testing Hypotheses about Individual Variables

There are numerous occasions when marketing researchers are called upon to compare univariate sample statistics against preconceived standards. In our hypothesis testing example in the previous section, the analyst was asked to determine if the sample results provided sufficient evidence that more than 20% of the population (i.e., the standard) would prefer a certain product. In other situations, an analyst might need to compare the mean customer satisfaction score for a particular department store against the overall mean satisfaction score for all department stores in the chain, or to determine if the characteristics of sample respondents match those of the overall population from which the sample was drawn. Each of these examples calls for a researcher to test a hypothesis about a univariate measure.

Chi-Square Goodness-of-Fit Test for Frequencies

A breakfast food manufacturer has recently developed a new cereal called Score. Through single source scanner data for its existing cereals, the manufacturer found that for every package of cereal sold to a household with no children, three packages were sold to households with children and two packages were sold to retirement households (households with at least one spouse of retirement age). The researchers were careful that each household was categorized into only one category. The manufacturer wishes to see if this same tendency will hold with this new cereal, since a change in consumption patterns could have significant marketing communication implications. The manufacturer therefore decides to conduct a market test

8 Describe the chi-square goodness-of-fit test and compare it to the Kolmogorov-Smirnov test.

to determine the relative frequencies with which different household categories purchase the new cereal.

Suppose that, in an appropriate test market, over a one-week period, 1,200 boxes of the new cereal are sold and that the distribution of sales by household category is as follows:

Number Buying per Household Category

no children	children	retirement	Total
240	575	385	1,200

As some quick multiplication would show, these figures do not match the pattern established earlier with other cereal brands. Does this preliminary evidence indicate that the firm should expect a change in the purchase patterns of different types of households with Score?

This is the type of problem for which the **chi-square goodness-of-fit test** is ideally suited. (Note that chi, χ, is a Greek letter that rhymes with sky.) The variable of interest has been broken into k mutually exclusive categories ($k = 3$ in the example), and each observation logically falls into one of the k classes or cells. In short, this is simply a frequency analysis for a variable representing type of household. The trials (purchases) are independent, and the sample size is large.

All that is necessary to use the test is to calculate the expected number of cases that would fall in each category and to compare the expected number with the observed number actually falling in the category, using the equation

$$\chi^2 = \sum_{i=1}^{k} \frac{[O_i - E_i]^2}{E_i}$$

where

- O_i is the observed number of cases falling in the ith category
- E_i is the expected number of cases falling in the ith category
- k is the number of categories

The expected number falling into a category is generated from the null hypothesis, which in this case is that the composition of sales of Score by household type will follow the manufacturer's normal sales pattern (that is, for every package purchased by a household with no children, three packages will be purchased by households with children, and two packages will be purchased by retirement households). In terms of the proportion of all sales, that means that one-sixth of the sales could be expected to be to households with no children, one-half to households with children, and one-third to retirement households if sales of the new cereal follow traditional patterns. If the 1,200 boxes sold in test market followed the normal or expected pattern, then 200 ($1/6 \times 1,200$) would have been sold to households with no children, 600 ($1/2 \times 1,200$) households with children, and 400 ($1/3 \times 1,200$) to retirement households. How does the observed pattern compare with the expected pattern? The appropriate χ^2 statistic is computed as

---

chi-square goodness-of-fit test
A statistical test to determine whether some observed pattern of frequencies corresponds to an expected pattern.

Calculating confidence intervals is one way to avoid misinterpreting the results of hypothesis testing procedures.

PART 6:
Data Analysis

$$\chi^2 = \frac{(240-200)^2}{200} + \frac{(575-600)^2}{600} + \frac{(385-400)^2}{400} = 9.60$$

The chi-square distribution is completely determined by its degrees of freedom, v. The term *degrees of freedom* refers to the number of things that can vary independently, and for the chi-square test degrees of freedom is one less than the number of categories ($v = k - 1$), or $v = 3 - 1 = 2$ in the breakfast cereal example.[13]

Suppose the researcher has chosen a significance level of $\alpha = 0.05$ for this test. The tabled value of χ^2 for two degrees of freedom and $\alpha = 0.05$ is 5.99 (see Table 2 in the Appendix at the end of the book). Since the calculated value ($\chi^2 = 9.60$) is larger, the conclusion is that the probability that we could obtain differences this large—if the null hypothesis were true—is less than .05. Rather, the preliminary market-test results suggest that sales of Score will follow a different pattern than is typical. In particular, sales to families with no children are higher than expected. The null hypothesis of sales in the ratio of 1:3:2 is rejected.

The chi-square test outlined here is an approximate test.[14] The approximation is relatively good if, as a rule of thumb, the expected number of cases in each category is five or more, although this value can be as low as 1 for some situations.[15]

Kolmogorov-Smirnov Test

The **Kolmogorov-Smirnov test** is similar to the chi-square goodness-of-fit test in that it uses a comparison between observed and expected frequencies to determine whether observed results are in accord with a stated null hypothesis. But the Kolmogorov-Smirnov test is used with ordinal-level measures and takes advantage of the ordinal nature of the data.

Consider, for example, a manufacturer of cosmetics who is testing four different shades of a foundation compound: very light, light, medium, and dark. The company has hired a marketing research firm to determine whether any distinct preference exists toward either extreme. If so, the company will manufacture only the preferred shades. Otherwise, it will market all shades. Suppose that in a sample of 100, 50 persons prefer the very light shade, 30 the light shade, 15 the medium shade, and 5 the dark shade. Do these results indicate some kind of preference?

Since shade represents a natural ordering, the Kolmogorov-Smirnov test can be used to test the preference hypothesis. The test involves specifying the cumulative distribution function that would occur under the null hypothesis and comparing that with the observed cumulative distribution function. The point at which the two functions show the maximum difference is determined, and the value of this deviation is the test statistic.

The null hypothesis for the cosmetic manufacturer would be that there is no preference for the various shades. Thus it would be expected that 25 percent of the sample would prefer each shade. The cumulative distribution function resulting from this assumption is presented in the last column of Exhibit 20.7.

Kolmogorov-Smirnov test
A statistical test used with ordinal data to determine whether some observed pattern of frequencies corresponds to some expected pattern; also used to determine whether two independent samples have been drawn from the same population or from populations with the same distribution.

Exhibit 20.7

Observed and Theoretical Cumulative Distributions of Foundation Compound Preference

Shade	Observed Number	Observed Proportion	Observed Cumulative Proportion	Theoretical Proportion	Theoretical Cumulative Proportion
Very light	50	0.50	0.50	0.25	0.25
Light	30	0.30	0.80	0.25	0.50
Medium	15	0.15	0.95	0.25	0.75
Dark	5	0.05	1.00	0.25	1.00

Kolmogorov-Smirnov D, which is equal to the absolute value of the maximum deviation between the observed cumulative proportion and the theoretical cumulative proportion, is $0.80 - 0.50 = 0.30$. If the researcher chooses an $\alpha = 0.05$, the critical value of D for large samples is given by the formula

$$D = \frac{1.36}{\sqrt{n}}$$

where n is the sample size. In our case of a sample size of 100, the critical value is 0.136. Calculated D ($D = 0.30$) exceeds the critical value, and thus the null hypothesis of no preference among shades is rejected. The data indicate a statistically significant preference for the lighter shades.

You may have noticed that the hypothesis of no preference could also have been tested with the chi-square goodness-of-fit test. When the data are ordinal, however, the Kolmogorov-Smirnov test is the preferred procedure. It is more powerful than chi-square in almost all cases, is easier to compute, and does not require a certain minimum expected frequency in each cell as does the chi-square test.

Z-test for Comparing Sample Proportion against a Standard

9 *Discuss the process for comparing a proportion against a standard.*

In our earlier discussion of hypothesis testing we used an example in which a company planned to introduce a new product only if more than 20% of consumers could be expected to prefer it. Recall that we calculated a z statistic to test the hypothesis using the following formulas:

$$z = \frac{p - \pi}{\sigma_p} \qquad\qquad \sigma_p = \sqrt{\frac{\pi(1 - \pi)}{n}}$$

where p = proportion of consumers who preferred the new product in the sample, π = the proportion standard to be achieved, σ_p = the standard error of the proportion and n = number of respondents in the sample. We then found the probability of obtaining the z statistic if the null hypothesis were true and compared that probability to the significance level of the test (often, $\alpha = 0.05$) to determine whether or not to reject the null hypothesis.

Suppose that the company was particularly concerned about the strength of the leading competing product in the category and added a second constraint on the decision to introduce the new product. That is, even if the new product achieved the threshold level of preference among consumers, the company decided not to introduce the product if more than 50% of consumers still preferred the competing product. In this case, the null and alternative hypotheses are as follows:

$$H_0: \pi > 0.50$$
$$H_a: \pi \le 0.50$$

The results of the study indicated that 290 of the 625 sample respondents preferred the competing product, so $p = 290/625 = 0.46$. Thus, it appears that less than 50% of consumers will prefer the competing product after introduction of the new product, but we must determine whether or not the sample proportion (0.46) is statistically distinct from the standard (0.50). Accordingly,

$$\sigma_p = \sqrt{\frac{0.50(1 - 0.50)}{625}} = 0.02$$

and

$$z = \frac{0.46 - 0.50}{0.02} = -2.00$$

Figure 20.4

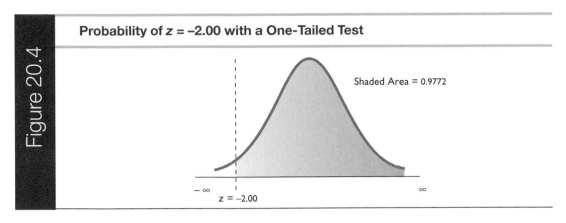

Probability of z = –2.00 with a One-Tailed Test

Shaded Area = 0.9772

$-\infty$

$z = -2.00$

∞

The probability of occurrence of a z value of –2.00 is found from standard tabled values of areas under the normal curve in Table 1 in the Appendix at the end of the book. Figure 20.4 indicates the probability of the occurrence of a z value as low as –2.00, given that the null hypothesis is true. This probability turns out to be 0.0228, the area to the left of the shaded area. Because this probability is lower than the significance level of the test established by the researchers ($\alpha = 0.05$), the researchers would reject the null hypothesis and tentatively accept the alternative hypothesis that after introduction of the new product, the proportion of consumers preferring the competing product is 50% or less.

Z-test for Comparing Sample Mean against a Standard

When the variable to be compared against a standard is a continuous measure, the analyst can take advantage of greater statistical power by working with the mean of the variable and comparing it against a standard just as we did with categorical measures in the previous sections. The task is a bit more complex, however, because we must consider (a) whether the variance of the variable in the population is known or unknown; (b) whether the distribution of the variable in the population is normal (or at least symmetrical) or asymmetrical; and (c) whether the sample size is small ($n \leq 30$) or large ($n > 30$). Technically Speaking 20.2 outlines the appropriate test statistic under various conditions. For sake of brevity, we will illustrate only the common situation in which the variance of the variable in the population is unknown and the distribution of the variable in the population is assumed to be at least symmetrical.

To illustrate the comparison of a sample mean to a standard when the sample size is small, consider a supermarket chain that is thinking about adding a new product to the shelves of its associated stores. Since many products must compete for limited shelf space, the store has determined that it must sell 100 units per week in each store in order for the item to be sufficiently profitable to warrant handling it. Suppose that the research department decides to investigate the item's turnover by putting it in a random sample of ten stores for a limited period of time. Suppose further that the average sales per store per week were as shown in Exhibit 20.8.

10 *Describe the appropriate tests for comparing a mean against a standard for (a) small samples and (b) large samples.*

Exhibit 20.8

Store Sales of Trial Product per Week

Store i	Sales X_i	Store i	Sales X_i
1	86	6	93
2	97	7	132
3	114	8	116
4	108	9	105
5	123	10	120

Testing Hypotheses about a Single Mean

	σ Known	σ Unknown
Distribution of variable in parent population is normal or symmetrical.	Small n: Use $z = \dfrac{\bar{x} - \mu}{\sigma_{\bar{x}}}$	Small n: Use $$t = \frac{\bar{x} - \mu}{s_{\bar{x}}}$$ where $$s_{\bar{x}} = \hat{s} / \sqrt{n}$$ and $$\hat{s} = \sqrt{\frac{\sum_{i=1}^{n}(X_i - \bar{x})^2}{n - 1}}$$ and refer to t table for $n - 1$ degrees of freedom.
	Large n: Use $z = \dfrac{\bar{x} - \mu}{\sigma_{\bar{x}}}$	Large n: Since the t distribution approaches the normal as n increases, use $$z = \frac{\bar{x} - \mu}{s_{\bar{x}}}$$ for $n > 30$.
Distribution of variable in parent population is asymmetrical.	Small n: There is no theory to support the parametric test. Either one must transform the variate so that it is normally distributed and then use the z test, or one must use a distribution-free statistical test.	Small n: There is no theory to support the parametric test. Either one must transform the variate so that it is normally distributed and then use the t test, or one must use a distribution-free statistical test.
	Large n: If the sample is large enough so that the central-limit theorem is operative, use $$z = \frac{\bar{x} - \mu}{\sigma_{\bar{x}}}$$	Large n: If sample is large enough so that (1) the central-limit theorem is operative and (2) ŝ is a close estimate of σ, use $$z = \frac{\bar{x} - \mu}{s_{\bar{x}}}$$

Because the population variance of sales per store is unknown and has to be estimated, the t test is the correct test if the distribution of sales is approximately normal. The normality assumption seems reasonable and could be checked using one of the goodness-of-fit tests. The little sales evidence available does not indicate any real asymmetry, so let us assume that the normality assumption is satisfied.

A one-tailed test is appropriate, because it is only when the sales per store per week reach at least 100 units that the product will be introduced on a national scale. The null and alternate hypotheses are

$$H_0: \mu < 100$$
$$H_a: \mu \geq 100$$

and suppose the significance level is set at $\alpha = 0.05$. From the data in Exhibit 20.8, we can calculate that mean sales in units of the product across the 10 test stores is 109.4 and that the sample standard deviation is 14.4. The t statistic is calculated using the following formula:

$$t = \frac{\bar{x} - \mu}{s_{\bar{x}}}$$

where $\bar{x}$ is the sample mean, μ is the population standard, and $s_{\bar{x}}$ is the standard error of the mean, which is estimated as follows:

$$s_{\bar{x}} = \frac{s}{\sqrt{n}}$$

where s is the sample standard deviation and n is the sample size. Thus, the standard error of the mean is calculated to be $14.4 / \sqrt{10} = 4.55$. Further calculations yield:

$$t = \frac{109.4 - 100}{4.55} = 2.07$$

Critical t as read from the t table with $v = n - 1 = 9$ degrees of freedom is 1.833 ($\alpha = .05$). (See Table 3 in the appendix at the end of the book.) Thus, the obtained t value exceeds the critical value and we can reject the null hypothesis. It is unlikely that the stores in the sample would have averaged sales of 109.4 units if the sales per store in the population were indeed less than 100 units per week.

Suppose that company management was still nervous about the product and decided to conduct a larger-scale test. The product was placed in 50 stores this time, with a resulting sample mean and sample standard deviation of 108.7 and 14.2, respectively. As noted in Technically Speaking 20.2, with large n the z distribution becomes appropriate; the test statistic is calculated as follows:

$$z = \frac{\bar{x} - \mu}{s_{\bar{x}}}$$

The estimated standard error of the mean is $s_{\bar{x}} = 14.2 / \sqrt{50} = 2.01$, and the test statistic is

$$z = \frac{108.7 - 100}{2.01}$$

and is referred to a normal table. Calculated z is greater than critical $z = 1.645$ for $\alpha = 0.05$, and the same conclusion is warranted as from the initial test. The product could be expected to sell at the rate of 100 units or more per store per week.

ETHICAL dilemma 20.1

A manufacturer of aspirin had its marketing research department conduct a national survey among doctors to investigate what common household remedies doctors would most likely recommend when treating a patient with a cold. The question asked doctors to pick the one product they would most likely prescribe for their patients from among the choices Advil, Tylenol, aspirin, or none of the above. The distribution of responses was as follows:

Advil	*100*
Tylenol	*100*
Aspirin	*200*
None of the above	*600*
Total	*1,000*

The firm used the results of the survey as a basis for an extensive ad campaign that claimed, "In a national survey, doctors recommended aspirin two to one over Advil and Tylenol as the medicine they would most likely recommend to their patients suffering from colds."

- *Was the firm's claim legitimate?*
- *Was it ethical for the firm to omit reporting the number of doctors that expressed no preference?*
- *What would be the fairest way to state the ad claim? Do you think stating the claim in this way would be as effective as stating it in the way the firm did?*

Frito-Lay set research objectives of developing guidelines for managing television advertising and setting priorities for advertising campaigns. The company focused on television advertising because it receives the bulk of Frito-Lay's advertising budget.

The research plan was to test a series of hypotheses that an ad would produce increased sales. Researchers assigned Behaviorscan households randomly to "ad" or "no ad" conditions. Frito-Lay tested ads that were already approved during the company's regular media-planning process. Each household assigned to the "ad" condition received the ads in the media plan. Households in the "no ad" condition received public service announcements in place of Frito-Lay's TV ads.

The experiment lasted four years, during which Frito-Lay tested each brand's advertising in at least two markets for 12 months. At the end of the four years, the company learned that 57 percent of its advertisments resulted in sales increases that were significantly larger in the "ad" households than in the "no ad" households. Frito-Lay's experience resembled Wanamaker's retailing career—half its advertising worked. The research data would help Frito-Lay decide which half was working.

Frito-Lay's advertising produced many results similar to Lodish's study of historical data. In 88 percent of the cases when ad content introduced something new, such as a new brand or new product features, the ad led to significant sales increases. In all but one case, the impact on sales was noticeable within the first three months. Not only were results rapid, they also tended to last. A follow-up study found that the ads producing a gain in the short term also had a long-term effect, approximately doubling the short-term sales increase. The average short-term impact of an effective ad was a 15 percent increase in sales.

The research also looked at advertising weight—the amount and frequency of the advertising. The data showed that 61 percent of Frito-Lay's advertising was not responsive to weight changes (changes in weight for that advertising did not explain changes in sales). Marketers could apply that result by testing specific ads to see whether lowering the advertising weight resulted in a sales decline in the test market. If not, the marketer could save money by lowering the frequency of those ads.

Frito-Lay learned some other important lessons as well. One is that its ads should deliver "news." Another lesson is to test ads and target spending on the most effective ads. A 15 percent boost in sales for a big consumer-products company like Frito-Lay amounts to millions of dollars. Spending hundreds of thousands of dollars to choose the right advertising is a logical management decision. With data from services such as Behaviorscan, Frito-Lay can say, "We know which half of our advertising works." ■

Source: This research is described in Leonard Lodish, "When Do Commercials Boost Sales?" *Financial Times* (August 7, 2002), downloaded from the Dow Jones Interactive Publications Library, http://www.nrstg2s.djnr.com.

Summary

Learning Objective 1
Distinguish between univariate and multivariate analyses.
Univariate analyses are conducted on individual variables, while multivariate analyses involve multiple variables.

Learning Objective 2
Describe frequency analysis.
A frequency analysis, or one-way tabulation, is a univariate technique that involves counting the number of responses that fall into various response categories.

Learning Objective 3
Explain the various ways in which frequency analysis can be used.
Frequency analysis can be used (1) to communicate the results of a study, (2) to determine the degree of item nonresponse, (3) to locate blunders, (4) to locate outliers, and (5) to determine the empirical distribution of the variable in question.

Learning Objective 4
Discuss confidence intervals for proportions.
The confidence interval is the range within which the true proportion in the population (π) will fall, with a given level of confidence (usually 95% confidence). The confidence interval is equal to the sample proportion (p) plus or minus estimated sampling error.

Learning Objective 5
Describe commonly used descriptive statistics.
The most commonly used descriptive statistics for continuous measures (interval- or ratio-level measures) are the mean, or arithmetic average, and the standard deviation. The mean is a measure of central tendency while the standard deviation provides a convenient measure of the dispersion of responses.

Learning Objective 6
Discuss confidence intervals for means.
The confidence interval is the range within which the true mean value for the population (μ) will fall, with a given level of confidence (usually 95%). The confidence interval is equal to the sample mean ($\bar{x}$) plus or minus estimated sampling error.

Learning Objective 7
List the steps involved in hypothesis testing.
The steps in hypothesis testing include:
1. Specify null and alternative hypotheses
2. Choose the appropriate test statistic
3. Specify significance (α) level for the test
4. Compute value of test statistic based on sample data
5. Determine probability of test statistic given true null hypothesis
6. Compare obtained probability with specified significance level

Learning Objective 8
Describe the chi-square goodness-of-fit test and compare it to the Kolmogorov-Smirnov test.
The chi-square goodness-of-fit test is a univariate analysis in which the frequency distribution obtained on a categorical variable is compared against a standard to determine if the obtained frequency is statistically different from the standard. The Kolmogorov-Smirnov test is a similar, but more powerful, univariate analysis that can be applied if the categories are ordinal in nature.

Learning Objective 9
Discuss the process for comparing a proportion against a standard.
A sample proportion is compared against a standard by calculating a z statistic, finding the probability of obtaining this level of z given a true null hypothesis, and comparing the obtained probability with the significance level of the test.

Learning Objective 10
Describe the appropriate tests for comparing a mean against a standard for (a) small samples and (b) large samples.
For small samples ($n < 30$), a sample mean is compared against a standard by calculating a t statistic, finding the probability of the obtained t statistic given a true null hypothesis, and comparing the obtained probability with the significance level of the test. For large samples, the process is similar, except that a z statistic is calculated instead of the t statistic.

Key Terms

categorical measures (page 537)

frequency analysis (page 537)

outlier (page 540)

histogram (page 541)

frequency polygon (page 541)

cumulative distribution function (page 542)

confidence interval (page 543)

continuous measures (page 544)

descriptive statistics (page 545)

sample mean (page 545)

sample standard deviation (page 546)

median split (page 547)

cumulative percent breakdown (page 547)

two-box technique (page 547)

hypotheses (page 549)

null hypothesis (page 549)

alternative hypothesis (page 549)

significance level (α) (page 552)

p-value (page 552)

power (page 553)

chi-square goodness-of-fit test (page 556)

Kolmogorov-Smirnov test (page 557)

Review Questions

1. What types of variables might be analyzed with frequency analysis?
2. What is an outlier?
3. With how many digits should percentages be reported?
4. What is a histogram? A frequency polygon? What information do they provide?
5. What is the cumulative distribution function? Of what value is it?
6. Why do analysts often construct confidence intervals? What is their purpose?
7. What type of error do confidence intervals take into account?
8. How do continuous measures differ from categorical measures? Which type offers analysts more statistical power in analyses?
9. What are the most commonly used descriptive statistics?
10. Why must the distribution of responses be taken into account when deciding which type of "average" to present?
11. Why might an analyst choose to convert a continuous measure to a categorical measure?
12. What is a two-box? A median split? A cumulative percentage breakdown?
13. What is the difference between the null and alternative hypotheses?
14. Why can a hypothesis be rejected, but never fully accepted?
15. What is the difference between a one-tailed test and a two-tailed test of statistical significance? When would each be appropriate?
16. What is a *p*-value? Do researchers typically want to obtain higher or lower p-values?
17. Is a *statistically* significant result necessarily *managerially* significant? Why or why not?
18. What is the basic use of a chi-square goodness-of-fit test? How is the value of the test statistic calculated? How are the expected frequencies determined?
19. If the data are ordinal and the analyst wishes to determine whether the observed frequencies correspond to some expected pattern, what statistical test is appropriate? What is the basic procedure to follow in implementing this test?
20. What is the appropriate test statistic for making inferences about a population proportion?
21. What is the appropriate test statistic for making inferences about a population mean when the population variance is unknown and the sample is small? Suppose that the population variance is unknown, but the sample is large. What is the appropriate procedure then?

Discussion Questions, Problems, and Projects

1. A large manufacturer of electronic components for automobiles once conducted a study to determine the average value of electronic components per automobile. Personal interviews were conducted with a random sample of 400 respondents. The following information was secured with respect to each subject's "main" vehicle when he or she had more than one.

Average Dollar Value of Electronic Equipment per Automobile

Dollar Value of Electronic Equipment	Number of Automobiles
Less than or equal to $50	35
$51 to $100	40
$101 to $150	55
$151 to $200	65
$201 to $250	65
$251 to $300	75
$301 to $350	40
$351 to $400	20
More than $400	5
Total number of automobiles	400

(a) Convert the above information into percentages.

(b) Compute the cumulative percentages.

(c) Prepare a histogram and frequency polygon with the average value of electronic equipment on the X axis and the absolute frequency on the Y axis.

(d) Graph the empirical cumulative distribution function with the average value on the X axis and the relative frequency on the Y axis.

(e) Locate the median, first sample quartile, and third sample quartile on the cumulative distribution function graphed in Part (d) of this project.

2. Compute the 95% confidence interval for the percentage of automobiles with more than $250 worth of electronics in them using the information in the previous question.

3. Suppose that the researchers had originally asked an open-ended question about the dollar value of the electronics in the automobile, and that respondents had provided these values. If the mean value in the sample were $234 with standard deviation of $76, construct the 95% confidence interval for the mean value in the population.

4. A large publishing house recently conducted a survey to assess the reading habits of senior citizens. The company published four magazines specifically tailored to suit the needs of senior citizens. Management hypothesized that there were no differences in the preferences for the magazines. A sample of 1,600 senior citizens interviewed in the city of Albuquerque, New Mexico, indicated the following preferences for the four magazines:

Publication	Frequency of Preference
1. *Golden Years*	350
2. *Maturation*	500
3. *High Serenity*	450
4. *Time of Living*	300
Total	1,600

Management needs your expertise to determine whether there are differences in senior citizens' preferences for the magazines.

(a) State the null and alternate hypotheses.

(b) How many degrees of freedom are there?

(c) What is the chi-square critical table value at the 5 percent significance level?

(d) What is the calculated χ^2 value? Show all your calculations.

(e) Should the null hypothesis be rejected? Explain.

5. Management of the publishing house was particularly concerned about *Time of Living*. This magazine had been introduced almost 20 years prior, but had begun slipping in circulation about 5 years ago. A "facelift" for the magazine had helped a little a year ago, but rising costs were threatening the remaining profits in the magazine. A recent analysis indicated that at current circulation rates, the title was barely breaking even. Knowing that it sometimes takes time for changes and improvements to be noticed by the market, management decided prior to the survey that if at least 20% of the market preferred the magazine to its three siblings in the publishing house, they would continue the title for another year.

(a) State the null and alternative hypotheses.

(b) What is the calculated z statistic? Show all your calculations.

(c) Should the null hypothesis be rejected with a significance level of .05? Explain.

6. Silken-Shine Company is a medium-sized manufacturer of shampoo. During the past years the company has increased the number of variations of its shampoo from three to five to increase its market share. Management conducted a survey to compare sales of Silken-Shine shampoo with sales of Rapunzel and So-Soft, its two major competitors. A sample of 1,800 housewives indicated the following frequencies with respect to most recent shampoo purchased:

Shampoo	Number Buying
1. Silken-Shine	425
2. Rapunzel	1,175
3. So-Soft	200
Total	1,800

Experience had indicated that three times as many households preferred Rapunzel to Silken-Shine and that, in turn, twice as many households preferred Silken-Shine to So-Soft. Management wants to determine if the historic tendency still holds, given that Silken-Shine Company has increased the range of shampoos available.

(a) State the null and alternate hypotheses.

(b) How many degrees of freedom are there?

(c) What is the chi-square critical table value at the 5 percent significance level?

(d) What is the calculated χ^2 value? Show all your calculations.

(e) Should the null hypothesis be rejected? Explain.

7. A manufacturer of music cassettes wants to test four different cassettes varying in tape length: 30 minutes, 60 minutes, 90 minutes, and 120 minutes. The company has hired you to determine whether customers show any distinct preference toward either extreme. If there is a preference toward any extreme, the company will manufacture only cassettes of the preferred length; otherwise, it plans to market cassettes of all four lengths. A sample of 1,000 customers indicated the following preferences:

Tape Length	Frequency of Preference
30 minutes	150
60 minutes	250
90 minutes	425
120 minutes	175
Total	1,000

PART 6:

Data Analysis

(a) State the null and alternate hypotheses.
(b) Compute the Kolmogorov-Smirnov D by completing the following table:

Tape Length	Observed Number	Observed Proportion	Observed Cumulative Proportion	Theoretical Proportion	Theoretical Cumulative Proportion
30 minutes					
60 minutes					
90 minutes					
120 minutes					

(c) Compute the critical value of D at $\alpha = 0.05$. Show your calculations.
(d) Would you reject the null hypothesis? Explain.
(e) What are the implications for management?
(f) Explain why the Kolmogorov-Smirnov test would be used in this situation.

8. Liberty Foods markets vegetables in six different sized cans: A, B, C, D, E, and F. Through the years the company has observed that sales of all its vegetables in the six can sizes are in the proportion 6;4;2;1.5;1.5;1, respectively. In other words, for every 1 case of size F that is sold, 6 cases of size A, 4 of size B, 2 of size C, 1.5 of size D, and 1.5 of size E are also sold.

The marketing manager would like the sales data for a new canned vegetable—pureed carrots—compared with the pattern for the rest of Liberty's product line to see if there is any difference. Based on a representative sample of 600 cases of pureed carrots, he observes that 30 percent were Size A, 20 percent B, 10 percent C, 10 percent D, 15 percent E, and 15 percent F.

(a) The marketing manager has asked you to determine whether the pureed carrots' sales pattern is similar to the pattern for other vegetables by using the chi-square goodness-of-fit test. Show all your calculations clearly.
(b) You are now asked to determine the above with the use of the Kolmogorov-Smirnov test. Show all your calculations clearly.
(c) What can you conclude from the use of the two test statistics? Are your results from the two tests conflicting or similar?
(d) Which test statistic would you prefer? Why?

9. Suppose the sponsor of the car ownership study presented in this chapter had decided to begin offering financing for car purchases, but only if at least 25% of the market could be expected to finance a car purchase (anything less would not produce enough lending volume to make the effort profitable). Because the venture would require considerable resources, the sponsor wants to be very certain before proceeding.
(a) What significance level (α) would you recommend for the test? Why?
(b) What are the null and alternative hypotheses?
(c) Based on the information in Exhibit 20.2, calculate the appropriate test statistic.
(d) With $\alpha = .01$, would you reject the null hypothesis?

10. The manager of the Budget Department Store recently increased the store's use of in-store promotions in an attempt to increase the proportion of entering customers who made a purchase. The effort was prompted by a study made a year ago that showed 65 percent of a sample of 1,000 parties entering the store made no purchase. A recent sample of 900 parties contained 635 who made no purchases. Management is wondering whether there has been a change in the proportion of entering parties who make a purchase.
(a) State the null and alternate hypotheses.
(b) What is the calculated value? Show your calculations clearly.
(c) Based on your results, would you reject the null hypothesis? Explain.

11. A medium-sized manufacturer of paper products was planning to introduce a new line of tissues, hand towels, and toilet paper. However, management had stipulated that the new products should be introduced only if average monthly purchases per household would be $2.50 or more. The product was market tested, and the diaries of the 100 panel households living in the test market area were checked. They indicated that average monthly purchases were $3.10 per household with

a standard deviation of $0.50. Management is wondering what decision it should make and has asked for your recommendation.

(a) State the null and alternate hypotheses.

(b) Is the sample size considered large or small?

(c) Which test should be used? Why?

(d) At the 5 percent level of significance, would you reject the null hypothesis? Support your answer with the necessary calculations.

12. The president of a chain of department stores had promised the managers of the various stores a bonus of 8 percent if the average monthly sales per store increased $300,000 or more. A random sample of 12 stores yielded the following sales increases:

Store	Sales	Store	Sales
1	$320,000	7	$380,000
2	$230,000	8	$280,000
3	$400,000	9	$420,000
4	$450,000	10	$360,000
5	$280,000	11	$440,000
6	$320,000	12	$320,000

The president is wondering whether this random sample of stores indicates that the population of stores has reached the goal. (Assume the distribution of the variable in the parent population is normal.)

(a) State the null and alternate hypotheses.

(b) Is the sample size considered small or large?

(c) Which test should be used? Why?

(d) Would you reject the null hypothesis at the 5 percent level of significance? Support your conclusion with the necessary calculations.

NFO Research, Inc. (NFO), recently conducted a study of the ground caffeinated coffee market because several of its clients operate in this market. The study was undertaken with several objectives in mind, including the identification of benefits that consumers seek and the comparison of consumer opinions regarding several of the brands offered in the market.

The questionnaire in Figure 12.2 (pages 288–290) was designed to accomplish these objectives. This questionnaire was mailed to 400 individuals previously identified as consumers of ground caffeinated coffee (personally drinking at least one cup per day). Of those mailed out, 328 were returned; 299 of these were judged to be usable responses.

The data collected from these consumers are stored in a free-field format (space delimited) ASCII file named "coffee.dat" on the product support Web site. The coding format of the data is shown below. Missing data are coded –99 for all items and should be disregarded for all analyses. While the data included are basically the data collected, some items or responses were generated to complete the data set.

13. (a) Produce a histogram for the age variable. Does it appear that anything has been obviously miscoded? If so, explain.

(b) Produce a histogram for the variable "brand used most often" (VAR9). Determine an estimate of market share for the various brands based on this data set, assuming these were the only brands available.

(c) Do the data suggest that the market share for Maxwell House Regular is equal to 15%? Calculate the appropriate z statistic to test the following hypotheses:
$$H_0: \pi = .15$$
$$H_a: \pi \neq .15$$

(d) Suppose that the following table was an accurate representation of market share for these brands from the previous year:

Brand	Market Share
Folgers	39%
Hills Brothers	7
Maxwell House Regular	15
Maxwell House Mstr Blend	12
Yuban	5
Other	22

Do the study results suggest that market shares may be changing from the previous year? Perform a chi-square goodness-of-fit test to find out.

14. (a) Calculate the mean and standard deviation of the overall rating for Hills Bros. coffee (VAR18).

(b) Construct the 95% confidence interval for the mean rating of Hills Bros. coffee.

(c) Which test statistic would be appropriate to test the hypothesis that the mean rating of Hills Bros. coffee is at least 6.0, assuming an unknown population variance?

(d) If the null hypothesis were true (that is, the mean rating of Hills Bros. coffee within the population is less than 6.0), what is the probability that the mean rating you calculated for the sample could have been obtained?

CODING FORMAT FOR NFO COFFEE STUDY

Question Number	Variable (Variable Number)	Coding Specification
—	Questionnaire ID (VAR1)	—
1	Usual Method of Preparation (VAR2)	1 = automatic drip 2 = electric percolator 3 = stove-top percolator 4 = stove-top dripolator
2a	Ever Use: Folgers (VAR3) Hills Bros. (VAR4) Maxwell House Regular (VAR5) Maxwell House Master Blend (VAR6) Yuban (VAR7) Other (VAR8)	0 = no 1 = yes
2b	Brand Used Most Often (VAR9)	1 = Folgers 2 = Hills Bros. 3 = Maxwell House Regular 4 = Maxwell House Master Blend 5 = Yuban 6 = Other
2c	On Hand: Folgers (VAR10) Hills Bros. (VAR11) Maxwell House Regular (VAR12) Maxwell House Master Blend (VAR13) Yuban (VAR14) Other (VAR15)	0 = no 1 = yes
2d	Brand Will Buy Next (VAR16)	1 = Folgers 2 = Hills Bros. 3 = Maxwell House Regular 4 = Maxwell House Master Blend 5 = Yuban 6 = Other
2e	Overall Rating: Folgers (VAR17) Hills Bros. (VAR18)	Rating 1–10, where 1 = dislike it extremely

		Maxwell House Regular (VAR19)		10 = like it extremely
		Maxwell House Master Blend (VAR20)		
		Yuban (VAR21)		
		Other (VAR22)		

3   Add Nothing (VAR23)   0 = no

Add Dairy Creamer (VAR24)   1 = yes

Add Nondairy Creamer (VAR25)

Add Sugar (VAR26)

Add Artificial Sweetener (VAR27)

Add Something Else (VAR28)

4   Are You Primary Coffee Purchaser (VAR29)?   0 = no

     1 = yes

5   Importance Ratings, 0–10, where   0 = not at all important

     Rich Taste (VAR30)   10 = extremely important

Always Fresh (VAR31)

Gets Day Off to Good Start (VAR32)

Full-Bodied Taste (VAR33)

Rich Aroma in the Cup (VAR34)

Good Value for the Money (VAR35)

Best Coffee in the Morning (VAR36)

Rich Aroma in the Can/Bag (VAR37)

Smooth Taste (VAR38)

Highest Quality Coffee (VAR39)

Premium Brand (VAR40)

Not Bitter (VAR41)

Coffee That Brightens Day Most (VAR42)

Cost More Than Other Brands (VAR43)

Strong Taste (VAR44)

Has No Aftertaste (VAR45)

Economy Brand (VAR46)

Rich Aroma While Brewing (VAR47)

Best Ground Coffee Available (VAR48)

Enjoy Drinking with Meal (VAR49)

Cost Less Than Other Brands (VAR50)

Special Coding Instruction, Question 6

All variables are rating scales coded 0–10, where

     0 = does not describe at all

   10 = describes completely

Variable	Folgers Var. No.	Hills Bros. Var. No.	Maxwell House Regular Var. No.	Maxwell House Master Blend Var. No.	Yuban Var. No.
Rich Taste	VAR51	VAR72	VAR93	VAR114	VAR135
Always Fresh	VAR52	VAR73	VAR94	VAR115	VAR136
Good Start	VAR53	VAR74	VAR95	VAR116	VAR137
Full-Bodied Taste	VAR54	VAR75	VAR96	VAR117	VAR138
Rich Aroma/Cup	VAR55	VAR76	VAR97	VAR118	VAR139
Good Value	VAR56	VAR77	VAR98	VAR119	VAR140
Best Coffee in A.M.	VAR57	VAR78	VAR99	VAR120	VAR141
Rich Aroma/Can	VAR58	VAR79	VAR100	VAR121	VAR142
Smooth Taste	VAR59	VAR80	VAR101	VAR122	VAR143
Highest Quality	VAR60	VAR81	VAR102	VAR123	VAR144
Premium Brand	VAR61	VAR82	VAR103	VAR124	VAR145
Not Bitter	VAR62	VAR83	VAR104	VAR125	VAR146

PART 6:

Data Analysis

Brightens Day Most	VAR63	VAR84	VAR105	VAR126	VAR147
Cost More	VAR64	VAR85	VAR106	VAR127	VAR148
Strong Taste	VAR65	VAR86	VAR107	VAR128	VAR149
No Aftertaste	VAR66	VAR87	VAR108	VAR129	VAR150
Economy Brand	VAR67	VAR88	VAR109	VAR130	VAR151
Rich Aroma/Brewing	VAR68	VAR89	VAR110	VAR131	VAR152
Best Available	VAR69	VAR90	VAR111	VAR132	VAR153
Enjoy with Meal	VAR70	VAR91	VAR112	VAR133	VAR154
Cost Less	VAR71	VAR92	VAR113	VAR134	VAR155

Question Number	Variable (Variable Number)	Coding Specifications
7a	Gender (VAR156)	1 = male
		2 = female
7b	Age (VAR157)	Actual Age Coded

Suggested Additional Readings

Most of the statistical tests discussed in this chapter can be found in any introductory statistics text, and readers are encouraged to refer to the text they used in their introductory statistics course for more details on any of the methods that are discussed.

For more on the interpretation of "averages," see Darrell Huff, *How to Lie with Statistics* (New York: Norton, 1954).

Chapter 21

Data Analysis: Analyzing Multiple Variables Simultaneously

Learning Objectives

1   *Explain the purpose and importance of cross tabulation.*

2   *Describe how percentages should be calculated for a two-way cross-tab.*

3   *Describe how one determines if there is a statistically significant relationship between two categorical variables in a cross-tabulation table.*

4   *Describe a technique for comparing two proportions from independent groups.*

5   *Discuss two techniques for examining associations among ordinal variables.*

6   *Explain two techniques for comparing groups on dependent variables assessed on continuous measures.*

7   *Explain the difference between an independent sample t-test for means and a paired sample t-test for means.*

8   *List three advantages of using analysis of variance versus conducting a series of t-tests to examine differences across groups.*

9   *Discuss two techniques for determining the degree of association between two continuous measures.*

10   *Describe how multiple regression differs from simple regression.*

arketers of fragrances confront a special challenge. As you might expect, the scent of a perfume or cologne is what consumers say they consider most when making a purchase decision. So how does a marketer bring fragrance buyers into contact with a scent they might like?

Enter Vertis Direct Marketing Services. This company, based in Baltimore, Maryland, provides marketers with a variety of services related to planning and preparation of advertisements, magazine inserts, and direct mail—those brochures, coupons, and other advertisements you get in your mail every week. The company also sponsors a variety of research projects, including its annual Customer Focus survey of consumer behavior. As part of the Customer Focus project, researchers ask consumers about their purchase and use of fragrances. Of course, Vertis hopes to work with fragrance companies to apply the results in their marketing campaigns.

Imagine that you work for a company planning a marketing program for a brand of perfume or cologne. General results from the Customer Focus survey suggest not only some approaches to take, but also more questions to answer. According to the 2001 survey of 2,000 U.S. adults, 79 percent say a product's scent is the most important factor they consider in choosing a fragrance to buy.

One way fragrance marketers can take a scent to their customers is by placing scented strips of paper in magazine advertisements. This approach seems reasonable, since 68 percent of fragrance wearers told researchers they had read a magazine during the past week. Among adults who sniffed a scent strip during the previous three months, 61 percent said the scent strip was somewhat or very helpful in choosing a fragrance. Not everyone likes to scratch and sniff, though. Out of all the adults surveyed, just 22 percent said they had purchased a fragrance due to a fragrance strip in a print ad.

Another way to expose consumers to a scent would be to include scent strips in direct-mail advertising. The Customer Focus survey provides some encouragement for this approach as well. In the survey, 73 percent of the respondents said they read direct mail at least occasionally.

As a marketing planner for a fragrance company, you might want to explore these numbers further with a Vertis sales representative. If so, you should formulate additional questions. Your questions might be aimed at learning more about the buying behavior of the consumers most likely to buy your brand. You might also have some questions about certain groups' media behavior—which magazines they read, for example.

Discussion Issues

1. To plan a marketing effort for a particular brand of perfume or cologne, what subgroups of consumers would you want to know more about?

2. What are some more specific questions you would want to answer?

3. In using the results of research conducted by a firm that wants to sell you a service, what issues should you consider? What are some pros and cons of this source of research? ■

The previous chapter demonstrated various approaches for analyzing individual variables. While such univariate analyses are sometimes sufficient for providing the information necessary for a research problem, analysts often encounter situations in which multiple variables must be taken into account in the same analysis. In many ways, multivariate analyses allow researchers a closer look at their data than is possible with univariate analyses. For instance, suppose that in an awareness test for a new ice cream shop, 58% of survey respondents could name the shop in an aided recall task. Closer analysis revealed several insights, however. Only 45% of male respondents could name the shop, compared with 71% of female respondents. Further, age also seemed to be related to awareness: 65% of respondents 30 years old and younger could name the shop, while only 46% of those over 30 years old could do so. The researcher who stopped with the univariate analysis result (i.e., 58% correct in aided recall task) would miss potentially important managerial insights about the relationships between gender and awareness and age and awareness.

In this chapter, we present a number of commonly used multivariate analysis techniques. As with all types of analysis, the level of measurement used with the variables to be analyzed largely determines the types of analytic approaches that are appropriate. The chapter includes three general categories of analyses: those involving categorical measures, those involving both categorical and continuous measures, and those involving continuous measures. For more information about these or other multivariate techniques, the reader is encouraged to consult one of the many multivariate statistics texts that are available (see "Suggestions for Further Reading" at the end of this chapter).

Regardless of the particular type of analysis, when the analysis is based on a sample appropriately drawn from a population it is possible to test the statistical significance of the result. That is, we can use the hypothesis testing procedure outlined in the previous chapter to determine the probability of obtaining the given result in the sample if, in fact, there were no relationship between the variables in the population. Rather than focus on the calculation of the test statistics, however, in most cases we prefer to demonstrate how they are applied in practice. Any good statistical software package can compute the test values for the inferential statistics we discuss.

Analyses Involving Categorical Measures

Two-Way Cross Tabulations

1 *Explain the purpose and importance of cross tabulation.*

cross tabulation
A multivariate technique used for studying the relationship between two or more categorical variables. The technique considers the joint distribution of sample elements across variables.

Cross tabulation is an important tool for studying the relationships between two (or more) categorical variables. It is clearly the most used multivariate data-analysis technique in applied marketing research. Many marketing research studies go no further than simple cross tabulations between two variables at a time (i.e., "two-way" cross tabs). Because they are so commonly used, both researchers and managers need to understand how cross tabulations are developed and interpreted.

In cross tabulation, we usually seek to investigate the influence of one variable (the independent variable) on another variable (the dependent variable). In effect, the respondents are divided into subgroups based on the independent variable in order to see how the dependent variable varies from group to group. For example, consider again the car ownership data from Exhibit 20.1 (page 539). Suppose that the client, an automobile manufacturer, was considering whether or not to offer financing to purchasers of its products. Exhibit 20.2 (page 540) showed that 30% of respondents overall had financed their most recent automobile purchase. The client, however, is particularly interested in whether or not people who own vans are more or less likely to finance auto purchases compared with people who don't own vans. Because we are looking for a potential relationship between two categorical variables, van ownership (yes or no) and financing the most recent car purchase (yes or no), cross tabulation is an appropriate analytic technique.

Exhibit 21.1 presents SPSS (Statistical Package for the Social Sciences) output for the two-way classification of the sample families by van ownership (i.e., VAN) and whether or not the most recent automobile purchase was financed (i.e., FINANCE). Note initially the marginal totals for each variable: 20 respondents owned a van (80 did not), and 30 had financed the

Exhibit 21.1

Financing the Purchase by Van Ownership: SPSS Output

			FINANCE		
			YES	NO	Total
VAN	YES	Count	3	17	20
		% within VAN	15.0%	85.0%	100.0%
		% within FINANCE	10.0%	24.3%	20.0%
		% of Total	3.0%	17.0%	20.0%
	NO	Count	27	53	80
		% within VAN	33.8%	66.3%	100.0%
		% within FINANCE	90.0%	75.7%	80.0%
		% of Total	27.0%	53.0%	80.0%
Total		Count	30	70	100
		% within VAN	30.0%	70.0%	100.0%
		% within FINANCE	100.0%	100.0%	100.0%
		% of Total	30.0%	70.0%	100.0%

most recent car purchase (70 did not). The marginal totals represent the frequencies (one-way tabs) for each of the variables independently. We are more interested, however, in the joint distribution of the two variables. Because there are two levels for each of the variables being considered there are four possible combinations when both variables are considered together ($2 \times 2 = 4$). These combinations are represented by four cells in the cross tabulation. In this case, 3 respondents owned a van and financed their most recent car purchase, 17 owned a van but did not finance the most recent car purchase, 27 did not own a van but did finance the car purchase, and 53 neither owned a van nor financed the car purchase. But what does this mean? Does it appear that there is some connection between owning a van and financing auto purchases?

© AP/Wide World Photos

As noted in Chapter 20, percentages are incredibly useful for interpreting results. Each of the cells in Exhibit 21.1 contains three different percentages that differ depending upon what number is used as the denominator in the calculation of the percentage. The first percentage in each cell, sometimes called the "row percentage" is calculated using the row total as the denominator. For example, consider the cell representing respondents who neither own a van nor financed the car purchase. The row percentage is 66% (i.e., 53/80 = .663). The next percentage in each cell is the column percentage and is calculated using the column total as the denominator. Thus, for those who don't own a van and didn't finance their most recent auto purchase, the column percentage is 76% (i.e., 53/70 = .757). The final percentage shown in each cell is the total percentage; it uses the total number of respondents as the denominator. Thus, for the same cell, the total percentage is 53% (i.e., 53/100 = .530).

The obvious question is "Which percentage should I use?" To answer this question, the analyst must consider which of the variables being studied is the independent variable (cause) and which is the dependent variable (effect). Percentages are always calculated in the direction of the causal variable. That is, the marginal totals for the causal variable are always

Cross tabulation can aid researchers in determining whether there is a relationship between two variables—for example, whether van ownership and financing are linked, and if so, how.

2 *Describe how percentages should be calculated for a two-way cross-tab.*

Exhibit 21.2

Financing the Purchase by Van Ownership

Own Van?	FINANCE MOST RECENT AUTO PURCHASE?		
	Yes	No	Total
Yes	3 (15%)	17 (85%)	20 (100%)
No	27 (34%)	53 (66%)	80 (100%)
Total	30	70	100

used as the denominator when calculating percentages in cross tabulations. In Exhibit 21.1, is it more likely that financing the most recent car purchase caused the family to own a van, or that owning a van caused the family to finance the car purchase? The latter is more plausible, making van ownership the "causal" variable. Because the different levels of the causal variable (van ownership, yes or no) are represented by the rows in the cross tabulation, the row percentages should be used. Exhibit 21.2 demonstrates one method of presenting these results in a research report.

Now back to the original question: Does it appear that people who own vans are more or less likely to finance auto purchases compared with people who don't own vans? Is van ownership related to financing auto purchases? Looking only at the row percentages in Exhibit 21.1, can you detect a different pattern of responses for the two groups (i.e., those who own vans vs. those who do not own vans)? For this sample, families that own vans are less likely to have financed their most recent car purchase compared with families that do not own vans (15% vs. 34%, respectively, had financed the purchase). Thus, it appears that van ownership might be negatively related to financing car purchases. We will address how to determine whether or not this relationship is likely to be true for the population (as opposed to the sample) in the following section.

Cross tabulations work equally well with continuous measures that have been recast as categorical measures. Although recasting continuous measures into categories almost always results in the loss of information and lowered statistical power, managers will often find it easy to interpret and use results from a cross tabulation analysis. Consider the question of the relationship between the number of cars that a family owns and family income. To keep the example simple, suppose the analyst is simply interested in determining if a family above average in income is more likely to own two or more cars than a family below average in income. Suppose further that we knew that $37,500 is the median income in the overall population and that we used this income value to separate the families in the sample into two groups, those with below-average and those with above-average incomes.

Exhibit 21.3 presents the two-way classification of the sample families by income and number of cars. Looking at the marginal totals, we see that 74 families have one car, while 26 families have two cars or more. Further, 54 families fall into the below-average income group using the $37,500 cutoff; 46 families fall into the above-average income group. These results suggest that the sample is fairly representative of the population with respect to income. Notice also that percentages are calculated in the direction of the causal factor (income) across levels of the effect variable (number of cars) based on the logic that income might influence the number of cars a family owns, but the number of cars owned could not cause the level of income.

Does the number of cars depend on income? It certainly seems so on the basis of Exhibit 21.3, since 20 (44%) of the sample families in the upper-income group own two or more cars, compared with only 6 (11%) of the sample families with below-average income. Because we are working with a sample, however, we must consider whether or not this result could have been caused by chance if there were no real relationship between the variables in the population.

Exhibit 21.3

Number of Cars Family Owns by Family Income			
	NUMBER OF CARS		
	1	**2 or More**	**Total**
Less than $37,500	48 (89%)	6 (11%)	54 (100%)
More than $37,500	26 (57%)	20 (44%)	46 (100%)
Total	74	26	100

Testing for Statistical Significance

The hypothesis testing procedure outlined in the previous chapter applies to multivariate analyses as well as to univariate analyses: hypotheses are specified, an inferential test statistic is computed, and the test statistic is compared to a critical value to determine if the result is statistically significant. There are numerous statistical tests that can be applied to cross tabulation results to test for statistical significance. Two of the more commonly used tests are the Pearson chi-square test of independence and Cramer's V.

The **Pearson chi-square test of independence** assesses the degree to which the two variables in a cross tabulation analysis are independent of one another. Note that the Pearson chi-square test does not measure the degree of association between variables, but instead is used to test the null hypothesis that the variables are independent. Though we omit the details, the chi-square test is conceptually similar to the chi-square goodness-of-fit test described in Chapter 20, except that expected frequencies are determined jointly using the marginal totals for both variables in the cross tabulation. The Pearson chi-square value can range from zero to some upper value limited by sample size and the distribution of cases across the cells. The chi-square value, degrees of freedom for the chi-square test, and the p-value are provided in the output for standard statistical analysis software packages. For the analysis of financing the purchase by van ownership presented in Exhibit 21.2, the Pearson chi-square value is 2.697, on 1 degree of freedom, and the associated p-value is .102. Thus, if these variables are truly independent of one another in the population, the probability that we could have obtained a chi-square value of this magnitude is greater than 10% and we choose not to reject the null hypothesis that the variables are independent. The chi-square value for the number of cars by family income (see Exhibit 21.3) is 13.526 on 1 degree of freedom, and the p-value is less than .001. Therefore, if income and the number of cars a family owns were unrelated in the population, the likelihood that we could have obtained a chi-square value this large is less than one in a thousand, and we can reject the null hypothesis of independence and tentatively accept the alternative hypothesis that the variables are not independent of one another.

While the chi-square test indicates whether two variables are independent, it does not measure the strength of association when they are dependent. Numerous approaches have been developed to measure the strength of the relationship between two categorical variables. One of the more popular measures is **Cramer's V,** which is scaled to range between 0 and 1, with higher values representing a stronger relationship between the variables. For example, consider again the possible relationship between family income and the number of cars a family owns (Exhibit 21.3). The chi-square test indicated that the two variables are not independent; Cramer's V for the analysis is equal to .368, an indication of a moderate degree of association between the variables. (For comparison, Cramer's V for the cross tabulation of financing the most recent purchase by van ownership is only .164.)

Presenting Tabular Data

Tabular results for commercial marketing research studies are often presented using banners. A **banner** is a series of cross tabulations between a criterion or dependent variable and several

3 *Describe how one determines if there is a statistically significant relationship between two categorical variables in a cross-tabulation table.*

Pearson chi-square test of independence
A commonly-used statistic for testing the null hypothesis that categorical variables are independent of one another.

Cramer's V
A statistic used to measure the strength of relationship between categorical variables.

banner
A series of cross tabulations between a criterion, or dependent variable, and several (sometimes many) explanatory variables in a single table.

Exhibit 21.4

Banner Format for Car Ownership Data

Question: How many cars does your family own?

	Total Sample	INCOME		FAMILY SIZE	
		Less than $37,500	More than $37,500	4 or Less	5 or More
Total	100	54	46	78	22
	(100)	(100)	(100)	(100)	(100)
1	75	48	27	70	5
	(75)	(89)	(59)	(90)	(23)
2	23	6	17	8	15
	(23)	(11)	(37)	(10)	(68)
3	2	0	2	0	2
	(2)	(0)	(4)	(0)	(9)

(sometimes many) explanatory variables in a single table on a single page. The dependent variable, or phenomenon to be explained, typically serves as the row variable, which is also known as the *stub*. The predictor or explanatory variables serve as the column variables, with each category of these variables serving as a banner point. Exhibit 21.4 shows what the banner format might look like for the car ownership study. Although only two explanatory variables are shown, many more could be. The top line in each row of the table indicates the absolute number possessing the characteristic, whereas the second line indicates the percentage. All percentages have been rounded to zero decimal places in keeping with recommended practice.

There are several advantages of banner tables. First, they allow a great amount of information to be conveyed in a very limited space. Second, their display format makes it easy for nonresearch managers to understand. Managers simply need to look at how the responses to the actual questions that were asked are distributed. A difficulty with these tables is that they tend to hide relationships in which it is necessary to consider several variables simultaneously (e.g., the joint effect of income and family size on multiple car ownership). They consequently make it more difficult to probe alternative explanations for what is producing the results. Banners also make it more difficult to detect data errors caused by improper coding or editing. Although popular, they should not be considered as a substitute for careful cross-tabulation analysis but more as an efficient form of data presentation.

Independent Samples Z-test for Proportions

4 *Describe a technique for comparing two proportions from independent groups.*

It is also possible to directly test for differences between two population proportions. For example, suppose a manufacturer of electric razors is interested in comparing male college students and male nonstudents in terms of their use of electric razors. Suppose random samples of 100 male students and 100 male nonstudents in Austin, Texas, are selected and their use of electric razors is determined. Suppose further that 30 of these students and 20 of these nonstudents regularly shave using electric razors. Does this evidence indicate that a significantly higher percentage of male college students than male nonstudents use electric razors?

Before we proceed with the analysis to answer this question, we must cross one hurdle: the samples from each population must be large enough so that the analytic technique is appropriate. What is large enough? The number of "successes" (i.e., males using electric razors) and "failures" (i.e., males not using electric razors) in each group (i.e., student vs. nonstudent) should be greater than 10. In other words, if these data were arranged in a cross tabulation, the minimum cell size required is 11 per cell. In our example, we find that for college students, 30 were successes and 70 were failures on the characteristic of interest; for nonstudents, successes and failures were 20 and 80, respectively. Therefore, the sample sizes from the two populations may be considered large enough to use the z-test to compare proportions.[1]

Since we are interested in determining whether the two parent-population proportions are different, we test the null hypothesis that they are the same (i.e., $\pi_1 = \pi_2$). To test this hypothesis, we calculate a z statistic to determine the probability that we could have obtained a difference in proportions this large in our samples (i.e., $0.30 - 0.20 = 0.10$) if there truly were no difference in the proportions in the parent populations. Because this is an independent samples test and, accordingly, the data from the two samples may exist in separate data files, we demonstrate how the z statistic is calculated by hand. Although the formula looks a little involved, the calculations are actually quite simple:

$$z = \frac{(p_1 - p_2) - (\pi_1 - \pi_2)}{\sigma_{p_1 - p_2}}$$

where p_1 is the proportion from the first sample; p_2 is the proportion from the second sample; and $\sigma_{p_1 - p_2}$ is the standard error of the difference in the two sample proportions. Because $\pi_1 - \pi_2 = 0$ in this case (remember that the null hypothesis proposes no difference in proportions in the parent populations), the one question that still remains in the calculation of z is, what does $\sigma_{p_1 - p_2}$ equal?

The standard error of the difference in sample proportions is estimated by $s^2_{p_1 - p_2}$, where

$$s_{p_1 - p_2} = \sqrt{pq \left(\frac{1}{n_1} + \frac{1}{n_2}\right)}$$

and

$$p = \frac{\text{total number of successes in the two samples}}{\text{total number of observations in the two samples}}$$

$$q = 1 - p$$

For the example,

$$p = \frac{30 + 20}{100 + 100} = \frac{50}{200} = 0.25$$

$$q = 1 - 0.25 = 0.75$$

$$s_{p_1 - p_2} = \sqrt{(0.25)(0.75)\left(\frac{1}{100} + \frac{1}{100}\right)} = 0.061$$

Calculated z is found as follows:

$$z = \frac{(0.30 - 0.20) - 0}{0.061} = \frac{0.100}{0.061} = 1.64$$

while critical $z = 1.96$ for $\alpha = 0.05$. Thus, the calculated value of z does not exceed the critical value of z; the probability that the difference we observed in the sample proportions could have been obtained if there were no differences in the population proportions is greater than 0.05. Based on the sample evidence, we cannot conclude that there is a difference in the proportion of male college students and male nonstudents using electric razors.

Adding Variables to an Analysis

MOST OF THE EXAMPLES IN THIS CHAPTER EXAMINE RELATIONSHIPS BETWEEN only two variables at a time. Unfortunately, life is usually a bit more complicated than that. A particular dependent variable will almost always be influenced by more than one independent variable, and the effect of one independent variable on the dependent variable may well be influenced, or modified, by some third variable. Recall from Chapter 6 that one of the requirements for establishing causality is the elimination of other possible causes. For this reason alone, the research analyst should consider how a particular bivariate relationship might change with the introduction of a third variable. The bivariate analysis may initially indicate the existence or nonexistence of a relationship between the variables. The introduction of a third variable may result in no change in the initial conclusion, or it may indicate that a substantial change is in order.

For example, suppose one purpose of the car ownership study discussed earlier is to determine the characteristics of families who financed the purchase of their automobiles. Consider the cross tabulation of installment debt versus education of the household head. The following table results when the families included in Exhibit 20.1 are classified into one of two educational categories—those with a high school education or less and those with some college training.

Thus, based on the bivariate cross-tabs analysis, it appears that there is no relationship between education and installment debt; the percentage of families with outstanding car debt is 30 percent in each case. Consider what happens, however, when income (divided into two categories) is also considered in the analysis. A clear picture of the relationship among the three variables considered simultaneously can be developed by reporting the percentage of families who financed the car purchase in each of the categories. (The complement, 100 minus the percentage, then indicates the proportion not financing the car purchase.)

For below-average incomes, the presence of installment debt increases with education.

Financed Car Purchase by Education of Household Head

Education of Household Head	FINANCED CAR PURCHASE?		
	Yes	No	Total
High school or less	24 (30%)	56 (70%)	80 (100%)
Some college	6 (30%)	14 (70%)	20 (100%)

Spearman rank-order correlation coefficient
A technique for determining the degree of association between two ordinal, or rank-ordered, variables.

Spearman Rank-Order Correlation Coefficient

Sometimes a marketing research analyst needs to determine the degree of association between two ordinal measures. The **Spearman rank-order correlation coefficient (Spearman's rho)** is ideal for determining the degree of association between two rank-ordered series.[2] Suppose, for instance, that a company sells its products through 15 different distributors and wishes to determine whether there is any association between the overall performance of a distributor and the distributor's level of service. Using many different measures of performance (e.g., sales, market share, sales growth, profit) and service quality (e.g., customer complaints, customer compliments, service turnaround records), the marketing research department is able to rank the distributors from 1 to 15 on each of the two dimensions. Exhibit 21.5 contains the ranks of the company's 15 distributors with respect to each of the two variables.

Financed Car Purchase by Education of Household Head and Income			
	INCOME		
Education of Household Head	Less than $37,500	More than $37,500	Total
High school or less	12%	58%	30%
Some college	40%	27%	30%

For above-average incomes, installment debt decreases with education. The effect of education was hidden in the original bivariate analysis because the effects canceled each other. When income is also considered, the relationship of installment debt to education is quite pronounced. This is an example of *spurious noncorrelation;* that is, the analyst would have concluded that there was no relationship between two variables when in fact a strong relationship existed—but was hidden until the third variable was included in the analysis. It is also possible that a bivariate analysis can suggest that a relationship exists between two variables when in fact there is none. Instead, one or both variables may simply be related to a third variable and the relationship will disappear when that variable is taken into account. This situation represents *spurious correlation* between the two original variables.

Thus, a conclusion can change dramatically when a third variable is added to an analysis. This is true for any type of analysis, not just bivariate cross-tabs. You may have paused to ask yourself, Why stop with three variables? Would the conclusion change with the addition of a fourth variable? A fifth? Indeed it might. The problem is that we never really know for sure when to stop introducing variables. The conclusion is always susceptible to change with the introduction of the "right" variable or variables. The analyst is always in the position of inferring that a relationship exists. Later research may demonstrate that the inference was incorrect. This is why the accumulation of studies, rather than a single study, supporting a particular relationship is so vital to the advancement of knowledge. The development of sound theory is also critical to determining which variables should be related to other variables and when to stop putting more variables into an analysis. ■

Exhibit 21.5

Distributor Performance

Distributor	Service Quality Ranking X_i	Overall Performance Ranking Y_i	Ranking Difference $D_i = X_i - Y_i$	Difference Squared D_i^2
1	6	8	−2	4
2	2	4	+2	4
3	13	12	+1	1
4	1	2	−1	1
5	7	10	−3	9
6	4	5	−1	1
7	11	9	+2	4
8	15	13	+2	4
9	3	1	+2	4
10	9	6	+3	9
11	12	14	−2	4
12	5	3	+2	4
13	14	15	−1	1
14	8	7	+1	1
15	10	11	−1	

$$\sum_{i=1}^{15} d_i^2 = 52$$

These types of analyses often involve only a few objects (15 in this example) and it is about as easy to calculate the Spearman rank-order correlation coefficient by hand as to input the data into the computer for analysis. The calculation is straightforward:

$$r_s = 1 - \frac{6\sum_{i=1}^{n} d_i^2}{n(n^2 - 1)}$$

where X_i = service quality ranking for the ith distributor; Y_i = performance ranking for the ith distributor; n = total number of distributors; and $d_i = X_i - Y_i^3$. In the example at hand,

$$\sum_{i=1}^{15} d_i^2 = 52$$

and

$$r_s = 1 - \frac{6(52)}{15(15^2 - 1)} = 1 - \frac{312}{3,360} = 0.907$$

Because the Spearman rank-order correlation coefficient can range from -1 (indicating that the rankings on the two attributes are exactly opposite one another) to $+1$ (indicating that the rankings are identical for the two attributes), the obtained value of 0.907 indicates a strong positive relationship between service quality and overall performance.

In our example, there were only 15 distributors in the entire population and we had rankings for all of them. In this situation (i.e., complete information on the population) there is no sampling error and it is unnecessary to use inferential statistics and hypothesis tests: the results are what they are. Much of the time, however, we are forced to work with only a sample drawn from the population. Suppose, for example, that the company employed 150 distributors and the 15 distributors shown in Exhibit 21.5 were randomly drawn from the population. Now it becomes important to determine whether or not a rank-order correlation of this magnitude could likely have been obtained if there were no relationship between the variables in the population. The null hypothesis for the example would be that there is no association between service level and overall distributor performance, while the alternate hypothesis would suggest there is a relationship. The null hypothesis that $r_s = 0$ can be tested by referring to tables of critical values of r_s or, when the number of sample objects is greater than 10, by calculating the t statistic

$$t = r_s \sqrt{\frac{n-2}{1 - r_s^2}}$$

which is referred to a t table for $v = n - 2$ degrees of freedom. Calculated t is

$$t = 0.907 \sqrt{\frac{15 - 2}{1 - (0.907)^2}} = 7.77$$

while critical t for $\alpha = 0.05$ and $v = 13$ degrees of freedom is 2.16. Calculated t exceeds critical t, and the null hypothesis of no relationship is rejected. Overall distributor performance is related to service quality level. On the basis of the sample of 15 distributors, we could conclude that the relationship is statistically significant.

PART 6:
Data Analysis

Coefficient of Concordance

Spearman's rank-order correlation coefficient is concerned with the correlation between two sets of rankings of n objects. What would happen, however, if we needed to analyze the association among three or more sets of rankings of n objects or individuals? When there are three or more sets of rankings, **Kendall's coefficient of concordance,** W, can be used to examine the association among the rankings.

One particularly important use of the coefficient of concordance is in examining interjudge reliability. Imagine that a computer equipment manufacturer wanted to evaluate its domestic sales branch managers. To accomplish this task, the company asked the vice president in charge of marketing, the general sales manager, and the marketing research department to rank the company's ten branch managers from best to worst (Exhibit 21.6).

The coefficient of concordance, W, is easy to calculate by hand using the following formula,

$$W = \frac{\sum_{i=1}^{n}(R_i - \bar{R})^2}{\frac{1}{12}\,k^2\,(n^3 - n)}$$

where R_i = the sum of ranks for object$_i$; $\bar{R}$ = average sum of ranks across all objects; k = number of sets of rankings; and n = number of objects being ranked. The coefficient of concordance can range from 0 to 1; the larger the value, the greater the agreement among the evaluations. For the example,

$$\bar{R} = \frac{\sum_{i=1}^{n} R_i}{n} = \frac{13 + 7 + \ldots + 23}{10} = \frac{165}{10} = 16.5$$

$$W = \frac{(13 - 16.5)^2 + (7 - 16.5)^2 + \ldots + (23 - 16.5)^2}{\frac{1}{12}\,(3^2)(10^3 - 10)} = \frac{720.50}{742.50} = 0.97$$

When examining interjudge reliability, it is likely that the objects or individuals being evaluated make up the entire population of such objects or individuals, as is the case for our

Kendall's coefficient of concordance
A technique for determining the degree of association between three or more ordinal variables.

Exhibit 21.6

Branch Manager Rankings

Branch Manager	RANK ADVOCATED BY			Sum of Ranks R_i
	Vice-President of Marketing	General Sales Manager	Marketing Research Department	
A	4	4	5	13
B	3	2	2	7
C	9	10	10	29
D	10	9	9	28
E	2	3	3	8
F	1	1	1	3
G	6	5	4	15
H	8	7	7	22
I	5	6	6	17
J	7	8	8	23

example. However, if the objects to be evaluated are a sample drawn from the population, it is possible to test for the statistical significance of the result. The significance of W can be examined by using special tables when the number of objects ranked is small (in particular, when $n \leq 7$). When there are more than seven objects, the coefficient of concordance is approximately chi-square distributed where $\chi^2 = k(n - 1) W$, with $v = n - 1$ degrees of freedom. The null hypothesis is that there is no agreement among the rankings, while the alternate hypothesis is that there is some agreement. For an assumed $\alpha = 0.05$, critical χ^2 for $v = n - 1 = 9$ degrees of freedom is 16.92, while calculated χ^2 is

$$\chi^2 = k\,(n-1)W = 3\ (9)\,(0.97) = 26.20$$

Calculated χ^2 exceeds critical χ^2, and the null hypothesis of no agreement is rejected, because there indeed is agreement. Further, the agreement is good, as is evidenced by the calculated coefficient of concordance. The calculated value of W of 0.970 suggests that while the agreement in the ranks is not perfect, it is certainly good. The marketing vice-president, the general sales manager, and the marketing research department are applying essentially the same standards in ranking the branch managers.

Kendall has suggested that the best estimate of the true ranking of n objects is provided by the order of the various sums of ranks, R_j, when W is significant.[4] Thus, the best estimate of the true ranking of the sales managers is that F is doing the best job, B the next best job, and C the poorest job.

Analyses Involving Categorical and Continuous Measures

6 *Explain two techniques for comparing groups on dependent variables assessed on continuous measures.*

Researchers commonly encounter situations in which an interval- or ratio-level outcome measure must be compared across levels of one or more categorical independent variables. For instance, imagine that a brand manager wanted to know whether men and women held different attitudes toward her brand or that a research manager for a small hospital chain wanted to compare patient perceptions of service quality across the three different hospitals in the chain. In these and many other cases, the task is to test for differences across groups (i.e., men vs. women; hospital A patients vs. hospital B patients vs. hospital C patients) on some important variable assessed using a continuous measure (i.e., attitude toward the brand; perceptions of service quality). In this section, we present two related techniques for examining differences of these types, the independent samples t-test for means and the analysis of variance. It is important to note that these techniques only apply to situations in which there is at least the potential for a causal relationship between one or more categorical independent variables and a continuous dependent variable. More sophisticated techniques are required to analyze the reverse situation (i.e., continuous independent variable(s) and categorical dependent variable).

In this section we also consider the situation in which a researcher wants to compare mean scores for variables provided by the same group of respondents. For example, suppose that a department store had a sample of its customers rate the quality of its merchandise in two general categories, clothing and accessories, using the same "very poor" to "very good" rating scale, and that everyone evaluated both categories. Department store managers were interested in determining whether the quality of its clothing was superior to the judged quality of the accessories that they offered. The appropriate analysis, the paired sample t-test for means, is presented in this section.

Independent Samples *T*-test for Means

7 *Explain the difference between an independent sample t-test for means and a paired sample t-test for means.*

A manufacturer of floor waxes recently developed a new wax. The company is considering two different containers for the wax, one plastic and one metal. The company decides to make the final determination on the basis of a limited sales test in which the plastic containers are

PART 6:
Data Analysis

introduced in a random sample of ten stores and the metal containers are introduced in an *independent,* or separate, random sample of ten stores. Thus, we have a categorical independent variable (type of container) measured on two levels that we believe might influence a continuous dependent variable (sales). The test results are presented in Exhibit 21.7.

Using a calculator we can quickly discover that mean store sales for wax sold is 403.0 units per store for the plastic containers and 390.3 units per store for the metal containers. Can we conclude that the company should choose the plastic container? Not yet. As usual, we must test to determine how likely it is that we could have obtained these *sample* results (a difference of about 13 units per store) if there really were no difference in sales in the overall *population* from which the samples were drawn. The company has decided to use the 0.05 level of significance ($\alpha = 0.05$) for this test.

The test statistic, *t*, can be easily obtained using any statistical software package. In this case, an analysis using SPSS produces a calculated *t*-value of 1.558 with 18 degrees of freedom (d.f. = total sample size for analysis – 2 = 20 – 2 = 18). The associated p-value, using

© Terri L. Miller/E-Visual Communications, Inc.

a two-tailed test (recall that we are testing whether or not the mean sales levels are equal, not whether one exceeds the other), is equal to 0.137. Thus, if there really were no difference in sales for the two types of containers in the population, the probability that we could have obtained a difference of 13.3 units per store in our sample ($p = 0.137$) is considerably greater than the level of significance adopted by the company ($p < 0.05$), and we cannot conclude that the plastic container will do better than the metal container based on the evidence at hand.

Simply comparing mean store sales of a product is not enough—the researcher must also determine the likelihood that the sample results would also be obtained in the overall population.

Exhibit 21.7	Store Sales of Floor Wax in Units		
	Store	Plastic Container	Metal Container
	1	432	—
	2	360	—
	3	397	—
	4	408	—
	5	417	—
	6	380	—
	7	422	—
	8	406	—
	9	400	—
	10	408	—
	11	—	365
	12	—	405
	13	—	396
	14	—	390
	15	—	404
	16	—	372
	17	—	378
	18	—	410
	19	—	383
	20	—	400

independent
samples *t*-test

A commonly-used tech-
nique used to determine
whether two groups differ
on some characteristic
assessed on a continuous
measure.

The **independent samples *t*-test** is so fundamental to marketing research that it warrants closer examination. With a small sample size, the *t*-test can be calculated easily by hand. Assuming that the distribution of the dependent variable in each population is normal (a slightly modified technique is required if the distribution is very non-normal), the *t*-value is calculated as follows:

$$t = \frac{(\bar{x}_1 - \bar{x}_2 - (\mu_1 - \mu_2)}{s_{\bar{x}_1 - \bar{x}_2}}$$

where $\bar{x}_1$ is the sample mean for the first group, $\bar{x}_2$ is the sample mean for the second group, μ_1 is the population mean for the first group, μ_2 is the population mean for the second group (note that μ_1 and μ_2 are assumed to be equal under the null hypothesis), and $s_{\bar{x}_1 - \bar{x}_2}$ is the estimated error of the test statistic. The estimated error is calculated by

$$s_{\bar{x}_1 - \bar{x}_2} = \sqrt{\hat{s}^2 \left(\frac{1}{n_1} + \frac{1}{n_2}\right)}$$

where $\hat{s}^2$ is the pooled sample variance (we assume that the two parent-population variances are equal)[5], n_1 is the sample size for the first group, and n_2 is the sample size for the second group. In turn, $\hat{s}^2$ is calculated as

$$\hat{s}^2 = \frac{\sum_{i=1}^{n_1}(X_{i1} - \bar{x}_1)^2 + \sum_{i=1}^{n_2}(X_{i2} - \bar{x}_2)^2}{(n_1 + n_2 - 2)}$$

where X_{i1} is the value of X for the ith sample element in the first group and X_{i_2} is the value of X for the ith sample element in the second group.

Applying these formulas to the data reported in Exhibit 21.7, we find the pooled sample variance by

$$\hat{s}^2 = \frac{(432.0 - 403.0)^2 + (360.0 - 403.0)^2 + \ldots + (383.0 - 390.3)^2 + (400.0 - 390.3)^2}{10 + 10 - 2} = 332.1$$

and the estimated error of the test statistic is thus

$$s_{\bar{x}_1 - \bar{x}_2} = \sqrt{332.1\left(\frac{1}{10} + \frac{1}{10}\right)} = 8.15$$

and the calculated *t*-value equals

$$\text{calculated } t = \frac{(403.0 - 390.3) - (0)}{8.15} = 1.56$$

This is the same value of t produced by the SPSS analysis reported above. However, when performing t-tests by hand, it is necessary to compare the obtained value of t to a critical value of t obtained from a t table for 18 degrees of freedom in order to determine whether or not the results are statistically significant (the p-value is provided directly in the computer output). For our example, the critical value of t corresponding to a two-tailed test and a desired significance level of 0.05 is t = 2.101. Because the *t*-value calculated from the results of the empirical analysis is less than the critical value, we cannot reject the null hypothesis that the means are equal in the population.

Paired Sample *T*-test for Means

The independent samples *t*-test for means always compares mean scores for the same variable measured in two separate groups. What happens when a researcher needs to compare two means when both measures are provided by the same sample? The analyst will use the **paired sample *t*-test** for means. For instance, advertising researchers might be interested in determining whether attitude toward a brand increases after consumers watch a 30-second ad for the brand. The researchers would measure attitude toward the brand *both before and after* showing the 30-second ad and then compare mean scores across the consumers in the study. In this situation, the continuous dependent variable is the measure of brand attitude and the categorical independent variable is time of measurement (i.e., before vs. after).

Another common situation that calls for the use of the paired sample *t*-test arises when researchers take the same measure and apply it to different objects. For example, suppose that a local grocery store wanted to compare consumers' overall perceptions of its prices vs. overall perceptions of prices for a nearby competitor. Researchers might prepare a questionnaire that includes measures designed to assess perception of prices on a 1–10 rating scale for each of the two stores and then collect data from a sample of community residents. The continuous dependent variable is perception of price and the categorical independent variable is the store (i.e., local store vs. competitor).

As with the independent samples *t*-test, the paired sample *t*-test is common in marketing research and is easy to calculate by hand when the number of cases is small. To illustrate, consider a manufacturer and retailer of camping equipment that wished to study consumer color preferences for a sleeping bag it had recently developed. The company was uncertain whether consumers would prefer bright colors or more subdued earth tones for the new line of sleeping bags. Instead of simply polling potential consumers about their opinions on color, the company decided to perform a market test by introducing both brightly-colored and earth tone bags into five randomly selected stores and examine actual sales patterns over a three-month period. The sales per store are presented in Exhibit 21.8.

A quick look at the sales of the different colored bags per store allows a couple of observations. First, bright colors outsold earth tones in each of the 5 stores. Second, differences in units sold between the two colors of bags were not that large. The mean units sold for bright colors and earth tones were 50.2 and 45.2, respectively, in the sample. The key question: Do these data present sufficient evidence to indicate that consumers prefer brightly-colored sleeping bags?

If we were to apply the procedures of the previous section (i.e., the independent samples *t*-test), we would find that the difference in units sold is not statistically significant. This test would be inappropriate, however, because the samples providing the sales data are obviously *not* independent. Sales of bright-colored and earth-colored bags are definitely related, since they are both found in the same stores. Note how this example differs from the floor wax example, in which the metal containers were placed in one sample of stores and the plastic containers were located in an independent sample of stores. We need a procedure that takes into account the fact that the observations are related.

paired sample *t*-test
A technique for comparing two means when scores for both variables are provided by the same sample.

Exhibit 21.8

Store Sales of Sleeping Bags

Store	Bright Colors	Earth Colors
1	64	56
2	72	66
3	43	39
4	22	20
5	50	45

The appropriate procedure is the paired sample t-test, sometimes called the t-test for related samples. The procedure begins by calculating d_i, the difference between sales of the bright-colored bags and the earth-colored bags for each of the five stores. Thus,

$$d_1 = 64 - 56 = 8$$
$$d_2 = 72 - 66 = 6$$
$$d_3 = 43 - 39 = 4$$
$$d_4 = 22 - 20 = 2$$
$$d_5 = 50 - 45 = 5$$

Now calculate the mean difference by averaging the individual store-to-store differences

$$\bar{d} = \frac{\sum\limits_{i=1}^{n} d_i}{n} = \frac{8 + 6 + 4 + 2 + 5}{5} = 5.0$$

and the standard deviation of the difference by determining the sum of the deviations around the mean squared, specifically

$$s_d \sqrt{\frac{\sum\limits_{i=1}^{n} (d_i - \bar{d})^2}{n - 1}} = \sqrt{\frac{20}{4}} = 2.24$$

The test statistic is the sample mean difference minus the hypothesized population mean difference, divided by the standard deviation of the difference divided by the square root of the sample size

$$t = \frac{\bar{d} - D}{s_d / \sqrt{n}}$$

where D is the difference that is expected under the null hypothesis. In this case, because there is no reason why one color would be expected to sell better than the other, the appropriate null hypothesis is that there is no difference, making $D = 0$. Calculated t is therefore

$$t = \frac{5.0 - 0}{2.24 / \sqrt{5}} = 5.0$$

This value is referred to a t table for $v = $ (sample size $-$ 1) degrees of freedom; thus, $v = 5 - 1 = 4$. The critical value of t for $v = 4$ and $\alpha = 0.05$ is 2.776, and we can therefore reject the null hypothesis of no difference. The sample evidence indicates that the bright-colored sleeping bags are likely to outsell the earth-colored ones.

Analysis of Variance (ANOVA)

8 *List three advantages of using analysis of variance versus conducting a series of t-tests to examine differences across groups.*

The t-test is a useful tool for comparing means between two groups. What happens, though, when there are more than two groups to be compared, or when there is more than one categorical independent variable to be considered? In these situations, the analyst might resort to a series of t-tests, taking two groups at a time for one independent variable at a time, but such a strategy would be inefficient, would increase the likelihood of making a type I error (i.e., rejecting a true null hypothesis), and wouldn't allow for the joint effects of the independent variables. Fortunately, there is a better way.

PART 6:
Data Analysis

The **analysis of variance (ANOVA)** has the distinct advantage of being applicable when there are more than two means being compared. The basic idea underlying the analysis of variance is that the parent-population variance can be estimated from the sample in several ways, and comparisons among these estimates tell us a great deal about the population. If the null hypothesis of no differences across groups is true (i.e., scores on the dependent variable are unaffected by which category the member of the sample belongs to), the following three estimates of the population variance should be equal:

1. The *total variation,* computed by comparing each of the individual scores on the continuous dependent variable (across all groups) with the overall mean score.
2. The *between-group variation,* computed by comparing each of the group means with the overall mean score.
3. The *within-group variation,* computed by comparing each of the individual scores with the mean of its own group.

If, however, the null hypothesis is not true, and there is a difference in the mean scores across the groups, then the between-group variation should produce a higher estimate than the within-group variation, which considers only the variation within groups and is independent of differences between groups.

As an example, one of the authors has been working with an automobile dealership to better understand factors related to customer loyalty. Among other things, we wanted to determine variables that might lead to higher levels of consumer commitment to a continued relationship with the dealership. One possibility is that the level of existing relationship (some customers currently drive cars purchased from the dealership, while others don't and presumably only visit the dealership for service) might influence the level of commitment to the dealership. Consumer commitment was measured via four Likert-type items; an index score was computed by taking the average across the four items, with scores ranging from 1 to 7. Type of relationship was assessed on a single-item scale that asked respondents whether or not they or a close family member were currently driving a vehicle purchased from the dealership. Thus, we have a continuous dependent variable (consumer commitment, which we labeled COMMIT in analyses) and a categorical independent variable measured on two levels (type of relationship: currently driving a car purchased from the dealership vs. not currently driving a car purchased from the dealership—we labeled this variable CURRAUTO). In ANOVA, the independent variables are typically called *factors,* and the different levels of the independent variable are referred to as *treatment levels.*

Using a systematic sample of the dealership's customer database and a mail survey, we obtained 397 usable responses for this analysis. For the 285 respondents who currently drove a car purchased from the dealership, the mean commitment score was 4.3, while the mean commitment score for 112 customers who did not drive a car obtained from the dealership was 3.7. Based on the sample results, it appears that type of existing relationship does influence consumer commitment, but is this difference statistically significant? In other words, can we safely conclude that the result is likely to be true for all customers of the dealership?

To find the answer, the researcher can use the analysis of variance. Using SPSS to analyze the data, we obtained the ANOVA table presented in Exhibit 21.9. Looking at the "mean square" column allows an insight into the size of the between-group variation relative to the within-group variation. The mean square for the between-group variation (representing the independent variable CURRAUTO) is 30.981 and is over 10 times larger than the mean square for the within-group variation (represented as "residual" in the table). For ANOVA, the inferential test statistic is the F-statistic ($F = 10.667$). The final column presents the p-value associated with the test statistic and represents the likelihood of obtaining the sample results (i.e., commitment = 4.3 for current drivers vs. commitment = 3.7 for non-drivers) if there were truly no difference in the parent-population scores. Because $p < 0.05$, we conclude that customers who currently drive cars purchased from the dealership are indeed more committed to the dealership than are customers who do not currently drive cars purchased from the dealership.

Exhibit 21.9

SPSS ANOVA Table for Consumer Commitment Study

ANOVA[a,b]

			Sum of Squares	df	Mean Square	F	Sig.
			Unique Method				
COMMIT	Main Effects	CURRAUTO	30.981	1	30.981	10.667	.001
	Model		30.981	1	30.981	10.667	.001
	Residual		1147.219	395	2.904		
	Total		1178.200	396	2.975		

[a] COMMIT by CURRAUTO
[b] All effects entered simultaneously

It would have been a simple matter to perform an independent samples t-test to arrive at the same conclusion since there were only two groups in the previous example. However, the ANOVA applies equally well when there are more than two treatment levels (i.e., groups) or more than one factor (i.e., independent variable). For example, based on prior research, we believed that the level of satisfaction of the respondents would also influence the level of consumer commitment. Simply put, respondents who were more satisfied with the dealership should report higher levels of commitment to the dealership. To test this proposition, we measured respondents' satisfaction using a 10-item scale and used a median split to group respondents into two groups, those with lower levels of satisfaction and those with higher levels of satisfaction.

factorial design
An ANOVA analysis that includes two or more categorical independent variables.

In ANOVA, a **factorial design** allows a researcher to examine simultaneously the effects of two or more independent variables. For our example, there are two different treatment levels for each factor, or four different treatments in all since they can be used in combination. Exhibit 21.10 presents mean commitment scores for the four different treatments. Consider what this table tells us. First, we can see that the overall commitment score across all respondents was 4.1. While this univariate result is interesting, can we learn more about consumer commitment by adding additional variables to the analysis? The answer is a resounding "yes!" We can see the independent effects of satisfaction and whether or not the respondent drives a car purchased from the dealership on the level of consumer commitment by examining the "total" column or row corresponding to the factors. Respondents in the lower satisfaction group had a mean commitment score of 3.4, while those in the higher satisfaction group had a mean score of 4.8; the scores for those driving a vehicle purchased from the dealership vs. those who did not were reported earlier and can be found in the bottom row of the table. Thus, it appears that both driving a car obtained from the dealership and being more satisfied

Exhibit 21.10

Mean Commitment Scores for Four Groups

	CURRENTLY DRIVE CAR FROM DEALERSHIP?					
Satisfaction Level	No	(n)	Yes	(n)	Total	(n)
Lower	3.2	(61)	3.6	(132)	3.4	(193)
Higher	4.3	(51)	5.0	(153)	4.8	(204)
Total	3.7	(112)	4.3	(285)	4.1	(397)

with the dealership lead to higher levels of commitment. Third, the table allows us to see the joint effects of the two independent variables on commitment scores. We observe, for instance, that we obtain the lowest mean commitment score for those who are dissatisfied and don't drive a car purchased from the dealership, while the highest mean commitment score is produced by the opposite conditions.

Exhibit 21.11 contains the ANOVA table produced by an SPSS analysis. With both factors in the analysis, we see that each produces a significant effect on the dependent variable, consumer commitment. For CURRAUTO, the variable representing whether or not the respondent drives a car obtained from the dealership, $F = 8.666$; for SAT2, the variable representing satisfaction in two groups, $F = 52.262$. Each of these test statistics is statistically significant at $\alpha = 0.05$, so we can conclude that both variables influence commitment in the parent-populations.

There is an additional important piece of information contained in the ANOVA table shown in Exhibit 21.11. As addressed in Technically Speaking 21.1, the introduction of a second independent variable makes it possible to determine if the two independent variables interact in their influence on the dependent variable. For instance, suppose we hypothesized that for "service-only" customers (i.e., those not driving an automobile purchased from the dealership), satisfaction would exert a stronger effect upon commitment than for customers who purchased their vehicles from the dealership because of the variety of options available for automotive service. In effect, because of the range of options available, consumer commitment for service-only customers might be especially sensitive to the effects of satisfaction with a particular option. If such an interaction effect is present, we would expect to see substantially larger differences between mean commitment scores for the lower and higher satisfaction groups in the first column in Exhibit 21.10 compared with the second column (i.e., those not driving a car from the dealership vs. those who are driving a car from the dealership). As it turns out, in the sample results (Exhibit 21.10), the difference between mean satisfaction scores for the higher vs. lower satisfaction groups is actually a little bit greater for those who currently drive vehicle purchased from the dealer. A look at the ANOVA table in Exhibit 21.11, however, reveals that this difference could easily have been obtained by chance ($F = 0.545$; $p = .461$) if there were really no interaction between the two independent variables in the parent-populations. Therefore, we can conclude that the variables exert independent influences on commitment; it is unlikely that the variables interact in the population.

Exhibit 21.11

SPSS ANOVA Table for Two-Way Consumer Commitment Study

ANOVA[a,b]

COMMIT			Unique Method				
			Sum of Squares	df	Mean Square	F	Sig.
COMMIT	Main Effects	(Combined)	160.726	2	80.363	32.505	.000
		CURRAUTO	21.424	1	21.424	8.666	.003
		SAT2	129.211	1	129.211	52.262	.000
	2-Way Interactions	CURRAUTO* SAT2	1.347	1	1.347	.545	.461
	Model		206.567	3	68.856	27.850	.000
	Residual		971.633	393	2.472		
	Total		1178.200	396	2.975		

[a] COMMIT by CURRAUTO, SAT2
[b] All effects entered simultaneously

Analyses Involving Continuous Measures

9 *Discuss two techniques for determining the degree of association between two continuous measures.*

The first two sections of this chapter have examined relationships in which at least one of the variables involved in the analysis was a categorical measure. What happens when both variables in a bivariate analysis are measured on continuous scales? Suppose a researcher wanted to determine if there was a relationship between salespeople's years of experience and annual sales per salesperson. Similarly, a company might be interested in knowing whether or not there is a relationship between household income and units purchased per household for its product within a certain market segment. In this section, we discuss two closely related analyses involving continuous measures, the correlation coefficient and simple regression analysis. We also overview multiple regression analysis, a technique used to investigate the nature of the relationship between two or more predictor variables and a continuous outcome variable.

Pearson Product-Moment Correlation Coefficient

The correlation coefficient is a fundamental building block of data analysis. Most people seem to have a basic understanding of what it means when someone says that two things are "correlated." Though they may not understand the technical details, there is an implicit understanding that the two concepts, events, or ideas somehow "go together," that there is some sort of association between them. As one thing changes, so does the other. People intuitively understand the basic concept because life is full of examples. For example, as temperatures rise, the average amount of clothing worn decreases; as family incomes rise, the size of the family house increases; as study time increases, so often do exam scores.

Pearson product-moment correlation coefficient

A statistic that indicates the degree of linear association between two continuous variables. The correlation coefficient can range from –1 to +1.

The **Pearson product-moment correlation coefficient** provides a means of quantifying the degree of association between two continuous variables. Consider the manufacturer of a ballpoint pen, Click, which is interested in investigating the effectiveness of the firm's marketing efforts. The company uses wholesalers to distribute Click, and supplements their efforts with company sales representatives and spot television advertising. The company plans to use annual territory sales as its measure of effectiveness. These data and information on the number of sales representatives serving a territory are readily available in company records. The other characteristics to which the manufacturer seeks to relate sales—television spot advertising and wholesaler efficiency—are more difficult to determine. To obtain information on television spot advertising in a territory, researchers must analyze advertising schedules and study area coverage by channel to determine what areas each broadcast might reach. Wholesaler efficiency requires rating the wholesalers on a number of criteria and aggregating the ratings into an overall measure of wholesaler efficiency, where 4 is outstanding, 3 is good, 2 is average, and 1 is poor. Because of the time and expense required to generate these advertising and distribution characteristics, the company has decided to analyze only a sample of sales territories. The data for a simple random sample of 40 territories are contained in Exhibit 21.12.

scatter diagram

A graphic technique in which a sample element's scores on two variables are used to position the element on a graph so that the nature of the relationship between the variables can be observed.

Initially, the company simply wants to determine if there is any relationship between TV spot advertising and annual sales. This relationship might be investigated in several ways. One very obvious way is to simply plot sales and number of TV spots on a graph known as a **scatter diagram,** or scatter plot. Figure 21.1 contains the plot. An "eyeball" analysis suggests that sales increase as the number of television spots per month increases. While the scatter plot gives us an idea about the potential relationship between two variables, a much more precise measure of association is provided by the Pearson product-moment correlation coefficient. The formula for this correlation coefficient is

$$r = \frac{\sum_{i=1}^{n}(X_i - \bar{x})(Y_i - \bar{y})}{(n-1)s_x s_y}$$

Exhibit 21.12

Territory Data for Click Ballpoint Pens

Territory	Sales (in Thousands) Y	Advertising (TV Spots per Month) X_1	Number of Sales Representatives X_2	Wholesaler Efficiency Index X_3
005	260.3	5	3	4
019	286.1	7	5	2
033	279.4	6	3	3
039	410.8	9	4	4
061	438.2	12	6	1
082	315.3	8	3	4
091	565.1	11	7	3
101	570.0	16	8	2
115	426.1	13	4	3
118	315.0	7	3	4
133	403.6	10	6	1
149	220.5	4	4	1
162	343.6	9	4	3
164	644.6	17	8	4
178	520.4	19	7	2
187	329.5	9	3	2
189	426.0	11	6	4
205	343.2	8	3	3
222	450.4	13	5	4
237	421.8	14	5	2
242	245.6	7	4	4
251	503.3	16	6	3
260	375.7	9	5	3
266	265.5	5	3	3
279	620.6	18	6	4
298	450.5	18	5	3
306	270.1	5	3	2
332	368.0	7	6	2
347	556.1	12	7	1
358	570.0	13	6	4
362	318.5	8	4	3
370	260.2	6	3	2
391	667.0	16	8	2
408	618.3	19	8	2
412	525.3	17	7	4
430	332.2	10	4	3
442	393.2	12	5	3
467	283.5	8	3	3
471	376.2	10	5	4
488	481.8	12	5	2

where X_i and Y_i are the number of TV spots and territory sales (in thousands) for the ith territory; $\bar{x}$ and $\bar{y}$ are the mean number of TV spots and mean territory sales (in thousands) across the 40 territories; n is the number of territories; and s_x and s_y are the standard deviations for number of TV spots and territory sales, respectively. The numerator in the formula, called the "cross-products sum," establishes the degree of covariation between the two variables. Because this quantity can be easily altered by changing sample size or by changing units of analysis, the covariance is adjusted for sample size (to get a sense of the average degree of covariation per territory) and by each of the standard deviations for the two variables of interest (to make the

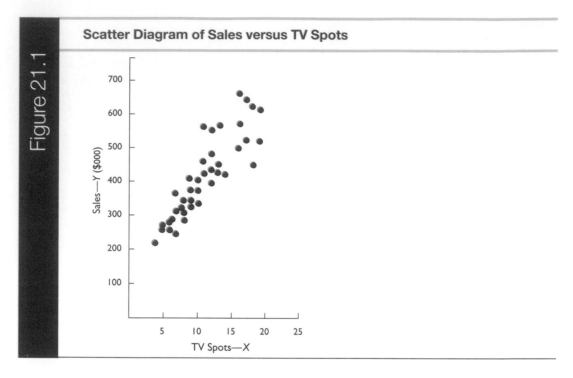

Figure 21.1

Scatter Diagram of Sales versus TV Spots

resulting correlation coefficient unitless). The Pearson product-moment correlation coefficient can range from -1 (representing perfect negative linear correlation) to $+1$ (representing perfect positive linear correlation). In practice, it is rare for correlations to approach -1 or $+1$.

For the manufacturer of Click pens, the correlation coefficient is determined as follows. The cross-products sum is equal to 18,300.95, the standard deviations of number of TV spots and sales per territory are 4.31 and 123.78, respectively, and there are 40 territories providing data.

$$r = \frac{18,300.95}{(39)(4.31)(123.78)} = 0.88$$

Accordingly, we have evidence of a strong relationship between the number of TV advertising spots and annual sales per territory in the sample data. The larger question is whether or not there is an association between the variables in the population of sales territories, not just within the sample territories. It is easy to test the null hypothesis of no relationship against the alternative hypothesis by calculating the test statistic *t:*

$$t = r\sqrt{\frac{n-2}{1-r^2}} = 0.88\sqrt{\frac{40-2}{1-(0.88)^2}} = 11.31$$

Degrees of freedom for the test are equal to $n - 2 = 38$, and assuming $\alpha = 0.05$, the critical value of t is about 2.03. Thus, because calculated t is greater than the critical value of t, we reject the null hypothesis of no relationship between number of TV spots and sales.

We have demonstrated the calculation of the correlation coefficient (and the associated test statistic) to demonstrate the basic concepts involved in this often-used analytic technique. As a practical matter, correlation coefficients are virtually always calculated using statistical software. Exhibit 21.13 presents SPSS output for the correlation between sales (SALES) and TV spots (NUMSPOTS). Notice that the output provides the correlation coefficient, the corresponding p-value (Sig.), and the number of cases in the analysis (N). By default, the SPSS program assumes a two-tailed test, which is appropriate for testing the null hypothesis that the

Exhibit 21.13

SPSS Output for the Correlation of Sales and TV Spots

CORRELATIONS			Numspots	Sales
Pearson Correlation	NUMSPOTS		1.000	.880**
	SALES		.880**	1.000
Sig. (2-tailed)	NUMSPOTS		.	.000
	SALES		.000	.
N	NUMSPOTS		40	40
	SALES		40	40

** Correlation is significant at the 0.01 level (2-tailed).

correlation does not differ from 0 in either direction (positive or negative). One-tailed tests are readily available if the researcher has proposed a directional hypothesis.

Before going further, it is important that we offer some words of caution about the correlational techniques (including regression) presented in this chapter. First, the correlation coefficient only assesses the strength of the *linear relationship* between two variables. Look again at the scatter diagram for the relationship between number of TV spots and sales for the different sales territories (Figure 21.1). The relationship between the variables seems to be relatively steady; that is, equal increases in number of TV spots (say, from 5 to 10 and from 10 to 15) are associated with about equal changes in sales for the entire diagram. A straight line drawn through the points could provide a good summary of the relationship between TV spots and sales. When two variables are related to one another, there is usually a linear component to their relationship, and the correlation coefficient will usually provide a reasonable summary of the relationship. There are situations, however, in which there can be a very strong nonlinear relationship between variables that cannot be reflected in the correlation coefficient. Figure 21.2 presents a number of different scatter diagrams and their associated correlation coefficients. In diagram I, there is obviously a very strong relationship between the X and Y variables. The relationship, however, is completely nonlinear and produces a correlation coefficient equal to 0. Consider also diagram B: although there is a linear component to the relationship ($r = 0.60$) indicating generally increasing Y values as X increases, a curved line would better describe the relationship between the variables. Different analytic approaches are required to capture the nonlinear components of relationships between variables. In any event, we advise the research analyst to examine the bivariate scatter diagrams to understand the general relationship between the variables rather than simply assume that the relationship is linear.

The second caution concerns the distinction between correlation and causation. Sometimes researchers assume a causal relationship between two variables when calculating correlation or regression coefficients. Researchers often use the terms *dependent* (criterion) and *independent* (predictor) *variables* to describe the different variables in a correlation or regression analysis. The use of these terms, however, stems from the mathematical functional relationship between the variables and is in no way related to the dependence of one variable on another in a causal sense based on the mathematics. For example, while the techniques may show a strong association between high income and a tendency to take winter vacations in the Caribbean, it would be a mistake to assume that having a high income *causes* a person to head south when the thermometer plummets. A high income may have enabled—but certainly not caused—someone to take a winter vacation. Similarly, if we were to determine the average price of Bibles and the total number of people in prison over the past 100 years we would almost certainly find a significant positive correlation. Would we be able to conclude, then, that people stopped buying (and reading) Bibles as prices increased and as a result were more likely to embark on lives of crime? The association between these variables more likely represents spurious correlation (see Technically Speaking 21.1).

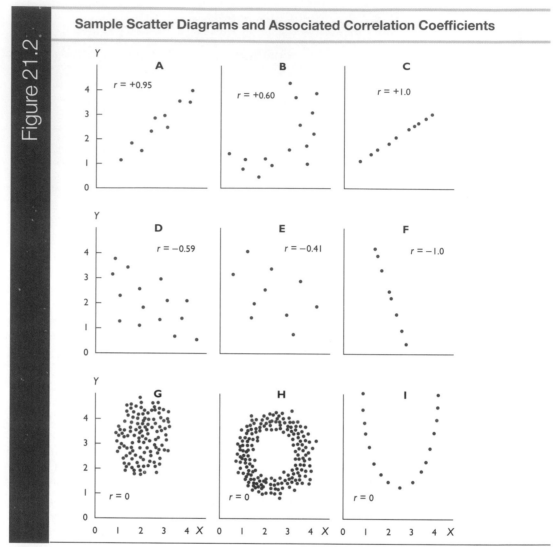

Sample Scatter Diagrams and Associated Correlation Coefficients

Source: Ronald E. Frank, Alfred A. Kuehn, and William F. Massy, *Quantitative Techniques in Marketing Analysis* (Homewood, Ill.: Richard D. Irwin, Inc., 1962), p. 71. Used with permission.

simple regression
A statistical technique used to derive an equation that relates a single continuous dependent variable to a single independent variable.

There is nothing in correlation analysis, or any other mathematical procedure, that can be used to establish causality. All these procedures can do is measure the nature and degree of association or covariation between variables. While there must be covariation between two variables in order for one to cause the other, the presence of covariation does not imply causation of itself. Statements of causality must come from underlying knowledge and theories about the phenomena under investigation. They do not come from the mathematics.[6] In Research Window 21.1, the former director of marketing research at General Mills urges researchers to look beyond the vast amounts of data they devote their energies to collecting and consider the theory that directs marketing inquiry. Research Window 21.2 presents a similar argument for the importance of theory. Without the theory, the mathematics is useless.

Simple Regression

Simple regression provides a means for getting at the functional form or nature of the relationship between two variables, an independent or predictor variable and a dependent or criterion variable. Usually the researcher has reason to believe that the predictor variable somehow influences the criterion variable (keeping in mind that the mathematics alone can-

PART 6:
Data Analysis

The Importance of Theory in Marketing Research

If marketing researchers want to acquire true marketing "knowledge" they should devote more time and effort to developing and validating marketing theories, according to Lawrence D. Gibson, former director of marketing research, General Mills, Inc., Minneapolis.

"There's a funny notion around that theories are vague, ephemeral, and useless, and data are nice, hard, real things. And that somehow knowledge is associated with facts and data. This is nonsense. Knowledge is an interrelated set of validated theories and established facts, not just facts. In marketing, we are profoundly ignorant of what we're doing because we're woefully short on theory while we're drowning in data."

Deploring the lack of validated marketing theories and the overabundance of marketing "facts," Gibson quoted the scientist, R. B. Braithwaite: "The world is not made up of empirical facts with the addition of the laws of nature. What we call the laws of nature are simply theories, the conceptual devices by which we organize our empirical knowledge and predict the future."

And he quoted Albert Einstein: "The grand aim of all science is to cover the maximum number of empirical facts, by logical deduction, into the smallest number of axioms, axioms which represent that remainder which is not comprehended."

In other words, Gibson said, "the axioms and theories are not our knowledge, they are our ignorance. They're part of the problem we assume away." A theory, he said, is how "scientists choose to organize their knowledge and perceptions of the world. Theories are pretty well laid out, simplistic,

general, have predicted usefulness, and fit the facts.

"Theory is basic to what data you choose to collect," he said. "You can't observe all the veins of all the leaves of all the branches of all the trees of all the forests in the world. You've got to choose what facts you choose to observe, and you're going to be guided in some sense by some kind of theory. And when you turn around to use the data, you're also going to be guided by theory. It will have a profound effect on what you do."

This shows up in the way researchers go about analyzing different kinds of data. For example, when working with observational data, people simply don't realize the weak theoretical ground on which they stand. They wander around the data, merrily trying to find out what makes sense.

"Perhaps you've seen some fairly typical versions of this. The creative analyst looks at the data and the survey and they don't make sense. 'Make sense' means the findings are congenial to his prior judgment. But the world isn't working the way he thought it was supposed to be working.

"So he cross-tabs by big cities versus little cities. Still doesn't make sense. But he is very creative, and observes there are more outer-directed people in big cities than in little cities, so he now cross-tabs by inner-directed versus outer-directed by city size, and—lo and behold—he finds out he was right all along!

"Now, obviously, as long as you keep analyzing when you don't like what you see, and stop analyzing when you do like what you see, the world always will look to you the way it's supposed to look. You'll never learn anything." ■

Source: Larry Gibson, "Marketing Research Needs Validated Theories," *Marketing News* 17 (January 21, 1983), p. 14. Reprinted with permission from *Marketing News* published by the American Marketing Association, Chicago, IL 60606. For an example of the danger associated with continuing to analyze data when you don't like what you see, see Ralph T. King, Jr., "The Tale of a Dream Drug and Data Dredging," *The Wall Street Journal* (February 7, 1995), pp. B1, B6.

not prove causation), although this does not have to be the case. For example, the goal might simply be to predict the value of the criterion, given the level of the predictor value, with no concern about the issue of causation.

Consider again the manufacturer of Click pens. If the company wanted to determine if there is a relationship between number of sales representatives assigned per territory and annual sales in a territory, researchers might simply develop a scatter diagram and look at the relationship (Figure 21.3) or they might calculate the correlation coefficient between the variables. Researchers might also use simple regression analysis, in which a line is mathematically fit to the data. Figure 21.3 suggests that it would be possible to summarize the relationship between sales and number of sales representatives by drawing a straight line through the data points to represent the "average" relationship between the variables. One could then enter

Walkup's Laws of Statistics

Law No. 1

Everything correlates with everything, especially when the same individual defines the variables to be correlated.

Law No. 2

It won't help very much to find a good correlation between the variable you are interested in and some other variable that you don't understand any better.

Law No. 3

Unless you can think of a logical reason why two variables should be connected as cause and effect, it doesn't help much to find a correlation between them. In Columbus, Ohio, the mean monthly rainfall correlates very nicely with the number of letters in the names of the months! ■

the graph with the number of sales representatives and then read off the average level of sales expected for that number of representatives. Naturally, different researchers would likely draw different lines through the scatter diagram. The issue, then, is determining how to find the best fitting line for the data.

The most common mathematical procedure for determining the best line is known as the *ordinary least-squares (OLS)* approach. Unless there is a perfect linear relationship between two variables (virtually impossible in practice), the data points will not all lie along a single line, resulting in deviations between the actual data points and the line itself (which, in effect, represents predicted values of the dependent variable for different levels of the independent variable). The OLS approach identifies the line that minimizes the sum of the squared deviations about the line. This best-fitting line is symbolized as

$$Y_i = \alpha + \beta X_i + \epsilon_i$$

where Y_i is the level of sales in the ith territory, X_i is the number of sales reps in the ith territory, ϵ_i is the error associated with the ith observation, α is the β intercept, and b is the slope coefficient. The best-fitting line for the data determined through the OLS procedure is

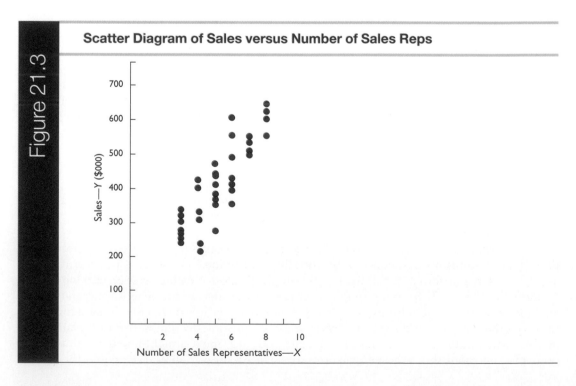

Figure 21.3

Scatter Diagram of Sales versus Number of Sales Reps

known as the regression line. Note that the error term is part and parcel of the model. It represents a failure to include all factors related to the dependent variable in the model, the fact that there is an unpredictable element in human behavior, and the condition that there are errors of measurement.[7] This probabilistic model allows for the fact that the Y value is not uniquely determined for a given X_i value. Instead, all that is determined for a given X_i value is the "average value" of Y. Individual values can be expected to fluctuate above and below this average.

Although estimates for α and β can be calculated by hand, it is much more common to conduct regression analyses using a computer.[8] Using the data in Exhibit 21.11 for sales (Y) and number of sales reps per territory (X), it turns out that the intercept term (α) is 80.1 and the slope (β) is 66.2, based on the information contained in the "Coefficients" section of the SPSS output for the analysis (Exhibit 21.14). The equation is plotted in Figure 21.4. The slope of the line (β) indicates how much we can expect Y (sales) to change for every 1 unit change in X (number of sales representatives). So, for each additional sales rep in a territory, we can expect an increase in sales of $66,200. Keep in mind, however, that this is only an estimate of what is going on in the population based on our particular sample of 40 territories. We still must determine if this result is statistically significant or whether it could have occurred by chance. To do this, one simply needs to look at the final two columns in the "Coefficients" section of the SPSS output to see that the t-value associated with the independent variable NUMREPS is equal to 11.6 and that the likelihood of obtaining a β coefficient of 66.2 if there were truly no relationship between number of representatives and sales is less than .001. Thus, we conclude that the number of sales representatives in a territory is related to total sales in that territory.

Exhibit 21.14

Simple Regression Analysis Output from SPSS

MODEL SUMMARY

Model	R	R Square	Adjusted R Square	Std. Error of the Estimate
1	.882[a]	.778	.773	59.016

[a] Predictors: (Constant), NUMREPS

ANOVA[b]

Model		Sum of Squares	df	Mean Square	F	Sig.
1	Regression	465161.13	1	465161.13	133.556	.000[a]
	Residual	132349.55	38	3482.883		
	Total	597510.67	39			

[a] Predictors: (Constant), NUMREPS
[b] Dependent Variable: SALES

COEFFICIENTS[a]

Model		Unstandardized Coefficients		Standardized Coefficients		
		B	Std. Error	Beta	t	Sig.
1	(Constant)	80.141	30.141		2.659	.011
	NUMREPS	66.244	5.732	.882	11.557	.000

[a] Dependent Variable: SALES

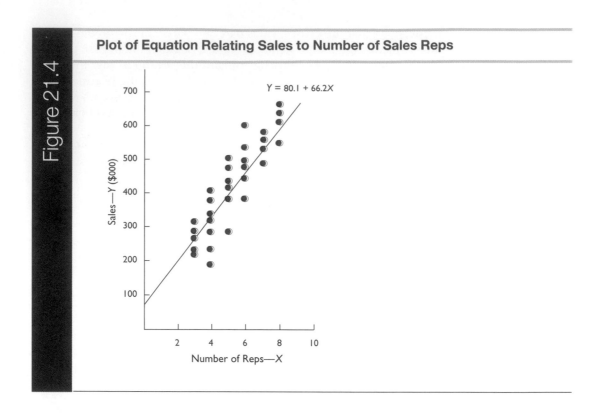

Figure 21.4

Plot of Equation Relating Sales to Number of Sales Reps

$Y = 80.1 + 66.2X$

Sales—Y ($000)

Number of Reps—X

We should note one other important statistic in the regression analysis output at this point. Analysts typically want to gauge how well a particular predictor variable (or set of predictor variables, as we will see in the following section) does at predicting the outcome variable. A commonly used measure for this purpose is R^2, the **coefficient of determination,** which represents the relative proportion of the total variation in the outcome variable (sales in this case) that can be accounted for by the predictor variable in the regression. This value is presented in the "Model Summary" section of the SPSS output. In this case, with a single predictor variable (number of representatives), we are able to explain about 78% of the variation in sales per territory.

Multiple Regression

With simple regression, we examined the relationship between a single predictor variable and an outcome variable. **Multiple regression** analysis allows the introduction of additional variables, so that the regression equation reflects the values of several rather than one predictor variable. Why add additional variables? The goal is to improve our ability to predict, or explain, the outcome variable.

We have seen that the number of sales representatives in a territory is strongly related to the level of sales for the territory. Can we improve our ability to predict sales by including additional variables? The choice of additional variables to include should be based on theory and reasoning; it is not a matter of whim or whimsy on the part of the analyst. The researcher would decide if there were any other pieces of information available that might help predict sales for the territories. Earlier, we saw that there is a significant positive correlation between advertising level (number of TV spots) and sales and—importantly—it seems reasonable to expect that increases in the level of advertising might lead to increases in sales, so advertising is one variable that might be added. We also have information about the efficiency of the wholesalers who also sell and distribute Click pens in each territory. Presumably, more efficient wholesalers should produce higher levels of sales than less efficient ones. The regression equation including all three predictor variables is

coefficient of determination

A measure representing the relative proportion of the total variation in the dependent variable that can be explained or accounted for by the fitted regression equation.

10 *Describe how multiple regression differs from simple regression.*

multiple regression

A statistical technique used to derive an equation that relates a single continuous dependent variable to two or more independent variables.

$$Y_i = \alpha + \beta_1 X_{1i} + \beta_2 X_{2i} + \beta_3 X_{3i} + \epsilon_i$$

where X_{1i}, X_{2i}, and X_{3i} are the values for number of reps, number of TV ads, and wholesaler efficiency index for the ith territory, respectively; and β_1, β_2, and β_3 are the regression coefficients corresponding to the three variables. Each of the regression coefficients is called a coefficient of partial regression and represents the average change in the outcome or criterion variable per unit change in the associated predictor variable, holding all other predictor variables constant. We will discuss what this means shortly.

Before running the multiple regression analysis, we need to look at the bivariate scatterplot for the relationship between wholesaler efficiency index (WEI) and sales (the bivariate plots for number of TV spots and number of sales reps were presented in Figures 21.1 and 21.3, respectively). Judging from Figure 21.5, it is not clear what relationship may exist between WEI and sales, if any exists at all. There does not appear to be any particular pattern to the placement of observations.

With most statistical software packages it is quite easy to perform the multiple regression analysis. The SPSS analysis output is presented in Exhibit 21.15. The resulting regression equation is

$$Y = 31.4 + 41.3\,X_1 + 12.9\,X_2 + 11.5\,X_3$$

but before attempting to interpret it we must determine whether or not the overall model is statistically significant (because we are working with a sample). With simple regression it was only necessary to test the significance of the single beta coefficient to determine whether or not the model was significant. With multiple regression, it is mandatory that all predictors be taken into account simultaneously to establish the statistical significance of the overall model. The model is tested via the F statistic found in the ANOVA section of the computer output. The overall model is tested on the basis of the amount of variance in the dependent variable that can be explained by the regression relative to the variation in the dependent variable that cannot be explained. In this case, the F statistic equals 89.471 and the corresponding p-value

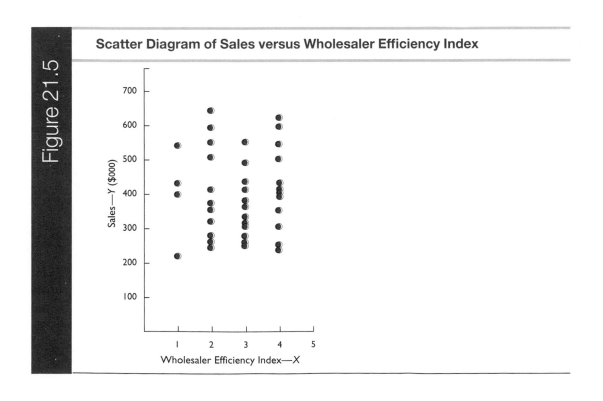

Scatter Diagram of Sales versus Wholesaler Efficiency Index

Figure 21.5

Exhibit 21.15

Multiple Regression Analysis Output from SPSS

MODEL SUMMARY

Model	R	R Square	Adjusted R Square	Std. Error of the Estimate
1	.939[a]	.882	.872	44.304

[a] Predictors: (Constant), WEI, NUMSPOTS, NUMREPS

ANOVA[b]

Model		Sum of Squares	df	Mean Square	F	Sig.
1	Regression	526849.11	3	175616.37	89.471	.000[a]
	Residual	70661.569	36	1962.821		
	Total	597510.67	39			

[a] Predictors: (Constant), WEI, NUMSPOTS, NUMREPS
[b] Dependent Variable: SALES

COEFFICIENTS[a]

Model		Unstandardized Coefficients		Standardized Coefficients		
		B	Std. Error	Beta	t	Sig.
1	(Constant)	31.382	34.083		.921	.363
	NUMREPS	41.316	7.260	.550	5.691	.000
	NUMSPOTS	12.931	2.730	.450	4.737	.000
	WEI	11.486	7.670	.091	1.497	.143

[a] Dependent Variable: SALES

© CORBIS

multicollinearity
A condition said to be present in a multiple regression analysis when the independent variables are correlated among themselves.

is less than .001, so we are safe in concluding that there is a statistically significant linear relationship between sales and the predictor variables, number of television spots, number of sales representatives, and wholesaler efficiency index.

One additional consideration is necessary before interpreting the individual components of the regression equation. A key assumption of multiple regression is that the independent variables are independent of one another; there must not be high levels of correlation between predictors. When data result from a survey rather than an experiment (where the researcher has more control), the assumption is often violated, because many variables of interest in marketing vary together. For instance, higher incomes are typically associated with higher education levels. Thus, predicting purchase behavior using both income and education would likely violate the assumption that the predictor variables are independent of one another. **Multicollinearity** is said to be present in a multiple regression problem when the predictor variables are correlated among themselves. The higher the level of intercorrelation among the predictor variables, the worse the problem becomes.

Assuming the multicollinearity assumption is satisfied, the coefficients of partial regression—the individual β coefficients corresponding to the predictor variables in the regression equation—can be interpreted as the average change in the criterion variable associated with a unit change in the appropriate predictor variable *while holding the other predictor variables constant*. Thus, assuming there is no multicollinearity, $\beta_1 = 41.3$ indicates that on the average, an increase of $41,300 in sales can be expected with each additional sales rep in the territory if the number of TV spots and WEI are not changed.

The slope coefficients can also be tested individually for their statistical significance in a multiple regression problem given that the overall function is significant. The *t*-test is again used, although the validity of the procedure is highly dependent on the multicollinearity that exists within the data. Is multicollinearity a problem in our dataset? Consider again the simple regression of sales on number of sales reps we presented in the previous section: the slope was equal to 66.2. Thus, when the number of TV spots and WEI were not considered, the average change in sales associated with an additional sales rep was $66,200. Yet when number of TV spots and WEI were considered, the average change in sales associated with an additional sales rep was only $41,300. Part of the sales effect that we were attributing to number of reps was apparently due to either (or both) number of TV spots or WEI. We were thus overstating the impact of adding sales reps to territories. This example demonstrates how the coefficient of partial regression works: the coefficient represents the degree of relationship between the predictor and the outcome variable *when the effects of other predictors are also taken into account*. The example also demonstrates a situation in which multicollinearity may be a problem. It turns out that the correlation between number of sales reps in a territory and number of TV spots equals 0.78.

Let's assume that multicollinearity were not a problem. Looking at the *t*-values associated with the three predictors (see Exhibit 21.15) we see that number of sales reps and number of TV spots are significant predictors of sales in a territory, but that WEI is not (the p-value, the probability that we could have seen an effect of this magnitude if there truly were no relationship between WEI and sales, is greater than 0.05). This result for WEI is consistent with what we observed in the scatter diagram shown in Figure 21.5 and, unless there is a compelling theoretical reason for further consideration of WEI, we would be about as well off to eliminate this variable from further analyses.

Unfortunately, in the presence of multicollinearity, very little meaning can be attached to the coefficients of partial regression. The equation may still be quite useful for prediction, however, assuming conditions are stable. That is, it may be used to predict sales in the territories for given levels of television spots, number of sales reps, and level of WEI if the relationships among the variables can be expected to continue.[9] The partial regression coefficients should

ETHICAL dilemma 21.1

The newly appointed analyst in the firm's marketing research department was given the responsibility of developing a method by which market potential for the firm's products could be estimated by small geographic areas. The analyst went about the task by gathering as much secondary data as he could. He then ran a series of regression analyses using the firm's sales as the criterion and the demographic factors as predictors. He realized that several of the predictors were highly correlated (e.g., average income in the area and average educational level), but he chose to ignore this fact when presenting the results to management.

- *What is the consequence when the predictors in a regression equation are highly correlated?*

- *Is a research analyst ethically obliged to learn all he or she can about a particular technique before applying it to a problem in order to avoid incorrectly interpreting the results?*

- *Is a research analyst ethically obliged to advise those involved to be cautious in interpreting results because of violations of the assumptions in the method used to produce the results?*

- *What are the researcher's responsibilities if management has no interest in the technical details by which the results are achieved?*

not be used, however, as the basis for making marketing strategy decisions when significant multicollinearity is present.[10]

Just as we used the coefficient of determination as a measure of closeness of the relationship between the predictor variable and outcome variable in simple regression, we can calculate the **coefficient of multiple determination** in multiple regression analyses. Also symbolized by R^2, the coefficient of multiple determination represents the proportion of variation in the outcome variable that is accounted for by the covariation in the predictor variables. As presented in Exhibit 21.15, R^2 for the current example is .882. This means that 88% of the variation in sales is associated with variation in televison spots, number of sales reps, and WEI (though we suspect that WEI adds very little to improving the fit of the regression line).

As a final note to our discussion of regression, we should point out that regression is a robust analytic tool that can also be used when one or more independent variables are categorical as opposed to continuous variables. In fact, the analysis of variance discussed earlier in the chapter is actually just a special case of regression analysis in which all of the predictor variables are categorical. The analysis, including the testing of interaction effects, could easily be performed in multiple regression analysis. Such analysis, however, goes beyond the intended scope of this book. Interested students can learn more about these or other techniques by reading a good multivariate statistics text.

looking back...

As the planner of a marketing campaign for a fragrance, you can use overall patterns in consumer behavior to help you develop questions. An obvious place to start is to break down the data according to whether your target customer is male or female. Also, a particular brand may target consumers in a certain age bracket, income range, or ethnic group. Finally, heavy users of a product are likely to be the company's most profitable customers, so they are worth extra study.

The information released by Vertis from its Customer Focus study sheds some light on these topics of interest. For example, you could create cross tabulations of age group versus use of a scent strip in making a purchase decision. Based on data from Vertis, part of your cross tabulation would include these percentages:

Purchase Based on a Scent Strip?*

	Yes	No
Generation Y	36%	64%
Generation X	24%	76%
Baby Boomers	23%	77%

*n = 2,000 U.S. adults

According to the data, use of scent strips in magazines seems to be more appealing for reaching the youngest group of adults (Generation Y). Similar cross tabulations show differences in usage among ethnic groups. African Americans are most likely (at 35 percent) to use scent strips for purchase decisions, and this group also is most likely (at 79 percent) to wear perfume or cologne.

PART 6:
Data Analysis

Let's say your target group of consumers is Generation Y, so the data increase your interest in using scent strips. You therefore want to see more data on which magazines this age group reads. You probably also want data on which magazines are read by heavy users of fragrances. According to Vertis, women who spend over $50 a year for perfume read several kinds of magazines. For example, 38 percent read fashion and style magazines, 35 percent read home and garden magazines, and 29 percent read arts and entertainment magazines. As the buyer of a perfume ad, you might conclude that fashion and style magazines are the logical media choice, since they reach the largest share of heavy consumers. Or you might opt to place an ad in home and garden magazines, because you would reach a share that is almost as large and your ad would stand out more.

This level of information is just the beginning for a well-informed decision. If you choose, you can work with a representative from a company like Vertis to get customized cross tabulations about your brand and market segment. Of course, unlike the data gleaned from news releases, customized information is not free, and the service provider has an incentive to present the information in a light that makes the services seem valuable. Along with knowing how to interpret the data, users of marketing research need to consider the source of the data and develop working relationships with trusted sources. ■

Sources: Sandra Yin, "The Nose Knows," *American Demographics* (February 2002), downloaded from EBSCOhost; Vertis, "Vertis Customer Focus 2002 Survey Identifies Trends among Fragrance Shoppers," news release, October 16, 2002, Vertis Web site, http://www.vertisinc.com.

Summary

Learning Objective 1
Explain the purpose and importance of cross tabulation.
Cross tabulation is the most commonly used multivariate technique. Its purpose is to study the relationships among and between categorical variables.

Learning Objective 2
Describe how percentages should be calculated for a two-way cross-tab.
In a two-way cross-tab analysis, percentages should be calculated using the marginal totals for the independent variable as the denominator. Thus, percentages are calculated in the direction of the causal variable.

Learning Objective 3
Describe how one determines if there is a statistically significant relationship between two categorical variables in a cross-tabulation table.
The Pearson chi-square test of independence is used to determine whether or not two categorical variables are independent of one another. Cramer's *V* is used to obtain an indication of the strength of the relationship between the categorical variables.

Learning Objective 4
Describe a technique for comparing two proportions from independent groups.
The independent samples z-test for proportions is used to test for differences between two population proportions. Provided that sample sizes are large enough (i.e., more than 10 successes and failures in each group), a z-statistic can be calculated and compared against a critical value of z to determine if the observed difference in population proportions is statistically significant.

Learning Objective 5
Discuss two techniques for examining associations among ordinal variables.
When there are only two ordinal variables, the Spearman rank-order correlation coefficient is appropriate for assessing the degree of association between the rank-order variables. Spearman's rho can range from –1 to +1. When there are three or more ordinal variables, Kendall's coefficient of concordance provides a measure of association between the ordinal variables; its value can range from 0 to 1.

Learning Objective 6

Explain two techniques for comparing groups on dependent variables assessed on continuous measures.
When there are only two groups, the independent samples *t*-test is used to determine if the mean score on the dependent variable for one group is significantly different than the mean score for the second group. If there are more than two groups, the analysis of variance technique, which compares the variance in dependent variable scores within groups with the variance in dependent variable scores between groups, is appropriate.

Learning Objective 7

Explain the difference between an independent sample t-test for means and a paired sample t-test for means.
In the independent samples *t*-test, mean scores on the dependent variable are compared for different groups of respondents. In a paired sample *t*-test, mean scores on two different variables (measured on similar scales) are compared across a single group (i.e., all respondents provide scores on both variables).

Learning Objective 8

List three advantages of using analysis of variance versus conducting a series of t-tests to examine differences across groups.
The ANOVA technique (a) would be more efficient, requiring fewer computations; (b) would decrease the likelihood of a Type I error; and (c) would consider the joint effects of different independent variables.

Learning Objective 9

Discuss two techniques for determining the degree of association between two continuous measures.
One approach is to calculate the Pearson product-moment correlation coefficient, which assesses the degree of linear association between the variables. Another approach is to use simple regression, a technique in which a mathematical equation is derived that relates a dependent variable to an independent variable.

Learning Objective 10

Describe how multiple regression differs from simple regression.
Simple regression and multiple regression differ in that only one independent variable is used to predict the dependent variable in simple regression, whereas more than one independent variable is included in multiple regression.

Key Terms

cross tabulation (page 574)

Pearson chi-square test of independence (page 577)

Cramer's *V* (page 577)

banner (page 577)

Spearman rank-order correlation coefficient (page 580)

Kendall's coefficient of concordance (page 583)

independent samples *t*-test (page 586)

paired sample *t*-test (page 587)

analysis of variance (ANOVA) (page 589)

factorial design (page 590)

Pearson product-moment correlation coefficient (page 592)

scatter diagram (page 592)

simple regression (page 596)

coefficient of determination (page 600)

multiple regression (page 600)

multicollinearity (page 602)

coefficient of multiple determination (page 604)

Review Questions

1. What is the proper procedure for investigating the following hypotheses using cross-tabulation analysis?
   (a) Consumption of Product X depends on a person's income.
   (b) Consumption of Product X depends on a person's education.
2. Illustrate the procedure from Question 1 with data of your own choosing; that is, develop the tables, fill in the assumed numbers, and indicate the conclusions to be drawn from each table.
3. How do you explain the condition in which a two-way cross tabulation of Variables X and Y revealed no relationship between X and Y, but the introduction of Z revealed a definite relationship between X and Y?
4. How do you test whether two parent-population proportions differ?
5. What is the difference between regression analysis and correlation analysis?
6. Suppose that an analyst wished to make an inference about the slope coefficient in a regression model. What is the appropriate procedure? What does it mean if the null hypothesis is rejected? If it is not rejected?
7. What is the correlation coefficient, and what does it measure? What is the coefficient of determination, and what does it measure?
8. What is a coefficient of partial regression, and what does it measure? What condition must occur for the usual interpretation to apply? What happens if this condition is not satisfied?
9. What is the coefficient of multiple determination?

Discussion Questions, Problems, and Projects

1. A social organization was interested in determining if there were various demographic characteristics that might be related to people's propensity to contribute to charities. The organization was particularly interested in determining if individuals 40 years of age or over were more likely to contribute larger amounts than individuals under 40. The average contribution in the population was $1,500, and this figure was used to form two groups based on a median-split. The following table presents a two-way classification of the number of individuals by contributions and age.

Exhibit 1

Personal Contributions by Age

Personal Contribution	AGE		
	39 or Less	40 or More	Total
Less than or equal to $1,500	79	50	129
More than $1,500	11	60	71
Total	90	110	200

(a) Does the amount of personal contributions depend on age? Generate a table for a report that communicates the relevant information.

2. A large toy manufacturer wants to determine the characteristics of families who have purchased a new electronic game that is designed and marketed for all age groups. Management needs your assistance in interpreting the following two cross-classification tables.
   (a) What does Exhibit 1 indicate? Explain and show calculations where necessary.
   (b) What does Exhibit 2 indicate? Have your conclusions changed or remained the same? Explain.

Purchased Electronic Games versus Number of Children

Exhibit 1

| Number of Children | PURCHASED ELECTRONIC GAMES | | |
	Yes	No	Total
Less than or equal to 1	63	87	150
More than 1	21	29	50

Purchased Electronic Games versus Number of Children and Age of Head of Household

Exhibit 2

| Number of Children | AGE OF HEAD OF HOUSEHOLD | | |
	Less than or Equal to 45	More than 45	Total
Less than or equal to 1	14%	46%	42%
More than 1	38%	19%	42%

3. To better understand the marketplace, researchers working on the car ownership project (see data in Exhibit 20.1) conducted a cross-tab analysis of the relationship between the region of the country where the respondent lived (i.e., north or south) and the respondent's lifestyle orientation (i.e., liberal or conservative) and developed the following table:

Region by Lifestyle Orientation

Exhibit 1

| Region | LIFESTYLE ORIENTATION | | |
	Liberal	Conservative	Total
North	38	22	60
	(63)	(37)	(100)
South	17	23	40
	(43)	(58)	(100)
Total	55	45	100

(a) What does the exhibit indicate about the relationship between region and lifestyle orientation?

(b) The researchers chose to report row percentages; was this a good choice? Why or why not?

(c) The Pearson chi-square value for the analysis equals 4.209, on 1 degree of freedom, and $p = .040$. What does this indicate?

(d) Cramer's V for the analysis equals .205. What does this indicate?

4. Suppose that the researchers on the car ownership project (see data in Exhibit 20.1) wished to test whether or not the proportion of people with a liberal lifestyle was significantly different for those living in the north versus those living in the south. The researchers knew that 63% of sample respondents living in the north and 43% of sample respondents living in the south described themselves as "liberal" (see exhibit for previous question). The researchers decided to apply the z-test for proportions to test the null hypothesis that the proportions were not different in the population.

(a) What condition must be met for the z-test to be appropriate? Is this condition satisfied in the current scenario?

(b) Does the sample provide evidence that the proportion of people with a liberal lifestyle differs depending upon region at the .05 significance level?

5. Footsense is a chain of shoe stores located in the southwestern part of the U.S. The CEO believes that customer service is probably related to total sales at the stores and has asked you, the newly-hired assistant marketing research director, to determine if this is so. Coming up with sales data is no problem; determining how to assess the level of customer service in the stores is another matter. Significant time and money would be required to obtain customer service ratings on each store. Instead, you decide to randomly select 12 stores and have the director of training—who spends time in each store and is familiar with all the store managers—rank the stores according to her perceptions of the level of customer service provided. Her rankings, along with sales rankings, are provided for each of the 12 stores in the following exhibit:

Exhibit 1

Customer Service and Sales Ranking by Store

Store	Customer Service Rank	Sales Rank
1	6	4
2	3	5
3	8	9
4	1	3
5	5	6
6	11	8
7	10	12
8	12	11
9	2	2
10	9	7
11	7	10
12	4	1

(a) Calculate the Spearman rank-order correlation coefficient. Does it appear that there may be a relationship between the level of customer service and sales performance?
(b) Determine if your results are statistically significant and would thus hold for the entire population of stores ($\alpha = .05$).

6. Alvin Whitby is director of sales for a manufacturer of steel building materials. He has noticed that the three salespeople in a particular sales territory are producing vastly differing levels of sales, and he suspects that this may be due to differences in the salespeople's ability to identify likely prospects. One of the salespeople is able to convert nearly 25% of sales calls into purchase orders, while the other two are successful only about 10% of the time. To determine if the salespeople are using different criteria in choosing prospects, Alvin decided to try a test. He randomly selected 10 prospects from the territory and put detailed information about each prospect (but no names) on separate cards. He then asked each of the three salespeople to put the prospect cards in order from most promising to least promising. The exhibit provides the resulting rank orders for the three salespeople:

Exhibit 1

Rank Order of Prospects by Salesperson

Prospect	SALESPERSON		
	A	B	C
1	8	7	5
2	1	6	3
3	9	8	9
4	4	4	7
5	6	2	1
6	7	5	8
7	2	9	2
8	3	3	6
9	10	10	10
10	5	1	4

(a) Calculate Kendall's coefficient of concordance and determine the degree of association among the rankings. Does it appear that the salespeople may be using different criteria in the selection of prospects?

(b) Determine if your results are statistically significant and would likely hold for the entire population of prospects ($\alpha = .05$).

7. Come-and-Go Company, a large multi-office travel agency in Portland, Oregon, wants to study consumer preferences for two different versions of a packaged tour to New England. Other providers offer the tours, and although they cost about the same, they include stops in different cities. Because Come-and-Go only wants to offer a single tour package (they would be eligible for volume discounts from either provider, but they don't believe they could achieve sufficient volume with either provider if they tried to offer both), they have decided to conduct a market test. They randomly selected five of their offices and offered only Packaged Tour I in those offices. Then they randomly selected five additional offices and offered only Packaged Tour II in those offices. After six months, the following number of packaged tours had been sold in each of the offices:

Office	Packaged Tour I	Packaged Tour II
1	90	
2	70	
3	120	
4	110	
5	60	
6		100
7		60
8		80
9		90
10		80

The management of Come-and-Go needs your assistance to determine whether there is a difference in preference for the two tours.

(a) State the null and alternate hypotheses.

(b) What test would you use? Why?

(c) What is the calculated value of the test statistic? Show your calculations.

(d) What is the critical tabled value at the 5 percent significance level?

(e) Would you reject the null hypothesis? Explain.

(f) What can the management of Come-and-Go Company conclude about preferences for the two tours?

8. Wet Noodle, a manufacturer of fresh refrigerated pasta products, is unhappy with sales of its products. Management suspects that sales might improve if the product were displayed in a freestand-

ing refrigerated case next to the dry pasta, rather than in the dairy case as it is now. To test this assumption, the marketing research department has arranged for six stores that currently carry Wet Noodle to allow placement of the freestanding case in addition to the regular display. Packages have been specially bar-coded so sales generated from each display can be tracked. After a three-week trial period, the following sales figures are assembled:

Store	New Display	Old Display
1	230	195
2	187	185
3	250	220
4	157	130
5	99	80
6	295	245

(a) What is the appropriate test to determine if the two displays differ in effectiveness?
(b) State the null and alternate hypotheses.
(c) What is the value of the test statistic?
(d) If $\alpha = 0.05$, what is your conclusion?

9. The creative shop at Impact Advertising developed two different approaches, labeled A and B, for a new direct mail solicitation for a major client. In order to test the effectiveness of the different solicitations, the research department was directed to conduct a test mailing. Two independent random samples of size $n = 2,000$ were selected, and after a one-month waiting period, the number of orders received from each sample was tabulated. Approach A resulted in 257 orders, and Approach B generated 230 orders.
(a) What is the appropriate test to determine if Approach A and Approach B differ in effectiveness?
(b) State the null and alternate hypotheses.
(c) What is the value of the test statistic?
(d) If $\alpha = .05$, what is your conclusion?

10. Plaza AutoMall is a medium-sized automobile dealership located in a small city in the southeastern U.S. The dealership sells and services new and pre-owned automobiles. In recent months, revenues from the automotive servicing side of the business have been flat, while revenues from new car sales have been rising. The owner suspects that part of the service and repair business may have shifted to a new auto repair shop that opened about a year ago on the other side of town. The new repair shop is much more conveniently located for consumers who live on that side of town. To better understand the perceptions and behaviors of the dealership's customer base (i.e., those who had purchased a car from the dealership) regarding auto servicing, the owner brought in a team of researchers. The researchers developed a mail questionnaire that asked respondents the percentage of times they use Plaza AutoMall for auto repairs (assessed on a 0% to 100% scale). The researchers also coded the return envelopes so that they could determine in which section of town the respondent resides (the city can easily be divided into three well-defined areas, which the researchers coded A, B, and C). The questionnaire was sent to a random sample of the dealership's customer base. Mean scores on the dependent variable were as follows: region A (where the dealership is located) = 93; region B = 82; and region C (where the competing auto repair shop is located) = 70. The researchers utilized the analysis of variance technique to determine if the difference in these means is statistically significant, producing the following ANOVA table:

ANOVA Table

Source	Sum of Squares	df	Mean Square	F	Sig.
Between Groups	3934.103	2	1967.051	2.057	.136
Within Groups	59290.513	62	956.299		
Total	63224.615	64			

(a) Assuming $\alpha = .05$, can the researchers reject the null hypothesis of no difference across groups? Why or why not?

(b) Suppose that the researchers were willing to change the level of significance to $\alpha = .15$; would your answer to part (a) change? What would be the consequences for Type I error? Explain.

11. The researchers working with Plaza AutoMall decided to take a closer look at the data. In addition to information about region where the respondent was located (see previous question), they also knew whether or not the respondent had purchased a new or pre-owned car from Plaza. Mean scores (representing the percentage of times the respondent uses the dealership for auto repairs, assessed on a 0% to 100% scale) broken down by region and type of car are as follows:

	TYPE OF CAR	
Region	New Car	Pre-owned Car
A	92	96
B	90	63
C	95	50
(n = 65)		

An analysis of variance produced the following ANOVA table:

ANOVA Table

Source	Sum of Squares	df	Mean Square	F	Sig.
MAIN EFFECTS					
Region	2555.532	2	1277.766	1.505	.230
Type of Car	4676.456	1	4676.456	5.509	.022
INTERACTION					
Region by Type of Car	4531.600	2	2265.800	2.669	.078
Within Groups	50082.456	59	848.855		
Total	63224.615	64			

(a) Examine closely the mean scores reported above for the six combinations of region and type of car. Based on these results, does it appear that there is a relationship between region and the proportion of times owners take their cars to Plaza for repair? If so, what is the nature of this relationship?

(b) Explain the ANOVA table. What can you conclude about the effects of region and type of car on the proportion of times owners take their cars to Plaza for repair?

12. The chancellor of Enormous State University has decided that ESU needs to develop a new marketing plan in order to attract the best students. The objective is to attract students who will have the best chance of graduating within four years of their matriculation. The administration has assigned you, the associate vice-chancellor, the responsibility for carrying out this project. You have decided that, as part of the research to be performed in designing the new marketing plan, it would be helpful to know what, if any, characteristics possessed by high school seniors are associated with success in college. You decide that a multiple-regression approach seems to be the way to proceed. Your task is simplified by the existence of a large, comprehensive database that contains the results of several broad-based surveys of high school seniors, many of whom later attended ESU. However, you know that simply mining the database is not likely to be much help. Accordingly, your first task is to develop a theory of why students succeed in college. After explaining your theory, specify the dependent variable and predictor variables that you will use in the regression equation. How serious a problem is multicollinearity in the data likely to be, given your objective?

13. The Crystallo Bottling Company, which provides glass bottles to various soft drink manufacturers, has the following information pertaining to the number of cases per shipment and the corresponding transportation costs:

Number of Cases per Shipment	Transportation Costs in Dollars
1,500	200
2,200	260
3,500	310
4,300	360
5,800	420
6,500	480
7,300	540
8,200	630
8,500	710
9,800	730

The marketing manager is interested in studying the relationship between the number of cases per shipment and the transportation costs. Your assistance is needed.

(a) Plot the transportation costs as a function of the number of cases per shipment.

(b) Interpret the scatter diagram.

(c) Calculate the Pearson product-moment correlation coefficient.

(d) Does it appear that there is a relationship between number of cases and transportation costs? Explain.

14. The marketing manager at the Crystallo Bottling Company is studying the relationship between number of cases per shipment and transportation costs. An analysis of the data from the previous question produced the following simple regression output:

COEFFICIENTS[a]

Model		Unstandardized Coefficients		Standardized Coefficients		
		B	Std. Error	Beta	t	Sig.
1	(Constant)	87.000	25.984		3.348	.010
	CASES	6.545E-02	.004	.985	15.981	.000

[a] Dependent Variable: TRANCOST
$R^2 = .970$

Thus, the regression equation is: $Y = 0.065X + 87.000$

(a) What is the interpretation of the slope coefficient?

(b) Does it appear that number of cases per shipment influences transportation cost?

(c) If so, how strong is the relationship between the variables?

15. The marketing manager of Crystallo Bottling Company is considering multiple-regression analysis with the number of cartons per shipment and the size of cartons as predictor variables and transportation costs as the dependent variable (refer to the previous two problems). He has devised the following regression equation:

$$Y = -3.95X_1 + 24.44X_2 - 41.44$$

where X_1 is the number of cartons per shipment and X_2 is the size of the cartons.

(a) Interpret each of the values in the regression equation.

(b) Is multiple regression appropriate in this situation? If yes, why? If no, why not?

Refer to the NFO Research, Inc., coffee study described on pages 288–290 in Chapter 12 (the codebook is on pages 569–571 in Chapter 20) for the following problems.

16. Perform a cross-tabulation analysis of "brand used most often" with "age," when the age variable has been recorded into the following categories:

35 years or less
36–45 years
46–59 years
60 years or more

(a) Does it appear that there is a relationship between age and brand used most often?

(b) If so, how strong is the relationship between age and brand used most often?

 17. Compare the overall ratings (from question 2 of the survey) of Folgers and Yuban. Is there a difference in the ratings for the two brands of coffee ($\alpha = 0.05$)? If so, which brand is rated more highly?

 18. Compute a "taste" index score on the following features of question 6 of the survey for Maxwell House Regular: rich taste, always fresh, full-bodied taste, smooth taste, not bitter, has no aftertaste. Is there a difference in this overall score for individuals who add nothing to their coffee versus those who do add something ($\alpha = 0.05$)?

 19. Use simple regression to investigate the association between the predictor variable age (as a continuous variable) and the dependent variable "value" index score composed of the following attributes from question 6 for Maxwell House Regular: good value for the money, economy brand, costs less than other brands.

 20. Using multiple regression, investigate the association between respondents' overall rating of Maxwell House Regular and the following predictor variables: the "taste" index score for Maxwell House Regular (see question 18), the "value" index score for the brand (see question 19), and the repondent's age.

Suggested Additional Readings

Many of the statistical tests discussed in this chapter can be found in any introductory statistics text, and readers are encouraged to refer to the text they used in their introductory statistics course for more details on any of the methods that are discussed.

For especially insightful discussions of the use of cross-tabulation analysis to reveal the underlying patterns in data, see the classic works Hans Zeisel, *Say It with Figures,* 5th ed. (New York: Harper and Row, 1968).

Ottar Helevik, *Introduction to Causal Analysis: Exploring Survey Data by Cross-tabulation,* 2nd ed. (Cambridge, Mass.: Scandinavian University Press, 1995).

For a detailed discussion of analysis of variance, see Geoffrey Keppel, *Design and Analysis: A Researcher's Handbook,* 3rd ed. (Englewood Cliffs, N.J.: Prentice-Hall, 1991).

For a detailed discussion of regression and correlation analysis, see Jacob Cohen and Patricia Cohen, *Applied Multiple Regression/Correlation Analysis for the Behavioral Sciences,* 2nd ed. (Mahwah, N.J.: Lawrence Erlbaum, 1983).

Melissa A. Hardy, *Regression with Dummy Variables* (Thousand Oaks, Calif.: Sage Publications, 1993).

Thomas P. Ryan, *Modern Regression Methods* (New York: Wiley, 1996).

John Neter, Michael H. Kutner, and William Wasserman, *Applied Linear Regression Models,* 2nd ed. (Burr Ridge, Ill.: Irwin, McGraw Hill, 1996).

Thomas H. Wonnacott and Ronald J. Wonnacott, *Regression: A Second Course in Statistics* (Malabar, Fla.: Robert E. Krieger Publishing Co., 1986).

The sixth stage in the research process is to analyze and interpret the data. All the earlier steps in the research process were undertaken to support this search for meaning. Most data analysis begins with the preliminary steps of editing, coding, and tabulating the data. The results are often analyzed further to determine if the differences are statistically significant, or if there is any correlation between the variables.

CARA researchers had begun their study with two objectives:

1. Identify business decision makers' attitudes toward the advertising media of newspaper, radio, and television.
2. Identify business decision makers' attitudes toward the advertising sales representatives of those media.

In analyzing the data collected from the questionnaires, researchers calculated the percentage of respondents who agreed that their sales representatives possessed the attributes listed on the questionnaire and who agreed that the categories of advertising media were characterized by the listed items. They calculated this by determining the two-box proportion: the proportion of the total number of respondents that checked the "strongly agree" or "agree" category for each item.

Business Decision Makers' Attitudes Toward Advertising Media

CARA researchers found that the characteristics of television advertising that garnered the highest percentage of agreement were (1) that the ads reached many people (86 percent), (2) that they built up recognition (80 percent), and (3) that people paid attention (67 percent). The highest categories for radio advertising were that (1) the ads reached many people (73 percent), (2) they built up recognition (67 percent), and (3) they were easy to buy (54 percent). Respondents agreed that newspaper ads (1) were easy to monitor (77 percent), (2) built up recognition (70 percent), (3) reached many people (70 percent), and (4) were easy to buy (70 percent). The items on which respondents expressed the lowest percentage of agreement for television advertising were that (1) few repeats were necessary (20 percent), and (2) the ads were not costly (10 percent). For radio advertising, the items of lowest agreement were that (1) the ads were not costly (34 percent) and (2) few repeats were necessary (17 percent). For newspaper advertising the lowest categories were that (1) the ads were creative (27 percent) and (2) few repeats were necessary (27 percent).

Business Decision Makers' Attitudes Toward Advertising Sales Representatives

When analyzing the data, CARA researchers found that 68 percent, 62 percent, and 62 percent of respondents felt their television sales representatives were cooperative, knowledgeable, and available, respectively, and these represented the items with the highest percentage of agreement in this category. For radio representatives, the highest percentage of agreement was found concerning their cooperation (72 percent), ability to quickly place ads (68 percent), and availability (64 percent). The highest rated items for newspaper representatives were cooperation (73 percent), the ability to place ads quickly (64 percent), and reliability (62 percent). The items with the lowest percent of agreement for television sales representatives were creativity (42 percent), awareness of client's customers (40 percent), and follow-through (37 percent). For radio representatives, the lowest items were follow-through (35 percent), awareness of client's customers (43 percent), and knowledgeability (28 percent). Follow-through, awareness, and knowledgeability were also the lowest items for newspaper representatives, with, respectively, 33 percent, 30 percent, and 29 percent of respondents agreeing.

Importance Scales

A chi-square test of independence was used to test whether respondents differed on the number of times they checked a given attribute or characteristic and to see whether these frequencies differed from the theoretical (expected) frequencies. Comparisons of the observed and expected frequencies for each individual attribute of sales representatives and characteristic of advertising media indicated that no significant differences existed between respondents who were decision makers and respondents who were not. The same type of comparison also revealed no significant differences between respondents who were owners and/or managers and those who were not.

A chi-square goodness-of-fit test was used to assess whether respondents ascribed different values to the attributes and characteristics listed in the sales-representatives and advertising-media sections of the study. Significant differences were found in the observed and expected frequencies of the attributes of sales representatives (Exhibit 1). Not all attributes were rated equally important. Figure 1 portrays graphically the number of times each attribute was chosen as one of the three most important attributes. The most important attributes were creativity, knowledge about the client's business, concern about particular advertising needs, and an orientation toward results. The least important attributes were sincerity, concern about follow-through, a willingness to work hard, availability, ability to place ads quickly, and cooperation.

Significant differences were also noted when the observed and expected frequencies of the characteristics of advertising media were tested (Exhibit 2). The hypothesis that each of the characteristics was of equal importance was rejected. Figure 2 displays the observed frequencies

Exhibit 1

Chi-Square Test: Attributes of Sales Representatives

Item No.	1	2	3	4	5	6	7	8	9	10	11	12
Observed Frequencies	75	98	28	122	15	8	47	99	17	1	5	23
Expected Frequencies	All cells = 43.83			df = 1		$\chi^2 = 444.35$[a]						

[a]Statistically significant, $p = 0.001$.

Figure 1

Number of Times an Attribute Was Chosen as One of the Three Most Important

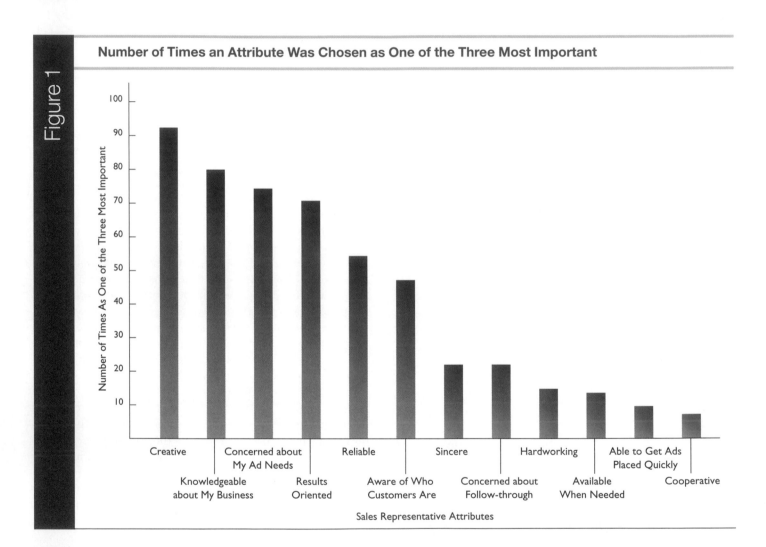

Exhibit 2

Chi-Square Test: Characteristics of Advertising

Item No.	1	2	3	4	5	6	7	8	9	10	11	12
Observed Frequencies	91	54	23	73	80	11	17	18	75	13	48	23
Expected Frequencies	All cells = 43.83			df = 11		$\chi^2 = 222.67$[a]						

[a]Statistically significant, $p = 0.001$.

associated with each characteristic. The most important characteristics were whether the ads improved sales volume, whether they built recognition of the business, whether they were costly, and whether people paid attention to them. The least important characteristics were whether the ads were of high quality, whether there was evidence that the ads reached a known market, whether they were creative, whether repetition was necessary for effectiveness, whether they were easy to monitor, and whether the ad-buying process was difficult.

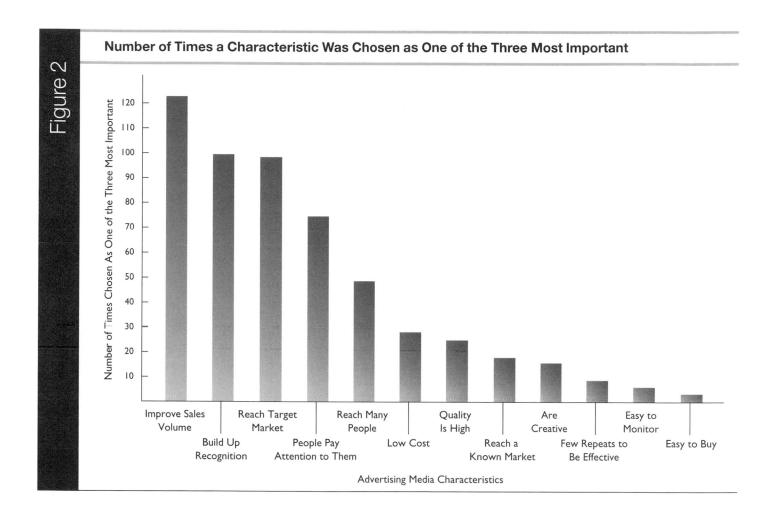

Figure 2

Number of Times a Characteristic Was Chosen as One of the Three Most Important

Advertising Media Characteristics

Case • 6.1

Wisconsin Power & Light (C)[1]

In response to the current consumer trend towards increased environmental sensitivity, Wisconsin Power & Light (WP&L) adopted several high-visibility environmental initiatives. These environmental programs fell under the BuySmart umbrella of WP&L's Demand-Side Management Programs and were intended to foster the conservation of energy among WP&L's residential, commercial, and industrial customers. Examples of specific programs include: Appliance Rebates, Energy Analysis, Weatherization Help, and the Home Energy Improvement Loan (HEIL) program. All previous marketing research and information gathering focused primarily on issues from the customers' perspective, such as an evaluation of net program impacts in terms of energy and demand savings and an estimation of the levels of free ridership (individuals who would have undertaken the conservation actions promoted by the program, even if there was no program in place). In addition, a study has been designed and is currently being conducted to evaluate and identify customer attitudes and opinions concerning the design, implementation, features, and delivery of the residential programs. Having examined the consumer perspective, WP&L's next objective is to focus on obtaining information from other participants in the programs, namely employees and lenders.

WP&L's immediate research focus is to undertake a study of the Home Energy Improvement Loan (HEIL) program of the BuySmart umbrella. The HEIL program was introduced in 1987 and was designed to make low-interest-rate financing available to residential gas and electric WP&L customers for conservation and weatherization measures. The low-interest guaranteed loans are delivered through WP&L account representatives in conjunction with participating financial institutions and trade allies. The procedures for obtaining a loan begin with an energy "audit" of the interested customer's residence to determine the appropriate conservation measures. Once the customer decides on which measures to have installed, the WP&L representative assists in arranging low-interest-rate financing through one of the participating local banking institutions. At the completion of the projects, WP&L representatives conduct an inspection of the work by checking a random sample of participants. Conservation measures eligible under the HEIL program include the installation of natural gas furnaces/boilers, automatic vent dampers, intermittent ignition devices, heat pumps, and heat pump water heaters. Eligible structural improvements include the addition of attic/wall/basement insulation, storm windows and doors, sillbox insulation, window weather-stripping, and caulking.

Purpose

The primary goal of the current study is to identify ways of improving the HEIL program from the lenders' point of view. Specifically, the following issues need to be addressed:

- Identify the lenders' motivation for participating in the program.
- Determine how lenders get their information regarding various changes/updates in the program.
- Identify how lenders promote the program.
- Assess the current program with respect to administrative and program features.
- Determine the type of credit analysis conducted by the lenders.
- Identify ways of minimizing the default rate from the lenders' point of view.
- Assess the lenders' commitment to the program.
- Identify lenders' opinions of the overall program.
- Identify if the reason for loan inactivity in some lending institutions is due to lack of a customer base.

Methodology

WP&L decided to use a telephone survey of participating lending institutions to collect the data for their study. WP&L referenced two lists of lending institutions, which were supplied by their residential marketing staff, in order to select the sample for the survey. A total of 124 participating lending institutions were identified. However, one of the lists was shorter than the other by 15 names. Specifically, the names of some of the branches of major banks were not enumerated on one of the lists. Nevertheless, all 124 institutions, including the 15 discrepant ones, were included in the pool of names from which the sample was drawn.

The sample pool was stratified into three groups based on loan activity in the previous calendar year, as follows:

Group	Number of Lenders	Loan Activity
1	44	0 loans
2	40	1 to 7 loans
3	40	8 to 54 loans

[1]The contributions of Kavita Maini and Paul Metz to the development of this case are gratefully acknowledged as is the permission of Wisconsin Power & Light to use the material included.

The final sample for the survey consisted of 20 systematically chosen lenders from Groups 2 and 3, and 10 randomly chosen institutions from Group 1. The 40 institutions selected from among Groups 2 and 3 formed the sample base in which WP&L was most interested (each of these 40 institutions demonstrated loan activity in the past year). Consequently, WP&L used a systematic selection procedure for this key group in order to ensure that the sample was representative of the population and to improve the statistical efficiency of the sample. The sample size ($n = 40$) was based on judgment. The 10 randomly selected institutions from Group 1 were chosen primarily to explore the hypothesized reasons for zero-loan activity. These 10 zero-loan lenders received a shortened version of the telephone survey that focused only on their lack of activity.

All the districts within WP&L's service territory were notified two weeks in advance that a survey was going to be conducted. A survey was designed to address the research objectives and included both closed- and open-ended questions. The survey was pretested and modified prior to final administration. All interviewing was conducted over a one-week period by a project manager and research assistant, both employees of WP&L's marketing department.

One of the open-ended questions in the survey asked lenders to identify the benefits gained by participating in the HEIL program. The actual wording of the question follows:

Q.6 Does your bank benefit in any way by participating in this program?
1 Yes
2 No

Q.7 Would you please explain your answer?

Data from this question, it was hypothesized, could be used to address several of the aforementioned research objectives. First, the responses would provide qualitative insights into the lenders' motivation for participating in the program. Second, they would help explain lenders' level of commitment to the program as well as help identify reasons why banks promote (or fail to promote) the HEIL program. Finally, the benefits cited could provide WP&L with an understanding of the lenders' overall opinion of the program. Exhibit 1 contains a list of the verbatim responses to this open-ended question.

Questions

1. Synthesize the verbatim responses by developing a set of codes and then grouping them into categories that would help WP&L understand the perceived benefits of the HEIL program.
2. What advantages does the researcher gain by coding open-ended data?
3. What recommendations would you make to WP&L about the HEIL program based on what the open-ended data suggest?

Exhibit 1

Verbatim Responses Regarding the Benefits Conveyed to Lenders by Participation in the HEIL Program

1. We acquire a new loan customer. The customer likes the fact that the loan is guaranteed.
2. It's good public relations to be associated with WP&L. Also, we have nothing to lose on it. It is a risk-free program.
3. It fulfills the CRA (Credit Reinvestment Act) requirement.
4. We got some new customers. People from other towns cannot get into the HEIL program from their bank.
5. We make some money through the buydown.
6. We have access to more customers and can therefore cross-sell other services. We stay competitive this way. It's also good PR to be associated with WP&L.
7. We provide another service to the customer. It helps us to stay competitive.
8. We improve on customer service by providing an additional service. It helps us stay competitive.
9. We can provide another service. We have also built customer contact a lot more.
10. We earn interest income. Customers look on us more favorably because this program is really good.
11. We got some new customers. In addition, the HEIL program helps us make more loans, which is helping us to make revenue.
12. We get money out of the interest buydowns.
13. Another service to provide our customers.
14. It is an added service that enriches our offerings. People come back for other loans.
15. If fulfills CRA. Also, good public relations to be associated with WP&L.
16. It fulfills CRA. Also, more loans implies more income for the bank and a higher proportion can be reinvested back into the community.
17. Another service to provide our customers.
18. It fulfills CRA.
19. Another service to provide for our customers.
20. Good public relations.

continued

Exhibit 1

Verbatim Responses Regarding the Benefits Conveyed to Lenders by Participation in the HEIL Program (*continued*)

21. We can provide another service to our customers.
22. We got some new customers.
23. It's good for our customers.
24. No benefits anymore. There are so many restrictions. There should be more types of options.
25. We are in it for the CRA.
26. We can provide another service to our customers.
27. No benefits because too many good options are excluded.
28. It fulfills the CRA requirement. We are providing the customers a service that has very good rates.
29. We got some new customers.
30. Financially, we get more money by lending without the program.
31. We provide another service to our customers.
32. We are in it for the CRA.
33. We get money through the buydowns.
34. We gain new customers.
35. Good public relations.
36. We provide another service and it allows us to help people who really need the loan.
37. We provide another service to our clients and community.
38. It helps us provide another service to our clients and community.
39. We don't have a high enough volume to be able to say that there has been a benefit.
40. We provide another service to our customers.

Case • 6.2

Young Ideas Publishing Company (B)

Young Ideas Publishing Company was founded three years ago by Linda Halley and her business partner, Teresa Martinez. Thus far, the company has published two novels, *Illusions of Summer* and *Ultimate Choices*, both of which were written by Halley. The novels address several controversial social and political topics and are targeted toward high-school-age teenagers (ages 15 to 18 years). Both books have received critical praise but have not fared well commercially. Distributors have been unwilling to carry the books, believing that no real market demand exists for novels of this type. Halley, however, maintains that her novels would appeal to teens, particularly "nonconformist" teens—by her definition, teens who take an interest in social and political issues.

In an effort to generate insights into the local teen market, Halley has retained the services of a young marketing researcher. A research project has been designed to focus on the potential demand for the product among teens as well as potential marketing-mix elements. A questionnaire has been designed and administered to 166 teens in the target age group. A portion of the questionnaire is shown in Exhibit 1; note that a scale to measure the nonconformity construct is included.

Questions

1. Items 13 through 25 in Exhibit 1 attempt to measure nonconformity. Define "nonconformity" based on these items. How well do these items tap into the construct? What other items could (or should) have been included?

2. Analyze the data in the file "young" using cross-tabulations or other analyses. Summarize your findings and make recommendations. Include descriptions of the student market in general, the most likely student market for books of this nature (if one exists), and the "nonconformist" student market.

Exhibit 1

Partial Questionnaire/Coding

The following is a portion of a questionnaire administered to teens ages 15 to 18 years. The questionnaire was designed to gather information and opinions pertaining to reading habits, subject matter preferences, and related issues. Codes are shown in parentheses.

NOTE: Nonresponses were coded as "9" or "99."

For the first group of questions, respondents were asked to check the appropriate box.

1. On average, how many books do you read for pleasure outside of school in one month?
   - (0) ☐ Less than one
   - (1) ☐ One
   - (2) ☐ Two
   - (3) ☐ Three
   - (4) ☐ Four
   - (5) ☐ Five
   - (6) ☐ Six
   - (7) ☐ I never read any.

2. In the last 12 months, where have you usually gotten the books you have read for pleasure?
   - (0) ☐ I never read any.
   - (1) ☐ Public library
   - (2) ☐ School library
   - (3) ☐ Home
   - (4) ☐ Borrow from another person
   - (5) ☐ Book store
   - (6) ☐ Store other than book store
   - (7) ☐ Book club
   - (8) ☐ Mail order other than book club
   - (9) ☐ Receive as gifts
   - (10) ☐ Other

3. On average, what would you pay for a new paperback book?
   - (1) ☐ Less than $3.00
   - (2) ☐ $3.00 to $3.99
   - (3) ☐ $4.00 to $4.99
   - (4) ☐ $5.00 to $5.99
   - (5) ☐ $6.00 to $6.99
   - (6) ☐ $7.00 to $7.99
   - (7) ☐ $8.00 or more

continued

Exhibit 1

Partial Questionnaire/Coding (*continued*)

In the following section, the teens were asked to judge the importance of various features of books in their decision process of purchasing a book.

	Very Important	Somewhat Important	Neither Important nor Unimportant	Somewhat Unimportant	Very Unimportant
4. The story description	(1) ☐	(2) ☐	(3) ☐	(4) ☐	(5) ☐
5. The author	(1) ☐	(2) ☐	(3) ☐	(4) ☐	(5) ☐
6. The price	(1) ☐	(2) ☐	(3) ☐	(4) ☐	(5) ☐

Next, respondents were asked to circle the appropriate number corresponding to how likely they were to read books within various subject-matter categories. Actual number coded.

	Extremely Likely			Neither Likely nor Unlikely			Extremely Unlikely
7. Science fiction	1	2	3	4	5	6	7
8. Humor/comedy	1	2	3	4	5	6	7
9. Mystery/suspense	1	2	3	4	5	6	7
10. Political	1	2	3	4	5	6	7
11. Romance	1	2	3	4	5	6	7
12. Social issues/problems	1	2	3	4	5	6	7

To determine the degree to which a teen was "nonconformist," he/she was asked to indicate his/her level of agreement with each of the following statements. Actual number coded.

	Strongly Agree	Agree	Disagree	Strongly Disagree
13. When I make decisions, I like to get other people's opinions.	1	2	3	4
14. I would lead a demonstration for a social cause if I felt strongly about it.	1	2	3	4
15. I fit in well with society.	1	2	3	4
16. I respect the opinions of most adults.	1	2	3	4
17. I like to try to change society.	1	2	3	4
18. It's important to me that I fit in well with other students my age.	1	2	3	4
19. I would participate in a local/national campaign to promote a candidate who represented my views.	1	2	3	4
20. My lifestyle is different than most students my own age.	1	2	3	4
21. I keep up with current events.	1	2	3	4
22. I don't like to call attention to myself.	1	2	3	4
23. If I feel strongly about something, I need to make my statement even if my friends disagree.	1	2	3	4
24. I try to avoid conflict with my parents.	1	2	3	4
25. Keeping up with the trends is important to me.	1	2	3	4

Exhibit 1

Partial Questionnaire/Coding (*continued*)

Finally, two of the classification questions from the questionnaire are presented.

26. What is your age? _____ years old.
    [actual age was coded]

27. Are you male or female?
    (1) __ Male
    (2) __ Female

Case • 6.3

Office of Student Financial Services (B)[1]

As part of a quality service initiative (QSI) program at a midwestern university, the Office of Student Affairs fielded a questionnaire designed to ascertain the level of satisfaction that undergraduate students had with the various student services provided on campus. Among its findings, which were distributed to all the relevant departments on campus, was that the Office of Student Financial Services (OSFS) was one of the lowest ranking departments. Susan Solacy, director of the OSFS, raised several issues that she felt were problematic with the QSI survey:

1. The QSI survey had only one question that pertained directly to satisfaction with the OSFS, and thus it may have provided a distorted view of what students were actually feeling. Moreover, the question may have captured dissatisfaction with issues over which the OSFS has no control, in that the majority of the funding guidelines regarding scholarships, grants, and loans are established by the federal government. Given that the role of the OSFS is simply to execute the procedures set forth at the national level, it controls neither the amount of aid available nor the amount allocated to each applicant. In addition, the application processing time is also out of the OSFS's jurisdiction, as the materials are submitted by the students directly to the federal government.
2. All the questions in the QSI survey were structured (close-ended). This may have caused respondents to feel that they needed to provide an answer even when they did not have an opinion on the issue. This may be the case in this instance as historically only about 30 percent of the student body applies for financial aid through the OSFS. However, almost all the students completing the QSI survey had responded to the question regarding satisfaction with the OSFS.

Methodology

Susan felt that it was necessary to address any misconceptions that may have arisen from the QSI findings. She therefore elected to develop her own study dealing specifically with the OSFS. The objectives of the study were to:

1. Determine the relative importance of the services provided by the OSFS that are listed in Exhibit 1, and
2. Ascertain the level of satisfaction with these services.

Susan hired several marketing research students to develop a mail questionnaire that would address the factors that contribute to the level of satisfaction with the OSFS. The direction provided to the students was based upon Susan's ten years experience with the OSFS, and several financial aid surveys from other universities which dealt with many of the same issues with which the OSFS is concerned.

To address the objectives set forth by Susan, the student marketing research team developed the mail questionnaire that appears in Exhibit 2. It contains five-point Likert scale items designed to ascertain the level of satisfaction students have with the various services provided by the OSFS, and the helpfulness of its staff. Of the 5,000 questionnaires mailed to students who had applied for financial aid within the last 12 months, 943 usable surveys were returned. Regarding the analysis, the OSFS has historically been most interested in looking at the two-box score, along with its cumulative percentage. This two-box score is obtained by simply combining the agree and strongly agree responses for each of the Likert scale items. For example, for Question 14 ("I have no problem with picking up any financial aid check"), the two-box score frequency is 448 and the two-box cumulative percentage is 48%.

Exhibit 3 provides a tabulation of the rankings of all services provided by the OSFS. This summary of frequencies is based on Question 35, which asks students to identify the five most important services provided by the OSFS (1 = most important, 2 = second most important, through 5 = fifth most important).

Questions

1. On the basis of Exhibit 3, what do students feel are the most important services provided by the OSFS?
2. Using the two-box percentage for the relevant five-point Likert scale items as a guide along with the raw data supplied by your instructor, are there any facets within the three most important services that are especially problematic?
3. Based upon the cross tabulation of most important services provided by OSFS (Question 35) with student classification (Question 42), are there any differences among the student classes regarding the most important services provided by the OSFS?
4. Given that the OSFS has limited resources, what would you recommend to Susan if you were part of the student marketing research team?

[1]The contributions of Neeraj Bhardawaj to the development of this case are gratefully acknowledged.

Exhibit 1

Services Provided by OSFS

Application process

Dispensing checks

Scholarships

Federal work-study

Loans

Fee waivers

Federal Pell Grants

Summer financial aid

Study abroad

Student job center

Exhibit 2

OSFS Survey

INSTRUCTIONS: Please read the statements below and select the responses that best describe your experience with the Office of Student Financial Services (OSFS)

	Strongly Disagree (1)	Disagree (2)	Neutral (3)	Agree (4)	Strongly Agree (5)
Application Process					
1. OSFS provided me with adequate information about my rights and responsibilities involved in the financial aid process.	____	____	____	____	____
2. The application instructions are clear, concise, and easy to understand.	____	____	____	____	____
3. Information concerning filing procedures and deadlines is clearly presented in the instruction sheet.	____	____	____	____	____
4. After filing the application, I always receive follow-up letters from OSFS informing me what documents are received, which are required to complete the application, and what forms are submitted incorrectly.	____	____	____	____	____
5. I open all mail from OSFS as soon as I receive it.	____	____	____	____	____
6. The follow-up letters I receive are useful in making sure I submit requested documents on time.	____	____	____	____	____
7. I usually get notified about missing documents just before deadlines.	____	____	____	____	____
8. OSFS does a good job in keeping track of my application process and informing me of my current status.	____	____	____	____	____
9. I do most of the job of keeping track of my own financial status by calling or visiting OSFS.	____	____	____	____	____
10. Not being able to fill out forms correctly is my biggest problem with the financial aid process.	____	____	____	____	____
11. Not being able to submit requested documents on time is my biggest problem with the financial aid application process.	____	____	____	____	____
12. OSFS mislocating submitted documents is the biggest problem with the financial aid application process.	____	____	____	____	____
13. I feel I am overwhelmed by the complexity of the entire financial aid process.	____	____	____	____	____

continued

Exhibit 2

OSFS Survey (*continued*)

	Strongly Disagree (1)	Disagree (2)	Neutral (3)	Agree (4)	Strongly Agree (5)

Receiving Checks

Please answer question 14 only if you received financial aid checks.

14. I have no problems with picking up my financial aid check. _____ _____ _____ _____ _____

General Information

15. How do you get most of your financial aid questions answered? (Please circle only one answer.)
    a. Telephone
    b. Walk ins/Counter help
    c. Appointments with counselors
    d. Financial aid publications
    e. Fellow students
    f. Public information sessions
    g. Other financial assistance agencies (banks, governments, etc.)
    h. High school counselor
    i. Other: _____

16. I prefer to contact OSFS by:

	Strongly Disagree (1)	Disagree (2)	Neutral (3)	Agree (4)	Strongly Agree (5)
a. Telephone	_____	_____	_____	_____	_____
b. Walk ins/Counter help	_____	_____	_____	_____	_____
c. Appointments with counselors	_____	_____	_____	_____	_____
d. Financial aid publications	_____	_____	_____	_____	_____
e. Fellow students	_____	_____	_____	_____	_____
f. Public information sessions	_____	_____	_____	_____	_____
g. Other financial assistance agencies (banks, governments, etc.)	_____	_____	_____	_____	_____
h. High school counselor	_____	_____	_____	_____	_____
i. Other	_____	_____	_____	_____	_____

17. How many times have you called OSFS in the past year (circle one)?
    a. 0–5
    b. 6–10
    c. 11–15
    d. More than 15

18. In reference to your telephone experience with the OSFS:

	Strongly Disagree (1)	Disagree (2)	Neutral (3)	Agree (4)	Strongly Agree (5)
a. The person was informative.	_____	_____	_____	_____	_____
b. The person was courteous.	_____	_____	_____	_____	_____
c. The person did not clearly explain the information.	_____	_____	_____	_____	_____
d. I received correct information pertaining to my file.	_____	_____	_____	_____	_____
e. I usually wait on hold for less than 5 minutes.	_____	_____	_____	_____	_____
f. OSFS was easily accessible by telephone (not busy).	_____	_____	_____	_____	_____

19. I rely on the FINFONE service to check on the status of my financial aid. _____ _____ _____ _____ _____

20. The FINFONE service provided the information needed. _____ _____ _____ _____ _____

Exhibit 2

OSFS Survey (*continued*)

21. How many times have you visited OSFS in the past year (circle one)?
    a. 0–5
    b. 6–10
    c. 11–15
    d. More than 15

	Strongly Disagree (1)	Disagree (2)	Neutral (3)	Agree (4)	Strongly Agree (5)
22. In reference to your experience with the front desk personnel:					
a. The person was informative.	_____	_____	_____	_____	_____
b. The person was courteous.	_____	_____	_____	_____	_____
c. The person did not clearly explain the information.	_____	_____	_____	_____	_____
d. I received correct information pertaining to my file.	_____	_____	_____	_____	_____
e. The person was efficient.	_____	_____	_____	_____	_____
f. I usually wait in line for less than 5 minutes.	_____	_____	_____	_____	_____
23. I rely on OSFS publications for financial aid information.	_____	_____	_____	_____	_____
24. In reterence to the publication(s) read:					
a. The material was informative.	_____	_____	_____	_____	_____
b. The material was confusing.	_____	_____	_____	_____	_____
c. The material was complete.	_____	_____	_____	_____	_____
d. The material was sent in a timely manner when requested.	_____	_____	_____	_____	_____
e. I usually find the information I need.	_____	_____	_____	_____	_____

Counselors

25. Have you seen a counselor at the OSFS?
    (1) No (If no, please skip to question 27.)
    (2) Yes

	Strongly Disagree (1)	Disagree (2)	Neutral (3)	Agree (4)	Strongly Agree (5)
26. a. It was easy to reach the counselor by phone.	_____	_____	_____	_____	_____
b. The counselor did not return my phone calls promptly.	_____	_____	_____	_____	_____
c. It was easy to get in to see a counselor.	_____	_____	_____	_____	_____
d. The counselor(s) spent enough time on me.	_____	_____	_____	_____	_____
e. The counselor(s) was (were) friendly and courteous.	_____	_____	_____	_____	_____
f. The counselor(s) was (were) knowledgeable about my financial aid concerns.	_____	_____	_____	_____	_____
g. The counselor(s) did not explain the information clearly.	_____	_____	_____	_____	_____
h. I received the necessary information during the FIRST visit.	_____	_____	_____	_____	_____
i. Overall, the counselor(s) was (were) helpful.	_____	_____	_____	_____	_____

continued

Exhibit 2

OSFS Survey (*continued*)

	Strongly Disagree (1)	Disagree (2)	Neutral (3)	Agree (4)	Strongly Agree (5)

Scholarships

Please answer questions in this section if your interaction with OSFS involved scholarships. (Otherwise, skip to question 28.)

27. a. The OSFS provided helpful publications and information on applying for scholarships.
    b. The services provided by the Scholarship Office in the OSFS were useful to me.
    c. The personnel in the office were unable to answer questions I asked concerning scholarships.
    d. The amount of scholarships available through the OSFS were adequate.

Federal Work-Study

Please answer questions in this section if your interaction with OSFS involved federal work-study. (Otherwise, skip to question 29.)

28. a. The OSFS provided helpful publications and information on opportunities for federal work-study.
    b. The services regarding federal work-study provided by the OSFS were useful to me.
    c. The personnel in the office were unable to answer questions I asked concerning federal work-study.
    d. The amount of federal work-study available through the OSFS was adequate.

Loans

Please answer questions in this section if your interaction with OSFS involved loans. (Otherwise, skip to question 30.)

29. a. The OSFS provided helpful publications and information on opportunities for loans.
    b. The service provided by the Loan Office of OSFS was useful to me.
    c. The personnel in the office were unable to answer questions I asked concerning loans.
    d. The amount of loans available through OSFS was adequate.
    e. The office was accurate and effective in servicing the loans (for example, informing when checks were in, payments, debt information.

Few Waivers

Please answer questions in this section if your interaction with OSFS involved fee waivers. (Otherwise, skip to question 31.)

30. a. The OSFS provided helpful information on fee waivers.

Exhibit 2

OSFS Survey (*continued*)

	Strongly Disagree (1)	Disagree (2)	Neutral (3)	Agree (4)	Strongly Agree (5)
b. The personnel in the office were unable to answer questions I asked concerning fee waivers.	_____	_____	_____	_____	_____
c. The services for fee waivers provided by OSFS were useful to me.	_____	_____	_____	_____	_____

Federal Pell Grants

Please answer questions in this section if your interaction with OSFS involved federal Pell Grants. (Otherwise, skip to question 32.)

31. a. The OSFS provided helpful publications and information on applying for federal Pell Grants.	_____	_____	_____	_____	_____
b. The service provided by the Pell Grant Office of OSFS was useful to me.	_____	_____	_____	_____	_____
c. The personnel in the office were unable to answer questions I asked concerning federal Pell Grants.	_____	_____	_____	_____	_____
d. The amount of federal Pell Grants available through the OSFS was adequate.	_____	_____	_____	_____	_____

Summer Financial Aid

Please answer questions in this section if your interaction with OSFS involved summer financial aid. (Otherwise, skip to question 33.)

32. a. The OSFS provided helpful publications and information on applying for summer financial aid.	_____	_____	_____	_____	_____
b. The personnel in the office were unable to answer questions I asked concerning summer financial aid.	_____	_____	_____	_____	_____
c. The amount of summer financial aid available through the OSFS was adequate.	_____	_____	_____	_____	_____

Study Abroad

Please answer questions in this section if your interaction with OSFS involved study abroad. (Otherwise, skip to question 34.)

33. a. The OSFS provided helpful publications and information on applying for study abroad.	_____	_____	_____	_____	_____
b. The personnel in the office were unable to answer questions I asked concerning study abroad.	_____	_____	_____	_____	_____
c. The amount of aid available for study abroad through the OSFS was adequate.	_____	_____	_____	_____	_____

Student Job Center

Please answer questions in this section if your interaction with OSFS involved the student job center. (Otherwise, skip to question 35.)

34. a. The OSFS provided helpful publications and information on applying for jobs.	_____	_____	_____	_____	_____
b. The service provided by the Student Job Center of the OSFS was useful to me.	_____	_____	_____	_____	_____
c. The personnel in the office were unable to answer questions I asked concerning jobs.	_____	_____	_____	_____	_____
d. The amount of job opportunities available through the Student Job Center was adequate.	_____	_____	_____	_____	_____

continued

Exhibit 2

OSFS Survey (*continued*)

35. The following is a list of some of the services provided by the OSFS.

Please identify what you feel are the five most important services by placing "1" in front of the most important service, "2" in front of the second most important service, "3" in front of the third most important service, "4" in front of the fourth most important service, and "5" in front of the fifth most important service.

_____ a. Assistance in filling out financial aid forms
_____ b. Assistance with scholarship information
_____ c. The federal work-study program
_____ d. Assistance in obtaining loans
_____ e. Assistance with fee waivers
_____ f. Obtaining federal Pell Grants
_____ g. Assistance in obtaining summer financial aid
_____ h. The Study Abroad program
_____ i. Receiving a financial aid award in a timely fashion
_____ j. The FINFONE telephone service
_____ k. Loan servicing (for example, informing when checks are in, payments, debt information)
_____ l. Speed in obtaining financial aid check
_____ m. Counselor assistance
_____ n. Receiving printed informational material
_____ o. Other (please specify) _____

Please Circle or Complete as Appropriate

36. Gender:
    (1) Female
    (2) Male

37. Age:_____

38. Marital Status:
    (1) Single
    (2) Married

39. a. Do you have any children?
    (1) No (if no, please skip to question 40)
    (2) Yes
    b. If you have children, please circle the appropriate reply.
    (1) 1 to 3 children
    (2) 4 to 6 children
    (3) 7 or more children

40. Did you complete the entire financial aid process?
    (1) No
    (2) Yes

41. Did you receive financial aid through OSFS?
    (1) No
    (2) Yes

42. Year of study:
    (1) Freshman
    (2) Sophomore
    (3) Junior
    (4) Senior
    (5) Other

43. How often did you have contact with OSFS during a calendar year?
    (1) 0–5
    (2) 6–10
    (3) 11–15
    (4) More than 15

Thank you very much for your assistance!

Exhibit 3

Ranking of Services Provided by OSFS (Summary of Question 35)

Question	Service	FREQUENCY RANKING OF SERVICES					
		1st	2nd	3rd	4th	5th	Not Ranked
35a	Assistance in filling out financial aid forms	191	117	73	78	80	404
35b	Assistance with scholarship information	101	85	87	71	47	552
35c	The federal work-study program	26	38	41	53	50	735
35d	Assistance in obtaining loans	112	117	98	73	74	469
35e	Assistance with fee waivers	4	13	25	29	29	843
35f	Obtaining federal Pell Grants	102	98	65	73	41	564
35g	Assistance in obtaining summer financial aid	3	10	26	19	35	850
35h	The Study Abroad Program	7	16	14	24	32	850
35i	Receiving a financial aid award in a timely fashion	134	114	105	110	89	391
35j	The FINFONE telephone service *	23	34	36	47	73	730
35k	Loan servicing	61	76	103	102	84	517
35l	Speed in obtaining financial aid check	62	98	98	99	83	503
35m	Counselor assistance	36	56	73	64	73	641
35n	Receiving printed information material	52	46	66	62	93	624
35o	Other	13	3	2	2	17	906

*FINFONE is a 24-hour touchtone system that students can call to check on the status of their financial aid applications. The information is part of Dean of Student Affairs Magnus Pym's Quality Service Initiative Program that enables students to have their most frequently asked questions about all the student services provided on campus to be answered by a preprogrammed telephone system.

Case • 6.4

Transitional Housing, Inc. (B)[1]

Transitional Housing Inc. (THI) is a nonprofit organization located in Madison, Wisconsin. THI provides assistance to homeless and very low income individuals and families in finding emergency shelter, food, employment, transitional housing, and affordable apartment housing (see Case 1.2, Transitional Housing, Inc. [A], for more details). As part of its planning, the board of directors of THI was interested in finding ways to improve the organization's services. They decided to assemble a task force to evaluate THI's current facilities and services, and to determine what future facilities and services it should provide.

Methodology

The task force was assembled in February. After evaluating external information on the homeless situation in Dane County and internal information on THI, the task force submitted a proposal to the board outlining their methodology and time frame (Exhibit 1). The proposal consisted of three surveys, conducted on the organization's paid staff, volunteers, and guests (the homeless staying at THI or using its facilities/services).

Given the exploratory nature of the research project, the task force decided to use a nonprobability convenience sample for guests and volunteers, and a census for the small number of staff members. Three separate questionnaires were used, with volunteers and staff being surveyed using self-administered questionnaires and guests being surveyed using structured in-person interviews.

Questionnaire

The initial research done by the task force suggested several areas of interest, including the need for adding staff members and services at the drop-in shelter, and the addition of personal sleeping and storage areas for guests. However, in order to create more directed questions, separate focus groups were conducted with staff, volunteers,

and guests. Individual survey questions were based on the focus group responses.

The final questionnaire was broken out into four sections: physical facilities, current services, potential future services, and demographics (Exhibit 2). Most questions for the three surveys were identical. Exceptions included demographic questions that were unique for guests, staff, and volunteers, and physical facilities questions that were applicable only to guests.

Both closed- and open-ended questions were asked to all three groups. After all the questionnaires were complete, open-ended responses were evaluated to determine representative categories. A coding sheet was then created to facilitate data entry (Exhibit 3). A total of 68 guests, 33 volunteers, and 11 staff members completed questionnaires. Two of the volunteer surveys were discarded due to incomplete responses. The raw data are contained in file THI.dat.

Questions

1. One of the research objectives was to determine what new services are needed by the homeless men. Which survey questions best address this research objective? Why?
2. Using the data provided, run one-way tabulations (i.e., frequency analyses) on the survey questions you recommended in Question 1. Discuss the general findings from these tabulations.
3. Run cross tabulations on the survey questions you recommended in Question 1 against the type of respondent. Are there significant differences among guests, volunteers, and staff? If yes, what are the implications for THI's board of directors?
4. What recommendations would you make to THI based on your findings? Why?

[1]The contributions of Monika Wingate to the development of this case are gratefully acknowledged.

Exhibit 1

Research Proposal to Transitional Housing

Purpose and Limits of the Project:

THI is interested in knowing how their services enable them to meet community needs and if the services are aiding the clients in their struggle to "get out of the loop." Specifically, Transitional Housing, Inc. (THI), would like to address the following questions:

1. What are the needs of the homeless community?
2. Are current services meeting the homeless community's needs?
3. How could the needs of the homeless community be better met?

As discussed in earlier meetings, this project will focus on the services provided by the Drop-In Shelter and the Hospitality House, as it is used in conjunction with the Drop-In Shelter.

Data Sources and Research Methodology:

The primary source of data collection will be through the use of a questionnaire. Focus groups will be conducted in order to facilitate development of the questions asked of the target populations. Secondary data collection sources will include statistics on the current homeless population in Dane County, and internal information provided by THI such as statistics of the guest services and previous/simultaneous studies conducted by THI.

The target population to be surveyed are current guests (at the Drop-In Shelter and Hospitality House), staff, volunteers, and previous guests of the Drop-In Shelter or Hospitality House who are currently in Transitional Housing. Sample sizes for the target population will be determined as follows:

- The current guest sample will be based on the number of guests staying at the Drop-In Shelter on two separate nights.
- The staff and volunteers sample sizes will be based on the number of years of service to the organization and will be adjusted for sample population mortality.
- The previous guests sample will be taken from the actual number of guests currently in one of the Transitional Housing facilities who were previous guests of the Drop-In Shelter and/or Hospitality House.

These groups were chosen because they are representative of the population who use THI services and who administer them.

Estimate of Time and Personnel Requirements:

The study will be conducted by the five research team members. Additional personnel may be required for administration of the questionnaire. They will be recruited from the THI volunteer base not included in the sample population. The projected time frame for the project is listed below:

- Focus groups and questionnaire development: 4–5 weeks
- Sample selection: 1 week
- Administration of the survey: 3–4 weeks
- Analysis of data and presentation to agency: 2 weeks

Exhibit 2

Questionnaires

GUEST QUESTIONNAIRE

Physical Facilities of the Drop-In Shelter:

The following questions relate to potential future facilities of the Drop-In Shelter. Please circle the number which most closely represents your opinion of the need for the following facilities.

	Definitely Needed	Needed	Neutral	Not Needed	Definitely Not Needed
1. Personal storage areas	1	2	3	4	5
2. Study areas	1	2	3	4	5
3. Library	1	2	3	4	5
4. Separate areas for guests with contagious diseases (e.g., flu, cold, etc.)	1	2	3	4	5
5. Wheelchair accessibility	1	2	3	4	5

6. Often there is limited funding, and choices on where to spend these funds must be made. Please rank the following items in order of importance using 1 through 5 (1 being most important and 5 being least important). Please use each number only once.

    ____ Personal storage areas
    ____ Study areas
    ____ Library
    ____ Separate areas for guests with contagious diseases
    ____ Wheelchair accessibility

7. If the option existed for you to stay in a room by yourself for the night, what is the most that you would be willing (and able) to pay for this room? (CHECK HIGHEST AMOUNT YOU WOULD BE WILLING TO PAY)

    ____ $2–$3 per night
    ____ $4–$5 per night
    ____ $6–$8 per night
    ____ More than $8 per night
    ____ I would not be willing to pay for my own room (skip to question 10)

8. If the option existed for you to stay in a room by yourself for the night, what is the farthest you would be willing to walk from the Capitol?

    ____ under 1 block
    ____ 1–2 blocks
    ____ 3–4 blocks
    ____ 5–6 blocks
    ____ 7–8 blocks

If the option existed for you to stay in a room by yourself for the night, the following list of features are items that might be included in such a facility. On a scale of 1 to 5, where 1 is "very important" and 5 is "not at all important," please rate the need for the following facilities.

	Very Important	Somewhat Important	Neutral	Not Very Important	Not at All Important
9. Personal storage areas in the room	1	2	3	4	5
10. Cafeteria/food service	1	2	3	4	5
11. Private bathroom	1	2	3	4	5

12. What other features, if any, do you think should be included in this type of facility?

_____
_____
_____

Exhibit 2

Questionnaires (*continued*)

13. Would you be willing to pay for personal storage facilities at the Drop-In Shelter if they were available?
    ____ Yes
    ____ No

Services at the Drop-In Shelter

The questions in this section of the survey relate to the services available to guests of the Drop-In Shelter. The first section relates to services that are already provided at the Drop-In Shelter. The second section relates to potential services that may be provided at the Drop-In Shelter in the future.

Current Services

14. I find the social worker at the Drop-In Shelter helpful.

Strongly Agree	Agree	Neutral	Disagree	Strongly Disagree
1	2	3	4	5

15. There are enough social workers available to meet the guests' needs.

Strongly Agree	Agree	Neutral	Disagree	Strongly Disagree
1	2	3	4	5

IF GUEST ANSWERS WITH A 4 OR 5: How many social workers do you think would be better? ____

16. How do you think the counseling services could be improved, if at all, to better serve the needs of the Drop-In Shelter guests?
    _____
    _____
    _____

17. I find the medical services at the Drop-In Shelter useful.

Strongly Agree	Agree	Neutral	Disagree	Strongly Disagree
1	2	3	4	5

18. There are enough staff people available for the medical services to meet the guests' needs.

Strongly Agree	Agree	Neutral	Disagree	Strongly Disagree
1	2	3	4	5

19. How do you think the medical services could be improved, if at all, to better serve the needs of the Drop-In Shelter guests?
    _____
    _____
    _____

20. There are enough staff people available for the legal services to meet the guests' needs.

Strongly Agree	Agree	Neutral	Disagree	Strongly Disagree
1	2	3	4	5

21. How do you think the legal services could be improved, if at all, to better serve the needs of the Drop-In Shelter guests?

22. One mental health worker (like Axel) is enough to meet the guests' needs.

Strongly Agree	Agree	Neutral	Disagree	Strongly Disagree
1	2	3	4	5

23. How do you think the mental health services could be improved, if at all, to better serve the needs of the Drop-In Shelter guests?
    _____
    _____
    _____

continued

Questionnaires (continued)

24.   There are enough volunteers available to meet the guests' needs.

Strongly Agree	Agree	Neutral	Disagree	Strongly Disagree
1	2	3	4	5

Potential Future Services

The following questions relate to potential future services of the Drop-In Shelter. Please circle the number which most closely represents your opinion of the need for the following services.

	Definitely Needed	Needed	Neutral	Not Needed	Definitely Not Needed
25. On-duty drug and alcohol counselor	1	2	3	4	5
26. Dental services	1	2	3	4	5
27. Optical services	1	2	3	4	5
28. Tutors for guests	1	2	3	4	5
29. Assistance with social service agencies	1	2	3	4	5
30. Seasonal clothing	1	2	3	4	5
31. Interview clothing	1	2	3	4	5
32. Haircuts	1	2	3	4	5

33.   Are there any services that are offered during the day by the Hospitality House that you would like offered at the Drop-In Shelter at night?

_____

_____

34.   What other services do you think should be offered at the Drop-In Shelter?

_____

_____

Demographics Section:

35.   On average, how many times a week do you stay at the Drop-In Shelter?
  ____ once a week or less
  ____ 2–3 times a week
  ____ 4–5 times a week
  ____ 6–7 times a week

36.   Which months during the year do you usually stay at the Drop-In Shelter? (CHECK ALL THAT APPLY)
  ____ January   ____ July
  ____ February   ____ August
  ____ March   ____ September
  ____ April   ____ October
  ____ May   ____ November
  ____ June   ____ December

37.   On average, how many times a week do you visit the Hospitality House?
  ____ I don't use the Hospitality House
  ____ Only once per week
  ____ 2–3 times a week
  ____ 4–5 times a week
  ____ 6–7 times a week

38.   If you do not use the Hospitality House when you stay at the Drop-In Shelter, why not?
  (DO NOT READ LIST; CHECK ALL THAT APPLY)
  ____ Not applicable, I use the HH.
  ____ Too crowded/I don't feel safe.
  ____ Too far.
  ____ Don't like staff.
  ____ Don't feel it meets my service needs.
  ____ Don't want to participate in clean-up.

Exhibit 2

Questionnaires (*continued*)

_____ Not open on weekends.

_____ Don't know about Holiday House.

_____ Other _____

VOLUNTEER QUESTIONNAIRE

Questions 1–6 are identical to Guest Questions 1–6
Questions 7–27 are identical to Guest Questions 14–34

Demographics Section:

28. How many years have you been a volunteer at the Drop-In Shelter?

_____ This is my first night volunteering at the Drop-In Shelter.

_____ 1 year or less

_____ 2–3 years

29. On average, how often do you volunteer at the Drop-In Shelter?

_____ At least once a month

_____ 4 times a year

_____ 2 times a year

_____ Once a year

_____ Less than once a year

30. How did you initially come to volunteer at the Drop-In Shelter?

_____ Church group

_____ Work group

_____ Mandatory community service for a university class

_____ Mandatory community service for some other reason

_____ Personal interest

_____ Other

31. What volunteer shift do you normally work?

_____ Breakfast

_____ 8 pm to midnight

_____ midnight to 4 am

STAFF QUESTIONNAIRE

Questions 1–6 are identical to Guest Questions 1–6
Questions 7–27 are identical to Guest Questions 14–34

Demographics Section:

28. How long have you worked for Transitional Housing, Inc.?

_____ Less than 1 year

_____ 1–2 years

_____ 3–4 years

_____ 5 or more years

29. At which THI facility do you work?

_____ Hospitality House

_____ Drop-In Shelter

30. Are you a full-time or part-time employee?

_____ Full-time

_____ Part-time

Exhibit 3

THI Coding Scheme (for fixed field text format)

Column(s)	Question	Contents
1–3	N/A	Questionnaire I.D.
4	N/A	Type: 1 - Guest
		2 - Volunteer
		3 - Staff
5	1	Personal storage
6	2	Study areas
	3	Library
8	4	Separate areas for guests with contagious diseases
9	5	Wheelchair accessibility
10	6a	Personal storage
11	6b	Study areas
12	6c	Library
13	6d	Separate areas
14	6e	Wheelchair accessibility
15	7 (G14)	Social worker helpful
16	8a (G15a)	Enough social workers
17	8b (G15b)	How many social workers
18–19, 20–21	9 (G16)	Counseling services improved OPEN-ENDED (2 ideas)
		01 - Make guess aware of counseling services
		02 - More individual one-on-one (case) interaction
		03 - Should give referrals
		04 - More structured and enforced rules
		05 - Better trained/new staff
		06 - More AODA counseling
		07 - Be available more often
		08 - Job opportunities advice
		09 - More time with social workers
		10 - Better help with handicapped/special needs
		11 - Other
22	10 (G17)	Medical Services Helpful
23	11 (G18)	Enough Medical Staff
24–25, 26–27	12 (G19)	Medical Services Improved OPEN-ENDED (2 ideas)
		01 - Services offered more often
		02 - Better trained people or "real" doctors/nurses
		03 - More medicine available
		04 - Offer dental care
		05 - Offer eye doctor services
		06 - Better equipment and/or facilities (clinic)
		07 - Keep medical records of guests
		08 - Get rid of it—use other existing programs
		09 - Offer medical tests (TB, etc.)
		10 - Offer more staff—more doctors
		11 - More emphasis on preventive medicine
		12 - Other
28	13 (G20)	Enough Staff-Legal Services
29, 30	14 (G21)	Legal Services Improved OPEN-ENDED (2 ideas)
		1 - Longer appointments—more time with lawyers
		2 - More staff (lawyers) available
		3 - Offered more nights (accessibility)
		4 - Schedule lawyers ahead of time by appt.
		5 - Give guests info about legal rights, rental, etc.
		6 - Other
31	15 (G22)	One Mental Health Worker Is Enough
32, 33	16 (G23)	Mental Health Services Improved OPEN-ENDED (2 ideas)
		1 - Awareness (communicate availability to guests)

PART 6:
Data Analysis

Exhibit 3

THI Coding Scheme (for fixed field text format) (*continued*)

Column(s)	Question	Contents
		2 - Offer classes
		3 - Network with existing agencies (referrals)
		4 - More staff (one-female; one-male)
		5 - Separate the mentally ill
		6 - More individual counseling
		7 - More hours of service
		8 - More structured rules at Drop-In
		9 - Other
34	17 (G24)	Enough volunteers available
35	18 (G25)	On-duty drug and alcohol counselor
36	19 (G26)	Dental services
37	20 (G27)	Optical services
38	21 (G28)	Tutors for guests
39	22 (G29)	Assistance with social service agencies
40	23 (G30)	Seasonal clothing
41	24 (G31)	Interview clothing
42	25 (G32)	Haircuts
43–44, 45–46, 47–48	26 (G33)	Any services offered at Hospitality House that could be offered? (OPEN-ENDED) (Maximum 3 ideas)
		01 - Doesn't use Hospitality House/Unaware
		02 - Counseling services
		03 - Job listings
		04 - Telephone and/or long distance
		05 - Drug/alcohol referrals
		06 - More staff available
		07 - Newspaper
		08 - Computer/typewriter access
		09 - Mailboxes
		10 - Bus tickets/transportation
		11 - Rental/housing lists
		12 - Activities/game room
		13 - Cooking facilities
		14 - Nothing/should use Hospitality House
		15 - Other
49–50, 51–52, 53–54, 55–56	27 (G34)	What Other Services Should Be Offered? (Maximum: 4 ideas)
		01 - More laundry facilities (and ironing board)
		02 - Daily newspaper
		03 - More counseling services
		04 - More showers/sinks
		05 - Additional entertainment
		06 - Bible study
		07 - Answering/message service
		08 - Telephone
		09 - Chiropractor
		10 - Better ventilation
		11 - More beds
		12 - Drug/alcohol treatment
		13 - Better food and more variety
		14 - Enforce rules (drinking)
		15 - Extended shelter hours in winter
		16 - VCR/movies/stereo
		17 - Offer Bible counseling/priests
		18 - Skills training/jobs
		19 - Check for weapons
		20 - Transportation (bus passes)

continued

Exhibit 3

THI Coding Scheme (for fixed field text format) (*continued*)

Column(s)	Question	Contents
		21 - More blankets
		22 - More staff (more accommodating staff)
		23 - Mailing address/mail service
		24 - Other
GUEST-ONLY QUESTIONS: (For volunteer and staff, put spaces in)		
57	G7	Own room by yourself willing to pay
58	G8	Own room—farthest willing to walk
59	G9	Personal storage
60	G10	Cafeteria/food service
61	G11	Private bathroom
62–63, 64–65	G12	What other features should be included? OPEN-ENDED (2 ideas)
		01 - Warm blankets
		02 - A good bed
		03 - TV
		04 - Radio/stereo
		05 - Kitchenette
		06 - Telephone
		07 - Social room
		08 - Separate smoking room
		09 - Laundry facilities
		10 - Job training courses
		11 - Games/entertainment
		12 - Counseling services (all types)
		13 - Workout facilities/gym
		14 - Good ventilation
		15 - Refrigerator
		16 - First aid
		17 - Rules/policies enforcement
		18 - Other
66	G13	Would you be willing to pay for personal storage facilities . . . ?
67	G35	On average, how many times a week do you stay . . . ?
68–69, 70–71,	G36	Which months during the year?
72–73, 74–75		01 - January 07 - July
76–77, 78–79		02 - February 08 - August
ROW 2: 1–2,		03 - March 09 - September
3–4, 5–6, 7–8,		04 - April 10 - October
9–10, 11–12		05 - May 11 - November
(12 possible months)		06 - June 12 - December
ROW 2:		
13	G37	On average, how many times a week do you visit HH?
14–15, 16–17	G38	If you do not use HH, why not? (2 ideas)
		01 - N/A; I use HH
		02 - Too crowded
		03 - Don't feel safe
		04 - Don't like staff
		05 - Don't feel meets service needs
		06 - Don't want to take part in clean-up
		07 - Not open on weekends
		08 - Don't know about HH
		09 - Busy doing other things
		10 - Should have area for sleeping
		11 - Too far away
		12 - Too noisy
		13 - Other

Exhibit 3

THI Coding Scheme (for fixed field text format) (*continued*)

Column(s)	Question	Contents
VOLUNTEER-ONLY QUESTIONS: (For guests and staff, put in spaces)		
18	V28	How many years have you been a volunteer?
19	V29	On average, how often . . . ?
20	V30	How did you initially come to volunteer at the Drop-In?
21	V31	What volunteer shift do you work?
STAFF-ONLY QUESTIONS: (For guests and volunteers, put in spaces)		
22	S28	How long have you worked for?
23	S29	At which THI facility . . . ?
24	S30	Are you full-time/part-time?

Case • 6.5

Fabhus, Inc.

Fabhus, Inc., a manufacturer of prefabricated homes located in Atlanta, Georgia, had experienced steady, sometimes spectacular, growth since its founding in the early 1950s. In recent years, however, things have not been so rosy, with sales dropping about 20% from their high point three years earlier, in spite of a very attractive interest-rate environment for home building.

In an attempt to offset the decline in sales, company management decided to use marketing research to get a better perspective on their customers so that they could better target their marketing efforts. After much discussion, the members of the executive committee finally determined that the following questions would be important to address in this research effort.

1. What is the demographic profile of the typical Fabhus customer?
2. What initially attracts these customers to a Fabhus home?
3. Do Fabhus home customers consider other factory-built homes when making their purchase decision?
4. Are Fabhus customers satisfied with their homes? If they are not, what particular features are unsatisfactory?

Method

The research firm that was called in on the project suggested conducting a mail survey to past buyers. Preliminary discussions with management revealed that Fabhus had the greatest market penetration near its factory. As one moved farther from the factory, the share of the total new housing business that went to Fabhus declined. The company suspected that this might result from the higher prices of the units due to shipping charges. Fabhus relied on a zone-price system in which prices were based on the product delivered at the construction site.

Local dealers actually supervised construction. Each dealer had pricing latitude and could charge more or less than Fabhus's suggested list price. Individual dealers were responsible for seeing that customers were satisfied with their Fabhus home, although Fabhus also had a toll-free number that customers could call if they were not satisfied with the way their dealer handled the construction or if they had problems moving in.

Considering the potential impact distance and dealers might have, the research team thought it was important to sample purchasers in the various zones as well as customers of the various dealers. Since Fabhus's records of houses sold were kept by zone and by date sold within zone, sample respondents were selected in the following way: First, the registration cards per zone were counted. Second, the sample size per zone was determined so that the number of respondents per zone was proportionate to the number of homes sold in the zones. Third, a sample interval, k, was chosen for each zone, a random start between 1 and k was generated, and every kth record was selected. The mail questionnaire shown in Exhibit 1 was sent to the 423 households selected.

A cover letter informing Fabhus's customers of the general purpose of the survey accompanied the questionnaire, and a new one-dollar bill was included with each survey as an incentive to respond. Further, the anonymity of the respondents was guaranteed by enclosing a self-addressed postage-paid postcard in the survey. Respondents were asked to mail the postcard when they mailed their survey. All those who had not returned their postcards in two weeks were sent a notice reminding them that their survey had not been returned. The combination of incentives, guaranteed anonymity, and follow-up prompted the return of 342 questionnaires for an overall response rate of 81 percent.

Questions

1. Using the data in the file "FABHUS" and analytic techniques of your own choosing, address as best you can the objectives that prompted the research effort in the first place.
2. Do you think the research design was adequate for the problems posed? Why or why not?

Exhibit 1

Factory-Built Home Owners Survey

1. How did you first learn of the factory-built home that you bought? (check one, please)

   ☐ Friend or relative   ☐ Direct mail
   ☐ Another customer   ☐ Newspaper
   ☐ Realtor   ☐ Radio
   ☐ Model home   ☐ TV
   ☐ Yellow pages   ☐ Don't remember
   ☐ National magazine   ☐ Other _____
                                       (please specify)

2. Did you own the land your home is on before you first visited your home builder?

   ☐ Yes   ☐ No

3. How long have you lived in your home? _____ years

4. Where did you live before purchasing your factory-built home? (please check one)

   ☐ Rented a house, apartment, or mobile home
   ☐ Owned a mobile home
   ☐ Owned a conventionally built home
   ☐ Owned another factory-built home
   ☐ Other _____
              (please specify)

5. Please rate your overall level of satisfaction with your home. (please check one)

   ☐ Very satisfied
   ☐ Somewhat satisfied
   ☐ Somewhat dissatisfied
   ☐ Very dissatisfied

6. How important to you were each of the following considerations in purchasing your factory-built home?
   (please check one space for each item)

Considerations	Extremely Important	Important	Slightly Important	Not Important
Investment value	____	____	____	____
Quality	____	____	____	____
Price	____	____	____	____
Energy features	____	____	____	____
Dealer	____	____	____	____
Exterior style	____	____	____	____
Floor plan	____	____	____	____
Interior features	____	____	____	____
Delivery schedule	____	____	____	____

7. Below, please list any other homes you looked at before purchasing the home you chose. Please state the reason you did not purchase the other home.

Name of Home	Factory-Built?		Reason for Not Purchasing
_____	☐ Yes	☐ No	_____
_____	☐ Yes	☐ No	_____
_____	☐ Yes	☐ No	_____
_____	☐ Yes	☐ No	_____

Now we would like you to please tell us about yourself and your family.

8. How many children do you have living at home? _____ children

9. What is the age of the head of your household? (check one, please)

   ☐ Under 20   ☐ 35–44   ☐ 55–64
   ☐ 20–24   ☐ 45–54   ☐ 65 or over
   ☐ 25–34

continued

Exhibit 1

Factory-Built Home Owners Survey (*continued*)

10. What is the occupation of the head of the household? (check one, please)

☐ Professional or official   ☐ Labor or machine operator
☐ Technical or manager   ☐ Foreman
☐ Proprietor   ☐ Service worker
☐ Farmer   ☐ Retired
☐ Craftsperson   ☐ Other _____
☐ Clerical or sales   (please specify)

11. Which of the following categories includes your family's total annual income? (check one, please)

☐ Less than $20,000   ☐ $50,000-$59,999
☐ $20,001-$29,999   ☐ $60,000-$69,999
☐ $30,000-$39,999   ☐ $70,000-$79,999
☐ $40,000-$49,999   ☐ $80,000 or over

12. Is the spouse of the head of the household employed? (check one, please)

☐ Spouse employed full-time   ☐ Spouse not employed
☐ Spouse employed part-time   ☐ Not married

One final question:

13. Would you recommend your particular factory-built home to someone interested in building a new home?

☐ Yes   ☐ No

Thank you very much for completing this survey.
Your help in this study is greatly appreciated.

Case • 6.6

Telecard.com (B)

Teresa Morgan, Steve Morrison and Maria Carlotti, friends and co-workers at a large Chicago-based advertising agency, had formed an Internet start-up company, Telecard.com, approximately 15 months earlier to sell prepaid long distance telephone services. As detailed in Telecard.com (A), the firm was off to a rocky start, with initial capital nearly depleted and no profits expected soon, based on operating results from the first year. Three months into the second year, revenues were up somewhat but still considerably below the costs being incurred.

Telecard.com offers one basic service, prepaid long distance telephone. The service is only accessible via the company's Web site. Customers go to the Web site, select a calling plan and number of minutes they wish to purchase, provide a credit card number and email address, and then receive the appropriate long distance access numbers via an email message. The Telecard.com Web site is easy to navigate, the long distance telephone rates are good, and the service is available around-the-clock from any computer connected to the Internet.

Initially, the Telecard.com partners assumed that their customers would be business professionals much like themselves who needed a convenient way to make personal long distance calls when away from home (e..g., at the office; while traveling). Based on comments left by customers on the Web site, however, it appeared that at least some of their customers were college students who used the prepaid long distance while at school. The partners quickly realized that a college student target market made sense in several ways. Students are often on limited budgets. Intrastate long distance and collect calls are often among the most expensive forms of long distance telephone service available (*inter*state long distance is often the least expensive), yet they are often the most needed, because most students don't move that far away from home to attend college. When they also considered that (a) young people are among the most Internet-savvy, and (b) virtually all college students have Internet access at school, the partners thought they might have begun to see a way to make their business grow and become successful.

Marketing Research

At the suggestion of a friend in the research department of the ad agency, Teresa connected with a group of students at a nearby university for help with marketing research. She believed that the students would have good insight into the student market. Besides that, they worked for free as part of a class assignment. After considerable discussion, the students and the partners arrived at two research problems to be addressed. The first was to determine the size of the potential market among college students enrolled at the university. The second was to investigate the best methods of promoting prepaid long distance to students.

Exploratory Research. With research problems in hand, the students began conducting several types of exploratory research. For example, two students went to the university library to learn all they could about trends in long distance telephone service, particularly with respect to prepaid long distance and younger consumers. In addition, they searched for examples of companies that had been successful in marketing other types of products and services to young people using the Internet. A second set of research students gathered together a dozen students from the university and conducted a quasi-focus group in an attempt to uncover students' feelings about purchasing products and services over the Internet. Still another group of research students passed out informal surveys to students in various cafeterias across campus. The surveys assessed such things as students' favorite radio stations, newspapers, etc.; amount of time spent surfing the net per week; and average amount spent per month on long distance telephone services. Based on their exploratory research, the student researchers found that (a) increasing amounts of prepaid long distance are purchased each year and analysts expect the trend to continue; (b) most students have not purchased products/services over the Internet, though they believe that they will in the near future; (c) most students spend $10 or more each month on long distance; and (d) the only media vehicle that most students claim to use regularly is the school's daily newspaper. On the basis of these exploratory results, Teresa and her partners decided that it would be worthwhile for the research team to proceed with descriptive research.

Descriptive Research. The student researchers elected to collect primary data from local university students using a communication method. Unfortunately, the researchers did not have access to a complete mailing list of all students, and only those who lived on-campus were listed in the student telephone directory. Because most off-campus students tended to live in houses and apartments near campus (and on-campus students lived in group housing), the researchers decided to use the residential drop-off method in which they would drop surveys off in selected neighborhoods and dormitories and return to pick up the completed forms a couple of hours later. To select areas for dropping off surveys, the researchers used area sampling. That is, they noted the locations of all appropriate living units on a city map (including campus), grouped the living units into approximately 20 equal-sized clusters, and then randomly selected three clusters within which to distribute surveys to all units, with a maximum of one student respondent per unit. When distributing the surveys, the researchers were to note all addresses of "not-at-homes" and attempt to reach these addresses again the following evening. The students figured that they needed to drop off 450 surveys to reach their desired sample size of 200. Overall, about 6,000 students attend the university.

Based on what they had learned from their exploratory research, the researchers developed a written survey form that they believed would provide insights into the research problems. The survey included 29 questions and is presented in Exhibit 1. The associated codebook is presented in Exhibit 2.

After concluding their data collection, the researchers discovered that a total of 437 units were located within the areas randomly selected. The disposition of the 437 units were as follows: 171 completed interviews, 141 ineligibles (no students at the address), 49 refusals, and 76 not-at-homes (after two tries).

Questions

1. Discuss options for different methods of data collection in this situation. Do you agree with the researchers' decision to use the residential drop-off method? Why or why not? (Hint: Think about the assumptions that must be made for this method to provide a probabilistic sample.)
2. Critique the data collection form developed by the researchers.
3. Using the information provided, calculate the response rate for the survey.
4. Assuming that the method of sampling and its application were appropriate, to what population may the students draw inferences?
5. What percentage of sample respondents report an interest in prepaid long distance telephone service? What is the 95% confidence interval?
6. Provide a reasonable estimate of the *maximum* potential market (both number of users and minutes of prepaid long distance sold) for Telecard.com at this university. Explain your estimation process carefully.
7. Based on the survey results, which advertising medium might best reach potential purchasers of Telecard.com services?

Exhibit 1

Telecard.com Questionnaire

PART A

(1) Are you currently enrolled in college? ☐ Yes ☐ No

(2) Do you make long distance calls? ☐ Yes ☐ No

(3) On average, how much money do you spend on long distance in a month?

☐ 0–15 ☐ 16–30 ☐ 31–45 ☐ 46–60 ☐ 61–75 ☐ 76–90 ☐ 91 and above

(4) Do you compare long distance rates? ☐ Yes ☐ No

(5) Do you make long distance calls outside the United States? ☐ Yes ☐ No

(6) In the past month, approximately how many long-distance phone calls have you made?

☐ 0–10 ☐ 11–20 ☐ 21–30 ☐ 31–40 ☐ 41–50 ☐ 51–60 ☐ 61 and above

(7) Check how many minutes your average long-distance phone call lasts:

☐ 0–10 ☐ 11–20 ☐ 21–30 ☐ 31–40 ☐ 41–50
☐ 51–60 ☐ 61–70 ☐ 71–80 ☐ 81–90 ☐ over 91

PART B

(1) Circle all the following that you currently use for long distance calls:

local telephone service   cell phone   pay phone   calling card
prepaid calling card   dial pad (Internet long distance calls)   other   none

(2) Circle which one of the services from above you use the most?

local telephone service   cell phone   pay phone   dial pad   calling card   prepaid calling card   other   none

(3) Are you a member of a phone company long-distance calling program? ☐ Yes ☐ No

(4) Are you interested in prepaid long distance? ☐ Yes ☐ No

(5) When purchasing prepaid phone cards, circle how many minutes you buy at a time.

Never purchased   1–20 min.   21–40 min.   41–60 min.   61–90 min.   91 or more

(6) Do you have a credit card? ☐ Yes ☐ No

(7) Do you have a debit card? ☐ Yes ☐ No

(8) Do you have access to the Internet? ☐ Yes ☐ No

PART C

(1) Do you have a personal email address? ☐ Yes ☐ No

(2) Circle how important you think that security is when buying a product on the Web?

very Important   1   2   3   4   5   6   7   not very important

(3) On average, how many times per day do you access the Web (i.e. Internet)? _____ times

(4) On average, how much time do you spend on the Web each time you access it? _____ minutes

(5) How many times in the past month have you bought a product off a Web site? _____ times

(6) Have you ever purchased a product after seeing an advertisement for it on the Internet?

☐ Yes ☐ No

(7) What two radio stations do you listen to the most? _____ and _____

(8) Where do you listen to the radio?

☐ home ☐ work ☐ school ☐ car ☐ outside activities

(9) Circle all the times that apply to when you listen to the radio:

7am–12pm   1pm–6pm   7pm–12am   1am–6am

(10) Have you ever purchased a product after hearing an advertisement for it on the radio?

☐ Yes ☐ No

PART D

(1) Approximately how many hours of TV do you watch per week? _____ hrs of TV per week

(2) Circle all time frames during which you watch TV at least 3 times per week.

7am–12pm   1pm–6pm   7pm–12am   1am–6am

(3) Circle all of these that you read on a daily basis.

Magazine   College Newspaper   Local Newspaper   State Newspaper
National Newspaper   None

(4) Circle all of the following methods that you think are good ways to advertise to you.

Magazine   College Newspaper   Local Newspaper
State Newspaper   Radio   Television   Internet   Other _____

Exhibit 2

Telecard.com Codebook

Columns	Variable Name	Description	
1–3	ID	Respondent identification number	
4	ENROLLED	Currently enrolled in college	1=yes 2=no
5	LONGDIST	Does respondent make long distance calls?	1=yes 2=no
6	SPEND	How much spent on long distance in a month?	
		1=0–15	
		2=16–30	
		3=31–45	
		4=40–60	
		5=61–75	
		6=76–90	
		7=91 or more	
7	COMPARE	Does respondent compare rates?	1=yes 2=no
8	INTER	Does respondent place calls outside US?	1=yes 2=no
9	NUMCALLS	Number of calls made in past month	
		1=0–10	
		2=11–20	
		3=21–30	
		4=31–40	
		5=41–50	
		6=51–60	
		7=61 or more	
10–11	CALLMIN	How long average long-distance call lasts in minutes?	
		1=0–10	
		2=11–20	
		3=21–30	
		4=31–40	
		5=41–50	
		6=51–60	
		7=61–70	
		8=71–80	
		9=81–90	
		10=over 91	
12	MED1	(What is used to make calls?) local calls	1=yes 0=no
13	MED2	cell phone	1=yes 0=no
14	MED3	pay phone	1=yes 0=no
15	MED4	calling card	1=yes 0=no
16	MED5	prepaid calling card	1=yes 0=no
17	MED6	dial pad	1=yes 0=no
18	MED7	other	1=yes 0=no
19	MED8	none	1=yes 0=no
20	MOST	Which service method is used the most?	
		1=local	
		2=cell phone	
		3=pay phone	
		4=dial pad	
		5=calling card	
		6=prepaid calling card	
		7=other	
		8=none	
21	MEMBER	Is respondent a member of a phone company long distance calling program?	1=yes 2=no
22	INTEREST	Is respondent interested in prepaid long distance?	1=yes 2=no

PART 6:
Data Analysis

Exhibit 2

Telecard.com Codebook (*continued*)

Columns	Variable Name	Description	
23	PURCHASE	Minutes purchased on prepaid phone cards at a time	
		1=never purchased	
		2=1–20	
		3=21–40	
		4=41–60	
		5=61–90	
		6=91 or more	
24	CREDIT	Does respondent have a credit card?	1=yes 2=no
25	DEBIT	Does respondent have a debit card?	1=yes 2=no
26	INTERNET	Does respondent have Internet access?	1=yes 2=no
27	EMAIL	Does respondent have a personal email address?	1=yes 2=no
28	SECURITY	How important security is when buying product on Web. Security importance (1–7)	
29–30	ACCESS	Average number of times respondent accesses Web per day	
31–32	TIME	Average time spent on Web in minutes each time accessed	
33–34	PRODUCT	Number of times a product has been bought off a Web site in past month	
35	ADVER	Has respondent purchased a product after seeing advertisement on Internet?	1=yes 2=no
36–39	STATION1	First radio station, coded by frequency, no decimals	
40	AMFM1	Is first radio station AM or FM?	1=AM 2=FM
41–44	STATION2	Second radio station, coded by frequency, no decimals	
45	AMFM2	Is second radio station AM or FM?	1=AM 2=FM
46	WHERE1	(Where does respondent listen to radio?) home	1=yes 0=no
47	WHERE2	work	1=yes 0=no
48	WHERE3	school	1=yes 0=no
49	WHERE4	car	1=yes 0=no
50	WHERE5	outside activities	1=yes 0=no
51	RADTIME1	(Time when respondent listens to radio) 7am-12pm	1=yes 0=no
52	RADTIME2	1pm–6pm	1=yes 0=no
53	RADTIME3	7pm–12am	1=yes 0=no
54	RADTIME4	1am–6pm	1=yes 0=no
55	HEARAD	Has respondent purchased a product after hearing advertisement on radio?	1=yes 2=no
56–57	HOURS	Approximately how many hours of TV watched per week	
58	WATIME	(Time when respondent watches TV) 7am–12pm	1=yes 0=no
59	WATIME2	1pm–6pm	1=yes 0=no
60	WATIME3	7pm–12am	1=yes 0=no
61	WATIME4	1am–6am	1=yes 0=no
62	READ1	(What respondent reads on a daily basis?) magazine	1=yes 0=no
63	READ2	college newspaper	1=yes 0=no
64	READ3	local newspaper	1=yes 0=no
65	READ4	state newspaper	1=yes 0=no
66	READ5	national newspaper	1=yes 0=no
67	READ6	none	1=yes 0=no
68	ADMETH01	(Which method is best to advertise to respondent?) magazine	1=yes 0=no
69	ADMETH02	college newspaper	1=yes 0=no
70	ADMETH03	local newspaper	1=yes 0=no
71	ADMETH04	state newspaper	1=yes 0=no
72	ADMETH05	radio	1=yes 0=no
73	ADMETH06	television	1=yes 0=no
74	ADMETH07	Internet	1=yes 0=no
75	ADMETH08	other	1=yes 0=no

MISSING DATA: All columns with missing data are coded using a space if respondent failed to answer question.

Case • 6.7

Marty's Department Store

Bethany Tate was nervous. As the general manager of the local Marty's, a regional department store chain based in the southwest U.S., she was apprehensive about lackluster sales growth at her store over the most recent quarter. The problem, she believed, was the nearby presence of Naples Clothing Co., a nationally-known specialty retailer of clothing that had opened about six months ago. She expected sales to be flat while the new Naples store went through its honeymoon period with shoppers, but she didn't expect it to last this long.

Marty's Department Store

The Marty's chain was founded in 1967 in Scottsdale, Arizona. The company currently operates 113 stores across a dozen southwestern states. In general, the company's strategy is to locate stores in strip malls in small to medium-sized cities in an attempt to avoid direct competition with larger retailers in regional shopping centers. Compared with similarly sized regional department store chains, Marty's typically performs rather poorly, with lower than average revenue growth and much higher than average cost structure.

The local store had been a bright spot for the company. Located in a small university city (population 43,000, including 15,000 students), the store enjoyed steady sales growth since its opening four years earlier. The store offers most types of goods usually found in department stores, with the bulk of sales revenues coming from clothing. The store prides itself on offering the most complete range of clothing for the whole family available locally. Like all Marty's stores, the local store sells several national brands as well as its own private label brand. The store normally runs at least one price promotion per month in an attempt to emphasize its attractive prices. Until recently, the store's primary local competitors included a nationally known department store, a locally-owned department store, and several small specialty clothing stores.

Bethany Tate had managed the store for the past two years. She had been a management trainee with the company for only two months when the local store's original manager left the company to work for a competitor. Although company policy is for all general managers to have been with the company at least a year before being placed in their own stores, the district manager liked Bethany a lot and believed she had the qualities necessary to be successful in the retailing industry. Although she was young and relatively inexperienced (this was her first job after

graduating from college with a marketing degree), she was bright, worked very hard, and people seemed to enjoy working with her, even employees twice her age. For the first 18 months, everything had gone smoothly, despite Bethany's unspoken fears of getting in over her head. Things began to change when Naples came to town.

Naples Clothing Co.

The Naples Clothing Co. chain has been in existence barely 10 years, yet routinely outperforms virtually all other specialty clothing chains. The company sells only its own brand of casual clothes, which it manufactures in various locations around the world. The clothing line is extremely popular at the present time; the Naples Clothing Co. name and logo appear on millions of articles of clothing in current use. In many cases, wearers become walking advertisements for the company. The company emphasizes reasonable everyday prices, with occasional price promotions, particularly on overstocked or out-of-season merchandise.

Initially, the company's strategy was to locate in newer strip malls in cities of 400,000 and above. The company often opened 2–4 stores (or more) in these cities. With increasing success, however, the company has begun to locate in selected smaller communities. The stores are uniform in design, appearance, and merchandise selection (with some small regional differences). The stores feature an open, no-frills layout, which helps keep costs low. There are currently 524 Naples Clothing Co. outlets in the United States, with the company opening about 80 new stores per year.

Marketing Research

Bethany Tate was convinced that her revenues were suffering due to the popularity of Naples Clothing Co., particularly among college students. Worse, she realized that she had no real idea what college students thought about her store. Recognizing the need for more information, she convinced her district manager to allow her to hire a local research company to determine consumer perceptions of both Marty's Department Store and Naples Clothing Co. among younger consumers. The company was interested in the results, because they expected to be competing with Naples Clothing Co. in more and more markets.

The research company and Bethany agreed to focus on three key areas in their research with young consumers:

(1) identifying the attributes of retail stores deemed most important, (2) determining perceptions of Marty's, and (3) determining perceptions of Naples Clothing Co. for comparison purposes. After some preliminary exploratory research, the research company developed a one-page (front and back) survey to be administered to local residents between the ages of 18 and 25 (Exhibit 1; the codebook is presented in Exhibit 2). An area sample was used, and surveys were dropped off at each residence within randomly selected clusters. A total of 208 usable questionnaires were received from eligible respondents.

Questions

1. Did this research result from planned or unplanned change? Is the research discovery- or strategy-oriented? Explain.
2. Suppose that the mean score for "good service" is 4.1 on the 5-point "definitely no–definitely yes" scale (see survey). What can you conclude from this information? How might this score be given more meaning? Explain.
3. How important are the various attributes of retail stores to young consumers in this market? Present your answer using (a) mean scores and standard deviations, and (b) two-boxes. Technically speaking, can Bethany conclude that service is more important than atmosphere to these consumers?
4. In terms of service quality and employee helpfulness, do perceptions of Marty's Department Store differ for those who have visited the store versus those who have not? What would your results mean to Bethany Tate, if anything?
5. Overall, how does Marty's Department Store compare with Naples Clothing Co. on key attributes? Are any differences statistically significant? If so, what do they mean?

Exhibit 1

Marty's Questionnaire

PART I

1. Please rate how important each of the following items are to you for retail stores on a scale of 1 to 5, where "1" is "not important" and "5" is "very important":

	Not Important				Very Important
Service	1	2	3	4	5
Merchandise quality	1	2	3	4	5
Merchandise variety	1	2	3	4	5
Price	1	2	3	4	5
Atmosphere	1	2	3	4	5
Convenience	1	2	3	4	5
Value of brand name	1	2	3	4	5
Merchandise style	1	2	3	4	5

2. Please rate Naples Clothing Co. on each of the following characteristics on a scale of 1 to 5, where "1" is "definitely NO" and "5" is definitely YES:

	Definitely NO				Definitely YES
Good service	1	2	3	4	5
Good quality	1	2	3	4	5
Good variety	1	2	3	4	5
Low price	1	2	3	4	5
Appealing atmosphere	1	2	3	4	5
Convenient location	1	2	3	4	5
Brand name is appealing	1	2	3	4	5
Stylish products	1	2	3	4	5
Good value	1	2	3	4	5
Good reputation	1	2	3	4	5
Fun to shop	1	2	3	4	5
Helpful employees	1	2	3	4	5

Have you visited the local Naples Clothing Co.? ☐ Yes ☐ No

continued

Exhibit 1

Marty's Questionnaire (*continued*)

3. Please rate Marty's Department Store on each of the following characteristics on a scale of 1 to 5, "1" being definitely NO and "5" being definitely YES.

	Definitely NO				Definitely YES
Good service	1	2	3	4	5
Good quality	1	2	3	4	5
Good variety	1	2	3	4	5
Low price	1	2	3	4	5
Appealing atmosphere	1	2	3	4	5
Convenient location	1	2	3	4	5
Brand name is appealing	1	2	3	4	5
Stylish products	1	2	3	4	5
Good value	1	2	3	4	5
Good reputation	1	2	3	4	5
Fun to shop	1	2	3	4	5
Helpful employees	1	2	3	4	5

Have you visited the local Marty's Department Store?   ☐ Yes   ☐ No

PART II

1. What do you perceive as the average age of a typical person who shops at local Naples Clothing Co.
   _____ years old
2. What do you perceive as the average age of a typical person who shops at the local Marty's Department Store?
   _____ years old
3. Approximately how many times in the past month have you shopped at the following:
   a. local Marty's Department Store
   _____ times
   b. local Naples Clothing Co.
   _____ times
4. Approximately how many times in the past month have you seen an advertisement for Naples Clothing Co. on the following forms of media?
   Television: _____ times
   Print (newspaper and magazine): _____ times
   Radio: _____ times
5. Approximately how many times in the past month have you seen an advertisement for Marty's Department Store on the following forms of media?
   Television: _____ times
   Print (newspaper and magazine): _____ times
   Radio: _____ times
6. Approximately how much money do you spend on clothing each month?
   $_____

Thank you for your time.

Exhibit 2

Marty's Codebook

Columns	Variable Name/Description		
1–4	ID	SURVEY ID#	
5	GEN	Gender	1=male 2=female
6	IMP1	Retail Store Attribute Importance - item 1	1–5; Not Important, Very Important
7	IMP2	Retail Store Attribute Importance - item 2	1–5; Not Important, Very Important
8	IMP3	Retail Store Attribute Importance - item 3	1–5; Not Important, Very Important
9	IMP4	Retail Store Attribute Importance - item 4	1–5; Not Important, Very Important
10	IMP5	Retail Store Attribute Importance - item 5	1–5; Not Important, Very Important
11	IMP6	Retail Store Attribute Importance - item 6	1–5; Not Important, Very Important
12	IMP7	Retail Store Attribute Importance - item 7	1–5; Not Important, Very Important
13	IMP8	Retail Store Attribute Importance - item 8	1–5; Not Important, Very Important
14	NAPLES1	Perceptions of Naples Clothing Co., item 1	1–5; Definitely NO, Definitely YES
15	NAPLES2	Perceptions of Naples Clothing Co., item 2	1–5; Definitely NO, Definitely YES
16	NAPLES3	Perceptions of Naples Clothing Co., item 3	1–5; Definitely NO, Definitely YES
17	NAPLES4	Perceptions of Naples Clothing Co., item 4	1–5; Definitely NO, Definitely YES
18	NAPLES5	Perceptions of Naples Clothing Co., item 5	1–5; Definitely NO, Definitely YES
19	NAPLES6	Perceptions of Naples Clothing Co., item 6	1–5; Definitely NO, Definitely YES
20	NAPLES7	Perceptions of Naples Clothing Co., item 7	1–5; Definitely NO, Definitely YES
21	NAPLES8	Perceptions of Naples Clothing Co., item 8	1–5; Definitely NO, Definitely YES
22	NAPLES9	Perceptions of Naples Clothing Co., item 9	1–5; Definitely NO, Definitely YES
23	NAPLES10	Perceptions of Naples Clothing Co., item 10	1–5; Definitely NO, Definitely YES
24	NAPLES11	Perceptions of Naples Clothing Co., item 11	1–5; Definitely NO, Definitely YES
25	NAPLES12	Perceptions of Naples Clothing Co., item 12	1–5; Definitely NO, Definitely YES
26	VISNAT	Visited Naples Clothing Co.?	1=yes, 2=no
27	MARTYS1	Perceptions of Marty's Department Store, item 1	1–5; Definitely NO, Definitely YES
28	MARTYS2	Perceptions of Marty's Department Store, item 2	1–5; Definitely NO, Definitely YES
29	MARTYS3	Perceptions of Marty's Department Store, item 3	1–5; Definitely NO, Definitely YES
30	MARTYS4	Perceptions of Marty's Department Store, item 4	1–5; Definitely NO, Definitely YES
31	MARTYS5	Perceptions of Marty's Department Store, item 5	1–5; Definitely NO, Definitely YES
32	MARTYS6	Perceptions of Marty's Department Store, item 6	1–5; Definitely NO, Definitely YES
33	MARTYS7	Perceptions of Marty's Department Store, item 7	1–5; Definitely NO, Definitely YES
34	MARTYS8	Perceptions of Marty's Department Store, item 8	1–5; Definitely NO, Definitely YES
35	MARTYS9	Perceptions of Marty's Department Store item 9	1–5; Definitely NO, Definitely YES
36	MARTYS10	Perceptions of Marty's Department Store, item 10	1–5; Definitely NO, Definitely YES
37	MARTYS11	Perceptions of Marty's Department Store, item 11	1–5; Definitely NO, Definitely YES
38	MARTYS12	Perceptions of Marty's Department Store, item 12	1–5; Definitely NO, Definitely YES
39	VISMARTY	Visited Marty's Department Store?	1=yes, 2=no
40–41	AGENAP	Naples average perceived age of customers	
42–43	AGEMART	Marty's average perceived age of customers	
44–45	SHOPMART	Marty's times shopped in last month	
46–47	SHOPNAP	Naples times shopped in last month	
48–49	NAPTV	Number of Naples advertisements seen on TV last month	
50–51	NAPPRINT	Number of Naples advertisements seen in print last month	
52–53	NAPRADIO	Number of Naples advertisements heard on radio last month	
54–55	MARTV	Number of Marty's advertisements seen on TV last month	
56–57	MARPRINT	Number of Marty's advertisements seen in print last month	
58–59	MARRADIO	Number of Marty's advertisements heard on radio last month	
60–62	MONEY	Average money spent on clothing each month	

Missing Data: Blank

Case • 6.8

A Picture Is Worth a Mega-Byte of Words: Census Data and Trends in Lifestyle Purchases

While it is always dangerous to make generalizations about people and their consumption behaviors, it is helpful to the marketer to have a sense of what people tend to buy as a function of some of their demographic characteristics. For example, household expenditures on furniture might be higher for younger people as they begin to set up house, and decline as the house is established. With these facts, and extrapolations of the likely sizes and timing of baby-booms and baby-busts, a furniture manufacturer could use this trend information to project market sizes, and to modify its product line (for example, bean bag chairs for college students, fine wood and upholstered furniture for older, wealthier consumers).

The data that follow were extracted from the Bureau of Labor Statistics[1] and reflect expenditures on various goods and services categories, broken down by the census age groups. Within each purchase category, the data have been calibrated so that a score of "100" means the age group spends about average on that category. Numbers that exceed 100 mean that the age group spends more on that category of purchases than the other age groups, and numbers that are less than 100 mean that age group spends less than other age groups. For example, people younger than 25 years old and those 65 years old or older spend less on food; people between the ages of 35–44 and 45–54 spend more. People aged 25–34 and 55–64 spend about the "average." Use these data to answer the questions that follow.

Questions

1. If you wanted to know whether expenditures on furniture and computers were correlated, why might the actual computation of a correlation coefficient be inappropriate, or at least not very compelling?

2. Plot these data with the age categories as the horizontal axis, and the different columns as profiles depicting the peaks and valleys of expenditures with age.
   a. Plot total spending by age and overlay that plot with the plots of food by age and women's apparel by age. What is the pattern of spending on these apparent basic necessities?
   b. Overlay the plots for furniture, computers, and health care by age. Generally speaking, what target age groups will you be aiming for if you are Scandinavian Design? Dell? A hospital network or health and life insurance company?
   c. Overlay the plot for entertainment expenditures by age with the plot for travel by age. How do we tend to amuse ourselves as younger versus older people?
   d. Finally, use whichever variables interest you and whatever plotting format you think will lend insight to creatively discover any other phenomenon in the data.

Age (in years)	Total Spending	Food	Women's Apparel	Furniture	Computers	Health Care	Entertainment	Travel
<25	59	74	62	55	60	30	62	47
25–34	99	101	85	105	98	67	109	83
35–44	129	134	119	147	119	96	141	98
45–54	130	128	145	126	161	111	123	143
55–64	105	101	120	107	103	122	95	136
65–74	77	69	87	64	55	149	73	102
75+	50	39	49	19	15	141	26	53

[1]For example, see "The New Consumer Paradigm," *American Demographics* (April 1999), pp. 50–58.

Case • 6.9

Joseph Machine Company

The Joseph Machine Company, which was named after its founder and longtime owner/manager Gerald Joseph, produced pumps and air compressors. Joseph Machine had for some time been concerned with improving the procedures by which its sales force was selected. The company had always hired engineering graduates for this work because an equipment sale demanded some technical sophistication on the part of the sales representatives. A sales representative must be able to respond to a customer's technical questions about the equipment, and also to explain how the customer's processing system might be better designed. Assuming that a prospective sales candidate had an engineering degree (mechanical or electrical degrees were preferred, but others were accepted as well), the hiring decision was made primarily on the basis of a personal interview with several executives in the company. Those doing the interviewing often disagreed as to what kinds of credentials and candidates were acceptable.

The company was interested in determining whether there were some more objective criteria that could be used in the hiring decision. An examination of sales performance literature suggested that a sales representative's personality and intellectual abilities are often primary determinants of success. The company therefore decided to administer personality and IQ tests to each of its sales representatives to determine whether there was any association between these characteristics and the representatives' performance. Total sales for the past year in relation to territory quota, expressed as an index, were to be used as the performance criterion, and Joseph Machine wished to control for any differences in performance that might be attributable to time on the job.

The data resulting from the investigation are shown in Exhibit 1.

Questions

1. Is there any relationship between a sales representative's performance and IQ? Performance and personality score?
2. Do the relationships change when time on the job is held constant?
3. What amount of performance can be attributed to all three factors considered simultaneously?
4. Evaluate your method of analysis and also evaluate the procedure being employed by Joseph Machine Company to improve its sales representative selection procedures.

Exhibit 1

Sales Representative	Performance Index	IQ Test	Personality Score	Time on the Job (in months)	Sales Representative	Performance Index	IQ Test	Personality Score	Time on the Job (in months)
1	122	130	86	78	21	99	116	69	53
2	105	100	62	48	22	102	113	82	89
3	103	93	85	81	23	98	109	81	75
4	95	81	72	62	24	100	86	68	71
5	97	98	78	98	25	99	92	61	74
6	106	114	68	63	26	99	92	75	79
7	100	87	79	72	27	113	81	71	87
8	115	82	67	85	28	114	103	79	84
9	78	115	70	59	29	110	114	76	106
10	101	114	64	55	30	98	92	83	109
11	115	92	84	117	31	92	105	81	80
12	120	81	84	103	32	106	81	79	85
13	88	89	56	49	33	103	81	84	95
14	110	82	87	110	34	111	85	55	67
15	96	92	82	77	35	102	98	54	61
16	93	85	65	60	36	102	84	74	83
17	92	85	70	74	37	88	109	65	45
18	103	114	64	82	38	105	85	66	93
19	121	85	83	115	39	94	91	62	64
20	95	99	84	102	40	108	81	79	63
					41	84	101	59	41

© Digital Vision/Getty Images

Part 7

Research Reports

Part 7 consists of one chapter and an epilogue. Chapter 22 first discusses one of the most important parts of the whole research process: the research report. The research report often becomes the standard by which the entire research effort is assessed, and it is important that the report contribute positively to the evaluation of the effort. Chapter 22 also discusses the criteria a research report should satisfy and the form a research report can follow so that it does contribute positively to the research effort. Chapter 22 then discusses how to deliver effective oral reports and also reviews some of the graphic devices that can be employed to communicate important findings more forcefully. The epilogue ties together the parts of the research process. It reinforces the points made early in the text, that the steps in the research process are highly interrelated and a decision made at one stage has implications for the others, by demonstrating the nature of some of these interrelationships.

Chapter 22

© Digital Vision/Getty Images

The Research Report

Learning Objectives

1   *Specify the fundamental criterion by which all research reports are evaluated.*

2   *Identify and discuss the four criteria that a report should meet if it is to communicate effectively with readers.*

3   *Outline the main elements that make up a standard report form.*

4   *Explain the kind of information contained in the summary.*

5   *Distinguish between a conclusion and a recommendation.*

6   *Describe the kind of information that should be contained in the introduction.*

7   *Describe the kind of information that should be contained in the body.*

8   *Describe the kind of information that should be contained in the appendix.*

9   *Specify the first rule to keep in mind when preparing an oral report.*

10   *Describe the two most common forms of organization for oral reports.*

11   *Discuss the key points a presenter should keep in mind regarding the use of visual aids.*

12   *Explain how the time allotted for an oral presentation should be organized.*

13   *Describe the circumstances in which a pie chart is most effective.*

14   *Explain the best use of a line chart.*

15   *Describe the circumstances in which a stratum chart is most effective.*

16   *Cite the reason bar charts are so widely used.*

17   *Describe the circumstances in which a grouped-bar chart is most effective.*

Three researchers—Martin Kinslow, Anita O'Reilly, and Margo Wirtz—were conferring online about a report and presentation they were preparing. The three had been coordinating a research project to guide development of a new vacuum cleaner. Their company, Superior Appliances, wanted a model ready for the International Appliance Fair two years down the road, and Superior wanted to demonstrate its continuing leadership in meeting consumers' needs. The research had included observational and survey studies aimed at uncovering consumers' likes and dislikes. In five weeks, Martin, Anita, and Margo were to present the findings to Superior's product development team assigned to the vacuum cleaner project.

"Can we focus on the oral presentation first, then put together detailed documents?" typed Anita.

"No," came back Margo's reply a few seconds later. "Peter and Francesca always want to study the full report before a presentation. They pore over every table so they can be ready with questions. We have to work on the report and the presentation at the same time."

"The report has to be ready at least a week before the presentation," added Martin. "We'll make it available to whoever wants it. Nobody will want it before the meeting except Peter and Francesca. We'll have some copies at the presentation, too. Usually a couple of other people pick up a copy. Dan will just listen to the presentation. He always zeros in on the key points."

"OK, so someone has to put together the tables for the written report while someone else starts on PowerPoint slides for the presentation," said Anita's next message.

"I'll do the slides," volunteered Martin. "Let's identify the key points."

"We have to compare the survey responses with the observations," responded Margo. "People say they want a vacuum cleaner that is easier to use. They complain about vacuuming stairs. When we watched them, they had strategies for that. The new design should take those strategies into account. Also, they want powerful cleaning, but they don't always measure power in the same way."

"Right. We'll make slides with graphs showing what consumers value and how they measure those features," replied Martin.

"Also myths about cleaning power," added Anita. "Put the key points in the graph and explain them in the oral presentation."

"I'll assemble the data into tables for the written report while Martin's doing that," said Margo. "Martin, send us copies of the graphs, so we can keep the keep the key points in mind. Anita, you're the best oral presenter—can you take the lead there?"

"OK, and I'll write commentary for the graphs," typed Anita. "We'll save that on Notes pages in PowerPoint, and we can use them as a starting point for the written report."

Discussion Issues

1. Why does the company require both a written report and an oral presentation of the research results?

2. How should the information provided by the written report differ from that in the oral report?

3. What characteristics can enhance the effectiveness of the slides, oral presentation, and written documents? ∎

A frustrated executive of a large corporation once remarked that "he is convinced reports are devices by which the informed ensure that the uninformed remain that way."[1] To avoid creating the kind of report that executive was thinking of requires considerable amounts of knowledge, skill, and attention to detail. If length were the criterion of importance of a chapter, there would be an inverse relationship between this chapter and the criterion.

This chapter is relatively short, but its subject is vital to the success of the research effort. Regardless of the sophistication displayed in other portions of the research process, the project is a failure if the research results are not communicated effectively.

Invariably, the communication of the research results is handled by the preparation of a written report and quite often through an oral report as well. The empirical evidence indicates that these research reports are one of the most important variables affecting the use of research information.[2] The research steps discussed in the preceding chapters of this text determine the content of the written and oral research reports, but since the reports are all that many executives will see of the project, they become the yardstick for evaluation. The writer and presenter must ensure that the reports inform without misinforming.

The reports must tell readers what they need and wish to know. Typically, executives must be convinced of the usefulness of the findings. They are more interested in results than methods. However, to act on the reports effectively, they must know enough about the methods that were used to recognize the methods' weaknesses and bounds of error. It is the researcher's responsibility to convey this information to the decision maker in sufficient detail and in understandable form.

In this chapter, we will offer some guidelines for developing successful research reports. In the first part of the chapter we will focus on the criteria by which written research reports are evaluated and the parts and forms of the written research report. In the latter part of the chapter, we discuss oral reports and some graphic means of presenting the results.

Research Report Evaluation Criteria

Specify the fundamental criterion by which all research reports are evaluated.

Research reports are evaluated by one fundamental criterion—how well they communicate with the reader. The "iron law" of marketing research holds, for example, that "people would rather live with a problem they cannot solve than accept a solution they cannot understand."[3] The reader is not only the reason that the report is prepared, but also the standard by which its success is measured. This means that the report must be tailor-made for its reader or readers, with due regard for their technical sophistication, their interest in the subject area, the circumstances under which they will read the report, and the use they will make of it.

The technical sophistication of the readers determines their capacity for understanding methodological decisions, such as experimental design, measurement device, sampling plan, analysis technique, and so on. Readers with little technical sophistication will more than likely take offense at the use of unexplained technical jargon. "The readers of your reports are busy people, and very few of them can balance a research report, a cup of coffee, and a dictionary at one time."[4] Unexplained jargon may even make such persons suspicious of the report writer. Researchers should try to be particularly sensitive to this hazard, because, being technical people, they may fail to realize that they are using technical language unless they remind themselves to watch for it.

While the readers' backgrounds and need for methodological detail will determine the upper limit for the technical content of the report, it is the readers' individual preferences that must guide the report writer.

Some executives prefer less to more. They want only the results, not a discussion on how the results were obtained nor any conclusions or recommendations. Other executives prefer just the opposite. They not only want a discussion of the results, but also detailed information on how the results were obtained as well as the researcher's conclusions, reasoning, and recommendations.

In a nutshell, the *audience determines the type of report,* and researchers need to make every effort to acquaint themselves with the *specific preferences* of their audiences. While the report writer may deviate from the preferences, the *deviations should be made with good reason and not from ignorance.*

The report writer's difficulties in tailoring the report are often compounded by the existence of several audiences. The marketing vice president might have a different technical capacity and level of interest than the product manager responsible for the product discussed in the report. There is no easy solution to this problem of "many masters." The researcher must recognize the potential differences that may arise and may have to exercise a great deal of ingenuity to reconcile them. Occasionally, a researcher may find it necessary to prepare several reports, each designed for a specific audience, although more often the conflicting demands can be satisfied by one report that contains both technical and nontechnical sections for different readers.

In the experience of Ron Sellers, president of Ellison Research, researchers can best tailor their reports if they have earlier asked their clients what they are looking for. Sellers recommends asking the people for whom the report will be prepared to answer a few questions:

- What are the five or ten most important items you want the study to focus on (for example, satisfaction with product quality, intent to buy from a competitor)?
- What do you hope the research will show?
- What do you think the research will show?

The report then would highlight comparisons between the actual results and the audience's hopes and expectations for the key data items. Such a focus is almost certain to be significant to the audience—and grab their attention.[5]

Writing Criteria

A report that achieves the goal of communicating effectively with readers is generally one that meets the specific criteria of completeness, accuracy, clarity, and conciseness.[6] These criteria are intimately related. An accurate report, for example, is also a complete report. For discussion purposes, however, it is helpful to discuss the criteria as if they were distinct.

 Identify and discuss the four criteria that a report should meet if it is to communicate effectively with readers.

Completeness

A report is **complete** when it provides all the information readers need in language they understand. This means that the writer must continually ask whether every question in the original assignment has been addressed. What alternatives were examined? What was found? An incomplete report implies that supplementary reports, which are annoying and delay action, will be forthcoming.

The report may be incomplete because it is too brief or too long. The writer may omit necessary definitions and short explanations. On the other hand, the report may be lengthy but not profound, due to a reluctance to waste any collected information. In a report full of nonvital information, the main issues are often lost in the clutter. Also, if the report is big, it may discourage readers from even attempting to digest its contents.

Readers are thus the key to determining completeness. Their interest and abilities determine what clarification should be added and what findings should be omitted. In general, the amount of detail should be proportionate to the amount of direct control users can exercise over the areas under discussion. For example, if the intended reader is a product's advertising manager, it would generally be wise to omit a lengthy discussion of possible improvements to production techniques.

This principle would have prevented some frustration if it had been applied to some research that a firm conducted for the Turner Entertainment Group. Turner had hired the firm to conduct studies to support the development of Web sites for some of its entities, which include TBS, TNT, and the Cartoon network. Having demonstrated its ability to provide useful

completeness
A criterion used to evaluate a research report; specifically, whether the report provides all the information readers need in language they understand.

information for Web site development, the research firm urged Turner to try a new service that involved collecting ongoing, real-time data from visitors to the Web sites, including their demographics, satisfaction, and media consumption habits. The research firm pointed out that these ongoing reports, based on 100 surveys per week, would enable Webmasters to tweak sites in response to the most recent feedback. However, the Webmasters were appalled at the idea of having to review a continuous stream of research reports and add to their already heavy workload of maintaining Web sites. Under those conditions, Turner backed away from the idea of real-time research reporting. Dan Coates, a member of the research firm, explains the decision this way: "Just because you can incorporate all of this stuff and create one large on-line report that encompasses everything, doesn't mean you should." Turner instead opted to receive research updates once or twice a year.[7]

Accuracy

The previously discussed steps in the research process are obviously vital to accuracy, but, given accurate input, the research report may generate inaccuracies because of carelessness in handling the data, illogical reasoning, or inept phrasing.[8] Thus, **accuracy** is another writing criterion. Exhibit 22.1 illustrates some examples of sources of inaccuracy in report writing.

The possession of advanced degrees is no safeguard against the hazards detailed in Exhibit 22.1. In fact, the more educated a person is, the more apt he or she may be to sink into the morass of excess verbiage. Consider the president of a major university who, in the late 1960s, wrote a letter to soothe anxious alumni after a spell of campus unrest. "You are probably aware," he began, "that we have been experiencing very considerable potentially explosive expressions of dissatisfaction on issues only partially related." He meant that the students had been hassling the university about different things.[9] In Research Window 22.1, Jock Elliott, chairman emeritus of the advertising agency Ogilvy & Mather, shows how one corporate vice president also sank into the quicksand of his own words.

accuracy
A criterion used to evaluate a research report; specifically, whether the reasoning in the report is logical and the information correct.

Exhibit 22.1

Some Examples of Sources of Inaccuracy in Report Writing

A. Simple Errors in Addition or Subtraction
"In the United States, 14 percent of the population has an elementary school education or less, 51 percent has attended or graduated from high school, and 16 percent has attended college."

An oversight such as this (14 + 51 + 16 does not equal 100 percent) can be easily corrected by the author, but not so easily by the reader, because he or she may not know if one or more of the percentage values is incorrect or if a category might have been left out of the tally.

B. Confusion between Percentages and Percentage Points
"The company's profits as a percentage of sales were 6.0 percent in 1997 and 8.0 percent in 2002. Therefore, they increased only 2.0 percent in five years."

In this example, the increase is, of course, 2.0 percentage points, or 33 percent.

C. Inaccuracy Caused by Grammatical Errors
"The reduction in the government's price supports for dairy products has reduced farm income $600 million to $800 million per year."

To express a range of reduction, the author should have written, "The reduction in the government's price supports for dairy products has reduced farm income $600–800 million per year."

D. Confused Terminology Resulting in Fallacious Conclusions
"The Joneses' household annual income increased from $10,000 in 1970 to $30,000 in 2000, thereby tripling the family's purchasing power."

While the Joneses' household income annual may have tripled in 30 years, the family's purchasing power certainly did not, as the cost of living, as measured by the consumer price index, more than tripled in the same period.

PART 7:
Research Reports

How to Write Your Way Out of a Job

Jock Elliott, the chairman emeritus of the Ogilvy & Mather advertising agency, is a man who appreciates good writing. After all, his business is built on his employees' ability to communicate with clients and consumers.

Elliott makes no bones about the importance of being able to write well in order to advance in a career. "As you sail along on your career," he writes, "bad writing acts as a sea anchor, pulling you back, good writing as a spinnaker, pulling you ahead."

In the following excerpt from an article he wrote, he tells about one prospective employee who sank beneath the waves, weighted down by the anchor of his own words.

"Last month I got a letter from a vice president of a major management consulting firm. Let me read you two paragraphs. The first:

Recently, the companies of our Marketing Services Group were purchased by one of the largest consumer research firms in the U.S. While this move well fits the basic business purpose and focus of the acquired MSG units, it is personally restrictive. I will rather choose to expand my management opportunities with a career move into industry.

"What he meant was: The deal works fine for my company, but not so fine for me. I'm looking for another job.

"Second paragraph:

The base of managerial and technical accomplishment reflected in my enclosed resumé may suggest an opportunity to meet a management need for one of your clients. Certainly my experience promises a most productive pace to understand the demands and details of any new situation I would choose.

"What he meant was: As you can see in my resumé, I've had a lot of good experience. I am a quick study. Do you think any of your clients might be interested in me?

"At least, that's what I think he meant.

"This fellow's letter reveals him as pompous. He may not be pompous. He may only be a terrible writer. But I haven't the interest or time to find out which. There are so many people looking for jobs who don't sound like pompous asses.

"Bad writing done him in—with me, at any rate." ■

Source: Jock Elliott, "How Hard It Is to Write Easily," *Viewpoint: By, For, and About Ogilvy & Mather* 2 (1980), p. 18. The use of jargon and imprecise expression have become so commonplace that computer programs that analyze grammar, readability, and sentence structure and suggest alternative wordings have been developed to deal with it. Microsoft Office 97, for example, contains a grammar checker, as do many of the most popular word processing programs. See Stephen H. Wildstrom, "Good Help Gets Easier to Find," *Business Week* (February 10, 1997), p. 21.

Inaccuracies also arise because of grammatical errors in punctuation, spelling, tense, subject and verb agreement, and so on.[10] Careful attention to detail in these areas is essential for any report writer.

Clarity

The writing criterion of **clarity** is probably failed more than any other. Clarity is produced by clear and logical thinking and precision of expression. When the underlying logic is fuzzy or the presentation imprecise, readers experience difficulty in understanding what they read. They may be forced to guess, in which case the corollary to Murphy's law applies: "If the reader is offered the slightest opportunity to misunderstand, he probably will."[11] Achieving clarity, however, requires effort.

The first, and most important, rule is that the report be well organized.[12] For this to happen, you must first clarify for yourself the purpose of your report and how you intend to accomplish writing it. Make an outline of your major points. Put the points in logical order and place the supporting details in their proper position. Tell the reader what you are going to cover in the report and then do what you said you were going to do. Use short paragraphs and short sentences. Do not be evasive or ambiguous; once you have decided what you want to say, come right out and say it. Choose your words carefully, making them as precise and understandable as possible. See Research Window 22.2 for some specific suggestions when choosing words.

clarity
A criterion used to evaluate a research report; specifically, whether the phrasing in the report is precise.

RESEARCH *Window*

22.2

Some Suggestions When Choosing Words for Marketing Research Reports

1. *Use short words.* Always use short words in preference to long words that mean the same thing.

Use this	Not this
Now	Currently
Start	Initiate
Show	Indicate
Finish	Finalize
Use	Utilize
Place	Position

2. *Avoid vague modifiers.* Avoid lazy adjectives and adverbs and use vigorous ones. Lazy modifiers are so overused in some contexts that they have become clichés. Select only those adjectives and adverbs that make your meaning precise.

Lazy modifiers	Vigorous modifiers
Very good	Short meeting
Awfully nice	Crisp presentation
Basically accurate	Baffling instructions
Great success	Tiny raise
Richly deserved	Moist handshake
Vitally important	Lucid recommendation

3. *Use specific, concrete language.* Avoid technical jargon. There is always a simple, down-to-earth word that says the same thing as the show-off fad word or the vague abstraction.

Jargon	Down-to-earth English
Implement	Carry out
Viable	Practical, workable
Suboptimal	Less than ideal
Proactive	Active
Bottom line	Outcome

4. *Write simply and naturally—the way you talk.* Use only those words, phrases, and sentences that you might actually say to your reader if you were face-to-face. If you wouldn't say it, if it doesn't sound like you, don't write it.

Stiff	Natural
The reasons are fourfold	There are four reasons
Importantly	The important point is
Visitation	Visit

5. *Strike out words you don't need.* Certain commonly used expressions contain redundant phrasing. Cut out the extra words.

Don't write	Write
Advance plan	Plan
Take action	Act
Study in depth	Study
Consensus of opinion	Consensus
Until such time as	Until

Source: Table adapted from Chapter 2 of *Writing That Works* by Kenneth Roman and Joel Raphaelson. Copyright © 1981 by Kenneth Roman and Joel Raphaelson. Reprinted by permission of HarperCollins Publishers Inc.

Do not expect your first draft to be satisfactory. Expect to rewrite it several times. When rewriting, attempt to reduce the length by half. That forces you to simplify and remove the clutter. It also forces you to think about every word and its purpose, to evaluate whether each word is helping you say what you wish to say. Jock Elliott has some very pointed comments on writing clearly:

> Our written and spoken words reflect what we are. If our words are brilliant, precise, well ordered and human, then that is how we are seen.
>
> When you write, you must constantly ask yourself: What am I trying to say? If you do this religiously, you will be surprised at how often you don't know what you are trying to say.
>
> You have to think before you start every sentence, and you have to think about every word.
>
> Then you must look at what you have written and ask: Have I said it? Is it clear to someone encountering the subject for the first time? If it's not, it is because some fuzz has worked its way into the machinery. The clear writer is a person clearheaded enough to see this stuff for what it is: fuzz.

It is not easy to write a simple declarative sentence. Here is one way to do it. Think what you want to say. Write your sentence. Then strip it of all adverbs and adjectives. Reduce the sentence to its skeleton. Let the verbs and nouns do the work.

If your skeleton sentence does not express your thoughts precisely, you've got the wrong verb or noun. Dig for the right one. Nouns and verbs carry the guns in good writing; adjectives and adverbs are decorative camp followers.[13]

Conciseness

Although the report must be complete, it must also be **concise.** This means that the writer must be selective in what is included. The researcher must avoid trying to impress the reader with all that has been found. If something does not pertain directly to the subject, it should be omitted. The writer must also avoid lengthy discussions of commonly known methods. Given that the material is appro-

" WE GOT THE ASPIRIN ACCOUNT! A STUDY SHOWED OUR ADS GIVE PEOPLE HEADACHES. "

© Harley Schwadron

priate, conciseness can still be violated by writing style. This commonly occurs when the writer is groping for the phrases and words that capture an idea. Instead of finally coming to terms with the idea, the writer writes around it, restating it several times, in different ways, hoping that repetition will overcome poor expression. Concise writing, on the other hand, is effective because "it makes maximum use of every word. . . . No word in a concise discussion can be removed without impairing or destroying the function of the whole composition. . . . To be concise is to express a thought completely and clearly in the fewest words possible."[14]

One helpful technique for ensuring that the report is concise is reading the draft aloud. This often reveals sections that should be pruned or rewritten.[15]

> Silent reading allows him [the writer] to skim over the familiar material and thus impose an artificial rapidity and structural simplicity on something that is in reality dense and tangled. The eye can grow accustomed to the appearance of a sentence, but it is much more difficult for the tongue, lips, and jaw to deal with what the eye might accept readily.

conciseness
A criterion used to evaluate a research report; specifically, whether the writing in the report is crisp and direct.

Forms of Report

The organization of the report influences all the criteria of report writing. While good organization cannot guarantee clarity, conciseness, accuracy, and completeness, poor organization can preclude them. There is no single acceptable organization for a report. Once again, the writer should be guided by the nature and needs of the reader in choosing the most appropriate format for the report. The following format is sufficiently flexible to allow the inclusion or exclusion of elements to satisfy particular needs:

3 *Outline the main elements that make up a standard report form.*

1. Title page
2. Table of contents
3. Summary
   a. Introduction
   b. Results
   c. Conclusions
   d. Recommendations

4. Introduction
5. Body
   a. Methodology
   b. Results
   c. Limitations
6. Conclusions and recommendations
7. Appendix
   a. Copies of data collection forms
   b. Detailed calculations supporting sample size, test statistics, and so on
   c. Tables not included in the body
   d. Bibliography

Title Page

The title page indicates the subject of the report, the name of the organization for whom the report is made, the name of the organization submitting it, and the date. If the report is done by one department within a company for another, the names of organizations or companies are replaced by those of individuals. Those for whom the report is intended are listed on the title page, as are the departments or people preparing the report. If a report is confidential, it is especially important to list on the title page the names of the individuals authorized to see it.

Table of Contents

The table of contents lists, in order of appearance, the divisions and subdivisions of the report with page references. In a short report, the table of contents may simply contain the main headings. The table of contents will also typically include tables and figures and the pages on which they may be found. For most reports, exhibits will be labeled as either tables or figures, with maps, diagrams, and graphs falling into the latter category.

Summary

Explain the kind of information contained in the summary.

The summary is the *most important* part of the report. It is the heart and core. Many executives will read only the summary. Others will read more, but even they will use the summary as a guide to those questions about which they would like more information.

The true summary is not an abstract of the whole report in which everything is restated in condensed form, nor is it a simple restatement of the subject, nor is it a brief statement of the significant results and conclusions. A true summary gives the high points of the entire body of the report. A properly written summary saves the time of busy executives without sacrificing their understanding. A good test of a summary is self-sufficiency. Can it stand on its own, or does it collapse without the full report?

A good summary contains the necessary background information as well as the important results and conclusions. Whether it contains recommendations is determined to an extent by the reader. Some managers prefer that the writer suggest appropriate action, while others prefer to draw their own conclusions on the basis of the evidence contained in the study. Although the good summary contains the necessary information, it will rarely be broken down through the use of headings and subheadings. The summary that requires such subdivisions is probably too long.

The summary begins with an introduction that should provide the reader with enough background to appreciate the results, conclusions, and recommendations of the study. The introduction should state who authorized the research and for what purpose. It should state explicitly the problems or hypotheses that guided the research.

Following the introduction should be a section in which the study's significant findings or results are presented. The results presented in the summary must agree, of course, with those in the body of the report, but only the key findings are presented here. A useful approach is to include one or several statements reporting what was found with regard to each problem or objective mentioned in the introduction.

The final two sections of the summary are conclusions and recommendations, which follow a discussion of the results. Conclusions and recommendations are not the same. A conclusion is an opinion based on the results. A recommendation is a suggestion as to appropriate future action.

Conclusions should be included in the summary section. The writer is in a much better position to base conclusions on the evidence than is the reader, as the writer has greater familiarity with the methods used to generate and analyze the data. The writer is at fault if conclusions are omitted and readers are allowed to draw their own. Recommendations, however, are another matter. Some managers simply prefer to determine the appropriate courses of action themselves and do not want the writer to offer recommendations. Others hold that the writer, being closest to the research, is in the best position to suggest a course of action. Increasingly, marketing researchers are being asked to interpret the findings in terms of what they mean to the business and to make recommendations as to appropriate courses of action.

5 *Distinguish between a conclusion and a recommendation.*

Introduction

Whereas in the summary the readers' interests are taken into account, in the report's formal introduction their education and experience are considered. The introduction provides the background information readers need to appreciate the discussion in the body of the report. Some form of introduction is almost always necessary. Its length and detail, however, depend upon the readers' familiarity with the subject, the report's approach to it, and the treatment of it. A report with wide distribution will generally require a more extensive introduction than a report for a narrow audience.

6 *Describe the kind of information that should be contained in the introduction.*

The introduction often serves to define unfamiliar terms or terms that are used in a specific way in the report. For instance, in a study of market penetration of a new product, the introduction might define the market and name the products and companies considered "competitors" in calculating the new product's market share.

The introduction may provide some pertinent history, answering such questions as the following: What similar studies have been conducted? What findings did they produce? What circumstances led to the present study? How was its scope and emphasis determined? Clearly, if readers are familiar with the history of this project and related research or the circumstances that inspired the current research, these items can be omitted. A report going to executives with little background in the particular product or service dealt with would probably have to include them.

The introduction should state the specific objectives of the research. If the project was part of a larger, overall project, this should be mentioned. Each of the subproblems or hypotheses should be explicitly stated. After reading the introduction, readers should know just what the report covers and what it omits. They should appreciate the overall problem and how the subproblems relate to it. They should be aware of the relationship between this study and other related work. And they should appreciate the need for the study and its importance. Through all of this, the introduction should serve to win the readers' confidence and dispel any prejudices they may have.

Body

The details of the research—its method, results, and limitations—are contained in the body of the report. One of the hardest portions of the report to write is that giving the details of the method. The writer has a real dilemma here. Sufficient information must be presented so that readers can appreciate the research design, data collection methods, sample procedures, and analysis techniques that were used without being bored or overwhelmed. Technical jargon,

7 *Describe the kind of information that should be contained in the body.*

which is often a succinct way of communicating a complex idea, should be omitted, since many in the audience will not understand it.

Readers must be told whether the design was exploratory, descriptive, or causal. They should also be told why the particular design was chosen and what its merits are in terms of the problem at hand. Readers should also be told whether the results are based on secondary or primary data. If primary, are they based on observation or questionnaire? And if the latter, were the questionnaires administered in person, or by mail, e-mail, fax, or telephone? Once again it is important to mention why the particular method was chosen. What were its perceived advantages over alternative schemes? This may mean discussing briefly the perceived weaknesses of the other data collection schemes that were considered.

Sampling is a technical subject, and the writer cannot usually hope to convey all the nuances of the sampling plan in the body of the report, but must be somewhat selective in this regard. At the very minimum, the researcher should answer the following questions:

1. How was the population defined? What were the geographical, age, sex, or other bounds?
2. What sampling units were used? Were they business organizations or business executives? Were they dwelling units, households, or individuals within a household? Why were these particular sampling units chosen?
3. How was the list of sampling units generated? Did this produce any weaknesses? Why was this method used?
4. Were any difficulties experienced in contacting designated sample elements? How were these difficulties overcome, and was bias introduced in the process?
5. Was a probability or nonprobability sampling plan used? Why? How was the sample actually selected? How large a sample was selected? Why was this size chosen?

In essence, the readers need to understand at least three things with respect to the sample: What was done? How was it done? Why was it done?

There is very little that can be said about the method of analysis when discussing research methods, since the results tend to show what has been done in this regard. It often proves quite useful, though, to discuss the method in general before detailing the results. Thus, if statistical significance is established through chi-square analysis, the writer might provide the general rationale and calculation procedure for the chi-square statistic, as well as the assumptions surrounding this test and how well the data supported the assumptions. This enables readers to separate what was found from how it was determined. The distinction may not only help the readers' understanding but also prevent repetition in the report. The procedure is outlined with its key components once, and the results are then simply reported in terms of these components.

The results section of the body of the report presents the findings of the study in some detail, often including supporting tables and figures, and accounts for the bulk of the report. The results need to address the specific problems posed and must be presented with some logical structure. The first of these requirements directs that information that is interesting but irrelevant in terms of the specific problems that guided the research be omitted. The second requirement directs that the tables and figures not be a random collection but reflect some psychological ordering.[16] This may mean ordering by subproblem, geographic region, time, or another criterion that served to structure the investigation.

Tables and figures should be used liberally when presenting the results. This is especially important in today's environment, where most clients are used to visual and even multimedia content, thanks to the ability of computer programs to translate data into charts and graphs. Clients will expect to see keys points illustrated clearly. At Ames Department Stores, for example, managers use their computers to look up colorful graphs displaying financial and merchandising data, as well as customer demographics and even weather data, rather than deciphering columns of numbers.[17] Similarly, the marketing team at NextCard, which offers credit cards strictly through online marketing via Web pages, tracks the performance of NextCard's online banner ads by watching a monitor in a San Francisco office. There, the performance of each ad is reported on a graph that uses colored lines to record the number of new accounts and new balances. The report is updated automatically every 15 minutes. If a line is trending downward, the marketing team must spring into action.[18]

While the tables in the appendix are complex, detailed, and apply to a number of problems, the tables in the body of the report should be simple summaries of this information. Each table should address only a single problem, and it should be specially constructed to shed maximum light on this problem. Guidelines for constructing tables follow:[19]

1. Order the columns or rows of the table by the marginal averages or some other measure of size. If there are many similar tables, keep the same order in each one.
2. Put the figures to be compared into columns rather than rows, and, if possible, put the larger numbers at the top of the columns.
3. Round the numbers to two effective digits.
4. For each table, give a brief verbal summary that will guide the reader to the main patterns and exceptions.

Exhibit 22.2 gives an example of how these guidelines can yield better tables.

Figures, like tables, should address only one subproblem. Further, they should be chosen carefully for the type of message they can most effectively convey. This subject will be discussed later in this chapter.

It is impossible to conduct the "perfect" study, because every study has its limitations. The researcher knows what the limitations of his or her efforts are, and these should not be hidden from the reader. Researchers sometimes fear that a frank admission of a study's limitations may diminish the reader's opinion of the quality of the research. Often the contrary is true. If some limitations are not stated and readers discover them, they may begin to question the whole report and assume a much more skeptical, critical posture than they would have had, had the limitations been stated explicitly. Stating them also allows the writer to discuss whether, and by how much, the limitations might bias the results. Their exclusion, and later discovery, encourages readers to draw their own conclusions in this regard.

When discussing the limitations, the writer should provide some idea of the accuracy with which the work was done. The writer should specifically discuss the sources of nonsampling error and the suspected direction of their biases. This often means that the researcher provides some limits by which the results are distorted due to these inaccuracies. Readers should be informed specifically as to how far the results can be generalized. To what populations can they be expected to apply? If the study was done in Miami, readers should be warned not to generalize the results to the southern states or all the states. The writer should provide the proper caveats for readers and not make them discover the weaknesses themselves. However, *the writer should not overstate the limitations either, but should assume a balanced perspective.*

© Eyewire/Getty Images

Most clients are used to visual content. This makes the use of tables, figures, and graphs especially important in presentations.

Conclusions and Recommendations

The results lead to the conclusions and recommendations. In this section, the writer shows the step-by-step development of the conclusions and states them in greater detail than in the summary. There should be a conclusion for each study objective or problem. One good strategy is to link the objectives and conclusions so closely that the reader—after reviewing the objectives—could turn directly to the conclusions to find a specific conclusion for each objective. If the study does not provide evidence sufficient to draw a conclusion about a problem, this should be explicitly stated.

Exhibit 22.2

Guidelines for Producing Better Tables

Table A displays some sales figures for a product being sold in ten U.S. cities. At first glance it seems fairly laid out, but look again. How would you summarize the information in the table to someone over the phone?

Table A
Quarterly Sales of Product Y in Ten Cities

City	SALES IN THOUSANDS OF DOLLARS			
	Quarter 1	Quarter 2	Quarter 3	Quarter 4
Atlanta	540.4	507.6	528.4	833.2
Chattanooga	68.9	64.0	55.4	64.5
Des Moines	65.7	61.1	52.9	61.5
Hartford	61.1	71.5	59.0	70.5
Indianapolis	153.2	162.8	122.8	185.7
Los Angeles	700.2	660.3	580.8	662.7
Miami	553.6	517.2	446.0	672.4
Omaha	78.3	72.8	63.0	73.3
Phoenix	196.8	227.6	198.5	235.2
San Antonio	168.2	179.3	166.9	207.1

The table seems to be a jumble when looked at more carefully. It appears that no thought was given to communicating what the numbers really mean. The main difficulty is that the cities for which the numbers are given are listed alphabetically. There is no apparent pattern in each column. Now look at the same information as presented in Table B.

Table B
Quarterly Sales of Product Y in Ten Cities Ordered by Population Size (Rounded and with Averages)

City	Quarter 1	Quarter 2	Quarter 3	Quarter 4	Average
Los Angeles	700	660	580	660	650
Miami	550	520	450	670	550
Atlanta	540	510	530	830	600
Phoenix	200	230	200	240	220
San Antonio	170	180	170	210	180
Indianapolis	150	160	120	190	160
Hartford	60	70	60	70	70
Omaha	80	70	60	70	70
Chattanooga	70	60	60	60	60
Des Moines	70	60	50	60	60
Average	260	250	230	310	260

Note how ordering the information by following the recommended steps improves the table's readability.

Table B's heading informs the reader that the cities are ordered by population size. Having this information and examining the table as it's laid out, we can begin to see major patterns emerge: the bigger the cities, the higher the sales, as might be expected. The single exception is Atlanta, where sales are relatively high given its population size.

Trends over time are also easier to see. Although not typical, the column averages help us see that sales in each city were relatively steady quarter by quarter, but that they were lower in Quarter 3 and larger in Quarter 4. We can also see that the fourth-quarter increases were largest in Miami and Atlanta.

The difference between Tables A and B is the difference between a good table and a poor one. In a good table, the patterns and exceptions should be obvious at a glance, at least once one knows what they are.

Next time you have trouble reading a table, ask yourself if the information could be better ordered. The fault may not be in your ability to comprehend the information but in the table itself.

Source: Adapted from A. S. C. Ehrenberg, "The Problem of Numeracy," *The American Statistician* 35 (May 1981), pp. 67–71. Reprinted from *The American Statistician.* Copyright 1981 by the American Statistical Association. All rights reserved.

Researchers' recommendations should follow the conclusions. In developing the recommendations, researchers need to focus on the value of the information that has been gathered. They need to interpret this information in terms of what it means for the business. One of the best ways of doing this is by offering specific recommendations as to the appropriate courses of action—along with reasons why—given the evidence. While not all managers want the researcher's recommendations, many do, and the researcher needs to be prepared to offer and support them.

Appendix

The appendix contains material that is too complex, too detailed, too specialized, or not absolutely necessary for the text. The appendix will typically contain as an exhibit a copy of the questionnaire or observation form used to collect the data. It will also contain any maps used to draw the sample, as well as any detailed calculations used to support the determination of the sample size and sample design. The appendix may include detailed calculations of test statistics and will often include detailed tables from which the summary tables in the body of the report were generated. The writer should recognize that the appendix will be read by only the most technically competent and interested reader. Therefore, the writer should not put material in the appendix if its omission from the body of the report would create gaps in the presentation.

8 Describe the kind of information that should be contained in the appendix.

Synopsis

Exhibit 22.3 can serve as a checklist of things to include in reports. The checklist reflects the guidelines that have been developed to evaluate research that is to be put to a public purpose. Public-purpose research can affect the interests of people and organizations who have had no part in its design, execution, or funding. Consequently, the criteria on which it is evaluated tend to be stricter than those applied to research done for private use. Still, the general issues and questions serve as useful criteria by which all research reports can be judged.

The Oral Report

In addition to the written report, most marketing research investigations require one or more oral reports. Often clients, or those in the company for whom the study is being undertaken, want progress reports during the course of the project. Almost always they require a formal oral report at the conclusion of the study. The principles surrounding the preparation and delivery of the oral report parallel those for the written report.

That means report preparers and presenters need to realize that many listeners will not truly understand the technical ramifications involved in research and certainly will not be able to judge whether the research done is "quality research." However, they can judge whether the research was presented in a professional, confidence-inspiring manner or in a disorganized, uninformed one. A quality presentation can disguise poor research, but quality research cannot improve a poor presentation.

Preparing the Oral Report

As we emphasized earlier, the first requirement is to know the audience. What is their technical level of sophistication? What is their involvement in the project? Their interest? Once again, researchers may want to present more detailed reports to those who are deeply involved in the project or who have a high level of technical sophistication than to those who are only slightly involved or interested.

Learning about the audience comes more naturally with the modern emphasis on teamwork. Kellogg, for example, has tried to improve new-product development by establishing cross-functional teams that bring together marketing researchers with food technologists and

9 Specify the first rule to keep in mind when preparing an oral report.

Checklist for Evaluating Research Reports

A. Origin: What Is Behind the Research
Does the report identify the organizations, divisions, or departments that initiated and paid for the research?
Is there a statement of the purpose of the research that says clearly what it was meant to accomplish?
Are the organizations that designed and conducted the research identified?

B. Design: The Concept and the Plan
Is there a full, nontechnical description of the research design?
Is the design consistent with the stated purpose for which the research was conducted?
Is the design evenhanded? That is, is it free of leading questions and other biases?
Have precautions been taken to avoid sequence or timing bias or other factors that might prejudice or distort the findings?
Does it address questions that respondents are capable of answering?
Is there a precise statement of the universe or population that the research is meant to represent?
Does the sampling frame fairly represent the population under study?
Does the report specify the kind of sample used and clearly describe the method of sample selection?
Does the report describe the plan for the analysis of the data?
Are copies of all questionnaire forms, field and sampling instructions, and other study materials available in the appendix or on file?

C. Execution: Collecting and Handling the Information
Does the report describe the data collection and data processing procedures?
Is there an objective report on the care with which the data were collected?
What procedures were used to minimize bias and ensure the quality of the information collected?

D. Stability: Sample Size and Reliability
Was the sample large enough to provide stable findings?
Are sampling error limits shown if they can be computed?
Are methods of calculating the sampling error described, or, if the error cannot be computed, is this stated and explained?
Does the treatment of sampling error limits make clear that they do not cover nonsampling error?
For the major findings, are the reported error tolerances based on direct analysis of the variability of the collected data?

E. Applicability: Generalizing the Findings
Does the report specify when the data were collected?
Does the report say clearly whether its findings do or do not apply beyond the direct source of the data?
Is it clear who is underrepresented by the research, or not represented at all?
If the research has limited application, is there a statement covering who or what it represents and the time or conditions under which it applies?

F. Meaning: Interpretations and Conclusions
Are the measurements described in simple and direct language?
Does it make logical sense to use such measurements for the purpose to which they are being put?
Are the actual findings clearly differentiated from the interpretation of the findings?
Have rigorous objectivity and sound judgment been exercised in interpreting the research findings?

G. Candor: Open Reporting and Disclosure
Is there a full and forthright disclosure of how the research was done?
Has the research been fairly presented?

Source: Adapted from *Guidelines for the Public Use of Market and Opinion Research* © 1981 by the Advertising Research Foundation. Adapted with permission.

engineers. The objective is to develop products that appeal to customers, and are financially and technologically feasible.[20] Researchers who are assigned to such teams should use their participation as an opportunity to learn the technical sophistication and interests of their teammates. This understanding should enable researchers to target their reports and increase their value to the team.

PART 7:
Research Reports

In general, it is better to err on the side of too little technical detail rather than too much. Executives want to hear and see what the information means to them as managers of marketing activities. What do the data suggest with respect to marketing actions? They can ask for the necessary clarification with respect to the technical details if they want it. Paco Underhill, noted for his use of observational research in stores, emphasizes marketing implications. In one instance, Underhill told a group of (mostly male) Wal-Mart executives that he could tell whether any of their stores had a male or female manager, based only on how recently the women's dressing room had been painted. Over the months following that meeting, Underhill says, he noticed a lot of newly painted dressing rooms at Wal-Mart stores.[21]

Another important consideration is how the presentation is organized. There are two popular forms of organization. Both begin by stating the general purpose of the study and the specific objectives that were addressed. They differ, however, with respect to when the conclusions are introduced. In the most popular structure, the conclusions are introduced after all of the evidence supporting a particular course of action is presented. This allows the presenter to build a logical case in sequential fashion. By progressively disclosing the facts, the presenter has the opportunity to deal with audience concerns and biases as they arise, and thus lead listeners to the conclusion that the case builds.

10 *Describe the two most common forms of organization for oral reports.*

In the alternative structure, conclusions are presented immediately after the purpose and main objectives. This structure tends to involve managers immediately in the findings. It not only gets them to think about what actions the results suggest, but also alerts them to pay close attention to the evidence supporting the conclusions. This format allows managers to evaluate the strength of the evidence supporting an action, since they know beforehand the conclusions that have been drawn from it.

The structure a presenter decides to use should depend on the particular company's style and preferences and on the presenter's own level of comfort with each form of organization. In either case, the evidence supporting the conclusions must be presented systematically, and the conclusions drawn must be consistent with the evidence.

A third important element in the effective oral presentation is the use of appropriate visual aids. Depending on the size of the group and the physical facilities in which the meeting is held, flip charts, transparencies, slides, and white boards can all be used to advantage, although increasingly most oral presentations make use of computer presentation software, such as Microsoft's PowerPoint. Presentation software allows the relatively easy preparation of many different, high quality kinds of exhibits from definitions, bulleted lists, maps, to various types of graphs. Moreover, presentation software allows the presenter to go forward or backward during the presentation or to focus on a particular point. It allows the use of various font sizes, font styles, and colors to create emphasis. It also allows the use of special effects such as the addition of sound or video tapes in the presentation or the use of fading, dissolving, progressively adding or deleting items in an exhibit, all of which can also create some desired emphasis. Increasingly, because of these capabilities, it is becoming more common to have 20–30 or more exhibits in an oral presentation.

11 *Discuss the key points a presenter should keep in mind regarding the use of visual aids.*

Another advantage of preparing the report using computer presentation software is that it can be placed easily on the company's intranet (or perhaps the Internet), where it can be accessed by those with proper authorization. By not being stuck in a file drawer, the research report is more likely to contribute to the company's key learnings or accumulated knowledge about some product or issue.

Regardless of how the visuals are prepared or which types are used, it is important to make sure they can be read by those in the back of the room. It is also important that they be kept simple so that they can be understood at a glance. Whenever possible, use figures rather than tables to make the points, as figures are more easily understood. In addition, obey the other principles of effective visual aid design listed in Research Window 22.3.

Delivering the Oral Report

Honor the time limit set for the meeting. Use no more than a third to a half of the time for the formal presentation. But be careful not to rush the presentation of the information contained

12 *Explain how the time allotted for an oral presentation should be organized.*

Keep them simple. Deliver complex ideas in a way your audience can understand. Present one point per exhibit, with as few words and lines as possible.

Use lots of exhibits as you talk, rather than lots of talk per exhibit. Less is more when you are speaking.

Use one minute per visual, then move on. Visuals should make their impact quickly.

Highlight and emphasize significant points using bullets, font sizes or styles, color, or by some other means.

Make the visuals easy to read. Use large, legible typefaces and limit the typefaces to one or two different ones and no more than three sizes.

Be careful with the use of color. While color can add interest and emphasis, it can also detract if used without planning. Plan your color scheme and use it faithfully throughout.

Build complexity. If you have a complicated concept to communicate, start with the ground level and use three or four exhibits to complete the picture.

Prepare copies of exhibits. Hand them to the audience before or after your presentation. If people have to take notes, they won't be watching or listening closely.

Number the pages in the handout. You will have a better reference for discussion or a question-and-answer period. ∎

ETHICAL dilemma 22.2

A colleague confides in you: "I've just run a survey for a restaurant owner who is planning to open a catering service for parties, weddings, and the like. He wanted to know the best way to advertise the new service. In the questionnaire, I asked respondents where they would expect to see advertisements for catering facilities, and the most common source was the newspaper. I now realize that my question only established where people are usually exposed to relevant ads, not where they would like to see relevant ads or where they could most productively be exposed to an ad. All we know is where other caterers advertise! Yet I'm sure my client will interpret my findings as meaning that the newspaper is the most effective media vehicle. Should I make the limitations of the research explicit?"

- *What are the costs of making the limitations of the research explicit?*

- *What are the costs of not doing so?*

- *Isn't promoting the correct use of the research one of the researcher's prime obligations?*

in the charts. Remember, the audience is seeing them for the first time. Order your presentation in such a way that there is enough time to both present and discuss the most critical findings. Reserve the remaining time for questions and further discussion.

One of the unique benefits of the oral presentation is that it allows interaction. A question-and-answer period may be the most important part of your presentation. It allows you to clear up any confusion that may have arisen during the course of your talk, to emphasize points that deserve special attention, and to get a feeling for the issues that are of particular concern or interest to your audience. The nature of the questions raised during a progress report may help you structure your final report to best advantage.

Researcher Michele Holleran has experienced these benefits first hand at small to midsized companies, where her audience is apt to include a marketing director or vice president who sees the research in terms of the company's overall objectives. For example, she presented the results of a multifaceted study to management of a company that makes products for home builders. The study addressed a variety of issues, from what the company's advertising should emphasize to how the company's product mix should be expanded. The researchers managed to combine the findings of interviews and focus groups into a single report. In their oral presentation, the researchers emphasized what they concluded were the key pieces of information. They summarized what they learned, then asked the managers how it fit with what they already knew. The result was an interactive presentation, with all the parties contributing knowledge. At various points, managers asked the researchers to document findings that were counter to their expectations. Through this process, the company's management abandoned some misconceptions about the market and developed several growth strategies.[22]

When delivering the message, use the time-honored principles of public speaking: Keep the presentation simple and uncluttered so that the audience does not have to backtrack mentally to think about what was said, and choose words and sentences that are appropriate for the tongue. That means spoken speech, your usual vocabulary, and simple phrases.[23]

Graphic Presentation of the Results

The old adage that a picture is worth a thousand words is equally true for business reports. A picture, called a *graphic illustration* in the case of the research report, can indeed be worth a thousand words when it is appropriate to the presentation and well designed. When inappropriate or poorly designed, such an illustration may actually detract from the value of the written or oral research report. In this section, we will review briefly some of the most popular forms of graphics and when each is best used.[24]

In a research report, graphic illustration generally involves the presentation of quantities in graph form. To be effective, it must be more than simply converting a set of numbers into a drawing; the picture must give the readers an accurate understanding of the comparisons or relationships that they would otherwise have to search for in the numbers in the report and perhaps fail to see. If well done, the graphic illustration will give the readers this understanding more quickly, more forcefully, more completely, and more accurately than could be done in any other way.[25]

Graphic presentation is not the only way to present quantitative information, nor is it always the best. Sometimes text and tables are better used. Graphics should be used only when they serve the purpose better than do these other modes. Written textual material is generally the most useful in explaining, interpreting, and evaluating results, while tables are particularly good for providing emphasis and for vivid demonstrations of important findings. Particularly since some readers tend to shy away from a graphic presentation as "too technical," it should be used with discretion and designed with care.

At one time graphic presentation was expensive and often delayed the presentation of reports because the visuals had to be drawn by graphic artists. Computer graphics have changed that. The development of computer software for graphically portraying the results of a study now makes the preparation of visuals fast and inexpensive. There is no longer any excuse for not using graphics when appropriate.

There are three basic kinds of graphics: charts that show how much, maps that show where, and diagrams that show how. Since charts are generally the most useful of the three types, the following discussion focuses on some of the more common chart types.

Pie Chart

13 *Describe the circumstances in which a pie chart is most effective.*

pie chart
A circle representing a total quantity and divided into sectors, with each sector showing the size of the segment in relation to that total.

Probably one of the more familiar charts, the **pie chart** is simply a circle divided into sections, with each of the sections representing a portion of the total. Since the sections are presented as part of a whole, or total, the pie chart is particularly effective for depicting relative size or emphasizing static comparisons. Figure 22.1 (resulting from the data of Exhibit 22.4), for instance, shows the breakdown of personal consumption expenditures by major category for 2001. The conclusion is obvious. Expenditures for services account for the largest proportion of total consumption expenditures. Further, expenditures for services and nondurable goods completely dwarf expenditures for durable goods.

Figure 22.1 has three slices, and it is easy to interpret. Had the information been broken into finer categories (for example, if the separate components of durable and nondurable goods had been depicted), a greater number of sections would have been required. Although more information would have been conveyed, emphasis would have been lost. As a rule of thumb, no more than six slices should be generated; the division of the pie should start at the twelve o'clock position; the sections should be arrayed clockwise in decreasing order of magnitude; and the exact percentages should be provided on the graph.

Figure 22.1

Personal Consumption Expenditures by Major Category for 2001

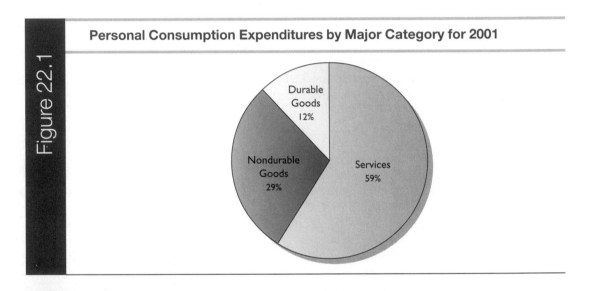

Exhibit 22.4

Personal Consumption Expenditures for 1990–2001 (billions of dollars)

Year	Total Personal Consumption Expenditures	Durable Goods	Nondurable Goods	Services
1990	3,659.3	480.3	1,193.7	1,983.3
1991	3,887.7	446.1	1,251.5	2,190.1
1992	4,095.8	480.4	1,290.7	2,324.7
1993	4,378.2	538.0	1,339.2	2,501.0
1994	4,628.4	591.5	1,394.3	2,642.7
1995	4,957.7	608.5	1,475.8	2,873.4
1996	5,207.6	634.5	1,534.7	3,038.4
1997	5,433.7	657.4	1,619.9	3,156.7
1998	5,856.0	693.2	1,708.5	3,454.3
1999	6,246.5	755.9	1,830.1	3,660.5
2000	6,683.7	803.9	1,972.9	3,906.9
2001	6,987.0	835.9	2,041.3	4,109.9

Source: Survey of Current Business

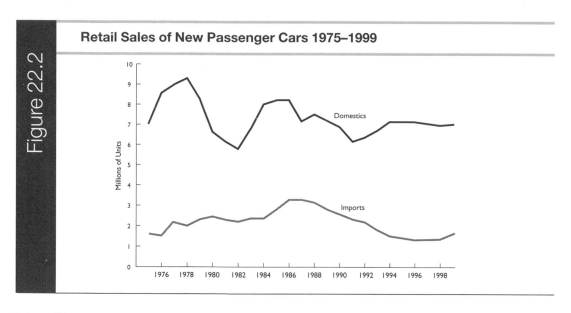

Figure 22.2

Retail Sales of New Passenger Cars 1975–1999

Domestics

Imports

Millions of Units

1976 1978 1980 1982 1984 1986 1988 1990 1992 1994 1996 1998

Line Chart

The pie chart is a one-scale chart, which is why it is best used for static comparisons of a phenomenon at a point in time. The **line chart** is a two-dimensional chart that is particularly useful in depicting dynamic relationships such as time-series fluctuations of one or more series. For example, Figure 22.2 (produced from the data of Exhibit 22.5) shows that, for 1975–1999, new car sales of imports were subject to less fluctuation than were domestic sales.

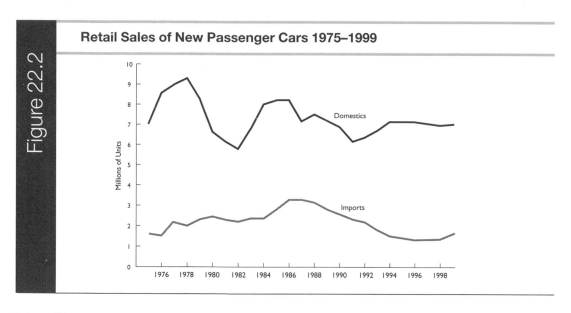

14 *Explain the best use of a line chart.*

line chart
A two-dimensional chart constructed on graph paper with the *X* axis representing one variable (typically time) and the *Y* axis representing another variable.

Exhibit 22.5

Retail Sales of New Passenger Cars (millions of units)

Year	Domestics	Imports	Total
1975	7.0	1.6	8.6
1976	8.5	1.5	10.0
1977	9.0	2.1	11.1
1978	9.2	2.0	11.2
1979	8.2	2.3	10.5
1980	6.6	2.4	9.0
1981	6.2	2.3	8.5
1982	5.8	2.2	8.0
1983	6.8	2.4	9.2
1984	8.0	2.4	10.4
1985	8.2	2.8	11.0
1986	8.2	3.2	11.4
1987	7.1	3.2	10.3
1988	7.5	3.1	10.6
1989	7.1	2.8	9.9
1990	6.9	2.6	9.5
1991	6.1	2.3	8.4
1992	6.3	2.1	8.4
1993	6.7	1.8	8.5
1994	7.3	1.7	9.0
1995	7.1	1.5	8.6
1996	7.2	1.3	8.5
1997	6.9	1.4	8.3
1998	6.7	1.4	8.1
1999	7.0	1.7	8.7

Source: Statistical Abstract of the United States.

Source: © Jon Feingersh/The Stock Market

The line chart is probably used even more often than the pie chart. It is typically constructed on graph paper with the *X* axis representing time and the *Y* axis representing values of the variable or variables. When more than one variable is presented, it is recommended that the lines for different items be distinctive in color or form (dots and dashes in suitable combinations) with identification of the different forms given in a legend.

Stratum Chart

The **stratum chart** serves in some ways as a dynamic pie chart, in that it can be used to show relative emphasis by sector (for example, quantity consumed by user class) and change in relative emphasis over time. The stratum chart consists of a set of line charts whose quantities are grouped together (or a total that is broken into its components). It is also called a *stacked line chart*. For example, Figure 22.3 (resulting from the data of Exhibit 22.4) shows personal consumption expenditures by major category for the 1990–2001 period. The lowest line shows the expenditures just for services; the second lowest line shows the total expenditures for services plus nondurable goods. Personal consumption expenditures for nondurable goods are thus shown by the area between the two lines. So it is with the remaining area. We would need multiple pie charts (one for each year) to capture the same information, and the message would not be as obvious.

The *X* axis typically represents time in the stratum chart, and the *Y* axis again captures the value of the variables. The use of color or distinctive cross-hatching is strongly recommended to distinguish the various components in the stratum chart. As was true for the pie chart, no more than six components should be depicted in a stratum chart.

Bar Chart

The **bar chart** can be either a one-scale or a two-scale chart. This feature, plus the many other variations it permits, probably accounts for its wide use. Figure 22.4, for example, is a one-scale chart. It also shows personal consumption expenditures by major category at a single point in time. Figure 22.4 presents the same information as Figure 22.1 but is, in at least one respect, more revealing; it not only offers some appreciation of the relative expenditures by major category, but also indicates the magnitude of the expenditures by category. Given the total amount of personal consumption expenditures for 2001, readers could, of course, also generate this information from the pie chart. However, it would involve additional calculations on their part.

Figure 22.5, on the other hand, is a two-scale bar chart. It uses the data contained in Exhibit 22.5 and shows total automobile sales for the period 1976–1998. The *Y* axis represents quantity, and the *X* axis, time.

Figures 22.4 and 22.5 show that the bar chart can be drawn either vertically or horizontally. When emphasis is on the change in the variable through time, the vertical form is preferred, with the *X* axis as the time axis. When time is not a variable, either the vertical or the horizontal form is used.

Bar Chart Variations

As previously suggested, bar charts are capable of great variation. One variation is to convert them to **pictograms.** Instead of using the length of the bar to capture quantity, amounts are shown by piles of dollars for income, pictures of cars for automobile production, people in a

A line chart is a two-dimensional chart printed on graph paper or produced electronically on a computer with each of two axes representing one variable. This form of chart, such as the growth chart seen in the photo, is commonly used for oral presentations during business meetings.

stratum chart
A set of line charts in which quantities are aggregated or a total is disaggregated so that the distance between two lines represents the amount of some variable.

15 *Describe the circumstances in which a stratum chart is most effective.*

16 *Cite the reason bar charts are so widely used.*

Figure 22.3

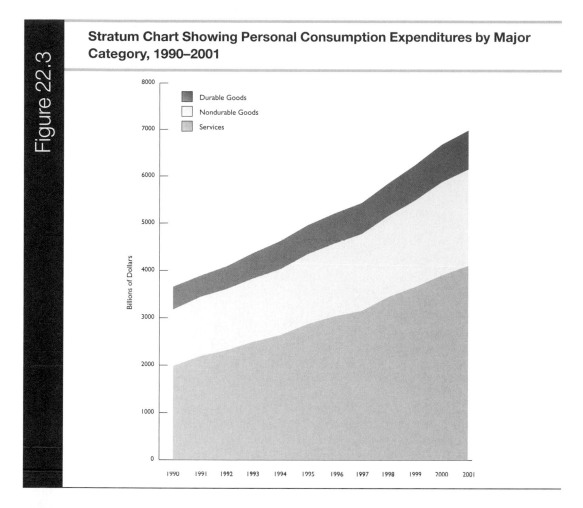

Stratum Chart Showing Personal Consumption Expenditures by Major Category, 1990–2001

Figure 22.4

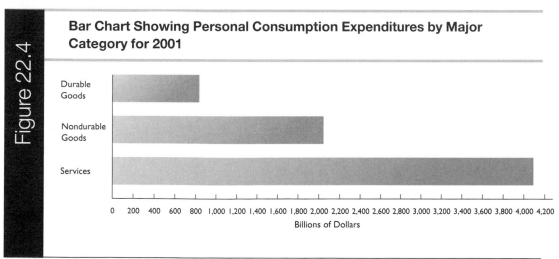

Bar Chart Showing Personal Consumption Expenditures by Major Category for 2001

bar chart
A chart in which the relative lengths of the bars show relative amounts of variables or objects.

pictogram
A bar chart in which pictures represent amounts—for example, piles of dollars for income, pictures of cars for automobile production, people in a row for population.

row for population, and so on. This can be a welcome change of pace for the reader if there are a number of graphs in the report. However, pictograms are especially susceptible to perceptual distortions. Report users have to be especially careful when reading them so that they are not led to incorrect conclusions.

A variation of the basic bar chart—the grouped-bar chart—can be used to capture the change in two or more series through time. Figure 22.6, for example, shows the change in consumption expenditures by the three major categories for the period 1990–2001. Just as

Describe the circumstances in which a grouped-bar chart is most effective.

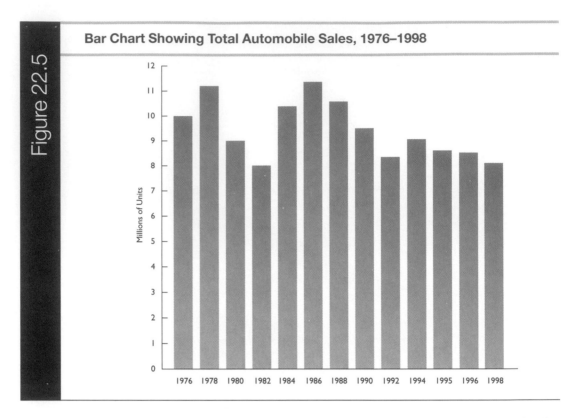

Figure 22.5

Bar Chart Showing Total Automobile Sales, 1976–1998

distinctive symbols are effective in distinguishing the separate series in a line chart, distinctive coloring and/or cross-hatching is equally helpful in a grouped-bar chart.

There is also a bar chart equivalent to the stratum chart—the divided-bar chart or, as it is sometimes called, the stacked-bar chart. Its construction and interpretation are similar to those for the stratum chart. Figure 22.7, for example, is a divided-bar chart of personal consumption expenditures by major category. It shows both total and relative expenditures through time, and it makes use of distinctive color for each component.

ETHICAL dilemma 22.4

You are preparing to deliver the final report to top management to make the case that your new advertising campaign has increased sales dramatically in trial areas. Your conceptual arguments on behalf of the new campaign are very convincing, but although there has been a consistent rise in sales in trial areas, the bar charts look rather disappointing: 61,500 units the first month, 61,670 units the next, 61,820 the next. Why, the increase is barely visible! Then you realize how much more exciting your results would look if the Y axis were broken above the origin so that the plots started at 50,000 units.

• *Where does salesmanship stop and deception start?*

Maps

Maps focus attention on geographic areas. When used for the geographic display of quantitative or statistical information, they are usually called *data maps*.

Data maps are especially suited to the presentation of rates, ratios, and frequency distribution data by areas. In constructing data maps, the quantity of interest is typically broken into groups, and cross-hatching, shading, or color is used to display the numerical group in which each area belongs. In general, it is helpful to keep the group intervals approximately equal and to use a limited number of shadings—four to seven and certainly no more than ten. Moreover, the shadings should run progressively from light to dark, and all areas should have some shading. Leaving an area blank or white tends to weaken its importance. For example, Figure 22.8 shows how employment, a sign of economic vitality, grew over a ten-year period in various countries.

Research Window 22.4 offers some suggestions on using graphics in presentations.

Figure 22.6

Grouped Bar Chart Showing Personal Consumption Expenditures by Major Category, 1990–2001

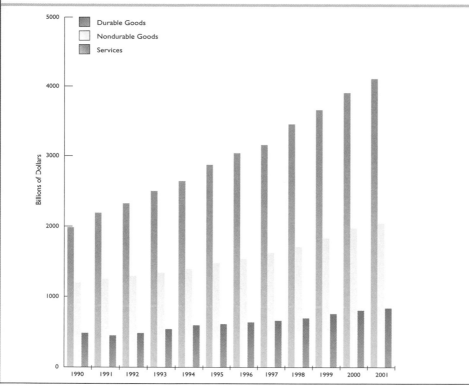

Figure 22.7

Divided Bar Chart Showing Personal Consumption Expenditures by Major Category, 1990–2000

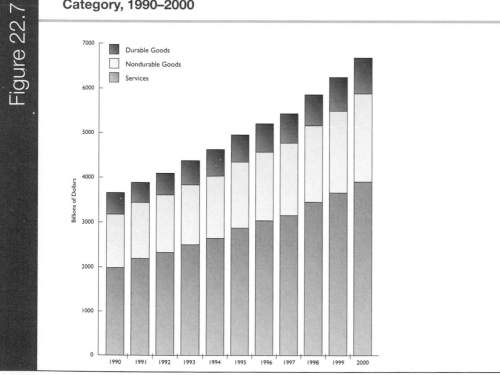

Putting Graphics to Use

Word slides

- Keep word slides brief; use key words only.
- Use bullets and color to highlight key points.
- Break up the information to make a series of slides (a progressive or "build" series). Use color to show the new line added to each slide.

Tabular slides

- Use tabular slides to show lists.
- Keep items as brief as possible; arrange them to fill the slide area so the type can be as large as possible.

Box charts

- Use box charts for organization charts, flow charts.
- Simplify to keep them legible.
- Break up complex charts into a series. (Show flow chart divided by time periods; show organization chart with the overall chart and departmental "close-up.")

Bar charts

- Use bar charts for data arranged in segments (by month, year, etc.).
- Choose vertical or horizontal bars (both within horizontal slide format).

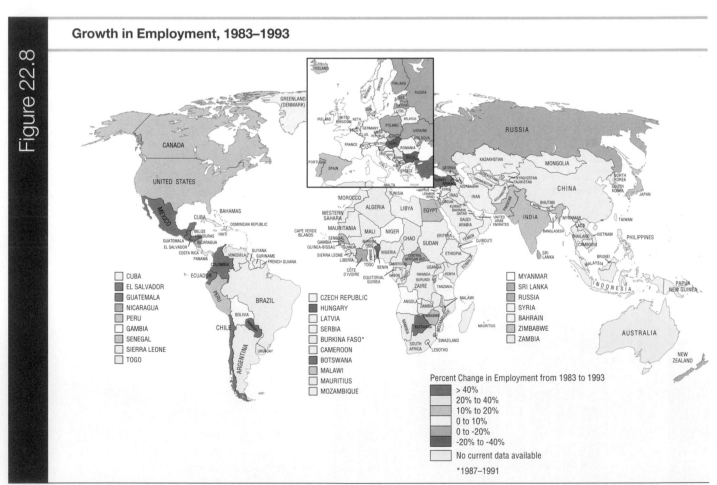

Figure 22.8

Growth in Employment, 1983–1993

Source: Michael R. Czinkota, Ilkka A. Ronkainene and Michael H. Moffett, *International Business*, 4th ed. (Forth Worth, Tex.: The Dryden Press, 1996).

- Add drop shadows for dimensional bars.
- Show complex facts clearly by using multiple or segmented bars.
- Divide extensive data into a progressive disclosure series.

Pie charts
- Use pie charts to emphasize the relationship of the parts to the whole.
- Select single pie or double pie.
- Consider options such as drop shadow for dimensional effect, pulled-out slices, etc.
- Arrange the slices to make your point most effectively.

- Divide the slice into a series if that improves effectiveness.

Line graphs and area graphs
- Use line graphs and area graphs to display trends or continuous data.
- Decide whether line graph or area graph shows your point better.
- Select baseline and scale for maximum effectiveness.
- Use call-outs to identify key points in graph.
- Divide extensive data into a series of graphs. ■

Source: Leslie Blumberg, "For Graphic Presentations, Managers Focus on Slides," *Data Management* (May 1983), p. 22.

looking back...

Twenty days after their online meeting, researchers Martin Kinslow, Anita O'Reilly, and Margo Wirtz felt satisfied with their reports. Martin had created a series of PowerPoint slides illustrating key points of the oral presentation to be given by Anita. Anita had written summary notes for each slide, which would be saved in Notes format for future reference. Backing up these efforts was a lengthy written report, the work of Margo with input from her two colleagues. The three of them reviewed their efforts.

Martin was clicking through the slides on his notebook computer. "After the title page, we have our main idea," he said. "I pulled it from the summary page of Margo's report: 'Consumers say a superior vacuum offers superior strength and superior ease of use.' The rest of the presentation details attitudes about those two measures of quality."

"It's the right message, but we have to cut some words from that first slide," responded Margo. "We want to avoid wordiness so the visuals support Anita's talk. If she just reads the slides, we'll lose our audience." They edited the image until it contained only enough language to signify the two-pronged focus on strength and ease of use.

The group continued editing as they reviewed slides detailing consumers' attitudes and behavior. Bar graphs compared the features male and female consumers valued. For example, with regard to a vacuum cleaner's power, 82 percent of men said power was the most important measure of a vacuum cleaner's quality, whereas only 61 percent of women rated power as most important. Another graph identified the features consumers associate with cleaning power. When focus groups compared actual vacuum cleaners, they rated the loudest and heaviest models "most powerful." In her presentation, Anita planned to point out that these features are not accurate measures of power. A large majority of women complained that their current vacuum cleaner was too heavy. Superior could make a lighter vacuum cleaner, but its advertising would have to teach consumers that a lighter vacuum can be equally powerful.

Based on their adjustments to the slide presentation, the three also edited the more detailed written report. The one-page summary at the beginning of the report covered most of the points from the oral presentation. It was followed by an in-depth discussion of the research methods and results. Tables contrasted the attitudes the research subjects expressed with the actual behaviors observed in visits to subjects' homes. Cross tabulations compared vacuum usage and consumer attitudes among men and women and among consumers in different geographic areas. This level of detail would not interest every manager but would be essential for answering questions later and for preparing future research efforts. ■

Source: Based on ideas from Stephen B. Wilcox, "Ethnography as a Product Development Tool," *Appliance Manufacturer* (July 2001), downloaded from EBSCOhost.

Summary

Learning Objective 1
Specify the fundamental criterion by which all research reports are evaluated.
Research reports are evaluated by one fundamental criterion—communication with the reader. The reader is the reason that the report is prepared and also the standard by which its success is measured.

Learning Objective 2
Identify and discuss the four criteria that a report should meet if it is to communicate effectively with readers.
A report that achieves the goal of communicating effectively with readers is generally one that meets the specific criteria of completeness, accuracy, clarity, and conciseness.

Learning Objective 3
Outline the main elements that make up a standard report form.
A standard report generally contains the following elements: title page, table of contents, summary, introduction, body, conclusions and recommendations, and appendix.

Learning Objective 4
Explain the kind of information contained in the summary.
A true summary gives the high points of the entire body of the report, including necessary background information, as well as important results and conclusions.

Learning Objective 5
Distinguish between a conclusion and a recommendation.
A conclusion is an opinion based on the results. A recommendation is a suggestion as to appropriate future action.

Learning Objective 6
Describe the kind of information that should be contained in the introduction.
An introduction provides background information, defines unfamiliar terms, outlines pertinent history, and states the specific objectives of the research. Through all this, the introduction should serve to win the readers' confidence and dispel any prejudices they may have.

Learning Objective 7
Describe the kind of information that should be contained in the body.
The details of the research are contained in the body of the report. This includes details of method, results, and limitations.

Learning Objective 8
Describe the kind of information that should be contained in the appendix.
The appendix contains material that is too complex, too detailed, too specialized, or not absolutely necessary for the text. The appendix will typically contain as an exhibit a copy of the questionnaire or observation form used to collect the data.

Learning Objective 9
Specify the first rule to keep in mind when preparing an oral report.
As with written reports, the first rule when preparing an oral report is to know your audience.

Learning Objective 10
Describe the two most common forms of organization for oral reports.
There are two popular forms of organization for oral reports. Both begin by stating the general purpose of the study and the specific objectives that were addressed. In the most popular struc-

ture, the conclusions are introduced after all of the evidence supporting a particular course of action is presented. This allows the presenter to build a logical case in sequential fashion. In the alternative structure, conclusions are presented immediately after the purpose and main objectives. This format allows managers to evaluate the strength of the evidence supporting an action, since they know beforehand the conclusions that have been drawn from it.

Learning Objective 11

Discuss the key points a presenter should keep in mind regarding the use of visual aids.

The visual aids used in an oral report should be easily understood and easily seen by those in the back of the room.

Learning Objective 12

Explain how the time allotted for an oral presentation should be organized.

Honor the time limit set for the meeting. Use no more than a third to a half of the time for the formal presentation. Reserve the remaining time for questions and discussion.

Learning Objective 13

Describe the circumstances in which a pie chart is most effective.

A pie chart is a one-scale chart, which is particularly effective in communicating a static comparison.

Learning Objective 14

Explain the best use of a line chart.

A line chart is a two-dimensional chart that is particularly useful in depicting dynamic relationships such as time-series fluctuations of one or more series.

Learning Objective 15

Describe the circumstances in which a stratum chart is most effective.

A stratum chart is in some ways a dynamic pie chart, in that it can be used to show relative emphasis by sector and change in relative emphasis over time.

Learning Objective 16

Cite the reason bar charts are so widely used.

The bar chart can be either a one-scale or a two-scale chart. This feature, plus the many other variations it permits, probably accounts for its wide use.

Learning Objective 17

Describe the circumstances in which a grouped-bar chart is most effective.

A variation of the basic bar chart, the grouped-bar can be used to capture the change in two or more series through time.

Key Terms

completeness (page 661)
accuracy (page 662)
clarity (page 663)
conciseness (page 665)
pie chart (page 676)

line chart (page 677)
stratum chart (page 678)
bar chart (page 679)
pictogram (page 679)

Review Questions

1. What is the fundamental report criterion? Explain.
2. What is meant by the report criteria of completeness, accuracy, clarity, and conciseness?
3. On the one hand, it is argued that the research report must be complete and, on the other, that it must be concise. Are these two objectives incompatible? If so, how do you reconcile them?
4. What is the essential content of each of the following parts of the research report?
   (a) title page
   (b) table of contents

(c) summary

(d) introduction

(e) body

(f) conclusions and recommendations

(g) appendix

5. What are the key considerations in preparing an oral report?

6. What is a pie chart? For what kinds of information is it particularly effective?

7. What is a line chart? For what kinds of information is it generally used?

8. What is a stratum chart? For what kinds of information is it particularly appropriate?

9. What is a bar chart? For what kinds of problems is it effective?

10. What is a pictogram?

11. What is a grouped bar chart? When is it used?

12. What is a data map? For what kinds of information is it particularly effective?

Discussion Questions, Problems, and Projects

1. It should be clear from your reading of this chapter that a professional marketing researcher must possess a well-developed ability to write effectively. Many colleges and universities offer a variety of programs designed to help students hone their writing skills. These programs may take a variety of forms, such as writing labs, special seminars, word-processing tutorials, one-on-one writing tutors, and regular written communication classes. Prepare a research report of the resources available at your school that can be used to enhance written communication skills. Assume that your report will be furnished to incoming first-year students as part of their orientation materials. Be sure to structure your report in the manner presented in this chapter.

2. The owner of a medium-sized home-building center specializing in custom-designed and do-it-yourself bathroom supplies requested the Liska and Leigh Consulting Firm to prepare a report on the customer profile of the bathroom design segment of the home-improvement market. Evaluate the following excerpts from the report:

Research report excerpts

The customer market for the company can be defined as the do-it-yourself and bathroom design segments. A brief profile of each follows.

The do-it-yourself (DIY) market consists of individuals in the 25–45 age-group living in a single dwelling. DIY customers are predominantly male, although an increasing number of females are becoming active DIY customers. The typical DIY customer has an income in excess of $20,000 and the median income is $22,100 with a standard deviation of 86. The DIY customer has an increasing amount of leisure time, is strongly value- and convenience-conscious, and displays an increasing desire for self-gratification.

The mean age of the custom bathroom design segment is 41.26 and the annual income is in the range of $25,000 to $35,000. The median income is $29,000 with a standard deviation of 73. The custom bathroom design customers usually live in a single dwelling. The wife is more influential and is the prime decision maker about bathroom designs.

3. Discuss the difference between conclusions and recommendations in research reports.

4. Assume that Wendy's International, Inc., wants to diversify into another fast food area. You are required to prepare a brief report for the company executives outlining an attractive opportunity. In preparing the report, go through the following steps:

(a) Decide on the particular fast food area you think is most appropriate.

(b) Collect secondary data relating to the area and analyze consumption trends over the past five years (or ten years).

(c) Decide on the outline of the report and its various sections.

(d) Develop the appropriate tables and charts to support your analysis.

(e) Write the report.

5. Describe the information that should be contained in the summary, and discuss why this is the most important part of the research report.

6. In presenting a report to a group of grocery store managers, a researcher stated the following: "The data from the judgment sample of 10 grocery stores was analyzed and the results show that the 95 percent confidence interval for average annual sales in the population of grocery stores is $1,000,000 ± $150,000."
   (a) As far as the audience is concerned, what is wrong with this statement?
   (b) Rewrite the statement. Be sure to include all the relevant information while correcting the problem.

7. Your marketing research firm is preparing the final written report on a research project commissioned by a major manufacturer of lawn mowers. One objective of the project was to investigate seasonal variations in sales, both on an aggregate basis and by each of the company's sales regions individually. Your client is particularly interested in the width of the range between maximum and minimum seasonal sales. Exhibit 1 was submitted by one of your junior analysts. Critique the table and prepare a revision suitable for inclusion in your report.

Exhibit 1

Seasonal Sales Variation

| Sales Region | SALES IN THOUSANDS OF DOLLARS | | | |
	Spring	Summer	Fall	Winter
Northeast	120.10	140.59	50.90	30.00
East-central	118.80	142.70	61.70	25.20
Southeast	142.00	151.80	134.20	100.10
Midwest	100.20	139.42	42.90	20.00
South-central	80.77	101.00	90.42	78.20
Plains	95.60	120.60	38.50	19.90
Southwest	105.40	110.50	101.60	92.10
Pacific	180.70	202.41	171.54	145.60

8. The management of the Seal-Tight Company, a manufacturer of metal cans, has presented you with the following information:

THE SEAL-TIGHT COMPANY:
A COMPARATIVE STATEMENT OF PROFIT AND LOSS FOR THE FISCAL YEARS 1998–2002

	1998	1999	2000	2001	2002
Net sales	$40,000,000	$45,000,000	$48,000,000	$53,000,000	$55,000,000
Cost and expenses Cost of goods sold	$28,000,000	$32,850,000	$33,600,000	$39,750,000	$40,150,000
Selling and admin. expenses	4,000,000	4,500,000	4,800,000	5,300,000	5,500,000
Depreciation	1,200,000	1,350,000	1,440,000	1,590,000	1,650,000
Interest	800,000	900,000	960,000	1,060,000	1,100,000
	$34,000,000	$39,600,000	$40,800,000	$47,700,000	$48,400,000
Profits from operations	6,000,000	5,400,000	7,200,000	5,300,000	6,600,000
Estimates taxes	$2,400,000	$2,160,000	$2,880,000	$2,120,000	$2,640,000
Net profits	$3,600,000	$3,240,000	$4,320,000	$3,180,000	$3,960,000

(a) Develop a visual aid to present the company's distribution of sales revenues in 1998.
(b) Develop a visual aid that would compare the change in the net profit level with the change in the net sales level.

(c) Develop a visual aid that will present the following expenses (excluding cost of goods sold) over the five-year period: selling and administration expenses and depreciation and interest expenses.

(d) The management of Seal-Tight has the following sales data relating to its two major competitors.

	1998	1999	2000	2001	2002
Metalmax Co.	$35,000,000	$40,000,000	$42,000,000	$45,000,000	$48,000,000
Superior Can Co.	$41,000,000	$43,000,000	$45,000,000	$46,000,000	$48,000,000

You are required to prepare a visual aid to facilitate the comparison of the sales performance of Seal-Tight Company with its major competitors.

9. Most universities and colleges offer a wide variety of computer graphics software for student use in campus microcomputer labs. Investigate the availability of graphics software on your campus. Prepare a report outlining your findings. Be sure to include the following information for each available package:
    (a) Name of package and basic capabilities
    (b) Location(s) of access point(s)
    (c) Times available for use
    (d) Name of contact person(s) for further information
    (e) Any special skills required for use and availability of training if needed
    (f) Access fees, if any
    (g) Hard-copy formats available (e.g., dot matrix printers, laser printers, color plotters, transparencies, slides)
10. Visit your school's library and find examples of each of the graphic illustrations described in this chapter. Look for these in such publications as *Business Week, Fortune, Newsweek,* and *The Wall Street Journal.* Make a copy of each chart and critique it, using the criteria noted in the text. For example, does the pie chart you found exceed the recommended maximum number of divisions? Are the exact percentages displayed? In each case, is the chart appropriate for its intended purpose, or would another type of chart be more informative? Are there any changes you might recommend if the chart were to be used in an oral presentation?

Suggested Additional Readings

For excellent, succinct treatments of how to write better, see Edward P. Bailey, *The Plain English Approach to Business Writing,* rev. ed. (New York: Oxford University Press, 1997).

Raymond Vincent Lesikar and John D. Petit, Jr., *Report Writing for Business,* 10th ed. (Chicago: Irwin, 1998).

Pneena P. Sageev, *Helping Research Write—So Managers Can Understand,* 2nd ed. (Columbus, Ohio: Batelle Press, 1994).

William Strunk, Jr. and E. B. White, *The Elements of Style,* 4th ed. (Boston: Allyn and Bacon, 2000).

William Zinsser, *On Writing Well,* 6th ed. (New York: Harper and Row, 1998).

For excellent discussions of how to make effective oral presentations, see Jan D'Arcy, *Technically Speaking: Proven Ways to Make Your Next Presentation a Success* (New York: AMACOM, 1992).

Rudolph F. Verderber, *The Challenge of Effective Speaking,* 12th ed. (Belmont, Calif.: Wadsworth Publishing Company, 2003).

For discussion of how to develop effective graphics, see Gary T. Henry, *Graphing Data: Techniques for Display and Analysis* (Thousand Oaks, Calif.: Sage Publications, 1994).

Edward R. Tufte, *The Visual Display of Quantitative Information,* 2nd ed. (Cheshire, Conn.: Graphics Press, 2001).

Anders Wallgren, et al., *Graphing Statistics and Data: Creating Better Charts* (Thousand Oaks, Calif.: Sage Publications, 1996).

Leland Wilkinson, *SYGRAPH* (Evanston, Ill.: Systat, Inc., 1990), especially pp. 38–61.

Epilogue

THE SUBJECT OF MARKETING RESEARCH CAN BE APPROACHED in a number of ways. In this book we have used a *project emphasis* as the basis for our discussion. Using this perspective, we focused on how to define a problem and then develop the research needed to answer it. Because we have broken the research process down into components small enough to be discussed in the space of a chapter, it may seem to be a series of disconnected bits and pieces. However, as pointed out in Chapter 3, the research process is anything but a set of disconnected parts. All the steps are highly interrelated, and a decision made at one stage has implications for the others as well. Now that we have closely examined each of the individual components of the research process, in this epilogue we will look once again at how they work together. We will also review some of the key decisions that must be made as the process unfolds.

A research project should not be viewed as an end in itself. Projects arise because managerial problems need solving. The problems themselves may concern the identification of market opportunities, the evaluation of alternative courses of action, or control of marketing operations. Since these activities, in turn, are the essence of the managerial function, research activity can also be viewed from the broader perspective of the firm's marketing intelligence system. Chapter 2, therefore, focused on the nature and present status of the supply of marketing intelligence.

The Research Process Revisited

Earlier in this text, we suggested that marketing research involves the systematic gathering, recording, and analyzing of data about problems relating to the marketing of goods and services. We pointed out that these activities are logically viewed as a sequence of steps called the research process. The stages of the process were identified as follows:

1. Formulate the problem.
2. Determine the research design.
3. Determine the data collection method.
4. Design the data collection forms.
5. Design the sample and collect the data.
6. Analyze and interpret the data.
7. Prepare the research report.

The decision problem logically comes first. It dictates the research problem and design of the project. However, the transition from problem to project is not an automatic one. It is not unusual for a researcher to go from problem specification to tentative research design and then back to problem respecification and modified research design. This back-and-forth process is perfectly natural, and, in fact, reflects one of the researcher's more important roles: to help to define and redefine the problem so that it can be researched, and, more important, answer the decision maker's problem.

While this task might appear to be simple in principle, in practice it can be formidable, as it requires a clear specification of objectives, alternatives, and environmental constraints and influences. The decision maker may not readily provide these to the researcher, who then must dig them out in order to design effective research.

In some cases research may not even be necessary. If the decision maker's views are so strongly held that no amount of information might change them, the research will be wasted. It is up to the researcher to determine this before, rather than after, conducting the research. Often this can be accomplished by asking "what if" questions. What if consumer reaction to the product concept is overwhelmingly favorable? What if it is unfavorable? What if it is only slightly favorable? If the decision maker indicates that he or she will make the same decision in each case, there may be important objectives that have never been explicitly stated. This is a critical finding. Every research project should have one or more objectives, and one should not proceed to the other steps in the process until these can be explicitly stated.

It is also important to ask at this point whether the anticipated benefits of the research are likely to exceed the expected costs. It is a mistake to assume that simply because something might change as a result of the research, the research is warranted. It may be that the likelihood of finding something that might warrant a change in the decision is so remote that the research still will be wasted. Researchers and decision makers alike constantly need to ask: Why should this research be conducted? What could we possibly find out that we do not already know? Will the expected benefits from the research exceed its costs? If the answers indicate research, then the question logically turns to, what kind?

If the problem cannot be formulated as some specific "if-then" conjectural relationships, exploratory research is in order. The primary purpose of exploratory research is gathering some ideas and insights into the phenomenon. The output of an exploratory study will not be answers but more specific questions or statements of tentative relationships. The search for such insights demands a flexible research design. Structured questionnaires and probability sampling plans are not used in exploratory research, since the emphasis is not on gathering summary statistics but on gaining insight into the problem. The personal interview is much more appropriate than the telephone interview, and that in turn is more appropriate than a mail survey, since the unstructured question is most useful in the experience survey. Interviewees should be handpicked because they can provide the wanted information. In such cases, a convenience or judgment sample is very much in order, whereas it would be completely out of place in descriptive or causal research. Focus groups can also be productive.

The researcher may also want to conduct a survey of the literature or an analysis of selected cases. These steps can be advantageous in exploratory research, particularly if the researcher remembers that the goal of exploratory research is to discover ideas and tentative explanations of the phenomenon, and not to fix on one idea as being the sole definitive explanation. The analysis of published data may be particularly productive if it reveals sharp contrasts or other striking features that may help to illuminate the reasons behind the phenomenon under investigation.

If exploratory research has succeeded in generating one or more specific hypotheses to be investigated, the next research step would logically be descriptive or causal research. The design the researcher actually selects depends largely on how convinced he or she is that the tentative explanation is indeed the correct explanation for the phenomenon. Of course, the feasibility and cost of conducting an experiment are also important factors in determining research design. While experiments typically provide more convincing proof of causal relationships, they also usually cost more then descriptive designs. This is one of the reasons why descriptive designs are the most commonly employed type in marketing research.

Whereas exploratory designs are flexible, descriptive designs are rigid. Descriptive designs demand a clear specification of the who, what, when, where, how, and why of the research before data collection begins. They generally employ structured questionnaires or scales because these forms provide advantages in coding and tabulating. In descriptive designs, the emphasis is on generating an accurate picture of the relationships between and among variables. Probability sampling plans are desirable, but if the sample is to be drawn using nonprobabilistic methods, it is important that a quota sample be used. Descriptive studies typically rely heavily on cross-tabulation analysis or other means of investigating the association among variables, such as regression analysis, although the emphasis can also be on the search for differences. The great majority of descriptive studies are cross-sectional, although some do use longitudinal information.

Experiments are the best means we have for making inferences about cause-and-effect relationships, since, if designed properly, they provide the most compelling evidence regarding concomitant variation, time order of occurrence of variables, and elimination of other factors. A key feature of the experiment is that the researcher is able to control who will be exposed to the experimental stimulus (the presumed cause). Depending on the nature of the experiment, subjects may be individual consumers, members of panels, or other elements from the population of interest. Sampling plays little role in experiments other than in determining which objects are going to be assigned to which treatment conditions.

Because the goal is to test a specific relationship, causal designs also demand a clear specification of what is to be measured and how it is to be measured. Structured data collection instruments such as questionnaires and scales are often used. Researchers also rely heavily on the observation method for collecting data, because this method tends to produce more objective and accurate information.

The major objective in analyzing experimental results is to determine if there are differences between those exposed to the experimental stimulus and those not exposed. Although researchers generally use analysis of variance to investigate and measure these differences, other techniques (for example, the t test for the difference in means of independent or correlated samples) are used as well.

The previous paragraphs should indicate how significantly the steps are interrelated and, in particular, how the basic nature of the research design implies a number of things with respect to the structure of the data collection form, design of the sample, collection, and analysis of the data. A decision about appropriate research does not completely determine the latter considerations, of course, but simply suggests their basic nature. The analyst still has to determine their specific format. For example, is the structured questionnaire to be disguised or undisguised? Is the probability sample to be simple, stratified, or cluster? How large a sample is needed? Does the data collection instrument dictate a data-analysis procedure for nominal, ordinal, interval, or ratio data? These questions, too, will be determined in large part by the way the research question is framed, although the ingenuity displayed by the designer of the research will determine their final form. The researcher will have to balance the various sources of error that can arise in the process when determining this final form. In effecting this balance, the researcher must be concerned with assessing and minimizing total error; this often means assuming additional error in one of the parts of the process so that total error can be decreased.

Appendix

TABLE 1 CUMULATIVE STANDARD UNIT NORMAL DISTRIBUTION

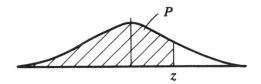

Values of P corresponding to Z for the normal curve. Z is the standard normal variable. The value of P for $-Z$ equals one minus the value of P for $+Z$, (e.g., the P for -1.62 equals $1 - .9474 = .0526$).

Z	.00	.01	.02	.03	.04	.05	.06	.07	.08	.09
.0	.5000	.5040	.5080	.5120	.5160	.5199	.5239	.5279	.5319	.5359
.1	.5398	.5438	.5478	.5517	.5557	.5596	.5636	.5675	.5714	.5753
.2	.5793	.5832	.5871	.5910	.5948	.5987	.6026	.6064	.6103	.6141
.3	.6179	.6217	.6255	.6293	.6331	.6368	.6406	.6443	.6480	.6517
.4	.6554	.6591	.6628	.6664	.6700	.6736	.6772	.6808	.6844	.6879
.5	.6915	.6950	.6985	.7019	.7054	.7088	.7123	.7157	.7190	.7224
.6	.7257	.7291	.7324	.7357	.7389	.7422	.7454	.7486	.7517	.7549
.7	.7580	.7611	.7642	.7673	.7704	.7734	.7764	.7794	.7823	.7852
.8	.7881	.7910	.7939	.7967	.7995	.8023	.8051	.8078	.8106	.8133
.9	.8159	.8186	.8212	.8238	.8264	.8289	.8315	.8340	.8365	.8389
1.0	.8413	.8438	.8461	.8485	.8508	.8531	.8554	.8577	.8599	.8621
1.1	.8643	.8665	.8686	.8708	.8729	.8749	.8770	.8790	.8810	.8830
1.2	.8849	.8869	.8888	.8907	.8925	.8944	.8962	.8980	.8997	.9015
1.3	.9032	.9049	.9066	.9082	.9099	.9115	.9131	.9147	.9162	.9177
1.4	.9192	.9207	.9222	.9236	.9251	.9265	.9279	.9292	.9306	.9319
1.5	.9332	.9345	.9357	.9370	.9382	.9394	.9406	.9418	.9429	.9441
1.6	.9452	.9463	.9474	.9484	.9495	.9505	.9515	.9525	.9535	.9545
1.7	.9554	.9564	.9573	.9582	.9591	.9599	.9608	.9616	.9625	.9633
1.8	.9641	.9649	.9656	.9664	.9671	.9678	.9686	.9693	.9699	.9706
1.9	.9713	.9719	.9726	.9732	.9738	.9744	.9750	.9756	.9761	.9767
2.0	.9772	.9778	.9783	.9788	.9793	.9798	.9803	.9808	.9812	.9817
2.1	.9821	.9826	.9830	.9834	.9838	.9842	.9846	.9850	.9854	.9857
2.2	.9861	.9864	.9868	.9871	.9875	.9878	.9881	.9884	.9887	.9890
2.3	.9893	.9896	.9898	.9901	.9904	.9906	.9909	.9911	.9913	.9916
2.4	.9918	.9920	.9922	.9925	.9927	.9929	.9931	.9932	.9934	.9936
2.5	.9938	.9940	.9941	.9943	.9945	.9946	.9948	.9949	.9951	.9952
2.6	.9953	.9955	.9956	.9957	.9959	.9960	.9961	.9962	.9963	.9964
2.7	.9965	.9966	.9967	.9968	.9969	.9970	.9971	.9972	.9973	.9974
2.8	.9974	.9975	.9976	.9977	.9977	.9978	.9979	.9979	.9980	.9981
2.9	.9981	.9982	.9982	.9983	.9984	.9984	.9985	.9985	.9986	.9986
3.0	.9987	.9987	.9987	.9988	.9988	.9989	.9989	.9989	.9990	.9990
3.1	.9990	.9991	.9991	.9991	.9992	.9992	.9992	.9992	.9993	.9993
3.2	.9993	.9993	.9994	.9994	.9994	.9994	.9994	.9995	.9995	.9995
3.3	.9995	.9995	.9995	.9996	.9996	.9996	.9996	.9996	.9996	.9997
3.4	.9997	.9997	.9997	.9997	.9997	.9997	.9997	.9997	.9997	.9998

Source: Paul E. Green, *Analyzing Multivariate Data* (Chicago: Dryden Press, 1978).

TABLE 2 SELECTED PERCENTILES OF THE χ^2 DISTRIBUTION

Values of χ^2 corresponding to P

ν	$\chi^2_{.005}$	$\chi^2_{.01}$	$\chi^2_{.025}$	$\chi^2_{.05}$	$\chi^2_{.10}$	$\chi^2_{.90}$	$\chi^2_{.95}$	$\chi^2_{.975}$	$\chi^2_{.99}$	$\chi^2_{.995}$
1	.000039	.00016	.00098	.0039	.0158	2.71	3.84	5.02	6.63	7.88
2	.0100	.0201	.0506	.1026	.2107	4.61	5.99	7.38	9.21	10.60
3	.0717	.115	.216	.352	.584	6.25	7.81	9.35	11.34	12.84
4	.207	.297	.484	.711	1.064	7.78	9.49	11.14	13.28	14.86
5	.412	.554	.831	1.15	1.61	9.24	11.07	12.83	15.09	16.75
6	.676	.872	1.24	1.64	2.20	10.64	12.59	14.45	16.81	18.55
7	.989	1.24	1.69	2.17	2.83	12.02	14.07	16.01	18.48	20.28
8	1.34	1.65	2.18	2.73	3.49	13.36	15.51	17.53	20.09	21.96
9	1.73	2.09	2.70	3.33	4.17	14.68	16.92	19.02	21.67	23.59
10	2.16	2.56	3.25	3.94	4.87	15.99	18.31	20.48	23.21	25.19
11	2.60	3.05	3.82	4.57	5.58	17.28	19.68	21.92	24.73	26.76
12	3.07	3.57	4.40	5.23	6.30	18.55	21.03	23.34	26.22	28.30
13	3.57	4.11	5.01	5.89	7.04	19.81	22.36	24.74	27.69	29.82
14	4.07	4.66	5.63	6.57	7.79	21.06	23.68	26.12	29.14	31.32
15	4.60	5.23	6.26	7.26	8.55	22.31	25.00	27.49	30.58	32.80
16	5.14	5.81	6.91	7.96	9.31	23.54	26.30	28.85	32.00	34.27
18	6.26	7.01	8.23	9.39	10.86	25.99	28.87	31.53	34.81	37.16
20	7.43	8.26	9.59	10.85	12.44	28.41	31.41	34.17	37.57	40.00
24	9.89	10.86	12.40	13.85	15.66	33.20	36.42	39.36	42.98	45.56
30	13.79	14.95	16.79	18.49	20.60	40.26	43.77	46.98	50.89	53.67
40	20.71	22.16	24.43	26.51	29.05	51.81	55.76	59.34	63.69	66.77
60	35.53	37.48	40.48	43.19	46.46	74.40	79.08	83.30	88.38	91.95
120	83.85	86.92	91.58	95.70	100.62	140.23	146.57	152.21	158.95	163.64

Source: Adapted with permission from *Introduction to Statistical Analysis,* 2nd ed., by W. J. Dixon and F. J. Massey, Jr., © 1957 McGraw-Hill.

TABLE 3 UPPER PERCENTILES OF THE t DISTRIBUTION

ν $\backslash$ $1-\alpha$	.75	.90	.95	.975	.99	.995	.9995
1	1.000	3.078	6.314	12.706	31.821	63.657	636.619
2	.816	1.886	2.920	4.303	6.965	9.925	31.598
3	.765	1.638	2.353	3.182	4.541	5.841	12.941
4	.741	1.533	2.132	2.776	3.747	4.604	8.610
5	.727	1.476	2.015	2.571	3.365	4.032	6.859
6	.718	1.440	1.943	2.447	3.143	3.707	5.959
7	.711	1.415	1.895	2.365	2.998	3.499	5.405
8	.706	1.397	1.860	2.306	2.896	3.355	5.041
9	.703	1.383	1.833	2.262	2.821	3.250	4.781
10	.700	1.372	1.812	2.228	2.764	3.169	4.587
11	.697	1.363	1.796	2.201	2.718	3.106	4.437
12	.695	1.356	1.782	2.179	2.681	3.055	4.318
13	.694	1.350	1.771	2.160	2.650	3.012	4.221
14	.692	1.345	1.761	2.145	2.624	2.977	4.140
15	.691	1.341	1.753	2.131	2.602	2.947	4.073
16	.690	1.337	1.746	2.120	2.583	2.921	4.015
17	.689	1.333	1.740	2.110	2.567	2.898	3.965
18	.688	1.330	1.734	2.101	2.552	2.878	3.922
19	.688	1.328	1.729	2.093	2.339	2.861	3.883
20	.687	1.325	1.725	2.086	2.528	2.845	3.850
21	.686	1.323	1.721	2.080	2.518	2.831	3.819
22	.686	1.321	1.717	2.074	2.508	2.819	3.792
23	.685	1.319	1.714	2.069	2.500	2.807	3.767
24	.685	1.318	1.711	2.064	2.492	2.797	3.745
25	.684	1.316	1.708	2.060	2.485	2.787	3.725
26	.684	1.315	1.706	2.056	2.479	2.779	3.707
27	.684	1.314	1.703	2.052	2.473	2.771	3.690
28	.683	1.313	1.701	2.048	2.467	2.763	3.674
29	.683	1.311	1.699	2.045	2.462	2.756	3.659
30	.683	1.310	1.697	2.042	2.457	2.750	3.646
40	.681	1.303	1.684	2.021	2.423	2.704	3.551
60	.679	1.296	1.671	2.000	2.390	2.660	3.460
120	.677	1.289	1.658	1.980	2.358	2.617	3.373
∞	.674	1.282	1.645	1.960	2.326	2.576	3.291

ν = degrees of freedom

Source: Taken from Table III of R. A. Fisher and F. Yates: *Statistical Tables for Biological, Agricultural, and Medical Research,* published by Longman Group UK Ltd., London, 1974.

TABLE 4 Selected Percentiles of the *F* Distribution

$F_{.90(v_1, v_2)}$ $\alpha = 0.1$

v_1 = degrees of freedom for numerator

v_2 = degrees of freedom for denominator

v_2 \ v_1	1	2	3	4	5	6	7	8	9	10	12	15	20	24	30	40	60	120	∞
1	39.86	49.50	53.59	55.83	57.24	58.20	58.91	59.44	59.86	60.19	60.71	61.22	61.74	62.00	62.26	62.53	62.79	63.06	63.33
2	8.53	9.00	9.16	9.24	9.29	9.33	9.35	9.37	9.38	9.39	9.41	9.42	9.44	9.45	9.46	9.47	9.47	9.48	9.49
3	5.54	5.46	5.39	5.34	5.31	5.28	5.27	5.25	5.24	5.23	5.22	5.20	5.18	5.18	5.17	5.16	5.15	5.14	5.13
4	4.54	4.32	4.19	4.11	4.05	4.01	3.98	3.95	3.94	3.92	3.90	3.87	3.84	3.83	3.82	3.80	3.79	3.78	3.76
5	4.06	3.78	3.62	3.52	3.45	3.40	3.37	3.34	3.32	3.30	3.27	3.24	3.21	3.19	3.17	3.16	3.14	3.12	3.10
6	3.78	3.46	3.29	3.18	3.11	3.05	3.01	2.98	2.96	2.94	2.90	2.87	2.84	2.82	2.80	2.78	2.76	2.74	2.72
7	3.59	3.26	3.07	2.96	2.88	2.83	2.78	2.75	2.72	2.70	2.67	2.63	2.59	2.58	2.56	2.54	2.51	2.49	2.47
8	3.46	3.11	2.92	2.81	2.73	2.67	2.62	2.59	2.56	2.54	2.50	2.46	2.42	2.40	2.38	2.36	2.34	2.32	2.29
9	3.36	3.01	2.81	2.69	2.61	2.55	2.51	2.47	2.44	2.42	2.38	2.34	2.30	2.28	2.25	2.23	2.21	2.18	2.16
10	3.29	2.92	2.73	2.61	2.52	2.46	2.41	2.38	2.35	2.32	2.28	2.24	2.20	2.18	2.16	2.13	2.11	2.08	2.06
11	3.23	2.86	2.66	2.54	2.45	2.39	2.34	2.30	2.27	2.25	2.21	2.17	2.12	2.10	2.08	2.05	2.03	2.00	1.97
12	3.18	2.81	2.61	2.48	2.39	2.33	2.28	2.24	2.21	2.19	2.15	2.10	2.06	2.04	2.01	1.99	1.96	1.93	1.90
13	3.14	2.76	2.56	2.43	2.35	2.28	2.23	2.20	2.16	2.14	2.10	2.05	2.01	1.98	1.96	1.93	1.90	1.88	1.85
14	3.10	2.73	2.52	2.39	2.31	2.24	2.19	2.15	2.12	2.10	2.05	2.01	1.96	1.94	1.91	1.89	1.86	1.83	1.80
15	3.07	2.70	2.49	2.36	2.27	2.21	2.16	2.12	2.09	2.06	2.02	1.97	1.92	1.90	1.87	1.85	1.82	1.79	1.76
16	3.05	2.67	2.46	2.33	2.24	2.18	2.13	2.09	2.06	2.03	1.99	1.94	1.89	1.87	1.84	1.81	1.78	1.75	1.72
17	3.03	2.64	2.44	2.31	2.22	2.15	2.10	2.06	2.03	2.00	1.96	1.91	1.86	1.84	1.81	1.78	1.75	1.72	1.69
18	3.01	2.62	2.42	2.29	2.20	2.13	2.08	2.04	2.00	1.98	1.93	1.89	1.84	1.81	1.78	1.75	1.72	1.69	1.66
19	2.99	2.61	2.40	2.27	2.18	2.11	2.06	2.02	1.98	1.96	1.91	1.86	1.81	1.79	1.76	1.73	1.70	1.67	1.63
20	2.97	2.59	2.38	2.25	2.16	2.09	2.04	2.00	1.96	1.94	1.89	1.84	1.79	1.77	1.74	1.71	1.68	1.64	1.61
21	2.96	2.57	2.36	2.23	2.14	2.08	2.02	1.98	1.95	1.92	1.87	1.83	1.78	1.75	1.72	1.69	1.66	1.62	1.59
22	2.95	2.56	2.35	2.22	2.13	2.06	2.01	1.97	1.93	1.90	1.86	1.81	1.76	1.73	1.70	1.67	1.64	1.60	1.57
23	2.94	2.55	2.34	2.21	2.11	2.05	1.99	1.95	1.92	1.89	1.84	1.80	1.74	1.72	1.69	1.66	1.62	1.59	1.55
24	2.93	2.54	2.33	2.19	2.10	2.04	1.98	1.94	1.91	1.88	1.83	1.78	1.73	1.70	1.67	1.64	1.61	1.57	1.53
25	2.92	2.53	2.32	2.18	2.09	2.02	1.97	1.93	1.89	1.87	1.82	1.77	1.72	1.69	1.66	1.63	1.59	1.56	1.52
26	2.91	2.52	2.31	2.17	2.08	2.01	1.96	1.92	1.88	1.86	1.81	1.76	1.71	1.68	1.65	1.61	1.58	1.54	1.50
27	2.90	2.51	2.30	2.17	2.07	2.00	1.95	1.91	1.87	1.85	1.80	1.75	1.70	1.67	1.64	1.60	1.57	1.53	1.49
28	2.89	2.50	2.29	2.16	2.06	2.00	1.94	1.90	1.87	1.84	1.79	1.74	1.69	1.66	1.63	1.59	1.56	1.52	1.48
29	2.89	2.50	2.28	2.15	2.06	1.99	1.93	1.89	1.86	1.83	1.78	1.73	1.68	1.65	1.62	1.58	1.55	1.51	1.47
30	2.88	2.49	2.28	2.14	2.05	1.98	1.93	1.88	1.85	1.82	1.77	1.72	1.67	1.64	1.61	1.57	1.54	1.50	1.46
40	2.84	2.44	2.23	2.09	2.00	1.93	1.87	1.83	1.79	1.76	1.71	1.66	1.61	1.57	1.54	1.51	1.47	1.42	1.38
60	2.79	2.39	2.18	2.04	1.95	1.87	1.82	1.77	1.74	1.71	1.66	1.60	1.54	1.51	1.48	1.44	1.40	1.35	1.29
120	2.75	2.35	2.13	1.99	1.90	1.82	1.77	1.72	1.68	1.65	1.60	1.55	1.48	1.45	1.41	1.37	1.32	1.26	1.19
∞	2.71	2.30	2.08	1.94	1.85	1.77	1.72	1.67	1.63	1.60	1.55	1.49	1.42	1.38	1.34	1.30	1.24	1.17	1.00

continued

TABLE 4 SELECTED PERCENTILES OF THE *F* DISTRIBUTION (continued)

$F_{.95}(v_1, v_2)$ $\alpha = 0.05$

v_1 = degrees of freedom for numerator

v_2 \ v_1	1	2	3	4	5	6	7	8	9	10	12	15	20	24	30	40	60	120	∞
1	161.4	199.5	215.7	224.6	230.2	234.0	236.8	238.9	240.5	241.9	243.9	245.9	248.0	249.1	250.1	251.1	252.2	253.3	254.3
2	18.51	19.00	19.16	19.25	19.30	19.33	19.35	19.37	19.38	19.40	19.41	19.43	19.45	19.45	19.46	19.47	19.48	19.49	19.50
3	10.13	9.55	9.28	9.12	9.01	8.94	8.89	8.85	8.81	8.79	8.74	8.70	8.66	8.64	8.62	8.59	8.57	8.55	8.53
4	7.71	6.94	6.59	6.39	6.26	6.16	6.09	6.04	6.00	5.96	5.91	5.86	5.80	5.77	5.75	5.72	5.69	5.66	5.63
5	6.61	5.79	5.41	5.19	5.05	4.95	4.88	4.82	4.77	4.74	4.68	4.62	4.56	4.53	4.50	4.46	4.43	4.40	4.36
6	5.99	5.14	4.76	4.53	4.39	4.28	4.21	4.15	4.10	4.06	4.00	3.94	3.87	3.84	3.81	3.77	3.74	3.70	3.67
7	5.59	4.74	4.35	4.12	3.97	3.87	3.79	3.73	3.68	3.64	3.57	3.51	3.44	3.41	3.38	3.34	3.30	3.27	3.23
8	5.32	4.46	4.07	3.84	3.69	3.58	3.50	3.44	3.39	3.35	3.28	3.22	3.15	3.12	3.08	3.04	3.01	2.97	2.93
9	5.12	4.26	3.86	3.63	3.48	3.37	3.29	3.23	3.18	3.14	3.07	3.01	2.94	2.90	2.86	2.83	2.79	2.75	2.71
10	4.96	4.10	3.71	3.48	3.33	3.22	3.14	3.07	3.02	2.98	2.91	2.85	2.77	2.74	2.70	2.66	2.62	2.58	2.54
11	4.84	3.98	3.59	3.36	3.20	3.09	3.01	2.95	2.90	2.85	2.79	2.72	2.65	2.61	2.57	2.53	2.49	2.45	2.40
12	4.75	3.89	3.49	3.26	3.11	3.00	2.91	2.85	2.80	2.75	2.69	2.62	2.54	2.51	2.47	2.43	2.38	2.34	2.30
13	4.67	3.81	3.41	3.18	3.03	2.92	2.83	2.77	2.71	2.67	2.60	2.53	2.46	2.42	2.38	2.34	2.30	2.25	2.21
14	4.60	3.74	3.34	3.11	2.96	2.85	2.76	2.70	2.65	2.60	2.53	2.46	2.39	2.35	2.31	2.27	2.22	2.18	2.13
15	4.54	3.68	3.29	3.06	2.90	2.79	2.71	2.64	2.59	2.54	2.48	2.40	2.33	2.29	2.25	2.20	2.16	2.11	2.07
16	4.49	3.63	3.24	3.01	2.85	2.74	2.66	2.59	2.54	2.49	2.42	2.35	2.28	2.24	2.19	2.15	2.11	2.06	2.01
17	4.45	3.59	3.20	2.96	2.81	2.70	2.61	2.55	2.49	2.45	2.38	2.31	2.23	2.19	2.15	2.10	2.06	2.01	1.96
18	4.41	3.55	3.16	2.93	2.77	2.66	2.58	2.51	2.46	2.41	2.34	2.27	2.19	2.15	2.11	2.06	2.02	1.97	1.92
19	4.38	3.52	3.13	2.90	2.74	2.63	2.54	2.48	2.42	2.38	2.31	2.23	2.16	2.11	2.07	2.03	1.98	1.93	1.88
20	4.35	3.49	3.10	2.87	2.71	2.60	2.51	2.45	2.39	2.35	2.28	2.20	2.12	2.08	2.04	1.99	1.95	1.90	1.84
21	4.32	3.47	3.07	2.84	2.68	2.57	2.49	2.42	2.37	2.32	2.25	2.18	2.10	2.05	2.01	1.96	1.92	1.87	1.81
22	4.30	3.44	3.05	2.82	2.66	2.55	2.46	2.40	2.34	2.30	2.23	2.15	2.07	2.03	1.98	1.94	1.89	1.84	1.78
23	4.28	3.42	3.03	2.80	2.64	2.53	2.44	2.37	2.32	2.27	2.20	2.13	2.05	2.01	1.96	1.91	1.86	1.81	1.76
24	4.26	3.40	3.01	2.78	2.62	2.51	2.42	2.36	2.30	2.25	2.18	2.11	2.03	1.98	1.94	1.89	1.84	1.79	1.73
25	4.24	3.39	2.99	2.76	2.60	2.49	2.40	2.34	2.28	2.24	2.16	2.09	2.01	1.96	1.92	1.87	1.82	1.77	1.71
26	4.23	3.37	2.98	2.74	2.59	2.47	2.39	2.32	2.27	2.22	2.15	2.07	1.99	1.95	1.90	1.85	1.80	1.75	1.69
27	4.21	3.35	2.96	2.73	2.57	2.46	2.37	2.31	2.25	2.20	2.13	2.06	1.97	1.93	1.88	1.84	1.79	1.73	1.67
28	4.20	3.34	2.95	2.71	2.56	2.45	2.36	2.29	2.24	2.19	2.12	2.04	1.96	1.91	1.87	1.82	1.77	1.71	1.65
29	4.18	3.33	2.93	2.70	2.55	2.43	2.35	2.28	2.22	2.18	2.10	2.03	1.94	1.90	1.85	1.81	1.75	1.70	1.64
30	4.17	3.32	2.92	2.69	2.53	2.42	2.33	2.27	2.21	2.16	2.09	2.01	1.93	1.89	1.84	1.79	1.74	1.68	1.62
40	4.08	3.23	2.84	2.61	2.45	2.34	2.25	2.18	2.12	2.08	2.00	1.92	1.84	1.79	1.74	1.69	1.64	1.58	1.51
60	4.00	3.15	2.76	2.53	2.37	2.25	2.17	2.10	2.04	1.99	1.92	1.84	1.75	1.70	1.65	1.59	1.53	1.47	1.39
120	3.92	3.07	2.68	2.45	2.29	2.17	2.09	2.02	1.96	1.91	1.83	1.75	1.66	1.61	1.55	1.50	1.43	1.35	1.25
∞	3.84	3.00	2.60	2.37	2.21	2.10	2.01	1.94	1.88	1.83	1.75	1.67	1.57	1.52	1.46	1.39	1.32	1.22	1.00

v_2 = degrees of freedom for denominator

continued

TABLE 4 Selected Percentiles of the *F* Distribution (continued)

$F_{.975}(\nu_1, \nu_2)$ α = 0.025

ν₁ = degrees of freedom for numerator

ν₂ \ ν₁	1	2	3	4	5	6	7	8	9	10	12	15	20	24	30	40	60	120	∞
1	647.8	799.5	864.2	899.6	921.8	937.1	948.2	956.7	963.3	968.6	976.7	984.9	993.1	997.2	1001	1006	1010	1014	1018
2	38.51	39.00	39.17	39.25	39.30	39.33	39.36	39.37	39.39	39.40	39.41	39.43	39.45	39.46	39.46	39.47	39.48	39.49	39.50
3	17.44	16.04	15.44	15.10	14.88	14.73	14.62	14.54	14.47	14.42	14.34	14.25	14.17	14.12	14.08	14.04	13.99	13.95	13.90
4	12.22	10.65	9.98	9.60	9.36	9.20	9.07	8.98	8.90	8.84	8.75	8.66	8.56	8.51	8.46	8.41	8.36	8.31	8.26
5	10.01	8.43	7.76	7.39	7.15	6.98	6.85	6.76	6.68	6.62	6.52	6.43	6.33	6.28	6.23	6.18	6.12	6.07	6.02
6	8.81	7.26	6.60	6.23	5.99	5.82	5.70	5.60	5.52	5.46	5.37	5.27	5.17	5.12	5.07	5.01	4.96	4.90	4.85
7	8.07	6.54	5.89	5.52	5.29	5.12	4.99	4.90	4.82	4.76	4.67	4.57	4.47	4.42	4.36	4.31	4.25	4.20	4.14
8	7.57	6.06	5.42	5.05	4.82	4.65	4.53	4.43	4.36	4.30	4.20	4.10	4.00	3.95	3.89	3.84	3.78	3.73	3.67
9	7.21	5.71	5.08	4.72	4.48	4.32	4.20	4.10	4.03	3.96	3.87	3.77	3.67	3.61	3.56	3.51	3.45	3.39	3.33
10	6.94	5.46	4.83	4.47	4.24	4.07	3.95	3.85	3.78	3.72	3.62	3.52	3.42	3.37	3.31	3.26	3.20	3.14	3.08
11	6.72	5.26	4.63	4.28	4.04	3.88	3.76	3.66	3.59	3.53	3.43	3.33	3.23	3.17	3.12	3.06	3.00	2.94	2.88
12	6.55	5.10	4.47	4.12	3.89	3.73	3.61	3.51	3.44	3.37	3.28	3.18	3.07	3.02	2.96	2.91	2.85	2.79	2.72
13	6.41	4.97	4.35	4.00	3.77	3.60	3.48	3.39	3.31	3.25	3.15	3.05	2.95	2.89	2.84	2.78	2.72	2.66	2.60
14	6.30	4.86	4.24	3.89	3.66	3.50	3.38	3.29	3.21	3.15	3.05	2.95	2.84	2.79	2.73	2.67	2.61	2.55	2.49
15	6.20	4.77	4.15	3.80	3.58	3.41	3.29	3.20	3.12	3.06	2.96	2.86	2.76	2.70	2.64	2.59	2.52	2.46	2.40
16	6.12	4.69	4.08	3.73	3.50	3.34	3.22	3.12	3.05	2.99	2.89	2.79	2.68	2.63	2.57	2.51	2.45	2.38	2.32
17	6.04	4.62	4.01	3.66	3.44	3.28	3.16	3.06	2.98	2.92	2.82	2.72	2.62	2.56	2.50	2.44	2.38	2.32	2.25
18	5.98	4.56	3.95	3.61	3.38	3.22	3.10	3.01	2.93	2.87	2.77	2.67	2.56	2.50	2.44	2.38	2.32	2.26	2.19
19	5.92	4.51	3.90	3.56	3.33	3.17	3.05	2.96	2.88	2.82	2.72	2.62	2.51	2.45	2.39	2.33	2.27	2.20	2.13
20	5.87	4.46	3.86	3.51	3.29	3.13	3.01	2.91	2.84	2.77	2.68	2.57	2.46	2.41	2.35	2.29	2.22	2.16	2.09
21	5.83	4.42	3.82	3.48	3.25	3.09	2.97	2.87	2.80	2.73	2.64	2.53	2.42	2.37	2.31	2.25	2.18	2.11	2.04
22	5.79	4.38	3.78	3.44	3.22	3.05	2.93	2.84	2.76	2.70	2.60	2.50	2.39	2.33	2.27	2.21	2.14	2.08	2.00
23	5.75	4.35	3.75	3.41	3.18	3.02	2.90	2.81	2.73	2.67	2.57	2.47	2.36	2.30	2.24	2.18	2.11	2.04	1.97
24	5.72	4.32	3.72	3.38	3.15	2.99	2.87	2.78	2.70	2.64	2.54	2.44	2.33	2.27	2.21	2.15	2.08	2.01	1.94
25	5.69	4.29	3.69	3.35	3.13	2.97	2.85	2.75	2.68	2.61	2.51	2.41	2.30	2.24	2.18	2.12	2.05	1.98	1.91
26	5.66	4.27	3.67	3.33	3.10	2.94	2.82	2.73	2.65	2.59	2.49	2.39	2.28	2.22	2.16	2.09	2.03	1.95	1.88
27	5.63	4.24	3.65	3.31	3.08	2.92	2.80	2.71	2.63	2.57	2.47	2.36	2.25	2.19	2.13	2.07	2.00	1.93	1.85
28	5.61	4.22	3.63	3.29	3.06	2.90	2.78	2.69	2.61	2.55	2.45	2.34	2.23	2.17	2.11	2.05	1.98	1.91	1.83
29	5.59	4.20	3.61	3.27	3.04	2.88	2.76	2.67	2.59	2.53	2.43	2.32	2.21	2.15	2.09	2.03	1.96	1.89	1.81
30	5.57	4.18	3.59	3.25	3.03	2.87	2.75	2.65	2.57	2.51	2.41	2.31	2.20	2.14	2.07	2.01	1.94	1.87	1.79
40	5.42	4.05	3.46	3.13	2.90	2.74	2.62	2.53	2.45	2.39	2.29	2.18	2.07	2.01	1.94	1.88	1.80	1.72	1.64
60	5.29	3.93	3.34	3.01	2.79	2.63	2.51	2.41	2.33	2.27	2.17	2.06	1.94	1.88	1.82	1.74	1.67	1.58	1.48
120	5.15	3.80	3.23	2.89	2.67	2.52	2.39	2.30	2.22	2.16	2.05	1.94	1.82	1.76	1.69	1.61	1.53	1.43	1.31
∞	5.02	3.69	3.12	2.79	2.57	2.41	2.29	2.19	2.11	2.05	1.94	1.83	1.71	1.64	1.57	1.48	1.39	1.27	1.00

ν₂ = degrees of freedom for denominator

continued

TABLE 4 SELECTED PERCENTILES OF THE *F* DISTRIBUTION (continued)

$F_{.99}(\nu_1, \nu_2)$ $\alpha = 0.01$

ν_1 = degrees of freedom for numerator

ν_2	1	2	3	4	5	6	7	8	9	10	12	15	20	24	30	40	60	120	∞
1	4052	4999.5	5403	5625	5764	5859	5928	5982	6022	6056	6106	6157	6209	6235	6261	6287	6313	6339	6366
2	98.50	99.00	99.17	99.25	99.30	99.33	99.36	99.37	99.39	99.40	99.42	99.43	99.45	99.46	99.47	99.47	99.48	99.49	99.50
3	34.12	30.82	29.46	28.71	28.24	27.91	27.67	27.49	27.35	27.23	27.05	26.87	26.69	26.60	26.50	26.41	26.32	26.22	26.13
4	21.20	18.00	16.69	15.98	15.52	15.21	14.98	14.80	14.66	14.55	14.37	14.20	14.02	13.93	13.84	13.75	13.65	13.56	13.46
5	16.26	13.27	12.06	11.39	10.97	10.67	10.46	10.29	10.16	10.05	9.89	9.72	9.55	9.47	9.38	9.29	9.20	9.11	9.02
6	13.75	10.92	9.78	9.15	8.75	8.47	8.26	8.10	7.98	7.87	7.72	7.56	7.40	7.31	7.23	7.14	7.06	6.97	6.88
7	12.25	9.55	8.45	7.85	7.46	7.19	6.99	6.84	6.72	6.62	6.47	6.31	6.16	6.07	5.99	5.91	5.82	5.74	5.65
8	11.26	8.65	7.59	7.01	6.63	6.37	6.18	6.03	5.91	5.81	5.67	5.52	5.36	5.28	5.20	5.12	5.03	4.95	4.86
9	10.56	8.02	6.99	6.42	6.06	5.80	5.61	5.47	5.35	5.26	5.11	4.96	4.81	4.73	4.65	4.57	4.48	4.40	4.31
10	10.04	7.56	6.55	5.99	5.64	5.39	5.20	5.06	4.94	4.85	4.71	4.56	4.41	4.33	4.25	4.17	4.08	4.00	3.91
11	9.65	7.21	6.22	5.67	5.32	5.07	4.89	4.74	4.63	4.54	4.40	4.25	4.10	4.02	3.94	3.86	3.78	3.69	3.60
12	9.33	6.93	5.95	5.41	5.06	4.82	4.64	4.50	4.39	4.30	4.16	4.01	3.86	3.78	3.70	3.62	3.54	3.45	3.36
13	9.07	6.70	5.74	5.21	4.86	4.62	4.44	4.30	4.19	4.10	3.96	3.82	3.66	3.59	3.51	3.43	3.34	3.25	3.17
14	8.86	6.51	5.56	5.04	4.69	4.46	4.28	4.14	4.03	3.94	3.80	3.66	3.51	3.43	3.35	3.27	3.18	3.09	3.00
15	8.68	6.36	5.42	4.89	4.56	4.32	4.14	4.00	3.89	3.80	3.67	3.52	3.37	3.29	3.21	3.13	3.05	2.96	2.87
16	8.53	6.23	5.29	4.77	4.44	4.20	4.03	3.89	3.78	3.69	3.55	3.41	3.26	3.18	3.10	3.02	2.93	2.84	2.75
17	8.40	6.11	5.18	4.67	4.34	4.10	3.93	3.79	3.68	3.59	3.46	3.31	3.16	3.08	3.00	2.92	2.83	2.75	2.65
18	8.29	6.01	5.09	4.58	4.25	4.01	3.84	3.71	3.60	3.51	3.37	3.23	3.08	3.00	2.92	2.84	2.75	2.66	2.57
19	8.18	5.93	5.01	4.50	4.17	3.94	3.77	3.63	3.52	3.43	3.30	3.15	3.00	2.92	2.84	2.76	2.67	2.58	2.49
20	8.10	5.85	4.94	4.43	4.10	3.87	3.70	3.56	3.46	3.37	3.23	3.09	2.94	2.86	2.78	2.69	2.61	2.52	2.42
21	8.02	5.78	4.87	4.37	4.04	3.81	3.64	3.51	3.40	3.31	3.17	3.03	2.88	2.80	2.72	2.64	2.55	2.46	2.36
22	7.95	5.72	4.82	4.31	3.99	3.76	3.59	3.45	3.35	3.26	3.12	2.98	2.83	2.75	2.67	2.58	2.50	2.40	2.31
23	7.88	5.66	4.76	4.26	3.94	3.71	3.54	3.41	3.30	3.21	3.07	2.93	2.78	2.70	2.62	2.54	2.45	2.35	2.26
24	7.82	5.61	4.72	4.22	3.90	3.67	3.50	3.36	3.26	3.17	3.03	2.89	2.74	2.66	2.58	2.49	2.40	2.31	2.21
25	7.77	5.57	4.68	4.18	3.85	3.63	3.46	3.32	3.22	3.13	2.99	2.85	2.70	2.62	2.54	2.45	2.36	2.27	2.17
26	7.72	5.53	4.64	4.14	3.82	3.59	3.42	3.29	3.18	3.09	2.96	2.81	2.66	2.58	2.50	2.42	2.33	2.23	2.13
27	7.68	5.49	4.60	4.11	3.78	3.56	3.39	3.26	3.15	3.06	2.93	2.78	2.63	2.55	2.47	2.38	2.29	2.20	2.10
28	7.64	5.45	4.57	4.07	3.75	3.53	3.36	3.23	3.12	3.03	2.90	2.75	2.60	2.52	2.44	2.35	2.26	2.17	2.06
29	7.60	5.42	4.54	4.04	3.73	3.50	3.33	3.20	3.09	3.00	2.87	2.73	2.57	2.49	2.41	2.33	2.23	2.14	2.03
30	7.56	5.39	4.51	4.02	3.70	3.47	3.30	3.17	3.07	2.98	2.84	2.70	2.55	2.47	2.39	2.30	2.21	2.11	2.01
40	7.31	5.18	4.31	3.83	3.51	3.29	3.12	2.99	2.89	2.80	2.66	2.52	2.37	2.29	2.20	2.11	2.02	1.92	1.80
60	7.08	4.98	4.13	3.65	3.34	3.12	2.95	2.82	2.72	2.63	2.50	2.35	2.20	2.12	2.03	1.94	1.84	1.73	1.60
120	6.85	4.79	3.95	3.48	3.17	2.96	2.79	2.66	2.56	2.47	2.34	2.19	2.03	1.95	1.86	1.76	1.66	1.53	1.38
∞	6.63	4.61	3.78	3.32	3.02	2.80	2.64	2.51	2.41	2.32	2.18	2.04	1.88	1.79	1.70	1.59	1.47	1.32	1.00

ν_2 = degrees of freedom for denominator

Source: Adapted with permission from *Biometrika Tables for Statisticians,* Vol. 1, 2nd ed., edited by E. S. Pearson and H. O. Hartley, Cambridge University Press, 1958.

Endnotes

Chapter 1

1. For more information on these examples, see Patricia Sellers, "Birth of a Rib Joint," *Fortune* (April 29, 2002), pp. 187–189; Brian O'Keefe, "Meet Your New Neighborhood Grocer," *Fortune* (May 13, 2002), pp. 93–96; Patricia Leigh Brown, "Cinematography and Chilling Out? That's Scouting," *New York Times* (downloaded from http://www.nytimes.com, May 13, 2002); Joshua Macht, "The New Market Research," *Inc.* (July 1998), pp. 87–94; and Julian Lee, "Can Levi's Ever Be Cool Again?" *Marketing* (downloaded from http://www.marketing.haynet.com, June 3, 1999).

2. Gilbert A. Churchill, Jr., and J. Paul Peter, *Marketing: Creating Value for Customers,* 2nd ed. (Burr Ridge, Ill.: Irwin/McGraw-Hill, 1998), p. 15.

3. Peter D. Bennett, ed., *Dictionary of Marketing Terms,* 2nd ed. (Chicago: American Marketing Association, 1995), p. 169.

4. "How McDonald's Conquered the UK," *Marketing* (downloaded from http://www.marketing.haynet.com, June 3, 1999).

5. Lawrence C. Lockley, "History and Development of Marketing Research," Section 1, p. 4, in Robert Ferber, ed., *Handbook of Marketing Research,* Copyright © 1974 by McGraw-Hill, 1974. Used with permission of McGraw-Hill Book Company.

6. For a detailed treatment of the development of marketing research, see Robert Bartels, *The Development of Marketing Thought* (Homewood, Ill.: Richard D. Irwin, 1962), pp. 106–124, or Jack J. Honomichl, *Marketing Research People: Their Behind-the-Scenes Stories* (Chicago: Crain Books, 1984), especially Part II on pages 95–184.

7. Downloaded from the Dentsu Web site (http://www.dentsu.com), July 2, 2002.

8. Downloaded from the McCann-Erickson WorldGroup Web site (http://www.mccann.com), July 2, 2002.

9. Jack Honomichl, "Honomichl Top 50," *Marketing News* (June 10, 2002), p. H4.

10. Jack Honomichl, "Honomichl Global Top 25," *Marketing News* (August 19, 2002), p. H3.

11. "Economists and Market and Survey Researchers," *Occupational Outlook Handbook.* 2002–2003 edition (Washington, D.C.: Bureau of Labor Statistics), pp. 239–241, downloaded from http://www.bls.gov/oco/home.htm, July 2, 2002).

Chapter 2

1. Robert J. Williams, "Marketing Intelligence Systems: A DEW Line for Marketing Men," *Business Management* (January 1966), p. 32.

2. Peter D. Bennett, ed., *Dictionary of Marketing Terms,* 2nd ed. (Chicago: American Marketing Association, 1995), p. 167.

3. Ibid., p. 77.

4. Nielsen//Net Ratings, "March 2002 Global Internet Index Average Usage" (downloaded from http://www.netratings.com on June 7, 2002).

5. Statistics on size of Internet downloaded from the Online Computer Library Center, Inc. (http://wcp.oclc.org), July 10, 2002.

6. Eldon Y. Li, Raymond McLeod Jr., and John C. Rogers, "Marketing Information Systems in *Fortune* 500 Companies: A Longitudinal Analysis of 1980, 1990, and 2000," *Information & Management* (38, 2001), pp. 307–322.

7. Jeremy Kahn, "Wal-Mart Goes Shopping in Europe," *Fortune* (June 7, 1999), pp. 105–106; Wal-Mart Web site (http://www.walmartstores.com, downloaded June 27, 2002).

8. Information downloaded from Intelliseek Web site (http://www.intelliseek.com), June 27, 2002, and from the Invisible Web site (http://www.invisibleweb.com), July 11, 2002; "Lycos Aligns with IntelliSeek to Reveal the Invisible Web Catalog—The Largest Collection of Searchable Databases" (Lycos press release, downloaded from http://biz.yahoo.com on June 7, 1999).

9. Laura Mazur, "Laxity May Lead to New Laws on Internet Privacy," *Marketing* (June 13, 2002), downloaded via ProQuest Direct, June 27, 2002. See also Daniel Tynan, "How to Take Back your Privacy," *PC World* (June 2002), downloaded via ProQuest Direct, June 28, 2002.

10. Thea Singer, "Sharer Beware," *Inc. Technology* (March 16, 1999), pp. 38–40.

11. John D. C. Little and Michael N. Cassettari, *Decision Support Systems for Marketing Managers* (New York: American Management Association, 1984), p. 14. See also Peter S.H. Leeflang and Dick R. Wittink, "Marketing Decisions Based on Econometric Models," *Marketing Research* (Spring 2002), pp. 19–22.

12. Little and Cassettari, p. 15.

13. James Studnicki, Frank V. Murphy, Donna Malvey, Robert A. Costello, Stephen L. Luther, and Dennis C. Werner, "Toward a Population Health Delivery System: First Steps in Performance Measurement," *Health Care Management Review* (Winter 2002), pp. 76–95.

14. For more information, see Berend Wierenga and Gerrit H. Van Bruggen, "Developing a Customized Decision-Support System for Brand Managers," *Interfaces* (May–June 2001), pp. S128–S145; S. Kanungo, S. Sharma, and P.K. Jain, "Evaluation of a Decision Support System for Credit Management Decisions," *Decision Support Systems* (30, 2001), pp. 419–436; R. Jeffrey Thieme, Michael Song, and Roger J. Calantone, "Artificial Neural Network Decision Support Systems for New Product Development Project Selection," *Journal of Marketing Research* (November 2000), pp. 499–507; and Jehoshua Eliashberg, Jedid-Jah Jonker, Mohanbir S. Sawhney, and Berend Wierenga, "MOVIEMOD: An Implementable Decision-Support System for Prerelease Market Evaluation of Motion Pictures," *Marketing Science* (Summer 2000), pp. 226–243.

15. For a general discussion of the history of expert systems, see David Brown, "'Intelligent' Systems?" *Information World Review* (November 2001), downloaded via ProQuest Direct, July 11, 2002.

16. Laurie Hays, "Using Computers to Decide Who Might Buy a Gas Grill," *The Wall Street Journal* (August 16, 1994), pp. B1, B6. See also John Verity, "Silicon and Software that Mine for Gold," *Business Week* (September 5, 1994), p. 62.

17. Tom Field, "Great Expectations," *CIO Magazine* (May 1, 1999, downloaded from the CIO Web site, http://www.cio.com, June 7, 1999).

18. Thomas A. Stewart, "Telling Tales at BP Amoco," *Fortune* (June 7, 1999), pp. 220, 222, 224.

19. Stowe Boyd, "The Role of the Chief Knowledge Officer," *Knowledge Management Review* (September/October 1998, downloaded from the Modus Operandi Web site, http://www.modusoperandi.com, June 7, 1999).

Chapter 3

1. Walter B. Wentz, *Marketing Research: Management and Methods* (New York: Harper and Row, 1972), pp. 19–24. For insights into Frito-Lays program strategy for marketing research, see Robert Johnson, "In the Chips: At Frito-Lay, the Consumer Is an Obsession," *The Wall Street Journal,* (March 22, 1991), pp. B1–B2; Robert Frank, "Frito-Lay Devours Snack-Food Business," *The Wall Street Journal,* (October 27, 1995), pp. B1, B4; Chad Rubel, "Research Results Must Justify Brand Spending," *Marketing News* 30 (February 26, 1996), p. 12; "Anatomy of a Success Story," *Progressive Grocer* (July 1997), pp. 16–18.

2. Joseph R. Hochstim, "Practical Uses of Sampling Surveys in the Field of Labor Relations," *Proceedings of the Conference on Business Application of Statistical Sampling Methods* (Monticello, Ill.: The Bureau of Business Management, University of Illinois, 1950), pp. 181–182. As should be obvious from the example, researchers need to access both constituencies (dogs *and* dogs' purchasing agents) when assessing the appeal of a product like dog food. See Nancy J. Church, "Get the Dog's Opinion When Researching Dog Food," *Marketing News* 22 (August 29, 1988), p. 41, for suggestions on how to go about this.

3. Robert A. Cooke, *Ethics in Business: A Perspective* (Chicago: Arthur Andersen, 1988), p. 2. See also Lawrence B. Chonko, *Ethical Decision Making in Marketing* (Thousand Oaks, Calif.: Sage Publications, 1995).

Chapter 4

1. Frederick Allen, *Secret Formula* (New York: HarperCollins Publishers, Inc., 1994).

2. Ibid, pg. 401.

3. Jeff Ousborne, "The 25 Dumbest Business Decisions of All Time," *MBA Jungle* 1 (May 2001), pp. 64–70.

4. Wayne A. Lemburg, "Past AMA President Hardin, Head of Market Facts, Looks Back at the Early Days of Marketing Research," *Marketing News* 20 (December 19, 1986), p. 9.

5. Cliff Edwards, "A Look at the Century's Hyped Products," *Chicago Tribune* (June 13, 1999), sec. 5, p. 12.

6. Ann Marie Kerwin, "'*Fortune*' Eyes Its Own Spinoff on Technology," *Advertising Age* (June 28, 1999), p. 2.

7. Andrew Kupfer, "Why the Bounce at Rubbermaid," *Fortune* 115 (April 13, 1987), pp. 77–78; Zachary Schiller, "At Rubbermaid, Little Things Mean a Lot," *Business Week* (November 11, 1991), p. 126; Marshall Loeb, "How to Grow a New Product Every Day," *Fortune* 130 (November 14, 1994), pp. 269–270; "Rubbermaid—Another Day, Another Product," *Chief Executive* (July/August 1995), pp. 12–13; Lee Smith, "Rubbermaid Goes Thump," *Fortune* 132 (October 2, 1995), pp. 90–104.

8. Alan R. Andreasen, "'Backward' Market Research," *Harvard Business Review* 63 (May/June 1985), p. 176.

9. Russell L. Ackoff, *Scientific Method* (New York: John Wiley, 1962), p. 71.

10. Andreasen, "'Backward' Market Research," p. 180.

11. Gordon Fairclough, "Campbell's Recipe for Higher Profit: Reheat Soup Sales," *The Wall Street Journal* (May 19, 1999), p. B6.

12. Paul W. Conner, "'Research Request Step' Can Enhance Use of Results," *Marketing News* 19 (January 4, 1985), p. 41; Charles D. Cowan, "Write Your Questions Down before You Pay for Your Research," *Marketing Research: A Magazine of Management & Applications* 4 (March 1992), pp. 65–68.

13. Lawrence H. Blagman, "Managing Information," in Presentations from the 9th Annual Marketing Research Conference (Chicago: American Marketing Association, 1988), p. 134.

14. J. Paul Peter and James H. Donnelly, *A Preface to Marketing Management,* 9th ed. (Burr-Ridge, Ill.: McGraw-Hill Higher Education, 2003), pp. 30–31.

15. The American Marketing Association, Marketing Research Association, Council for Marketing and Opinion Research, American Association for Public Opinion Research, and the Council of American Survey Research Organizations each offer ethical guidelines for researchers.

16. Kevin J. Clancy and Peter C. Krieg, "Surviving Death Wish Research," *Marketing Research: A Magazine of Management & Applications* 13 (Winter 2001), p. 9.

17. William I. Zangwill, "When Customer Research is a Lousy Idea," *The Wall Street Journal* (March 8, 1993), p. A12. See also Justin Martin, "Ignore Your Customer," *Fortune* (May 1, 1995), pp. 121–126.

18. For a list of the criteria used by Dow Brands, Inc., see Robert M. Smith, "Research Provider Partnerships: Do They Consider the Client's Real Needs?" *Marketing Research: A Magazine of Management & Applications* 4 (June 1992), pp. 24–26.

19. For a discussion of the extent of partnering as well as the factors that are most important in successful partnering relationships, see Paul Boughton, "Marketing Research Partnerships: A Strategy for the '90s," *Marketing Research: A Magazine of Management & Applications* 4 (December 1992), pp. 8–12.

Chapter 5

1. Claire Selltiz, Lawrence S. Wrightsman, and Stuart W. Cook, *Research Methods in Social Relations,* 3rd ed. (New York: Holt, Rinehart and Winston, 1976), pp. 90–91. See also Fred N. Kerlinger, *Foundations of Behavioral Research,* 4th ed. (New York: Holt, Rinehart and Winston, 1999). David A. deVaus, *Research Design in Social Research* (Thousand Oaks, CA.: Sage Publications, 2000).

2. The basic purposes are those suggested by Selltiz, Wrightsman, and Cook, *Research Methods.*

3. See Kerlinger, *Foundations of Behavioral Research,* for a discussion of the criteria of good hypotheses and of the value of hypotheses in guiding research.

4. Selltiz, Wrightsman, and Cook, *Research Methods,* p. 91.

5. Steven P. Galante, "More Firms Quiz Customers for Clues About Competi-

tion," *The Wall Street Journal* (March 3, 1986), p. 17. See also Thomas L'egare, "Acting on Customer Feedback," *Marketing Research: A Magazine of Management & Applications* 8 (Spring 1996), pp. 46–51.

6. Bob Deierlein, "A New Louisville Slugger," *Beverage World* 114 (June 1995), pp. 116–117.

7. Selltiz, Wrightsman, and Cook, *Research Methods,* p. 94.

8. Selltiz, Wrightsman, and Cook suggest that it is often useful in an exploratory study to orient questions toward "what works." That is, they recommend that questions be of the following form: "If (a given effect) is desired, what influences or what methods will, in your experience, be most likely to produce it?" (p. 95).

9. Joshua Macht, "The New Market Research," *Inc.* (July 1998), pp. 87–94.

10. Tim Neenan, "007's BMW Z3," *Ward's Auto World* 32 (March 1996), pp. 75–76.

11. David L. Morgan, *Planning Focus Groups* (Thousand Oaks, CA.: Sage Publications, 1997).

12. See Richard A. Krueger, *Moderating Focus Groups* (Thousand Oaks, CA.: Sage Publications, 1997); Holly Edmonds, *The Focus Group Research Handbook* (Chicago: American Marketing Association, 1999) for discussion of the skills needed by moderators and how to go about selecting them. See Thomas L. Greenbaum, *Moderating Focus Groups* (Thousand Oaks, CA.: Sage Publications, 2000) for discussion of how to go about moderating focus groups.

13. Robert K. Yin, *Case Study Research: Design and Methods* (Thousand Oaks, Calif.: Sage Publications, 1994); Robert E. Stake, *The Art of Case Study Research* (Thousand Oaks, Calif.: Sage Publications, 1993).

14. Jeremy Main, "How to Steal the Best Ideas Around," *Fortune* 126 (October 19, 1992), pp. 102–106. See also Douglas Brownlie, "The Conduct of Marketing Audits," *Industrial Marketing Management* 25 (January 1996), pp. 11–22; Subra Balakrishnan, "Benefits of Customer and Competitive Orientations in Industrial Markets," *Industrial Marketing Management* 25 (July 1996), pp. 257–269.

15. Dean Takahashi, "Doing Fieldwork in the High-Tech Jungle," *The Wall Street Journal* (October 27, 1998), pp. B1, B22. For discussion of the basics of the ethnographic methods, see Craig J. Thompson, "Interpreting Consumers: A Hermeneutical Framework for Deriving Marketing Insights from the Texts of Consumers' Consumption Stories," *Journal of Marketing Research* 34 (November 1997), pp. 438–455; Hy Mariampolski, "The Power of Ethnography," *Journal of the Market Research Society* 41 (January 1999), pp. 75–86.

Chapter 6

1. Brian Wansink and Seymour Sudman, "Selecting a Consumer Panel Service," *Quirk's Marketing Research Review* (May 2002), p. 32. See also Thomas T. Semon, "Marketing Research Needs Basic Research," *Marketing News* (March 14, 1994), p. 12.

2. Robert Ferber, Donald F. Blankertz, and Sidney Hollander, Jr., *Marketing Research* (New York: Ronald Press, 1964), p. 171.

3. Hans Zeisel, *Say It With Figures,* 5th ed. (New York: Harper and Row, 1968), pp. 200–239, has a highly readable version of the analyses that can be performed with panel data. See also Steven E. Finkel, *Causal Analysis with Panel Data* (Thousand Oaks, Calif.: Sage Publications, 1995); Gregory B. Markus, *Analyzing Panel Data* (Thousand Oaks, Calif.: Sage Publications, 1979); Scott Menard, *Longitudinal Research* (Thousand Oaks, Calif.: Sage Publications, 1991); and Seymour Sudman and Brian Wansink, *Consumer Panels,* 2d ed. (Chicago: American Marketing Association, 2002).

4. See Sudman and Wansink, *Consumer Panels,* pp. 45–68. See also B. Golany, F. Y. Phillips, and J. J. Rousseau, "Few-Wave vs. Continuous Consumer Panels: Some Issues of Attrition, Bias, and Variance," *International Journal of Research in Marketing* 8 (September 1991), pp. 273–280.

5. "Mail Panels vs. General Samples: How Similar and How Different," *Research on Research,* No. 59 (Chicago: Market Facts, Inc., undated).

6. Sudman and Wansink, *Consumer Panels,* pp. 45–68.

7. "Mail Panels vs. General Samples: How Similar and How Different," *Research on Research,* No. 59 (Chicago: Market Facts, Inc., undated).

8. John R. Nevin, "Using Controlled Experiments to Estimate and Analyze Brand Demand," unpublished Ph.D. Dissertation, University of Illinois, 1972. See also John R. Nevin, "Laboratory Experiments for Estimating Consumer Demand: A Validation Study," *Journal of Marketing Research* 11 (August 1974), pp. 261–268. For comparison of consumer choice processes in a laboratory versus an actual grocery store, see Raymond R. Burke, Barbara E. Kahn, and Leonard M. Lodish, "Comparing Dynamic Consumer Choice in Real and Computer-Simulated Environments," *Journal of Consumer Research* 19 (June 1992), pp. 71–82.

9. Laboratory and field experiments typically play complementary roles in providing managerially useful marketing information. For a discussion of their respective roles, see Alan G. Sawyer, Parker M. Worthing, and Paul E. Sendak, "The Role of Laboratory Experiments to Test Marketing Strategies," *Journal of Marketing* 43 (Summer 1979), pp. 60–67.

10. "Test and Learn," *Marketing Management* (May/June, 2002), p. 22.

11. For a general discussion of how the usefulness of experimental results is affected by the researcher's treatment of unmanipulated background factors in the experiment, see John G. Lynch, Jr., "On the External Validity of Experiments in Consumer Research," *Journal of Consumer Research* 9 (December 1982), pp. 225–244. See also Raymond R. Burke, Bari A. Harlam, Barbara E. Kahn, and Leonard M. Lodish, "Comparing Dynamic Consumer Choice in Real and Computer-Simulated Environments," *Journal of Consumer Research* 19 (June 1992), pp. 71–82.

12. Alvin R. Achenbaum, "Market Testing: Using the Marketplace as a Laboratory," in Robert Ferber, ed., *Handbook of Marketing Research* (New York: McGraw-Hill, 1974), pp. 4–31 to 4–54. See also James F. Donues, "Marketplace Measurement: The Evolution of Market Testing," *Journal of Advertising Research* 27 (December 1987/January 1988), pp. RC3–RC5; Madhav N. Segal and J. S. Johar, "On Improving the Effectiveness of Test Marketing Decisions," *European Journal of Marketing* 26 (No. 4, 1992), pp. 21–33.

13. Omar L. Gallaga, "Blockbuster Video Tests Rental of Desktop-Computer Games," *Austin American-Statesman* (April 26, 1999, downloaded from Dow Jones Publications Library at the Dow Jones Web site, http://www.dowjones.com, August 4, 1999).

14. "Test Marketing: What's in Store," *Sales and Marketing Management* 128 (March 15, 1982), pp. 57–85. See also Richard Gibson, "Pinning Down Costs of Product Introductions," *The Wall Street Journal* (November 26, 1990), p. B1.

15. Kathleen Deveny, "Failure of Its Oven Lovin' Cookie Dough Shows Pillsbury Pitfalls of New Products," *The Wall Street Journal* (June 17, 1993), pp. B1, B8.

16. Gabriele Stern, "GM Expands Its Experiment to Improve Cadillac's Distribution, Cut Inefficiency," *The Wall Street Journal* (February 8, 1995), p. A12.

17. There are several references that provide useful overviews of marketing's use of experiments in general and test markets in particular. See, for example, David M. Gardner and Russell W. Belk, *A Basic Bibliography on Experimental Design in Marketing* (Chicago: American Marketing Association, 1980); John R. Dickinson, *The Bibliography of Marketing Research Methods*, 3rd ed. (Lexington, Mass.: Lexington Books, 1990), pp. 148–150.

18. "To Test or Not to Test Seldom the Question," *Advertising Age* 55 (February 20, 1984), pp. M10–M11.

19. Annetta Miller and Karen Springen, "Egg Rolls for Peoria," *Newsweek* (October 12, 1992), pp. 59–60.

20. Suzanne Vranica, "P&G Puts Two Cleaning Products on Its New Marketing Fast Track," *The Wall Street Journal* (May 18, 1999, downloaded from Dow Jones Publications Library at the Dow Jones Web site, http://www.dowjones.com, August 4, 1999).

21. The first problem is found in Lynn G. Reiling, "Consumer Misuse Mars Sampling for Sunlight Dishwashing Liquid," *Marketing News* 16 (September 3, 1982), pp. 1 and 12; the second problem is discussed in Annetta Miller and Dody Tsiantor, "A Test for Market Research," *Newsweek* 110 (December 28, 1987), pp. 32–33.

22. Lee Gomes, "It Sounded So Good . . . : The History of Consumer Electronics Is Littered with Failure," *The Wall Street Journal* (June 15, 1998, downloaded from Dow Jones Publications Library at the Dow Jones Web site, http://www.dowjones.com, August 7, 1999).

23. Jim Carlton, "Apple Drops Newton, an Idea Ahead of Its Time," *The Wall Street Journal* (March 2, 1998, downloaded from Dow Jones Publications Library at the Dow Jones Web site, http://www.dowjones.com, August 7, 1999).

24. Jim Miller and Sheila Lundy, "Test Marketing Plugs Into the Internet," *Consumer Insight* (Spring 2002), pp. 20–23; "Simulated Test Marketing Winning Acceptance," *Marketing News* 19; Allan D. Shocker and William G. Hall, "Pretest Market Models: A Critical Evaluation," *Journal of Product Innovation Management* 3 (September 1986), pp. 86–107; Kevin J. Clancy and Robert S. Shulman, "It's Better to Fly a New Product Simulator than Crash the Real Thing," *Planning Review* 20 (July/August 1992), pp. 10–17; Christopher Power, "Will It Sell in Podunk? Hard to Say," *Business Week* (August 10, 1992), pp. 46–47; Burke, Harlam, Kahn, and Lodish, "Comparing Dynamic Consumer Choice in Real and Computer-Simulated Environments," pp. 71–82; Kevin J. Clancy, Robert S. Schulman, and Marianne Wolf, *Simulated Test Marketing: Technology for Launching Successful New Products* (New York: Lexington Books, 1994).

25. Miller and Lundy, p.23.

26. Jack Neff, "Is Testing the Answer?" *Advertising Age* (July 9, 2001), p.13.

Chapter 7

1. Robert Ferber and P. J. Verdoorn, *Research Methods in Economics and Business* (New York: Macmillan, 1962), p. 208.

2. David W. Stewart and Michael A. Kamins, *Secondary Research: Information Sources and Methods*, 2nd ed. (Thousand Oaks, Calif.: Sage Publications, 1993), p. 130.

3. Jacob has a particularly helpful discussion on the various errors that are present in published data and what remedies are available to the analyst for treating these errors. See Herbert Jacob, *Using Published Data: Errors and Remedies* (Thousand Oaks, Calif.: Sage Publications, 1984).

4. Phaedra Hise, "Grandma Got Run Over by Bad Research," *Inc.* (January 1998), p. 27.

5. *The Chicago Tribune*, September 19, 1960. If there had not been a cult of "baseball superfans whose passion is to dig up obscure facts about the erstwhile national pastime," the error might never have been discovered. See "You May Not Care but 'Nappie' Lajoie Batted .422 in 1901," *The Wall Street Journal* (September 13, 1974), p. 1.

6. Larry P. Stanek, "Keeping Focused on the Consumer While Managing Tons of Information," in *Presentations from the 9th Annual Marketing Research Conference* (Chicago: American Marketing Association, 1988), pp. 66–67.

7. The figure and surrounding discussion are adapted from Stewart and Kamins, *Secondary Research.*

8. Fred Vogelstein, "Looking For a Dot-Com Winner? Search No Further," *Fortune* (May 27, 2002), pp. 65–68.

Chapter 8

1. Eric Schine, "Computer Maps Pop Up All Over the Map," *Business Week* (July 26, 1993), pp. 75–76.

2. "GIS for Business: Chase Manhattan Bank," downloaded from http://www.gis.com, June 24, 2002.

3. Pamela DeSmidt, "Claritas for Market Demographic Analysis," *Database* (June 1, 1999, downloaded from the Northern Light Internet site, http://www.northernlight.com, August 16, 1999). See also the Claritas Web site (http://www.cluster2.claritas.com).

4. For discussion of some of the marketing insights made possible by the availability of geodemographic data, see Howard Schlossberg, "Census Bureau's TIGER Seen as a Roaring Success," *Marketing News* 24 (April 30, 1990), p. 2; Richard K. Thomas and Russell J. Kirchner, *Desktop Marketing: Lessons From America's Best* (Ithaca, N.Y.: American Demographic Books, 1991); Diane Crispell, *The Insider's Guide to Demographic Know How* (Burr Ridge, Ill.: Irwin Professional Publishing, 1992).

5. Downloaded from the NPD Foodworld Web site (http://npdfoodworld.com), April 7, 2003.

6. Downloaded from the NPD Group Web site (http://www.npd.com), April 7, 2003.

7. "Information Resources, Inc. Enhances BehaviorScan," news release from Information Resources, Inc., (October 29, 2001; downloaded from http://www.infores.com, June 12, 2002).

8. Ken Greenberg, "Using Panels to Understand the Consumer," *Consumer Insight* (Spring 2002), pp. 16–18, 28; downloaded from the Nielsen Web site, http://www.acneilsen.com, June 12, 2002; *Nielsen Household Panel* (Northbrook, Ill.: A. C.

Nielsen Company, undated). For a specific example of the use of Homescan, see "Using the Numbers," *Progressive Grocer* 75 (May 1996), pp. 117–123.

9. Greenberg, pg. 28; Priscilla Donegan, "Completing the Picture," *Grocery Headquarters* (April 1999), pp. 100–102.

10. "Study Predicts Bigger Impact by Single-Source Data," *Marketing News* 22 (February 1, 1988), p. 13. See also John Phillip Jones, "Single-Source Begins to Fulfill Its Promise," *Journal of Advertising Research* 35 (May/June 1995), pp. 9–16.

11. Rick Wartzman, "A Push to Probe Buying Habits in Latino Homes," *The Wall Street Journal* (August 5, 1999, downloaded from Dow Jones Publications Library at the Dow Jones Web site, http://www.dowjones.com, August 10, 1999).

12. "What's New for the Portable People Meter," downloaded from the Arbitron Web site, http://www.arbitron.com, June 26, 2002.

13. Information downloaded from http://www.roperasw.com/products/starch, June 26, 2002. See also *Starch Readership Report: Scope, Method, and Use* (Mamaroneck, N.Y.: Starch INRA Hooper, undated).

14. Information downloaded from the Simmons Web site, http://www.smrb.com, June 26, 2002.

15. "About Mediamark Research, Inc.," downloaded from the company's Web site, http://www.mriplus.com, June 26, 2002.

Chapter 9

1. Terry Lefton, "Ups and Downs: 18–49 Men," *Brandweek* (May 10, 1999), pp. S12–S14; Carol M. Morgan and Doran J. Levy, "Where the Bucks Are," *Brandweek* (November 30, 1998), pp. 20–28.

2. Harry Webber, *Divide and Conquer: Target Your Customers through Market Segmentation* (New York: Wiley, 1998).

3. Two collections that are especially relevant to marketers and consumer behavior researchers are: Gordon C. Bruner II and Paul J. Hensel, *Marketing Scales Handbook: A Compilation of Multi-Item Measures* (Chicago: AMA, 1994) and William O. Bearden and Richard G. Netemeyer, *Handbook of Marketing Scales,* 2nd ed. (Thousand Oaks, CA: Sage Publications, 1999).

4. Frito-Lay Profiles Salty Snack Consumers," *Supermarket News* (March 18, 1996), p. 39.

5. One of the more popular AIO inventories is the 300-question set that appears in William D. Wells and Douglas Tigert, "Activities, Interests, and Opinions," *Journal of Advertising Research* 11 (August 1971), pp. 27–35. See Qimei Chen and William D. Wells, "Attitude Toward the Site," *Journal of Advertising Research* (September/October 1999), pp. 27–37 for an example in which a Web site is evaluated. For a general review of the origins, development, and thrust of lifestyle and psychographic research, see William D. Wells, ed., *Life Style and Psychographics* (Chicago: American Marketing Association, 1974). For evidence regarding the reliability and validity of psychographic inventories, see Thabet A. Edris and A. Meidan, "On the Reliability of Psychographic Research: Encouraging Signs for Measurement Accuracy and Methodology in Consumer Research," *European Journal of Marketing* 24 (No. 3, 1990), pp. 23–41; Faye W. Gilbert and William E. Warren, "Psychographic Constructs and Demographic Segments," *Psychology & Marketing* 12 (May 1995), pp. 223–237.

6. Allana Sullivan, "Mobil Bets Drivers Pick Cappuccino over Low Prices," *The Wall Street Journal* (January 30, 1995), pp. B1, B4.

7. The original VALS was a typology of the American population developed to provide a model of societal values; see Arnold Mitchell, *The Nine American Lifestyles* (New York: Macmillan, 1983). It has been supplanted in the United States by VALS2, which is more focused on predicting consumer behavior. SRI International runs the proprietary VALS2; see http://www.sri.com. Another value-based classification scheme is the List of Values (LOV); for example, see Lynn R. Kahle, Sharon E. Beatty, and Pamela Homer, "Alternative Measurement Approaches to Consumer Values: The List of Values (LOV) and Values and Life Style (VALS)," *Journal of Consumer Research* 13 (December 1986), pp. 405–409; Wagner A. Kamakura and Thomas P. Novak, "Value-System Segmentation: Exploring the Meaning of LOV," *Journal of Consumer Research* 19 (June 1992), pp. 119–132; Lynn R. Kahle, Gregory Rose, and Aviv Shoham, "Findings of LOV Throughout the World, and Other Evidence of Cross-National Consumer Psychographics," *Journal of EuroMarketing* 8 (1999), pp. 1–13.

8. For a general discussion of the role of attitude in consumer behavior, see J. Paul Peter and Jerry C. Olson, *Consumer Behavior,* 6th ed. (Burr Ridge, IL: Irwin/McGraw-Hill, 2002), especially Chapter 6.

9. "Ford's Focus: Aim for Young Drivers," *Chicago Tribune* (August 13, 1999), sec. 3, p. 3.

10. Asher Koriat, Morris Goldsmith, and Ainat Pansky, "Toward a Psychology of Memory Accuracy," *Annual Review of Psychology* 51 (2000), pp. 481–537; Myra A. Fernandes and Morris Moscovitch, "Divided Attention and Memory," *Journal of Experimental Psychology: General* 129, no. 2 (June 2000), pp. 155–176; Terri E. Cameron and William E. Hockley, "The Revelation Effect for Item and Associative Recognition," *Memory and Cognition* 28, no. 2 (March 2000), pp. 176–183; William P. Wallace, Christine P. Malone, and Alison D. Spoo, "Implicit Word Activation During Prerecognition Processing," *Psychonomic Bulletin and Review* 7, no. 1 (March 2000), pp. 149–157; Luigi Castelli and Cristina Zogmaister, "The Role of Familiarity in Implicit Memory Effects," *European Journal of Social Psychology* 30 (March/April 2000), pp. 223–234; Jeffrey N. Rouder, Roger Ratcliff, and Gail McKoon, "A Neural Network Model of Implicit Memory for Object Recognition," *Psychological Science* 11 (January 2000), pp. 13–19; Stephen J. Hellebusch, "Survey May Not Measure True Awareness," *Marketing News* (September 27, 1999), p. 28; Rolf Reber, P. Winkielman, and Norbert Schwarz, "Effects of Perceptual Fluency on Affective Judgments," *Psychological Science* 29, no. 1 (1998), pp. 45–48.

11. Albert C. Bemmaor, "Predicting Behavior from Intention-to-Buy Measures: The Parametric Case," *Journal of Marketing Research* 32 (May 1995), pp. 176–191; William J. Infosino, "Forecasting New Product Sales from Likelihood of Purchase Ratings," *Marketing Science* 5 (Fall 1986), p. 375.

12. Shira Levine, "Clicking on the Customer," *America's Network* 104 (April 1, 2000) pp. 86–92.

Chapter 10

1. Formally, the procedure is known as content analysis. See Robert P. Weber, *Basic Content Analysis* 2nd ed. (Thousand Oaks, Calif.: Sage, 1990); Matthew B. Miles and A. Michael Huberman, *Qualitative Data Analysis,* 2nd ed. (Thousand

Oaks, Calif.: Sage, 1994). For examples, see David W. Stewart and Girish N. Punj, "Effects of Using a Nonverbal (Musical) Cue on Recall and Playback of Television Advertising," *Journal of Business Research* 42, no. 1 (May 1998), pp. 39–51; Thomas J. Richards and Lyn Richards, "Using Computers in Qualitative Research," in Norman K. Denzin and Yvonna S. Lincoln, eds., *Collecting and Interpreting Qualitative Materials* (Thousand Oaks, Calif.: Sage Publications, 1998), pp. 211–245.

2. Thomas J. Reynolds and Johnathan Gutman, "Laddering Theory, Method, Analysis and Interpretation," *Journal of Advertising Research* 26 (February/March 1988), pp. 11–31; Fred Langerak, Ed Peelen, and Ed Nijssen, "A Laddering Approach to the Use of Methods and Techniques to Reduce the Cycle Time of New-to-the-Firm Products," *Journal of Product Innovation Management* 16 (March 1999), pp. 173–182; Frenkel ter Hofstede, Anke Audenaert, Jan-Benedict E. M. Steenkamp, and Michael Wedel, "An Investigation into the Association Pattern Technique as a Quantitative Approach to Measuring Means-End Chains," *International Journal of Research in Marketing* 15 (February 1998), pp. 37–50; Jeffrey F. Durgee, Gina Colarelli O'Connor, and Robert W. Veryzer, "Observations: Translating Values into Product Wants," *Journal of Advertising Research* 36 (November/December 1996), pp. 90–100.

3. Fred N. Kerlinger, *Foundations of Behavioral Research,* 4th ed. (New York: Holt, Rinehart and Winston, 1999). See also Sidney J. Levy, *Brands, Consumers, Symbols, and Research* (Thousand Oaks, Calif: Sage Publications, 1999); Paul E. Meehl, "The Dynamics of 'Structured" Personality Tests," *Journal of Clinical Psychology* 56, no. 3 (March 2000), pp. 367–373; Marvin Leibowitz, *Interpreting Projective Drawings* (Philadelphia: Brunner/Mazel, 1999); R. W. Kamphaus, Martha D. Petoskey, and Ellen W. Rowe, "Current Trends in Psychological Testing of Children," *Professional Psychology: Research and Practice* 31, no. 2 (April 2000), pp. 155–164.

4. Sidney J. Levy, "Interpreting Consumer Methodology: Structural Approach to Consumer Behavior Focuses on Story Telling," *Marketing Management* 2 (1994), pp. 4–14; Teresa Fagulha, "The Once-Upon-A-Time Test": in Richard Henry Dana, ed., *Handbook of Cross-Cultural and Multicultural Personality Assessment,* (Mahwah, N.J.: Lawrence Earlbaum Associates, 2000), pp. 515–536.

5. Jeffrey Pope, *How Cultural Differences Affect Multi-Country Research* (Minneapolis, M.N.: Custom Research, Inc., 1991); V. Kumar, *International Marketing Research* (Upper Saddle River, N.J.: Prentice Hall, 2000).

6. Andrew Beutmueller, "Stepping Out," *Communications International* (April 2000), pp. 44–47; Iain Noble, Nick Moon, and Dominic McVey, "Bringing It All Back Home . . . Using RDD Telephone Methods for Large-Scale Social Policy and Opinion Research in the UK," *Journal of the Market Research Society* 41 (April 1998), pp. 93–120.

7. Richard Pothoff, "Some Generalizations of the Mitofsky-Waksberg Technique of Random Digit Dialing," *Journal of the American Statistical Association* 82 (June 1987), pp. 409–418; David H. Wilson, Gary J. Starr, Anne W. Taylor, and Eleonora Dal Grande, "Random Digit Dialing and Electronic White Pages Samples Compared," *Australian and New Zealand Journal of Public Health* 23 (December 1999), pp. 627–633.

8. Jon A. Yorgey, "Reaching Expectant and New Mums," *Target Marketing* 23 (March 2000), pp. 60–63.

9. All those who think unsolicited mail is a bother, however, can contact the Direct Marketing Association (http://www.the-dma.org), a trade group of over 4,600 direct-mail marketing firms (commercial and non-media, U.S. and 53 nations abroad), and that organization will remove the name from every member's list.

10. For general discussions of the mall intercept as a data-collection technique, see Alan J. Bush, Ronald F. Bush, and Henry C. K. Chen, "Method of Administration Effects in Mall Intercept Interviews," *Journal of the Market Research Society* 33 (October 1991), pp. 309–319.

11. The weighting technique was suggested by Seymour Sudman, "Improving the Quality of Shopping Center Sampling," *Journal of Marketing Research* 17 (November 1980), pp. 423–431. For empirical assessments of the usefulness of the weighting, see Clifford Nowell and Linda P. Stanley, "Length-Biased Sampling in Mall Intercept Surveys," *Journal of Marketing Research* 28 (November 1991), pp. 475–479. For information on the relationship between mall shopping behavior and various demographic characteristics, see Abhil Roy, "Correlates of Mall Visit Frequency," *Journal of Retailing* 70 (Summer 1994), pp. 139–161; Kiran Karanda, "Who Shops at Factory Outlets and Why?: An Exploratory Study," *Journal of Marketing Theory and Practice* 8 (Fall 2000), pp. 29–42.

12. Randy Minkoff, "Matters of Opinion: Foot Soldiers of Marketing Research Battle for a Moment of Your Time in the Mall," *Chicago Tribune* (July 5, 1998, downloaded from the Dow Jones Publications Library at http://www.dowjones.com, August 4, 1999).

13. Roger A. Kerin and Robert A. Peterson, "Scheduling Telephone Interviews," *Journal of Advertising Research* 23 (April/May 1983), pp. 41–47; Peter Tuckel and Trish Shukers, "The Answering Machine Dilemma," *Marketing Research* 9 (Fall 1997), pp. 4–9; Michael W. Link and Robert W. Oldendick, "Call Screening: Is It Really a Problem for Survey Research?" *Public Opinion Quarterly* 63 (Winter 1999), pp. 577–589.

14. Researchers suggest inversely weighting responses as a function of household size; see Andrew Gelman and Thomas C. Little, "Improving on Probability Weighting for Household Size," *Public Opinion Quarterly* 62 (Fall 1998), pp. 398–404.

15. See Paul L. Erdos, *Professional Mail Surveys* (Malabar, F.L.: Kreiger, 1983); Donald A. Dillman. "The Design and Administration of Mail Surveys," *Annual Review of Sociology* 17 (1991), pp. 225–249; Pamela J. Alreck and Robert B. Settle, *The Survey Research Handbook,* 2nd ed. (Chicago: Irwin, 1995); Thomas W. Mangione, *Mail Surveys: Improving the Quality* (Thousand Oaks, Calf.: Sage Publications, 1995) for discussions of the problem of sample control in mail surveys and what can be done to overcome respondent resistance.

16. Seymour Sudman and Edward Blair, "Sampling in the 21st Century," *Journal of the Academy of Marketing Science* 27 (Spring 1999), pp. 269–277; Tracy L. Tuten, Michael Bosnjak, and Wolfgang Bandilla, "Banner-Advertised Web Surveys," *Marketing Research* 11 (Spring 2000), pp. 16–21. In business-to-business surveys, the content of the survey is the clearest determinant of response rates and data quality. Day of week that the survey is sent had little effect; see Thomas V. Greer, Nuchai Chuch-

inprakam, and Sudhindra Seshadri, "Likelihood of Participating in Mail Survey Research," *Industrial Marketing Management* 29 (March 2000), pp. 97–119.

17. Edith D. De Leeuw, Joop J. Hox, and Ger Smijkers, "The Effect of Computer-Assisted Interviewing on Data Quality: A Review," *Journal of the Market Research Society* 37 (October 1995), pp. 325–344.

18. William E. Saris, *Computer-Assisted Interviewing* (Thousand Oaks, Calif.: Sage Publications, 1991). For an annotated bibliography, see Edith D. De Leeuw and Joop J. Hox, "Computer Assisted Data Collection: Data Quality and Costs: An Annotated Bibliography," *The Survey Statistician* 32 (1995), pp. 5–10.

Chapter 11

1. Paco Underhill, *Why We Buy: The Science of Shopping* (New York: Touchstone, 2000), p. 18.

2. Michael J. McCarthy, "James Bond Hits the Supermarket: Stores Snoop on Shoppers' Habits to Boost Sales," *The Wall Street Journal* (August 25, 1993), pp. B1, B5.

3. Bill Abrams, *The Observational Research Handbook: Understanding How Consumers Live with Your Product* (Chicago: AMA and NTC, 2000), p. 105.

4. Faith Russell, "Dangerous Intersections," *Marketing News* (February 28, 2000), p. 18.

5. Dieter Huckerstein and Robert Duboff, "Hilton Hotels," *Cornell Hotel and Restaurant Administration Quarterly* (August 1999), pp. 28–38; Paula Kephart, "The Spy in Aisle 3," *American Demographics* 18 (May 1996), pp. 16, 19.

6. For insight into some of the many ingenious ways that have been developed to make indirect measurements by observation, see Eugene J. Webb, Donald T. Campbell, and Richard D. Dwartz, eds., *Unobtrusive Measures* (Thousand Oaks, Calif.: Sage Publications, 1999).

7. Tony Case, "Getting Personal," *Brandweek* 41 (March 6, 2000), pp. M52–M54.

8. Roberta Bernstein, "Food for Thought," *American Demographics* 22 (May 2000), pp. 39–42.

9. Joshua Macht, "The New Market Research," *Inc.* 20 (July 1998), pp. 86–94.

10. Bob Becker, "Take Direct Route When Data-Gathering," *Marketing News* 33 (September 27, 1999), pp. 29, 31; Kendra

Parker, "How Do You Like Your Beef?" *American Demographics* 22 (January 2000), pp. 35–37.

11. Phil Guarisco, "How GM Targets 'Mature' Market Niche," *Advertising Age* 64 (January 11, 1993), p. 26.

12. Betsy Stewart, "Multimedia Market Research," *Marketing Research* 11 (Fall 1999), pp. 14–18; Glen L. Urban, et al., "Information Acceleration: Validation and Lessons from the Field," *Journal of Marketing Research* 34 (February 1997), pp. 143–153; Fareena Sultan and Gloria Barczak, "Turning Marketing Research High-Tech," *Marketing Management* 8 (Winter 1999), pp. 25–29.

13. Glenn Withiam, "Hilton's Vacation Station Conducts Toy Research," *Cornell Hotel and Restaurant Administration Quarterly* 40 (December 1999), p. 15.

14. Russell W. Belk, "Multimedia Approaches to Qualitative Data," in Barbara B. Stern, ed., *Representing Consumers: Voices, Views and Visions* (New York: Routledge, 1998), pp. 308–338; Christina Hughes, "From Field Notes to Dissertation," in Norman K. Denzin and Yvonna S. Lincoln, eds., *Collecting and Interpreting Qualitative Materials* (Thousand Oaks, Calif.: Sage Publications, 1998), pp. 35–46.

15. Priscilla A. LaBarbera and Joel D. Tucciarone, "GSR Reconsidered: A Behavior-Based Approach to Evaluating and Improving the Sales Potency of Advertising," *Journal of Advertising Research* 35 (September/October 1995), pp. 33–53.

16. Lee S. Weinblatt, "The Evolution of Technology in Pre-Testing," *Marketing Research* (Spring 1994), pp. 42–45; Rik Pieters, Edward Rosbergen, and Michel Wedel, "Visual Attention to Repeated Print Advertising," *Journal of Marketing Research* 36 (November 1999), pp. 424–438; Arthur F. Kramer, Sowon Hahn, David E. Irwin, and Jan Theeuwes, "Age Differences in the Control of Looking Behavior," *Psychological Science* 11 (May 2000), pp. 210–217.

17. For general discussions of the use of response latency measures, see John N. Bassili and Joseph F. Fletcher, "Response-Time Measurement in Survey Research," *Public Opinion Quarterly* 55 (Fall 1991), pp. 331–346; I. Koch and J. Hoffmann, "Patterns, Chunks, and Hierarchies in Serial Reaction-Time Tasks," *Psychological Research* 63 (2000), pp. 22–35.

18. Nancy Nischwonger and Claude R. Martin, "On Using Voice Analysis in Marketing Research," *Journal of Marketing Research* 18 (August 1981), pp. 350–355; Dirk Michaelis, Matthias Froehlich, and Hans Werner Strube, "Selection and Combination of Acoustic Features for the Description of Pathologic Voices," *Journal of the Acoustical Society of America* 103, no. 3 (March 1998), pp. 1628–1639.

Chapter 12

1. This procedure is adapted from one suggested by Arthur Kornhauser and Paul B. Sheatsley, "Questionnaire Construction and Interview Procedure," in Claire Selltiz, Lawrence S. Wrightsman, and Stuart W. Cook, *Research Methods in Social Relations*, 3rd ed. (New York: Holt, Rinehart and Winston, 1976), pp. 541–573. See also Arlene Fink, *How to Design Surveys* (Thousand Oaks, Calif.: Sage Publications, 1995).

2. Murray Simon, "Face/Off: A Pharmaceutical Projection Technique," *Quirk's Marketing Research Review* (December 1998), pp. 39–41.

3. Chris Grecco and Hal King, "Of Browsers and Plug-Ins: Researching Web Surfers' Technological Capabilities," *Quirk's Marketing Research Review* (July 1999), pp. 58–62.

4. These questions were suggested by Kornhauser and Sheatsley, "Questionnaire Construction." For a systematic treatment of questionnaire construction, see the classic work by Stanley L. Payne, *The Art of Asking Questions* (Princeton, N.J.: Princeton University Press, 1978). Other good general sources are Seymour Sudman and Norman M. Bradburn, *Asking Questions: A Practical Guide to Questionnaire Design* (San Francisco: Jossey-Bass, 1982); William Foddy, *Constructing Questions for Interviews and Questionnaires* (New York: Cambridge University Press, 1993); Robert A. Peterson, *Constructing Effective Questionnaires* (Thousand Oaks, Calif.: Sage Publications, 1999).

5. Sam Gill, "How Do You Stand on Sin?" *Tide* 21 (March 14, 1947), p. 72.

6. In a subsequent replication of the study on the Metallic Metals Act almost 40 years later, 64 percent of those interviewed had a definite opinion on the nonexistent act. See Daniel T. Seymour, "Numbers Don't Lie–Do They?" *Business*

Horizons 27 (November/December 1984), pp. 36–37. There are a number of other examples in the literature that report findings of people having opinions about totally fictional issues like the Metallic Metals Act. See, for example, Del I. Hawkins and Kenneth A. Coney, "Uninformed Response Error in Survey Research," *Journal of Marketing Research* 18 (August 1981), pp. 370–374; Kenneth C. Schneider, "Uninformed Response Rates in Survey Research: New Evidence," *Journal of Business Research* 13 (August 1985), pp. 153–162; George F. Bishop, Alfred J. Tuchfarber, and Robert W. Oldendick, "Opinions on Fictitious Issues: The Pressure to Answer Survey Questions," *Public Opinion Quarterly* 50 (Summer 1986), pp. 240–250; Arthur Sterngold, Rex H. Warland, and Robert O. Herrmann, "Do Surveys Overstate Public Concern?" *Public Opinion Quarterly* 58 (Summer 1994), pp. 255–263. The phenomenon is not unique to opinions. It also applies when measuring brand awareness, where it has been observed that the more plausible sounding a brand name, the more likely consumers are to claim they are aware of it even though it does not exist. See "'Spurious Awareness' Alters Brand Tests," *The Wall Street Journal* (September 13, 1984), p. 29; Eric R. A. N. Smith and Peverill Squire, "The Effects of Prestige Names in Question Wording," *Public Opinion Quarterly* 54 (Spring 1990), pp. 97–116.

7. Howard Schuman and Stanley Presser, "The Assessment of 'No Opinions' in Attitude Surveys," in Karl F. Schnessler, ed., *Sociological Methodology, 1979* (San Francisco: Jossey-Bass, 1979), pp. 241–275; George F. Bishop, Robert W. Oldendick, and Alfred J. Tuchfarber, "Effects on Filter Questions in Public Opinion Surveys," *Public Opinion Quarterly* 47 (Winter 1983), pp. 528–546; Otis Dudley Duncan and Magnus Stenbeck, "No Opinion or Not Sure?" *Public Opinion Quarterly* 52 (Winter 1988), pp. 513–525; Robert O. Herrmann, "Comparing Alternative Question Forms for Assessing Consumer Concerns," *The Journal of Consumer Affairs* 32 (Summer 1998), pp. 13–29.

8. Bruce Buchanan and Donald G. Morrison, "Sampling Properties of Rate Questions with Implications for Survey Research," *Marketing Science* 6 (Summer 1987), pp. 286–298; Scot Burton and Edward Blair, "Task Conditions, Response Formulation Processes, and Response Accuracy for Behavioral Frequency Questions in Surveys," *Public Opinion Quarterly* 55 (Spring 1991), pp. 50–79; Richard Nadeau and Richard G. Niemi, "Educated Guesses: The Process of Answering Factual Knowledge Questions in Surveys," *Public Opinion Quarterly* 59 (Fall 1995), pp. 323–346.

9. Graham Kalton and Howard Schuman, "The Effect of the Question on Survey Responses: A Review," *Journal of the Royal Statistical Society, Series A,* 145 (Part I, 1982), pp. 44–45; William A. Cook, "Telescoping and Memory's Other Tricks," *Journal of Advertising Research* 27 (February/March 1987), pp. RC5–RC8; Norman M. Bradburn, Lance J. Rip, and Steven K. Shevell, "Answering Autobiographical Questions: The Impact of Memory and Inference on Surveys," *Science* 236 (April 10, 1987), pp. 157–161; McKee J. McClendon, "Acquiescence and Recency Response Order Effects in Interview Surveys," *Sociological Methodology and Research* 20 (August 1991), pp. 60–103; Howard Schuman and Stanley Presser, *Questions and Answers in Attitude Surveys: Experiments on Question Form, Wording, and Context* (Thousand Oaks, Calif.: Sage Publications, 1996).

10. Lee Valeriano Lourdes, "Marketing: Western Firms Poll Eastern Europeans to Discern Tastes of Nascent Consumers," *The Wall Street Journal* (April 27, 1992), p. B1.

11. Stella M. Hopkins, "Furniture Makers Start Asking Customers What They Want," *Charlotte* (N.C.) *Observer* (October 12, 1998, downloaded from Dow Jones Publications Library, Dow Jones Web site, http://www.dowjones.com, August 16, 1999).

12. For general treatments on how to handle sensitive questions, see Kent H. Marquis et al., *Response Errors in Sensitive Topic Surveys: Estimates, Effects, and Correction Options* (Santa Monica, Calif.: Rand Corporation, 1981); Claire M. Renzetti and Raymond M. Lee, eds., *Researching Sensitive Topics* (Thousand Oaks, Calif.: Sage Publications, 1992); Raymond M. Lee, *Doing Research on Sensitive Topics* (Thousand Oaks, Calif.: Sage Publications, 1993).

13. James E. Reinmuth and Michael D. Geurts, "The Collection of Sensitive Information Using a Two-Stage Randomized Response Model," *Journal of Marketing Research* 12 (November 1975), pp. 402–407; Donald E. Stem, Jr., and R. Kirk Steinhorst, "Telephone Interview and Mail Questionnaire Applications of the Randomized Response Model," *Journal of the American Statistical Association* 79 (September 1984), pp. 555–564; James Alan Fox and Paul E. Tracy, *Randomizing Response: A Method for Sensitive Surveys* (Beverly Hills, Calif.: Sage Publications, 1986); U. N. Umesh and Robert A. Peterson," "A Critical Evaluation of the Randomized Response Model: Applications, Validations, and Research Agenda," *Sociological Methods and Research* 20 (August 1991), pp. 104–138; Robert P. Berrens, Alok K. Bohara and Joe Kerkvliel, "A Randomized Response Approach to Dichotomous Choice Contingent Valuation," *American Journal of Agricultural Economics* 79 (February 1997), pp. 252–266.

14. Kalton and Schuman, "The Effect of the Question on Survey Responses: A Review," pp. 51–52; Gail S. Poe et al., "Don't Know Box in Factual Questions in a Mail Questionnaire: Effects on Level and Quality of Response," *Public Opinion Quarterly* 52 (Summer 1988), pp. 212–222; Mikael Gilliam and Donald Granberg, "Should We Take Don't Know for an Answer," *Public Opinion Quarterly* 57 (Fall 1993), pp. 348–357.

15. National Public Radio, "All Things Considered" (September 7, 1999, summary and audio downloaded from the NPR Web site, http://www.npr.org, September 9, 1999); National Public Radio, "Americans Willing to Pay for Improving Schools," NPR Web site (http://www.npr.org, downloaded September 9, 1999); "NPR/Kaiser/Kennedy School Education Survey," NPR Web site (http://www.npr.org, downloaded September 9, 1999).

16. Hadley Cantril and Edreta Fried, *Gauging Public Opinion* (Princeton, N.J.: Princeton University Press, 1944), Chapter 1, as reported in Payne, *The Art of Asking Questions,* p. 93. For a discussion of how to take account of people's information processing abilities when designing questionnaires, see Seymour Sudman, Norman M. Bradburn and Norbert Schwarz, *Thinking about Answers: The Application of Cognitive Process to Survey Methodology* (San Francisco, Calif.: Jossey-Bass, 1996).

17. Norbert Schwarz, Hans J. Hippler, Brigitte Deutsch, and Fritz Strack, "Response Scales: Effect of Category Range on Reported Behavior and Comparative Judgments," *Public Opinion Quarterly* 49 (Fall 1985), pp. 388–395; Norbert Schwarz et al., "The Range of Response Alternatives May Determine the Meaning of the Question: Further Evidence on Information Functions of Response Alternatives," *Social Cognition* 6 (No. 2, 1988), pp. 107–117; Eric A. Greenleaf, "Measuring Extreme Response Style," *Public Opinion Quarterly* 56 (Fall 1992), pp. 328–351.

18. Two of the best discussions of this are to be found in Payne, *The Art of Asking Questions,* and Howard Schuman and Stanley Presser, *Questions and Answers in Attitude Surveys* (Orlando, Fla.: Academic Press, 1981), especially pp. 56–77. See also Donald A. Dillman et al., "Effects of Category Order on Answers in Mail and Telephone Surveys," *Rural Sociology* (Winter 1995), pp. 674–687.

19. For a review of the literature on the quality of questionnaire data, including item omission, see Robert A. Peterson and Roger A. Kerin, "The Quality of Self-Report Data: Review and Synthesis," in Ben Enis and Kenneth Roering, eds., *Annual Review of Marketing* 1981 (Chicago: American Marketing Association, 1981), pp. 5–20. See also Floyd Jackson Fowler, Jr., "How Unclear Terms Affect Survey Data," *Public Opinion Quarterly* 56 (Summer 1992), pp. 218–231.

20. Sudman and Bradburn, *Asking Questions,* p. 1.

21. Gonzalo R. Soruco, "Sampling and Non-sampling Errors in Hispanic Population Telephone Surveys," *Applied Marketing Research* 29 (Summer 1989), pp. 11–15; Patrice Braus, "What Does 'Hispanic' Mean?" *American Demographics* 15 (June 1993), pp. 46–49, 58.

22. E. Noelle-Neumann, "Wanted: Rules for Wording Structural Questionnaires," *Public Opinion Quarterly* 34 (Summer 1970), p. 200; Philip Gendall and Janet Hoek, "A Question of Wording," *Marketing Bulletin* 1 (May 1990), pp. 25–36.

23. Donald J. Messmer and Daniel T. Seymour, "The Effects of Branching on Item Nonresponse," *Public Opinion Quarterly* 46 (Summer 1982), pp. 270–277.

24. Sudman and Bradburn, *Asking Questions,* pp. 223–227.

25. For examples, see Charles S. Mayer and Cindy Piper, "A Note on the Importance of Layout in Self-Administered Questionnaires," *Journal of Marketing Research* 19 (August 1982), pp. 390–391; Maria Elena Sanchez, "Effects of Questionnaire Design on the Quality of Survey Data," *Public Opinion Quarterly* 56 (Summer 1992), pp. 206–217.

26. Each of the parts listed in Research Window 12.4 is discussed in detail in Paul L. Erdos, *Professional Mail Surveys* (Melbourne, Fla.: Robert E. Krieger Publishing Co., 1983), pp. 101–117. See also Linda B. Bourque and Eve P. Fiedler, *How to Conduct Self-Administered and Mail Surveys* (Thousand Oaks, Calif.: Sage Publications, 1995).

27. A. Regula Herzog and Jerald G. Bachman, "Effects of Questionnaire Length on Response Quality," *Public Opinion Quarterly* 45 (Winter 1981), pp. 549–559; David Jobber, "An Examination of the Effects of Questionnaire Factors on Response to an Industrial Mail Survey," *International Journal of Research on Marketing* 6 (December 1989), pp. 129–140; Andrew G. Bean and Michale J. Rozkowski, "The Long and Short of It," *Marketing Research: A Magazine of Management & Applications* 7 (Winter 1995), pp. 21–26.

28. These elementary steps, which are involved in the processing of all questionnaires, are discussed in Chapter 19.

29. Payne's book, *The Art of Asking Questions,* is particularly good in this regard. Chapter 13, for example, is devoted to the development of a passable question. When one considers that an entire chapter can be devoted to the development of one passable question (not a great question, mind you), one can appreciate the need for reexamining each question under a microscope for its potential implications. See also Sudman and Bradburn, *Asking Questions,* which has recommendations specific to the type of question being asked (e.g., opinions versus demographic characteristics) and Floyd J. Fowler, Jr., *Improving Survey Questions* (Thousand Oaks, Calif.: Sage Publications, 1995).

30. Linda Kirby, "Bloopers," *Newspaper Research Council* (January/February 1989), p. 1.

31. Shelby D. Hunt, Richard D. Sparkman, Jr., and James B. Wilcox, "The Pretest in Survey Research: Issues and Preliminary Findings," *Journal of Marketing Research* 19 (May 1982), pp. 265–275. Ruth N. Bolton, Randall G. Chapman, and John M. Zych, "Pretesting Alternative Survey Administration Designs," *Applied Marketing Research* 30 (No. 3, 1990), pp. 8–13; Nina Reynolds, Adamantios Diamantopoulus, and Bodo Schlegelmich, "Pretesting in Questionnaire Design: A Review of the Literature and Suggestions for Further Research," *Journal of the Market Research Society* 35 (April 1993), pp. 171–182. For discussion of some of the things the Department of Commerce pretested as it prepared for the 2000 Census, see John Pierson, "Preparing for 2000, Census Bureau Tests Carrots vs. Sticks," *The Wall Street Journal* (May 2, 1996), pp. B1, B9.

Chapter 13

1. Peter D. Bennett, ed., *Dictionary of Marketing Terms,* 2nd ed. (Chicago: American Marketing Association, 1995), p. 173.

2. Our classification follows that of Stanley S. Stevens, "Mathematics, Measurement and Psychophysics," in Stanley S. Stevens, ed., *Handbook of Experimental Psychology* (New York: John Wiley, 1951), the most accepted classification in the social sciences.

3. Elia Kacapyr, "Money Isn't Everything," *American Demographics* 18 (July 1996), pp. 10–11; Elia Kacapyr, "The Well-Being Index," *American Demographics* 18 (February 1996), pp. 32–35, 43.

4. Tom J. Brown, John C. Mowen, D. Todd Donavan, and Jane W. Licata, "The Customer Orientation of Service Workers: Personality Trait Effects on Self- and Supervisor Performance Ratings," *Journal of Marketing Research* 39 (February 2002), pp. 110–119.

5. These differences are adapted from Claire Selltiz, Lawrence S. Wrightsman, and Stuart W. Cook, *Research Methods in Social Relations,* 3rd ed. (New York: Holt, Rinehart and Winston, 1976), pp. 164–168. See also Duane F. Alwin and David J. Jackson, "Measurement Models for Response Errors in Surveys: Issues and Applications," in Karl F. Schuessler, ed., *Sociological Methodology* 1980 (San Francisco: Jossey-Bass, 1979), pp. 69–119; Frank E. Saal, Ronald G. Downey, and Mary Anne Lakey, "Rating the Ratings: Assessing the Psychometric Quality of Ratings Data," *Psychological Bulletin* 88 (September 1980), pp. 413–428; Ellen J. Wentland and Kent W. Smith, *Survey*

Responses: An Evaluation of Their Validity (San Diego, Calif.: Academic Press, 1993).

6. Eunkyu Lee, Michael Y. Hu, and Rex S. Toh, "Are Consumer Survey Results Distorted? Systematic Impact of Behavioral Frequency and Duration on Survey Response Errors," *Journal of Marketing Research* 37 (February 2000), pp. 125–133.

7. Tom Benemann, "Feds Announce Collection of Information on E-Commerce," *Forbes* (June 8, 1999, downloaded from the Forbes Web site, http://www.forbes.com, June 8, 1999).

8. Selltiz, Wrightsman, and Cook, *Research Methods*, p. 169.

9. For detailed discussion of the conceptual relationships that should exist among the various indicators of reliability and validity and an empirical assessment of the evidence, see J. Paul Peter and Gilbert A. Churchill, Jr., "The Relationship among Research Design Choices and Psychometric Properties of Rating Scales: A Meta-Analysis," *Journal of Marketing Research* 23 (February 1986), pp. 1–10. See also Mark S. Litwin, *How to Measure Survey Reliability and Validity* (Thousand Oaks, Calif.: Sage Publications, 1995).

10. See Gilbert A. Churchill, Jr., "A Paradigm for Developing Better Measures of Marketing Constructs," *Journal of Marketing Research* 16 (February 1979), pp. 64–73, for a procedure that can be used to construct scales having construct validity. See J. Paul Peter, "Construct Validity: A Review of Basic Issues and Marketing Practices," *Journal of Marketing Research* 18 (May 1981), pp. 133–145, for an in-depth discussion of the notion of construct validity. See also Robert DeVellis, *Scale Development: Theory and Applications* (Thousand Oaks, Calif.: Sage Publications, 1991).

11. One convenient way of establishing the convergent and discriminant validity of a measure is through the multitrait-multimethod matrix of Campbell and Fiske. See Donald T. Campbell and Donald W. Fiske, "Convergent and Discriminant Validation by the Multitrait-Multimethod Matrix," *Psychological Bulletin* 56 (1959), pp. 81–105. For an example of its use, see Ronald E. Goldsmith and Janelle Emmert, "Measuring Product Category Involvement: A Multi-trait-Multimethod Study," *Journal of Business Research* 23 (December 1991), pp. 363–371.

12. See J. Paul Peter, "Reliability: A Review of Psychometric Basics and Recent Marketing Practices," *Journal of Marketing Research* 16 (February 1979), pp. 6–17, for a detailed treatment of the issue of reliability in measurement. See Gilbert A. Churchill, Jr., and J. Paul Peter, "Research Design Effects on the Reliability of Rating Scales: A Meta-Analysis," *Journal of Marketing Research* 21 (February 1984), pp. 360–375, for an empirical assessment of the factors that seem to affect the reliability of rating scales.

13. For a general discussion of the measurement of interjudge reliability, see William D. Perreault, Jr., and Laurence E. Leigh, "Reliability of Nominal Data Based on Qualitative Judgments," *Journal of Marketing Research* 26 (May 1989), pp. 135–148; Marie Adele Hughes and Dennis E. Garrett, "Intercoder Reliability Estimation Approaches in Marketing: A Generalizability Theory Framework for Quantitative Data," *Journal of Marketing Research* 27 (May 1990), pp. 185–195. See also Roland T. Rust and Bruce Cooil, "Reliability Measures for Qualitative Data: Theory and Implications," *Journal of Marketing Research* 31 (February 1994), pp. 1–14.

14. Food Marketing Institute (FMI), "Shoplifting Remains Top Challenge for the Supermarket Industry," news release (May 3, 1998, downloaded from the FMI Web site, http://www.fmi.org, September 28, 1999); Steve Weinstein, "Loss Leaders," *Progressive Grocer* (September 1998), pp. 57–65.

15. The procedure is adapted from Gilbert A. Churchill, Jr., "A Paradigm," pp. 64–73.

16. Mary Jo Bitner, Bernard H. Booms, and Mary Stanfield Tetreault, "The Service Encounter: Diagnosing Favorable and Unfavorable Incidents," *Journal of Marketing* 54 (January 1990), pp. 71–84. See also Mary Jo Bitner, Bernard H. Booms, and Lois A. Mohr, "Critical Service Encounters: The Employee's Viewpoint," *Journal of Marketing* 58 (October 1994), pp. 95–106.

17. See Churchill, "A Paradigm," for detailed discussion of which coefficients should be used and the rationale for their use.

Chapter 14

1. Chester Dawson, "The Zen of Nissan," *BusinessWeek* (July 22, 2002), pp. 46–49.

2. Louise Lee, "Why Levi's Still Looks Faded," *BusinessWeek* (July 22, 2002), pp. 54–55.

3. This classification of approaches is taken from Stuart W. Cook and Claire Selltiz, "A Multiple Indicator Approach to Attitude Measurement," *Psychological Bulletin* 62 (1964), pp. 36–55. See also Dagmar Krebs and Peter Schmidt, eds., *New Directions in Attitude Measurement* (Berlin: Walter de Gruyter, 1993).

4. Hugh Graham, "Annals of Marketing: Don't Go Changin'," *Globe and Mail* (September 25, 1998, downloaded from Dow Jones Publications Library at the Dow Jones Web site, http://www.dowjones.com, August 10, 1999).

5. The scale was first proposed by Rensis Likert, "A Technique for the Measurement of Attitudes," *Archives of Psychology*, No. 140 (1932).

6. Albert R. Wildt and Michael B. Mazis, "Determinants of Scale Response: Label versus Position," *Journal of Marketing Research* 15 (May 1978), pp. 261–267; H. H. Friedman and J. R. Liefer, "Label versus Position in Rating Scales," *Journal of the Academy of Marketing Science* (Spring 1981), pp. 88–92; Norbert Schwarz et al., "Rating Scales: Numeric Values May Change the Meanings of Scale Labels," *Public Opinion Quarterly* 55 (Winter 1991), pp. 570–582; Colm O'Muircheartaigh, George D. Gaskell, and Daniel B. Wright, "Weighing Anchors: Verbal and Numerical Labels for Response Scales," *Journal of Official Statistics* 11 (1995), pp. 295–307.

7. Charles E. Osgood, George J. Suci, and Percy H. Tannenbaum, *The Measurement of Meaning* (Champaign, Ill.: University of Illinois Press, 1957).

8. One study that compared the performance of the Stapel scale with that of the semantic-differential found basically no difference between the results produced by, or respondents' ability to use, each. See Del I. Hawkins, Gerald Albaum, and Roger Best, "Stapel Scale or Semantic Differential in Marketing Research," *Journal of Marketing Research* 11 (August 1974), pp. 318–322. See also Grahame R. Dowling, "Measuring Corporate Images: A Review of Alternative Approaches," *Journal of Business Research* 17 (August 1988), pp. 27–34.

9. Gregory D. Upah and Steven C. Cosmas, "The Use of Telephone Dials as Attitudes Scales," *Journal of the Academy of Marketing Science* (Fall 1980), pp. 416–426; Bar-

bara Loken et al., "The Use of 0–10 Scales in Telephone Surveys," *Journal of the Market Research Society* 29 (July 1987), pp. 353–362.

10. Eli P. Cox III, "The Optimal Number of Response Alternatives for a Scale: A Review," *Journal of Marketing Research* 17 (November 1980), pp. 407–422. For discussion of the issue of number of scale points specifically with respect to customer satisfaction measurement, see the special session "Scales: A Weighty Debate," *Marketing Research: A Magazine of Management & Applications* 9 (Fall 1994), pp. 6–33.

11. Joel Herche and Brian Engelland, "Reversed-Polarity Items and Scale Unidimensionality," *Journal of the Academy of Marketing Science* 24 (Fall 1996), pp. 366–374.

12. Gilbert A. Churchill, Jr., and J. Paul Peter, "Research Design Effects on the Reliability of Rating Scales: A Meta-Analysis," *Journal of Marketing Research* 21 (November 1984), pp. 360–375.

13. Irvine Clarke III, "Global Marketing Research: Is Extreme Response Style Influencing your Results?" *Journal of International Consumer Marketing* 12 (4, 2000), pp. 91–110.

14. Churchill and Peter, "Research Design Effects on the Reliability of Rating Scales: A Meta-Analysis."

15. See Tom J. Brown, "Using Norms to Improve the Interpretation of Service Quality Measures," *Journal of Services Marketing* 11 (1, 1997), pp. 66–80.

16. "American Customer Satisfaction Index," ACSI Web site (http://www.theacsi.org, downloaded July 26, 2002).

17. Glen L. Urban and John R. Hauser, *Design and Marketing of New Products,* 2nd ed. (Englewood Cliffs, N.J.: Prentice-Hall, 1993). For discussion of the usefulness of various techniques for answering these questions, see Michael D. Johnson and Elania J. Hudson, "On the Perceived Usefulness of Scaling Techniques in Market Analysis," *Psychology & Marketing* 13 (October 1996), pp. 653–675.

18. See Marian Garcia Martinez, Zulema Aragones, and Nigel Poole, "A Repositioning Strategy for Olive Oil in the UK Market," *Agribusiness* 18 (Spring 2002), pp. 163–180; Jerry Wind, Paul E. Green, Douglas Shifflet, and Marsha Scarbrough, "Courtyard by Marriott: Designing a Hotel Facility with Consumer-Based Marketing Models," *Interfaces* 19 (Jan/Feb 1989), pp. 25–47.

Chapter 15

1. The fact that sample information is used to gauge the accuracy of the census has embroiled the Census Bureau in a debate about whether census counts should be adjusted on the basis of the sample results. For discussion of the controversy surrounding the 2000 census, see Gina Kolata, "Ideas and Trends: Down for the Count; Why Some Numbers Are Only Very Good Guesses," *The New York Times* (March 11, 2001), p. D1; Eric Schmitt, "U.S. Census Bureau Rejects Revision to Nation's Tally," *The New York Times* (March 2, 2001), p. A1.

2. Cyndee Miller, "Researching Children Isn't Kids Stuff Anymore," *Marketing News* 24 (September 3, 1990), p. 32.

3. Seymour Sudman, "Applied Sampling," in Peter H. Rossi, James D. Wright, and Andy B. Anderson, eds., *Handbook of Survey Research* (Orlando: Academic Press, 1983), p. 145–194. See also "SSI Lowers the Cost of Finding Rare Groups," *The Frame* (October 1991), p. 3.

4. Julie Johnsson, "Writing a New Policy," *Crain's Chicago Business* (June 7, 1999), pp. E47, E49.

5. Jack Neff, "P&G Enlists 13-Year-Olds in Summer Intern Jobs," *Advertising Age* (June 28, 1999), p. 20.

6. The technique was originally suggested by Leo A. Goodman, "Snowball Sampling," *Annals of Mathematical Statistics* 32 (1961), pp. 148–170.

7. Seymour Sudman, *Applied Sampling* (San Francisco: Academic Press, 1976), p. 10. For discussion of the makeup of the CPI, see "Is the CPI Accurate? Ask the Federal Sleuths Who Get the Numbers," *The Wall Street Journal* (January 16, 1997), pp. A1, A6.

8. Catherine Marsh and Elinor Scarbrough, "Testing Nine Hypotheses About Quota Sampling," *Journal of the Market Research Society* 32 (October 1990), pp. 485–506; John Curtice and Nick Sparrow, "How Accurate Are Traditional Quota Opinion Polls?" *Journal of the Market Research Society* 39 (July 1997), pp. 443–448.

9. In the example at hand, the sample is 10 percent of the population, since the procedure specifies samples of size $n = 2$ be drawn from a population of size $N = 20$. In a situation such as this, in which the sample is a relatively large part of the population, the correct

formula relating the two variances contains an additional term. Specifically it equals

$$\sigma_{\bar{x}}^2 = \frac{\sigma^2}{n} \frac{N-n}{N-1}$$

The additional term $\frac{N-n}{N-1}$ is called the *finite population correction factor.* It is, of course, close to 1 when the population is very large in comparison to the sample, and can then safely be ignored. The variance of mean incomes for the example using the formula turns out to be

$$\sigma_{\bar{x}}^2 = \frac{5,320,000}{2} \frac{20-2}{20-1} = 2,520,000$$

10. There are two major errors to avoid when using random-number tables: (1) starting at a given place because one knows the distribution of numbers at that place, and (2) discarding a sample because it does not "look right" in some sense and continuing to use random numbers until a "likely looking" sample is selected. Sudman, "Applied Sampling," p. 165.

11. Malcolm W. Browne, "Coin-Tossing Computers Found to Show Subtle Bias," *The New York Times* (January 13, 1993), pp. B5–B6.

Chapter 16

1. Cecelia Blalock, "Selling Sales," *Grocery Headquarters* (December 1998), pp. 43–46.

2. Joseph Rydholm, "On the Front Line of On-Line," *Quirk's Marketing Research Review* (July 1998, downloaded from the *Quirk's* Web site, http://www.quirks.com, August 13, 1999).

3. Earl R. Babbie, *The Practice of Social Research,* 9th ed. (Belmont, Calif. Wadsworth Publishing, 2001), Chapter 7.

4. R. L. Polk and Company, in Taylor, Michigan, publishes some 1,400 directories for most medium-sized cities in the range of 50,000 to 800,000 people. The directories contain both an alphabetical list of names and businesses and a street address directory of households. While the alphabetic list can contain a large percentage of inaccurate listings at any one time, the address directory is reasonably accurate since it omits only new construction after the directory is published. The directories are revised every two or three years.

5. *U.S. Census of Housing: Vol. III, City Blocks,* HC(3)—No. (city number).

6. Those interested in pursuing the subject further should see one of the excellent books on the subject, such as William G. Cochran, *Sampling Techniques,* 3rd ed. (New York: John Wiley, 1977); Morris H. Hansen, William N. Hurwitz, and William G. Madow, *Sample Survey Methods and Theory, Vol. I, Methods and Applications* (New York: John Wiley, 1993); Gary T. Henry, *Practical Sampling* (Thousand Oaks, Calif. Sage Publications, 1990); Leslie Kish, *Survey Sampling* (New York: John Wiley, 1995); Paul S. Levy and Stanley Lemeshow, *Sampling of Populations: Methods and Applications,* 3rd ed. (New York: John Wiley and Sons, Inc., 1999); Richard L. Schaeffer and William Mendenhall, *Elementary Survey Sampling,* 5th ed. (Belmont, Calif.: Wadsworth Publishing Company, 1996).

Chapter 17

1. The problem would be of interest to the tourist industry, and it also could be of interest to the division of state government concerned with economic development. The problem was chosen because the availability of a list of population elements allows a simple random sample to be selected.

2. The variable z more correctly equals 1.96 for a 95 percent confidence interval. The approximation $z = 2$ is used since it simplifies the calculations.

3. See Raphael Gillett, "Confidence Interval Construction by Stein's Method: A Practical and Economical Approach to Sample Size Determination," *Journal of Marketing Research* 26 (May 1989), pp. 237–240, for discussion of how the pilot study results can be used not only to develop an estimate of the population variance but also to produce an estimate of the population mean corresponding to the specified confidence level and desired interval size.

4. Ted Gregory, "Suburbanites a Study in Optimism," *Chicago Tribune* (August 29, 1999), sec. 1, pp. 1, 16.

5. The strict requirement is that $n\pi$ must be above a certain level if the normal curve is to provide a good approximation to the binomial, where π is the population proportion and n is the sample size. Some books hold that $n\pi$ must be

greater than 5, while others suggest that the product must be greater than 10.

6. The 5 percent correction factor is not a hard-and-fast rule. Some books contend that the finite population correction factor should be ignored if the sample includes no more than 10 percent of the population. Ignoring the finite population correction will result in overestimating the standard error of estimate.

7. See, for example, Morris H. Hansen, William N. Hurwitz, and William G. Madow, *Sample Survey Methods and Theory, Vol. 1* (New York: John Wiley, 1993); Paul S. Levy and Stanley Lemeshaw, *Sampling of Populations: Methods and Applications,* 3rd ed. (New York: John Wiley and Sons, Inc., 1999).

8. Computer-based expert systems that rely on artificial intelligence techniques also exist for determining sample size. These systems guide the researcher through a series of questions about the needed degree of confidence, precision, variability, and so on, and, based on the answers, perform the tedious computations concerning the needed sample size. See, for example, Ex-Sample, which is available from the Idea Works in Columbia, Missouri.

9. Chapter 19 discusses the procedures for setting up and analyzing cross-classification tables so that the proper inferences can be drawn.

10. Seymour Sudman, *Applied Sampling* (San Francisco: Academic Press, 1976), p. 30.

Chapter 18

1. Frederick Mosteller, "Nonsampling Errors," *Encyclopedia of Social Sciences* (New York: Macmillan, 1968), p. 113.

2. W. H. Williams, "How Bad Can 'Good' Data Really Be?" *The American Statistician* 32 (May 1978), p. 61. See also Judith T. Lessler and William D. Kalsbeek, *Nonsampling Errors in Surveys* (New York: John Wiley and Sons, Inc., 1992).

3. See, for example, Ronald Andersen, Judith Kasper, Martin R. Frankel, and Associates, *Total Survey Error* (San Francisco: Jossey-Bass, 1979), or Henry Assael and John Keon, "Nonsampling vs. Sampling Errors in Survey Research," *Journal of Marketing* 46 (Spring 1982), pp. 114–123.

4. Leslie Kish, *Survey Sampling* (New York: John Wiley, 1995), Chapter 13, "Biases and Nonsampling Errors," is particularly

recommended for discussion of the biases arising from nonobservation.

5. Jane M. Sheppard, "2001 Respondent Cooperation and Industry Study: Overview and Trends." The Council for Marketing and Opinion Research, 2001.

6. T. De Maio, "Refusals: Who, Where, and Why," *Public Opinion Quarterly* 44 (Summer 1980), pp. 223–233. See also Jolene M. Strubbe, Jerome B. Kernan, and Thomas J. Grogan, "The Refusal Problem in Telephone Surveys," *Journal of Marketing Research* 26 (June/July 1986), pp. 29–37; Kathy E. Green, "Sociodemographic Factors and Mail Survey Response," *Psychology & Marketing* 13 (March 1996), pp. 171–184.

7. *Respondent Cooperation and Industry Image Survey* (Port Jefferson, N.Y.: The Council for Marketing and Opinion Research, 1996), pp. 36-37.

8. There are several studies that contain data about when particular types of individuals are likely to be home. See, for example, M. F. Weeks, B. L. Jones, R. E. Folsum, Jr., and C. H. Benrud, "Optimal Times to Contact Sample Households," *Public Opinion Quarterly* 44 (Spring 1980), pp. 101–114; Michael F. Weeks, Richard W. Kulka, and Stephanie A. Pierson, "Optimal Call Scheduling for a Telephone Survey," *Public Opinion Quarterly* 51 (Winter 1987), pp. 540–549.

9. *CMOR Industry Image Study* (Port Jefferson, N.Y.: The Council for Marketing and Opinion Research, 2001).

10. W. Edwards Deming, "On a Probability Mechanism to Attain an Economic Balance between the Resultant Error of Response and the Bias of Nonresponse," *Journal of the American Statistical Association* 48 (December 1953), pp. 766–767. See also Benjamin Lipstein, "In Defense of Small Samples," *Journal of Advertising Research* 15 (February 1975), pp. 33–40; William C. Dunkelburg and George S. Day, "Nonresponse Bias and Callbacks in Sample Surveys," *Journal of Marketing Research* 10 (May 1973), pp. 160–168; Lorna Opatow, "Some Thoughts about How Interview Attempts Affect Survey Results," *Journal of Advertising Research* 31 (February/March 1991), pp. RC6–RC9.

11. James T. Massey, Charles Wolter, Siu Chong Wan, and Karen Liu, "Optimum Calling Patterns for Random Digit Dialed Telephone Surveys," paper pre-

sented at the American Statistical Association Meetings, 1996.

12. Ronald M. Weiers, *Marketing Research,* 2nd Edition (Englewood Cliffs, N.J.: Prentice Hall, 1988), pp. 213–217.

13. Art Shulman, "War Stories: True-Life Tales in Marketing Research," *Quirk's Marketing Research Review* (December 1998), p. 16.

14. Beth Clarkson, "Research and the Internet: A Winning Combination," *Quirk's Marketing Research Review* (July 1999), pp. 46, 48–51.

15. Seymour Sudman, Norman Bradburn, Ed Blair, and Carol Stocking, "Modest Expectations: The Effects of Interviewers' Prior Expectations and Response," *Sociological Methods & Research* 6 (November 1977), pp. 177–182; Eleanor Singer, Martin R. Frankel, and Marc B. Glassman, "The Effect of Interviewer Characteristics and Expectations on Response," *Public Opinion Quarterly* 47 (Spring 1983), pp. 68–83; Stanley Presser and Shanyang Zhao, "Attributes of Questions and Interviewers as Correlates of Interviewing Performance," *Public Opinion Quarterly* 56 (Summer 1992), pp. 236–240.

16. L. L. Guest, "A Study of Interviewer Competence," *International Journal of Opinion and Attitude Research* 1 (March 1947), pp. 17–30; P. Davis and A. Scott, "The Effect of Interviewer Variance on Domain Comparisons," *Survey Methodology* 21 (1995), pp. 99–106; Pamela Kiecker and James E. Nelson, "Do Interviewers Follow Survey Instructions?" *Journal of the Market Research Society* 38 (April 1996), pp. 161–176.

17. W. A. Belson, "Increasing the Power of Research to Guide Advertising Decisions," *Journal of Marketing* 29 (April 1965), p. 38. See also Martin Collins and Bob Butcher, "Interviewer and Clustering Effects in an Attitude Survey," *Journal of the Market Research Society* 25 (January 1983), pp. 39–58.

18. Benjamin Lipstein, "In Defense of Small Samples," *Journal of Advertising Research* 15 (February 1975), pp. 33–40.

19. The reader who believes that analysis errors should be no problem should see Mosteller, "Nonsampling Errors," in which he devotes 9 of 19 pages to the discussion of potential errors in analysis. See also John G. Keane, "Questionable Statistics," *American Demographics* 7 (June 1985), pp. 18–21. Paul Lavrakas, "To Err Is Human," *Marketing Research: A Magazine of Management & Applications* 8 (Spring 1996), pp. 30–36.

20. "On the Definition of Response Rates," *CASRO Special Report* (Port Jefferson, N.Y.: The Council of American Survey Research Organizations, 1982). See also M. A. Hidiroglu, J. D. Drew, and G. B. Gray, "A Framework for Measuring and Reducing Nonresponse in Surveys," *Survey Methodology* 19 (1993), pp. 81–94.

21. Peter H. Reingen and Jerome B. Kernan, "Compliance with an Interview Request: A Foot-in-the-Door, Self-Perception Interpretation," *Journal of Marketing Research* 14 (1977), pp. 365-369.

Chapter 19

1. Lourdes Lee Valeriano, "Marketing: Western Firms Poll Eastern Europeans to Discern Tastes of Nascent Consumers," *The Wall Street Journal* (April 27, 1992), p. B1.

2. Art Shulman, "War Stories: True-Life Tales in Marketing Research," *Quirk's Marketing Research Review* (December 1998), p. 16.

3. Valeriano, "Marketing: Western Firms Poll," p. B1.

4. Some writers would make the specification of categories part of the editing rather than the coding function. Its placement in one or the other function is not nearly as important as the recognition that it is an extremely critical step with significant ramifications for the whole research effort.

5. Carol Matlack, "What Unites Europe? Delayed Flights," *Business Week* (August 2, 1999), pp. 98, 100.

6. For discussion of a set of indices that can be used to investigate coder reliability as well as to determine which questions might prove to be particularly troublesome, see Martin Collins and Graham Kalton, "Coding Verbatim Answers to Open Questions," *Journal of the Market Research Society* 22 (October 1980), pp. 239–247; William D. Perreault, Jr., and Laurence E. Leigh, "Reliability of Nominal Data Based on Qualitative Judgments," *Journal of Marketing Research* 26 (May 1989), pp. 135–148.

7. Philip S. Siedl, "Coding," in Robert Ferber, ed., *Handbook of Marketing Research* (New York: McGraw-Hill, 1974), pp. 2–178 to 2–199. This article provides an excellent overview of the issues that arise in coding data and how they can be handled. See also Linda B. Bourque and Virginia A. Clark, *Processing Data: The Survey Example* (Thousand Oaks, Calif.: Sage Publications, 1992).

8. David W. Stewart, "Filling the Gap: A Review of the Missing Data Problem," unpublished manuscript, provides an excellent review of the literature on the problem of missing data, including various methods for eliminating cases and estimating answers. On the basis of this review, he concludes several things: Missing data points should be estimated regardless of whether the data are missing randomly or nonrandomly; for very small amounts of missing data, almost any of the estimation procedures work reasonably well; when larger amounts of data are missing and the average intercorrelation of variables is .20 or less, the substitution of the mean seems to work best; and when the average intercorrelation of the variables exceeds .20, a regression or principal-components procedure is the preferred choice when linearity among the variables may be assumed. For a study that empirically examines the question of whether or not missing items are random, see Richard M. Durand, Hugh J. Guffey, Jr., and John M. Planchon, "An Examination of the Random versus Nonrandom Nature of Item Omissions," *Journal of Marketing Research* 20 (August 1983), pp. 305–313. See also Roderick J. A. Little and Philip J. Smith, "Editing and Imputation for Quantitative Survey Data," *Journal of the American Statistical Association* 82 (March 1987), pp. 58–68; Roderick J. Little and Donald B. Rubin, "The Analysis of Social Science Data with Missing Values," *Sociological Methods and Research* 18 (November 1989), pp. 292–326; Philip L. Roth, "Missing Data: A Conceptual Review for Applied Psychologists," *Personnel Psychology* 47 (Autumn 1994), pp. 537–560.

Chapter 20

1. See the classic book by Hans Zeisel, *Say It with Figures,* 5th ed. (New York: Harper and Row, 1968), pp. 16–17, for conditions that would support reporting percentages with decimal-place accuracy.

2. Box and whisker plots can also be used to get a sense for the distribution of

the variable. They possess the attractive feature of including information about the variable mean, median, 25th and 75th percentiles, and outliers. For a discussion of how they are constructed, see "Graphic Displays of Data: Box and Whisker Plots," *Research on Research*, No. 17 (Chicago: Market Facts, Inc., undated).

3. See the classic book by Darrell Huff, *How to Lie with Statistics* (New York: Norton, 1954).

4. Robert J. Lavidge, "How to Keep Well-Intentioned Research from Misleading New-Product Planners," *Marketing News* 18 (January 6, 1984), p. 8. The more recent evidence suggests consumers want their sauces hot. See Kathleen Deveny, "Rival Hot Sauces Are Breathing Fire at Market Leader Tabasco," *The Wall Street Journal* (January 7, 1993), pp. B1, B6.

5. Bayesian statistical theory assumes a different posture with respect to hypothesis testing than does classical statistics. Because classical statistical significance-testing procedures are much more commonly used in marketing research, however, only the basic elements underlying classical statistical theory are presented here.

6. The authors express their appreciation to Dr. B. Venkatesh, of Burke Marketing Institute, for suggesting this example to illustrate the rationale behind the framing of hypotheses.

7. The binomial distribution tends toward the normal distribution for a fixed π as sample size increases. The tendency is most rapid when $\pi = 0.5$. With sufficiently large samples, normal probabilities may be used to approximate binomial probabilities with π's in this range. As π departs from 0.5 in either direction, the normal approximation becomes less adequate, although it is generally held that the normal approximation may be used safely if the smaller of $n\pi$ or $n(1 - \pi)$ is 10 or more. If this condition is not satisfied, binomial probabilities can either be calculated directly or found in tables that are readily available. In the example, $n\pi = 625(0.2) = 125$, and $n(1 - \pi) = 500$, and thus there is little question about the adequacy of the normal approximation to binomial probabilities.

8. For an excellent discussion of some of the most common misinterpretations of classical significance tests and some recommendations on how to surmount the problems, see Alan G. Sawyer and J. Paul Peter, "The Significance of Statistical Significance Tests in Marketing Research," *Journal of Marketing Research* 20 (May 1983), pp. 122–133. See also Jacob Cohen, "Things I Have Learned (So Far)," *American Psychologist* 45 (December 1990), pp. 1304–1312; Jacob Cohen, "The Earth is Round (p,.05)," *American Psychologist* 49 (December 1994), pp. 997–1003.

9. Lee J. Cronbach and R. E. Snow, *Aptitudes and Instructional Methods: A Handbook for Research on Interactions* (New York: Irvington, 1977), p. 52.

10. Sawyer and Peter, "The Significance," p. 123. For other useful discussions of what statistical tests of significance mean, see Mick Alt and Malcolm Brighton, "Analyzing Data or Telling Stories?" *Journal of the Market Research Society* 23 (October 1981), pp. 209–219; Siu L. Chow, *Statistical Significance: Rationale, Validity, and Utility* (Thousand Oaks, Calif.: Sage Publications, 1996).

11. Sawyer and Peter, "The Significance," p. 125.

12. Mary G. Natrella, "The Relation between Confidence Intervals and Tests of Significance," *American Statistician* 14 (1960), p. 22. See also G. R. Dawling and P. K. Walsh, "Estimating and Reporting Confidence Intervals for Marketing Opinion Research," *European Research* 13 (July 1985), pp. 130–133; Charles Cowan, "Testing versus Description: Confidence Intervals and Hypothesis Testing," *Marketing Research: A Magazine of Management & Applications* 2 (September 1990), pp. 59–61.

13. If we know the total number of packages sold and the number of packages sold for two of the three categories, the number of packages sold in the third category is fixed and cannot vary independently.

14. The correct distribution to test the hypothesis is the hypergeometric. The hypergeometric distribution, however, is unwieldy for anything but very small samples. The chi-square distribution approximates the hypergeometric for large sample sizes. For a discussion of this point as well as the other conditions surrounding a goodness-of-fit test, see Leonard A. Marascuilo and Maryellen McSweeney, *Nonparametric and Distribution Free Methods for the Social Sciences* (Belmont, Calif.: Brooks/Cole, 1977),

pp. 243–248. See also Wayne W. Daniel, *Applied Nonparametric Statistics*, 2d ed. (Boston: PWS-Kent Publishing, 1990); Jean D. Gibbons, *Nonparametric Statistics: An Introduction* (Thousand Oaks, Calif.: Sage Publications, 1992).

15. W. G. Cochran, "The χ^2 Test of Goodness of Fit," *Annuals of Mathematical Statistics* 23 (1952), pp. 315–345.

Chapter 21

1. In general, for the normal approximation to the exact binomial distribution of sample proportions to apply, np and nq should be greater than 10 for each sample, where p is the proportion of "successes" in the sample, q is the proportion of "failures" in the sample, and n is the sample size.

2. The Spearman rank correlation coefficient is a shortcut version of the product-moment correlation coefficient, in that both coefficients produce the same estimates of the strength of association between two sets of ranks. The rank correlation coefficient is easy to conceptualize and calculate, so it is often used when the data are ranked. See Jum C. Nunnally and Ira H. Bernstein, *Psychometric Theory*, 3rd ed. (New York: McGraw-Hill, Inc., 1994) pp. 131–132.

3. See Leonard A Marascuilo and Maryellen McSweeney, *Nonparametric and Distribution-Free Methods for the Social Sciences* (Belmont, Calif.: Brooks/Cole, 1977), pp. 250–251. See also Maurice G. Kendall and Jean D. Gibbons, *Rank Correlation Methods*, 5th ed. (New York: Oxford University Press, 1990); Jean D. Gibbons, *Nonparametric Measures of Association* (Thousand Oaks, Calif.: Sage Publications, 1993).

4. M. G. Kendall, *Rank Correlation Methods* (London: Griffin, 1948), p. 87.

5. If the two parent-population variances cannot be assumed to be equal, the standard error used in the calculation of t is

$$S_{\bar{x}_1 - \bar{x}_2} = \sqrt{\frac{\hat{s}_1^{\,2}}{n_1} + \frac{\hat{s}_2^{\,2}}{n_2}}$$

where $\hat{s}_1^{\,2}$ is the variance of the dependent variable for the first sample, and $\hat{s}_2^{\,2}$ is the variance of the dependent variable for the second sample.

6. See the classic little book by Darrell Huff, *How to Lie with Statistics* (New York:

Norton, 1954), pp. 87–99, for a discussion of this point using some rather humorous anecdotes.

7. Strictly speaking, the regression model requires that errors of measurement be associated only with the dependent variable and that the predictor variables be measured without error. See Thomas H. Wonnacott and Ronald J. Wonnacott, *Regression: A Second Course in Statistics* (Malabar, Fla.: Robert E. Krieger Publishing Co., 1986), pp. 293–299, for a discussion of the problems and solutions when the predictor variables also have an error component. In order to correctly apply the inferential test statistics, it is also necessary that errors (i.e., residuals) associated with the dependent variable are normally distributed.

8. For those who would like to try solving for each of these values, the formulas are

$$\hat{\alpha} = \bar{y} - \hat{\beta}\bar{x}_1$$

$$\hat{\beta} = \frac{n\sum_{i=1}^{n} X_i Y_i - \left(\sum_{i=1}^{n} X_i\right)\left(\sum_{i=1}^{n} Y_i\right)}{n\sum_{i=1}^{n} X_i^2 - \left(\sum_{i=1}^{n} X_i\right)^2}$$

where

$$\bar{y} = \sum_{i=1}^{n} \frac{Y_i}{n} \text{ and } \bar{x} = \sum_{i=1}^{n} \frac{X_i}{n}$$

9. There are some things that the analyst faced with multicollinear data can do. See R. R. Hocking, "Developments in Linear Regression Methodology: 1959–1982," *Technometrics* 25 (August 1983), pp. 219–230, and Ronald D. Snee, "Discussion," *Technometrics* 25 (August 1983), pp. 230–237, for a discussion of the problem and some alternative ways of handling it. See also Charlotte H. Mason and William D. Perreault, Jr., "Collinearity, Power and Interpretation of Multiple Regression Analysis," *Journal of Marketing Research* 28 (August 1991), pp. 268–280; R. Carter Hill, Phillip A. Cartwright, and Julia F. Arbaugh, "The Use of Biased Predictors in Marketing Research," *International Journal of Forecasting* 7 (November 1991), pp. 271–282; Peter Kennedy, *A Guide to Econometrics*, 3rd ed. (Cambridge, Mass.: The MIT Press, 1992), pp. 176–187; George C. S. Wang, "How to Handle Multicollinearity in Regression Modeling," *Journal of Business Forecasting* 15 (Spring 1996), pp. 23–27.

10. There is another interpretation danger in the example that was not discussed. It is not unreasonable to assume that both the number of sales representatives serving a territory and the number of television spots per month were both determined on the basis of territorial potential. If this is the case, the implied causality is reversed or at least confused; instead of the number of sales representatives and number of television spots determining sales, sales in a sense (potential sales anyway) determine the former qualities, and they in turn could be expected to affect realized sales. If this is actually the case, the coefficient-estimating procedure needs to take into account the two-way "causation" among the variables. See Wonnacott and Wonnacott, *Regression*, pp. 284–292, for a discussion of the problems and the logic underlying the estimation of simultaneous equation systems.

Chapter 22

1. William J. Gallagher, *Report Writing for Management* (Reading, MA: Addison-Wesley, 1969), p. 1. Much of this introductory section is also taken from this excellent book. See also Pnenna Sageev, *Helping Researchers Write, So Managers Can Understand* (Columbus, Ohio: Batelle Press, 1995).

2. The other variables are the extent of interaction that researchers have with managers, the research objectives, the degree of surprise in the results, and the stage of the product or service in its life cycle. See Rohit Deshpande and Gerald Zaltman, "A Comparison of Factors Affecting Researcher and Manager Perceptions of Market Research Use," *Journal of Marketing Research* 21 (February 1984), pp. 32–38. The understandability of the research report also affects managers' trust and that, in turn, affects what they do with the information. See, for example, Christine Moorman, Rohit Deshpande, and Gerald Zaltman, "Factors Affecting Trust in Market Research Relationships," *Journal of Marketing* 57 (January 1993), pp. 81–101; Kent Grayson and Tim Ambler, "The Dark Side of Long-Term Relationships in Marketing Services," *Journal of Marketing Research* 3 (February 1999), pp. 132–41.

3. Walter B. Wentz, *Marketing Research: Management, Method, and Cases,* 2nd ed. (New York: Harper and Row, 1979), p. 61. See also Edward P. Bailey and Philip A. Powell, *The Practical Writer,* 6th ed. (Orlando, Fla.: Harcourt Brace College Publishers, 1994).

4. Stewart Henderson Britt, "The Communication of Your Research Findings," in Robert Ferber, ed., *Handbook of Marketing Research* (New York: McGraw-Hill, 1974), pp. 1–90. See also Edward P. Bailey, *The Plain English Approach to Business Writing,* rev. ed. (New York: Oxford University Press, 1997).

5. Ron Sellers, "Interpreting Research Data: It All Depends on the Context," *Quirk's Marketing Research Review* (January 1998, downloaded from the *Quirk's* Web site, http://www.quirks.com, October 27, 1999).

6. Gallagher, *Report Writing*, p. 78.

7. Joseph Rydholm, "Are We Getting Ahead of Ourselves?" *Quirk's Marketing Research Review* (July 1999), pp. 19, 95–97.

8. See Gallagher, *Report Writing*, pp. 80–83, for a number of examples that display some of the inaccuracies that may arise. The examples are particularly interesting because they have been extracted from actual company reports.

9. Taken from William Zinsser, *On Writing Well*, 6th ed. (New York: Harper and Row, 1998), pp. 7–8, a modern classic for writers that is as helpful as it is fun to read.

10. Gallagher, *Report Writing*, Chapter 10, "Reviewing for Accuracy: Grammar," pp. 156–177, has examples of how these inaccuracies can confuse and misinform.

11. Gallagher, *Report Writing*, p. 83.

12. Kenneth Roman and Joel Raphaelson, *Writing That Works* (New York: Harper and Row, 1981). This book gives some excellent advice on how to write more effective reports, memos, letters, and speeches. The little book by William Strunk, Jr., and E. B. White, *The Elements of Style,* 4th ed. (Boston: Allyn and Bacon, 2000), is a classic on how to write clearly.

13. Jock Elliott, "How Hard It Is to Write Easily," *Viewpoint: By, For, and About Ogilvy & Mather* 2 (1980), p. 18. See also Edward P. Bailey, *Plain English at Work—A Guide to Writing and Speaking* (New York: Oxford University Press, 1996).

14. Gallagher, *Report Writing*, p. 87.

15. Ibid., p. 84.

16. See Gallagher, *Report Writing*, pp. 50–68, for a discussion of the psychological order of things in research reports.

17. Jean Thilmany, "Ames' Gains," *Executive Technology* (May 1999), pp. 14–15.

18. "6: Direct Marketing: NextCard," *Fortune* (May 24, 1999), pp. 122–123.

19. See A. S. C. Ehrenberg, "Rudiments of Numeracy," *Journal of the Royal Statistical Society,* Series A, 140 (1977), pp. 277–297, and A. S. C. Ehrenberg, "The Problem of Numeracy," *American Statistician* 35 (May 1981), pp. 67–71, for particularly informative discussions using examples of how adherence to these principles can dramatically improve readers' abilities to comprehend the information being presented in tables. For an empirical assessment of how various countries compare with respect to numeracy, see Alan Wells, "International Numeracy Survey," *Management Services* 43 (August 1999), pp. 14–16.

20. Alex Taylor III, "Kellogg Cranks Up Its Idea Machine," *Fortune* (July 5, 1999, downloaded from the Northern Light Web site, http://www.northern-light.com, August 6, 1999).

21. Paco Underhill, *Why We Buy: The Science of Shopping* (New York: Simon & Schuster, 1999), p. 241.

22. Michele Holleran, "Research Should Be Integrated and Lead to Strategic Decision-Making," *Quirk's Marketing Research Review* (June 1998, downloaded from the *Quirk's* Web site, http://www.quirks.com, October 27, 1999).

23. There are a number of excellent books available on making effective oral presentations. See, for example, Thomas Leech, *How to Prepare, Stage, and Deliver Winning Presentations* (New York: American Management Association, 1993). Dorothy Sarnoff, *Make the Most of Your Best: A Complete Program for Presenting Yourself and Your Ideas with Confidence and Authority* (Garden City, N.Y.: Doubleday, 1983); Jan D'Arcy, *Technically Speaking: Proven Ways to Make Your Next Presentation a Success* (New York: AMACOM, 1992); Rudolph F. Verderber, *The Challenge of Effective Speaking*, 12th ed. (Belmont, Calif.: Wadsworth Publishing Company, 2003).

24. The presentation should by no means include all the graph forms that could be used, but rather just some of the more common ones. Those interested in more detail should see William S. Cleveland, *The Elements of Graphing Data* (Boca Raton, Fla.: CRC Press LLC, 1994); Edward R. Tufte, *The Visual Display of Quantitative Information,* 2nd ed. (Cheshire, Conn.: Graphics Press, 2001); Edward R. Tufte, *Envisioning Information* (Cheshire, Conn.: Graphics Press, 1991).

25. For suggestions as to how best present statistical data, see Gary T. Henry, *Graphing Data: Techniques for Display and Analysis* (Thousand Oaks, Calif.: Sage Publications, 1994); Anders Wallgren, et al., *Graphing Statistics and Data: Creating Better Charts* (Thousand Oaks, Calif.: Sage Publications, 1996).

Glossary

accuracy A criterion used to evaluate a research report; specifically, whether the reasoning in the report is logical and the information correct.

administrative control A term applied to studies relying on questionnaires and referring to the speed, cost, and control of the replies afforded by the mode of administration.

advocacy research Research conducted to support a position rather than to find the truth about an issue.

ALCA Model A model especially useful in early stages of problem formulation in which researchers *ask* questions, *listen* carefully to responses, *clarify* the situation by asking additional questions, and *analyze* available information about the situation.

alternative hypothesis The hypothesis that a proposed result is true for the population.

analysis of selected cases Intensive study of selected examples of the phenomenon of interest.

analysis of variance (ANOVA) A statistical technique used with a continuous dependent variable and one or more categorical independent variables.

area sampling A form of cluster sampling in which areas (for example, census tracts, blocks) serve as the primary sampling units. The population is divided into mutually exclusive and exhaustive areas using maps, and a random sample of areas is selected. If all the households in the selected areas are used in the study, it is one-stage area sampling; if the areas themselves are subsampled with respect to households, the procedure is two-stage area sampling.

attitude An individual's preference, inclination, views, or feelings toward some phenomenon.

awareness/knowledge Insight into, or understanding of facts about, some object or phenomenon.

banner A series of cross tabulations between a criterion, or dependent variable, and several (sometimes many) explanatory variables in a single table.

bar chart A chart in which the relative lengths of the bars show relative amounts of variables or objects.

behavior What subjects have done or are doing.

benchmarking Using organizations that excel at some function as sources of ideas for improvement.

blunder An error that arises during editing, coding, or data entry.

branching question A technique used to direct respondents to different places in a questionnaire, based on their response to the question at hand.

categorical measures A commonly used expression for nominal and ordinal measures.

causal research Research design in which the major emphasis is on determining cause-and-effect relationships.

census A complete canvass of a population.

central-limit theorem A theorem that holds that if simple random samples of size n are drawn from a parent population with mean μ and variance σ^2, then when n is large, the sample mean $\bar{x}$ will be approximately normally distributed with mean equal to μ and variance equal to σ^2/n. The approximation will become more and more accurate as n becomes larger.

central-office edit Thorough and exacting scrutiny and correction of completed data collection forms, including a decision about what to do with the data.

chi-square goodness-of-fit test A statistical test to determine whether some observed pattern of frequencies corresponds to an expected pattern.

clarity A criterion used to evaluate a research report; specifically, whether the phrasing in the report is precise.

cluster sample A probability sample distinguished by a two-step procedure in which (1) the parent population is divided into mutually exclusive and exhaustive subsets, and (2) a random sample of subsets is selected. If the investigator then uses all the population elements in the selected subsets for the sample, the procedure is one-stage cluster sampling; if a sample of elements is selected probabilistically from the subsets, the procedure is two-stage cluster sampling.

codebook A book that contains explicit directions about how data from data collection forms are to be coded in the data file.

coding The technical procedure by which raw data are categorized or transformed into symbols; it involves specifying the alternative categories or classes into which the responses are to be placed and assigning code numbers to the classes.

coefficient of determination A measure representing the relative proportion of the total variation in the dependent variable that can be explained or accounted for by the fitted regression equation.

coefficient of multiple determination In multiple regression analysis, the proportion of variation in the dependent variable that is explained or accounted for by the covariation in the independent variables.

communication A method of data collection involving questioning of respondents to secure the desired information, using a data collection instrument called a questionnaire.

comparative-ratings scale A scale requiring subjects to make their ratings as a series of relative judgments or comparisons rather than as independent assessments.

completeness A criterion used to evaluate a research report; specifically, whether the report provides all the information readers need in language they understand.

composite measure A measure designed to provide a comprehensive assessment of an object or phenomenon, with items to assess all relevant aspects or dimensions.

computer-assisted interviewing (CAI) The conduct of surveys using computers to manage the sequence of questions and where the answers are recorded electronically through the use of a keyboard.

conceptual definition A definition in which a given construct is defined in terms of other constructs in the set, sometimes in the form of an equation that expresses the relationship among them.

conciseness A criterion used to evaluate a research report; specifically, whether the writing in the report is crisp and direct.

confidence The degree to which one can feel confident that an estimate approximates the true value.

confidence interval A projection of the range within which a population parameter will lie at a given level of confidence based on a statistic obtained from a probabilistic sample.

conjoint analysis A technique in which respondents' utilities or valuations of attributes are inferred from the preference they express for various combinations of these attributes.

constant-sum method A type of comparative-ratings scale in which an individual is instructed to divide some given sum among two or more attributes on some basis such as importance or favorability.

construct validity Assessment of how well the instrument captures the construct, concept, or trait it is supposed to be measuring.

contact rate (C) A measure used to evaluate and compare the effectiveness of interviewers in making contact with designated respondents; C-number of sample units contacted divided by total number of eligible sample units approached.

content validity The adequacy with which the important aspects of the characteris-

tic are captured by the measure; it is sometimes called *face validity*.

continuous measures A commonly used expression for interval and ratio measures.

continuous panel A fixed sample of respondents who are measured repeatedly over time with respect to the same variables.

contrived setting Subjects are observed in an environment that has been specially designed for recording their behavior.

controlled test market An entire test program conducted by an outside service in a market in which it can guarantee distribution.

convenience sample A nonprobability sample that is sometimes called an *accidental sample* because those included in the sample enter by accident, in that they just happen to be where the study is being conducted when it is being conducted.

Cramer's V A statistic used to measure the strength of relationship between categorical variables.

cross-sectional study Investigation involving a sample of elements selected from the population of interest that are measured at a single point in time.

cross tabulation A multivariate technique used for studying the relationship between two or more categorical variables. The technique considers the joint distribution of sample elements across variables.

cumulative distribution function A function that shows the number of cases having a value less than or equal to a specified quantity; the function is generated by connecting points representing the given combinations of X's (values) and Y's (cumulative frequencies) with straight lines.

cumulative percent breakdown A technique for converting a continuous measure into a categorical measure. The categories are formed based on the cumulative percentages obtained in a frequency analysis.

data system The part of a decision support system that includes the processes used to capture and the methods used to store data coming from a number of external and internal sources.

decision problem The problem facing the decision maker for which the research is intended to provide answers.

decision support system (DSS) A coordinated collection of data, systems, tools, and techniques with supporting software and hardware, by which an organization gathers and interprets relevant information from business and the environment and turns it into a basis for marketing decisions.

deontology An ethical or moral reasoning framework that focuses on the welfare of the individual and that uses means, intentions, and features of an act itself in judging its ethicality; sometimes referred to as the rights, or entitlements, model.

depth interview An unstructured personal interview in which the interviewer attempts to get the subject to talk freely and to express his or her true feelings.

derived population A population of all possible distinguishable samples that could be drawn from a parent population under a specific sampling plan.

descriptive research Research design in which the major emphasis is on determining the frequency with which something occurs or the extent to which two variables covary.

descriptive statistics Statistics that describe the distribution of responses on a variable. The most commonly used descriptive statistics are the mean and standard deviation.

dialog system The part of a decision support system that permits users to explore the databases by employing the system models to produce reports that satisfy their particular information needs. Also called *language system*.

dichotomous question A fixed-alternative question in which respondents are asked to indicate which of two alternative responses most closely corresponds to their position on a subject.

discontinuous panel A fixed sample of respondents who are measured repeatedly over time but on variables that change from measurement to measurement.

discovery-oriented decision problem A decision problem that typically seeks to answer "what" or "why" questions about a problem/opportunity. The focus is generally on generating useful information.

disguise The amount of knowledge about the purpose of a study communicated to the respondent. An undisguised questionnaire, for example, is one in which the purpose of the research is obvious.

disguised observation The subjects are not aware that they are being observed.

disproportionate stratified sample A stratified sample in which the individual strata or subsets are sampled in relation to both their size and their variability; strata exhibiting more variability are sampled more than proportionately to their relative size, while those that are very homogeneous are sampled less than proportionately.

double-barreled question A question that calls for two responses and thereby creates confusion for the respondent.

double-entry Data entry procedure in which data are entered separately by two people in two data files and the data files are compared for discrepancies.

dummy table A table that will be used to catalog the collected data.

editing Inspection and correction, if necessary, of each questionnaire or observation form.

electrical/mechanical observation An electrical or mechanical device observes a phenomenon and records the events that take place.

email survey A questionnaire both sent and returned by email.

ethics A concern with the development of moral standards by which situations can be judged; applies to all situations in which there can be actual or potential harm of any kind to an individual or group.

ethnographic methods The detailed observation of consumers during their ordinary daily lives using direct observations, interviews, and video and audio recordings.

experience survey Interviews with people knowledgeable about the general subject being investigated.

experiment Scientific investigation in which an investigator manipulates and controls one or more indepent variables and observes the degree to which the dependent variables change.

expert system A computer-based, artificial intelligence system that attempts to model how experts in the area process information to solve the problem at hand.

exploratory research Research design in which the major emphasis is on gaining ideas and insights; it is particularly helpful in breaking broad, vague problem statements into smaller, more precise subproblem statements.

external data Data that originate outside the organization for which the research is being done.

external validity A criterion by which an experiment is evaluated; the extent to which the observed experimental effect can be generalized to other populations and settings.

eye camera A device used by researchers to study a subject's eye movements while he or she is reading advertising copy.

factorial design An ANOVA analysis that includes two or more categorical independent variables.

faxed survey A questionnaire faxed to a respondent and, when completed, returned to the research sponsor by fax.

field edit A preliminary edit, typically conducted by a field supervisor, which is designed to detect the most glaring omissions and inaccuracies in a completed data collection instrument.

field experiment Research study in a realistic situation in which one or more independent variables are manipulated by the experimenter under as carefully controlled conditions as the situation will permit.

fixed sample A sample for which size is determined *a priori* and needed information is collected from the designated elements.

fixed-alternative questions Questions in which the responses are limited to stated alternatives.

focus group An interview conducted among a small number of individuals simultaneously; the interview relies more on group discussion than on directed questions to generate data.

frequency analysis A count of the number of cases that fall into each category when the categories are based on one variable.

frequency polygon A figure obtained from a histogram by connecting the midpoints of the bars of the histogram with straight lines.

funnel approach An approach to question sequencing that gets its name from its shape, starting with broad questions and progressively narrowing down the scope.

galvanometer A device used to measure the emotion induced by exposure to a particular stimulus by recording changes in the electrical resistance of the skin associated with the minute degree of sweating that accompanies emotional arousal; in marketing research, the stimulus is often specific advertising copy.

geodemography The availability of demographic, consumer-behavior, and lifestyle data by arbitrary geographic boundaries that are typically quite small.

global measure A measure designed to provide an overall assessment of an object or phenomenon, typically using one or two items.

graphic-ratings scale A scale in which individuals indicate their ratings of an attribute by placing a check at the appropriate point on a line that runs from one extreme of the attribute to the other.

halo effect A problem that arises in data collection when there is carryover from one judgment to another.

histogram A form of bar chart on which the values of the variable are placed along the abscissa, or X axis, and the absolute frequency or relative frequency of occurrence of the values is indicated along the ordinate, or Y axis.

human observation Individuals are trained to systematically observe a phenomenon and to record on the observational form the specific events that take place.

hypothesis A statement that specifies how two or more measurable variables are related.

hypothetical construct A concept used in theoretical models to explain how things work. Hypothetical constructs include such things as attitudes, personality, and intentions—things that cannot be seen but that are useful in theoretical explanations.

implicit alternative An alternative answer that is not expressed in a question's options.

implicit assumption A problem that occurs when a question is not framed so as to explicitly state the consequences, and thus it elicits different responses from individuals who assume different consequences.

incidence The percent of the general population or group that qualifies for inclusion in the sample using some criteria.

independent samples *t*-test A commonly-used technique used to determine whether two groups differ on some characteristic assessed on a continuous measure.

indirect techniques Methods of assessing attitudes that use unstructured or partially structured stimuli, such as word-association tests, sentence-completion tests, storytelling, and so on.

information control A term applied to studies using questionnaires and concerning the amount and accuracy of the information that can be obtained from respondents.

intentions Anticipated or planned future behavior.

internal data Data that originate within the organization for which the research is being done.

internal validity A criterion by which an experiment is evaluated; the focus is on obtaining evidence demonstrating that the variation in the dependent variable was the result of exposure to the treatment, or experimental, variable.

interval scale Measurement in which the assigned numbers legitimately allow the comparison of the size of the differences among and between members.

item nonresponse A source of nonsampling error that arises when a respondent agrees to an interview but refuses, or is unable, to answer specific questions.

itemized-ratings scale A scale distinguished by the fact that individuals must indicate their ratings of an attribute or object by selecting the response category that best describes their position on the attribute or object.

judgment sample A nonprobability sample that is often called a *purposive sample*; the sample elements are hand-picked because they are expected to serve the research purpose.

Kendall's coefficient of concordance A technique for determining the degree of association between three or more ordinal variables.

knowledge management The systematic collection of employee knowledge about customers, products, and the marketplace.

Kolmogorov-Smirnov test A statistical test used with ordinal data to determine whether some observed pattern of frequencies corresponds to some expected pattern; also used to determine whether two independent samples have been drawn from the same population or from populations with the same distribution.

laboratory experiment Research investigation in which investigators create a situation with exact conditions in order to control some variables, and manipulate others.

leading question A question framed so as to give the respondent a clue as to how he or she should answer.

line chart A two-dimensional chart constructed on graph paper with the *X* axis representing one variable (typically time) and the *Y* axis representing another variable.

literature search A search of statistics, trade journal articles, other articles, magazines, newspapers, and books for data or insight into the problem at hand.

longitudinal study Investigation involving a fixed sample of elements that is measured repeatedly through time.

mail questionnaire A questionnaire administered by mail to designated respondents under an accompanying cover letter. The respondents return the questionnaire by mail to the research organization.

mall intercept A method of data collection in which interviewers in a shopping mall stop or interrupt a sample of those passing by to ask them if they would be willing to participate in a research study; those who agree are typically taken to an interviewing facility that has been set up in the mall, where the interview is conducted.

market testing (test-marketing) A controlled experiment done in a limited but carefully selected sector of the marketplace; its aim is to predict the sales or profit consequences, either in absolute or relative terms, of one or more proposed marketing actions.

marketing ethics The principles, values, and standards of conduct followed by marketers.

marketing information system (MIS) A set of procedures and methods for the regular, planned collection, analysis, and presentation of information for use in making marketing decisions.

marketing research The function that links the consumer to the marketer through information—information used to identify and define marketing problems; generate, refine, and evaluate marketing actions; monitor marketing performance; and improve understanding of marketing as a process.

measurement Rules for assigning numbers to objects to represent quantities of attributes.

median split A technique for converting a continuous measure into a categorical measure with two approximately equal-sized groups. The groups are formed by "splitting" the continuous measure at its median value.

model system The part of a decision support system that includes all the routines that allow the user to manipulate the data so as to conduct the kind of analysis the individual desires.

motive A need, a want, a drive, a wish, a desire, an impulse, or any inner state that energizes, activates, or moves and that directs or channels behavior toward goals.

multichotomous question A fixed-alternative question in which respondents are asked to choose the alternative that most closely corresponds to their position on the subject.

multicollinearity A condition said to be present in a multiple regression analysis when the independent variables are correlated among themselves.

multidimensional scaling An approach to measurement in which people's perceptions of the similarity of objects and their preferences among the objects are measured, and these relationships are plotted in a multidimensional space.

multiple regression A statistical technique used to derive an equation that relates a single continuous dependent variable to two or more independent variables.

natural setting Subjects are observed in the environment where the behavior normally takes place.

nominal scale Measurement in which numbers are assigned to objects or classes of objects solely for the purpose of identification.

noncoverage error Nonsampling error that arises because of a failure to include some units, or entire sections, of the defined target population in the sampling frame.

nonprobability sample A sample that relies on personal judgment in the element selection process and therefore prohibits estimating the probability that any population element will be included in the sample.

nonresponse error Nonsampling error that represents a failure to obtain information from some elements of the population that were selected and designated for the sample.

nonsampling error Error that arises in research and that is not due to sampling; nonsampling error can occur because of errors in conception, logic, interpretation of replies, statistics, arithmetic, analyzing, coding, or reporting.

normative standard A comparative standard used to provide meaning to raw scale scores.

not-at-homes Nonsampling error that arises when replies are not secured from some designated sampling units because the respondents are not at home when the interviewer calls.

null hypothesis The hypothesis that a proposed result is not true for the population. Researchers typically attempt to reject the null hypothesis in favor of some alternative hypothesis.

observation A method of data collection in which the situation of interest is watched and the relevant facts, actions, or behaviors are recorded.

open-ended question A question that respondents are free to answer in their own words rather than being limited to choosing from among a set of alternatives.

operational definition A definition of a construct that describes the operations to be carried out in order for the construct to be measured empirically.

opinion Verbal expression of an attitude.

ordinal scale Measurement in which numbers are assigned to data on the basis of some order (for example, more than, greater than) of the objects.

outlier An observation so different in magnitude from the rest of the observations that the analyst chooses to treat it as a special case.

p-value The probability of obtaining a given result if in fact the null hypothesis were true in the population. A result is regarded as statistically significant if the p-value is less than the chosen significance level of the test.

paired sample *t*-test A technique for comparing two means when scores for both variables are provided by the same sample.

parameter A fixed characteristic or measure of a parent, or target, population.

parent population The totality of cases that conform to some designated specifications; also called a *target population*.

Pearson chi-square test of independence A commonly-used statistic for testing the null hypothesis that categorical variables are independent of one another.

Pearson product-moment correlation coefficient A statistic that indicates the degree of linear association between two continuous variables. The correlation coefficient can range from –1 to +1.

people meter A device used to measure when a television is on, to what channel it is tuned, and who in the household is watching it.

performance of objective tasks A method of assessing attitudes that rests on the presumption that a subject's performance of a specific assigned task (for example, memorizing a number of facts) will depend on the person's attitude.

personal interview Direct, face-to-face conversation between a representative of the research organization, the interviewer, and a respondent, or interviewee.

personality Normal patterns of behavior exhibited by an individual; the attributes, traits, and mannerisms that distinguish one individual from another.

physiological reaction A method of assessing attitudes in which the researcher monitors the subject's response, by electrical or mechanical means, to the controlled introduction of some stimuli.

pictogram A bar chart in which pictures represent amounts—for example, piles of dollars for income, picture of cars for automobile production, people in a row for population.

pie chart A circle representing a total quantity and divided into sectors, with each sector showing the size of the segment in relation to that total.

plus-one sampling A technique used in studies employing telephone interviews, in which a single, randomly determined digit is added to numbers selected from the telephone directory.

population The totality of cases that conform to some designated specifications.

power The probability of correctly rejecting a false null hypothesis.

precision The degree of error in a study, or the size of the estimating interval. *Absolute precision* is expressed as within plus or minus so many units. *Relative precision* is expressed relative to the level of the estimate of the parameter.

predictive validity The usefulness of the measuring instrument as a predictor of some other characteristic or behavior of the individual; it is sometimes called *criterion-related validity.*

pretest Use of a questionnaire (or observation form) on a trial basis in a small pilot study to determine how well the questionnaire (or observation form) works.

primary data Information collected specifically for the investigation at hand.

primary source The originating source of secondary data.

probability sample A sample in which each target population element has a known, nonzero chance of being included in the sample.

probability-proportional-to-size sampling A form of cluster sampling in which a fixed number of second-stage units is selected from each first-stage unit. The probabilities associated with the selection of each first-stage unit are in turn variable because they are directly related to the relative sizes of the first-stage units.

program strategy A company's philosophy of how marketing research fits into its marketing plan.

project strategy The design of individual marketing research studies that are to be conducted.

projective method The term used to describe questionnaires containing ambiguous stimuli that force subjects to rely on their own emotions, needs, motivations, attitudes, and values in framing a response.

proportionate stratified sample A stratified sample in which the number of observations in the total sample is allocated among the strata in proportion to the relative number of elements in each stratum in the population.

psychographic analysis A technique that investigates how people live, what interests them, and what they like; it is also called *lifestyle analysis,* since it relies on a number of statements about a person's AIO—activities (A), interests (I), and opinions (O).

quota sample A nonprobability sample chosen in such a way that the proportion of sample elements possessing certain characteristics is approximately the same as the proportion of the elements with the characteristics in the target population; each field-worker is assigned a quota that specifies the characteristics of the people he or she is to contact.

random error Error in measurement due to transient aspects of the person or measurement situation and which affects the measurement in irregular ways.

random-digit dialing A technique used in studies using telephone interviews, in which the numbers to be called are randomly generated.

randomized-response model An interviewing technique in which potentially embarrassing and relatively innocuous questions are paired, and the question the respondent answers is randomly determined but is unknown to the interviewer.

ratio scale Measurement that has a natural, or absolute, zero and therefore allows the comparison of absolute magnitudes of the numbers.

recall loss A type of error caused by a respondent's forgetting that an event happened at all.

refusals Nonsampling error that arises because some designated respondents refuse to participate in the study.

reliability Ability of a measure to obtain similar scores for the same object, trait, or construct across time, across different evaluators, or across the items forming the measure.

research design The framework or plan for a study that guides the collection and analysis of the data.

research problem A restatement of the decision problem in research terms.

research process The sequence of steps in the design and implementation of a research study, including problem formulation, determination of research design, determination of data collection method, design of data collection forms, design of the sample and collection of the data, analysis and interpretation of the data, and preparation of the research report.

research proposal A written statement that describes the marketing problem, the purpose of the study, and a detailed outline of the research methodology.

Research Request Agreement The initial step that sets the research process in motion; this statement, which is prepared by the researcher after meeting with the decision maker, summarizes the problem and the information that is needed to address it.

response latency The amount of time a respondent deliberates before answering a question.

response rate The number of completed interviews with responding units divided by the number of eligible responding units in the sample.

response set bias A problem that arises when respondents answer questionnaire items in a similar way without thinking about the items.

reverse scaling A technique in which some of the items on a multi-item scale are written so that the most positive responses are at the opposite end of the scale from where they would normally appear.

sample Selection of a subset of elements from a larger group of objects.

sample mean The arithmetic average value of the responses on a variable.

sample standard deviation A measure of the variation of responses on a variable. The standard deviation is the square root of the calculated variance on a variable.

sample survey Cross-sectional study in which the sample is selected to be representative of the target population and in which the emphasis is on the generation of summary statistics such as averages and percentages.

sampling control The term applied to studies relying on questionnaires and concerning the researcher's dual abilities to direct the inquiry to a designated respondent and to secure the desired cooperation from that respondent.

sampling distribution The distribution of values of some statistic calculated for each possible distinguishable sample that could be drawn from a parent population under a specific sampling plan.

sampling error The difference between the observed values of a variable and the long-run average of the observed values in repetitions of the measurement.

sampling frame The list of sampling units from which a sample will be drawn; the list could consist of geographic areas, institutions, individuals, or other units.

sampling units Nonoverlapping collections of elements from the population.

scanner An electronic device that automatically reads the Universal Product Code imprinted on a product, looks up the price in an attached computer, and instantly prints the description and price of the item on the cash register receipt.

scatter diagram A graphic technique in which a sample element's scores on two variables are used to position the element on a graph so that the nature of the relationship between the variables can be observed.

secondary data Information or statistics not gathered for the immediate study at hand but for some other purpose.

secondary source A source of secondary data that did not originate the data but rather secured them from another source.

self-report A method of assessing attitudes in which individuals are asked directly for their beliefs about or feelings toward an object or class of objects.

semantic-differential scale A self-report technique for attitude measurement in which the subjects are asked to check which cell between a set of bipolar adjectives or phrases best describes their feelings toward the object.

sentence completion A questionnaire containing a number of sentences that subjects are directed to complete with the first words that come to mind.

sequential sample A sample formed on the basis of a series of successive decisions. If the evidence is not conclusive after a small sample is taken, more observations are taken; if it is still inconclusive after these additional observations, still more observations are taken. At each stage a decision is made as to whether more information should be collected or whether the evidence is sufficient to draw a conclusion.

significance level (∝) The acceptable level of Type I error selected by the researcher, usually set at 0.05. Type I error is the probability of rejecting the null hypothesis when it is actually true for the population.

simple regression A statistical technique used to derive an equation that relates a single continuous dependent variable to a single independent variable.

simulated test market (STM) A study in which consumer ratings are obtained along with likely or actual purchase data often obtained in a simulated store environment; the data are fed into computer models to produce sales and market share predictions.

single-source data Data that allow researchers to link together purchase behavior, household characteristics, and advertising exposure at the household level.

snake diagram A diagram that connects the average responses to a series of semantic-differential statements, thereby depicting the profile of the object or objects being evaluated.

snowball sample A judgment sample that relies on the researcher's ability to locate an initial set of respondents with the desired characteristics; these individuals are then used as informants to identify still others with the desired characteristics.

Spearman rank-order correlation coefficient A technique for determining the degree of association between two ordinal, or rank-ordered, variables.

split ballot A technique used to combat response bias in which one phrasing is used for a question in one half of the questionnaires while an alternative phrasing is used in the other one half of the questionnaires.

standard test market A test market in which the company sells the product through its normal distribution channels.

Stapel scale A self-report technique for attitude measurement in which respondents are asked to indicate how accurately each of a number of statements describes the object of interest.

statistic A characteristic or measure of a sample.

statistical efficiency A measure used to compare sampling plans; one sampling plan is said to be superior (more statistically efficient) to another if, for the same size sample, it produces a smaller standard error of estimate.

storytelling A questionnaire method of data collection relying on a picture stimulus such as a cartoon, photograph, or drawing, about which the subject is asked to tell a story.

strategy-oriented decision problem A decision problem that typically seeks to answer "how" questions about a problem/opportunity. The focus is generally on selecting alternative courses of action.

stratified sample A probability sample that is distinguished by a two-step procedure in which (1) the parent population is divided into mutually exclusive and exhaustive subsets, and (2) a simple random sample of elements is chosen independently from each group or subset.

stratum chart A set of line charts in which quantities are aggregated or a total is disaggregated so that the distance between two lines represents the amount of some variable.

structure The degree of standardization imposed on the data collection instrument.

structured observation The problem has been defined precisely enough so that the behaviors that will be observed can be specified beforehand, as can the categories that will be used to record and analyze the situation.

summated-ratings scale A self-report technique for attitude measurement in which respondents are asked to indicate their degree of agreement or disagreement with each of a number of statements; a subject's attitude score is the total obtained by summing over the items in the scale.

systematic error Error in measurement that is also known as constant error since it affects the measurement in a constant way.

systematic sample A form of cluster sampling in which every kth element in the population is designated for inclusion in the sample after a random start.

tabulation The procedure by which the cases that fall into each of a number of categories are counted.

teleology An ethical or moral reasoning framework that focuses on society and the net consequences that an action may have. If the net result of benefits minus all costs is positive, the act is morally acceptable; if the net result is negative, the act is not morally acceptable.

telephone interview Telephone conversation between a representative of the research organization, the interviewer, and a respondent, or interviewee.

telescoping error A type of error resulting from the fact that most people remember an event as having occurred more recently than it did.

Thematic Apperception Test (TAT) A copyrighted series of pictures about which the subject is asked to tell stories.

two-box technique A technique for converting an interval-level rating scale into a categorical measure usually used for presentation purposes. The percentage of respondents choosing one of the top two positions on a rating scale is reported.

undisguised observation The subjects are aware that they are being observed.

unstructured observation The problem has not been specifically defined, so a great deal of flexibility is allowed the observers in terms of what they note and record.

validity The extent to which differences in scores on a measuring instrument reflect true differences among individuals, groups, or situations in the characteristic that it seeks to measure, or true differences in the same individual, group, or situation from one occasion to another, rather than systematic or random errors.

voice-pitch analysis Analysis that examines changes in the relative frequency of the human voice that accompany emotional arousal.

word association A questionnaire containing a list of words to which respondents are instructed to reply with the first word that comes to mind.

Index

Data collection methods, 42, 263
Data file building, 520, 524–525
Data maps, 680
Data mining, 30, 31
Data Sources for Business and Market Analysis, 183
Data systems, 25, 28, 36
Data warehouses, 25
Data Warehousing Institute, 33
Day-after recall, 213
"Death wish" research, 69
Decision Analyst, Inc., 133
Decision error, 554
Decision problem, 62
 research problem *versus*, 63, 64, 73
Decision support systems, 22, 23, 25–31, 35
 components of, 26, 36
 data systems, 25, 28
 dialog systems, 30–31
 model systems, 28–29
Degree of confidence, 452, 453, 463, 464
Degree of precision, 451, 453, 456, 463, 464, 545
Degrees of freedom, 557, 594
Del Monte, 130
Demographic/socioeconomic characteristics, 209, 220, 304
Dentsu, 11, 12
Deontological ethics, 51
Deontological model
 questions applying to, 49
Deontology, 48
Dependent variables, 120, 574, 580, 585, 595
Depth interview, 227–228
Derived population, 410–413, 423, 430
 distribution of estimates in, 415
 with simple random selection, 412
Descriptive research, 42, 90, 91, 104, 105, 109, 110–112, 134, 263, 282, 518, 692
Descriptive statistics, 545–546, 563
Descriptive studies, 112, 692
Diagrams, 675
Dialing attempts results, 237
Dialog, 173
Dialog systems, 30–31, 36
Diaries, 195, 200
Diary panels, 192–193, 205, 471, 493
Dichotomous questions, 295–297, 315
Digital music, 276
Direct observation, 251
Directories in Print, 171, 186
Directory of Corporate Affiliations, 182
Discontinuous panels, 112, 113, 135
Discovery-oriented decision problems, 62, 63, 65, 73
Discriminant validity, 335
Disguise, 225, 243
Disguised observation, 251

Disproportionate stratified sample, 435, 436, 445
Dissertation Abstracts International, 185
Distribution of sample means, 415
Divided-bar chart, 680, 681
Dole, 127
Domain sampling model, 337
"Don't know" option, 292, 293, 359, 481
Double-barreled questions, 301
Double-entry of data, 526
DowJones, 173
Dreese, Mike, 28
DSS. *See* Decision support systems
Dubin, Janet, 349
Dubin Market Research, 349
Dummy tables, 111, 112, 134, 283, 287, 461
Dun & Bradstreet, 27
Dun's Business Locator, 189

E

Eastman Kodak, 102
e-commerce, 15, 237
Economic and statistical information, 183–184
Economic Census, 181
Economic censuses, 180
Economic Indicators, 183
Economic Report of the President, 183
Editing, 43, 44, 515–518
Editor and Publisher Market Guide, 183
Einstein, Albert, 597
Electrical/mechanical observation, 256
Electronic security systems industry data sources, 172
Electronic test markets, 130
Eligibility percentage (E%), 488
Elliott, Jock, 662, 663, 664
Ellison Research, 661
email
 questionnaires, 235, 237, 238, 240
 surveys, 231, 244, 486
Encyclopedia of Associations, 171, 186
Encyclopedia of Business Information Sources, 172, 184
Enterprise resource planning, 32, 36
Environmental differences, 8
EPM Communications, 174
Equal Credit Opportunity Act, 506
Equal-interval scales, 545
ERP. *See* Enterprise resource planning
Errors, 693
 classification/assessment of, 332–336, 338
 in hypothesis testing, 550, 552, 553, 554, 555
 population mean estimates, 411
 in report writing, 662
 sampling, 433
 statistical, 418

ESOMAR (European Society for Opinion and Marketing), 285
Esperilla, Jorge, 174
Estimates size classification, 415
Ethical dilemmas
 anonymity, 310, 480
 attitude measurement, 356
 cinema experiment, 124
 coercive recruitment of participants, 408
 credit card information, 193
 dealership recommendations, 170
 employee survey, 361
 exploratory research, 92
 field experiment, 123
 hypothesis testing, 561
 laboratory experiment, 259
 mail study, 218
 measurement scale issues, 328, 339
 observation, 217, 258
 oral presentation (visual aids), 675, 680
 panel of households, 202
 perceptual map, 69
 personal/telephone interviews, 234
 price increase, 310
 questionnaire design, 283
 regression analysis, 603
 research limitations, 674
 sample representation, 441
 sample size, 461
 telephone surveys, 489
 test marketing, 453
 use of competitor's information, 101, 173
 women's banking program, 63
Ethics, 46
Ethnic groups
 in Nielsen Media Research samples, 201
 and observation methods, 253
Ethnographic marketing research, 253, 254
Ethnographic methods, 102
Ethnographic research, 103
Ethnography, 103, 256
European EAN–13 code, 194
Experience surveys, 94–95, 140
Experimentation
 as causal research, 120, 122–123
 future and problems of, 125–128
 role in marketing research, 124–125
Experiments, 120
 internal and external validity of, 123–124
 types of, 122
Expert systems, 29
Exploratory research, 41, 42, 90, 91, 92, 104, 109, 140, 263, 283
 analysis of selected cases, 100–102, 105
 experience surveys, 94–95, 105
 focus groups, 95–99, 105
 literature searches, 93–94, 105
 primary purpose of, 692
 types of, 93